STREET ATLAS
Lincolnshire

First published in 2003 by

Philip's, a division of
Octopus Publishing Group Ltd
2–4 Heron Quays, London E14 4JP

First edition 2003
Second impression with revisions 2004

ISBN 0-540-08340-2 (spiral)

© Philip's 2004

Ordnance Survey®

This product includes mapping data licensed
from Ordnance Survey® with the permission of
the Controller of Her Majesty's Stationery Office.
© Crown copyright 2004. All rights reserved.
Licence number 100011710.

Printed and bound in Spain
by Cayfosa-Quebecor

Contents

III **Key to map symbols**

IV **Key to map pages**

VI **Route planning**

X **Administrative and Postcode boundaries**

1 **Street maps** at 1¾ inches to 1 mile

178 **Street maps** at 3½ inches to 1 mile

234 **Street map of Lincoln city centre**
at 7 inches to 1 mile

235 **Index** of towns and villages

238 **Index** of streets, hospitals, industrial estates, railway
stations, schools, shopping centres, universities
and places of interest

Digital Data

The exceptionally high-quality mapping found in this atlas is available as digital data in TIFF
format, which is easily convertible to other bitmapped (raster) image formats.

The index is also available in digital form as a standard database table. It contains all the details
found in the printed index together with the National Grid reference for the map square in which
each entry is named.

For further information and to discuss your requirements, please contact Philip's on
020 7644 6932 or james.mann@philips-maps.co.uk

Symbol	Description
(22a)	**Motorway** with junction number
	Primary route – dual/single carriageway
	A road – dual/single carriageway
	B road – dual/single carriageway
	Minor road – dual/single carriageway
	Other minor road – dual/single carriageway
	Road under construction
	Tunnel, covered road
	Rural track, private road or narrow road in urban area
	Gate or obstruction to traffic (restrictions may not apply at all times or to all vehicles)
	Path, bridleway, byway open to all traffic, road used as a public path
	Pedestrianised area
DY7	**Postcode boundaries**
	County and unitary authority boundaries
	Railway, tunnel, railway under construction
	Tramway, tramway under construction
	Miniature railway
(Walsall)	**Railway station**
	Private railway station
(South Shields)	**Metro station**
	Tram stop, tram stop under construction
	Bus, coach station

Abbr	Full	Abbr	Full	Abbr	Full
Acad	**Academy**	Inst	**Institute**	Recn Gd	**Recreation Ground**
Allot Gdns	**Allotments**	Ct	**Law Court**		
Cemy	**Cemetery**	L Ctr	**Leisure Centre**	Resr	**Reservoir**
C Ctr	**Civic Centre**	LC	**Level Crossing**	Ret Pk	**Retail Park**
CH	**Club House**	Liby	**Library**	Sch	**School**
Coll	**College**	Mkt	**Market**	Sh Ctr	**Shopping Centre**
Crem	**Crematorium**	Meml	**Memorial**	TH	**Town Hall/House**
Ent	**Enterprise**	Mon	**Monument**	Trad Est	**Trading Estate**
Ex H	**Exhibition Hall**	Mus	**Museum**	Univ	**University**
Ind Est	**Industrial Estate**	Obsy	**Observatory**	Wks	**Works**
IRB Sta	**Inshore Rescue Boat Station**	Pal	**Royal Palace**	YH	**Youth Hostel**
		PH	**Public House**		

Symbol	Description
◆	**Ambulance station**
◆	**Coastguard station**
◆	**Fire station**
◆	**Police station**
✚	**Accident and Emergency entrance to hospital**
H	**Hospital**
+	**Place of worship**
i	**Information Centre** (open all year)
P	**Parking**
P&R	**Park and Ride**
PO	**Post Office**
Ⓧ	**Camping site**
	Caravan site
▶	**Golf course**
✕	**Picnic site**
Prim Sch	**Important buildings, schools, colleges, universities and hospitals**
River Ouse	**Tidal water, water name**
	Non-tidal water – lake, river, canal or stream
	Lock, weir, tunnel
	Woods
	Built up area
Church	**Non-Roman antiquity**
ROMAN FORT	**Roman antiquity**
87	**Adjoining page indicators and overlap bands**
228	The colour of the arrow and the band indicates the scale of the adjoining or overlapping page (see scales below)

■ The small numbers around the edges of the maps identify the 1 kilometre National Grid lines

■ The dark grey border on the inside edge of some pages indicates that the mapping does not continue onto the adjacent page

The scale of the maps on the pages numbered in blue is 5.52 cm to 1 km • 3½ inches to 1 mile • 1: 18103	0 — ¼ — ½ — ¾ — 1 mile / 0 — 250m — 500m — 750m — 1 kilometre
The scale of the maps on pages numbered in green is 2.76 cm to 1 km • 1¾ inches to 1 mile • 1: 36206	0 — ¼ — ½ — ¾ — 1 mile / 0 — 250m 500m 750m 1kilometre
The scale of the maps on the pages numbered in red is 11.04 cm to 1 km • 7 inches to 1 mile • 1: 9051.4	0 — 220 yards — 440 yards — 660 yards — ½ mile / 0 — 125m — 250m — 375m — ½ kilometre

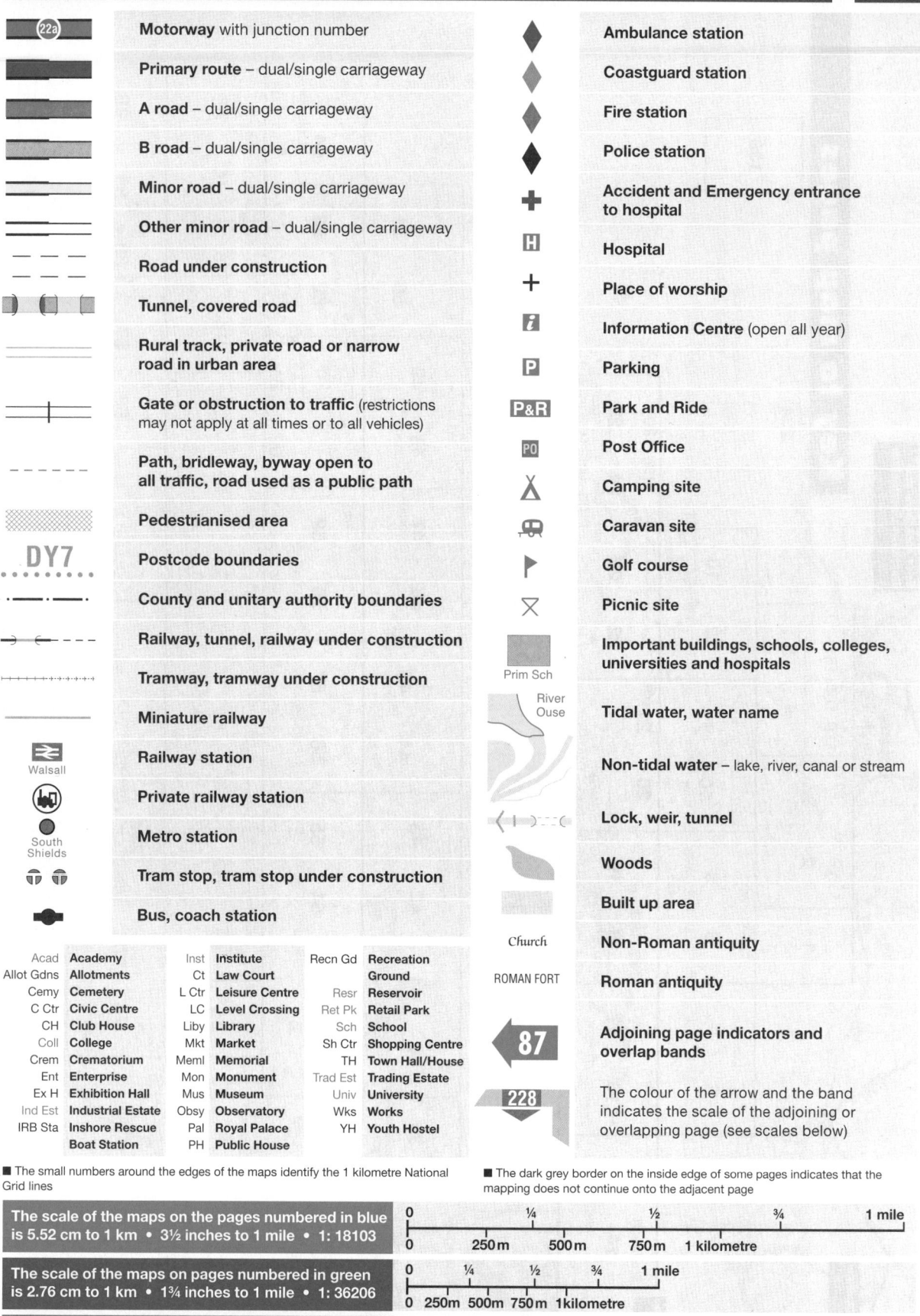

Key to map pages

138	Map pages at 1¾ inches to 1 mile
234	Map pages at 7 inches to 1 mile
180	Map pages at 3½ inches to 1 mile

East Yorkshire and Northern Lincolnshire
STREET ATLAS

North Yorkshire
STREET ATLAS

South Yorkshire
STREET ATLAS

Nottinghamshire
STREET ATLAS

Kingston upon Hull

Scunthorpe

Grimsby

Cleethorpes

Lincoln

Louth

Skegness

Mablethorpe

Gainsborough

Doncaster

Worksop

Retford

Mansfield

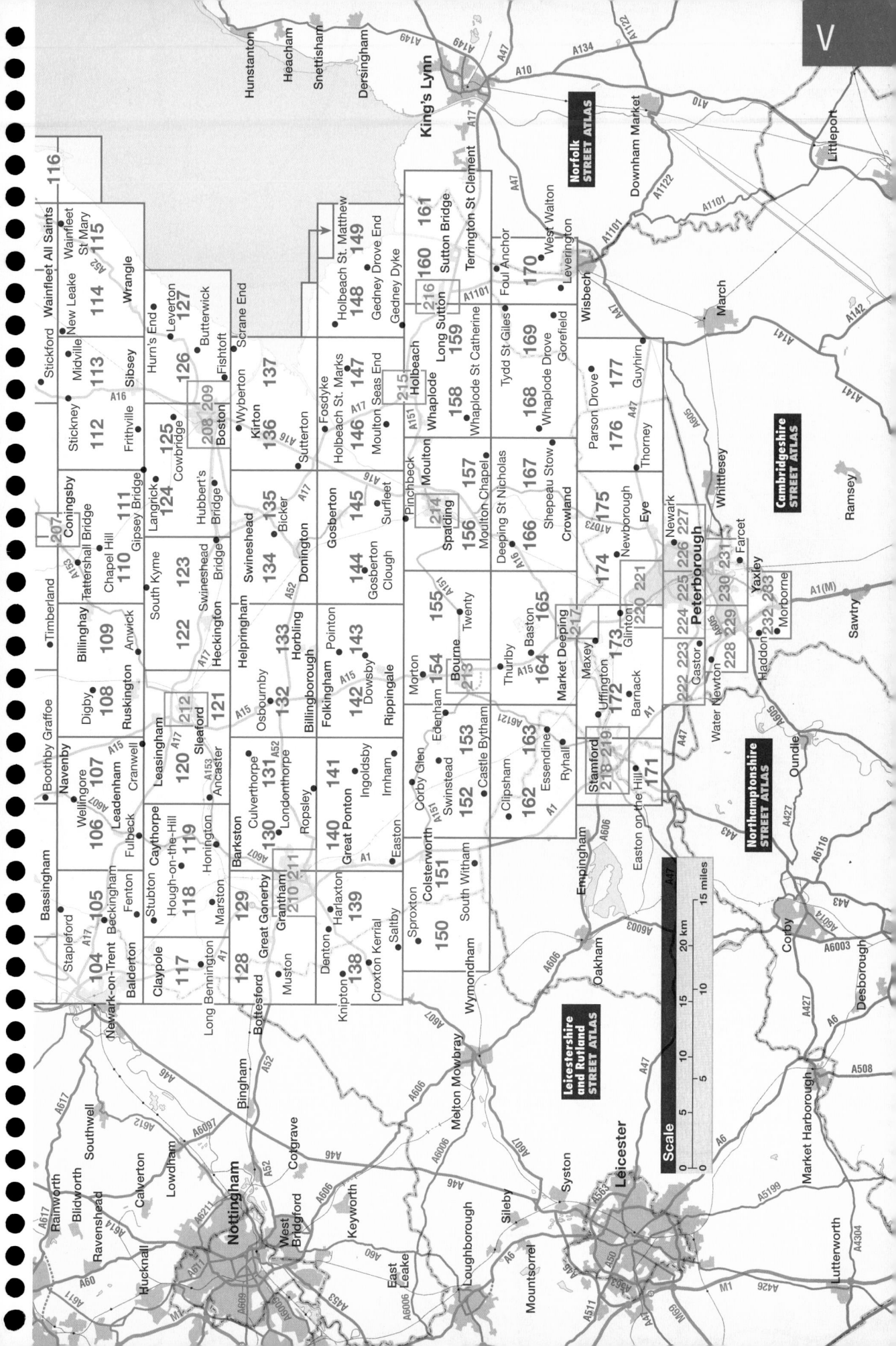
V
Scale
0 5 10 15 20 km
0 5 10 15 miles
Leicestershire and Rutland STREET ATLAS
Northamptonshire STREET ATLAS
Cambridgeshire STREET ATLAS
Norfolk STREET ATLAS
Nottingham
Leicester
Peterborough
King's Lynn
Newark-on-Trent
Grantham
Sleaford
Boston
Spalding
Stamford
Bourne
Market Deeping
Wisbech
Melton Mowbray
Loughborough
Oakham
Corby
Market Harborough
March
Whittlesey
Holbeach
Long Sutton
Sutton Bridge
Coningsby
Bingham
West Bridgford
Southwell
Hucknall
Lutterworth
Oundle
Downham Market
Hunstanton
Heacham
Snettisham
Dersingham
Littleport
Ramsey
Sawtry
Yaxley
104 105 106 107 108 109 110 111 112 113 114 115 116
117 118 119 120 121 122 123 124 125 126 127
128 129 130 131 132 133 134 135 136 137
138 139 140 141 142 143 144 145 146 147 148 149
150 151 152 153 154 155 156 157 158 159 160 161
162 163 164 165 166 167 168 169 170
171 172 173 174 175 176 177
207 208 209 210 211 212 213 214 215 216 217 218 219 220 221
222 223 224 225 226 227 228 229 230 231 232 233

Route planning
Scale
0 5 10 km
0 1 2 3 4 5 6 miles
North Lincolnshire
HUMBER
Humber Bridge
Kingston upon Hull
Goole
Scunthorpe
Doncaster
Gainsborough
Lincoln
RETFORD
Worksop
Thorne
Hatfield
Armthorpe
Epworth
Crowle
Brigg
Barton-upon-Humber
Barrow upon Humber
Winterton
Broughton
Messingham
Scotter
Kirton in Lindsey
Hibaldstow
Bawtry
Tickhill
Harworth
Blyth
Beckingham
Tuxford
Ollerton
Boughton
Edwinstowe
Market Warsop
Saxilby
North Hykeham
Waddington
Bassingham
Collingham
Sutton on Trent
Nettleham
Washingborough
Faldingworth
Cottingham
Hessle
Anlaby
North Ferriby
South Cave
North Cave
Gilberdyke
Snaith
Carlton
Stainforth
Bessacarr
New Rossington
Laughton Forest
Redcliff Channel
Read's Island
M62
M18
M180
M181
A1(M)
A15
A18
A46
A57
A63
A159
A161
A614
A631

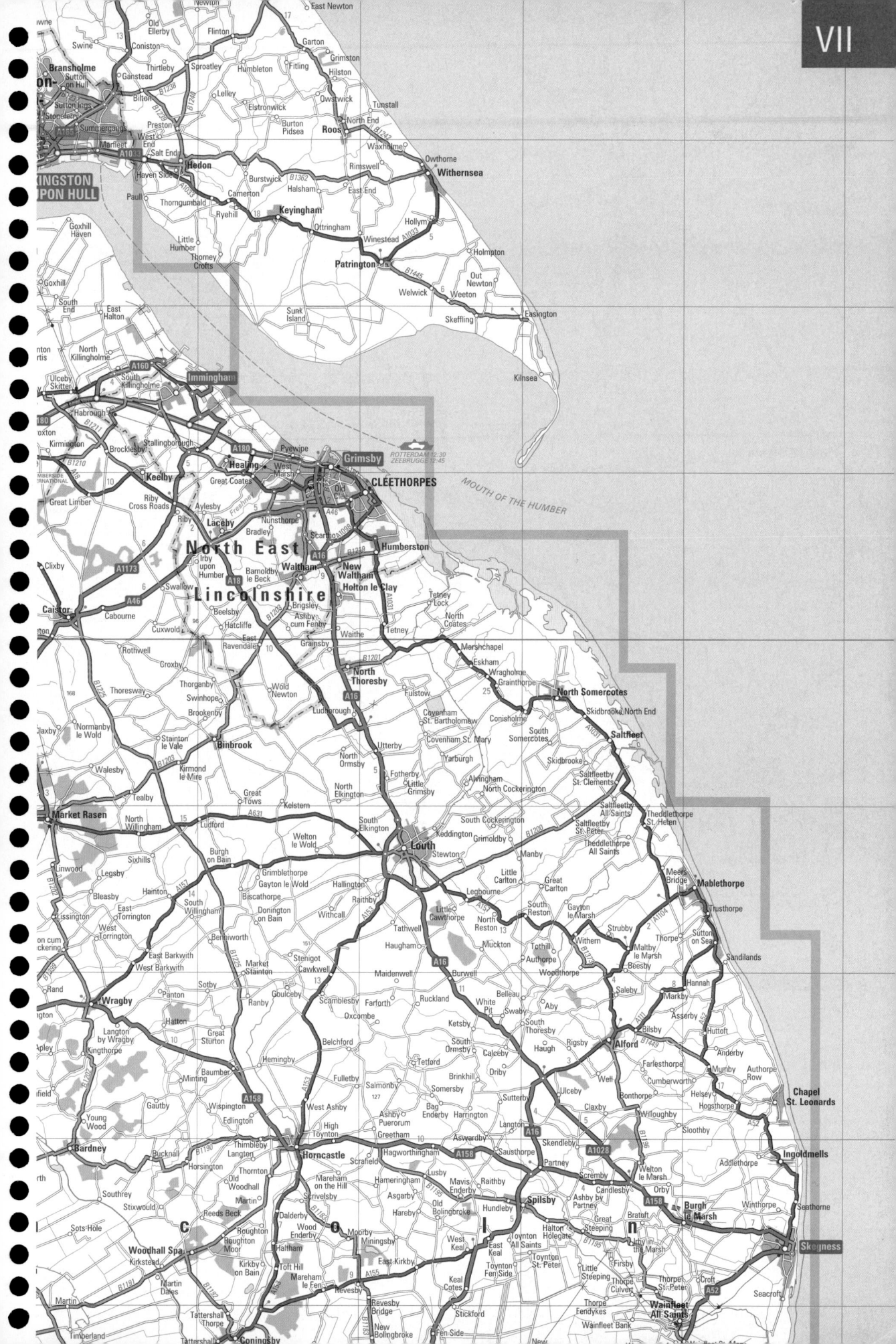
KINGSTON UPON HULL
Hedon
Withernsea
Keyingham
Patrington
Roos
Easington
Kilnsea
Immingham
Grimsby
CLEETHORPES
MOUTH OF THE HUMBER
ROTTERDAM 12:30
ZEEBRUGGE 12:45
North East Lincolnshire
Humberston
Waltham
New Waltham
Holton le Clay
Laceby
Healing
Keelby
Caistor
Market Rasen
Binbrook
North Thoresby
North Somercotes
Saltfleet
Louth
Mablethorpe
Sutton on Sea
Sandilands
Alford
Chapel St. Leonards
Ingoldmells
Skegness
Wragby
Bardney
Horncastle
Woodhall Spa
Spilsby
Burgh le Marsh
Wainfleet All Saints
Coningsby
Tattershall

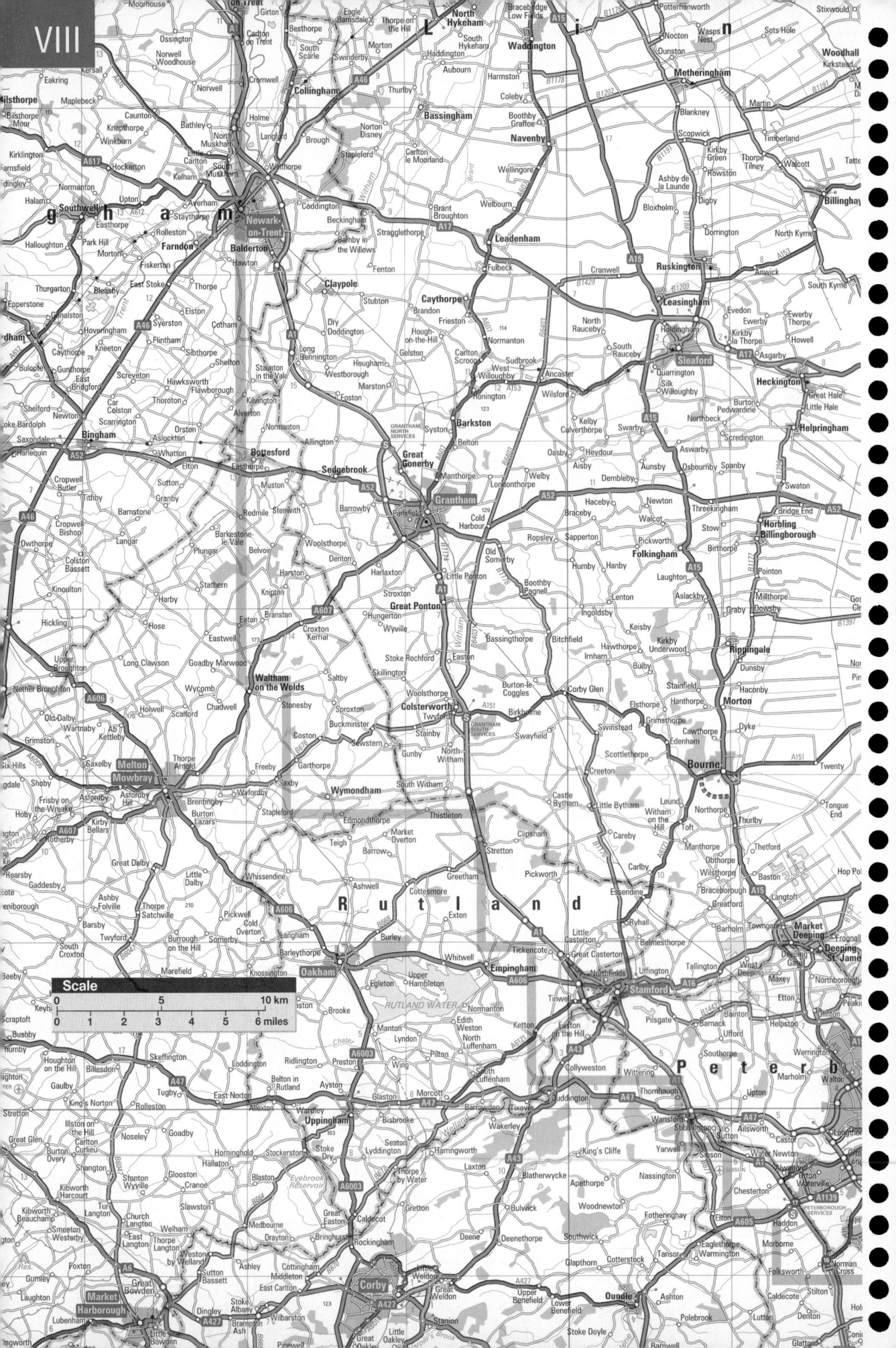
Scale
0 5 10 km
0 1 2 3 4 5 6 miles
Newark-on-Trent
Balderton
Farndon
Southwell
Bingham
Collingham
North Hykeham
South Hykeham
Waddington
Bassingham
Navenby
Wellingore
Leadenham
Fulbeck
Caythorpe
Claypole
Long Bennington
Barkston
Syston
Great Gonerby
Grantham
Sedgebrook
Bottesford
Metheringham
Martin
Timberland
Walcott
Billinghay
Digby
Dorrington
Ruskington
Leasingham
Sleaford
Heckington
Helpringham
Ancaster
Wilsford
Folkingham
Billingborough
Horbling
Rippingale
Morton
Bourne
Corby Glen
Colsterworth
Great Ponton
Little Ponton
Waltham on the Wolds
Melton Mowbray
Wymondham
Castle Bytham
Little Bytham
Market Deeping
Deeping St. James
Stamford
Empingham
Oakham
Rutland
Rutland Water
Uppingham
Corby
Oundle
Market Harborough
Tallington
Uffington
Ryhall
Great Casterton
Little Casterton
Essendine
Greetham
Cottesmore
Exton
Langham
Whissendine
Wansford
Sutton
Ailsworth
Castor
Alwalton
Orton Waterville
Peterborough Services
Elton
Fotheringhay
Nassington
King's Cliffe
Duddington
Collyweston
Easton on the Hill
Ketton
Tinwell
Barrowden
Morcott
Glaston
Wing
Preston
Manton
Lyndon
Edith Weston
North Luffenham
South Luffenham
Normanton
Egleton
Upper Hambleton
Whitwell
Burley
Barleythorpe
Knossington
Somerby
Burrough on the Hill
Tilton
Billesdon
Skeffington
Tugby
East Norton
Allexton
Belton in Rutland
Ridlington
Ayston
Wardley
Bisbrooke
Seaton
Lyddington
Stoke Dry
Caldecott
Rockingham
Gretton
Harringworth
Laxton
Bulwick
Blatherwycke
Deene
Deenethorpe
Southwick
Apethorpe
Woodnewton
Glapthorn
Cotterstock
Tansor
Eaglethorpe
Warmington
Morborne
Folksworth
Norman Cross
Stilton
Caldecote
Lutton
Polebrook
Ashton
Stoke Doyle
Benefield
Upper Benefield
Lower Benefield
Great Weldon
Little Weldon
Stanion
Great Oakley
Little Oakley
Cottingham
Middleton
East Carlton
Ashley
Sutton Bassett
Weston by Welland
Great Bowden
Lubenham
Little Bowden
Dingley
Brampton Ash
Wilbarston
Stoke Albany
Medbourne
Drayton
Bringhurst
Great Easton
Blaston
Hallaton
Horninghold
Stockerston
Eyebrook Reservoir
Glooston
Cranoe
Slawston
Welham
Church Langton
East Langton
Thorpe Langton
Tur Langton
Kibworth Harcourt
Kibworth Beauchamp
Smeeton Westerby
Foxton
Gumley
Laughton
Stonton Wyville
Shangton
Noseley
Goadby
Rolleston
Illston on the Hill
Carlton Curlieu
Burton Overy
Great Glen
Houghton on the Hill
Gaulby
King's Norton
Stretton
Keyham
Scraptoft
Bushby
Beeby
South Croxton
Twyford
Barsby
Ashby Folville
Thorpe Satchville
Gaddesby
Rearsby
Great Dalby
Little Dalby
Pickwell
Cold Overton
Burton Lazars
Kirby Bellars
Asfordby
Asfordby Hill
Frisby on the Wreake
Hoby
Rotherby
Shoby
Saxelby
Grimston
Wartnaby
Ab Kettleby
Old Dalby
Holwell
Scalford
Thorpe Arnold
Brentingby
Wyfordby
Stapleford
Freeby
Saxby
Garthorpe
Coston
Sproxton
Buckminster
Sewstern
Stonesby
Chadwell
Wycomb
Goadby Marwood
Eastwell
Eaton
Branston
Knipton
Croxton Kerrial
Long Clawson
Hose
Harby
Stathern
Upper Broughton
Nether Broughton
Hickling
Kinoulton
Colston Bassett
Plungar
Barkestone-le-Vale
Belvoir
Redmile
Stenwith
Woolsthorpe
Denton
Harlaxton
Harston
Stroxton
Hungerton
Wyville
Stoke Rochford
Skillington
Easton
Woolsthorpe
Twyford
Stainby
Gunby
North Witham
South Witham
Thistleton
Edmondthorpe
Market Overton
Teigh
Barrow
Ashwell
Stretton
Clipsham
Pickworth
Careby
Carlby
Witham on the Hill
Toft
Lound
Manthorpe
Obthorpe
Thurlby
Northorpe
Wilsthorpe
Braceborough
Greatford
Barholm
Baston
Langtoft
Thetford
Tongue End
Twenty
Dyke
Cawthorpe
Edenham
Grimsthorpe
Elsthorpe
Hanthorpe
Stainfield
Haconby
Dunsby
Kirkby Underwood
Hawthorpe
Irnham
Bulby
Swinstead
Scottlethorpe
Creeton
Swayfield
Birkholme
Burton-le-Coggles
Bitchfield
Bassingthorpe
Ingoldsby
Keisby
Lenton
Boothby Pagnell
Humby
Hanby
Laughton
Aslackby
Graby
Dowsby
Millthorpe
Pointon
Birthorpe
Stow
Threekingham
Walcot
Newton
Pickworth
Sapperton
Ropsley
Haceby
Braceby
Old Somerby
Cold Harbour
Londonthorpe
Manthorpe
Belton
Welby
Oasby
Heydour
Aisby
Dembleby
Aunsby
Osbournby
Spanby
Swaton
Bridge End
Aswarby
Scredington
Northbeck
Burton Pedwardine
Great Hale
Little Hale
Kelby
Culverthorpe
Swarby
Quarrington
Silk Willoughby
South Rauceby
North Rauceby
Holdingham
Evedon
Ewerby
Ewerby Thorpe
Kirkby la Thorpe
Asgarby
Howell
Cranwell
South Kyme
North Kyme
Anwick
Bloxholm
Ashby de la Launde
Rowston
Kirkby Green
Scopwick
Blankney
Thorpe Tilney
Dunston
Nocton
Potterhanworth
Wasps Nest
Sots Hole
Stixwould
Woodhall
Kirkstead
Tattershall
Bracebridge Low Fields
Harmston
Coleby
Boothby Graffoe
Thurlby
Aubourn
Haddington
Morton
Swinderby
South Scarle
Besthorpe
Girton
Eagle Barnsdale
Thorpe on the Hill
Carlton on Trent
Cromwell
Norwell
Norwell Woodhouse
Ossington
Moorhouse
Kersall
Eakring
Bilsthorpe
Maplebeck
Caunton
Knapthorpe
Winkburn
Kirklington
Farnsfield
Hockerton
Normanton
Halam
Upton
Easthorpe
Rolleston
Staythorpe
Averham
Kelham
South Muskham
North Muskham
Bathley
Little Carlton
Holme
Langford
Winthorpe
Brough
Norton Disney
Stapleford
Carlton le Moorland
Brant Broughton
Welbourn
Stragglethorpe
Beckingham
Barnby in the Willows
Coddington
Fenton
Hawton
Thorpe
East Stoke
Elston
Syerston
Flintham
Sibthorpe
Cotham
Shelton
Hawksworth
Flawborough
Staunton in the Vale
Kilvington
Alverton
Orston
Thoroton
Screveton
Car Colston
Scarrington
Aslockton
Whatton
Elton
Normanton
Allington
Muston
Easthorpe
Sutton
Granby
Barnstone
Langar
Tithby
Cropwell Butler
Cropwell Bishop
Owthorpe
Saxondale
Shelford
Newton
East Bridgford
Kneeton
Hoveringham
Caythorpe
Gunthorpe
Gonalston
Epperstone
Thurgarton
Bleasby
Fiskerton
Morton
Halloughton
Park Hill
Dry Doddington
Stubton
Brandon
Hough-on-the-Hill
Frieston
Gelston
Carlton Scroop
Normanton
Sudbrook
West Willoughby
Honington
Hougham
Westbourgh
Marston
Foston
Barrowby
Earlsfield
Grantham North Services
Grantham South Services
Peterborough Services
A1
A15
A17
A46
A52
A153
A151
A16
A6
A43
A47
A427
A605
A606
A607
A1139
A6003
A617
B1429
B1202
B1178
B1191
B1188
B1209
B1394
B1177
B1397
B6403
B1174
B1176
B676
B668
B1443
B1525
Trent
Witham
Brant
Eye
Chater
Welland
Eyebrook
Wreake
Harper's Brook

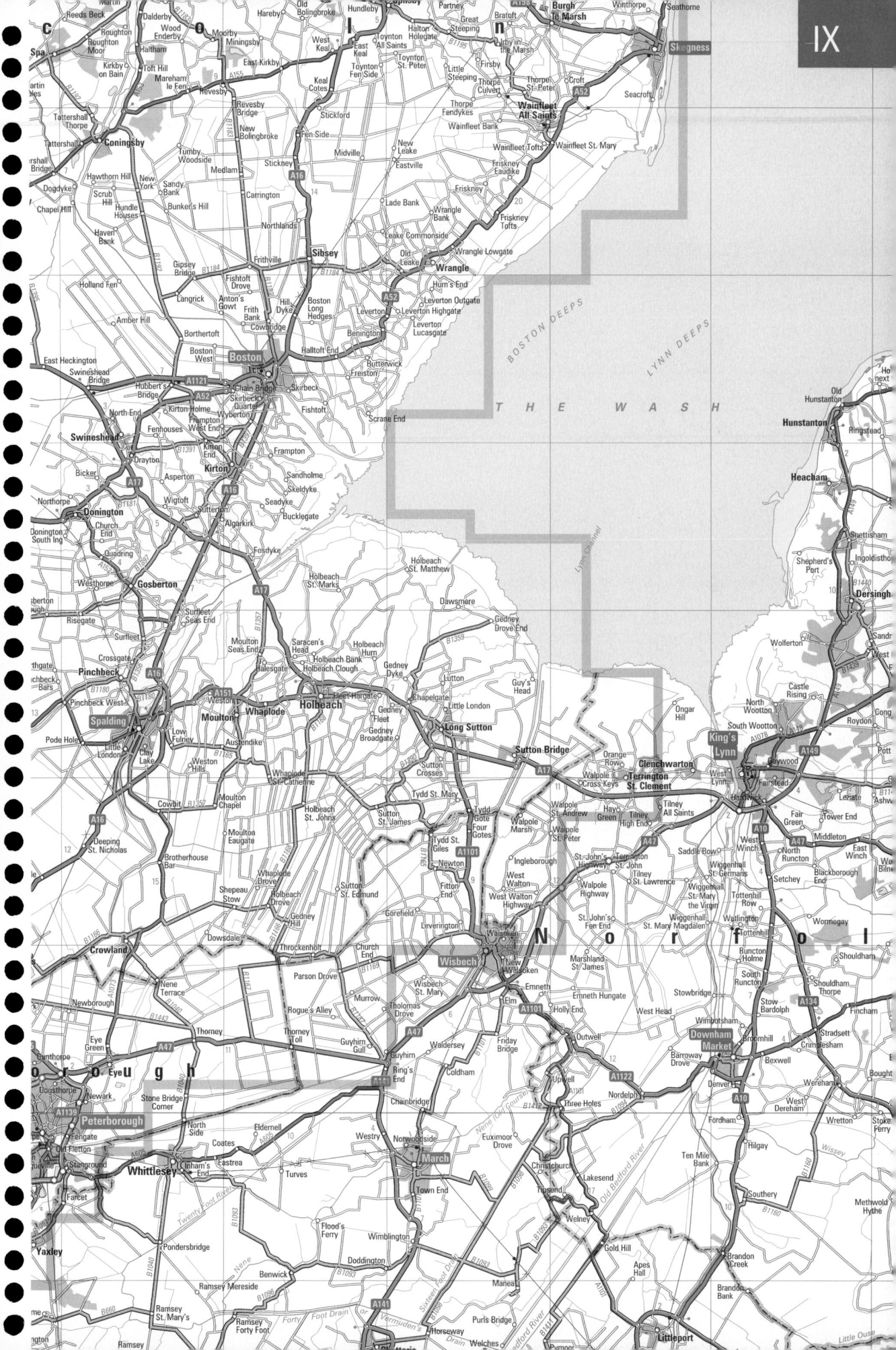
Skegness
Burgh le Marsh
Winthorpe
Seathorne
Partney
Spilsby
Hundleby
Old Bolingbroke
Hareby
Halton Holegate
Great Steeping
Bratoft
Irby in the Marsh
Firsby
Toynton All Saints
Toynton St. Peter
Toynton Fen Side
East Keal
West Keal
Keal Cotes
Little Steeping
Thorpe Culvert
Thorpe St. Peter
Croft
Seacroft
Wainfleet All Saints
Wainfleet Bank
Wainfleet Tofts
Wainfleet St. Mary
Thorpe Fendykes
Stickford
New Leake
Eastville
Midville
Stickney
Friskney Eaudike
Friskney
Friskney Tofts
Lade Bank
Wrangle Bank
Leake Commonside
Old Leake
Wrangle
Wrangle Lowgate
Hurn's End
Leverton Outgate
Leverton Highgate
Leverton
Leverton Lucasgate
Benington
Butterwick
Freiston
Fishtoft
Skirbeck
Scrane End
Sibsey
Northlands
Carrington
Revesby
Revesby Bridge
New Bolingbroke
Moorby
Miningsby
East Kirkby
Dalderby
Wood Enderby
Haltham
Mareham le Fen
Toft Hill
Kirkby on Bain
Roughton
Roughton Moor
Reeds Beck
Tattershall Thorpe
Tattershall
Coningsby
Tumby Woodside
Medlam
Hawthorn Hill
New York
Sandy Bank
Bunker's Hill
Dogdyke
Scrub Hill
Hundle Houses
Chapel Hill
Haven Bank
Holland Fen
Gipsey Bridge
Frithville
Fishtoft Drove
Langrick
Anton's Gowt
Frith Bank
Hill Dyke
Boston Long Hedges
Cowbridge
Amber Hill
Borthertoft
Boston West
Boston
Halltoft End
East Heckington
Swineshead Bridge
Hubbert's Bridge
Chain Bridge
Skirbeck Quarter
Wyberton
Kirton Holme
Frampton West End
Frampton
North End
Fenhouses
Swineshead
Drayton
Kirton End
Kirton
Bicker
Asperton
Sandholme
Skeldyke
Seadyke
Bucklegate
Wigtoft
Sutterton
Algarkirk
Northorpe
Donington
Church End
Donington South Ing
Quadring
Fosdyke
Westhorpe
Gosberton
Surfleet Seas End
Surfleet
Risegate
Holbeach St. Matthew
Holbeach St. Marks
Dawsmere
Gedney Drove End
Moulton Seas End
Saracen's Head
Holbeach Bank
Holbeach Hurn
Holbeach Clough
Halesgate
Crossgate
Pinchbeck
Pinchbeck Bars
Pinchbeck West
Spalding
Weston
Moulton
Whaplode
Holbeach
Fleet Hargate
Gedney Dyke
Gedney Fleet
Gedney Broadgate
Lutton
Chapelgate
Little London
Long Sutton
Guy's Head
Sutton Bridge
Pode Hole
Little London
Low Fulney
Austendike
Clay Lake
Weston Hills
Whaplode St. Catherine
Sutton Crosses
Tydd St. Mary
Cowbit
Moulton Chapel
Holbeach St. Johns
Sutton St. James
Tydd Gote
Four Gotes
Tydd St. Giles
Newton
Moulton Eaugate
Deeping St. Nicholas
Brotherhouse Bar
Whaplode Drove
Holbeach Drove
Shepeau Stow
Sutton St. Edmund
Gedney Hill
Fitton End
Gorefield
Leverington
Dowsdale
Throckenholt
Crowland
Church End
Parson Drove
Wisbech
Walsoken
New Walsoken
Wisbech St. Mary
Murrow
Tholomas Drove
Rogue's Alley
Nene Terrace
Newborough
Thorney
Thorney Toll
Guyhirn Gull
Guyhirn
Ring's End
Eye Green
Eye
Gunthorpe
Dogsthorpe
Newark
Peterborough
Fengate
Old Fletton
Stanground
Farcet
Yaxley
Stone Bridge Corner
North Side
Coates
Eldernell
Whittlesey
Inham's End
Eastrea
Turves
Westry
Norwoodside
March
Town End
Chainbridge
Coldham
Waldersey
Friday Bridge
Elm
Emneth
Emneth Hungate
Holly End
Outwell
Upwell
Three Holes
Nordelph
Euximoor Drove
Christchurch
Tipsend
Lakesend
Welney
Flood's Ferry
Wimblington
Doddington
Benwick
Pondersbridge
Ramsey Mereside
Ramsey St. Mary's
Ramsey Forty Foot
Ramsey
Manea
Purls Bridge
Horseway
Welches Dam
Gold Hill
Apes Hall
Littleport
Brandon Creek
Brandon Bank
Southery
Hilgay
Ten Mile Bank
Fordham
Denver
Downham Market
Bexwell
Barroway Drove
Stow Bridge
West Head
Wimbotsham
Broomhill
Stow Bardolph
Runcton Holme
South Runcton
Shouldham
Shouldham Thorpe
Fincham
Stradsett
Crimplesham
Wereham
West Dereham
Wretton
Stoke Ferry
Methwold Hythe
Wormegay
Watlington
Tottenhill
Tottenhill Row
Setchey
Blackborough End
North Runcton
West Winch
Middleton
East Winch
Tower End
Fair Green
Leziate
Saddle Bow
Wiggenhall St. Germans
Wiggenhall St. Mary the Virgin
Wiggenhall St. Mary Magdalen
St. John's Fen End
Walpole Highway
Tilney St. Lawrence
Terrington St. John
St. John's Highway
West Walton
West Walton Highway
Ingleborough
Walpole St. Peter
Walpole Marsh
Walpole St. Andrew
Hay Green
Tilney High End
Tilney All Saints
Walpole Cross Keys
Terrington St. Clement
Clenchwarton
Orange Row
Ongar Hill
West Lynn
King's Lynn
Hardwick
Fairstead
Gaywood
South Wootton
North Wootton
Castle Rising
Roydon
Wolferton
Dersingham
Ingoldisthorpe
Shepherd's Port
Snettisham
Heacham
Hunstanton
Old Hunstanton
Ringstead
THE WASH
BOSTON DEEPS
LYNN DEEPS
Lynn Channel
Norfolk
Twenty Foot River
Old Bedford River
Forty Foot Drain
Sixteen Foot Drain
Nene
Wissey
Little Ouse
A16
A17
A52
A151
A1121
A47
A1101
A141
A1122
A10
A149
A148
A1078
A134
A605
A1139
A158
A155
A153

X

East Riding of Yorkshire

SE | TA
HU3
HU10
HU2
HU9
Anlaby
Kingston upon Hull
Broomfleet HU15 Brough
HU14
North Ferriby
HU13 HU4 HU1
Alkborough DN18
Barton-upon-Humber
Barrow-upon-Humber
DN14
Garthorpe Winterton DN19
DN15 Appleby
Ulceby DN40 Immingham
DN39 DN41
Stainforth Thorne Crowle North Lincolnshire Healing DN31 Grimsby
DN8 Scunthorpe Broughton DN38 Keelby DN32 Cleetethorpes
DN17 DN34
Hatfield DN7 Belton DN16 Brigg Barnetby DN33 DN35
DN3 Edenthorpe Messingham DN20 le Wold Grasby Laceby Humberston
Wroot Hibaldstow Waltham Holton le Clay
SE Epworth DN9 Scotter North Kelsey LN7 Caistor NE Lincs DN36
Haxey Kirton in Lindsey South Kelsey DN37
SK North Thoresby
DN10 Walkeringham LN21 Binbrook North Somercotes
Beckingham Hemswell Osgodby Tealby Utterby
Gainsborough West Lindsey Market Rasen Ludford LN11 Louth Manby LN12
DN22 Faldingworth LN8 Hainton Legbourne Mablethorpe
Marton Ingham Welton Wragby Goulceby Burwell Sutton on Sea
Rampton LN1 Saxilby LN2 Nettleham Lincolnshire East Lindsey LN13
NG24 LN3 Cherry Willingham Belchford Tetford Alford
Harby Lincoln Washingborough LN9 Hogsthorpe Chapel St Leonards
North Scarle Lincoln Bardney Horncastle Hagworthingham Ingoldmells
Besthorpe LN6 Branston Spilsby PE25
NG23 Swinderby Waddington LN10 Ravesby PE23 Burgh le Marsh Skegness
Collingham Bassingham Woodhall Spa PE24
Metheringham Wainfleet All Saints
Navenby North Kesteven Timberland Coningsby Stickney
Nottinghamshire Newark-on-Trent LN5 Billinghay LN4 PE22 Wrangle
NG24 Leadenham South Kyme Sibsey
Balderton Ruskington PE21
Claypole Caythorpe Sleaford Heckington Boston Butterwick
Long Bennington Marston Swineshead PE20 Kirton
NG32 Barkston NG34 Helpringham Boston
Bottesford Great Gonerby Horbling Donington Holbeach St Matthew
Sedgebrook Grantham NG31 Billingborough Gosberton Fosdyke
Harlaxton Ropsley Folkingham Pinchbeck South Holland
Knipton Great Ponton NG33 Rippingale Whaplode Holbeach
LE14 Corby Glen South Kesteven PE10 Spalding Moulton Long Sutton Sutton Bridge PE34
Sproxton Colsterworth Bourne PE11 Tydd St Giles PE12 Terrington St Clement
Wymondham Thurlby Cowbit PE14
LE15 Clipsham Hop Pole Gorefield West Walton
Ryhall Market Deeping Crowland Gedney Hill PE13 Norfolk
PE9 Deeping St James Church End Wisbech
Stamford PE6 Thorney Guyhirn
PE8 Helpston PE4 Eye TF
Wittering PE3 PE1 TL
PE5 Castor
PE8 PE2 Peterborough
PE7 Yaxley Cambridgeshire

Leicestershire

Administrative and Postcode boundaries

- County and unitary authority boundaries
- District boundaries
- Postcode boundaries
- Area covered by this atlas

Scale
0   10   20   30 km
0   5   10   15   20 miles

SP | TL
TF | TL

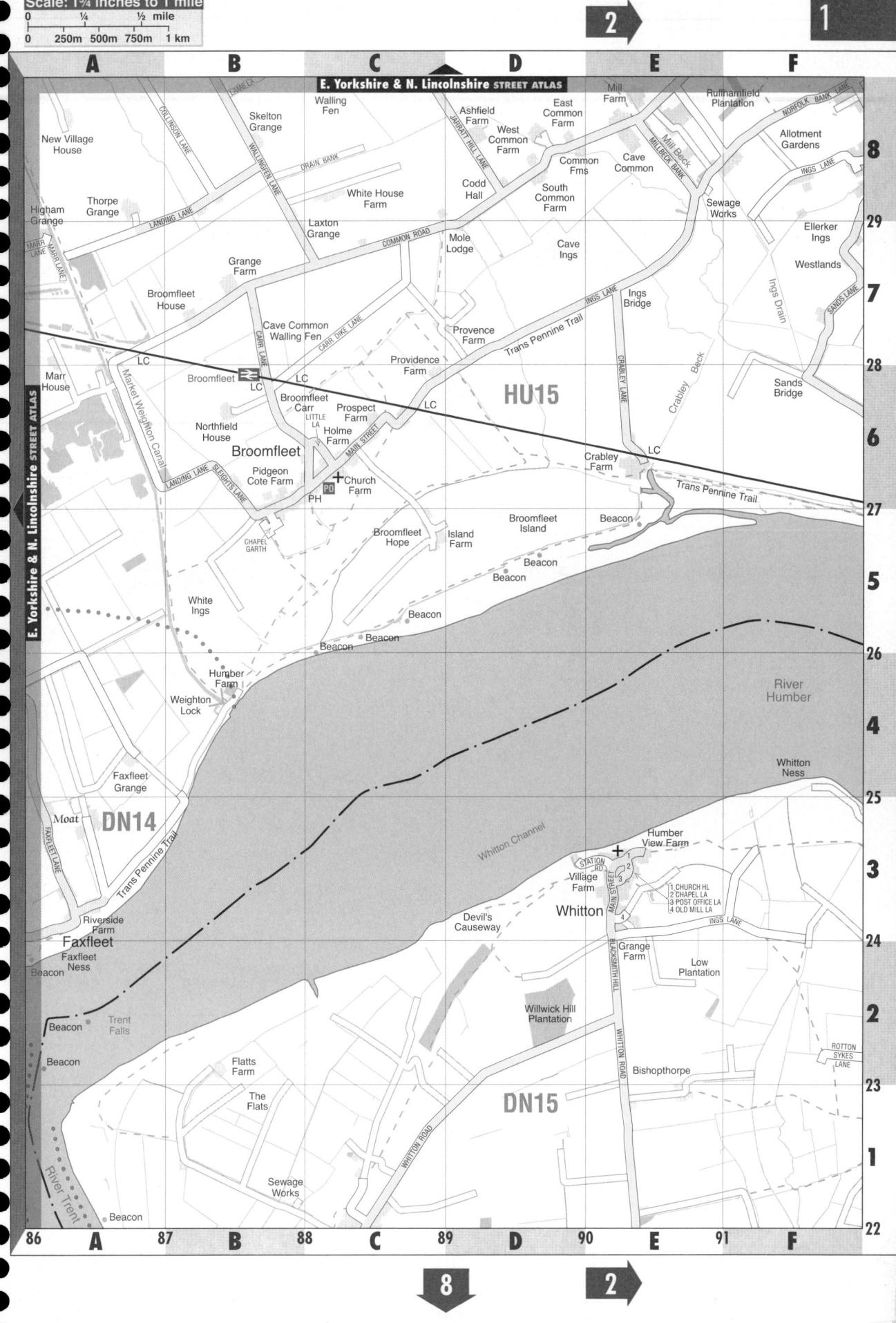
Scale: 1¾ inches to 1 mile
E. Yorkshire & N. Lincolnshire STREET ATLAS
Broomfleet
Whitton
Faxfleet
HU15
DN14
DN15
River Humber
Trans Pennine Trail
Whitton Channel
River Trent
Trent Falls
New Village House
Skelton Grange
Walling Fen
Ashfield Farm
East Common Farm
Mill Farm
Ruffhamfield Plantation
West Common Farm
Allotment Gardens
Thorpe Grange
Higham Grange
White House Farm
Codd Hall
Common Fms
Cave Common
South Common Farm
Sewage Works
Laxton Grange
Mole Lodge
Cave Ings
Ellerker Ings
Westlands
Grange Farm
Broomfleet House
Ings Bridge
Cave Common Walling Fen
Provence Farm
Providence Farm
Marr House
Sands Bridge
Broomfleet Carr
Prospect Farm
Holme Farm
Northfield House
Pidgeon Cote Farm
Church Farm
Crabley Farm
Broomfleet Island
Broomfleet Hope
Island Farm
Beacon
White Ings
Humber Farm
Weighton Lock
Whitton Ness
Faxfleet Grange
Moat
Humber View Farm
Village Farm
Devil's Causeway
Riverside Farm
Faxfleet Ness
Grange Farm
Low Plantation
Willwick Hill Plantation
Flatts Farm
The Flats
Bishopthorpe
Sewage Works
Market Weighton Canal
Crabley Beck
Mill Beck
Ings Drain
1 CHURCH HL
2 CHAPEL LA
3 POST OFFICE LA
4 OLD MILL LA

2
8
2

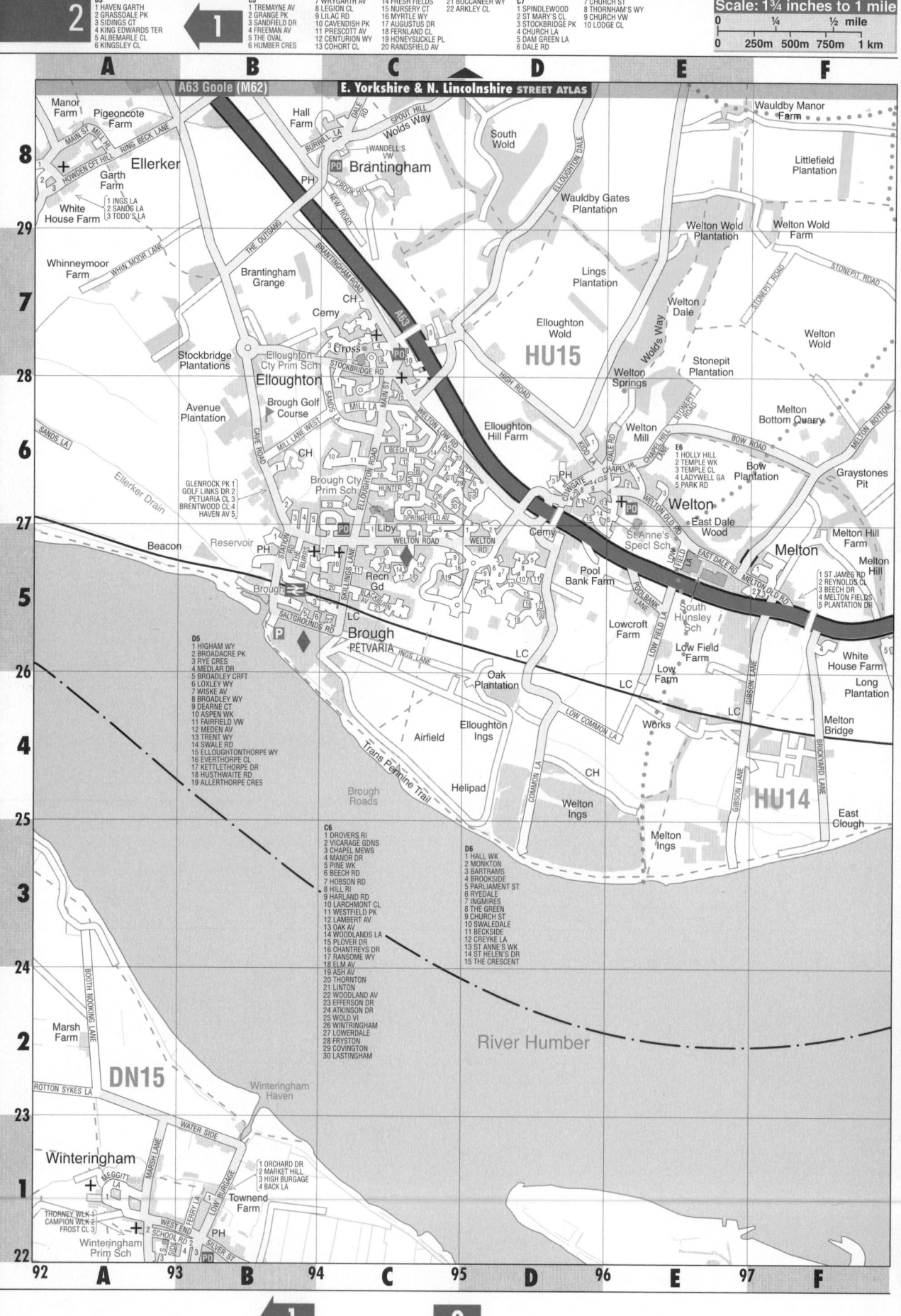

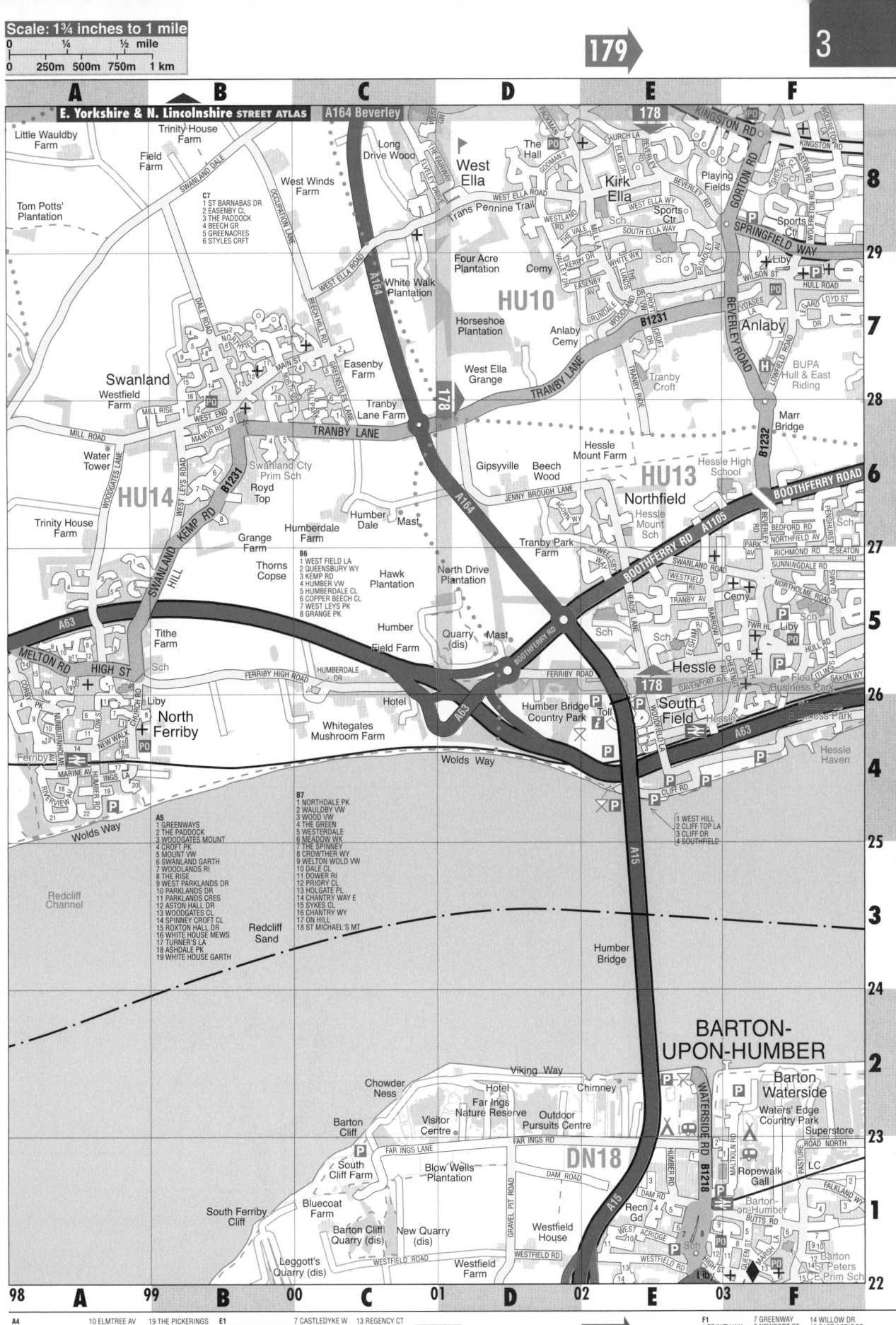

Scale: 1¾ inches to 1 mile

0   ¼   ½   mile

0   250m   500m   750m   1 km

E. Yorkshire & N. Lincolnshire STREET ATLAS   A164 Beverley

Map labels and features:

Little Wauldby Farm

Trinity House Farm

Field Farm

Tom Potts' Plantation

Long Drive Wood

West Ella

The Hall

Kirk Ella

Playing Fields

Sports Ctr

KINGSTON RD

Kingston Rd

178

Trans Pennine Trail

HU10

Four Acre Plantation

Cemy

Sports Ctr

SPRINGFIELD WAY

Anlaby

White Walk Plantation

Horseshoe Plantation

Anlaby Cemy

BEVERLEY ROAD

C7
1 ST BARNABAS DR
2 EASENBY CL
3 THE PADDOCK
4 BEECH GR
5 GREENACRES
6 STYLES CRFT

West Winds Farm

West Ella Grange

Tranby Croft

BUPA Hull & East Riding

Swanland

Westfield Farm

Easenby Farm

Tranby Lane Farm

TRANBY LANE

Marr Bridge

B1232

Water Tower

HU14

Swanland Cty Prim Sch

Royd Top

Humber Dale

Mast

Hessle Mount Farm

Gipsyville

Beech Wood

HU13

Hessle High School

Northfield

BOOTHFERRY ROAD

Trinity House Farm

Grange Farm

Thorns Copse

Humberdale Farm

JENNY BROUGH LANE

Hessle Mount Sch

Tranby Park Farm

Cemy

B6
1 WEST FIELD LA
2 QUEENSBURY WY
3 KEMP RD
4 HUMBER VW
5 HUMBERDALE CL
6 COPPER BEECH CL
7 WEST LEYS PK
8 GRANGE PK

Hawk Plantation

North Drive Plantation

Humber Field Farm

Quarry (dis)

Mast

Hessle

A63

Tithe Farm

MELTON RD   HIGH ST

FERRIBY HIGH ROAD

HUMBERDALE DR

FERRIBY ROAD

Humber Bridge Country Park

Toll

South Field

178

Business Park

Waterside Business Park

Liby

North Ferriby

Hotel

Hessle Haven

Whitegates Mushroom Farm

Wolds Way

Ferriby

MARINE AV

RIVERVIEW

B7
1 NORTHDALE PK
2 WAULDBY VW
3 WOOD VW
4 THE GREEN
5 WESTERDALE
6 MEADOW WK
7 THE SPINNEY
8 CROWTHER WY
9 WELTON WOLD VW
10 DALE CL
11 DOWER RI
12 PRIORY CL
13 HOLGATE PL
14 CHANTRY WAY E
15 SYKES CL
16 CHANTRY WY
17 ON HILL
18 ST MICHAEL'S MT

CLIFF RD

1 WEST HILL
2 CLIFF TOP LA
3 CLIFF DR
4 SOUTHFIELD

Wolds Way

Redcliff Channel

A5
1 GREENWAYS
2 THE PADDOCK
3 WOODGATES MOUNT
4 CROFT PK
5 MOUNT VW
6 SWANLAND GARTH
7 WOODLANDS RI
8 THE RISE
9 WEST PARKLANDS DR
10 PARKLANDS DR
11 PARKLANDS CRES
12 ASTON HALL DR
13 WOODGATES CL
14 SPINNEY CROFT CL
15 ROXTON HALL DR
16 WHITE HOUSE MEWS
17 TURNER'S LA
18 ASHDALE PK
19 WHITE HOUSE GARTH

Redcliff Sand

Humber Bridge

A15

BARTON-UPON-HUMBER

Barton Waterside

Waters' Edge Country Park

Superstore

Chowder Ness

Viking Way

Hotel

Chimney

WATERSIDE RD

B1218

Ropewalk Gall

FALKLAND WY

Far Ings Nature Reserve

Outdoor Pursuits Centre

Barton Cliff

Visitor Centre

DN18

Barton-on-Humber

South Cliff Farm

FAR INGS LANE

FAR INGS RD

Blow Wells Plantation

DAM ROAD

Recn Gd

St Peters CE Prim Sch

Bluecoat Farm

HUMBER RD

South Ferriby Cliff

Barton Cliff Quarry (dis)

New Quarry (dis)

GRAVEL PIT ROAD

Westfield House

WEST ACRIDGE

Leggott's Quarry (dis)

WESTFIELD ROAD

Westfield Farm

WESTFIELD RD

A4
1 SANDS CT
2 READING ROOM YARD
3 SCHOOL LA
4 WOOD DR
5 NUNBURNHOLME AV
6 BEECH DR
7 CHURCH AV
8 WILSON CL
9 TRIANGLE DR
10 ELMTREE AV
11 COLLIER CL
12 EAST MOUNT
13 THE TRIANGLE
14 PARKFIELD AV
15 WEST VW
16 SELWYN AV
17 THE RIDINGS
18 DERWENT AV
19 THE PICKERINGS
20 OLD POND PL
21 SOUTHFIELD DR
22 REDCLIFF DR

E1
1 BARRACLOUGH'S LA
2 ROPERY LA
3 STABLE LA
4 HAVEN RD
5 VICTORIA DR
6 COUNCIL TER
7 CASTLEDYKE W
8 FLEETGATE
9 OVERTON CT
10 PONDS WY
11 WESTERN DR
12 MALTBY LA
13 REGENCY CT
14 WOOD CL

F1
1 TRINITY WK
2 VICTORY WY
3 HARRIER RD
4 NURSERY CL
5 QUEEN'S AV
6 SEDGE CL
7 GREENWAY
8 NEWPORT ST
9 WHISTON WY
10 TREECE GDNS
11 FINKLE LA
12 EAST GR
13 SOUTERGATE
14 WILLOW DR
15 EAST ACRIDGE

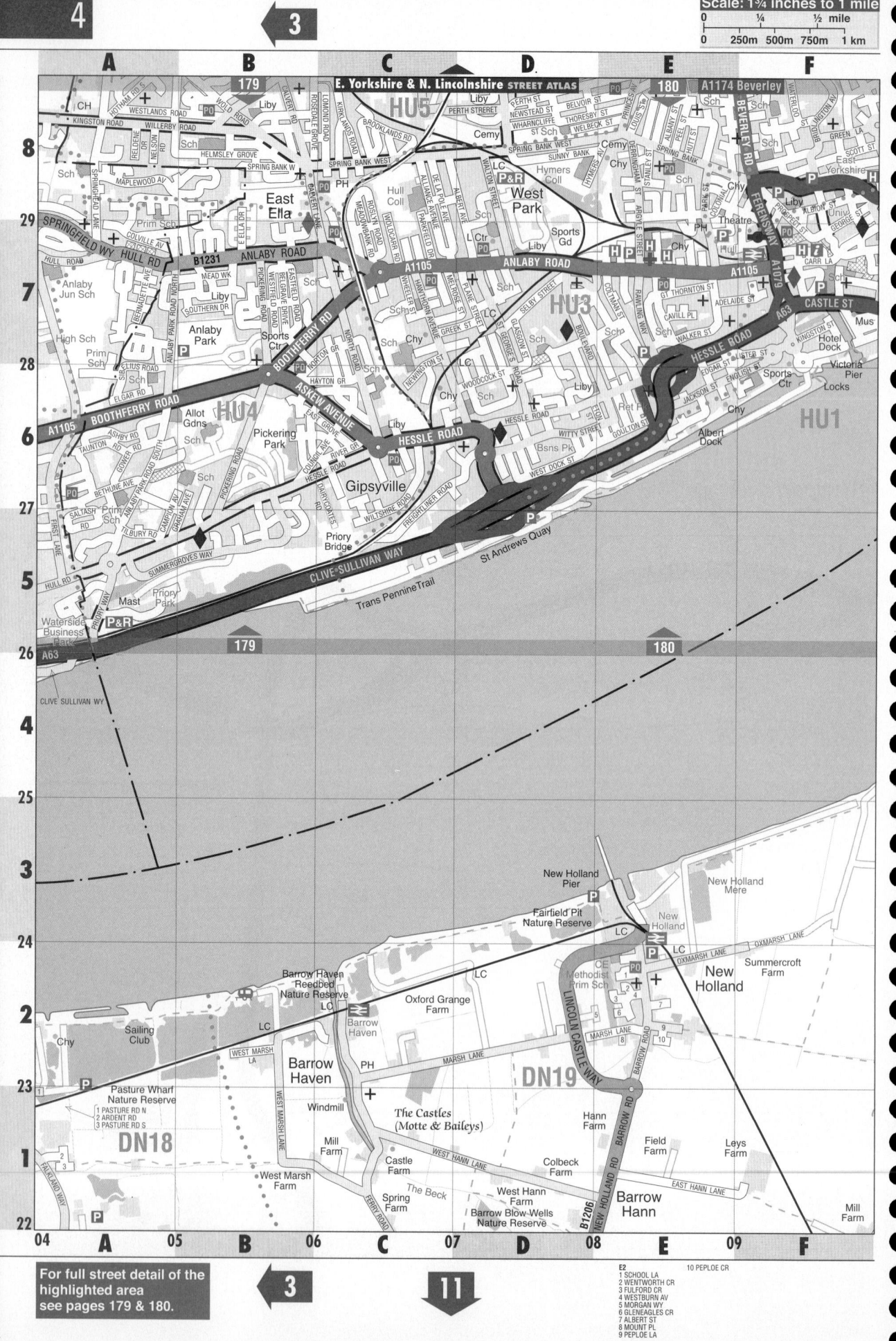

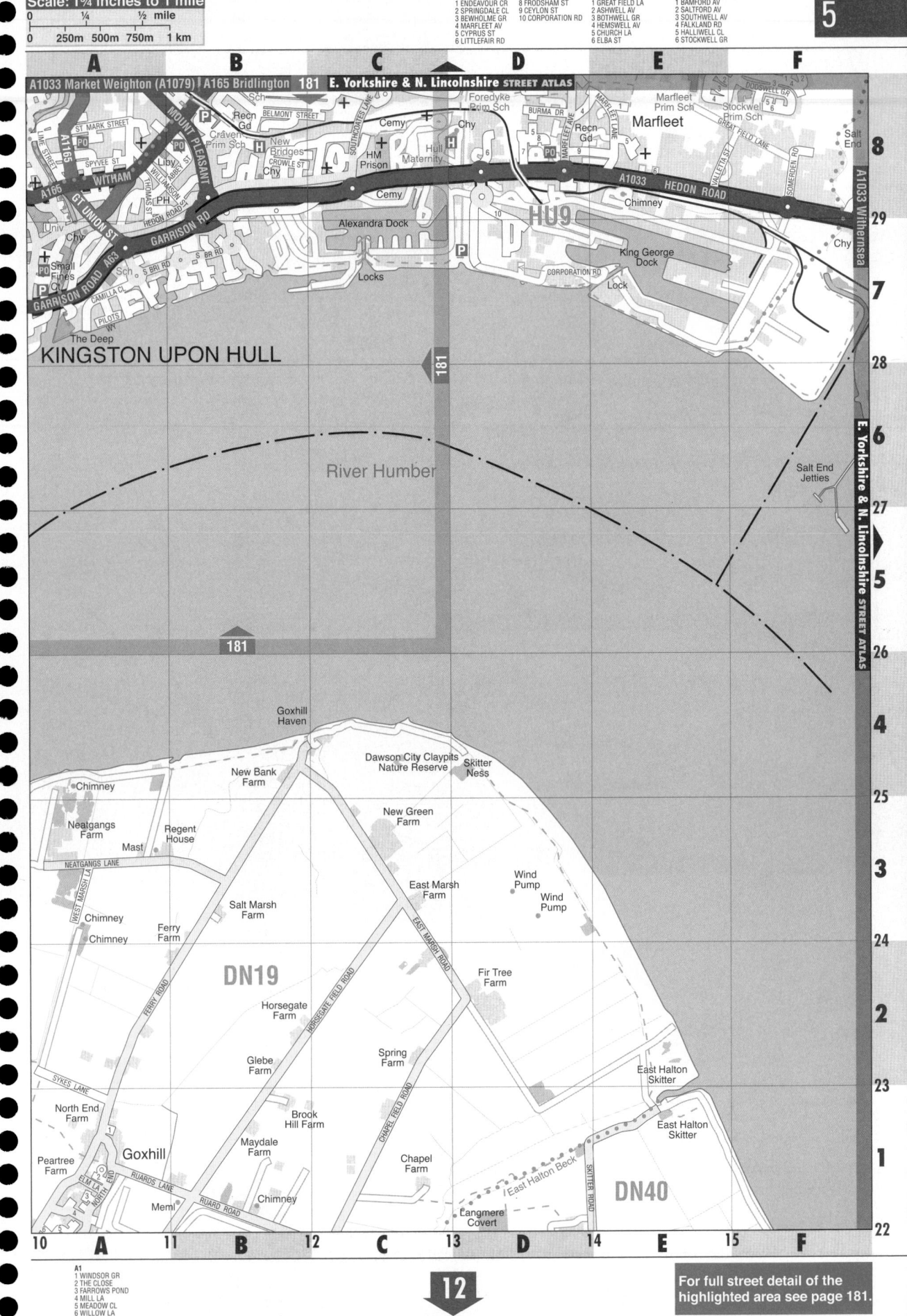

Scale: 1¾ inches to 1 mile

0   ¼   ½ mile
0   250m 500m 750m 1 km

D8
1 ENDEAVOUR CR
2 SPRINGDALE CL
3 BEWHOLME GR
4 MARFLEET AV
5 CYPRUS ST
6 LITTLEFAIR RD

7 DELHI ST
8 FRODSHAM ST
9 CEYLON ST
10 CORPORATION RD

E8
1 GREAT FIELD LA
2 ASHWELL AV
3 BOTHWELL GR
4 HEMSWELL AV
5 CHURCH LA
6 ELBA ST

F8
1 BAMFORD AV
2 SALTFORD AV
3 SOUTHWELL AV
4 FALKLAND RD
5 HALLIWELL CL
6 STOCKWELL GR

7 TOWER HOUSE LA

A1033 Market Weighton (A1079)   A165 Bridlington   181   E. Yorkshire & N. Lincolnshire STREET ATLAS

E. Yorkshire & N. Lincolnshire STREET ATLAS

KINGSTON UPON HULL

River Humber

Marfleet

HU9

Alexandra Dock

King George Dock

Salt End

Salt End Jetties

The Deep

Goxhill Haven

New Bank Farm

Dawson City Claypits Nature Reserve

Skitter Ness

Chimney

Neatgangs Farm

Regent House

New Green Farm

Mast

Salt Marsh Farm

East Marsh Farm

Wind Pump

Wind Pump

Chimney

Ferry Farm

Chimney

DN19

Fir Tree Farm

Horsegate Farm

Glebe Farm

Spring Farm

East Halton Skitter

East Halton Skitter

North End Farm

Brook Hill Farm

Maydale Farm

Chapel Farm

DN40

Peartree Farm

Goxhill

Meml

Ruard Road

Chimney

Langmere Covert

East Halton Beck

For full street detail of the highlighted area see page 181.

A1
1 WINDSOR GR
2 THE CLOSE
3 FARROWS POND
4 MILL LA
5 MEADOW CL
6 WILLOW LA

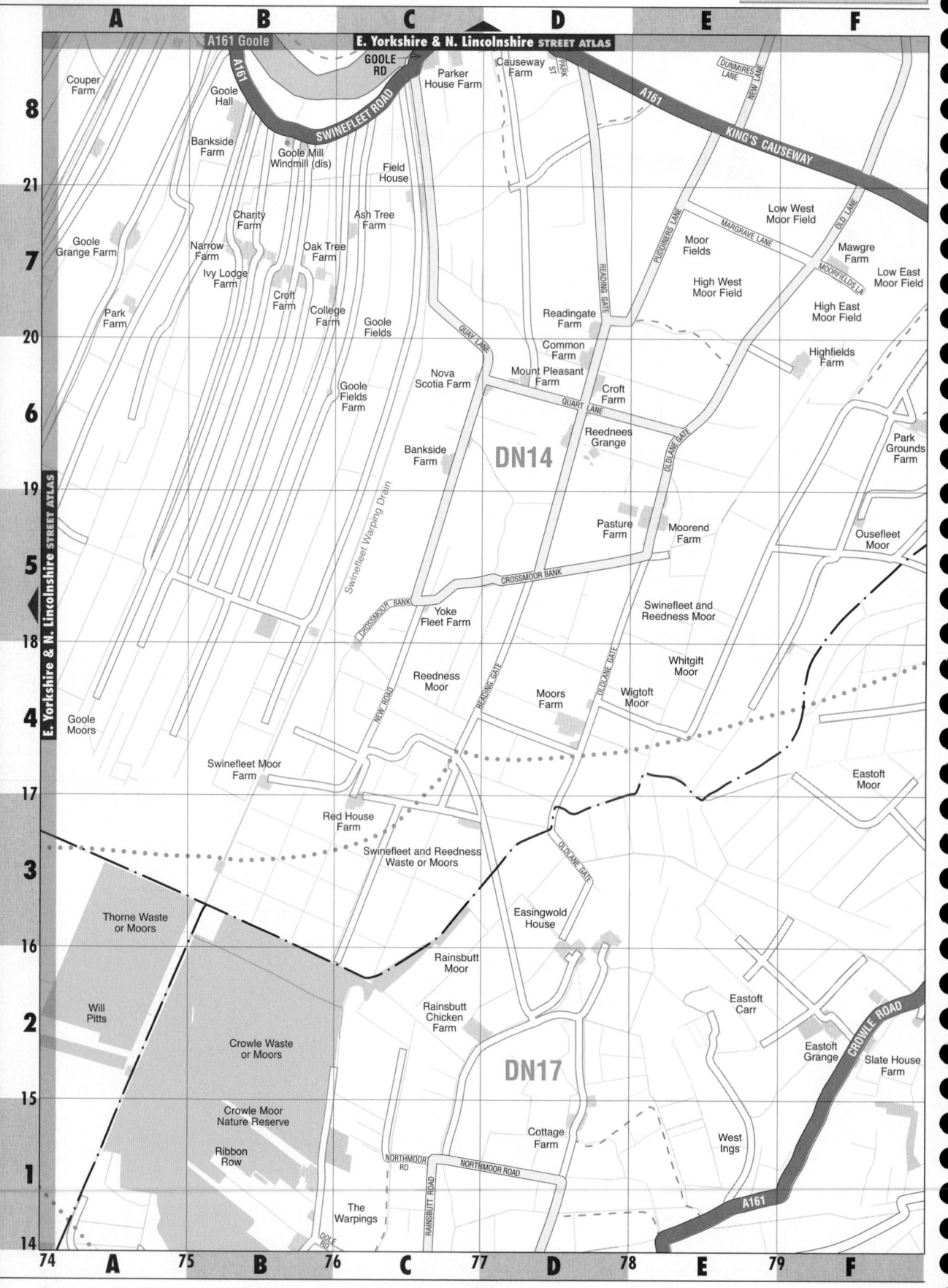

E. Yorkshire & N. Lincolnshire STREET ATLAS

A161 Goole

GOOLE RD

Couper Farm

Goole Hall

Bankside Farm

Goole Mill Windmill (dis)

SWINEFLEET ROAD

Parker House Farm

Causeway Farm

PARK ST

DUNMIRES LANE

NEW LANE

A161

KING'S CAUSEWAY

Field House

Charity Farm

Ash Tree Farm

Goole Grange Farm

Narrow Farm

Oak Tree Farm

Ivy Lodge Farm

Croft Farm

College Farm

Goole Fields

Park Farm

Goole Fields Farm

Nova Scotia Farm

Bankside Farm

Swinefleet Warping Drain

QUAY LANE

READING GATE

PUDDINERS LANE

MARGRAVE LANE

OLD LANE

Low West Moor Field

Moor Fields

Mawgre Farm

Low East Moor Field

High West Moor Field

MOORFIELDS LA

Readingate Farm

Common Farm

Mount Pleasant Farm

Croft Farm

High East Moor Field

Highfields Farm

QUART LANE

Reednees Grange

OLDLANE GATE

Park Grounds Farm

DN14

Pasture Farm

Moorend Farm

Ousefleet Moor

CROSSMOOR BANK

Yoke Fleet Farm

C CROSSMOOR BANK

Swinefleet and Reedness Moor

Goole Moors

Reedness Moor

NEW ROAD

READING GATE

Moors Farm

OLDLANE GATE

Wigtoft Moor

Whitgift Moor

Swinefleet Moor Farm

Red House Farm

Swinefleet and Reedness Waste or Moors

OLD LANE GATE

Eastoft Moor

Thorne Waste or Moors

Easingwold House

Rainsbutt Moor

Eastoft Carr

CROWLE ROAD

Will Pitts

Crowle Waste or Moors

Rainsbutt Chicken Farm

DN17

Eastoft Grange

Slate House Farm

Crowle Moor Nature Reserve

Cottage Farm

West Ings

Ribbon Row

NORTHMOOR RD

NORTHMOOR ROAD

RAINSBUTT ROAD

The Warpings

GOOLE RD

A161

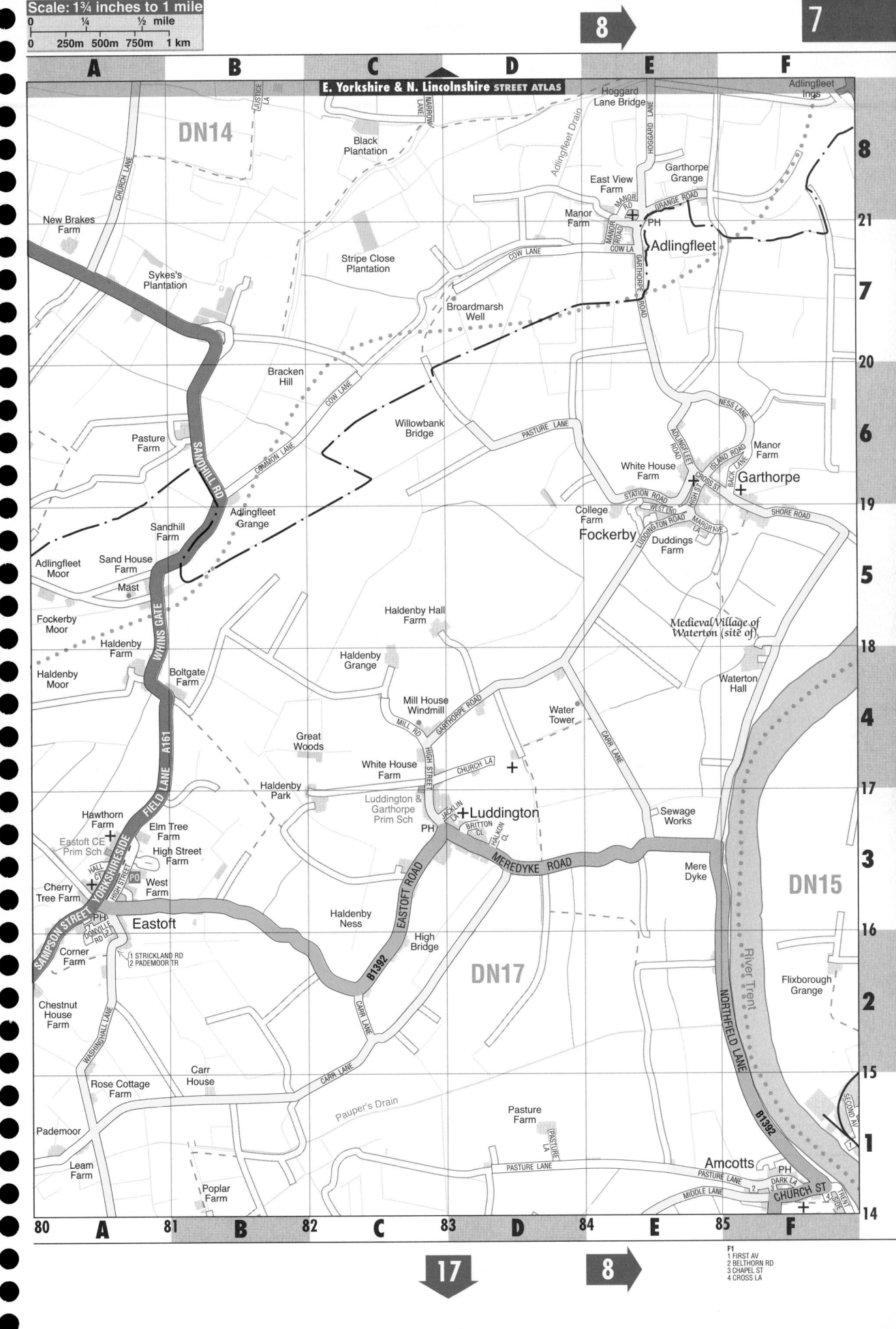

Scale: 1¾ inches to 1 mile

0 ¼ ½ mile
0 250m 500m 750m 1 km

E. Yorkshire & N. Lincolnshire STREET ATLAS

DN14

New Brakes Farm

Sykes's Plantation

Black Plantation

Stripe Close Plantation

Broardmarsh Well

Hoggard Lane Bridge

Adlingfleet Ings

East View Farm

Garthorpe Grange

Manor Farm

PH

Adlingfleet

21

Pasture Farm

Bracken Hill

Willowbank Bridge

COW LANE

PASTURE LANE

NESS LANE

White House Farm

Manor Farm

Garthorpe

College Farm

Fockerby

Duddings Farm

Medieval Village of Waterton (site of)

Sandhill Farm

Adlingfleet Grange

Sand House Farm

Adlingfleet Moor

Mast

Fockerby Moor

Haldenby Farm

Haldenby Moor

Boltgate Farm

Haldenby Hall Farm

Haldenby Grange

Mill House Windmill

Water Tower

Waterton Hall

Great Woods

White House Farm

Haldenby Park

Luddington & Garthorpe Prim Sch

Luddington

Sewage Works

Hawthorn Farm

Eastoft CE Prim Sch

Elm Tree Farm

High Street Farm

Mere Dyke

DN15

Cherry Tree Farm

West Farm

Eastoft

Haldenby Ness

High Bridge

DN17

Flixborough Grange

Corner Farm

1 STRICKLAND RD
2 PADEMOOR TR

Chestnut House Farm

Rose Cottage Farm

Carr House

Pauper's Drain

Pasture Farm

Pademoor

Leam Farm

Poplar Farm

Amcotts

Pasture Lane

Middle Lane

CHURCH ST

CHURCH LANE

MEREDYKE ROAD

EASTOFT ROAD

CARR LANE

NORTHFIELD LANE

River Trent

B1392

WHINS GATE

FIELD LANE A161

SANDHILL RD

CHURCH LANE

SAMPSON STREET

YORKSHIRESIDE

WASHINGHALL LANE

GARTHORPE ROAD

STATION ROAD

LUDDINGTON ROAD

HIGH STREET

80   81   82   83   84   85

F1
1 FIRST AV
2 BELTHORN RD
3 CHAPEL ST
4 CROSS LA

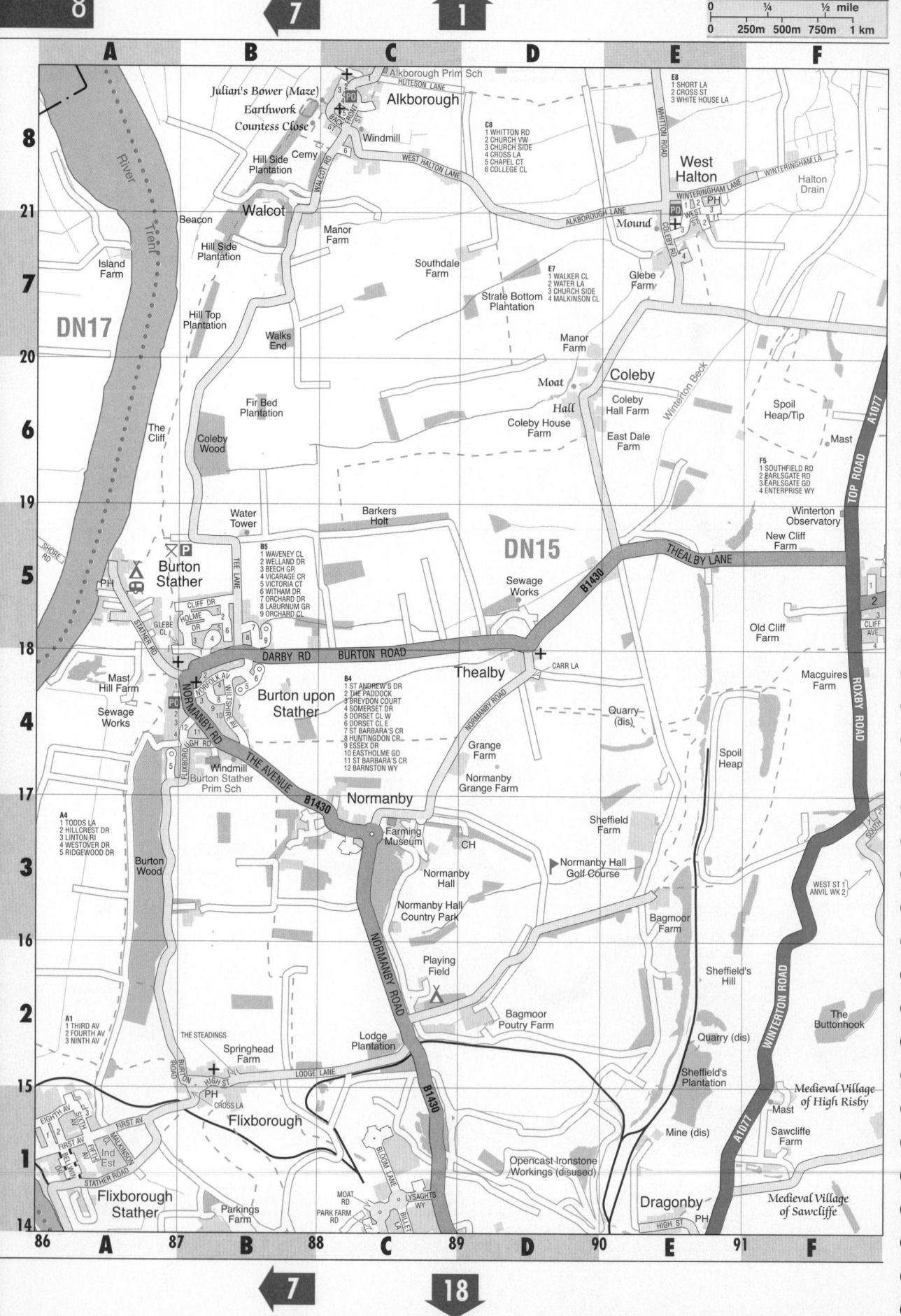

7
1
Scale: 1¾ inches to 1 mile
0 ¼ ½ mile
0 250m 500m 750m 1 km
A B C D E F
Alkborough Prim Sch
Julian's Bower (Maze)
Earthwork
Countess Close
Alkborough
HUTESON LANE
BACK ST
FRONT ST
Windmill
Cemy
Hill Side Plantation
WALCOT RD
WEST HALTON LANE
C8
1 WHITTON RD
2 CHURCH VW
3 CHURCH SIDE
4 CROSS LA
5 CHAPEL CT
6 COLLEGE CL
E8
1 SHORT LA
2 CROSS ST
3 WHITE HOUSE LA
WHITTON ROAD
West Halton
WINTERINGHAM LANE
WINTERINGHAM LA
Halton Drain
ALKBOROUGH LANE
Mound
COLEBY RD
WEST ST
PH
River Trent
Beacon
Walcot
Manor Farm
Island Farm
Hill Side Plantation
Southdale Farm
E7
1 WALKER CL
2 WATER LA
3 CHURCH SIDE
4 MALKINSON CL
Glebe Farm
Strate Bottom Plantation
DN17
Hill Top Plantation
Walks End
Manor Farm
Moat
Coleby
Hall
Coleby Hall Farm
Winterton Beck
Fir Bed Plantation
Coleby House Farm
East Dale Farm
Spoil Heap/Tip
Mast
A1077
TOP ROAD
The Cliff
Coleby Wood
F5
1 SOUTHFIELD RD
2 EARLSGATE RD
3 EARLSGATE GD
4 ENTERPRISE WY
Barkers Holt
Winterton Observatory
Water Tower
SHORE RD
DN15
New Cliff Farm
THEALBY LANE
B1430
Burton Stather
B5
1 WAVENEY CL
2 WELLAND DR
3 BEECH GR
4 VICARAGE CR
5 VICTORIA CT
6 WITHAM DR
7 ORCHARD DR
8 LABURNUM GR
9 ORCHARD CL
TEE LANE
Sewage Works
PH
CLIFF DR
HOLME DR
GLEBE CL
STATHER RD
Old Cliff Farm
CLIFF AVE
DARBY RD
BURTON ROAD
Thealby
CARR LA
Macguires Farm
Mast Hill Farm
NORFOLK AV
WILTSHIRE AV
Burton upon Stather
B4
1 ST ANDREW'S DR
2 THE PADDOCK
3 BREYDON COURT
4 SOMERSET DR
5 DORSET CL W
6 DORSET CL E
7 ST BARBARA'S CR
8 HUNTINGDON CR
9 ESSEX DR
10 EASTHOLME GD
11 ST BARBARA'S CR
12 BARNSTON WY
NORMANBY ROAD
Quarry (dis)
ROXBY ROAD
Sewage Works
NORMANBY RD
HIGH RD
FLIXBOROUGH RD
THE AVENUE
Grange Farm
Spoil Heap
Windmill
Burton Stather Prim Sch
Normanby Grange Farm
A4
1 TODDS LA
2 HILLCREST DR
3 LINTON RI
4 WESTOVER DR
5 RIDGEWOOD DR
Normanby
Farming Museum
CH
Sheffield Farm
SOUTH
Burton Wood
Normanby Hall
Normanby Hall Golf Course
WEST ST 1
ANVIL WK 2
Normanby Hall Country Park
Bagmoor Farm
NORMANBY ROAD
Playing Field
Sheffield's Hill
WINTERTON ROAD
A1
1 THIRD AV
2 FOURTH AV
3 NINTH AV
THE STEADINGS
Springhead Farm
Lodge Plantation
Bagmoor Poutry Farm
The Buttonhook
Quarry (dis)
BURTON ROAD
HIGH ST
LODGE LANE
Sheffield's Plantation
Medieval Village of High Risby
PH
CROSS LA
EIGHTH AV
SIXTH AV
FIRST AV
Flixborough
Mast
MALKINSON CL
FIFTH AV
Ind Est
BELLWIN DR
STATHER ROAD
Mine (dis)
Sawcliffe Farm
BLOOM LANE
Opencast Ironstone Workings (disused)
Flixborough Stather
MOAT RD
PARK FARM RD
LYSAGHTS WY
BILLET LA
Parkings Farm
Dragonby
PH
HIGH ST
Medieval Village of Sawcliffe
86 A 87 B 88 C 89 D 90 E 91 F
7
18

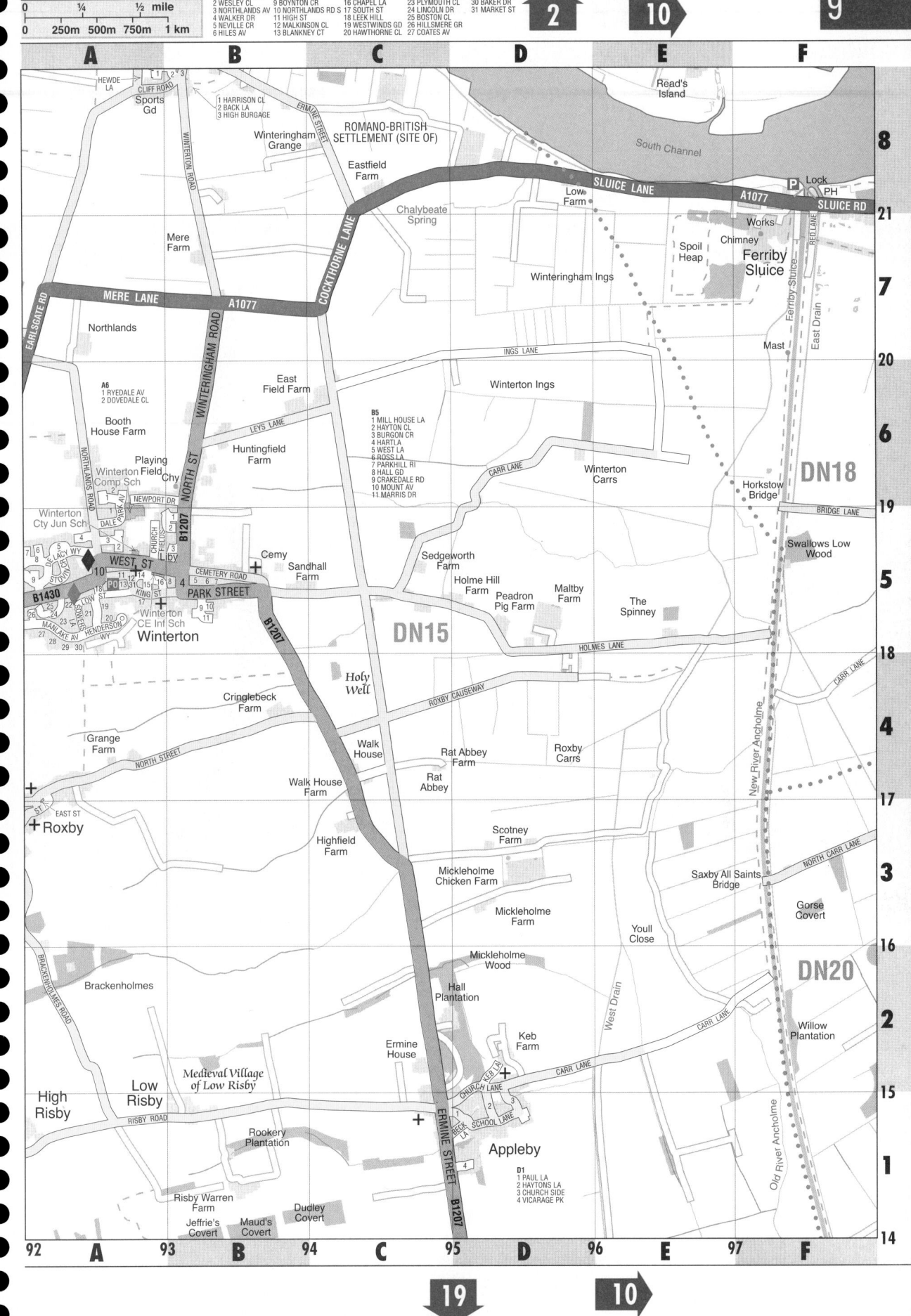

Scale: 1¾ inches to 1 mile

0   ¼   ½ mile
0   250m 500m 750m 1 km

A5
1 FARNDALE WY
2 WESLEY CL
3 NORTHLANDS AV
4 WALKER DR
5 NEVILLE DR
6 HILES AV

7 MARMION DR
8 TEANBY DR
9 BOYNTON CR
10 NORTHLANDS RD S
11 HIGH ST
12 MALKINSON CL
13 BLANKNEY CT

14 CHURCH SIDE
15 QUEEN ST
16 CHAPEL LA
17 SOUTH ST
18 LEEK HILL
19 WESTWINDS GD
20 HAWTHORNE CL

21 MALKINSON CL
22 WATERLOW DR
23 PLYMOUTH CL
24 LINCOLN DR
25 BOSTON CL
26 HILLSMERE GR
27 COATES AV

28 BENNETT DR
29 DRIFFIL WY
30 BAKER DR
31 MARKET ST

HEWDE LA
CLIFF ROAD
Sports Gd
WINTERTON ROAD
1 HARRISON CL
2 BACK LA
3 HIGH BURGAGE
ERMINE STREET
Winteringham Grange
ROMANO-BRITISH SETTLEMENT (SITE OF)
Eastfield Farm
Read's Island
South Channel
Low Farm
SLUICE LANE
A1077
P Lock
PH
SLUICE RD
Works
Chimney
Ferriby Sluice
21

Chalybeate Spring
Winteringham Ings
Spoil Heap
COCKTHORNE LANE
Mere Farm
Winterton Ings
Ferriby Sluice
RED LANE
East Drain

EARLSGATE RD
MERE LANE   A1077
Northlands
INGS LANE
Mast
20

A6
1 RYEDALE AV
2 DOVEDALE CL
East Field Farm
Winterton Ings
DN18
7

WINTERINGHAM ROAD
Booth House Farm
LEYS LANE
Huntingfield Farm
B5
1 MILL HOUSE LA
2 HAYTON CL
3 BURGON CR
4 HARTLA
5 WEST LA
6 ROSS LA
7 PARKHILL RI
8 HALL GD
9 CRAKEDALE RD
10 MOUNT AV
11 MARRIS DR
CARR LANE
Winterton Carrs
Horkstow Bridge
BRIDGE LANE
19

Playing Field
Winterton Comp Sch
Chy
NORTH ST
NEWPORT DR
Winterton Cty Jun Sch
DALE
PARK AV
Cemy
Sedgeworth Farm
Swallows Low Wood

WEST ST
CHURCH FIELDS
by
CEMETERY ROAD
Sandhall Farm
Holme Hill Farm
Maltby Farm
5

B1430
PO
KING ST
HENDERSON WY
PARK STREET
Peadron Pig Farm
The Spinney
New River Ancholme

MAIDLAKE AV
Winterton CE Inf Sch
Winterton
B1207
DN15
HOLMES LANE
18

Cringlebeck Farm
Holy Well
ROXBY CAUSEWAY
CARR LANE
4

Grange Farm
NORTH STREET
Walk House
Rat Abbey Farm
Roxby Carrs
17

EAST ST
Roxby
Walk House Farm
Rat Abbey
Scotney Farm
Saxby All Saints, Bridge
NORTH CARR LANE
Gorse Covert
3

Highfield Farm
Mickleholme Chicken Farm
Youll Close
DN20
16

Mickleholme Farm
Brackenholmes
Mickleholme Wood
WEST DRAIN
CARR LANE
Willow Plantation
2

BRACKENHOLMES ROAD
Hall Plantation
Keb Farm
KEB LA
Old River Ancholme
15

Ermine House
CHURCH LANE
High Risby
Low Risby
Medieval Village of Low Risby
RISBY ROAD
SCHOOL LANE
BECK LA
Appleby

Rookery Plantation
ERMINE STREET
D1
1 PAUL LA
2 HAYTONS LA
3 CHURCH SIDE
4 VICARAGE PK
1

Risby Warren Farm
Jeffrie's Covert
Maud's Covert
Dudley Covert
B1207
14

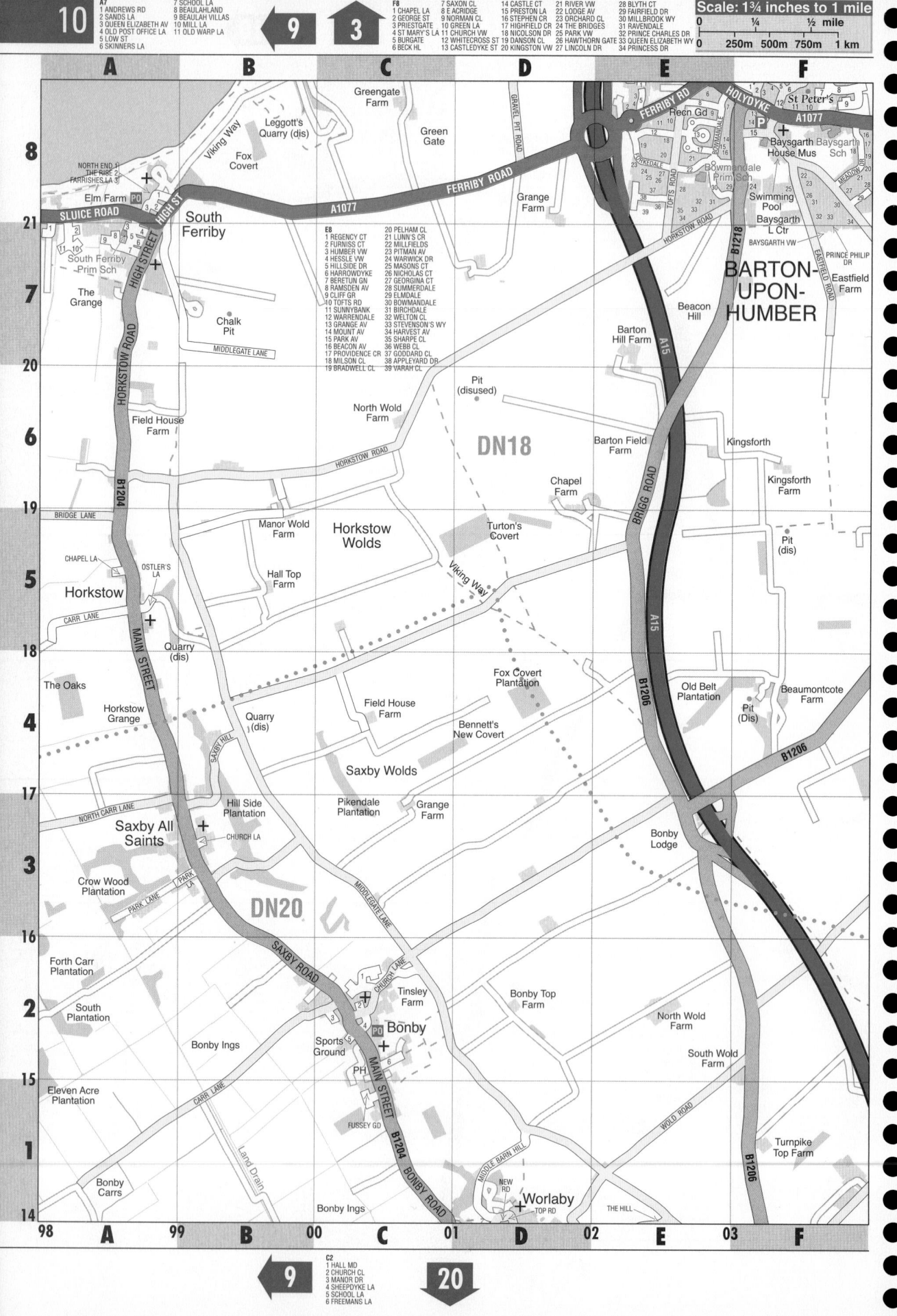

A7
1 ANDREWS RD
2 SANDS LA
3 QUEEN ELIZABETH AV
4 OLD POST OFFICE LA
5 LOW ST
6 SKINNERS LA
7 SCHOOL LA
8 BEAULAHLAND
9 BEAULAH VILLAS
10 MILL LA
11 OLD WARP LA

9

3

F8
1 CHAPEL LA
2 GEORGE ST
3 PRIESTGATE
4 ST MARY'S LA
5 BURGATE
6 BECK HL
7 SAXON CL
8 E ACRIDGE
9 NORMAN CL
10 GREEN LA
11 CHURCH VW
12 WHITECROSS ST
13 CASTLEDYKE ST
14 CASTLE CT
15 PRESTON LA
16 STEPHEN CR
17 HIGHFIELD CR
18 NICOLSON CR
19 DANSON CL
20 KINGSTON VW
21 RIVER VW
22 LODGE AV
23 ORCHARD CL
24 THE BRIDGES
25 PARK VW
26 HAWTHORN GATE
27 LINCOLN DR
28 BLYTH CT
29 FAIRFIELD DR
30 MILLBROOK WY
31 RAVENDALE
32 PRINCE CHARLES DR
33 QUEEN ELIZABETH WY
34 PRINCESS DR

E8
1 REGENCY CT
2 FURNISS CT
3 HUMBER VW
4 HESSLE VW
5 HILLSIDE DR
6 HARROWDYKE
7 BERETUN GN
8 RAMSDEN AV
9 CLIFF GR
10 TOFTS RD
11 SUNNYBANK
12 WARRENDALE
13 GRANGE AV
14 MOUNT AV
15 PARK AV
16 BEACON AV
17 PROVIDENCE CR
18 MILSON CL
19 BRADWELL CL
20 PELHAM CL
21 LUNN'S CR
22 MILLFIELDS
23 PITMAN AV
24 WARWICK DR
25 MASONS CT
26 NICHOLAS CT
27 GEORGINA CT
28 SUMMERDALE
29 ELMDALE
30 BOWMANDALE
31 BIRCHDALE
32 WELTON CL
33 STEVENSON'S WY
34 HARVEST AV
35 SHARPE CL
36 WEBB CL
37 GODDARD DR
38 APPLEYARD DR
39 VARAH CL

9

C2
1 HALL MD
2 CHURCH CL
3 MANOR DR
4 SHEEPDYKE LA
5 SCHOOL LA
6 FREEMANS LA

20

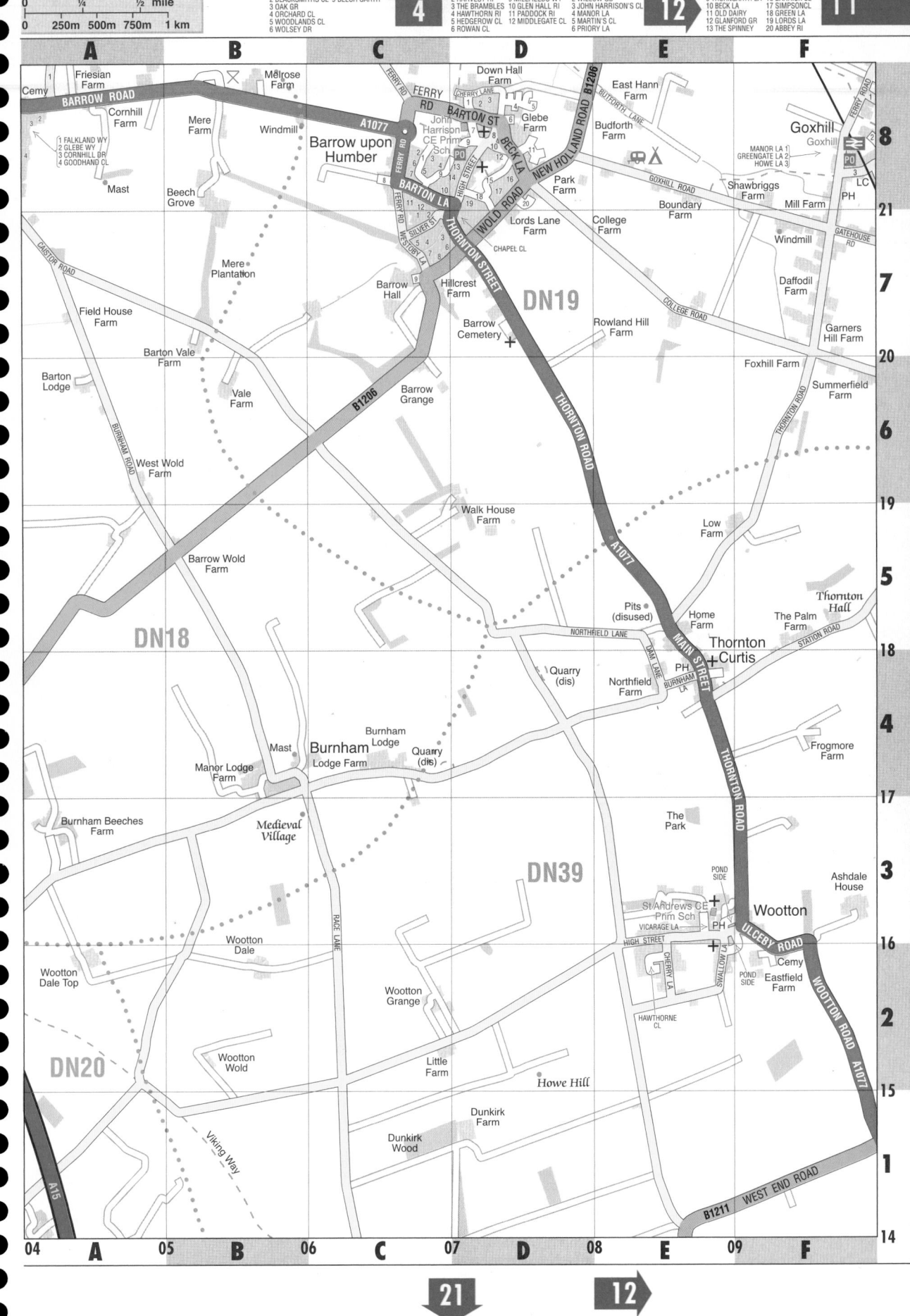

C7
1 HIGHFIELDS
2 BLACKSMITHS CL
3 OAK GR
4 ORCHARD CL
5 WOODLANDS CL
6 WOLSEY DR
7 PARK VIEW CL
8 FEATHER LA
9 BEECH GARTH

C8
1 CHESTNUT RI
2 HARVEST RI
3 THE BRAMBLES
4 HAWTHORN RI
5 HEDGEROW CL
6 ROWAN CL
7 SCHOFIELD CL
8 MILL LA
9 MILLFIELDS WY
10 GLEN HALL RI
11 PADDOCK CL
12 MIDDLEGATE CL

D8
1 NORTH ST
2 WILLOW GD
3 JOHN HARRISON'S CL
4 MANOR LA
5 MARTIN'S CL
6 PRIORY LA
7 NORTH ST
8 CROSS ST
9 THORNGARTH LA
10 BECK LA
11 OLD DAIRY
12 GLANFORD GR
13 THE SPINNEY
14 THE GR
15 PALMER LA
16 BARRICK CL
17 SIMPSONCL
18 GREEN LA
19 LORDS LA
20 ABBEY RI

4   12

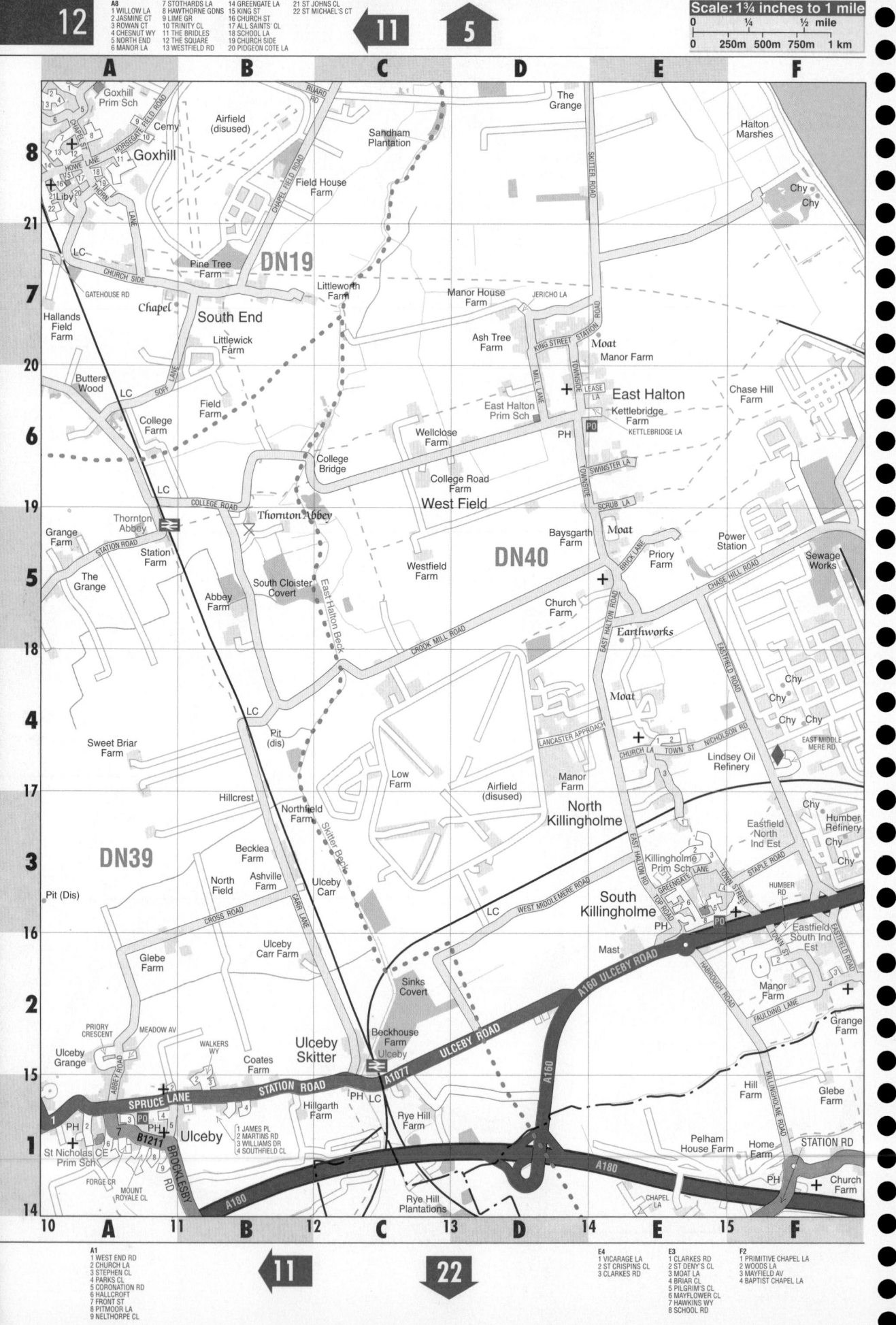

A8
1 WILLOW LA
2 JASMINE CT
3 ROWAN CT
4 CHESNUT WY
5 NORTH END
6 MANOR LA

7 STOTHARDS LA
8 HAWTHORNE GDNS
9 LIME GR
10 TRINITY CL
11 THE BRIDLES
12 THE SQUARE
13 WESTFIELD RD

14 GREENGATE LA
15 KING ST
16 CHURCH ST
17 ALL SAINTS' CL
18 SCHOOL LA
19 CHURCH SIDE
20 PIDGEON COTE LA

21 ST JOHNS CL
22 ST MICHAEL'S CT

11
5

DN19
Goxhill Prim Sch
Cemy
Goxhill
Airfield (disused)
The Grange
Sandham Plantation
Halton Marshes
Chy Chy

Field House Farm
Howe Lane
Liby

Pine Tree Farm
Littleworth Farm
Manor House Farm
JERICHO LA
Moat
Manor Farm
Chase Hill Farm

Hallands Field Farm
Chapel
South End
Littlewick Farm
Ash Tree Farm
East Halton
KING STREET
STATION ROAD

Butters Wood
Field Farm
Wellclose Farm
East Halton Prim Sch
Kettlebridge Farm
KETTLEBRIDGE LA
PH
PO
LEASE LA

College Farm
College Bridge
College Road Farm
West Field
SWINSTER LA
Moat

Grange Farm
Thornton Abbey
College Road
DN40
Baysgarth Farm
Moat
Power Station
SCRUB LA

The Grange
Station Farm
STATION ROAD
Westfield Farm
Priory Farm
BRICK LANE
Sewage Works

Abbey Farm
South Cloister Covert
Church Farm
Earthworks
CHASE HILL ROAD
EASTFIELD ROAD

Sweet Briar Farm
Pit (dis)
CROOK MILL ROAD
Moat
Chy Chy
Chy Chy
EAST MIDDLE MERE RD

Hillcrest
Northfield Farm
Low Farm
Airfield (disused)
Manor Farm
LANCASTER APPROACH
CHURCH LA
TOWN ST
NICHOLSON RD
Lindsey Oil Refinery

DN39
Becklea Farm
North Field
Ashville Farm
Ulceby Carr
North Killingholme
Killingholme Prim Sch
GREENGATE LA
STAPLE RD
Eastfield North Ind Est
Humber Refinery
Chy Chy
Chy

Pit (Dis)
CROSS ROAD
CARR LANE
LC
WEST MIDDLEMERE ROAD
South Killingholme
PH
PO
TOWN STREET
HUMBER RD
Eastfield South Ind Est

Glebe Farm
Ulceby Carr Farm
Sinks Covert
Mast
HARROLD RD
Manor Farm
Grange Farm

PRIORY CRESCENT
MEADOW AV
WALKERS WY
A160 ULCEBY ROAD
FAULDING LANE

Ulceby Grange
Coates Farm
Ulceby Skitter
Beckhouse Farm Ulceby
ULCEBY ROAD
A160
Hill Farm
Glebe Farm
KILLINGHOLME ROAD

ABBEY ROAD
SPRUCE LANE
STATION ROAD
A1077
PH LC
Hillgarth Farm
Rye Hill Farm
STATION RD
Church Farm

PH
B1211
Ulceby
1 JAMES PL
2 MARTINS RD
3 WILLIAMS DR
4 SOUTHFIELD CL
Pelham House Farm
Home Farm
PH

St Nicholas CE Prim Sch
FORGE CR
MOUNT ROYALE CL
BROCKLESBY RD
A180
Rye Hill Plantations
A180
CHAPEL LA

A1
1 WEST END RD
2 CHURCH LA
3 STEPHEN CL
4 PARKS CL
5 CORONATION RD
6 HALLCROFT
7 FRONT ST
8 PITMOOR LA
9 NELTHORPE CL

E4
1 VICARAGE LA
2 ST CRISPINS CL
3 CLARKES RD

E3
1 CLARKES RD
2 ST DENY'S CL
3 MOAT LA
4 BRIAR CL
5 PILGRIM'S CL
6 MAYFLOWER CL
7 HAWKINS WY
8 SCHOOL RD

F2
1 PRIMITIVE CHAPEL LA
2 WOODS LA
3 MAYFIELD AV
4 BAPTIST CHAPEL LA

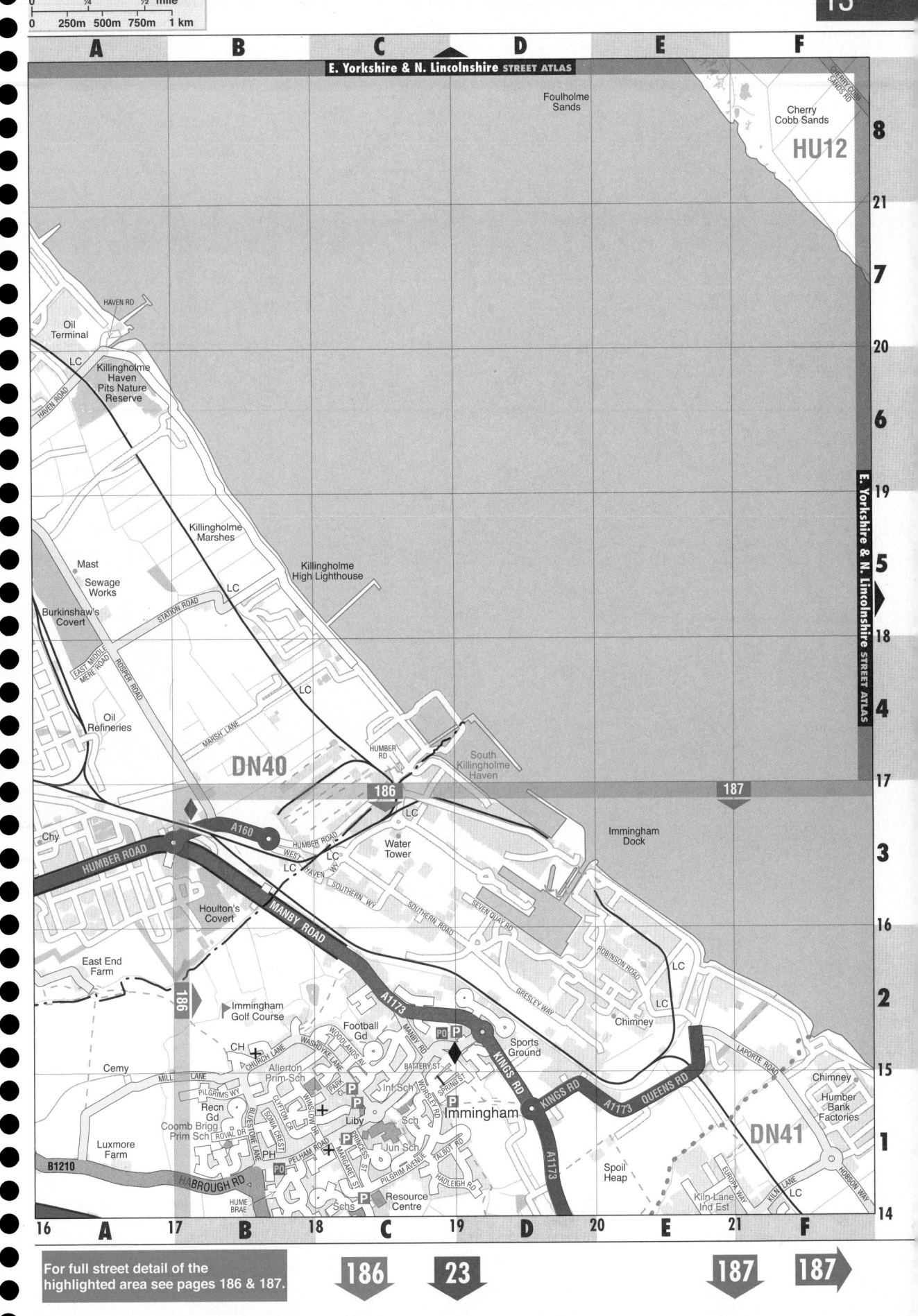

E. Yorkshire & N. Lincolnshire STREET ATLAS

E. Yorkshire & N. Lincolnshire STREET ATLAS

Foulholme
Sands

Cherry
Cobb Sands

HU12

Oil
Terminal

HAVEN RD

LC

HAVEN ROAD

Killingholme
Haven
Pits Nature
Reserve

Killingholme
Marshes

Killingholme
High Lighthouse

Mast

Sewage
Works

STATION ROAD

LC

Burkinshaw's
Covert

EAST MIDDLE
MERE ROAD

ROSPER ROAD

LC

MARSH LANE

LC

Oil
Refineries

DN40

HUMBER
RD

South
Killingholme
Haven

Immingham
Dock

186

Chy

A160

HUMBER ROAD

HUMBER ROAD

WEST HAVEN

LC

LC

LC

Water
Tower

SOUTHERN WY

SOUTHERN ROAD

SEVEN QUAY RD

187

LC

Houlton's
Covert

MANBY ROAD

186

ROBINSON ROAD

GRESLEY WAY

LC

LC

East End
Farm

Immingham
Golf Course

Football
Gd

A1173

WOODLANDS AV

MANBY RD

PO P

Chimney

Cemy

CH

CHURCH LANE

WASHDYKE LANE

PARK CL

BATTERY ST

Sports
Ground

KINGS RD

Sports
Ground

Chimney

DN41

MILL LANE

Allerton
Prim Sch

CLIFTON RD

Inf Sch

PRESLEY RD

SPRING ST

P

KINGS RD

A1173   QUEENS RD

LAPORTE ROAD

Humber
Bank
Factories

PILGRIMS WY

Recn
Gd

WINSLOW DR

SONIA CREST

Liby

Sch

Immingham

Luxmore
Farm

Coomb Brigg
Prim Sch

ROYAL DR

BLUESTONE AVE

Jun Sch

TALBOT RD

A1173

Spoil
Heap

EUROPA WAY

KILN LANE

HOBSON WAY

LC

B1210

PH

PELHAM ROAD

MARGARET ST

PRINCESS ST

PILGRIM AVENUE

HADLEIGH RD

Kiln Lane
Ind Est

HABROUGH RD

PO

Resource
Centre

Schs

Kiln Lane
Ind Est

HUME
BRAE

For full street detail of the
highlighted area see pages 186 & 187.

186   23   187 187

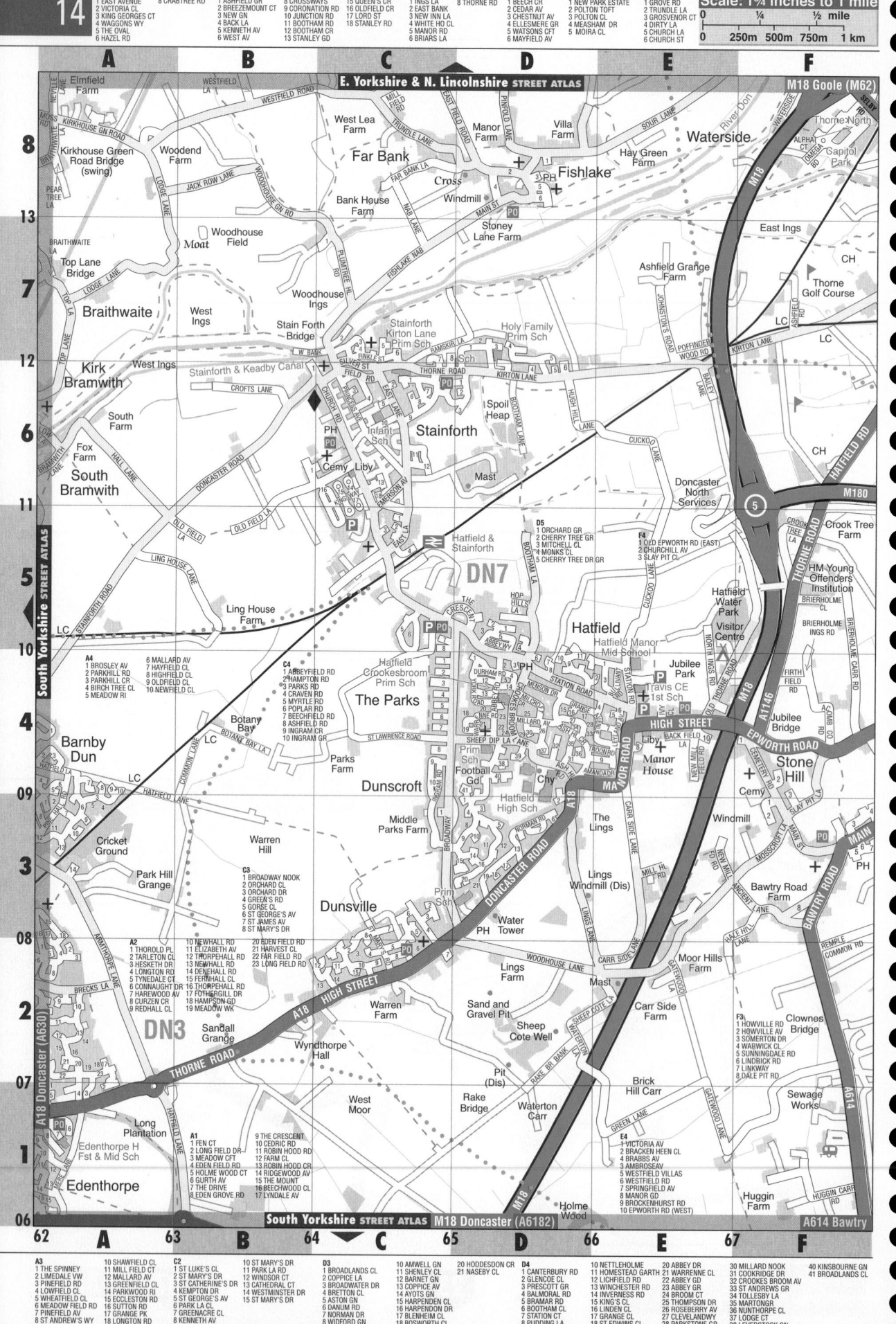
C5
1 EAST AVENUE
2 VICTORIA CL
3 KING GEORGES CT
4 WAGGONS WY
5 THE OVAL
6 HAZEL RD
7 NORWOOD RD
8 CRABTREE RD
C6
1 ASHFIELD GR
2 BREEZEMOUNT CT
3 NEW GN
4 BACK LA
5 KENNETH AV
6 WEST AV
7 NUTFIELDS GR
8 CROSSWAYS
9 CORONATION RD
10 JUNCTION RD
11 BOOTHAM RD
12 BOOTHAM CR
13 STANLEY GD
14 DUKE ST
15 QUEEN'S CR
16 OLDFIELD CR
17 LORD ST
18 STANLEY RD
C7
1 INGS LA
2 EAST BANK
3 NEW INN LA
4 WHITE HO CL
5 MANOR RD
6 BRIARS LA
7 HOLME GD
8 THORNE RD
D6
1 BEECH CR
2 CEDAR AV
3 CHESTNUT AV
4 ELLESMERE GR
5 WATSONS CFT
6 MAYFIELD AV
D7
1 NEW PARK ESTATE
2 POLTON TOFT
3 POLTON CL
4 MEASHAM DR
5 MOIRA CL
D8
1 GROVE RD
2 TRUNDLE LA
3 GROSVENOR CT
4 DIRTY LA
5 CHURCH LA
6 CHURCH ST
Scale: 1¾ inches to 1 mile
0 ¼ ½ mile
0 250m 500m 750m 1 km
E. Yorkshire & N. Lincolnshire STREET ATLAS
M18 Goole (M62)
South Yorkshire STREET ATLAS
M18 Doncaster (A6182)
A614 Bawtry
A18 Doncaster (A630)
Fishlake
Far Bank
Waterside
Stainforth
Hatfield
Braithwaite
Kirk Bramwith
South Bramwith
The Parks
Dunscroft
Dunsville
Barnby Dun
Edenthorpe
Stone Hill
DN7
DN3
Thorne Golf Course
HM Young Offenders Institution
Hatfield Water Park
Doncaster North Services
A4
1 BROSLEY AV
2 PARKHILL RD
3 PARKHILL CR
4 BIRCH TREE CL
5 MEADOW RI
6 MALLARD AV
7 HAYFIELD CL
8 HIGHFIELD CL
9 OLDFIELD CL
10 NEWFIELD CL
C4
1 ABBEYFIELD RD
2 HAMPTON RD
3 PARKS RD
4 CRAVEN RD
5 MYRTLE RD
6 POPLAR RD
7 BEECHFIELD RD
8 ASHFIELD RD
9 INGRAM CR
10 INGRAM GR
D5
1 ORCHARD GR
2 CHERRY TREE GR
3 MITCHELL CL
4 MONKS CL
5 CHERRY TREE DR GR
F4
1 OLD EPWORTH RD (EAST)
2 CHURCHILL AV
3 SLAY PIT CL
C3
1 BROADWAY NOOK
2 ORCHARD CL
3 ORCHARD DR
4 GREEN'S RD
5 GORSE CL
6 ST GEORGE'S AV
7 ST JAMES AV
8 ST MARY'S DR
A2
1 THOROLD PL
2 TARLETON CL
3 HESKETH DR
4 LONGTON RD
5 TYNEDALE CT
6 CONNAUGHT DR
7 HAREWOOD AV
8 CURZEN CR
9 REDHALL CL
10 NEWHALL RD
11 ELIZABETH AV
12 THORPEHALL RD
13 NEWHALL RD
14 DENEHALL RD
15 FERNHALL CL
16 THORPEHALL RD
17 FOTHERGILL DR
18 HAMPSON GD
19 MEADOW WK
20 EDEN FIELD RD
21 HARVEST CL
22 FAR FIELD RD
23 LONG FIELD RD
F3
1 HOWVILLE RD
2 HOWVILLE AV
3 SOMERTON DR
4 WARWICK CL
5 SUNNINGDALE RD
6 LINDRICK RD
7 LINKWAY
8 DALE PIT RD
A1
1 FEN CT
2 LONG FIELD DR
3 MEADOW CFT
4 EDEN FIELD RD
5 HOLME WOOD CT
6 GURTH AV
7 THE DRIVE
8 EDEN GROVE RD
9 THE CRESCENT
10 CEDRIC RD
11 ROBIN HOOD RD
12 FARM CL
13 ROBIN HOOD CR
14 RIDGEWOOD AV
15 THE MOUNT
16 BEECHWOOD CL
17 LYNDALE AV
E4
1 VICTORIA AV
2 BRACKEN HEEN CL
4 BRABBS AV
3 AMBROSEAV
5 WESTFIELD VILLAS
6 WESTFIELD RD
7 SPRINGFIELD AV
8 MANOR GD
9 BROCKENHURST RD
10 EPWORTH RD (WEST)
A3
1 THE SPINNEY
2 LIMEDALE VW
3 PINEFIELD RD
4 LOWFIELD CL
5 WHEATFIELD CL
6 MEADOW FIELD RD
7 PINEFIELD AV
8 ST ANDREW'S WY
9 HEATHFIELD CL
10 SHAWFIELD CL
11 MILL FIELD CT
12 MALLARD AV
13 GREENFIELD CL
14 PARKWOOD RI
15 ECCLESTON RD
16 SUTTON RD
17 GRANGE PK
18 LONGTON RD
C2
1 ST LUKE'S CL
2 ST MARY'S DR
3 ST CATHERINE'S DR
4 KEMPTON DR
5 ST GEORGE'S AV
6 PARK LA CL
7 GREENACRE CL
8 KENNETH AV
9 HAWTHORNE AV
10 ST MARY'S DR
11 PARK LA RD
12 WINDSOR CT
13 CATHEDRAL CT
14 WESTMINSTER DR
15 ST MARY'S DR
D3
1 BROADLANDS CL
2 COPPICE LA
3 BROADWATER DR
4 BRETTON CL
5 ASTON GN
6 DANUM RD
7 NORMAN DR
8 WIDFORD GN
9 BROADWATER DR
10 AMWELL GN
11 SHENLEY CL
12 BARNET GN
13 COPPICE AV
14 AYOTS GN
15 HARPENDEN CL
16 HARPENDEN DR
17 BLENHEIM CL
18 BOSWORTH CL
19 MILE END AV
20 HODDESDON CR
21 NASEBY CL
D4
1 CANTERBURY RD
2 GLENCOE CL
3 PRESCOTT GR
4 BALMORAL RD
5 BRAMAR RD
6 BOOTHAM CL
7 STATION CT
8 PUDDING LA
9 HUND OAK DR
10 NETTLEHOLME
11 HOMESTEAD GARTH
12 LICHFIELD RD
13 WINCHESTER RD
14 INVERNESS RD
15 KING'S CL
16 LINDEN CL
17 GRANGE CL
18 ST EDWINS CL
19 ST EDWINS DR
20 ABBEY DR
21 WARRENNE CL
22 ABBEY GD
23 ABBEY GR
24 BROOM CT
25 THOMPSON DR
26 ROSEBERRY AV
27 CLEVELANDWY
28 PARKSTONE GR
29 WHITE HO CL
30 MILLARD NOOK
31 COOKRIDGE DR
32 CROOKES BROOM AV
33 ST ANDREWS GR
34 TOLLESBY LA
35 MARTONGR
36 NUNTHORPE CL
37 LODGE CT
38 LEVERSTOCK GN
39 OAKLAND AV
40 KINSBOURNE GN
41 BROADLANDS CL

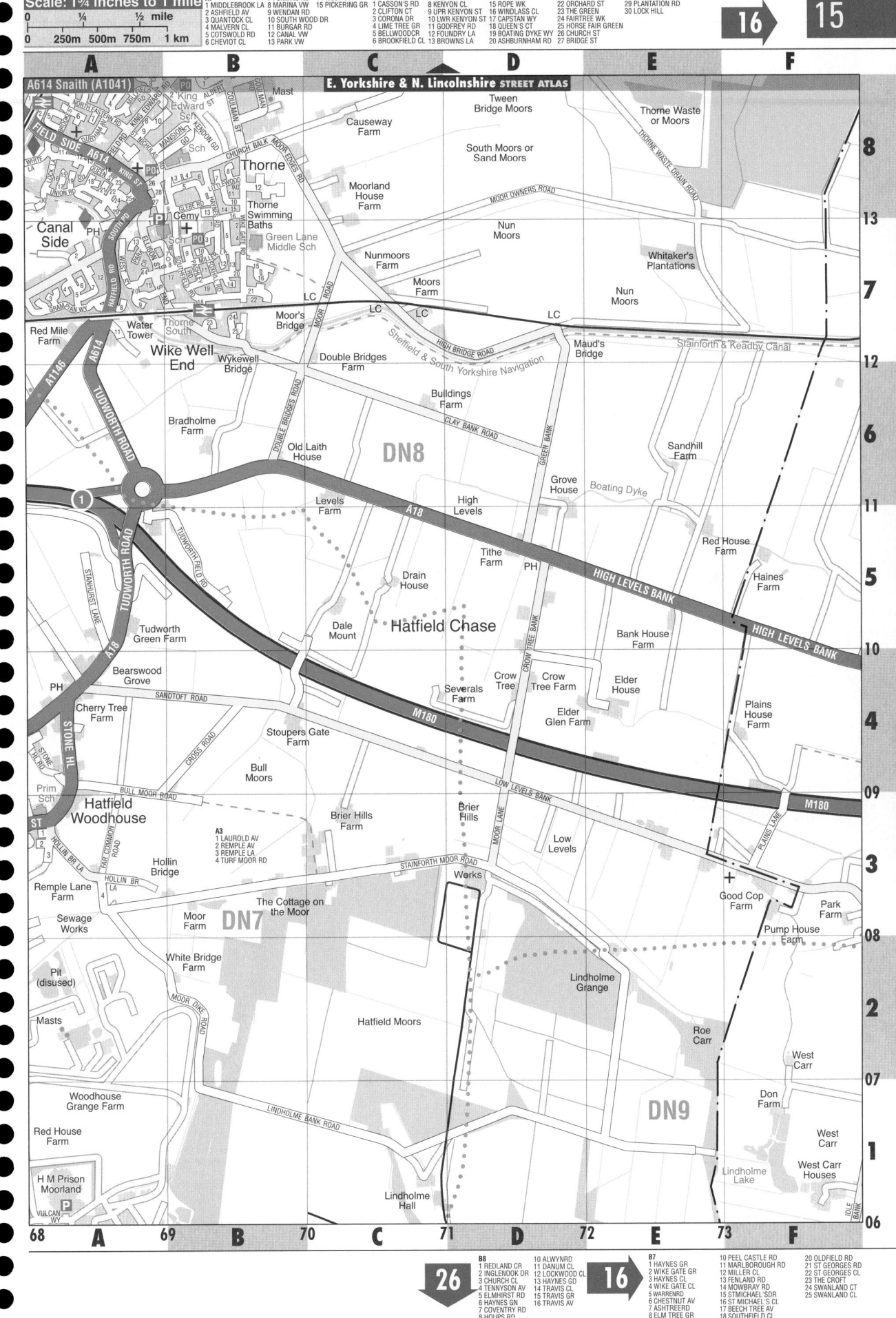

A7
1 MIDDLEBROOK LA
2 ASHFIELD AV
3 QUANTOCK CL
4 MALVERN CL
5 COTSWOLD RD
6 CHEVIOT CL

7 PENNINE RD
8 MARINA VW
9 WENDAN RD
10 SOUTH WOOD DR
11 BURGAR RD
12 CANAL VW
13 PARK VW

14 WEST CT
15 PICKERING GR

A8
1 CASSON'S RD
2 CLIFTON CT
3 CORONA DR
4 LIME TREE GR
5 BELLWOODCR
6 BROOKFIELD CL

7 FOSTER RD
8 KENYON CL
9 UPR KENYON ST
10 LWR KENYON ST
11 GODFREY RD
12 FOUNDRY LA
13 BROWNS LA

14 CHAPEL LA
15 ROPE WK
16 WINDLASS CL
17 CAPSTAN WY
18 QUEEN'S CT
19 BOATING DYKE WY
20 ASHBURNHAM WY

21 BELLE VUE TR
22 ORCHARD ST
23 THE GREEN
24 FAIRTREE WK
25 HORSE FAIR GREEN
26 CHURCH ST
27 BRIDGE ST

28 STONEGATE
29 PLANTATION RD
30 LOCK HILL

E. Yorkshire & N. Lincolnshire STREET ATLAS

Map labels:
A614 Snaith (A1041)
Thorne
Canal Side
Thorne Swimming Baths
Green Lane Middle Sch
Causeway Farm
Tween Bridge Moors
South Moors or Sand Moors
Moorland House Farm
Thorne Waste or Moors
Nunmoors Farm
Nun Moors
Whitaker's Plantations
Nun Moors
Moors Farm
Red Mile Farm
Water Tower
Thorne South
Moor's Bridge
Wike Well End
Wykewell Bridge
Double Bridges Farm
Maud's Bridge
Stainforth & Keadby Canal
Sheffield & South Yorkshire Navigation
High Bridge Road
Bradholme Farm
Buildings Farm
Clay Bank Road
Green Bank
Grove House
Sandhill Farm
DN8
Old Laith House
Levels Farm
High Levels
Red House Farm
Boating Dyke
A18
Haines Farm
Tithe Farm
PH
HIGH LEVELS BANK
Drain House
Crow Tree Bank
Tudworth Green Farm
Dale Mount
Hatfield Chase
Crow Tree
Crow Tree Farm
Bank House Farm
Elder House
Bearswood Grove
Severals Farm
M180
Elder Glen Farm
Plains House Farm
HIGH LEVELS BANK
Cherry Tree Farm
Sandtoft Road
Stoupers Gate Farm
Stanhurst Lane
Tudworth Road
Tudworthfield Rd
Cross Road
Bull Moors
Low Levels Bank
M180
Hatfield Woodhouse
Bull Moor Road
Brier Hills Farm
Brier Hills
Moor Lane
Low Levels
Plains Lane
Hollin Br La
Hollin Bridge
Far Common Road
Remple Lane Farm
DN7
Moor Farm
The Cottage on the Moor
Stainforth Moor Road
Works
Good Cop Farm
Park Farm
Pump House Farm
Sewage Works
White Bridge Farm
Lindholme Grange
Pit (disused)
Moor Dike Road
Hatfield Moors
Roe Carr
West Carr
Masts
Don Farm
Woodhouse Grange Farm
Lindholme Bank Road
DN9
West Carr
Red House Farm
Lindholme Lake
West Carr Houses
H M Prison Moorland
Vulcan Wy
Lindholme Hall
Idle Bank

A3
1 LAUROLD AV
2 REMPLE AV
3 REMPLE LA
4 TURF MOOR RD

Grid columns: A 68 69 B 70 C 71 D 72 E 73 F

Grid rows: 8 13 7 12 6 11 5 10 4 09 3 08 2 07 1 06

26 ◀   16 ▶

B8
1 REDLAND CR
2 INGLENOOK DR
3 CHURCH CL
4 TENNYSON AV
5 ELMHIRST RD
6 HAYNES GN
7 COVENTRY RD
8 HOUPS RD
9 TITHE BARN LA

10 ALWYNRD
11 DANUM CL
12 LOCKWOOD CL
13 HAYNES GD
14 WIKE GATE CL
15 TRAVIS CL
16 TRAVIS AV

B7
1 HAYNES GR
2 WIKE GATE GR
3 HAYNES CL
4 WIKE GATE CL
5 WARRENRD
6 CHESTNUT AV
7 ASHTREERD
8 ELM TREE GR
9 PEEL HL RD

10 PEEL CASTLE RD
11 MARLBOROUGH RD
12 MILLER CL
13 FENLAND RD
14 MOWBRAY RD
15 STMICHAEL SDR
16 ST MICHAEL'S CL
17 BEECH TREE AV
18 SOUTHFIELD CL
19 AXHOLME GN

20 OLDFIELD RD
21 ST GEORGES RD
22 ST GEORGES CL
23 THE CROFT
24 SWANLAND CT
25 SWANLAND CL

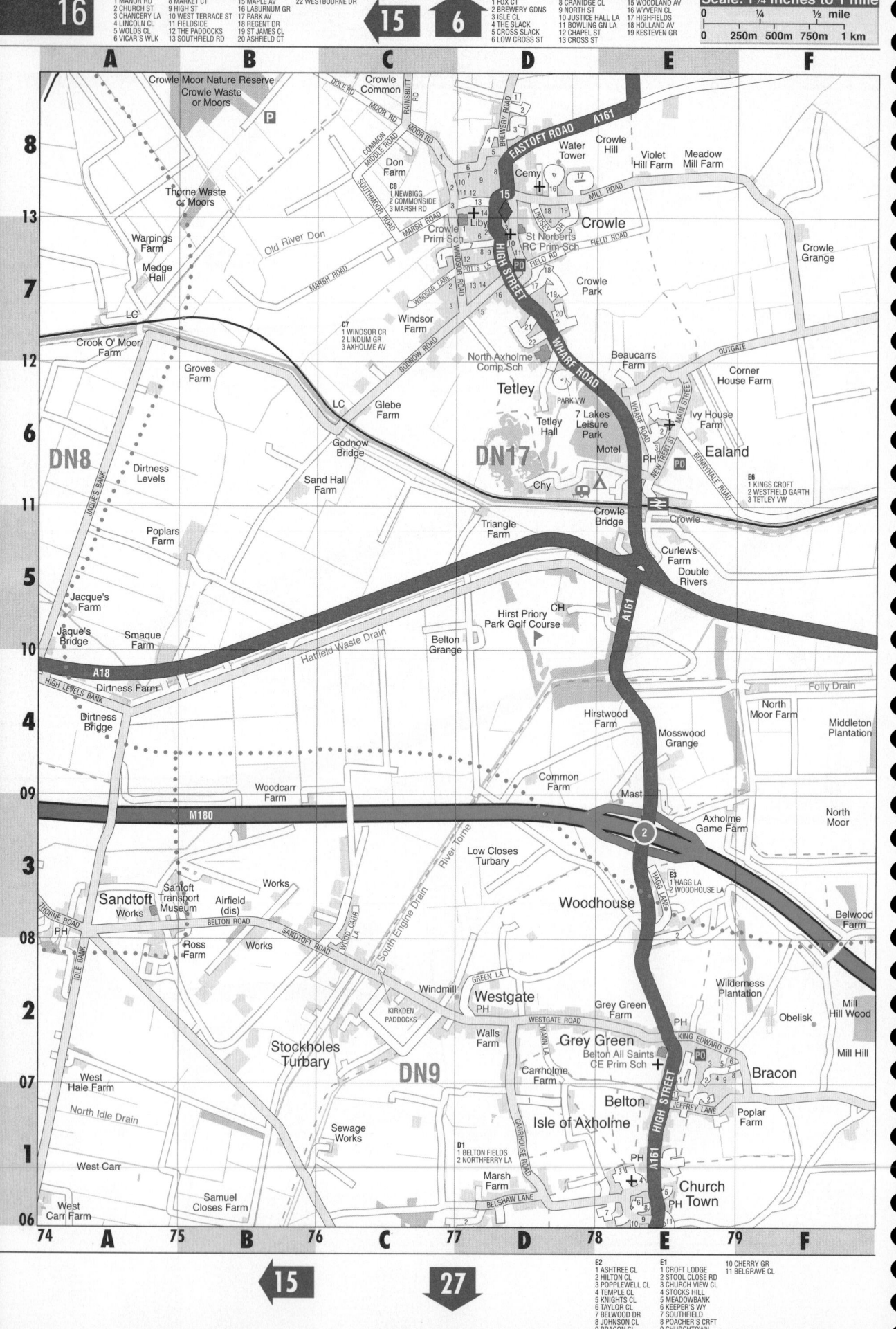

D7
1 MANOR RD
2 CHURCH ST
3 CHANCERY LA
4 LINCOLN CL
5 WOLDS CL
6 VICAR'S WLK

7 JOHNSON'S LA
8 MARKET CT
9 HIGH ST
10 WEST TERRACE ST
11 FIELDSIDE
12 THE PADDOCKS
13 SOUTHFIELD RD

14 CROWLAND RD
15 MAPLE AV
16 LABURNUM GR
17 PARK AV
18 REGENT DR
19 ST JAMES CL
20 ASHFIELD CT

21 MULBERRY DR
22 WESTBOURNE DR

D8
1 FOX CT
2 BREWERY GDNS
3 ISLE CL
4 THE SLACK
5 CROSS SLACK
6 LOW CROSS ST

7 COX LA
8 CRANIDGE CL
9 NORTH ST
10 JUSTICE HALL LA
11 BOWLING GN LA
12 CHAPEL ST
13 CROSS ST

14 PRINTING OFFICE LA
15 WOODLAND AV
16 WYVERN CL
17 HIGHFIELDS
18 HOLLAND AV
19 KESTEVEN GR

Crowle Moor Nature Reserve
Crowle Waste or Moors
Crowle Common

Thorne Waste or Moors
Don Farm

C8
1 NEWBIGG
2 COMMONSIDE
3 MARSH RD

Crowle
Water Tower
Crowle Hill
Violet Hill Farm
Meadow Mill Farm

Warpings Farm
Medge Hall
Old River Don

Crowle Prim Sch
St Norberts RC Prim Sch
Crowle Park
Crowle Grange

C7
1 WINDSOR CR
2 LINDUM GR
3 AXHOLME AV

Crook O' Moor Farm
Windsor Farm
Beaucarrs Farm
Corner House Farm

Groves Farm
Glebe Farm
North Axholme Comp Sch
Ivy House Farm

DN8
Tetley
7 Lakes Leisure Park
Ealand

Dirtness Levels
Godnow Bridge
Tetley Hall
DN17
Motel

E6
1 KINGS CROFT
2 WESTFIELD GARTH
3 TETLEY VW

Poplars Farm
Sand Hall Farm
Crowle Bridge
Crowle

Jacque's Farm
Triangle Farm
Curlews Farm
Double Rivers

Jaque's Bridge
Smaque Farm
Hirst Priory Park Golf Course

A18
Belton Grange
Folly Drain

Dirtness Farm
Hatfield Waste Drain
Hirstwood Farm
North Moor Farm
Middleton Plantation

Dirtness Bridge
Mosswood Grange

Common Farm
Mast
North Moor

M180
Axholme Game Farm

Woodcarr Farm
River Torne
Low Closes Turbary
Woodhouse

E3
1 HAGG LA
2 WOODHOUSE LA

Sandtoft
Santoft Transport Museum
Airfield (dis)
Works
Belwood Farm

BELTON ROAD
Ross Farm
Works
Windmill
Wilderness Plantation

Westgate
Grey Green Farm
Obelisk
Mill Hill Wood

Stockholes Turbary
Walls Farm
Grey Green
Belton All Saints CE Prim Sch
Mill Hill

DN9
Carrholme Farm
Bracon

West Hale Farm
Belton
Poplar Farm

North Idle Drain
Isle of Axholme

D1
1 BELTON FIELDS
2 NORTHFERRY LA

Sewage Works

West Carr
Marsh Farm
Church Town

West Carr Farm
Samuel Closes Farm
BELSHAW LANE

E2
1 ASHTREE CL
2 HILTON CL
3 POPPLEWELL CL
4 TEMPLE CL
5 KNIGHTS CL
6 TAYLOR CL
7 BELWOOD DR
8 JOHNSON CL
9 BRACON CL

E1
1 CROFT LODGE
2 STOOL CLOSE RD
3 CHURCH VIEW CL
4 STOCKS HILL
5 MEADOWBANK
6 KEEPER'S WY
7 SOUTHFIELD
8 POACHER'S CRFT
9 CHURCHTOWN

10 CHERRY GR
11 BELGRAVE CL

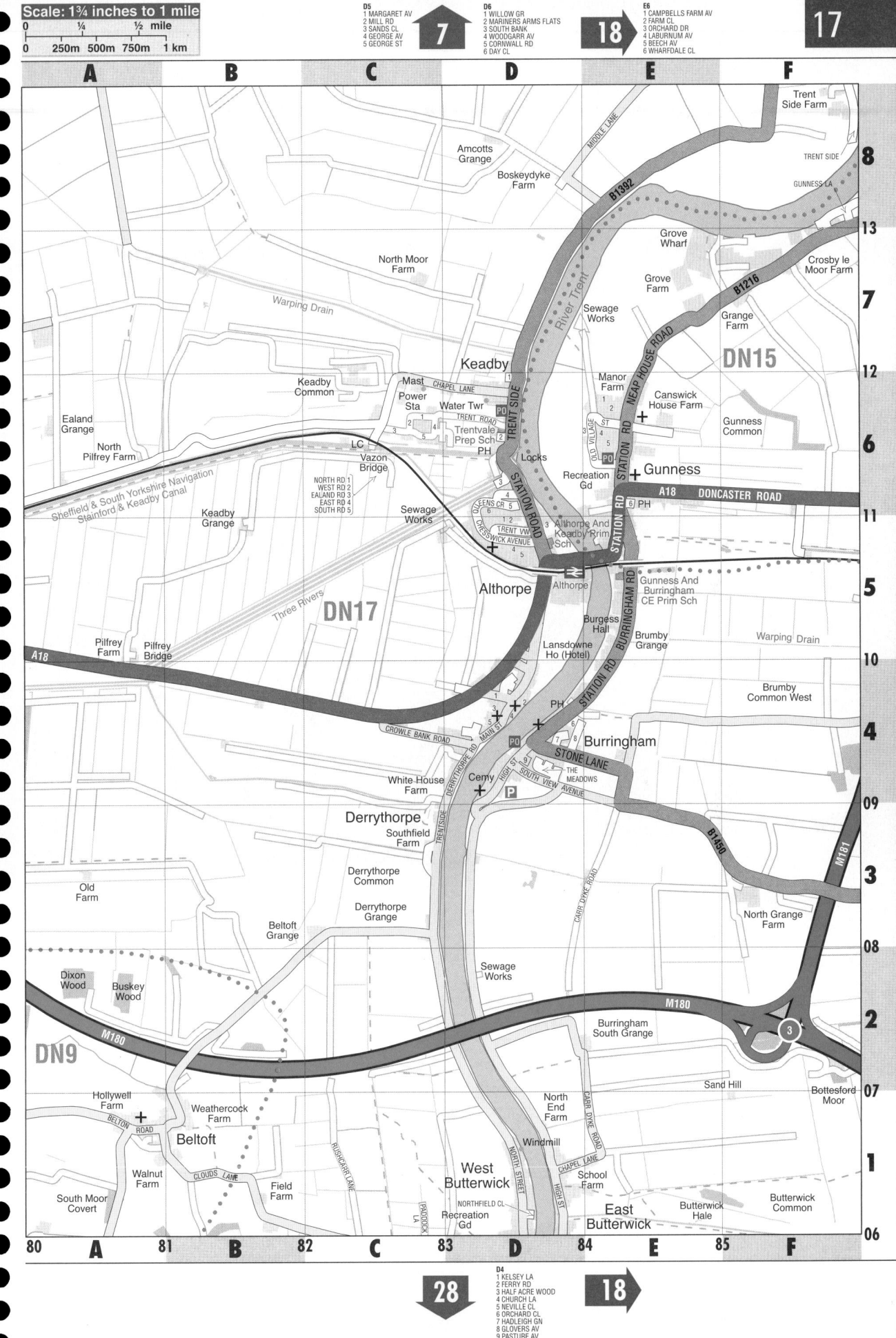

D5
1 MARGARET AV
2 MILL RD
3 SANDS CL
4 GEORGE AV
5 GEORGE ST

7

D6
1 WILLOW GR
2 MARINERS ARMS FLATS
3 SOUTH BANK
4 WOODGARR AV
5 CORNWALL RD
6 DAY CL

18

E6
1 CAMPBELLS FARM AV
2 FARM CL
3 ORCHARD DR
4 LABURNUM AV
5 BEECH AV
6 WHARFDALE CL

Trent Side Farm

TRENT SIDE

8

GUNNESS LA

13

A B C D E F

Amcotts Grange

Boskeydyke Farm

North Moor Farm

Warping Drain

B1392

River Trent

Grove Wharf

Crosby le Moor Farm

Grove Farm

B1216

Grange Farm

7

Keadby

DN15

12

Keadby Common

Ealand Grange

North Pilfrey Farm

Keadby Common

Mast
Power Sta

Chapel Lane

Water Twr

TRENT ROAD

Trentvale Prep Sch

PH

Manor Farm

VILLAGE ST

NEAP HOUSE ROAD

Canswick House Farm

Gunness Common

6

Sheffield & South Yorkshire Navigation
Stainford & Keadby Canal

Keadby Grange

LC

Vazon Bridge

NORTH RD 1
WEST RD 2
EALAND RD 3
EAST RD 4
SOUTH RD 5

Sewage Works

QUEENS CR

CHESWICK AVENUE

TRENT VW

Locks

PO

OLD

STATION RD

PO

Recreation Gd

STATION RD

+ Gunness

PH

A18 DONCASTER ROAD

11

DN17

Three Rivers

Althorpe And Keadby Prim Sch

Althorpe

Althorpe

Gunness And Burringham CE Prim Sch

Warping Drain

5

A18

Pilfrey Farm

Pilfrey Bridge

Burgess Hall

Lansdowne Ho (Hotel)

BURRINGHAM RD

Brumby Grange

STATION RD

Brumby Common West

10

CROWLE BANK ROAD

PH

Burringham

DERRYTHORPE RD

MAIN ST

PO

STONE LANE

Brumby Common West

B1450

M181

09

White House Farm

Cemy +

P

HIGH ST

SOUTH VIEW AVENUE

THE MEADOWS

CARR DYKE ROAD

4

Derrythorpe

Southfield Farm

TRENTSIDE

North Grange Farm

3

Old Farm

Derrythorpe Common

Derrythorpe Grange

Beltoft Grange

08

Dixon Wood

Buskey Wood

Sewage Works

M180

Burringham South Grange

2

DN9

M180

BELTON ROAD

+

Hollywell Farm

Weathercock Farm

Sand Hill

Bottesford Moor

07

Beltoft

CLOUDS LANE

RUSKCARR LANE

Field Farm

North End Farm

CARR DYKE ROAD

Windmill

CHAPEL LANE

School Farm

HIGH ST

1

Walnut Farm

West Butterwick

NORTH STREET

Butterwick Hale

Butterwick Common

South Moor Covert

PADDOCK LA

NORTHFIELD CL

Recreation Gd

East Butterwick

06

80 A 81 B 82 C 83 D 84 E 85 F

28

D4
1 KELSEY LA
2 FERRY RD
3 HALF ACRE WOOD
4 CHURCH LA
5 NEVILLE CL
6 ORCHARD CL
7 HADLEIGH GN
8 GLOVERS AV
9 PASTURE AV

18

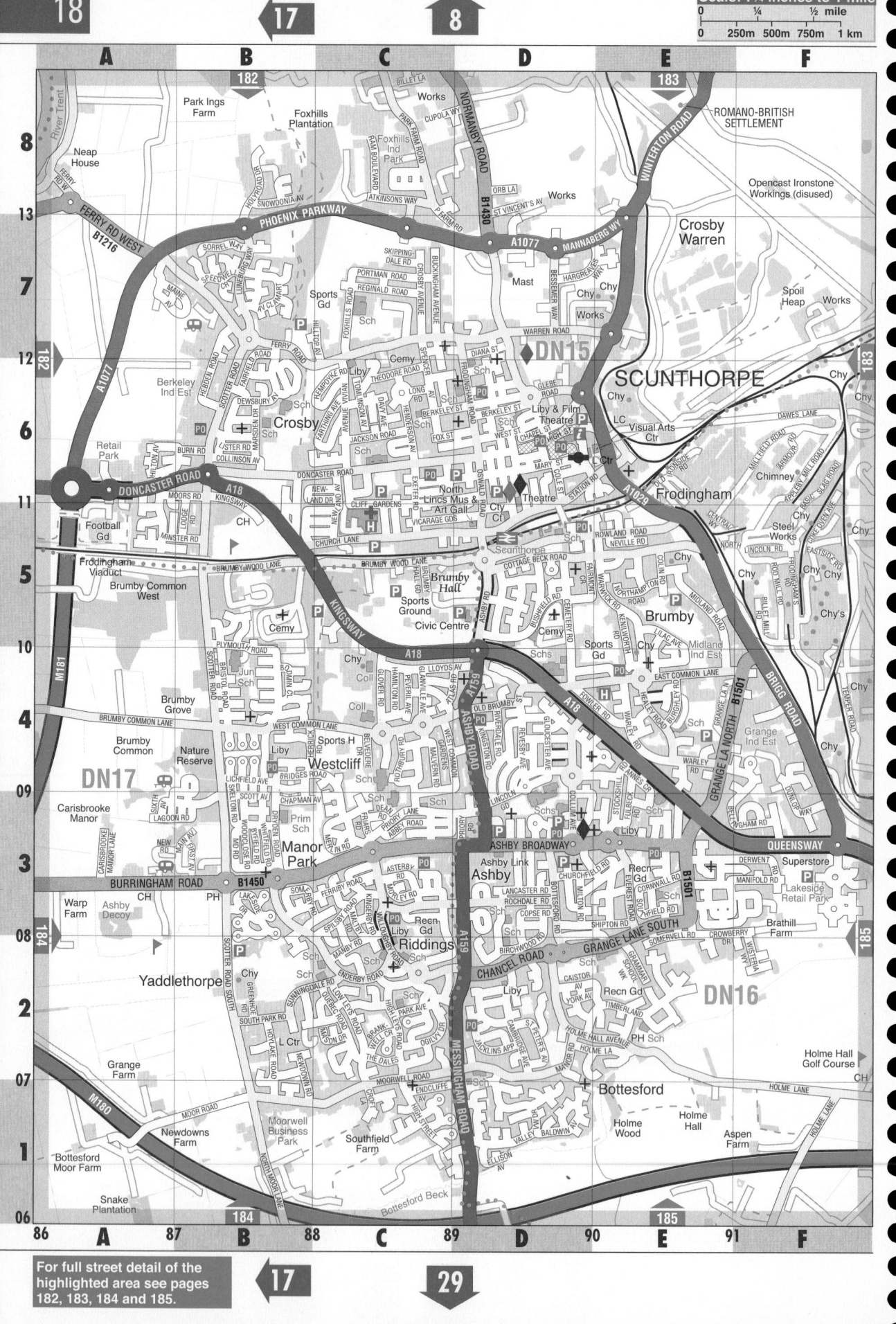

Scale: 1¾ inches to 1 mile

0   ¼   ½   mile
0   250m 500m 750m 1 km

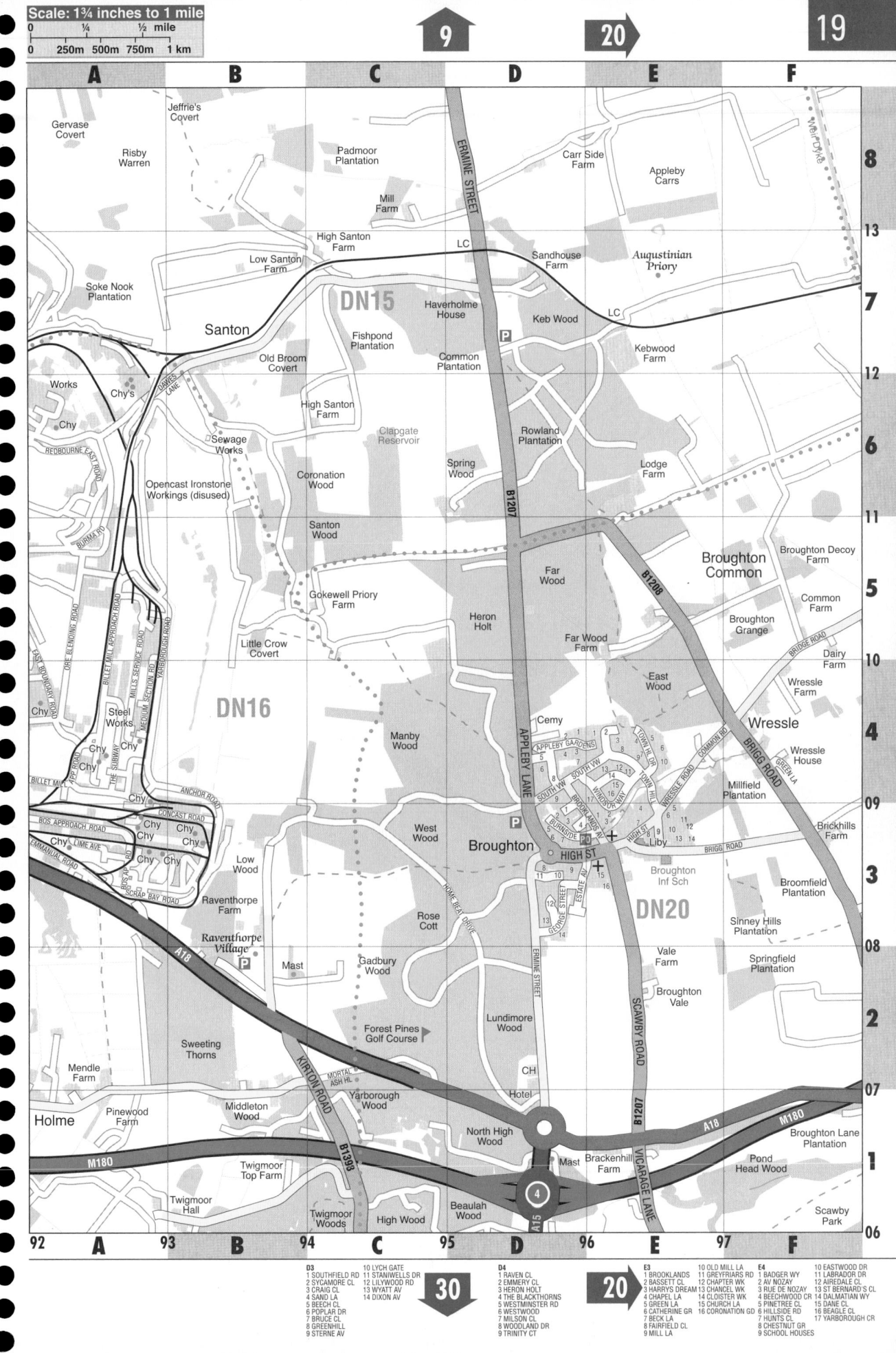

A   B   C   D   E   F

8
13
7
12
6
11
5
10
09
4
3
08
2
07
1
06

Gervase Covert
Jeffrie's Covert
Risby Warren
Padmoor Plantation
Carr Side Farm
Appleby Carrs

High Santon Farm
Sandhouse Farm
Augustinian Priory

Soke Nook Plantation
Low Santon Farm
DN15
Haverholme House
Keb Wood
LC

Santon
Fishpond Plantation
Common Plantation
Kebwood Farm

Works
Chy's
Old Broom Covert
High Santon Farm
Clapgate Reservoir
Rowland Plantation
Lodge Farm

Chy
Sewage Works
Coronation Wood
Spring Wood
Broughton Common
Broughton Decoy Farm

Opencast Ironstone Workings (disused)
Santon Wood
Far Wood
B1208
Broughton Grange
Common Farm

BURMA RD
Gokewell Priory Farm
Heron Holt
Far Wood Farm
East Wood
Broughton Common
Dairy Farm
Wressle Farm

DN16
Little Crow Covert
Manby Wood
Cemy
Wressle
Wressle House

Steel Works
Chy
Chy
West Wood
Broughton
HIGH ST
Liby
Millfield Plantation
Brickhills Farm

Chy
Chy
Low Wood
Rose Cott
Broughton Inf Sch
DN20
Broomfield Plantation

Raventhorpe Farm
Gadbury Wood
Sinney Hills Plantation
Springfield Plantation

Raventhorpe Village
Mast
Lundimore Wood
Vale Farm
Broughton Vale

A18
Sweeting Thorns
Forest Pines Golf Course
CH
Hotel

Mendle Farm
Middleton Wood
Yarborough Wood
North High Wood
Mast
Brackenhill Farm
A18
M180
Broughton Lane Plantation
Pond Head Wood

Holme
Pinewood Farm
KIRTON ROAD
MORTAL ASH HL
Twigmoor Top Farm
Beaulah Wood
4
A15
Scawby Park

M180
Twigmoor Hall
B1393
Twigmoor Woods
High Wood

92   93   94   95   96   97

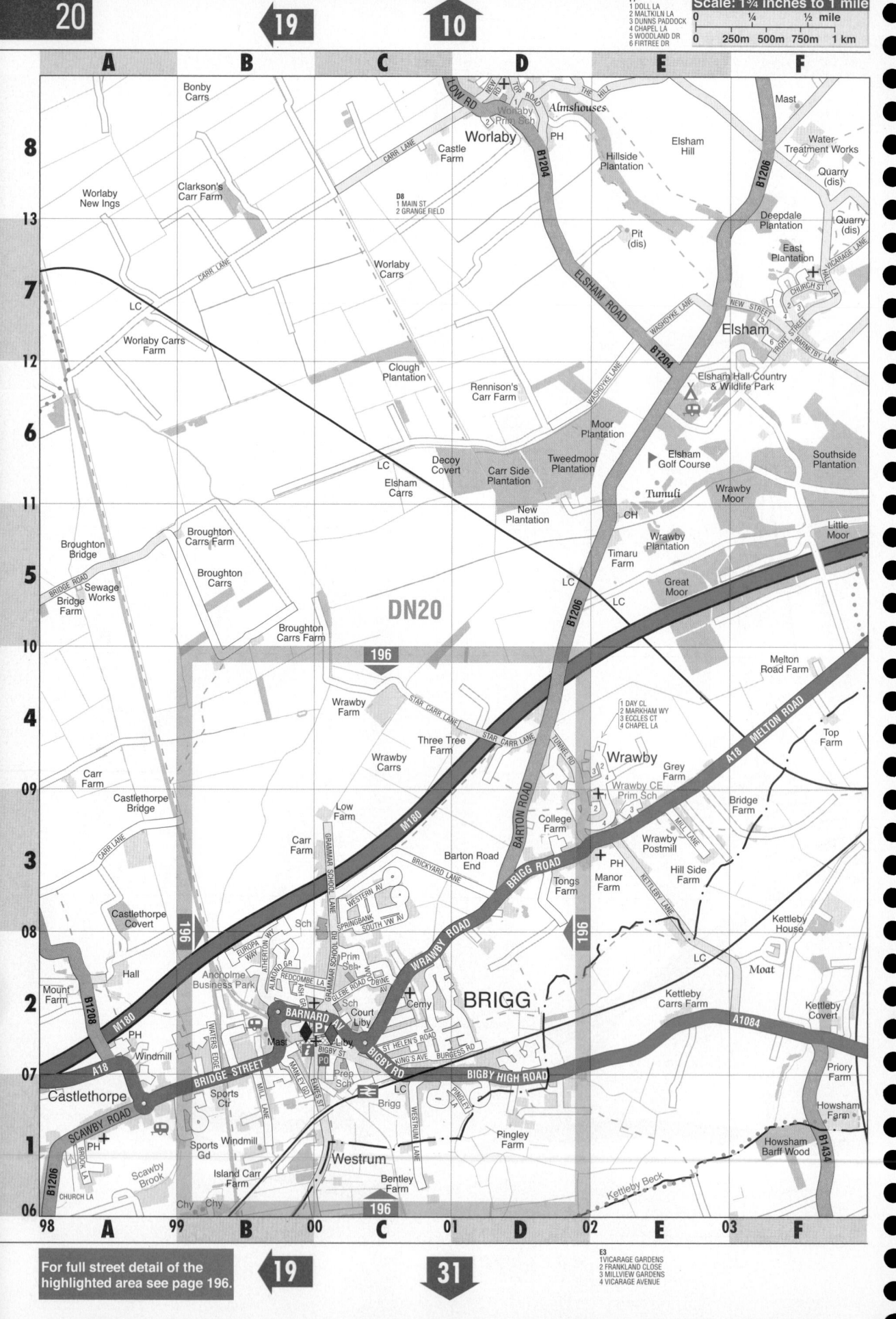

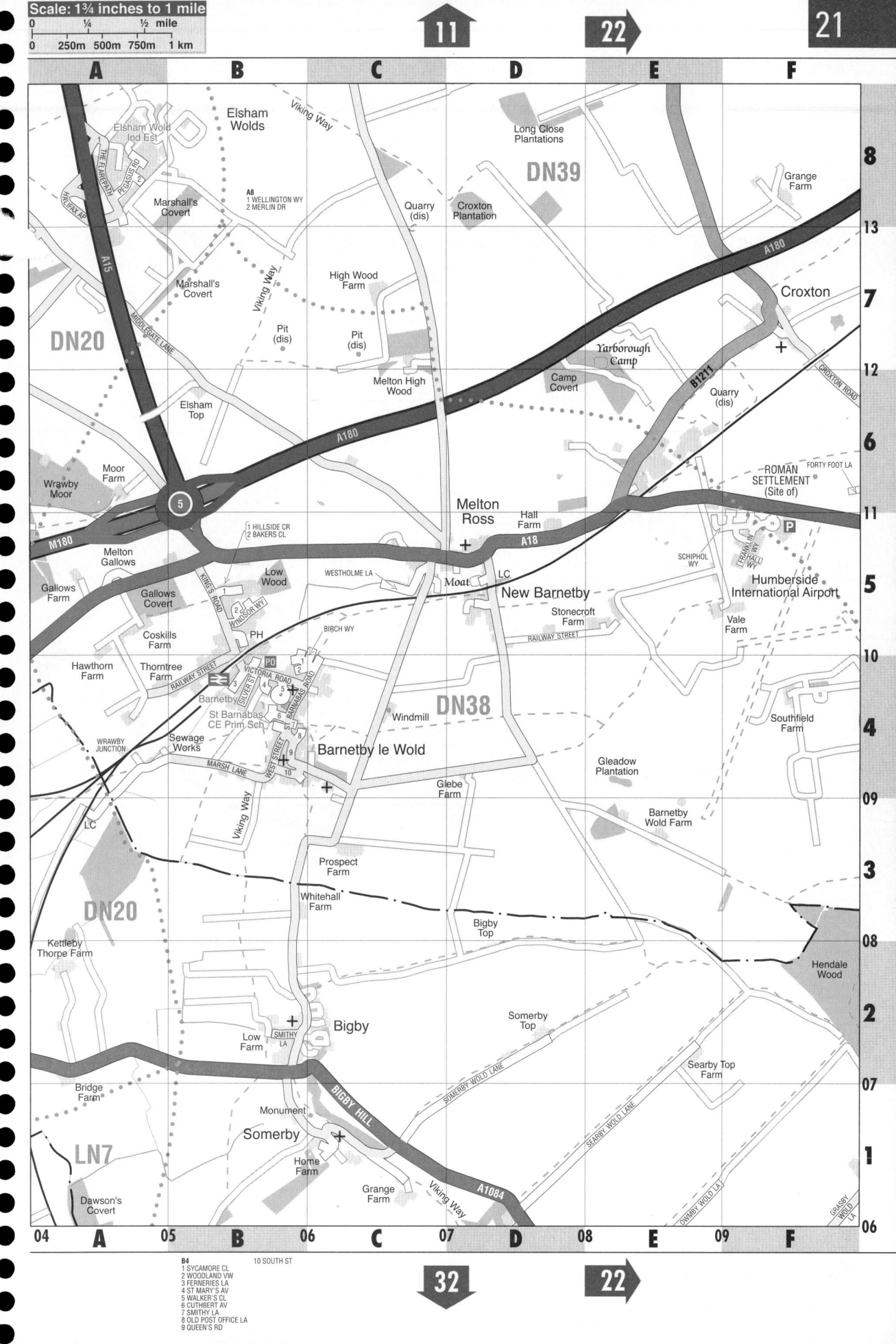

Scale: 1¾ inches to 1 mile
11
22
Elsham Wold Ind Est
Elsham Wolds
Viking Way
Long Close Plantations
DN39
Grange Farm
Marshall's Covert
A8
1 WELLINGTON WY
2 MERLIN DR
Quarry (dis)
Croxton Plantation
A15
A180
High Wood Farm
Marshall's Covert
Croxton
DN20
Pit (dis)
Pit (dis)
Yarborough Camp
Camp Covert
Melton High Wood
Elsham Top
B1211
Quarry (dis)
CROXTON ROAD
Moor Farm
Wrawby Moor
ROMAN SETTLEMENT (Site of)
FORTY FOOT LA
Melton Ross
Hall Farm
M180
A18
1 HILLSIDE CR
2 BAKERS CL
Melton Gallows
Low Wood
WESTHOLME LA
Moat
LC
New Barnetby
SCHIPHOL WY
FRANKLIN WY
HALL WY
Humberside International Airport
Gallows Farm
Gallows Covert
KING'S ROAD
WINDSOR WY
Stonecroft Farm
Vale Farm
Coskills Farm
PH
BIRCH WY
RAILWAY STREET
Hawthorn Farm
Thorntree Farm
PO
VICTORIA ROAD
BARNABAS ROAD
Barnetby
SILVER ST
St Barnabas CE Prim Sch
Windmill
DN38
Southfield Farm
WRAWBY JUNCTION
Sewage Works
WEST STREET
Barnetby le Wold
MARSH LANE
Gleadow Plantation
Glebe Farm
Viking Way
LC
Barnetby Wold Farm
Prospect Farm
DN20
Whitehall Farm
Bigby Top
Kettleby Thorpe Farm
Hendale Wood
Somerby Top
Bigby
Low Farm
SMITHY LA
Searby Top Farm
Bridge Farm
BIGBY HILL
SOMERBY WOLD LANE
SEARBY WOLD LANE
Monument
Somerby
LN7
Home Farm
Grange Farm
Viking Way
A1084
OWMBY WOLD LA
Dawson's Covert
GRASBY WOLD LA
04 05 06 07 08 09
A B C D E F
06 07 08 09 10 11 12 13
1 2 3 4 5 6 7 8
B4
1 SYCAMORE CL
2 WOODLAND VW
3 FERNERIES LA
4 ST MARY'S AV
5 WALKER'S CL
6 CUTHBERT AV
7 SMITHY LA
8 OLD POST OFFICE LA
9 QUEEN'S RD
10 SOUTH ST
32
22

A   **B**

A180

B1211

BROCKLESBY ROAD

8

Quarry (dis)

Pelham Farm

Mast

Vale House Farm

LC

13

Ladypits Plantation

LC

Mark Cooper's Wood

Major Wood

Granny Wood

Waterhill Wood

Washdyke Wood

Ulceby Chase Farm

DN39

Newsham Lodge

Thomas Wood

Carr Leys Wood

New Farm

7

Chase Wood

Irongate Wood

Pond Close Wood

Horns Wood

Rough Pasture Wood

12

Rumley Marsh Wood

Betty Holmes Wood

Spur Plat Wood

Sewage Works

Kirmington

Sewage Works

Brocklesby Park

PO

Brocklesby

Priory (Cistercian Nuns)

6

Kirmington CE Prim Sch

HIGH STREET

PH

EAST END

HABROUGH LANE

LIMBER ROAD

11

A18

B1210

The Paddocks

Primrose Hill

BROCKLESBY ROAD

B1211

Home Farm

Little Limber

Miller's Wood

5

CROXTON ROAD

Keelby Grange

Cross

DN41

Mill Mound

10

Bluegate Wood

Little Limber Grange

4

Mausoleum Woods

Brocklesby Park Prim Sch

09

Mausoleum

Town End

Cottagers Dale Wood

PO

HIGH STREET

3

GRASBY ROAD

PH

Grange

Coneygreen Wood

CHURCH LA

Great Limber

Pit (dis)

08

A18

Hendale Wood

Pimlico Farm

Pit (dis)

Limber Hill Wood

2

Pit (dis)

Limber Hill Farm

Grasby Bottoms

07

DN37

DN38

GRASBY WOLD LANE

1

Halliday Hill

Maux Hall

Pit (dis)

Greenlands Farm

Great Limber Grange

06

Pit (dis)

10   **A**   **11**   **B**   **12**   **C**   **13**   **D**   **14**   **E**   **15**   **F**

For full street detail of the highlighted area see pages 186 & 187.

← **21**

↓ **33**

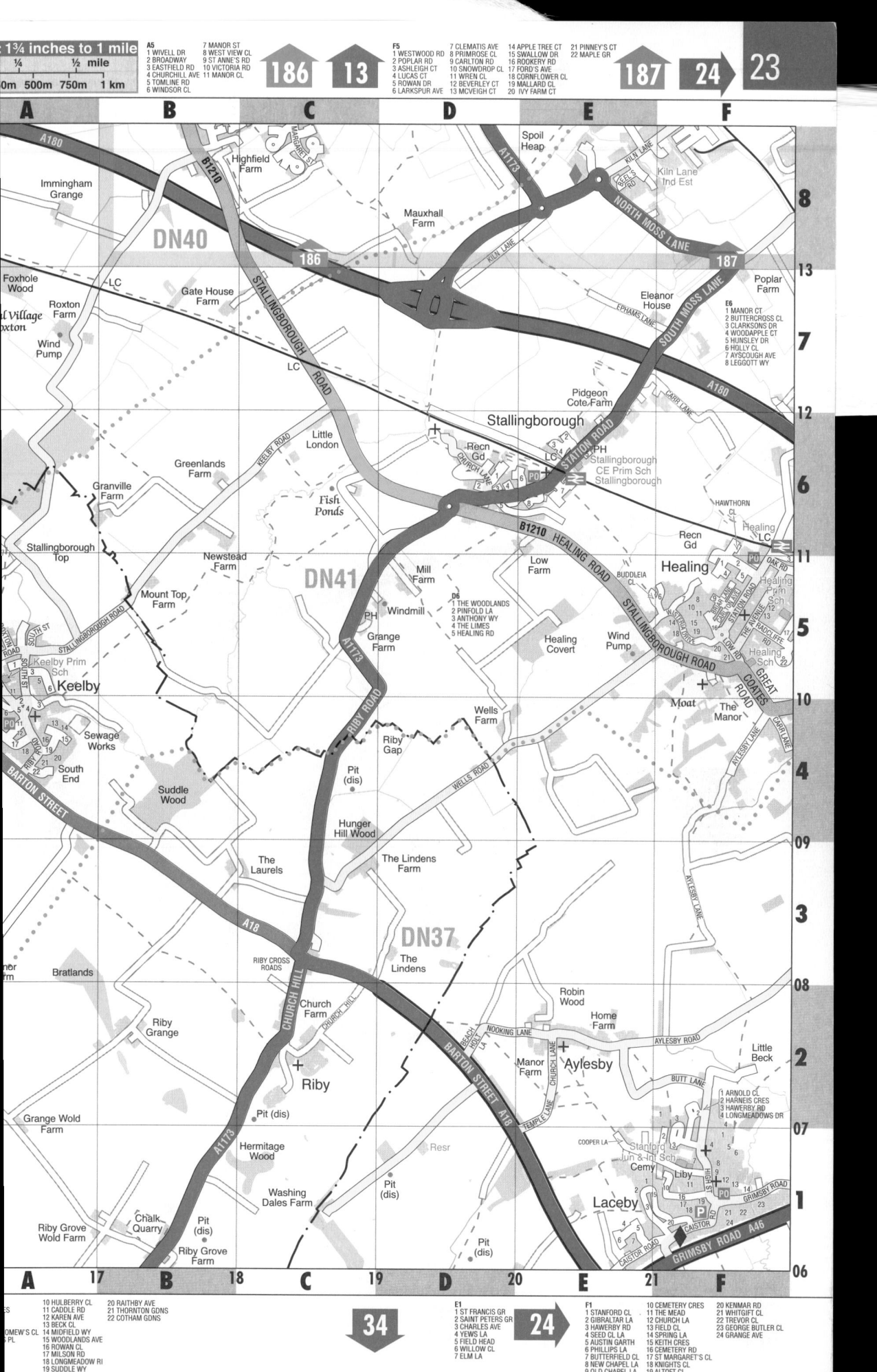

A5
1 WIVELL DR
2 BROADWAY
3 EASTFIELD RD
4 CHURCHILL AVE
5 TOMLINE RD
6 WINDSOR CL

7 MANOR ST
8 WEST VIEW CL
9 ST VICTORIA RD
10 VICTORIA RD
11 MANOR CL

186

13

F5
1 WESTWOOD RD
2 POPLAR RD
3 ASHLEIGH CT
4 LUCAS CT
5 ROWAN DR
6 LARKSPUR AVE

7 CLEMATIS AVE
8 PRIMROSE CL
9 CARLTON RD
10 SNOWDROP CL
11 WREN CL
12 BEVERLEY CT
13 MCVEIGH CT

14 APPLE TREE CT
15 SWALLOW DR
16 ROOKERY RD
17 FORD'S AVE
18 CORNFLOWER CL
19 MALLARD CL
20 IVY FARM CT

21 PINNEY'S CT
22 MAPLE GR

187

24

23

8

DN40

186

13

Immingham
Grange

Highfield
Farm

Mauxhall
Farm

Spoil
Heap

North Moss Lane

Kiln Lane
Ind Est

187

Foxhole
Wood

LC

Gate House
Farm

Eleanor
House

Poplar
Farm

Ephams Lane

South Moss Lane

E6
1 MANOR CT
2 BUTTERCROSS CL
3 CLARKSONS CL
4 WOODAPPLE CT
5 HUNSLEY DR
6 HOLLY CL
7 AYSCOUGH AVE
8 LEGGOTT WY

7

Roxton
Farm

Wind
Pump

LC

A180

Stallingborough Road

Pidgeon
Cote Farm

12

Granville
Farm

Keelby Road

Little
London

Greenlands
Farm

Fish
Ponds

Stallingborough

Recn
Gd

Church Lane

Station Road

PH
Stallingborough
CE Prim Sch
Stallingborough

PO

Healing
LC

6

Stallingborough
Top

Newstead
Farm

DN41

Mill
Farm

Low
Farm

Buddleia
CL

Healing

Recn
Gd

PO

Hawthorn
CL

Oak Rd

Healing
Prim
Sch

5

Mount Top
Farm

Stallingborough Road

PH

Windmill

D6
1 THE WOODLANDS
2 PINFOLD LA
3 ANTHONY WY
4 THE LIMES
5 HEALING RD

Healing
Covert

Wind
Pump

Radcliffe
Rd

The Avenue

Healing
Sch

Keelby Prim
Sch

Grange
Farm

A1173

Riby Road

Stallingborough Road

Great Coates Road

South St

Keelby

Sewage
Works

Wells
Farm

Moat

The
Manor

Aylesby Lane

Carr Lane

10

PO

South
End

Riby
Gap

Pit
(dis)

Wells Road

09

Barton Street

Suddle
Wood

Hunger
Hill Wood

The
Laurels

The Lindens
Farm

Rylesby Lane

4

Bratlands

A18

The Lindens

DN37

Robin
Wood

Home
Farm

Aylesby Road

Little
Beck

3

Riby Cross
Roads

Church Hill

Church
Farm

Nooking Lane

Manor
Farm

Church Lane

Aylesby

Butt Lane

F1
1 ARNOLD CL
2 HARNEIS CRES
3 HAWERBY RD
4 LONGMEADOWS DR

08

Riby
Grange

Church Hill

Riby

Beach Holt La

Barton Street A18

Temple Lane

Cooper La

Stanford
Jun & Inf Sch

Liby

P

Grimsby Road

2

Grange Wold
Farm

A1173

Pit (dis)

Hermitage
Wood

Resr

Laceby

PO

07

Riby Grove
Wold Farm

Chalk
Quarry

Pit
(dis)

Washing
Dales Farm

Pit
(dis)

Pit
(dis)

Caistor Rd

Grimsby Road A46

Caistor Road

1

Riby Grove
Farm

06

A

17

B

18

C

19

D

20

E

21

F

10 HULBERRY CL
11 CADDLE RD
12 KAREN AVE
13 BECK CL
14 MIDFIELD WY
15 WOODLANDS AVE
16 ROWAN CL
17 MILSON RD
18 LONGMEADOW RI
19 SUDDLE WY

20 RAITHBY AVE
21 THORNTON GDNS
22 COTHAM GDNS

34

24

E1
1 ST FRANCIS GR
2 SAINT PETERS GR
3 CHARLES AVE
4 YEWS LA
5 FIELD HEAD
6 WILLOW CL
7 ELM LA

F1
1 STANFORD CL
2 GIBRALTAR LA
3 HAWERBY RD
4 SEED CL LA
5 AUSTIN GARTH
6 PHILLIPS LA
7 BUTTERFIELD CL
8 NEW CHAPEL LA
9 OLD CHAPEL LA

10 CEMETERY CRES
11 THE MEAD
12 CHURCH LA
13 FIELD CL
14 SPRING LA
15 KEITH CRES
16 CEMETERY RD
17 ST MARGARET'S CL
18 KNIGHTS CL
19 ALTOFT CL

20 KENMAR RD
21 WHITGIFT CL
22 TREVOR CL
23 GEORGE BUTLER CL
24 GRANGE AVE

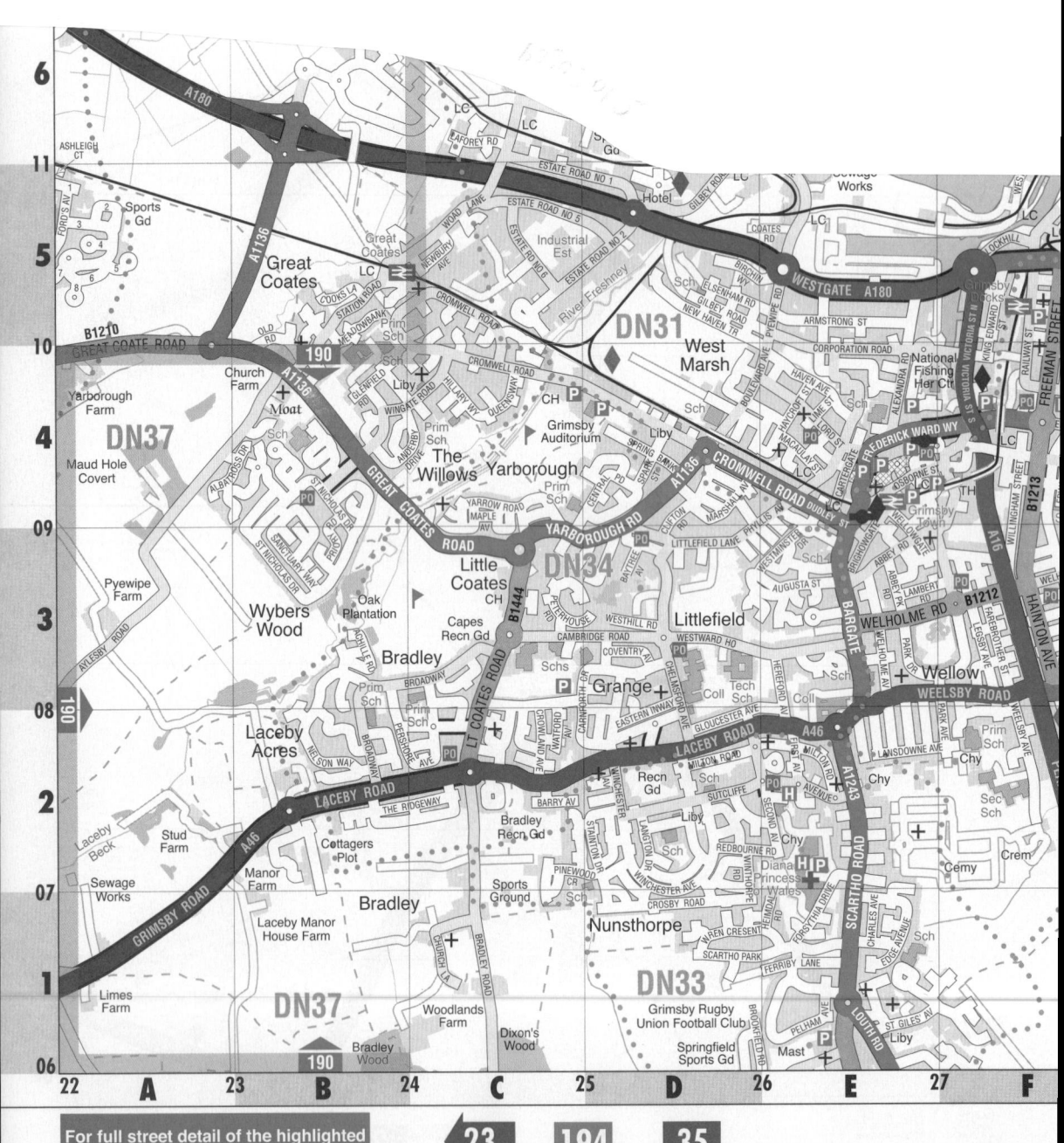

For full street detail of the highlighted areas see pages 187, 188, 190 & 191.

23   194   35

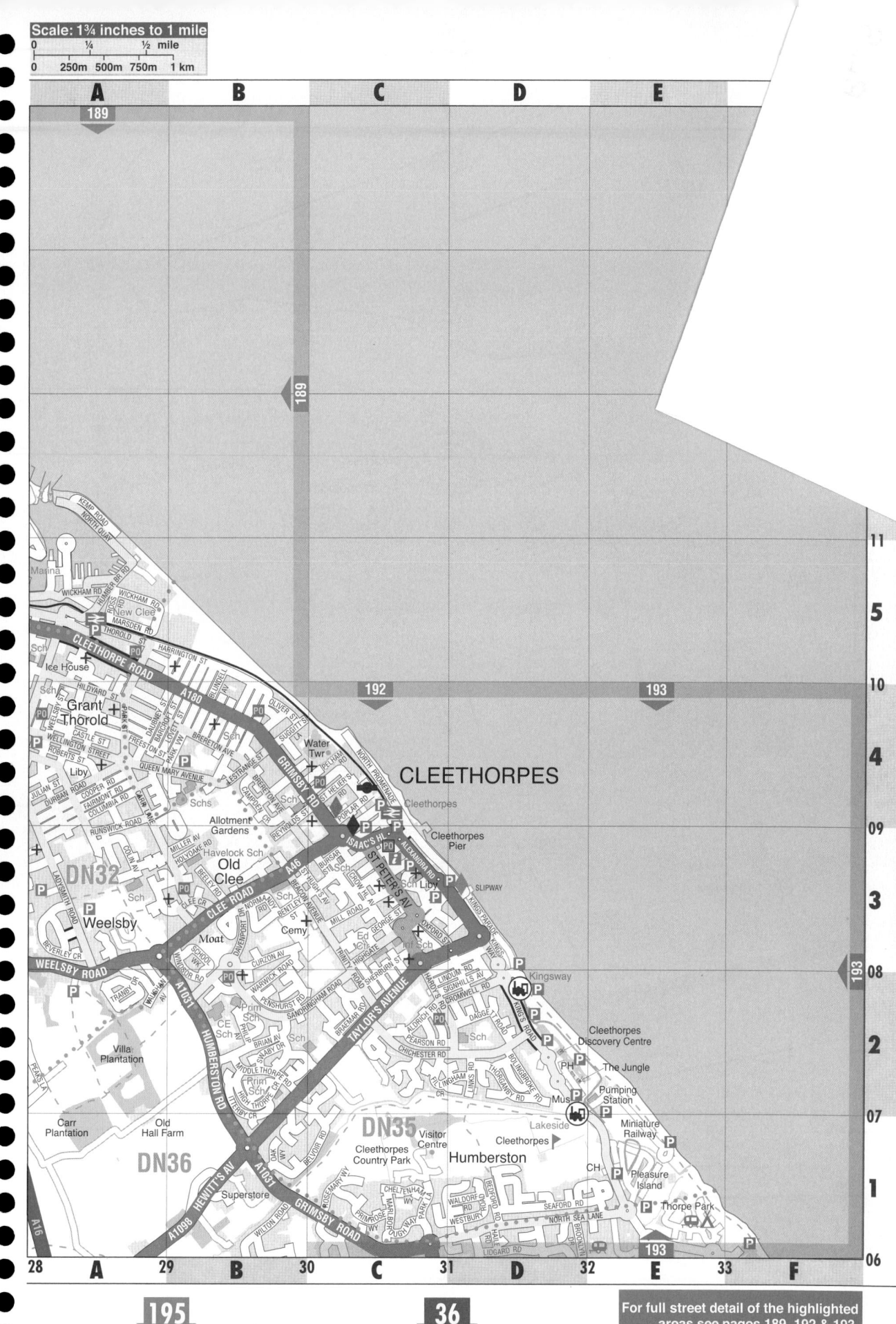

Scale: 1¾ inches to 1 mile

0   ¼   ½ mile

0   250m 500m 750m 1 km

189
189
192
193
193
195
36
For full street detail of the highlighted areas see pages 189, 192 & 193.

CLEETHORPES

A B C D E F

28 29 30 31 32 33

11 5 10 4 09 3 08 2 07 1 06

KEMP ROAD
NORTH QUAY
Marina
WICKHAM RD
WICKHAM RD
New Clee
MARSDEN RD
THOROLD ST
HARRINGTON ST
CLEETHORPE ROAD
Ice House
HILDYARD ST
Grant Thorold
A180
CASTLE ST
WELLINGTON STREET
ROBERTS ST
Liby
JULIAN ST
DURBAN RD
COOPER RD
FAIRMONT RD
COLUMBIA RD
RUNSWICK RD
MILLER AV
HOLYOAKE RD
DN32
Havelock Sch
Old Clee
Schs
LADYSMITH ROAD
Weelsby
BEVERLEY CR
CLEE RD
Moat
WEELSBY ROAD
CLEE ROAD
A46
Cemy
SCHOOL
DAVENPORT
CURZON AV
Villa Plantation
HUMBERSTON RD
ITTERBY CR
PEARS LA
Carr Plantation
Old Hall Farm
DN36
A1098
A16
HEWIT'S AV
A1031
Superstore
OAK WY
BELVOIR RD
WILTON ROAD
GRIMSBY ROAD
ROSE MARY WY
PRIMROSE WY
MARLBOROUGH WY
CHELTENHAM
WALDORF RD
BEDFORD RD
WESTBURY
PARK LA
LIDGARD RD
HALE RD
SEAFORD RD
NORTH SEA LANE
BROOKLYN
DN35
Cleethorpes Country Park
Visitor Centre
Humberston
Lakeside
Cleethorpes
CH
Pleasure Island
Thorpe Park
Miniature Railway
Pumping Station
Mus
The Jungle
PH
Cleethorpes Discovery Centre
Kingsway
KINGS ROAD
SIGNHILLS AV
LINDUM RD
CROMWELL RD
BOLINGBROKE RD
MORGAN'S RD
DAGGETT RD
LINKS RD
FLEMINGHAM RD
CR
PEARSON RD
CHICHESTER RD
BRAEMAR RD
AIDRICH RD
TAYLOR'S AVENUE
SANDRINGHAM ROAD
PENSHURST RD
WARWICK ROAD
BRIAN AV
SAXBY DR
MIDDLE THORPE RD
NORTH THORPE RD
PRIM Sch
CE Sch
HIGHGATE
SHERBORN ST
GEORGE ST
Ed Sch
Inf Sch
MILL ROAD
BURSAR
ST PETER'S AV
ISAAC'S HL
CLEETHORPES
Cleethorpes Pier
SLIPWAY
KINGS PARADE
Sch Liby
BRADFORD AV
ALEXANDRA RD
NORTH PROMENADE
Water Twr
PELHAM RD
ST HELEN'S AV
OLIVER ST
SUGGITT'S
POPLAR RD
REYNOLDS ST
Allotment Gardens
QUEEN MARY AVENUE
GRIMSBY RD
FREESTON ST
PARK ST
LOVETT ST
BARCROFT
CAMPDEN
BRERETON AV
BLUNDELL
CARR LANE

A8
1 CUNNINGHAM RD
2 GIBSON RD
3 HAMPDEN CR
4 VARSITY CL

15

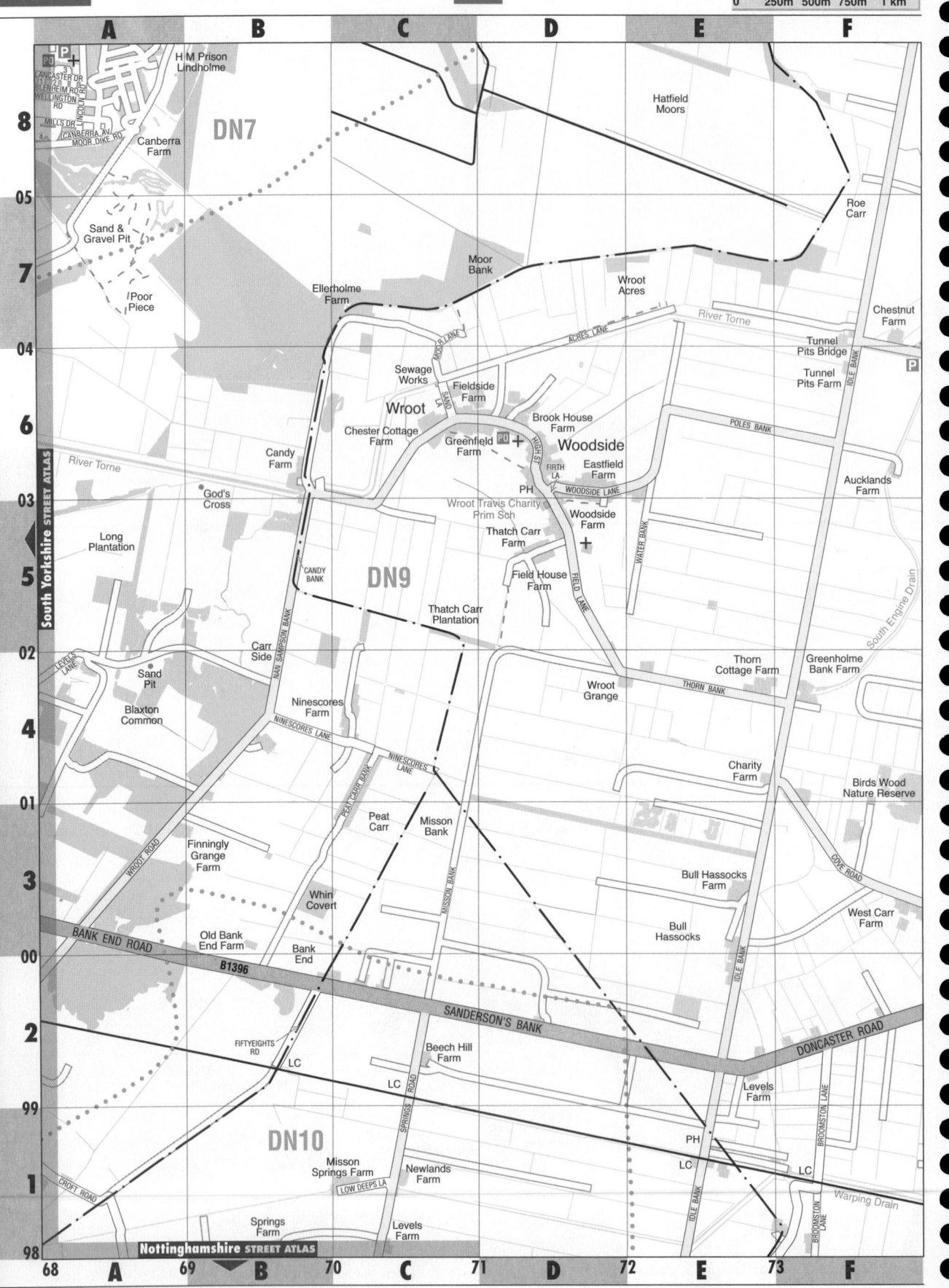

South Yorkshire STREET ATLAS

DN7

H M Prison
Lindholme

Canberra
Farm

Sand &
Gravel Pit

Poor
Piece

River Torne

Long
Plantation

God's
Cross

Hatfield
Moors

Roe
Carr

Moor
Bank

Wroot
Acres

Ellerholme
Farm

River Torne

Chestnut
Farm

Tunnel
Pits Bridge

Tunnel
Pits Farm

Acres Lane

Sewage
Works

Fieldside
Farm

Wroot

Chester Cottage
Farm

Candy
Farm

Greenfield
Farm

Brook House
Farm

Woodside

Firth
La

Eastfield
Farm

Poles Bank

Aucklands
Farm

Wroot Travis Charity
Prim Sch

PH

Woodside Lane

Thatch Carr
Farm

Woodside
Farm

DN9

CANDY
BANK

Thatch Carr
Plantation

Field House
Farm

Water Bank

South Engine Drain

Carr
Side

Sand
Pit

Blaxton
Common

Ninescores
Farm

Ninescores Lane

Thorn
Cottage Farm

Wroot
Grange

Thorn Bank

Greenholme
Bank Farm

Charity
Farm

Birds Wood
Nature Reserve

Ninescores
Lane

Peat Carr
Bank

Peat
Carr

Misson
Bank

Bull Hassocks
Farm

West Carr
Farm

Finningly
Grange
Farm

Wroot Road

Whin
Covert

Bull
Hassocks

Cove Road

Bank End Road

Old Bank
End Farm

Bank
End

Levels
Lane

B1396

Sanderson's Bank

Doncaster Road

Fiftyeights
Rd

LC

Beech Hill
Farm

Levels
Farm

Broomston Lane

DN10

Misson
Springs Farm

LC

Springs Road

Newlands
Farm

PH

LC

LC

Idle Bank

Croft Road

Low Deeps La

Springs
Farm

Levels
Farm

Warping Drain

Broomston
Lane

39

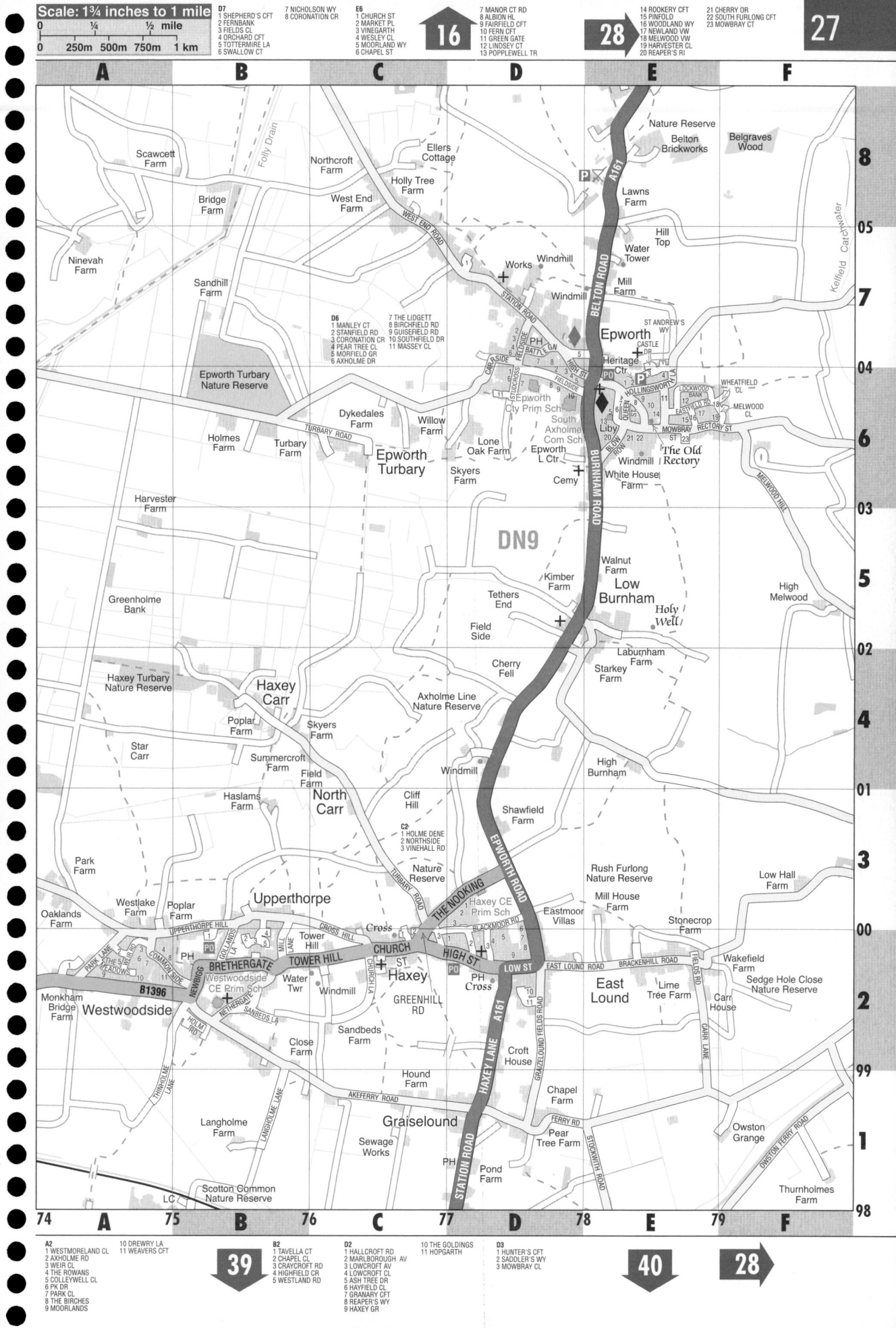

Scale: 1¾ inches to 1 mile
0 ¼ ½ mile
0 250m 500m 750m 1 km
D7
1 SHEPHERD'S CFT
2 FERNBANK
3 FIELDS CL
4 ORCHARD CFT
5 TOTTERMIRE LA
6 SWALLOW CT
7 NICHOLSON WY
8 CORONATION CR
E6
1 CHURCH ST
2 MARKET PL
3 VINEGARTH
4 WESLEY CL
5 MOORLAND WY
6 CHAPEL ST
16
7 MANOR CT RD
8 ALBION HL
9 FAIRFIELD CFT
10 FERN CFT
11 GREEN GATE
12 LINDSEY CT
13 POPPLEWELL TR
28
14 ROOKERY CFT
15 PINFOLD
16 WOODLAND WY
17 NEWLAND VW
18 MELWOOD VW
19 HARVESTER CL
20 REAPER'S RI
21 CHERRY OR
22 SOUTH FURLONG CFT
23 MOWBRAY CT
27
A B C D E F
Nature Reserve
Belton Brickworks
Belgraves Wood
Scawcett Farm
Ellers Cottage
Northcroft Farm
Folly Drain
Holly Tree Farm
Bridge Farm
West End Farm
Lawns Farm
A161
Hill Top
WEST END ROAD
Ninevah Farm
Water Tower
Works
Windmill
Kelfield Catchwater
Sandhill Farm
Mill Farm
Windmill
BELTON ROAD
STATION ROAD
D6
1 MANLEY CT
2 STANFIELD RD
3 CORONATION CR
4 PEAR TREE CL
5 MORFIELD GR
6 AXHOLME DR
7 THE LIDGETT
8 BIRCHFIELD RD
9 GUISEFIELD RD
10 SOUTHFIELD DR
11 MASSEY CL
Epworth
ST ANDREW'S WY
CASTLE DR
PH
BATTLE GN
HIGH ST
FIELDSIDE
Heritage Ctr
CARRSIDE
PO
HOLLINGSWORTH LA
WHEATFIELD CL
Epworth Turbary Nature Reserve
STUDCROSS
Epworth Cty Prim Sch
LOCKWOOD BANK
EASTFIELD RD
MELWOOD CL
QUEEN ST
Dykedales Farm
Willow Farm
South Axholme Com Sch
Liby
MOWBRAY ST
RECTORY ST
Holmes Farm
TURBARY ROAD
Turbary Farm
Lone Oak Farm
Epworth Turbary
Epworth L Ctr
BLOW ROW
Windmill
The Old Rectory
Skyers Farm
Cemy
White House Farm
BURNHAM ROAD
MELWOOD HILL
Harvester Farm
DN9
Walnut Farm
Kimber Farm
Low Burnham
High Melwood
Greenholme Bank
Tethers End
Holy Well
Field Side
Laburnham Farm
Cherry Fell
Starkey Farm
Haxey Turbary Nature Reserve
Haxey Carr
Axholme Line Nature Reserve
Poplar Farm
Skyers Farm
Star Carr
Summercroft Farm
Windmill
High Burnham
Field Farm
Haslams Farm
North Carr
Cliff Hill
Shawfield Farm
C2
1 HOLME DENE
2 NORTHSIDE
3 VINEHALL RD
Park Farm
Nature Reserve
Rush Furlong Nature Reserve
Low Hall Farm
EPWORTH ROAD
TURBARY ROAD
Westlake Farm
Poplar Farm
Upperthorpe
THE NOOKING
Haxey CE Prim Sch
Mill House Farm
Oaklands Farm
Eastmoor Villas
Stonecrop Farm
UPPERTHORPE HILL
CROSS HILL
Cross
BLACKMOOR RD
GOLLANDS LA
MILL LANE
Tower Hill
PARK LANE
THE MEADOWS
WEIR RD
COMMONSIDE
PH
PO
CHURCH
HIGH ST
Wakefield Farm
BRETHERGATE
TOWER HILL
ST
LOW ST
EAST LOUND ROAD
BRACKENHILL ROAD
FIELDS RD
NEWBIGG
CHURCH LA
Haxey
PO
PH
Cross
Sedge Hole Close Nature Reserve
B1396
Westwoodside CE Prim Sch
Water Twr
Windmill
East Lound
Lime Tree Farm
Monkham Bridge Farm
Westwoodside
NETHERGATE
GREENHILL RD
Carr House
SANBEDS LA
HOLM RD
A161
Sandbeds Farm
GRAIZELOUND FIELDS ROAD
CARR LANE
Close Farm
Croft House
THINHOLME LANE
Hound Farm
HAXEY LANE
AKEFERRY ROAD
Chapel Farm
LANGHOLME LANE
Langholme Farm
Graiselound
FERRY RD
Pear Tree Farm
Owston Grange
Sewage Works
STOCKWITH ROAD
OWSTON FERRY ROAD
PH
STATION ROAD
Pond Farm
Scotton Common Nature Reserve
LC
Thurnholmes Farm
8 05 7 04 6 03 5 02 4 01 3 00 2 99 1 98
74 75 76 77 78 79
A2
1 WESTMORELAND CL
2 AXHOLME RD
3 WEIR CL
4 THE ROWANS
5 COLLEYWELL CL
6 PK DR
7 PARK CL
8 THE BIRCHES
9 MOORLANDS
10 DREWRY LA
11 WEAVERS CFT
39
B2
1 TAVELLA CT
2 CHAPEL CL
3 CRAYCROFT RD
4 HIGHFIELD CR
5 WESTLAND RD
D2
1 HALLCROFT RD
2 MARLBOROUGH AV
3 LOWCROFT AV
4 LOWCROFT CL
5 ASH TREE DR
6 HAYFIELD CL
7 GRANARY CFT
8 REAPER'S WY
9 HAXEY GR
10 THE GOLDINGS
11 HOPGARTH
D3
1 HUNTER'S CFT
2 SADDLER'S WY
3 MOWBRAY CL
40
28

28
27
17
D8
1 FARM LA
2 THE CROFT
3 SCHOOL LA
4 PARKLANDS
Scale: 1¾ inches to 1 mile
0   ¼   ½   mile
0   250m 500m 750m 1 km

A   B   C   D   E   F

Sealings Wood
Clouds Lane Farm
CLOUDS LA
WEST ST
PARK VIEW TER 1
ULYETT LA 2
West Butterwick CE Prim Sch
PO
PH
East Butterwick
Bonito Farm

8

West Butterwick
MESSINGHAM ROAD
Highfield Farm

SAND ROAD
Sewage Works
Common Farm
Glebe Farm
HIGH STREET
SOUTH STREET
Poplar Grove Farm
Hollywood Farm

05

DARBHOLME CRESCENT
SOUTH FIELD DRAIN
Ings Farm
West Grange

7

Sand House Farm

04

Newlands
DARBHOLME CRESCENT
Messingham Ings
DN17
River Trent
Trentings Farm
Black Bank Farm

6

Barlings Farm
NORTH CARR ROAD

03

Newlands Farm
CARR DYKE BK
South Ewster Livery Farm
Barlings House Farm

Kelfield Grange
Walnut Tree Farm
Susworth PH
Castle House Farm

5

Priory (remains of)
DN9
Low Melwood Farm
Moat
Melwood Park

02

Riverdale Farm
Cote House Farm
Middlemoor Farm
Glebe Farm
SUSWORTH ROAD

4

BLACKDYKES ROAD
Drainhead Farm
Kelfield
Grove Farm
South Ings
Tuetoes Hills
P

01

Mount Pleasant Farm
EPWORTH RD
MELWOOD VW
Owston Ferry
GAUTRY LANE
Ings Farm
Kelfield Grange
South Carr
Warren Farm

3

Cemy
St Martins CE Prim Sch
BAGSBY ROAD
Windmill Farm
1 CROFT'S LA
2 MARKET PL
EAST FERRY ROAD
Hardwick Grange Farm

New Farm
BURNHAM ROAD
EAST LOUND RD CHURCH ST
War Meml
PH
NORTH STREET
Ferry Barrier Bank

00

Castle Hill Motte & Bailey
PO
SILVER ST
SOUTH STREET
HIGH STREET
East Ferry
Pin Hill
Hardwick Hill
Scotton Common
Laughton Woods

2

Chimney
STATION ROAD
DN21

99

Windmill
Redgate Farm
Laughton Lodge
Whitestone Farm

1

Lady Croft Farm
EAST FERRY RD
Jenny Hurn
Hornsey Hill
Jerry's Bog

98

MEYNELL ST
HORNSEY HILL ROAD

80 A 81 B 82 C 83 D 84 E 85 F

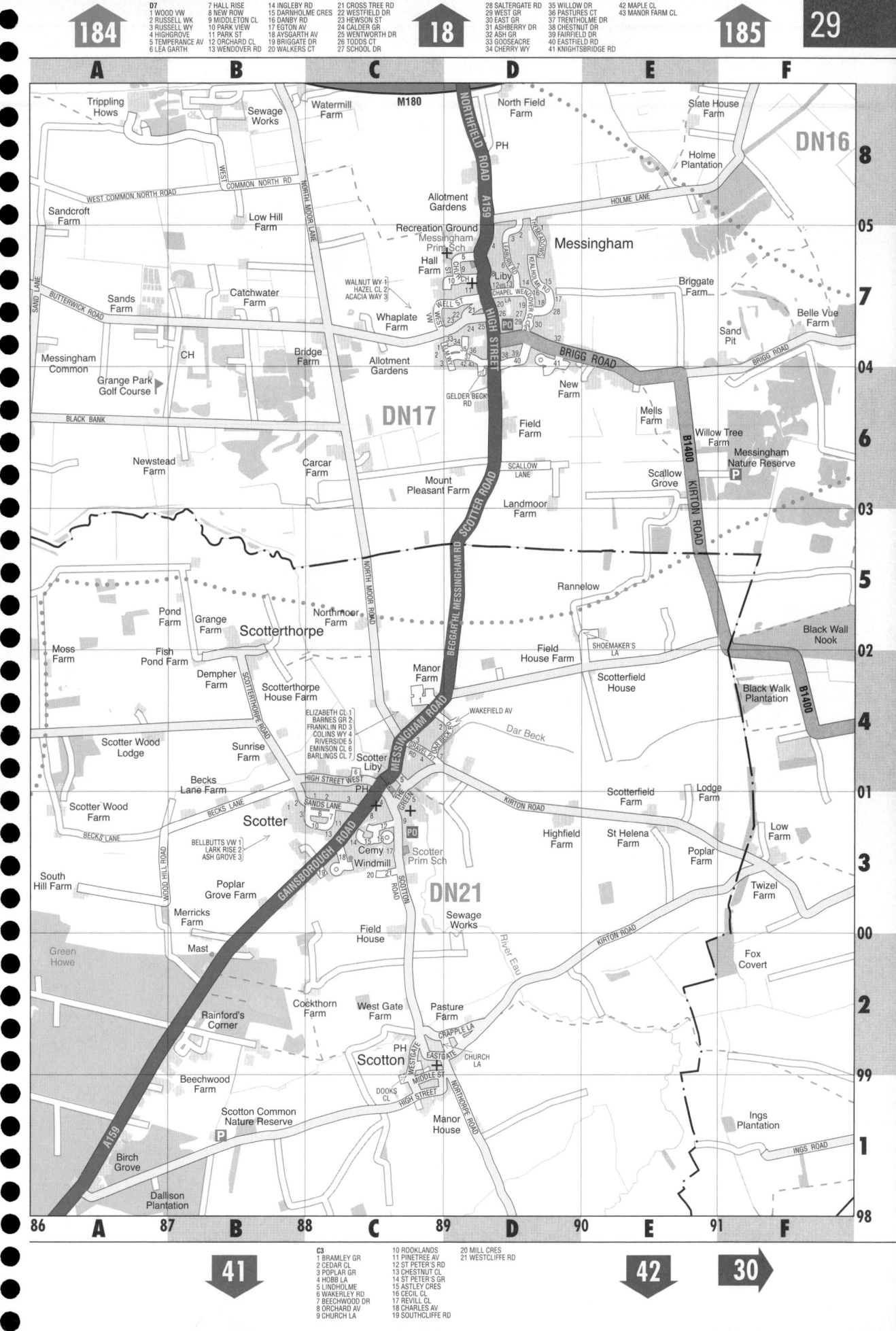

184
18
185
29
D7
1 WOOD VW
2 RUSSELL WK
3 RUSSELL WY
4 HIGHGROVE
5 TEMPERANCE AV
6 LEA GARTH
7 HALL RISE
8 NEW ROW
9 MIDDLETON CL
10 PARK VIEW
11 PARK ST
12 ORCHARD CL
13 WENDOVER RD
14 INGLEBY RD
15 DARNHOLME CRES
16 DANBY RD
17 EGTON AV
18 AYSGARTH AV
19 BRIGGATE DR
20 WALKERS CT
21 CROSS TREE RD
22 WESTFIELD DR
23 HEWSON ST
24 CALDER GR
25 WENTWORTH DR
26 TODDS CT
27 SCHOOL DR
28 SALTERGATE RD
29 WEST GR
30 EAST GR
31 ASHBERRY DR
32 ASH GR
33 GOOSEACRE
34 CHERRY WY
35 WILLOW DR
36 PASTURES CT
37 TRENTHOLME DR
38 CHESTNUT DR
39 FAIRFIELD DR
40 EASTFIELD RD
41 KNIGHTSBRIDGE RD
42 MAPLE CL
43 MANOR FARM CL
A
B
C
D
E
F
M180
Trippling Hows
Sewage Works
Watermill Farm
NORTHFIELD ROAD
North Field Farm
Slate House Farm
PH
DN16
Holme Plantation
8
WEST COMMON NORTH ROAD
NORTH MOOR LANE
A159
Allotment Gardens
HOLME LANE
Sandcroft Farm
Low Hill Farm
Recreation Ground
Messingham Prim Sch
05
Messingham
Hall Farm
Liby
Briggate Farm
WALNUT WY 1
HAZEL CL 2
ACACIA WAY 3
Catchwater Farm
Sands Farm
SAND LANE
BUTTERWICK ROAD
Whaplate Farm
HIGH STREET
PO
7
Belle Vue Farm
Sand Pit
BRIGG ROAD
Messingham Common
CH
Bridge Farm
Allotment Gardens
04
Grange Park Golf Course
GELDER BECK RD
New Farm
BLACK BANK
DN17
Field Farm
Mells Farm
Willow Tree Farm
B1400
6
Messingham Nature Reserve
Newstead Farm
Carcar Farm
Mount Pleasant Farm
SCALLOW LANE
SCOTTER ROAD
Scallow Grove
P
KIRTON ROAD
Landmoor Farm
03
5
Rannelow
Pond Farm
Grange Farm
Northmoor Farm
NORTH MOOR ROAD
MESSINGHAM RD
BEGGAR HL
Scotterthorpe
Black Wall Nook
Moss Farm
Fish Pond Farm
SHOEMAKER'S LA
Field House Farm
02
Dempher Farm
SCOTTERTHORPE ROAD
Scotterthorpe House Farm
Manor Farm
Scotterfield House
Black Walk Plantation
ELIZABETH CL 1
BARNES GR 2
FRANKLIN RD 3
COLINS WY 4
RIVERSIDE 5
EMINSON CL 6
BARLINGS CL 7
WAKEFIELD AV
Dar Beck
4
Scotter Wood Lodge
Sunrise Farm
MESSINGHAM ROAD
GRAVEL PIT RD
DAR BECK RD
Scotter Liby
HIGH STREET WEST
Becks Lane Farm
PH
THE GREEN
Scotterfield Farm
Lodge Farm
01
SANDS LANE
BECKS LANE
Scotter Wood Farm
Scotter
KIRTON ROAD
Low Farm
BECKS' LANE
BELLBUTTS VW 1
LARK RISE 2
ASH GROVE 3
PO
Highfield Farm
St Helena Farm
WOOD HILL ROAD
GAINSBOROUGH ROAD
Cemy
Windmill
Scotter Prim Sch
Poplar Farm
3
South Hill Farm
Poplar Grove Farm
SCOTTON ROAD
DN21
Twizel Farm
Merricks Farm
Sewage Works
Field House
00
Mast
Green Howe
River Eau
KIRTON ROAD
Fox Covert
Cockthorn Farm
West Gate Farm
Pasture Farm
2
Rainford's Corner
CRAPPLE LA
PH
WESTGATE
EASTGATE
CHURCH LA
Scotton
99
Beechwood Farm
MIDDLE ST
DOOKS CL
HIGH STREET
NORTHORPE ROAD
Scotton Common Nature Reserve
Manor House
Ings Plantation
A159
P
1
INGS ROAD
Birch Grove
Dallison Plantation
98
86
87
88
89
90
91
41
C3
1 BRAMLEY GR
2 CEDAR CL
3 POPLAR GR
4 HOBB LA
5 LINDHOLME
6 WAKERLEY RD
7 BEECHWOOD DR
8 ORCHARD AV
9 CHURCH LA
10 ROOKLANDS
11 PINETREE AV
12 ST PETER'S RD
13 CHESTNUT CL
14 ST PETER'S GR
15 ASTLEY CRES
16 CECIL CL
17 REVILL CL
18 CHARLES AV
19 SOUTHCLIFFE RD
20 MILL CRES
21 WESTCLIFFE RD
42
30

← 29

E8		7 ST MARTIN'S CR		F7		F8		7 WILLOW GR

E8
1 VICARAGE LA
2 OLD VICARAGE PK
3 MANOR DR
4 ST MARTIN'S RD
5 ST JOAN'S DR
6 ST JAMES'S RD

7 ST MARTIN'S CR
8 COACH HOUSE GDNS
9 CHURCH ST
10 CHAPEL LA
11 INGRAM GDNS
12 BEECHWOOD DR

↑ 19

F7
1 WALNUT DR
2 ST HYBALD'S GR
3 SWANNACKS VW
4 SUTTON PL

F8
1 PARK LA
2 THE ROOKERY
3 MILL CROFT
4 MEADOW VALE
5 OAK AV
6 CEDAR CL

7 WILLOW GR
8 LARCH GR
9 KINGS CT
10 LIDGETT CL

Scale: 1¾ inches to 1 mile

0 — ¼ — ½ mile
0 — 250m — 500m — 750m — 1 km

Grid columns: A B C D E F

DN16
DN17
DN20
DN21

Scotch Wood
Gull Ponds
Twigmoor Woods
Manton Warren
High Wood
Top Farm
Scawby
Scawby Hall
Cemy
Bowers Wood
Twigmoor Grange
Moor Farm
Messingham Lane
West Street
Scawby Prim Sch
Windmill
Black Hoe Plantation
Greetwell Hall Farm
Greetwell
Welburn Plantation
Scawby Grange
Main St
Sturton
Sewage Works
Broom Plantation
Brigg Road
Greetwell Hall
Aldham Plantation
Sturton Lane
Railway Plantation
New Farm
Middle Manton
Stonepit Wood
Station Farm
Station

1 MANTON CT
2 CASTLE KEEP
3 TRAFFORDS WY
4 BRIGG RD

America Wood
Manor Farm
Staniwells Farm
Settlement
Manton Lane
B1207
Manton
South Farm
Sand Lane
Newlands Farm
B1398
West Street
PH
Grange Farm

F5
1 WOODS MW
2 COTTAGE CL
3 PELHAM VW
4 HUNTS LA
5 BECK SIDE
6 BARNSIDE
7 CHURCH ST
8 FORD LA
9 STATION RD
10 COCKETTS LA
11 DICKINSON CL
12 RUSHTONS WY
13 EAST ST
14 OLD SCHOOL DR
15 MEADOW CT
16 ST ALBANS CL

Cleatham Hall Farm
Cleatham Hall
Quarry Fields Farm
Quarry (dis)
Gainsthorpe Road West
Gainsthorpe Road East
Old Home Farm
Wood Home Farm
Mill Road
Tumulus
Manton Road
PH
Chy
Medieval Village of Gainsthorpe
Cliff Farm
New Cleatham House Farm
Cleatham
Quarry (dis)
Gainsthorpe Farm
Northwood Farm
Redbourne Road
B1206
Mount Pleasant Farm
DN21
Kirton Tunnel
Kirton Road
Low Farm
Cleatham Road
B1400
Sweet Hills

ST GEORGE'S CT 1
ST ANDREW'S CL 2
PARK LA 3
SCHOOL LA 4

Redbourne
Carr Lane
Station Farm
Kirton Lindsey
Mast
Northcliff Farm
North Cliff Road
Stonepit Plantation
High Street
PH
1 BECK LA
2 VICARAGE LA
3 THE FALCONERS
Hall
Mount Pleasant Windmill
Grange Farm
Redbourne Park
Station Road
B1398
Liby
Kirton in Lindsey
King Edward St
Redbourne Mere
B1206
Springcliff Farm
Redbourne Mere
Redbourne Mere
Ings Farm
Cemy
Ings Road
PH
Huntcliff Comp Sch
1 MILL LA
2 BIRCHAM CR
3 LINCOLN CR
Cliff Farm
Pyewipe House
Sewage Works
Moat Manor Farm
B1398
Kirton Lindsey Prim Sch
Clay Lane
York Rd
Mast

92 93 94 95 96 97

B1
1 ORCHARD CL
2 HIGHFIELD DR
3 EAST DALE DR
4 WHITEWELL CL
5 GROVE ST
6 DARWIN ST
7 CHURCH ST
8 SUNNY HLL
9 SPA HLL
10 UNICORN RW
11 GEORGE ST
12 SYLVESTER ST
13 MARCH ST
14 TORKSEY ST
15 TURNER ST
16 ST ANDREW'S ST
17 OLD SCHOOL YD
18 HIGH ST
19 WESLEY ST
20 WRAY ST
21 CORNWALL ST
22 MOAT HOUSE RD
23 TRAIN GATE
24 WEST CROSS ST
25 EAST CROSS ST
26 DUNSTAN HILL
27 SOUTH CLIFF RD
28 PARK HILL
29 DUNSTAN VILLAS
30 CORNWALL ST
31 LOWFIELD CL
32 GAINSBOROUGH RD
33 FAIRFIELDS

B2
1 RICHDALE AV
2 WEST-DALE CR
3 SOUTH-DALE CL
4 NORTH-DALE CL

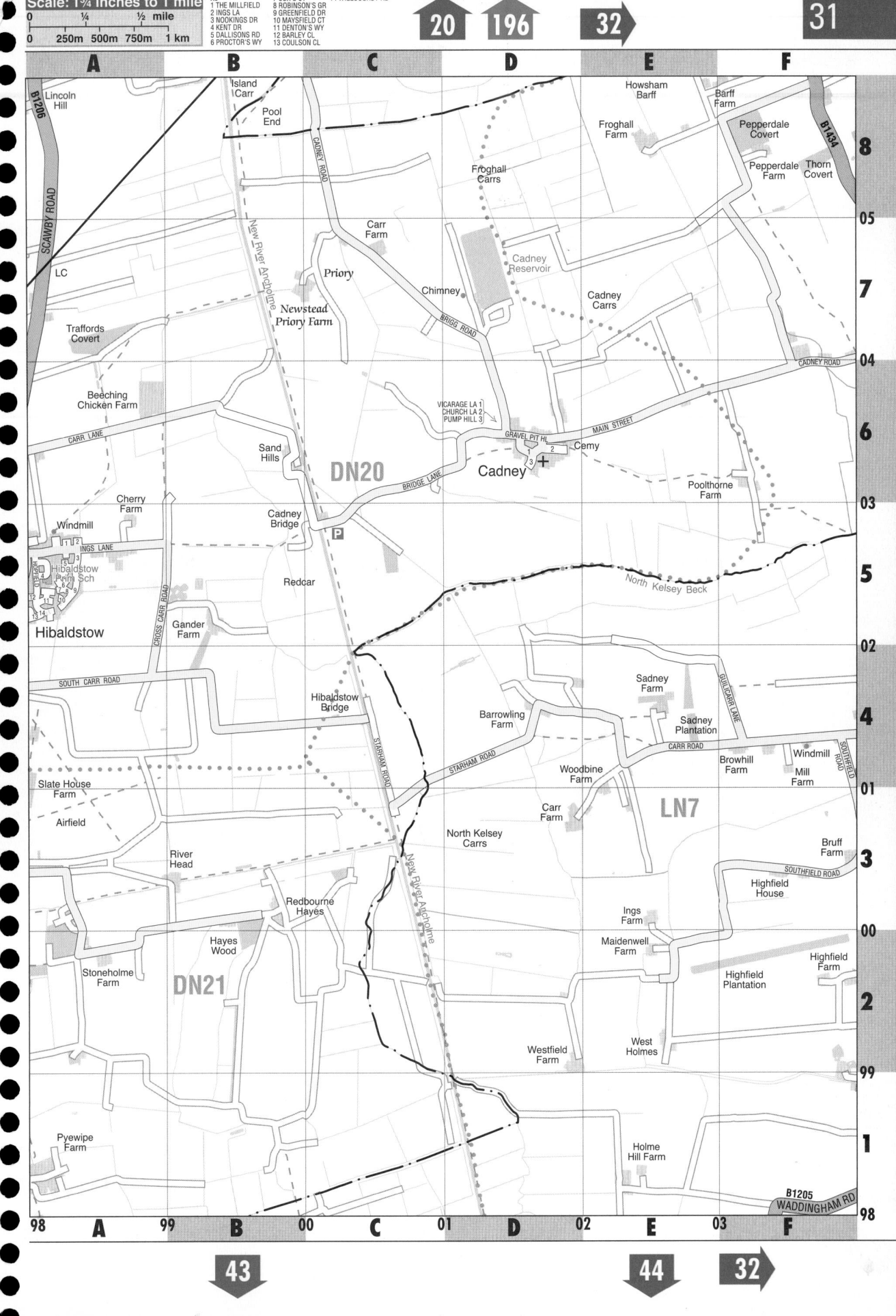

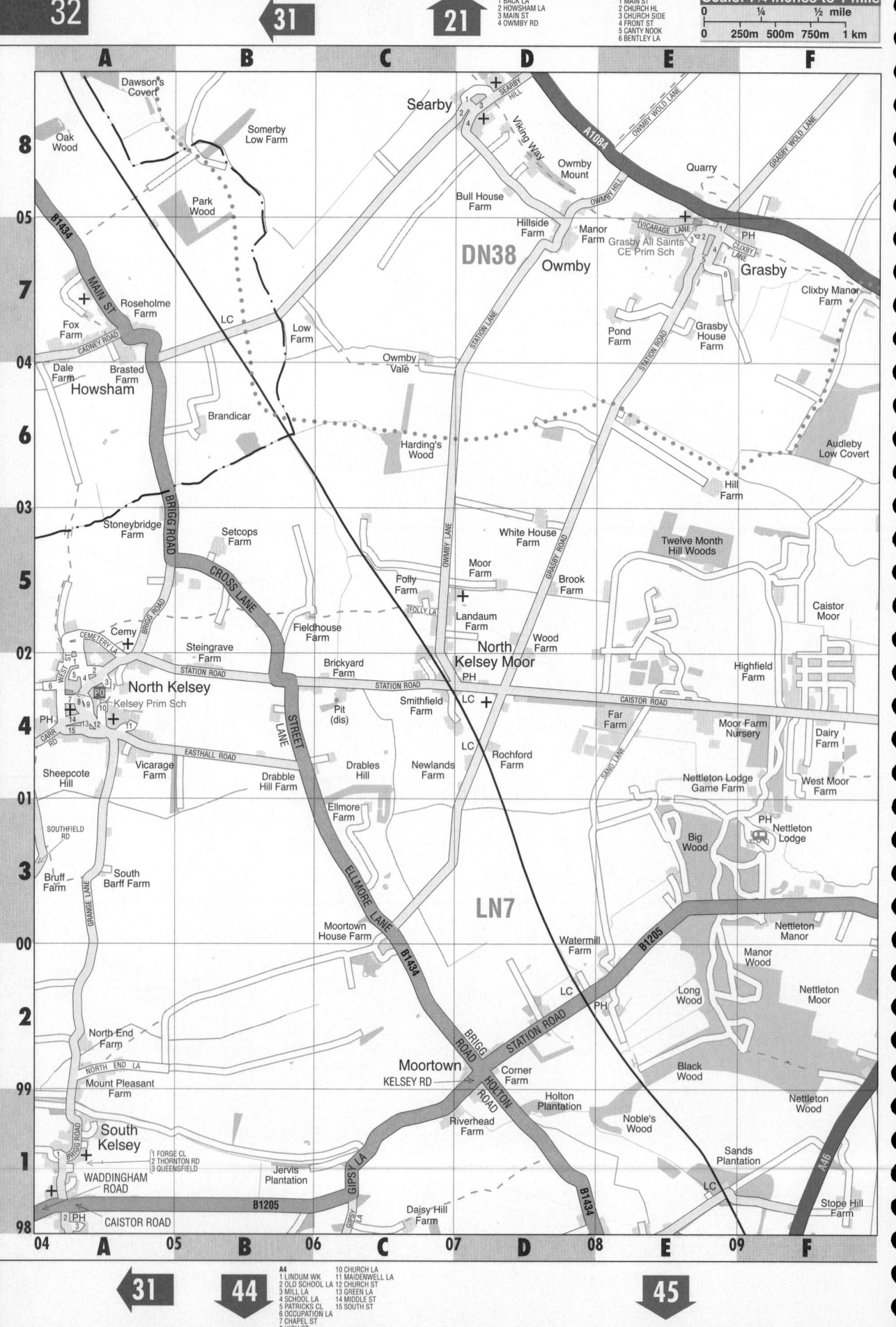

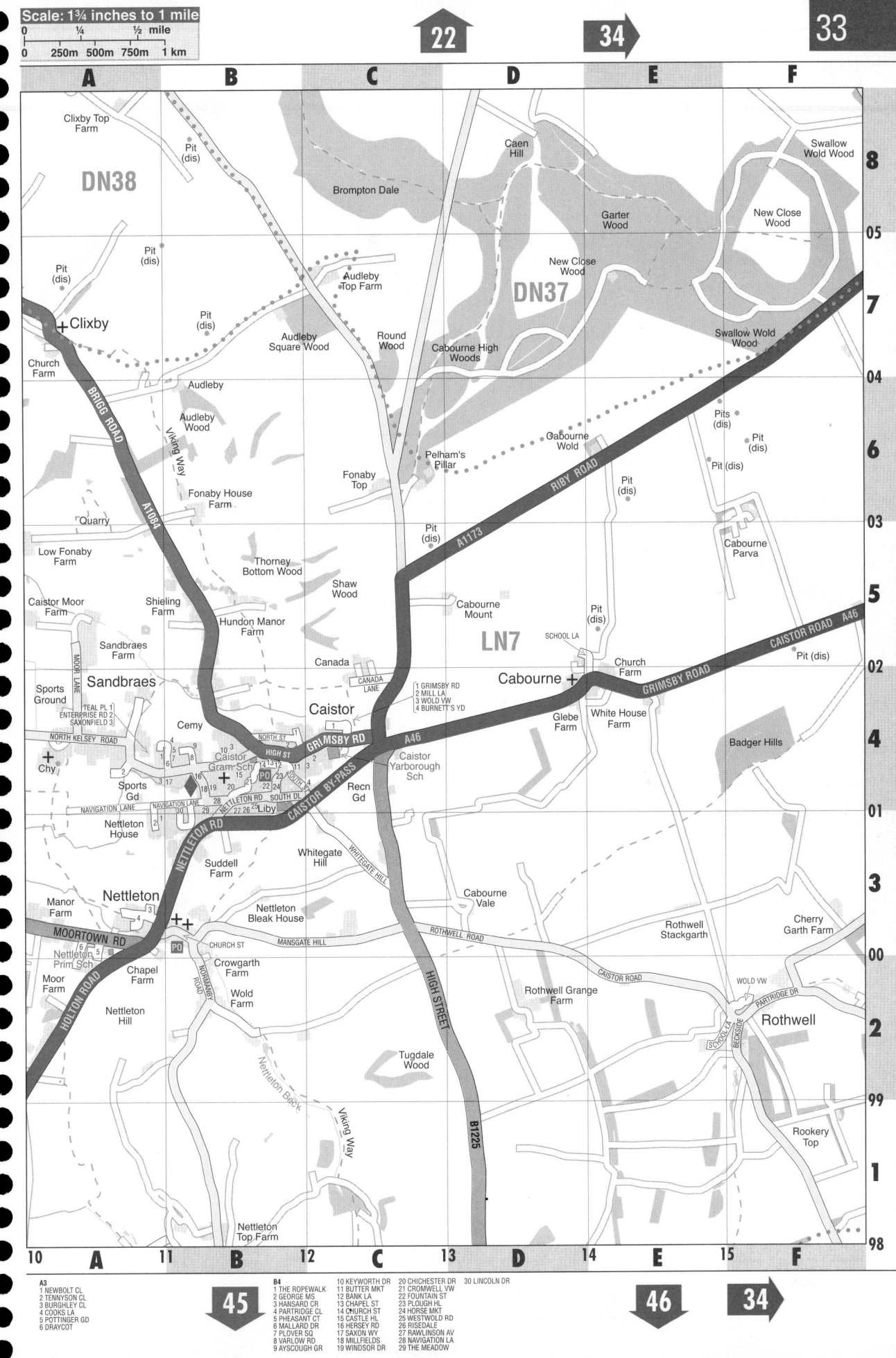

Scale: 1¾ inches to 1 mile

0   ¼   ½ mile
0   250m   500m   750m   1 km

A   B   C   D   E   F

Clixby Top Farm

DN38

Pit (dis)

Pit (dis)

Pit (dis)

Pit (dis)

Brompton Dale

Caen Hill

Audleby Top Farm

Garter Wood

New Close Wood

Swallow Wold Wood

8

05

+ Clixby

Pit (dis)

Audleby Square Wood

Round Wood

New Close Wood

DN37

Swallow Wold Wood

7

04

Church Farm

Audleby

Audleby Wood

Cabourne High Woods

Cabourne Wold

Pelham's Pillar

Pit (dis)

Pit (dis)

Pits (dis)

Pit (dis)

6

03

BRIGG ROAD

A1084

Viking Way

Fonaby House Farm

Quarry

Fonaby Top

Fonaby Top

Pit (dis)

RIBY ROAD

A1173

Pit (dis)

Cabourne Parva

Low Fonaby Farm

Thorney Bottom Wood

Shaw Wood

Cabourne Mount

Pit (dis)

5

02

Caistor Moor Farm

Shieling Farm

Hundon Manor Farm

LN7

Cabourne +

Church Farm

CAISTOR ROAD   A46

Pit (dis)

Sandbraes Farm

Canada

SCHOOL LA

Badger Hills

MOOR LANE

Sports Ground

Sandbraes

CANADA LANE

Caistor

1 GRIMSBY RD
2 MILL LA
3 WOLD VW
4 BURNETT'S YD

GRIMSBY ROAD

4

01

TEAL PL 1
ENTERPRISE RD 2
SAXONFIELD 3

NORTH KELSEY ROAD

+ Chy

Cemy

NORTH ST

HIGH ST

GRIMSBY RD

A46

Caistor By-Pass

Glebe Farm

White House Farm

Caistor Gram-Sch

PO

Caistor Yarborough Sch

Recn Gd

Sports Gd

NETTLETON RD

SOUTH DL

Liby

NAVIGATION LANE

Navigation Lane

NETTLETON RD

Nettleton House

Suddell Farm

Whitegate Hill

WHITEGATE HILL

Cabourne Vale

3

00

Manor Farm

Nettleton

Nettleton Bleak House

ROTHWELL ROAD

Rothwell Stackgarth

Cherry Garth Farm

MOORTOWN RD

++

CHURCH ST

MANSGATE HILL

CAISTOR ROAD

Rothwell Grange Farm

WOLD VW

Rothwell

2

PO

Crowgarth Farm

Nettleton Prim Sch

NORMANBY ROAD

PARTRIDGE DR

SCHOOL LA

BECKSIDE

HOLTON ROAD

Moor Farm

Chapel Farm

Wold Farm

HIGH STREET

Nettleton Hill

Nettleton Beck

Tugdale Wood

99

Viking Way

B1225

Rookery Top

Nettleton Top Farm

98

10   A   11   B   12   C   13   D   14   E   15   F

A3
1 NEWBOLT CL
2 TENNYSON CL
3 BURGHLEY CL
4 COOKS LA
5 POTTINGER GD
6 DRAYCOT

B4
1 THE ROPEWALK
2 GEORGE MS
3 HANSARD CR
4 PARTRIDGE CL
5 PHEASANT CT
6 MALLARD DR
7 PLOVER SQ
8 VARLOW RD
9 AYSCOUGH GR
10 KEYWORTH DR
11 BUTTER MKT
12 BANK LA
13 CHAPEL ST
14 CHURCH ST
15 CASTLE HL
16 HERSEY RD
17 SAXON WY
18 MILLFIELDS
19 WINDSOR DR
20 CHICHESTER DR
21 CROMWELL VW
22 FOUNTAIN ST
23 PLOUGH HL
24 HORSE MKT
25 WESTWOLD RD
26 RISEDALE
27 RAWLINSON AV
28 NAVIGATION LA
29 THE MEADOW
30 LINCOLN DR

33
23

Scale: 1¾ inches to 1 mile

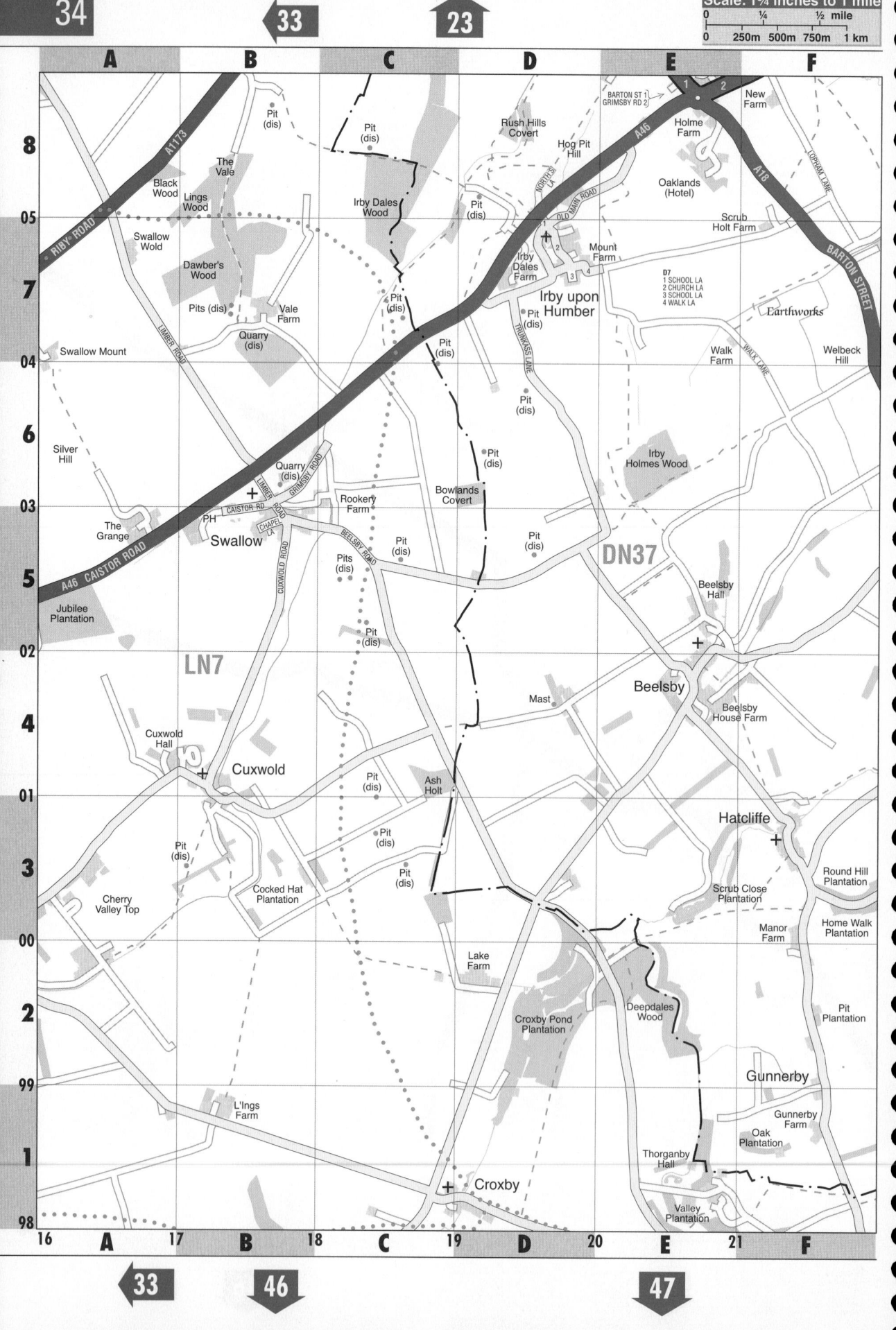
A
B
C
D
E
F
8
05
7
04
6
03
5
02
4
01
3
00
2
99
1
98
16
17
18
19
20
21
BARTON ST 1
GRIMSBY RD 2
New Farm
Holme Farm
Pit (dis)
Rush Hills Covert
Hog Pit Hill
A1173
The Vale
Black Wood
Lings Wood
Irby Dales Wood
Oaklands (Hotel)
A46
A18
LOPHAM LANE
NORTH'S LA
OLD MAIN ROAD
RIBY ROAD
Swallow Wold
Scrub Holt Farm
Mount Farm
Irby Dales Farm
Dawber's Wood
BARTON STREET
D7
1 SCHOOL LA
2 CHURCH LA
3 SCHOOL LA
4 WALK LA
Irby upon Humber
Pits (dis)
Vale Farm
Earthworks
Quarry (dis)
LIMBER ROAD
TRUNKASS LANE
Swallow Mount
Walk Farm
WALK LANE
Welbeck Hill
Silver Hill
Irby Holmes Wood
GRIMSBY ROAD
Bowlands Covert
Rookery Farm
CAISTOR RD
PH
The Grange
CHAPEL LA
Swallow
CUXWOLD ROAD
BEELSBY ROAD
DN37
A46 CAISTOR ROAD
Jubilee Plantation
Beelsby Hall
LN7
Mast
Beelsby
Beelsby House Farm
Cuxwold Hall
Cuxwold
Ash Holt
Hatcliffe
Round Hill Plantation
Scrub Close Plantation
Cherry Valley Top
Cocked Hat Plantation
Home Walk Plantation
Manor Farm
Lake Farm
Deepdales Wood
Croxby Pond Plantation
Pit Plantation
Gunnerby
L'Ings Farm
Gunnerby Farm
Oak Plantation
Thorganby Hall
Croxby
Valley Plantation

33
46
47

A B C D E F

Mill Farm
New Road
Manor Top Farm
CH
Top Farm
New Road
P

Bradley Wood
Nature Reserve
Bradley Gairs
Dixons Wood

Springfield Rd
Fairfield Prim Sch
Waltham Rd
A1243
Scartho
Sports Gd
Low Farm
Mast

M.O. Dr
Springfield Prim Sch
Grimsby Road
DN33
B1203
Southern Wk

Netherwood Dairy
Netherwood Farm
Grove Farm
Rosedale
Team Gate Drain

Waltham Recreation Gd
Fairway
Sch
Danesfield Ave
Station Road
DN36
Toll Bar Farm
Louth Rd
Toll Bar Sec Sch
B1219
Grove Farm
Louth Road
A16
Waltham House Farm

8
05
7
04
6
03
5
02
4
01

New Farm
Barnoldby le Beck
PH
Waltham Road
Grange Farm
Manor House
Bedlam Hill
B5
1 THE PADDOCKS
2 OLD MAIN RD
3 CHAPEL LA

Marian Way
Woodhall Drive
Sunningdale
Archer Rd
Barnoldby Rd
Westfield Road
Sterling Cl
PO
P
Liby
PH
Cemy
Skinners Lane
High Street
Brigsley Road
Norman Corner
Waltham Windmill
Waltham Mus of Rural Life
Waltham Grove
Grove Lane
Ings Lane
Poplar Farm
Mast
Cheapside Road
CH
Waltham Windmill Golf Course

DN37
Waltham Rd
Mushroom Farm
Brigsley Top
Brigsley Top Farm
194
195
Cheapside Farm
Briar Farm
Hillside Farm

Top Farm
Hatcliffe Top
Old Farm
Oak Plantation
Round Plantation
Hatcliffe Plantation
A18

Moorhouse Farm
Waithe Beck
Moor House
B1203
GREEN LA 1
CHURCH LA 2
Brigsley
Waithe Lane
Bratton House Farm

Ashby Hill
Ashby Hill
Shaws Farm
Ashby Lane
Hall Farm
POST OFFICE LA
Ashby cum Fenby
Main Road
Chapel La
Third Lane
PO

Farfield Plantation
Ravendale Top Farm
Ravendale Field Plantation
Ashby Hill Top Farm
Roberts Farm
Homefield Farm
Waithe Top
Grainsby Healing

West Ravendale
Priory Farm
Brownlow's Bottom Plantation
Mount Gate Plantation
East Ravendale CE Prim Sch
THE AVENUE
East Ravendale
Barton Street
Fenby Wood
Grainsby
DN36
Manor Farm

Ravendale Farm
Target Plantation
Fenby Top Wood
Grainsby Lane

Corner Plantation
Woodbine House
Petterhills
B1203
A18
Hawerby Hall Farm
Grainsby Grange

00
3
2
99
1
98

22 23 24 25 26 27
A B C D E F

For full street detail of the highlighted area see pages 194 and 195.

47 48 36

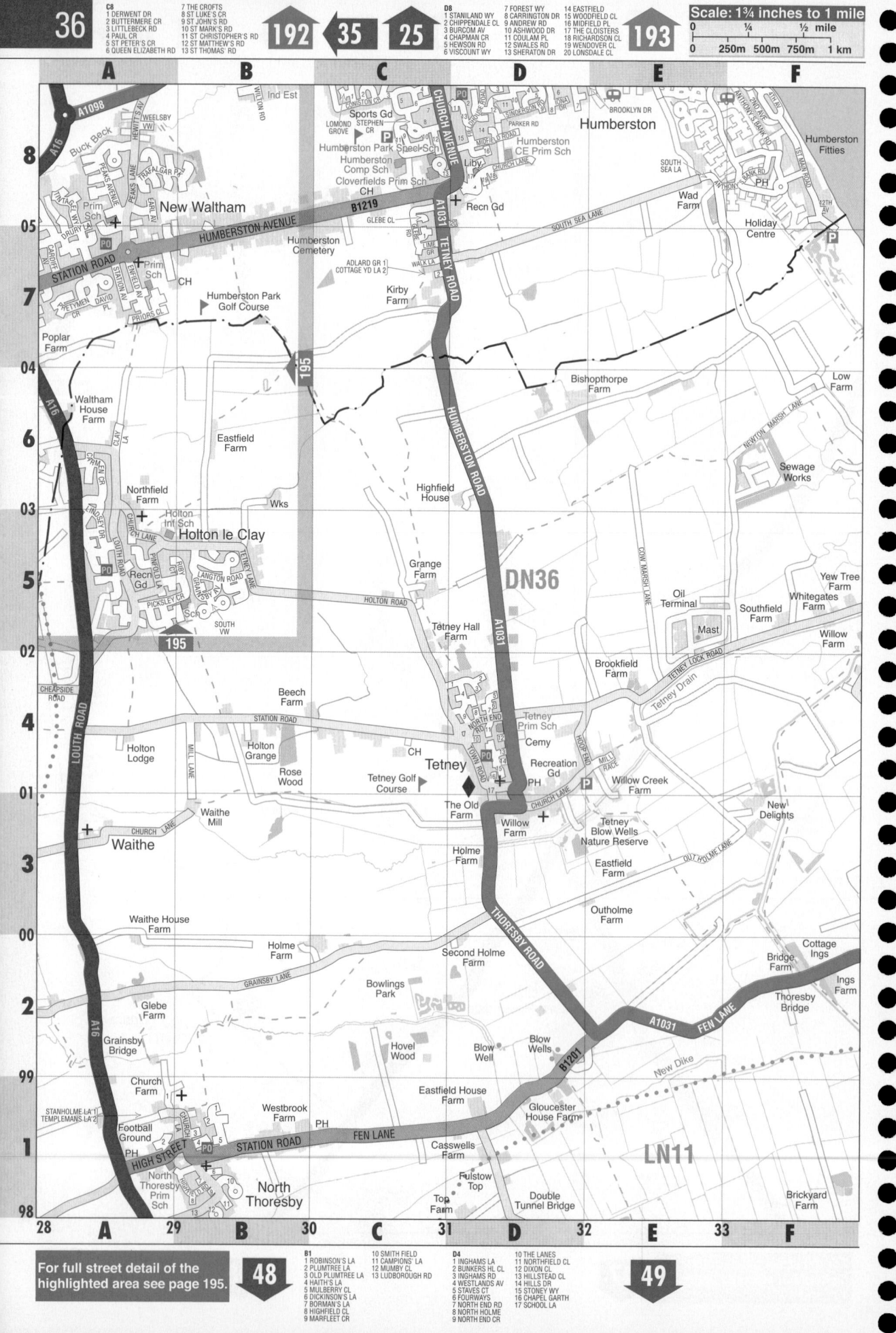
36
C8
1 DERWENT DR
2 BUTTERMERE CR
3 LITTLEBECK RD
4 PAUL CR
5 ST PETER'S CR
6 QUEEN ELIZABETH RD
7 THE CROFTS
8 ST LUKE'S CR
9 ST JOHN'S RD
10 ST MARK'S RD
11 ST CHRISTOPHER'S RD
12 ST MATTHEW'S RD
13 ST THOMAS' RD
192
35
25
D8
1 STANILAND WY
2 CHIPPENDALE CL
3 BURCOM AV
4 CHAPMAN CR
5 HEWSON RD
6 VISCOUNT WY
7 FOREST WY
8 CARRINGTON DR
9 ANDREW RD
10 ASHWOOD DR
11 COULAM PL
12 SWALES RD
13 SHERATON DR
14 EASTFIELD
15 WOODFIELD CL
16 MIDFIELD PL
17 THE CLOISTERS
18 RICHARDSON CL
19 WENDOVER CL
20 LONSDALE CL
193
Scale: 1¾ inches to 1 mile
0 ¼ ½ mile
0 250m 500m 750m 1 km
A B C D E F
8
05
7
04
6
03
5
02
4
01
3
00
2
99
1
98
28 29 30 31 32 33
A1098
A16
Buck Beck
WEELSBY VW
New Waltham
Prim Sch
PO
HUMBERSTON AVENUE
STATION ROAD
B1219
Prim Sch
CH
Humberston Park Golf Course
PRIORS CL
Ind Est
WILTON RD
Sports Gd
LOMOND GROVE
STEPHEN CR
Humberston Park Speel Sch
Humberston Comp Sch
Cloverfields Prim Sch
CH
CHURCH AVENUE
Liby
Recn Gd
A1031 TETNEY ROAD
GLEBE CL
Humberston Cemetery
ADLARD GR 1
COTTAGE YD LA 2
WALK LA
Kirby Farm
Humberston
PARKER RD
MIDFIELD ROAD
CHURCH LANE
Humberston CE Prim Sch
BROOKLYN DR
SOUTH SEA LANE
SOUTH SEA LA
Wad Farm
ANTHONY'S BANK RD
PH
Holiday Centre
Humberston Fitties
1ST MAIN RD
12TH AV
P
Poplar Farm
195
Waltham House Farm
Eastfield Farm
Bishopthorpe Farm
Low Farm
NEWTON MARSH LANE
Sewage Works
HUMBERSTON ROAD
Highfield House
Northfield Farm
Holton Inf Sch
Holton le Clay
CHURCH LANE
Wks
LOUTH ROAD
Recn Gd
PO
LANGTON ROAD
TETNEY LANE
PICKSLEY CR
Sch
SOUTH VW
Grange Farm
DN36
HOLTON ROAD
COW MARSH LANE
Oil Terminal
Mast
Southfield Farm
Whitegates Farm
Yew Tree Farm
Willow Farm
Tetney Hall Farm
A1031
Brookfield Farm
TETNEY LOCK ROAD
Tetney Drain
CHEAPSIDE ROAD
LOUTH ROAD
Beech Farm
STATION ROAD
Holton Lodge
MILL LANE
Holton Grange
Rose Wood
CH
Tetney
Tetney Golf Course
NORTH END RD
TOWN ROAD
Tetney Prim Sch
Cemy
Recreation Gd
PH
HOOP END
MILL RACE
Willow Creek Farm
The Old Farm
CHURCH LANE
Willow Farm
Tetney Blow Wells Nature Reserve
New Delights
Waithe Mill
CHURCH LANE
Waithe
Holme Farm
Eastfield Farm
OUT HOLME LANE
Outholme Farm
Waithe House Farm
THORESBY ROAD
Holme Farm
Second Holme Farm
GRAINSBY LANE
Bowlings Park
Glebe Farm
A16
Grainsby Bridge
Hovel Wood
Blow Well
Blow Wells
B1201
A1031 FEN LANE
Bridge Farm
Cottage Ings
Thoresby Bridge
Ings Farm
New Dike
Church Farm
STANHOLME LA 1
TEMPLEMANS LA 2
Football Ground
PH
HIGH STREET
CHURCH LA
PO
STATION ROAD
Westbrook Farm
PH
FEN LANE
Eastfield House Farm
Gloucester House Farm
Casswells Farm
LN11
North Thoresby Prim Sch
North Thoresby
Fulstow Top
Top Farm
Double Tunnel Bridge
Brickyard Farm
For full street detail of the highlighted area see page 195.
48
B1
1 ROBINSON'S LA
2 PLUMTREE LA
3 OLD PLUMTREE LA
4 HAITH'S LA
5 MULBERRY CL
6 DICKINSON'S LA
7 BORMAN'S LA
8 HIGHFIELD CL
9 MARFLEET CR
10 SMITH FIELD
11 CAMPIONS' LA
12 MUMBY CL
13 LUDBOROUGH RD
D4
1 INGHAMS LA
2 BUNKERS HL CL
3 INGHAMS RD
4 WESTLANDS AV
5 STAVES CT
6 FOURWAYS
7 NORTH END RD
8 NORTH HOLME
9 NORTH END CR
10 THE LANES
11 NORTHFIELD CL
12 DIXON CL
13 HILLSTEAD CL
14 HILLS DR
15 STONEY WY
16 CHAPEL GARTH
17 SCHOOL LA
49

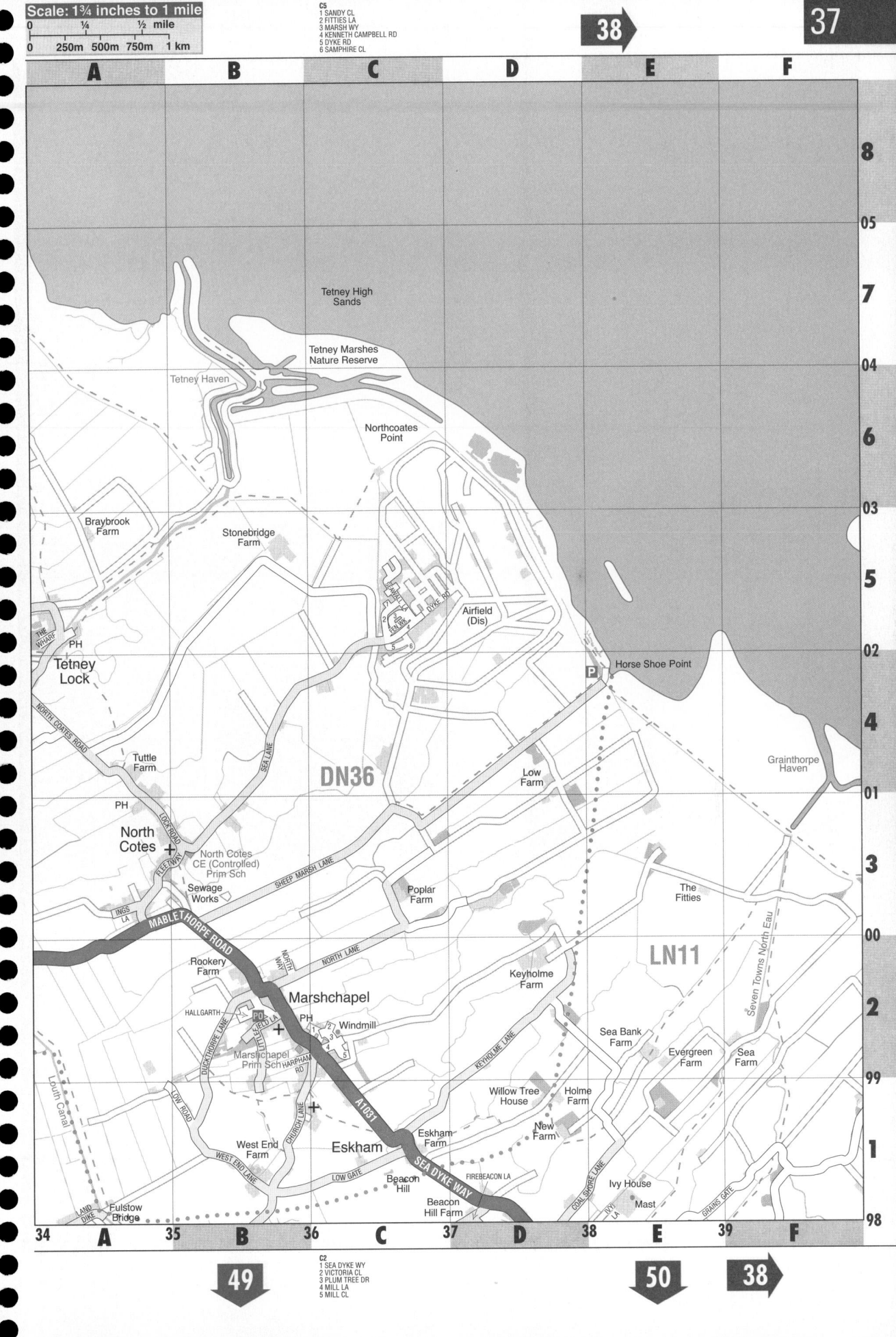

Scale: 1¾ inches to 1 mile

0   ¼   ½   mile
0   250m   500m   750m   1 km

38

C5
1 SANDY CL
2 FITTIES LA
3 MARSH WY
4 KENNETH CAMPBELL RD
5 DYKE RD
6 SAMPHIRE CL

8

05

7

Tetney High
Sands

Tetney Marshes
Nature Reserve

04

Tetney Haven

Northcoates
Point

6

03

Braybrook
Farm

Stonebridge
Farm

5

Airfield
(Dis)

02

THE
WHARF

PH

Horse Shoe Point
P

Tetney
Lock

NORTH COTES ROAD

4

Tuttle
Farm

DN36

SEA LANE

Low
Farm

Grainthorpe
Haven

01

PH

North
Cotes

North Cotes
CE (Controlled)
Prim Sch

Sewage
Works

SHEEP MARSH LANE

Poplar
Farm

The
Fitties

3

LOCK ROAD

FLEETWAY

INGS
LA

MABLETHORPE ROAD

NORTH
WAY

NORTH LANE

Keyholme
Farm

LN11

Seven Towns North Eau

00

Rookery
Farm

KEYHOLME LANE

Sea Bank
Farm

Evergreen
Farm

Sea
Farm

2

HALLGARTH

Marshchapel

PO

PH

Windmill

DUCKTHORPE LANE

LITTLE LA

Marshchapel
Prim Sch

SHARPHAM
RD

Willow Tree
House

Holme
Farm

99

LOW ROAD

CHURCH LANE

Eskham

A1031

West End
Farm

WEST END LANE

New
Farm

COAL SHORE LANE

Louth Canal

Eskham
Farm

SEA DYKE WAY

FIREBEACON LA

IVY
LA

Ivy House

Mast

GRAINS GATE

1

LOW GATE

Beacon
Hill

LAND
DIKE

Fulstow
Bridge

Beacon
Hill Farm

98

34   A   35   B   36   C   37   D   38   E   39   F

49

C2
1 SEA DYKE WY
2 VICTORIA CL
3 PLUM TREE DR
4 MILL LA
5 MILL CL

50   38

37

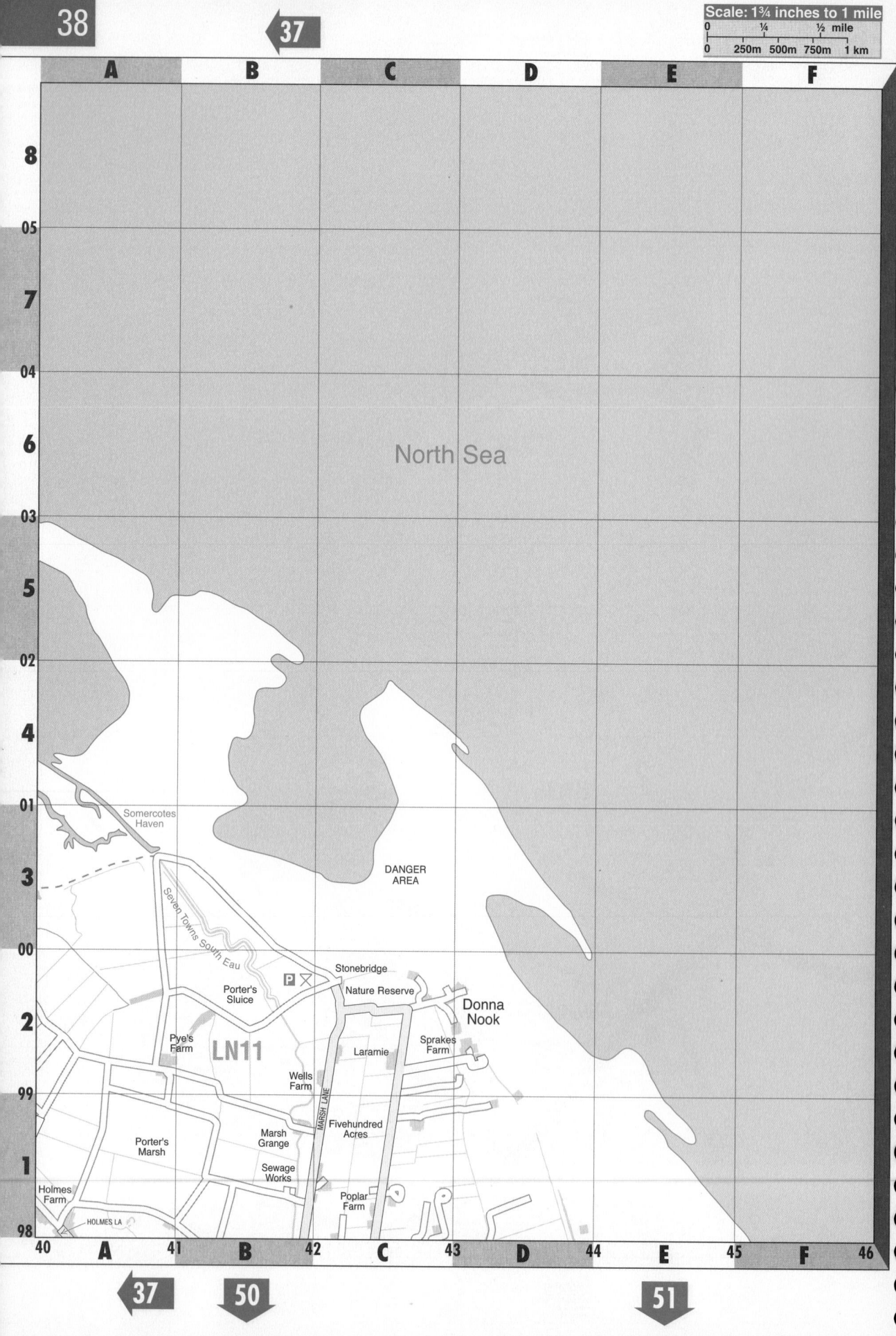

	A	B	C	D	E	F

North Sea

Somercotes
Haven

DANGER
AREA

Seven Towns South Eau

P ✕   Stonebridge
Nature Reserve

Porter's
Sluice

Donna
Nook

Pye's
Farm

LN11   Sprakes
                 Farm

Laramie

Wells
Farm

MARSH LANE

Porter's
Marsh

Marsh
Grange   Fivehundred
              Acres

Sewage
Works

Holmes
Farm   Poplar
                        Farm

HOLMES LA

37   50   51

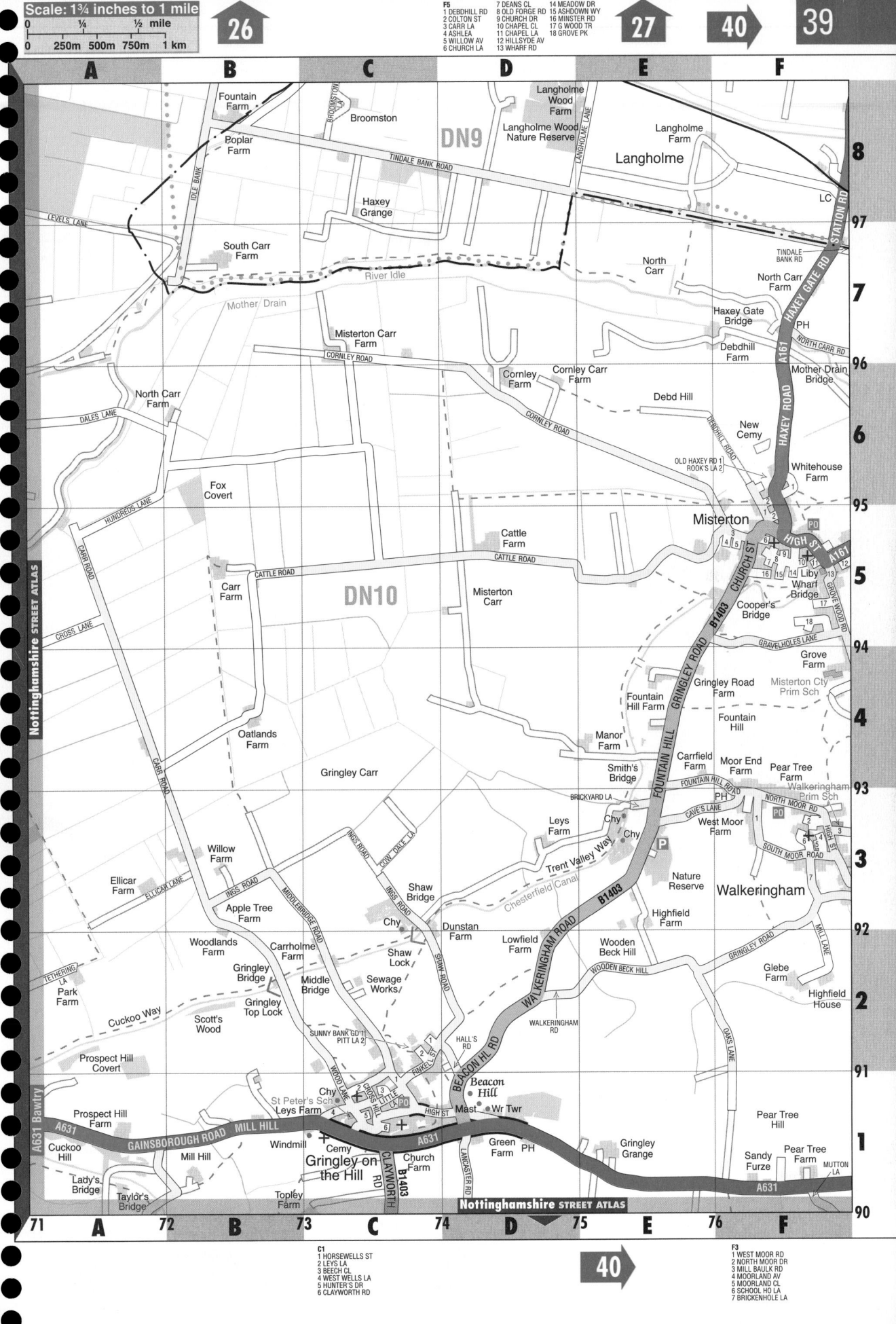

Scale: 1¾ inches to 1 mile
0
¼
½ mile
0
250m 500m 750m 1 km
26
F5
1 DEBDHILL RD
2 COLTON ST
3 CARR LA
4 ASHLEA
5 WILLOW AV
6 CHURCH LA
7 DEANS CL
8 OLD FORGE RD
9 CHURCH DR
10 CHAPEL CL
11 CHAPEL LA
12 HILLSYDE AV
13 WHARF RD
14 MEADOW DR
15 ASHDOWN WY
16 MINSTER RD
17 G WOOD TR
18 GROVE PK
27
40
39
A
B
C
D
E
F
Fountain Farm
Broomston
BROOMSTON LA
Langholme Wood Farm
Langholme Wood Nature Reserve
LANGHOLME LANE
Langholme Farm
Langholme
DN9
Poplar Farm
IDLE BANK
TINDALE BANK ROAD
Haxey Grange
LEVELS LANE
LC
STATION RD
South Carr Farm
River Idle
North Carr
TINDALE BANK RD
North Carr Farm
HAXEY GATE RD
Mother Drain
Misterton Carr Farm
Haxey Gate Bridge
PH
NORTH CARR RD
CORNLEY ROAD
Debdhill Farm
A161
Cornley Farm
Cornley Carr Farm
Mother Drain Bridge
North Carr Farm
Debd Hill
DALES LANE
CORNLEY ROAD
DEBDHILL ROAD
New Cemy
HAXEY ROAD
OLD HAXEY RD 1
ROOK'S LA 2
Whitehouse Farm
Fox Covert
HUNDREDS LANE
Misterton
PO
Cattle Farm
HIGH ST
CHURCH ST
CARR ROAD
CATTLE ROAD
CATTLE ROAD
Liby
Carr Farm
DN10
Misterton Carr
Wharf Bridge
Cooper's Bridge
GROVE WOOD RD
CROSS LANE
B1403
GRAVELHOLES LANE
Grove Farm
GRINGLEY ROAD
Gringley Road Farm
Misterton Cty Prim Sch
Fountain Hill Farm
Fountain Hill
Oatlands Farm
Manor Farm
FOUNTAIN HILL
Carrfield Farm
Moor End Farm
Pear Tree Farm
Gringley Carr
Smith's Bridge
FOUNTAIN HILL ROAD
Walkeringham Prim Sch
CARR ROAD
BRICKYARD LA
PH
NORTH MOOR RD
CAVE'S LANE
West Moor Farm
PO
Leys Farm
Chy
Chy
HIGH ST
INGS ROAD
COW DALE LA
P
Trent Valley Way
SOUTH MOOR ROAD
Willow Farm
Ellicar Farm
ELLICAR LANE
INGS ROAD
INGS ROAD
Shaw Bridge
Chesterfield Canal
Nature Reserve
Walkeringham
B1403
MIDDLEBRIDGE ROAD
Apple Tree Farm
Chy
Dunstan Farm
Highfield Farm
WALKERINGHAM ROAD
Lowfield Farm
Wooden Beck Hill
MILL LANE
GRINGLEY ROAD
Woodlands Farm
Carrholme Farm
Shaw Lock
SHAW ROAD
TETHERING LA
Gringley Bridge
Middle Bridge
Sewage Works
WOODEN BECK HILL
Glebe Farm
Park Farm
Gringley Top Lock
Highfield House
Cuckoo Way
Scott's Wood
WALKERINGHAM RD
SUNNY BANK GD 1
PITT LA 2
HALL'S RD
OAKS LANE
Prospect Hill Covert
FINKELL ST
BEACON HL RD
Beacon Hill
A631 Bawtry
Chy
St Peter's Sch
CROSS HILL
LITTLE LA
WOOD LANE
Leys Farm
PO
HIGH ST
Mast
Wr Twr
Prospect Hill Farm
A631
MILL HILL
GAINSBOROUGH ROAD
Windmill
Cemy
A631
Pear Tree Hill
Cuckoo Hill
Mill Hill
Gringley on the Hill
CLAYWORTH RD
B1403
Church Farm
Green Farm
PH
LANCASTER RD
Gringley Grange
Sandy Furze
Pear Tree Farm
MUTTON LA
A631
Lady's Bridge
Taylor's Bridge
Topley Farm
Nottinghamshire STREET ATLAS
Nottinghamshire STREET ATLAS
71
72
73
74
75
76
90
91
92
93
94
95
96
97
1
2
3
4
5
6
7
8
C1
1 HORSEWELLS ST
2 LEYS LA
3 BEECH CL
4 WEST WELLS LA
5 HUNTER'S DR
6 CLAYWORTH RD
40
F3
1 WEST MOOR RD
2 NORTH MOOR DR
3 MILL BAULK RD
4 MOORLAND AV
5 MOORLAND CL
6 SCHOOL HO LA
7 BRICKENHOLE LA

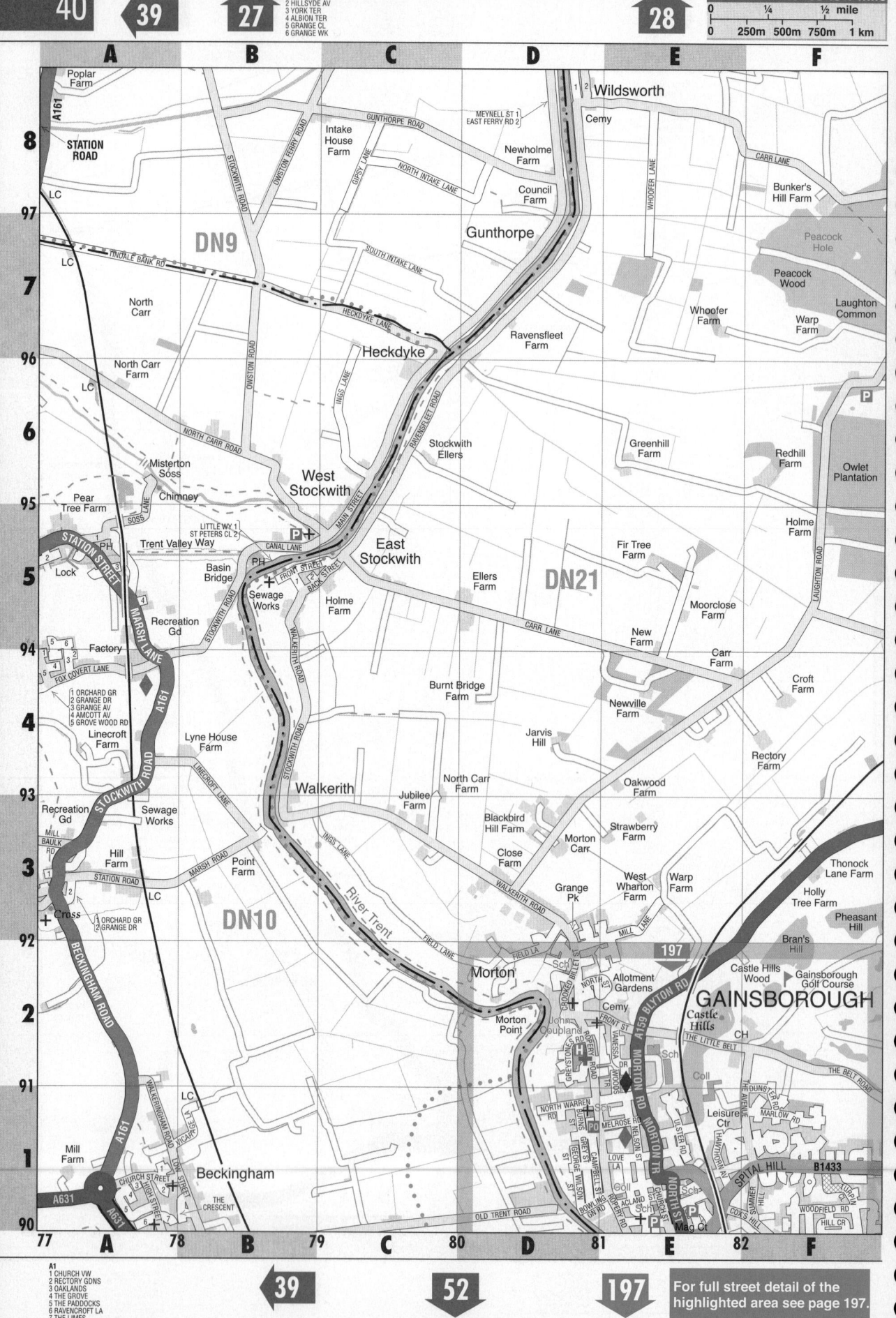

A5
1 STATION RD
2 HILLSYDE AV
3 YORK TER
4 ALBION TER
5 GRANGE CL
6 GRANGE WK

Scale: 1¾ inches to 1 mile
0   ¼   ½ mile
0   250m   500m   750m   1 km

A   B   C   D   E   F

8

Poplar Farm

A161

STATION ROAD

Wildsworth

MEYNELL ST 1
EAST FERRY RD 2

Cemy

Intake House Farm

GUNTHORPE ROAD

GYPSY LANE

NORTH INTAKE LANE

Newholme Farm

CARR LANE

WHOOFER LANE

97

LC

DN9

Gunthorpe

Council Farm

Bunker's Hill Farm

Peacock Hole

TINDALE BANK RD

SOUTH INTAKE LANE

Peacock Wood

7

North Carr

OWSTON FERRY ROAD

STOCKWITH ROAD

HECKDYKE LANE

Whoofer Farm

Warp Farm

Laughton Common

96

North Carr Farm

LC

Heckdyke

INGS LANE

Ravensfleet Farm

West Stockwith

Stockwith Ellers

Greenhill Farm

Redhill Farm

Owlet Plantation

6

NORTH CARR ROAD

RAVENSFLEET ROAD

P

95

Misterton Soss

Chimney

Pear Tree Farm

SOSS LANE

MAIN STREET

Holme Farm

LAUGHTON ROAD

LITTLE WY 1
ST PETERS CL 2

Trent Valley Way

CANAL LANE

East Stockwith

DN21

Fir Tree Farm

STATION STREET

PH

LC

Lock

2

MARSH LANE

Basin Bridge

PH

FRONT STREET

BACK STREET

Sewage Works

Ellers Farm

Moorclose Farm

Holme Farm

5

Recreation Gd

STOCKWITH ROAD

Holme Farm

CARR LANE

New Farm

Carr Farm

94

Factory

FOX COVERT LANE

WALKERITH ROAD

Burnt Bridge Farm

Newville Farm

Croft Farm

1 ORCHARD GR
2 GRANGE DR
3 GRANGE AV
4 AMCOTT AV
5 GROVE WOOD RD

A161

4

Linecroft Farm

Lyne House Farm

LINECROFT LANE

Jarvis Hill

Oakwood Farm

Rectory Farm

93

Recreation Gd

STOCKWITH ROAD

Sewage Works

Walkerith

Jubilee Farm

North Carr Farm

Blackbird Hill Farm

Strawberry Farm

MILL BAULK RD

INGS LANE

Morton Carr

Thonock Lane Farm

3

Hill Farm

STATION ROAD

LC

MARSH LANE

Point Farm

WALKERITH ROAD

Close Farm

Grange Pk

West Wharton Farm

Warp Farm

Holly Tree Farm

Pheasant Hill

Cross

1 ORCHARD GR
2 GRANGE DR

DN10

River Trent

Bran's Hill

92

BECKINGHAM ROAD

FIELD LANE

Morton

Sch

197

Castle Hills Wood

Gainsborough Golf Course

GAINSBOROUGH

Allotment Gardens

Cemy

Castle Hills

A159 BLYTTON RD

2

Morton Point

John Coupland

North St

Front St

THE LITTLE BELT

CH

Coll

THE BELT ROAD

Mill Farm

A161

LC

WALKERINGHAM ROAD

VICAR LA

NORTH WARREN

BURNS

MELROSE RD

NELSON ST

Sch

MORTON RD / MORTON TR

Sch

Leisure Ctr

THE AVENUE

THE YOUNG

MARLOW RD

1

91

Beckingham

THE CRESCENT

OLD TRENT ROAD

H

NORTH ST

Coll

SPITAL HILL

B1433

WOODFIELD RD

HILL CR

90

A631

A631

Mag Ct

P

77   A   78   B   79   C   80   D   81   E   82   F

A1
1 CHURCH VW
2 RECTORY GDNS
3 OAKLANDS
4 THE GROVE
5 THE PADDOCKS
6 RAVENCROFT LA
7 THE LIMES

For full street detail of the highlighted area see page 197.

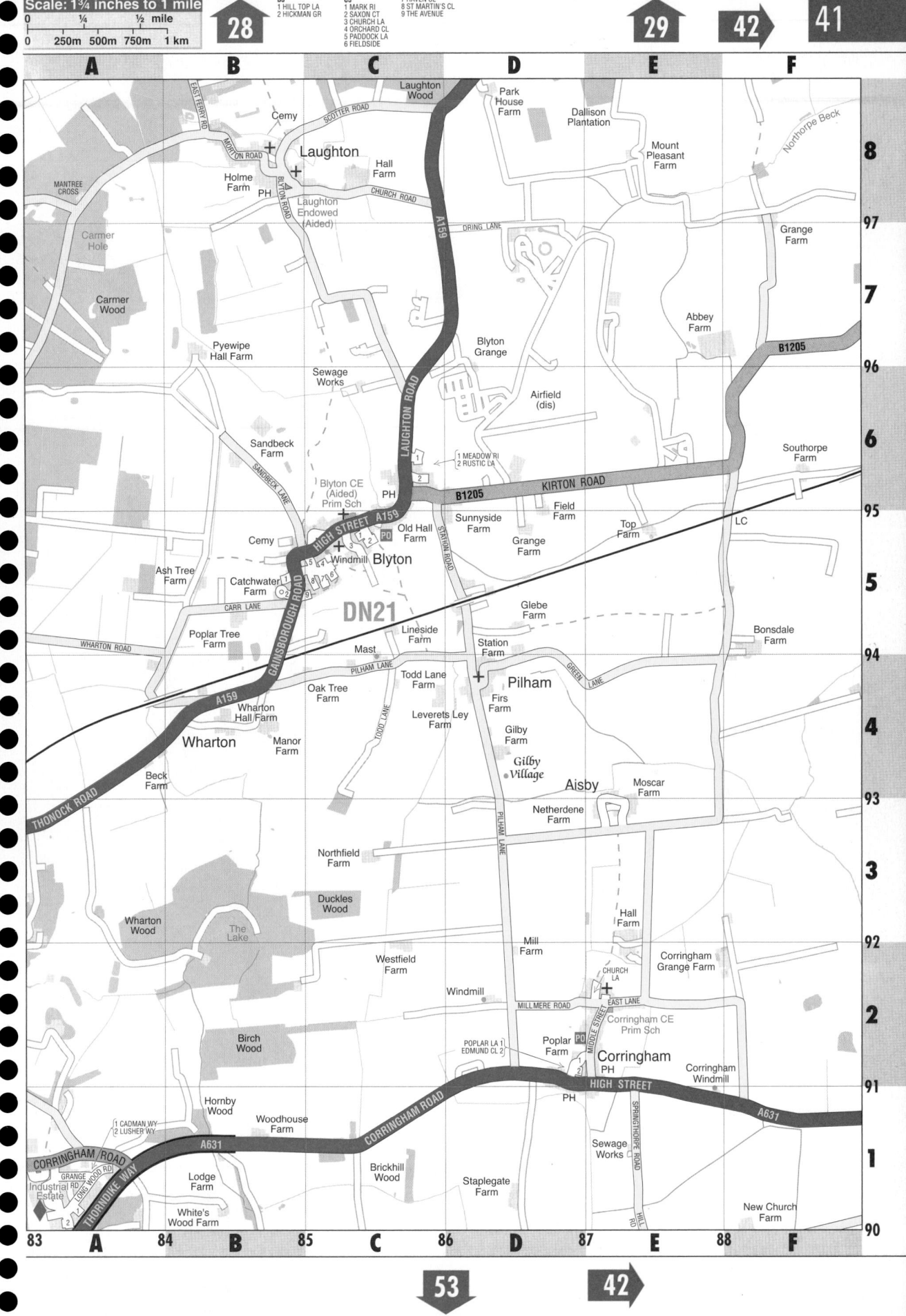

B5
1 HILL TOP LA
2 HICKMAN GR

C5
1 MARK RI
2 SAXON CT
3 CHURCH LA
4 ORCHARD CL
5 PADDOCK LA
6 FIELDSIDE

7 HAVEN CL
8 ST MARTIN'S CL
9 THE AVENUE

A   B   C   D   E   F

Laughton Wood
Park House Farm
Dallison Plantation
Northorpe Beck

Cemy
Laughton
Mount Pleasant Farm
8

EAST FERRY RD
SCOTTER ROAD
Hall Farm
97

Holme Farm
MORTON ROAD
Laughton Endowed (Aided)
CHURCH ROAD
DRING LANE
Grange Farm
B1205

Mantree Cross
PH
BLYTON ROAD
7

Carmer Hole
Blyton Grange
Abbey Farm
96

Carmer Wood
A159
Blyton Grange
6

Pyewipe Hall Farm
Airfield (dis)
Southorpe Farm

Sewage Works
LAUGHTON ROAD
95

Sandbeck Farm
1 MEADOW RI
2 RUSTIC LA
B1205   KIRTON ROAD
LC

SANDBECK LANE
Blyton CE (Aided) Prim Sch
PH
Sunnyside Farm
Field Farm
Top Farm
5

Ash Tree Farm
Cemy
HIGH STREET   A159
PO
Old Hall Farm
Grange Farm
Bonsdale Farm

GAINSBOROUGH ROAD
Windmill   Blyton
STATION ROAD
94

Catchwater Farm
CARR LANE
DN21
Lineside Farm
Glebe Farm

Poplar Tree Farm
Mast
Station Farm

WHARTON ROAD
PILHAM LANE
GREEN LANE

Oak Tree Farm
Todd Lane Farm
Pilham
4

A159
Wharton Hall Farm
Leverets Ley Farm
Firs Farm

Wharton
Manor Farm
TODD LANE
Gilby Farm

Beck Farm
Gilby Village
Aisby
Moscar Farm
93

THONOCK ROAD
Netherdene Farm
PILHAM LANE

Northfield Farm
3

Duckles Wood
Hall Farm
92

Wharton Wood
The Lake
Westfield Farm
Mill Farm
Corringham Grange Farm

Birch Wood
Windmill
CHURCH LA
EAST LANE
2

MILLMERE ROAD
Corringham CE Prim Sch
Corringham Windmill

POPLAR LA 1
EDMUND CL 2
Poplar Farm
PO
MIDDLE STREET
Corringham
PH

Hornby Wood
HIGH STREET
PH
A631
91

1 CADMAN WY
2 LUSHER WY
Woodhouse Farm
CORRINGHAM ROAD
SPRINGTHORPE ROAD

Lodge Farm
Brickhill Wood
Sewage Works

CORRINGHAM ROAD
A631
Staplegate Farm
HILL RD
New Church Farm

Industrial Estate
GRANGE RD
LONG WOOD RD
THORNDIKE WAY
White's Wood Farm
1

83   A   84   B   85   C   86   D   87   E   88   F   90

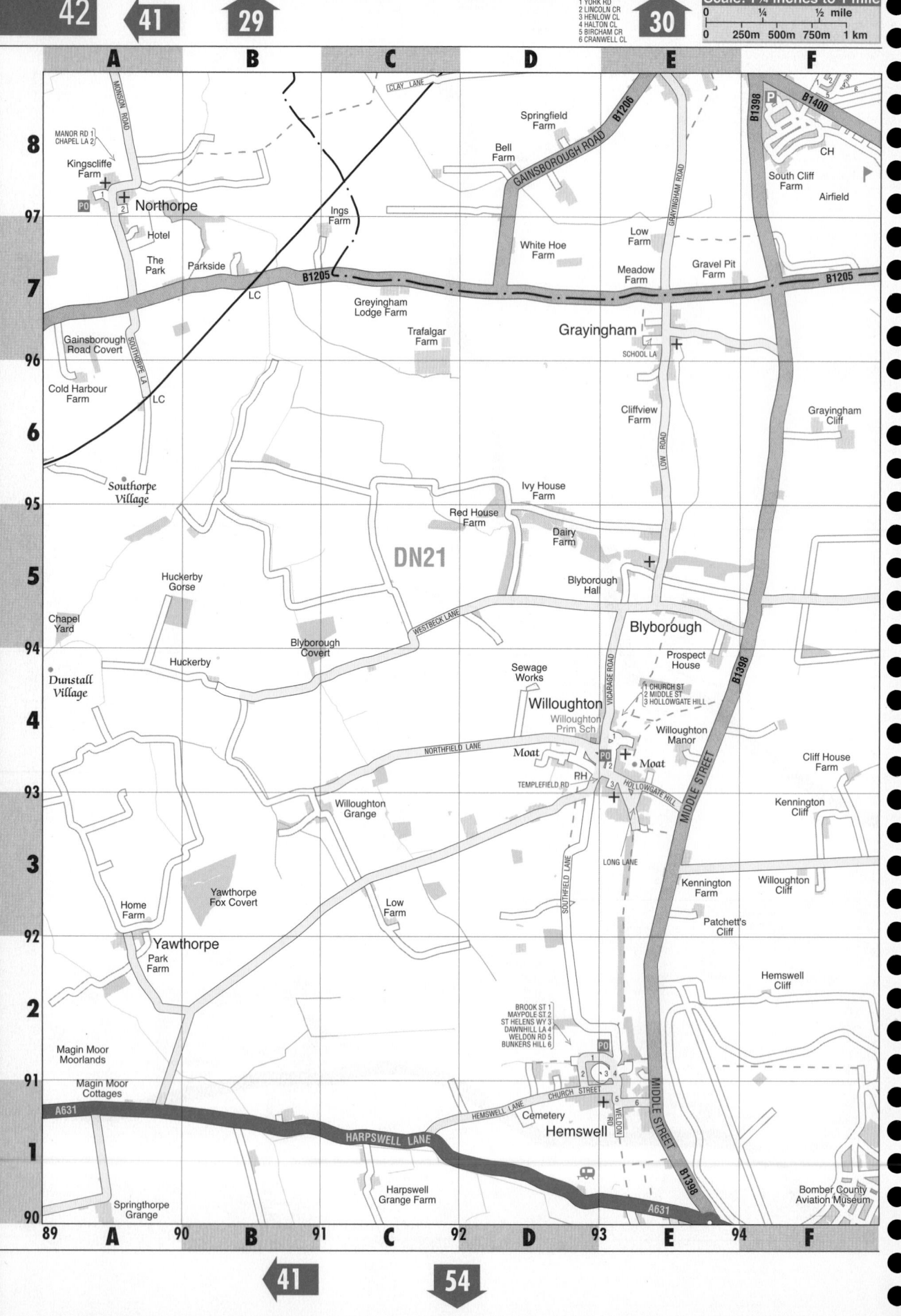

42
41
29
30

F8
1 YORK RD
2 LINCOLN CR
3 HENLOW CL
4 HALTON CL
5 BIRCHAM CR
6 CRANWELL CL

Scale: 1¾ inches to 1 mile
0   ¼   ½   mile
0   250m 500m 750m 1 km

MONSON ROAD
CLAY LANE

Springfield Farm
GAINSBOROUGH ROAD
B1206
P
B1398
B1400

MANOR RD 1
CHAPEL LA 2
Kingscliffe Farm
Bell Farm
CH
South Cliff Farm
Airfield

PO
Northorpe

Hotel
Ings Farm
White Hoe Farm
Low Farm
Gravel Pit Farm
B1205

The Park
Parkside
B1205
LC
Meadow Farm

Greyingham Lodge Farm
Grayingham

SOUTHORPE LA
Gainsborough Road Covert
Trafalgar Farm
SCHOOL LA

Cold Harbour Farm
LC
Cliffview Farm
Grayingham Cliff

LOW ROAD

Southorpe Village
Ivy House Farm
Red House Farm
Dairy Farm

Huckerby Gorse
DN21
Blyborough Hall

Chapel Yard
Blyborough Covert
Blyborough

Dunstall Village
Huckerby
Prospect House
B1398

WESTBECK LANE
Sewage Works
1 CHURCH ST
2 MIDDLE ST
3 HOLLOWGATE HILL

Willoughton
Willoughton Prim Sch
Willoughton Manor
Cliff House Farm

VICARAGE ROAD
NORTHFIELD LANE
Moat
PO
Moat
Kennington Cliff

Home Farm
Willoughton Grange
RH
TEMPLEFIELD RD
MIDDLE STREET

Yawthorpe Fox Covert
Low Farm
SOUTHFIELD LANE
LONG LANE
Kennington Farm
Willoughton Cliff

Yawthorpe
Park Farm
Patchett's Cliff

Magin Moor Moorlands
Hemswell Cliff

Magin Moor Cottages
BROOK ST 1
MAYPOLE ST 2
ST HELENS WY 3
DAWNHILL LA 4
WELDON RD 5
BUNKERS HILL 6
PO

A631
HARPSWELL LANE
HEMSWELL LANE
CHURCH STREET
Cemetery
Hemswell
WELDON RD
MIDDLE STREET
B1398

Springthorpe Grange
Harpswell Grange Farm
A631
Bomber County Aviation Museum

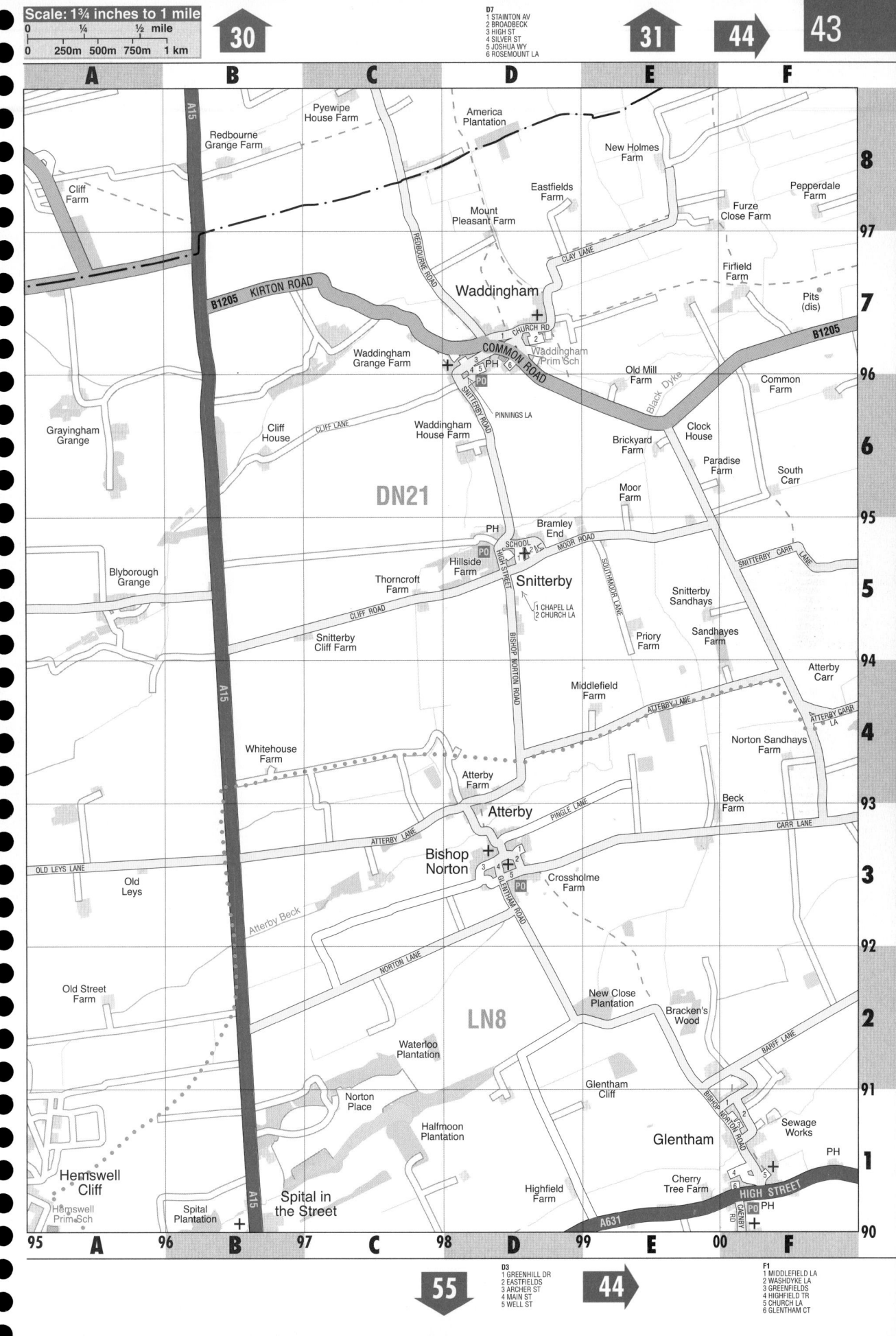

Scale: 1¾ inches to 1 mile
0 ¼ ½ mile
0 250m 500m 750m 1 km
30
D7
1 STAINTON AV
2 BROADBECK
3 HIGH ST
4 SILVER ST
5 JOSHUA WY
6 ROSEMOUNT LA
31
44
43
A
B
C
D
E
F
Pyewipe House Farm
America Plantation
Redbourne Grange Farm
New Holmes Farm
Cliff Farm
Eastfields Farm
Pepperdale Farm
Mount Pleasant Farm
Furze Close Farm
CLAY LANE
REDBOURNE ROAD
Firfield Farm
KIRTON ROAD
B1205
Waddingham
Pits (dis)
CHURCH RD
COMMON ROAD
Waddingham Prim Sch
Waddingham Grange Farm
PH
PO
Old Mill Farm
Common Farm
Black Dyke
PINNINGS LA
SNITTERBY ROAD
Grayingham Grange
Cliff House
CLIFF LANE
Waddingham House Farm
Clock House
Brickyard Farm
Paradise Farm
South Carr
DN21
Moor Farm
Bramley End
SCHOOL LA
MOOR ROAD
SOUTHMOOR LANE
Hillside Farm
SNITTERBY CARR LANE
Blyborough Grange
Thorncroft Farm
HIGH STREET
Snitterby
1 CHAPEL LA
2 CHURCH LA
Snitterby Sandhays
CLIFF ROAD
Snitterby Cliff Farm
Priory Farm
Sandhayes Farm
BISHOP NORTON ROAD
Atterby Carr
Middlefield Farm
ATTERBY LANE
ATTERBY CARR LA
A15
Whitehouse Farm
Norton Sandhays Farm
Atterby Farm
Atterby
PINGLE LANE
Beck Farm
CARR LANE
ATTERBY LANE
OLD LEYS LANE
Bishop Norton
Old Leys
Crossholme Farm
GLENTHAM ROAD
Atterby Beck
NORTON LANE
Old Street Farm
New Close Plantation
Bracken's Wood
LN8
BARFF LANE
Waterloo Plantation
Glentham Cliff
Norton Place
Halfmoon Plantation
Sewage Works
Glentham
Hemswell Cliff
Spital in the Street
Cherry Tree Farm
Highfield Farm
HIGH STREET
A631
CAENBY RD
Hemswell Prim Sch
Spital Plantation
8
97
7
96
6
95
5
94
4
93
3
92
2
91
1
90
95
96
97
98
99
00
55
D3
1 GREENHILL DR
2 EASTFIELDS
3 ARCHER ST
4 MAIN ST
5 WELL ST
44
F1
1 MIDDLEFIELD LA
2 WASHDYKE LA
3 GREENFIELDS
4 HIGHFIELD TR
5 CHURCH LA
6 GLENTHAM CT

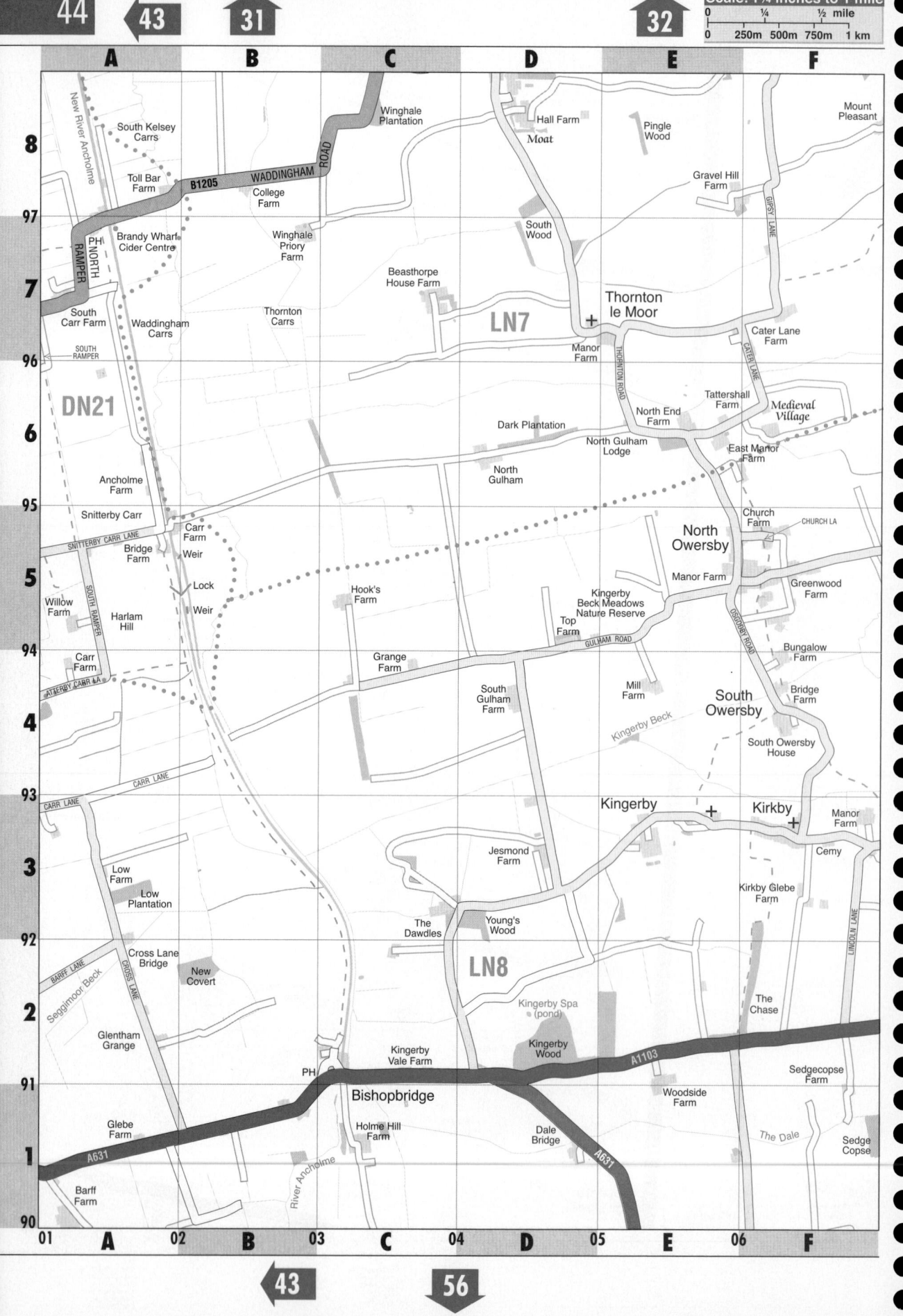

A B C D E F

8

New River Ancholme

South Kelsey Carrs

Winghale Plantation

Hall Farm

Moat

Pingle Wood

Mount Pleasant

Toll Bar Farm

B1205 WADDINGHAM ROAD

College Farm

Gravel Hill Farm

97

PH NORTH RAMPER

Brandy Wharf Cider Centre

Winghale Priory Farm

South Wood

GIPSY LANE

7

South Carr Farm

Waddingham Carrs

Thornton Carrs

Beasthorpe House Farm

LN7

Thornton le Moor

Cater Lane Farm

SOUTH RAMPER

Manor Farm

THORNTON ROAD

CATER LANE

96

DN21

Dark Plantation

North End Farm

Tattershall Farm

Medieval Village

6

Ancholme Farm

North Gulham Lodge

North Gulham

East Manor Farm

95

Snitterby Carr

Carr Farm

Weir

Church Farm

CHURCH LA

North Owersby

SNITTERBY CARR LANE

Bridge Farm

Lock

Hook's Farm

Kingerby Beck Meadows Nature Reserve

Manor Farm

Greenwood Farm

5

SOUTH RAMPER

Willow Farm

Weir

Top Farm

OSGODBY ROAD

Harlam Hill

Bungalow Farm

94

Carr Farm

Grange Farm

South Gulham Farm

GULHAM ROAD

Mill Farm

South Owersby

Bridge Farm

ATTERBY CARR LA

South Owersby House

4

Kingerby Beck

93

CARR LANE

CARR LANE

Kingerby

Kirkby

Manor Farm

3

Low Farm

Jesmond Farm

Cemy

Low Plantation

Kirkby Glebe Farm

BARFF LANE

CROSS LANE

Cross Lane Bridge

New Covert

Young's Wood

LINCOLN LANE

92

The Dawdles

LN8

Kingerby Spa (pond)

The Chase

2

Seggimoor Beck

Glentham Grange

Kingerby Wood

A1103

Sedgecopse Farm

91

PH

Kingerby Vale Farm

Bishopbridge

A631

Woodside Farm

The Dale

Glebe Farm

Holme Hill Farm

Dale Bridge

A631

Sedge Copse

1

A631

River Ancholme

Barff Farm

90

01 A 02 B 03 C 04 D 05 E 06 F

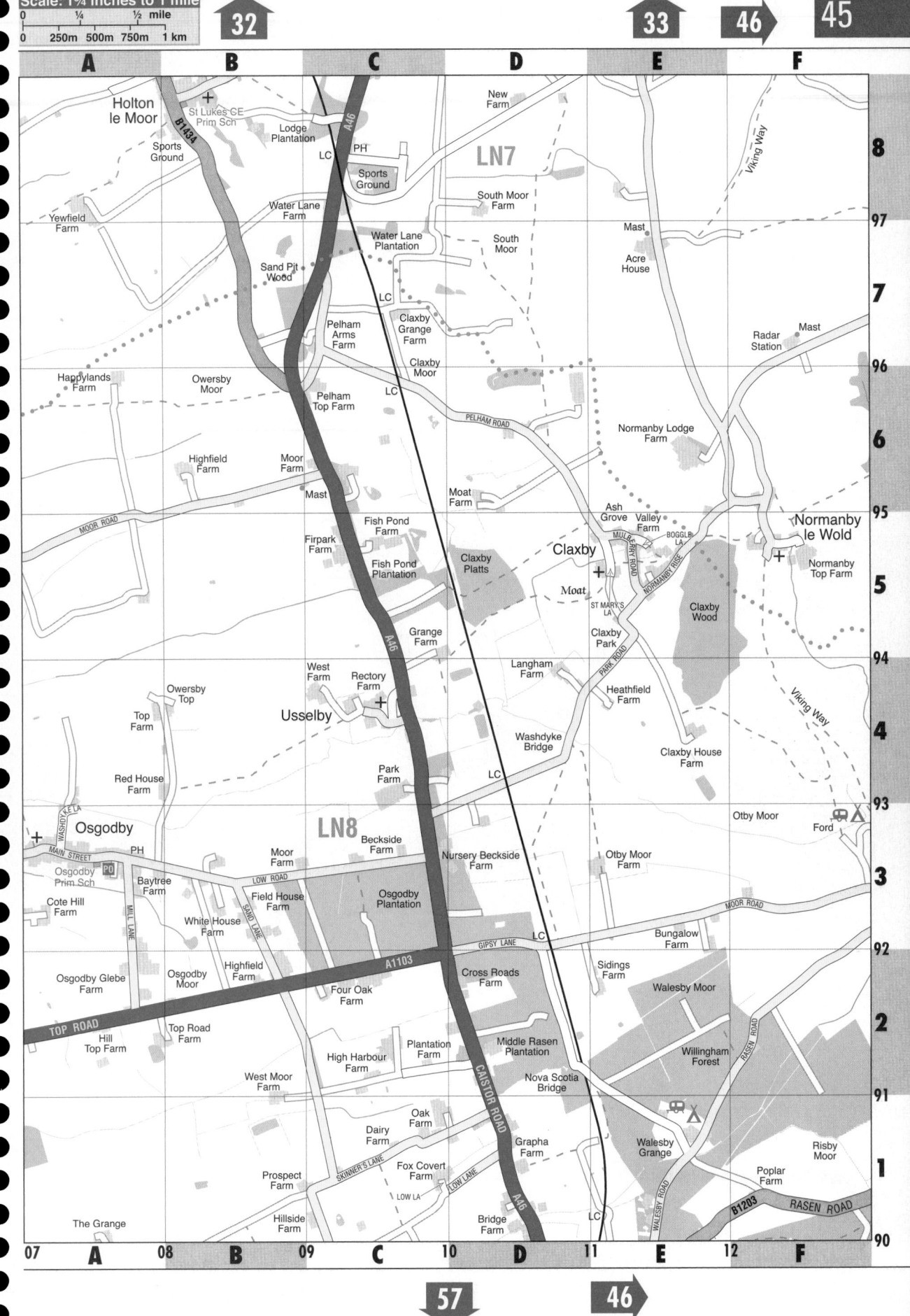
Scale: 1¾ inches to 1 mile
0 ¼ ½ mile
0 250m 500m 750m 1 km
32
33
46
A B C D E F
Holton le Moor
St Lukes CE Prim Sch
B1434
A46
Lodge Plantation
New Farm
Sports Ground
PH
LC
LN7
Viking Way
South Moor Farm
Yewfield Farm
Water Lane Farm
Water Lane Plantation
South Moor
Mast
Acre House
Sand Pit Wood
LC
Claxby Grange Farm
Pelham Arms Farm
Radar Station
Mast
Happylands Farm
Owersby Moor
Claxby Moor
Pelham Top Farm
LC
PELHAM ROAD
Normanby Lodge Farm
Highfield Farm
Moor Farm
Mast
Moat Farm
MOOR ROAD
Fish Pond Farm
Ash Grove
Valley Farm
Normanby le Wold
Firpark Farm
Claxby
MULBERRY ROAD
BOGGLE LA
NORMANBY RISE
Normanby Top Farm
Fish Pond Plantation
Claxby Platts
Moat
ST MARY'S LA
Claxby Wood
Grange Farm
A46
Claxby Park
PARK ROAD
West Farm
Rectory Farm
Langham Farm
Heathfield Farm
Owersby Top
Top Farm
Usselby
Viking Way
Washdyke Bridge
Claxby House Farm
Red House Farm
Park Farm
LC
WASHDYKE LA
Osgodby
LN8
Otby Moor
Ford
MAIN STREET
PH
Beckside Farm
Moor Farm
Nursery Beckside Farm
Otby Moor Farm
Osgodby Prim Sch
PO
Baytree Farm
LOW ROAD
Cote Hill Farm
Field House Farm
Osgodby Plantation
MOOR ROAD
MILL LANE
SAND LANE
White House Farm
Bungalow Farm
GIPSY LANE
LC
Osgodby Glebe Farm
Osgodby Moor
Highfield Farm
A1103
Cross Roads Farm
Sidings Farm
Walesby Moor
Four Oak Farm
TOP ROAD
Hill Top Farm
Top Road Farm
Middle Rasen Plantation
Plantation Farm
Willingham Forest
RASEN ROAD
High Harbour Farm
West Moor Farm
CAISTOR ROAD
Nova Scotia Bridge
Oak Farm
Dairy Farm
Grapha Farm
Walesby Grange
Risby Moor
Prospect Farm
SKINNER'S LANE
Fox Covert Farm
Poplar Farm
LOW LA
LOW LANE
B1203
RASEN ROAD
WALESBY ROAD
A46
The Grange
Hillside Farm
Bridge Farm
LC
07 08 09 10 11 12
98 97 96 95 94 93 92 91 90
8 7 6 5 4 3 2 1
57
46

45
33
34

Scale: 1¾ inches to 1 mile

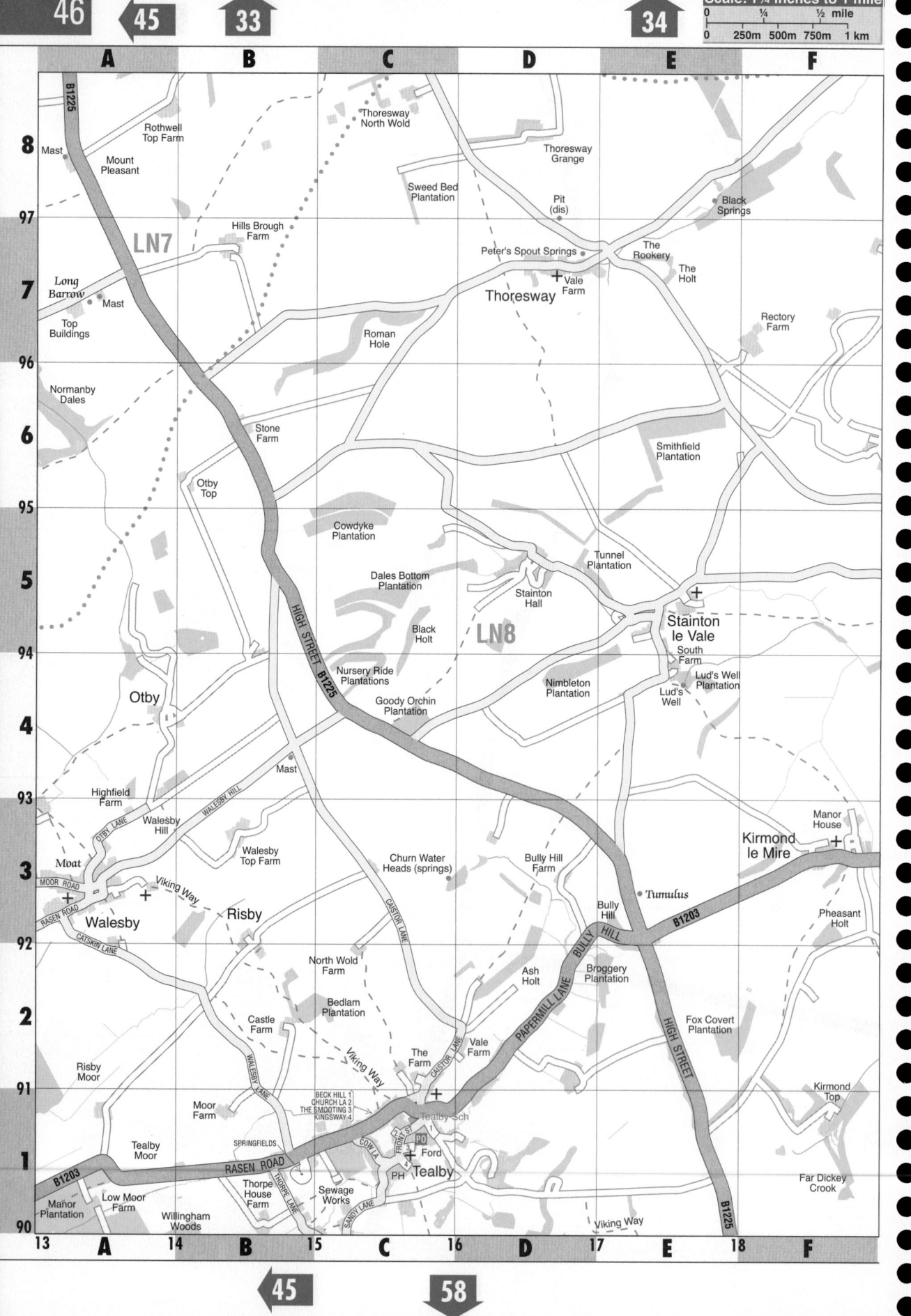

Rothwell Top Farm
Mast
Mount Pleasant
Thoresway North Wold
Thoresway Grange
Sweed Bed Plantation
Pit (dis)
Black Springs
Hills Brough Farm
LN7
Peter's Spout Springs
The Rookery
The Holt
Long Barrow
Mast
Top Buildings
Vale Farm
Thoresway
Rectory Farm
Roman Hole
Normanby Dales
Stone Farm
Smithfield Plantation
Otby Top
Cowdyke Plantation
Dales Bottom Plantation
Tunnel Plantation
Stainton Hall
Stainton le Vale
Black Holt
LN8
South Farm
HIGH STREET
B1225
Nursery Ride Plantations
Nimbleton Plantation
Lud's Well Plantation
Lud's Well
Otby
Goodv Orchin Plantation
Mast
Highfield Farm
Walesby Hill
WALESBY HILL
OTBY LANE
Walesby Top Farm
Churn Water Heads (springs)
Bully Hill Farm
Manor House
Kirmond le Mire
Moat
MOOR ROAD
Viking Way
Risby
Walesby
RASEN ROAD
CAISTOR LANE
Tumulus
Bully Hill
BULLY HILL
B1203
Pheasant Holt
CATSKIN LANE
North Wold Farm
Ash Holt
Broggery Plantation
Bedlam Plantation
Castle Farm
PAPERMILL LANE
Fox Covert Plantation
Risby Moor
Viking Way
The Farm
Vale Farm
WALESBY LANE
Kirmond Top
BECK HILL 1
CHURCH LA 2
THE SMOOTHING 3
KINGSWAY 4
Moor Farm
Tealby Sch
FRONT ST
PO
COW LA
SPRINGFIELDS
Ford
Tealby Moor
RASEN ROAD
THORPE LANE
PH
Tealby
B1203
Far Dickey Crook
Manor Plantation
Low Moor Farm
Thorpe House Farm
Sewage Works
SANDY LANE
Willingham Woods
Viking Way
B1225

45
58

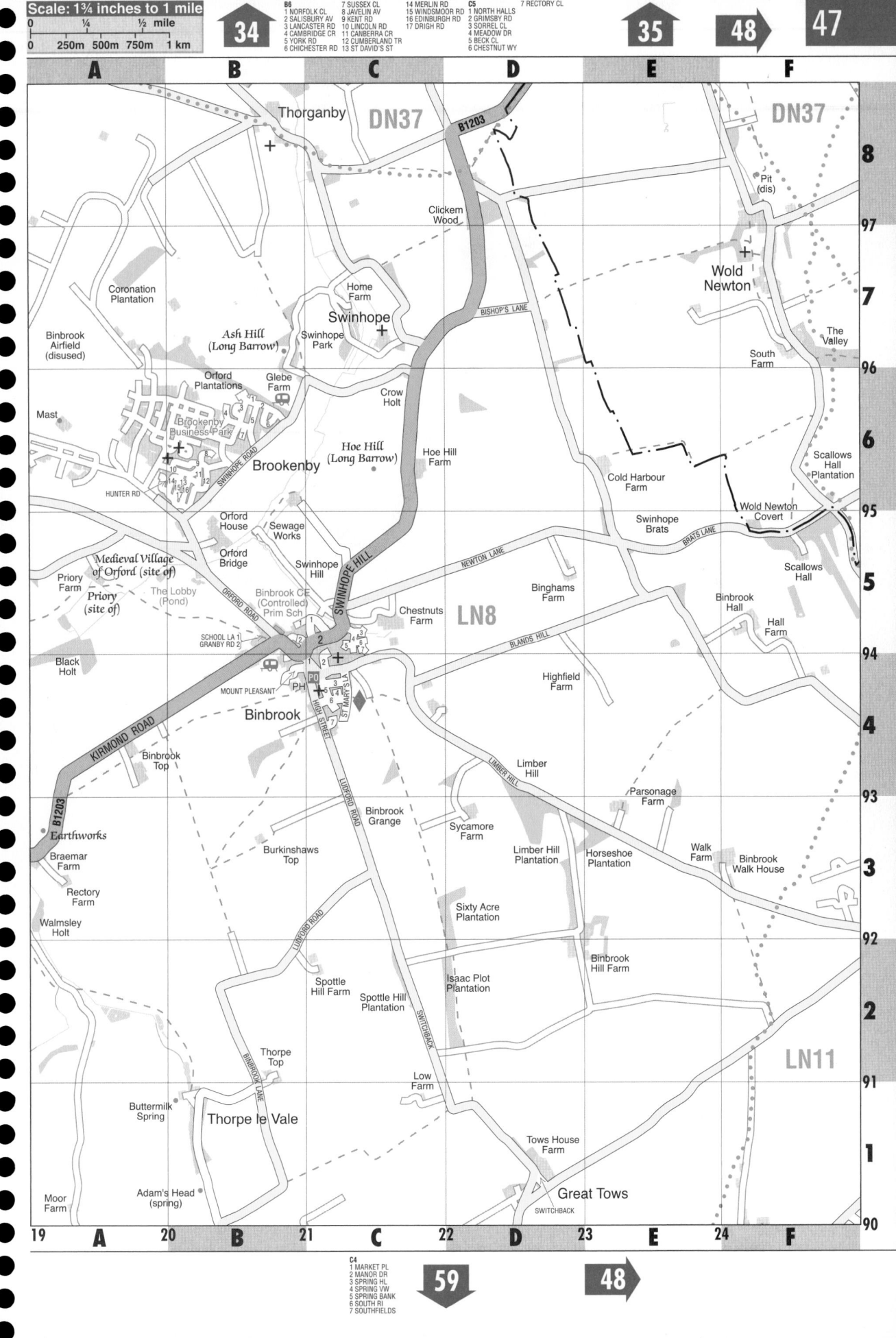

Scale: 1¾ inches to 1 mile
0 ¼ ½ mile
0 250m 500m 750m 1 km
34
35
48
B6
1 NORFOLK CL
2 SALISBURY AV
3 LANCASTER RD
4 CAMBRIDGE CR
5 YORK RD
6 CHICHESTER RD
7 SUSSEX CL
8 JAVELIN AV
9 KENT RD
10 LINCOLN RD
11 CANBERRA CR
12 CUMBERLAND TR
13 ST DAVID'S ST
14 MERLIN RD
15 WINDSMOOR RD
16 EDINBURGH RD
17 DRIGH RD
C5
1 NORTH HALLS
2 GRIMSBY RD
3 SORREL CL
4 MEADOW DR
5 BECK CL
6 CHESTNUT WY
7 RECTORY CL
A B C D E F
Thorganby
DN37
B1203
Clickem Wood
Pit (dis)
Wold Newton
Coronation Plantation
Home Farm
Swinhope
BISHOP'S LANE
Binbrook Airfield (disused)
Ash Hill (Long Barrow)
Swinhope Park
The Valley
South Farm
Orford Plantations
Glebe Farm
Crow Holt
Mast
Brookenby Business Park
Hoe Hill (Long Barrow)
Hoe Hill Farm
Scallows Hall Plantation
Brookenby
SWINHOPE ROAD
HUNTER RD
Cold Harbour Farm
Wold Newton Covert
Orford House
Sewage Works
Swinhope Brats
BRATS LANE
Orford Bridge
NEWTON LANE
Medieval Village of Orford (site of)
Swinhope Hill
SWINHOPE HILL
Scallows Hall
Priory Farm
The Lobby (Pond)
Binbrook CE (Controlled) Prim Sch
Binghams Farm
Binbrook Hall
Priory (site of)
ORFORD ROAD
Chestnuts Farm
LN8
Hall Farm
SCHOOL LA 1
GRANBY RD 2
BLANDS HILL
Black Holt
MOUNT PLEASANT
PH
PO
Highfield Farm
Binbrook
HIGH STREET
ST MARY'S LA
KIRMOND ROAD
Binbrook Top
Limber Hill
LIMBER HILL
Parsonage Farm
LUDFORD ROAD
Binbrook Grange
Sycamore Farm
Earthworks
Braemar Farm
Burkinshaws Top
Limber Hill Plantation
Horseshoe Plantation
Walk Farm
Binbrook Walk House
Rectory Farm
Sixty Acre Plantation
Walmsley Holt
LUDFORD ROAD
Binbrook Hill Farm
Spottle Hill Farm
Spottle Hill Plantation
Isaac Plot Plantation
SWITCHBACK
Thorpe Top
BINBROOK LANE
LN11
Low Farm
Buttermilk Spring
Thorpe le Vale
Tows House Farm
Moor Farm
Adam's Head (spring)
Great Tows
SWITCHBACK
8 97 7 96 6 95 5 94 4 93 3 92 2 91 1 90
19 20 21 22 23 24
C4
1 MARKET PL
2 MANOR DR
3 SPRING HL
4 SPRING VW
5 SPRING BANK
6 SOUTH RI
7 SOUTHFIELDS
59
48

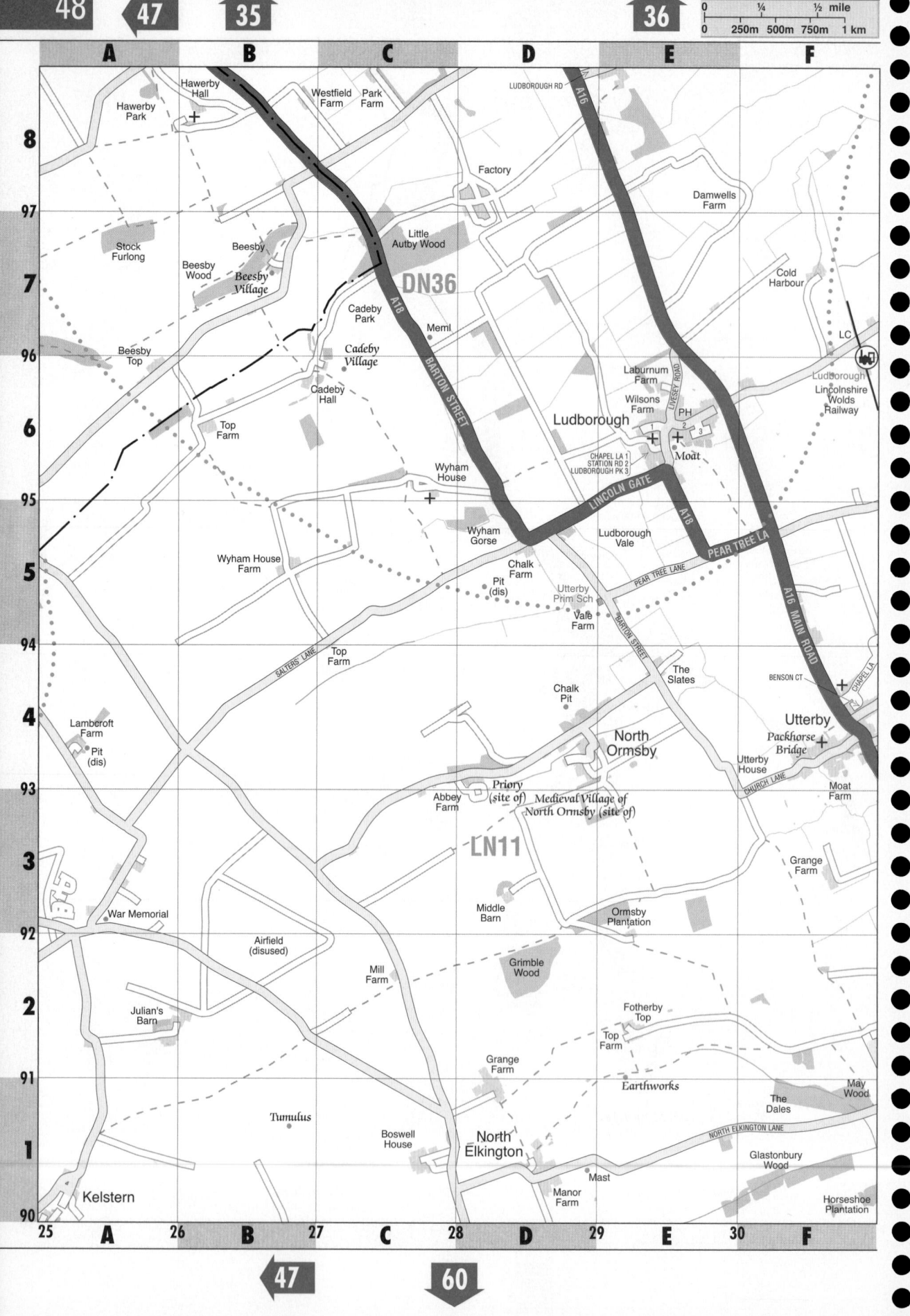

Scale: 1¾ inches to 1 mile

0   ¼   ½   mile
0   250m   500m   750m   1 km

A   B   C   D   E   F

8

Hawerby
Hall

Hawerby
Park

Westfield
Farm

Park
Farm

LUDBOROUGH RD

A16

97

Stock
Furlong

Beesby
Wood

Beesby

Factory

Damwells
Farm

7

Little
Autby Wood

DN36

A18

Cold
Harbour

Beesby
Village

Cadeby
Park

Meml

LC

96

Beesby
Top

Cadeby
Village

BARTON STREET

Ludborough
Lincolnshire
Wolds
Railway

Cadeby
Hall

Laburnum
Farm

LIVESEY ROAD

6

Top
Farm

Wilsons
Farm

Ludborough

PH
2
3

CHAPEL LA 1
STATION RD 2
LUDBOROUGH PK 3

Moat

Wyham
House

95

LINCOLN GATE

A18

Ludborough
Vale

PEAR TREE LA

Wyham
Gorse

Chalk
Farm

Pit
(dis)

PEAR TREE LANE

A16 MAIN ROAD

5

Wyham House
Farm

Utterby
Prim Sch

Vale
Farm

BARTON STREET

Benson Ct

CHAPEL LA

94

SALTERS LANE

Top
Farm

Chalk
Pit

The
Slates

Utterby

4

Lambcroft
Farm

North
Ormsby

Packhorse
Bridge

Pit
(dis)

Utterby
House

CHURCH LANE

Moat
Farm

93

Abbey
Farm

Priory
(site of)

Medieval Village of
North Ormsby (site of)

3

LN11

Grange
Farm

War Memorial

Middle
Barn

Ormsby
Plantation

92

Airfield
(disused)

Mill
Farm

Grimble
Wood

2

Julian's
Barn

Fotherby
Top

Top
Farm

Grange
Farm

91

Earthworks

The
Dales

May
Wood

1

Tumulus

Boswell
House

North
Elkington

NORTH ELKINGTON LANE

Glastonbury
Wood

Mast

90

Kelstern

Manor
Farm

Horseshoe
Plantation

25   A   26   B   27   C   28   D   29   E   30   F

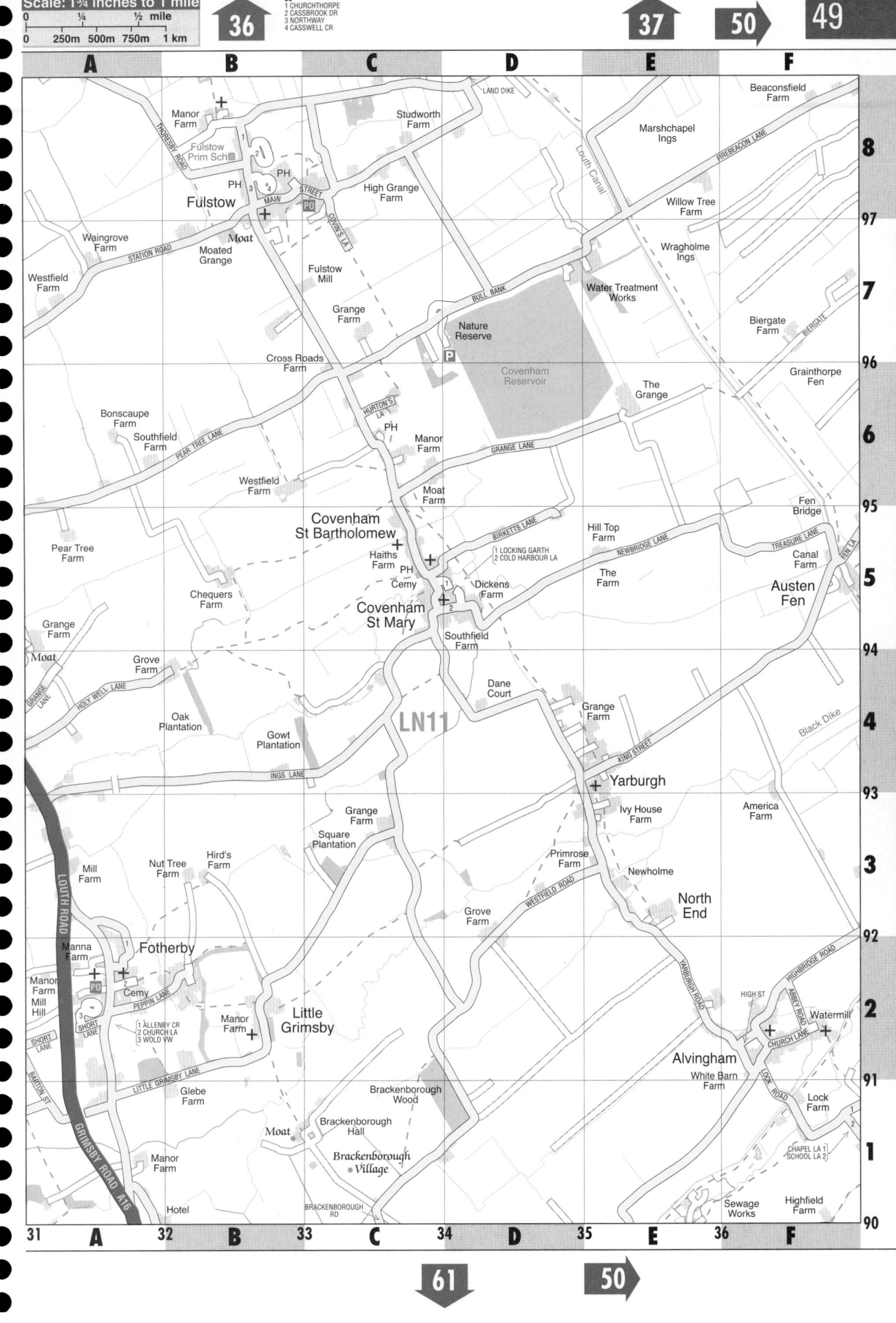

Scale: 1¾ inches to 1 mile

0   ¼   ½   mile
0   250m 500m 750m   1 km

36

B8
1 CHURCHTHORPE
2 CASSBROOK DR
3 NORTHWAY
4 CASSWELL CR

37

50

49

A   B   C   D   E   F

8
97
7
96
6
95
5
94
4
93
3
92
2
91
1
90

Beaconsfield Farm
Marshchapel Ings
LAND DIKE
Louth Canal
FIREBEACON LANE
Willow Tree Farm
Wragholme Ings
Water Treatment Works
Biergate Farm
BIERGATE
Grainthorpe Fen
Studworth Farm
High Grange Farm
Manor Farm
Fulstow Prim Sch
THRESER ROAD
MAIN STREET
COVIN'S LA
PH
PH
PO
Fulstow
Moat
Moated Grange
Waingrove Farm
STATION ROAD
Westfield Farm
Fulstow Mill
Grange Farm
BULL BANK
Nature Reserve
P
Covenham Reservoir
The Grange
Fen Bridge
Cross Roads Farm
PEAR TREE LANE
Bonscaupe Farm
Southfield Farm
Westfield Farm
HURTON'S LA
PH
Manor Farm
Moat Farm
GRANGE LANE
TREASURE LANE
Canal Farm
FEN LA
Pear Tree Farm
Covenham St Bartholomew
Haiths Farm
PH
Cemy
BIRKETTS LANE
1 LOCKING GARTH
2 COLD HARBOUR LA
Hill Top Farm
NEWBRIDGE LANE
The Farm
Austen Fen
Chequers Farm
Covenham St Mary
1
2
Dickens Farm
Grange Farm
Grove Farm
Southfield Farm
GRANGE LANE
HOLY WELL LANE
Moat
Oak Plantation
Gowt Plantation
INGS LANE
LN11
Dane Court
Grange Farm
KING STREET
Black Dike
Yarburgh
4
America Farm
Ivy House Farm
Mill Farm
Nut Tree Farm
Hird's Farm
Grange Farm
Square Plantation
Primrose Farm
Newholme
North End
WESTFIELD ROAD
LOUTH ROAD
Manna Farm
Fotherby
PO
Cemy
PEPPIN LANE
1 ALLENBY CR
2 CHURCH LA
3 WOLD VW
Manor Farm
Little Grimsby
Grove Farm
YARBURGH ROAD
HIGHBRIDGE ROAD
HIGH ST
ABBEY ROAD
Watermill
Manor Farm Mill Hill
SHORT LANE
SHORT LANE
BARTON ST
Glebe Farm
LITTLE GRIMSBY LANE
CHURCH LANE
Alvingham
White Barn Farm
LOCK ROAD
Lock Farm
GRIMSBY ROAD A16
Moat
Brackenborough Wood
Brackenborough Hall
Brackenborough Village
CHAPEL LA 1
SCHOOL LA 2
Manor Farm
Hotel
BRACKENBOROUGH RD
Sewage Works
Highfield Farm

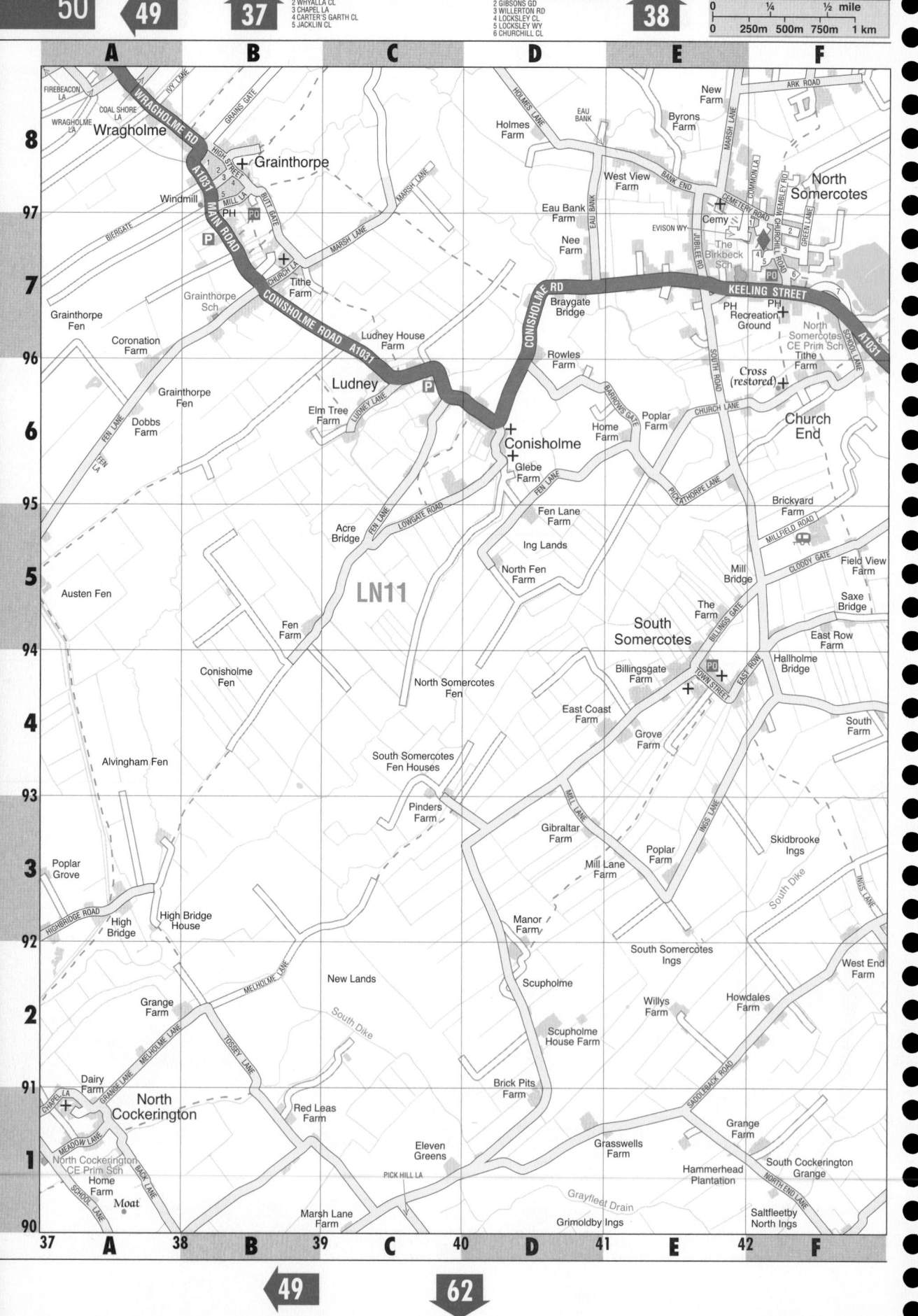

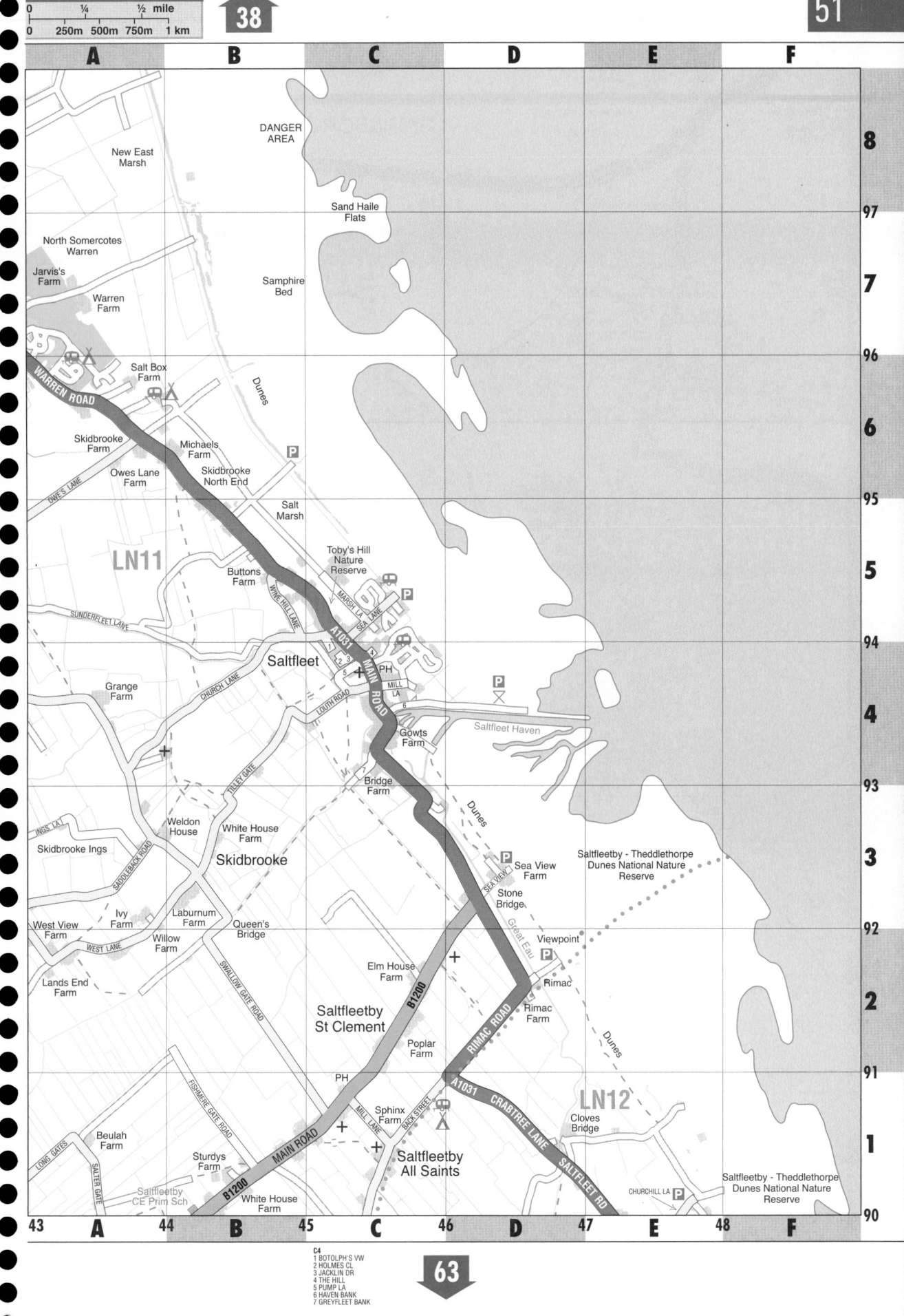

Scale: 1¾ inches to 1 mile

0   ¼   ½ mile

0   250m   500m   750m   1 km

38

DANGER AREA

New East Marsh

Sand Haile Flats

North Somercotes Warren

Samphire Bed

Jarvis's Farm

Warren Farm

WARREN ROAD

Salt Box Farm

Dunes

Skidbrooke Farm

Michaels Farm

Owes Lane Farm

Skidbrooke North End

OWES LANE

Salt Marsh

LN11

Buttons Farm

Toby's Hill Nature Reserve

WINE HILL LANE

MARSH LA

SEA LANE

SUNDERFLEET LANE

A1031

Saltfleet

CHURCH LANE

Grange Farm

MAIN ROAD

PH

1
2   3
5
6

MILL LA

LOUTH ROAD

Saltfleet Haven

Gowts Farm

TILLEY GATE

INGS LA

Skidbrooke Ings

Weldon House

White House Farm

Skidbrooke

Bridge Farm

Dunes

SADDLEBACK ROAD

Sea View Farm

Saltfleetby - Theddlethorpe Dunes National Nature Reserve

SEA VIEW

West View Farm

Ivy Farm

Laburnum Farm

Queen's Bridge

Stone Bridge

WEST LANE

Willow Farm

SWALLOW GATE ROAD

Elm House Farm

Great Eau

Viewpoint

Rimac

Lands End Farm

B1200

Rimac Farm

RIMAC ROAD

Dunes

Saltfleetby St Clement

Poplar Farm

PH

LN12

FENMERE GATE ROAD

MILL LANE

Sphinx Farm

BACK STREET

A1031

CRABTREE LANE

Cloves Bridge

SALTFLEET RD

Beulah Farm

MAIN ROAD

Saltfleetby All Saints

Saltfleetby - Theddlethorpe Dunes National Nature Reserve

LONG GATES

SALTER GATE

Sturdys Farm

B1200

White House Farm

Saltfleetby CE Prim Sch

CHURCHILL LA

43   44   45   46   47   48

A   B   C   D   E   F

8   97   7   96   6   95   5   94   4   93   3   92   2   91   1   90

C4
1 BOTOLPH'S VW
2 HOLMES CL
3 JACKLIN DR
4 THE HILL
5 PUMP LA
6 HAVEN BANK
7 GREYFLEET BANK

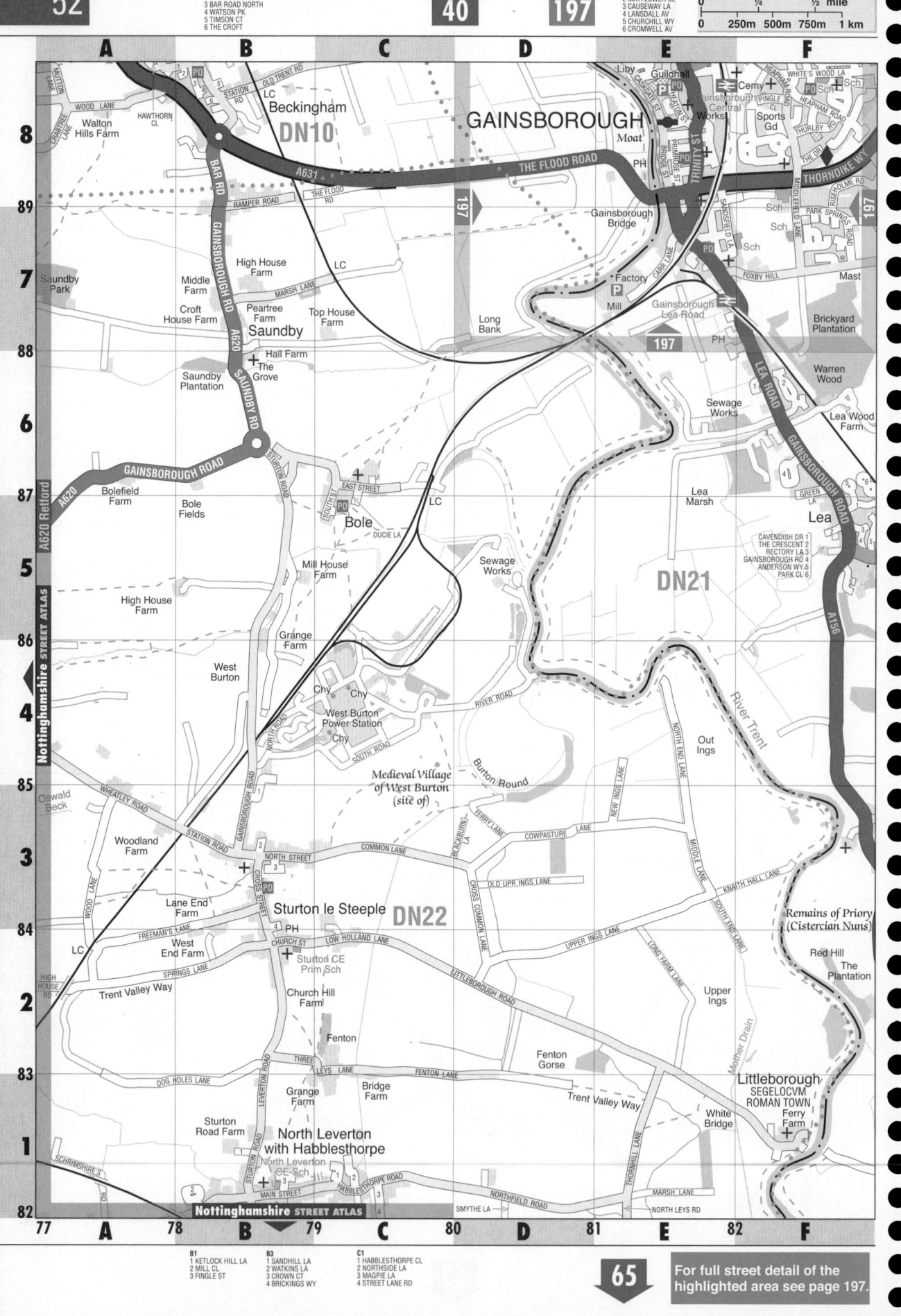

B8
1 HIGH ST
2 THE MEADOWS
3 BAR ROAD NORTH
4 WATSON PK
5 TIMSON CT
6 THE CROFT

7 BAR ROAD SOUTH

40   197

F6
1 COPPER BEECH CL
2 MAYFLOWER CL
3 CAUSEWAY LA
4 LANSDALL AV
5 CHURCHILL WY
6 CROMWELL AV

Scale: 1¾ inches to 1 mile
0   ¼   ½   mile
0   250m 500m 750m   1 km

DN10

Beckingham

GAINSBOROUGH

Walton Hills Farm

Saundby Park

Middle Farm

High House Farm

Croft House Farm

Peartree Farm

Top House Farm

Saundby

Hall Farm
The Grove

Saundby Plantation

Bolefield Farm

Bole Fields

Bole

Mill House Farm

High House Farm

Grange Farm

West Burton

Medieval Village of West Burton (site of)

West Burton Power Station

Woodland Farm

Lane End Farm

Sturton le Steeple

West End Farm

Church Hill Farm

Fenton

Grange Farm

Bridge Farm

Sturton Road Farm

North Leverton with Habblesthorpe

DN22

DN21

Lea

Lea Marsh

Sewage Works

Warren Wood

Lea Wood Farm

Brickyard Plantation

Out Ings

Upper Ings

Remains of Priory (Cistercian Nuns)

Red Hill
The Plantation

Littleborough
SEGELOCVM
ROMAN TOWN

Ferry Farm

White Bridge

Fenton Gorse

Long Bank

Sewage Works

Gainsborough Bridge

Moat

Guildhall

Gainsborough Lea Road

Mill

Factory

CAVENDISH DR 1
THE CRESCENT 2
RECTORY LA 3
GAINSBOROUGH RD 4
ANDERSON WY 5
PARK CL 6

77   A   78   B   79   C   80   D   81   E   82   F

B1
1 KETLOCK HILL LA
2 MILL CL
3 FINGLE ST

B3
1 SANDHILL LA
2 WATKINS LA
3 CROWN CT
4 BRICKINGS WY

C1
1 HABBLESTHORPE CL
2 NORTHSIDE LA
3 MAGPIE LA
4 STREET LANE RD

65

For full street detail of the highlighted area see page 197.

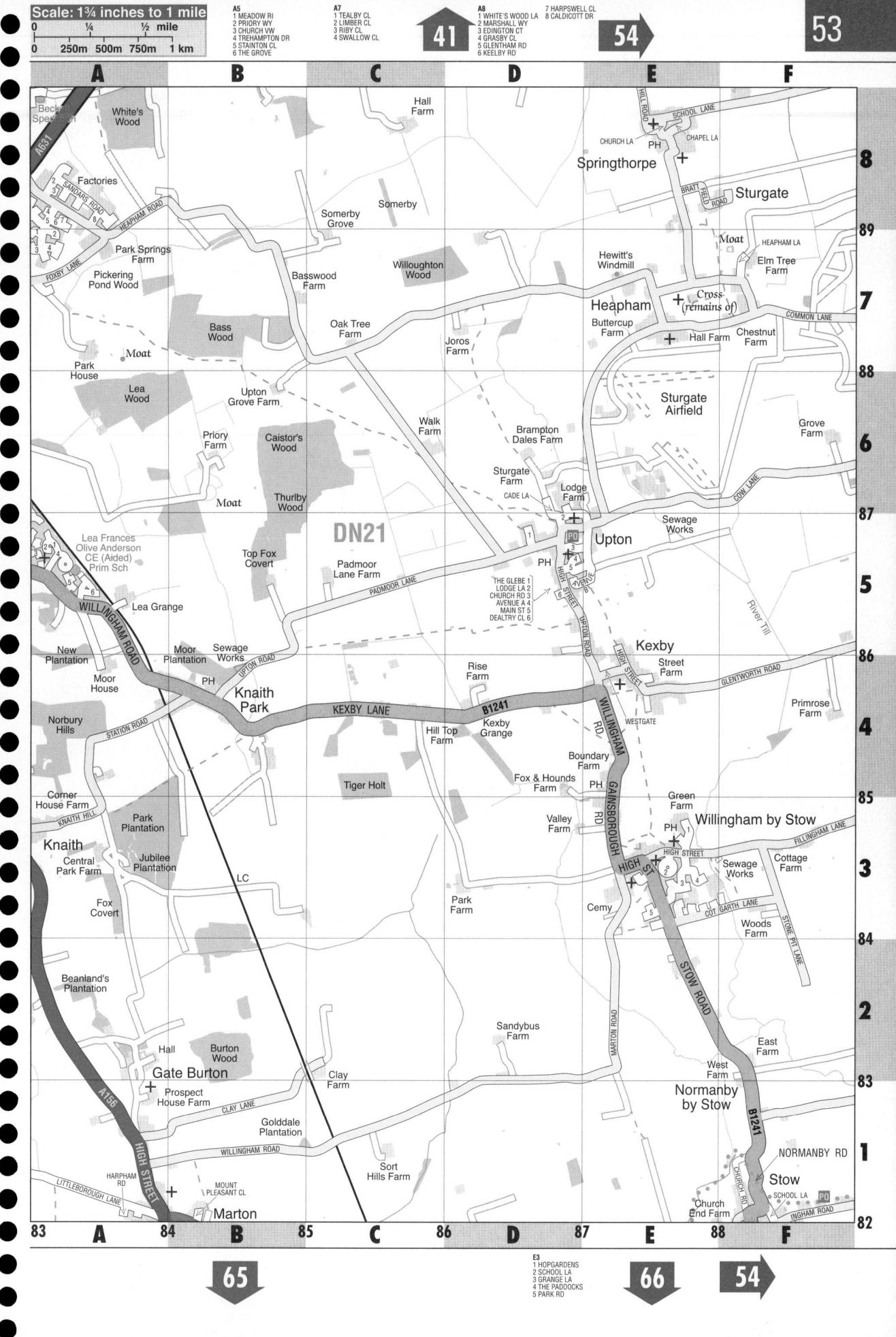

Scale: 1¾ inches to 1 mile

0   ¼   ½   mile
0   250m 500m 750m 1 km

A5
1 MEADOW RI
2 PRIORY WY
3 CHURCH VW
4 TREHAMPTON DR
5 STAINTON CL
6 THE GROVE

A7
1 TEALBY CL
2 LIMBER CL
3 RIBY CL
4 SWALLOW CL

A8
1 WHITE'S WOOD LA
2 MARSHALL WY
3 EDINGTON CT
4 GRASBY CL
5 GLENTHAM RD
6 KEELBY RD

7 HARPSWELL CL
8 CALDICOTT DR

41

54

53

Becket
Spectacn

A651

White's
Wood

Hall
Farm

Springthorpe

HILL ROAD
SCHOOL LANE
CHURCH LA
PH
CHAPEL LA

Sturgate

BRATT
FIELD
ROAD

8

Factories

SANDARS ROAD

Somerby
Grove

Somerby

HEAPHAM ROAD

FOXBY LANE

Park Springs
Farm

Willoughton
Wood

Hewitt's
Windmill

Moat

HEAPHAM LA
Elm Tree
Farm

89

Pickering
Pond Wood

Basswood
Farm

Heapham

Buttercup
Farm

Hall Farm

Cross
(remains of)

COMMON LANE

Chestnut
Farm

7

Moat

Bass
Wood

Oak Tree
Farm

Joros
Farm

Sturgate
Airfield

Grove
Farm

88

Park
House

Lea
Wood

Upton Grove Farm

Walk
Farm

Brampton
Dales Farm

6

Priory
Farm

Caistor's
Wood

Sturgate
Farm

Lodge
Farm

COW LANE

Moat

Thurlby
Wood

CADE LA

PO

Sewage
Works

87

DN21

Top Fox
Covert

Padmoor
Lane Farm

PADMOOR LANE

PH

Upton

River Till

Lea Frances
Olive Anderson
CE (Aided)
Prim Sch

THE GLEBE 1
LODGE LA 2
CHURCH RD 3
AVENUE A 4
MAIN ST 5
DEALTRY CL 6

AVENUE

HIGH STREET

Kexby

5

WILLINGHAM ROAD

Lea Grange

New
Plantation

Moor
Plantation

Sewage
Works

UPTON ROAD

UPTON ROAD

Street
Farm

GLENTWORTH ROAD

86

Moor
House

PH

Knaith
Park

KEXBY LANE

Rise
Farm

B1241

HIGH STREET

WESTGATE

Primrose
Farm

4

Norbury
Hills

STATION ROAD

Hill Top
Farm

Kexby
Grange

WILLINGHAM RD

Corner
House Farm

Tiger Holt

Boundary
Farm

Fox & Hounds
Farm

PH

Green
Farm

Willingham by Stow

FILLINGHAM LANE

85

KNAITH HILL

Park
Plantation

Valley
Farm

GAINSBOROUGH RD

PH

HIGH STREET

Cottage
Farm

Knaith

Central
Park Farm

Jubilee
Plantation

LC

HIGH ST

Cemy

STONE PIT LANE

COT GARTH LANE

Woods
Farm

3

Fox
Covert

84

Beanland's
Plantation

MARTON ROAD

STOW ROAD

2

Sandybus
Farm

East
Farm

Hall

Burton
Wood

West
Farm

Gate Burton

A156

Prospect
House Farm

CLAY LANE

Clay
Farm

Normanby
by Stow

B1241

NORMANBY RD

83

Golddale
Plantation

WILLINGHAM ROAD

Stow

CHURCH RD

SCHOOL LA

PO

1

HIGH STREET

LITTLEBOROUGH LANE

HARPHAM
RD

MOUNT
PLEASANT CL

Sort
Hills Farm

Church
End Farm

INGHAM ROAD

Marton

82

83   A   84   B   85   C   86   D   87   E   88   F

65

E3
1 HOPGARDENS
2 SCHOOL LA
3 GRANGE LA
4 THE PADDOCKS
5 PARK RD

66

54

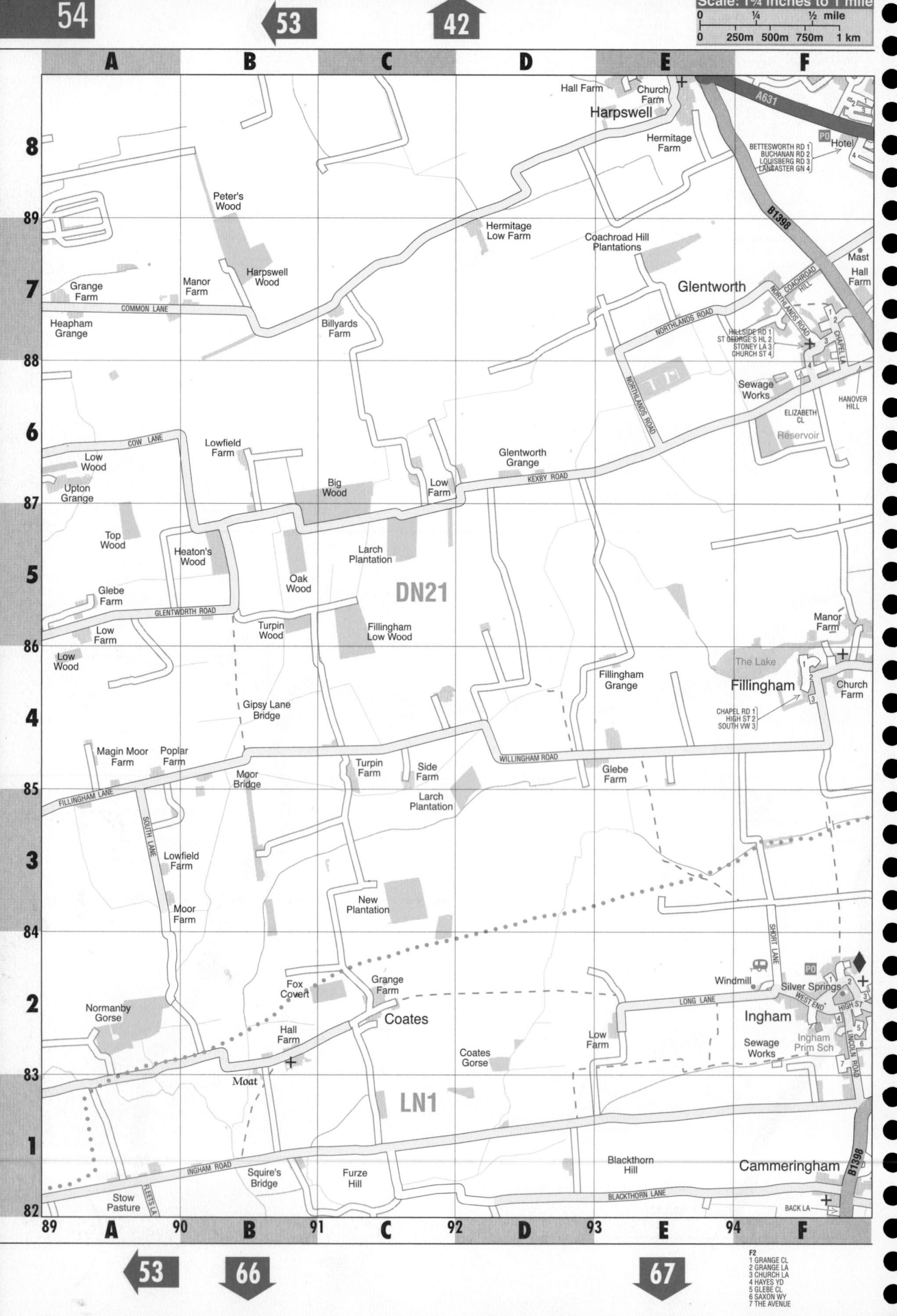

A   B   C   D   E   F

8

Hall Farm   Church Farm   Harpswell

Hermitage Farm

BETTESWORTH RD 1
BUCHANAN RD 2
LOUISBERG RD 3
LANCASTER GN 4

Hotel

A631

B1398

89

Peter's Wood

Hermitage Low Farm

Coachroad Hill Plantations

Mast
Hall Farm

7

Grange Farm

Manor Farm

Harpswell Wood

Glentworth

COACHROAD HILL

NORTHLANDS ROAD

CHAPEL LA

COMMON LANE

Billyards Farm

HILLSIDE RD 1
ST GEORGE'S HL 2
STONEY LA 3
CHURCH ST 4

Heapham Grange

88

NORTHLANDS ROAD

Sewage Works

HANOVER HILL

ELIZABETH CL

6

COW LANE

Low Wood

Lowfield Farm

Big Wood

Low Farm

Glentworth Grange

KEXBY ROAD

Reservoir

Upton Grange

87

Top Wood

Heaton's Wood

Larch Plantation

DN21

5

Oak Wood

Manor Farm

Glebe Farm

GLENTWORTH ROAD

Turpin Wood

Fillingham Low Wood

Low Farm

The Lake

86

Low Wood

Fillingham Grange

Fillingham

Church Farm

CHAPEL RD 1
HIGH ST 2
SOUTH VW 3

Gipsy Lane Bridge

4

Magin Moor Farm

Poplar Farm

Turpin Farm

Side Farm

WILLINGHAM ROAD

Glebe Farm

85

FILLINGHAM LANE

Moor Bridge

Larch Plantation

3

SOUTH LANE

Lowfield Farm

84

Moor Farm

New Plantation

SHORT LANE

Windmill

Silver Springs

2

Normanby Gorse

Fox Covert

Grange Farm

LONG LANE

Ingham

WEST END

HIGH ST

Hall Farm

Coates

Low Farm

Sewage Works

Ingham Prim Sch

LINCOLN ROAD

83

Moat

Coates Gorse

LN1

1

FLEETS LA

Blackthorn Hill

Cammeringham

B1398

Stow Pasture

INGHAM ROAD

Squire's Bridge

Furze Hill

BLACKTHORN LANE

BACK LA

82

89   A   90   B   91   C   92   D   93   E   94   F

F2
1 GRANGE CL
2 GRANGE LA
3 CHURCH LA
4 HAYES YD
5 GLEBE CL
6 SAXON WY
7 THE AVENUE

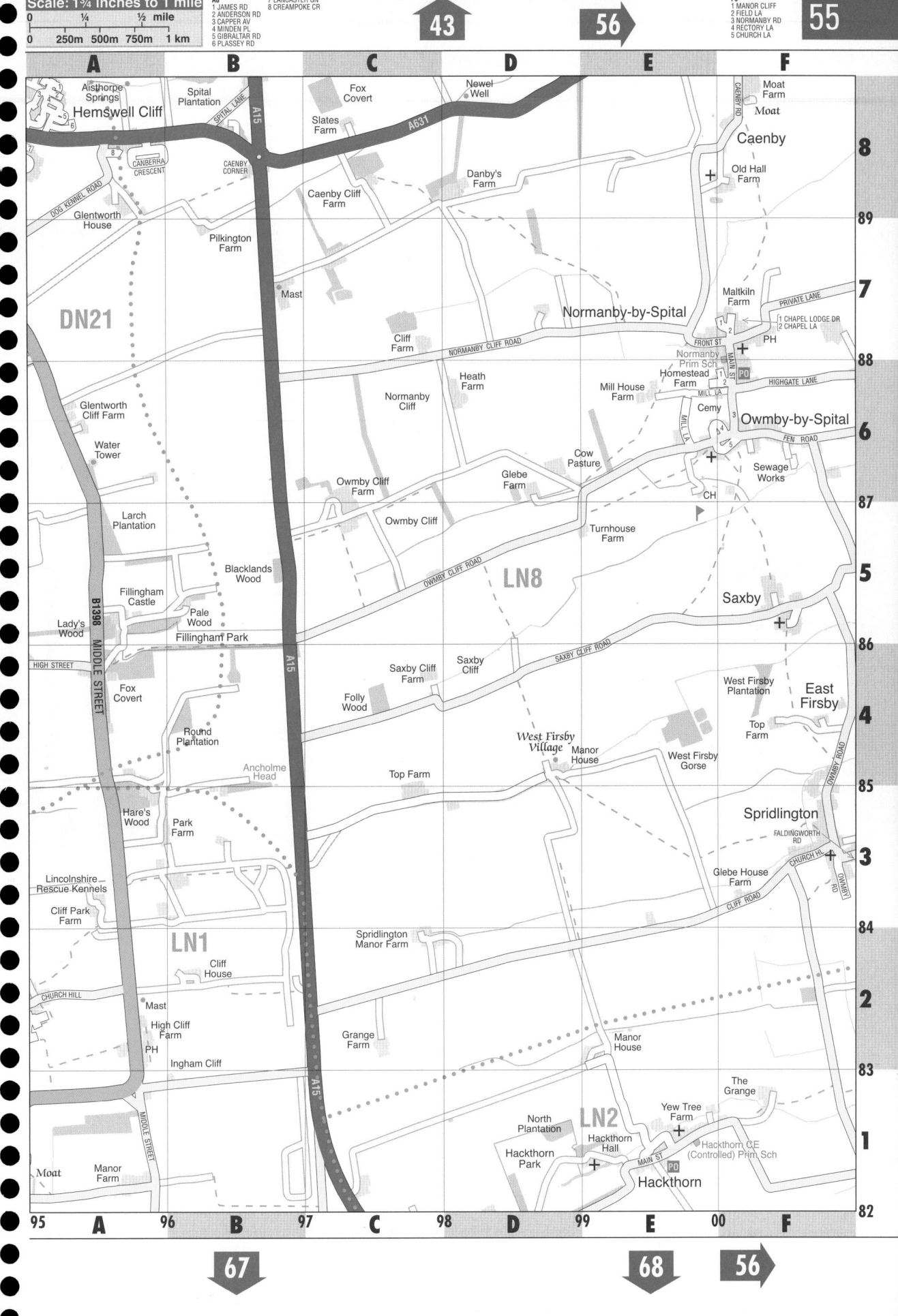

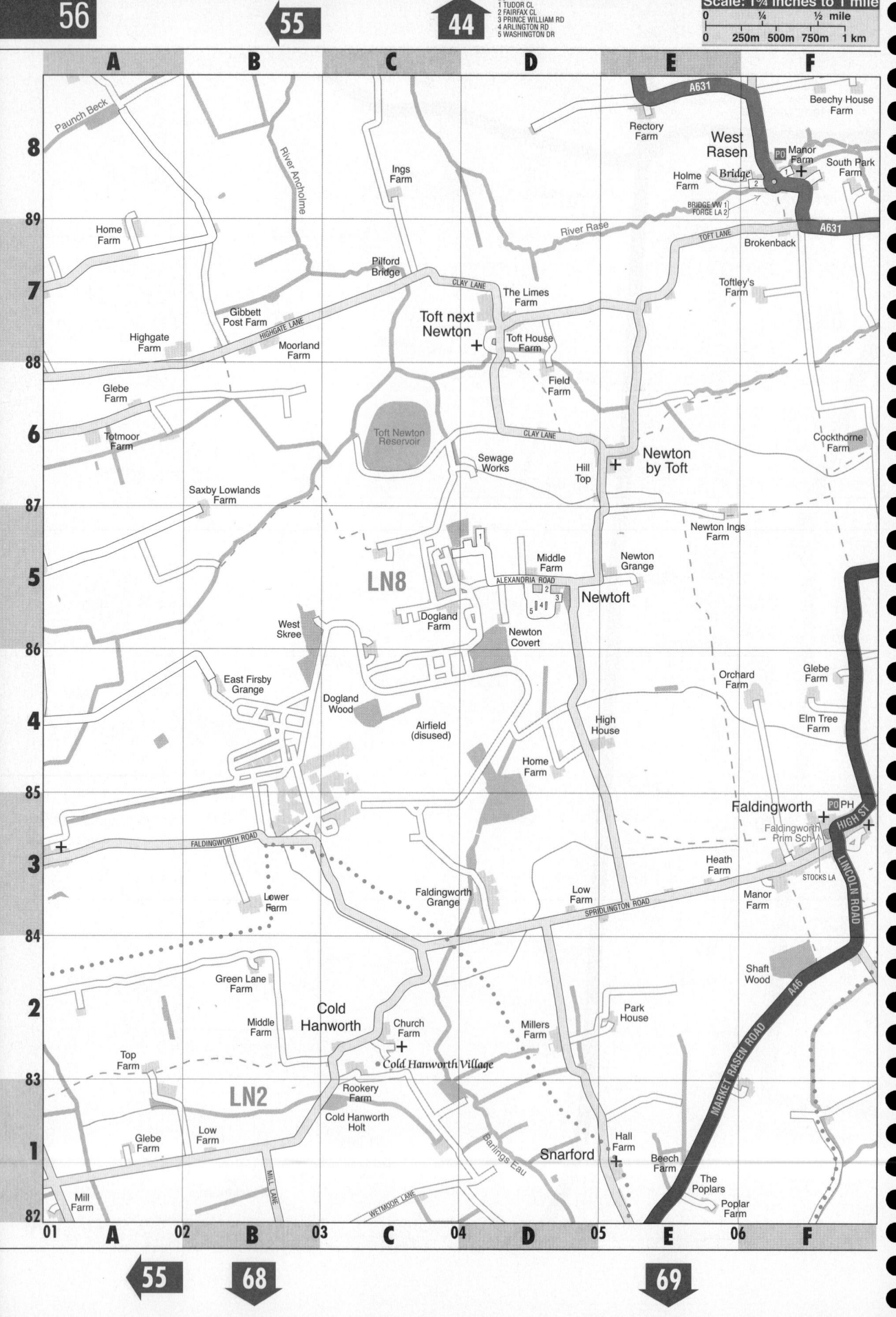

D5
1 TUDOR CL
2 FAIRFAX CL
3 PRINCE WILLIAM RD
4 ARLINGTON RD
5 WASHINGTON DR

Scale: 1¾ inches to 1 mile
0   ¼   ½   mile
0 250m 500m 750m 1 km

A B C D E F

A631
Beechy House Farm
Rectory Farm
West Rasen
PO Manor Farm
South Park Farm
Holme Farm
Bridge
BRIDGE WW 1
FORGE LA 2
A631

8

Paunch Beck

Ings Farm

River Ancholme

Pilford Bridge

CLAY LANE
Toft next Newton
The Limes Farm
River Rase
TOFT LANE
Brokenback
Toftley's Farm

89

Home Farm

Gibbett Post Farm
HIGHGATE LANE
Highgate Farm
Moorland Farm

Toft House Farm

7

88

Glebe Farm
Totmoor Farm

Toft Newton Reservoir

Field Farm
CLAY LANE

Newton by Toft
Cockthorne Farm

6

Saxby Lowlands Farm

Sewage Works
Hill Top

Newton Ings Farm

87

LN8

Middle Farm
ALEXANDRIA ROAD
2
3
5 4
Newtoft
Newton Grange

5

West Skree

Dogland Farm

Newton Covert

Orchard Farm
Glebe Farm

86

East Firsby Grange
Dogland Wood

Airfield (disused)

High House
Elm Tree Farm

4

Home Farm

85

FALDINGWORTH ROAD
Faldingworth
PO PH
Faldingworth Prim Sch
HIGH ST

3

Lower Farm

Faldingworth Grange

Low Farm
SPRIDLINGTON ROAD
Heath Farm
STOCKS LA
Manor Farm
LINCOLN ROAD

84

Green Lane Farm

Shaft Wood
A46

2

Middle Farm
Cold Hanworth
Church Farm
Millers Farm
Park House

Top Farm

Cold Hanworth Village
MARKET RASEN ROAD

83

LN2

Rookery Farm
Cold Hanworth Holt
Barlings Eau
Snarford
Hall Farm
Beech Farm
The Poplars
Poplar Farm

1

Glebe Farm
Low Farm
MILL LANE

Mill Farm
WETMOOR LANE

82

01 A 02 B 03 C 04 D 05 E 06 F

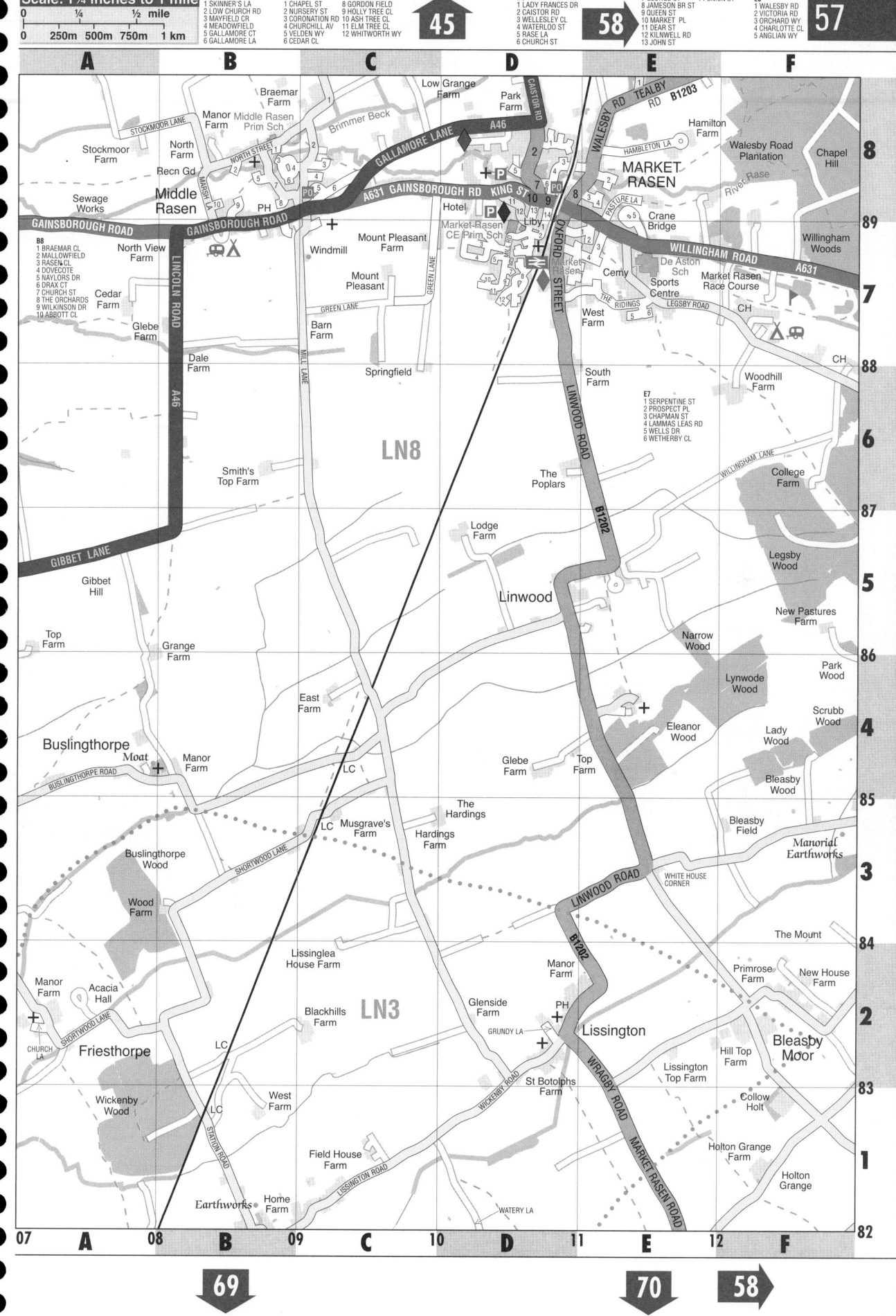

Scale: 1¾ inches to 1 mile

0   ¼   ½ mile
0   250m 500m 750m 1 km

C8
1 SKINNER'S LA
2 LOW CHURCH RD
3 RASEN CL
4 MAYFIELD CR
5 GALLAMORE CT
6 GALLAMORE LA

D7
1 CHAPEL ST
2 NURSERY ST
3 CORONATION RD
4 CHURCHILL AV
5 VELDEN WY
6 CEDAR CL

7 OAK TREE CL
8 GORDON FIELD
9 HOLLY TREE CL
10 ASH TREE CL
11 ELM TREE CL
12 WHITWORTH WY

D8
1 LADY FRANCES DR
2 CAISTOR RD
3 WELLESLEY CL
4 WATERLOO ST
5 RASE LA
6 CHURCH ST

7 GEORGE ST
8 JAMESON BR ST
9 QUEEN ST
10 MARKET PL
11 DEAR ST
12 KILNWELL RD
13 JOHN ST

14 UNION ST

E8
1 WALESBY RD
2 VICTORIA RD
3 ORCHARD WY
4 CHARLOTTE CL
5 ANGLIAN WY

45

58

57

A   B   C   D   E   F

STOCKMOOR LANE
Stockmoor Farm
Sewage Works
Middle Rasen
North Farm
Manor Farm
Braemar Farm
Middle Rasen Prim Sch
NORTH STREET
MARSH LANE
Recn Gd
PH
PO
Brimmer Beck
Low Grange Farm
Park Farm
GALLAMORE LANE
A46
CASTOR RD
WALESBY RD
TEALBY RD
B1203
Hamilton Farm
Walesby Road Plantation
Chapel Hill
8

GAINSBOROUGH ROAD
A631 GAINSBOROUGH RD
KING ST
MARKET RASEN
HAMBLETON LA
HAMBLETON LA
River Rase
89

B8
1 BRAEMAR CL
2 MALLOWFIELD
3 RASEN CL
4 DOVECOTE
5 NAYLORS DR
6 DRAX ST
7 CHURCH ST
8 THE ORCHARDS
9 WILKINSON DR
10 ABBOTT CL

North View Farm
Cedar Farm
Glebe Farm
Windmill
Mount Pleasant Farm
Mount Pleasant
GREEN LANE
Hotel
Market Rasen CE Prim Sch
Crane Bridge
Cemy
De Aston Sch
WILLINGHAM ROAD
A631
Willingham Woods
Sports Centre
Market Rasen Race Course
CH
7

LINCOLN ROAD
A46
Dale Farm
GREEN LANE
Barn Farm
Springfield
LN8
West Farm
THE RIDINGS
LEGSBY ROAD
CH
7

South Farm
Woodhill Farm
88

E7
1 SERPENTINE ST
2 PROSPECT PL
3 CHAPMAN ST
4 LAMMAS LEAS RD
5 WELLS DR
6 WETHERBY CL

6

MILL LANE
Smith's Top Farm
The Poplars
WILLINGHAM LANE
LINWOOD ROAD
B1202
College Farm
87

GIBBET LANE
Gibbet Hill
Lodge Farm
Linwood
Legsby Wood
5

Top Farm
Grange Farm
East Farm
Narrow Wood
Lynwode Wood
New Pastures Farm
Park Wood
86

Buslingthorpe
Moat
Manor Farm
BUSLINGTHORPE ROAD
LC
Glebe Farm
Top Farm
Eleanor Wood
Lady Wood
Scrubb Wood
Bleasby Wood
4

LC
Musgrave's Farm
The Hardings
Hardings Farm
Bleasby Field
Manorial Earthworks
85

Buslingthorpe Wood
SHORTWOOD LANE
LINWOOD ROAD
WHITE HOUSE CORNER
3

Wood Farm
B1202
The Mount
84

Manor Farm
Acacia Hall
SHORTWOOD LANE
Lissinglea House Farm
LN3
Blackhills Farm
Glenside Farm
PH
GRUNDY LA
Manor Farm
Lissington
Primrose Farm
New House Farm
Bleasby Moor
2

CHURCH LA
Friesthorpe
LC
St Botolphs Farm
Hill Top Farm
Lissington Top Farm
Collow Holt
83

Wickenby Wood
STATION ROAD
LC
West Farm
WICKENBY ROAD
WRAGBY ROAD
MARKET RASEN ROAD
Holton Grange Farm
Holton Grange
1

Earthworks
Field House Farm
Home Farm
LISSINGTON ROAD
WATERY LA
82

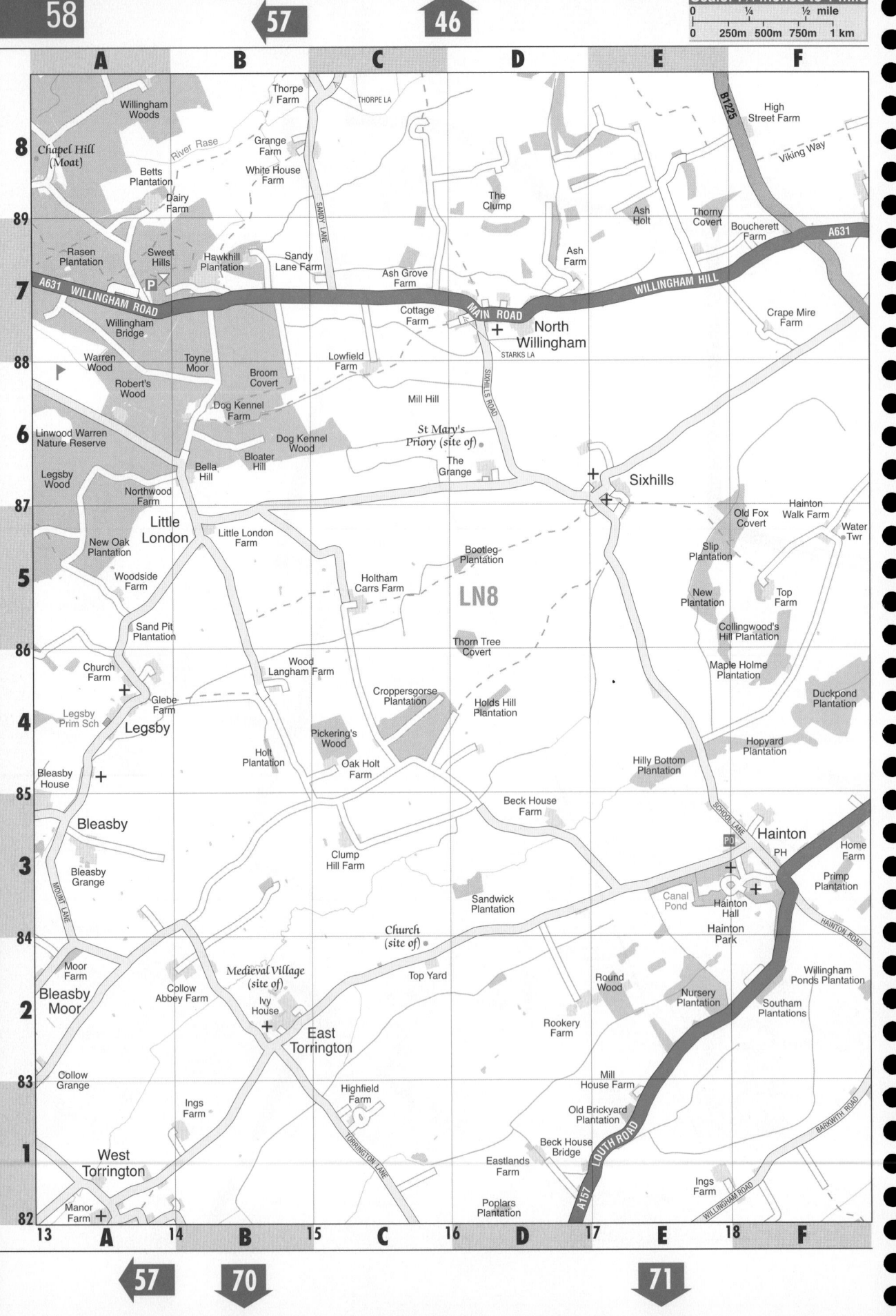

57
46

Scale: 1¾ inches to 1 mile
0   ¼   ½ mile
0   250m   500m   750m   1 km

8
Willingham Woods
Chapel Hill (Moat)
Betts Plantation
Dairy Farm
Thorpe Farm
THORPE LA
Grange Farm
White House Farm
The Clump
High Street Farm
Viking Way

89
Rasen Plantation
Sweet Hills
Hawkhill Plantation
Sandy Lane Farm
Ash Grove Farm
Ash Holt
Ash Farm
Thorny Covert
Boucherett Farm
A631

7
A631 WILLINGHAM ROAD
Willingham Bridge
Toyne Moor
Lowfield Farm
Cottage Farm
MAIN ROAD
North Willingham
WILLINGHAM HILL
Crape Mire Farm

88
Warren Wood
Robert's Wood
Broom Covert
Mill Hill
STARKS LA
SIXHILLS ROAD

6
Linwood Warren Nature Reserve
Legsby Wood
Dog Kennel Farm
Bella Hill
Bloater Hill
Dog Kennel Wood
St Mary's Priory (site of)
The Grange
Sixhills
Hainton Walk Farm
Water Twr
Old Fox Covert
Slip Plantation

87
Northwood Farm
Little London
New Oak Plantation
Little London Farm
Woodside Farm
Holtham Carrs Farm
Bootleg Plantation
LN8
New Plantation
Top Farm
Collingwood's Hill Plantation

5
Sand Pit Plantation
Thorn Tree Covert
Maple Holme Plantation
Duckpond Plantation

86
Church Farm
Wood Langham Farm
Croppersgorse Plantation
Holds Hill Plantation
Hopyard Plantation

4
Legsby Prim Sch
Glebe Farm
Legsby
Holt Plantation
Pickering's Wood
Oak Holt Farm
Hilly Bottom Plantation

85
Bleasby House
Beck House Farm
SCHOOL LANE
Hainton
Home Farm

3
Bleasby
Bleasby Grange
MOUNT LANE
Clump Hill Farm
Sandwick Plantation
PD
PH
Canal Pond
Hainton Hall
Hainton Park
Primp Plantation
HAINTON ROAD

84
Moor Farm
Church (site of)
Medieval Village (site of)
Top Yard
Round Wood
Nursery Plantation
Willingham Ponds Plantation

2
Bleasby Moor
Collow Abbey Farm
Ivy House
East Torrington
Rookery Farm
Southam Plantations

83
Collow Grange
Ings Farm
Highfield Farm
Mill House Farm
Old Brickyard Plantation
LOUTH ROAD
BARKWITH ROAD

1
West Torrington
TORRINGTON LANE
Eastlands Farm
Beck House Bridge
Ings Farm
A157
WILLINGHAM ROAD

82
Manor Farm
Poplars Plantation

13 A 14 B 15 C 16 D 17 E 18 F

57
70
71

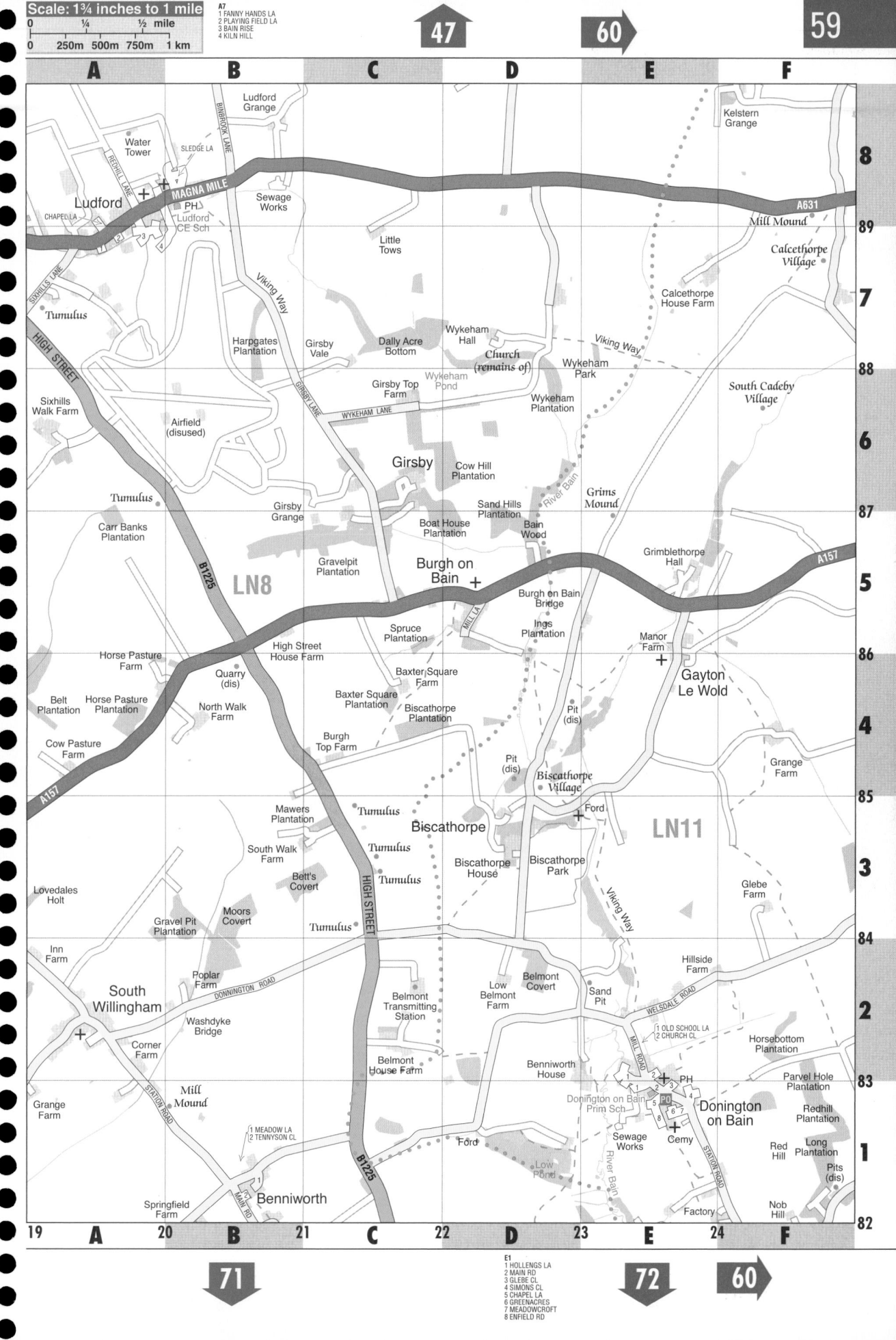
Scale: 1¾ inches to 1 mile
0 ¼ ½ mile
0 250m 500m 750m 1 km
A7
1 FANNY HANDS LA
2 PLAYING FIELD LA
3 BAIN RISE
4 KILN HILL
47
60
Ludford Grange
Water Tower
SLEDGE LA
BINBROOK LANE
MAGNA MILE
Ludford
PH
Ludford CE Sch
CHAPEL LA
REDHILL LANE
Sewage Works
Little Tows
Kelstern Grange
A631
Mill Mound
Calcethorpe Village
Calcethorpe House Farm
SIXHILLS LANE
Tumulus
Viking Way
HIGH STREET
Harpgates Plantation
Girsby Vale
Dally Acre Bottom
Wykeham Hall
Church (remains of)
Wykeham Pond
Wykeham Park
Girsby Top Farm
GIRSBY LANE
WYKEHAM LANE
South Cadeby Village
Sixhills Walk Farm
Airfield (disused)
Wykeham Plantation
Girsby
Cow Hill Plantation
River Bain
Grims Mound
Tumulus
Sand Hills Plantation
Girsby Grange
Boat House Plantation
Bain Wood
Carr Banks Plantation
Grimblethorpe Hall
A157
B1225
LN8
Gravelpit Plantation
Burgh on Bain
Burgh on Bain Bridge
MILL LA
Spruce Plantation
Ings Plantation
Manor Farm
High Street House Farm
Horse Pasture Farm
Quarry (dis)
Baxter Square Farm
Gayton Le Wold
Belt Plantation
Horse Pasture Plantation
North Walk Farm
Baxter Square Plantation
Biscathorpe Plantation
Pit (dis)
Burgh Top Farm
Cow Pasture Farm
Pit (dis)
Biscathorpe Village
Grange Farm
A157
Mawers Plantation
Tumulus
Ford
Biscathorpe
LN11
South Walk Farm
Tumulus
Biscathorpe House
Biscathorpe Park
Bett's Covert
Tumulus
HIGH STREET
Lovedales Holt
Glebe Farm
Gravel Pit Plantation
Moors Covert
Tumulus
Inn Farm
Hillside Farm
Poplar Farm
DONNINGTON ROAD
Belmont Covert
South Willingham
Low Belmont Farm
Sand Pit
Belmont Transmitting Station
WELSDALE ROAD
Washdyke Bridge
1 OLD SCHOOL LA
2 CHURCH CL
Corner Farm
Horsebottom Plantation
Belmont House Farm
Benniworth House
MILL ROAD
PH
Parvel Hole Plantation
Mill Mound
STATION ROAD
Grange Farm
Donington on Bain Prim Sch
PO
Donington on Bain
Redhill Plantation
1 MEADOW LA
2 TENNYSON CL
Ford
Sewage Works
Cemy
Red Hill
Long Plantation
B1225
Low Pond
River Bain
STATION ROAD
Pits (dis)
Benniworth
MAIN RD
Springfield Farm
Factory
Nob Hill
A B C D E F
8 7 6 5 4 3 2 1
89 88 87 86 85 84 83 82
19 20 21 22 23 24
E1
1 HOLLENGS LA
2 MAIN RD
3 GLEBE CL
4 SIMONS CL
5 CHAPEL LA
6 GREENACRES
7 MEADOWCROFT
8 ENFIELD RD
71
72
60

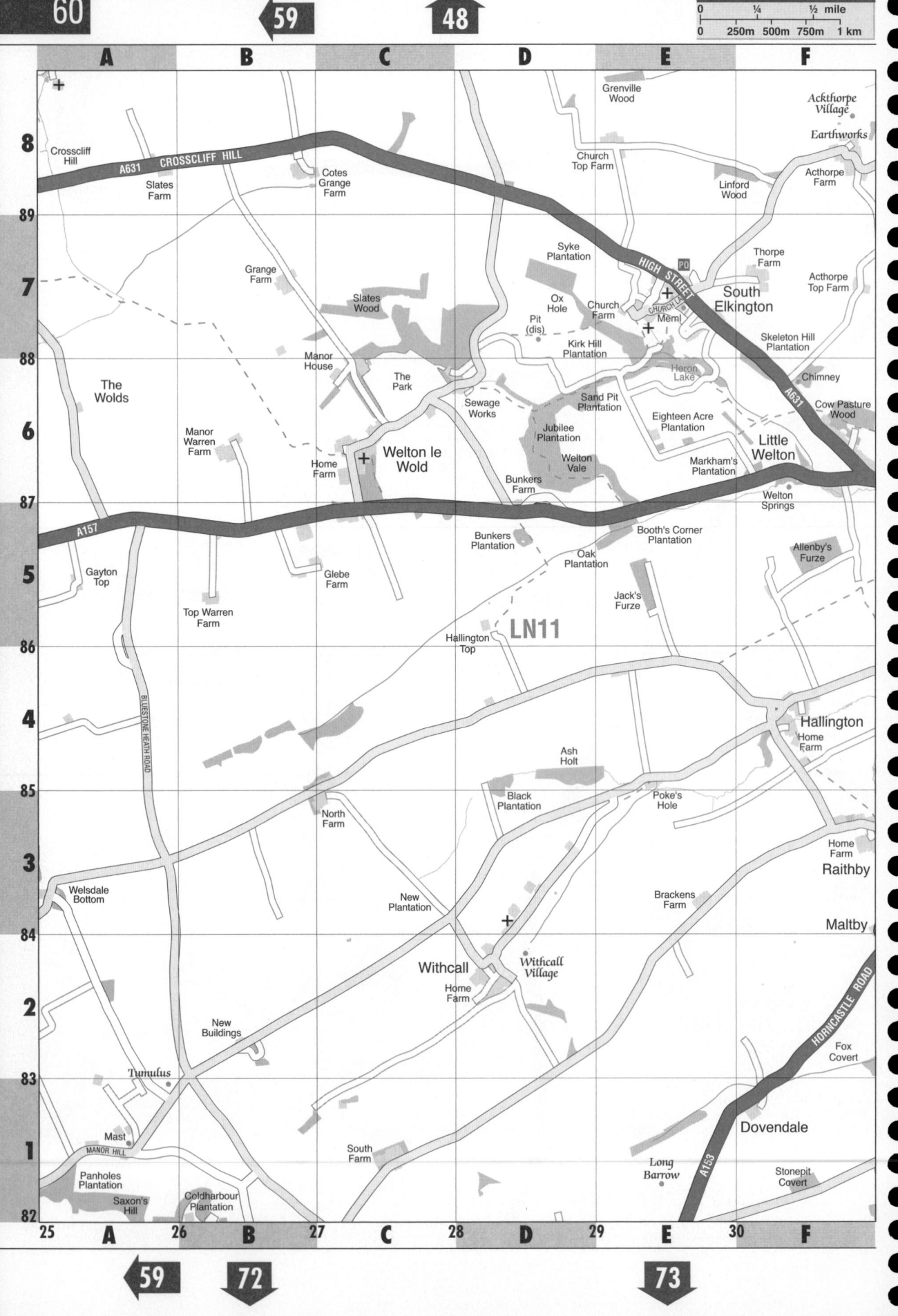

59
48

Scale: 1¾ inches to 1 mile

0   ¼   ½ mile
0   250m   500m   750m   1 km

A   B   C   D   E   F

Grenville Wood

Ackthorpe Village

Earthworks

Crosscliff Hill

A631 CROSSCLIFF HILL

Slates Farm

Cotes Grange Farm

Church Top Farm

Linford Wood

Acthorpe Farm

Grange Farm

Syke Plantation

HIGH STREET

PO

Thorpe Farm

Acthorpe Top Farm

South Elkington

Slates Wood

Ox Hole

Church Farm

Pit (dis)

Meml

CHURCH LN

Skeleton Hill Plantation

The Wolds

Manor House

The Park

Kirk Hill Plantation

Heron Lake

Chimney

A631

Cow Pasture Wood

Sewage Works

Sand Pit Plantation

Manor Warren Farm

Welton le Wold

Jubilee Plantation

Eighteen Acre Plantation

Little Welton

Home Farm

Welton Vale

Markham's Plantation

Welton Springs

Bunkers Farm

A157

Bunkers Plantation

Booth's Corner Plantation

Gayton Top

Oak Plantation

Allenby's Furze

Glebe Farm

Jack's Furze

Top Warren Farm

LN11

Hallington Top

Bluestone Heath Road

Hallington

Home Farm

Ash Holt

North Farm

Black Plantation

Poke's Hole

Home Farm

Welsdale Bottom

Raithby

New Plantation

Brackens Farm

Maltby

Withcall

Withcall Village

New Buildings

Home Farm

Horncastle Road

Tumulus

Fox Covert

Mast

MANOR HILL

South Farm

Dovendale

Panholes Plantation

Long Barrow

A153

Stonepit Covert

Saxon's Hill

Coldharbour Plantation

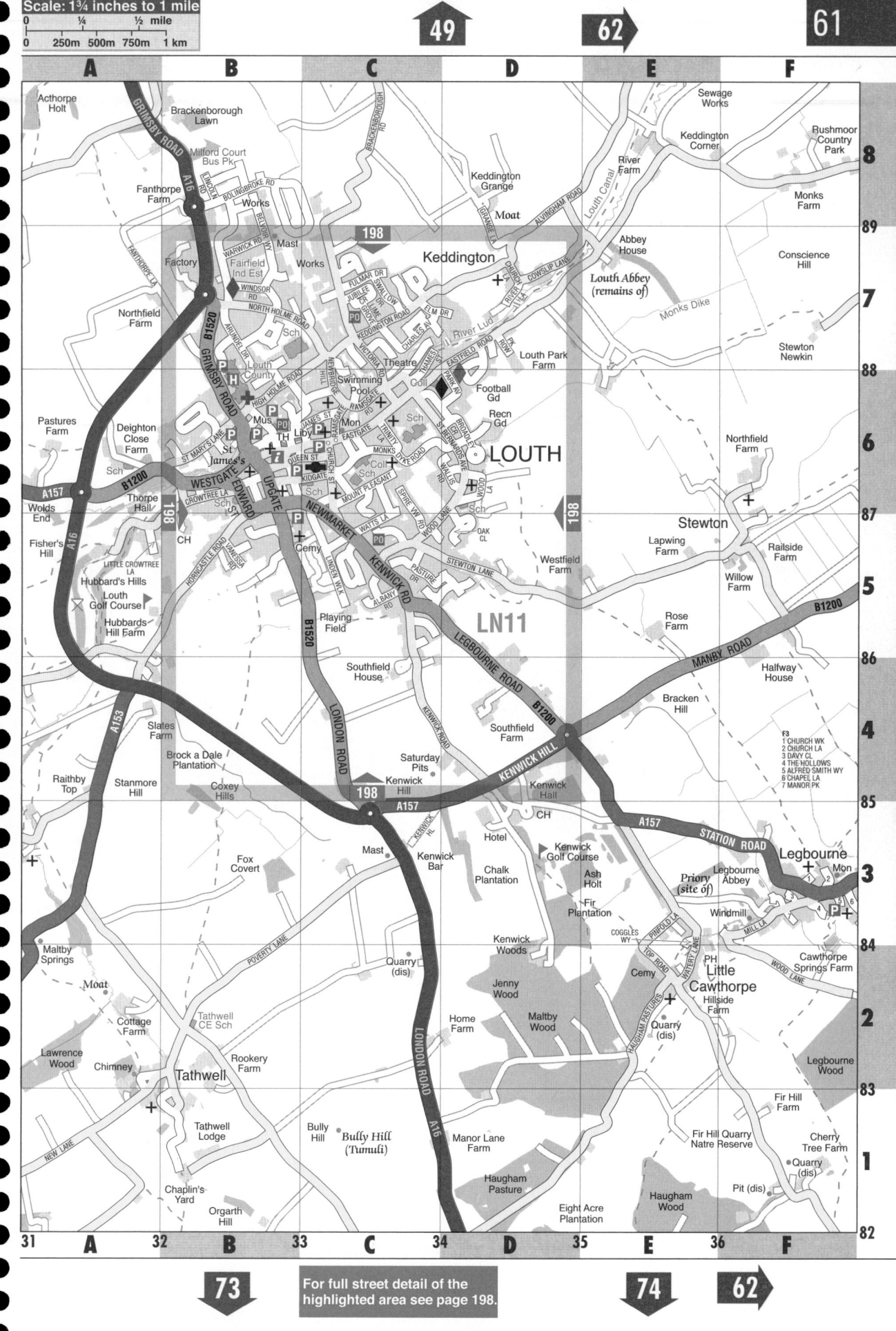

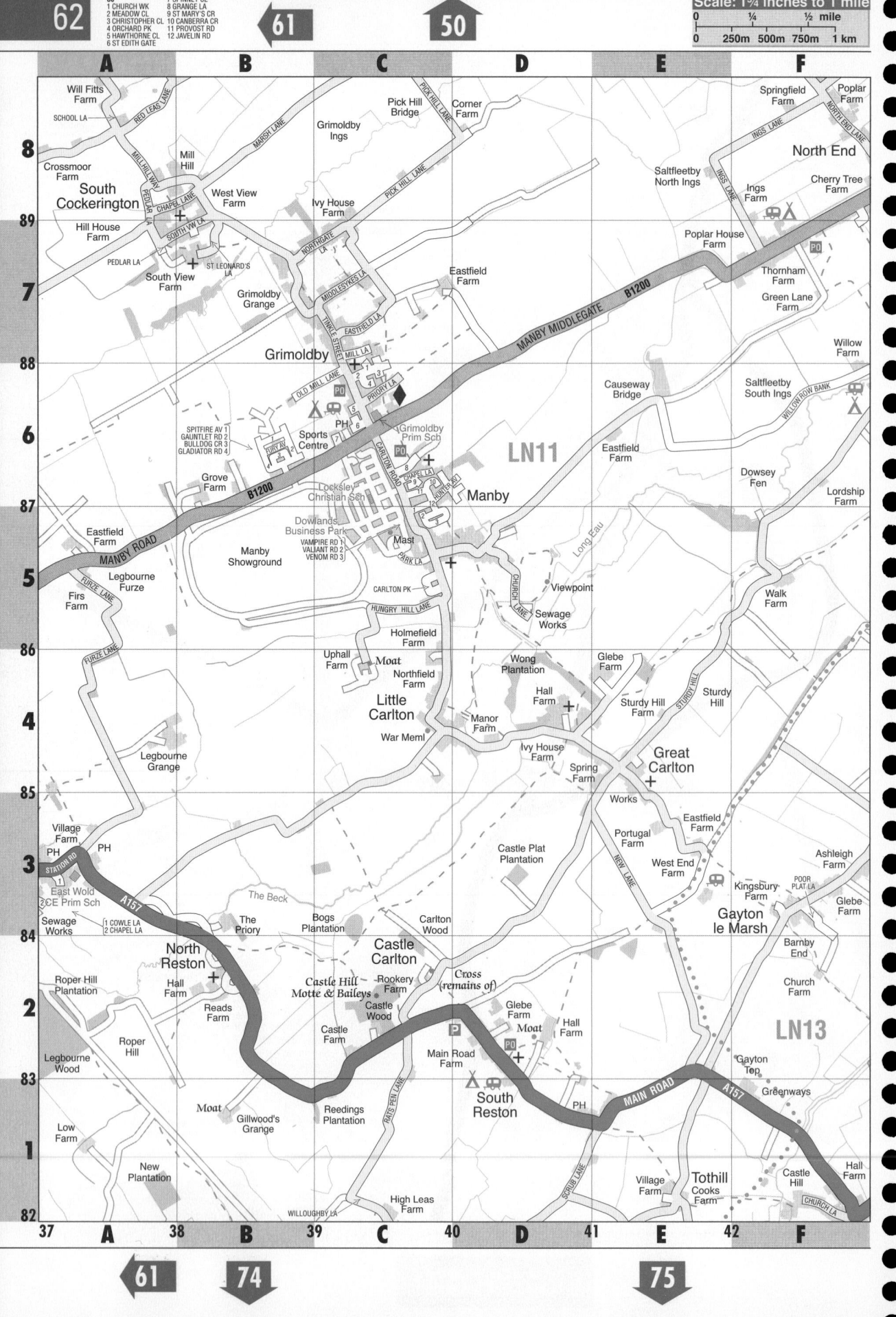

62

C6
1 CHURCH WK
2 MEADOW CL
3 CHRISTOPHER CL
4 ORCHARD PK
5 HAWTHORNE CL
6 ST EDITH GATE
7 SPINNEY CL
8 GRANGE LA
9 ST MARY'S CR
10 CANBERRA CR
11 PROVOST RD
12 JAVELIN RD

61

50

Scale: 1¾ inches to 1 mile
0   ¼   ½ mile
0   250m 500m 750m 1 km

A   B   C   D   E   F

8
89
7
88
6
87
5
86
4
85
3
84
2
83
1
82

Will Fitts Farm
SCHOOL LA
RED LEAS LANE
MILL HILL WAY
MARSH LANE
Crossmoor Farm
South Cockerington
Mill Hill
PEDLAR LA
CHAPEL LANE
SOUTH VW RD
Hill House Farm
West View Farm
PEDLAR LA
South View Farm
St LEONARD'S LA
NORTHGATE LA
MIDDLESYKES LA
TINCE STREET
EASTFIELD LA
Grimoldby Grange
Grimoldby Ings
Pick Hill Bridge
PICK HILL LANE
Corner Farm
Grimoldby Ings
Ivy House Farm
Eastfield Farm
Springfield Farm
Poplar Farm
INGS LANE
NORTH END LANE
North End
Saltfleetby North Ings
Cherry Tree Farm
Ings Farm
Poplar House Farm
PO
Thornham Farm
Green Lane Farm
B1200
MANBY MIDDLEGATE
Grimoldby
OLD MILL LANE
MILL LA
PO
PRIORY LA
PH
1 2 3 4 5 6
SPITFIRE AV 1
GAUNTLET RD 2
BULLDOG CR 3
GLADIATOR RD 4
FURY AV
Sports Centre
Grimoldby Prim Sch
CARLTON ROAD
CHAPEL LA
7 8 9 10 11 12
HUNTER RD
Manby
LN11
Causeway Bridge
Eastfield Farm
Willow Farm
Saltfleetby South Ings
WILLOW ROW BANK
Grove Farm
B1200
MANBY ROAD
Locksley Christian Sch
Dowlands Business Park
VAMPIRE RD 1
VALIANT RD 2
VENOM RD 3
Mast
PARK LA
PO
Dowsey Fen
Lordship Farm
Eastfield Farm
Firs Farm
Legbourne Furze
FURZE LANE
CARLTON PK
Long Eau
Viewpoint
CHURCH LANE
Sewage Works
Walk Farm
FURZE LANE
HUNGRY HILL LANE
Holmefield Farm
Uphall Farm
Moat
Northfield Farm
Wong Plantation
Hall Farm
Glebe Farm
Sturdy Hill Farm
STURDY HILL
Sturdy Hill
Legbourne Grange
Little Carlton
War Meml
Manor Farm
Ivy House Farm
Great Carlton
Ashleigh Farm
Spring Farm
Works
Glebe Farm
Village Farm
PH
PH
STATION RD
A157
East Wold CE Prim Sch
1 COWLE LA
2 CHAPEL LA
Sewage Works
The Beck
Castle Plat Plantation
NEW LANE
Portugal Farm
West End Farm
Kingsbury Farm
POOR PLAT LA
Glebe Farm
Gayton le Marsh
Barnby End
LN13
Church Farm
Roper Hill Plantation
North Reston
Hall Farm
Reads Farm
The Priory
Bogs Plantation
Carlton Wood
Castle Carlton
Castle Hill Motte & Baileys
Rookery Farm
Cross (remains of)
Glebe Farm
Moat
Hall Farm
Main Road Farm
PO
Gayton Top
Greenways
A157
Legbourne Wood
Roper Hill
Castle Wood
Castle Farm
RATS PEN LANE
Reedings Plantation
South Reston
PH
MAIN ROAD
Low Farm
Moat
Gillwood's Grange
New Plantation
WILLOUGHBY LA
High Leas Farm
SCRUB LANE
Village Farm
Tothill
Cooks Farm
Castle Hill
CHURCH LA
Hall Farm

37   38   39   40   41   42
A   B   C   D   E   F

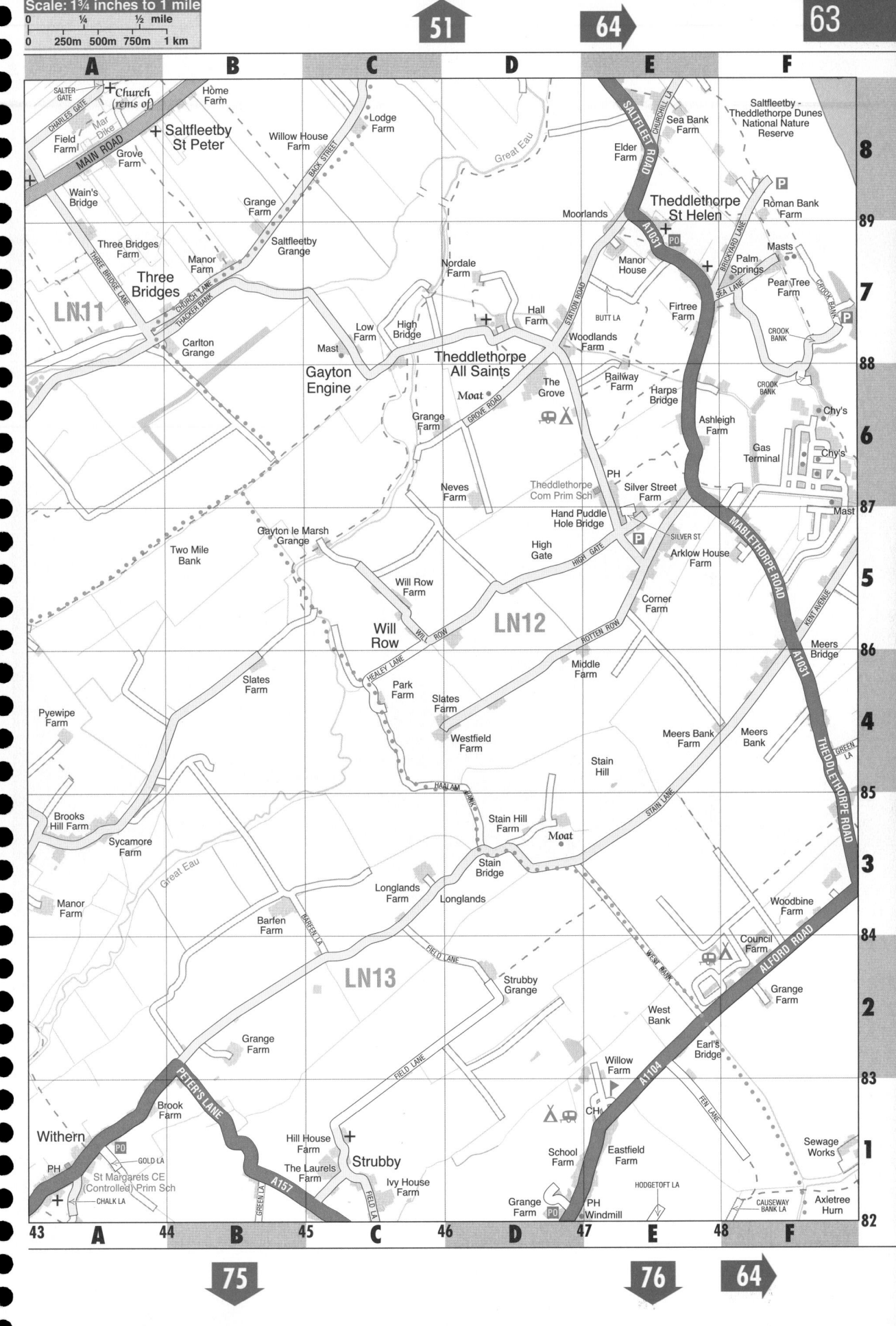
Scale: 1¾ inches to 1 mile
0 ¼ ½ mile
0 250m 500m 750m 1 km
51
64
A B C D E F
8 7 6 5 4 3 2 1
89 88 87 86 85 84 83 82
43 44 45 46 47 48
Salter Gate
Church (rems of)
Home Farm
Charles Gate
Mar Dike
Field Farm
Main Road
Saltfleetby St Peter
Grove Farm
Wain's Bridge
Lodge Farm
Willow House Farm
Back Street
Grange Farm
Great Eau
Saltfleet Road
Churchill La
Sea Bank Farm
Saltfleetby - Theddlethorpe Dunes National Nature Reserve
Elder Farm
Theddlethorpe St Helen
Roman Bank Farm
Moorlands
A1031
Three Bridges Farm
Three Bridge Lane
Saltfleetby Grange
Manor Farm
Three Bridges
Church Lane
Thacker Bank
LN11
Nordale Farm
Manor House
Brickyard Lane
Masts
Palm Springs
Sea Lane
Pear Tree Farm
Crook Bank
Station Road
Butt La
Firtree Farm
Hall Farm
Low Farm
High Bridge
Carlton Grange
Mast
Woodlands Farm
Theddlethorpe All Saints
Gayton Engine
Moat
The Grove
Railway Farm
Harps Bridge
Grove Road
Grange Farm
Ashleigh Farm
Chy's
Gas Terminal
Neves Farm
PH
Theddlethorpe Com Prim Sch
Silver Street Farm
Hand Puddle Hole Bridge
Silver St
Gayton le Marsh Grange
Two Mile Bank
High Gate
Arklow House Farm
Mablethorpe Road
Will Row Farm
Corner Farm
Kent Avenue
Will Row
LN12
Rotten Row
Meers Bridge
Healey Lane
Slates Farm
Middle Farm
Park Farm
Pyewipe Farm
Westfield Farm
Meers Bank Farm
Meers Bank
Stain Hill
Green La
Theddlethorpe Road
Haalam Bank
Stain Lane
Brooks Hill Farm
Stain Hill Farm
Sycamore Farm
Stain Bridge
Longlands Farm
Longlands
Woodbine Farm
Manor Farm
Barfen Farm
Barfen La
Council Farm
Field Lane
Alford Road
LN13
West Bank
Strubby Grange
Grange Farm
Grange Farm
Earl's Bridge
Willow Farm
A1104
Peter's Lane
Brook Farm
Fen Lane
CH
Withern
Hill House Farm
Strubby
School Farm
Eastfield Farm
Sewage Works
Gold La
St Margarets CE (Controlled) Prim Sch
The Laurels Farm
Ivy House Farm
Chalk La
A157
Green La
Hodgetoft La
Causeway Bank La
Axletree Hurn
Windmill
PO
75
76
64

B5
1 CAMBRIDGE RD N
2 LINKS AV
3 CAMBRIDGE RD S
4 IVEL GR
5 WHITEHEAD CL
6 IVEL CL

63

Scale: 1¾ inches to 1 mile

0   ¼   ½   mile
0   250m 500m 750m   1 km

A   B   C   D   E   F

8
89
7
88
6
87
5
86
4
85
3
84
2
83
1
82

Saltfleetby - Theddlethorpe Dunes National Nature Reserve

North End Farm
PH
MEERS BANK
The Seal Sanctuary & Nature Centre
POPLAR AV 1
CHALFONT AV 2
KENT AVE
GREEN LANE
GOLF ROAD
QUEBEC ROAD
PO
P
The Dunes Family Entertainment Centre
Fun Fair
Mablethorpe Community Prim Sch
Mon
Liby
Olde Curiosity Mus
HIGH STREET
VICTORIA RD
MABLETHORPE
Mablethorpe Hall
Moat
ALFORD ROAD
A1104
PH
LN12
CHURCH LANE
Art Gall
The Tennyson High Sch
SEAHOLME ROAD
Seahaven Springs
PH
Poplar Farm
AQUA DR 1
MARIAN AV 2
MEDINA GD 3
CHAMPION WY 4
Trusthorpe
Masts
Masts
SUTTON RD
Bourne Farm
A52
Bambers Farm
Bamber's Bridge
Elder Farm
NORTH ROAD
Sewage Works
Bridge Farm
Crossing Farm
MILL LANE
Thorpe Farm
WHITE PIT LA
FEN LA
MAIN STREET
TRUSTHORPE ROAD
Thorpe
Trusthorpe Hall
Boswell Farm
HIGHGATE

C3
1 QUEENS PK CL
2 NEWSTEAD RD
3 DYMOKE CL
4 BROOKE DR
5 DYMOKE RD
6 ARDEN CL

C2
1 MILL FIELD
2 PARKINSON'S WY
3 JAMES AV
4 ST PETER'S LA
5 BRAY AV
6 ETON RD

A4
1 THE FAIRWAY
2 THE DRIVE
3 ENTERPRISE RD
4 LYLE CL
5 THE GREEN
6 JACKLIN CR
7 EAGLE CL

1 PARK RD E
2 CROMER AV
3 HIGH ST
4 PROMENADE
5 YORK RD

49   A   50   B   51   C   52   D   53   E   54   F   55

A3
1 ORCHARD WY
2 ORCHARD CL
3 CHURCH RD
4 MALBOROUGH DR
5 OAKHAM AV
6 WINCHESTER DR
7 CHELTENHAM WY

B3
1 MAXWELL DR
2 KNOWLE ST
3 KENSINGTON GD
4 STANLEY AV
5 NELSON RD
6 PARKLANDS
7 MAYFLOWER WY
8 TRENCHARD RD
9 THE STRAND
10 STRAND CL
11 HAMMOND CT
12 FOXE END
13 PARK AV
14 PARRY RD
15 VYNER CL
16 RIPON PL
17 ANCASTER RD
18 HARRIS BD
19 MARINA RD
20 KING ST
21 ELM AV
22 MARIAN AV
23 HARLEQUIN DR
24 TOWER CL

B4
1 LONG ACRE
2 ST ANDREWS RD
3 SHERWOOD RD
4 RUGBY RD
5 MALVERN RD
6 HARROW RD
7 REPTON RD
8 QUEENSWAY
9 SOMERSBY AV
10 FITZWILLIAM ST
11 WELLINGTON AV
12 CHAUCER AV
13 RUSKIN RD
14 KINGSLEY RD
15 CHARLES WRIGHT CL
16 TENNYSON AV
17 TENNYSON RD
18 HIGH ST
19 ADMIRALTY RD
20 STATION RD
21 ALEXANDRA RD
22 ALEXANDRA PK

C1
1 ASHLEY CL
2 HALL LEAS DR
3 TRUSTHORPE RD
4 HIGHGATE CL
5 HIGHFIELD AV
6 PARK VIEW
7 UPPINGHAM RD
8 OUNDLE RD
9 GROVE RD
10 PARK RD WEST
11 WILLOUGHBY RD
12 MARINE AV
13 HARDING CL

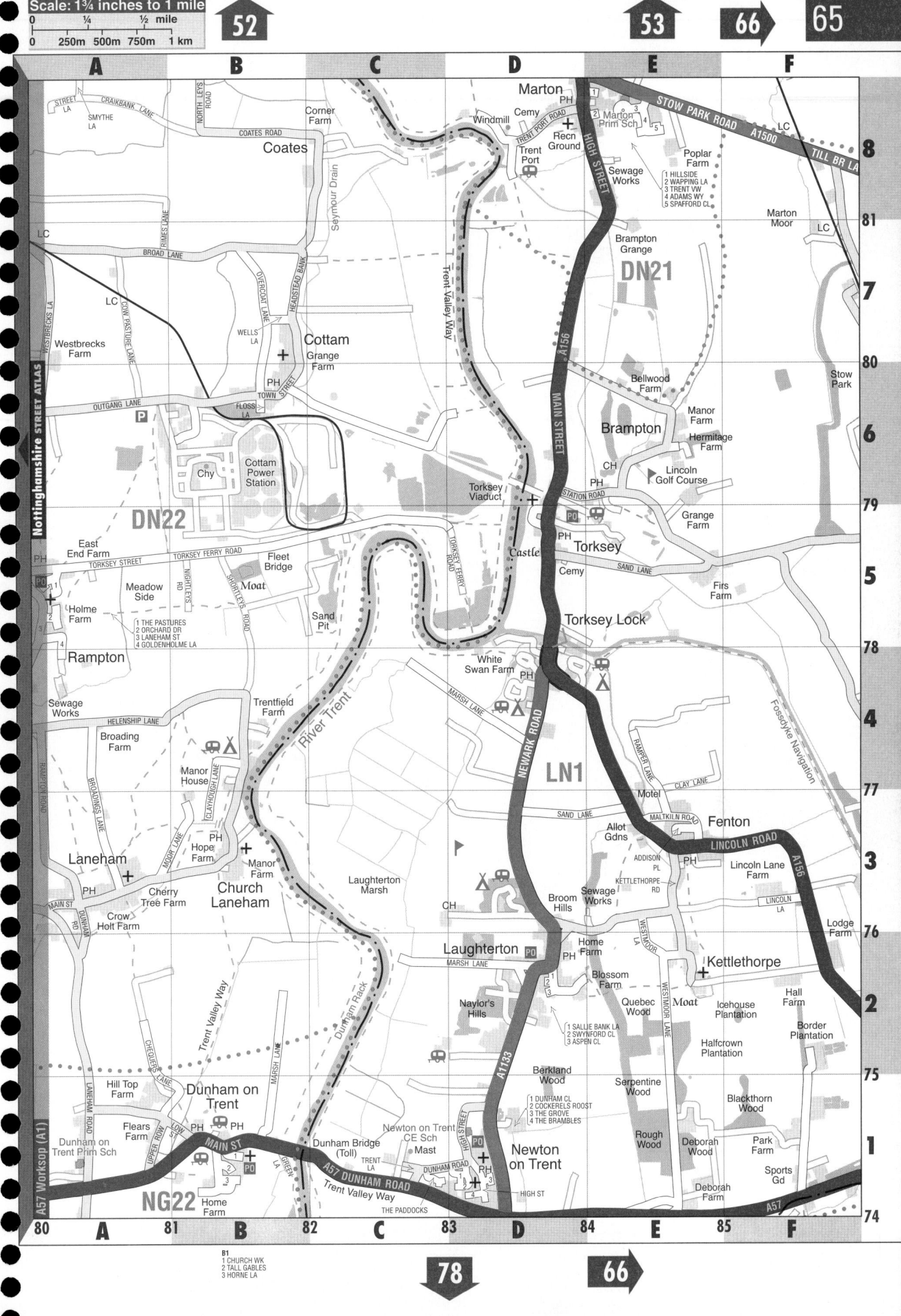

A   B   C   D   E   F

8
81
7
80
6
79
5
78
4
77
3
76
2
75
1
74

Nottinghamshire STREET ATLAS

STREET LA   CRAIKBANK LANE
SMYTHE LA
NORTH LEYS ROAD
Corner Farm
COATES ROAD
Coates
Seymour Drain
Windmill
Marton
Cemy   PH
Trent Port Road
Trent Port
Recn Ground
Marton Prim Sch
STOW PARK ROAD   A1500
LC   TILL BR LA

1 HILLSIDE
2 WAPPING LA
3 TRENT VW
4 ADAMS WY
5 SPAFFORD CL
Poplar Farm
Sewage Works

Brampton Grange
DN21
Marton Moor
LC

LC
BROAD LANE
RIMES LANE
LC
OVERCOAT LANE
HEADSTEAD BANK
WELLS LA
COW PASTURE LANE
WESTBRECKS LA
Westbrecks Farm
OUTGANG LANE
P
Cottam
Grange Farm
PH   TOWN STREET
FLOSS LA
Trent Valley Way
A156
MAIN STREET
Bellwood Farm
Manor Farm
Hermitage Farm
Brampton
CH
PH   STATION ROAD
Lincoln Golf Course
Grange Farm
Torksey
Firs Farm

DN22
Chy
Cottam Power Station
Torksey Viaduct
PO
Castle
Cemy
PH
Torksey
SAND LANE

East End Farm
TORKSEY STREET   TORKSEY FERRY ROAD
Fleet Bridge
Meadow Side
Moat
1 THE PASTURES
2 ORCHARD DR
3 LANEHAM ST
4 GOLDENHOLME LA
Sand Pit
NIGHTLEYS RD
SHORLEYS ROAD
TORKSEY FERRY ROAD
River Trent
Torksey Lock
Fossdyke Navigation

PH
PO
Holme Farm
4
Rampton

Sewage Works
HELENSHIP LANE
Broading Farm
BROADINGS LANE
Manor House
CLAYHOUGH LANE
Trentfield Farm
White Swan Farm
PH
MARSH LANE
NEWARK ROAD
LN1
RAMPER LANE
CLAY LANE
Motel
SAND LANE
MALTKILN RD
Fenton
LINCOLN ROAD
A156
Lincoln Lane Farm
LINCOLN LA

Laneham
MOOR LANE
PH   Hope Farm
DUNHAM ROAD
RAMPTON ROAD
Manor Farm
Church Laneham
Cherry Tree Farm
PH
Crow Holt Farm
Laughterton Marsh
CH
Broom Hills
Allot Gdns
ADDISON PL
PH
KETTLETHORPE RD
Sewage Works
WESTMOOR LA
Lodge Farm

Hill Top Farm
LANEHAM ROAD
CHEQUERS LANE
Trent Valley Way
MARSH LANE
Dunham Rack
MARSH LANE
Laughterton
PO
PH   Home Farm
Blossom Farm
1
2
3
Quebec Wood
Moat
Kettlethorpe
Icehouse Plantation
Hall Farm
Border Plantation

Dunham on Trent
PH
Flears Farm
UPPER ROW
LOW ROW
GREEN LA
MAIN ST
PO
Dunham Bridge (Toll)
Newton on Trent CE Sch
Mast
TRENT LA
HIGH STREET
Naylor's Hills
1 SALLIE BANK LA
2 SWYNFORD CL
3 ASPEN CL
A1133
Berkland Wood
1 DUNHAM CL
2 COCKERELS ROOST
3 THE GROVE
4 THE BRAMBLES
Serpentine Wood
Halfcrown Plantation
Blackthorn Wood
Park Farm

A57 Worksop (A1)
Dunham on Trent Prim Sch
Home Farm
NG22
A57 DUNHAM ROAD
Trent Valley Way
THE PADDOCKS
DUNHAM ROAD
Newton on Trent
HIGH ST
Rough Wood
Deborah Wood
Deborah Farm
Sports Gd
A57

66

←65

↑53

↑54

Scale: 1¾ inches to 1 mile
0   ¼   ½   mile
0   250m 500m 750m 1 km

C7
1 THE BEECHES
2 SCHOOL LA
3 ST HUGH'S TR
4 STRETTON CL
5 VILLAGE FARM DR
6 LARNERS FIELDS

C8
1 CHURCH RD
2 SCHOOL LA
3 INGHAM RD
4 SOUTH DR
5 ST MARY'S CR

D7
1 HAWTHORN WK
2 ASHFIELD
3 MANOR FARM DR
4 TWITCHELL
5 THE CLOSE
6 SWAN DR

7 MEDWAY
8 THE UPPER CLOSE
9 BRADWAY
10 KISGATE
11 EASTFIELD

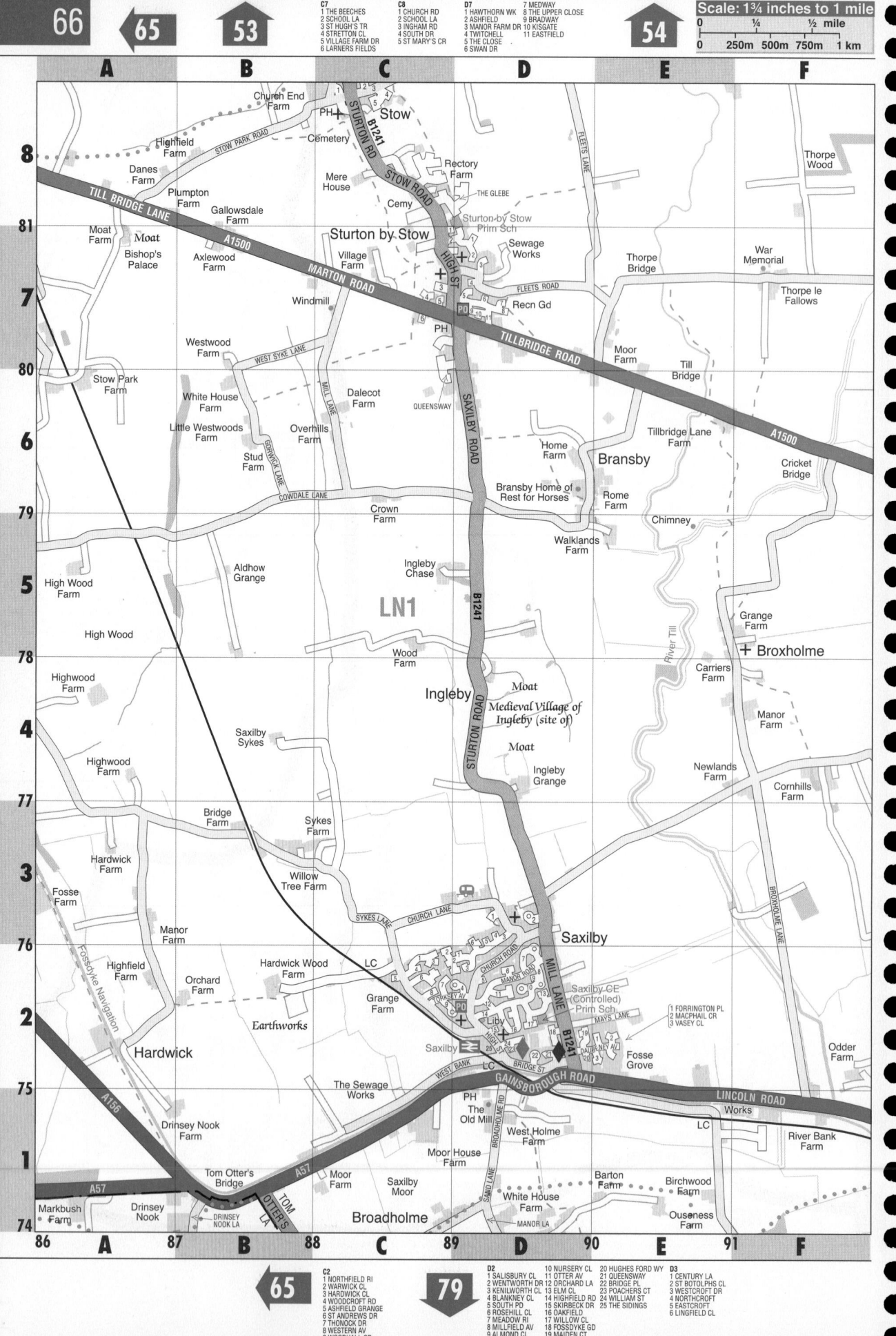

C2
1 NORTHFIELD RI
2 WARWICK CL
3 HARDWICK CL
4 WOODCROFT DR
5 ASHFIELD GRANGE
6 ST ANDREWS DR
7 THONOCK DR
8 WESTERN AV
9 WOODHALL CR

D2
1 SALISBURY CL
2 WENTWORTH DR
3 KENILWORTH CL
4 BLANKNEY CL
5 SOUTH PD
6 ROSEHILL CL
7 MEADOW RI
8 MILLFIELD AV
9 ALMOND CL

10 NURSERY CL
11 OTTER AV
12 ORCHARD LA
13 ELM CL
14 HIGHFIELD RD
15 SKIRBECK DR
16 OAKFIELD
17 WILLOW CL
18 FOSSDYKE GD
19 MAIDEN CT

20 HUGHES FORD WY
21 QUEENSWAY
22 BRIDGE PL
23 POACHERS CT
24 WILLIAM ST
25 THE SIDINGS

D3
1 CENTURY LA
2 ST BOTOLPHS CL
3 WESTCROFT DR
4 NORTHCROFT
5 EASTCROFT
6 LINGFIELD CL

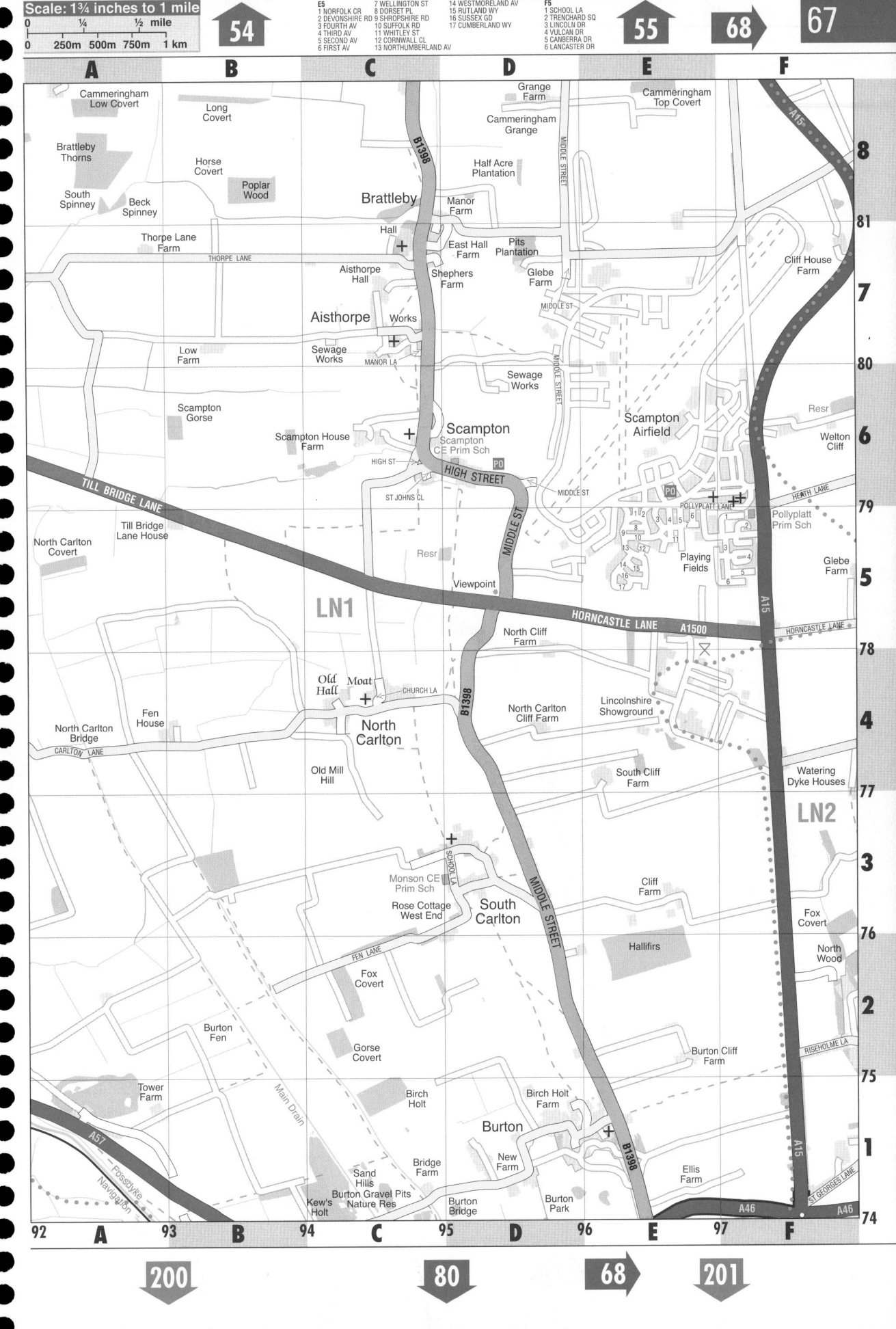
Cammeringham Low Covert
Long Covert
Brattleby Thorns
Horse Covert
Poplar Wood
South Spinney
Beck Spinney
Brattleby
Grange Farm
Cammeringham Grange
Cammeringham Top Covert
Half Acre Plantation
Manor Farm
Hall
East Hall Farm
Pits Plantation
Thorpe Lane Farm
THORPE LANE
Aisthorpe Hall
Shephers Farm
Glebe Farm
Cliff House Farm
Aisthorpe
Works
Low Farm
Sewage Works
MANOR LA
MIDDLE STREET
MIDDLE ST
Scampton Gorse
Scampton House Farm
Scampton
Scampton CE Prim Sch
PO
HIGH ST
HIGH STREET
ST JOHNS CL
Scampton Airfield
Resr
Welton Cliff
HEATH LANE
POLLYPLATT LANE
Pollyplatt Prim Sch
TILL BRIDGE LANE
Till Bridge Lane House
North Carlton Covert
Playing Fields
Glebe Farm
Viewpoint
LN1
HORNCASTLE LANE
A1500
North Cliff Farm
HORNCASTLE LANE
Old Hall
Moat
CHURCH LA
B1398
North Carlton
North Carlton Cliff Farm
Lincolnshire Showground
Fen House
North Carlton Bridge
CARLTON LANE
Old Mill Hill
South Cliff Farm
Watering Dyke Houses
LN2
SCHOOL LA
Monson CE Prim Sch
Rose Cottage West End
South Carlton
Cliff Farm
Fox Covert
Hallifirs
North Wood
FEN LANE
Fox Covert
Burton Fen
Gorse Covert
RISEHOLME LA
Burton Cliff Farm
Tower Farm
Main Drain
Birch Holt
Birch Holt Farm
Burton
A57
Fossdyke Navigation
Sand Hills
Burton Gravel Pits Nature Res
Kew's Holt
Bridge Farm
New Farm
Burton Bridge
Burton Park
Ellis Farm
A15
A46
ST GEORGES LANE
A B C D E F
8 81 7 80 6 79 5 78 4 77 3 76 2 75 1 74
92 93 94 95 96 97

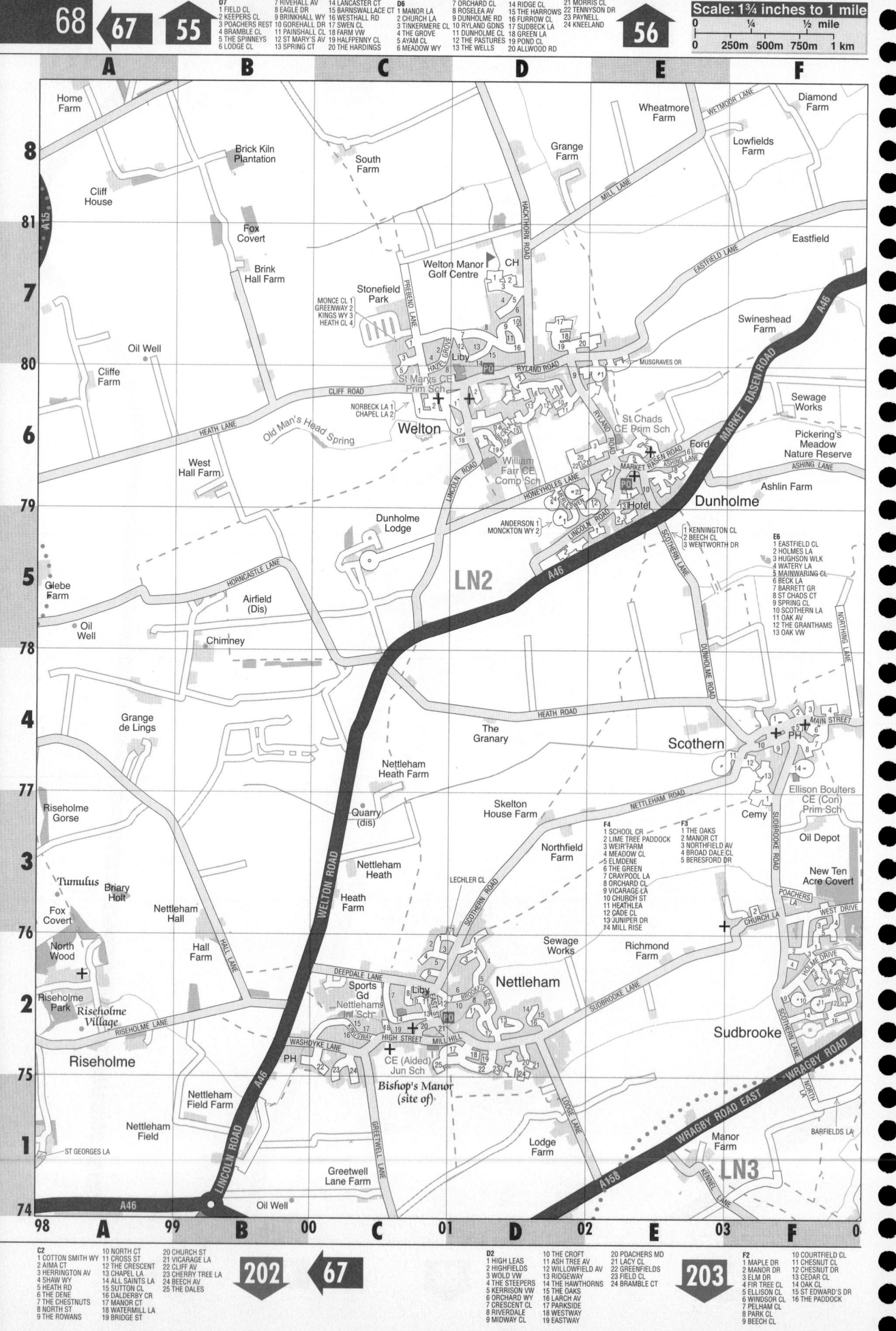

68 **67** **55**

D7
1 FIELD CL
2 KEEPERS CL
3 POACHERS REST
4 BRAMBLE CL
5 THE SPINNEYS
6 LODGE CL

7 RIVEHALL AV
8 EAGLE DR
9 BRINKHALL WY
10 GOREHALL DR
11 PAINSHALL CL
12 ST MARY'S AV
13 SPRING CT

14 LANCASTER CT
15 BARNSWALLACE CT
16 WESTHALL RD
17 SWEN CL
18 FARM VW
19 HALFPENNY CL
20 THE HARDINGS

D6
1 MANOR LA
2 CHURCH LA
3 TINKERMERE CL
4 THE GROVE
5 AYAM CL
6 MEADOW WY

7 ORCHARD CL
8 ROSELEA AV
9 DUNHOLME RD
10 RYLAND GDNS
11 DUNHOLME CL
12 THE PASTURES
13 THE WELLS

14 RIDGE CL
15 THE HARROWS
16 FURROW CL
17 SUDBECK LA
18 GREEN LA
19 POND CL
20 ALLWOOD RD

21 MORRIS CL
22 TENNYSON DR
23 PAYNELL
24 KNEELAND

56

Scale: 1¾ inches to 1 mile
0   ¼   ½ mile
0 250m 500m 750m 1 km

LN2

LN3

Home Farm
Cliff House
Brick Kiln Plantation
South Farm
Wheatmore Farm
WETMOOR LANE
Diamond Farm
Lowfields Farm

Cliffe Farm
Fox Covert
Brink Hall Farm
Grange Farm
Eastfield
EASTFIELD LANE

Oil Well
Stonefield Park
Welton Manor Golf Centre
CH
Swineshead Farm

MONCE CL 1
GREENWAY 2
KINGS WY 3
HEATH CL 4

St Marys CE Prim Sch
Liby
RYLAND ROAD
MUSGRAVES OR
Sewage Works

Cliff Farm
NORBECK LA 1
CHAPEL LA 2
CLIFF ROAD
Welton
HEATH LANE
Old Man's Head Spring

St Chads CE Prim Sch
Ford
Pickering's Meadow Nature Reserve
ASHING LANE
Ashlin Farm

West Hall Farm
William Farr CE Comp Sch
ANDERSON 1
MONCKTON WY 2
Hotel
Dunholme
MARKET RASEN ROAD

Dunholme Lodge
HORNCASTLE LANE
Airfield (Dis)

1 KENNINGTON CL
2 BEECH CL
3 WENTWORTH DR

E6
1 EASTFIELD CL
2 HOLMES LA
3 HUGHSON WLK
4 WATERY LA
5 MAINWARING CL
6 BECK LA
7 BARRETT GR
8 ST CHADS CT
9 SPRING CL
10 SCOTHERN LA
11 OAK AV
12 THE GRANTHAMS
13 OAK VW

Glebe Farm
Oil Well
Chimney

The Granary
HEATH ROAD
Scothern
PH
Ellison Boulters CE (Con) Prim Sch

Grange de Lings
Nettleham Heath Farm
NETTLEHAM ROAD
Cemy
Oil Depot

Riseholme Gorse
Quarry (dis)
Skelton House Farm

F4
1 SCHOOL CR
2 LIME TREE PADDOCK
3 WEIR FARM
4 MEADOW CL
5 ELMDENE
6 THE GREEN
7 CRAYPOOL LA
8 ORCHARD CL
9 VICARAGE LA
10 CHURCH ST
11 HEATHLEA
12 CADE CL
13 JUNIPER DR
14 MILL RISE

F3
1 THE OAKS
2 MANOR CT
3 NORTHFIELD AV
4 BROAD DALE CL
5 BERESFORD DR

New Ten Acre Covert

Tumulus
Briary Holt
Nettleham Heath
Heath Farm
Northfield Farm
POACHERS LA
WEST DRIVE

Fox Covert
Nettleham Hall
Sewage Works
Richmond Farm
CHURCH LA

North Wood
Hall Farm
DEEPDALE LANE
Sports Gd
Nettleham Inf Sch
Liby
Nettleham
HOLME DRIVE

Riseholme Park
Riseholme Village
RISEHOLME LANE
HIGH STREET
MILL HILL
Sudbrooke
SCOTHERN LANE

Riseholme
WASHDYKE LANE
PH
CE (Aided) Jun Sch
Bishop's Manor (site of)

ST GEORGES LA
Nettleham Field Farm
LODGE LANE
Lodge Farm
Manor Farm
BARFIELDS LA
WRAGBY ROAD

Nettleham Field
GREETWELL LANE
WRAGBY ROAD EAST
KENNEL LANE

Oil Well
Greetwell Lane Farm
A158

C2
1 COTTON SMITH WY
2 AIMA CT
3 HERRINGTON AV
4 SHAW WY
5 HEATH RD
6 THE DENE
7 THE CHESTNUTS
8 NORTH ST
9 THE ROWANS

10 NORTH CT
11 CROSS ST
12 THE CRESCENT
13 CHAPEL LA
14 ALL SAINTS LA
15 SUTTON CL
16 DALDERBY CR
17 MANOR CT
18 WATERMILL LA
19 BRIDGE ST

20 CHURCH ST
21 VICARAGE LA
22 CLIFF AV
23 CHERRY TREE LA
24 BEECH AV
25 THE DALES

202 **67**

D2
1 HIGH LEAS
2 HIGHFIELDS
3 WOLD VW
4 THE STEEPERS
5 KERRISON VW
6 ORCHARD WY
7 CRESCENT CL
8 RIVERDALE
9 MIDWAY CL

10 THE CROFT
11 ASH TREE AV
12 WILLOWFIELD AV
13 RIDGEWAY
14 THE HAWTHORNS
15 THE OAKS
16 LARCH AV
17 PARKSIDE
18 WESTWAY
19 EASTWAY

20 POACHERS MD
21 LACY CL
22 GREENFIELDS
23 FIELD CL
24 BRAMBLE CT

203

F2
1 MAPLE DR
2 HIGHFIELD
3 ELM DR
4 FIR TREE CL
5 ELLISON CL
6 WINDSOR CL
7 PELHAM CL
8 PARK CL
9 BEECH CL

10 COURTFIELD CL
11 CHESNUT CL
12 CHESNUT DR
13 CEDAR CL
14 OAK CL
15 ST EDWARD'S DR
16 THE PADDOCK

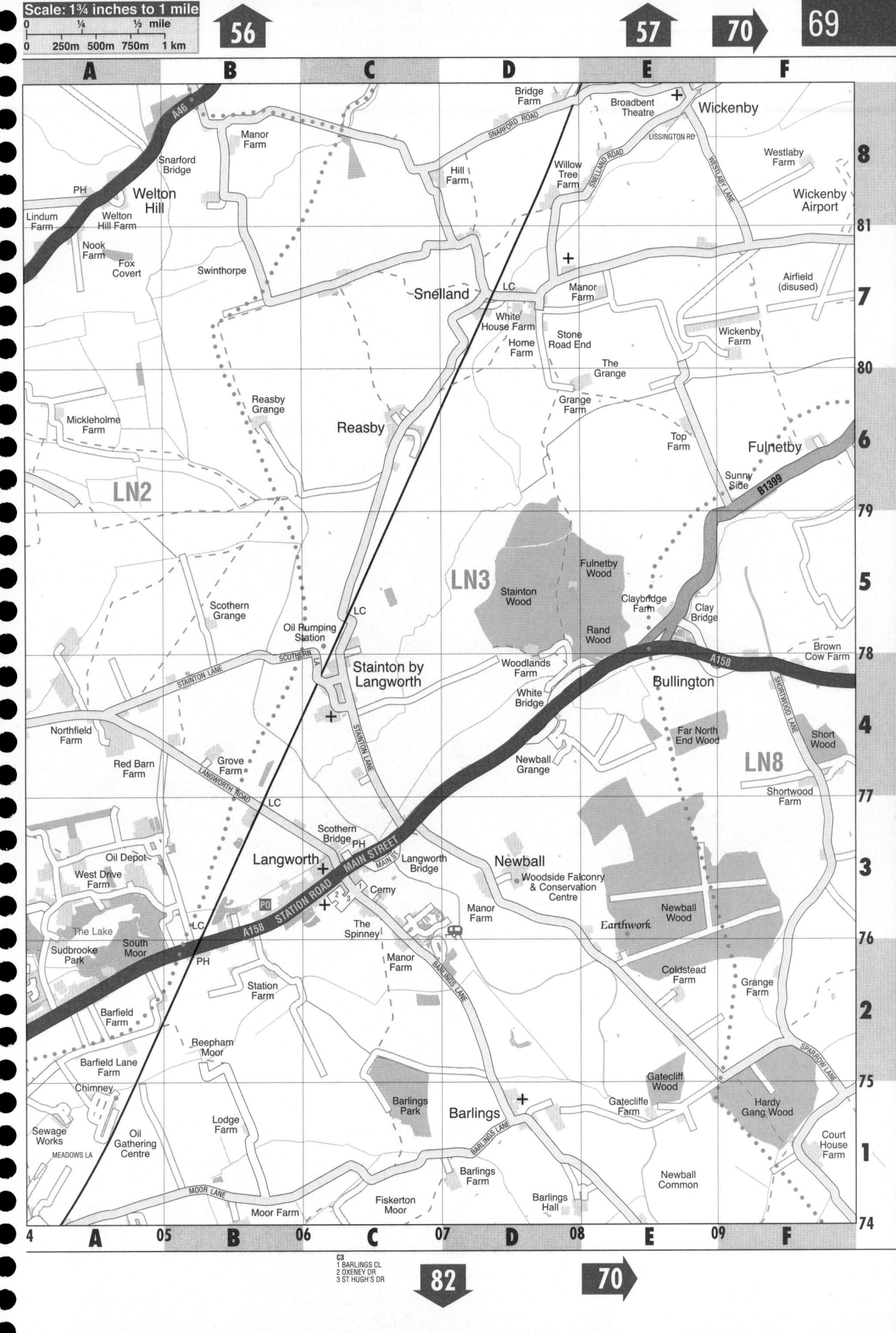
Scale: 1¾ inches to 1 mile
0 ¼ ½ mile
0 250m 500m 750m 1 km
56
57
70
Wickenby
Broadbent Theatre
Bridge Farm
Manor Farm
Snarford Bridge
Welton Hill
Welton Hill Farm
Lindum Farm
Nook Farm
Fox Covert
Swinthorpe
Hill Farm
Willow Tree Farm
Westlaby Farm
Wickenby Airport
Snelland
Manor Farm
Airfield (disused)
White House Farm
Home Farm
Stone Road End
The Grange
Wickenby Farm
Grange Farm
Reasby Grange
Reasby
Mickleholme Farm
Top Farm
Fulnetby
Sunny Side
LN2
LN3
Fulnetby Wood
Stainton Wood
Claybridge Farm
Clay Bridge
Rand Wood
Scothern Grange
Oil Pumping Station
Stainton by Langworth
Woodlands Farm
White Bridge
Bullington
Brown Cow Farm
Northfield Farm
Red Barn Farm
Grove Farm
Far North End Wood
Short Wood
Newball Grange
LN8
Shortwood Farm
Scothern Bridge
Langworth
Langworth Bridge
Oil Depot
West Drive Farm
Newball
Woodside Falconry & Conservation Centre
Cemy
Manor Farm
The Spinney
The Lake
Sudbrooke Park
South Moor
Newball Wood
Earthwork
Coldstead Farm
Manor Farm
Station Farm
Grange Farm
Barfield Farm
Reepham Moor
Barfield Lane Farm
Chimney
Gatecliff Wood
Gatecliffe Farm
Hardy Gang Wood
Barlings Park
Barlings
Lodge Farm
Sewage Works
Oil Gathering Centre
Court House Farm
Barlings Farm
Newball Common
Fiskerton Moor
Barlings Hall
Moor Farm
A46
A158
B1399
SNARFORD ROAD
LISSINGTON RD
SNELLAND ROAD
WESTLABY LANE
STAINTON LANE
SCOTHERN LA
STAINTON LANE
LANGWORTH ROAD
MAIN STREET
MAIN ST
STATION ROAD
SHORTWOOD LANE
BARLINGS LANE
SPARROW LANE
MOOR LANE
MEADOWS LA
PH
LC
PO
A B C D E F
8 81 7 80 6 79 5 78 4 77 3 76 2 75 1 74
4 05 06 07 08 09
82
70
C3
1 BARLINGS CL
2 OXENEY DR
3 ST HUGH'S DR

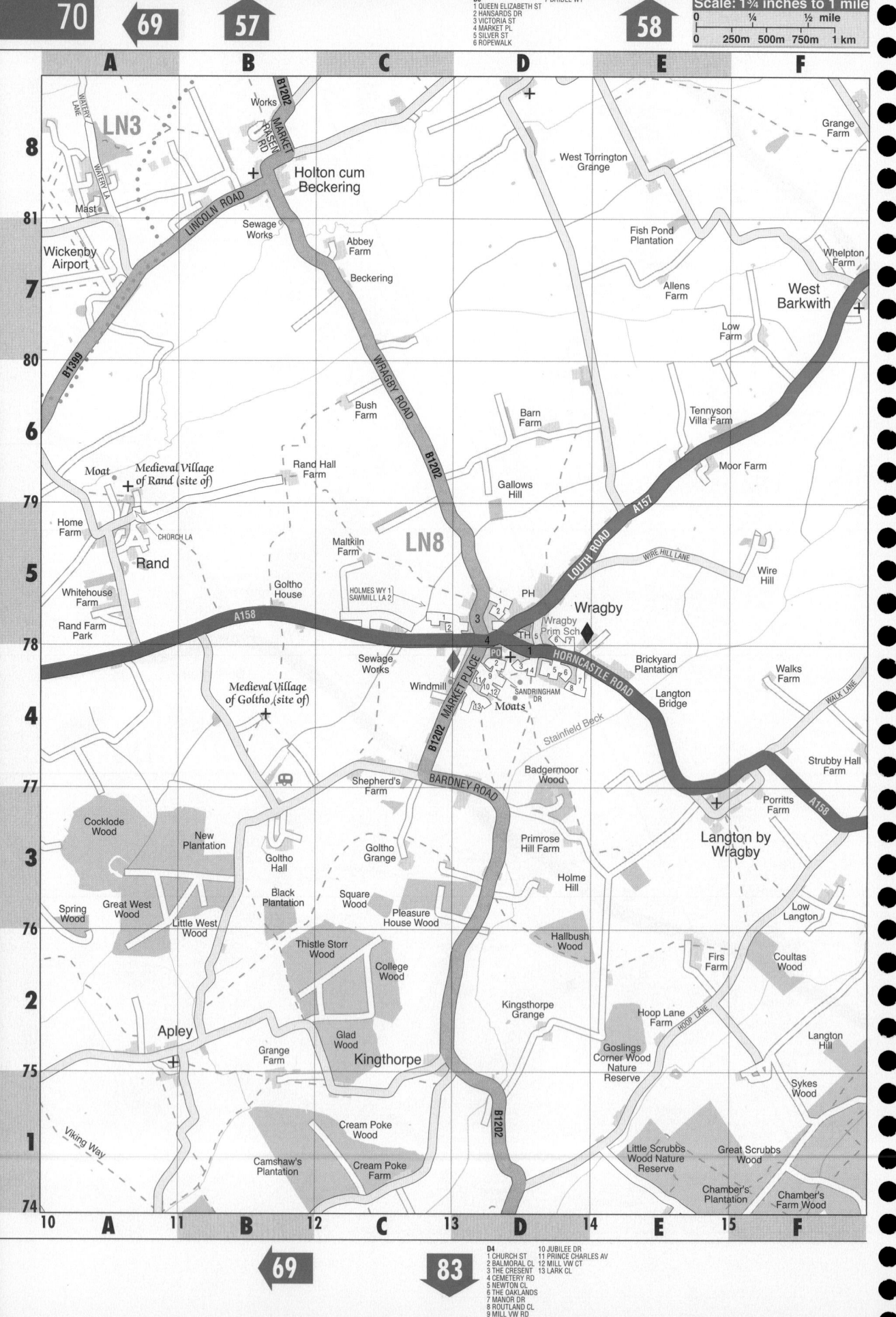

D5
1 QUEEN ELIZABETH ST
2 HANSARDS DR
3 VICTORIA ST
4 MARKET PL
5 SILVER ST
6 ROPEWALK
7 BRIDLE WY

Scale: 1¾ inches to 1 mile

0   ¼   ½   mile
0   250m   500m   750m   1 km

LN3

Works

B1202

MARKET RASEN RD

Watery Lane

Watery La

Holton cum Beckering

Mast

Wickenby Airport

LINCOLN ROAD

Sewage Works

Abbey Farm

Beckering

B1339

WRAGBY ROAD

Bush Farm

B1202

West Torrington Grange

Fish Pond Plantation

Allens Farm

Low Farm

Whelpton Farm

West Barkwith

Moat

Medieval Village of Rand (site of)

Rand Hall Farm

Barn Farm

Gallows Hill

Tennyson Villa Farm

Moor Farm

A157

Home Farm

CHURCH LA

Rand

LN8

Maltkiln Farm

LOUTH ROAD

WIRE HILL LANE

Wire Hill

Whitehouse Farm

Rand Farm Park

A158

Goltho House

HOLMES WY 1
SAWMILL LA 2

PH

Wragby

1
2

3

TH

Wragby Prim Sch
6 7

Brickyard Plantation

Walks Farm

Medieval Village of Goltho (site of)

Sewage Works

Windmill

MARKET PLACE

B1202

Moats

PO

1
4
9
10
12
13

3

SANDRINGHAM DR

5 6
8

7

HORNCASTLE ROAD

Langton Bridge

Strubby Hall Farm

WALK LANE

Shepherd's Farm

BARDNEY ROAD

Stainfield Beck

Badgermoor Wood

Porritts Farm

A158

Cocklode Wood

New Plantation

Goltho Hall

Goltho Grange

Square Wood

Primrose Hill Farm

Holme Hill

Langton by Wragby

Spring Wood

Great West Wood

Little West Wood

Black Plantation

Pleasure House Wood

Hallbush Wood

Firs Farm

Low Langton

Coultas Wood

Thistle Storr Wood

College Wood

Kingsthorpe Grange

Hoop Lane Farm

HOOP LANE

Langton Hill

Apley

Grange Farm

Glad Wood

Kingthorpe

Goslings Corner Wood Nature Reserve

Sykes Wood

Viking Way

Cream Poke Wood

B1202

Little Scrubbs Wood Nature Reserve

Great Scrubbs Wood

Camshaw's Plantation

Cream Poke Farm

Chamber's Plantation

Chamber's Farm Wood

D4
1 CHURCH ST
2 BALMORAL CL
3 THE CRESENT
4 CEMETERY RD
5 NEWTON CL
6 THE OAKLANDS
7 MANOR DR
8 ROUTLAND CL
9 MILL VW RD
10 JUBILEE DR
11 PRINCE CHARLES AV
12 MILL VW CT
13 LARK CL

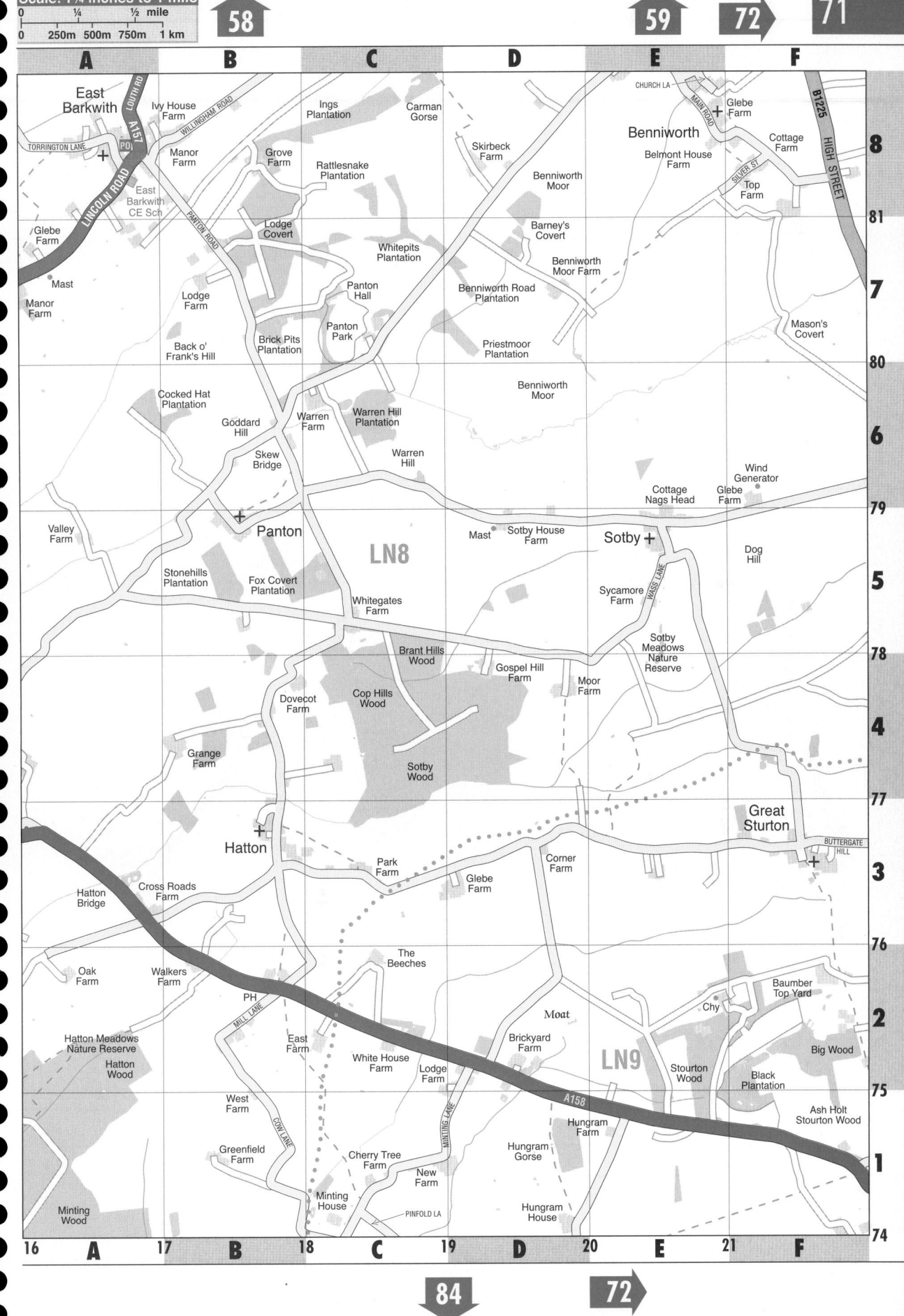

71 59 60

Scale: 1¾ inches to 1 mile

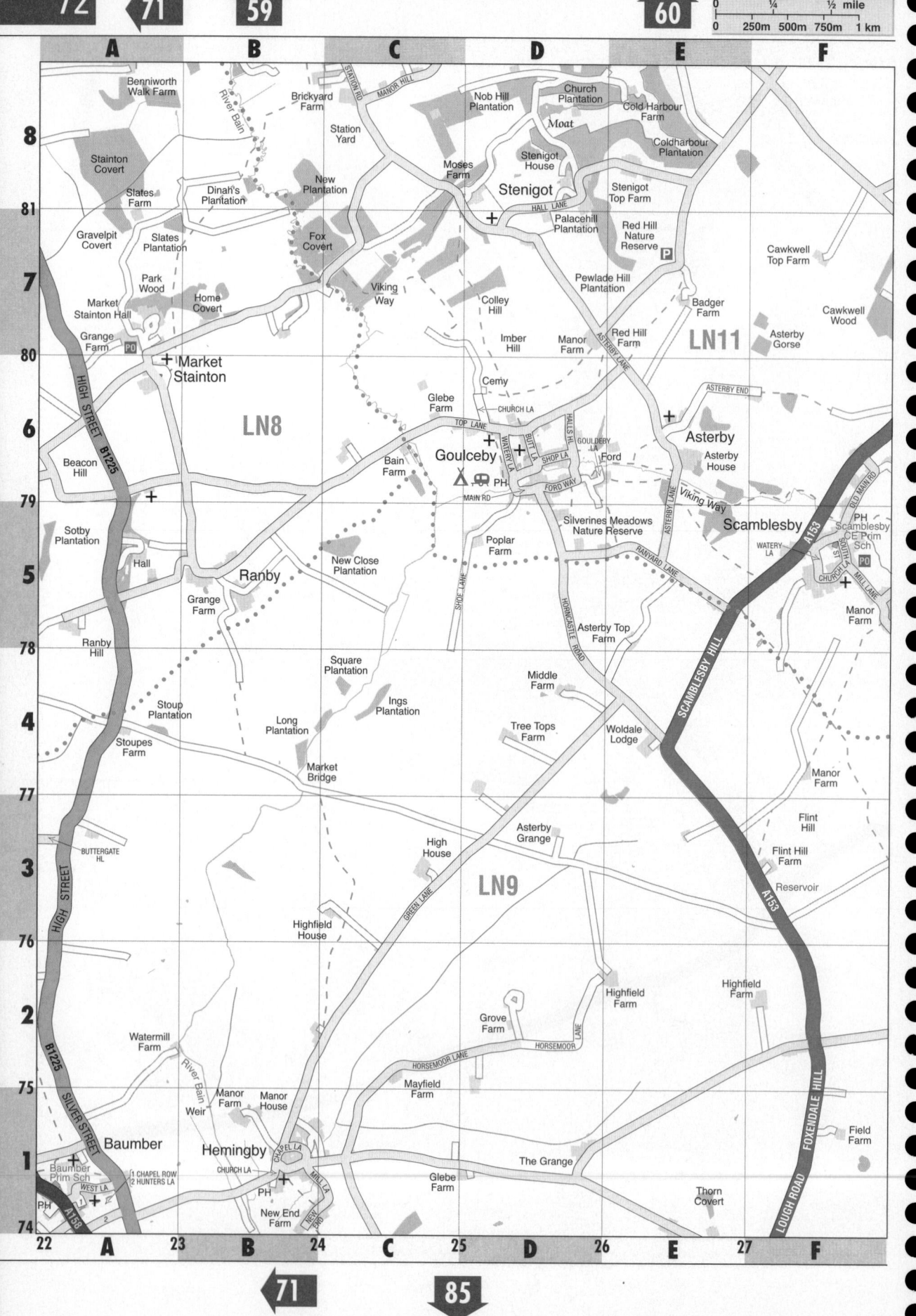

Benniworth Walk Farm
River Bain
Brickyard Farm
Station Yard
Nob Hill Plantation
Church Plantation
Cold Harbour Farm
Moat
Coldharbour Plantation
Stainton Covert
Moses Farm
Stenigot House
New Plantation
Slates Farm
Dinah's Plantation
Stenigot
Stenigot Top Farm
Hall Lane
Palacehill Plantation
Red Hill Nature Reserve
Gravelpit Covert
Slates Plantation
Fox Covert
Cawkwell Top Farm
Park Wood
Viking Way
Pewlade Hill Plantation
Market Stainton Hall
Home Covert
Colley Hill
Badger Farm
Cawkwell Wood
Grange Farm
Imber Hill
Manor Farm
Red Hill Farm
LN11
Asterby Gorse
Market Stainton
Asterby Lane
Cemy
Glebe Farm
Asterby End
Church La
LN8
Top Lane
Halls Hl
Asterby
Goulceby
Gouldeby La
Butt La
Asterby House
Watery La
Shop La
Ford
Beacon Hill
High Street
B1225
Bain Farm
PH
Ford Way
Main Rd
Viking Way
Silverines Meadows Nature Reserve
Scamblesby
Old Main Rd
PH
Scamblesby CE Prim Sch
Sotby Plantation
Poplar Farm
Watery La
A153
South St
Hall
New Close Plantation
Ranyard Lane
Ranby
Church La
Mill Lane
Grange Farm
Shoe Lane
Horncastle Road
Manor Farm
Asterby Top Farm
Ranby Hill
Square Plantation
Scamblesby Hill
Middle Farm
Stoup Plantation
Ings Plantation
Long Plantation
Tree Tops Farm
Woldale Lodge
Stoupes Farm
Market Bridge
Manor Farm
Flint Hill
Asterby Grange
Buttergate Hl
High House
Flint Hill Farm
LN9
Reservoir
Green Lane
Highfield House
Highfield Farm
Highfield Farm
Grove Farm
Watermill Farm
Horsemoor Lane
River Bain
Mayfield Farm
Manor Farm
Manor House
Weir
Foxendale Hill
Field Farm
Baumber
Hemingby
Chapel La
The Grange
Baumber Prim Sch
1 Chapel Row
2 Hunters La
Church La
Mill La
West La
Glebe Farm
Thorn Covert
A158
Silver Street
New End Farm
New End
Lough Road

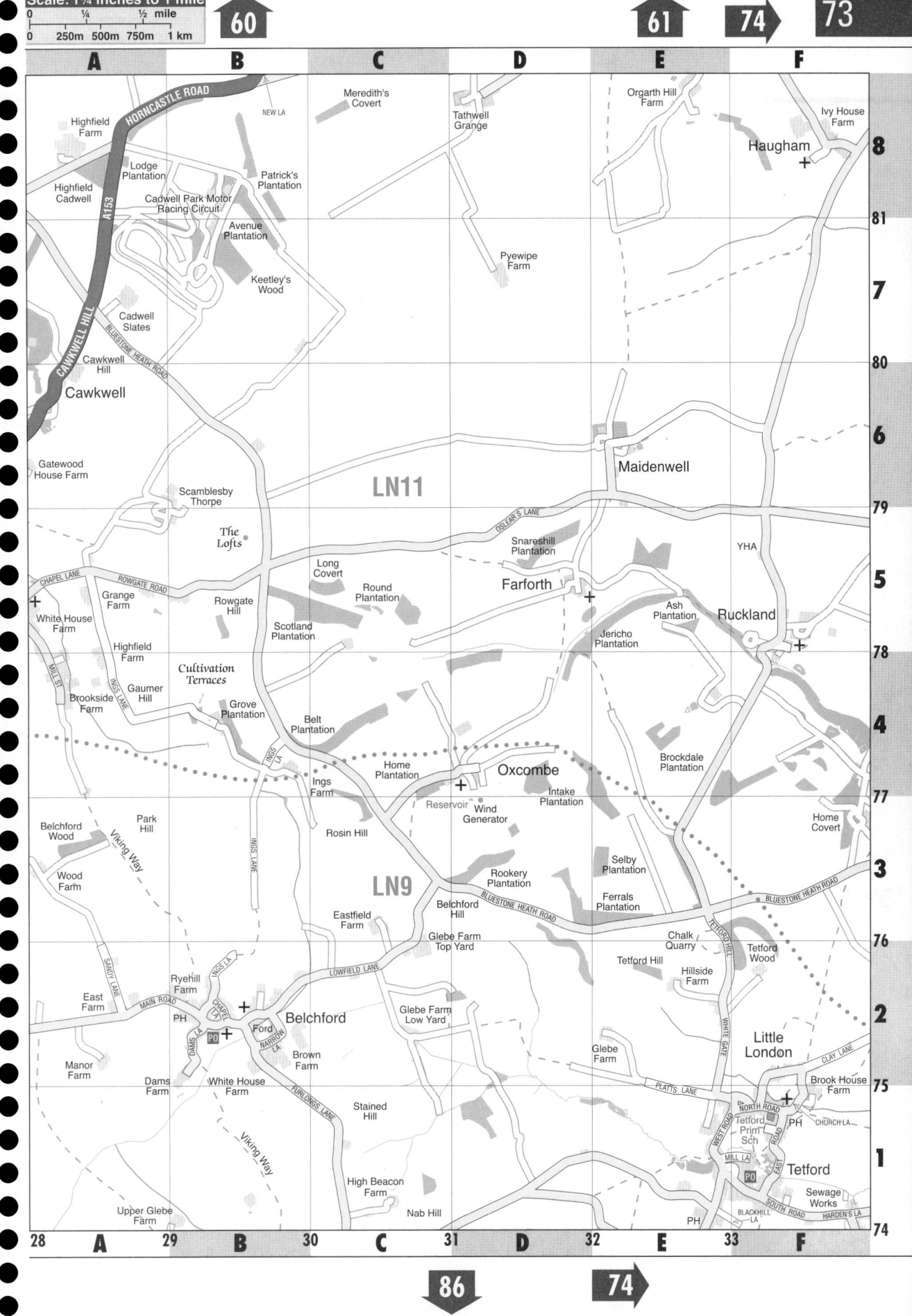

Map content (grid references and labels):

Scale: 1¾ inches to 1 mile
0 · ¼ · ½ · mile
0 · 250m · 500m · 750m · 1 km

Grid columns: A B C D E F
Grid rows: 8 81 7 80 6 79 5 78 4 77 3 76 2 75 1 74
Eastings: 28 29 30 31 32 33

Navigation markers: 60, 61, 74, 73 (top); 86, 74 (bottom)

Labels:
- Highfield Farm
- HORNCASTLE ROAD
- NEW LA
- Meredith's Covert
- Tathwell Grange
- Orgarth Hill Farm
- Ivy House Farm
- Haugham
- Lodge Plantation
- Patrick's Plantation
- Highfield Cadwell
- Cadwell Park Motor Racing Circuit
- A153
- Avenue Plantation
- Pyewipe Farm
- Keetley's Wood
- Cadwell Slates
- BLUESTONE HEATH ROAD
- Cawkwell Hill
- CAWKWELL HILL
- Cawkwell
- Gatewood House Farm
- Maidenwell
- Scamblesby Thorpe
- LN11
- OSLEAR'S LANE
- Snareshill Plantation
- The Lofts
- YHA
- Long Covert
- Round Plantation
- Farforth
- Ash Plantation
- Ruckland
- CHAPEL LANE
- ROWGATE ROAD
- Grange Farm
- Rowgate Hill
- Scotland Plantation
- Jericho Plantation
- White House Farm
- Highfield Farm
- Cultivation Terraces
- MILL ST
- INGS LANE
- Gaumer Hill
- Grove Plantation
- Belt Plantation
- Brookside Farm
- Brockdale Plantation
- Home Plantation
- Oxcombe
- Intake Plantation
- Ings Farm
- Reservoir
- Wind Generator
- Home Covert
- Belchford Wood
- Park Hill
- Rosin Hill
- Wood Farm
- Selby Plantation
- VIKING WAY
- Ferrals Plantation
- LN9
- Rookery Plantation
- Belchford Hill
- BLUESTONE HEATH ROAD
- Chalk Quarry
- Tetford Wood
- Eastfield Farm
- Glebe Farm Top Yard
- Tetford Hill
- Hillside Farm
- SANDY LANE
- LOWFIELD LANE
- TETFORD HILL
- East Farm
- MAIN ROAD
- Ryehill Farm
- INGS LA
- CHAPEL CL
- Belchford
- Glebe Farm Low Yard
- Glebe Farm
- WHITE GATE
- Little London
- CLAY LANE
- PH
- PO
- Ford
- NARROW LA
- Brown Farm
- DAMS LA
- PLATTS LANE
- Brook House Farm
- Manor Farm
- White House Farm
- FURLONGS LANE
- Stained Hill
- NORTH ROAD
- PH
- CHURCH LA
- WEST ROAD
- Tetford Prim Sch
- MILL LA
- EAST ROAD
- Viking Way
- High Beacon Farm
- Nab Hill
- PO
- Tetford
- Sewage Works
- Upper Glebe Farm
- SOUTH ROAD
- BLACKHILL LA
- HARDEN'S LA
- PH

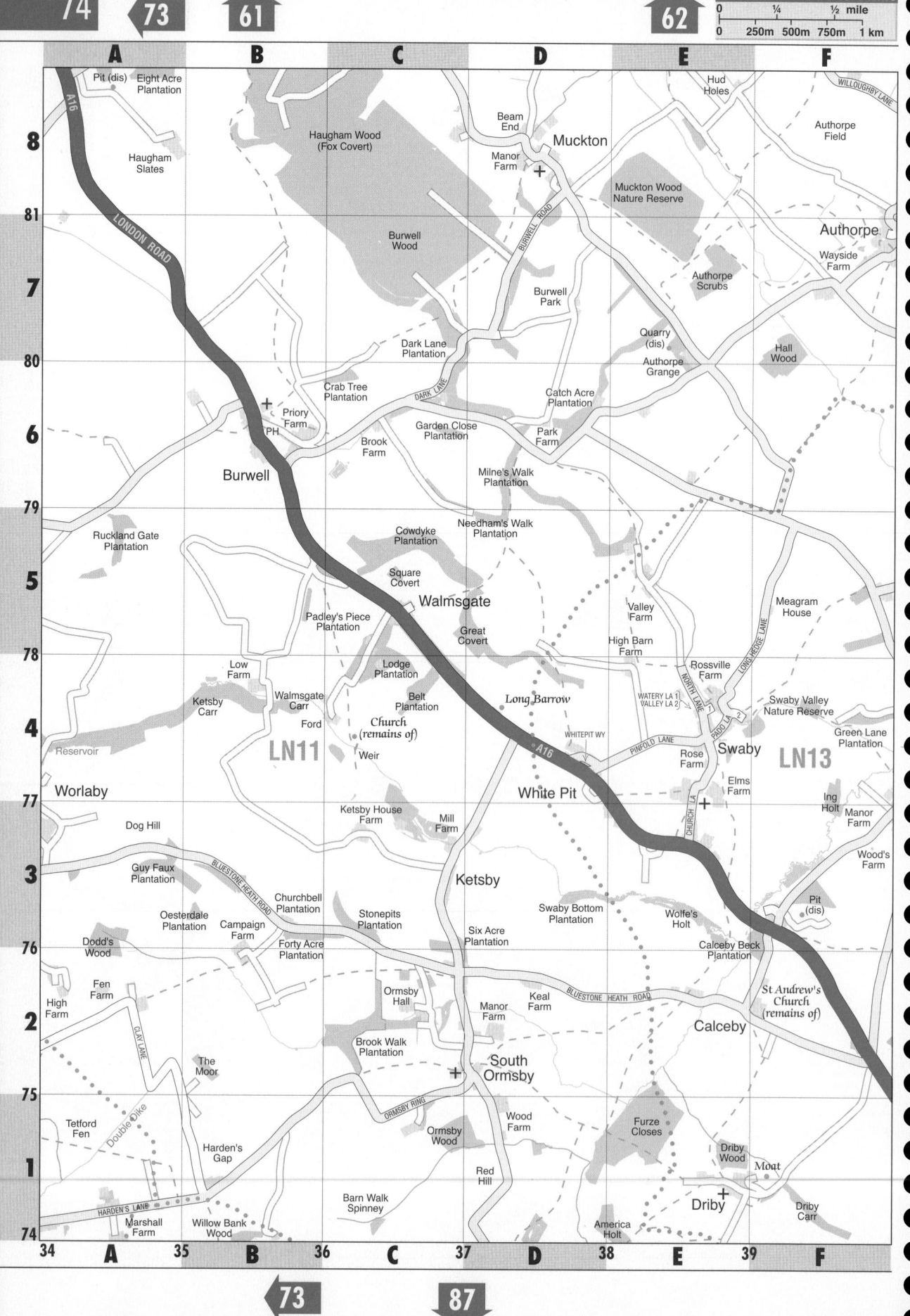

Scale: 1¾ inches to 1 mile

0   ¼   ½ mile
0   250m   500m   750m   1 km

A   **B**   **C**   **D**   **E**   **F**

Pit (dis)
Eight Acre Plantation
Haugham Wood (Fox Covert)
Hud Holes
WILLOUGHBY LANE
Authorpe Field

8

Beam End
Muckton
Manor Farm
Muckton Wood Nature Reserve

Haugham Slates

81

LONDON ROAD
Burwell Wood
BURWELL ROAD
Authorpe Scrubs
Authorpe
Wayside Farm

7

Burwell Park
Quarry (dis)
Hall Wood

80

Dark Lane Plantation
DARK LANE
Catch Acre Plantation
Authorpe Grange

Crab Tree Plantation
Priory Farm
PH
Garden Close Plantation
Park Farm

6

Burwell
Brook Farm
Milne's Walk Plantation

79

Ruckland Gate Plantation
Cowdyke Plantation
Needham's Walk Plantation

Square Covert
Valley Farm
Meagram House

5

Walmsgate
LONG HEDGE LANE

Padley's Piece Plantation
Great Covert
High Barn Farm
Rossville Farm
Swaby Valley Nature Reserve

78

Low Farm
Lodge Plantation
WATERY LA 1
VALLEY LA 2
NORTH LANE

Walmsgate Carr
Belt Plantation
Long Barrow
WHITEPIT WY
P400 LA
Green Lane Plantation

Ketsby Carr
Ford
Church (remains of)
A16
PINFOLD LANE
Rose Farm
Swaby

4

Reservoir
Weir
LN11
LN13

Worlaby
White Pit
Elms Farm
Ing Holt
Manor Farm

77

Dog Hill
Ketsby House Farm
Mill Farm
CHURCH LA
Wood's Farm

Guy Faux Plantation
BLUESTONE HEATH ROAD
Churchbell Plantation
Ketsby
Pit (dis)

3

Oesterdale Plantation
Campaign Farm
Stonepits Plantation
Six Acre Plantation
Swaby Bottom Plantation
Wolfe's Holt
Calceby Beck Plantation

Dodd's Wood
Forty Acre Plantation

76

Fen Farm
Ormsby Hall
Manor Farm
Keal Farm
BLUESTONE HEATH ROAD
St Andrew's Church (remains of)

High Farm
CLAY LANE
Brook Walk Plantation
Calceby

2

The Moor
South Ormsby
Wood Farm
Furze Closes
Driby Wood
Moat

Tetford Fen
DOUBLE DIKE
Harden's Gap
ORMSBY RING
Ormsby Wood
Red Hill
Driby
Driby Carr

1

HARDEN'S LANE
Marshall Farm
Willow Bank Wood
Barn Walk Spinney
America Holt

74

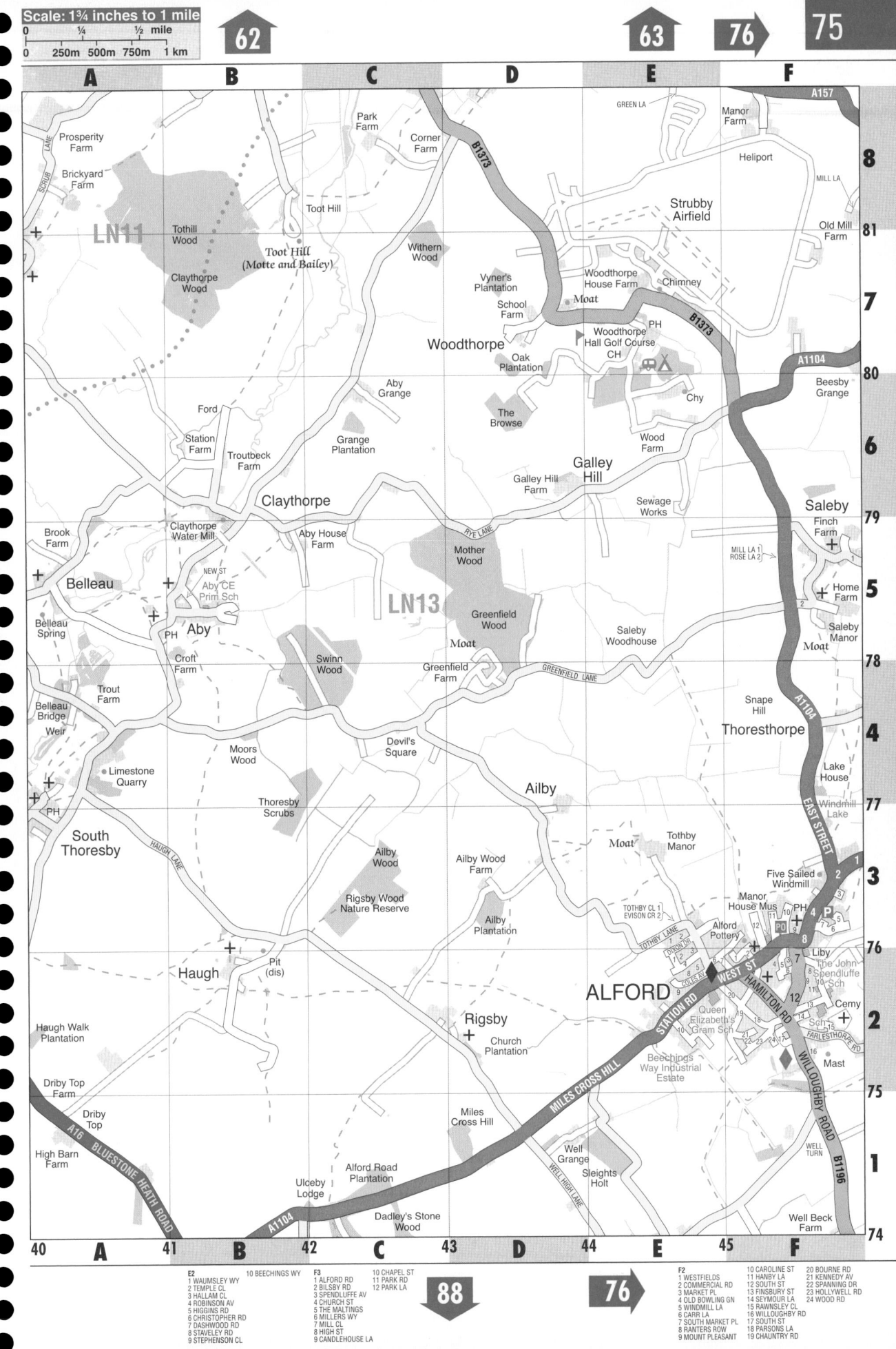

A157

Green La
Manor Farm
Heliport
MILL LA

8

Prosperity Farm
Brickyard Farm
SCRUB LANE
Park Farm
Corner Farm
B1373
Strubby Airfield

81

LN11
Tothill Wood
Toot Hill
Claythorpe Wood
Toot Hill (Motte and Bailey)
Withern Wood
Vyner's Plantation
Woodthorpe House Farm
Chimney
Moat
Woodthorpe Hall Golf Course CH
PH
B1373
Old Mill Farm

7

Woodthorpe
School Farm
Oak Plantation
Aby Grange
Grange Plantation
The Browse
Beesby Grange
A1104

80

Ford
Station Farm
Troutbeck Farm
Wood Farm
Chy

6

Claythorpe
Aby House Farm
RYE LANE
Galley Hill Farm
Galley Hill
Sewage Works
Saleby
Finch Farm

79

Brook Farm
Claythorpe Water Mill
NEW ST
Mother Wood
MILL LA 1
ROSE LA 2
Home Farm

5

Belleau
Aby CE Prim Sch
LN13
Greenfield Wood
Saleby Woodhouse
Saleby Manor
Moat

Belleau Spring
PH
Aby
Croft Farm
Swinn Wood
Moat
Greenfield Farm
GREENFIELD LANE

78

Trout Farm
Belleau Bridge Weir
Moors Wood
Devil's Square
Snape Hill
Thoresthorpe
A1104

4

Limestone Quarry
PH
Thoresby Scrubs
Ailby
Lake House

77

HAUGH LANE
South Thoresby
Ailby Wood
Ailby Wood Farm
Moat
Tothby Manor
EAST STREET
Windmill Lake
Five Sailed Windmill

3

Rigsby Wood Nature Reserve
Ailby Plantation
TOTHBY CL 1
EVISON CR 2
Manor House Mus
PH
P
PO

Haugh
Pit (dis)
Rigsby
Church Plantation
TOTHBY LANE
Alford Pottery
ALFORD
WEST ST
Liby
The John Spendluffe Sch
Cemy

76

Haugh Walk Plantation
STATION RD
Queen Elizabeth's Gram Sch
HAMILTON RD
WILLOUGHBY RD
FARLESTHORPE RD
Mast

2

Driby Top Farm
Driby Top
A16
BLUESTONE HEATH ROAD
Miles Cross Hill
MILES CROSS HILL
Beechings Way Industrial Estate
WELL HIGH LANE
Well Grange
Sleights Holt
WELL TURN
B1196

75

High Barn Farm
Ulceby Lodge
Alford Road Plantation
Miles Cross Hill
Well Beck Farm

1

Dadley's Stone Wood
A1104

74

40   41   42   43   44   45

A   B   C   D   E   F

E2
1 WAUMSLEY WY
2 TEMPLE CL
3 HALLAM CL
4 ROBINSON AV
5 HIGGINS RD
6 CHRISTOPHER RD
7 DASHWOOD RD
8 STAVELEY RD
9 STEPHENSON CL
10 BEECHINGS WY

F3
1 ALFORD RD
2 BILSBY RD
3 SPENDLUFFE AV
4 CHURCH ST
5 THE MALTINGS
6 MILLERS WY
7 MILL CL
8 HIGH ST
9 CANDLEHOUSE LA
10 CHAPEL ST
11 PARK RD
12 PARK LA

F2
1 WESTFIELDS
2 COMMERCIAL RD
3 MARKET PL
4 OLD BOWLING GN
5 WINDMILL LA
6 CARR LA
7 SOUTH MARKET PL
8 RANTERS ROW
9 MOUNT PLEASANT
10 CAROLINE ST
11 HANBY LA
12 SOUTH ST
13 FINSBURY ST
14 SEYMOUR LA
15 RAWNSLEY RD
16 WILLOUGHBY RD
17 SOUTH ST
18 PARSONS LA
19 CHAUNTRY RD
20 BOURNE RD
21 KENNEDY AV
22 SPANNING DR
23 HOLLYWELL RD
24 WOOD RD

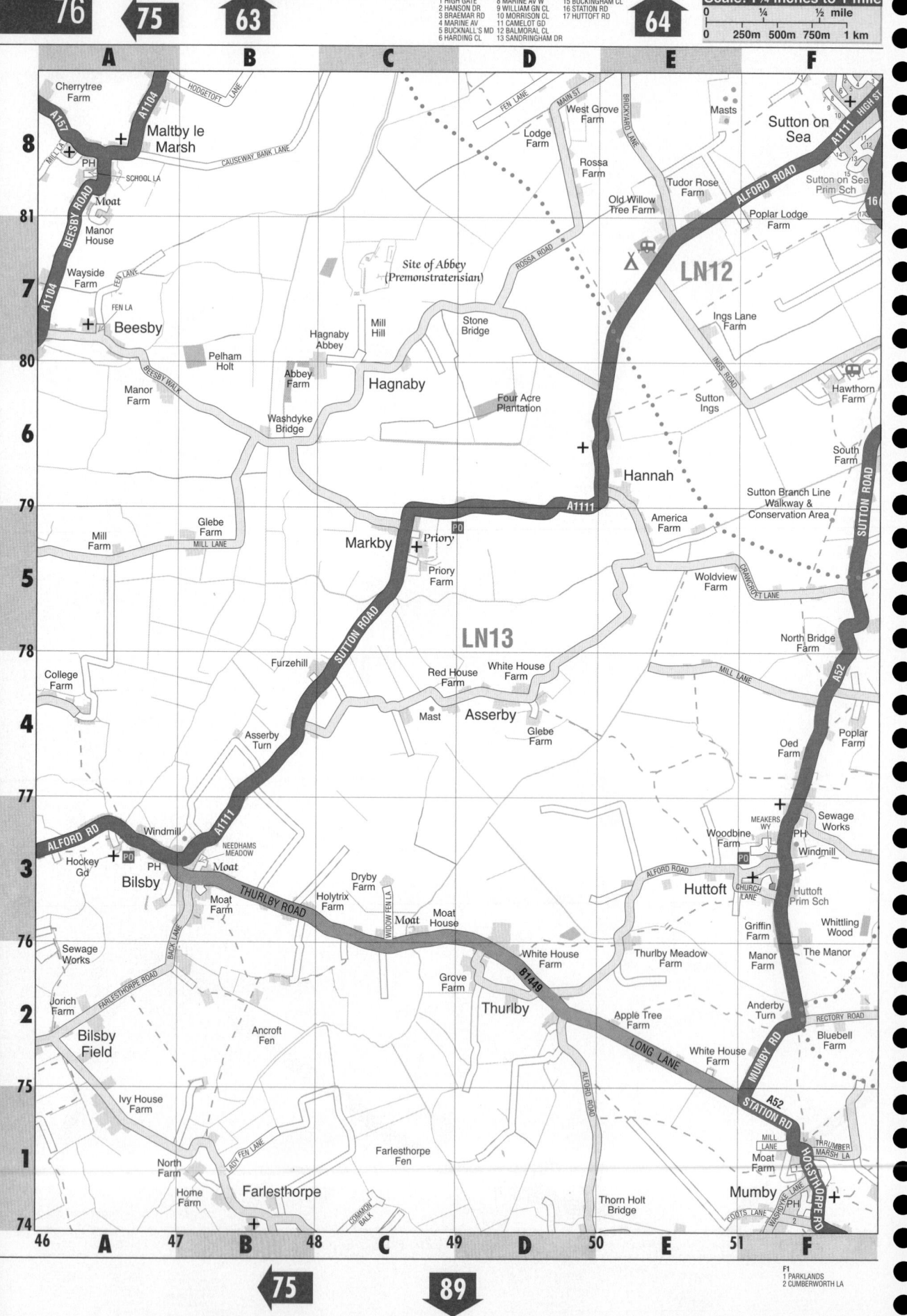
75
63
F8
1 HIGH GATE
2 HANSON DR
3 BRAEMAR RD
4 MARINE AV
5 BUCKNALL'S MD
6 HARDING CL
7 WILLIAM TOW CL
8 MARINE AV W
9 WILLIAM GN CL
10 MORRISON CL
11 CAMELOT GD
12 BALMORAL CL
13 SANDRINGHAM DR
14 HONEYSUCKLE CL
15 BUCKINGHAM CL
16 STATION RD
17 HUTTOFT RD
64
Scale: 1¾ inches to 1 mile
0 ¼ ½ mile
0 250m 500m 750m 1 km
A B C D E F
Cherrytree Farm
A157
A1104
HODGETOFT LANE
Maltby le Marsh
MILL LA
PH
SCHOOL LA
CAUSEWAY BANK LANE
FEN LANE
MAIN ST
West Grove Farm
Lodge Farm
BRICKYARD LANE
Masts
Sutton on Sea
A1111
HIGH ST
Rossa Farm
Tudor Rose Farm
ALFORD ROAD
Sutton on Sea Prim Sch
Moat
BEESBY ROAD
Manor House
Old Willow Tree Farm
Poplar Lodge Farm
Wayside Farm
FEN LANE
Site of Abbey (Premonstratensian)
ROSSA ROAD
LN12
FEN LA
Beesby
Mill Hill
Stone Bridge
Ings Lane Farm
Hagnaby Abbey
Pelham Holt
Manor Farm
BEESBY WALK
Abbey Farm
Hagnaby
INGS ROAD
Four Acre Plantation
Sutton Ings
Hawthorn Farm
Washdyke Bridge
South Farm
Hannah
Glebe Farm
A1111
Sutton Branch Line Walkway & Conservation Area
SUTTON ROAD
Mill Farm
MILL LANE
Markby
Priory
PO
America Farm
Priory Farm
Woldview Farm
CRAWCROFT LANE
SUTTON ROAD
LN13
North Bridge Farm
College Farm
Furzehill
Red House Farm
White House Farm
MILL LANE
A52
Mast
Asserby
Glebe Farm
Asserby Turn
Oed Farm
Poplar Farm
Windmill
NEEDHAMS MEADOW
A1111
ALFORD RD
Sewage Works
MEAKERS WY
Woodbine Farm
Hockey Gd
PO
PH
Moat
Bilsby
Windmill
Dryby Farm
ALFORD ROAD
Huttoft
CHURCH LANE
Huttoft Prim Sch
Moat Farm
THURLBY ROAD
Holytrix Farm
WIDOW FEN LA
Moat
Moat House
Griffin Farm
Whittling Wood
Sewage Works
BACK LANE
White House Farm
Thurlby Meadow Farm
The Manor
Manor Farm
FARLESTHORPE ROAD
Jorich Farm
Grove Farm
B1449
Thurlby
Anderby Turn
RECTORY ROAD
Bilsby Field
Ancroft Fen
Apple Tree Farm
Bluebell Farm
LONG LANE
MUMBY RD
White House Farm
ALFORD ROAD
Ivy House Farm
A52
STATION RD
MILL LANE
THRUMBER MARSH LA
Farlesthorpe Fen
North Farm
LADY FEN LANE
Moat Farm
HOGSTHORPE RD
Home Farm
Farlesthorpe
Thorn Holt Bridge
Mumby
WASHDYKE LANE
COMMON BALK
COOTS LANE
PH
46 47 48 49 50 51
F1
1 PARKLANDS
2 CUMBERWORTH LA
75
89

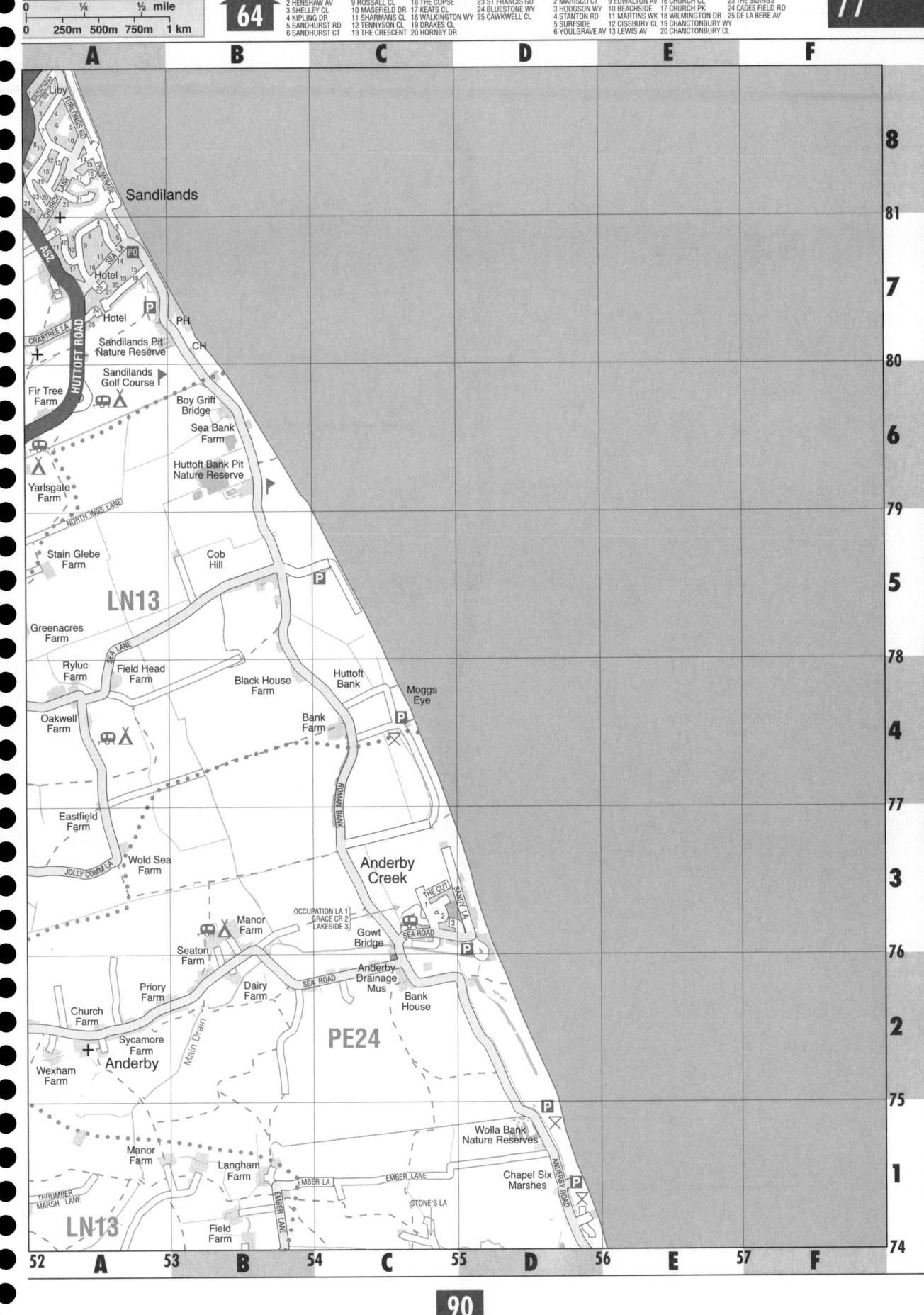

Scale: 1¾ inches to 1 mile

0   ¼   ½   mile
0 250m 500m 750m 1 km

64

A7	7 RUDYARD CL	14 GRANGE RD	21 WILYMAN CL	A8	7 HILLSIDE AV	14 CHURCH LA	21 LANSDOWNE DR
1 COMPER SWIFT CL	8 THE GLADE	15 SANDERS CL	22 SANDILANDS CL	1 MORELAND AV	8 QUEENS RD	15 DENNOR CL	22 LANDSDOWNE CL
2 HENSHAW AV	9 ROSSALL CL	16 THE COPSE	23 ST FRANCIS GD	2 MARISCO CT	9 EDWALTON AV	16 CHURCH CL	23 THE SIDINGS
3 SHELLEY CL	10 MASEFIELD DR	17 KEATS CL	24 BLUESTONE WY	3 HODGSON WY	10 BEACHSIDE	17 CHURCH PK	24 CADES FIELD RD
4 KIPLING DR	11 SHARMANS CL	18 WALKINGTON WY	25 CAWKWELL CL	4 STANTON RD	11 MARTINS WK	18 WILMINGTON DR	25 DE LA BERE AV
5 SANDHURST RD	12 TENNYSON CL	19 DRAKES CL		5 SURFSIDE	12 CISSBURY CL	19 CHANCTONBURY WY	
6 SANDHURST CT	13 THE CRESCENT	20 HORNBY DR		6 YOULGRAVE AV	13 LEWIS AV	20 CHANCTONBURY CL	

77

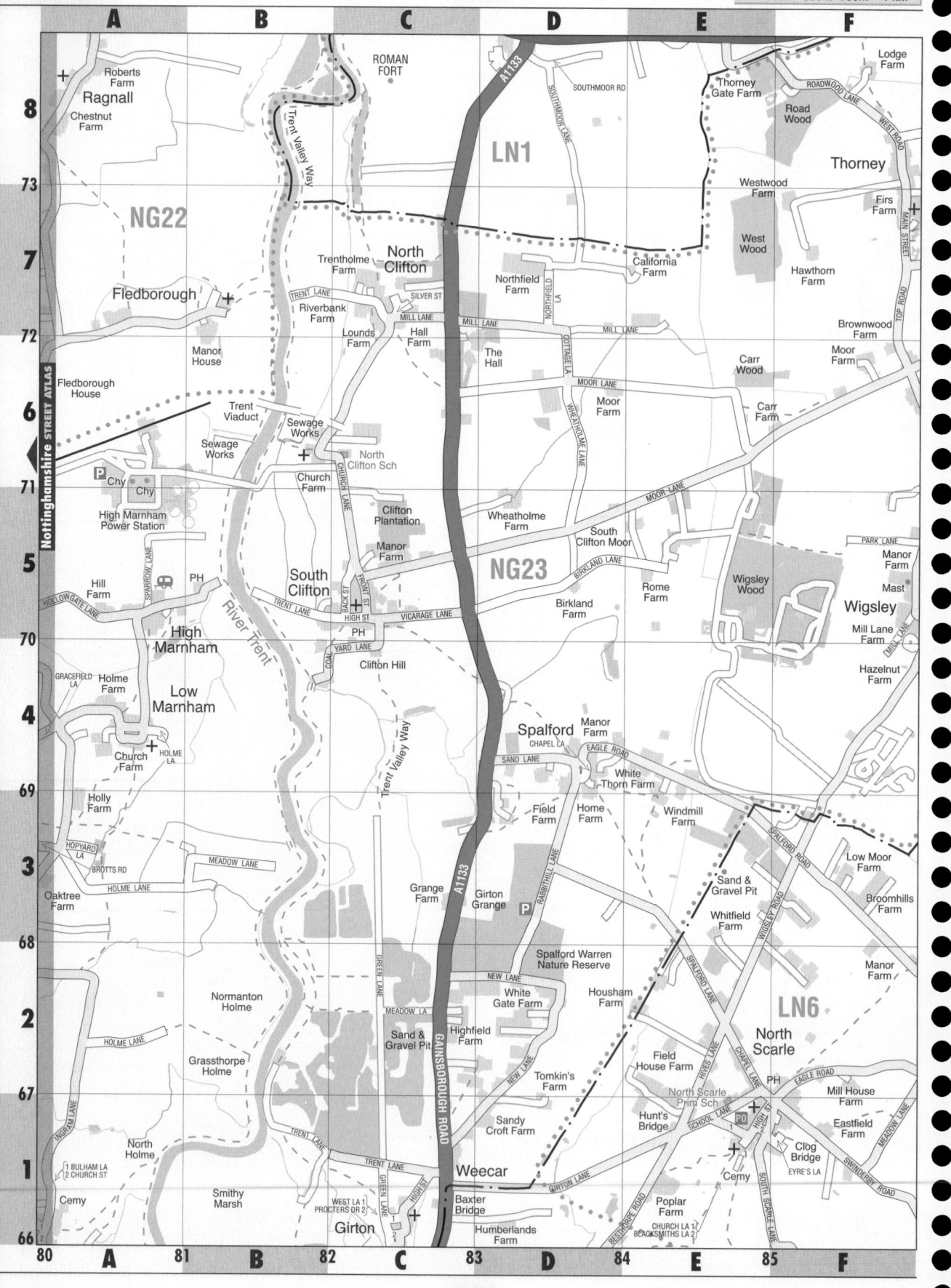

0   ¼   ½   mile
0   250m 500m 750m 1 km

A   B   C   D   E   F

8

ROMAN
FORT

Roberts
Farm

Ragnall

Chestnut
Farm

Lodge
Farm

Thorney
Gate Farm

ROADWOOD LANE

Road
Wood

WEST ROAD

SOUTHMOOR RD

A1133

LN1

73

NG22

Trent Valley Way

Thorney

Westwood
Farm

West
Wood

Firs
Farm

MAIN STREET

LOW ROAD

7

Fledborough

Trentholme
Farm

North
Clifton

Northfield
Farm

NORTHFIELD LA

California
Farm

Hawthorn
Farm

TRENT LANE

SILVER ST

MILL LANE

MILL LANE

Brownwood
Farm

72

Riverbank
Farm

Lounds
Farm

Hall
Farm

MILL LANE

COTTAGE LA

The
Hall

MOOR LANE

Carr
Wood

Moor
Farm

Manor
House

Moor
Farm

Carr
Farm

Fledborough
House

Trent Viaduct

Sewage
Works

WHEATHOLME LANE

6

Trent Viaduct

Sewage
Works

North
Clifton Sch

P

Chy

Chy

High Marnham
Power Station

Church
Farm

CHURCH LANE

Wheatholme
Farm

MOOR LANE

71

Clifton
Plantation

South
Clifton Moor

Park Lane

Manor
Farm

Mast

Manor
Farm

5

Hill
Farm

SPARROW LANE

PH

South
Clifton

Manor
Farm

FRONT ST

BIRKLAND LANE

Rome
Farm

Wigsley
Wood

Wigsley

HOLLOW GATE LANE

River Trent

TRENT LANE

HIGH ST

VICARAGE LANE

Birkland
Farm

Mill Lane
Farm

MILL LANE

70

High
Marnham

BACK ST

PH

YARD LANE

Hazelnut
Farm

GRACEFIELD LA

Holme
Farm

Low
Marnham

COAL LA

Clifton Hill

NG23

4

Holly
Farm

Church
Farm

HOLME LA

Spalford

CHAPEL LA

Manor
Farm

EAGLE ROAD

White
Thorn Farm

69

HOPYARD LA

BROTTS RD

MEADOW LANE

HOLME LANE

Trent Valley Way

Field
Farm

Home
Farm

Windmill
Farm

SPALFORD ROAD

Low Moor
Farm

Oaktree
Farm

Sand &
Gravel Pit

Whitfield
Farm

Broomhills
Farm

3

HOLME LANE

Normanton
Holme

GREEN LANE

Grange
Farm

A1133

Girton
Grange

P

RABBITHILL LANE

Spalford Warren
Nature Reserve

Housham
Farm

SPALFORD LANE

WISSEY ROAD

Manor
Farm

68

MEADOW LA

New Lane

White
Gate Farm

CHAPEL LANE

LN6

2

Grassthorpe
Holme

Sand &
Gravel Pit

GAINSBOROUGH ROAD

Highfield
Farm

NEW LANE

Field
House Farm

North
Scarle

PH

EAGLE ROAD

Mill House
Farm

67

JINGRAM LANE

North
Holme

TRENT LANE

Tomkin's
Farm

Sandy
Croft Farm

North Scarle
Prim Sch

Hunt's
Bridge

SCHOOL LANE

PO

HIGH ST

Eastfield
Farm

MEADOW LANE

Clog
Bridge

SWINDERBY ROAD

1

1 BULHAM LA
2 CHURCH ST

Cemy

Smithy
Marsh

TRENT LANE

GREEN LANE

HIGH ST

WEST LA 1
PROCTERS DR 2

Baxter
Bridge

Weecar

Humberlands
Farm

GIRTON LANE

BESTHORPE ROAD

Poplar
Farm

Cemy

EYRE'S LA

SOUTH SCARLE LANE

CHURCH LA 1
BLACKSMITHS LA 2

66

Girton

A   81   B   82   C   83   D   84   E   85   F

Nottinghamshire STREET ATLAS

Scale: 1¾ inches to 1 mile

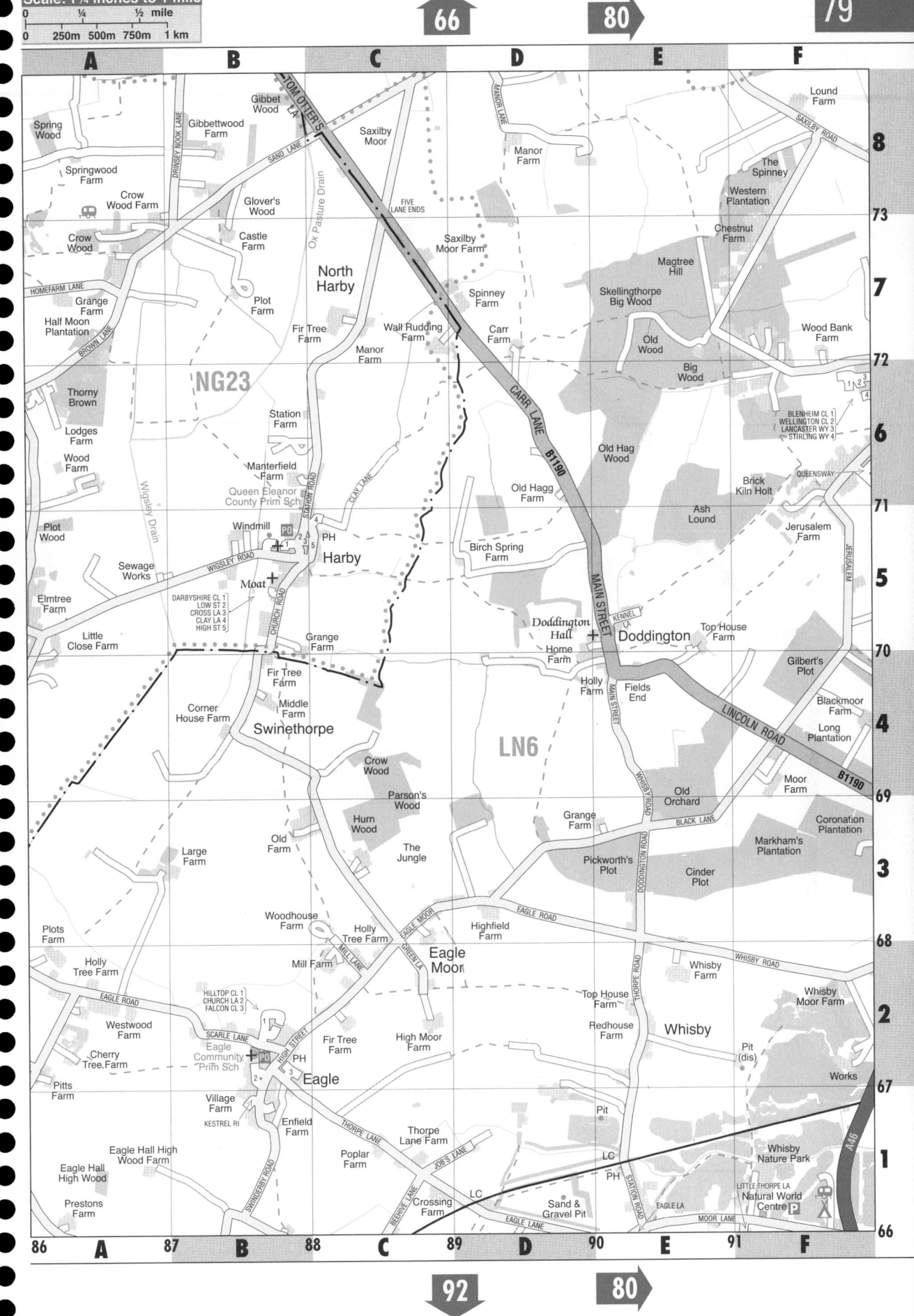

0 ¼ ½ mile
0 250m 500m 750m 1 km
66
80
A B C D E F
Spring Wood
Gibbettwood Farm
Gibbet Wood
TOM OTTER'S LA
Saxilby Moor
MANOR LANE
Manor Farm
Lound Farm
SAXILBY ROAD
The Spinney
Western Plantation
Springwood Farm
Crow Wood Farm
Glover's Wood
SAND LANE
DRINSEY NOOK LANE
FIVE LANE ENDS
Crow Wood
Castle Farm
Ox Pasture Drain
Saxilby Moor Farm
Chestnut Farm
Magtree Hill
North Harby
Skellingthorpe Big Wood
HOMEFARM LANE
Grange Farm
Half Moon Plantation
Plot Farm
Spinney Farm
Fir Tree Farm
Wall Rudding Farm
Carr Farm
Old Wood
Wood Bank Farm
BROWN LANE
Manor Farm
Big Wood
NG23
CARR LANE
Thorny Brown
BLENHEIM CL 1
WELLINGTON CL 2
LANCASTER WY 3
STIRLING WY 4
Station Farm
Lodges Farm
B1190
Old Hag Wood
Wood Farm
Manterfield Farm
QUEENSWAY
Brick Kiln Holt
Queen Eleanor County Prim Sch
Wigsley Drain
STATION ROAD
CLAY LANE
Old Hagg Farm
Ash Lound
Plot Wood
Windmill
PO
PH
Jerusalem Farm
Harby
Birch Spring Farm
Sewage Works
WIGSLEY ROAD
Moat
JERUSALEM
Elmtree Farm
DARBYSHIRE CL 1
LOW ST 2
CROSS LA 3
CLAY LA 4
HIGH ST 5
CHURCH ROAD
MAIN STREET
Doddington Hall
KENNEL LA
Doddington
Top House Farm
Little Close Farm
Grange Farm
Home Farm
Gilbert's Plot
Fir Tree Farm
Holly Farm
Fields End
Middle Farm
Blackmoor Farm
Corner House Farm
Swinethorpe
LINCOLN ROAD
Long Plantation
LN6
MAIN STREET
Crow Wood
Moor Farm
B1190
Parson's Wood
Old Orchard
WHISBY ROAD
Hurn Wood
Grange Farm
BLACK LANE
Coronation Plantation
Old Farm
The Jungle
Markham's Plantation
Large Farm
Pickworth's Plot
DODDINGTON ROAD
Cinder Plot
Woodhouse Farm
EAGLE ROAD
Plots Farm
Holly Tree Farm
EAGLE MOOR
Highfield Farm
Mill Farm
MILL LANE
GREEN LA
Eagle Moor
THORPE ROAD
Whisby Farm
WHISBY ROAD
Holly Tree Farm
EAGLE ROAD
HILLTOP CL 1
CHURCH LA 2
FALCON CL 3
Top House Farm
Whisby Moor Farm
Westwood Farm
SCARLE LANE
HIGH STREET
Fir Tree Farm
High Moor Farm
Redhouse Farm
Whisby
Cherry Tree Farm
Eagle Community Prim Sch
PO
PH
Pit (dis)
Eagle
Works
Pitts Farm
Village Farm
KESTREL RI
Enfield Farm
Pit
Thorpe Lane Farm
THORPE LANE
Eagle Hall High Wood Farm
Poplar Farm
JOB'S LANE
LC
Whisby Nature Park
Eagle Hall High Wood
SWINDERBY ROAD
PH
STATION ROAD
LITTLE THORPE LA
A46
Prestons Farm
BEEHIVE LANE
Crossing Farm
LC
Sand & Gravel Pit
EAGLE LA
Natural World Centre
P
EAGLE LANE
MOOR LANE
8 73 7 72 6 71 5 70 4 69 3 68 2 67 1 66
86 A 87 B 88 C 89 D 90 E 91 F
92
80

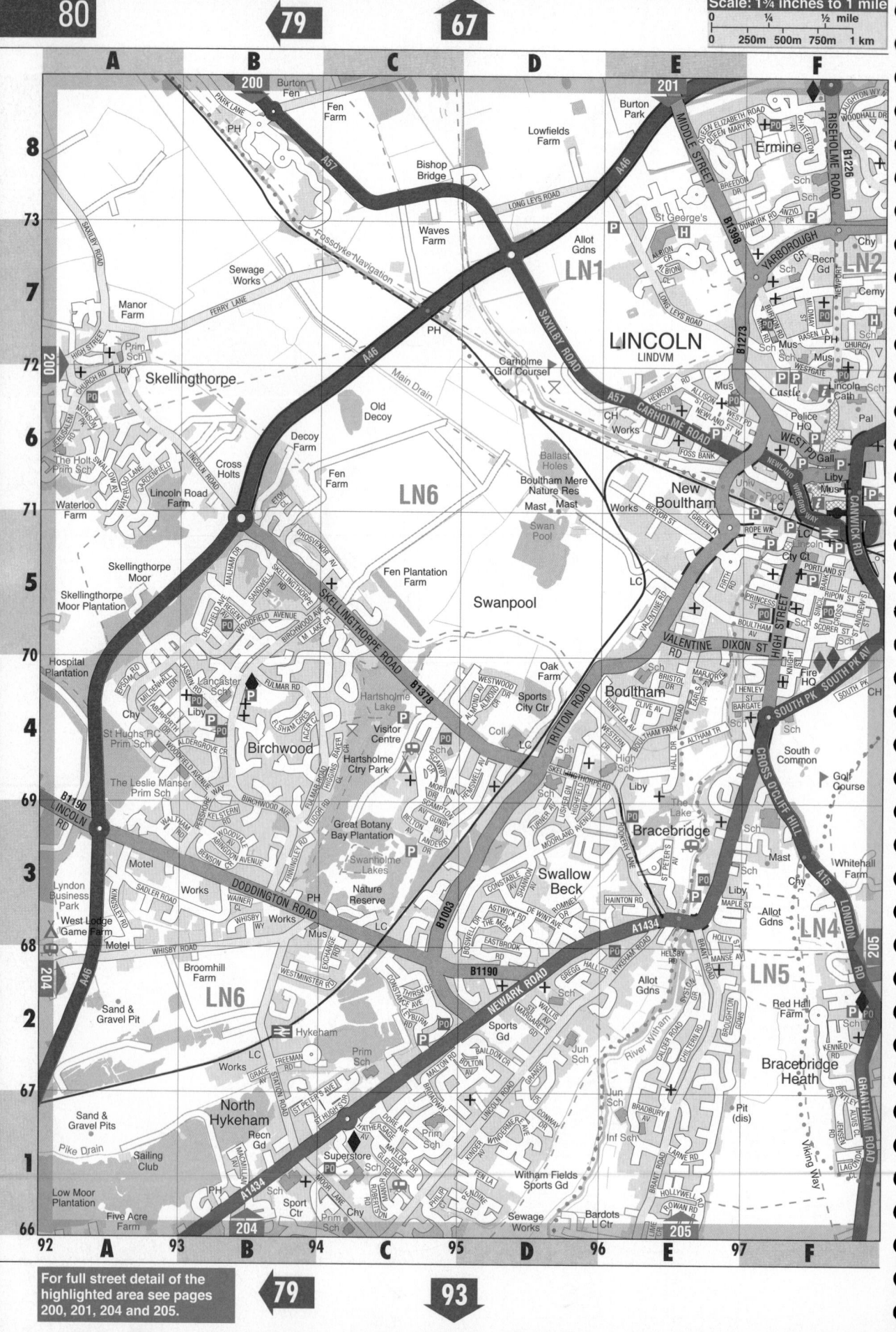

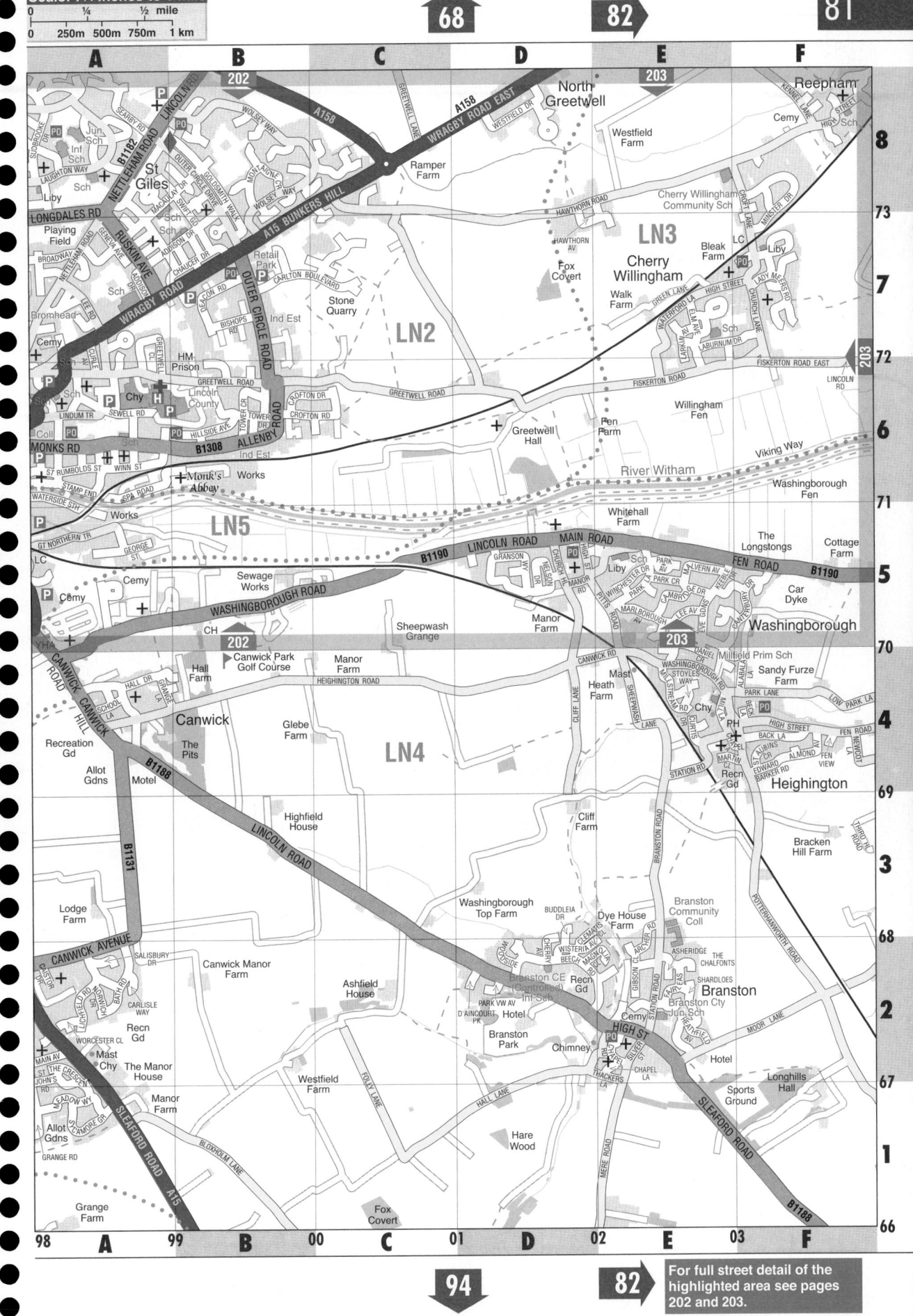

For full street detail of the highlighted area see pages 202 and 203.

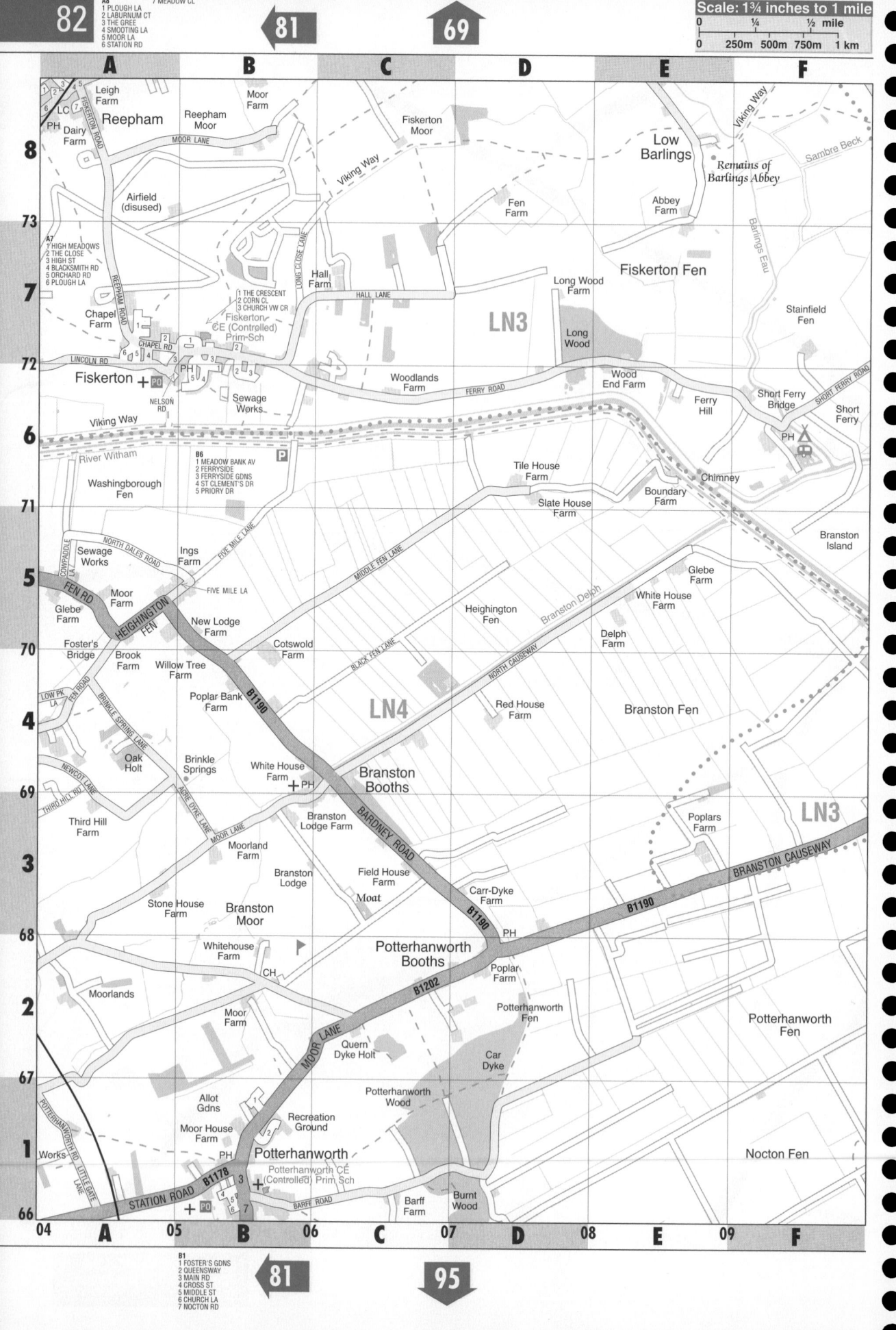

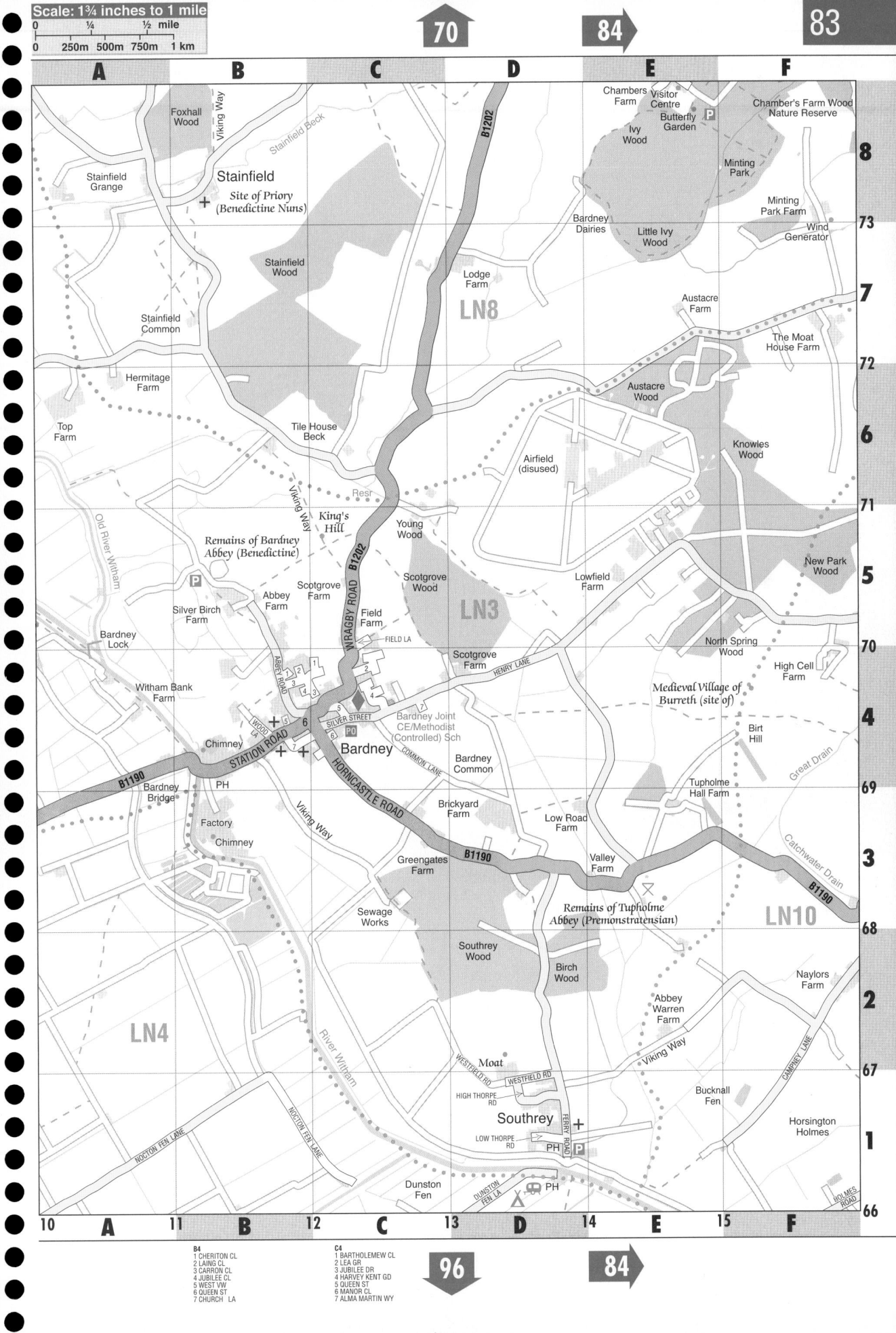

Scale: 1¾ inches to 1 mile

0   ¼   ½   mile
0   250m   500m   750m   1 km

A **B** **C** **D** **E** **F**

Foxhall Wood
Viking Way
Stainfield Beck
Stainfield Grange
Stainfield
Site of Priory (Benedictine Nuns)
Stainfield Wood
B1202
Chambers Farm
Visitor Centre
Butterfly Garden
P
Chamber's Farm Wood Nature Reserve
Ivy Wood
Minting Park
Bardney Dairies
Little Ivy Wood
Minting Park Farm
Wind Generator

8

73

Lodge Farm
LN8
Austacre Farm
The Moat House Farm

7

Stainfield Common
Hermitage Farm
Tile House Beck
Austacre Wood
Knowles Wood

72

Top Farm
Airfield (disused)

6

Old River Witham
Viking Way
Resr
King's Hill
Young Wood
Lowfield Farm
New Park Wood

71

Remains of Bardney Abbey (Benedictine)
P
Scotgrove Farm
Scotgrove Wood
B1202
WRAGBY ROAD
LN3

5

Silver Birch Farm
Abbey Farm
Field Farm
FIELD LA
North Spring Wood
High Cell Farm

70

Bardney Lock
ABBEY ROAD
Scotgrove Farm
Henry Lane
Medieval Village of Burreth (site of)

4

Witham Bank Farm
WOOD LA
1 2 3 4
5 6
SILVER STREET
PO
Bardney
Bardney Joint CE/Methodist (Controlled) Sch
Birt Hill
Great Drain

Chimney
STATION ROAD
7
COMMON LANE
Bardney Common
Tupholme Hall Farm

69

B1190
Bardney Bridge
PH
HORNCASTLE ROAD
Brickyard Farm
Low Road Farm
Valley Farm
Catchwater Drain
B1190

3

Factory
Chimney
Viking Way
Greengates Farm
B1190
Remains of Tupholme Abbey (Premonstratensian)
LN10

68

Sewage Works
Southrey Wood
Birch Wood
Naylors Farm

2

LN4
River Witham
Abbey Warren Farm
Viking Way
Bucknall Fen
CABBURY LANE

Moat
WESTFIELD RD
HIGH THORPE RD
WESTFIELD RD
FERRY ROAD
Horsington Holmes

67

NOCTON FEN LANE
NOCTON FEN LANE
Southrey
LOW THORPE RD
PH
P

1

Dunston Fen
DUNSTON FEN LA
PH
HOLMES ROAD

66

A 10 **A** 11 **B** 12 **C** 13 **D** 14 **E** 15 **F**

B4
1 CHERITON CL
2 LAING CL
3 CARRON CL
4 JUBILEE CL
5 WEST VW
6 QUEEN ST
7 CHURCH LA

C4
1 BARTHOLEMEW CL
2 LEA GR
3 JUBILEE DR
4 HARVEY KENT GD
5 QUEEN ST
6 MANOR CL
7 ALMA MARTIN WY

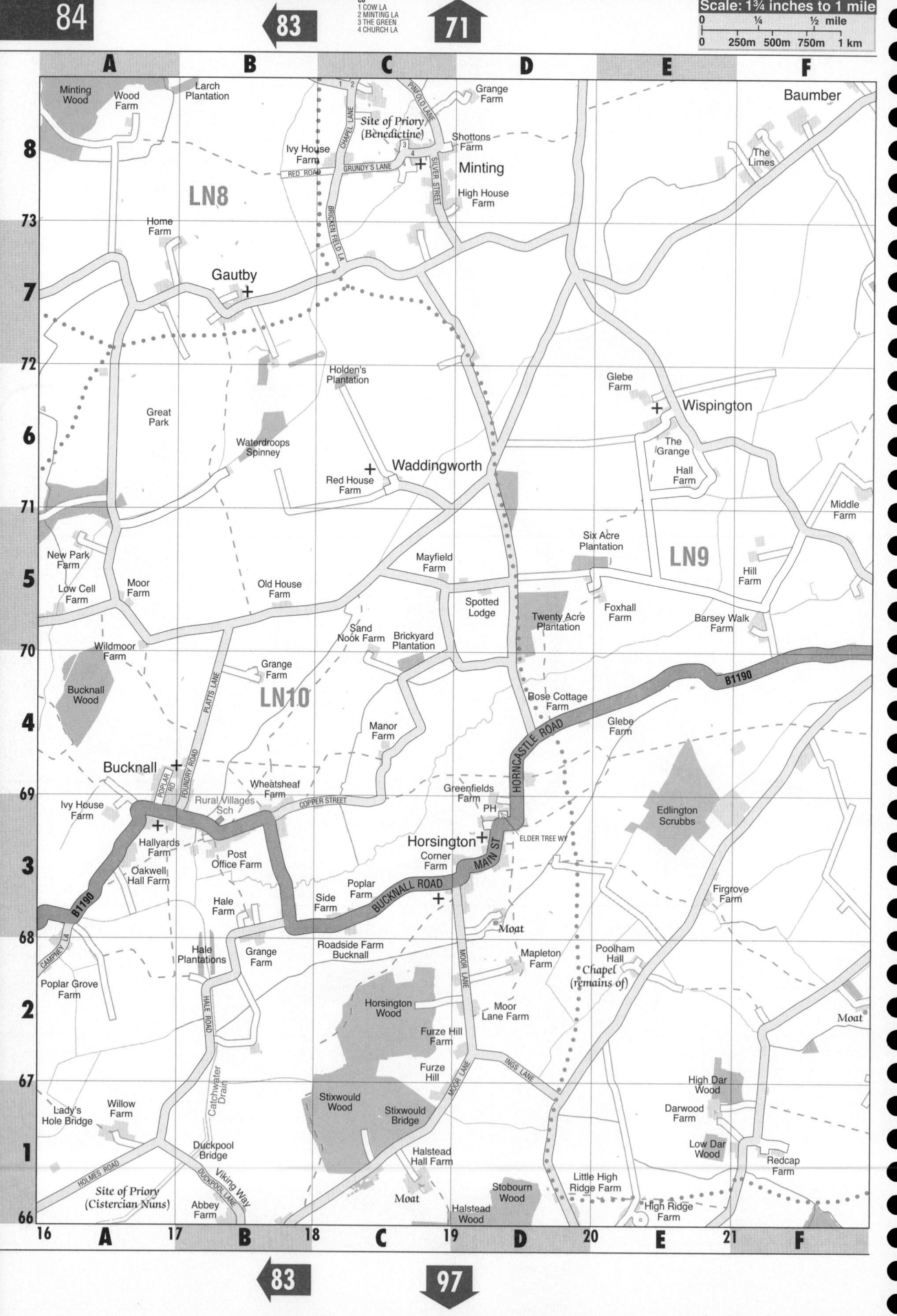

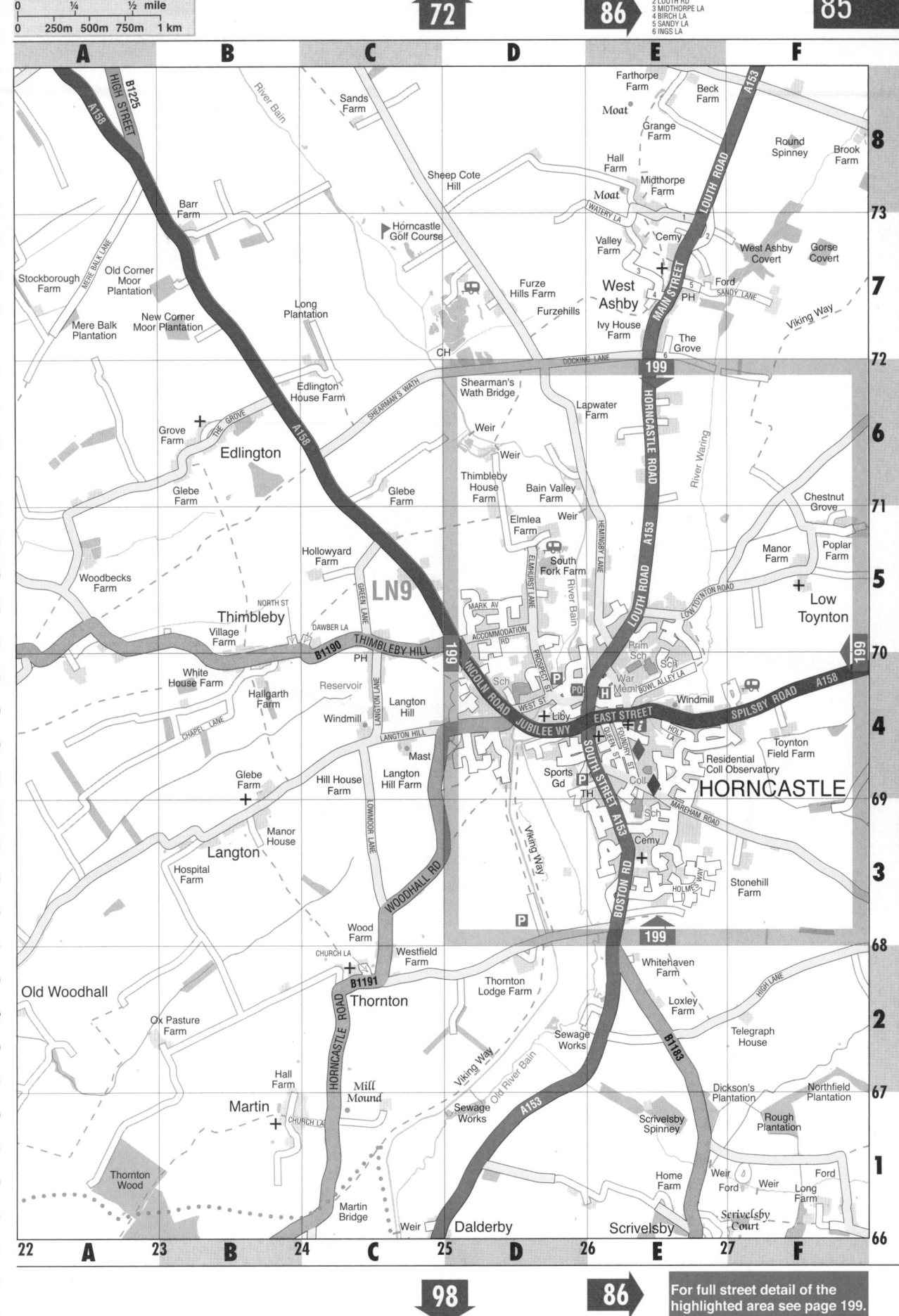

E7
1 WATERY LA
2 LOUTH RD
3 MIDTHORPE LA
4 BIRCH LA
5 SANDY LA
6 INGS LA

A   B   C   D   E   F

8
73
7
72
6
71
5
70
4
69
3
68
2
67
1
66

B1225
A158
HIGH STREET
Sands Farm
Sheep Cote Hill
Horncastle Golf Course
Farthorpe Farm
Beck Farm
Moat
Grange Farm
A153
Round Spinney
Brook Farm
Hall Farm
Midthorpe Farm
Barr Farm
River Bain
WATERY LA
LOUTH ROAD
Moat
Valley Farm
Cemy
West Ashby Covert
Gorse Covert
Stockborough Farm
Old Corner Moor Plantation
MERE BALK LANE
Long Plantation
West Ashby
Furze Hills Farm
Furzehills
MAIN STREET
PH
Ford
SANDY LANE
Mere Balk Plantation
New Corner Moor Plantation
Ivy House Farm
The Grove
Viking Way
CH
DOCKING LANE
199
Shearman's Wath Bridge
Lapwater Farm
THE GROVE
Edlington House Farm
SHEARMAN'S WATH
Weir
HORNCASTLE ROAD
River Waring
Grove Farm
Edlington
A158
Weir
Chestnut Grove
Glebe Farm
Glebe Farm
Thimbleby House Farm
Bain Valley Farm
A153
Manor Farm
Poplar Farm
Woodbecks Farm
Hollowyard Farm
LN9
Elmlea Farm
Weir
HEMINGBY LANE
South Fork Farm
Low Toynton
NORTH ST
GREEN LANE
LOUTH ROAD
LONG TOYNTON ROAD
Thimbleby
Village Farm
DAWBER LA
ELMHURST LANE
MARK AV
River Bain
Prim Sch
White House Farm
B1190
THIMBLEBY HILL
PH
ACCOMMODATION RD
PROSPECT ST
Sch
199
LINCOLN ROAD
A158
199
Hallgarth Farm
Reservoir
LANGTON LANE
Langton Hill
War Mem
BOWL ALLEY LA
Windmill
SPILSBY ROAD
CHAPEL LANE
Windmill
LANGTON HILL
Mast
WEST ST
JUBILEE WY
EAST STREET
HOLT LA
Toynton Field Farm
Glebe Farm
Hill House Farm
Langton Hill Farm
Sports Gd
SOUTH STREET
QUEEN ST
FOUNDRY ST
Residential Coll Observatory
HORNCASTLE
Langton
Manor House
LOWMOOR LANE
P
TH
Coll
MAREHAM ROAD
Sch
Hospital Farm
WOODHALL RD
Cemy
Viking Way
BOSTON RD
HOLMES WAY
Stonehill Farm
199
Wood Farm
Westfield Farm
Whitehaven Farm
HIGH LANE
CHURCH LA
B1191
Thornton Lodge Farm
Loxley Farm
Old Woodhall
HORNCASTLE ROAD
Thornton
Sewage Works
B1183
Telegraph House
Ox Pasture Farm
Viking Way
Old River Bain
Dickson's Plantation
Northfield Plantation
Hall Farm
Mill Mound
Sewage Works
A153
Scrivelsby Spinney
Rough Plantation
Martin
CHURCH LA
Home Farm
Weir
Ford
Weir
Ford
Long Farm
Thornton Wood
Martin Bridge
Weir
Dalderby
Scrivelsby
Scrivelsby Court

22   A   23   B   24   C   25   D   26   E   27   F   66

98
86
For full street detail of the highlighted area see page 199.

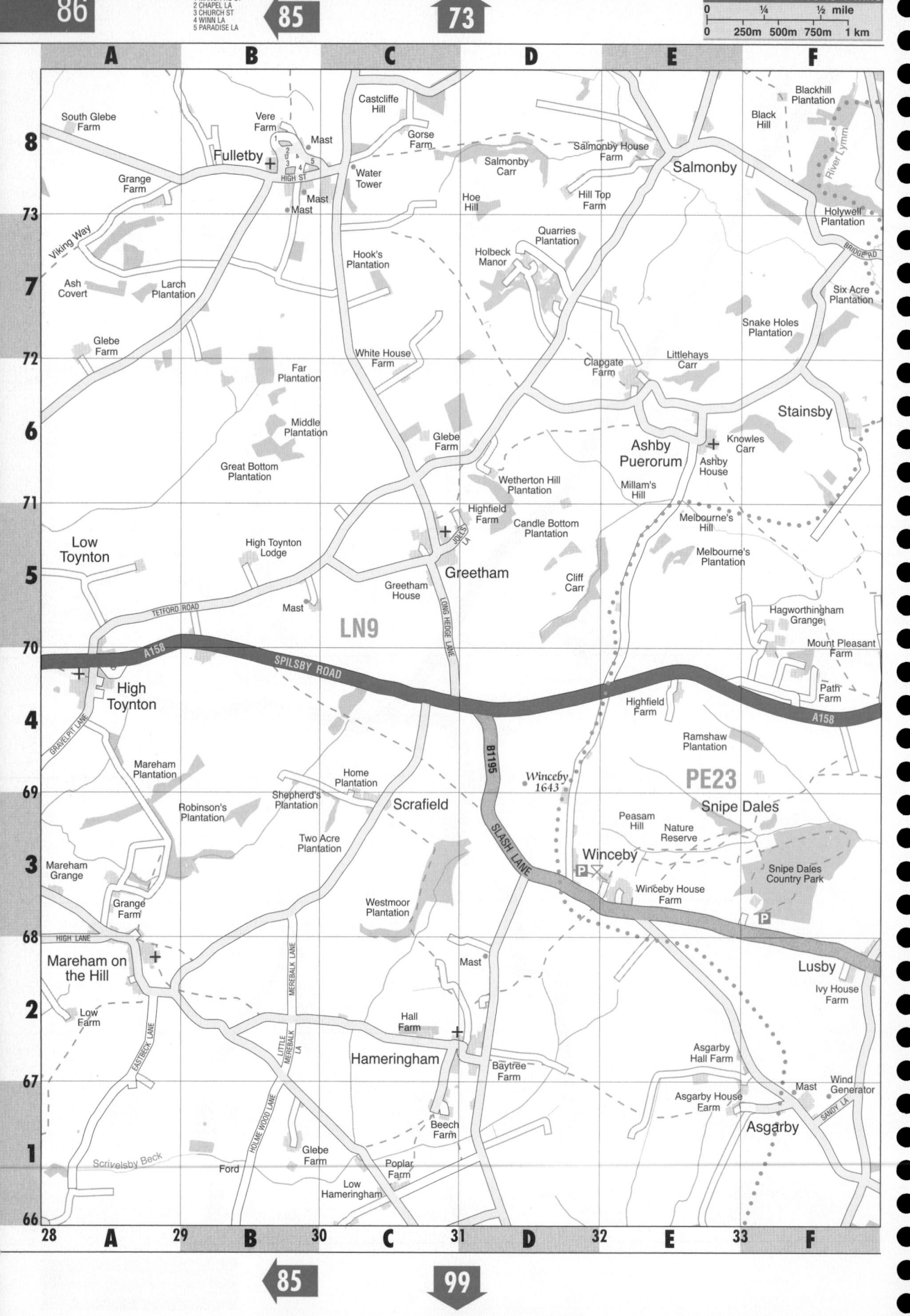

B8
1 MANOR HO ST
2 CHAPEL LA
3 CHURCH ST
4 WINN LA
5 PARADISE LA

85   73

Scale: 1¾ inches to 1 mile

| | A | B | C | D | E | F |

8
73
7
72
6
71
5
70
4
69
3
68
2
67
1
66

South Glebe Farm
Grange Farm
Viking Way
Ash Covert
Larch Plantation
Glebe Farm
Low Toynton
High Toynton Lodge
Mareham Plantation
Robinson's Plantation
Mareham Grange
Grange Farm
Mareham on the Hill
Low Farm

Vere Farm
Fulletby
HIGH ST
Mast
Mast
Mast
Far Plantation
Middle Plantation
Great Bottom Plantation
High Toynton Lodge
Mast
Shepherd's Plantation
Two Acre Plantation
Westmoor Plantation

Castcliffe Hill
Gorse Farm
Water Tower
Hoe Hill
Hook's Plantation
White House Farm
Glebe Farm
Greetham House
Greetham
Home Plantation
Scrafield
Mast
Hameringham
Baytree Farm
Beech Farm
Glebe Farm
Poplar Farm
Low Hameringham
Ford
Scrivelsby Beck

Salmonby House Farm
Salmonby Carr
Hill Top Farm
Quarries Plantation
Holbeck Manor
Wetherton Hill Plantation
Highfield Farm
Candle Bottom Plantation
Cliff Carr
Winceby 1643

Salmonby
Snake Holes Plantation
Clapgate Farm
Ashby Puerorum
Millam's Hill
Ashby House
Melbourne's Hill
Melbourne's Plantation
Highfield Farm
Ramshaw Plantation
Peasam Hill
Nature Reserve
Winceby
Winceby House Farm
Asgarby Hall Farm
Asgarby House Farm
Asgarby

Blackhill Plantation
Black Hill
Holywell Plantation
Six Acre Plantation
Littlehays Carr
Stainsby
Knowles Carr
Hagworthingham Grange
Mount Pleasant Farm
Path Farm
Snipe Dales
Snipe Dales Country Park
Lusby
Ivy House Farm
Mast
Wind Generator

LN9
Tetford Road
A158
Spilsby Road
Long Hedge Lane
High Toynton
Gravel Pit Lane
Mereball Lane
Little Mereball La
Holme Wood Lane
Eastbeck Lane
High Lane
Slash Lane
B1195
PE23
A158
River Lymm
Bridge Rd
Sandy La

28 A 29 B 30 C 31 D 32 E 33 F

85   99

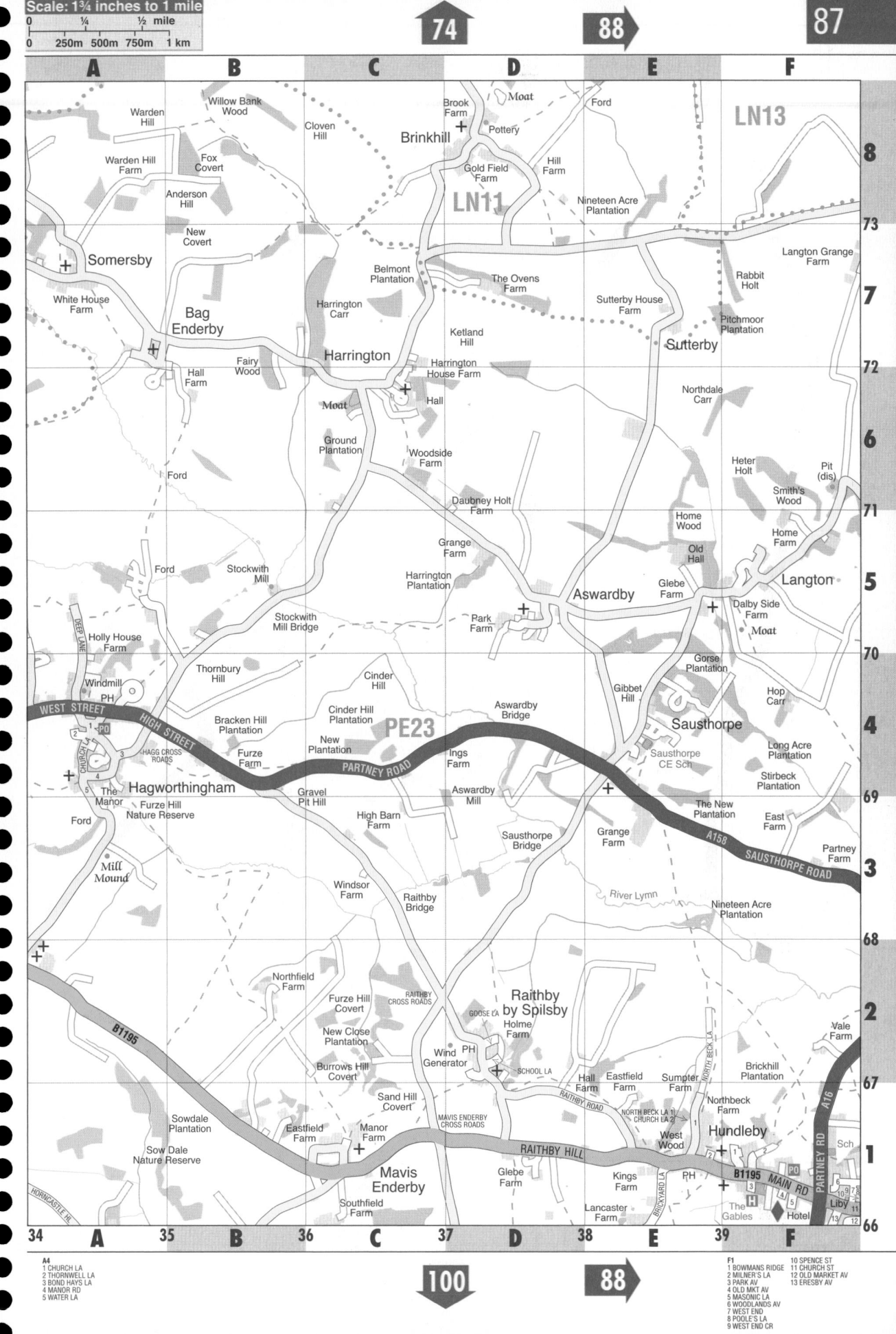

A   B   C   D   E   F

LN13

8

Warden
Hill

Willow Bank
Wood

Cloven
Hill

Brook
Farm

Moat

Ford

Warden Hill
Farm

Fox
Covert

Brinkhill

Pottery

Hill
Farm

Anderson
Hill

Gold Field
Farm

LN11

Nineteen Acre
Plantation

73

New
Covert

Langton Grange
Farm

7

Somersby

Belmont
Plantation

The Ovens
Farm

Sutterby House
Farm

Rabbit
Holt

White House
Farm

Bag
Enderby

Harrington
Carr

Pitchmoor
Plantation

Sutterby

72

Fairy
Wood

Harrington

Harrington
House Farm

Northdale
Carr

Hall
Farm

Moat

Hall

6

Ketland
Hill

Ground
Plantation

Woodside
Farm

Heter
Holt

Pit
(dis)

Ford

Daubney Holt
Farm

Smith's
Wood

Home
Wood

Home
Farm

71

Grange
Farm

Old
Hall

Langton

Ford

Stockwith
Mill

Harrington
Plantation

Park
Farm

Aswardby

Glebe
Farm

Dalby Side
Farm

5

Stockwith
Mill Bridge

Moat

Holly House
Farm

Thornbury
Hill

Cinder
Hill

Gorse
Plantation

70

Windmill
PH

Cinder Hill
Plantation

Aswardby
Bridge

Gibbet
Hill

Hop
Carr

4

WEST STREET

HIGH STREET

Bracken Hill
Plantation

PE23

Sausthorpe

Long Acre
Plantation

1

2

PO

New
Plantation

Furze
Farm

PARTNEY ROAD

Ings
Farm

Sausthorpe
CE Sch

Stirbeck
Plantation

HAGG CROSS
ROADS

3

Gravel
Pit Hill

Aswardby
Mill

The New
Plantation

East
Farm

69

5

The
Manor

Hagworthingham

Furze Hill
Nature Reserve

High Barn
Farm

Sausthorpe
Bridge

Grange
Farm

A158   SAUSTHORPE ROAD

Partney
Farm

Ford

Windsor
Farm

Raithby
Bridge

River Lymn

Nineteen Acre
Plantation

3

Mill
Mound

68

Northfield
Farm

RAITHBY
CROSS ROADS

Raithby
by Spilsby

Vale
Farm

2

B1195

Furze Hill
Covert

GOOSE LA

Holme
Farm

NORTH BECK LA

Brickhill
Plantation

New Close
Plantation

Wind
Generator

PH

SCHOOL LA

Hall
Farm

Eastfield
Farm

Sumpter
Farm

Northbeck
Farm

67

Burrows Hill
Covert

RAITHBY ROAD

NORTH BECK LA 1
CHURCH LA 2

West
Wood

Hundleby

A16

Sowdale
Plantation

Sand Hill
Covert

MAVIS ENDERBY
CROSS ROADS

Eastfield
Farm

Manor
Farm

Glebe
Farm

Kings
Farm

PH

B1195

PO

PARTNEY RD

Sch

Liby

1

HORNCASTLE HL

Sow Dale
Nature Reserve

Mavis
Enderby

RAITHBY HILL

MAIN RD

H

The
Gables

Hotel

Southfield
Farm

Lancaster
Farm

66

34   A   35   B   36   C   37   D   38   E   39   F

A4
1 CHURCH LA
2 THORNWELL LA
3 BOND HAYS LA
4 MANOR RD
5 WATER LA

F1
1 BOWMANS RIDGE
2 MILNER'S LA
3 PARK AV
4 OLD MKT AV
5 MASONIC LA
6 WOODLANDS AV
7 WEST END
8 POOLE'S LA
9 WEST END CR
10 SPENCE ST
11 CHURCH ST
12 OLD MARKET AV
13 ERESBY AV

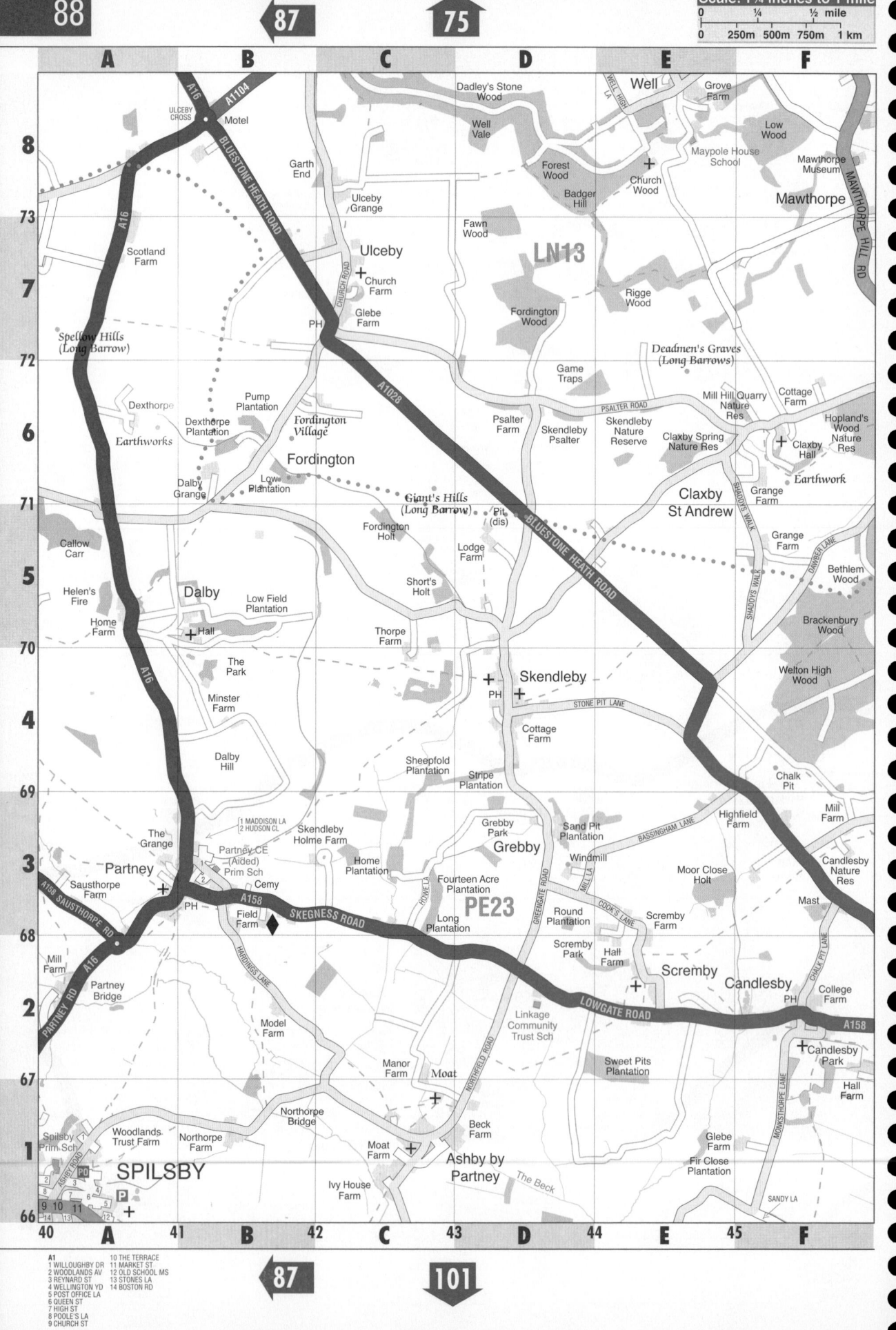

A   B   C   D   E   F

8

73

7

72

6

71

5

70

4

69

3

68

2

67

1

66

A1104

ULCEBY CROSS

Motel

BLUESTONE HEATH ROAD

A16

Garth End

Scotland Farm

Spellow Hills
(Long Barrow)

Dexthorpe

Earthworks

Dexthorpe Plantation

Pump Plantation

Fordington Village

Dalby Grange

Low Plantation

Fordington

CHURCH ROAD

Ulceby Grange

Ulceby

Church Farm

Glebe Farm

PH

A1028

Dadley's Stone Wood

Well Vale

Forest Wood

Badger Hill

Fawn Wood

LN13

Fordington Wood

Psalter Farm

Skendleby Psalter

PSALTER ROAD

Skendleby Nature Reserve

Game Traps

Well

Grove Farm

Low Wood

Maypole House School

Church Wood

Mawthorpe Museum

Mawthorpe

MAWTHORPE HILL RD

Rigge Wood

Deadmen's Graves
(Long Barrows)

Mill Hill Quarry Nature Res

Cottage Farm

Claxby Spring Nature Res

Hopland's Wood Nature Res

Claxby Hall

Earthwork

Callow Carr

Helen's Fire

Home Farm

Dalby

Hall

Low Field Plantation

Giant's Hills
(Long Barrow)

Fordington Holt

Short's Holt

Thorpe Farm

Pit (dis)

Lodge Farm

BLUESTONE HEATH ROAD

Claxby St Andrew

SHADDY'S WALK

DAWBER LANE

Grange Farm

Grange Farm

Bethlem Wood

Brackenbury Wood

A16

The Park

Minster Farm

Dalby Hill

Sheepfold Plantation

Stripe Plantation

Skendleby

PH

Cottage Farm

STONE PIT LANE

Welton High Wood

Chalk Pit

Mill Farm

The Grange

Partney

Sausthorpe Farm

PH

1 MADDISON LA
2 HUDSON CL

Partney CE (Aided) Prim Sch

Skendleby Holme Farm

Cemy

Field Farm

Home Plantation

Grebby Park

Grebby

Windmill

ROWE LA

PE23

Fourteen Acre Plantation

Long Plantation

Sand Pit Plantation

GREENGATE ROAD

MILL LA

BASSINGHAM LANE

Round Plantation

COOK'S LANE

Highfield Farm

Moor Close Holt

Scremby Farm

Candlesby Nature Res

Mast

A158

A158 SAUSTHORPE RD

SKEGNESS ROAD

Scremby Park

Hall Farm

Scremby

Candlesby

PH

College Farm

CHALK PIT LANE

PARTNEY RD

A16

Mill Farm

Partney Bridge

HARDINGS LANE

Model Farm

Manor Farm

Moat

NORTHFIELD ROAD

Linkage Community Trust Sch

LOWGATE ROAD

Sweet Pits Plantation

Candlesby Park

MONKSTHORPE LANE

Hall Farm

Spilsby Prim Sch

ASHBY ROAD

PO

SPILSBY

P

Woodlands Trust Farm

Northorpe Farm

Northorpe Bridge

Ivy House Farm

Moat Farm

Ashby by Partney

Beck Farm

The Beck

Glebe Farm

Fir Close Plantation

SANDY LA

40   A   41   B   42   C   43   D   44   E   45   F

A1
1 WILLOUGHBY DR
2 WOODLANDS AV
3 REYNARD ST
4 WELLINGTON YD
5 POST OFFICE LA
6 QUEEN ST
7 HIGH ST
8 POOLE'S LA
9 CHURCH ST
10 THE TERRACE
11 MARKET ST.
12 OLD SCHOOL MS
13 STONES LA
14 BOSTON RD

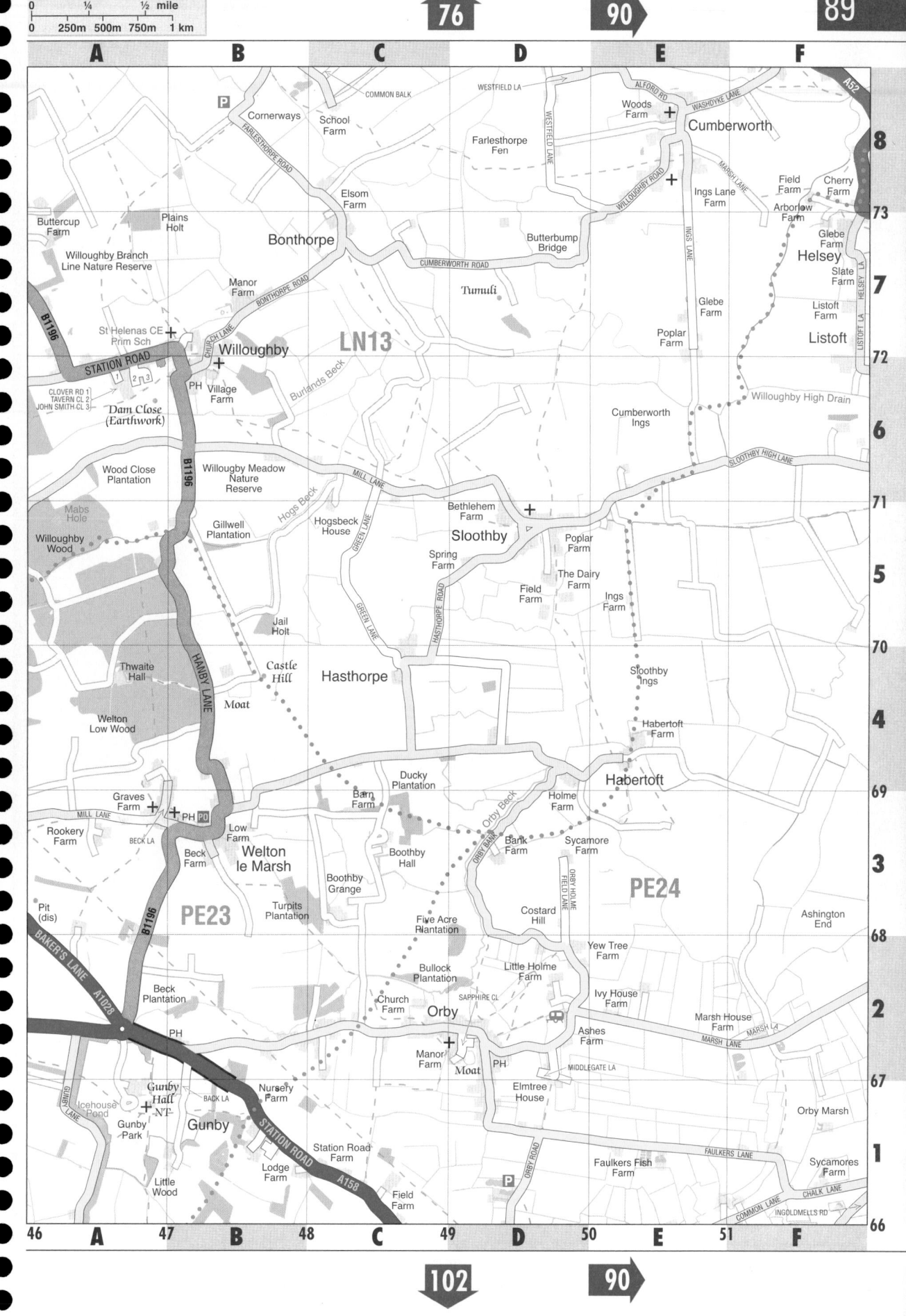

A52

8

WESTFIELD LA

Woods Farm

Cumberworth

ALFORD RD   WASHDYKE LANE

Common Balk

Cornerways   School Farm

Farlesthorpe Fen

Field Farm   Cherry Farm

73

Buttercup Farm   Plains Holt

Elsom Farm

Bonthorpe

Butterbump Bridge

Ings Lane Farm

Arborlow Farm   Glebe Farm

Helsey

Willoughby Branch Line Nature Reserve

Manor Farm

BONTHORPE ROAD

CUMBERWORTH ROAD

Slate Farm

7

St Helenas CE Prim Sch

Willoughby

Tumuli

LN13

Glebe Farm

Listoft Farm

Listoft

72

STATION ROAD   CHURCH LANE

PH   Village Farm

Burlands Beck

Poplar Farm

Willoughby High Drain

CLOVER RD 1   TAVERN CL 2   JOHN SMITH CL 3   Dam Close (Earthwork)

Cumberworth Ings

6

Wood Close Plantation

Willougby Meadow Nature Reserve

MILL LANE

SLOOTHBY HIGH LANE

Mabs Hole

Gillwell Plantation

Hogs Beck   Hogsbeck House

GREEN LANE

Bethlehem Farm

Sloothby

Poplar Farm

71

Willoughby Wood

Spring Farm

The Dairy Farm

Jail Holt

Field Farm

Ings Farm

5

HASTHORPE ROAD

Thwaite Hall

Castle Hill   Moat

Hasthorpe

Sloothby Ings

70

Welton Low Wood

HANBY LANE

Habertoft Farm

4

Ducky Plantation

Habertoft

Graves Farm   Barn Farm

Orby Beck

Holme Farm

69

MILL LANE   PH   PO

Rookery Farm   BECK LA

Beck Farm

Low Farm

Welton le Marsh

Boothby Hall

ORBY BANK

Bank Farm

Sycamore Farm

ORBY HOLME FIELD LANE

PE24

3

Pit (dis)

PE23

Boothby Grange

Turpits Plantation

Five Acre Plantation

Costard Hill

Ashington End

68

B1196

Beck Plantation

Bullock Plantation

Church Farm

Orby

Little Holme Farm

SAPPHIRE CL

Yew Tree Farm

Ivy House Farm

Marsh House Farm

MARSH LANE

2

BAKER'S LANE   A1028

PH

Manor Farm   Moat   PH

Ashes Farm

MIDDLEGATE LA

67

GUNBY LANE   Icehouse Pond

Gunby Hall NT   BACK LA

Nursery Farm

Elmtree House

1

Gunby Park

Gunby

STATION ROAD

Station Road Farm

ORBY ROAD

Faulkers Fish Farm

FAULKERS LANE

Orby Marsh

Little Wood

Lodge Farm

A158

Field Farm

Sycamores Farm

CHALK LANE

COMMON LANE   INGOLDMELLS RD

66

46   A   47   B   48   C   49   D   50   E   51   F

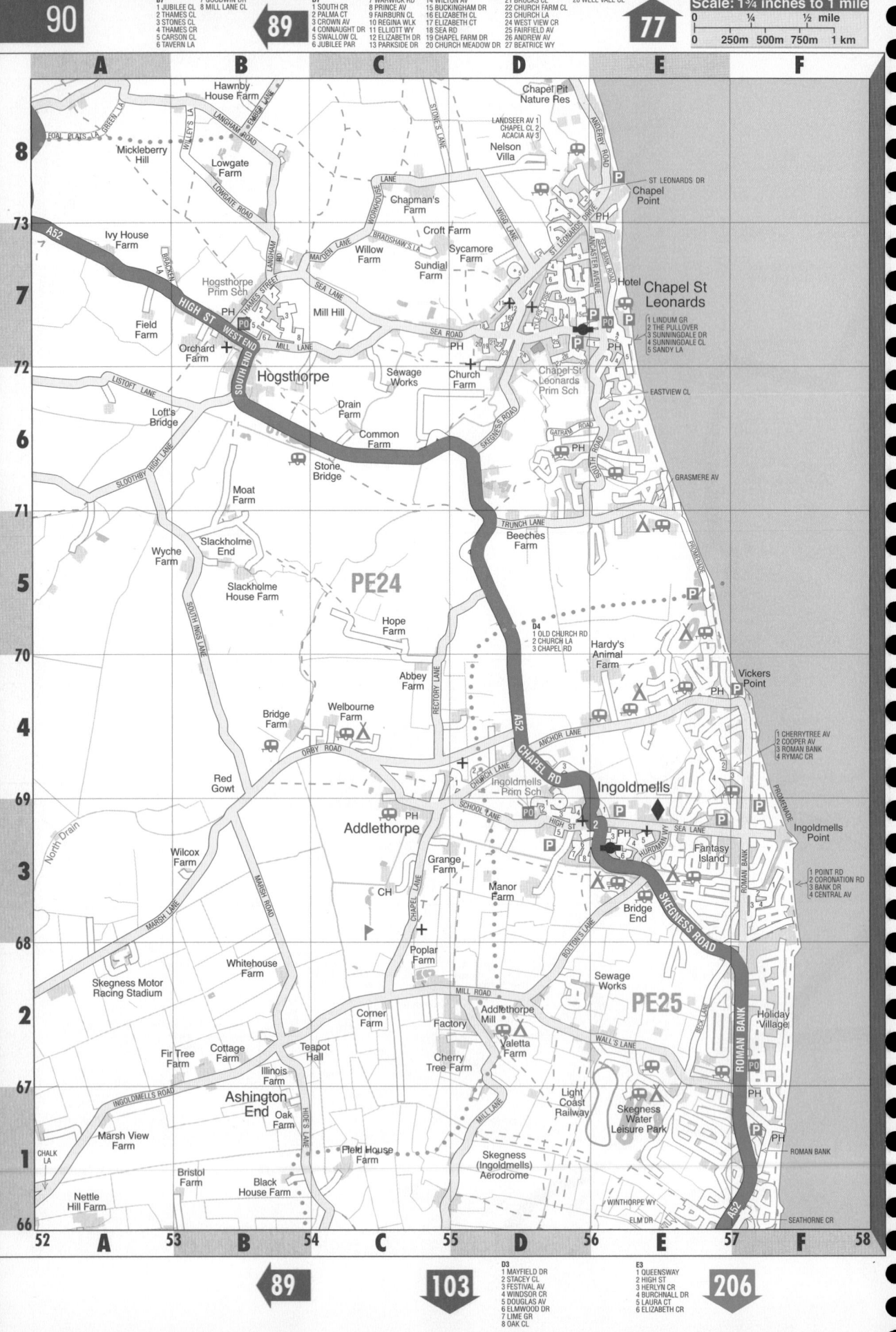

89

77

B7
1 JUBILEE CL
2 THAMES CL
3 STONES CL
4 THAMES CR
5 CARSON CL
6 TAVERN LA

7 GOODWIN DR
8 MILL LANE CL

D7
1 SOUTH CR
2 PALMA CT
3 CROWN AV
4 CONNAUGHT DR
5 SWALLOW CL
6 JUBILEE PAR

7 WARWICK RD
8 PRINCE AV
9 FAIRBURN CL
10 REGINA WLK
11 ELLIOTT WY
12 ELIZABETH DR
13 PARKSIDE DR

14 WILTON AV
15 BUCKINGHAM DR
16 ELIZABETH CL
17 ELIZABETH CT
18 SEA RD
19 CHAPEL FARM DR
20 CHURCH MEADOW DR

21 BROCKS CL
22 CHURCH FARM CL
23 CHURCH LA
24 WEST VIEW CR
25 FAIRFIELD AV
26 ANDREW AV
27 BEATRICE WY

28 WELL VALE CL

Scale: 1¾ inches to 1 mile
0   ¼   ½ mile
0   250m   500m   750m   1 km

Scale: 1¾ inches to 1 mile

Chapel Pit
Nature Res

LANDSEER AV 1
CHAPEL CL 2
ACACIA AV 3

Nelson
Villa

ST LEONARDS DR

Chapel
Point

Hawnby
House Farm

Mickleberry
Hill

Lowgate
Farm

Chapman's
Farm

Croft Farm

Willow
Farm

Sycamore
Farm

Sundial
Farm

Hotel

Chapel St
Leonards

1 LINDUM GR
2 THE PULLOVER
3 SUNNINGDALE DR
4 SUNNINGDALE CL
5 SANDY LA

Ivy House
Farm

Hogsthorpe
Prim Sch

Mill Hill

Field
Farm

PH

Orchard
Farm

Hogsthorpe

Drain
Farm

Sewage
Works

Church
Farm

Chapel St
Leonards
Prim Sch

EASTVIEW CL

LISTOFT LANE

Loft's
Bridge

Common
Farm

Stone
Bridge

GRASMERE AV

Moat
Farm

SLOOTHBY HIGH LANE

TRUNCH LANE

Beeches
Farm

Wyche
Farm

Slackholme
End

PE24

Slackholme
House Farm

Hope
Farm

PROMENADE

D4
1 OLD CHURCH RD
2 CHURCH LA
3 CHAPEL RD

Hardy's
Animal Farm

Vickers
Point

Abbey
Farm

Bridge
Farm

Welbourne
Farm

1 CHERRYTREE AV
2 COOPER AV
3 ROMAN BANK
4 RYMAC CR

Red
Gowt

Ingoldmells
Prim Sch

Ingoldmells

North Drain

Wilcox
Farm

Addlethorpe

PH

Ingoldmells
Point

Grange
Farm

CH

Manor
Farm

Fantasy
Island

1 POINT RD
2 CORONATION RD
3 BANK DR
4 CENTRAL AV

Bridge
End

Poplar
Farm

Skegness Motor
Racing Stadium

Whitehouse
Farm

Sewage
Works

PE25

Corner
Farm

Factory

Addlethorpe
Mill

Holiday
Village

Fir Tree
Farm

Cottage
Farm

Teapot
Hall

Valetta
Farm

WALL'S LANE

Illinois
Farm

Cherry
Tree Farm

Light
Coast
Railway

Skegness Water
Leisure Park

ROMAN BANK

Ashington
End

Oak
Farm

PH

CHALK
LA

Marsh View
Farm

Field House
Farm

Skegness
(Ingoldmells)
Aerodrome

ROMAN BANK

Nettle
Hill Farm

Bristol
Farm

Black
House Farm

WINTHORPE WY

ELM DR

SEATHORNE CR

89

103

D3
1 MAYFIELD DR
2 STACEY CL
3 FESTIVAL AV
4 WINDSOR CR
5 DOUGLAS AV
6 ELMWOOD DR
7 LIME GR
8 OAK CL

E3
1 QUEENSWAY
2 HIGH ST
3 HERLYN CR
4 BURCHNALL DR
5 LAURA CT
6 ELIZABETH CR

206

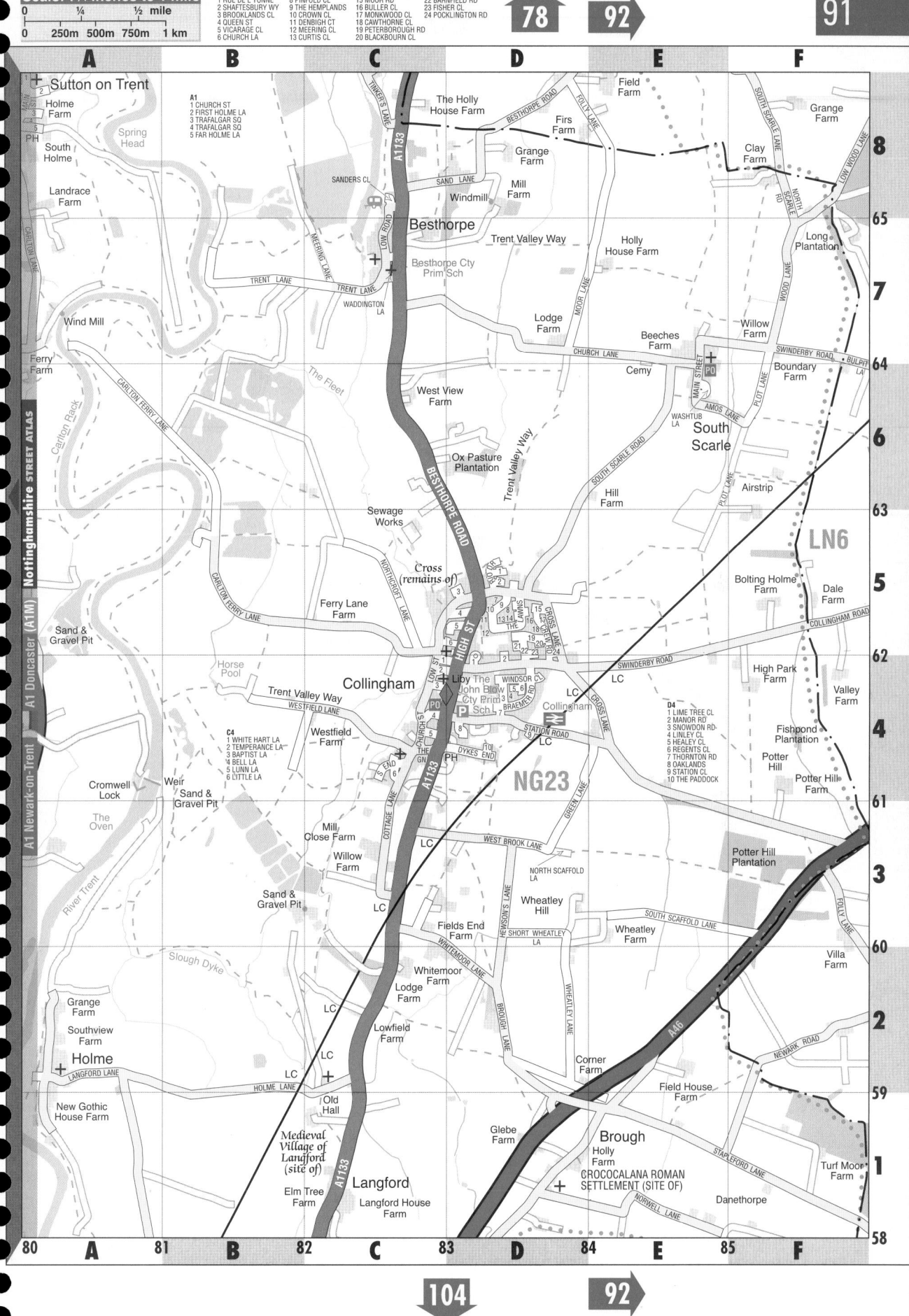
Scale: 1¾ inches to 1 mile
0 ¼ ½ mile
0 250m 500m 750m 1 km
D5
1 RUE DE L'YONNE
2 SHAFTESBURY WY
3 BROOKLANDS CL
4 QUEEN ST
5 VICARAGE CL
6 CHURCH LA
7 DEANE CL
8 PINFOLD CL
9 THE HEMPLANDS
10 CROWN CL
11 DENBIGH CT
12 MEERING CL
13 CURTIS CL
14 THE ROOKERY
15 MOOR RD
16 BULLER CL
17 MONKWOOD CL
18 CAWTHORNE CL
19 PETERBOROUGH RD
20 BLACKBOURN CL
21 FOSTER RD
22 BARNFIELD RD
23 FISHER CL
24 POCKLINGTON RD
78
92
A1
1 CHURCH ST
2 FIRST HOLME LA
3 TRAFALGAR SQ
4 TRAFALGAR SQ
5 FAR HOLME LA
Sutton on Trent
Holme Farm
South Holme
Spring Head
Landrace Farm
The Holly House Farm
Field Farm
Firs Farm
Grange Farm
Clay Farm
Mill Farm
Windmill
Besthorpe
Trent Valley Way
Holly House Farm
Long Plantation
Besthorpe Cty Prim Sch
Wind Mill
Lodge Farm
Beeches Farm
Willow Farm
Ferry Farm
Cemy
Boundary Farm
West View Farm
South Scarle
Ox Pasture Plantation
Hill Farm
Airstrip
Sewage Works
LN6
Cross (remains of)
Bolting Holme Farm
Dale Farm
Ferry Lane Farm
Sand & Gravel Pit
Horse Pool
Collingham
High Park Farm
Valley Farm
The John Blow Cty Prim Sch
Westfield Farm
Fishpond Plantation
Potter Hill
Potter Hill Farm
Cromwell Lock
Weir
Sand & Gravel Pit
NG23
The Oven
Mill Close Farm
Willow Farm
Potter Hill Plantation
Wheatley Hill
Wheatley Farm
Fields End Farm
Villa Farm
Whitemoor Farm
Lodge Farm
Grange Farm
Southview Farm
Lowfield Farm
Holme
Corner Farm
Field House Farm
Old Hall
New Gothic House Farm
Medieval Village of Langford (site of)
Glebe Farm
Brough
Holly Farm
CROCOCALANA ROMAN SETTLEMENT (SITE OF)
Turf Moor Farm
Langford
Elm Tree Farm
Langford House Farm
Danethorpe
C4
1 WHITE HART LA
2 TEMPERANCE LA
3 BAPTIST LA
4 BELL LA
5 LUNN LA
6 LITTLE LA
D4
1 LIME TREE CL
2 MANOR RD
3 SNOWDON RD
4 LINLEY CL
5 HEALEY CL
6 REGENTS CL
7 THORNTON RD
8 OAKLANDS
9 STATION CL
10 THE PADDOCK
A1 Doncaster (A1M)
A1 Newark-on-Trent
Nottinghamshire STREET ATLAS
104
92

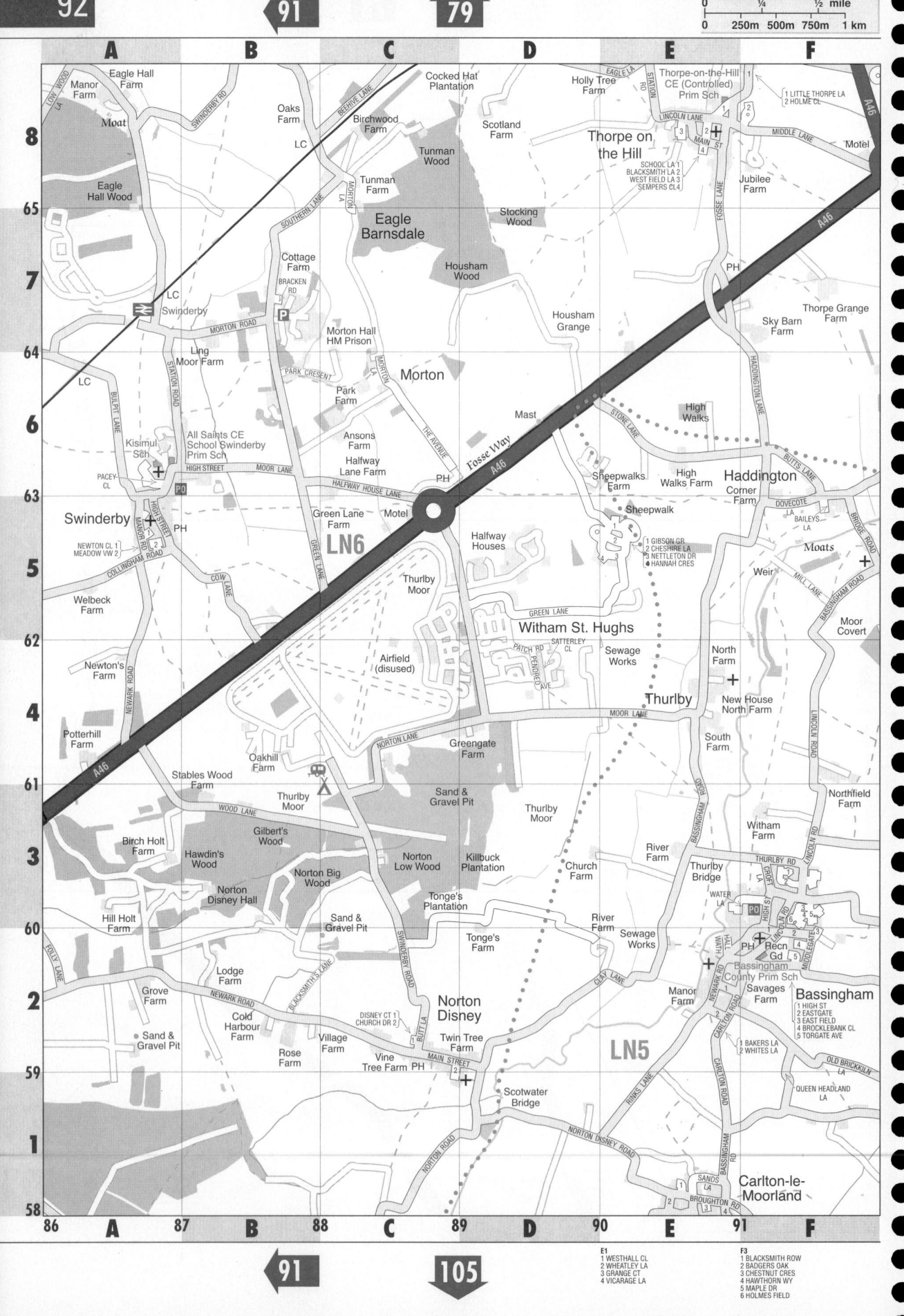
91
79
Scale: 1¾ inches to 1 mile
0 ¼ ½ mile
0 250m 500m 750m 1 km
A B C D E F
8 65 7 64 6 63 5 62 4 61 3 60 2 59 1 58
86 87 88 89 90 91
Manor Farm
Eagle Hall Farm
Moat
Eagle Hall Wood
Oaks Farm
Birchwood Farm
Cocked Hat Plantation
Holly Tree Farm
Thorpe-on-the-Hill CE (Controlled) Prim Sch
1 LITTLE THORPE LA
2 HOLME CL
Scotland Farm
Thorpe on the Hill
SCHOOL LA 1
BLACKSMITH LA 2
WEST FIELD LA 3
SEMPERS CL 4
Motel
Jubilee Farm
Tunman Wood
Tunman Farm
Eagle Barnsdale
Stocking Wood
Housham Wood
Cottage Farm
LC
Swinderby
Morton Hall HM Prison
Housham Grange
Sky Barn Farm
Thorpe Grange Farm
Ling Moor Farm
Morton
Park Farm
Mast
High Walks
Kisimul Sch
All Saints CE School Swinderby Prim Sch
Ansons Farm
Halfway Lane Farm
Fosse Way
A46
PH
Sheepwalks Farm
High Walks Farm
Haddington
Corner Farm
Swinderby
Green Lane Farm
Motel
Sheepwalk
1 GIBSON GR
2 CHESHIRE LA
3 NETTLETON DR
4 HANNAH CRES
NEWTON CL 1
MEADOW VW 2
LN6
Halfway Houses
Moats
Weir
Welbeck Farm
Thurlby Moor
Witham St. Hughs
Moor Covert
Newton's Farm
Airfield (disused)
Sewage Works
North Farm
Thurlby
New House North Farm
Potterhill Farm
Greengate Farm
South Farm
Oakhill Farm
Stables Wood Farm
Sand & Gravel Pit
Thurlby Moor
Northfield Farm
Witham Farm
Birch Holt Farm
Hawdin's Wood
Gilbert's Wood
Norton Low Wood
Killbuck Plantation
Church Farm
River Farm
Thurlby Bridge
Norton Big Wood
Norton Disney Hall
Tonge's Plantation
Hill Holt Farm
Sand & Gravel Pit
Tonge's Farm
River Farm
Sewage Works
Recn Gd
Bassingham County Prim Sch
Lodge Farm
Grove Farm
Cold Harbour Farm
Norton Disney
Manor Farm
Savages Farm
Bassingham
1 HIGH ST
2 EASTGATE
3 EAST FIELD
4 BROCKLEBANK CL
5 TORGATE AVE
Sand & Gravel Pit
DISNEY CT 1
CHURCH DR 2
Village Farm
Twin Tree Farm
LN5
1 BAKERS LA
2 WHITES LA
Rose Farm
Vine Tree Farm
Scotwater Bridge
QUEEN HEADLAND LA
Carlton-le-Moorland
E1
1 WESTHALL CL
2 WHEATLEY LA
3 GRANGE CT
4 VICARAGE LA
F3
1 BLACKSMITH ROW
2 BADGERS OAK
3 CHESTNUT CRES
4 HAWTHORN WY
5 MAPLE DR
6 HOLMES FIELD
91
105

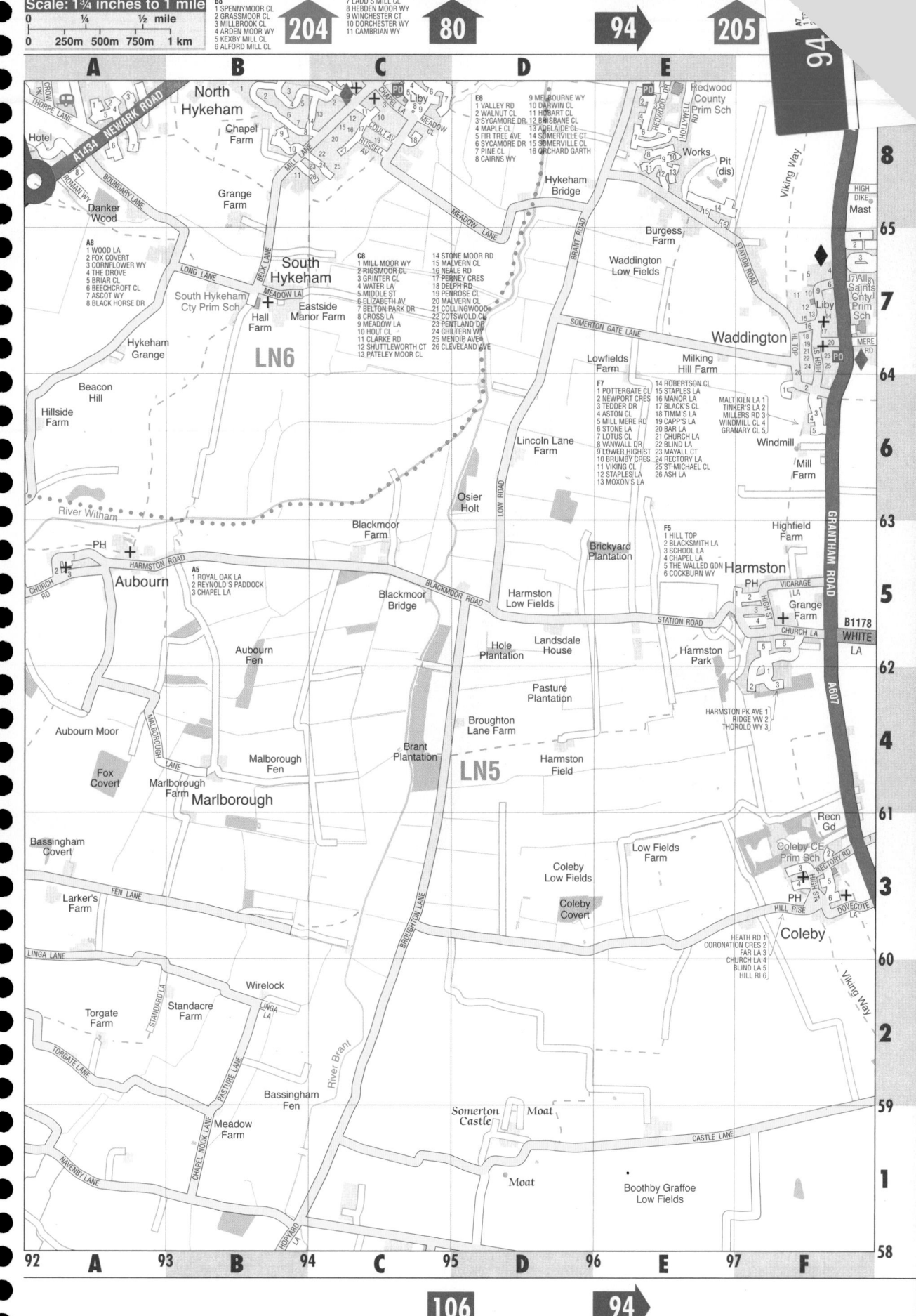

Scale: 1¾ inches to 1 mile
0 ¼ ½ mile
0 250m 500m 750m 1 km
B8
1 SPENNYMOOR CL
2 GRASSMOOR CL
3 MILLBROOK CL
4 ARDEN MOOR WY
5 KEXBY MILL CL
6 ALFORD MILL CL
7 LADD'S MILL CL
8 HEBDEN MOOR WY
9 WINCHESTER CT
10 DORCHESTER WY
11 CAMBRIAN WY
204
80
94
205
94
A
B
C
D
E
F
North Hykeham
Chapel Farm
Liby
Hotel
A1434 NEWARK ROAD
THORPE LANE
BOUNDARY LANE
ROMAN WY
MILL LANE
CHAPEL LA
COULT AV
RUSSELL AV
MEADOW CL
MEADOW LANE
E8
1 VALLEY RD
2 WALNUT CL
3 SYCAMORE DR
4 MAPLE CL
5 FIR TREE AVE
6 SYCAMORE DR
7 PINE CL
8 CAIRNS WY
9 MELBOURNE WY
10 DARWIN CL
11 HOBART CL
12 BRISBANE CL
13 ADELAIDE CL
14 SOMERVILLE CT
15 SOMERVILLE CL
16 ORCHARD GARTH
Redwood County Prim Sch
REDWOOD DR
HOLLYWELL RD
Works
Pit (dis)
Viking Way
Grange Farm
Danker Wood
Hykeham Bridge
HIGH DIKE
Mast
A8
1 WOOD LA
2 FOX COVERT
3 CORNFLOWER WY
4 THE DROVE
5 BRIAR CL
6 BEECHCROFT CL
7 ASCOT WY
8 BLACK HORSE DR
BECK LANE
LONG LANE
MEADOW LA
South Hykeham
South Hykeham Cty Prim Sch
Hall Farm
Eastside Manor Farm
C8
1 MILL MOOR WY
2 RIGSMOOR CL
3 GRINTER CL
4 WATER LA
5 MIDDLE ST
6 ELIZABETH AV
7 BELTON PARK DR
8 CROSS LA
9 MEADOW LA
10 HOLT CL
11 CLARKE RD
12 SHUTTLEWORTH CT
13 PATELEY MOOR CL
14 STONE MOOR RD
15 MALVERN CL
16 NEALE RD
17 PERNEY CRES
18 DELPH RD
19 PENROSE CL
20 MALVERN CL
21 COLLINGWOOD
22 COTSWOLD CL
23 PENTLAND DR
24 CHILTERN WY
25 MENDIP AVE
26 CLEVELAND AVE
BRANT ROAD
Burgess Farm
Waddington Low Fields
STATION ROAD
All Saints Cnty Prim Sch
Liby
Waddington
SOMERTON GATE LANE
HL TOP
HIGH ST
MERE RD
Hykeham Grange
LN6
Lowfields Farm
Milking Hill Farm
Beacon Hill
Hillside Farm
F7
1 POTTERGATE CL
2 NEWPORT CRES
3 TEDDER DR
4 ASTON CL
5 MILL MERE RD
6 STONE LA
7 LOTUS CL
8 VANWALL DR
9 LOWER HIGH ST
10 BRUMBY CRES
11 VIKING CL
12 STAPLES LA
13 MOXON'S LA
14 ROBERTSON CL
15 STAPLES LA
16 MANOR LA
17 BLACK'S CL
18 TIMM'S LA
19 CAPP'S LA
20 BAR LA
21 CHURCH LA
22 BLIND LA
23 MAYALL CT
24 RECTORY LA
25 ST MICHAEL CL
26 ASH LA
MALT KILN LA 1
TINKER'S LA 2
MILLERS RD 3
WINDMILL CL 4
GRANARY CL 5
Windmill
Lincoln Lane Farm
Mill Farm
Osier Holt
LOW ROAD
River Witham
Blackmoor Farm
Brickyard Plantation
F5
1 HILL TOP
2 BLACKSMITH LA
3 SCHOOL LA
4 CHAPEL LA
5 THE WALLED GDN
6 COCKBURN WY
Highfield Farm
GRANTHAM ROAD
PH
Aubourn
HARMSTON ROAD
CHURCH RD
A5
1 ROYAL OAK LA
2 REYNOLD'S PADDOCK
3 CHAPEL LA
Blackmoor Bridge
BLACKMOOR ROAD
Harmston Low Fields
Harmston
VICARAGE LA
Grange Farm
STATION ROAD
CHURCH LA
B1178
WHITE LA
Aubourn Fen
Hole Plantation
Landsdale House
Harmston Park
Pasture Plantation
HARMSTON PK AVE 1
RIDGE VW 2
THOROLD WY 3
A607
Aubourn Moor
MALBOROUGH LANE
Broughton Lane Farm
Brant Plantation
Fox Covert
Malborough Fen
LN5
Harmston Field
Marlborough Farm
Marlborough
Recn Gd
Bassingham Covert
Low Fields Farm
Coleby CE Prim Sch
RECTORY RD
Coleby Low Fields
Larker's Farm
FEN LANE
Coleby Covert
HIGH ST
DOVECOTE LA
HILL RISE
Coleby
BROUGHTON LANE
HEATH RD 1
CORONATION CRES 2
FAR LA 3
CHURCH LA 4
BLIND LA 5
HILL RI 6
LINGA LANE
Wirelock
Standacre Farm
STANDARD LA
LINGA LA
Torgate Farm
TORGATE LANE
PASTURE LANE
River Brant
Bassingham Fen
Somerton Castle
Moat
Meadow Farm
CHAPEL NOOK LANE
CASTLE LANE
NAVENBY LANE
Moat
Boothby Graffoe Low Fields
HOPYARD LA
8
65
7
64
6
63
5
62
4
61
3
60
2
59
1
58
92
93
94
95
96
97

106

94

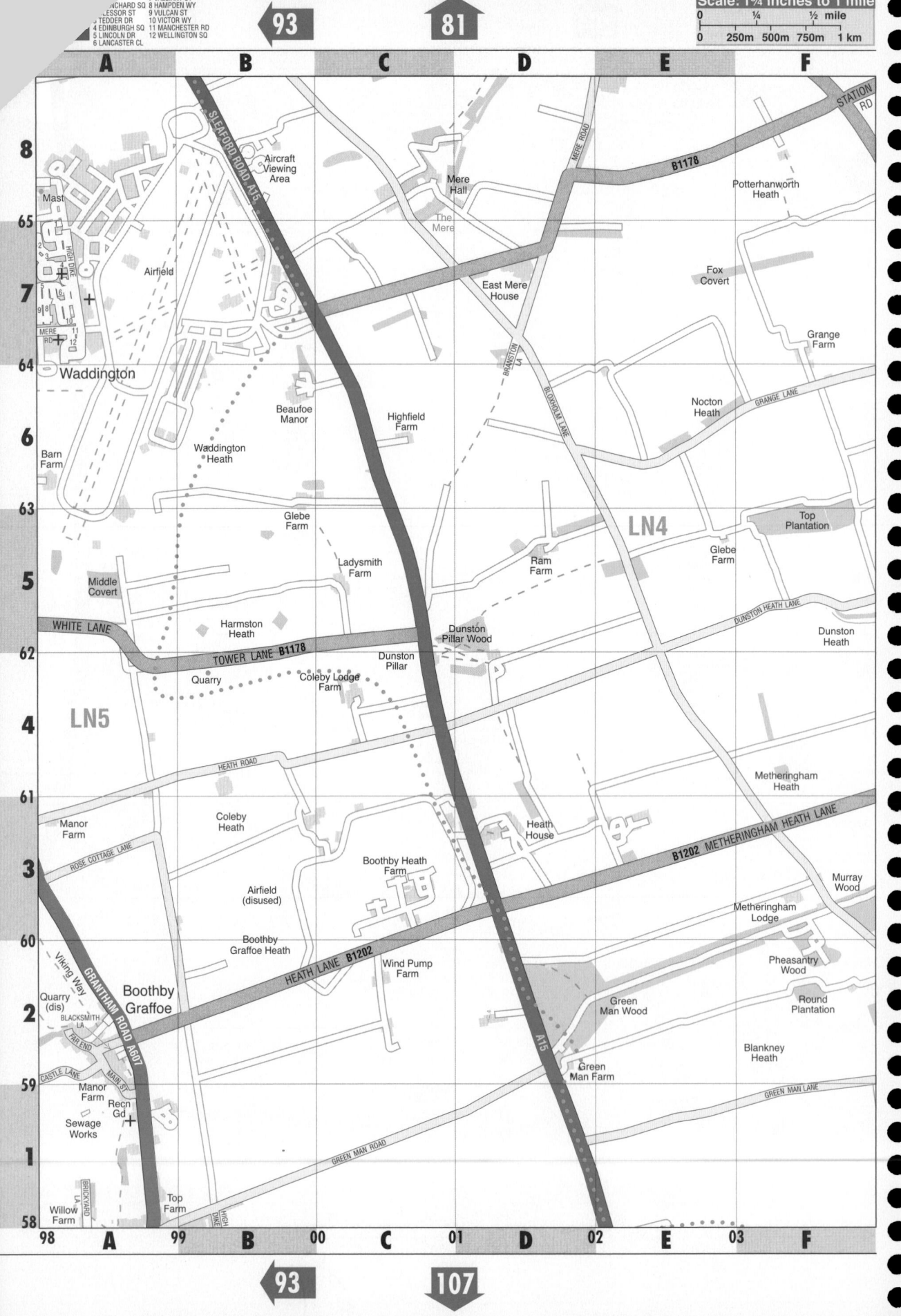

7 VALLIANT ST
8 HAMPDEN WY
9 VULCAN ST
10 VICTOR WY
11 MANCHESTER RD
12 WELLINGTON SQ
4 EDINBURGH SQ
5 LINCOLN DR
6 LANCASTER CL
93
81
Scale: 1¾ inches to 1 mile
0 ¼ ½ mile
0 250m 500m 750m 1 km
A B C D E F
8
65
7
64
6
63
5
62
4
61
3
60
2
59
1
58
98 99 00 01 02 03
SLEAFORD ROAD A15
Aircraft Viewing Area
Mere Hall
The Mere
MERE ROAD
B1178
STATION RD
Potterhanworth Heath
Mast
HIGH DIKE
MERE RD
Airfield
Waddington
East Mere House
Fox Covert
Grange Farm
BRANSTON LA
BLOXHOLM LANE
Nocton Heath
GRANGE LANE
Beaufoe Manor
Highfield Farm
Waddington Heath
Barn Farm
Glebe Farm
LN4
Top Plantation
Ladysmith Farm
Ram Farm
Glebe Farm
Middle Covert
WHITE LANE
Harmston Heath
Dunston Pillar Wood
DUNSTON HEATH LANE
Dunston Heath
TOWER LANE B1178
Dunston Pillar
Quarry
Coleby Lodge Farm
LN5
HEATH ROAD
Metheringham Heath
Manor Farm
Coleby Heath
Heath House
ROSE COTTAGE LANE
Boothby Heath Farm
B1202 METHERINGHAM HEATH LANE
Murray Wood
Airfield (disused)
Metheringham Lodge
Boothby Graffoe Heath
Viking Way
HEATH LANE B1202
Wind Pump Farm
Pheasantry Wood
GRANTHAM ROAD A607
Quarry (dis)
Boothby Graffoe
Green Man Wood
Round Plantation
BLACKSMITH LA
FAR END
A15
Blankney Heath
CASTLE LANE
MAIN ST
Green Man Farm
Manor Farm
Recn Gd
GREEN MAN LANE
Sewage Works
GREEN MAN ROAD
BRICKYARD LA
Top Farm
HIGH DIKE
Willow Farm
93
107

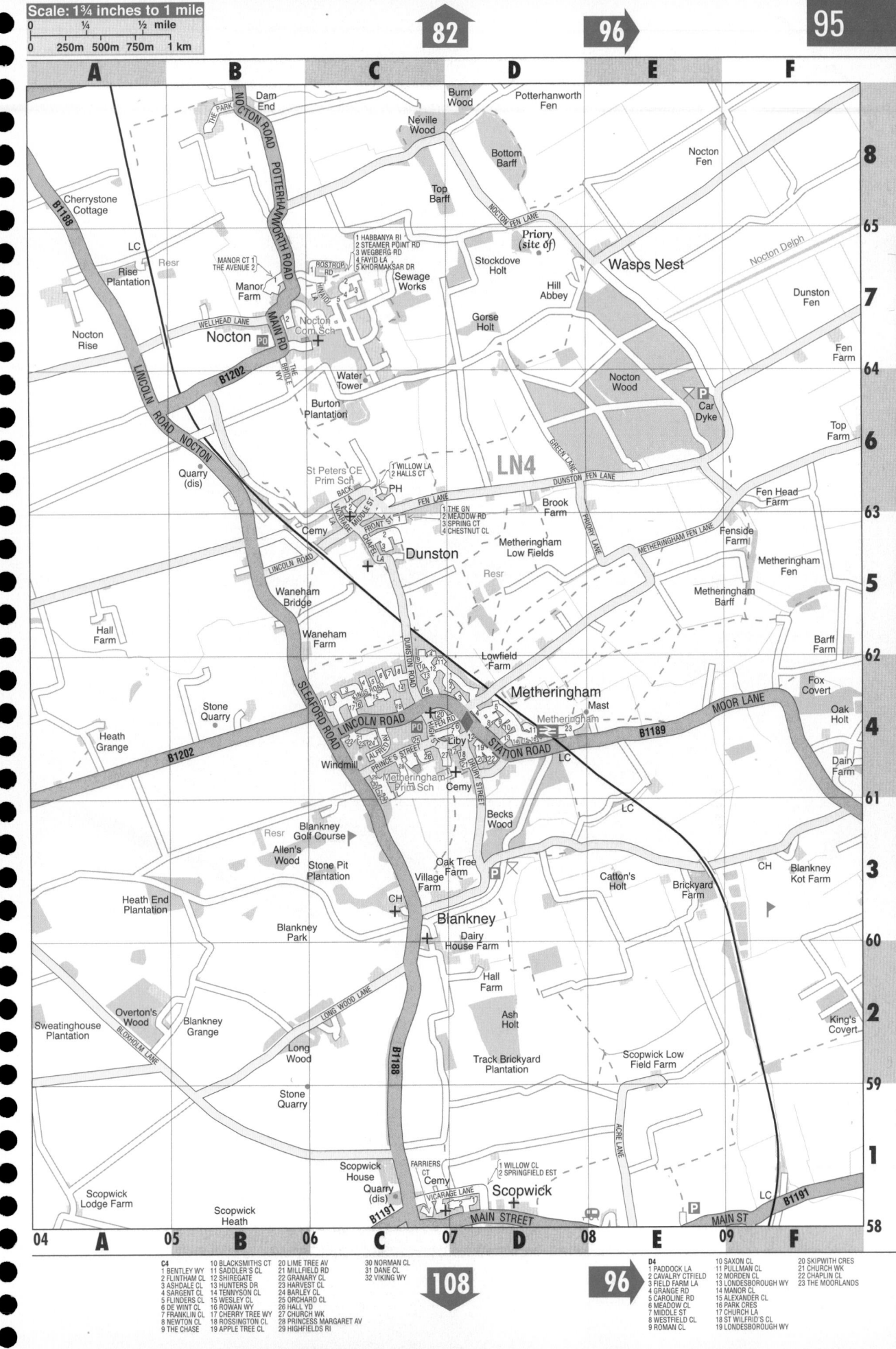

THE PARK
Dam End
Burnt Wood
Potterhanworth Fen
NOCTON ROAD
Neville Wood
Bottom Barff
Nocton Fen
8
B1188
Cherrystone Cottage
POTTERHANWORTH ROAD
Top Barff
NOCTON FEN LANE
65
LC
Resr
Rise Plantation
1 HABBANYA RI
2 STEAMER POINT RD
3 WEGBERG RD
4 FAYID LA
5 KHORMAKSAR DR
Priory (site of)
Wasps Nest
Nocton Delph
MANOR CT 1
THE AVENUE 2
ROSTROP RD
Sewage Works
Stockdove Holt
Dunston Fen
7
Manor Farm
Hill Abbey
Nocton Rise
WELLHEAD LANE
MAIN RD
Nocton Com Sch
Gorse Holt
Fen Farm
64
Nocton
B1202
THE BRIDGE WY
PQ
Water Tower
Nocton Wood
Car Dyke
P
LINCOLN ROAD NOCTON
Burton Plantation
GREEN LANE
Top Farm
6
Quarry (dis)
St Peters CE Prim Sch
1 WILLOW LA
2 HALLS CT
LN4
DUNSTON FEN LANE
Fen Head Farm
BACK LA
PH
FEN LANE
1 THE GN
2 MEADOW RD
3 SPRING CT
4 CHESTNUT CL
Brook Farm
PRIORY LANE
METHERINGHAM FEN LANE
Fenside Farm
63
Cemy
VICARAGE MIDDLE ST
FRONT ST
CHAPEL LA
Dunston
Metheringham Low Fields
Metheringham Fen
LINCOLN ROAD
Waneham Bridge
Resr
Metheringham Barff
5
Waneham Farm
Barff Farm
62
Hall Farm
DUNSTON ROAD
Lowfield Farm
Fox Covert
SLEAFORD ROAD
Stone Quarry
KINGS ROAD
Metheringham
Mast
MOOR LANE
Oak Holt
4
Heath Grange
B1202
LINCOLN ROAD
PQ
FEN RD
Metheringham
B1189
Dairy Farm
Windmill
PRINCE'S STREET
Liby
STATION ROAD
LC
ALFRETON
DRURY STREET
Metheringham Prim Sch
Cemy
LC
61
Resr
Blankney Golf Course
Becks Wood
LC
Allen's Wood
Stone Pit Plantation
CH
Blankney Kot Farm
3
Heath End Plantation
CH
Oak Tree Farm
Village Farm
P
Catton's Holt
Brickyard Farm
Blankney Park
Blankney
Dairy House Farm
60
BLOXHOLM LANE
Hall Farm
2
Sweatinghouse Plantation
Overton's Wood
Blankney Grange
LONG WOOD LANE
Ash Holt
King's Covert
Long Wood
B1188
Track Brickyard Plantation
Scopwick Low Field Farm
59
Stone Quarry
ACRE LANE
1
Scopwick House Quarry (dis)
FARRIERS CT
Cemy
1 WILLOW CL
2 SPRINGFIELD EST
LC
B1191
Scopwick Lodge Farm
Scopwick Heath
B1191
VICARAGE LANE
Scopwick
P
MAIN ST
MAIN STREET
LC
58

04   A   05   B   06   C   07   D   08   E   09   F

C4
1 BENTLEY WY
2 FLINTHAM CL
3 ASHDALE CL
4 SARGENT CL
5 FLINDERS CL
6 DE WINT CL
7 FRANKLIN CL
8 NEWTON CL
9 THE CHASE
10 BLACKSMITHS CT
11 SADDLER'S CL
12 SHIREGATE
13 HUNTERS DR
14 TENNYSON CL
15 WESLEY CL
16 ROWAN WY
17 CHERRY TREE WY
18 ROSSINGTON CL
19 APPLE TREE CL
20 LIME TREE AV
21 MILLFIELD RD
22 GRANARY CL
23 HARVEST CL
24 BARLEY CL
25 ORCHARD CL
26 HALL YD
27 CHURCH WK
28 PRINCESS MARGARET AV
29 HIGHFIELDS RI
30 NORMAN CL
31 DANE CL
32 VIKING WY

D4
1 PADDOCK LA
2 CAVALRY CTFIELD
3 FIELD FARM LA
4 GRANGE RD
5 CAROLINE RD
6 MEADOW CL
7 MIDDLE ST
8 WESTFIELD CL
9 ROMAN CL
10 SAXON CL
11 PULLMAN CL
12 MORDEN CL
13 LONDESBOROUGH WY
14 MANOR CL
15 ALEXANDER CL
16 PARK CRES
17 CHURCH LA
18 ST WILFRID'S CL
19 LONDESBOROUGH WY
20 SKIPWITH CRES
21 CHURCH WK
22 CHAPLIN CL
23 THE MOORLANDS

95
83
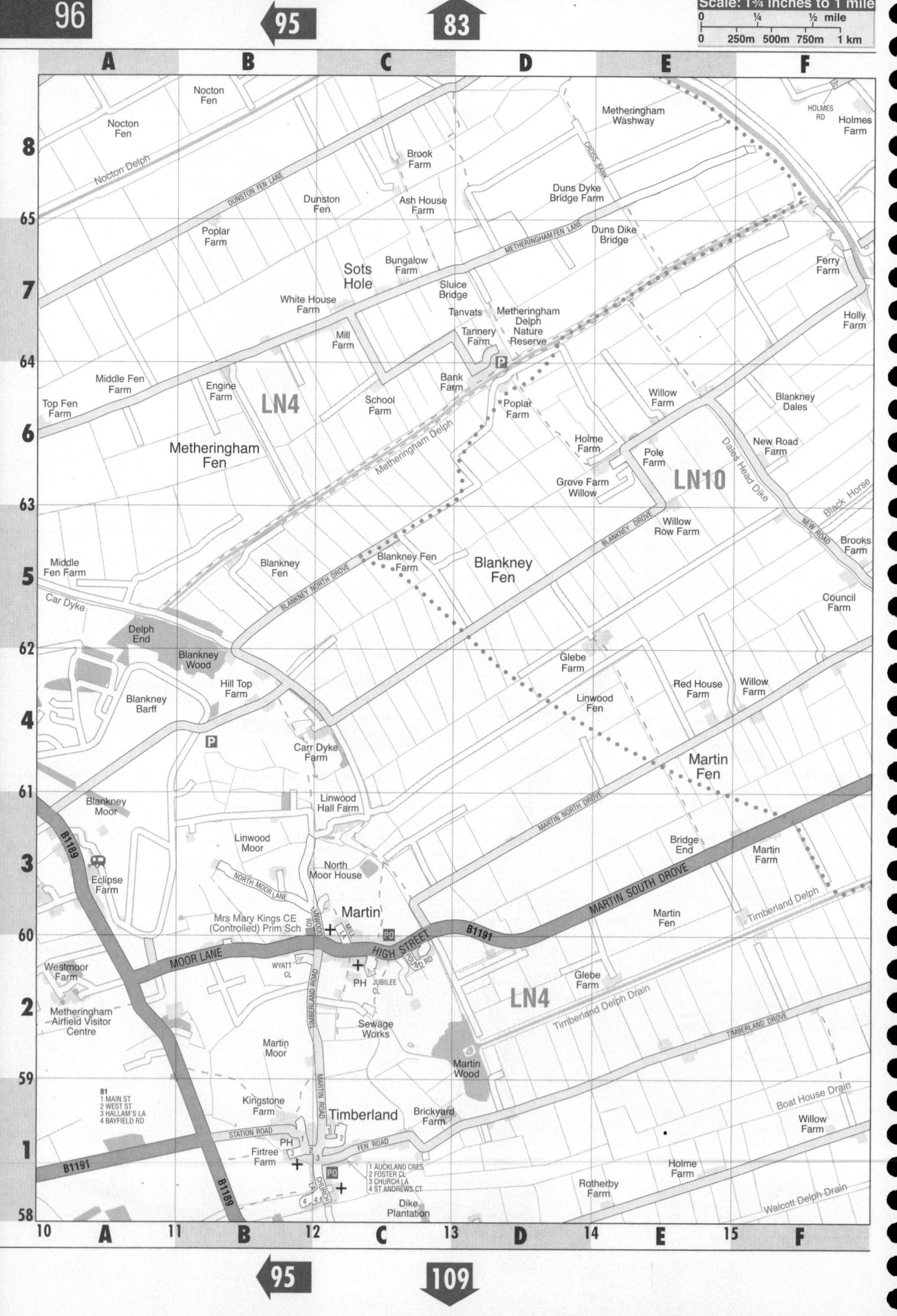
Scale: 1¾ inches to 1 mile
0 ¼ ½ mile
0 250m 500m 750m 1 km
A B C D E F
Nocton Fen
Nocton Fen
Nocton Delph
Metheringham Washway
HOLMES RD
Holmes Farm
CROSS BANK
Brook Farm
DUNSTON FEN LANE
Dunston Fen
Ash House Farm
Duns Dyke Bridge Farm
Poplar Farm
METHERINGHAM FEN LANE
Duns Dike Bridge
Bungalow Farm
Sots Hole
Sluice Bridge
Ferry Farm
White House Farm
Tanvats
Metheringham Delph Nature Reserve
Holly Farm
Mill Farm
Tannery Farm
Middle Fen Farm
Engine Farm
Bank Farm
Top Fen Farm
LN4
School Farm
Poplar Farm
Willow Farm
Blankney Dales
Metheringham Delph
Metheringham Fen
Holme Farm
Pole Farm
New Road Farm
Dales Head Dike
LN10
Grove Farm Willow
Black Horse
Willow Row Farm
BLANKNEY DROVE
NEW ROAD
Brooks Farm
Middle Fen Farm
Blankney Fen
Blankney Fen Farm
Blankney Fen
BLANKNEY NORTH DROVE
Car Dyke
Council Farm
Delph End
Blankney Wood
Glebe Farm
Hill Top Farm
Red House Farm
Willow Farm
Blankney Barff
Linwood Fen
Carr Dyke Farm
Martin Fen
Blankney Moor
Linwood Hall Farm
MARTIN NORTH DROVE
B1189
Linwood Moor
Bridge End
Martin Farm
Eclipse Farm
North Moor House
NORTH MOOR LANE
MARTIN SOUTH DROVE
Martin
Timberland Delph
Mrs Mary Kings CE (Controlled) Prim Sch
LINWOOD RD
MILL LA
PO
HIGH STREET
B1191
Martin Fen
MOOR LANE
WYATT CL
POUND RD
Westmoor Farm
PH
JUBILEE CL
Glebe Farm
TIMBERLAND ROAD
LN4
Timberland Delph Drain
Metheringham Airfield Visitor Centre
Sewage Works
TIMBERLAND DROVE
Martin Moor
Martin Wood
B1
1 MAIN ST
2 WEST ST
3 HALLAM'S LA
4 BAYFIELD RD
Kingstone Farm
MARTIN ROAD
Timberland
Brickyard Farm
Boat House Drain
Willow Farm
STATION ROAD
PH
FEN ROAD
Firtree Farm
B1191
PO
1 AUCKLAND CRES
2 FOSTER CL
3 CHURCH LA
4 ST ANDREWS CT
CHURCH LA
Holme Farm
Rotherby Farm
B1189
Dike Plantation
Walcott Delph Drain
8
65
7
64
6
63
5
62
4
61
3
60
2
59
1
58
10 11 12 13 14 15
A B C D E F
95
109

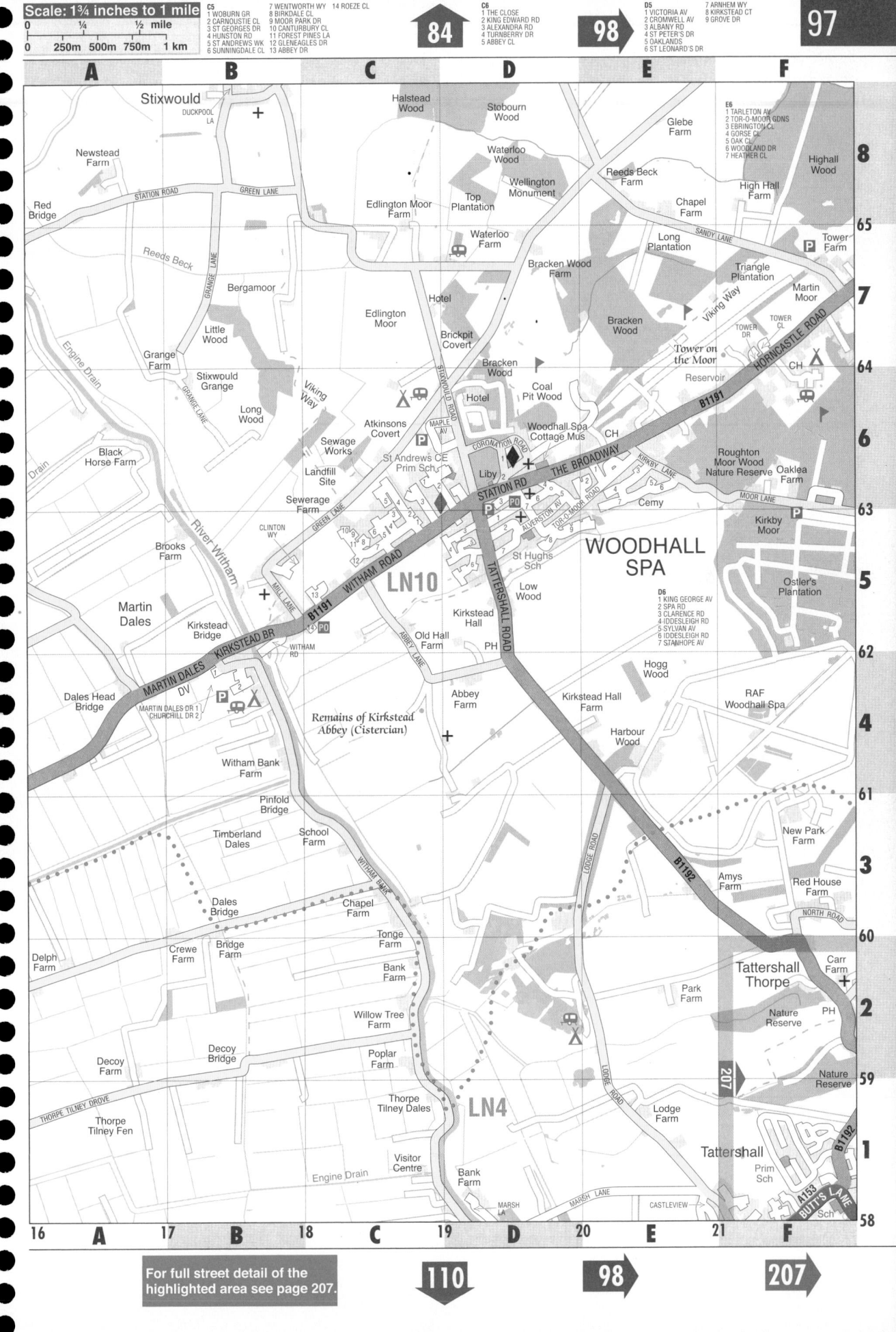

Scale: 1¾ inches to 1 mile

0   ¼   ½ mile

0   250m 500m 750m 1 km

84

98

C5
1 WOBURN GR
2 CARNOUSTIE CL
3 ST GEORGES DR
4 HUNSTON RD
5 ST ANDREWS WK
6 SUNNINGDALE CL
7 WENTWORTH WY
8 BIRKDALE CL
9 MOOR PARK DR
10 CANTURBURY CL
11 FOREST PINES LA
12 GLENEAGLES DR
13 ABBEY DR
14 ROEZE CL

C6
1 THE CLOSE
2 KING EDWARD RD
3 ALEXANDRA RD
4 TURNBERRY DR
5 ABBEY CL

D5
1 VICTORIA AV
2 CROMWELL AV
3 ALBANY RD
4 ST PETER'S DR
5 OAKLANDS
6 ST LEONARD'S DR
7 ARNHEM WY
8 KIRKSTEAD CT
9 GROVE DR

E6
1 TARLETON AV
2 TOR-O-MOOR GDNS
3 EBRINGTON CL
4 GORSE CL
5 OAK CL
6 WOODLAND DR
7 HEATHER CL

D6
1 KING GEORGE AV
2 SPA RD
3 CLARENCE RD
4 IDDESLEIGH RD
5 SYLVAN AV
6 IDDESLEIGH RD
7 STANHOPE AV

WOODHALL SPA

LN10

LN4

Stixwould

Martin Dales

Tattershall Thorpe

Tattershall

For full street detail of the highlighted area see page 207.

110

98

207

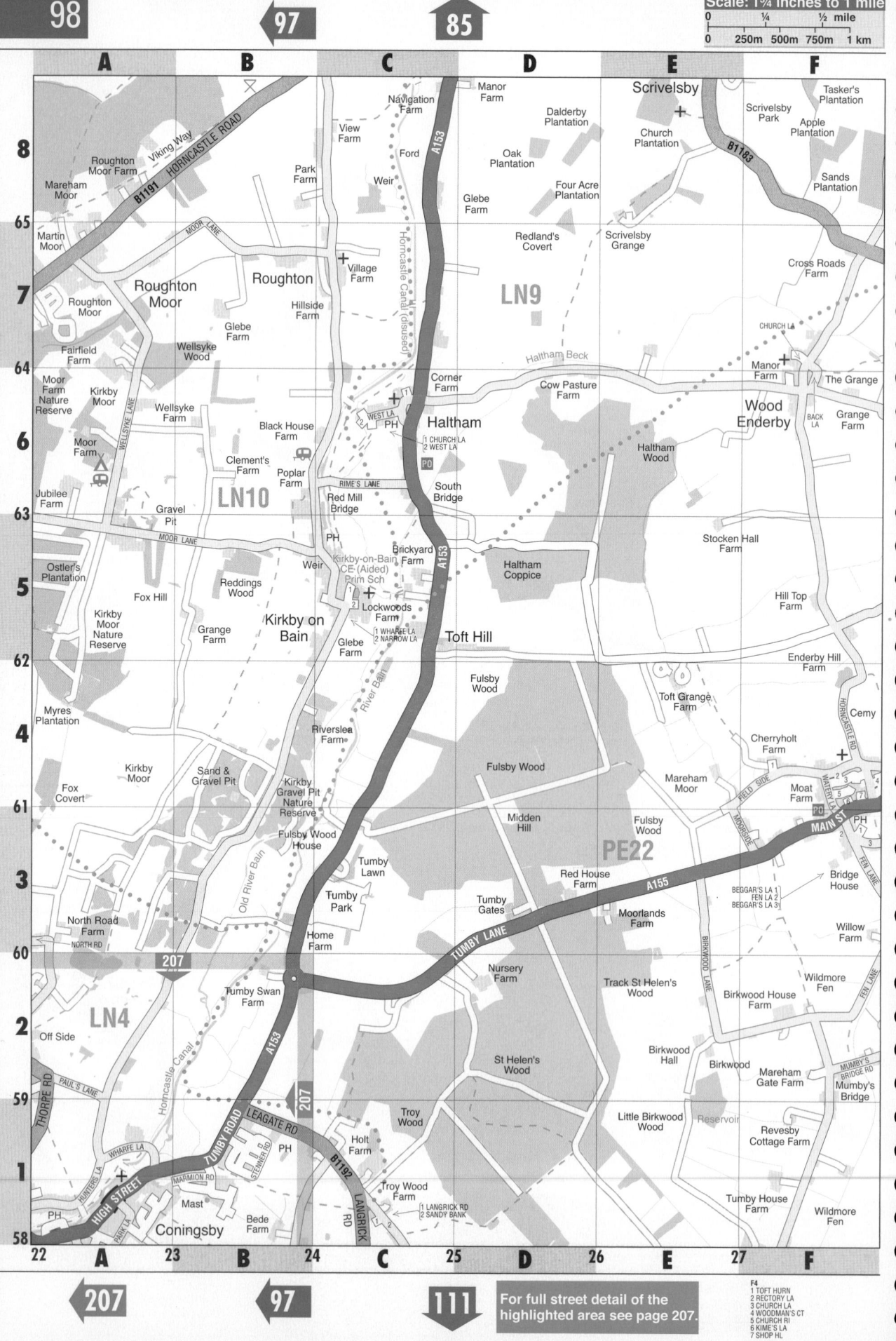

A   B   C   D   E   F

8

Viking Way

HORNCASTLE ROAD

Manor Farm

Scrivelsby

Tasker's Plantation

Navigation Farm

Dalderby Plantation

Scrivelsby Park

Apple Plantation

B1183

View Farm

Ford

Oak Plantation

Church Plantation

Sands Plantation

Roughton Moor Farm

Mareham Moor

B1191

Park Farm

Weir

Glebe Farm

Four Acre Plantation

65

Martin Moor

MOOR LANE

Village Farm

Redland's Covert

Scrivelsby Grange

Cross Roads Farm

7

Roughton Moor

Roughton

LN9

CHURCH LA

Manor Farm

The Grange

Fairfield Farm

Hillside Farm

Haltham Beck

Roughton Moor

Glebe Farm

Horncastle Canal (disused)

Wood Enderby

BACK LA

64

Moor Farm Nature Reserve

Kirkby Moor

Wellsyke Wood

Corner Farm

Cow Pasture Farm

Grange Farm

6

Moor Farm

WELLSYKE LANE

Wellsyke Farm

Black House Farm

WEST LA

Haltham

PH

1 CHURCH LA
2 WEST LA

Haltham Wood

Jubilee Farm

Clement's Farm

Poplar Farm

RIME'S LANE

PO

South Bridge

63

Gravel Pit

MOOR LANE

Red Mill Bridge

Brickyard Farm

Stocken Hall Farm

Ostler's Plantation

Reddings Wood

Weir

Kirkby-on-Bain CE (Aided) Prim Sch

A153

Haltham Coppice

Hill Top Farm

5

Fox Hill

Grange Farm

Kirkby on Bain

Lockwoods Farm

Toft Hill

Kirkby Moor Nature Reserve

LN10

Glebe Farm

1 WHARFE LA
2 NARROW LA

62

Myres Plantation

River Bain

Fulsby Wood

Enderby Hill Farm

4

Kirkby Moor

Sand & Gravel Pit

Kirkby Gravel Pit Nature Reserve

Riverslea Farm

Toft Grange Farm

HORNCASTLE RD

Cemy

Fox Covert

Fulsby Wood

Cherryholt Farm

61

Old River Bain

Fulsby Wood House

Midden Hill

Mareham Moor

Fulsby Wood

FIELD SIDE

Moat Farm

PO

MAIN ST

PH

Tumby Lawn

MOORSIDE

WATERY LA

FEN LANE

3

North Road Farm

NORTH RD

Tumby Park

Red House Farm

A155

BEGGAR'S LA 1
FEN LA 2
BEGGAR'S LA 3

Bridge House

207

Home Farm

Tumby Gates

Moorlands Farm

BIRKWOOD LANE

Willow Farm

60

Tumby Swan Farm

TUMBY LANE

Nursery Farm

Track St Helen's Wood

Birkwood House Farm

Wildmore Fen

FEN LANE

2

LN4

Off Side

Horncastle Canal

A153

207

St Helen's Wood

Birkwood Hall

Birkwood

Mareham Gate Farm

MUMBY'S BRIDGE RD

THORPE RD

PAUL'S LANE

TUMBY ROAD

LEAGATE RD

Troy Wood

Little Birkwood Wood

Reservoir

Revesby Cottage Farm

Mumby's Bridge

59

WHARFE LA

STEYNER RD

PH

B1192

Holt Farm

LANGRICK RD

Tumby House Farm

Wildmore Fen

1

HUNTERS LA

HIGH STREET

MARMION RD

PARK LA

Bede Farm

Troy Wood Farm

1 LANGRICK RD
2 SANDY BANK

PH

Mast

Coningsby

58

22   A   23   B   24   C   25   D   26   E   27   F

For full street detail of the highlighted area see page 207.

F4
1 TOFT HURN
2 RECTORY LA
3 CHURCH LA
4 WOODMAN'S CT
5 CHURCH RI
6 KIME'S LA
7 SHOP HL

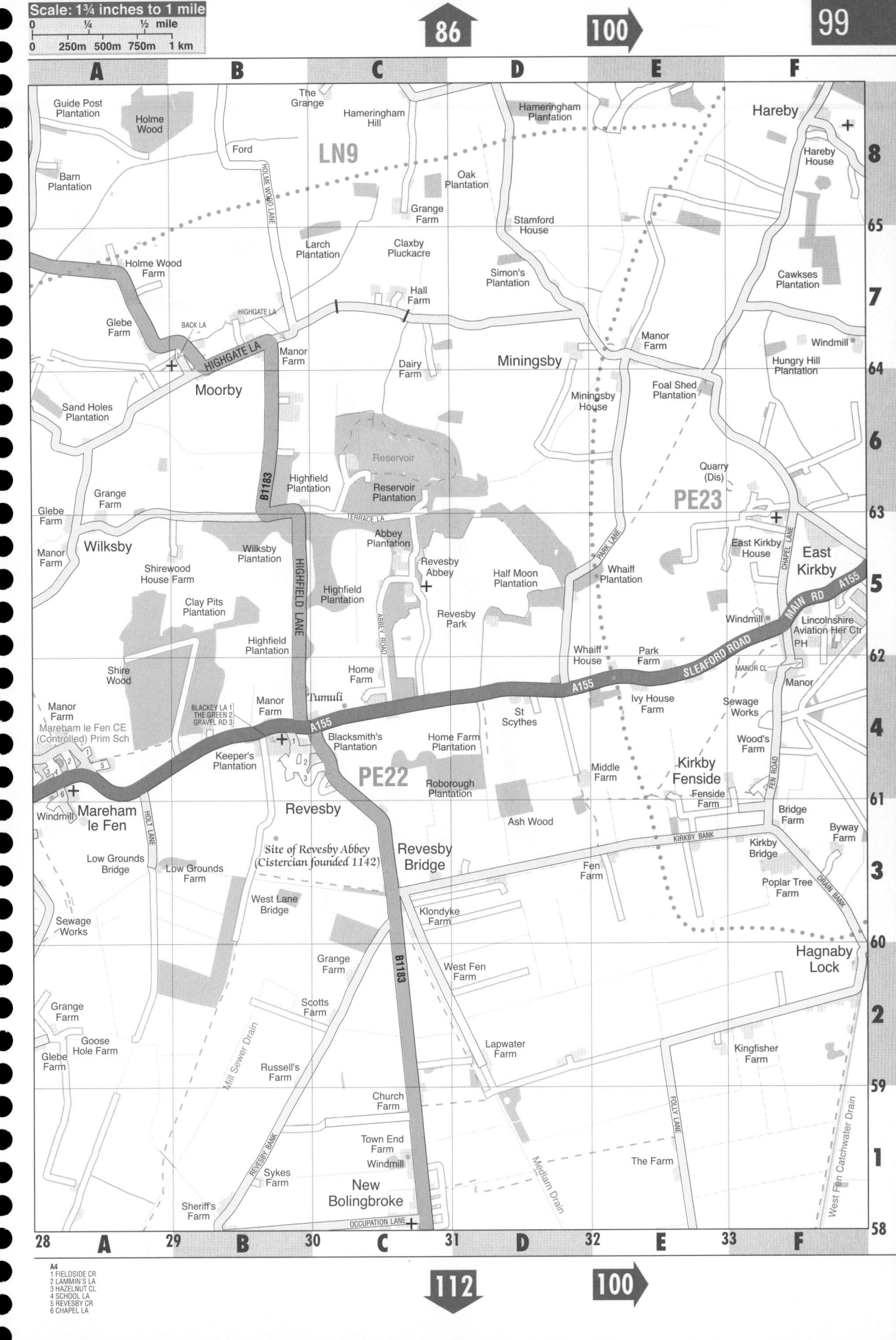

Scale: 1¾ inches to 1 mile

0   ¼   ½   mile
0   250m 500m 750m 1 km

A B C D E F

Guide Post Plantation
Holme Wood
The Grange
Hameringham Hill
Hameringham Plantation
Hareby
Hareby House

Barn Plantation
Ford
LN9
Oak Plantation
Stamford House
Cawkses Plantation

Holme Wood Farm
Larch Plantation
Claxby Pluckacre
Simon's Plantation
Windmill

Glebe Farm
BACK LA
HIGHGATE LA
Manor Farm
Hall Farm
Manor Farm
Miningsby
Hungry Hill Plantation

Moorby
Dairy Farm
Miningsby House
Foal Shed Plantation

Sand Holes Plantation
B1183
Reservoir
Quarry (Dis)
PE23

Grange Farm
Highfield Plantation
Reservoir Plantation
TERRACE LA
Whaiff Plantation
East Kirkby House

Glebe Farm
Wilksby
Wilksby Plantation
Abbey Plantation
Half Moon Plantation
East Kirkby
MAIN RD A155

Manor Farm
Shirewood House Farm
Highfield Plantation
Revesby Abbey
Revesby Park
Windmill
Lincolnshire Aviation Her Ctr PH

Clay Pits Plantation
ABBEY ROAD
SLEAFORD ROAD
MANOR CL

Shire Wood
Highfield Plantation
Home Farm
Whaiff House
Park Farm
Manor

Manor Farm
Mareham le Fen CE (Controlled) Prim Sch
BLACKEY LA 1
THE GREEN 2
GRAVEL RD 3
Manor Farm
Tumuli
A155
St Scythes
Ivy House Farm
Sewage Works
Wood's Farm

Keeper's Plantation
Blacksmith's Plantation
Home Farm Plantation
Middle Farm
Kirkby Fenside
FEN ROAD

Windmill
Mareham le Fen
HOLT LANE
Revesby
PE22
Roborough Plantation
Fenside Farm
Bridge Farm
Byway Farm

Low Grounds Bridge
Low Grounds Farm
Ash Wood
KIRKBY BANK
Kirkby Bridge
Poplar Tree Farm
DRAIN BANK

Sewage Works
Site of Revesby Abbey (Cistercian founded 1142)
Revesby Bridge
Fen Farm
Hagnaby Lock

Grange Farm
West Lane Bridge
Klondyke Farm
West Fen Farm

Grange Farm
Goose Hole Farm
Grange Farm
B1183
Scotts Farm

Glebe Farm
Lapwater Farm
Kingfisher Farm

Mill Sewer Drain
Russell's Farm
Church Farm
FOLLY LANE
West Fen Catchwater Drain

REVESBY BANK
Sykes Farm
Town End Farm
Windmill
Medlam Drain
The Farm

Sheriff's Farm
New Bolingbroke
OCCUPATION LANE

A4
1 FIELDSIDE CR
2 LAMMIN'S LA
3 HAZELNUT CL
4 SCHOOL LA
5 REVESBY CR
6 CHAPEL LA

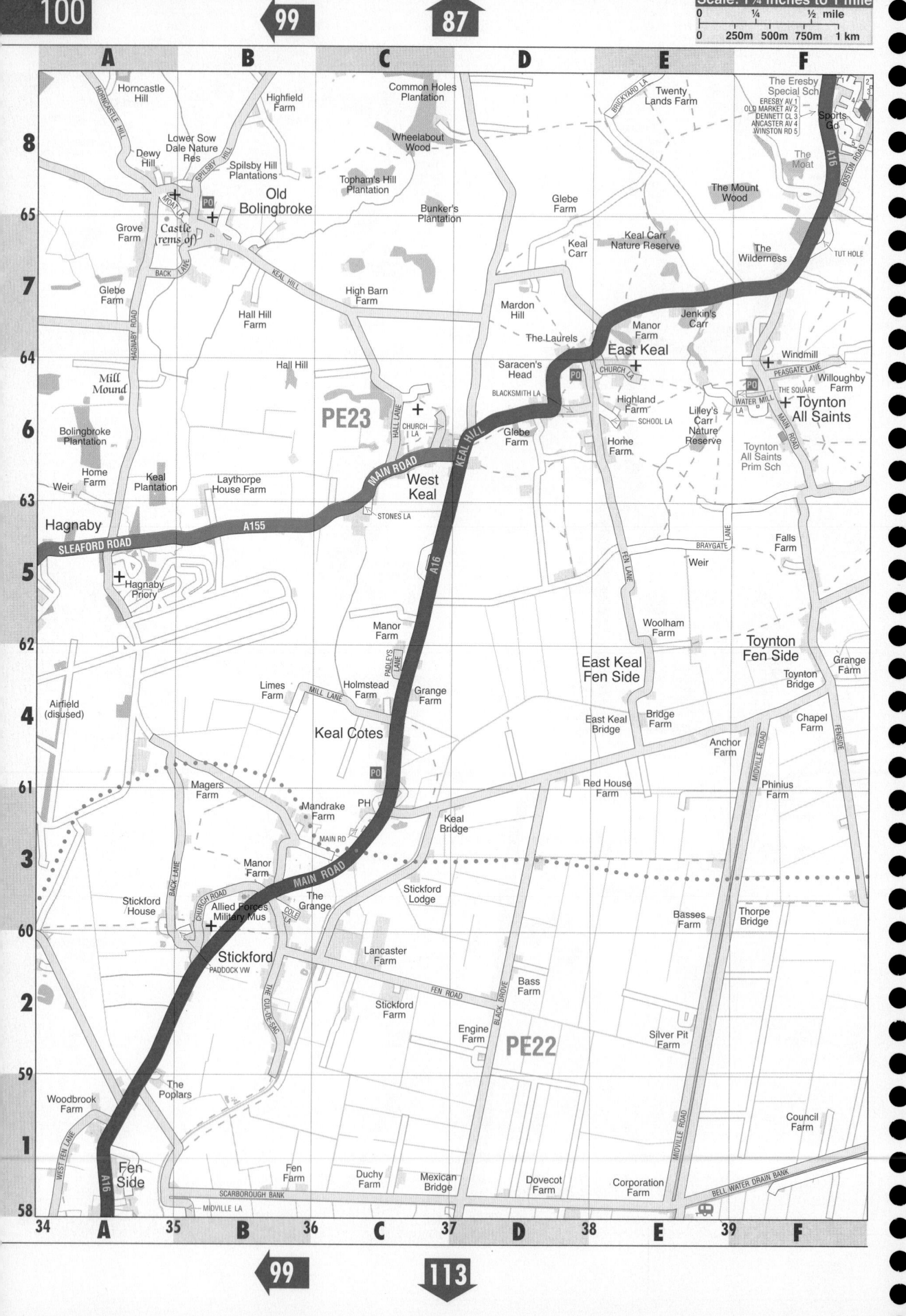

99
87

Scale: 1¾ inches to 1 mile

0   ¼   ½ mile
0   250m 500m 750m 1 km

A **B** **C** **D** **E** **F**

8

Horncastle Hill
Highfield Farm
Common Holes Plantation
Twenty Lands Farm
The Eresby Special Sch
ERESBY AV 1
OLD MARKET AV 2
DENNETT CL 3
ANCASTER AV 4
WINSTON RD 5
Sports Gd

Dewy Hill
Lower Sow Dale Nature Res
Spilsby Hill Plantations
Wheelabout Wood
The Moat

65
Grove Farm
Castle (rems of)
Old Bolingbroke
Topham's Hill Plantation
Bunker's Plantation
Glebe Farm
Keal Carr
Keal Carr Nature Reserve
The Mount Wood
The Wilderness
TUT HOLE

7
Glebe Farm
BACK LANE
KEAL HILL
High Barn Farm
Hall Hill Farm
High Barn Farm
Mardon Hill
The Laurels
Manor Farm
Jenkin's Carr
East Keal
Windmill
Willoughby Farm
PEASGATE LANE

64
Mill Mound
Hall Hill
PE23
Saracen's Head
BLACKSMITH LA
CHURCH LA
Water Mill
THE SQUARE
Toynton All Saints

6
Bolingbroke Plantation
Home Farm
Keal Plantation
Laythorpe House Farm
HALL LANE
CHURCH LA
MAIN ROAD
West Keal
KEAL HILL
Glebe Farm
Highland Farm
SCHOOL LA
Home Farm
Lilley's Carr Nature Reserve
Toynton All Saints Prim Sch
MAIN ROAD

63
Weir
Home Farm
Hagnaby
A155
STONES LA
A16
BRAYGATE
Falls Farm

5
SLEAFORD ROAD
Hagnaby Priory
FEN LANE
Weir
Toynton Fen Side

62
Manor Farm
PADLEYS LANE
East Keal Fen Side
Woolham Farm
Toynton Bridge
Grange Farm

4
Airfield (disused)
Limes Farm
MILL LANE
Holmstead Farm
Grange Farm
East Keal Bridge
Bridge Farm
Chapel Farm
MIDVILLE ROAD
FENSIDE

Keal Cotes
PO
Red House Farm
Anchor Farm
Phinius Farm

61
Magers Farm
Mandrake Farm
PH
Keal Bridge

3
BACK LANE
Manor Farm
MAIN RD
MAIN ROAD
Stickford Lodge
Stickford Lodge
Basses Farm
Thorpe Bridge

60
Stickford House
CHURCH ROAD
Allied Forces Military Mus
The Grange
COLE LA
Stickford
PADDOCK VW
Lancaster Farm
FEN ROAD
Bass Farm
BLACK GROVE

2
THE CUL-DE-SAC
Stickford Farm
Engine Farm
PE22
Silver Pit Farm
MIDVILLE ROAD

59
Woodbrook Farm
The Poplars
Council Farm

1
WEST FEN LANE
A16
Fen Side
Fen Farm
Duchy Farm
Mexican Bridge
Dovecot Farm
Corporation Farm
BELL WATER DRAIN BANK

58
SCARBOROUGH BANK
MIDVILLE LA

34 **A** 35 **B** 36 **C** 37 **D** 38 **E** 39 **F**

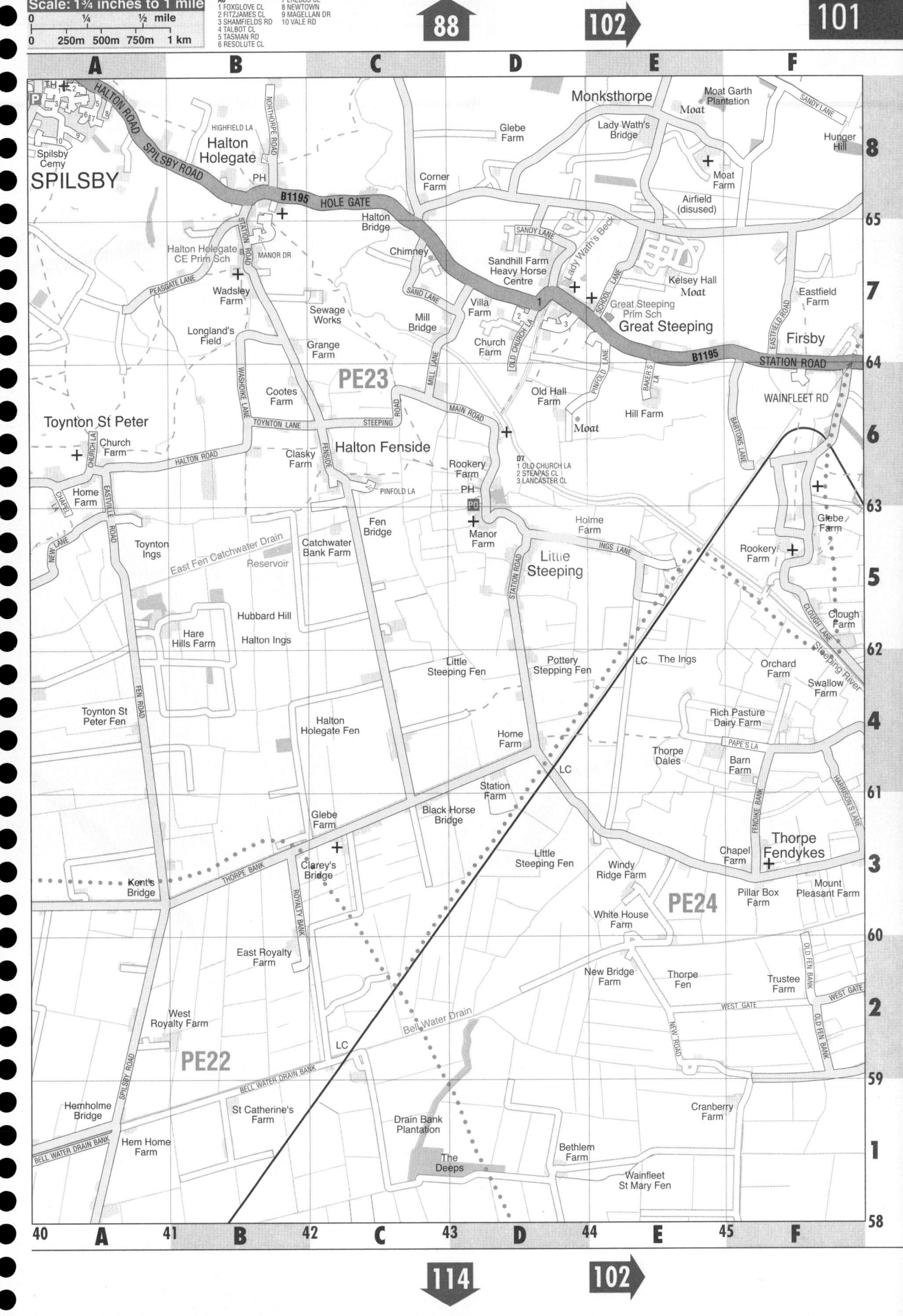
Scale: 1¾ inches to 1 mile
0 ¼ ½ mile
0 250m 500m 750m 1 km
A8
1 FOXGLOVE CL
2 FITZJAMES CL
3 SHAMFIELDS RD
4 TALBOT CL
5 TASMAN RD
6 RESOLUTE CL
7 EREBUS CL
8 NEWTOWN
9 MAGELLAN DR
10 VALE RD
88
102
SPILSBY
Spilsby Cemy
Halton Holegate
HALTON ROAD
SPILSBY ROAD
B1195
HOLE GATE
Monksthorpe
Moat Garth Plantation
Lady Wath's Bridge
Glebe Farm
Corner Farm
Moat Farm
Airfield (disused)
Hunger Hill
SANDY LANE
Halton Bridge
Chimney
Halton Holegate CE Prim Sch
Wadsley Farm
PEASGATE LANE
Sandhill Farm Heavy Horse Centre
Lady Wath's Beck
Kelsey Hall
Moat
Great Steeping Prim Sch
Great Steeping
Eastfield Farm
Firsby
STATION ROAD
Villa Farm
Mill Bridge
Sewage Works
Grange Farm
Longland's Field
Church Farm
PE23
Cootes Farm
Old Hall Farm
Hill Farm
WAINFLEET RD
Toynton St Peter
Church Farm
Clasky Farm
Halton Fenside
Rookery Farm
D7
1 OLD CHURCH LA
2 STEAPAS CL
3 LANCASTER CL
Home Farm
PINFOLD LA
Fen Bridge
Manor Farm
Holme Farm
Little Steeping
Glebe Farm
Rookery Farm
Toynton Ings
East Fen Catchwater Drain
Reservoir
Catchwater Bank Farm
Hubbard Hill
Hare Hills Farm
Halton Ings
Clough Farm
Steeping River
Little Steeping Fen
Pottery Stepping Fen
The Ings
Orchard Farm
Swallow Farm
Toynton St Peter Fen
Halton Holegate Fen
Home Farm
Rich Pasture Dairy Farm
Thorpe Dales
Barn Farm
Station Farm
Glebe Farm
Black Horse Bridge
Little Steeping Fen
Windy Ridge Farm
Chapel Farm
Thorpe Fendykes
Kent's Bridge
Clarey's Bridge
PE24
Pillar Box Farm
Mount Pleasant Farm
White House Farm
East Royalty Farm
New Bridge Farm
Thorpe Fen
Trustee Farm
West Royalty Farm
Bell Water Drain
PE22
BELL WATER DRAIN BANK
Hemholme Bridge
St Catherine's Farm
Drain Bank Plantation
Cranberry Farm
Hem Home Farm
The Deeps
Bethlem Farm
Wainfleet St Mary Fen
114
102

101
89

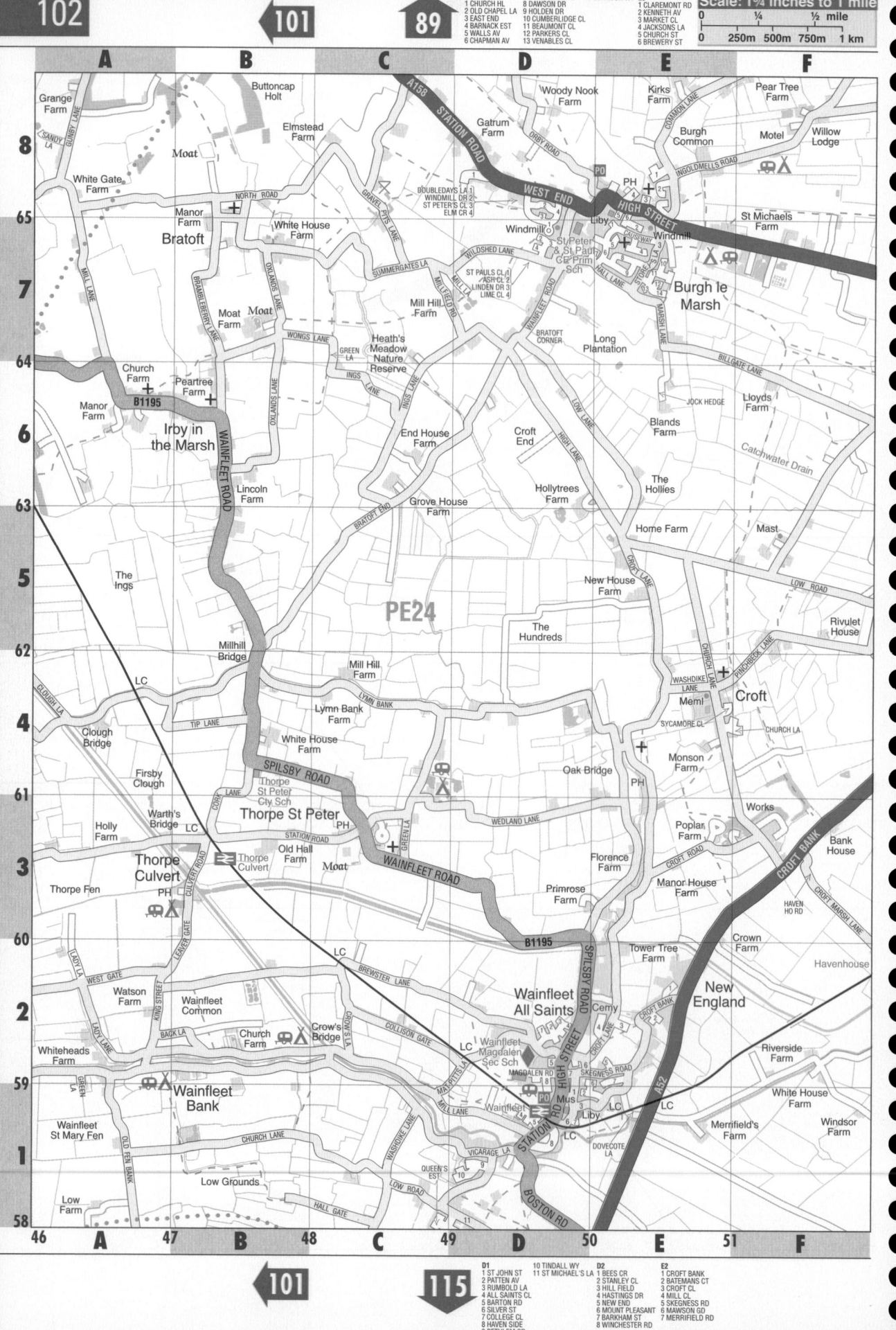
E7
1 CHURCH HL
2 OLD CHAPEL LA
3 EAST END
4 BARNACK EST
5 WALLS AV
6 CHAPMAN AV
7 THE PADDOCKS
8 DAWSON DR
9 HOLDEN DR
10 CUMBERLIDGE CL
11 BEAUMONT CL
12 PARKERS CL
13 VENABLES CL
14 JOHNSON WY
E8
1 CLAREMONT RD
2 KENNETH AV
3 MARKET CL
4 JACKSONS LA
5 CHURCH ST
6 BREWERY ST
Scale: 1¾ inches to 1 mile
0 ¼ ½ mile
0 250m 500m 750m 1 km
A B C D E F
Grange Farm
Buttoncap Holt
Woody Nook Farm
Kirks Farm
Pear Tree Farm
Elmstead Farm
Gatrum Farm
Burgh Common
Motel
Willow Lodge
White Gate Farm
Moat
NORTH ROAD
Manor Farm
Bratoft
White House Farm
STATION ROAD
WEST END
HIGH STREET
INGOLDMELLS ROAD
St Michaels Farm
Windmill
St Peter & St Paul CE Prim Sch
Burgh le Marsh
DOUBLEDAYS LA 1
WINDMILL DR 2
ST PETER'S CL 3
ELM CR 4
ST PAULS CL 1
ASH CL 2
LINDEN DR 3
LIME CL 4
Moat Farm
Mill Hill Farm
Heath's Meadow Nature Reserve
Long Plantation
BRATOFT CORNER
Church Farm
Peartree Farm
Manor Farm
B1195
Irby in the Marsh
WAINFLEET ROAD
End House Farm
Croft End
JOCK HEDGE
Lloyds Farm
Blands Farm
Catchwater Drain
Lincoln Farm
Grove House Farm
Hollytrees Farm
The Hollies
Home Farm
Mast
The Ings
PE24
New House Farm
The Hundreds
Rivulet House
Millhill Bridge
Mill Hill Farm
Croft
Lymn Bank Farm
White House Farm
Clough Bridge
Oak Bridge
Monson Farm
Firsby Clough
SPILSBY ROAD
Thorpe St Peter Cty Sch
Thorpe St Peter
Warth's Bridge
Holly Farm
Works
Poplar Farm
Bank House
Thorpe Culvert
Old Hall Farm
Florence Farm
Thorpe Fen
Manor House Farm
Primrose Farm
Crown Farm
Tower Tree Farm
Havenhouse
Watson Farm
Wainfleet Common
Wainfleet All Saints
New England
Church Farm
Crow's Bridge
Whiteheads Farm
Wainfleet Magdalen Sec Sch
Riverside Farm
Wainfleet Bank
White House Farm
Wainfleet St Mary Fen
Merrifield's Farm
Windsor Farm
Low Grounds
Low Farm
BOSTON RD
A52
46 47 48 49 50 51
D1
1 ST JOHN ST
2 PATTEN AV
3 RUMBOLD LA
4 ALL SAINTS CL
5 BARTON RD
6 SILVER ST
7 COLLEGE CL
8 HAVEN SIDE
9 BETHLEM CR
10 TINDALL WY
11 ST MICHAEL'S LA
D2
1 BEES CR
2 STANLEY CL
3 HILL FIELD
4 HASTINGS DR
5 NEW END
6 MOUNT PLEASANT
7 BARKHAM ST
8 WINCHESTER RD
E2
1 CROFT BANK
2 BATEMANS CT
3 CROFT CL
4 MILL CL
5 SKEGNESS RD
6 MAWSON GD
7 MERRIFIELD RD

101
115

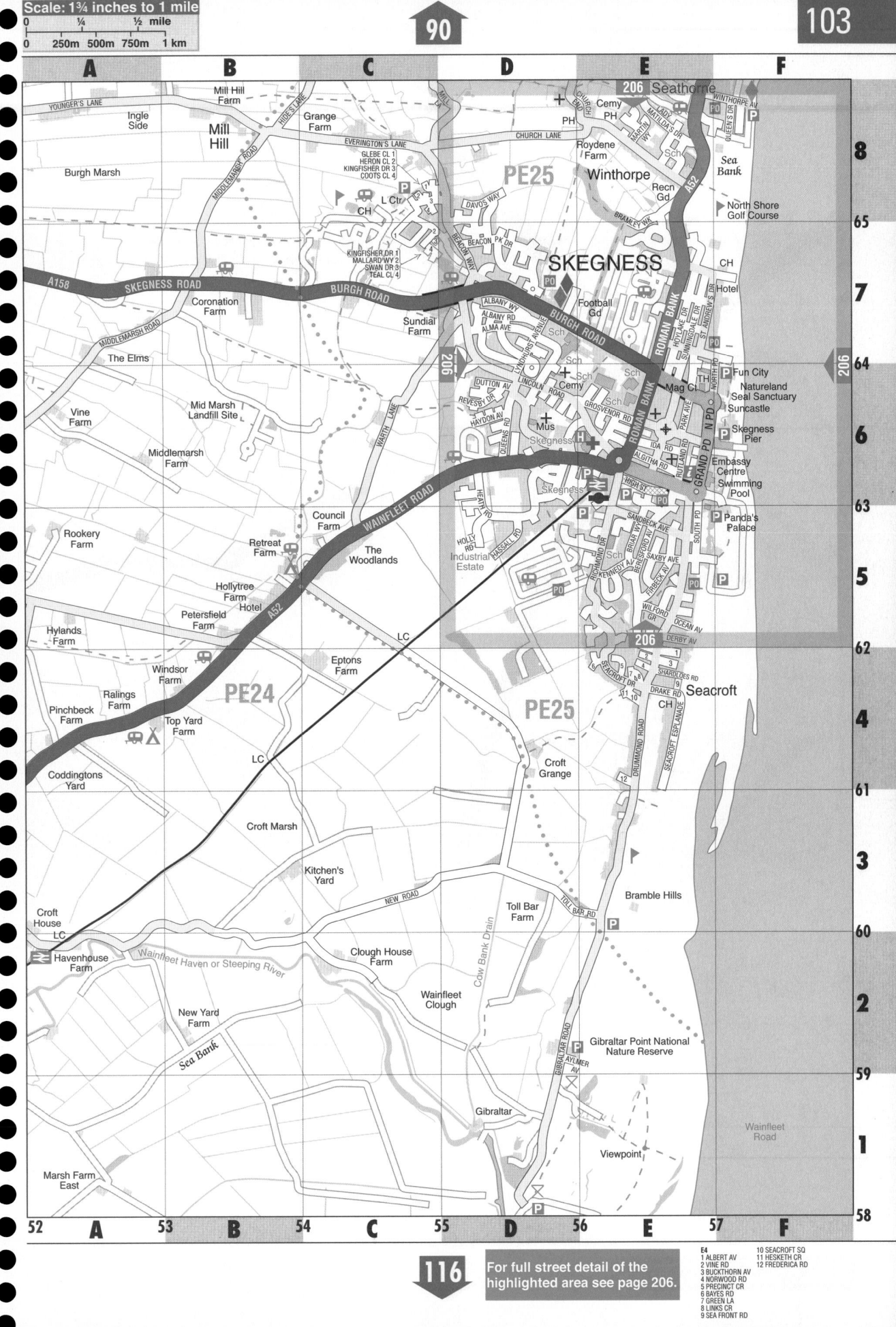

A   B   C   D   E   F

Younger's Lane
Mill Hill Farm
Ingle Side
Mill Hill
Burgh Marsh
HIDE'S LANE
Grange Farm
Everington's Lane
GLEBE CL 1
HERON DR 2
KINGFISHER DR 3
COOTS CL 4
MIDDLEMARSH ROAD
L Ctr
CH
Davos Way
PE25
Seathorne
206
Church End
Cemy
PH
Martin Wy
Lady Matilda's Dr
Sch
Queen's Dr
Winthorpe Av
Roydene Farm
Winthorpe
Recn Gd
Sea Bank
8
65

A158   SKEGNESS ROAD   BURGH ROAD
Coronation Farm
Sundial Farm
BEACON WAY
DAVOS WAY
BEACON PK DR
KINGFISHER DR 1
MALLARD WY 2
SWAN DR 3
TEAL CL 4
SKEGNESS
ALBANY WY
ALBANY RD
ALMA AVE
Football Gd
Sch
CH
Hotel
North Shore Golf Course
7
64
206

The Elms
MIDDLEMARSH ROAD
Vine Farm
Mid Marsh Landfill Site
Middlemarsh Farm
WARTH LANE
LYNDHURST AVENUE
DUTTON AV
206
Cemy
REVESBY DR
HAYDON AV
Mus
Skegness
LINCOLN ROAD
QUEENS RD
GROSVENOR ROAD
Sch
Sch
ROMAN BANK
HOYLAKE DR
SUMMINGDALE DR
ST ANDREWS DR
NORTH RD
Mag Ct
TH
Fun City
Natureland
Seal Sanctuary
Suncastle
Skegness Pier
PARK AVE
GRAND PDE
N PDE
6
64
206 Fun City

Rookery Farm
Council Farm
WAINFLEET ROAD
The Woodlands
Retreat Farm
HEATH RD
HOLLY RD
MASSALL RD
Industrial Estate
Skegness
RICHMOND DR
KENNEDY
BRIAR WY
SANDBECK AVE
BERESFORD AV
SAXBY AVE
SOUTH PD
IDA
ALGITHA RD
RUTLAND RD
RICHMOND DR
DERBY RD
Embassy Centre
Swimming Pool
Panda's Palace
63
5

Hollytree Farm Hotel
Petersfield Farm
A52
LC
Eptons Farm
WILFORD GR
OCEAN AV
206
Sch
1
3
SHARDLOES RD
DRAKE RD
SEACROFT DR
Seacroft
62

Hylands Farm
Windsor Farm
PE24
Pinchbeck Farm
Ralings Farm
Top Yard Farm
Croft Marsh
PE25
DRUMMOND ROAD
SEACROFT ESPLANADE
Croft Grange
12
CH
4

Coddingtons Yard
LC
Kitchen's Yard
NEW ROAD
Bramble Hills
3
61

Croft House
LC
Havenhouse Farm
Wainfleet Haven or Steeping River
Clough House Farm
Cow Bank Drain
Toll Bar Farm
TOLL BAR RD
60

New Yard Farm
Wainfleet Clough
GIBRALTAR ROAD
Gibraltar Point National Nature Reserve
AYLMER AV
2

Sea Bank
Gibraltar
59

Marsh Farm East
Viewpoint
Wainfleet Road
1
58

52   A   53   B   54   C   55   D   56   E   57   F

For full street detail of the highlighted area see page 206.

E4
1 ALBERT AV
2 VINE RD
3 BUCKTHORN AV
4 NORWOOD RD
5 PRECINCT CR
6 BAYES RD
7 GREEN LA
8 LINKS CR
9 SEA FRONT RD
10 SEACROFT SQ
11 HESKETH CR
12 FREDERICA RD

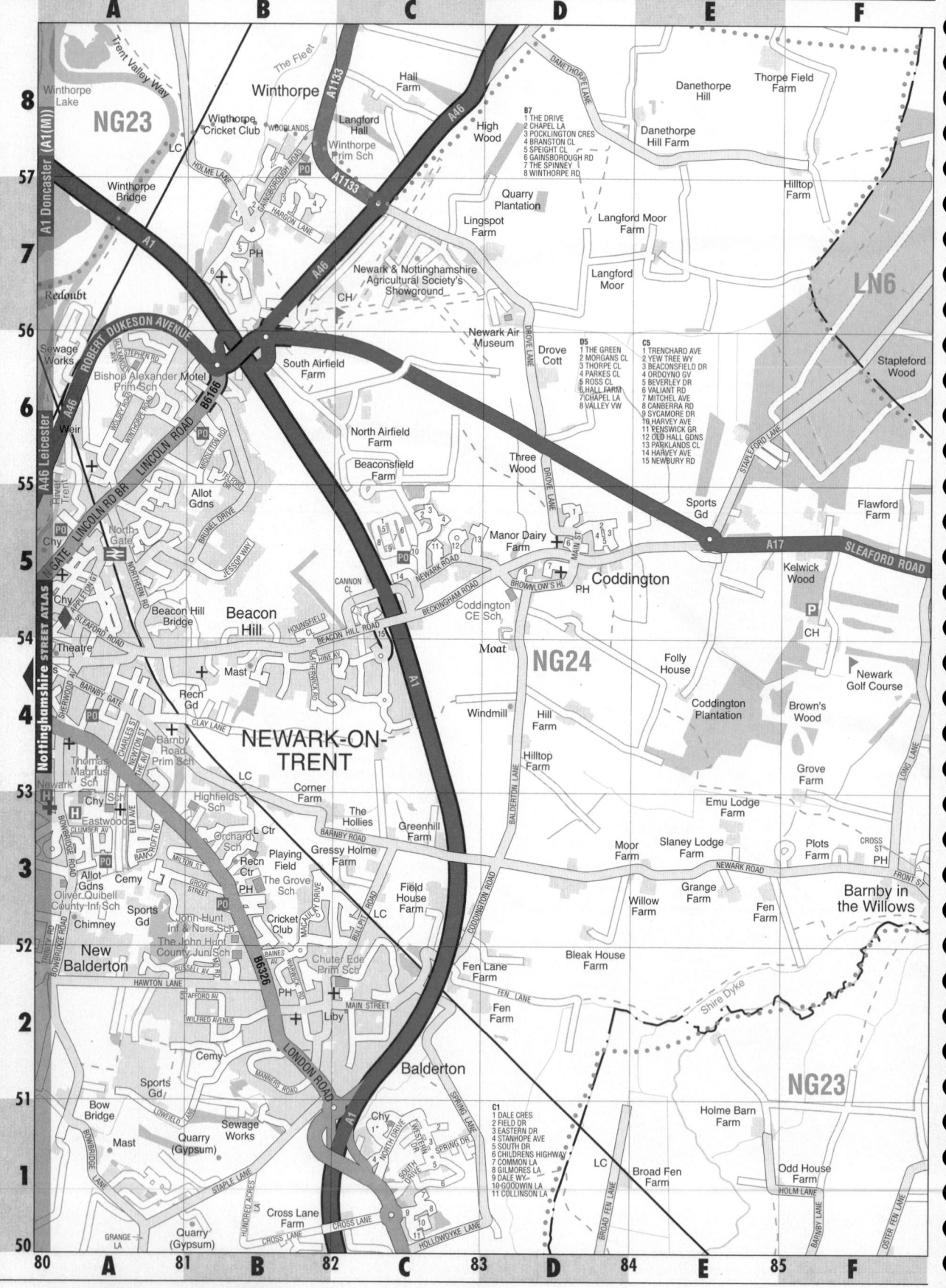

For full street detail of Newark see Philip's
STREET ATLAS of **Nottinghamshire**

Scale: 1¾ inches to 1 mile

92
106

E8
1 WHEATLEY LA
2 MANOR CT
3 VICARAGE LA
4 CHURCH ST
5 MANOR LA
6 CHURCH LA
7 SKAYMAN FLDS
8 MOORLAND CL

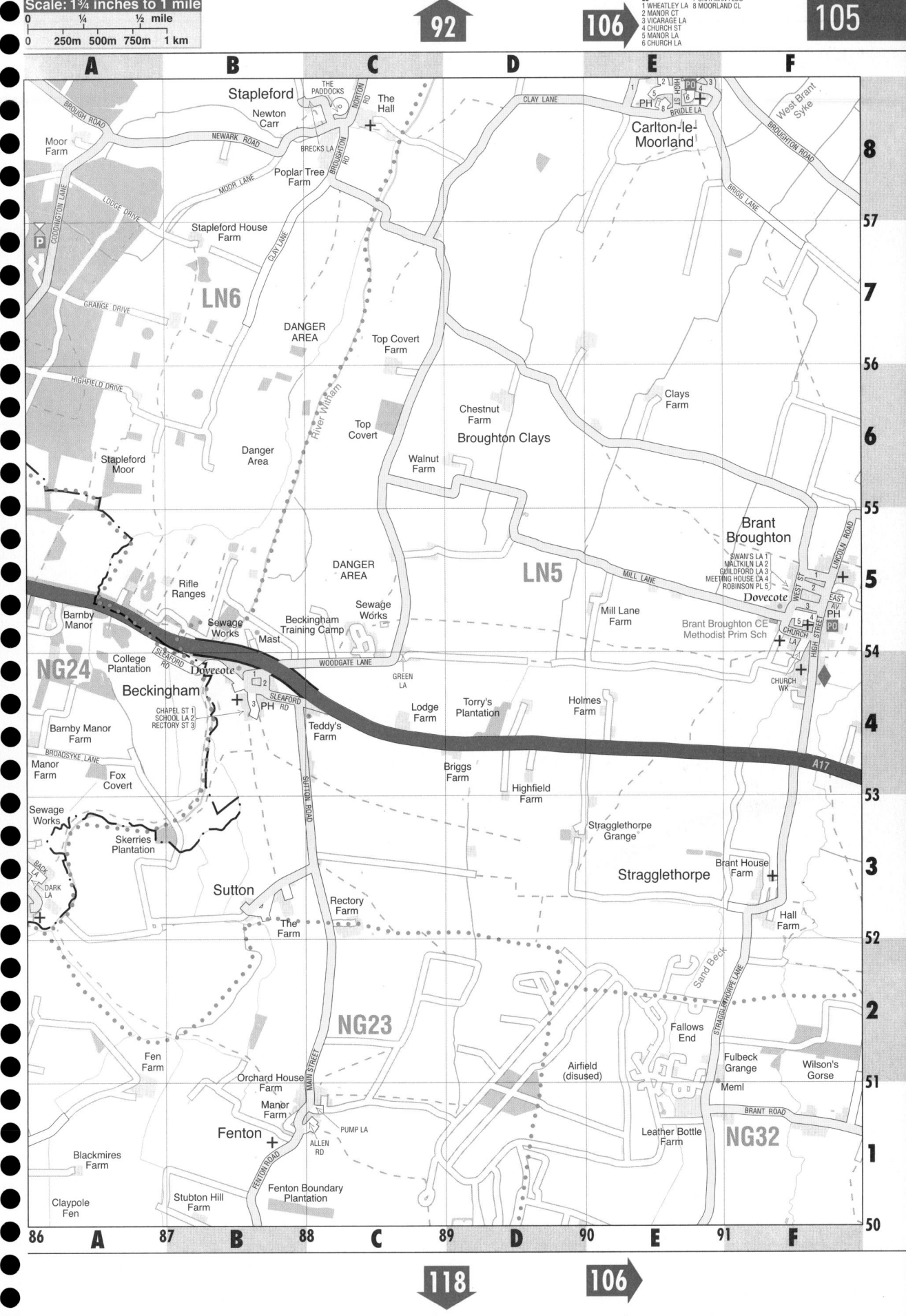

118
106

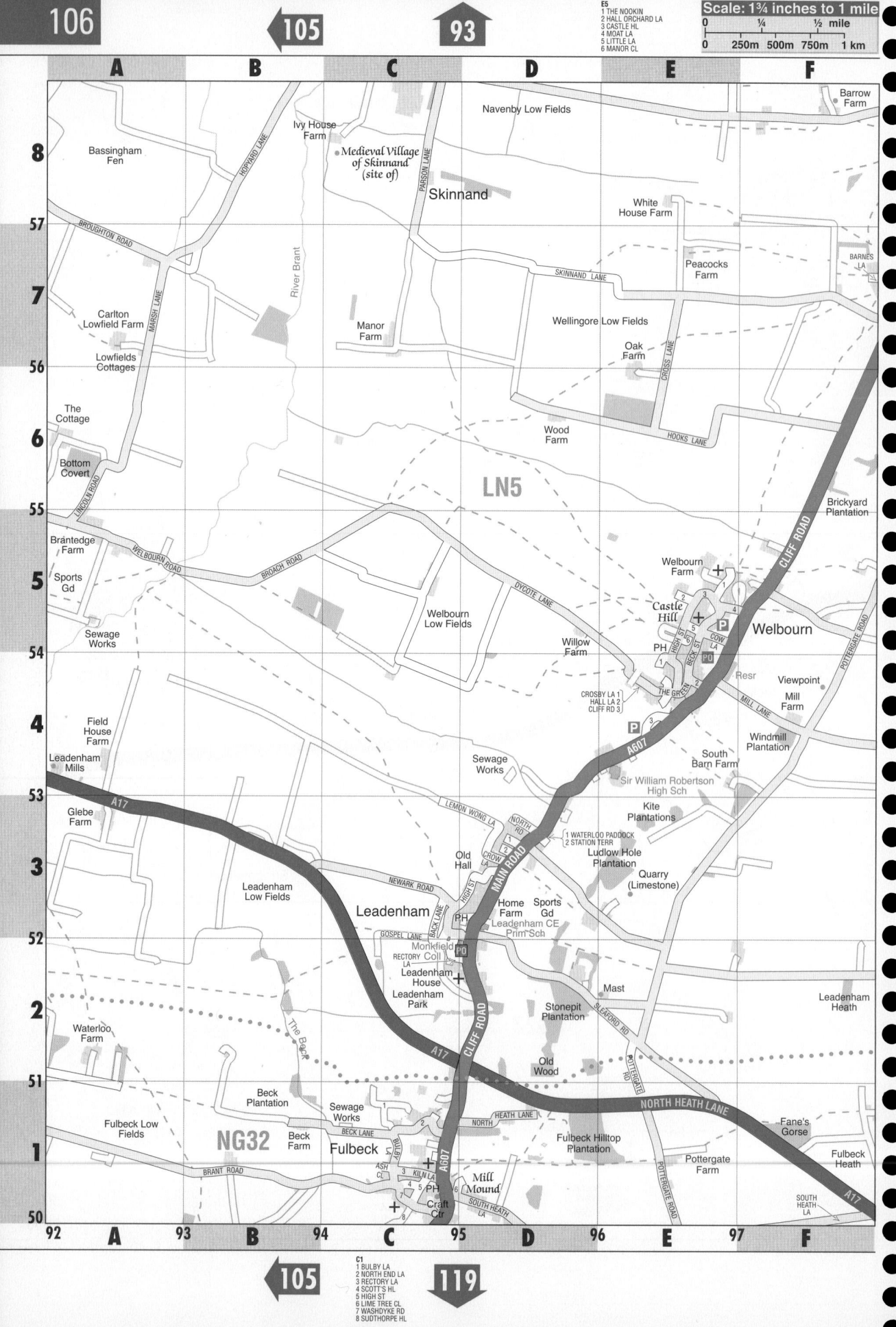

105
93

E5
1 THE NOOKIN
2 HALL ORCHARD LA
3 CASTLE HL
4 MOAT LA
5 LITTLE LA
6 MANOR CL

Scale: 1¾ inches to 1 mile

0   ¼   ½   mile
0   250m   500m   750m   1 km

A   B   C   D   E   F

Barrow Farm

8   Bassingham Fen   Ivy House Farm   Medieval Village of Skinnand (site of)   Navenby Low Fields

Skinnand   White House Farm   BARNES LA

57   BROUGHTON ROAD   Peacocks Farm

7   Carlton Lowfield Farm   River Brant   Manor Farm   SKINNAND LANE   Wellingore Low Fields

MARSH LANE   PARSON LANE   CROSS LANE   HOOKYARD LANE

56   Lowfields Cottages   Oak Farm

The Cottage   Wood Farm

6   Bottom Covert   LINCOLN ROAD   HOOKS LANE   Brickyard Plantation

55   Brantedge Farm   WELBOURN ROAD   BROACH ROAD   LN5   CLIFF ROAD

5   Sports Gd   DYCOTE LANE   Welbourn Farm   Welbourn

Sewage Works   Welbourn Low Fields   Willow Farm   Castle Hill   P   PO   POTTERGATE ROAD

54   PH   COW LA   Resr   Viewpoint   Mill Farm

CROSBY LA 1   MILL LANE   HALL LA 2   THE GREEN   CLIFF RD 3   Windmill Plantation

4   Field House Farm   Sewage Works   P   A607   South Barn Farm

Leadenham Mills   LEMON WONG LA   Sir William Robertson High Sch   Kite Plantations

53   A17   Glebe Farm   NORTH RD   1 WATERLOO PADDOCK   2 STATION TERR   Quarry (Limestone)

3   Leadenham Low Fields   Old Hall   CROW LA   MAIN ROAD   Ludlow Hole Plantation

NEWARK ROAD   BACK LANE   HIGH ST   Home Farm   Sports Gd   Mast

Leadenham   PH   Leadenham CE Prim Sch

52   GOSPEL LANE   Monkfield   PO   Stonepit Plantation   Leadenham Heath

RECTORY   Coll   LA   Leadenham House

2   Waterloo Farm   The Back   Leadenham Park   Old Wood   PH

CLIFF ROAD   SLEAFORD RD

51   A17   NORTH HEATH LANE

Beck Plantation   Sewage Works   HEATH LANE   Fane's Gorse

1   Fulbeck Low Fields   NG32   Beck Farm   BECK LANE   NORTH   Fulbeck Hilltop Plantation   Pottergate Farm   Fulbeck Heath

Fulbeck   A607   POTTERGATE ROAD   A17

BRANT ROAD   ASH CL   KILN LA   Mill Mound   SOUTH HEATH LA   SOUTH HEATH LA

50   PH   Craft Ctr

92   93   94   95   96   97

A   B   C   D   E   F

105
119

C1
1 BULBY LA
2 NORTH END LA
3 RECTORY LA
4 SCOTT'S HL
5 HIGH ST
6 LIME TREE CL
7 WASHDYKE RD
8 SUDTHORPE HL

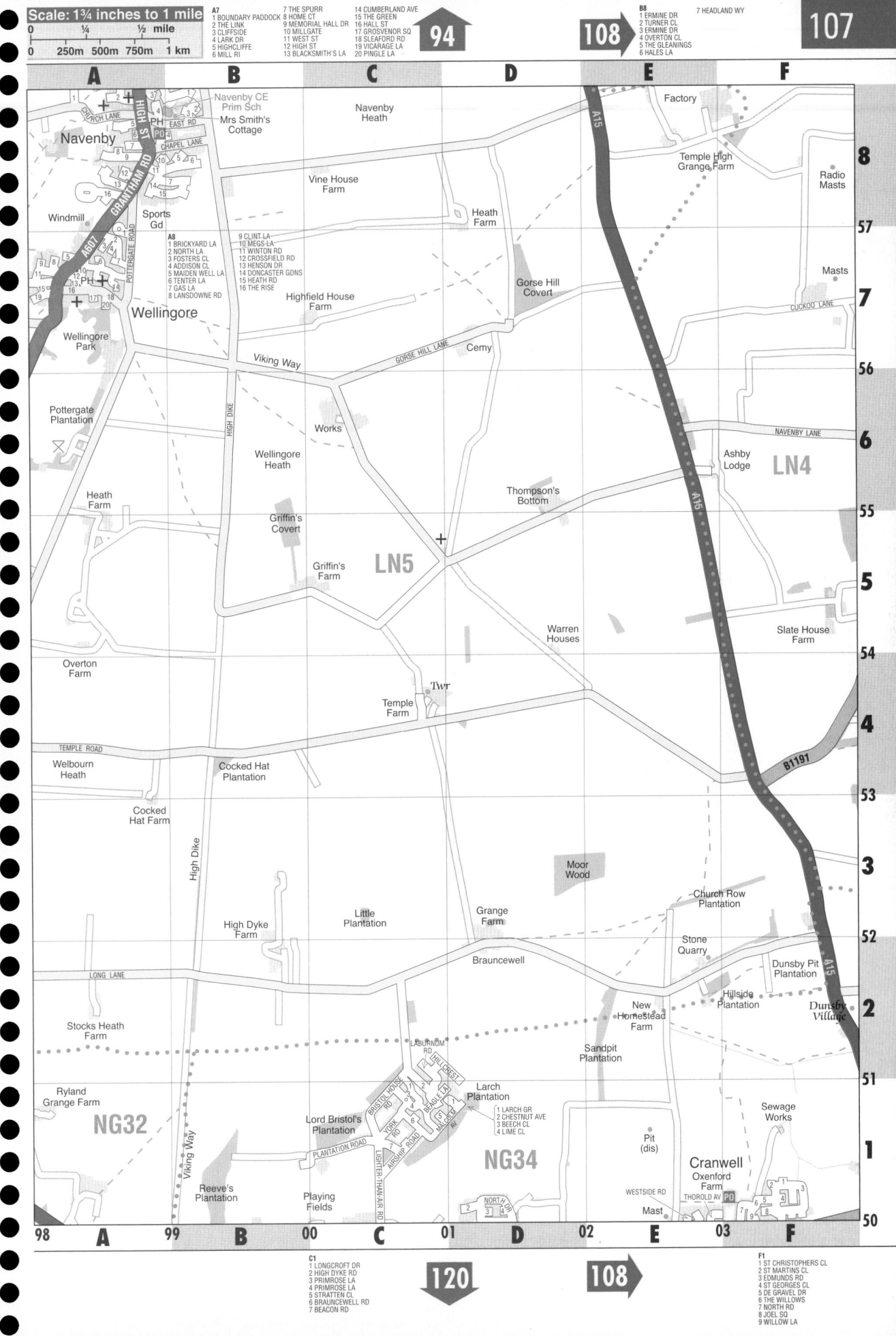

Scale: 1¾ inches to 1 mile

0   ¼   ½ mile
0 250m 500m 750m 1 km

A7
1 BOUNDARY PADDOCK
2 THE LINK
3 CLIFFSIDE
4 LARK DR
5 HIGHCLIFFE
6 MILL RI

7 THE SPUR
8 HOME CT
9 MEMORIAL HALL DR
10 MILLGATE
11 WEST ST
12 HIGH ST
13 BLACKSMITH'S LA

14 CUMBERLAND AVE
15 THE GREEN
16 HALL ST
17 GROSVENOR SQ
18 SLEAFORD RD
19 VICARAGE LA
20 PINGLE LA

94

108

B8
1 ERMINE DR
2 TURNER CL
3 ERMINE DR
4 OVERTON CL
5 THE GLEANINGS
6 HALES LA

7 HEADLAND WY

107

Navenby CE Prim Sch
Mrs Smith's Cottage

Navenby Heath

Factory

Temple High Grange Farm

Radio Masts

8

Navenby

PH
PO
EAST RD
CHAPEL LANE

Vine House Farm

Heath Farm

57

Windmill

Sports Gd

A8
1 BRICKYARD LA
2 NORTH LA
3 FOSTERS CL
4 ADDISON CL
5 MAIDEN WELL LA
6 TENTER LA
7 GAS LA
8 LANSDOWNE RD

9 CLINT LA
10 MEGS LA
11 WINTON RD
12 CROSSFIELD RD
13 HENSON DR
14 DONCASTER GDNS
15 HEATH RD
16 THE RISE

Gorse Hill Covert

Masts

7

Wellingore

Highfield House Farm

Ashby Lodge

LN4

Wellingore Park

Viking Way

Gorse Hill Lane

Cemy

CUCKOO LANE

56

NAVENBY LANE

Pottergate Plantation

Works

Wellingore Heath

Thompson's Bottom

A15

6

Heath Farm

Griffin's Covert

LN5

55

Griffin's Farm

Warren Houses

Slate House Farm

5

Overton Farm

54

Twr

Temple Farm

B1191

4

TEMPLE ROAD

Welbourn Heath

Cocked Hat Plantation

53

Cocked Hat Farm

Moor Wood

3

HIGH DIKE

Church Row Plantation

Stone Quarry

52

High Dyke Farm

Little Plantation

Grange Farm

Dunsby Pit Plantation

A15

LONG LANE

Brauncewell

New Homestead Farm

Hillside Plantation

Dunsby Village

2

Stocks Heath Farm

Sandpit Plantation

51

Ryland Grange Farm

NG32

LABURNUM RD
HILLCREST

Larch Plantation

Sewage Works

1

Lord Bristol's Plantation

(Larch box)
1 LARCH GR
2 CHESTNUT AVE
3 BEECH CL
4 LIME CL

NG34

Pit (dis)

Cranwell Oxenford Farm
THOROLD AV PO

Viking Way

PLANTATION ROAD

Reeve's Plantation

Playing Fields

WESTSIDE RD

Mast

50

C1
1 LONGCROFT DR
2 HIGH DYKE RD
3 PRIMROSE LA
4 PRIMROSE LA
5 STRATTEN CL
6 BRAUNCEWELL RD
7 BEACON RD

F1
1 ST CHRISTOPHERS CL
2 ST MARTINS CL
3 EDMUNDS RD
4 ST GEORGES CL
5 DE GRAVEL DR
6 THE WILLOWS
7 NORTH RD
8 JOEL SQ
9 WILLOW LA

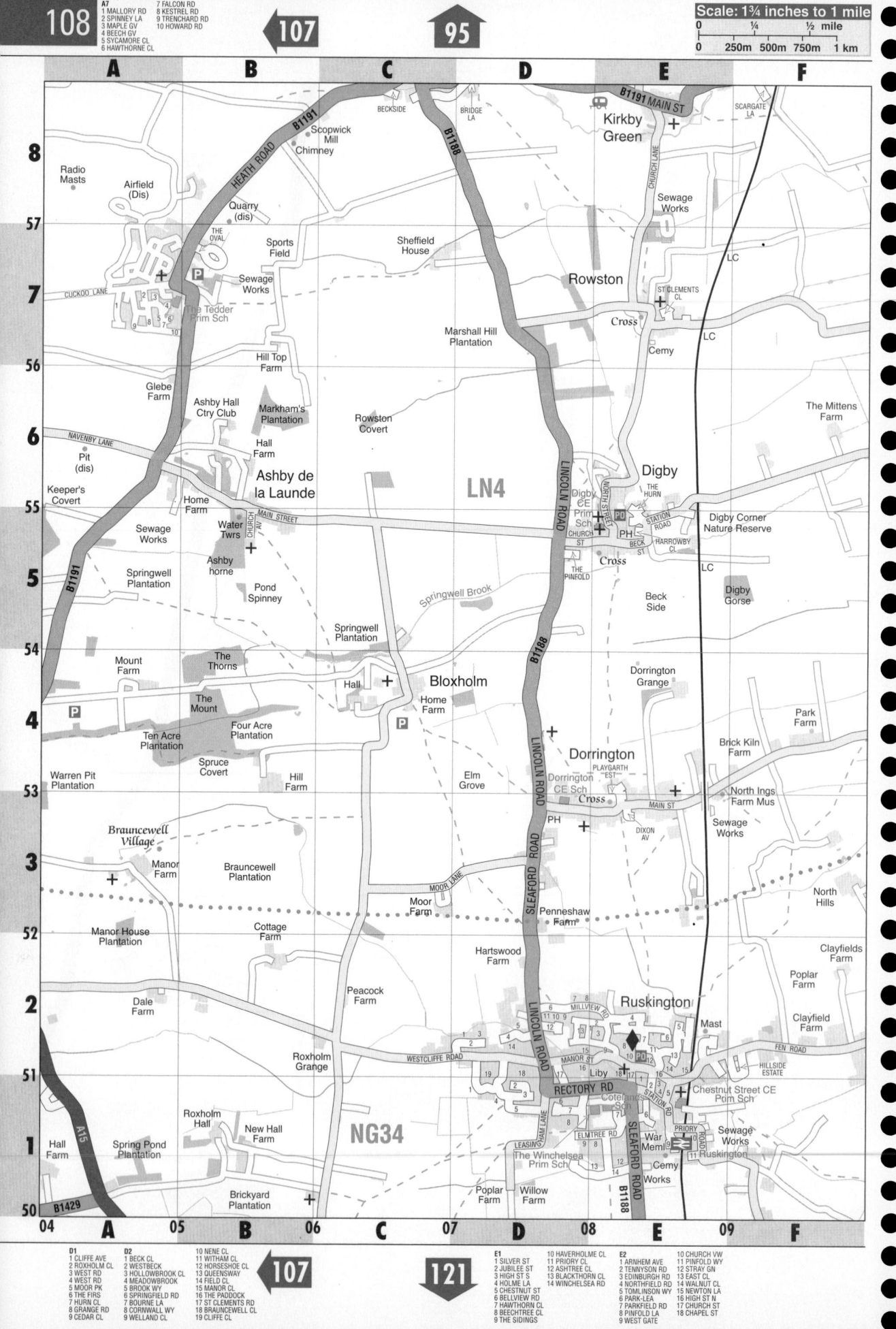
A7
1 MALLORY RD
2 SPINNEY LA
3 MAPLE GV
4 BEECH GV
5 SYCAMORE CL
6 HAWTHORNE CL
7 FALCON RD
8 KESTREL RD
9 TRENCHARD RD
10 HOWARD RD
107
95
Scale: 1¾ inches to 1 mile
0 ¼ ½ mile
0 250m 500m 750m 1 km
A B C D E F
8 57 7 56 6 55 5 54 4 53 3 52 2 51 1 50
BECKSIDE
BRIDGE LA
B1191 MAIN ST
Kirkby Green
SCARGATE LA
B1191
HEATH ROAD
Scopwick Mill
Chimney
B1188
CHURCH LANE
Radio Masts
Airfield (Dis)
Quarry (dis)
THE OVAL
Sports Field
Sheffield House
Sewage Works
LC
CUCKOO LANE
Sewage Works
The Tedder Prim Sch
Rowston
ST CLEMENTS CL
Cross
Marshall Hill Plantation
Cemy
LC
Hill Top Farm
Glebe Farm
Ashby Hall Ctry Club
Markham's Plantation
Rowston Covert
The Mittens Farm
NAVENBY LANE
Hall Farm
Pit (dis)
Ashby de la Launde
LN4
LINCOLN ROAD
NORTH STREET
Digby
THE HURN
Keeper's Covert
Home Farm
MAIN STREET
Digby CE Prim Sch
PO
STATION ROAD
Digby Corner Nature Reserve
Water Twrs
CHURCH AV
CHURCH ST
PH
BECK ST
HARROWBY CL
Sewage Works
Ashby horne
THE PINFOLD
Cross
LC
Springwell Plantation
Pond Spinney
Beck Side
Digby Gorse
Springwell Brook
B1191
Springwell Plantation
B1188
Mount Farm
The Thorns
Hall
Bloxholm
Dorrington Grange
Home Farm
The Mount
P
Park Farm
Four Acre Plantation
Ten Acre Plantation
Brick Kiln Farm
Dorrington
Spruce Covert
PLAYGARTH EST
Warren Pit Plantation
Hill Farm
Elm Grove
Dorrington CE Sch
North Ings Farm Mus
Cross
MAIN ST
PH
DIXON AV
Sewage Works
Braucewell Village
Manor Farm
Brauncewell Plantation
MOOR LANE
SLEAFORD ROAD
North Hills
Moor Farm
Penneshaw Farm
Manor House Plantation
Cottage Farm
Clayfields Farm
Hartswood Farm
Poplar Farm
Peacock Farm
Ruskington
MILLVIEW RD
Dale Farm
Mast
Clayfield Farm
Roxholm Grange
WESTCLIFFE ROAD
MANOR ST
Liby
PO
FEN ROAD
HILLSIDE ESTATE
RECTORY RD
STATION RD
Chestnut Street CE Prim Sch
Cotelands Sch
Roxholm Hall
New Hall Farm
NG34
LEASINGHAM LANE
ELMTREE RD
War Meml
PRIORY RD
Sewage Works
Ruskington
Hall Farm
Spring Pond Plantation
A15
The Winchelsea Prim Sch
Cemy
Works
Poplar Farm
Willow Farm
B1188
B1429
Brickyard Plantation
04 A 05 B 06 C 07 D 08 E 09 F
D1
1 CLIFFE AVE
2 ROXHOLM CL
3 WEST RD
4 WEST RD
5 MOOR PK
6 THE FIRS
7 HURN CL
8 GRANGE RD
9 CEDAR CL
D2
1 BECK CL
2 WESTBECK
3 HOLLOWBROOK CL
4 MEADOWBROOK
5 BROOK WY
6 SPRINGFIELD RD
7 BOURNE LA
8 CORNWALL WY
9 WELLAND CL
10 NENE CL
11 WITHAM CL
12 HORSESHOE CL
13 QUEENSWAY
14 FIELD CL
15 MANOR CL
16 THE PADDOCK
17 ST CLEMENTS RD
18 BRAUNCEWELL CL
19 CLIFFE CL
107
121
E1
1 SILVER ST
2 JUBILEE ST
3 HIGH ST S
4 HOLME LA
5 CHESTNUT ST
6 BELLVIEW RD
7 HAWTHORN CL
8 BEECHTREE CL
9 THE SIDINGS
10 HAVERHOLME CL
11 PRIORY CL
12 ASHTREE CL
13 BLACKTHORN CL
14 WINCHELSEA RD
E2
1 ARNHEM AVE
2 TENNYSON RD
3 EDINBURGH RD
4 NORTHFIELD RD
5 TOMLINSON WY
6 PARK-LEA
7 PARKFIELD RD
8 PINFOLD LA
9 WEST GATE
10 CHURCH VW
11 PINFOLD WY
12 STRAY GN
13 EAST CL
14 WALNUT CL
15 NEWTON LA
16 HIGH ST N
17 CHURCH ST
18 CHAPEL ST

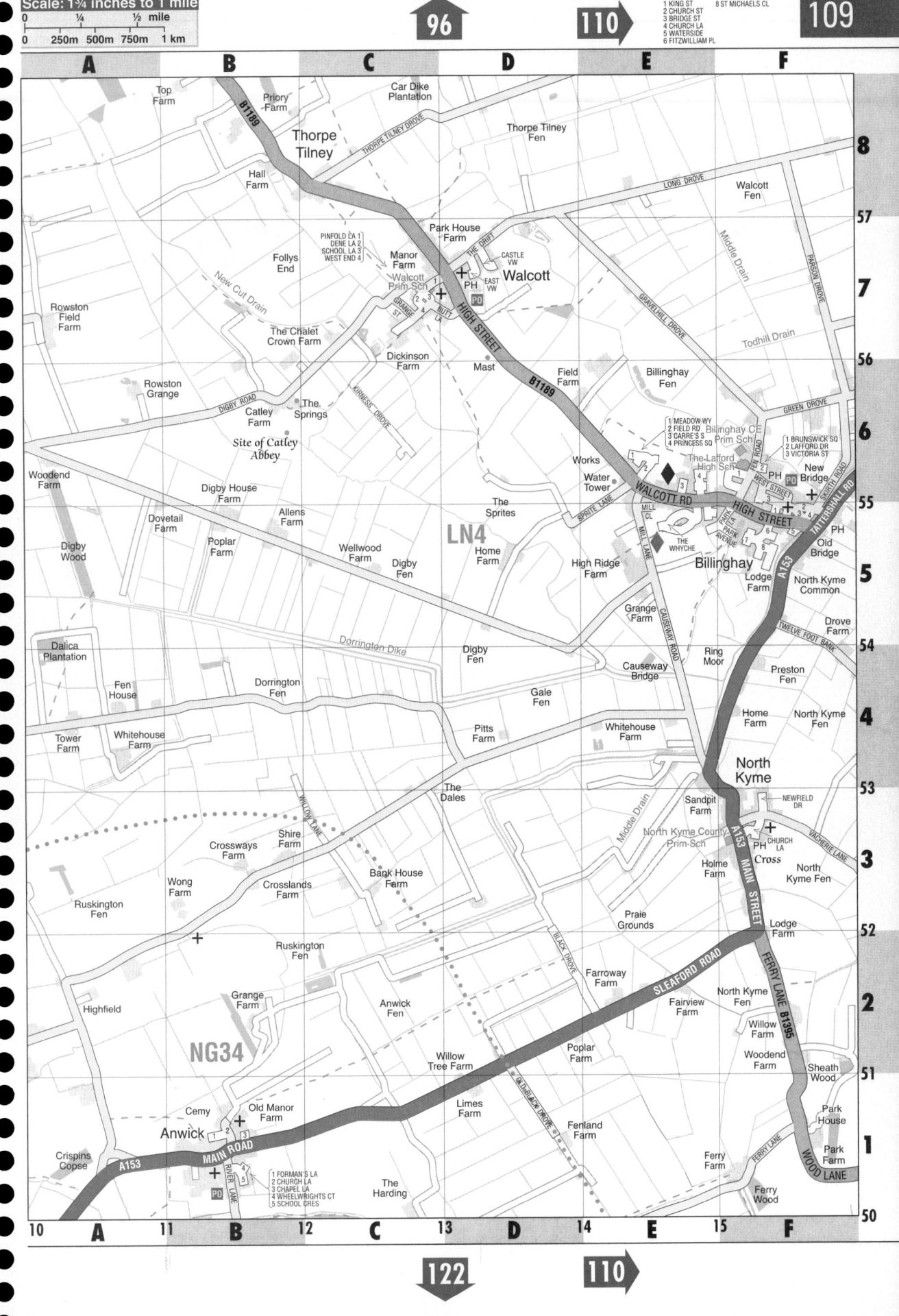
Scale: 1¾ inches to 1 mile
0 ¼ ½ mile
0 250m 500m 750m 1 km
96
110
F5
1 KING ST
2 CHURCH ST
3 BRIDGE ST
4 CHURCH LA
5 WATERSIDE
6 FITZWILLIAM PL
7 RING MOOR CL
8 ST MICHAELS CL
Top Farm
Priory Farm
Car Dike Plantation
Thorpe Tilney
THORPE TILNEY DROVE
Thorpe Tilney Fen
B1189
Hall Farm
LONG DROVE
Walcott Fen
Park House Farm
PINFOLD LA 1
DENE LA 2
SCHOOL LA 3
WEST END 4
Follys End
Manor Farm
THE DRIFT
CASTLE VW
EAST VW
Walcott
Walcott Prim Sch
PH
PO
HIGH STREET
GRANGE ST
BUTT LA
New Cut Drain
Rowston Field Farm
The Chalet Crown Farm
GRAVELHILL DROVE
Middle Drain
PARSON DROVE
Todhill Drain
Dickinson Farm
Mast
Rowston Grange
KIRKNESS DROVE
Field Farm
Billinghay Fen
DIGBY ROAD
Catley Farm
The Springs
Site of Catley Abbey
1 MEADOW WY
2 FIELD RD
3 CARRE'S S
4 PRINCESS SQ
Billinghay CE Prim Sch
GREEN DROVE
1 BRUNSWICK SQ
2 LAFFORD DR
3 VICTORIA ST
The Lafford High Sch
FEN ROAD
Works
Water Tower
WEST STREET
New Bridge
SKIRTH ROAD
Woodend Farm
Digby House Farm
The Sprites
WALCOTT RD
HIGH STREET
TATTERSHALL RD
SPRITE LANE
MILL CL
Dovetail Farm
Allens Farm
LN4
MILL LANE
THE WHYCHE
PARK LA
PARK AVENUE
Old Bridge
Digby Wood
Poplar Farm
Wellwood Farm
Digby Fen
Home Farm
High Ridge Farm
Billinghay
Lodge Farm
A153
North Kyme Common
Grange Farm
CAUSEWAY ROAD
Drove Farm
TWELVE FOOT BANK
Dalica Plantation
Dorrington Dike
Digby Fen
Ring Moor
Causeway Bridge
Preston Fen
Fen House
Dorrington Fen
Gale Fen
Home Farm
North Kyme Fen
Tower Farm
Whitehouse Farm
Pitts Farm
Whitehouse Farm
North Kyme
The Dales
Sandpit Farm
NEWFIELD DR
WILLOW LANE
Middle Drain
North Kyme County Prim Sch
CHURCH LA
VACHERIE LANE
Shire Farm
Crossways Farm
PH
Cross
Bank House Farm
Holme Farm
North Kyme Fen
Wong Farm
Crosslands Farm
MAIN STREET
Ruskington Fen
Praie Grounds
Lodge Farm
BLACK DROVE
Ruskington Fen
SLEAFORD ROAD
Farroway Farm
Grange Farm
Anwick Fen
North Kyme Fen
Fairview Farm
Highfield
FERRY LANE B1395
Willow Farm
NG34
Poplar Farm
Woodend Farm
Willow Tree Farm
Sheath Wood
Limes Farm
OLD BLACK DROVE
Cemy
Old Manor Farm
Park House
Anwick
Fenland Farm
MAIN ROAD
Crispins Copse
FERRY LANE
Ferry Farm
Park Farm
WOOD LANE
RIVER LANE
1 FORMAN'S LA
2 CHURCH LA
3 CHAPEL LA
4 WHEELWRIGHTS CT
5 SCHOOL CRES
The Harding
Ferry Wood
A B C D E F
8 7 6 5 4 3 2 1
57 56 55 54 53 52 51 50
10 11 12 13 14 15
122
110

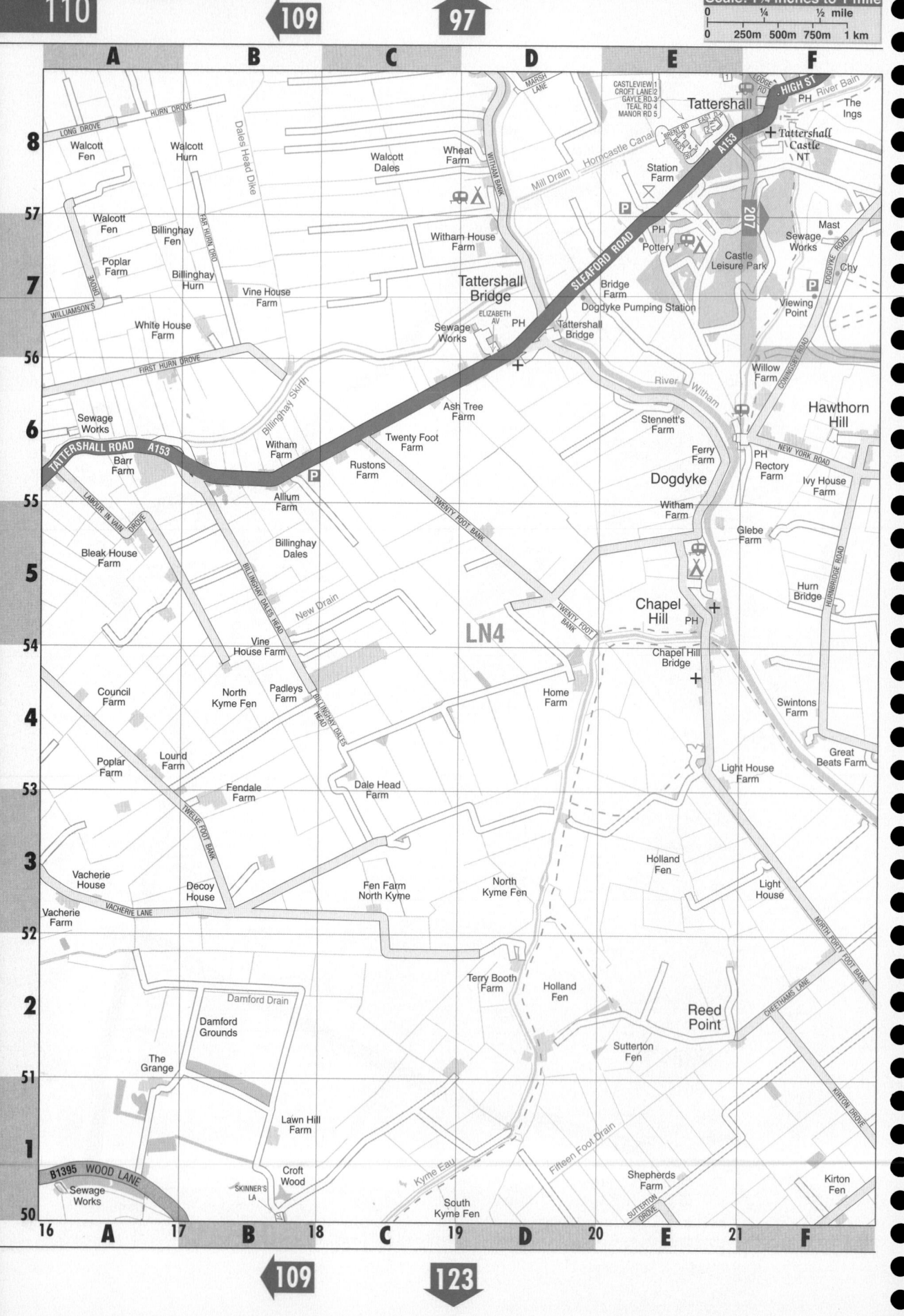

A   B   C   D   E   F

8

57

7

56

6

55

5

54

4

53

3

2

51

1

50

16   A   17   B   18   C   19   D   20   E   21   F

LONG DROVE

HURN DROVE

Walcott Fen

Walcott Hurn

Dales Head Dike

Walcott Dales

Wheat Farm

MARSH LANE

Tattershall

CASTLEVIEW 1
CROFT LANE 2
GAYLE RD 3
TEAL RD 4
MANOR RD 5

LODGE RD

HIGH ST

River Bain

The Ings

Walcott Fen

Billinghay Fen

FAR HURN DROD

Witham House Farm

WITHAM BANK

Mill Drain

Horncastle Canal

BRENT RD

EAST RD

A153

Tattershall Castle NT

Poplar Farm

Billinghay Hurn

Vine House Farm

Station Farm

P

SLEAFORD ROAD

PH

207

Mast

Sewage Works

WILLIAMSON'S

White House Farm

Tattershall Bridge

ELIZABETH AV

PH

Pottery

Castle Leisure Park

DOGDYKE ROAD

Chy

FIRST HURN DROVE

Sewage Works

Bridge Farm

Dogdyke Pumping Station

P

Viewing Point

Billinghay Skirth

Witham Farm

Tattershall Bridge

River   Witham

Willow Farm

CORNWALL ROAD

Hawthorn Hill

TATTERSHALL ROAD   A153

Barr Farm

Allium Farm

P

Ash Tree Farm

Twenty Foot Farm

Rustons Farm

Stennett's Farm

Ferry Farm

PH

Rectory Farm

NEW YORK ROAD

Ivy House Farm

LABOUR IN VAIN DROVE

Bleak House Farm

Billinghay Dales

BILLINGHAY DALES HEAD

New Drain

Dogdyke

Witham Farm

Glebe Farm

Hurn Bridge

HURNBRIDGE ROAD

Council Farm

North Kyme Fen

Vine House Farm

Padleys Farm

TWENTY FOOT BANK

LN4

Home Farm

Chapel Hill

TWENTY FOOT BANK

PH

Chapel Hill Bridge

Swintons Farm

Poplar Farm

Lound Farm

Fendale Farm

TWELVE FOOT BANK

Dale Head Farm

Light House Farm

Great Beats Farm

Vacherie House

Decoy House

VACHERIE LANE

Fen Farm North Kyme

North Kyme Fen

Holland Fen

Light House

NORTH FORTY FOOT BANK

Vacherie Farm

Damford Drain

Damford Grounds

Terry Booth Farm

Holland Fen

Reed Point

CHEETHAMS LANE

KIRTON DROVE

The Grange

Sutterton Fen

Lawn Hill Farm

B1395   WOOD LANE

Sewage Works

SKINNER'S LA

Croft Wood

Kyme Eau

Fifteen Foot Drain

South Kyme Fen

SUTTERTON DROVE

Shepherds Farm

Kirton Fen

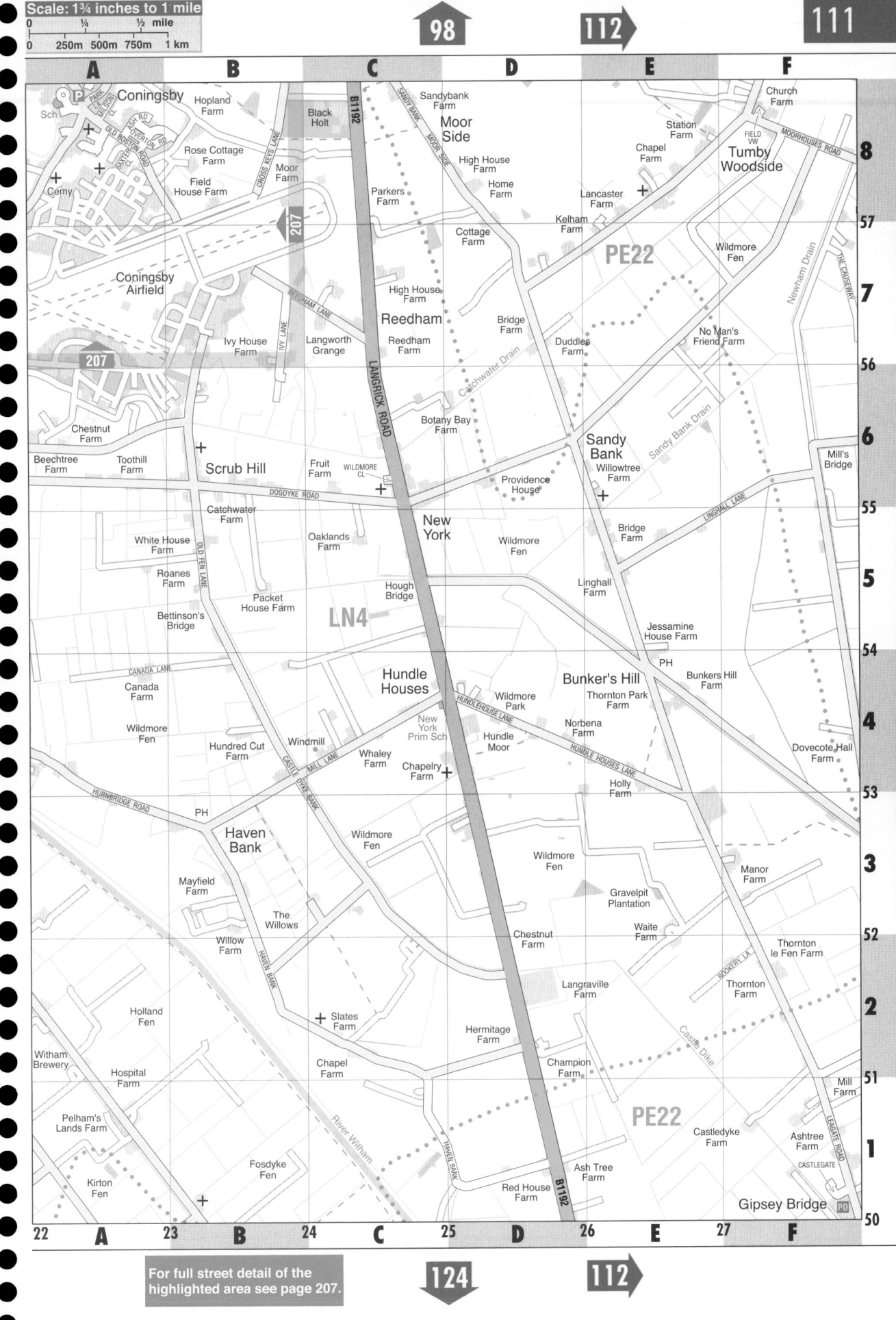

Scale: 1¾ inches to 1 mile

0   ¼   ½   mile
0 250m 500m 750m 1 km

A   B   C   D   E   F

Coningsby

P
PARK
LA
MH SCH
SCH RD
OLD BOSTON ROAD
BAXTER LA
OVERTON RD
CROSS KEYS LANE

Sch

Hopland Farm

Rose Cottage Farm

Field House Farm

Moor Farm

Cemy

B1192

Black Holt

Sandybank Farm

Moor Side

SANDY BANK

MOOR SIDE

Station Farm

FIELD VW

Church Farm

MOORHOUSES ROAD

8

Parkers Farm

High House Farm

Home Farm

Chapel Farm

Lancaster Farm

Tumby Woodside

THE CAUSEWAY

57

207

Coningsby Airfield

Cottage Farm

Kelham Farm

PE22

Wildmore Fen

Newham Drain

7

Ivy House Farm

REEDHAM LANE

IVY LANE

Langworth Grange

Reedham

High House Farm

Reedham Farm

Bridge Farm

LANGRICK ROAD

Duddles Farm

No Man's Friend Farm

56

207

Catchwater Drain

Botany Bay Farm

Sandy Bank Drain

Sandy Bank

Mill's Bridge

6

Beechtree Farm

Toothill Farm

Scrub Hill

Fruit Farm

WILDMORE CL

Providence House

Willowtree Farm

LINGHALL LANE

New York

55

White House Farm

DOGDYKE ROAD

Catchwater Farm

Oaklands Farm

Wildmore Fen

Bridge Farm

Roanes Farm

OLD FEN LANE

Packet House Farm

Hough Bridge

Linghall Farm

5

Bettinson's Bridge

LN4

Jessamine House Farm

54

CANADA LANE

Canada Farm

Hundle Houses

HUNDLEHOUSE LANE

Wildmore Park

Bunker's Hill

Thornton Park Farm

Bunkers Hill Farm

PH

4

Wildmore Fen

Hundred Cut Farm

Windmill

MILL LANE

CASTLE DYKE BANK

New York Prim Sch

Hundle Moor

Norbena Farm

HUNDLE HOUSES LANE

Dovecote Hall Farm

53

HURNBRIDGE ROAD

PH

Whaley Farm

Chapelry Farm

Holly Farm

Haven Bank

Wildmore Fen

Manor Farm

3

Mayfield Farm

HAVEN BANK

The Willows

Wildmore Fen

Gravelpit Plantation

Waite Farm

ROOKERY LA

Thornton le Fen Farm

52

Willow Farm

Chestnut Farm

Thornton Farm

Witham Brewery

Holland Fen

Slates Farm

Langraville Farm

Castle Dike

2

Hospital Farm

Chapel Farm

Hermitage Farm

Champion Farm

PE22

Castledyke Farm

Mill Farm

51

Pelham's Lands Farm

River Witham

HAVEN BANK

B1192

LEGATE ROAD

Ashtree Farm

CASTLEGATE

Kirton Fen

Fosdyke Fen

Red House Farm

Ash Tree Farm

Gipsey Bridge

PO

1

50

22   A   23   B   24   C   25   D   26   E   27   F   50

For full street detail of the highlighted area see page 207.

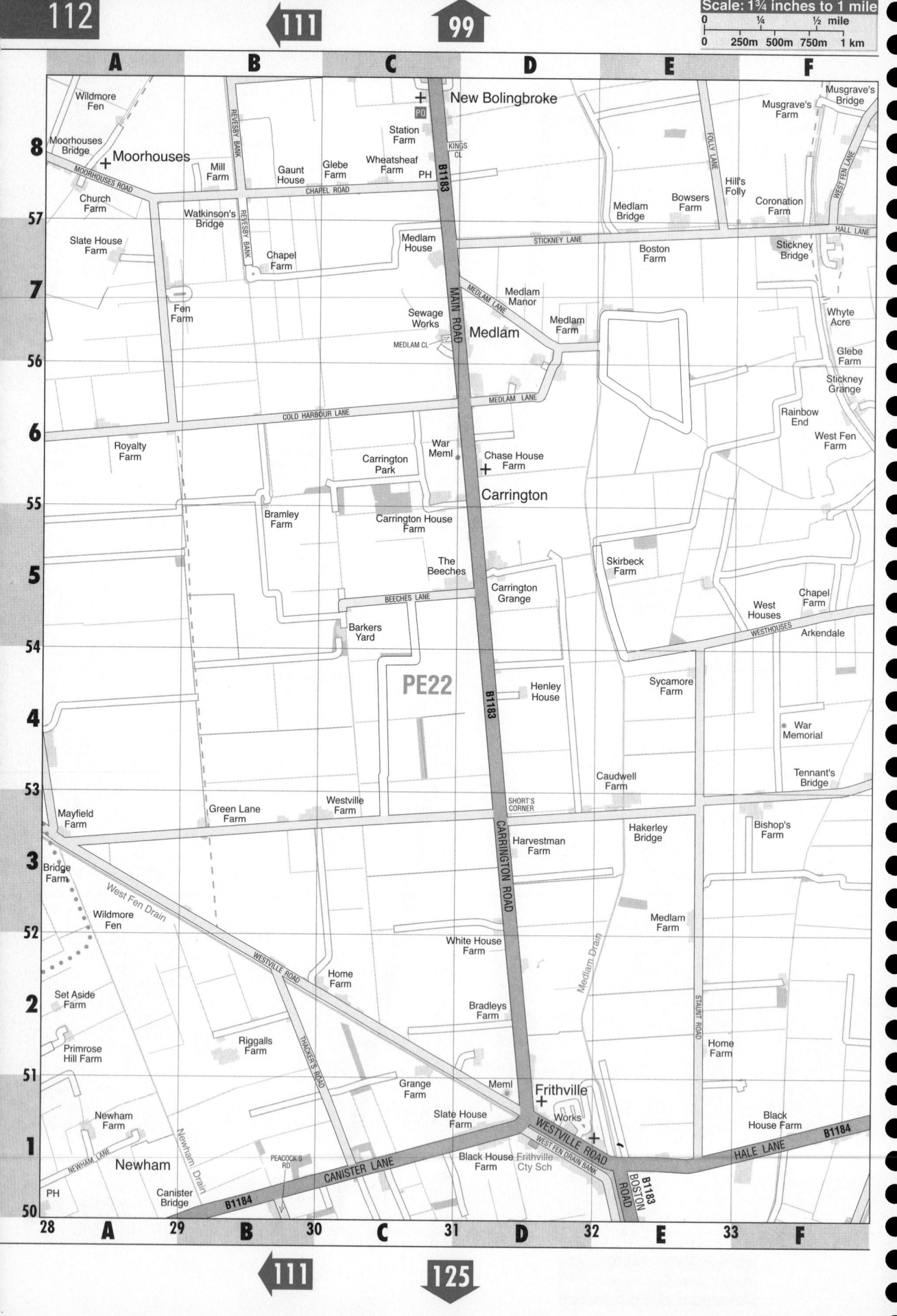

Scale: 1¾ inches to 1 mile
0   ¼   ½   mile
0   250m   500m   750m   1 km

A   B   C   D   E   F

New Bolingbroke

Wildmore Fen

Moorhouses Bridge

Moorhouses

MOORHOUSES ROAD

Church Farm

Slate House Farm

Mill Farm

Gaunt House

Glebe Farm

Station Farm

Wheatsheaf Farm
PH

CHAPEL ROAD

KINGS CL

PO

Musgrave's Bridge

Musgrave's Farm

FOLLY LANE

Hill's Folly

Coronation Farm

WEST FEN LANE

8

Watkinson's Bridge

Medlam House

Medlam Bridge

Bowsers Farm

HALL LANE

57

REVESBY BANK

REVESBY BANK

Chapel Farm

STICKNEY LANE

Boston Farm

Stickney Bridge

7

Fen Farm

Sewage Works

MEDLAM CL

Medlam

MEDLAM LANE

Medlam Manor

Medlam Farm

Whyte Acre

Glebe Farm

56

MAIN ROAD

MEDLAM LANE

Stickney Grange

COLD HARBOUR LANE

MEDLAM LANE

Rainbow End

West Fen Farm

6

Royalty Farm

Carrington Park

War Meml

Chase House Farm

Carrington

55

Bramley Farm

Carrington House Farm

The Beeches

Skirbeck Farm

West Houses

Chapel Farm

5

BEECHES LANE

Carrington Grange

WESTHOUSES

Arkendale

54

Barkers Yard

PE22

Henley House

Sycamore Farm

War Memorial

4

B1183

Caudwell Farm

Tennant's Bridge

53

Mayfield Farm

Green Lane Farm

Westville Farm

SHORT'S CORNER

Harvestman Farm

Hakerley Bridge

Bishop's Farm

3

Bridge Farm

West Fen Drain

CARRINGTON ROAD

Medlam Farm

Wildmore Fen

WESTVILLE ROAD

White House Farm

Medlam Drain

52

Set Aside Farm

Home Farm

Bradleys Farm

STAUNT ROAD

Home Farm

2

Primrose Hill Farm

Riggalls Farm

THACKER'S ROAD

Newham Drain

Grange Farm

Meml

Frithville

Works

Black House Farm

B1184

51

Newham Farm

Slate House Farm

WESTVILLE ROAD

HALE LANE

1

Newham

PEACOCK'S RD

Black House Farm

Frithville Cty Sch

WEST FEN DRAIN BANK

BOSTON ROAD

NEWHAM LANE

CANISTER LANE

Canister Bridge

B1184

Frithville Cty Sch

B1183

PH

50

28   A   29   B   30   C   31   D   32   E   33   F

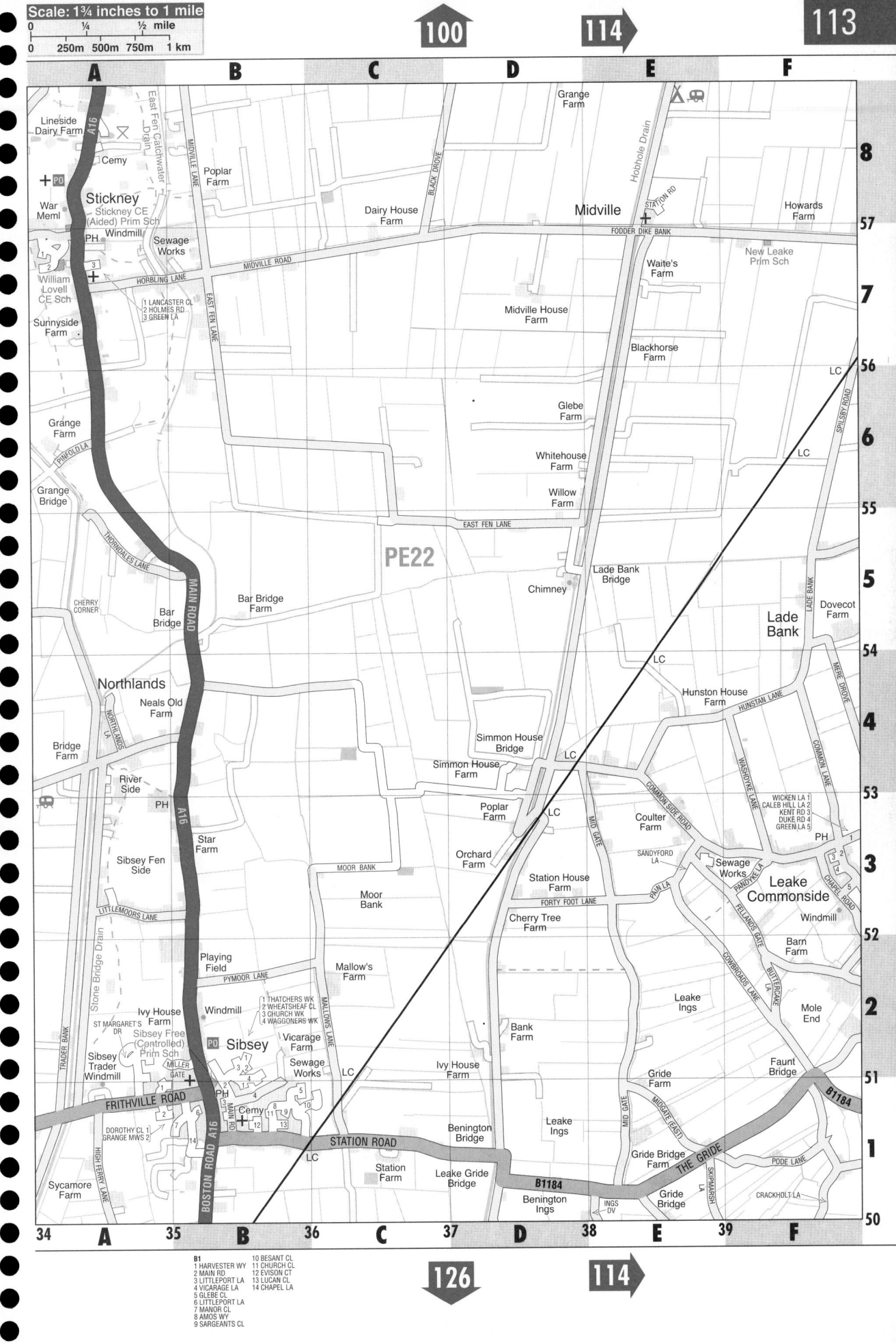

Scale: 1¾ inches to 1 mile

0   ¼   ½   mile
0   250m 500m 750m 1 km

100
114

A B C D E F

Grange Farm

Lineside Dairy Farm

Cemy

East Fen Catchwater Drain

Poplar Farm

Stickney

Stickney CE (Aided) Prim Sch

Windmill

War Meml

PO

Midville

Station Rd

Howards Farm

New Leake Prim Sch

PH

Dairy House Farm

Sewage Works

Horbling Lane

Midville Road

Fodder Dike Bank

William Lovell CE Sch

1 LANCASTER CL
2 HOLMES RD
3 GREEN LA

Sunnyside Farm

Waite's Farm

Midville House Farm

Blackhorse Farm

Hobhole Drain

Grange Farm

Glebe Farm

LC

Pinfold La

Whitehouse Farm

LC

Grange Bridge

Willow Farm

East Fen Lane

PE22

Thorndales Lane

Bar Bridge Farm

Chimney

Lade Bank Bridge

Lade Bank

Dovecot Farm

Main Road

Cherry Corner

Bar Bridge

Bar Bridge Farm

LC

Lade Bank

Mere Drive

Northlands

Neals Old Farm

Hunston House Farm

Hunstan Lane

Bridge Farm

River Side

PH

Simmon House Bridge

LC

Washdyke Lane

Common Lane

WICKEN LA 1
CALEB HILL LA 2
KENT RD 3
DUKE RD 4
GREEN LA 5

Star Farm

Sibsey Fen Side

Moor Bank

Simmon House Farm

Poplar Farm

LC

Coulter Farm

SANDYFORD LA

Sewage Works

Pandyke La

PH

Leake Commonside

Littlemoors Lane

Moor Bank

Orchard Farm

LC

Station House Farm

Forty Foot Lane

Windmill

Fellands Gate

Mid Gate

Common Side Road

Pan La

Playing Field

Pymoor Lane

Mallow's Farm

Cherry Tree Farm

Barn Farm

Combroads Lane

Buttercake Lane

Leake Ings

Mole End

Ivy House Farm

St Margaret's Dr

Windmill

Sibsey Free (Controlled) Prim Sch

PO

Sibsey

1 THATCHERS WK
2 WHEATSHEAF CL
3 CHURCH WK
4 WAGGONERS WK

Vicarage Farm

Bank Farm

Ivy House Farm

Gride Farm

Leake Ings

Faunt Bridge

Sibsey Trader Windmill

Sewage Works

LC

Frithville Road

PH

Cemy

Benington Bridge

Mid Gate

Mudgate (East)

Gride Bridge Farm

B1184

DOROTHY CL 1
GRANGE MWS 2

Boston Road A16

Main Rd

Station Road

LC

Leake Gride Bridge

B1184

Benington Ings

The Gride

Skipmarsh La

Pode Lane

Sycamore Farm

High Ferry Lane

Station Farm

Benington Ings

INGS DV

Gride Bridge

Crackholt La

B1
1 HARVESTER WY
2 MAIN RD
3 LITTLEPORT LA
4 VICARAGE LA
5 GLEBE CL
6 LITTLEPORT LA
7 MANOR CL
8 AMOS WY
9 SARGEANTS CL
10 BESANT CL
11 CHURCH CL
12 EVISON CT
13 LUCAN CL
14 CHAPEL LA

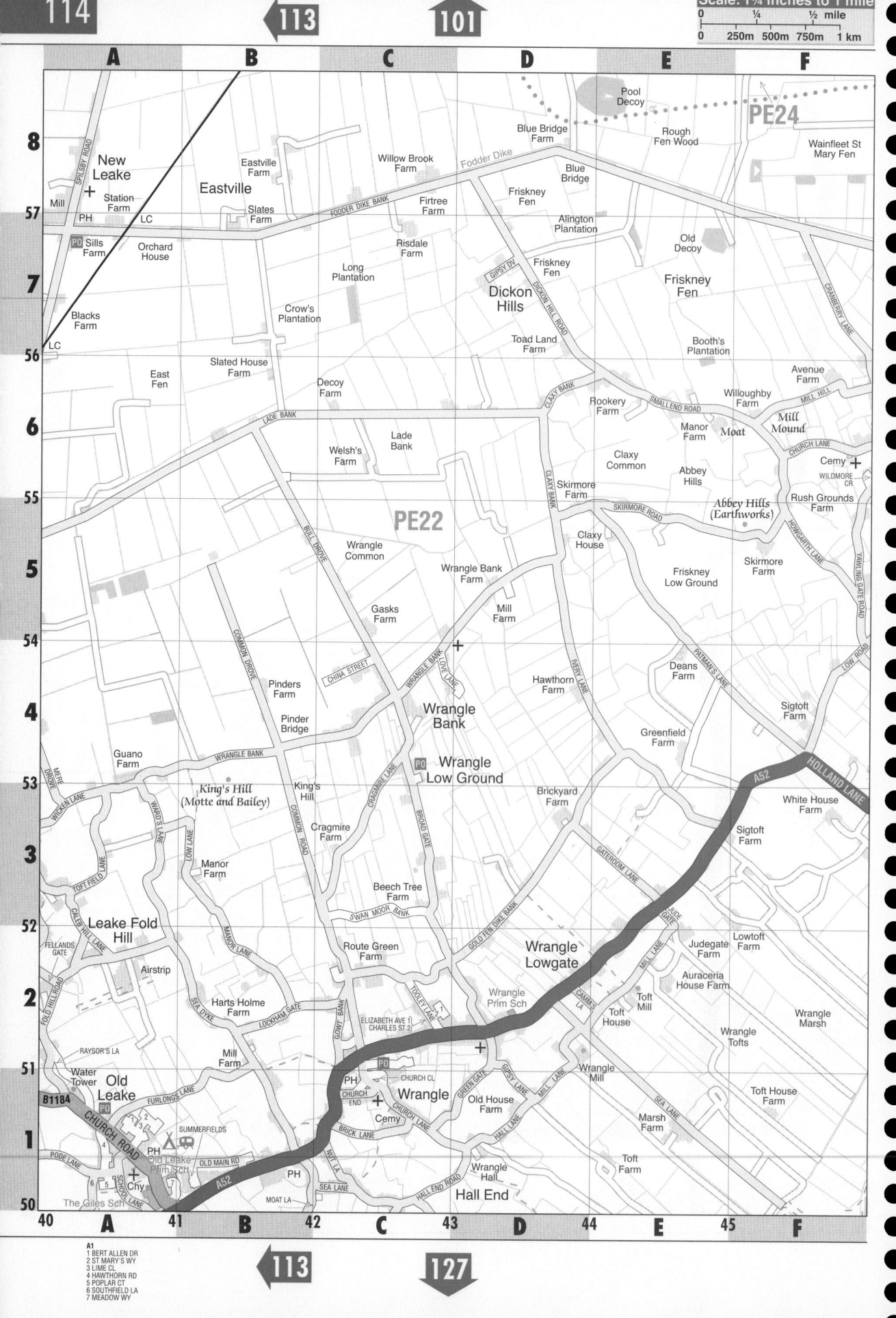

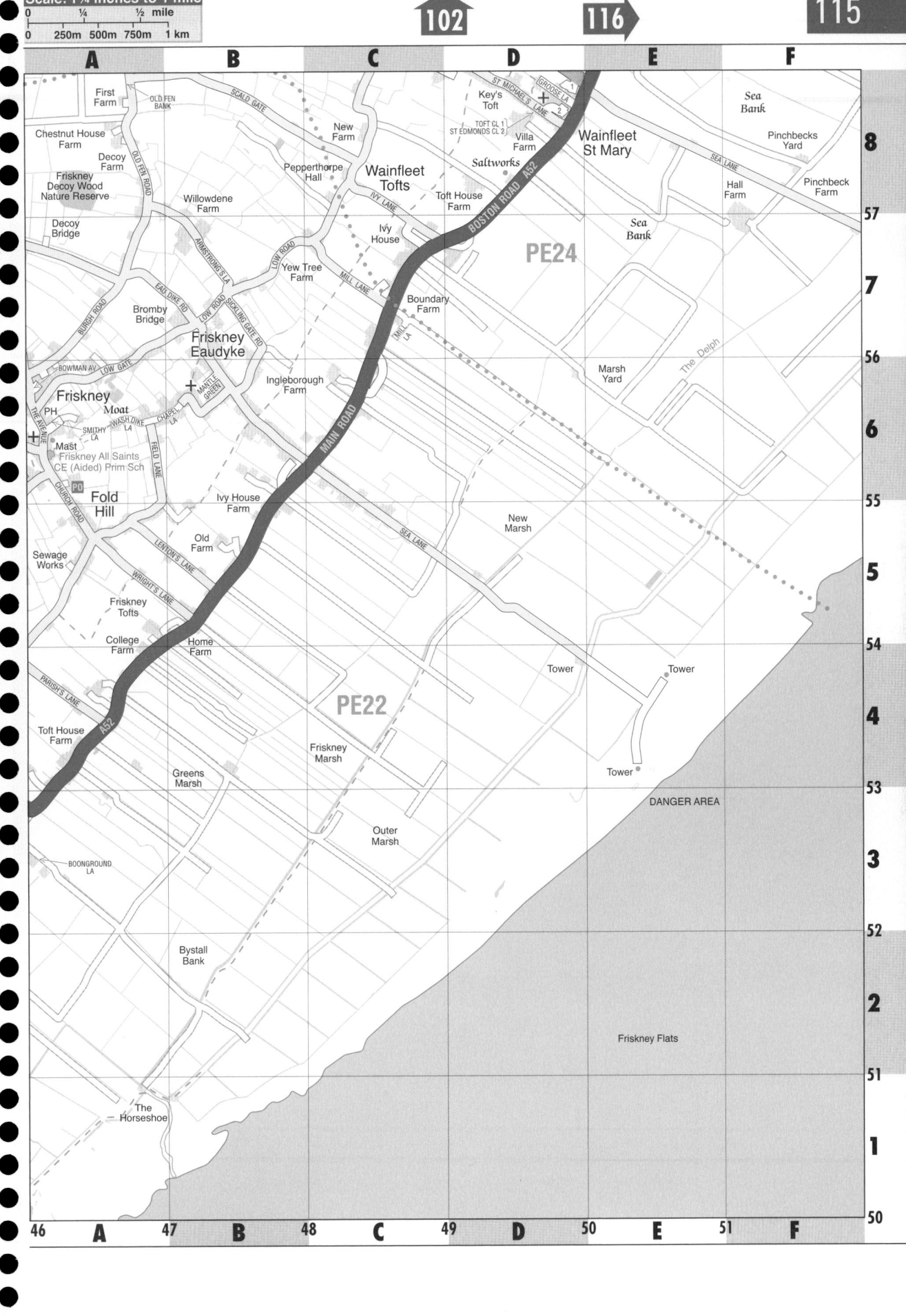

Scale: 1¾ inches to 1 mile

0   ¼   ½   mile
0   250m 500m 750m 1 km

102

116

A   B   C   D   E   F

First Farm
Old Fen Bank
Scald Gate
New Farm
St Michael's CE
Key's Toft
Sea Bank
Chestnut House Farm
Decoy Farm
Pepperthorpe Hall
TOFT CL 1
ST EDMONDS CL 2
Villa Farm
GROUSE LA
Wainfleet St Mary
Pinchbecks Yard
8
Friskney Decoy Wood Nature Reserve
Willowdene Farm
Wainfleet Tofts
Saltworks
Toft House Farm
BOSTON ROAD A52
Sea Lane
Hall Farm
Pinchbeck Farm
Decoy Bridge
OLD FEN ROAD
IVY LANE
Ivy House
PE24
Sea Bank
57
LOW ROAD
Yew Tree Farm
MILL LANE
ARMSTRONG'S LA
Bromby Bridge
EAU DIKE RD
LOW ROAD
SICKLING GATE RD
Boundary Farm
MILL LA
7
Friskney Eaudyke
The Delph
56
BURGH ROAD
BOWMAN AV
LOW GATE
Friskney
MANTLE GREEN
Ingleborough Farm
MAIN ROAD
Marsh Yard
6
Moat
WASH DIKE LA
CHAPEL LA
PH
SMITHY LA
FIELD LANE
Mast
Friskney All Saints CE (Aided) Prim Sch
55
THE AVENUE
PO
Fold Hill
Ivy House Farm
SEA LANE
New Marsh
5
CHURCH ROAD
Old Farm
LENTON'S LANE
Sewage Works
WRIGHT'S LANE
54
Friskney Tofts
Home Farm
Tower
Tower
College Farm
PE22
A52
Toft House Farm
PARISH'S LANE
Friskney Marsh
Tower
Tower
4
Greens Marsh
53
BOONGROUND LA
Outer Marsh
DANGER AREA
3
52
Bystall Bank
2
Friskney Flats
51
The Horseshoe
1
50

46   A   47   B   48   C   49   D   50   E   51   F

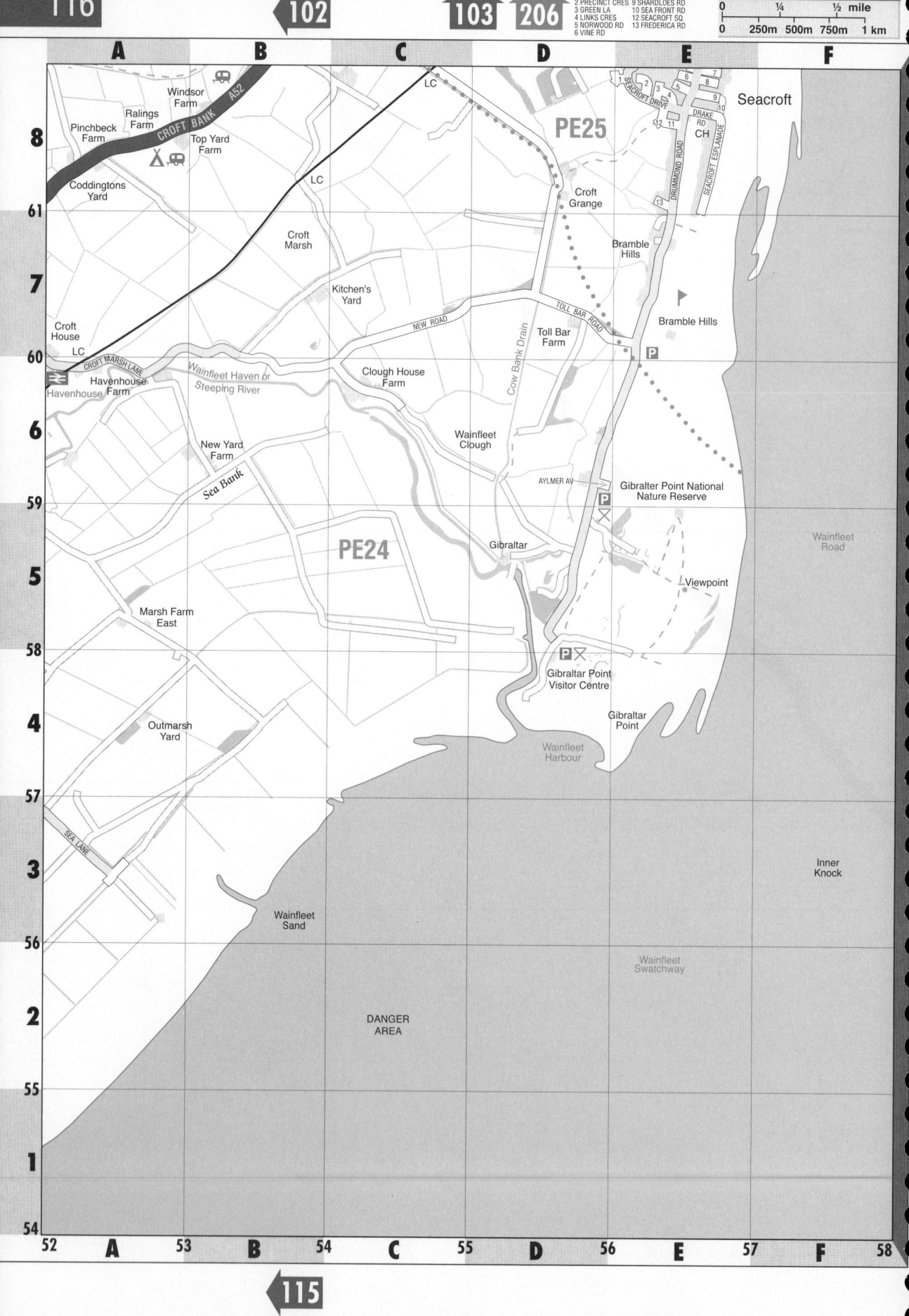

102

103 206

E8
1 BAYES RD   7 ALBERT AVE
2 PRECINCT CRES   8 BUCKTHORN AVE
3 GREEN LA   9 SHARDLOES RD
4 LINKS CRES   10 SEA FRONT RD
5 NORWOOD RD   11 SEACROFT SQ
6 VINE RD   12 SEACROFT SQ
                        13 FREDERICA RD

Scale: 1¾ inches to 1 mile
0   ¼   ½   mile
0   250m 500m 750m   1 km

PE25

Seacroft

Windsor Farm
Ralings Farm
Pinchbeck Farm
Top Yard Farm
CROFT BANK A52
Coddingtons Yard

Croft Marsh

Kitchen's Yard

Croft House
LC
Croft Marsh Lane
Havenhouse Farm
Havenhouse

Wainfleet Haven or Steeping River

New Road

Clough House Farm

Croft Grange
Bramble Hills
Bramble Hills
TOLL BAR ROAD
Toll Bar Farm
Cow Bank Drain

SEACROFT DRIVE
DRUMMOND ROAD
SEACROFT ESPLANADE
DRAKE RD
CH

New Yard Farm
Sea Bank

Wainfleet Clough

PE24

Marsh Farm East

Outmarsh Yard

AYLMER AV
Gibraltar

Gibralter Point National Nature Reserve

Viewpoint

Gibraltar Point Visitor Centre

Gibraltar Point

Wainfleet Harbour

Wainfleet Sand

DANGER AREA

Wainfleet Swatchway

Wainfleet Road

Inner Knock

Sea Lane

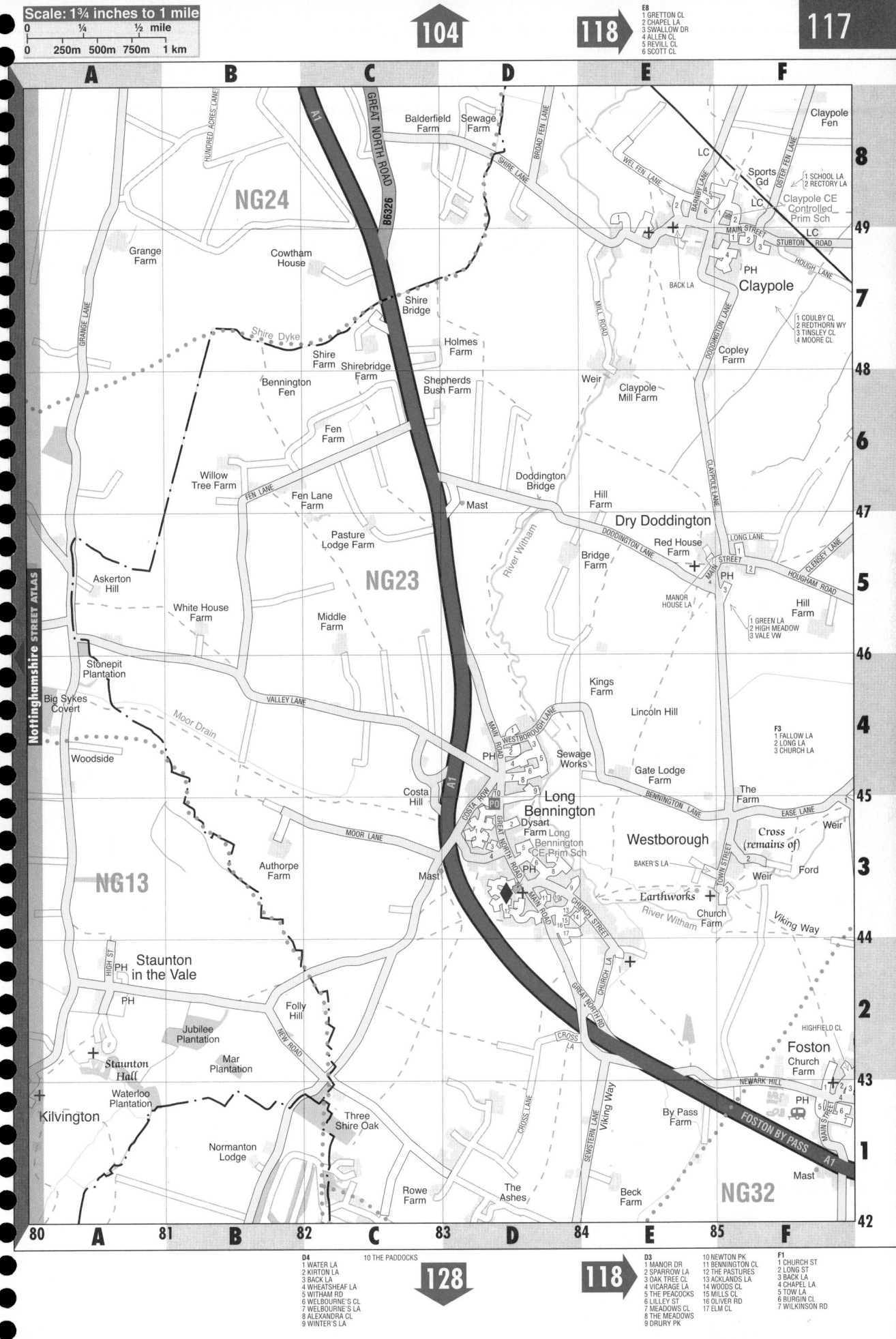

Scale: 1¾ inches to 1 mile

0   ¼   ½ mile
0   250m 500m 750m 1 km

104

118

117

E8
1 GRETTON CL
2 CHAPEL LA
3 SWALLOW DR
4 ALLEN CL
5 REVILL CL
6 SCOTT CL

Nottinghamshire STREET ATLAS

NG24

HUNDRED ACRES LANE

Balderfield
Farm

Sewage
Farm

GREAT NORTH ROAD

A1

B6326

BROAD FEN LANE

SHIRE LANE

WEL FEN LANE

OSTER FEN LANE

BARNBY LANE

Claypole
Fen

Sports
Gd

1 SCHOOL LA
2 RECTORY LA

LC

LC

Claypole CE
Controlled
Prim Sch

MAIN STREET

STUBTON ROAD

HOUGH LANE

LC

8

49

Grange
Farm

Cowtham
House

Shire
Bridge

Shire Dyke

BACK LA

PH

Claypole

DODDINGTON LANE

7

1 COULBY CL
2 REDTHORN WY
3 TINSLEY CL
4 MOORE CL

Shire
Farm

Shirebridge
Farm

Holmes
Farm

Shepherds
Bush Farm

Weir

Copley
Farm

48

Bennington
Fen

Fen
Farm

Doddington
Bridge

Hill
Farm

Claypole
Mill Farm

CLAYPOLE LANE

6

47

Willow
Tree Farm

FEN LANE

Fen Lane
Farm

Mast

RIVER WITHAM

DODDINGTON LANE

Dry Doddington

Red House
Farm

LONG LANE

CLENSEY LANE

MAIN STREET

HOUGHAM ROAD

PH

Pasture
Lodge Farm

NG23

Bridge
Farm

Hill
Farm

1 GREEN LA
2 HIGH MEADOW
3 VALE VW

5

Askerton
Hill

White House
Farm

Middle
Farm

MANOR
HOUSE LA

46

Stonepit
Plantation

VALLEY LANE

Kings
Farm

Lincoln Hill

F3
1 FALLOW LA
2 LONG LA
3 CHURCH LA

4

Big Sykes
Covert

Moor Drain

Gate Lodge
Farm

BENNINGTON LANE

The
Farm

EASE LANE

Weir

45

Woodside

Costa
Hill

A1

WESTBOROUGH LANE

MAIN ROAD

PH

COSTA ROW

Sewage
Works

Long
Bennington

Dysart
Farm Long
Bennington
CE Prim Sch

Westborough

Cross
(remains of)

TOWN STREET

Ford

3

MOOR LANE

PO

PH

BAKER'S LA

Weir

Authorpe
Farm

Mast

Earthworks

RIVER WITHAM

Church
Farm

Viking Way

44

NG13

HIGH ST

Staunton
in the Vale

PH

PH

NEW ROAD

Folly
Hill

CHURCH STREET

CHURCH LA

2

Jubilee
Plantation

Mar
Plantation

HIGHFIELD CL

Foston

Church
Farm

Staunton
Hall

CROSS LA

GREAT NORTH RD

NEWARK HILL

PH

43

Kilvington

Waterloo
Plantation

Three
Shire Oak

CROSS LANE

SEWSTERN LANE

VIKING WAY

By Pass
Farm

FOSTON BY PASS

MAIN STREET

A1

1

Normanton
Lodge

Rowe
Farm

The
Ashes

Beck
Farm

NG32

Mast

42

A   81   B   82   C   83   D   84   E   85   F

80   A   81   B   82   C   83   D   84   E   85   F

D4
1 WATER LA
2 KIRTON LA
3 BACK LA
4 WHEATSHEAF LA
5 WITHAM RD
6 WELBOURNE'S CL
7 WELBOURNE'S LA
8 ALEXANDRA CL
9 WINTER'S LA

10 THE PADDOCKS

128

118

D3
1 MANOR DR
2 SPARROW LA
3 OAK TREE CL
4 VICARAGE LA
5 THE PEACOCKS
6 LILLEY ST
7 MEADOWS CL
8 THE MEADOWS
9 DRURY PK

10 NEWTON PK
11 BENNINGTON CL
12 THE PASTURES
13 ACKLANDS LA
14 WOODS CL
15 MILLS CL
16 OLIVER RD
17 ELM CL

F1
1 CHURCH ST
2 LONG ST
3 BACK LA
4 CHAPEL LA
5 TOW LA
6 BURGIN CL
7 WILKINSON RD

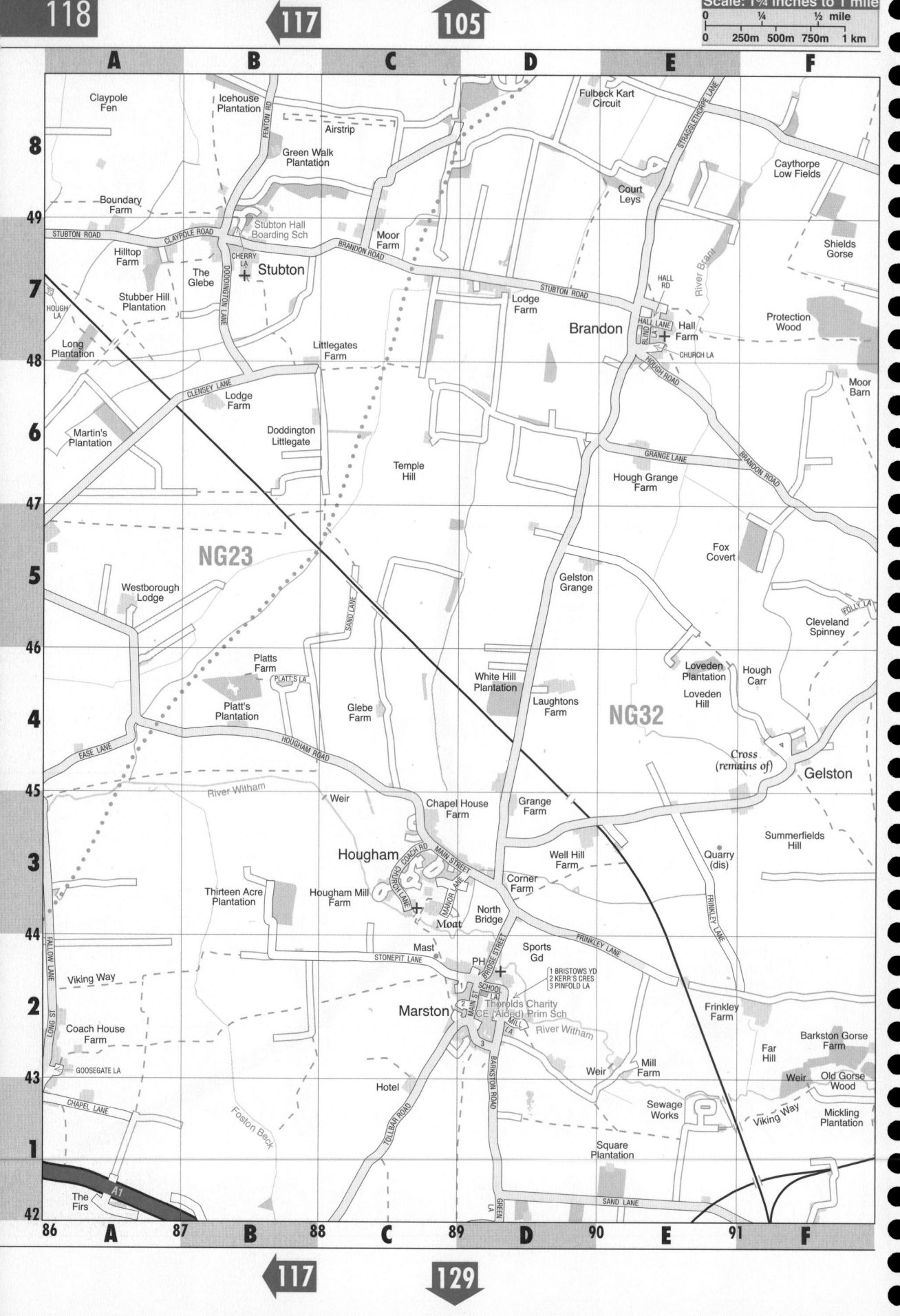

Scale: 1¾ inches to 1 mile

Claypole Fen

Icehouse Plantation

Airstrip

Fulbeck Kart Circuit

Court Leys

Caythorpe Low Fields

Boundary Farm

Green Walk Plantation

Stubton Road

Claypole Road

Stubton Hall Boarding Sch

Moor Farm

River Brant

Shields Gorse

Hilltop Farm

The Glebe

Cherry La

Stubton

Brandon Road

Stubton Road

Lodge Farm

Hall Rd

Brandon

Hall Lane

Blind La

Hall Farm

Protection Wood

Stubber Hill Plantation

Doddington Lane

Church La

Long Plantation

Hough La

Clensey Lane

Littlegates Farm

Lodge Farm

Hough Road

Moor Barn

Martin's Plantation

Doddington Littlegate

Grange Lane

Brandon Road

Temple Hill

Hough Grange Farm

NG23

Sand Lane

Fox Covert

Westborough Lodge

Gelston Grange

Cleveland Spinney

Folly La

Platts Farm

Platt's La

Loveden Plantation

Hough Carr

Glebe Farm

White Hill Plantation

Loveden Hill

Platt's Plantation

Laughtons Farm

NG32

Ease Lane

Hougham Road

Cross (remains of)

Gelston

River Witham

Weir

Chapel House Farm

Grange Farm

Summerfields Hill

Hougham

Coach Rd

Main Street

Well Hill Farm

Quarry (dis)

Fallow Lane

Thirteen Acre Plantation

Hougham Mill Farm

Church Lane

Manor Lane

Corner Farm

Frinkley Lane

Moat

North Bridge

Viking Way

Mast

Stonepit Lane

Bridge Street

Sports Gd

PH

1 BRISTOWS YD
2 KERR'S CRES
3 PINFOLD LA

Frinkley Farm

Lions St

Coach House Farm

Marston

School La

Main St

Mill La

Thorolds Charity CE (Aided) Prim Sch

River Witham

Far Hill

Barkston Gorse Farm

Goosegate La

Weir

Mill Farm

Weir

Old Gorse Wood

Chapel Lane

Hotel

Barkston Road

Tollbar Road

Foston Beck

Sewage Works

Viking Way

Mickling Plantation

The Firs

A1

Square Plantation

Green La

Sand Lane

106
120

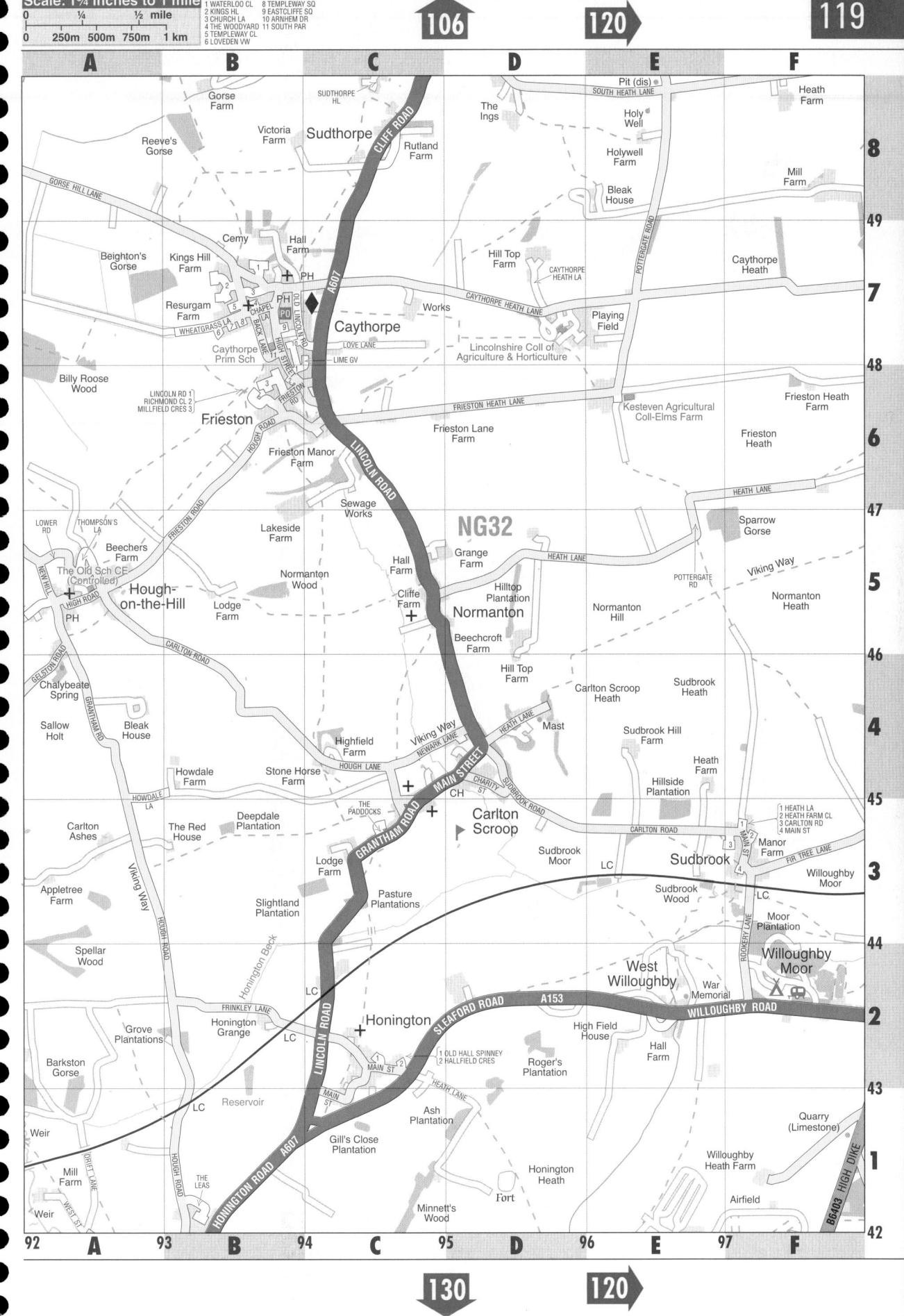
Scale: 1¾ inches to 1 mile
0 ¼ ½ mile
0 250m 500m 750m 1 km
B7
1 WATERLOO CL
2 KINGS HL
3 CHURCH LA
4 THE WOODYARD
5 TEMPLEWAY CL
6 LOVEDEN VW
7 SHERWOOD RI
8 TEMPLEWAY SQ
9 EASTCLIFFE SQ
10 ARNHEM DR
11 SOUTH PAR
A
B
C
D
E
F
8
49
7
48
6
47
5
46
4
45
3
44
2
43
1
42
92
93
94
95
96
97
Pit (dis)
SOUTH HEATH LANE
Heath Farm
Gorse Farm
SUDTHORPE HL
The Ings
Holy Well
Reeve's Gorse
Victoria Farm
Sudthorpe
CLIFF ROAD
Rutland Farm
Holywell Farm
Mill Farm
GORSE HILL LANE
Bleak House
POTTERGATE ROAD
Cemy
Hall Farm
Beighton's Gorse
Kings Hill Farm
Hill Top Farm
CAYTHORPE HEATH LA
Caythorpe Heath
PH
A607
Resurgam Farm
CHAPEL LA
BACK LANE
HIGH STREET
OLD LINCOLN RD
PO
Works
CAYTHORPE HEATH LANE
Playing Field
WHEATGRASS LA
Caythorpe
LOVE LANE
Caythorpe Prim Sch
LIME GV
Lincolnshire Coll of Agriculture & Horticulture
Billy Roose Wood
LINCOLN RD 1
RICHMOND CL 2
MILLFIELD CRES 3
FRIESTON RD
Frieston
FRIESTON HEATH LANE
Kesteven Agricultural Coll-Elms Farm
Frieston Heath Farm
Frieston Lane Farm
Frieston Heath
HOUGH ROAD
Frieston Manor Farm
LINCOLN ROAD
Sewage Works
HEATH LANE
FRIESTON ROAD
LOWER RD
THOMPSON'S LA
Lakeside Farm
NG32
Sparrow Gorse
Beechers Farm
Hall Farm
Grange Farm
HEATH LANE
NEW HILL
The Old Sch CE (Controlled)
Normanton Wood
POTTERGATE RD
Viking Way
HIGH ROAD
Hough-on-the-Hill
Cliffe Farm
Hilltop Plantation
Normanton Heath
PH
Lodge Farm
Normanton
Normanton Hill
Beechcroft Farm
GELSTON ROAD
CARLTON ROAD
Hill Top Farm
Chalybeate Spring
GRANTHAM RD
Carlton Scroop Heath
Sudbrook Heath
Sallow Holt
Bleak House
Viking Way
HEATH LANE
Mast
Highfield Farm
NEWARK LANE
Sudbrook Hill Farm
Howdale Farm
Stone Horse Farm
HOUGH LANE
MAIN STREET
CHARITY ST
Heath Farm
Hillside Plantation
HOWDALE LA
CH
SUDBROOK ROAD
Carlton Ashes
THE PADDOCKS
Deepdale Plantation
Carlton Scroop
CARLTON ROAD
1 HEATH LA
2 HEATH FARM CL
3 CARLTON RD
4 MAIN ST
The Red House
GRANTHAM ROAD
Sudbrook Moor
MAIN ST
Manor Farm
Lodge Farm
LC
Sudbrook
FIR TREE LANE
Willoughby Moor
Viking Way
Appletree Farm
Pasture Plantations
Sudbrook Wood
LC
Slightland Plantation
HOUGH ROAD
Moor Plantation
ROOKERY LANE
Spellar Wood
Honington Beck
Willoughby Moor
West Willoughby
War Memorial
LC
A153
SLEAFORD ROAD
WILLOUGHBY ROAD
FRINKLEY LANE
LINCOLN ROAD
Honington
Grove Plantations
Honington Grange
High Field House
LC
Hall Farm
1 OLD HALL SPINNEY
2 HALLFIELD CRES
Barkston Gorse
MAIN ST
Roger's Plantation
HEATH LANE
MAIN ST
Reservoir
LC
Ash Plantation
Quarry (Limestone)
Weir
A607
Gill's Close Plantation
Willoughby Heath Farm
B6403 HIGH DIKE
Mill Farm
DRIFT LANE
HOUGH ROAD
HONINGTON ROAD
Honington Heath
THE LEAS
WEST ST
Fort
Airfield
Weir
Minnett's Wood

130
120

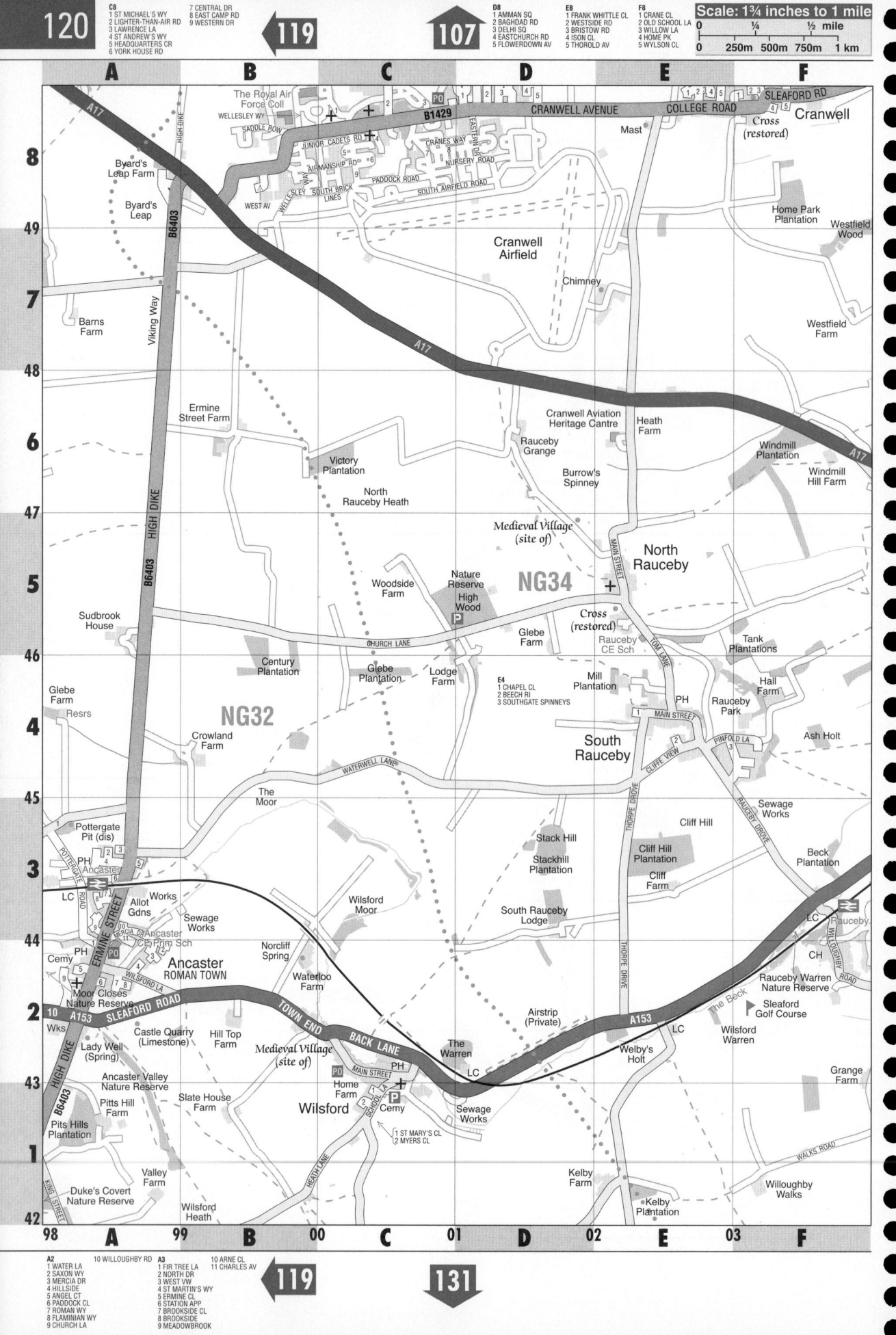
Cranwell
Cranwell Airfield
The Royal Air Force Coll
CRANWELL AVENUE
COLLEGE ROAD
SLEAFORD RD
B1429
A17
B6403
HIGH DIKE
Viking Way
Byard's Leap Farm
Byard's Leap
Barns Farm
Ermine Street Farm
Victory Plantation
North Rauceby Heath
Cranwell Aviation Heritage Centre
Rauceby Grange
Burrow's Spinney
Heath Farm
Home Park Plantation
Westfield Wood
Westfield Farm
Windmill Plantation
Windmill Hill Farm
Chimney
Mast
North Rauceby
NG34
NG32
Woodside Farm
Nature Reserve
High Wood
Sudbrook House
CHURCH LANE
Glebe Farm
Century Plantation
Glebe Plantation
Lodge Farm
Mill Plantation
Rauceby CE Sch
Tank Plantations
Hall Farm
Rauceby Park
South Rauceby
Crowland Farm
Ash Holt
WATERWELL LANE
The Moor
Pottergate Pit (dis)
Stack Hill
Stackhill Plantation
Cliff Hill
Cliff Hill Plantation
Cliff Farm
Sewage Works
Beck Plantation
Ancaster
ERMINE STREET
Allot Gdns
Works
Wilsford Moor
South Rauceby Lodge
Norcliff Spring
Waterloo Farm
Ancaster ROMAN TOWN
Moor Closes Nature Reserve
A153
SLEAFORD ROAD
TOWN END
BACK LANE
Castle Quarry (Limestone)
Lady Well (Spring)
Hill Top Farm
Medieval Village (site of)
The Warren
Airstrip (Private)
Welby's Holt
Wilsford Warren
Rauceby Warren Nature Reserve
Sleaford Golf Course
Ancaster Valley Nature Reserve
Pitts Hill Farm
Pits Hills Plantation
Slate House Farm
Wilsford
Home Farm
Sewage Works
Grange Farm
Valley Farm
Duke's Covert Nature Reserve
Wilsford Heath
Kelby Farm
Kelby Plantation
Willoughby Walks
WALKS ROAD
THORPE DROVE
RAUCEBY DROVE
TOM LANE
MAIN STREET
CLIFFE VIEW
PINFOLD LA
E4
1 CHAPEL CL
2 BEECH RI
3 SOUTHGATE SPINNEYS
1 ST MARY'S CL
2 MYERS CL

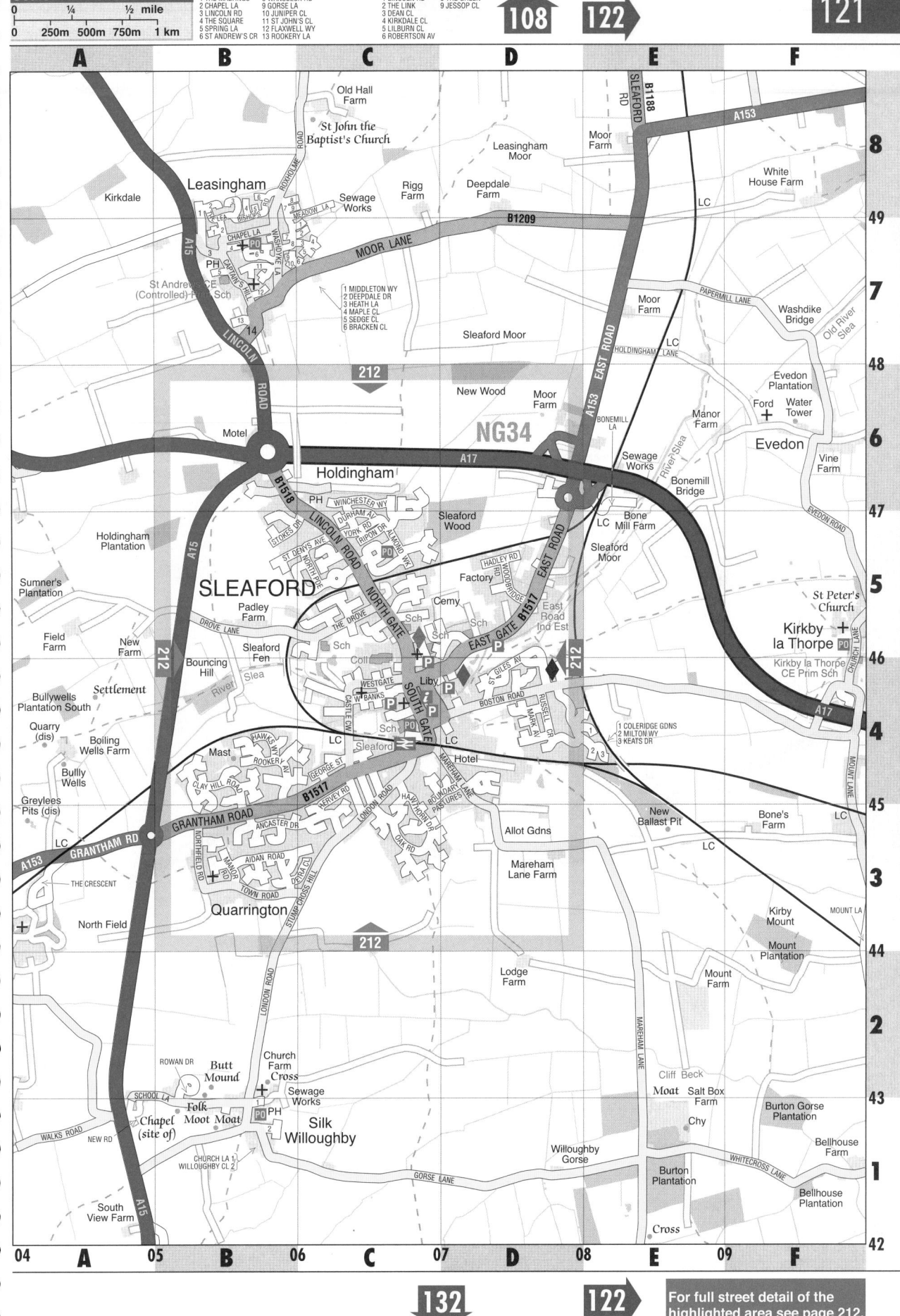

← 121   109

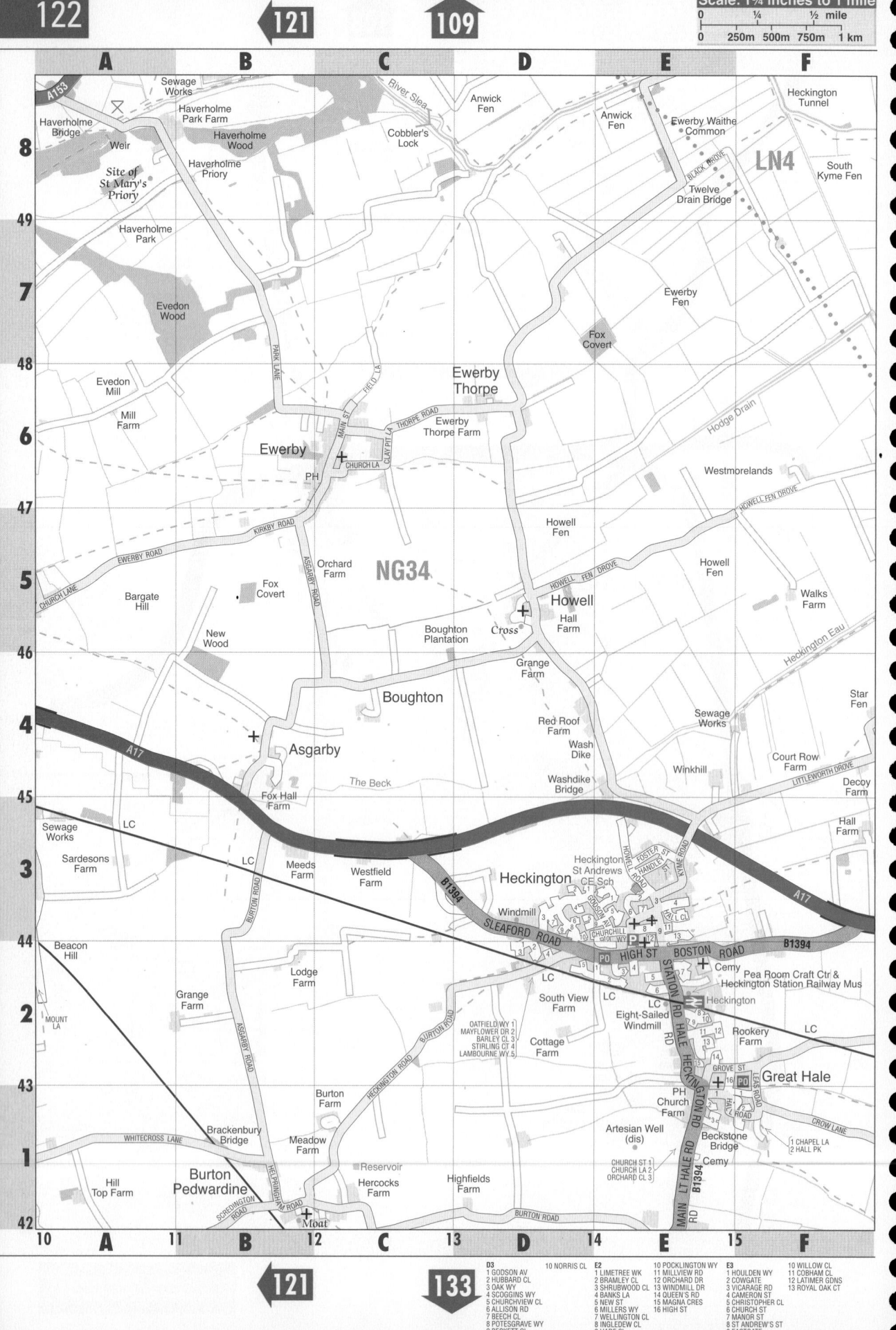

Scale: 1¾ inches to 1 mile

0   ¼   ½ mile
0   250m 500m 750m 1 km

A153
Haverholme Bridge
Sewage Works
Haverholme Park Farm
Haverholme Wood
River Slea
Anwick Fen
Anwick Fen
Cobbler's Lock
Ewerby Waithe Common
Heckington Tunnel

8

Site of St Mary's Priory
Weir
Haverholme Priory
LN4
South Kyme Fen

49

Haverholme Park
Evedon Wood
BLACK DROVE
Twelve Drain Bridge

7

Ewerby Fen

48

PARK LANE
FIELD LA
Fox Covert
Hodge Drain

Evedon Mill
Mill Farm
Ewerby Thorpe
THORPE ROAD
Ewerby Thorpe Farm
Westmorelands

6

Ewerby
CLAY PIT LA
MAIN ST
CHURCH LA
PH
HOWELL FEN DROVE

47

KIRKBY ROAD
Howell Fen

EWERBY ROAD
CHURCH LANE
ASGARBY ROAD
Orchard Farm
Fox Covert
NG34
Boughton Plantation
Cross
Howell
Hall Farm
HOWELL FEN DROVE
Howell Fen
Walks Farm

5

Bargate Hill
New Wood
Heckington Eau

46

Grange Farm
Star Fen

4

A17
Asgarby
The Beck
Red Roof Farm
Wash Dike
Washdike Bridge
Winkhill
Sewage Works
Court Row Farm
LITTLEWORTH DROVE
Decoy Farm

45

Fox Hall Farm
Hall Farm

Sewage Works
LC
Sardesons Farm
LC
BURTON ROAD
Meeds Farm
Westfield Farm
B1394
Heckington St Andrews CE Sch
FOSTER RD
HANDLEY
KYME ROAD
HOWELL ROAD
A17

3

Heckington
Windmill
SLEAFORD ROAD
LC CL
CHURCHILL
P
PO
HIGH ST
BOSTON ROAD
B1394
Cemy
Pea Room Craft Ctr & Heckington Station Railway Mus

44

Beacon Hill
Lodge Farm
South View Farm
LC
LC
STATION RD
Heckington
LC
Eight-Sailed Windmill
Rookery Farm
LC

2

MOUNT LA
Grange Farm
BURTON ROAD
ASGARBY ROAD
HECKINGTON ROAD
OATFIELD WY 1
MAYFLOWER DR 2
BARLEY CL 3
STIRLING CT 4
LAMBOURNE WY 5
Cottage Farm
HECKINGTON RD
GROVE ST
PH
Great Hale
PO
LEAS ROAD

43

Burton Farm
Church Farm
Artesian Well (dis)
HALE ROAD
PH
CROW LANE

WHITECROSS LANE
Brackenbury Bridge
Meadow Farm
Reservoir
Hercocks Farm
Highfields Farm
Beckstone Bridge
1 CHAPEL LA
2 HALL PK
Cemy

1

SCREDINGTON ROAD
HELPRINGHAM ROAD
Burton Pedwardine
CHURCH ST 1
CHURCH LA 2
ORCHARD CL 3
MAIN LT HALE RD
LT HALE RD
B1394

Hill Top Farm
Moat
BURTON ROAD

42

10   A   11   B   12   C   13   D   14   E   15   F

← 121   133

D3
1 GODSON AV
2 HUBBARD CL
3 OAK WY
4 SCOGGINS WY
5 CHURCHVIEW CL
6 ALLISON RD
7 BEECH CL
8 POTESGRAVE WY
9 BECKETT CL

10 NORRIS CL

E2
1 LIMETREE WK
2 BRAMLEY CL
3 SHRUBWOOD CL
4 BANKS LA
5 NEW ST
6 MILLERS WY
7 WELLINGTON CL
8 INGLEDEW CL
9 HARE CL

10 POCKLINGTON WY
11 MILLVIEW RD
12 ORCHARD DR
13 WINDMILL DR
14 QUEEN'S RD
15 MAGNA CRES
16 HIGH ST

E3
1 HOULDEN WY
2 COWGATE
3 VICARAGE RD
4 CAMERON ST
5 CHRISTOPHER CL
6 CHURCH ST
7 MANOR ST
8 ST ANDREW'S ST
9 EASTGATE

10 WILLOW CL
11 COBHAM CL
12 LATIMER GDNS
13 ROYAL OAK CT

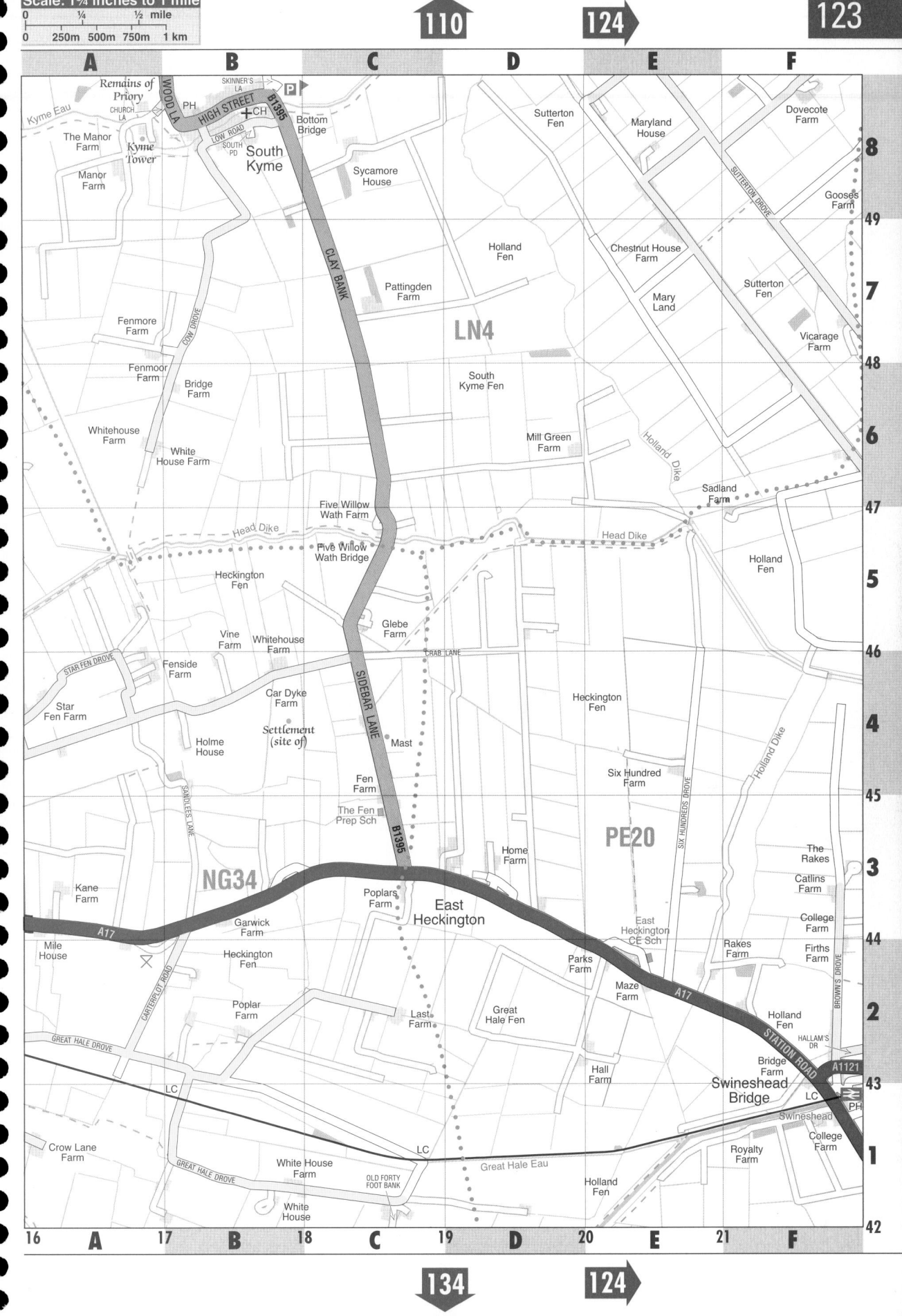
Scale: 1¾ inches to 1 mile
110
124
South Kyme
Remains of Priory
Kyme Tower
The Manor Farm
Manor Farm
Bottom Bridge
Sycamore House
Sutterton Fen
Maryland House
Dovecote Farm
Gooses Farm
Holland Fen
Chestnut House Farm
Mary Land
Sutterton Fen
Pattingden Farm
LN4
Vicarage Farm
Fenmore Farm
Fenmoor Farm
Bridge Farm
South Kyme Fen
Whitehouse Farm
White House Farm
Mill Green Farm
Sadland Farm
Five Willow Wath Farm
Five Willow Wath Bridge
Head Dike
Heckington Fen
Holland Fen
Glebe Farm
Vine Farm
Whitehouse Farm
Fenside Farm
Star Fen Farm
Car Dyke Farm
Settlement (site of)
Holme House
Mast
Heckington Fen
Six Hundred Farm
Fen Farm
The Fen Prep Sch
PE20
NG34
Home Farm
The Rakes
Catlins Farm
Kane Farm
Poplars Farm
East Heckington
Garwick Farm
East Heckington CE Sch
College Farm
Mile House
Heckington Fen
Parks Farm
Rakes Farm
Firths Farm
Maze Farm
Poplar Farm
Last Farm
Great Hale Fen
Holland Fen
Bridge Farm
Hall Farm
Swineshead Bridge
Crow Lane Farm
White House Farm
Royalty Farm
College Farm
Holland Fen
White House
Great Hale Eau
Swineshead
134
124

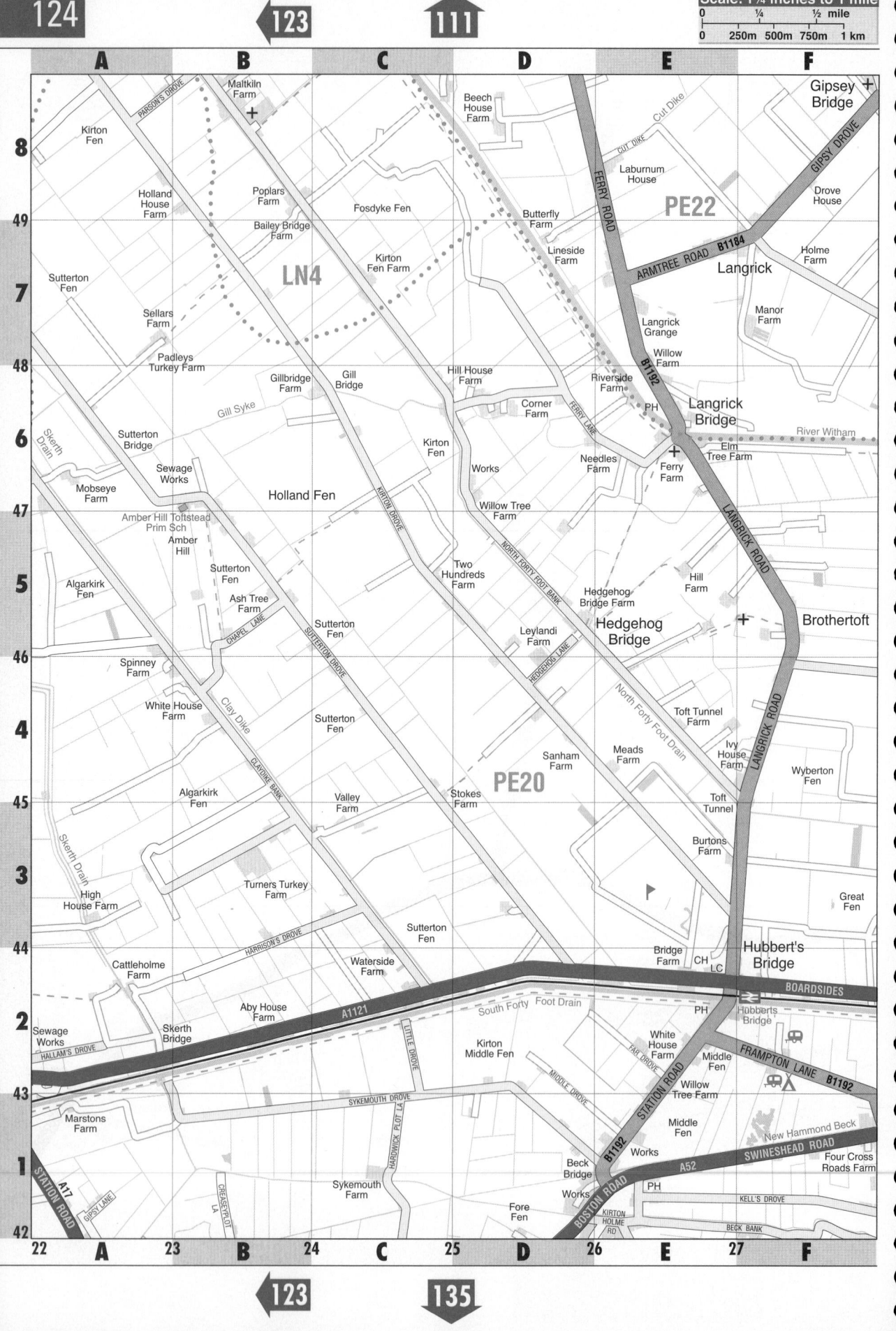

123
111

Scale: 1¾ inches to 1 mile

0   ¼   ½ mile
0   250m 500m 750m 1 km

A   B   C   D   E   F

Gipsy Bridge

Cut Dike

8

Kirton Fen

Maltkiln Farm

Beech House Farm

Ferry Road

Laburnum House

PE22

Drove House

GIPSY DROVE

49

Holland House Farm

Poplars Farm

Fosdyke Fen

Butterfly Farm

Armtree Road   B1184

Holme Farm

Langrick

LN4

Bailey Bridge Farm

Kirton Fen Farm

Lineside Farm

7

Sutterton Fen

Sellars Farm

Langrick Grange

Manor Farm

B1192

48

Padleys Turkey Farm

Gillbridge Farm

Gill Bridge

Hill House Farm

Willow Farm

Gill Syke

Riverside Farm

PH

Langrick Bridge

6

Skerth Drain

Sutterton Bridge

Kirton Fen

Corner Farm

Ferry Lane

River Witham

Elm Tree Farm

Mobseye Farm

Sewage Works

Works

Needles Farm

Ferry Farm

47

Holland Fen

Willow Tree Farm

Amber Hill Toftstead Prim Sch

Amber Hill

KIRTON DROVE

NORTH FORTY FOOT BANK

Hill Farm

5

Algarkirk Fen

Sutterton Fen

Two Hundreds Farm

Hedgehog Bridge Farm

Hedgehog Bridge

Brothertoft

Ash Tree Farm

CHAPEL LANE

Leylandi Farm

HEDGEHOG LANE

46

Spinney Farm

SUTTERTON DROVE

Sutterton Fen

North Forty Foot Drain

LANGRICK ROAD

Toft Tunnel Farm

4

White House Farm

Clay Dike

Sutterton Fen

Sanham Farm

Meads Farm

Ivy House Farm

Wyberton Fen

CLAYDIKE BANK

PE20

Toft Tunnel

45

Algarkirk Fen

Valley Farm

Stokes Farm

Burtons Farm

3

High House Farm

Skerth Drain

Turners Turkey Farm

Great Fen

HARRISON'S DROVE

44

Cattleholme Farm

Waterside Farm

Sutterton Fen

Bridge Farm   CH   LC

Hubbert's Bridge

BOARDSIDES

2

Sewage Works

Aby House Farm

Skerth Bridge

A1121

LITTLE DROVE

South Forty   Foot Drain

White House Farm

PH

Hubberts Bridge

FRAMPTON LANE   B1192

HALLAM'S DROVE

Kirton Middle Fen

STATION ROAD

TAE DROVE

Middle Fen

43

Marstons Farm

SYKEMOUTH DROVE

MIDDLE DROVE

Willow Tree Farm

Middle Fen

New Hammond Beck

STATION ROAD

A17

GIPSY LANE

HARDWICK PLOT LA

CREASEPLOT LA

Sykemouth Farm

B1192

Beck Bridge

BOSTON ROAD

Works

A52   SWINESHEAD ROAD

Four Cross Roads Farm

1

Fore Fen

Works

PH

KELL'S DROVE

KIRTON HOLME RD

BECK BANK

42

22   A   23   B   24   C   25   D   26   E   27   F

123
135

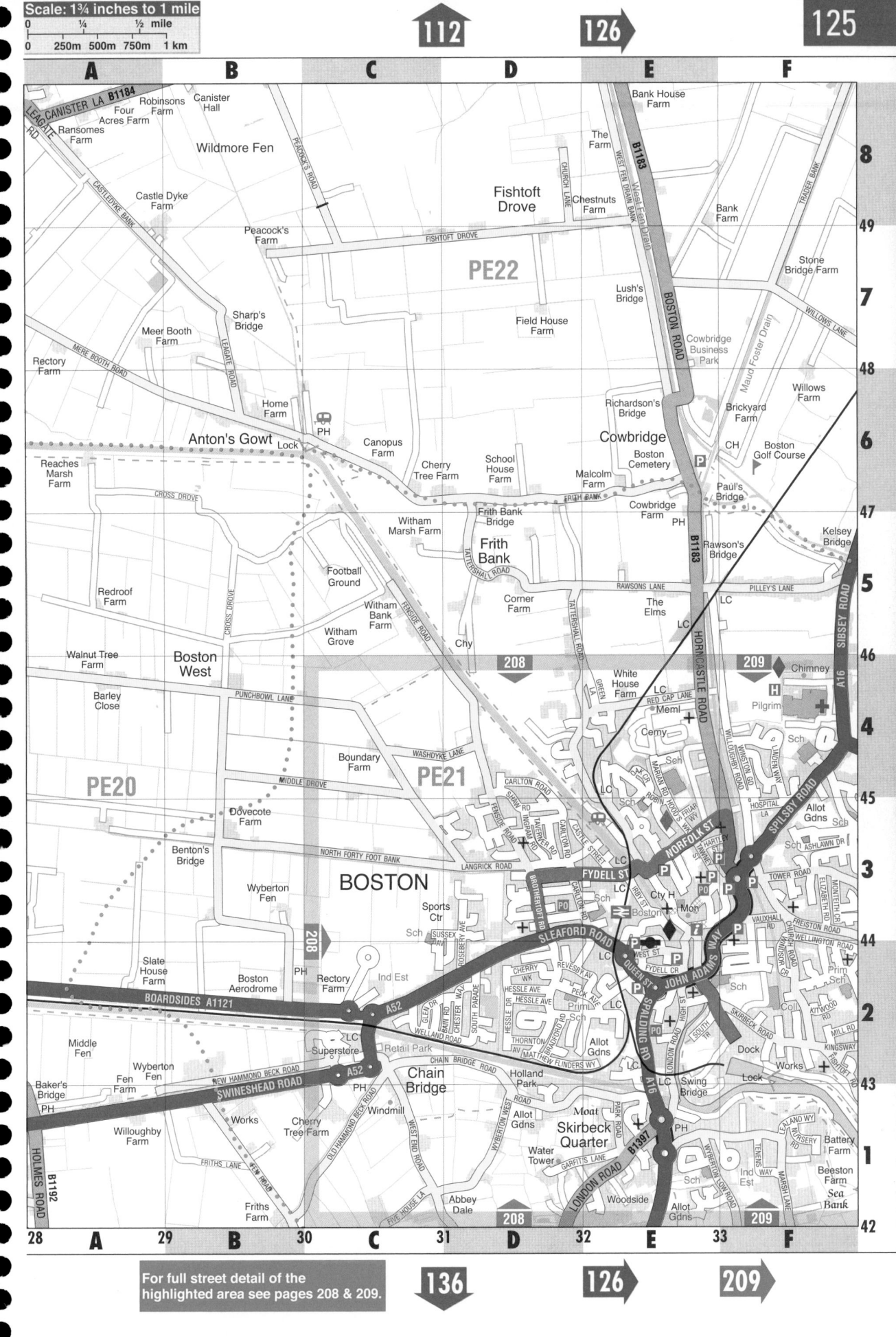

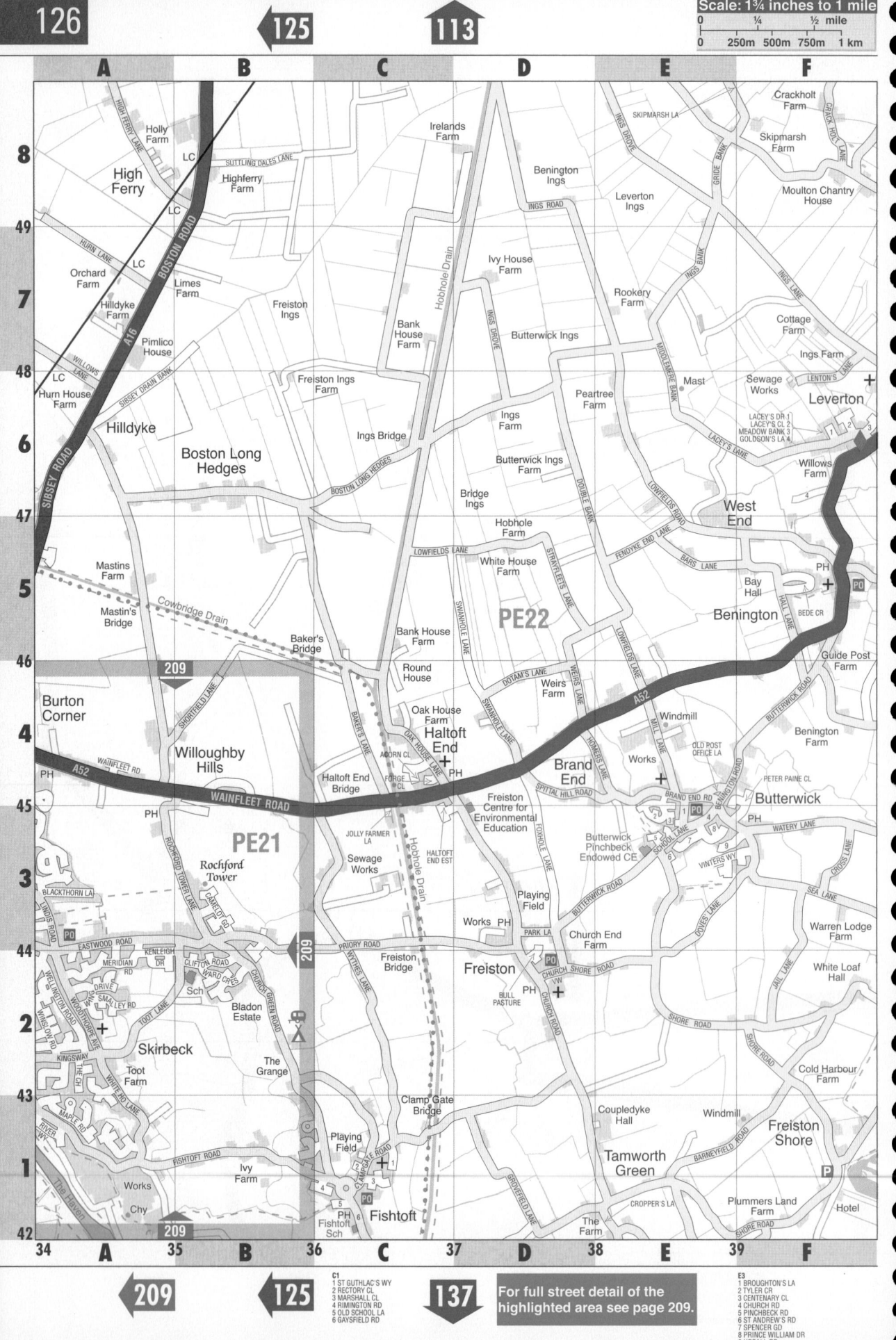

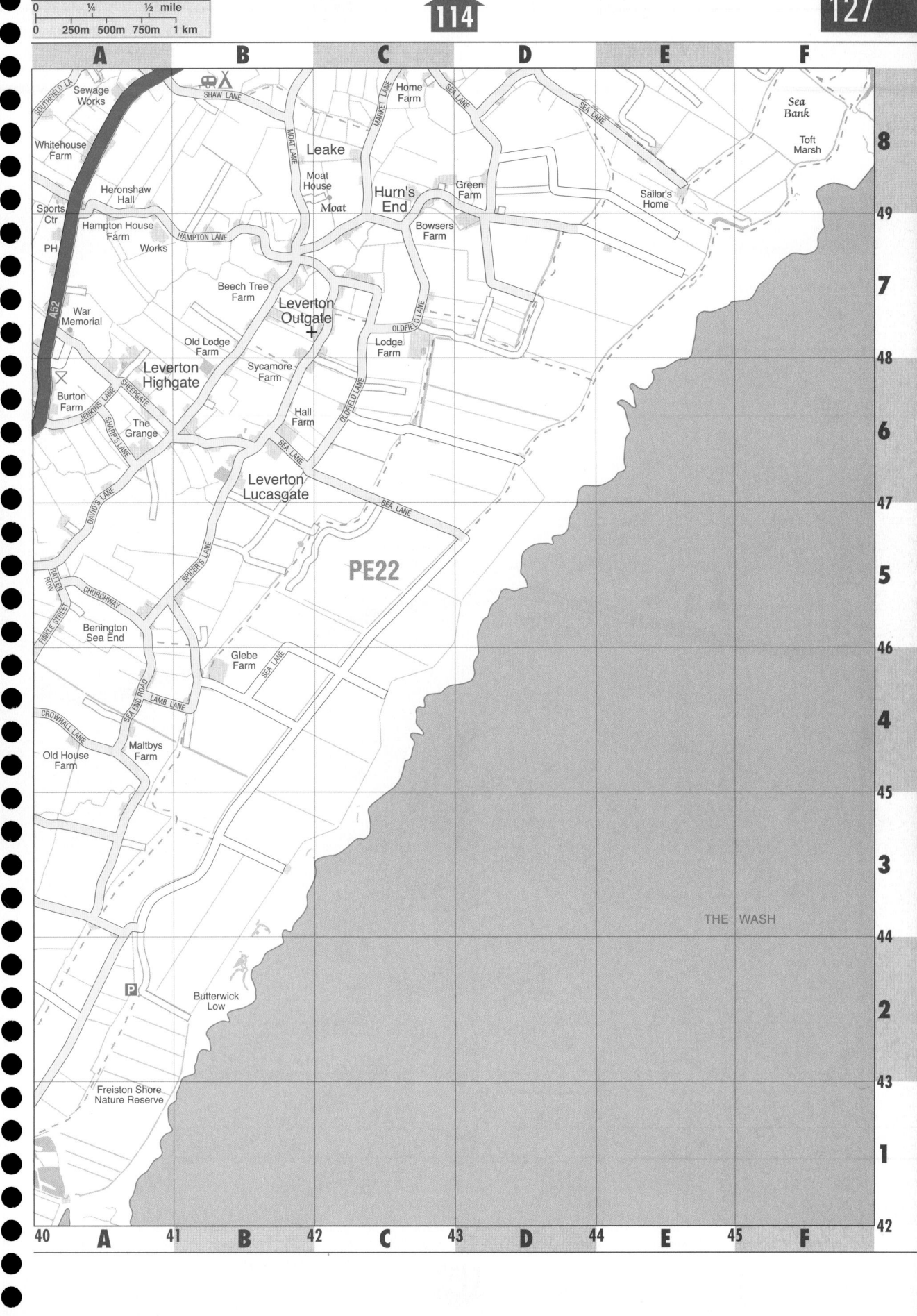

A   B   C   D   E   F

Southfield La
Sewage Works
Whitehouse Farm
Heronshaw Hall
Sports Ctr
PH
Hampton House Farm
Works
War Memorial
Old Lodge Farm
Leverton Highgate
Burton Farm
Jenkins Lane
Sharp's Lane
The Grange
Sheepgate
Beech Tree Farm
Leverton Outgate
Sycamore Farm
Hall Farm
Leverton Lucasgate
David's Lane
Churchway
Fendle Street
Fulten Row
Benington Sea End
Spicer's Lane
Glebe Farm
Sea Lane
Lamb Lane
Sea End Road
Crowhall Lane
Old House Farm
Maltbys Farm
P
Butterwick Low
Freiston Shore Nature Reserve

A52
HAMPTON LANE
MOAT LANE
SHAW LANE
Leake
Moat House
Moat
Hurn's End
Home Farm
MARKET LANE
SEA LANE
Green Farm
SEA LANE
Sea Bank
Toft Marsh
Sallor's Home
Bowsers Farm
OLDFIELD LANE
Lodge Farm
SEA LANE

PE22

THE   WASH

8
49
7
48
6
47
5
46
4
45
3
44
2
43
1
42

40   A   41   B   42   C   43   D   44   E   45   F

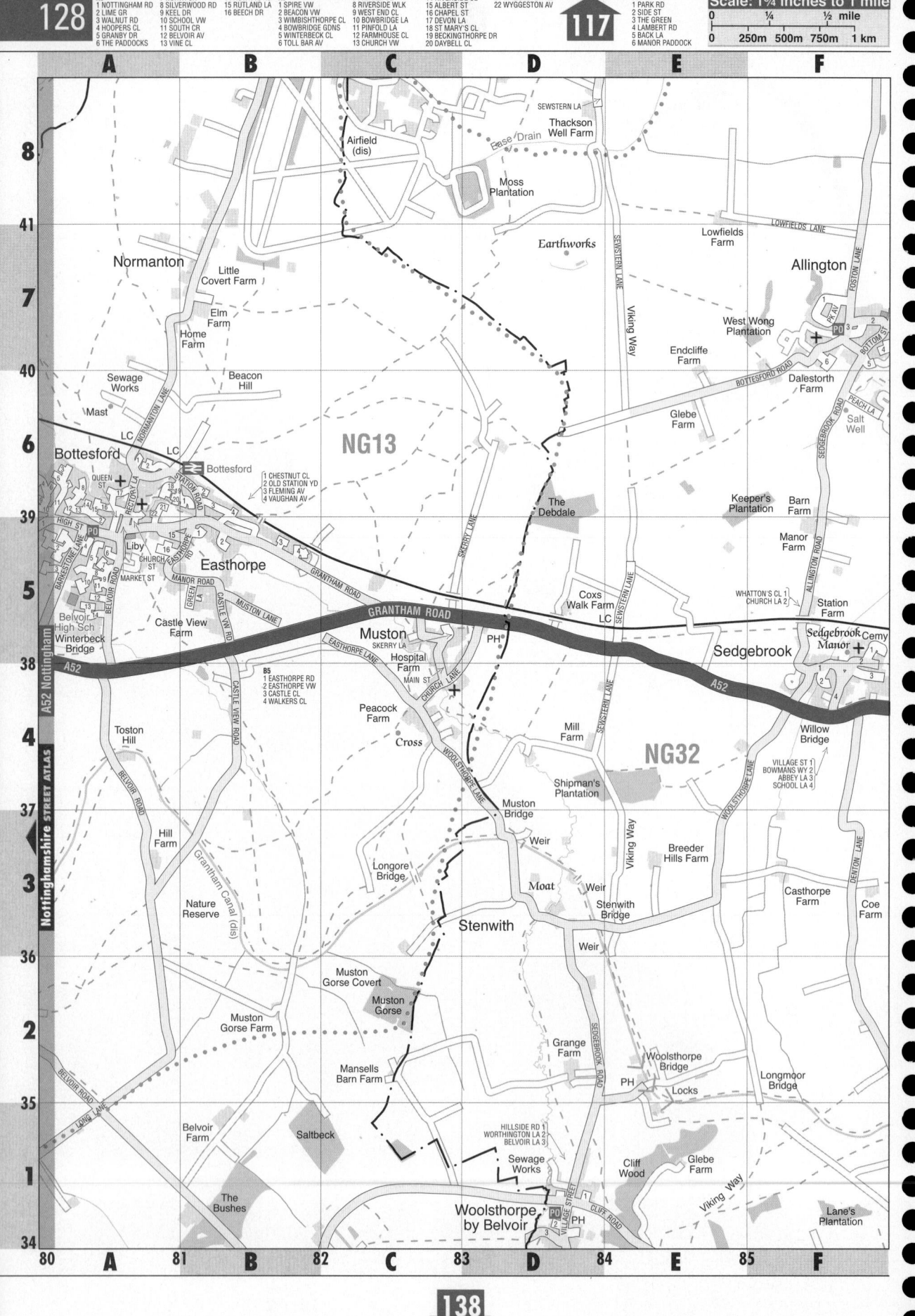

A5
1 NOTTINGHAM RD
2 LIME GR
3 WALNUT RD
4 HOOPERS CL
5 GRANBY DR
6 THE PADDOCKS

7 NORTH CR
8 SILVERWOOD RD
9 KEEL DR
10 SCHOOL VW
11 SOUTH CR
12 BELVOIR AV
13 VINE CL

14 HOWITTS RD
15 RUTLAND LA
16 BEECH DR

A6
1 SPIRE VW
2 BEACON VW
3 WIMBISHTHORPE CL
4 BOWBRIDGE GDNS
5 WINTERBECK CL
6 TOLL BAR AV

7 PINFOLD CL
8 RIVERSIDE WLK
9 WEST END CL
10 BOWBRIDGE LA
11 PINFOLD LA
12 FARMHOUSE CL
13 CHURCH VW

14 RIVERSIDE CL
15 ALBERT ST
16 CHAPEL ST
17 DEVON LA
18 ST MARY'S CL
19 BECKINGTHORPE DR
20 DAYBELL CL

21 WYGGESTON RD
22 WYGGESTON AV

F7
1 PARK RD
2 SIDE ST
3 THE GREEN
4 LAMBERT RD
5 BACK LA
6 MANOR PADDOCK

117

138

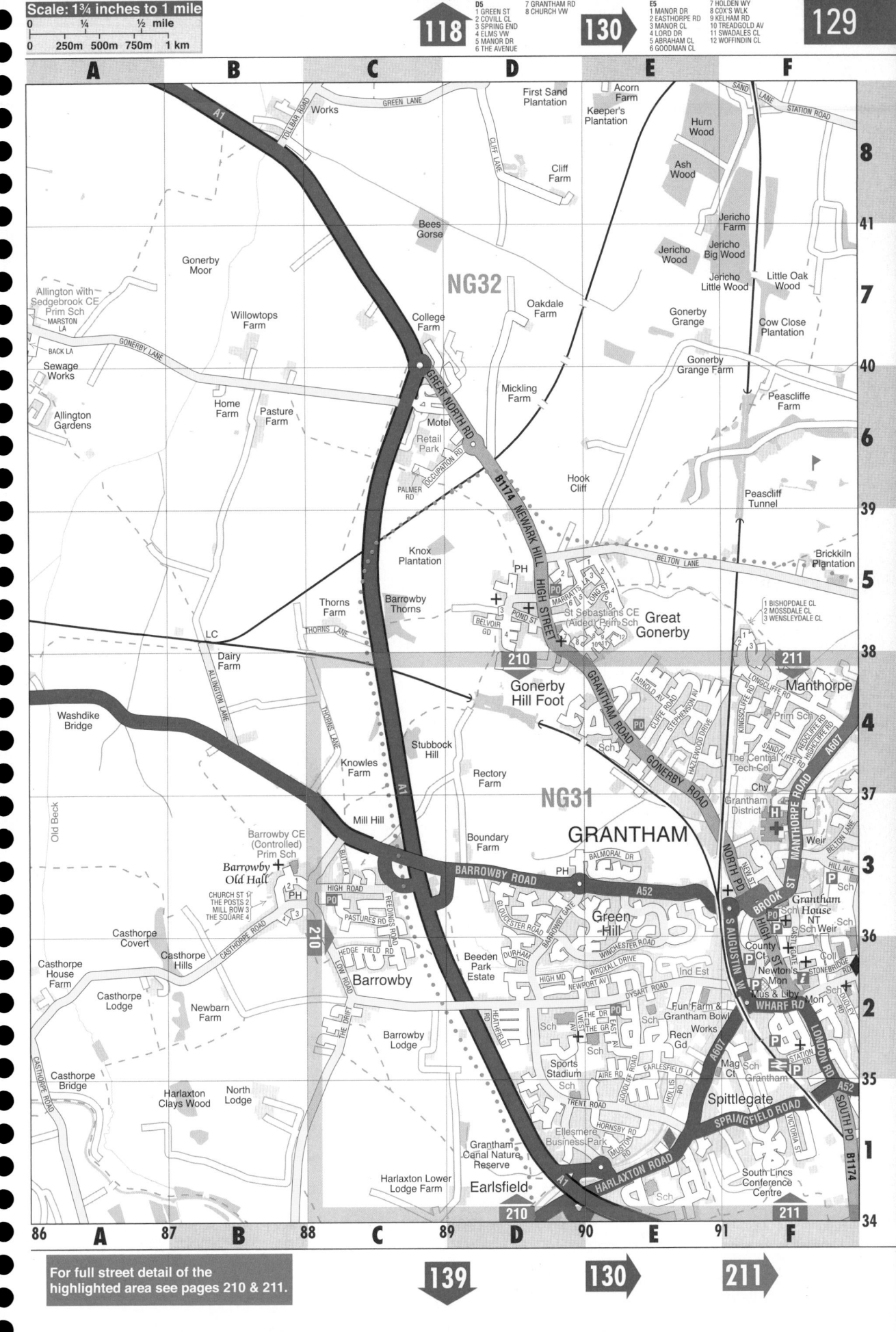

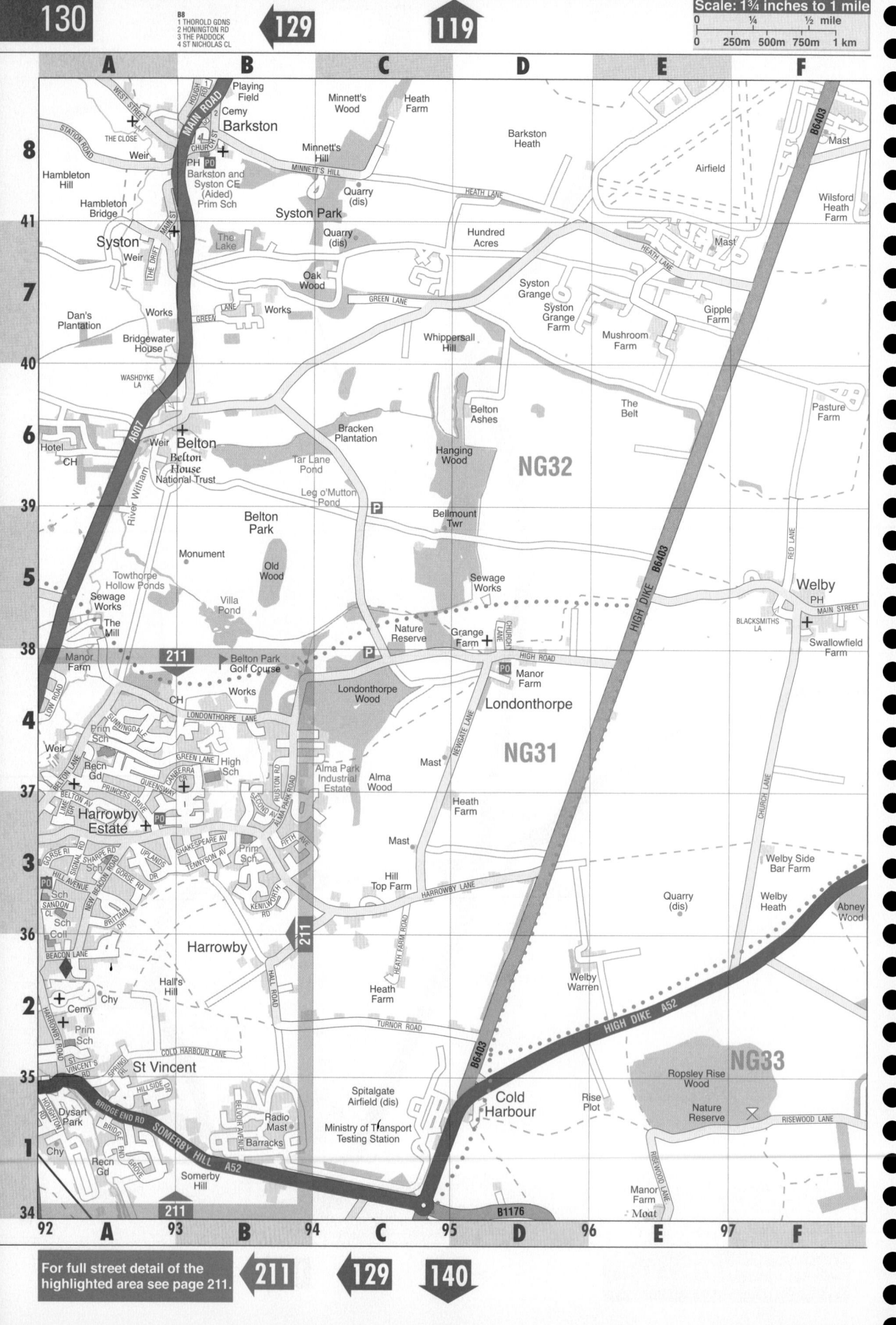

BB
1 THOROLD GDNS
2 HONINGTON RD
3 THE PADDOCK
4 ST NICHOLAS CL

129

119

Scale: 1¾ inches to 1 mile

0 ¼ ½ mile
0 250m 500m 750m 1 km

Column headers (top): A B C D E F

Row numbers (left): 8 41 7 40 6 39 5 38 4 37 3 36 2 35 1 34

West Street
THE CLOSE
Station Road
Weir
Hambleton Hill
Hambleton Bridge
Syston
Weir
The Drift
Dan's Plantation
Bridgewater House
Washdyke La
Green Lane
Works
Hotel
CH
Weir
A607
Belton
Belton House
National Trust
River Witham
Belton Park
Monument
Towthorpe Hollow Ponds
Sewage Works
The Mill
Villa Pond
Old Wood
Manor Farm
211
Belton Park Golf Course
Low Road
CH
Works
Londonthorpe Lane
Cunningdale
Prim Sch
Recn Gd
Belton Ln
Queensway
Canberra Cr
High Sch
Green Lane
Weir
Belton Av
Princess Drive
Harrowby Estate
PO
Gorse Ri
Signal
Sch
New Beacon Rd
Gorse Rd
Uplands Dr
Shakespeare Av
Tennyson Av
Sharpe Rd
Hill Avenue
PO
Sch
Sandon Cl
Sch Coll
Brittain Dr
Kenilworth Rd
Prim Sch
Shakespeare Av
Harrowby
211
Hall Road
Beacon Lane
Hall's Hill
Cemy
Chy
Prim Sch
Harrowby Road
Cold Harbour Lane
St Vincent's Rd
Spring Hill
St Vincent
Hillside Dr
Chy
Dysart Park
Bridge End Rd
Recn Gd
Bridge End Grove
Belvoir Avenue
Radio Mast
Barracks
Somerby Hill
A52
211
Somerby Hill

Main Road
Playing Field
Cemy
Barkston
Hough Rd
Church St
PH PO
Barkston and Syston CE (Aided) Prim Sch
Main St
Minnett's Hill
Minnett's Hill
Syston Park
Quarry (dis)
Quarry (dis)
Minnett's Wood
The Lake
Oak Wood
Green Lane
Works
Lane
Bracken Plantation
Belton Park
Tar Lane Pond
Leg o'Mutton Pond
P
Works
Alma Park Industrial Estate
Alma Wood
Fifth Ave
Second Av
Alma Park Road
Ruston Rd
Hill Top Farm
Turnor Road
Spitalgate Airfield (dis)
Ministry of Transport Testing Station
B1176

Heath Farm
Heath Lane
Barkston Heath
Hundred Acres
Whippersall Hill
Heath Lane
Green Lane
Belton Ashes
NG32
Hanging Wood
Bellmount Twr
Sewage Works
Nature Reserve
Grange Farm
High Road
Church Lane
Londonthorpe Wood
P
PO
Manor Farm
Newgate Lane
Londonthorpe
NG31
Mast
Heath Farm
Mast
Heath Farm Road
Harrowby Lane
Heath Farm
Cold Harbour

Airfield
Mast
Wilsford Heath Farm
Mast
Syston Grange
Syston Grange Farm
Gipple Farm
Mushroom Farm
The Belt
High Dike B6403
Red Lane
Pasture Farm
Welby
PH
Blacksmiths La
Main Street
Swallowfield Farm
Church Lane
Welby Side Bar Farm
Welby Heath
Quarry (dis)
Abney Wood
Welby Warren
High Dike A52
Rise Plot
Ropsley Rise Wood
NG33
Nature Reserve
Risewood Lane
Manor Farm Moat
Risewood Lane

B6403
Mast

Column letters (bottom): A B C D E F
Numbers (bottom): 92 93 94 95 96 97

For full street detail of the highlighted area see page 211.
211
129
140

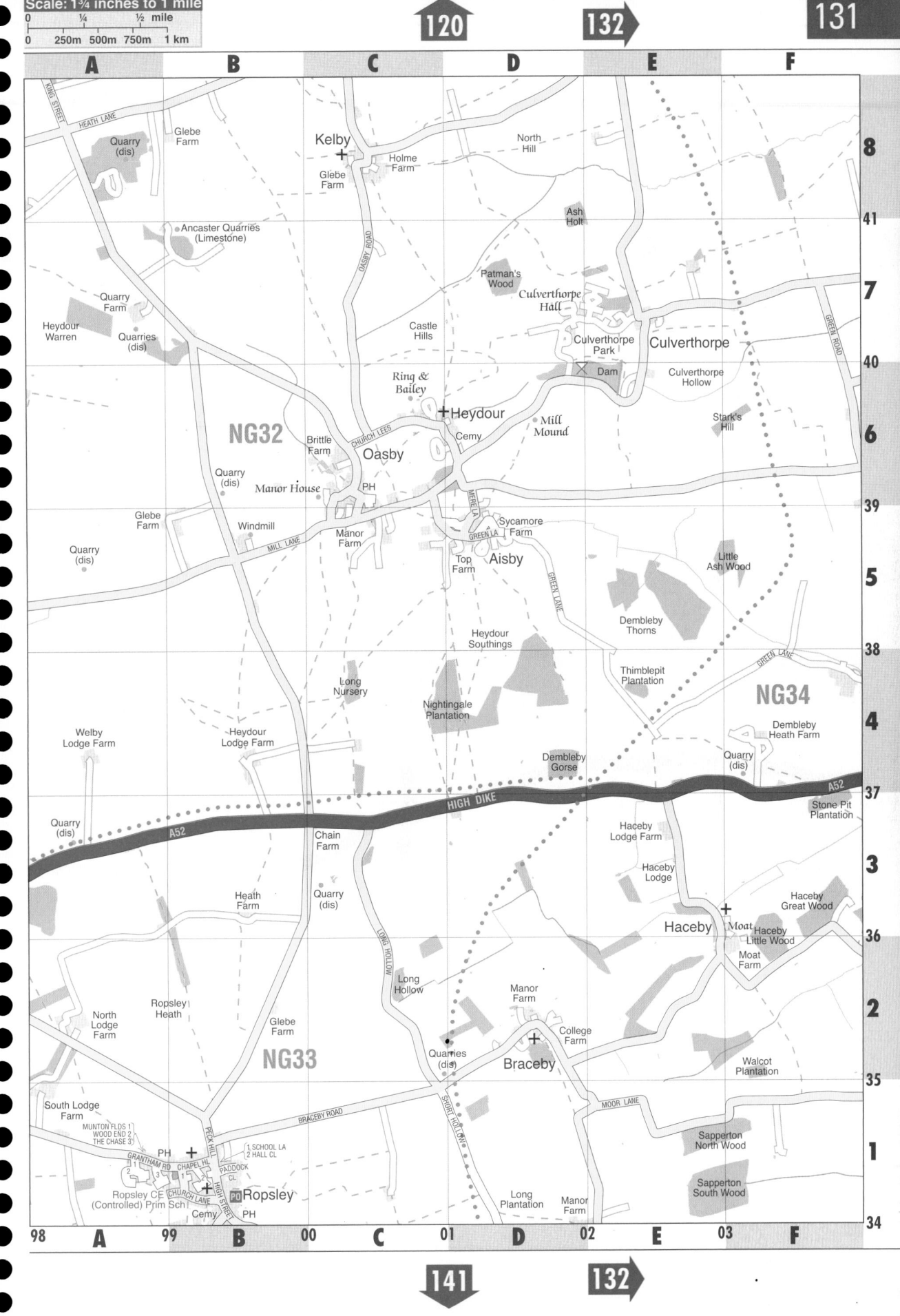

Scale: 1¾ inches to 1 mile

0   ¼   ½ mile
0 250m 500m 750m 1 km

120

132

131

A   B   C   D   E   F

KING STREET

HEATH LANE

Quarry
(dis)

Glebe
Farm

Kelby

Holme
Farm

North
Hill

8

41

Ancaster Quarries
(Limestone)

OASBY ROAD

Glebe
Farm

Patman's
Wood

Ash
Holt

Quarry
Farm

Castle
Hills

Culverthorpe
Hall

Culverthorpe

7

GREEN ROAD

Heydour
Warren

Quarries
(dis)

Culverthorpe
Park

Culverthorpe
Hollow

40

Ring &
Bailey

CHURCH LEES

Heydour

Mill
Mound

Stark's
Hill

NG32

Brittle
Farm

Cemy

6

Oasby

Quarry
(dis)

Manor House

PH

Sycamore
Farm

Little
Ash Wood

39

Glebe
Farm

Windmill

MILL LANE

Manor
Farm

MERE LA

GREEN LA

Aisby

GREEN LANE

Quarry
(dis)

Top
Farm

Dembleby
Thorns

5

Heydour
Southings

Thimblepit
Plantation

38

Long
Nursery

NG34

Nightingale
Plantation

Dembleby
Gorse

Dembleby
Heath Farm

Quarry
(dis)

4

Welby
Lodge Farm

Heydour
Lodge Farm

GREEN LANE

A52

37

Quarry
(dis)

HIGH DIKE

Stone Pit
Plantation

A52

Chain
Farm

Haceby
Lodge Farm

3

Heath
Farm

Quarry
(dis)

Haceby
Lodge

Haceby
Great Wood

LONG HOLLOW

Haceby

Moat

Haceby
Little Wood

36

Long
Hollow

Manor
Farm

Moat
Farm

North
Lodge
Farm

Ropsley
Heath

Glebe
Farm

College
Farm

Walcot
Plantation

2

NG33

SHORT HOLLOW

Quarries
(dis)

Braceby

35

South Lodge
Farm

BRACEBY ROAD

MOOR LANE

MUNTON FLDS 1
WOOD END 2
THE CHASE 3

GRANTHAM RD

PECK HILL

PH

1 SCHOOL LA
2 HALL CL

Sapperton
North Wood

1

CHAPEL HL

PADDOCK
CL

Ropsley CE
(Controlled) Prim Sch

CHURCH LANE

HIGH STREET

PO

Ropsley

Long
Plantation

Manor
Farm

Sapperton
South Wood

Cemy

PH

34

98   A   99   B   00   C   01   D   02   E   03   F

131
121

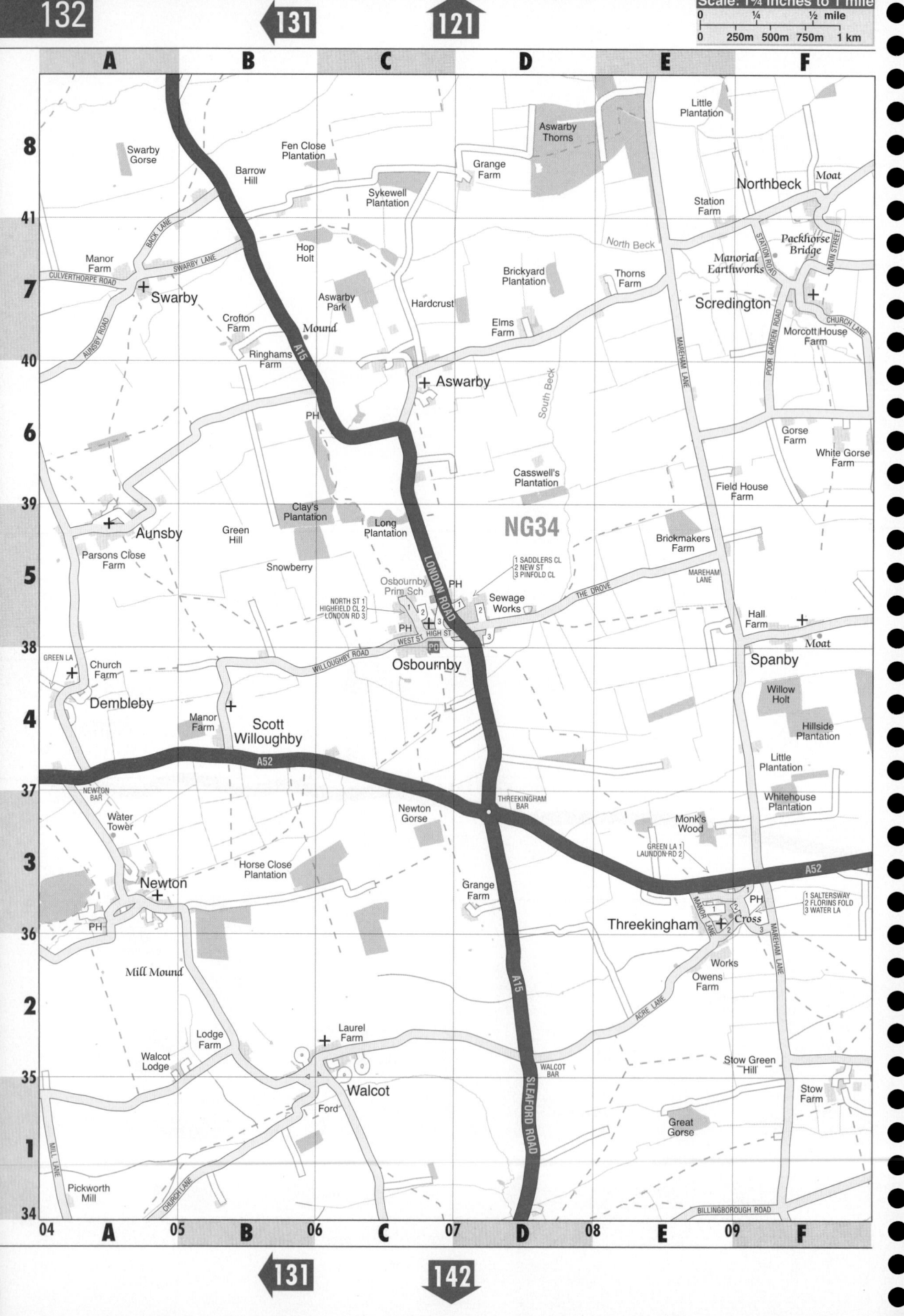
Scale: 1¾ inches to 1 mile
0 ¼ ½ mile
0 250m 500m 750m 1 km
A B C D E F
Swarby Gorse
Fen Close Plantation
Barrow Hill
Aswarby Thorns
Grange Farm
Little Plantation
Northbeck
Moat
Sykewell Plantation
Station Farm
North Beck
Packhorse Bridge
Manorial Earthworks
STATION ROAD
MAIN STREET
Manor Farm
CULVERTHORPE ROAD
BACK LANE
SWARBY LANE
Hop Holt
Brickyard Plantation
Thorns Farm
Swarby
Aswarby Park
Hardcrust
Scredington
Crofton Farm
Mound
Elms Farm
CHURCH LANE
Morcott House Farm
AUNSBY ROAD
Ringhams Farm
A15
POOR GARDEN ROAD
MAREHAM LANE
Aswarby
South Beck
PH
Gorse Farm
White Gorse Farm
Casswell's Plantation
Field House Farm
Clay's Plantation
Aunsby
Green Hill
Long Plantation
NG34
Brickmakers Farm
Parsons Close Farm
Snowberry
LONDON ROAD
1 SADDLERS CL
2 NEW ST
3 PINFOLD CL
MAREHAM LANE
Osbournby Prim Sch
PH
NORTH ST 1
HIGHFIELD CL 2
LONDON RD 3
Sewage Works
THE DROVE
Hall Farm
HIGH ST
WEST ST
PO
Moat
GREEN LA
Church Farm
WILLOUGHBY ROAD
Osbournby
Spanby
Willow Holt
Dembleby
Manor Farm
Scott Willoughby
Hillside Plantation
A52
Little Plantation
NEWTON BAR
THREEKINGHAM BAR
Whitehouse Plantation
Water Tower
Newton Gorse
Monk's Wood
GREEN LA 1
LAUNDON RD 2
A52
Horse Close Plantation
Newton
Grange Farm
PH
1 SALTERSWAY
2 FLORINS FOLD
3 WATER LA
MANOR LANE
Threekingham
Cross
PH
Mill Mound
A15
Works
Owens Farm
ACRE LANE
Laurel Farm
Lodge Farm
Walcot Lodge
WALCOT BAR
Stow Green Hill
Walcot
SLEAFORD ROAD
Stow Farm
Ford
Great Gorse
MILL LANE
Pickworth Mill
CHURCH LANE
BILLINGBOROUGH ROAD
8
41
7
40
6
39
5
38
4
37
3
36
2
35
1
34
04 05 06 07 08 09

131
142

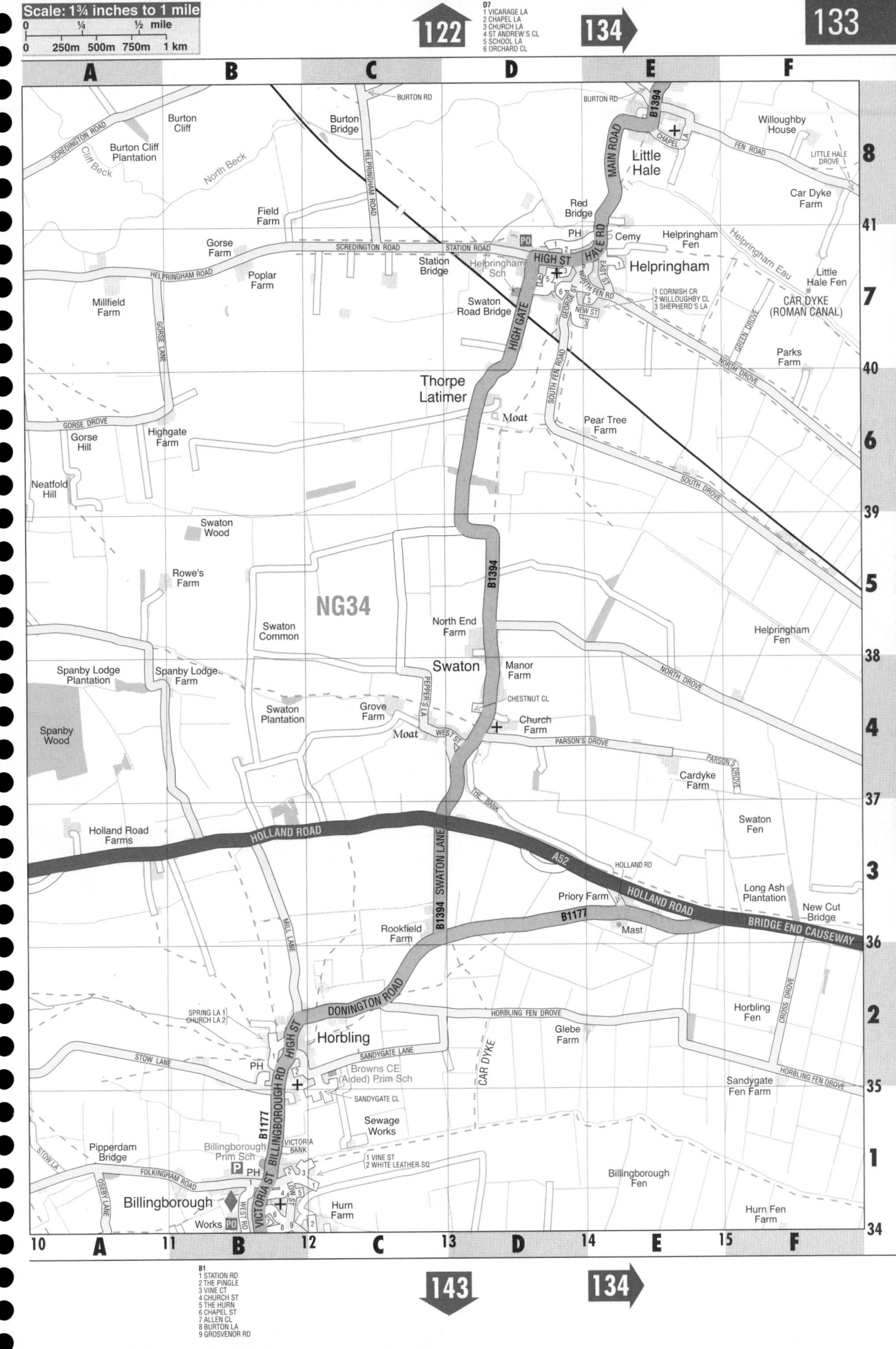

Scale: 1¾ inches to 1 mile

0 ¼ ½ mile
0 250m 500m 750m 1 km

122
134

D7
1 VICARAGE LA
2 CHAPEL LA
3 CHURCH LA
4 ST ANDREW'S CL
5 SCHOOL LA
6 ORCHARD CL

A B C D E F

Scredington Road
Cliff Beck
Burton Cliff
Burton Cliff Plantation
Burton Bridge
Burton Rd
North Beck
Helpringham Road
Burton Rd
Little Hale
B1394
Main Road
Chapel La
Willoughby House
Little Hale Drove

Field Farm
Scredington Road
Station Road
Station Bridge
PO
Red Bridge
PH
Hale Rd
Cemy
Helpringham Fen
Car Dyke Farm
41

Gorse Farm
Poplar Farm
Helpringham Sch
High St
East St
North Fen Rd
Helpringham
Helpringham Eau
Little Hale Fen

Helpringham Road
Swaton Road Bridge
1
2
George St
New St
1 CORNISH CR
2 WILLOUGHBY CL
3 SHEPHERD'S LA
CAR DYKE (ROMAN CANAL)
7

Millfield Farm
High Gate
3
Green Drove
Parks Farm

Gorse Lane
North Drove
40

Thorpe Latimer
South Fen Road
Pear Tree Farm
6

Gorse Drove
Moat
South Drove

Gorse Hill
Highgate Farm
39

Neatfold Hill
Swaton Wood
B1394
Helpringham Fen
5

Rowe's Farm
NG34
North End Farm
North Drove

Swaton Common
Swaton
38

Spanby Lodge Plantation
Spanby Lodge Farm
Manor Farm
4

Swaton Plantation
Grove Farm
Pepper's La
Chestnut Cl
Church Farm

Spanby Wood
Moat
West St
Parson's Drove
Parson's Drove
Cardyke Farm

Swaton Fen
37

Holland Road Farms
Holland Road
The Bank
A52
Holland Rd
Swaton Fen

Swaton Lane
B1394
Holland Road
3

Long Ash Plantation
New Cut Bridge

Priory Farm
B1177
Mast
Bridge End Causeway
36

Rookfield Farm
Mill Lane
Cross Drove

Donington Road
Horbling Fen Drove
Horbling Fen
2

Spring La 1
Church La 2
High St
Horbling
Glebe Farm

Stow Lane
Sandygate Lane
Car Dyke
Horbling Fen Drove

PH
Browns CE (Aided) Prim Sch
Sandygate Fen Farm
35

B1177
Billingborough Rd
Sandygate Cl
Sewage Works

Pipperdam Bridge
Billingborough Prim Sch
Victoria Bank
1 VINE ST
2 WHITE LEATHER SQ
Billingborough Fen
1

Folkingham Road
P
PH
West Rd
Stow La
Ousby Lane
Billingborough
Hurn Farm
Hurn Fen Farm

Works
PO
34

10 A 11 B 12 C 13 D 14 E 15 F

B1
1 STATION RD
2 THE PINGLE
3 VINE CT
4 CHURCH ST
5 THE HURN
6 CHAPEL ST
7 ALLEN CL
8 BURTON LA
9 GROSVENOR RD

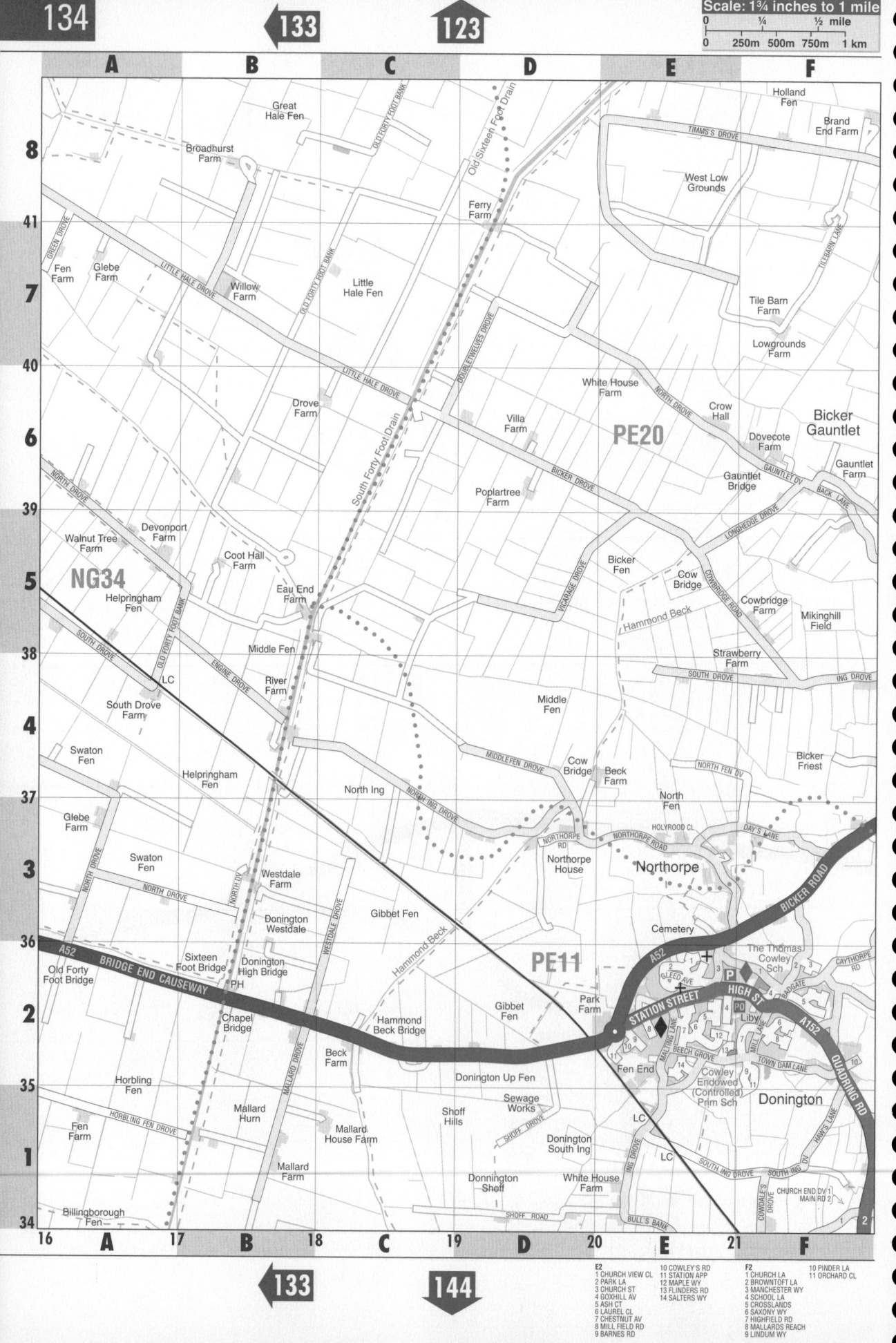

Scale: 1¾ inches to 1 mile

0   ¼   ½ mile
0   250m 500m 750m 1 km

A   B   C   D   E   F

8

41

7

40

6

39

5

38

4

37

3

36

2

35

1

34

16   17   18   19   20   21

Holland Fen
Brand End Farm
Great Hale Fen
Broadhurst Farm
West Low Grounds
Timms's Drove
Ferry Farm
Tile Barn Farm
Lowgrounds Farm
Fen Farm
Glebe Farm
Willow Farm
Little Hale Fen
White House Farm
Crow Hall
Bicker Gauntlet
Little Hale Drove
Drove Farm
Villa Farm
PE20
Dovecote Farm
Gauntlet Bridge
Gauntlet Farm
Back Lane
Poplartree Farm
Bicker Drove
Longhedge Drove
Cowbridge Farm
Mikinghill Field
Walnut Tree Farm
Devonport Farm
Coot Hall Farm
Bicker Fen
Cow Bridge
NG34
Helpringham Fen
Eau End Farm
Hammond Beck
Strawberry Farm
Middle Fen
South Drove
Ing Drove
South Drove Farm
River Farm
LC
Middle Fen
Bicker Friest
Swaton Fen
Helpringham Fen
North Ing
Middlefen Drove
Cow Bridge
Beck Farm
North Fen Dv
North Fen
Glebe Farm
Swaton Fen
North Drove
North Ing Drove
Holyrood Cl
Northorpe Rd
Day's Lane
North Drove
Westdale Farm
Gibbet Fen
Northorpe House
Northorpe Road
Northorpe
Bicker Road
Donington Westdale
Cemetery
The Thomas Cowley Sch
Caythorpe Rd
A52
Sixteen Foot Bridge
Donington High Bridge
Hammond Beck
PE11
Park Farm
A52
High St
Old Forty Foot Bridge
Bridge End Causeway
PH
Gleed Av
Station Street
Libby
A152
Chapel Bridge
Hammond Beck Bridge
Gibbet Fen
Beech Grove
Town Dam Lane
Fen End
Cowley Endowed (Controlled) Prim Sch
Donington
Quadring Rd
Horbling Fen
Beck Farm
Donington Up Fen
LC
Horbling Fen Drove
Mallard Hurn
Sewage Works
Shoff Hills
LC
Fen Farm
Mallard House Farm
Donington South Ing
White House Farm
Mallard Farm
Donnington Shoff
Shoff Road
Bull's Bank
Billingborough Fen
Cowdale's Drove
South Ing Drove
Church End Dv 1
Main Rd 2

E2
1 CHURCH VIEW CL
2 PARK LA
3 CHURCH ST
4 GOXHILL AV
5 ASH CT
6 LAUREL CL
7 CHESTNUT AV
8 MILL FIELD RD
9 BARNES RD
10 COWLEY'S RD
11 STATION APP
12 MAPLE WY
13 FLINDERS RD
14 SALTERS WY

F2
1 CHURCH LA
2 BROWNTOFT LA
3 MANCHESTER WY
4 SCHOOL LA
5 CROSSLANDS
6 SAXONY WY
7 HIGHFIELD RD
8 MALLARDS REACH
9 LINDUM WY
10 PINDER LA
11 ORCHARD CL

124
136

B7
1 COLE'S LA
2 LOCKTON CL
3 HILLCREST GDNS
4 MILNE GN
5 SARTHE CL
6 KING JOHNS RD
7 VIKING CL
8 MONKS RD
9 ADRIAN CL
10 CHEESE HILL
11 WESTFIELD DR
12 MILLHILL LA
13 CHURCH LA
14 BUTLER'S WY

C7
1 LA MILESSE WY
2 HAFF CL
3 CRAGG CL
4 ABBEY CR
5 TOWNFIELD LA
6 COWLEY CL

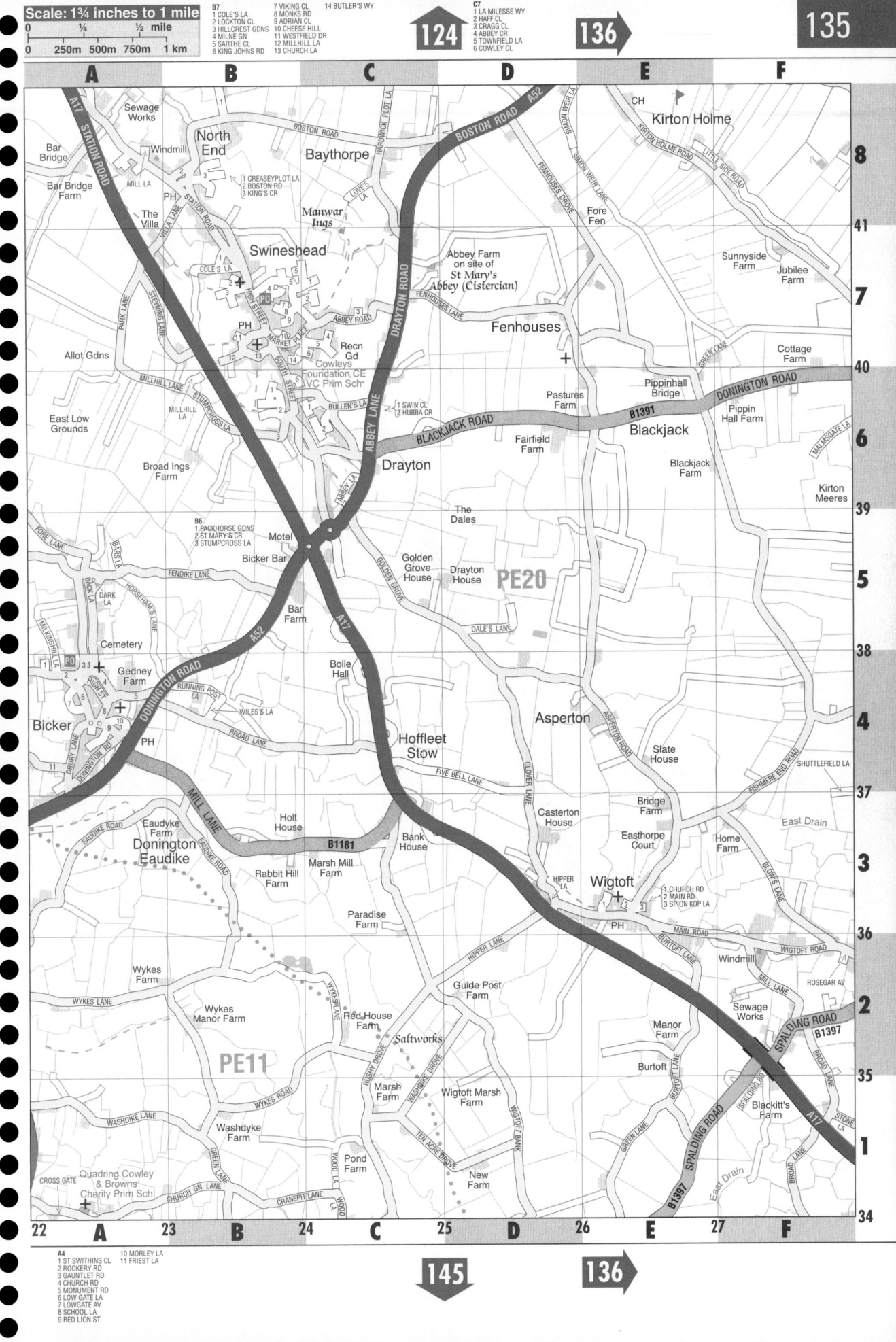

A4
1 ST SWITHINS CL
2 ROOKERY RD
3 GAUNTLET RD
4 CHURCH RD
5 MONUMENT RD
6 LOW GATE LA
7 LOWGATE AV
8 SCHOOL LA
9 RED LION ST
10 MORLEY LA
11 FRIEST LA

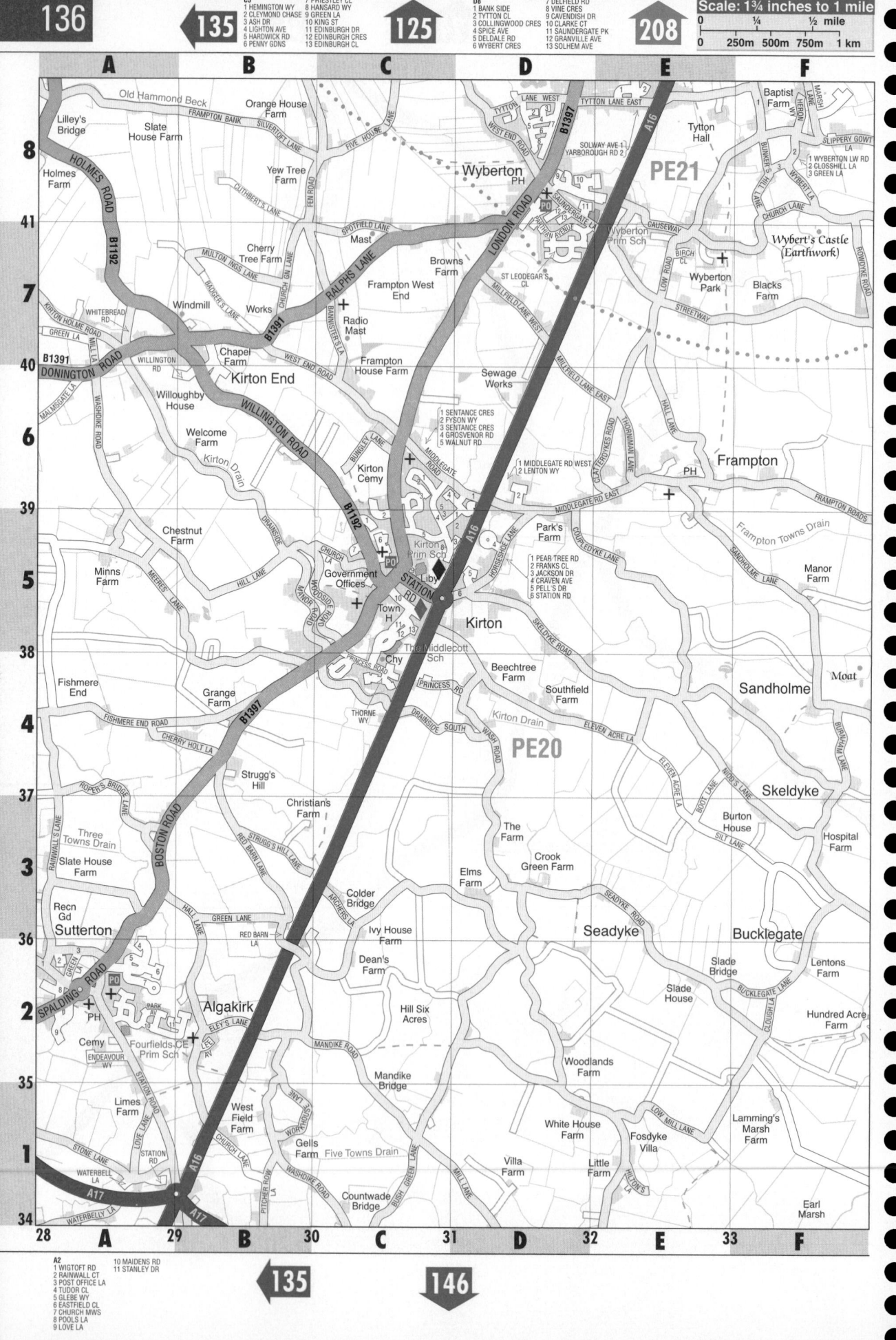
135
C5
1 HEMINGTON WY
2 CLEYMOND CHASE
3 ASH DR
4 LIGHTON AVE
5 HARDWICK RD
6 PENNY GDNS
7 PRIESTLEY CL
8 HANSARD WY
9 GREEN LA
10 KING ST
11 EDINBURGH DR
12 EDINBURGH CRES
13 EDINBURGH CL
125
D8
1 BANK SIDE
2 TYTTON CL
3 COLLINGWOOD CRES
4 SPICE AVE
5 DELDALE RD
6 WYBERT CRES
7 DELFIELD RD
8 VINE CRES
9 CAVENDISH DR
10 CLARKE CT
11 SAUNDERGATE PK
12 GRANVILLE AVE
13 SOLHEM AVE
208
Scale: 1¾ inches to 1 mile
0 ¼ ½ mile
0 250m 500m 750m 1 km
A B C D E F
Old Hammond Beck
Lilley's Bridge
Slate House Farm
Orange House Farm
FRAMPTON BANK
SILVERTOFT LANE
FIVE HOUSE LANE
Holmes Farm
HOLMES ROAD
Yew Tree Farm
CUTHBERT'S LANE
FEN ROAD
TYTTON LANE WEST
TYTTON LANE EAST
WEST END ROAD
B1397
SOLWAY AVE 1
YARBOROUGH RD 2
Wyberton
PH
PO
SAUNDERGATE LA
LONDON ROAD
A16
Tytton Hall
PE21
Baptist Farm
HERON WY
MARSH LANE
SLIPPERY GOWT LA
BUNKER'S HILL LANE
WYBERT LA
1 WYBERTON LW RD
2 CLOSSHILL LA
3 GREEN LA
CHURCH LANE
CAUSEWAY
Wyberton Prim Sch
Wybert's Castle (Earthwork)
ROWDYKE ROAD
BIRCH CL
LOW ROAD
Wyberton Park
Blacks Farm
STREETWAY
B1192
Cherry Tree Farm
MULTON INGS LANE
CHURCH GN LANE
SPOTFIELD LANE
Mast
RALPHS LANE
Browns Farm
Frampton West End
ST LEODEGAR'S CL
MILLFIELD LANE WEST
KIRTON HOLME ROAD
WHITEBREAD RD
Windmill
BADGER'S LANE
Works
B1391
BANNISTER'S LA
Radio Mast
GREEN LA
MILL LA
B1391
DONINGTON ROAD
WILLINGTON RD
Chapel Farm
WEST END ROAD
Frampton House Farm
Sewage Works
MILLFIELD LANE EAST
Kirton End
MALMSGATE LA
WASHDIKE ROAD
Willoughby House
WILLINGTON ROAD
1 SENTANCE CRES
2 FYSON WY
3 SENTANCE CRES
4 GROSVENOR RD
5 WALNUT RD
CLATTERDYKES ROAD
THORNIMAN LANE
HALL LANE
Welcome Farm
Kirton Drain
BUNGLEY LANE
MIDDLEGATE ROAD
Kirton Cemy
1 MIDDLEGATE RD WEST
2 LENTON WY
PH
Frampton
MIDDLEGATE RD EAST
FRAMPTON ROADS
DRAINSIDE
Chestnut Farm
B1192
Kirton Prim Sch
HORSESHOE LANE
Park's Farm
COUPLEDYKE LANE
Frampton Towns Drain
SANDHOLME LANE
CHURCH LA
1 PEAR TREE RD
2 FRANKS CL
3 JACKSON DR
4 CRAVEN AVE
5 PELL'S DR
6 STATION RD
Minns Farm
MEERES' LANE
HILL LANE
Government Offices
STATION RD
Liby
MANOR ROAD
WOODSIDE ROAD
Town H
Kirton
Manor Farm
SKELDYKE ROAD
The Middlecott Sch
Chy
PRINCESS ROAD
PRINCESS RD
Beechtree Farm
Southfield Farm
Moat
Fishmere End
Grange Farm
Sandholme
THORNE WY
DRAINSIDE SOUTH
Kirton Drain
FISHMERE END ROAD
B1397
WASH ROAD
ELEVEN ACRE LA
BURNHAM LANE
CHERRY HOLT LA
PE20
Strugg's Hill
ELEVEN ACRE LA
NIDD'S LANE
BOOT LANE
Skeldyke
ROPER'S BRIDGE LANE
Christian's Farm
RAINWALL'S LANE
Three Towns Drain
BOSTON ROAD
STRUGG'S HILL LANE
RED BARN LANE
The Farm
Burton House
SILT LANE
Hospital Farm
Slate House Farm
Crook Green Farm
Elms Farm
Colder Bridge
ARCHERS LA
SEADYKE ROAD
Recn Gd
Sutterton
HALL LANE
GREEN LANE
RED BARN LA
Ivy House Farm
Seadyke
Bucklegate
Dean's Farm
Slade Bridge
Lentons Farm
SPALDING ROAD
PO
Slade House
BUCKLEGATE LANE
CLOUGH LA
PH
Algakirk
PARK AV
Hill Six Acres
Hundred Acre Farm
ELEY'S LANE
Cemy
Fourfields CE Prim Sch
ENDEAVOUR WY
LEE AV
MANDIKE ROAD
Woodlands Farm
STATION ROAD
Mandike Bridge
Limes Farm
West Field Farm
WORKHOUSE LANE
White House Farm
LOW MILL LANE
Lamming's Marsh Farm
LOVE LANE
Fosdyke Villa
STONE LANE
STATION RD
CHURCH LANE
Gells Farm
Five Towns Drain
WATERBELL LA
A16
Villa Farm
Little Farm
HILTON'S LA
A17
WASHDIKE ROAD
PITCHER ROW LA
BUSH GREEN LANE
MILL LANE
Countwade Bridge
Earl Marsh
WATERBELLY LA
A17
28 29 30 31 32 33 34
35 1 36 2 37 3 38 4 39 5 40 6 41 7 8
A2
1 WIGTOFT RD
2 RAINWALL CT
3 POST OFFICE LA
4 TUDOR CL
5 GLEBE WY
6 EASTFIELD CL
7 CHURCH MWS
8 POOLS LA
9 LOVE LA
10 MAIDENS RD
11 STANLEY DR
135
146

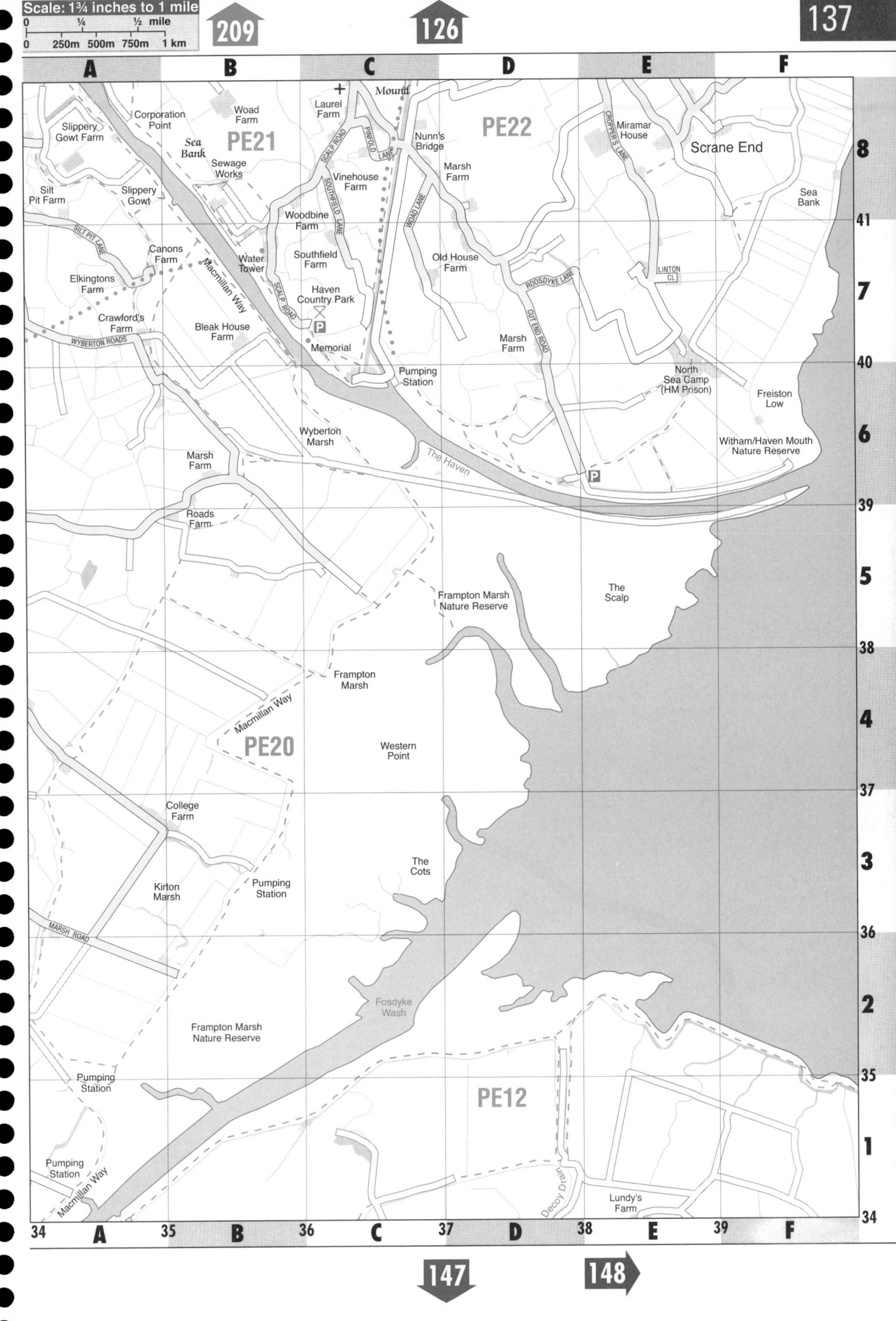
Scale: 1¾ inches to 1 mile
0 ¼ ½ mile
0 250m 500m 750m 1 km
209
126
A B C D E F
PE21
PE22
PE20
PE12
Mound
Laurel Farm
Woad Farm
Corporation Point
Slippery Gowt Farm
Sea Bank
Sewage Works
Scalp Road
Pinfold Lane
Nunn's Bridge
Miramar House
Cropper's Lane
Scrane End
Marsh Farm
Vinehouse Farm
Southfield Lane
Woad Lane
Silt Pit Farm
Slippery Gowt
Sea Bank
Woodbine Farm
Silt Pit Lane
Canons Farm
Water Tower
Southfield Farm
Old House Farm
Elkingtons Farm
Macmillan Way
Haven Country Park
Roosdyke Lane
Linton Cl
Crawford's Farm
Wyberton Roads
Bleak House Farm
Memorial
Cut End Road
Marsh Farm
Pumping Station
North Sea Camp (HM Prison)
Freiston Low
Wyberton Marsh
Witham/Haven Mouth Nature Reserve
Marsh Farm
The Haven
Roads Farm
The Scalp
Frampton Marsh Nature Reserve
Frampton Marsh
Macmillan Way
Western Point
College Farm
The Cots
Kirton Marsh
Pumping Station
Marsh Road
Fosdyke Wash
Frampton Marsh Nature Reserve
Pumping Station
Pumping Station
Macmillan Way
Decoy Drain
Lundy's Farm
8 41 7 40 6 39 5 38 4 37 3 36 2 35 1 34
34 35 36 37 38 39
147
148

Scale: 1¾ inches to 1 mile

0   ¼   ½   mile
0 250m 500m 750m 1 km

A   B   C   D   E   F

Leicestershire & Rutland STREET ATLAS

8

Belvoir
The Queen's Royal Lancers Museum
Woolsthorpe By Belvoir
The Ash Beds
Belvoir Castle
Cobleas Wood
Holy Well
Church Thorns
West Wong
Mausoleum
Belvoir Lower Lake
Kennel Wood
Young Oaks
1 CHAPEL HL
2 RECTORY LA
3 COBLEAS
P

33
Duchess Garden
Cemy

7
Old Park Wood
High Leys
Blackberry Hill
Knipton Pasture
Old Church Wood
Castle Farm
Manor Farm
Sir John's Belt
Carlisle Wood
Windsor Hill
Briery Wood
Belvoir Upper Lake
The Devon
Woolsthorpe Quarries
Viking Way
Socketwell Plantation
HARSTON ROAD

32
Jubilee Way
Terrace Hills
Frog Hollow
King's Wood
The Trout Pond
DENTON LANE
Denton Park
BELVOIR RD
MOOD LA

6
High Leys Farm
Granby Wood
Quarry (dis)
NURSERY LA 1
HNNS LA 2
CHURCH HL 3
THE OLD HL 4
Glebe Farm
KNIPTON LANE
Harston
NG32
Gallows Plantation
A607
THE DRIFT

31
Bunkers Wood
Knipton CE Prim Sch
Knipton
PH
PO
Big Wood
Black Fir Plantation
Top Ash Plantation
THE DRIFT

5
Reservoir Wood
Nursery Plantation
Harston Wood
Beasley's Wood
Hill Top Farm
Knipton Reservoir
CROXTON LANE
Hallam's Wood
Cedar Hill

30
Sewage Works
Croxton Banks
Coneygear Wood

4
Branston
Memorial
PH
Croxton Lodge Farm
Bluebell Wood
Croxton Kerrial
Tipping's Gorse
Home Farm
KNIPTON ROAD
THE ROCK
MIDDLE STREET
PH
Sewage Works
Croxton Kerrial CE Prim Sch
WALTHAM ROAD
SALTBY ROAD

29
MAIN STREET
A607
PO
THE NOOK 1
HIGHFIELD CR 2
House Hillside Farm
Tipping's Lodge
Eaton Grange

3
Bottom Farm
Lings Hill
Windmill Hill
Old Wood
Heath Farm
STATION ROAD
GREEN LANE

28
Top Farm
Lings Farm
Kennel Plantation
Swallow Hole Farm
Swallow Hole
Swallow Hole Covert

2
Lings Covert
Site of Abbey
Croxton Park
Saltby Lodge
CROXTON ROAD

27
The Moss
Lawn Hollow Plantation
Station Farm

1
Croxton Race Course (dis)
Bescaby Oaks
LE14
Cherry Tree Farm
Joey's Wood
Saltby
MARY LANE
PH
THE BUTTS
BACK ST

26
A607 Melton Mowbray
Leicestershire & Rutland STREET ATLAS
Bescaby
Medieval Village of Bescaby (site of)
Weir
Weir
Dairy Farm
Chalybeate Spring
Hawthorn Farm
STONESBY ROAD
MARY LA

80 A 81 B 82 C 83 D 84 E 85 F

D4
1 CHAPEL LA
2 CHURCH LA
3 THORPES LA
4 TOP RD
5 SCHOOL LA
6 SHIRES OR
7 MILL LA

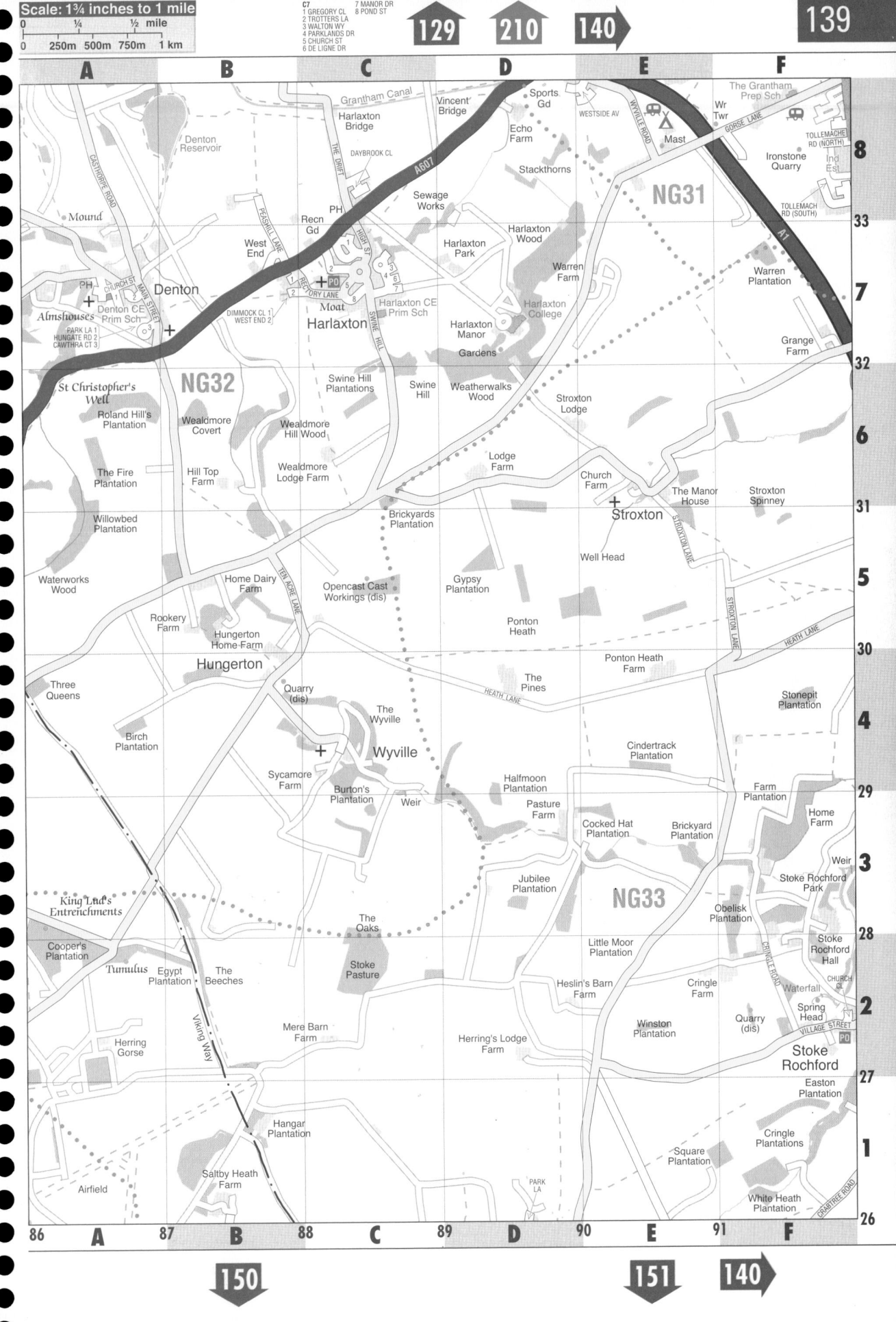

Scale: 1¾ inches to 1 mile

0   ¼   ½   mile
0   250m   500m   750m   1 km

C7
1 GREGORY CL   7 MANOR DR
2 TROTTERS LA   8 POND ST
3 WALTON WY
4 PARKLANDS DR
5 CHURCH ST
6 DE LIGNE DR

129   210   140

A   B   C   D   E   F

The Grantham Prep Sch
Grantham Canal
Vincent Bridge
Harlaxton Bridge
Sports Gd
WESTSIDE AV
Wr Twr
TOLLEMACHE RD (NORTH)
GORSE LANE
Echo Farm
Denton Reservoir
THE DRIFT
DAYBROOK CL
A607
Stackthorns
Mast
WYVILLE ROAD
Ironstone Quarry
Ind Est
8

Mound
PH
Recn Gd
Sewage Works
NG31
TOLLEMACHE RD (SOUTH)
A1
33

West End
PEASHILL LANE
Harlaxton Wood
Harlaxton Park
Warren Farm
Warren Plantation
7

PH
CHURCH ST
MAIN STREET
Denton
RECTORY LANE
PO
HIGH ST
Harlaxton CE Prim Sch
Harlaxton Wood
Harlaxton College
Almshouses
Denton CE Prim Sch
DIMMOCK CL 1
WEST END 2
Moat
Harlaxton
Harlaxton Manor
Gardens
Grange Farm
32

PARK LA 1
HUNGATE RD 2
CAWTHRA CT 3
St Christopher's Well
NG32
Swine Hill Plantations
SWINE HILL
Swine Hill
Weatherwalks Wood
Stroxton Lodge
6

Roland Hill's Plantation
Wealdmore Covert
Wealdmore Hill Wood
Lodge Farm
Church Farm
The Manor House
Stroxton Spinney
The Fire Plantation
Hill Top Farm
Wealdmore Lodge Farm
Stroxton
STROXTON LANE
31

Willowbed Plantation
Brickyards Plantation
Well Head
Waterworks Wood
Home Dairy Farm
TEN ACRE LANE
Opencast Cast Workings (dis)
Gypsy Plantation
Ponton Heath
STROXTON LANE
HEATH LANE
5

Rookery Farm
Hungerton Home Farm
Ponton Heath Farm
30

Hungerton
Quarry (dis)
The Pines
HEATH LANE
Stonepit Plantation
Three Queens
The Wyville
Cindertrack Plantation
Farm Plantation
4

Birch Plantation
Sycamore Farm
Wyville
Halfmoon Plantation
Home Farm
Weir
29

King Lud's Entrenchments
Burton's Plantation
Weir
Pasture Farm
Cocked Hat Plantation
Brickyard Plantation
Weir
Stoke Rochford Park
3

Cooper's Plantation
Jubilee Plantation
NG33
Obelisk Plantation
Stoke Rochford Hall
The Oaks
Little Moor Plantation
CRINGLE ROAD
CHURCH CT
28

Tumulus
Egypt Plantation
The Beeches
Stoke Pasture
Heslin's Barn Farm
Cringle Farm
Waterfall
Spring Head
VILLAGE STREET
2

Herring Gorse
VIKING WAY
Mere Barn Farm
Herring's Lodge Farm
Winston Plantation
Quarry (dis)
PO
Stoke Rochford
Easton Plantation
27

Hangar Plantation
PARK LA
Square Plantation
Cringle Plantations
1

Saltby Heath Farm
Airfield
White Heath Plantation
CRABTREE ROAD
26

86   A   87   B   88   C   89   D   90   E   91   F

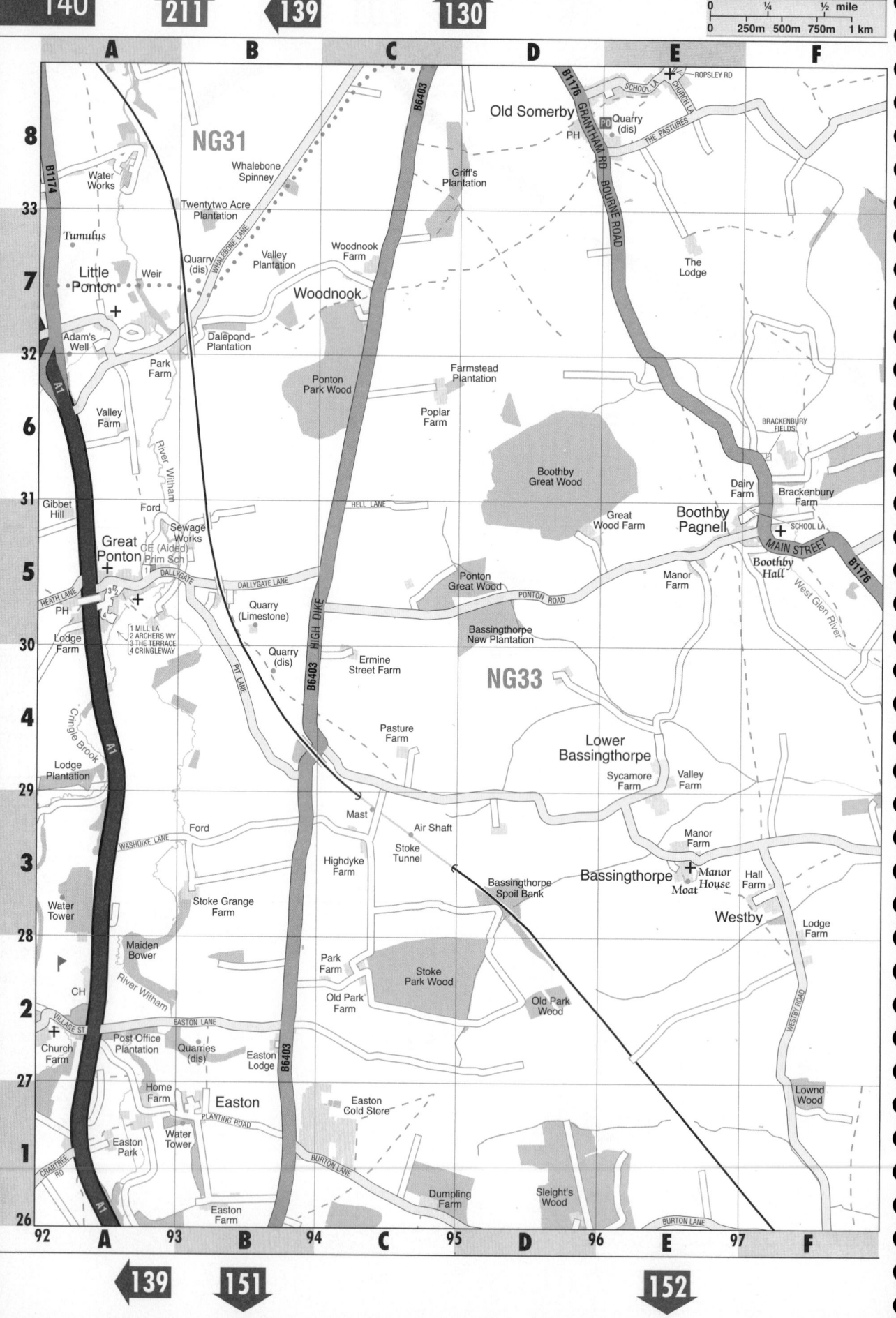

211
139
130

Scale: 1¾ inches to 1 mile
0   ¼   ½ mile
0   250m 500m 750m 1 km

A **B** **C** **D** **E** **F**

NG31

8

Whalebone Spinney

Water Works

Twentytwo Acre Plantation

33

Tumulus

Quarry (dis)

Valley Plantation

Woodnook Farm

Griff's Plantation

Old Somerby

Quarry (dis)

THE PASTURES

SCHOOL LA

ROPSLEY RD

CHURCH LA

PH

PO

GRANTHAM RD

BOURNE ROAD

7

Little Ponton

Weir

Woodnook

The Lodge

32

Adam's Well

Dalepond Plantation

Park Farm

Farmstead Plantation

BRACKENBURY FIELDS

6

Valley Farm

Ponton Park Wood

Poplar Farm

Boothby Great Wood

Dairy Farm

Brackenbury Farm

31

Gibbet Hill

Ford

River Witham

HELL LANE

Great Wood Farm

Boothby Pagnell

SCHOOL LA

MAIN STREET

B1176

5

Great Ponton

Sewage Works

CE (Aided) Prim Sch

DALLYGATE

DALLYGATE LANE

Ponton Great Wood

PONTON ROAD

Manor Farm

Boothby Hall

West Glen River

HEATH LANE

PH

Quarry (Limestone)

1 MILL LA
2 ARCHERS WY
3 THE TERRACE
4 CRINGLEWAY

30

Lodge Farm

Quarry (dis)

Ermine Street Farm

Bassingthorpe New Plantation

NG33

HIGH DYKE

PIT LANE

B6403

4

Cringle Brook

A1

Pasture Farm

Lower Bassingthorpe

Sycamore Farm

Valley Farm

29

Lodge Plantation

Mast

Air Shaft

Manor Farm

Ford

WASHDIKE LANE

Stoke Tunnel

Bassingthorpe

Manor Farm

Hall Farm

3

Highdyke Farm

Bassingthorpe Spoil Bank

Manor House

Moat

Westby

WESTBY ROAD

Water Tower

Stoke Grange Farm

Park Farm

Stoke Park Wood

Old Park Wood

Lodge Farm

28

Maiden Bower

Old Park Farm

CH

River Witham

EASTON LANE

2

Village St

Post Office Plantation

Quarries (dis)

Easton Lodge

Easton Cold Store

Lownd Wood

Church Farm

B6403

27

Home Farm

Easton

PLANTING ROAD

1

Easton Park

Water Tower

BURTON LANE

Dumpling Farm

Sleight's Wood

CRABTREE RD

A1

26

Easton Farm

BURTON LANE

92   A   93   B   94   C   95   D   96   E   97   F

139
151
152

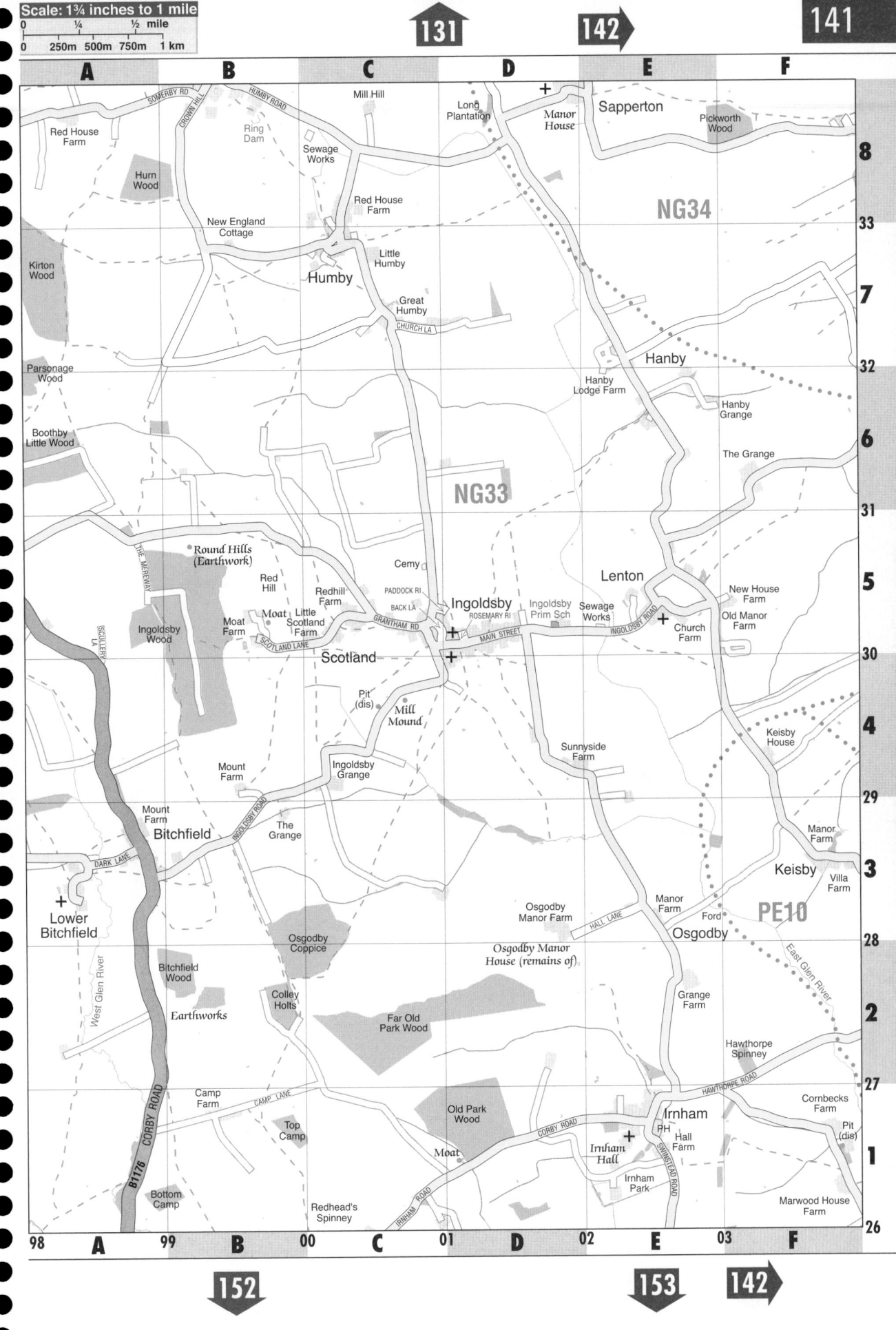

Scale: 1¾ inches to 1 mile

0   ¼   ½   mile
0 250m 500m 750m 1 km

Somerby Rd
Crown Hill
Humby Road
Mill Hill
Long Plantation
Manor House
Sapperton
Pickworth Wood

Red House Farm
Hurn Wood
Ring Dam
Sewage Works
Red House Farm

NG34

New England Cottage
Little Humby
Humby
Kirton Wood

Great Humby
Church La
Hanby

Parsonage Wood
Hanby Lodge Farm
Hanby Grange

Boothby Little Wood
NG33
The Grange

The Mereway
Round Hills (Earthwork)
Red Hill
Redhill Farm
Cemy
Paddock Ri
Back La
Ingoldsby
Rosemary Ri
Main Street
Ingoldsby Prim Sch
Sewage Works
Lenton
New House Farm
Old Manor Farm

Scollery La
Ingoldsby Wood
Moat Farm
Little Scotland Farm
Grantham Rd
Scotland Lane
Scotland
Church Farm
Ingoldsby Road

Pit (dis)
Mill Mound
Sunnyside Farm
Keisby House

Mount Farm
Ingoldsby Grange

Mount Farm
Bitchfield
Ingoldsby Road
The Grange
Manor Farm
Keisby
Villa Farm

Dark Lane
PE10

Lower Bitchfield
Osgodby Manor Farm
Manor Farm
Ford
Osgodby
East Glen River

West Glen River
Bitchfield Wood
Osgodby Coppice
Osgodby Manor House (remains of)
Hall Lane
Grange Farm

Earthworks
Colley Holts
Far Old Park Wood
Hawthorpe Spinney

Camp Farm
Camp Lane
Top Camp
Old Park Wood
Hawthorpe Road
Cornbecks Farm
Irnham
PH
Hall Farm
Pit (dis)

Corby Road
B1176
Bottom Camp
Moat
Irnham Hall
Irnham Park
Corby Road
Irnham Road
Swinstead Road
Marwood House Farm

Redhead's Spinney

141
132

D8
1 CHURCH LA
2 CHAPEL LA
3 TANNERY LA
4 SPRING LA
5 GREENFIELDS LA

Scale: 1¾ inches to 1 mile

0   ¼   ½   mile
0   250m 500m 750m 1 km

Folkingham

KIME CL 1
CHURCHFIELDS RD 2
LOW FARM DR 3

Castle
Earthworks

Moat

Little
Gorse

New
Bridge

Beacon
Hill

Pickworth

Village
Farm

SHEPTON
LA

Allot
Gdns

Low
Farm

Ford

Spring
Farm

BRICKYARD LANE

Water
Tower

Manor
Farm

Owens Barn
Farm

New
Covert

GREENFIELDS LANE

Pointon Cottage
Farm

Pickworth
Lodge Farm

South
Lodge

NG34

Laughton

West
Laughton

The
Chestnuts

Works

Lodge
Farm

Medieval Village of
West Laughton (site of)

Aslackby Castle
(site of)

Manor
Farm

NG33

AVELAND WAY

PH

Ford

AVELAND CL

Temple
Farm

TEMPLE RD

Aslackby

SOVEREIGN STREET

Airfield
(dis)

Keisby
Wood

Low Park
Farm

Graby

Manor
Farm

High Park
Farm

Temple
Wood

ASLACKBY ROAD

Milking
Bridge

Potash
Farm

Rippingale

Radio
Mast

Grange
Wood

Rippingale CE
(Controlled)
Prim-Sch

Sunny Bank
Farm

Hawthorpe

Hawthorne
Farm

BARNBERRY
WY

RIPPINGALE ROAD

Cemy

PH

HAWTHORPE ROAD

Rookery
Farm

Radio
Masts

Grange
Farm

Kirkby
Underwood

PINFOLD CL 1
BLANCHARD CL 2
MIDDLE ST 3
SCARBOROUGH CL 4
WENDOVER CL 5

Manor
Farm

Old Beck

CALLAN'S LANE

PE10

RINGSTONE CHASE

Bulby Hall
Wood

Moats

Callan's
Lane Wood

STANFIELD ROAD

Hall
Farm

Glebe
Farm

Studio Wood
Farm

Bulby

Manor
Farm

Pasture
Wood

Thorny
Wood

Row
Wood

Ringstone
Wood

Dunsby
Wood

Westwood
Farm

HIGH STREET

BILLINGBOROUGH ROAD

SLEAFORD RD

BOURNE ROAD

A15

MAREHAM LANE

WALCOT DR

WEST STREET

MILL LANE

FOLKINGHAM RD

VILLAGE ST

CHURCH LANE

CHURCH
FIELDS

PH

153
141
154

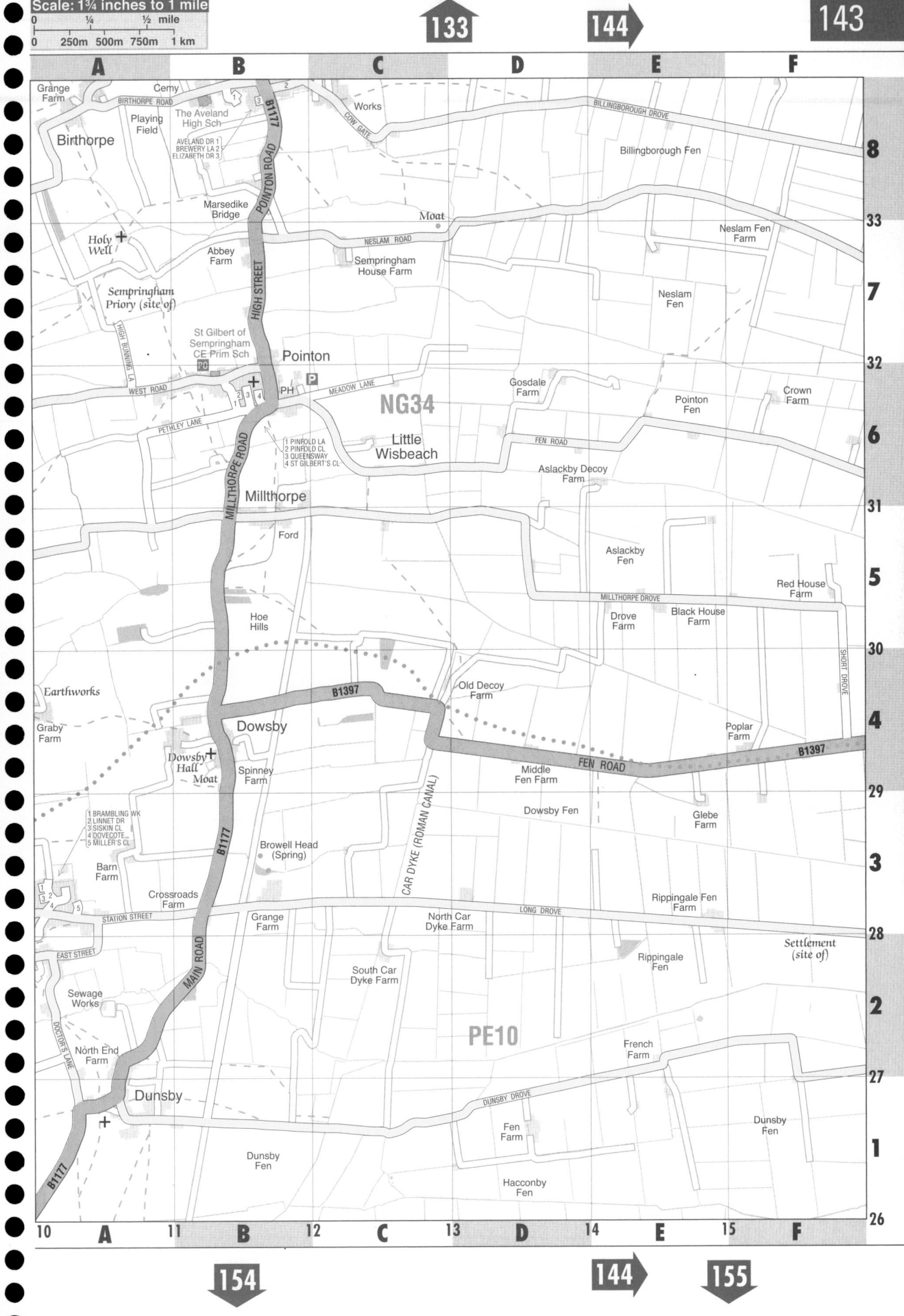
Scale: 1¾ inches to 1 mile
133
144
Birthorpe
Billingborough Fen
Neslam Fen Farm
Neslam Fen
Sempringham Priory (site of)
Pointon
NG34
Little Wisbeach
Millthorpe
Pointon Fen
Crown Farm
Gosdale Farm
Aslackby Decoy Farm
Aslackby Fen
Red House Farm
Drove Farm
Black House Farm
Hoe Hills
Old Decoy Farm
Dowsby
Dowsby Hall
Spinney Farm
Middle Fen Farm
Dowsby Fen
Glebe Farm
Poplar Farm
Browell Head (Spring)
Barn Farm
Crossroads Farm
Grange Farm
North Car Dyke Farm
Rippingale Fen Farm
Rippingale Fen
South Car Dyke Farm
PE10
French Farm
Dunsby
North End Farm
Sewage Works
Fen Farm
Dunsby Fen
Hacconby Fen
154
144
155

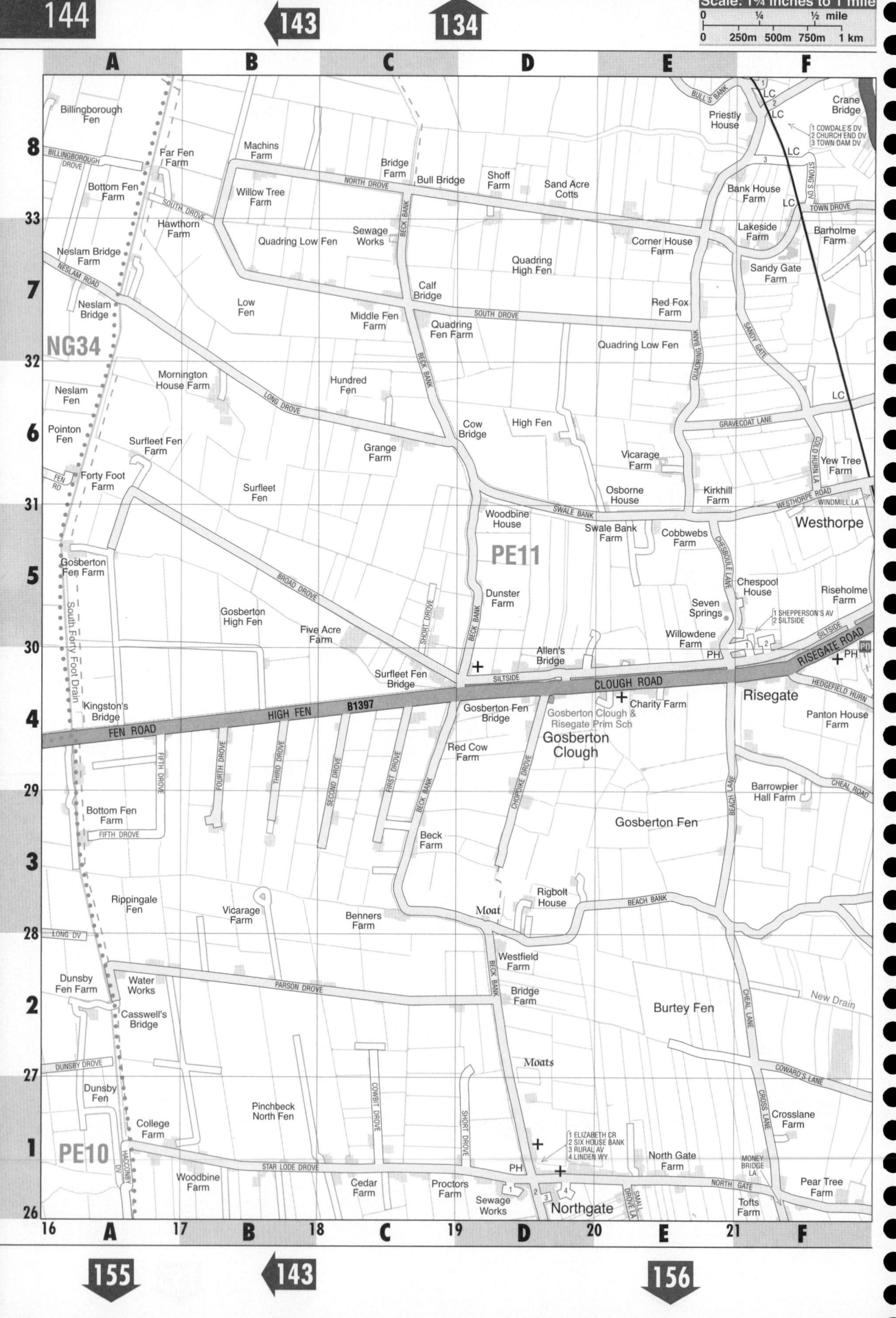

A   B   C   D   E   F

8   Billingborough Fen

Far Fen Farm

Machins Farm

Willow Tree Farm

Bridge Farm

Bull Bridge

Shoff Farm

Sand Acre Cotts

BULL'S BANK
Priestly House

Crane Bridge

1 COWDALE'S DV
2 CHURCH END DV
3 TOWN DAM DV

LC   LC   LC   LC

BILLINGBOROUGH DROVE

SOUTH DROVE

NORTH DROVE

Bottom Fen Farm

Hawthorn Farm

Quadring Low Fen

Sewage Works

Bank House Farm

Lakeside Farm

STONG'S AV   TOWN DROVE   Barholme Farm

33

Neslam Bridge Farm

NESLAM ROAD

Calf Bridge

Quadring High Fen

Corner House Farm

Sandy Gate Farm

7   Neslam Bridge

Low Fen

Middle Fen Farm

Quadring Fen Farm

SOUTH DROVE

Red Fox Farm

NG34

32   Neslam Fen

Mornington House Farm

Hundred Fen

QUADRING BANK

Quadring Low Fen

LC

LONG DROVE

Cow Bridge

High Fen

GRAVECOAT LANE

SANDY GATE   Yew Tree Farm

6   Pointon Fen

Surfleet Fen Farm

Grange Farm

BECK BANK

Vicarage Farm

COLD HURN LA   WESTHORPE ROAD   WINDMILL LA

FEN RD

Forty Foot Farm

Surfleet Fen

Osborne House

SWALE BANK

Kirkhill Farm

Westhorpe

31

Woodbine House

Swale Bank Farm

Cobbwebs Farm

CHESBOULE LANE

LC

5   Gosberton Fen Farm

BROAD DROVE

Gosberton High Fen

Five Acre Farm

PE11

Dunster Farm

Chespool House

Riseholme Farm

SHEPPERSON'S AV
SILTSIDE

SOUTH FORTY FOOT DRAIN

SHORT DROVE

BECK BANK

Seven Springs

Willowdene Farm

PH

RISEGATE ROAD   PO   PH

30   Kingston's Bridge

Surfleet Fen Bridge

Allen's Bridge

SILTSIDE

CLOUGH ROAD

Charity Farm

Risegate

HEDGEFIELD HURN

Panton House Farm

4   FEN ROAD   HIGH FEN   B1397

Gosberton Fen Bridge

Gosberton Clough & Risegate Prim Sch

Gosberton Clough

FIFTH DROVE   FOURTH DROVE   THIRD DROVE   SECOND DROVE   FIRST DROVE

Red Cow Farm

BECK BANK

CHOPDIKE DROVE

BEACH LANE   Barrowpier Hall Farm   CHEAL ROAD

29   Bottom Fen Farm

FIFTH DROVE

Beck Farm

Gosberton Fen

3   Rippingale Fen

Vicarage Farm

Benners Farm

Moat

Rigbolt House

BEACH BANK

28   LONG DV

Dunsby Fen Farm

Water Works

PARSON DROVE

Westfield Farm

2   Casswell's Bridge

BECK BANK

Bridge Farm

Burtey Fen

CHEAL LANE   New Drain

DUNSBY DROVE

COMBIT DROVE

SHORT DROVE

Moats

COWARD'S LANE

CROSS LANE   Crosslane Farm

27   Dunsby Fen

Pinchbeck North Fen

1 ELIZABETH CR
2 SIX HOUSE BANK
3 RURAL AV
4 LINDEN WY

MONEY BRIDGE LA

1   PE10

HACCONBY DV

College Farm

STAR LODE DROVE

Cedar Farm

Proctors Farm

PH

North Gate Farm

NORTH GATE   Pear Tree Farm

26   Woodbine Farm

Sewage Works

Northgate

SMALL DROVE LA

Tofts Farm

16   A   17   B   18   C   19   D   20   E   21   F

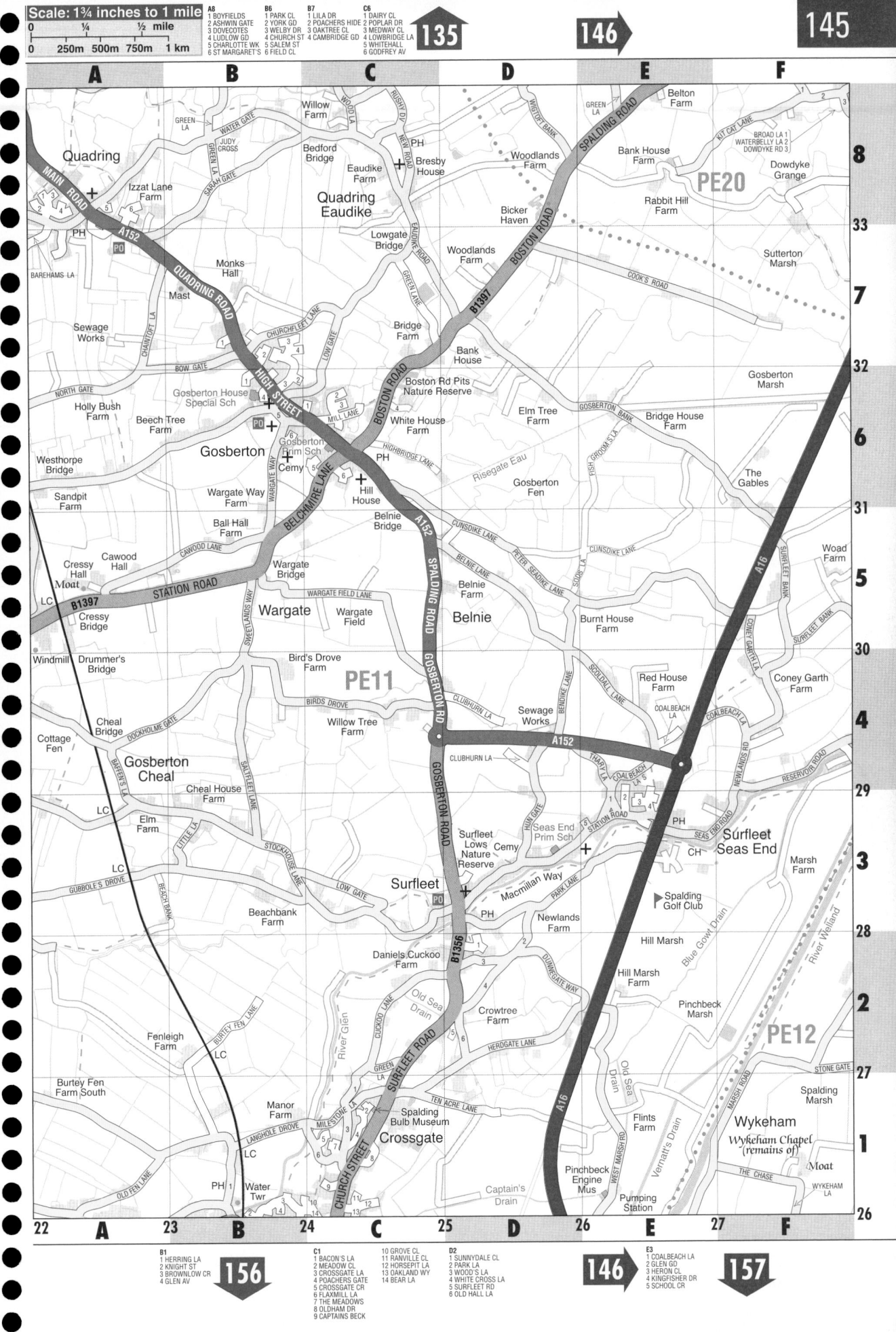

Scale: 1¾ inches to 1 mile
0 ¼ ½ mile
0 250m 500m 750m 1 km
A8
1 BOYFIELDS
2 ASHWIN GATE
3 DOVECOTES
4 LUDLOW GD
5 CHARLOTTE WK
6 ST MARGARET'S
B6
1 PARK CL
2 YORK GD
3 WELBY DR
4 CHURCH ST
5 SALEM ST
6 FIELD CL
B7
1 LILA DR
2 POACHERS HIDE
3 OAKTREE CL
4 CAMBRIDGE GD
C6
1 DAIRY CL
2 POPLAR DR
3 MEDWAY CL
4 LOWBRIDGE LA
5 WHITEHALL
6 GODFREY AV
135
146
145
A B C D E F
Quadring
MAIN ROAD
A152
QUADRING ROAD
HIGH STREET
Izzat Lane Farm
Monks Hall
Mast
Sewage Works
BAREHAMS LA
GREEN LA
WATER GATE
JUDY CROSS
SARAH GATE
Willow Farm
WOOD LA
RUSHY DY
NEW ROAD
Bedford Bridge
Eaudike Farm
Bresby House
Quadring Eaudike
Lowgate Bridge
EAUDIKE ROAD
GREEN LANE
Woodlands Farm
Bicker Haven
SPALDING ROAD
BOSTON ROAD
B1397
WIGTOFT BANK
Belton Farm
Bank House Farm
Rabbit Hill Farm
PE20
BROAD LA 1
WATERBELLY LA 2
DOWDYKE RD 3
KIT CAT LANE
Dowdyke Grange
Sutterton Marsh
COOK'S ROAD
Woodlands Farm
Bridge Farm
Bank House
CHURCHFLEET LANE
LOW GATE
CHAINTOFT LA
BOW GATE
NORTH GATE
Holly Bush Farm
Beech Tree Farm
Gosberton House Special Sch
Gosberton
Gosberton Prim Sch
Cemy
MILL LANE
Boston Rd Pits Nature Reserve
White House Farm
HIGHBRIDGE LANE
Hill House
Westhorpe Bridge
Sandpit Farm
Wargate Way Farm
WARGATE WAY
BELCHMIRE LANE
Ball Hall Farm
Elm Tree Farm
GOSBERTON BANK
Bridge House Farm
Gosberton Marsh
Risegate Eau
Gosberton Fen
FISH GROOM'S LA
The Gables
Belnie Bridge
CUNSDIKE LANE
PETER SEADIKE LANE
SODS LA
A16
SURFLEET BANK
Woad Farm
Cressy Hall
Moat
Cawood Hall
CAWOOD LANE
STATION ROAD
Wargate Bridge
SWEETLANDS WAY
WARGATE FIELD LANE
Wargate
Wargate Field
SPALDING ROAD
BELNIE LANE
Belnie Farm
Belnie
Burnt House Farm
CONEY GARTH LA
SURFLEET BANK
Cressy Bridge
LC
Windmill
Drummer's Bridge
Bird's Drove Farm
PE11
GOSBERTON RD
CLUBHURN LA
BIRDS DROVE
Willow Tree Farm
Sewage Works
BENDIKE LANE
SCOLDALL LANE
Red House Farm
Coney Garth Farm
COALBEACH LA
Cottage Fen
Cheal Bridge
DOCKHOLME GATE
Gosberton Cheal
BAFFEN'S LA
SALTFLEET LANE
Cheal House Farm
CLUBHURN LA
THARY LA
COALBEACH LA
NEWLANDS RD
RESERVOIR ROAD
Elm Farm
LITTLE LA
STOCKHOUSE LANE
GOSBERTON ROAD
Surfleet Lows Nature Reserve
Cemy
HUN GATE
Seas End Prim Sch
STATION ROAD
SEAS END ROAD
PH
CH
Surfleet Seas End
Marsh Farm
GUBBOLE'S DROVE
BEACH BANK
LOW GATE
Surfleet
Macmillan Way
PARK LANE
Spalding Golf Club
Beachbank Farm
Newlands Farm
Blue Gowt Drain
River Welland
Daniels Cuckoo Farm
B1356
DUNMEGATE WAY
Hill Marsh
Hill Marsh Farm
Old Sea Drain
CUCKOO LANE
River Glen
Crowtree Farm
Pinchbeck Marsh
PE12
Fenleigh Farm
BURTEY FEN LANE
HERDGATE LANE
SURFLEET ROAD
GREEN LA
Old Sea Drain
STONE GATE
MARSH ROAD
Burtey Fen Farm South
Manor Farm
TEN ACRE LANE
Spalding Bulb Museum
Spalding Marsh
MILESTONE LA
LANGHOLE DROVE
Crossgate
CHURCH STREET
Flints Farm
Vernatt's Drain
Wykeham
Wykeham Chapel (remains of)
Moat
OLD FEN LANE
Water Twr
Captain's Drain
Pinchbeck Engine Mus
WEST MARSH RD
Pumping Station
THE CHASE
WYKEHAM LA
8 33 7 32 6 31 5 30 4 29 3 28 2 27 1 26
22 23 24 25 26 27
B1
1 HERRING LA
2 KNIGHT ST
3 BROWNLOW CR
4 GLEN AV
156
C1
1 BACON'S LA
2 MEADOW CL
3 CROSSGATE LA
4 POACHERS GATE
5 CROSSGATE CR
6 FLAXMILL LA
7 THE MEADOWS
8 OLDHAM DR
9 CAPTAINS BECK
10 GROVE CL
11 RANVILLE CL
12 HORSEPIT LA
13 OAKLAND WY
14 BEAR LA
D2
1 SUNNYDALE CL
2 PARK LA
3 WOOD'S LA
4 WHITE CROSS LA
5 SURFLEET RD
6 OLD HALL LA
146
E3
1 COALBEACH LA
2 GLEN GD
3 HERON CL
4 KINGFISHER DR
5 SCHOOL CR
157

145
136
Scale: 1¾ inches to 1 mile

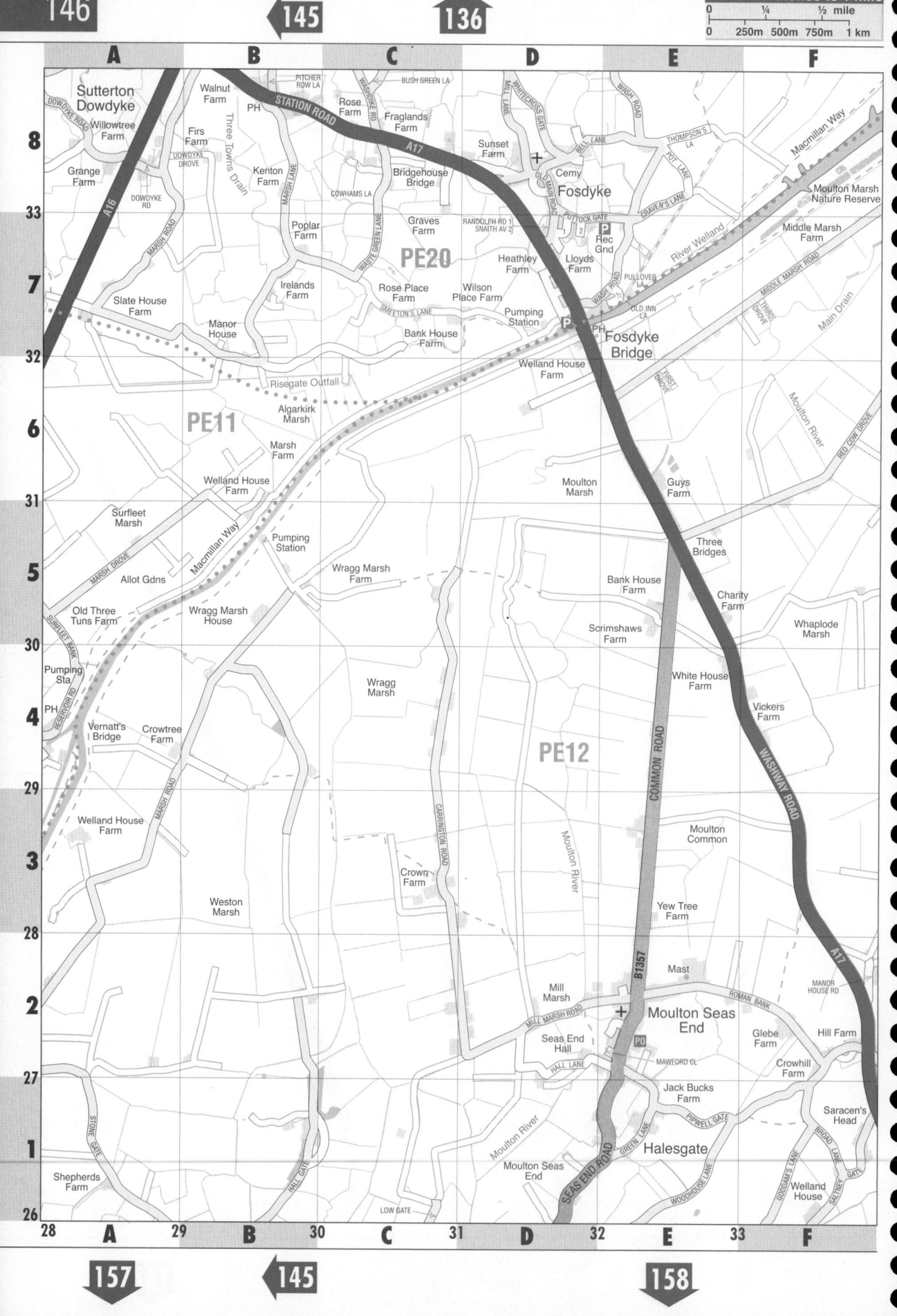
A
B
C
D
E
F
Sutterton Dowdyke
Walnut Farm
PH
PITCHER ROW LA
STATION ROAD
Rose Farm
WASHDIKE RD
BUSH GREEN LA
Fraglands Farm
MILL LANE
WHITECROSS GATE
WASH ROAD
DOWDYKE ROAD
Willowtree Farm
Firs Farm
Three Towns Drain
A17
Sunset Farm
BELL LANE
THOMPSON'S LA
Macmillan Way
DOWDYKE DROVE
Grange Farm
Kenton Farm
MARSH LANE
Bridgehouse Bridge
Cemy
OLD MAIN ROAD
Fosdyke
POT LANE
DOWDYKE RD
COWHAMS LA
Moulton Marsh Nature Reserve
A16
MARSH ROAD
Poplar Farm
Graves Farm
RANDOLPH RD
SNAITH AV
PUTTOCK GATE
CRAVEN'S LANE
Rec Gnd
River Welland
Middle Marsh Farm
PE20
WASTE GREEN LANE
Heathley Farm
Lloyds Farm
MIDDLE MARSH ROAD
Slate House Farm
Irelands Farm
Rose Place Farm
Wilson Place Farm
WASH ROAD
PULLOVER LA
SMEETON'S LANE
Pumping Station
OLD INN LA
THIRD DROVE
Main Drain
Manor House
Bank House Farm
PH
Fosdyke Bridge
Welland House Farm
Risegate Outfall
FIRST DROVE
Moulton River
PE11
Algarkirk Marsh
RED COW DROVE
Marsh Farm
Moulton Marsh
Guys Farm
Welland House Farm
Surfleet Marsh
Macmillan Way
Pumping Station
Three Bridges
MARSH DROVE
Wragg Marsh Farm
Bank House Farm
Allot Gdns
Charity Farm
Old Three Tuns Farm
Wragg Marsh House
Scrimshaws Farm
Whaplode Marsh
SURFLEET BANK
Pumping Sta
Wragg Marsh
White House Farm
PH
RESERVOIR RD
Vickers Farm
Vernatt's Bridge
Crowtree Farm
PE12
COMMON ROAD
WASHWAY ROAD
MARSH ROAD
Welland House Farm
CARRINGTON ROAD
Moulton Common
Moulton River
Crown Farm
Weston Marsh
Yew Tree Farm
B1357
Mast
A17
MANOR HOUSE RD
Mill Marsh
ROMAN BANK
MILL MARSH ROAD
Moulton Seas End
Seas End Hall
Glebe Farm
Hill Farm
PO
MAWFORD CL
HALL LANE
Crowhill Farm
Jack Bucks Farm
STONE GATE
PIPWELL GATE
Saracen's Head
Moulton River
GREEN LANE
Halesgate
BROAD LANE
HALL GATE
Moulton Seas End
SEAS END ROAD
GODDAM'S LANE
GATE
Shepherds Farm
WOODHOUSE LANE
Welland House
SALTNEY
LOW GATE
28
29
30
31
32
33
8
33
7
32
6
31
5
30
4
29
3
28
2
27
1
26

157
145
158

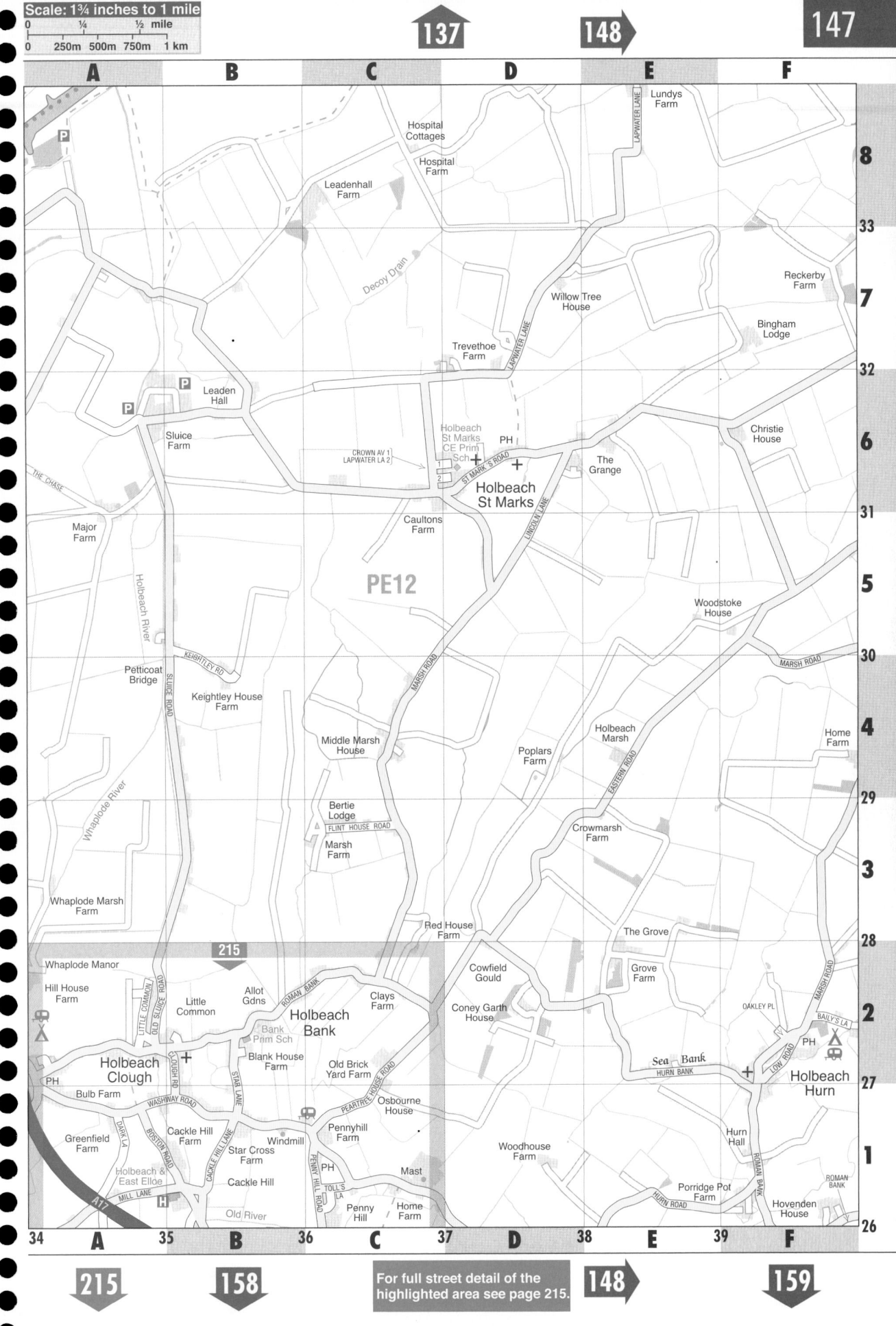

Scale: 1¾ inches to 1 mile

0 ¼ ½ mile
0 250m 500m 750m 1 km

A B C D E F

8

33

7

32

6

31

5

30

4

29

3

28

2

27

1

26

Lundys Farm
Hospital Cottages
Hospital Farm
Leadenhall Farm
Decoy Drain
Reckerby Farm
Willow Tree House
Bingham Lodge
Trevethoe Farm
LAPWATER LANE
Leaden Hall
Sluice Farm
THE CHASE
Holbeach St Marks CE Prim Sch
CROWN AV 1
LAPWATER LA 2
PH
Holbeach St Marks
Christie House
The Grange
Caultons Farm
Major Farm
PE12
LINCOLN LANE
Woodstoke House
Holbeach River
ST MARK'S ROAD
KEIGHTLEY RD
Petticoat Bridge
Keightley House Farm
SLUICE ROAD
MARSH ROAD
MARSH ROAD
Middle Marsh House
Holbeach Marsh
Poplars Farm
Home Farm
EASTERN ROAD
Whaplode River
Bertie Lodge
FLINT HOUSE ROAD
Marsh Farm
Crowmarsh Farm
Whaplode Marsh Farm
Red House Farm
The Grove
Whaplode Manor
215
Cowfield Gould
Grove Farm
Hill House Farm
Little Common
Allot Gdns
ROMAN BANK
Clays Farm
Coney Garth House
OAKLEY PL
BAILY'S LA
PH
Bank Prim Sch
Holbeach Bank
LITTLE COMMON
OLD SLUICE ROAD
Sea Bank
HURN BANK
Holbeach Hurn
Holbeach Clough
Blank House Farm
Old Brick Yard Farm
PEARTREE HOUSE ROAD
LOW ROAD
PH
Bulb Farm
STAR LANE
Osbourne House
MARSH ROAD
WASHWAY ROAD
Hurn Hall
Greenfield Farm
Cackle Hill Farm
Windmill
Pennyhill Farm
DARK LA
BOSTON ROAD
CACKLE HILL LANE
Star Cross Farm
PENNY HILL ROAD
PH
Mast
ROMAN BANK
Holbeach & East Elloe
Cackle Hill
TOLL'S LA
Woodhouse Farm
Porridge Pot Farm
HURN ROAD
A17
MILL LANE
H
Old River
Penny Hill
Home Farm
Hovenden House
ROMAN BANK

34 35 36 37 38 39
A B C D E F

For full street detail of the highlighted area see page 215.

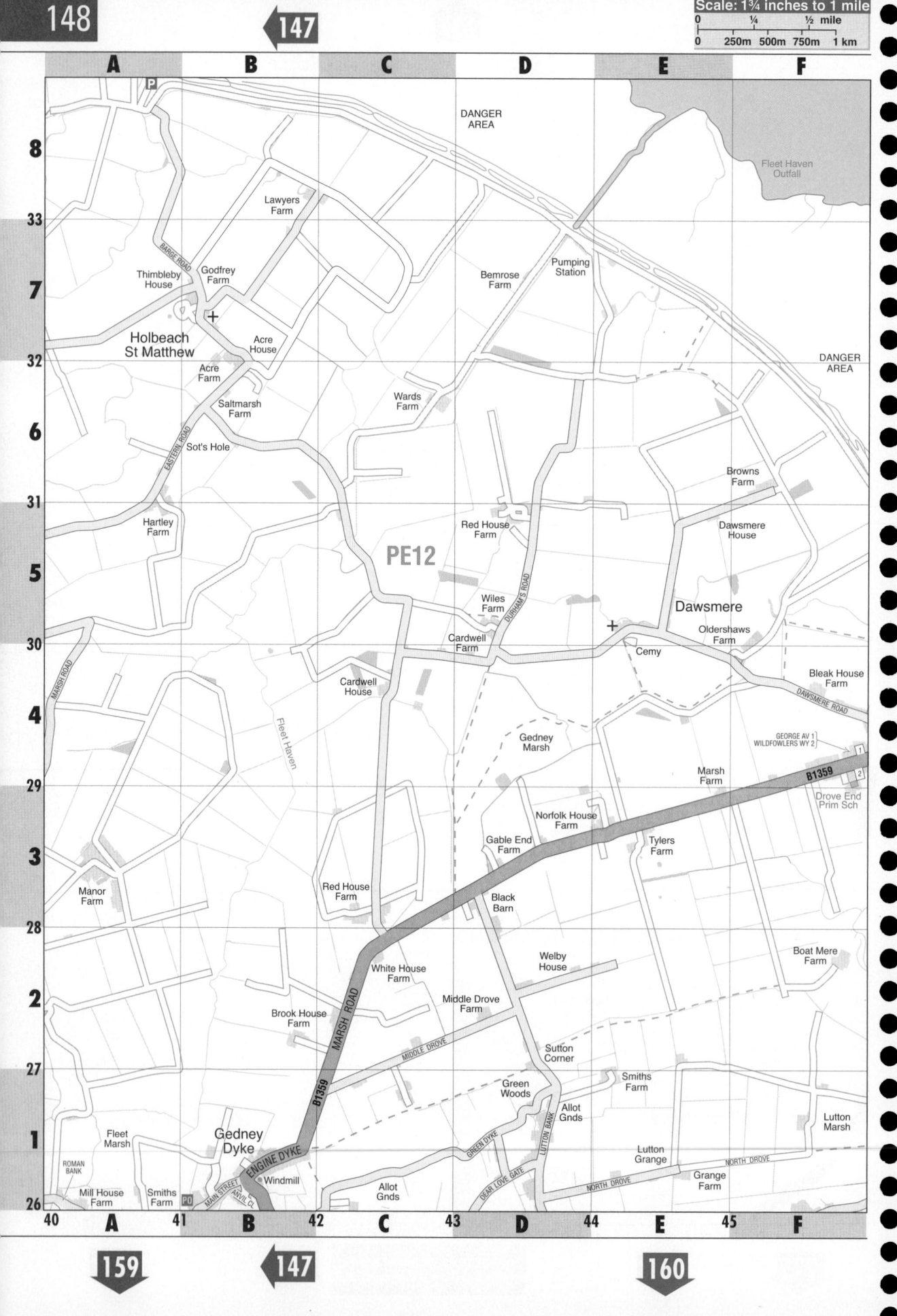

147

Scale: 1¾ inches to 1 mile

0   ¼   ½   mile
0   250m 500m 750m 1 km

DANGER
AREA

Fleet Haven
Outfall

Lawyers
Farm

Bemrose
Farm

Pumping
Station

BARGE ROAD

Thimbleby
House

Godfrey
Farm

DANGER
AREA

Holbeach
St Matthew

Acre
House

Acre
Farm

Wards
Farm

Browns
Farm

Saltmarsh
Farm

EASTERN ROAD

Sot's Hole

Dawsmere
House

Hartley
Farm

PE12

Red House
Farm

DURHAM'S ROAD

Wiles
Farm

Dawsmere

Oldershaws
Farm

MARSH ROAD

Cardwell
Farm

Cemy

Bleak House
Farm

Cardwell
House

DAWSMERE ROAD

Fleet Haven

Gedney
Marsh

GEORGE AV 1
WILDFOWLERS WY 2

Marsh
Farm

B1359

1

2

Drove End
Prim Sch

Norfolk House
Farm

Manor
Farm

Red House
Farm

Gable End
Farm

Tylers
Farm

Black
Barn

Boat Mere
Farm

White House
Farm

Welby
House

Brook House
Farm

MARSH ROAD

Middle Drove
Farm

MIDDLE DROVE

Sutton
Corner

Smiths
Farm

Lutton
Marsh

B1359

Green
Woods

Allot
Gnds

GREEN DYKE

LUTTON BANK

Fleet
Marsh

Gedney
Dyke

ENGINE DYKE

Lutton
Grange

NORTH DROVE

Grange
Farm

ROMAN
BANK

Mill House
Farm

Smiths
Farm

PO

MAIN STREET

ARVIL CL

Windmill

Allot
Gnds

BEAR LOVE GATE

NORTH DROVE

A B C D E F

8 33 7 32 6 31 5 30 4 29 3 28 2 27 1 26

40 A 41 B 42 C 43 D 44 E 45 F

159   147   160

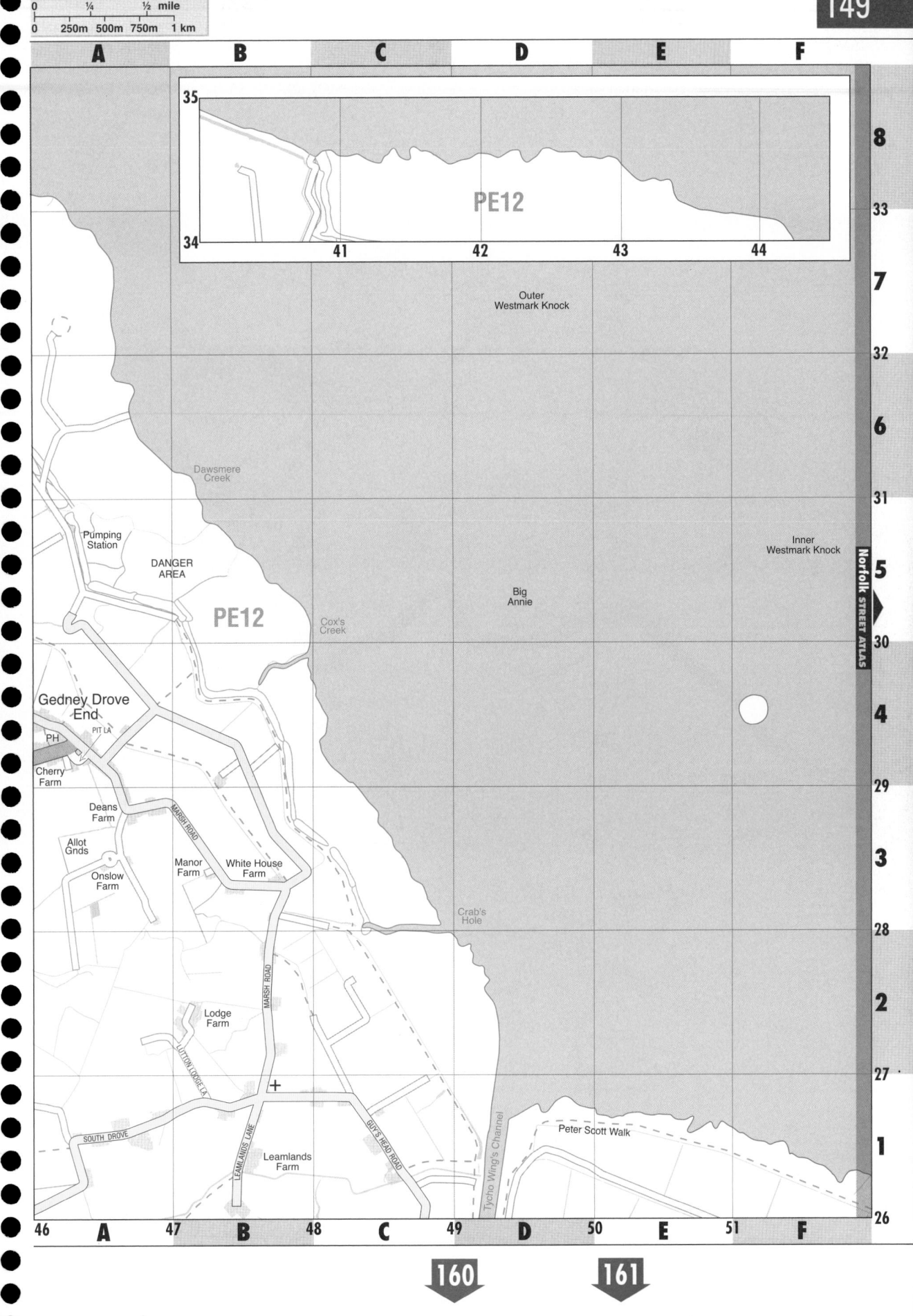

Scale: 1¾ inches to 1 mile
0   ¼   ½   mile
0   250m   500m   750m   1 km

PE12

PE12

Outer
Westmark Knock

Dawsmere
Creek

Pumping
Station

DANGER
AREA

Inner
Westmark Knock

PE12

Cox's
Creek

Big
Annie

Gedney Drove
End

PH   PIT LA

Cherry
Farm

Deans
Farm

Allot
Gnds

Onslow
Farm

Manor
Farm

White House
Farm

MARSH ROAD

Crab's
Hole

Lodge
Farm

LUTTON LODGE LA

MARSH ROAD

SOUTH DROVE

LEAMLANDS LANE

Leamlands
Farm

GUY'S HEAD ROAD

Tycho Wing's Channel

Peter Scott Walk

Norfolk STREET ATLAS

Scale: 1¾ inches to 1 mile
0   ¼   ½   mile
0   250m   500m   750m   1 km

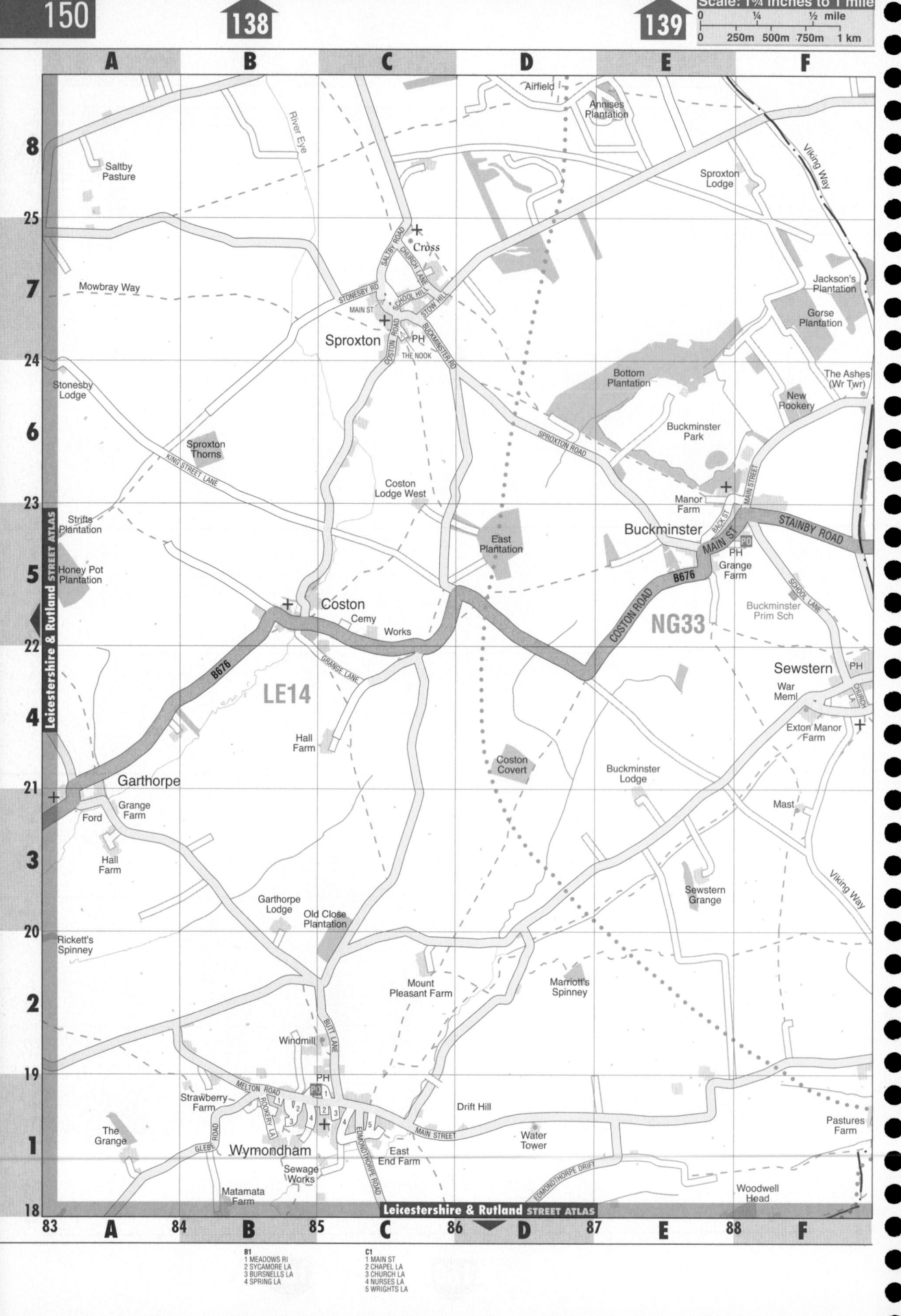

Leicestershire & Rutland STREET ATLAS

Grid letters (top): A B C D E F

Grid numbers (left): 8 25 7 24 6 23 5 22 4 21 3 20 2 19 1 18

River Eye

Airfield
Annises Plantation
Saltby Pasture
Sproxton Lodge
Mowbray Way
Cross
Jackson's Plantation
SALTBY ROAD
CHURCH LANE
Gorse Plantation
STONESBY RD
SCHOOL HILL
STOW HILL
MAIN ST
Sproxton
COSTON ROAD
BUCKMINSTER RD
PH
THE NOOK
Bottom Plantation
The Ashes (Wr Twr)
Stonesby Lodge
New Rookery
Buckminster Park
Sproxton Thorns
KING STREET LANE
SPROXTON ROAD
Coston Lodge West
Manor Farm
Buckminster
BACK ST
MAIN STREET
STAINBY ROAD
Strifts Plantation
East Plantation
PH
Grange Farm
PO
Honey Pot Plantation
B676
SCHOOL LANE
Buckminster Prim Sch
Coston
Cemy
Works
COSTON ROAD
NG33
GRANGE LANE
Sewstern
PH
B676
War Meml
CHURCH LA
LE14
Hall Farm
Exton Manor Farm
Garthorpe
Ford
Grange Farm
Coston Covert
Buckminster Lodge
Mast
Hall Farm
Garthorpe Lodge
Old Close Plantation
Sewstern Grange
Viking Way
Rickett's Spinney
Mount Pleasant Farm
Marriott's Spinney
BUTT LANE
Windmill
PH
PO
MELTON ROAD
ROOKERY LA
Strawberry Farm
Drift Hill
Pastures Farm
GLEBE ROAD
The Grange
EDMONDTHORPE ROAD
MAIN STREET
Water Tower
Wymondham
East End Farm
Sewage Works
EDMONDTHORPE DRIFT
Woodwell Head
Matamata Farm

Viking Way

Grid letters (bottom): 83 A 84 B 85 C 86 D 87 E 88 F

B1
1 MEADOWS RI
2 SYCAMORE LA
3 BURSNELLS LA
4 SPRING LA

C1
1 MAIN ST
2 CHAPEL LA
3 CHURCH LA
4 NURSES LA
5 WRIGHTS LA

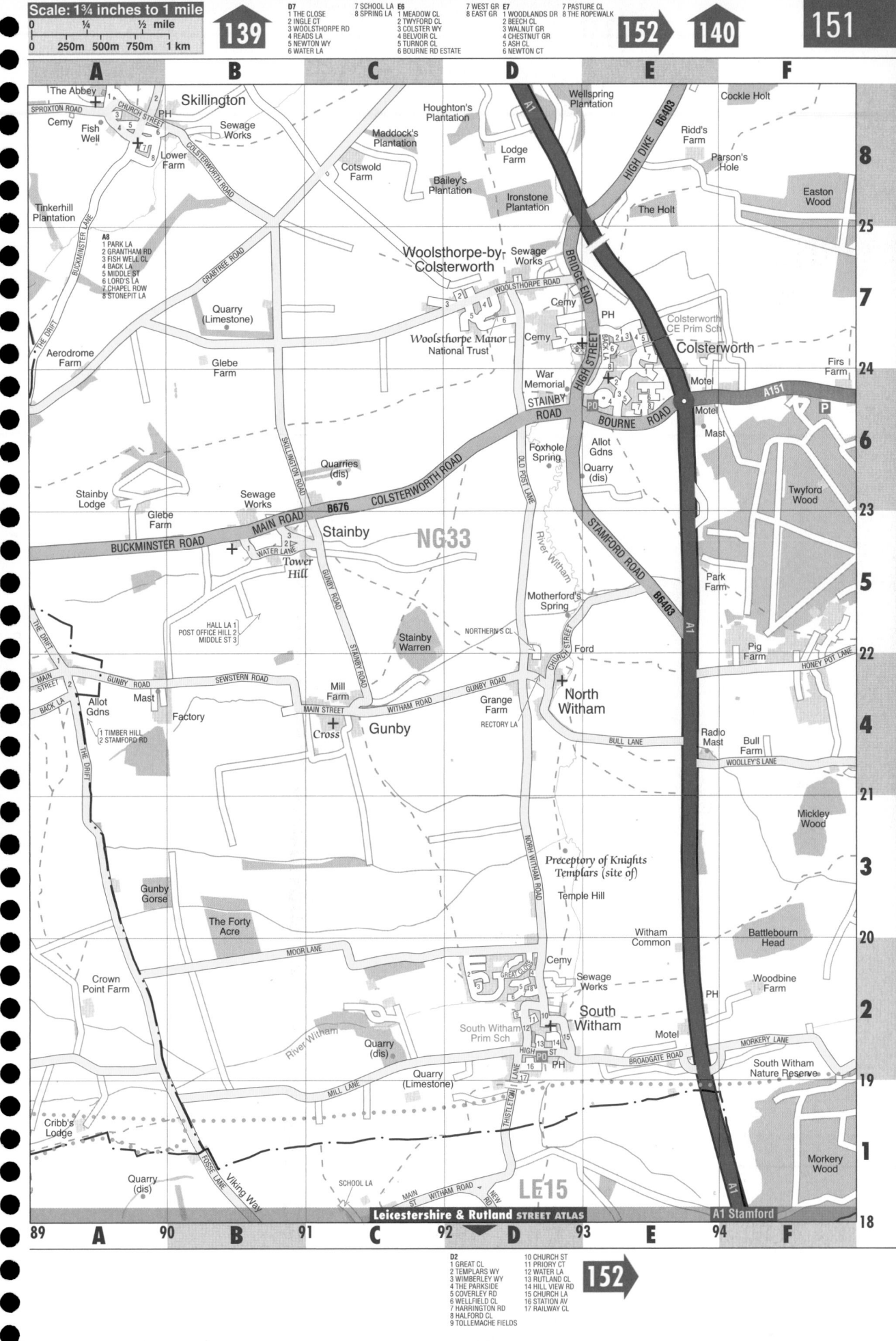

Scale: 1¾ inches to 1 mile
0 ¼ ½ mile
0 250m 500m 750m 1 km
139
D7
1 THE CLOSE
2 INGLE CT
3 WOOLSTHORPE RD
4 READS LA
5 NEWTON WY
6 WATER LA
7 SCHOOL LA
8 SPRING LA
E6
1 MEADOW CL
2 TWYFORD CL
3 COLSTER WY
4 BELVOIR CL
5 TURNOR CL
6 BOURNE RD ESTATE
7 WEST GR
8 EAST GR
E7
1 WOODLANDS DR
2 BEECH CL
3 WALNUT GR
4 CHESTNUT GR
5 ASH CL
6 NEWTON CT
7 PASTURE CL
8 THE ROPEWALK
152
140
151
A B C D E F
8
25
7
24
6
23
5
22
4
21
3
20
2
19
1
18
The Abbey
Skillington
SPROXTON ROAD
CHURCH STREET
PH
Cemy
Fish Well
Sewage Works
Lower Farm
COLSTERWORTH ROAD
Houghton's Plantation
Maddock's Plantation
Cotswold Farm
Bailey's Plantation
Lodge Farm
Ironstone Plantation
Wellspring Plantation
A1
B6403
HIGH DIKE
Cockle Holt
Ridd's Farm
Parson's Hole
The Holt
Easton Wood
Tinkerhill Plantation
BUCKMINSTER LANE
A8
1 PARK LA
2 GRANTHAM RD
3 FISH WELL CL
4 BACK LA
5 MIDDLE ST
6 LORD'S LA
7 CHAPEL ROW
8 STONEPIT LA
CRABTREE ROAD
Woolsthorpe-by-Colsterworth
Sewage Works
WOOLSTHORPE ROAD
BRIDGE END
Cemy
PH
Quarry (Limestone)
THE DRIFT
Aerodrome Farm
Glebe Farm
Woolsthorpe Manor
National Trust
Cemy
HIGH STREET
BACK LA
Colsterworth CE Prim Sch
Colsterworth
Firs Farm
War Memorial
Motel
A151
STAINBY ROAD
PO
BOURNE ROAD
Motel
Mast
Foxhole Spring
Allot Gdns
Quarry (dis)
Quarries (dis)
SKILLINGTON ROAD
OLD POST LANE
Twyford Wood
Stainby Lodge
Sewage Works
Glebe Farm
MAIN ROAD
B676
COLSTERWORTH ROAD
Stainby
NG33
BUCKMINSTER ROAD
WATER LANE
Tower Hill
River Witham
STAMFORD ROAD
GUNBY ROAD
Park Farm
Motherford's Spring
B6403
HALL LA 1
POST OFFICE HILL 2
MIDDLE ST 3
Stainby Warren
NORTHERN'S CL
Ford
CHURCH STREET
Pig Farm
HONEY POT LANE
MAIN STREET
GUNBY ROAD
SEWSTERN ROAD
STAINBY ROAD
GUNBY ROAD
BACK LA
Mast
Mill Farm
North Witham
Allot Gdns
Factory
MAIN STREET
WITHAM ROAD
Grange Farm
1 TIMBER HILL
2 STAMFORD RD
Cross
Gunby
RECTORY LA
BULL LANE
Radio Mast
Bull Farm
WOOLLEY'S LANE
Mickley Wood
NORTH WITHAM ROAD
Preceptory of Knights Templars (site of)
Temple Hill
Gunby Gorse
The Forty Acre
Witham Common
Battlebourn Head
MOOR LANE
Cemy
GREAT CLOSE
Crown Point Farm
Sewage Works
Woodbine Farm
PH
South Witham
South Witham Prim Sch
River Witham
Quarry (dis)
Motel
MORKERY LANE
BROADGATE ROAD
HIGH ST
PO
PH
South Witham Nature Reserve
Quarry (Limestone)
MILL LANE
THISTLETON LANE
Cribb's Lodge
Morkery Wood
FOSSE LANE
Viking Way
Quarry (dis)
SCHOOL LA
MAIN ST
WITHAM ROAD
NEW RD
LE15
Leicestershire & Rutland STREET ATLAS
A1 Stamford
89 90 91 92 93 94
D2
1 GREAT CL
2 TEMPLARS WY
3 WIMBERLEY WY
4 THE PARKSIDE
5 COVERLEY RD
6 WELLFIELD CL
7 HARRINGTON RD
8 HALFORD CL
9 TOLLEMACHE FIELDS
10 CHURCH ST
11 PRIORY CT
12 WATER LA
13 RUTLAND CL
14 HILL VIEW RD
15 CHURCH LA
16 STATION AV
17 RAILWAY CL
152

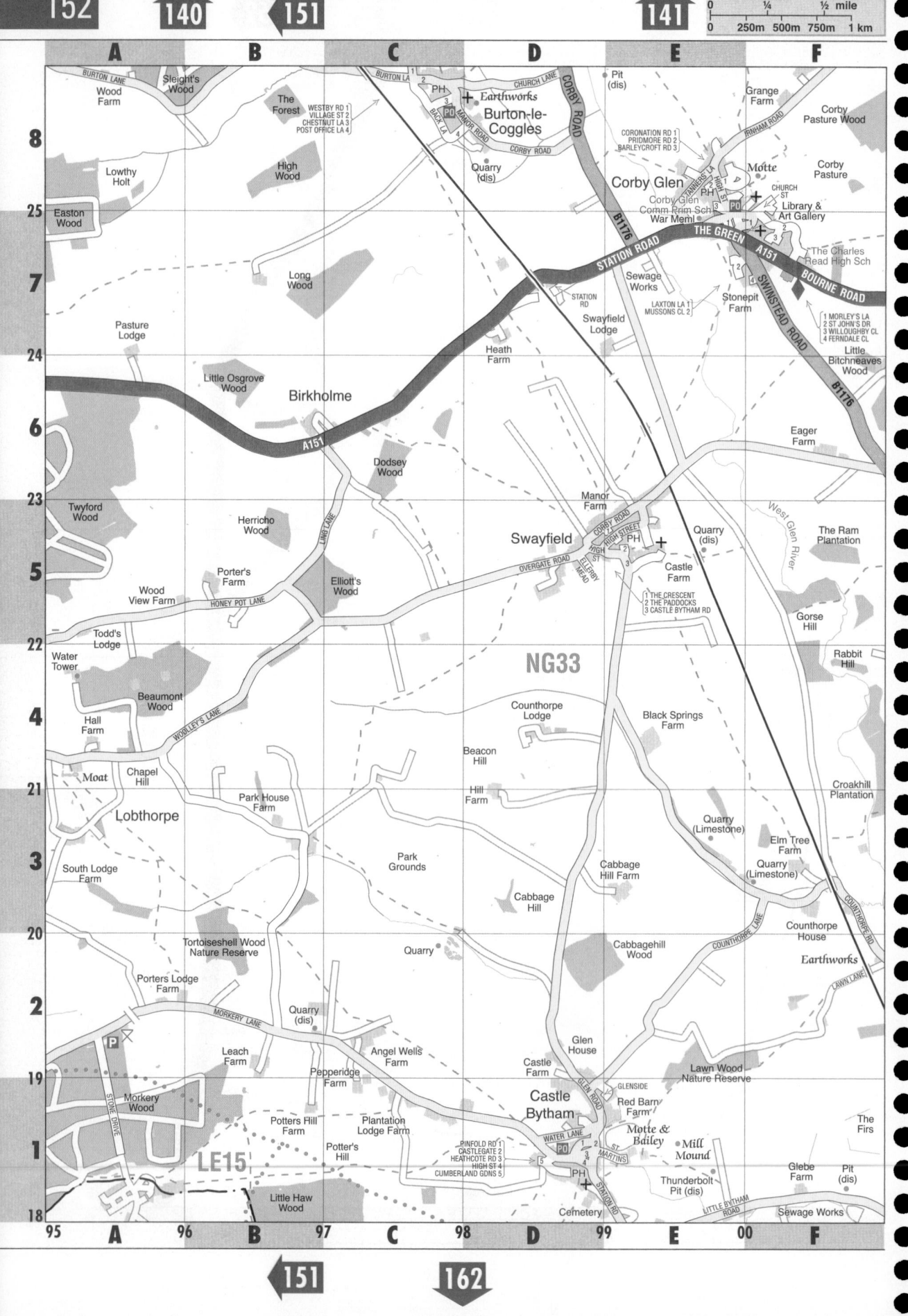

152

140
151
141

Scale: 1¾ inches to 1 mile
0   ¼   ½ mile
0   250m 500m 750m 1 km

A   B   C   D   E   F

BURTON LANE

Wood Farm

Sleight's Wood

The Forest

WESTBY RD 1
VILLAGE ST 2
CHESTNUT LA 3
POST OFFICE LA 4

BURTON LA

CHURCH LANE

PH

Earthworks

Burton-le-Coggles

CORBY ROAD

Pit (dis)

Grange Farm

Corby Pasture Wood

8

Lowthy Holt

High Wood

BLACK LA

MANOR ROAD

PO

CORBY ROAD

Quarry (dis)

CORONATION RD 1
PRIDMORE RD 2
BARLEYCROFT RD 3

IRNHAM ROAD

Corby Pasture

Corby Glen

Motte

25

Easton Wood

TANNERS LA

HIGH ST

Corby Glen Comm Prim Sch
War Meml

CHURCH ST

PO

Library & Art Gallery

7

Long Wood

B1176

STATION ROAD

Sewage Works

THE GREEN

A151

BOURNE ROAD

The Charles Read High Sch

Pasture Lodge

STATION RD

Swayfield Lodge

LAXTON LA 1
MUSSONS CL 2

Stonepit Farm

SWINSTEAD ROAD

1 MORLEY'S LA
2 ST JOHN'S DR
3 WILLOUGHBY CL
4 FERNDALE CL

Little Bitchneaves Wood

24

Little Osgrove Wood

Heath Farm

B1176

Birkholme

A151

6

Dodsey Wood

Manor Farm

Eager Farm

23

Twyford Wood

Herricho Wood

LING LANE

CORBY ROAD

Swayfield

HIGH ST

PH

Quarry (dis)

West Glen River

The Ram Plantation

5

Porter's Farm

Elliott's Wood

OVERGATE ROAD

ELLERBY MEAD

Castle Farm

1 THE CRESCENT
2 THE PADDOCKS
3 CASTLE BYTHAM RD

Gorse Hill

Wood View Farm

HONEY POT LANE

22

Todd's Lodge

NG33

Rabbit Hill

Water Tower

WOOLLEY'S LANE

Beaumont Wood

Counthorpe Lodge

Black Springs Farm

4

Hall Farm

Moat

Chapel Hill

Beacon Hill

Croakhill Plantation

21

Lobthorpe

Park House Farm

Hill Farm

Quarry (Limestone)

Elm Tree Farm

3

South Lodge Farm

Park Grounds

Cabbage Hill Farm

Quarry (Limestone)

Counthorpe House

20

Tortoiseshell Wood Nature Reserve

Quarry

Cabbage Hill

COUNTHORPE LANE

Cabbagehill Wood

COUNTHORPE RD

Earthworks

Porters Lodge Farm

MORKERY LANE

Quarry (dis)

LAWN LANE

2

P

Leach Farm

Angel Wells Farm

Castle Farm

Glen House

Lawn Wood Nature Reserve

The Firs

19

STONE DRIVE

Morkery Wood

Pepperidge Farm

GLEN ROAD

GLENSIDE

Red Barn Farm

1

Potters Hill Farm

Potter's Hill

Plantation Lodge Farm

PINFOLD RD 1
CASTLEGATE 2
HEATHCOTE RD 3
HIGH ST 4
CUMBERLAND GDNS 5

WATER LANE

PO

Castle Bytham

ST MARTINS

PH

STATION RD

Motte & Bailey

Mill Mound

Thunderbolt Pit (dis)

Glebe Farm

Pit (dis)

LE15

Little Haw Wood

Cemetery

LITTLE BYTHAM ROAD

Sewage Works

18

95   A   96   B   97   C   98   D   99   E   00   F

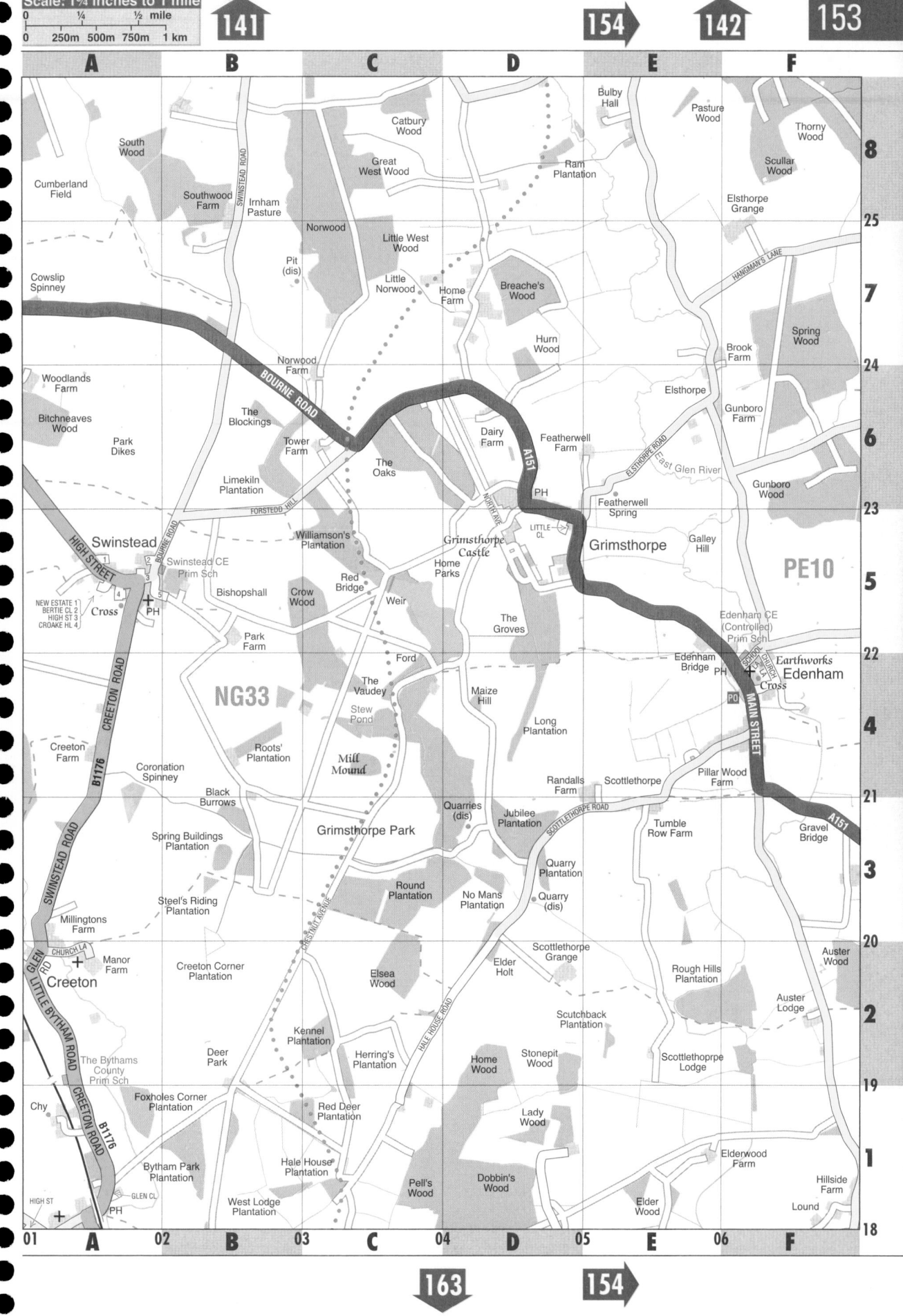

Scale: 1¾ inches to 1 mile

0   ¼   ½ mile
0   250m 500m 750m 1 km

141

154

142

153

A   B   C   D   E   F

8

25

7

24

6

23

5

22

4

21

20

3

2

19

1

18

01   A   02   B   03   C   04   D   05   E   06   F

Bulby Hall

Pasture Wood

Thorny Wood

Scullar Wood

South Wood

Catbury Wood

Elsthorpe Grange

Cumberland Field

Southwood Farm

Irnham Pasture

Great West Wood

Norwood

Little West Wood

Ram Plantation

HANGMAN'S LANE

Cowslip Spinney

Pit (dis)

Little Norwood

Home Farm

Breache's Wood

Spring Wood

Brook Farm

Woodlands Farm

Norwood Farm

BOURNE ROAD

Hurn Wood

Elsthorpe

Gunboro Farm

Bitchneaves Wood

The Blockings

Dairy Farm

Featherwell Farm

ELSTHORPE ROAD

East Glen River

Gunboro Wood

Park Dikes

Tower Farm

The Oaks

A151

NORTH FEN

PH

Featherwell Spring

Limekiln Plantation

FORSTEDD HILL

LITTLE CL

Galley Hill

PE10

Swinstead

HIGH STREET

BOURNE ROAD

Williamson's Plantation

Grimsthorpe Castle

Grimsthorpe

NEW ESTATE 1
BERTIE CL 2
HIGH ST 3
CROAKE HL 4

Swinstead CE Prim Sch

Red Bridge

Home Parks

Cross   PH

Bishopshall

Crow Wood

Weir

The Groves

Edenham CE (Controlled) Prim Sch

Edenham Bridge   PH

Earthworks

CREETON ROAD

Park Farm

Ford

SCHOOL LA
CHURCH LA

Cross   Edenham

NG33

The Vaudey

Maize Hill

PO

MAIN STREET

Creeton Farm

Roots' Plantation

Stew Pond

Long Plantation

Coronation Spinney

Mill Mound

SWINSTEAD ROAD

B1176

Black Burrows

Randalls Farm

Scottlethorpe

Pillar Wood Farm

A151

Grimsthorpe Park

Quarries (dis)

Jubilee Plantation

SCOTTLETHORPE ROAD

Tumble Row Farm

Gravel Bridge

Spring Buildings Plantation

Quarry Plantation

Millingtons Farm

Steel's Riding Plantation

CHESTNUT AVENUE

Round Plantation

No Mans Plantation

Quarry (dis)

Scottlethorpe Grange

Rough Hills Plantation

Auster Wood

CHURCH LA

Creeton Corner Plantation

Elsea Wood

Elder Holt

Scutchback Plantation

Scottlethoprpe Lodge

Auster Lodge

Chy

GLEN RD
LITTLE BYTHAM ROAD

Manor Farm

Creeton

HALE HOUSE ROAD

Kennel Plantation

Herring's Plantation

Home Wood

Stonepit Wood

The Bythams County Prim Sch

Deer Park

Lady Wood

Foxholes Corner Plantation

CREETON ROAD

Red Deer Plantation

Elderwood Farm

B1176

Bytham Park Plantation

Hale House Plantation

Pell's Wood

Dobbin's Wood

Hillside Farm

HIGH ST

PH

GLEN CL

West Lodge Plantation

Elder Wood

Lound

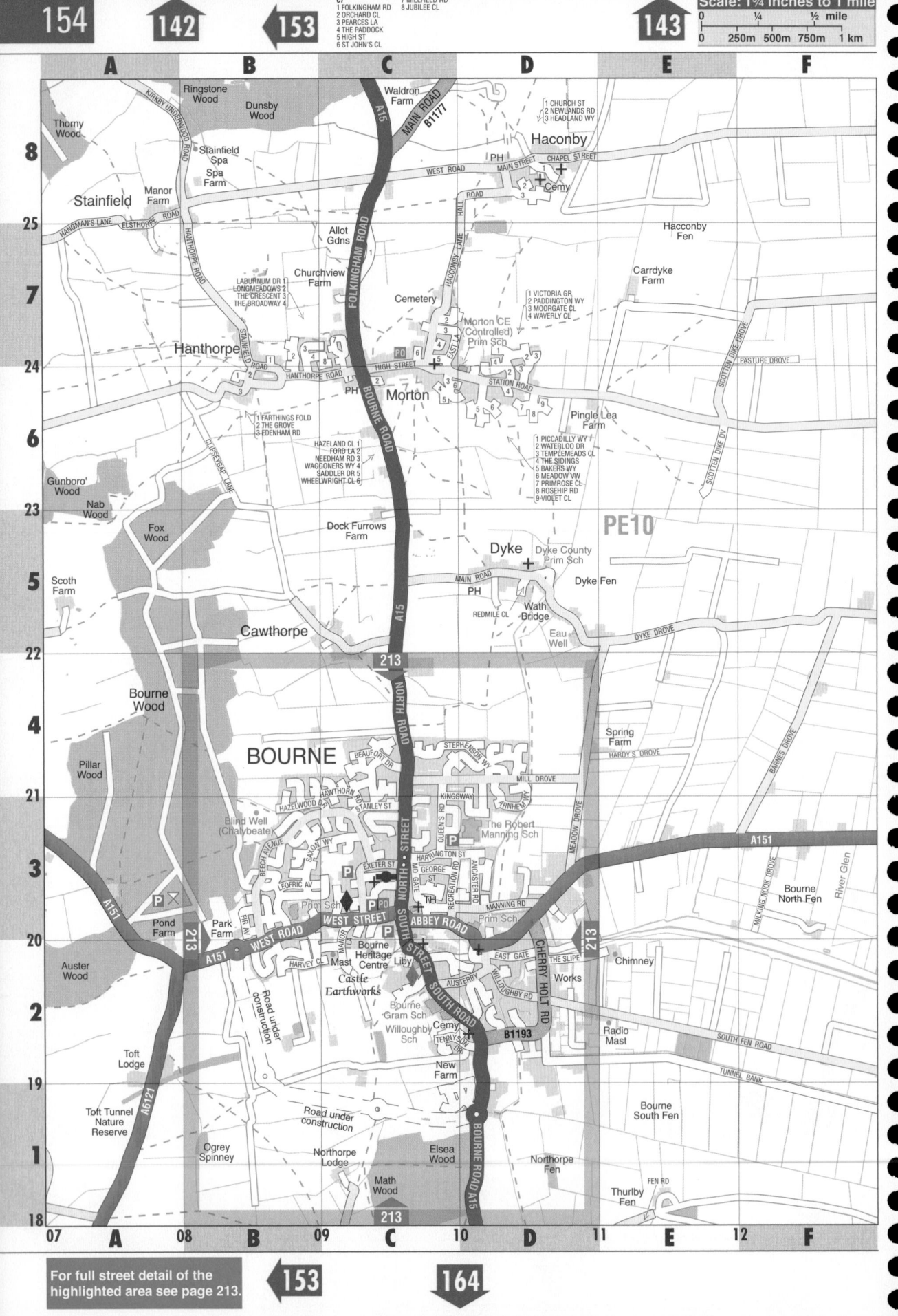

C7
1 FOLKINGHAM RD
2 ORCHARD CL
3 PEARCES LA
4 THE PADDOCK
5 HIGH ST
6 ST JOHN'S CL

7 MILLFIELD RD
8 JUBILEE CL

Scale: 1¾ inches to 1 mile
0   ¼   ½   mile
0   250m 500m 750m   1 km

Thorny Wood
Kirkby Underwood Road
Ringstone Wood
Dunsby Wood
Waldron Farm
MAIN ROAD
B1177
A15

1 CHURCH ST
2 NEWLANDS RD
3 HEADLAND WY

Haconby
PH
Main Street
Chapel Street
Cemy
WEST ROAD

Stainfield Spa
Spa Farm
Stainfield
Manor Farm
Hacconby Fen

Hangman's Lane
Elsthorpe Road
Hanthorpe Road

25
7
24
6
23
5
22
4
21
3
20
19
1
18

Allot Gdns
Churchview Farm
LABURNUM DR 1
LONGMEADOWS 2
THE CRESCENT 3
THE BROADWAY 4

Cemetery
Carrdyke Farm

1 VICTORIA GR
2 PADDINGTON WY
3 MOORGATE CL
4 WAVERLY CL

Morton CE (Controlled) Prim Sch

PASTURE DROVE
SCOTTEN DIKE DRIVE

Hanthorpe
Hanthorpe Road
High Street
PH
Morton
PO
EAST LA

Station Road
Pingle Lea Farm

1 FARTHINGS FOLD
2 THE GROVE
3 EDENHAM RD

HAZELAND CL 1
FORD LA 2
NEEDHAM RD 3
WAGGONERS WY 4
SADDLER DR 5
WHEELWRIGHT CL 6

1 PICCADILLY WY
2 WATERLOO DR
3 TEMPLEMEADS CL
4 THE SIDINGS
5 BAKERS WY
6 MEADOW VW
7 PRIMROSE CL
8 ROSEHIP RD
9 VIOLET CL

PE10

Gunboro' Wood
Nab Wood
Fox Wood

Dock Furrows Farm
Dyke
Dyke County Prim Sch
MAIN ROAD
PH
REDMILE CL
Wath Bridge
Dyke Fen
Eau Well
DYKE DROVE

Scoth Farm
Cawthorpe
213

Bourne Wood
NORTH ROAD

BOURNE
BEAUFORT DR
STEPHENSON WY
Spring Farm
HARDY'S DROVE
A151
River Glen

Pillar Wood
HAWTHORN RD
HAZELWOOD DR
STANLEY ST
Kingsway
MILL DROVE
TANHEW
The Robert Manning Sch
MEADOW DROVE
BARNES DROVE

Blind Well (Chalybeate)
SAXON WY
QUEEN'S RD
HARRINGTON ST
A151
Bourne North Fen

BEECH AVENUE
EXETER ST
ST GEORGE ST
RECREATION RD
ANCASTER RD
MANNING RD
Prim Sch
MILKING NOOK DROVE

LEOFRIC AV
FIR AV
Prim Sch
PO
TH
213
CHERRY HOLT RD

P
WEST STREET
SOUTH STREET
ABBEY ROAD
East Gate
THE SLIPE
Chimney

Park Farm
MANOR
HARVEY CL
WEST ROAD
A151
Bourne Heritage Centre
Liby
Mast
AUSTERBY
WILLOUGHBY RD
Works
Radio Mast

Auster Wood
Pond Farm
A151
Castle Earthworks
Bourne Gram Sch
Willoughby Sch
Cemy
TENNYSON DR
B1193
SOUTH FEN ROAD

Road under construction
Bourne South Fen
TUNNEL BANK

Toft Lodge
A6121
New Farm
FEN RD
Thurlby Fen

Toft Tunnel Nature Reserve
Ogrey Spinney
Northorpe Lodge
Road under construction
Northorpe
Elsea Wood
BOURNE ROAD A15
Northorpe Fen

Math Wood
213

For full street detail of the highlighted area see page 213.

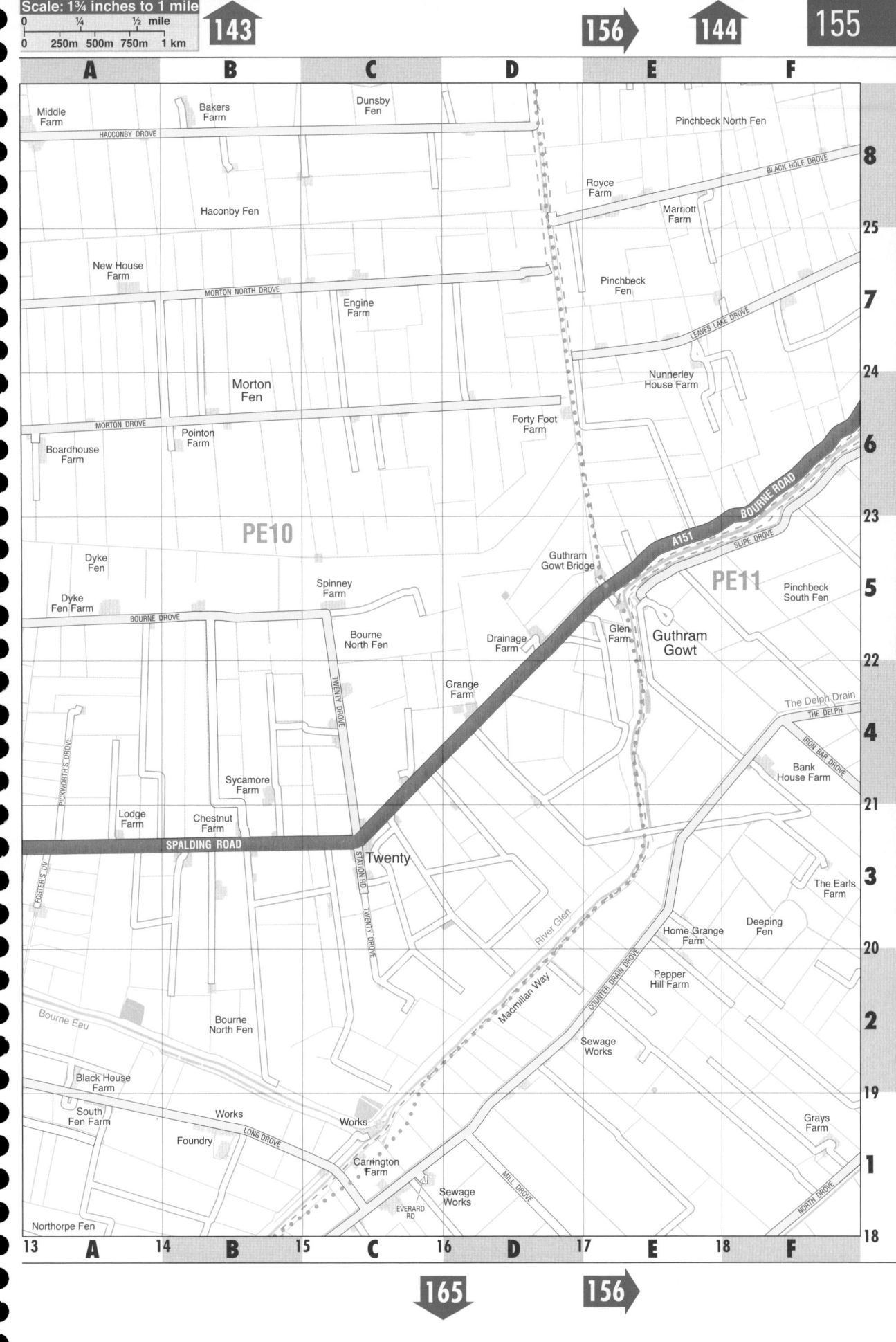

A   B   C   D   E   F

Middle Farm
HACCONBY DROVE
Bakers Farm
Dunsby Fen
Pinchbeck North Fen
BLACK HOLE DROVE
8

Haconby Fen
Royce Farm
Marriott Farm
25

New House Farm
MORTON NORTH DROVE
Engine Farm
Pinchbeck Fen
7

LEAVES LAKE DROVE

Morton Fen
Nunnerley House Farm
24

MORTON DROVE
Pointon Farm
Forty Foot Farm
6

Boardhouse Farm

PE10
Guthram Gowt Bridge
A151
BOURNE ROAD
SLIPE DROVE
23

Dyke Fen
Spinney Farm
PE11
Pinchbeck South Fen
5

Dyke Fen Farm
BOURNE DROVE
Bourne North Fen
Drainage Farm
Glen Farm
Guthram Gowt
22

TWENTY DROVE
Grange Farm
The Delph Drain
THE DELPH
4

PICKWORTH'S DROVE
IRON BAR DROVE
Bank House Farm

Sycamore Farm
21

Lodge Farm
Chestnut Farm
SPALDING ROAD
Twenty
The Earls Farm
3

STATION RD
FOSTER'S DIV
River Glen
Home Grange Farm
Deeping Fen
20

Macmillan Way
COUNTER DRAIN DROVE
Pepper Hill Farm

Bourne Eau
Bourne North Fen
Sewage Works
2

Black House Farm
19

South Fen Farm
Works
Works
Grays Farm
1

Foundry
LONG DROVE
MILL DROVE
NORTH DROVE

Carrington Farm
EVERARD RD
Sewage Works

Northorpe Fen
18

13   A   14   B   15   C   16   D   17   E   18   F

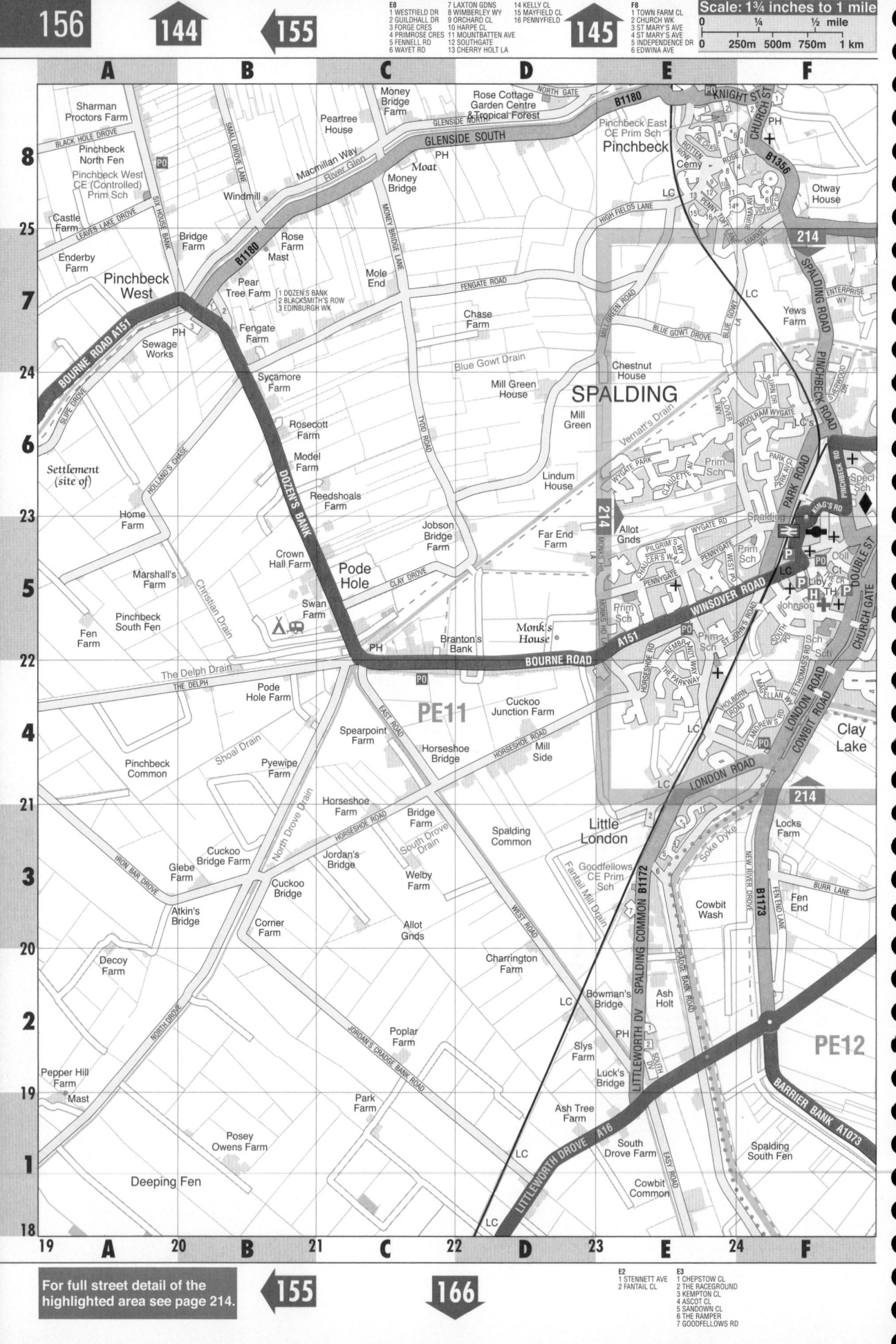

156

144

155

145

Scale: 1¾ inches to 1 mile
0   ¼   ½   mile
0   250m 500m 750m 1 km

E8
1 WESTFIELD DR
2 GUILDHALL DR
3 FORGE CRES
4 PRIMROSE CRES
5 FENNEL RD
6 WAYET RD

7 LAXTON GDNS
8 WIMBERLEY WY
9 ORCHARD CL
10 HARPE CL
11 MOUNTBATTEN AVE
12 SOUTHGATE
13 CHERRY HOLT LA

14 KELLY CL
15 MAYFIELD CL
16 PENNYFIELD

F8
1 TOWN FARM CL
2 CHURCH WK
3 ST MARY'S AVE
4 ST MARY'S AVE
5 INDEPENDENCE DR
6 EDWINA AVE

PINCHBECK

SPALDING

PE11

PE12

For full street detail of the
highlighted area see page 214.

155

166

E2
1 STENNETT AVE
2 FANTAIL CL

E3
1 CHEPSTOW CL
2 THE RACEGROUND
3 KEMPTON CL
4 ASCOT CL
5 SANDOWN CL
6 THE RAMPER
7 GOODFELLOWS RD

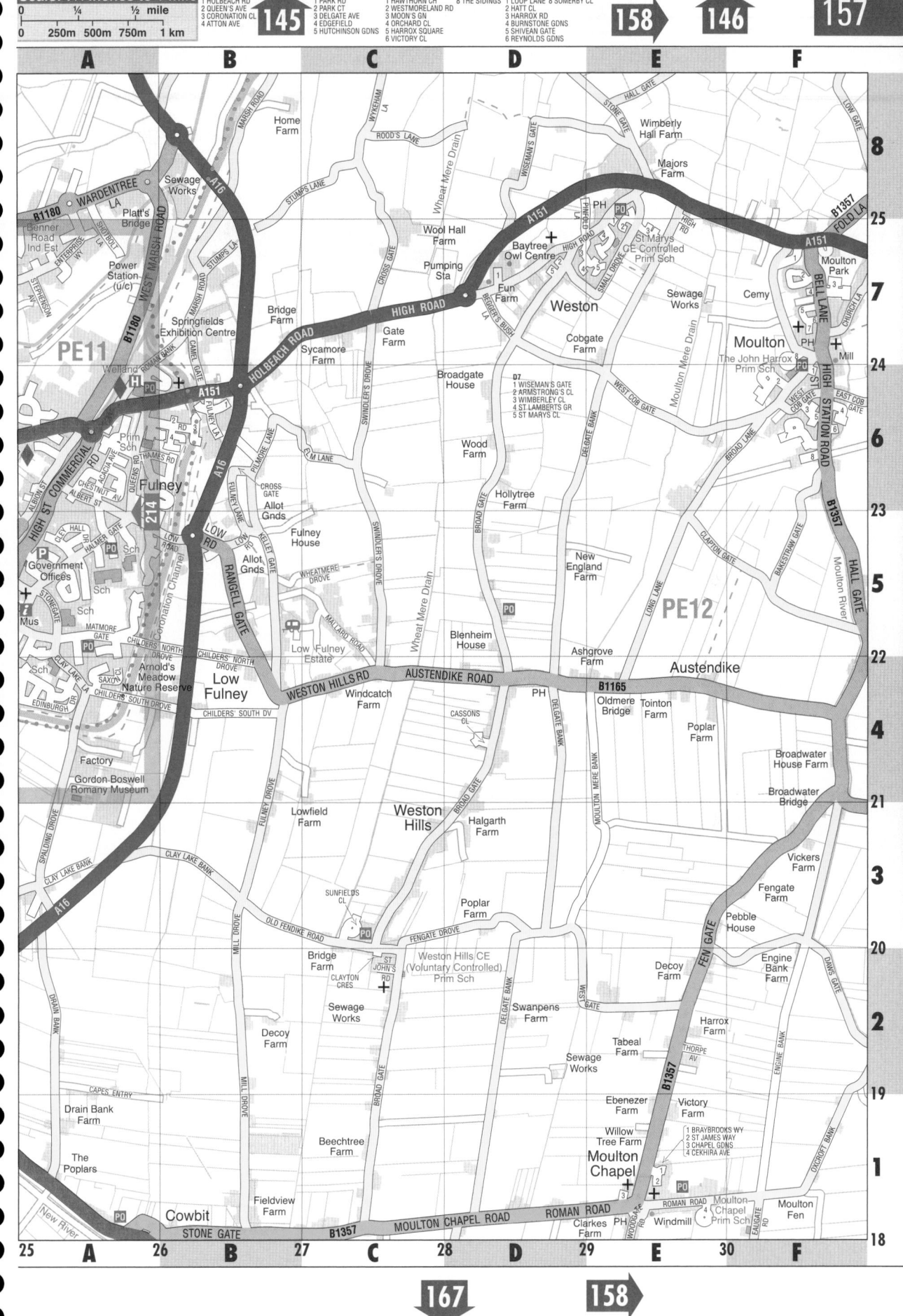

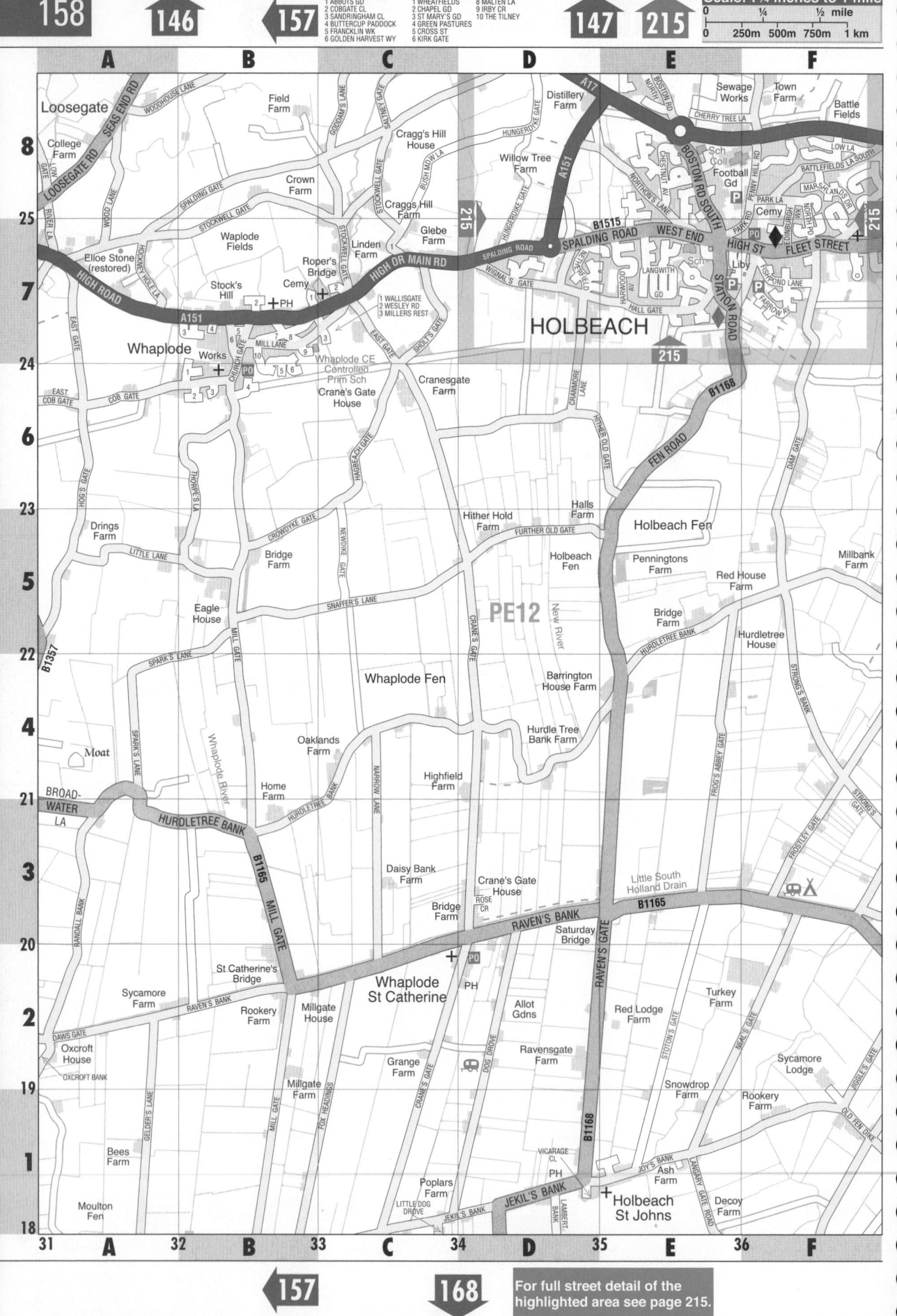

146
157
147
215

B6
1 ABBOTS GD
2 COBGATE CL
3 SANDRINGHAM CL
4 BUTTERCUP PADDOCK
5 FRANCKLIN WK
6 GOLDEN HARVEST WY

B7
1 WHEATFIELDS
2 CHAPEL GD
3 ST MARY'S GD
4 GREEN PASTURES
5 CROSS ST
6 KIRK GATE

7 MIDDLE RD
8 MALTEN LA
9 IRBY CR
10 THE TILNEY

Loosegate

College Farm

Field Farm

WOODHOUSE LANE

GODDAM'S LANE

STANLEY LANE

Cragg's Hill House

Willow Tree Farm

Distillery Farm

Sewage Works

Town Farm

Battle Fields

LOOSEGATE RD
SEAS END RD

SPALDING GATE

Crown Farm

Craggs Hill Farm

Glebe Farm

BUSH MDW LA

HUNGERDYKE GATE

BOSTON RD NORTH

CHERRY TREE LA

Sch Coll

Football Gd

MARSHLAND ST

BATTLEFIELDS LA SOUTH

LOW LA

STOCKWELL GATE

Waplode Fields

Linden Farm

STOCKWELL GATE

Roper's Bridge

Cemy

HIGH ROAD

Elloe Stone (restored)

HOCKEY HOLE LA

Stock's Hill

HIGH OR MAIN RD

SPALDING ROAD

WIGNAL'S GATE

SPALDING ROAD

WEST END

B1515

HARWOOD

LANGWITH GD

HALL GATE

WEST END

HIGH ST

FLEET STREET

SECOND LANE

FARROW

HOLBEACH

215

A151

PH

1 WALLISGATE
2 WESLEY RD
3 MILLERS REST

EAST GATE

SHOLT'S GATE

Whaplode CE Controlled Prim Sch

Cranesgate Farm

CRANMORE LANE

B1168

DAM GATE

Whaplode

Works

MILL LANE

Crane's Gate House

HAYBEACH GATE

Cranesgate Farm

HITHER OLD GATE

FEN ROAD

COB GATE

EAST COB GATE

THORPE'S LA

CROWDYKE GATE

NEWDIKE GATE

Hither Hold Farm

FURTHER OLD GATE

Halls Farm

Holbeach Fen

Penningtons Farm

Red House Farm

Millbank Farm

Drings Farm

LITTLE LANE

Bridge Farm

SNAFFER'S LANE

Holbeach Fen

Bridge Farm

Hurdletree House

B1357

Eagle House

MILL GATE

CRANE'S GATE

PE12

New River

HURDLETREE BANK

STRONG'S BANK

SPARK'S LANE

Whaplode Fen

Barrington House Farm

Moat

SPARK'S LANE

Whaplode River

HURDLETREE BANK

Oaklands Farm

NARROW LANE

Highfield Farm

Hurdle Tree Bank Farm

FROG'S ABBEY GATE

FROSTLEY GATE

STRONG'S GATE

BROAD-WATER LA

Home Farm

HURDLETREE BANK

HURDLETREE BANK

Daisy Bank Farm

Little South Holland Drain

B1165

MILL GATE

B1165

RANDALL BANK

Crane's Gate House

ROSE CR

Bridge Farm

RAVEN'S BANK

Saturday Bridge

RAVEN'S GATE

Sycamore Farm

St Catherine's Bridge

RAVEN'S BANK

Rookery Farm

Millgate House

Whaplode St Catherine

PO

PH

Allot Gdns

Red Lodge Farm

Turkey Farm

STOTON'S GATE

NEAL'S GATE

Oxcroft House

DAWS GATE

GELDER'S LANE

Grange Farm

CRANE'S GATE

Millgate Farm

FOX HEADINGS

Ravensgate Farm

DOG DRONE

Snowdrop Farm

Sycamore Lodge

JUGGLE'S GATE

OLD FEN DIKE

OXCROFT BANK

MILL GATE

VICARAGE CL

B1168

Rookery Farm

Bees Farm

Poplars Farm

PH

JOY'S BANK

Ash Farm

LANGARY GATE ROAD

Decoy Farm

Moulton Fen

LITTLE DOG DROVE

JEKIL'S BANK

JEKIL'S BANK

LAMBERT BANK

Holbeach St Johns

157
168

For full street detail of the highlighted area see page 215.

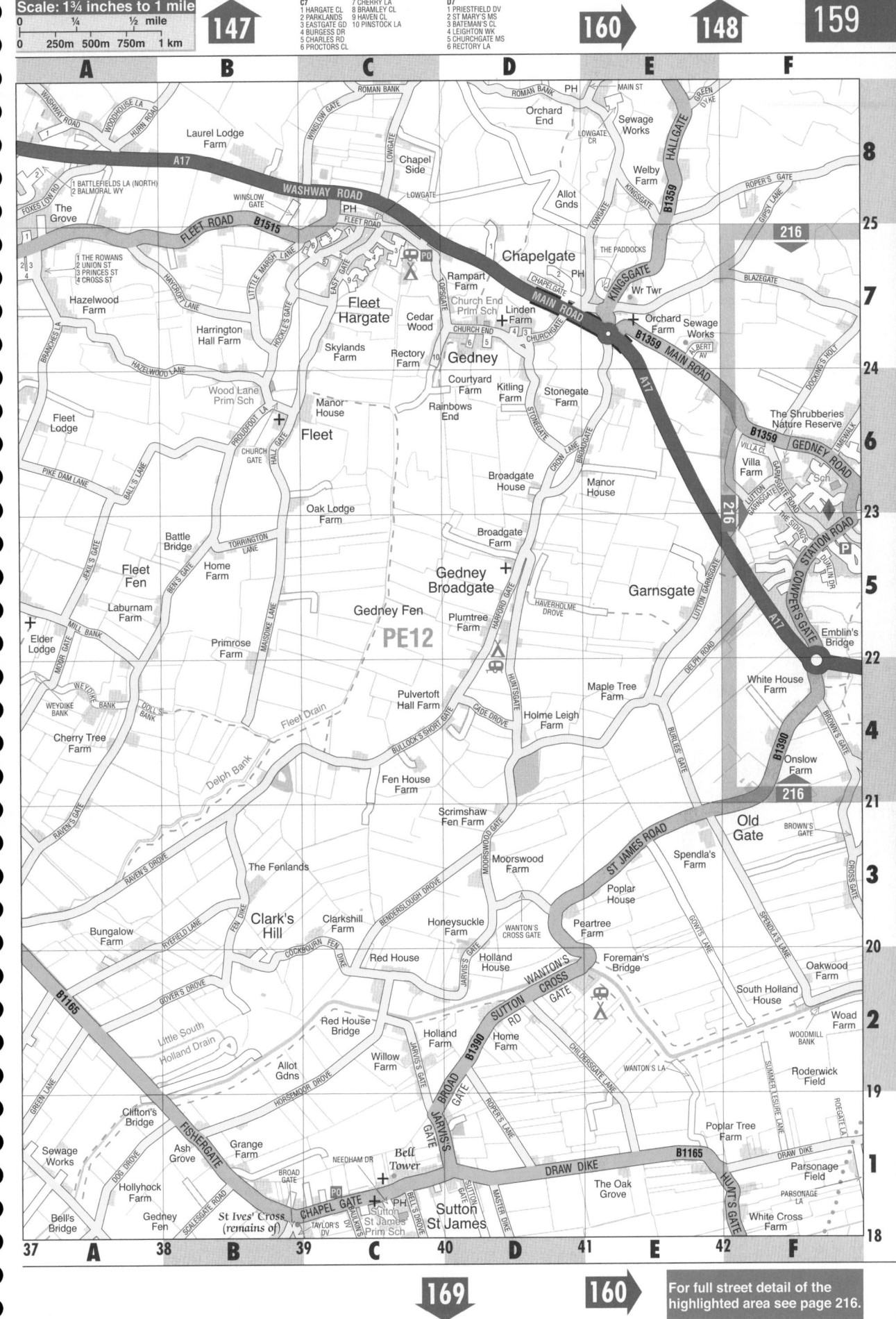

Scale: 1¾ inches to 1 mile

0   ¼   ½ mile
0   250m 500m 750m 1 km

147

C7
1 HARGATE CL
2 PARKLANDS
3 EASTGATE GD
4 BURGESS DR
5 CHARLES RD
6 PROCTORS CL

7 CHERRY LA
8 BRAMLEY CL
9 HAVEN CL
10 PINSTOCK LA

D7
1 PRIESTFIELD DV
2 ST MARY'S MS
3 BATEMAN'S CL
4 LEIGHTON WK
5 CHURCHGATE MS
6 RECTORY LA

160

148

159

A17 WASHWAY ROAD

FLEET ROAD B1515

Laurel Lodge Farm

Chapel Side

Lowgate

ROMAN BANK

Orchard End

Sewage Works

Welby Farm

HALLGATE

GREEN DYKE

MAIN ST

LOWGATE CR

Allot Gnds

KINGSGATE

B1359

ROPER'S GATE

GIPS LANE

216

The Grove

1 BATTLEFIELDS LA (NORTH)
2 BALMORAL WY

WINSLOW GATE

FLEET RD

PH

Chapelgate

WR TWR

THE PADDOCKS

BLAZEGATE

8

25

Hazelwood Farm

1 THE ROWANS
2 UNION ST
3 PRINCES ST
4 CROSS ST

Harrington Hall Farm

HACKLE'S GATE

EAST GATE

Fleet Hargate

Cedar Wood

Rampart Farm

Church End Prim Sch

CHURCH END

MAIN ROAD

CHAPELGATE

PH

Orchard Farm

Sewage Works

ALBERT AV

B1359

DOCKING'S HOLT

7

HAZELWOOD LANE

Skylands Farm

Rectory Farm

Linden Farm

Gedney

CHURCH END

Courtyard Farm

Kitling Farm

Stonegate Farm

A17

Villa Farm

VILLA CL

GARNSGATE ROAD

The Shrubberies Nature Reserve

B1359

GEDNEY ROAD

Sch

TIMEWALK

24

6

Fleet Lodge

Wood Lane Prim Sch

Manor House

CHURCH GATE

PROUDFOOT LA

HALL GATE

Fleet

Rainbows End

Broadgate House

CROW LANE

STONEGATE

BROADGATE

Manor House

216

STATION ROAD

THE SIDINGS

DUHLIN DR

P

23

PIKE DAM LANE

BRANCHES LA

Battle Bridge

Home Farm

TORRINGTON LANE

Oak Lodge Farm

Broadgate Farm

Gedney Broadgate

HARFORD GATE

LUTTON GARNSGATE

5

Fleet Fen

BEN'S GATE

Laburnam Farm

Primrose Farm

MAISDIKE LANE

Gedney Fen

PE12

Plumtree Farm

HUNTSGATE

HAVERHOLME DROVE

Garnsgate

DELPH ROAD

Emblin's Bridge

22

Elder Lodge

MOOR GATE

MILL BANK

WEYDIKE BANK

DOLL'S BANK

Fleet Drain

CADE DROVE

Pulvertoft Hall Farm

Maple Tree Farm

Holme Leigh Farm

BURLEIS GATE

White House Farm

BROWN'S GATE

B1390

Onslow Farm

216

4

21

Cherry Tree Farm

RAVEN'S GATE

Delph Bank

BULLOCK'S SHORT GATE

Fen House Farm

Scrimshaw Fen Farm

MOORSWOOD GATE

Old Gate

ST JAMES ROAD

Spendla's Farm

BROWN'S GATE

CROSS GATE

SPENDLA'S LANE

Bungalow Farm

RAVEN'S DROVE

The Fenlands

Clarkshill Farm

BENDERSLOUGH DROVE

Moorswood Farm

Honeysuckle Farm

WANTON'S CROSS GATE

Poplar House

Peartree Farm

GOWT'S LANE

3

20

FEN LANE

Clark's Hill

Red House

COCKBOURN FEN DIKE

Holland House

Foreman's Bridge

South Holland House

Oakwood Farm

Woad Farm

WOODMILL BANK

RYEFIELD LANE

SUTTON

CROSS

GATE

2

B1165

GOVER'S DROVE

Little South Holland Drain

Red House Bridge

Willow Farm

JARVIS'S GATE

Holland Farm

B1390

Home Farm

ROPER'S LANE

WANTON'S LA

CHILLERGATE LANE

SUMMER LEISURE LANE

Roderwick Field

ROGATE LA

19

GREEN LANE

Clifton's Bridge

FISHERGATE

Ash Grove

Grange Farm

HORSEMOOR DROVE

Allot Gdns

BROAD GATE

NEEDHAM DR

Bell Tower

BELL'S DROVE

MASTER DIKE

DRAW DIKE

B1165

Poplar Tree Farm

DRAW DIKE

Parsonage Field

PARSONAGE LA

1

Sewage Works

DOG DROVE

Hollyhock Farm

Gedney Fen

SCALESGATE ROAD

CHAPEL GATE

TAYLOR'S DV

PO

Sutton St James Prim Sch

PH

FAULKN'S GATE

St Ives' Cross (remains of)

Sutton St James

SUTTON GATE

The Oak Grove

HUNT'S GATE

White Cross Farm

18

Bell's Bridge

37 A 38 B 39 C 40 D 41 E 42 F

169

160

For full street detail of the highlighted area see page 216.

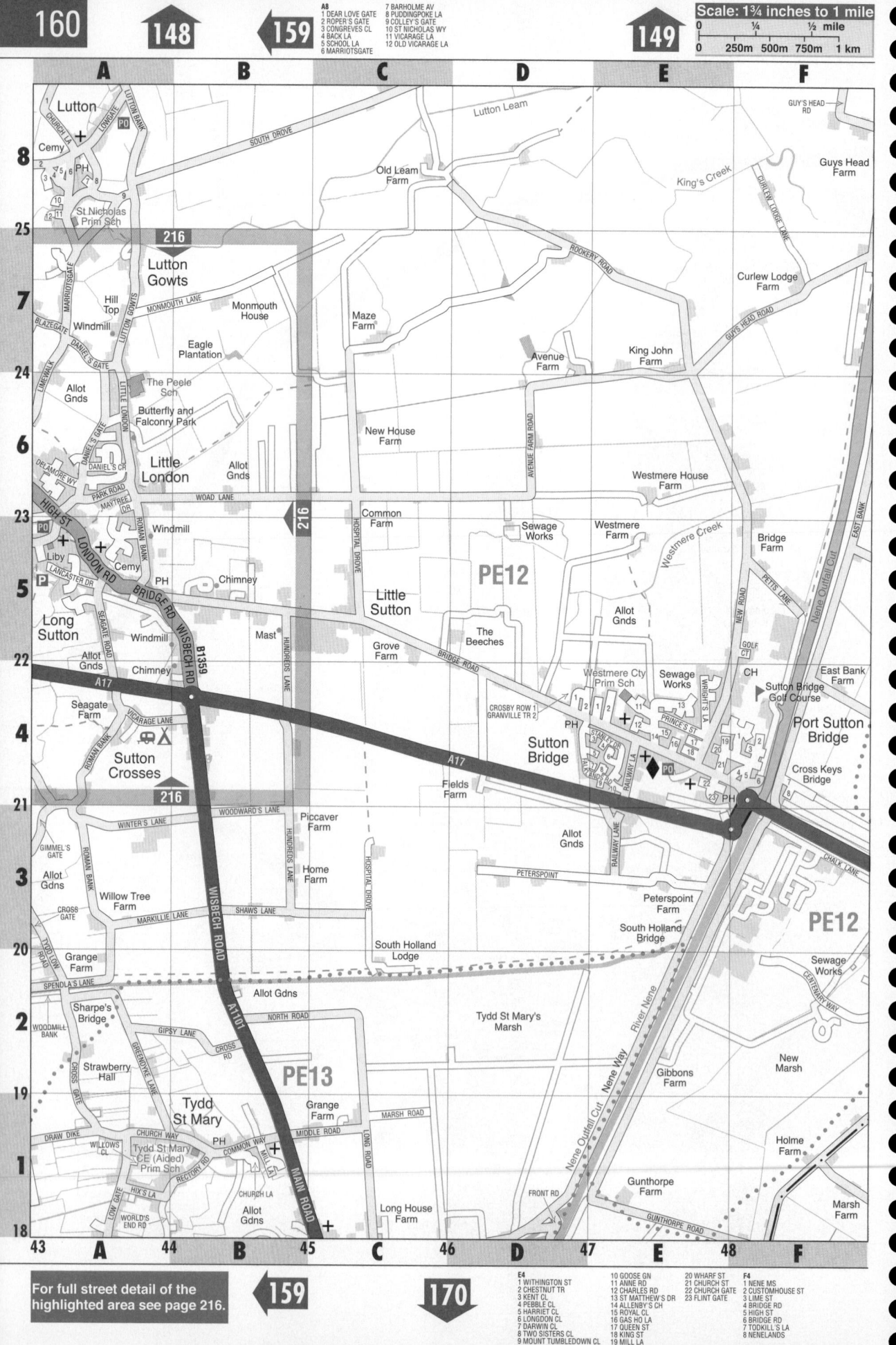

148
159
149

A8
1 DEAR LOVE GATE
2 ROPER'S GATE
3 CONGREVES CL
4 BACK LA
5 SCHOOL LA
6 MARRIOTSGATE

7 BARHOLME AV
8 PUDDINGPOKE LA
9 COLLEY'S GATE
10 ST NICHOLAS WY
11 VICARAGE LA
12 OLD VICARAGE LA

Scale: 1¾ inches to 1 mile
0   ¼   ½ mile
0   250m 500m 750m 1 km

Map labels (top to bottom, left to right):

Lutton
GUY'S HEAD RD
Lutton Leam
Cemy
Church La
Lowgate
PO
South Drove
Old Leam Farm
King's Creek
Guys Head Farm
PH
St Nicholas Prim Sch

216
Lutton Gowts
Rookery Road
Curlew Lodge Farm
Curlew Loose Lane
Guys Head Road

Hill Top
Windmill
Monmouth Lane
Monmouth House
Maze Farm
Avenue Farm
King John Farm
Marriotsgate
Little London Gowts

Blazegate
Eagle Plantation
The Peele Sch
New House Farm
Westmere House Farm
Allot Gnds
Butterfly and Falconry Park
Allot Gnds

Limewalk
Daniel's Gate
Little London
Daniel's Cr
Woad Lane
Common Farm
Sewage Works
Westmere Farm
Westmere Creek
Bridge Farm

Delmore Wy
Park Road
Maytree Dr
High St
PO
Liby
London Rd
Lancaster Dr
Cemy
Windmill
Chimney
Little Sutton
PE12
Allot Gnds
Golf Ct
East Bank
Nene Outfall Cut
New Road
Petts Lane

Long Sutton
Allot Gnds
Windmill
Chimney
Seagate Road
Mast
Hundreds Lane
Grove Farm
The Beeches
Bridge Road
Westmere Cty Prim Sch
Sewage Works
CH
East Bank Farm
Sutton Bridge Golf Course

A17
Seagate Farm
Vicarage Lane
Roman Bank
Bridge Rd
Wisbech Rd
B1359
Crosby Row 1
Granville Tr 2
PH
Prince's St
Wright's La
Port Sutton Bridge

Sutton Crosses
216
Fields Farm
Sutton Bridge
Railway Lane
PO
PH
Cross Keys Bridge
Chalk Lane
PE12

Gimmel's Gate
Winter's Lane
Woodward's Lane
Piccaver Farm
Allot Gnds
Roman Bank
Allot Gdns
Hundreds Lane
Home Farm
Hospital Drove
Peterspoint
Peterspoint Farm

Cross Gate
Willow Tree Farm
Markillie Lane
Shaws Lane
South Holland Lodge
South Holland Bridge

Tydd Low Road
Grange Farm
Spendla's Lane
Allot Gdns
Nene Way
River Nene
Sewage Works
Centenary Way

Woodmill Bank
Sharpe's Bridge
Gipsy Lane
North Road
Cross Rd
Tydd St Mary's Marsh
New Marsh
Gunthorpe Farm

Cross Gate
Strawberry Hall
Greendyke Lane
PE13
Grange Farm
Marsh Road
Gibbons Farm
Holme Farm

Draw Dike
Tydd St Mary
Church Way
Willows Cl
Tydd St Mary CE (Aided) Prim Sch
Rectory Rd
Common Way
Mill La
Middle Road
Long Road
Front Rd
Gunthorpe Farm
Marsh Farm

Low Gate
Hix's La
World's End Rd
Church La
Main Road
Allot Gdns
Long House Farm
Gunthorpe Road

For full street detail of the highlighted area see page 216.
159
170

E4
1 WITHINGTON ST
2 CHESTNUT TR
3 KENT CL
4 PEBBLE CL
5 HARRIET CL
6 LONGDON CL
7 DARWIN CL
8 TWO SISTERS CL
9 MOUNT TUMBLEDOWN CL

10 GOOSE GN
11 ANNE RD
12 CHARLES RD
13 ST MATTHEW'S DR
14 ALLENBY'S CH
15 ROYAL CL
16 GAS HO LA
17 QUEEN ST
18 KING ST
19 MILL LA

20 WHARF ST
21 CHURCH ST
22 CHURCH GATE
23 FLINT GATE

F4
1 NENE MS
2 CUSTOMHOUSE ST
3 LIME ST
4 BRIDGE RD
5 HIGH ST
6 BRIDGE RD
7 TODKILL'S LA
8 NENELANDS

43 A 44 B 45 C 46 D 47 E 48 F

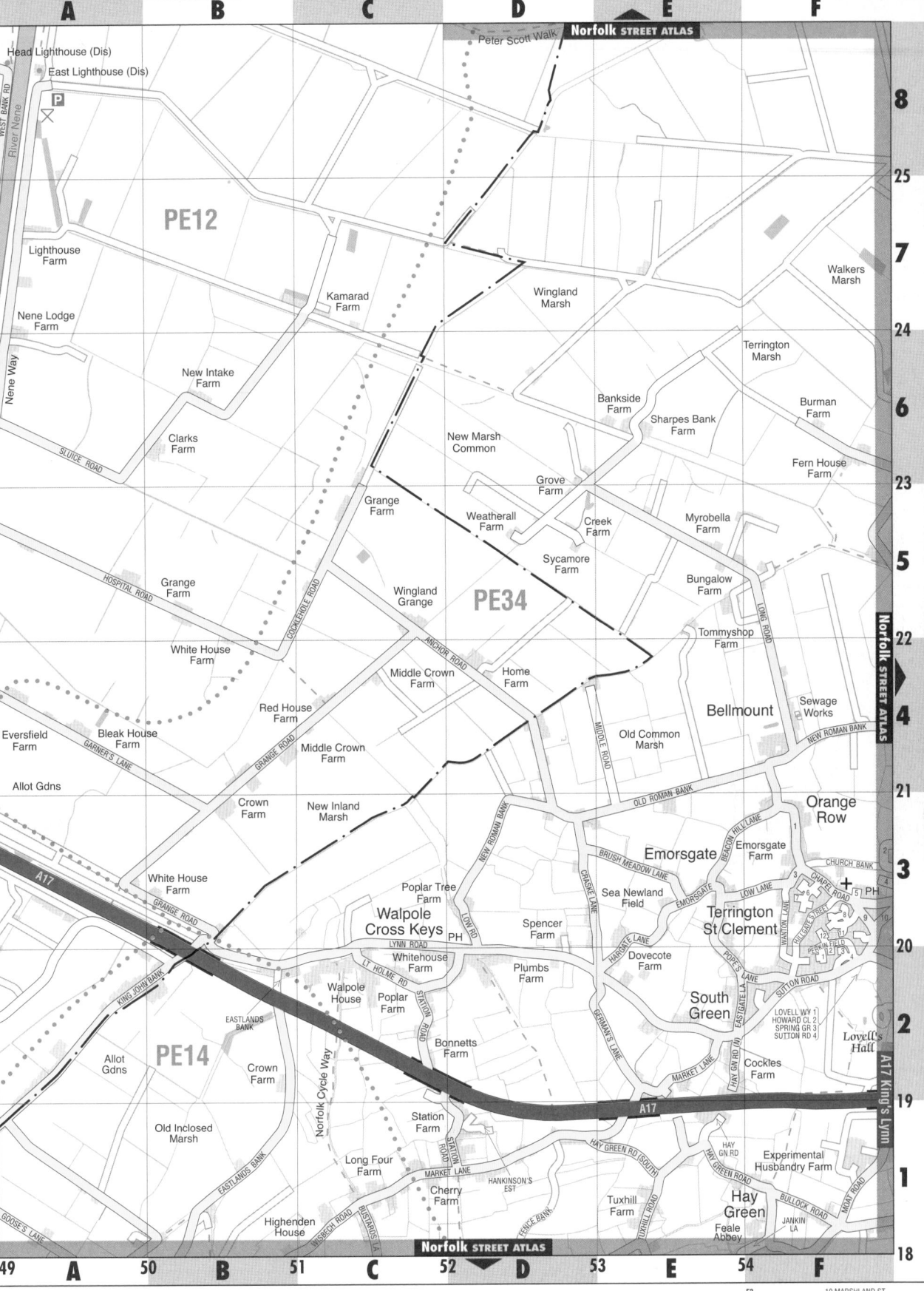

Scale: 1¾ inches to 1 mile

0   ¼   ½   mile
0 250m 500m 750m 1 km

149

161

Norfolk STREET ATLAS

PE12

PE34

PE14

Head Lighthouse (Dis)
East Lighthouse (Dis)
Lighthouse Farm
Nene Lodge Farm
New Intake Farm
Clarks Farm
Kamarad Farm
Wingland Marsh
Walkers Marsh
Terrington Marsh
Bankside Farm
Sharpes Bank Farm
Burman Farm
Fern House Farm
New Marsh Common
Grove Farm
Creek Farm
Myrobella Farm
Grange Farm
Weatherall Farm
Sycamore Farm
Bungalow Farm
Grange Farm
Wingland Grange
White House Farm
Middle Crown Farm
Home Farm
Tommyshop Farm
Bellmount
Sewage Works
Eversfield Farm
Bleak House Farm
Red House Farm
Middle Crown Farm
Old Common Marsh
Orange Row
Allot Gdns
Crown Farm
New Inland Marsh
Emorsgate
Emorsgate Farm
White House Farm
Poplar Tree Farm
Walpole Cross Keys
Sea Newland Field
Terrington St Clement
Whitehouse Farm
Spencer Farm
Plumbs Farm
Dovecote Farm
South Green
Walpole House
Poplar Farm
Bonnetts Farm
Cockles Farm
Lovell's Hall
Allot Gdns
Crown Farm
Norfolk Cycle Way
Station Farm
Station Farm
Old Inclosed Marsh
Long Four Farm
Cherry Farm
Hankinson's Est
Hay Green Rd (South)
Tuxhill Farm
Experimental Husbandry Farm
Hay Green
Highenden House
Feale Abbey

F3
1 ORANGE ROW RD
2 CHURCH BANK
3 ORANGE ROW
4 KING WILLIAM CL
5 WESLEY AV
6 THE SALTINGS
7 BRELLOWS HL
8 CAVE'S CL
9 WESLEY RD
10 MARSHLAND ST
11 WESLEY CL
12 FFOLKES DR

E8
1 LITTLE BYTHAM RD
2 REGAL GDNS
3 BYTHAM HEIGHTS

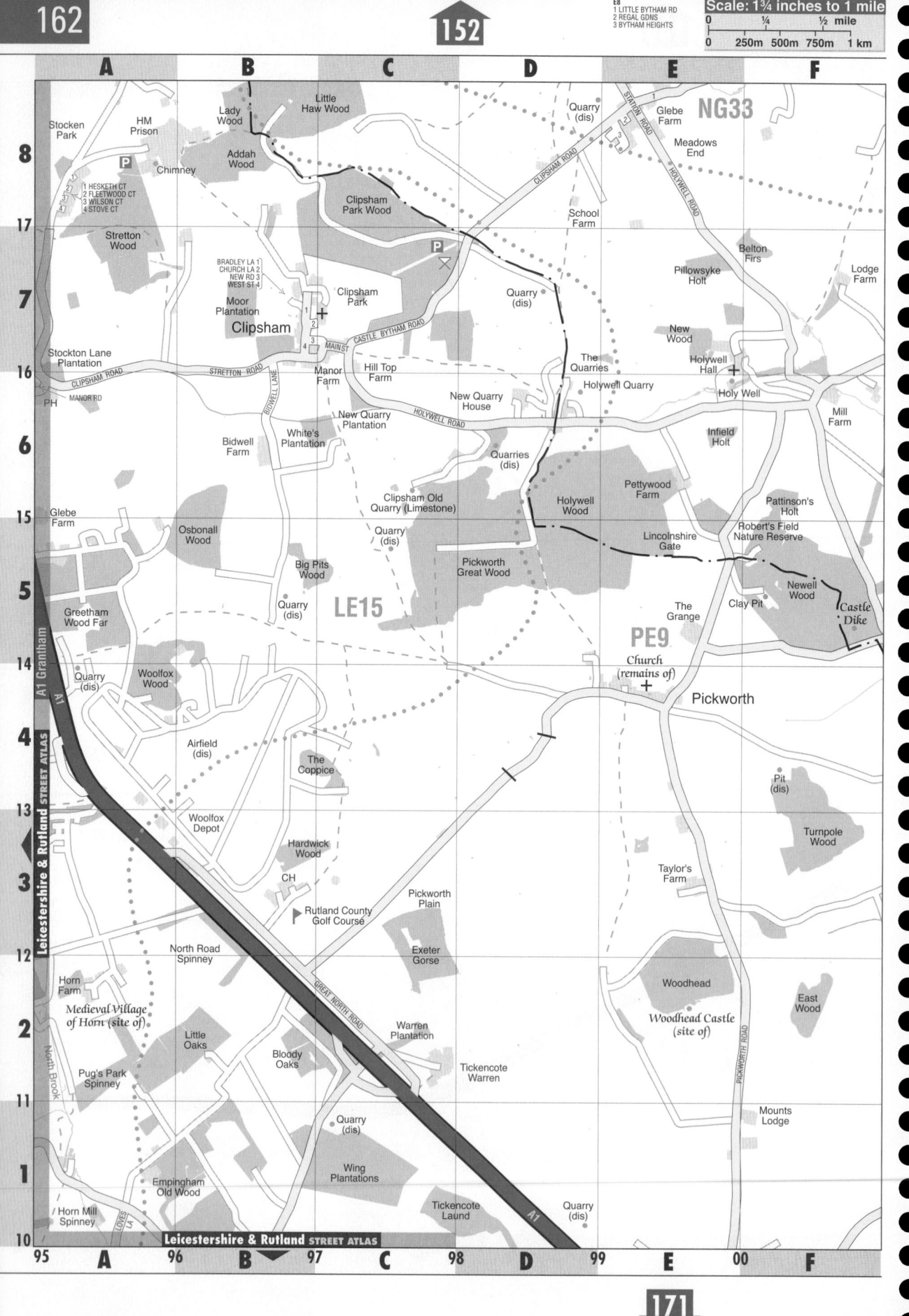

Stocken Park
HM Prison
Lady Wood
Little Haw Wood
Quarry (dis)
Glebe Farm
NG33
Chimney
Addah Wood
Meadows End
P
1 HESKETH CT
2 FLEETWOOD CT
3 WILSON CT
4 STOVE CT
Clipsham Park Wood
School Farm
Stretton Wood
Belton Firs
BRADLEY LA 1
CHURCH LA 2
NEW RD 3
WEST ST 4
Clipsham Park
P
Quarry (dis)
Pillowsyke Holt
Lodge Farm
Moor Plantation
Clipsham
New Wood
Stockton Lane Plantation
MAIN ST
CASTLE BYTHAM ROAD
The Quarries
Holywell Hall
Holy Well
CLIPSHAM ROAD
STRETTON ROAD
Manor Farm
Hill Top Farm
Holywell Quarry
Mill Farm
PH
MANOR RD
BIDWELL LANE
New Quarry Plantation
New Quarry House
HOLYWELL ROAD
Infield Holt
Bidwell Farm
White's Plantation
Quarries (dis)
Pettywood Farm
Pattinson's Holt
Glebe Farm
Osbonall Wood
Clipsham Old Quarry (Limestone)
Holywell Wood
Lincolnshire Gate
Robert's Field Nature Reserve
Big Pits Wood
Quarry (dis)
Pickworth Great Wood
The Grange
Clay Pit
Newell Wood
Castle Dike
Greetham Wood Far
Quarry (dis)
LE15
PE9
Quarry (dis)
Woolfox Wood
Church (remains of)
Pickworth
A1 Grantham
A1
Airfield (dis)
Pit (dis)
The Coppice
Turnpole Wood
Woolfox Depot
Hardwick Wood
CH
Taylor's Farm
North Road Spinney
Rutland County Golf Course
Pickworth Plain
Horn Farm
Exeter Gorse
Woodhead
East Wood
Medieval Village of Horn (site of)
Little Oaks
Warren Plantation
Woodhead Castle (site of)
PICKWORTH ROAD
North Brook
Pug's Park Spinney
Bloody Oaks
Tickencote Warren
GREAT NORTH ROAD
Mounts Lodge
Empingham Old Wood
Quarry (dis)
Wing Plantations
Horn Mill Spinney
LOVES LA
Tickencote Laund
Quarry (dis)
A1

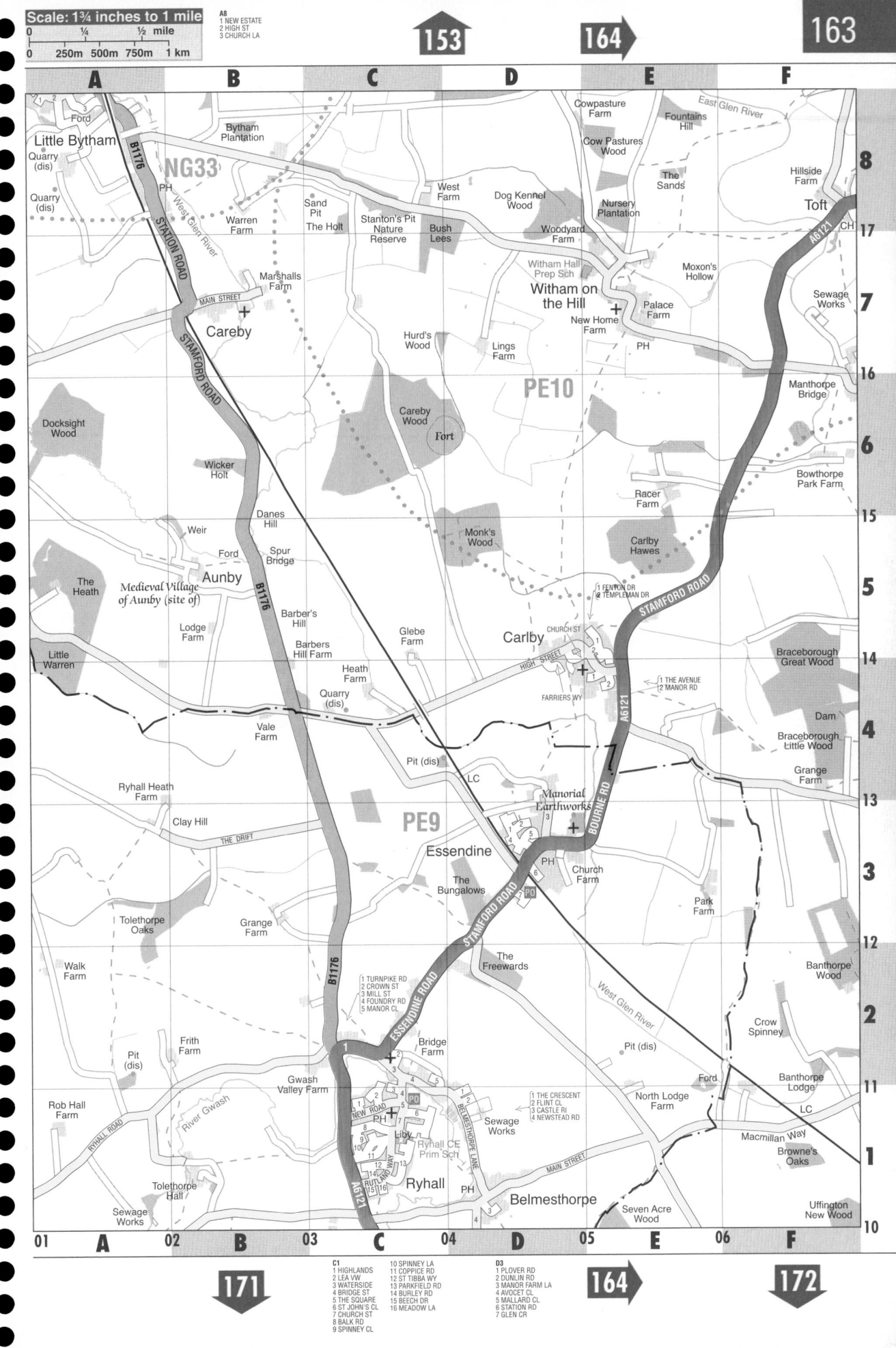

Scale: 1¾ inches to 1 mile

0 ¼ ½ mile
0 250m 500m 750m 1 km

A8
1 NEW ESTATE
2 HIGH ST
3 CHURCH LA

A B C D E F

Little Bytham
Quarry (dis)
Quarry (dis)
Ford
NG33
B1176
West Glen River
STATION ROAD
PH
Warren Farm
Sand Pit
The Holt
Bytham Plantation
West Farm
Stanton's Pit Nature Reserve
Bush Lees
Dog Kennel Wood
Cowpasture Farm
Cow Pastures Wood
Fountains Hill
The Sands
Woodyard Farm
Witham Hall Prep Sch
Nursery Plantation
Hillside Farm
Toft
A6121
CH
Sewage Works
Marshalls Farm
Careby
MAIN STREET
STAMFORD ROAD
Hurd's Wood
Witham on the Hill
New Home Farm
Palace Farm
PH
Moxon's Hollow
Lings Farm
PE10
Manthorpe Bridge
Docksight Wood
Wicker Holt
Careby Wood
Fort
Racer Farm
Bowthorpe Park Farm
Weir
Danes Hill
Ford
Spur Bridge
Monk's Wood
Carlby Hawes
Medieval Village of Aunby (site of)
Aunby
B1176
Barber's Hill
Glebe Farm
Carlby
CHURCH ST
1 FENTON DR
2 TEMPLEMAN DR
STAMFORD ROAD
Braceborough Great Wood
The Heath
Lodge Farm
Barbers Hill Farm
Heath Farm
HIGH STREET
1 THE AVENUE
2 MANOR RD
Dam
Little Warren
Quarry (dis)
FARRIERS WY
A6121
Braceborough Little Wood
Ryhall Heath Farm
Vale Farm
Pit (dis)
LC
Manorial Earthworks
BOURNE RD
Grange Farm
Clay Hill
THE DRIFT
PE9
Essendine
PH
Church Farm
Park Farm
Tolethorpe Oaks
Grange Farm
The Bungalows
STAMFORD ROAD
6
PO
Banthorpe Wood
Walk Farm
1 TURNPIKE RD
2 CROWN ST
3 MILL ST
4 FOUNDRY RD
5 MANOR CL
The Freewards
West Glen River
Crow Spinney
Frith Farm
Pit (dis)
ESSENDINE ROAD
B1176
Bridge Farm
1 THE CRESCENT
2 FLINT CL
3 CASTLE RI
4 NEWSTEAD RD
Pit (dis)
Ford
Banthorpe Lodge
LC
Rob Hall Farm
Gwash Valley Farm
NEW ROAD
PH
PO
Sewage Works
North Lodge Farm
Macmillan Way
Browne's Oaks
RYHALL ROAD
River Gwash
Liby
Ryhall CE Prim Sch
RUTLAND
BELMESTHORPE LANE
MAIN STREET
Tolethorpe Hall
A6121
Ryhall
PH
Belmesthorpe
Seven Acre Wood
Uffington New Wood
Sewage Works

8
17
7
16
6
15
5
14
4
13
3
12
2
11
1
10

01 A 02 B 03 C 04 D 05 E 06 F

C1
1 HIGHLANDS
2 LEA VW
3 WATERSIDE
4 BRIDGE ST
5 THE SQUARE
6 ST JOHN'S CL
7 CHURCH ST
8 BALK RD
9 SPINNEY CL
10 SPINNEY LA
11 COPPICE RD
12 ST TIBBA WY
13 PARKFIELD RD
14 BURLEY RD
15 BEECH DR
16 MEADOW LA

D3
1 PLOVER RD
2 DUNLIN RD
3 MANOR FARM LA
4 AVOCET CL
5 MALLARD CL
6 STATION RD
7 GLEN CR

163 213 154

C8
1 WOODSIDE CL
2 CAPPITT DR
3 ELSEA DR
4 ELIZABETH WY
5 BECK WY
6 THE CAUSEWAY

7 VIKING WY
8 THE KIPPINGS
9 THE PINGLES
10 LAWRANCE WY
11 PINFOLD CL
12 PRIORY CL
13 MAPLE AVE

14 CROWN LA
15 PARK VW

E5
1 BRUDENELL CL
2 ST JOHNS CL
3 BEDE RD
4 MERCIA GV
5 THETFORD AVE
6 CHARIOTS WY

7 CAESAR CL
8 APPIAN CL
9 FOSSE CL
10 HADRIAN DR
11 MANOR CL
12 MANOR DR
13 CARDYKE DR

Northorpe
West Farm
Northorpe Fen Farm
FEN ROAD
Northorpe Fen
NORTHORPE LANE
Woodside East
WOOD LANE
Thurlby
WATER
Thurlby Com Prim Sch
THE GREEN
PO
Mast
SWALLOW HILL
SWIFT WY
STATION ROAD
HIGH STREET
YHA
TUDOR CL
Elm Farm
St FIRMIN'S WY
CHURCH STREET
SHORT DROVE
LONG DROVE
MANTHORPE DROVE
LAWRENCE'S DV
Thurlby Fen
Thurlby Fen Nature Reserve
BASTON FEN DROVE
PE10
PH
MAIN ROAD
A15
Playing Field
Poplar Tree Farm
FAIRWAYS
Toft
A6121
Church Farm
Manthorpe
Home Farm
Cross Farm
OBTHORPE LANE
Dole Wood Nature Reserve
Park Wood
Macmillan Way
Red House Farm
HACK'S DROVE
Katesbridge Farm
Hack's Plantation
Manor Farm
Obthorpe
Obthorpe Lodge
Thetford House Farm
Thetford
Fringes Fen
Kate's Bridge Weir
Spa Lodge Farm
East Glen River
Fletland
Baston CE Prim Sch
Cemy
Works
Brook House Farm
Old Hall Farm
Wilsthorpe
Mill Farm
MALTBY DR 1
FRISBY CL 2
WHATTOFF WY 3
GREATFORD RD
Sand & Gravel Pit
Baston
PE6
Manor Farm
Church Farm
Braceborough
Macmillan Way
Kirkstone House Sch
Middle Field
Moat
Church Farm
Braceborough Great Wood
Lodge Farm
DEEPING ROAD
Windmill
PE9
Meadow Field
Truesdale Lodge
BOURNE ROAD
Stonehouse Farm
A15
EAST END
NEW ROAD
Bottom Meadow
Middle Field
Red Inn Field
MANOR CL 1
MOSSOP DR 2
SCOTT'S CL 3
TRUESDALE GDNS 4
Langtoft Prim Sch
PO
Cemy
PH
Banthorpe Wood
GREATFORD GD
Greatford
The Council Houses
MAIN STREET
Nook Field
W END
Langtoft
PETERBOROUGH ROAD
Dogkennel Plantation
Macmillan Way
Greatford Hall
PH
Manor Farm
Glen Farm
Shillingthorpe Park
West Glen River
Greatford Wood
Weir
Banks Farm
Parsonage Field
Bleak House Farm
STOWE ROAD
1 WHEATFIELD
2 AQUILA WY
3 BARLEYFIELD
4 WESTFIELD WY
Middle Field
Tithe Farm
West Field
Sand & Gravel Pit
Stowe Farm
PH
Barholm
Old Hall
Marsh Plantation
Beck Field
Sand & Gravel Pit
Greatford Cut
Far Field
Towngate
MILLFIELD RD
Great Maidens
Cank Wood
Cedar Plantation
Rectory Farm
Crown Farm
Mill Field
A16
Cow Pasture Plantation
Cow Pasture
Casewick Field

172   163   173

E4
1 SCHOOL LA
2 CHURCH ST
3 AVELAND WY
4 CLARE CT
5 DENSHIRE CT
6 COLTON CL
7 CHESHAM DR

F3
1 BARN OWL CL
2 LIME CL
3 DEER PK RD
4 CLOVEN ENDS
5 REEDMANS CL
6 MANOR WY
7 THE RIDES

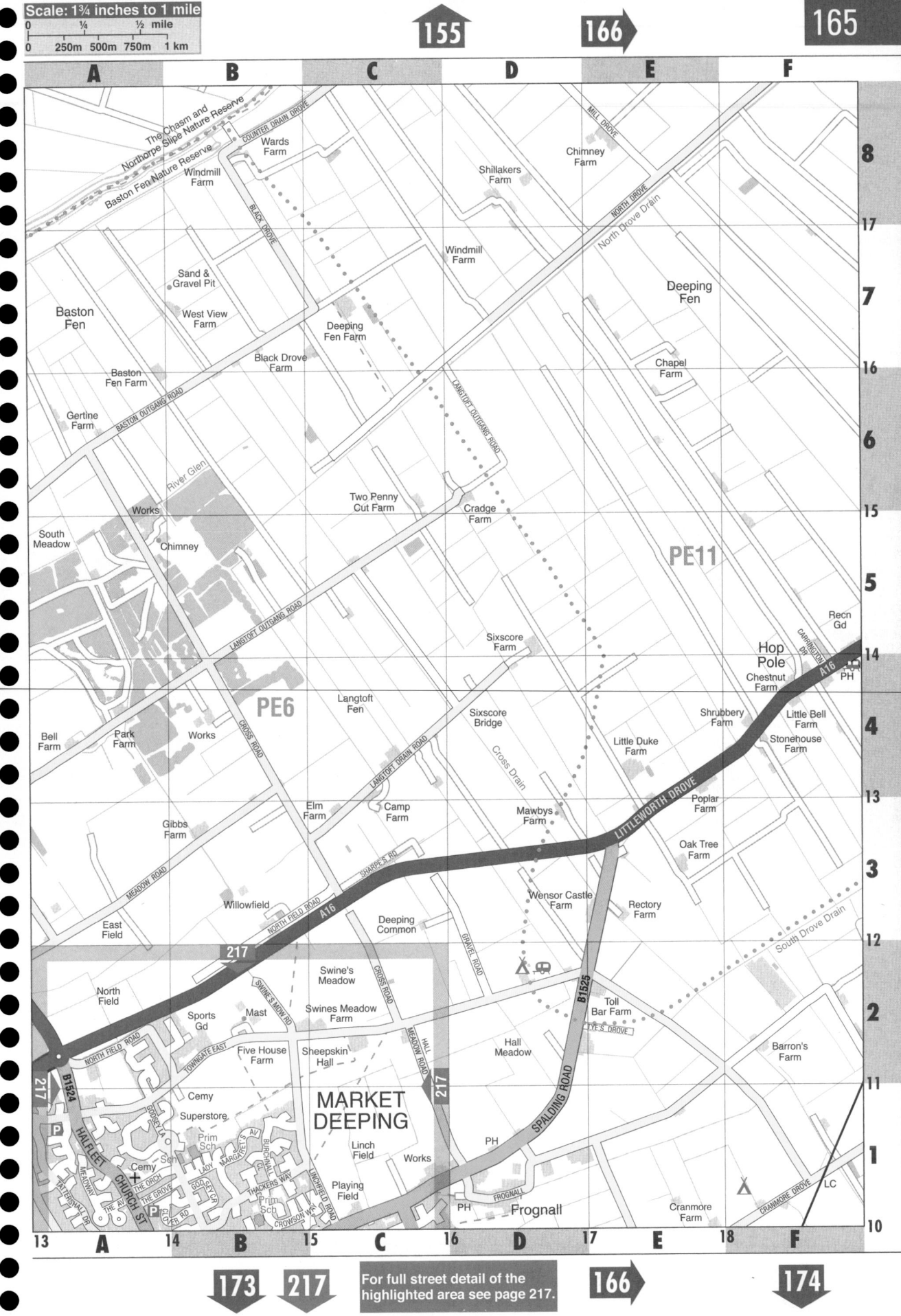

Scale: 1¾ inches to 1 mile

0   ¼   ½ mile
0 250m 500m 750m 1 km

155

166

165

A   B   C   D   E   F

The Chasm and
Northorpe Slipe Nature Reserve

Baston Fen Nature Reserve

COUNTER DRAIN DROVE

MILL DROVE

Wards Farm

Windmill Farm

BLACK DROVE

Shillakers Farm

Chimney Farm

NORTH DROVE

8

17

Sand & Gravel Pit

West View Farm

Windmill Farm

North Drove Drain

Deeping Fen

7

Baston Fen

Black Drove Farm

Deeping Fen Farm

Chapel Farm

16

Baston Fen Farm

BASTON OUTGANG ROAD

LANGTOFT OUTGANG ROAD

PE11

6

Gertine Farm

River Glen

Two Penny Cut Farm

Cradge Farm

15

Works

South Meadow

Chimney

Sixscore Farm

CARRINGTON DR

Recn Gd

Hop Pole

A16

14

LANGTOFT OUTGANG ROAD

PE6

Langtoft Fen

Sixscore Bridge

Chestnut Farm

Shrubbery Farm

Little Bell Farm

PH

5

CROSS ROAD

LANGTOFT DRAIN ROAD

Cross Drain

Little Duke Farm

Stonehouse Farm

4

Bell Farm

Park Farm

Works

Elm Farm

Camp Farm

Mawbys Farm

LITTLEWORTH DROVE

Poplar Farm

Oak Tree Farm

13

Gibbs Farm

MEADOW ROAD

SHARPE'S RD

NORTH FIELD ROAD

A16

Willowfield

Wensor Castle Farm

Rectory Farm

South Drove Drain

3

East Field

Deeping Common

GRAVEL ROAD

B1525

12

217

CROSS ROAD

North Field

Swine's Meadow

Swines Meadow Farm

MEADOW ROAD

HALL ROAD

Toll Bar Farm

LYE'S DROVE

Barron's Farm

2

Sports Gd

Mast

SWINE'S MDW RD

Hall Meadow

SPALDING ROAD

217

NORTH FIELD ROAD

TOWNGATE EAST

Five House Farm

Sheepskin Hall

B1524

11

Cemy

Superstore

MARKET DEEPING

Linch Field

Works

PH

1

HALF LEET

CHURCH ST

Prim Sch

LADY

GODSEY LA

MARGARET'S AV

BIRCHNALL CL

LINCHFIELD ROAD

Playing Field

Prim Sch

CROWSON WY

FROGNALL

PH

Frognall

Cranmore Farm

CRANMORE DROVE

LC

10

13   A   14   B   15   C   16   D   17   E   18   F   10

173   217

For full street detail of the highlighted area see page 217.

166

174

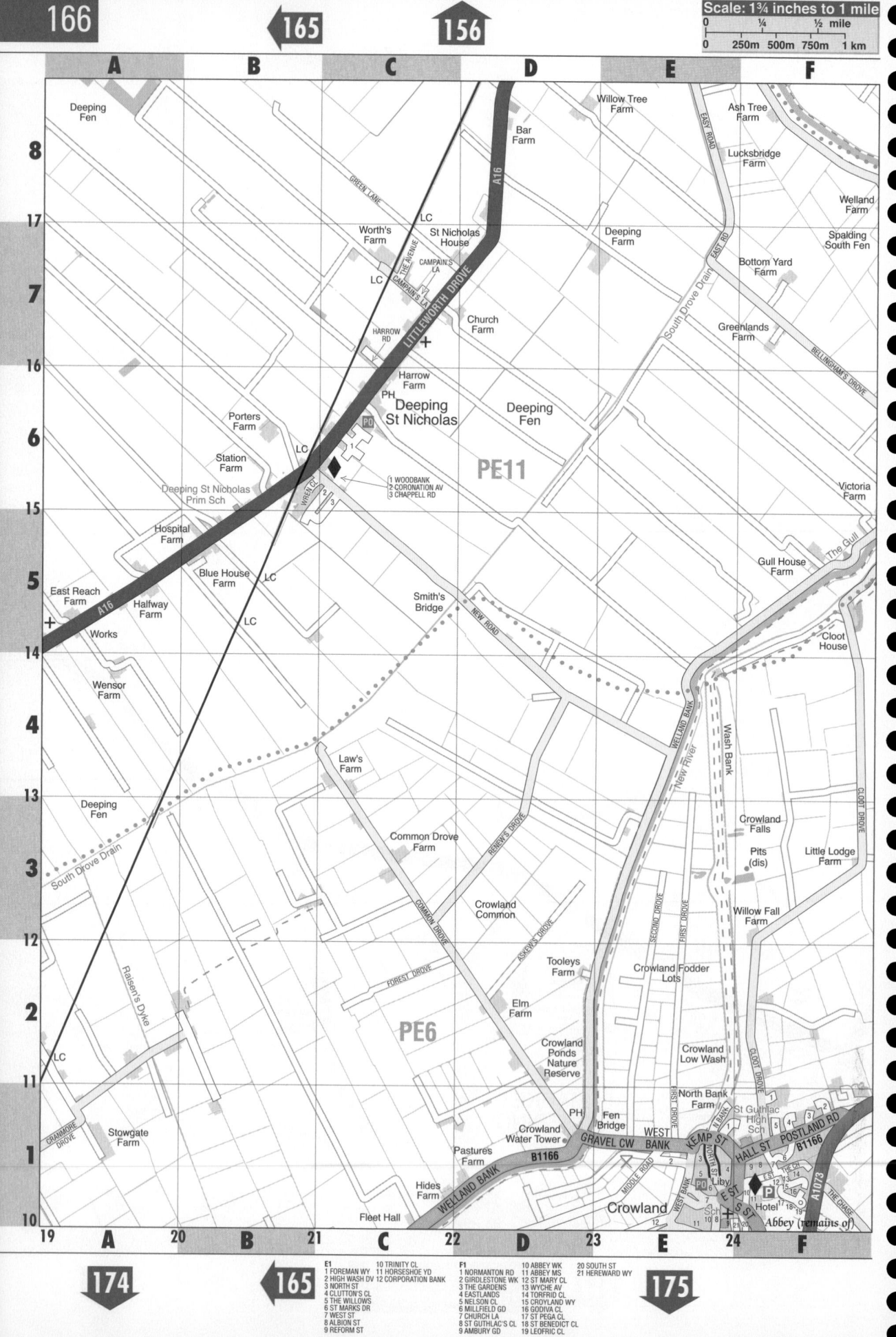

166

165

156

Scale: 1¾ inches to 1 mile
0   ¼   ½ mile
0   250m 500m 750m 1 km

A   B   C   D   E   F

8

17

7

16

6

15

5

14

4

13

3

12

2

11

10

Deeping Fen

Worth's Farm

St Nicholas House

Willow Tree Farm

Ash Tree Farm

Lucksbridge Farm

Welland Farm

Spalding South Fen

GREEN LANE

CAMPAIN'S LA

THE AVENUE

LITTLEWORTH DROVE

A16

LC

LC

LC

CAMPAIN'S LA

Church Farm

Deeping Farm

EASY ROAD

EAST RD

Bottom Yard Farm

Greenlands Farm

BELLINGHAM'S DROVE

SOUTH DROVE DRAIN

HARROW RD

Harrow Farm

PH

Deeping St Nicholas

Porters Farm

PO

Deeping Fen

PE11

Victoria Farm

Station Farm

1 WOODBANK
2 CORONATION AV
3 CHAPPELL RD

Deeping St Nicholas Prim Sch

WREN CL

1
2
3

Gull House Farm

THE GULL

Hospital Farm

Blue House Farm

LC

Smith's Bridge

NEW ROAD

Cloot House

East Reach Farm

A16

Halfway Farm

LC

WELLAND BANK

Works

Wash Bank

Wensor Farm

NEW RIVER

CLOOT DRIVE

Deeping Fen

SOUTH DROVE DRAIN

Law's Farm

Crowland Falls

Pits (dis)

Little Lodge Farm

Common Drove Farm

RENEW'S DROVE

Willow Fall Farm

Crowland Common

Raisin's Dyke

COMMON DROVE

FOREST DROVE

Crowland Fodder Lots

ASKEW'S DROVE

Tooleys Farm

PE6

Elm Farm

Crowland Ponds Nature Reserve

Crowland Low Wash

SECOND DROVE

FIRST DROVE

LC

North Bank Farm

FIRST DROVE

St Guthlac High Sch

NEWHAM

POSTLAND RD

KEMP ST

B1166

CRANMORE DROVE

Stowgate Farm

Crowland Water Tower

PH

Fen Bridge

WEST BANK

GRAVEL CW

HALL ST

NORTH ST

WEST BANK

PO

Liby

Pastures Farm

B1166

WELLAND BANK

Hides Farm

Fleet Hall

MIDDLE ROAD

SCH

THE CH

Hotel

P

A1073

THE CHASE

Crowland

Abbey (remains of)

19   20   21   22   23   24

A   B   C   D   E   F

E1
1 FOREMAN WY
2 HIGH WASH DV
3 NORTH ST
4 CLUTTON'S CL
5 THE WILLOWS
6 ST MARKS DR
7 WEST ST
8 ALBION ST
9 REFORM ST
10 TRINITY CL
11 HORSESHOE YD
12 CORPORATION BANK

F1
1 NORMANTON RD
2 GIRDLESTONE WK
3 THE GARDENS
4 EASTLANDS
5 NELSON CL
6 MILLFIELD GD
7 CHURCH LA
8 ST GUTHLAC'S CL
9 AMBURY GD
10 ABBEY WK
11 ABBEY MS
12 ST MARY CL
13 WYCHE AV
14 TORFRID CL
15 CROYLAND WY
16 GODIVA CL
17 ST PEGA CL
18 ST BENEDICT CL
19 LEOFRIC CL
20 SOUTH ST
21 HEREWARD WY

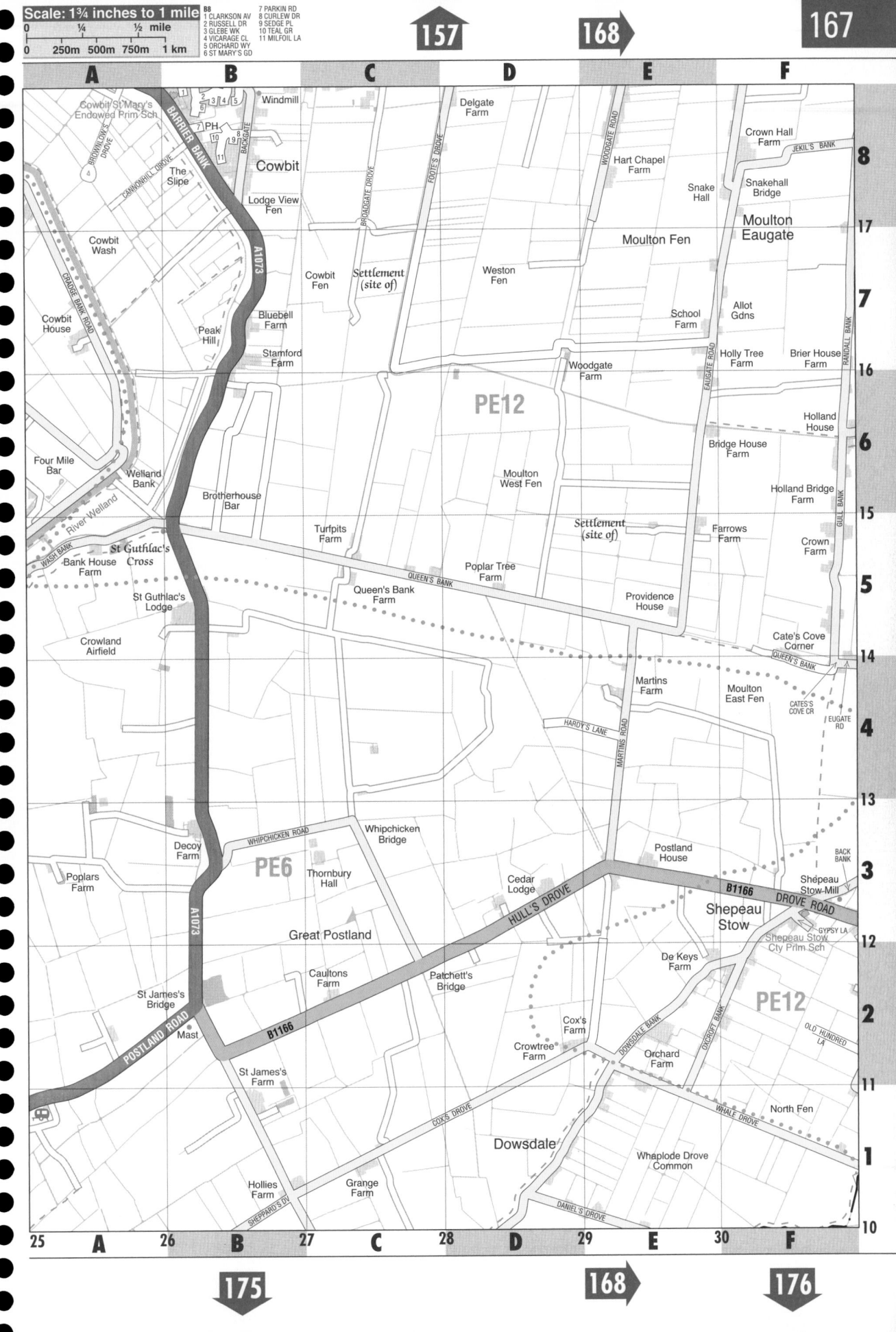
Scale: 1¾ inches to 1 mile
0 ¼ ½ mile
0 250m 500m 750m 1 km
B8
1 CLARKSON AV
2 RUSSELL DR
3 GLEBE WK
4 VICARAGE CL
5 ORCHARD WY
6 ST MARY'S GD
7 PARKIN RD
8 CURLEW DR
9 SEDGE PL
10 TEAL GR
11 MILFOIL LA
157
168
Cowbit St Mary's Endowed Prim Sch
Windmill
Cowbit
Delgate Farm
Crown Hall Farm
Hart Chapel Farm
Snake Hall
Snakehall Bridge
Moulton Eaugate
Moulton Fen
The Slipe
Lodge View Fen
Cowbit Wash
Cowbit Fen
Settlement (site of)
Weston Fen
School Farm
Allot Gdns
Cowbit House
Peak Hill
Bluebell Farm
Stamford Farm
Woodgate Farm
Holly Tree Farm
Brier House Farm
PE12
Holland House
Bridge House Farm
Four Mile Bar
Welland Bank
Brotherhouse Bar
Moulton West Fen
Holland Bridge Farm
River Welland
Turfpits Farm
Farrows Farm
Crown Farm
St Guthlac's Cross
Bank House Farm
Poplar Tree Farm
Queen's Bank Farm
St Guthlac's Lodge
Providence House
Crowland Airfield
Cate's Cove Corner
Martins Farm
Moulton East Fen
CATES'S COVE CR
EUGATE RD
Whipchicken Bridge
Postland House
Decoy Farm
PE6
Thornbury Hall
Cedar Lodge
Poplars Farm
Shepeau Stow Mill
BACK BANK
Shepeau Stow
Shepeau Stow Cty Prim Sch
Great Postland
De Keys Farm
Caultons Farm
Patchett's Bridge
St James's Bridge
Mast
Cox's Farm
Crowtree Farm
Orchard Farm
St James's Farm
North Fen
Dowsdale
Whaplode Drove Common
Hollies Farm
Grange Farm
BARRIER BANK
A1073
BACKGATE
BROWNLOWS DROVE
CANNONHILL DROVE
CRADGE BANK ROAD
BROADGATE DROVE
FOOTE'S DROVE
WOODGATE ROAD
EAUGATE ROAD
JEKIL'S BANK
RANDALL BANK
GULL BANK
WASH BANK
QUEEN'S BANK
HARDY'S LANE
MARTINS ROAD
WHIPCHICKEN ROAD
HULL'S DROVE
B1166
DROVE ROAD
GYPSY LA
DOWSDALE BANK
OXCROFT BANK
OLD HUNDRED LA
POSTLAND ROAD
WHALE DROVE
COX'S DROVE
SHEPPARD'S DV
DANIEL'S DROVE
A B C D E F
25 26 27 28 29 30
10 11 12 13 14 15 16 17
1 2 3 4 5 6 7 8
175
168
176

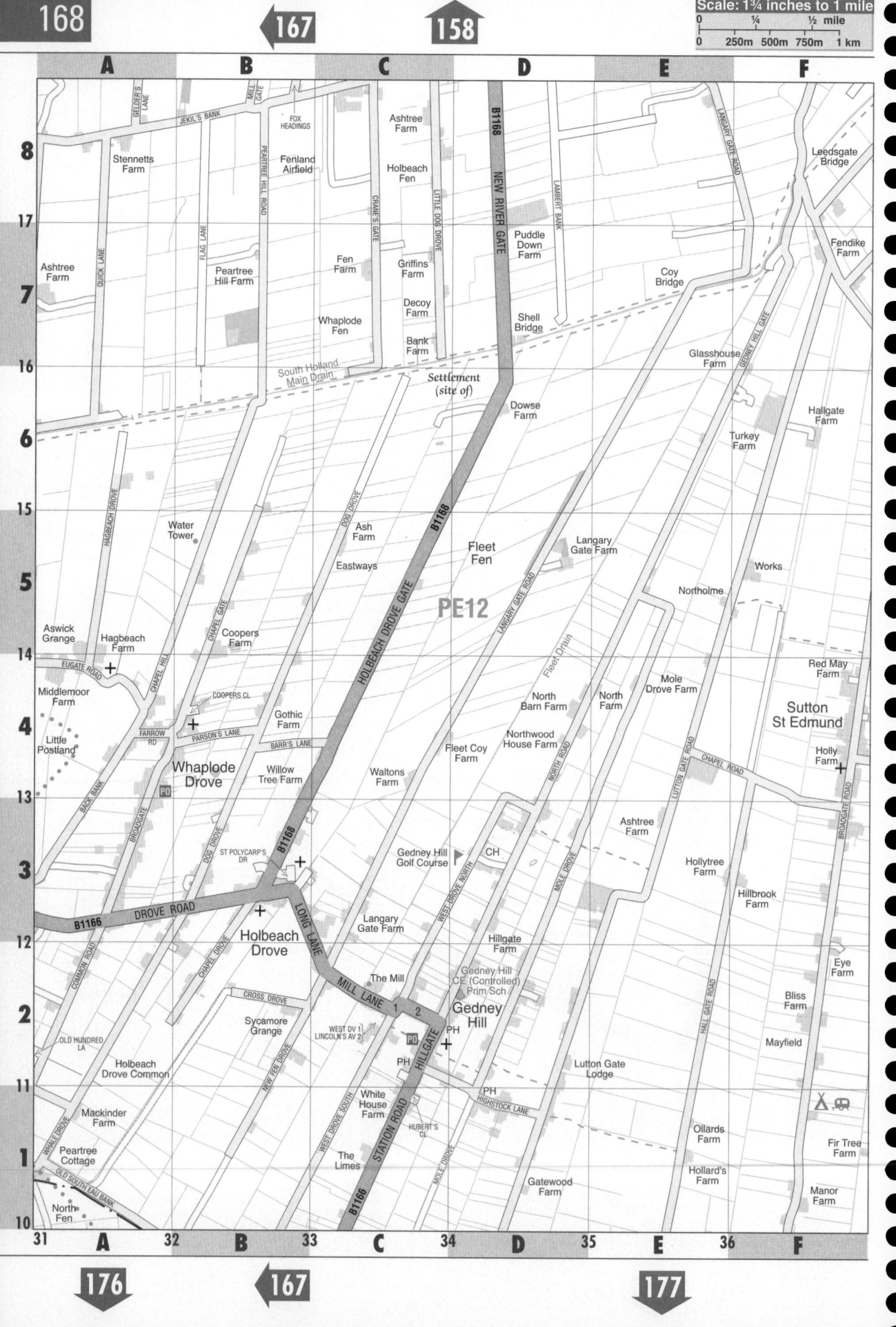

Scale: 1¾ inches to 1 mile

0   ¼   ½   mile
0   250m 500m 750m 1 km

A **B** **C** **D** **E** **F**

8

GELDER'S LANE

JEKIL'S BANK

MILL GATE

FOX HEADINGS

Stennetts Farm

Fenland Airfield

PEARTREE HILL ROAD

Ashtree Farm

Holbeach Fen

B1168

NEW RIVER GATE

LAMBERT BANK

Leedsgate Bridge

LANGARY GATE ROAD

17

QUICK LANE

FLAG LANE

Peartree Hill Farm

CRANE'S GATE

LITTLE DOG DROVE

Puddle Down Farm

Fendike Farm

GEDNEY HILL GATE

7

Ashtree Farm

Fen Farm

Griffins Farm

Decoy Farm

Shell Bridge

Coy Bridge

16

Whaplode Fen

Bank Farm

South Holland Main Drain

Settlement (site of)

Dowse Farm

Glasshouse Farm

Halgate Farm

6

HAGBEACH DROVE

Turkey Farm

15

Water Tower

DOG DROVE

Ash Farm

B1168

HOLBEACH DROVE GATE

Fleet Fen

Langary Gate Farm

LANGARY GATE ROAD

Works

5

Eastways

Northolme

CHAPEL GATE

PE12

Red May Farm

14

Aswick Grange

Hagbeach Farm

EUGATE ROAD

CHAPEL HILL

Coopers Farm

COOPERS CL.

Gothic Farm

Fleet Drain

North Barn Farm

North Farm

Mole Drove Farm

Sutton St Edmund

CHAPEL ROAD

Middlemoor Farm

FARROW RD

PARSON'S LANE

BARR'S LANE

Northwood House Farm

NORTH ROAD

LUTTON GATE ROAD

BROADGATE ROAD

Holly Farm

4

Little Postland

BACK BANK

Whaplode Drove

Willow Tree Farm

Waltons Farm

Fleet Coy Farm

13

BROADGATE

PO

DOG DROVE

St POLYCARP'S DR

B1168

Gedney Hill Golf Course

CH

Ashtree Farm

Hollytree Farm

Hillbrook Farm

3

B1166

DROVE ROAD

Holbeach Drove

CHAPEL DROVE

LONG LANE

Langary Gate Farm

WEST DROVE NORTH

MOLE DROVE

Hillgate Farm

Eye Farm

12

COMMON ROAD

CROSS DROVE

MILL LANE

The Mill

Gedney Hill CE (Controlled) Prim Sch

Bliss Farm

2

Sycamore Grange

NEW FEN DROVE

WEST DV 1 LINCOLN'S AV 2

1 2

PO

HILLGATE

Gedney Hill

PH

HALL GATE ROAD

Mayfield

Old Hundred LA

Holbeach Drove Common

PH

Lutton Gate Lodge

11

WHALE DROVE

Mackinder Farm

WEST DROVE SOUTH

STATION ROAD

White House Farm

HUBERT'S CL.

PH

HIGHSTOCK LANE

Ollards Farm

Fir Tree Farm

1

Peartree Cottage

OLD SOUTH EAU BANK

The Limes

B1166

MOLE DROVE

Gatewood Farm

Hollard's Farm

Manor Farm

10

North Fen

A 32 **B** 33 **C** 34 **D** 35 **E** 36 **F**

31

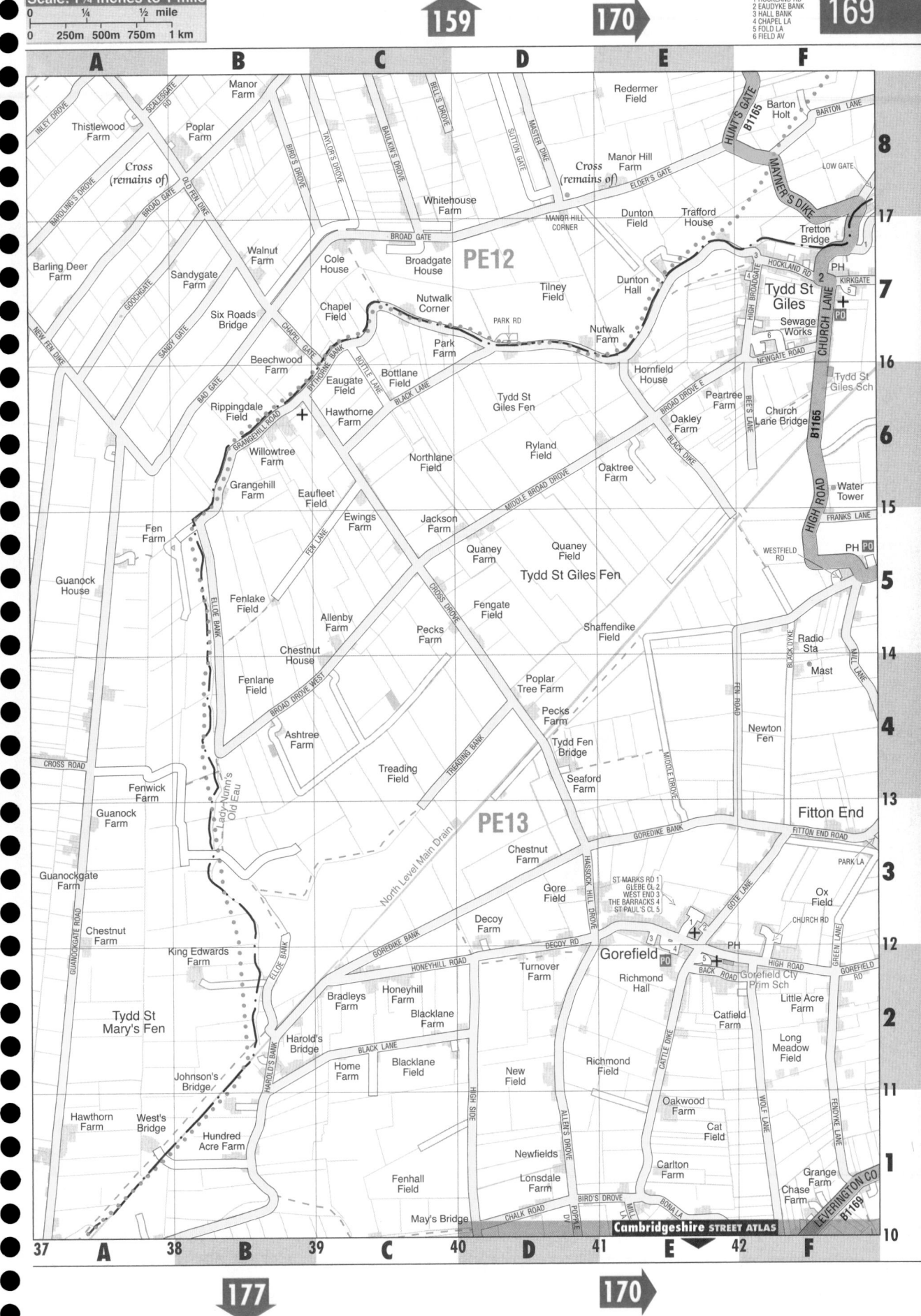

Scale: 1¾ inches to 1 mile

0   ¼   ½ mile
0   250m 500m 750m 1 km

159   170

169

F7
1 HOCKLAND RD
2 EAUDYKE BANK
3 HALL BANK
4 CHAPEL LA
5 FOLD LA
6 FIELD AV

A   B   C   D   E   F

8

17

Redermer Field

Barton Holt   BARTON LANE

B1165   HUNT'S GATE   MAYNER'S DIKE   LOW GATE

Manor Farm
Thistlewood Farm
INLEY DROVE
SCALESGATE RD

Poplar Farm

Manor Hill Farm

Cross (remains of)
BROAD GATE
OLD TEN DIKE
BARDING'S DROVE
BIRD'S DROVE
TAYLOR'S DROVE
BAULKIN'S DROVE
BELL'S DROVE
SUTTON GATE
MASTER DIKE

Cross (remains of)
ELDER'S GATE
Dunton Field
Trafford House

Walnut Farm
Whitehouse Farm

MANOR HILL CORNER

Tretton Bridge

17

Barling Deer Farm
GOOCHGATE
NEW FEN DIKE

Cole House
BROAD GATE

Broadgate House

PE12

Dunton Hall

HOCKLAND RD
3   PH
Tydd St Giles
1
4   2
KIRKGATE
5
PO

7

Sandygate Farm
SANDY GATE

Chapel Field
SANDY GATE
CHAPEL GATE

Nutwalk Corner

Tilney Field

HIGH BROADGATE
6   Sewage Works

7

Six Roads Bridge
BAD GATE

Beechwood Farm
BLYTHORNE BANK
BUTTLE LANE

Park Farm
PARK RD

Nutwalk Farm

NEWGATE ROAD

Church Lane Bridge
CHURCH LANE

Tydd St Giles Sch

16

Rippingdale Field
GRANGEHILL ROAD
+

Eaugate Field
Hawthorne Farm
Bottlane Field
BLACK LANE

Tydd St Giles Fen

Hornfield House
BROAD DROVE E
Peartree Farm
Oakley Farm
BEE'S LANE

Church
B1165

16

6

Willowtree Farm
Grangehill Farm

Eaufleet Field

Northlane Field

Ryland Field

Oaktree Farm
BLACK DIKE

HIGH ROAD
Water Tower
FRANKS LANE

6

15

Fen Farm
FEN LANE

Ewings Farm

Jackson Farm
MIDDLE BROAD DROVE

15

Guanock House

ELLOE BANK
Fenlake Field

Quaney Farm
Quaney Field

Tydd St Giles Fen

WESTFIELD RD
PH   PO

5

Allenby Farm
CROSS DROVE

Pecks Farm

Fengate Field

Shaffendike Field

BLACK DYKE
Radio Sta
Mast
MILL LANE

14

Chestnut House

FEN ROAD
Newton Fen

4

Fenlane Field
BROAD DROVE WEST

Ashtree Farm

Poplar Tree Farm
TREADING BANK

Pecks Farm

Tydd Fen Bridge

MIDDLE DROVE

4

CROSS ROAD

Fenwick Farm

Guanock Farm

LADY NUNN'S OLD EAU
ELLOE BANK

Treading Field

TREADING BANK

Seaford Farm

13

PE13

Fitton End

13

Guanockgate Farm
GUANOCKGATE ROAD

Chestnut Farm

North Level Main Drain

GOREDIKE BANK

Chestnut Farm

Gore Field
HASSOCK HILL DROVE

GOREDIKE BANK
FITTON END ROAD
PARK LA

Ox Field

3

King Edwards Farm
ELLOE BANK

Decoy Farm
DECOY RD

ST MARKS RD 1
GLEBE CL 2
WEST END 3
THE BARRACKS 4
ST PAUL'S CL 5
GOTE LANE
CHURCH RD

3   B
4
PH
5   +

Gorefield
PO
BACK ROAD
HIGH ROAD
Gorefield Cty Prim Sch
Little Acre Farm
GREEN LANE
GOREFIELD RD

12

Tydd St Mary's Fen

Bradleys Farm

HONEYHILL ROAD
Honeyhill Farm
Blacklane Farm

Turnover Farm

Richmond Hall

Catfield Farm

12

Johnson's Bridge
HAROLD'S BANK

Harold's Bridge

BLACK LANE
Home Farm

Blacklane Field

New Field

Richmond Field
CATTLE DIKE

Long Meadow Field

2

Hawthorn Farm
West's Bridge

ALLEN'S DROVE
HIGH SIDE

Oakwood Farm
WOLF LANE

Cat Field

FENDYKE LANE

11

Hundred Acre Farm

Fenhall Field

Newfields

Lonsdale Farm
BIRD'S DROVE

Carlton Farm
BONAL LA
MILL LANE
POPPLE DV

Grange Farm
Chase Farm
B1169
LEVERINGTON CO

1

May's Bridge
CHALK ROAD

10

37   A   38   B   39   C   40   D   41   E   42   F

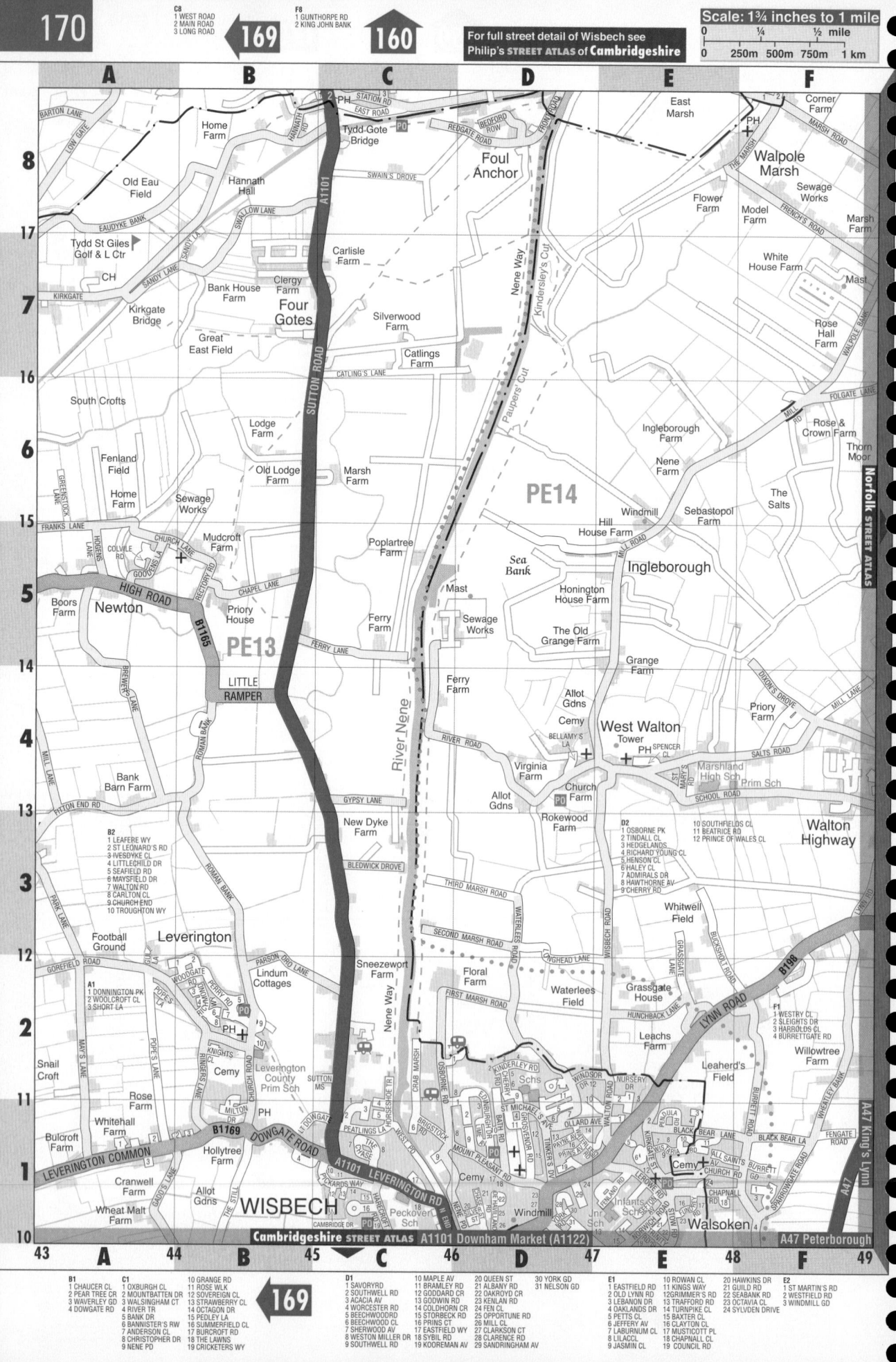

C8
1 WEST ROAD
2 MAIN ROAD
3 LONG ROAD
← 169

F8
1 GUNTHORPE RD
2 KING JOHN BANK
↑ 160

For full street detail of Wisbech see
Philip's STREET ATLAS of Cambridgeshire

Scale: 1¾ inches to 1 mile
0   ¼   ½ mile
0   250m 500m 750m 1 km

A   B   C   D   E   F

Norfolk STREET ATLAS

BARTON LANE
LOW GATE
Old Eau
Field
Home
Farm
Tydd-Gote
Bridge
STATION RD
EAST ROAD
PH
BEDFORD ROW
REDGATE ROAD
FRONT ROAD
East
Marsh
PH
Corner
Farm
MARSH ROAD
Walpole
Marsh
Foul
Anchor
THE MARSH
Sewage
Works

EAUDYKE BANK
HANNATH RD
SWAIN'S DROVE
FRENCH'S ROAD
Flower
Farm
Model
Farm
Marsh
Farm

Tydd St Giles
Golf & L Ctr
CH
KIRKGATE
Carlisle
Farm
Nene Way
Kindersley's Cut
White
House Farm
Mast

Kirkgate
Bridge
SANDY LANE
SWALLOW LANE
Bank House
Farm
Clergy
Farm
Four
Gotes
Silverwood
Farm
Paupers' Cut
FOLGATE LANE
Rose
Hall
Farm
WALPOLE BANK

Great
East Field
CATLING'S LANE
Catlings
Farm
Ingleborough
Farm
Nene
Farm
MILL RD
Rose &
Crown Farm
Thorn
Moor

South Crofts
GREENSTOCK LANE
Lodge
Farm
Old Lodge
Farm
Marsh
Farm
Windmill
Hill
House Farm
Sebastopol
Farm
The Salts

FRANKS LANE
Fenland
Field
Home
Farm
Sewage
Works
Mudcroft
Farm
Poplartree
Farm
Sea
Bank
Honington
House Farm
Ingleborough
PE14

HIGH ROAD
COLVILE
RD
CHURCH LANE
GOODS RD
CHAPEL LANE
Priory
House
Mast
Sewage
Works
The Old
Grange Farm
DIXON'S DROVE
MILL ROAD

Boors
Farm
Newton
PE13
B1165
RECTORY RD
Ferry
Farm
Grange
Farm
Priory
Farm

BREWERY LANE
FERRY LANE
River Nene
Ferry
Farm
Allot
Gdns
Cemy
West Walton
Tower
SPENCER CL
PH
SALTS ROAD

LITTLE
RAMPER
ROMAN BANK
RIVER ROAD
BELLAMY'S
LA
Church
Farm
MARSH'S
RD
SCHOOL ROAD
Marshland
High Sch
Prim Sch

Bank
Barn Farm
PITTON END RD
GYPSY LANE
Virginia
Farm
Allot
Gdns
Rokewood
Farm
Walton
Highway

MILL LANE
New Dyke
Farm
BLEDWICK DROVE
THIRD MARSH ROAD
WATERLEES
ROAD
WISBECH ROAD
D2
1 OSBORNE PK
2 TINDALL CL
3 HEDGELANDS
4 RICHARD YOUNG CL
5 HENSON CL
6 HALEY CL
7 ADMIRALS DR
8 HAWTHORNE AV
9 CHERRY RD
10 SOUTHFIELDS CL
11 BEATRICE RD
12 PRINCE OF WALES CL

B2
1 LEAFERE WY
2 ST LEONARD'S RD
3 IVESDYKE CL
4 LITTLECHILD DR
5 SEAFIELD RD
6 MAYSFIELD DR
7 WALTON RD
8 CARLTON CL
9 CHURCH END
10 TROUGHTON WY
Football
Ground
Leverington
PARK LANE
WOODGATE
PERRY RD
PARSON DRO LANE
Lindum
Cottages
Sneezewort
Farm
SECOND MARSH ROAD
Whitwell
Field
LONGHEAD LANE
Grassgate
House
Grassgate
Field
BUCKSMILL ROAD
B198
F1
1 WESTRY CL
2 SLEIGHTS DR
3 HARBOLDS CL
4 BURRETTGATE RD

GOREFIELD ROAD
A1
1 DONNINGTON PK
2 WOOLCROFT CL
3 SHORT LA
Nene Way
Floral
Farm
Waterlees
Field
FIRST MARSH ROAD
Leachs
Farm
Leaherd's
Field
WHENTSEY BANK
Willowtree
Farm

Snail
Croft
MAY'S LANE
POPE'S LANE
RINGERS LANE
KNIGHTS
MILTON
DR
Rose
Farm
Leverington
County Prim Sch
SUTTON
MS
CRAB MARSH
KINDERLEY RD
OSBORNE RD
Schs
WINDSOR
NURSERY
DR
WALTON ROAD
PENINSULA
BLACK BEAR LANE
Cemy
BURRETT
RD

Bulcroft
Farm
Whitehall
Farm
CHURCH ROAD
PH
DOWGATE
B1169
Hollytree
Farm
DOWGATE ROAD
A1101
LEVERINGTON RD
WEST DR
MOUNT PLEASANT RD
GROSVENOR
RD
OLLARD AVE
ALL SAINTS
CHURCH RD
Cemy
A47 King's Lynn
A47

LEVERINGTON COMMON
Cranwell
Farm
Wheat Malt
Farm
Allot
Gdns
THE STILL
GOOD'S LANE
WISBECH
PECKOVER
Sch
CAMBRIDGE DR
PO
Cemy
Windmill
PO
Inf
Sch
Infants
Sch
Walsoken
SPARROWGATE ROAD
FENGATE
ROAD

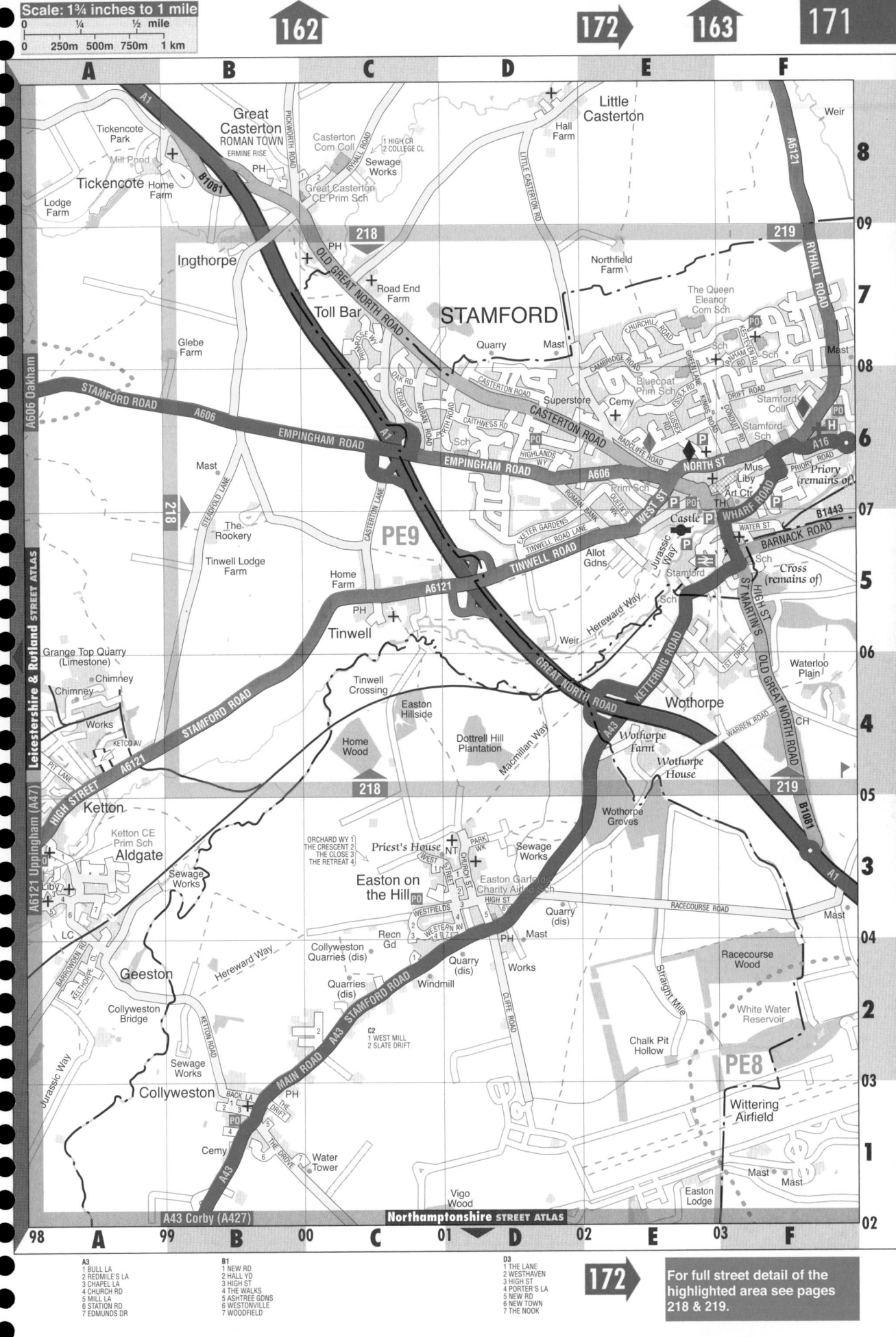

A   B   C   D   E   F

8   09   7   08   6   07   5   06   4   05   3   04   2   03   1   02

Tickencote Park
Mill Pond
Tickencote
Home Farm
Lodge Farm
Ingthorpe
Glebe Farm

Great Casterton
ROMAN TOWN
ERMINE RISE
Casterton Com Coll
1 HIGH CR
2 COLLEGE CL
Sewage Works
Great Casterton CE Prim Sch

Little Casterton
Hall Farm

Weir

Northfield Farm

The Queen Eleanor Com Sch

Toll Bar
Road End Farm
STAMFORD
Quarry
Mast

CHURCHILL ROAD
Bluecoat Prim Sch
Cemy
Stamford Coll

A606 Oakham
STAMFORD ROAD
A606
EMPINGHAM ROAD
Mast
218
The Rookery
Tinwell Lodge Farm

Superstore

Casterton Road
EMPINGHAM ROAD
A606

North St
Mus
Liby
Art Ctr
Castle
Priory (remains of)
B1443

PE9

Home Farm
PH
Tinwell

A6121
TINWELL ROAD
Weir

Allot Gdns
Jurassic Way
Stamford Sch

Hereward Way

Cross (remains of)
Waterloo Plain

Grange Top Quarry (Limestone)
Chimney
Chimney
Works
KETCO AV
A6121
PIT LANE
HIGH STREET
Ketton
Ketton CE Prim Sch
Aldgate
Liby
LC

Tinwell Crossing
Easton Hillside
Home Wood
Dottrell Hill Plantation

Macmillan Way

GREAT NORTH ROAD
KETTERING ROAD
Wothorpe

A43
Wothorpe Farm
Wothorpe House
219
B1081
A1
Wothorpe Groves

CH

218

ORCHARD WY 1
THE CRESCENT 2
THE CLOSE 3
THE RETREAT 4
Priest's House
NT
PARK WK
Easton on the Hill
WESTFIELDS
WESTERN AV
Recn Gd
Easton Garfords Charity Aitken Sch
HIGH ST
Quarry (dis)
Mast
Sewage Works

Racecourse Wood
RACECOURSE ROAD
Mast

A6121 Uppingham (A47)
BARROWDEN RD
KELTHORPE CL
Geeston
Collyweston Bridge
KETTON ROAD
Collyweston

Hereward Way

C2
1 WEST MILL
2 SLATE DRIFT

Collyweston Quarries (dis)
Quarries (dis)
Windmill
Quarry (dis)
Works

CLIFFE ROAD
Straight Mile
Chalk Pit Hollow
White Water Reservoir
PE8

Sewage Works
MAIN ROAD
STAMFORD ROAD
A43
PH
THE DRIFT
THE GROVE
PO
Cemy
Water Tower
A43

Vigo Wood

Wittering Airfield

Mast   Mast

Easton Lodge

Leicestershire & Rutland STREET ATLAS

A3
1 BULL LA
2 REDMILE'S LA
3 CHAPEL LA
4 CHURCH RD
5 MILL LA
6 STATION RD
7 EDMUNDS DR

B1
1 NEW RD
2 HALL YD
3 HIGH ST
4 THE WALKS
5 ASHTREE GDNS
6 WESTONVILLE
7 WOODFIELD

D3
1 THE LANE
2 WESTHAVEN
3 HIGH ST
4 PORTER'S LA
5 NEW RD
6 NEW TOWN
7 THE NOOK

For full street detail of the highlighted area see pages 218 & 219.

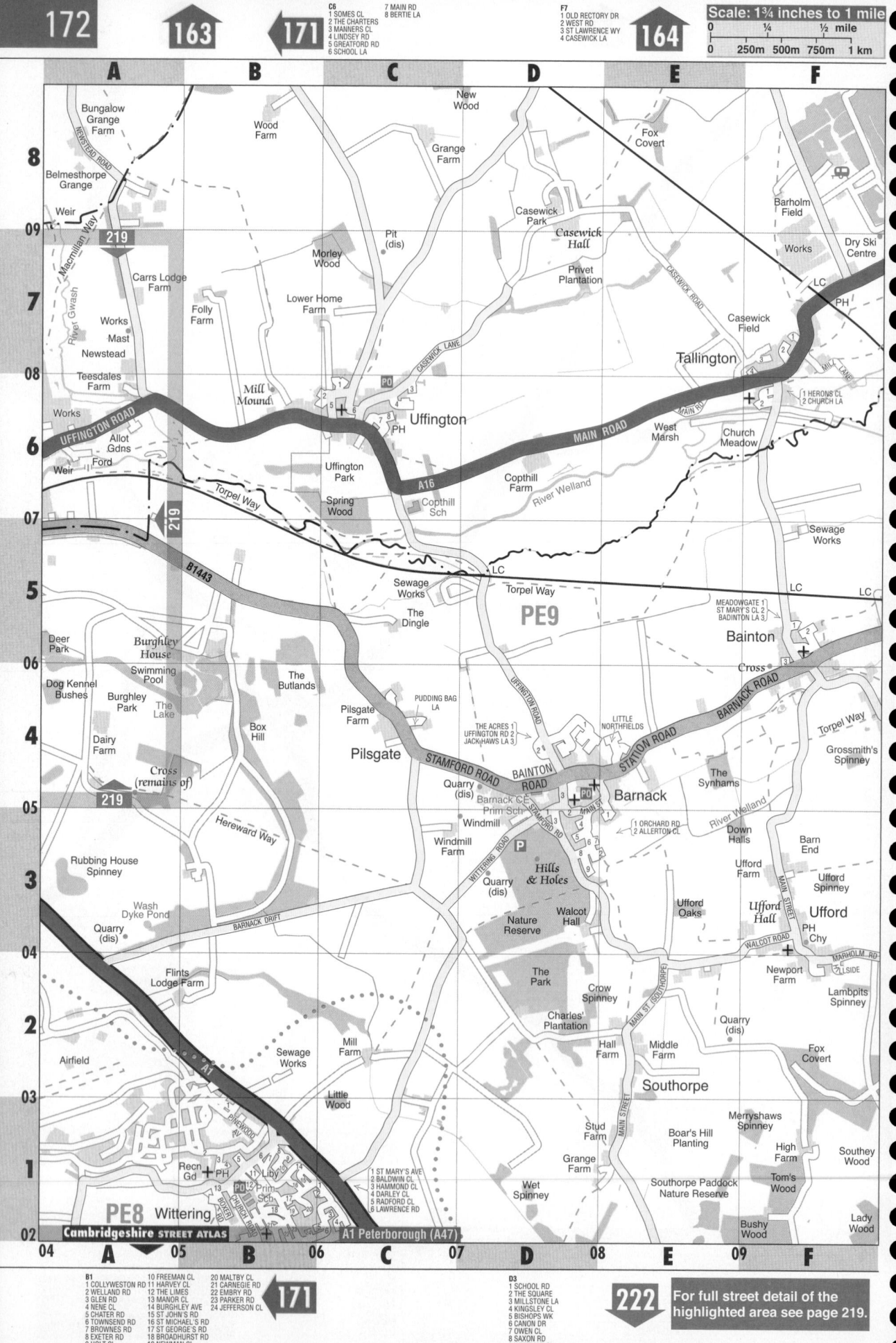

C6
1 SOMES CL
2 THE CHARTERS
3 MANNERS CL
4 LINDSEY RD
5 GREATFORD RD
6 SCHOOL LA

7 MAIN RD
8 BERTIE LA

F7
1 OLD RECTORY DR
2 WEST RD
3 ST LAWRENCE WY
4 CASEWICK LA

Scale: 1¾ inches to 1 mile
0   ¼   ½   mile
0   250m   500m   750m   1 km

Map labels

Bungalow Grange Farm
Belmesthorpe Grange
Weir
HEMPSTEAD ROAD
Macmillan Way
219
River Gwash
Carrs Lodge Farm
Works
Mast
Newstead
Teesdales Farm
Works
Weir
Ford
Allot Gdns
UFFINGTON ROAD
219
B1443
Deer Park
Dog Kennel Bushes
Burghley Park
Dairy Farm
Cross (remains of)
219
Rubbing House Spinney
Wash Dyke Pond
Quarry (dis)
Flints Lodge Farm
Airfield
A1
Sewage Works
PE8   Wittering
Recn Gd
PH
Lby
Prim Sch
PO
PINEWOOD AV
BAKER RD
CHURCH RD

Wood Farm
New Wood
Grange Farm
Pit (dis)
Morley Wood
Folly Farm
Lower Home Farm
Mill Mound
PO
Uffington
PH
Uffington Park
Spring Wood
CASEWICK LANE
Torpel Way
Copthill Sch
Sewage Works
The Dingle
Burghley House
Swimming Pool
The Lake
The Butlands
Box Hill
Pilsgate Farm
Pilsgate
STAMFORD ROAD
Hereward Way
BARNACK DRIFT
Mill Farm
Little Wood
1 ST MARY'S AVE
2 BALDWIN CL
3 HAMMOND CL
4 DARLEY CL
5 RADFORD CL
6 LAWRENCE RD

Fox Covert
Casewick Park
Casewick Hall
Privet Plantation
Tallington
CASEWICK ROAD
MAIN ROAD
A16
Copthill Farm
River Welland
West Marsh
Church Meadow
1 HERONS CL
2 CHURCH LA
PE9
Torpel Way
LC
Sewage Works
MEADOWGATE 1
ST MARY'S CL 2
BADINTON LA 3
Bainton
Cross
BARNACK ROAD
UFFINGTON ROAD
PUDDING BAG LA
THE ACRES 1
UFFINGTON RD 2
JACK HAWS LA 3
Little Northfields
STATION ROAD
Torpel Way
Grossmith's Spinney
The Synhams
Quarry (dis)
Barnack CE Prim Sch
Windmill
Windmill Farm
WITTERING ROAD
Quarry (dis)
Hills & Holes Nature Reserve
BAINTON ROAD
PO
Barnack
1 ORCHARD RD
2 ALLERTON CL
River Welland
Down Halls
Barn End
Ufford Farm
Ufford Spinney
Ufford Oaks
Ufford Hall
Ufford
PH
Chy
MAIN STREET
MARHOLM RD
LC SIDE
Walcot Hall
WALCOT ROAD
Newport Farm
Lambpits Spinney
The Park
Crow Spinney
Charles' Plantation
Hall Farm
Middle Farm
Quarry (dis)
Fox Covert
Southorpe
MAIN ST SOUTHORPE
Stud Farm
Grange Farm
Wet Spinney
Boar's Hill Planting
Southorpe Paddock Nature Reserve
MAIN STREET
Merryshaws Spinney
High Farm
Tom's Wood
Bushy Wood
Southey Wood
Lady Wood

B1
1 COLLYWESTON RD
2 WELLAND RD
3 GLEN RD
4 NENE CL
5 CHATER RD
6 TOWNSEND RD
7 BROWNES RD
8 EXETER RD
9 HOLT CL

10 FREEMAN CL
11 HARVEY CL
12 THE LIMES
13 MANOR CL
14 BURGHLEY AVE
15 ST JOHN'S RD
16 ST MICHAEL'S RD
17 ST GEORGE'S RD
18 BROADHURST RD
19 NEWMAN CL

20 MALTBY CL
21 CARNEGIE RD
22 EMBRY RD
23 PARKER RD
24 JEFFERSON CL

D3
1 SCHOOL RD
2 THE SQUARE
3 MILLSTONE LA
4 KINGSLEY CL
5 BISHOPS WK
6 CANON DR
7 OWEN CL
8 SAXON RD
9 WHITMAN CL

222   For full street detail of the highlighted area see page 219.

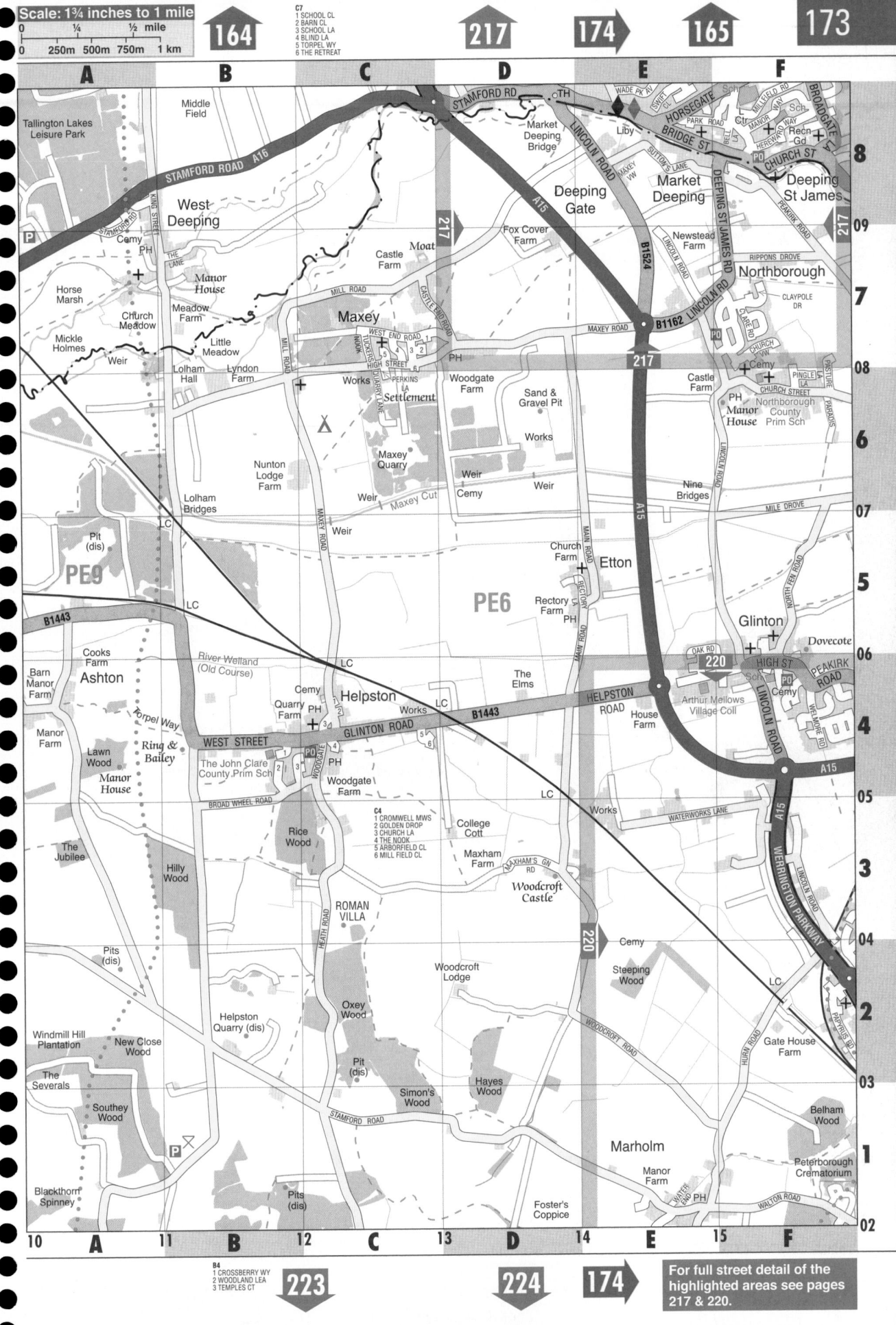

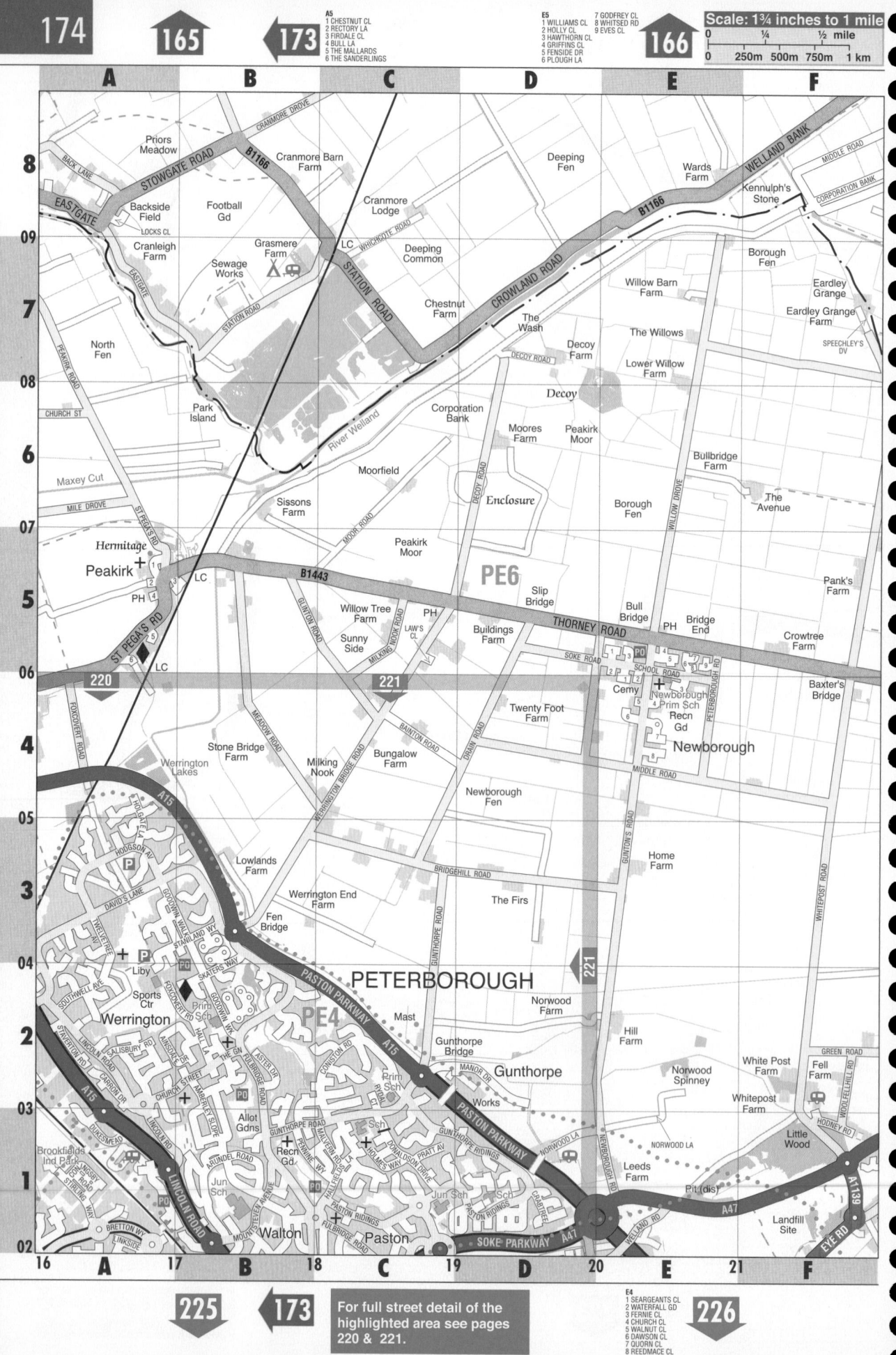

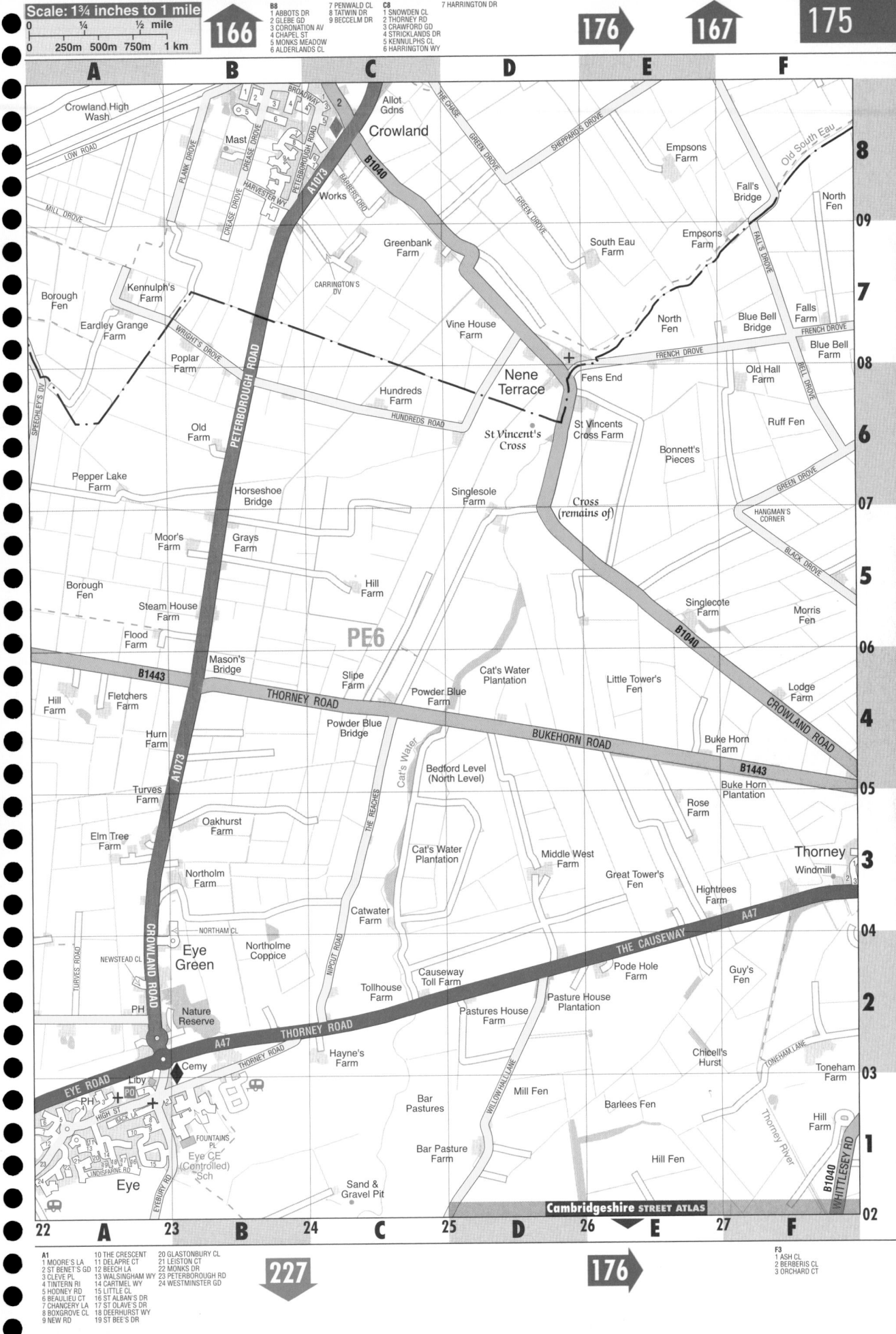
Scale: 1¾ inches to 1 mile
0 ¼ ½ mile
0 250m 500m 750m 1 km
166
176
167
175
B8
1 ABBOTS DR
2 GLEBE GD
3 CORONATION AV
4 CHAPEL ST
5 MONKS MEADOW
6 ALDERLANDS CL
7 PENWALD CL
8 TATWIN DR
9 BECCELM DR
C8
1 SNOWDEN CL
2 THORNEY RD
3 CRAWFORD GD
4 STRICKLANDS DR
5 KENNULPHS CL
6 HARRINGTON WY
7 HARRINGTON DR
Crowland High Wash
LOW ROAD
MILL DROVE
PLANK DROVE
CREASE DROVE
HARVESTER WY
PETERBOROUGH ROAD
BROADWAY
Mast
Allot Gdns
Crowland
THE CHASE
GREEN DROVE
SHEPPARD'S DROVE
B1040
A1073
Works
BARBERS DRO
Empsons Farm
Old South Eau
Fall's Bridge
North Fen
Empsons Farm
South Eau Farm
Greenbank Farm
CARRINGTON'S DV
FALL'S DROVE
Borough Fen
Kennulph's Farm
Eardley Grange Farm
WRIGHT'S DROVE
Poplar Farm
Vine House Farm
North Fen
Blue Bell Bridge
Falls Farm
FRENCH DROVE
Blue Bell Farm
Nene Terrace
Fens End
Old Hall Farm
BELL DROVE
Hundreds Farm
HUNDREDS ROAD
SPEECHLEY'S DV
Old Farm
St Vincent's Cross
St Vincents Cross Farm
Ruff Fen
Bonnett's Pieces
Pepper Lake Farm
Horseshoe Bridge
Singlesole Farm
Cross (remains of)
GREEN DROVE
HANGMAN'S CORNER
Moor's Farm
Grays Farm
BLACK DROVE
Borough Fen
Hill Farm
Steam House Farm
Singlecote Farm
Morris Fen
Flood Farm
PE6
B1040
Mason's Bridge
B1443
THORNEY ROAD
Slipe Farm
Cat's Water Plantation
Little Tower's Fen
Hill Farm
Fletchers Farm
Powder Blue Farm
Lodge Farm
CROWLAND ROAD
Hurn Farm
Powder Blue Bridge
BUKEHORN ROAD
Buke Horn Farm
Cat's Water
Bedford Level (North Level)
B1443
Turves Farm
THE REACHES
Buke Horn Plantation
Rose Farm
Oakhurst Farm
Elm Tree Farm
Cat's Water Plantation
Middle West Farm
Thorney
Windmill
Great Tower's Fen
Northolm Farm
Hightrees Farm
Catwater Farm
A47
NORTHAM CL
THE CAUSEWAY
TURVES ROAD
NEWSTEAD CL
Eye Green
Northolme Coppice
NIPCUT ROAD
Pode Hole Farm
Guy's Fen
CROWLAND ROAD
Causeway Toll Farm
Tollhouse Farm
Pasture House Plantation
PH
Nature Reserve
Pastures House Farm
THORNEY ROAD
A47
Hayne's Farm
WILLOW HALL LANE
Chicell's Hurst
TONEHAM LANE
Toneham Farm
Cemy
THORNEY ROAD
EYE ROAD
Liby
PO
PH
HIGH ST
BACK LA
Mill Fen
Bar Pastures
Barlees Fen
Hill Farm
Thorney River
FOUNTAINS PL
Eye CE (Controlled) Sch
LINDISFARNE RD
Bar Pasture Farm
Hill Fen
WHITTLESEY RD
B1040
Eye
EYEBURY RD
Sand & Gravel Pit
Cambridgeshire STREET ATLAS
A B C D E F
8 09 7 08 6 07 5 06 4 05 3 04 2 03 1 02
22 23 24 25 26 27
A1
1 MOORE'S LA
2 ST BENET'S GD
3 CLEVE PL
4 TINTERN RI
5 HODNEY RD
6 BEAULIEU CT
7 CHANCERY LA
8 BOXGROVE CL
9 NEW RD
10 THE CRESCENT
11 DELAPRE CT
12 BEECH LA
13 WALSINGHAM WY
14 CARTMEL WY
15 LITTLE CL
16 ST ALBAN'S DR
17 ST OLAVE'S DR
18 DEERHURST WY
19 ST BEE'S DR
20 GLASTONBURY CL
21 LEISTON CT
22 MONKS DR
23 PETERBOROUGH RD
24 WESTMINSTER GD
227
176
F3
1 ASH CL
2 BERBERIS CL
3 ORCHARD CT

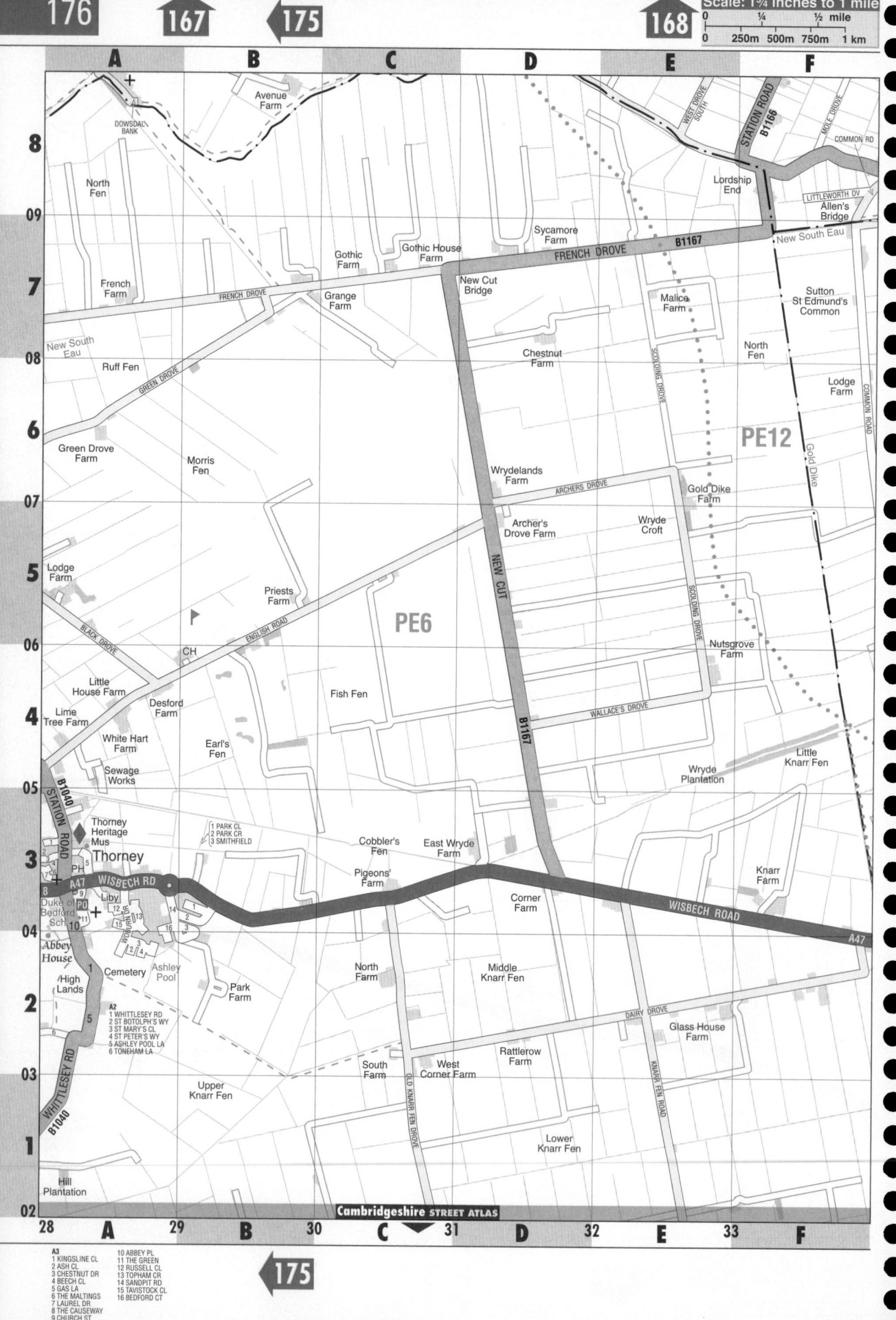

A   B   C   D   E   F

8

09

7

08

6

07

5

06

4

05

3

04

2

03

1

02

Avenue
Farm

DOWSDALE
BANK

North
Fen

WEST DROVE SOUTH

MOLE DROVE

STATION ROAD

B1166

COMMON RD

Lordship
End

LITTLEWORTH DV

Allen's
Bridge

Gothic
Farm

Gothic House
Farm

Sycamore
Farm

FRENCH DROVE

B1167

New South Eau

New Cut
Bridge

Sutton
St Edmund's
Common

French
Farm

FRENCH DROVE

Grange
Farm

Malice
Farm

North
Fen

New South
Eau

Ruff Fen

GREEN DROVE

Chestnut
Farm

SCOLDING DROVE

Lodge
Farm

COMMON ROAD

PE12

Green Drove
Farm

Morris
Fen

Wrydelands
Farm

ARCHERS DROVE

Gold Dike
Farm

Gold Dike

Lodge
Farm

Archer's
Drove Farm

Wryde
Croft

Priests
Farm

BLACK DROVE

ENGLISH ROAD

NEW CUT

Nutsgrove
Farm

CH

Little
House Farm

Desford
Farm

Fish Fen

SCOLDING DROVE

PE6

WALLACE'S DROVE

Lime
Tree Farm

White Hart
Farm

Earl's
Fen

B1167

Wryde
Plantation

Little
Knarr Fen

Sewage
Works

STATION ROAD

B1040

1 PARK CL
2 PARK CR
3 SMITHFIELD

Cobbler's
Fen

East Wryde
Farm

Knarr
Farm

Thorney
Heritage
Mus

Thorney

Pigeons'
Farm

WISBECH ROAD

A47

PH

A47   WISBECH RD

Liby

14

Corner
Farm

12   13
15
16   3

2   4

Duke of
Bedford
Sch

8

9

PO

10   11

WOBURN RD

Abbey
House

High
Lands

1

Cemetery

Ashley
Pool

Park
Farm

North
Farm

Middle
Knarr Fen

Glass House
Farm

5

A2
1 WHITTLESEY RD
2 ST BOTOLPH'S WY
3 ST MARY'S CL
4 ST PETER'S WY
5 ASHLEY POOL LA
6 TONEHAM LA

DAIRY DROVE

WHITTLESEY RD

B1040

Upper
Knarr Fen

South
Farm

West
Corner Farm

OLD KNARR FEN DROVE

Rattlerow
Farm

KNARR FEN ROAD

Lower
Knarr Fen

Hill
Plantation

28   A   29   B   30   C   31   D   32   E   33   F

175

A3
1 KINGSLINE CL
2 ASH CL
3 CHESTNUT DR
4 BEECH CL
5 GAS LA
6 THE MALTINGS
7 LAUREL DR
8 THE CAUSEWAY
9 CHURCH ST
10 ABBEY PL
11 THE GREEN
12 RUSSELL CL
13 TOPHAM CR
14 SANDPIT RD
15 TAVISTOCK CL
16 BEDFORD CT

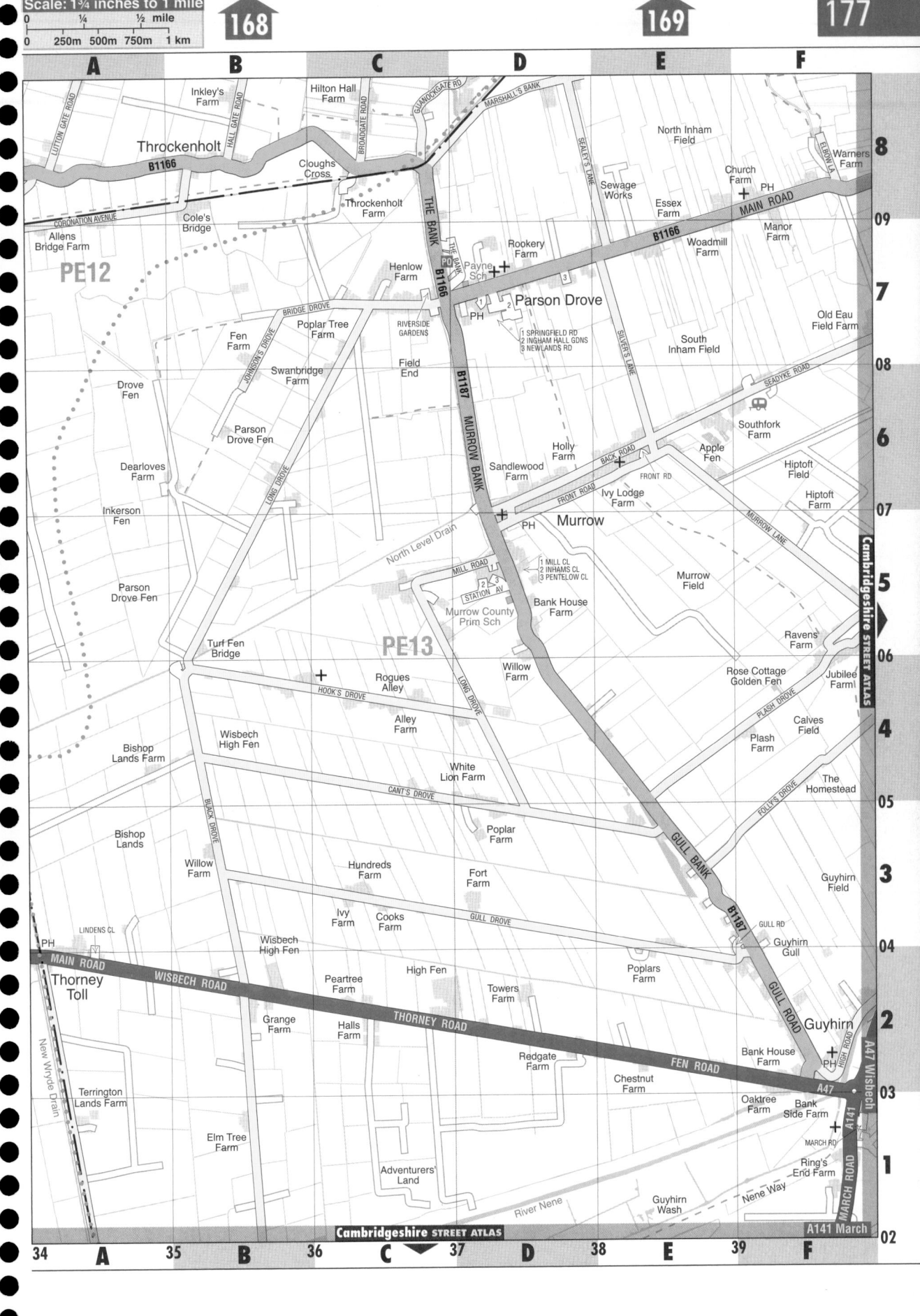
Scale: 1¾ inches to 1 mile
168
169
Throckenholt
Parson Drove
Murrow
Thorney Toll
Guyhirn
PE12
PE13
B1166
B1187
MAIN ROAD
WISBECH ROAD
THORNEY ROAD
FEN ROAD
GULL ROAD
GULL BANK
MURROW BANK
THE BANK
A47 Wisbech
A141 March
MARCH ROAD
North Level Drain
River Nene
Nene Way
New Wryde Drain
Cambridgeshire STREET ATLAS

E. Yorkshire & N. Lincolnshire STREET ATLAS

E7
1 CROMWELL CT
2 WOODHILL CL
3 NORWOOD CL
4 WAULDBY CL
5 WEETON WY

E8
1 COLLYNSON CL
2 SETTERWOOD GARTH
3 OAKDALE AV

A B C D E F

RIPLINGHAM RD

BIRKDALE CL

ANNANDALE ROAD

OLD ANNANDALE RD

B1232

PO

OVERTON

THE OVAL

MAPLE

PRUNUS AV

CHESTNUT DR

WOLFRETON LANE

WENTWORTH CLOSE

8

The Lunds

CH

ST ANDREW'S MOUNT

ELMS DRIVE

CHURCH MEADOWS

WOLFRETON

BEVERLEY RD

MARSHALL AV

THORNWOOD AV

KENWARDLY RD

KINGSTON ROAD

LINTHORPE GR

ASH

BROMWICH RD

SPRINGDALE

GANTON WY

West Ella

BRADS WALK

GODMAN'S LANE

HOGG LA

ALANWALL WY

SCHOOL LA

HONDALES

Kirk Ella

ODAMS S

JULIAN'S WELLS

GARTH

BLADONS

WILLOW DR

NORWOOD

Playing Field

GORTON ROAD

KING CHARLES

SAFFRONDALE

FORTY STEPS

BLACKTHORN LANE

HAZELBARROW RD

WOLFRETON ROAD

FORTY ACRE

THE AVENUE

Factory

Anlaby

7

WEST ELLA ROAD

Trans Pennine Trail

WEST ELLA ROAD

THE PADDOCKS

KIRK RI

KIRK RI

PINE MS

WESTLAND RD

MILL LANE

THE VALE

THE AVENUE

St Andrews Prim Sch

SOUTH ELLA DRIVE

WEST ELLA WAY

SOUTH ELLA WAY

EGGINTON CL

Wolfreton Sch

ALMA GR

CEDAR

WEST ELLA

THE LAWNS

BEVERLEY ROAD

Haltemprice Leisure Centre

P

SPRINGFIELD WAY

SAFFRONDALE

SPRINGFIELD WY

B1231

WINDSOR AVENUE

ST PETER'S RD

NORTH ST

Liby

RAYWELL CL
2 PENWITH CL
3 ORCHARD CL

29

Four Acre Plantation

Slight's Plantation

VALLEY DRIVE

DALESWAY

KARKWAY

KERRY DR

Cemy

GREEN CRES

WHITE WALK

SWANLAND

BUTTS CLOSE

MILL LANE

THE LINDS

FOUR ACRE CL

HU10

BROADLEY AV

CEDAR CL

GRANGE

WILSON ST

PRYME ST

OR WY

CAYLEY RD

Hull Road

6

The Grove

White Walk Plantation

HILL BROW

EASENBY AVE

DRYDALES

KERRY PIT WAY

COCK PIT CL

GRUNDALE

WOODLAND DRIVE

CROFT VIEW

TORCHIL CL

BARKWORTH CL

FIR TREES

B1232

LYNWOOD AVE

VOASES LA

BEECH LAWN

NORTH DR 1
WILSON ST 2

PO

LEGARD

LOYD STREET

MORTIMER DR

TISON GARTH

F6
1 HILDYARD CL
2 DALEHOUSE DR
3 STATHERS WK
4 NANDIKE CL
5 GRIMSTON RD
6 SYKES CL
7 ANLAFGATE
8 JULIAN'S WK

Horseshoe Plantation

Hut Plantation

Cemy

TRANBY LANE

B1231

CROFT DRIVE

TRANBY RIDE

TRANBY VW

BEVERLEY ROAD

LOWFIELD ROAD

LEGARD DRIVE

BUPA Hull & East Riding

5

West Ella Grange

TRANBY RIDE

Hull High Sch for Girls

H

28

Drydales

B1231

B1232

Marr Bridge

BEVERLEY ROAD

Low Field

4

BISHOP TEMPLE CT 1
KELSTON DR 2

THE WILLOWS

BOOTHFERRY ROAD

A1105

BRIGG DR

BEECH GR

ASH CL

Howden Pit (dis)

HU13

Hessle Lower Sch

THE BRAIDS

ASTRAL CL

ASTRAL RD

BARNETBY RD

E2
1 HALYCON AV
2 NORTHOLME CL
3 WESTBOURNE AV
4 THE CIRCLE
5 BRUNSWICK GR

JENNY BROUGH LANE

NORTHWOOD WY

TALL TREES

TRANBY MEADOWS

FOUNTAIN

ROSEMOUNT GRANGE

Hessle Mount Sch

HEMMINGWAY

BEVERLEY ROAD

ATHOLL AV

CROSSFIELD

CAMBRIDGE RD

BEDFORD RD

PENSHURST AVE

Hessle Penshurst Prim Sch

3

JENNY CL

Tranby Park

ACORN WY

HAWTHORNE RI

Hessle Mount

Park Ave

NORTHFIELD AVE

RICHMOND RD

SEATON RD

Northfield

MINIC

27

Tranby Park Farm

A164

Stockdove Wood

WEELSBY WY

HEADLANDS DR

Tranby Park Farm

SWANLAND HEADS RD

SWANLAND AV

SUNNINGDALE RD

COTTESMORE RD

2

North Drive Plantation

Hawk Plantation

BOOTHFERRY ROAD

A1105

Hessle High Sch

WESTFIELD RISE

HILLCREST

ELMSWOOD

HUMBAR VW

BARROW LANE

CALFONT CL

WOODHILL RI

TRANBY AVENUE

LAWNSWOOD

MARLBOROUGH AV

PEASEHOL

WESTBOURNE GR

TRINITY GR

NORTHGATE

All Saints CE Jun Sch

FLETCHER

THE

EAST GATE

BELVEDERE ROAD

1

Quarry (dis)

Mast

Factory

BOOTHFERRY ROAD A15

BARTON DR

ELSHAM DR

BRIDGEVIEW Sch

THORNTON CL

SALISBURY

THE SQUARE

SWINEGATE

Liby

PO

HULL ROAD

Humber Field Farm

A63

A15

A63

FERRIBY ROAD

FERRIBY ROAD

WOODHILL LA

DAVENPORT AVENUE

Hessle

GLADSTONE ST

CHESTNUT AVE

STATION ROAD

FERRY RD

SOUTHGATE

Factory

SAXON WAY

26

01 A 02 B C 03 D E F

E1
1 SPIRE VW
2 TOWER HL MS
3 VICARAGE LA
4 CLOWES CT
5 FISHWICK AV

F1
1 MARGARET GR
2 BISHOP BLUNT CL
3 BISHOP KEMPTHORNE CLO
4 BISHOP GURDON CL

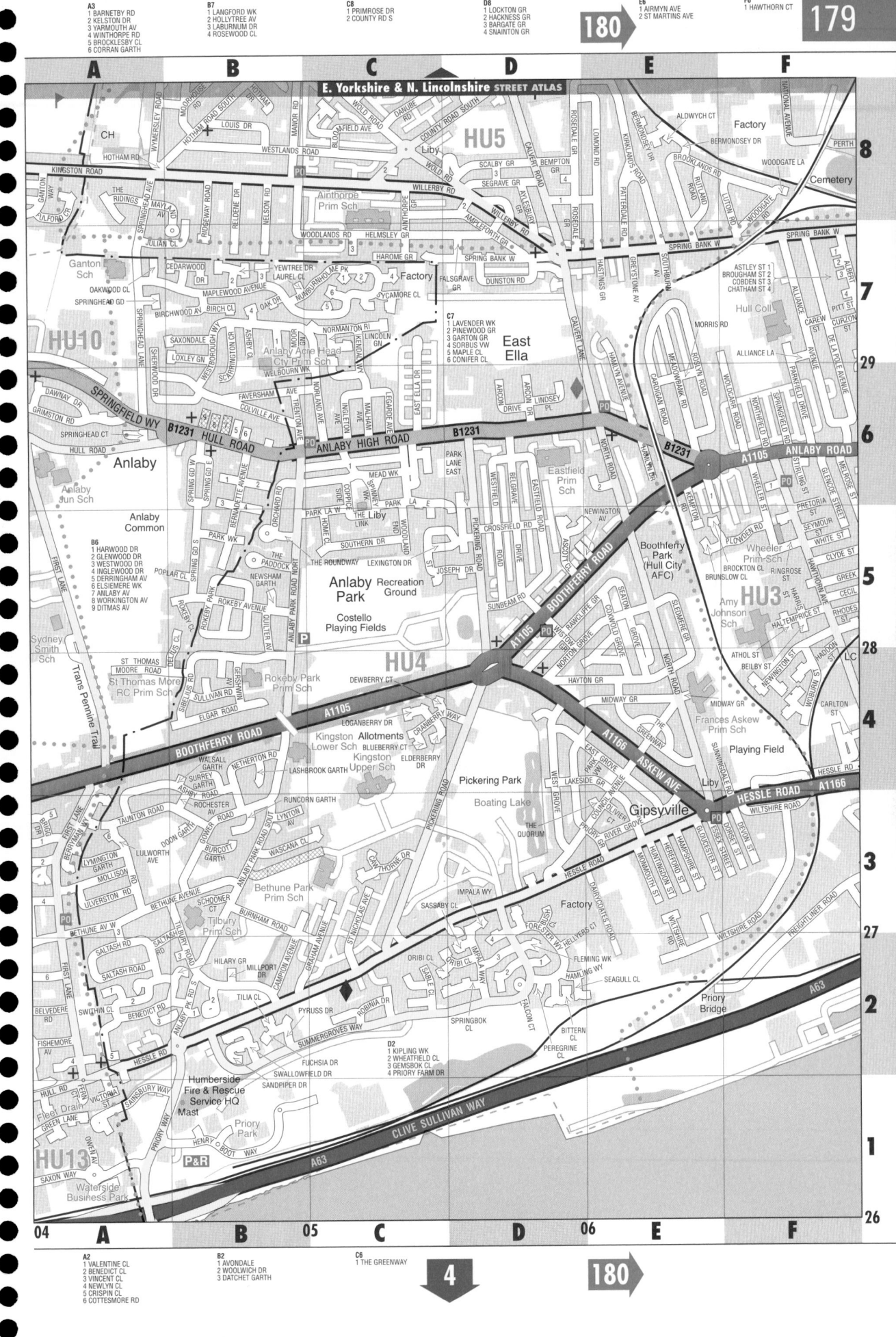

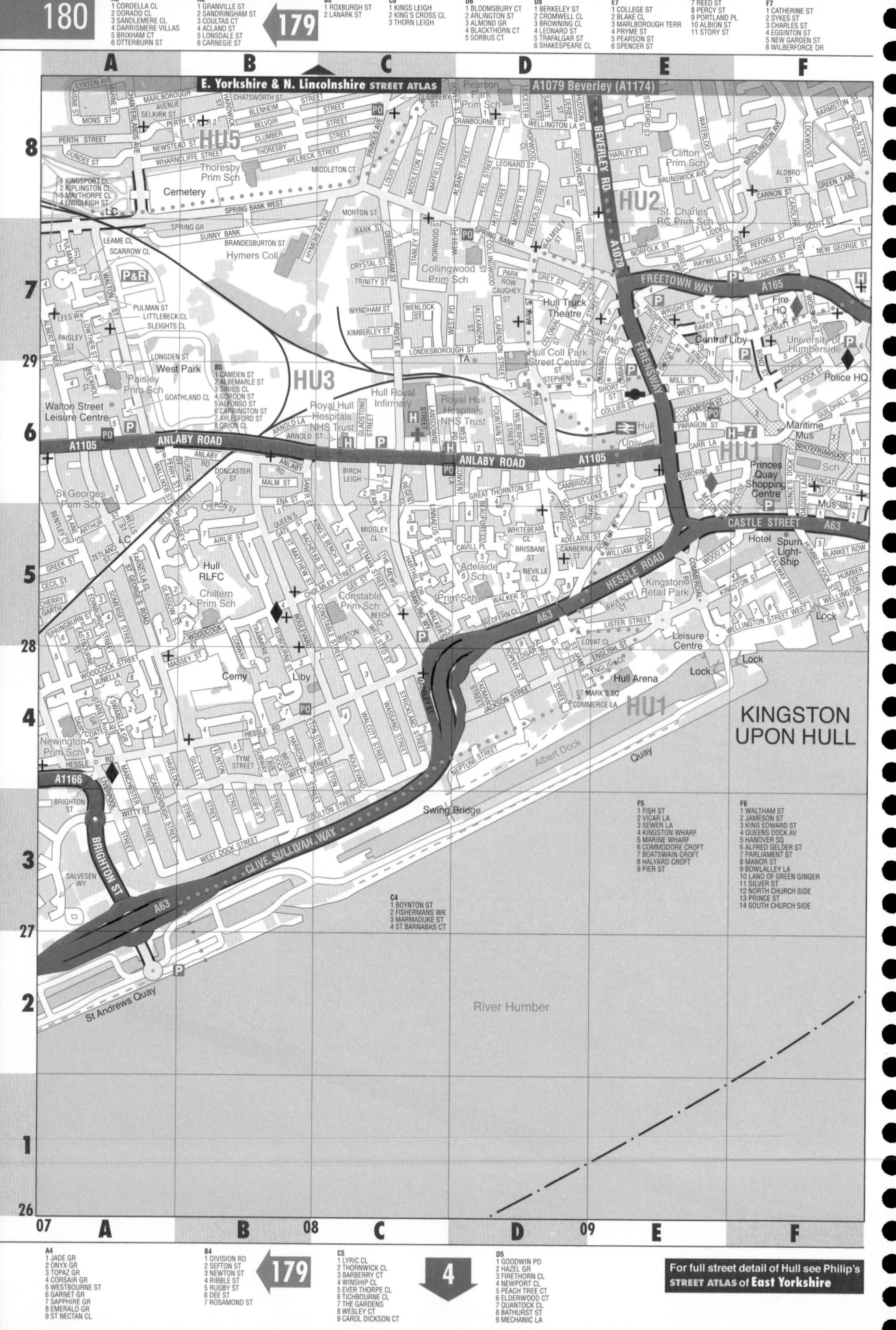

KINGSTON
UPON HULL

For full street detail of Hull see Philip's STREET ATLAS of East Yorkshire

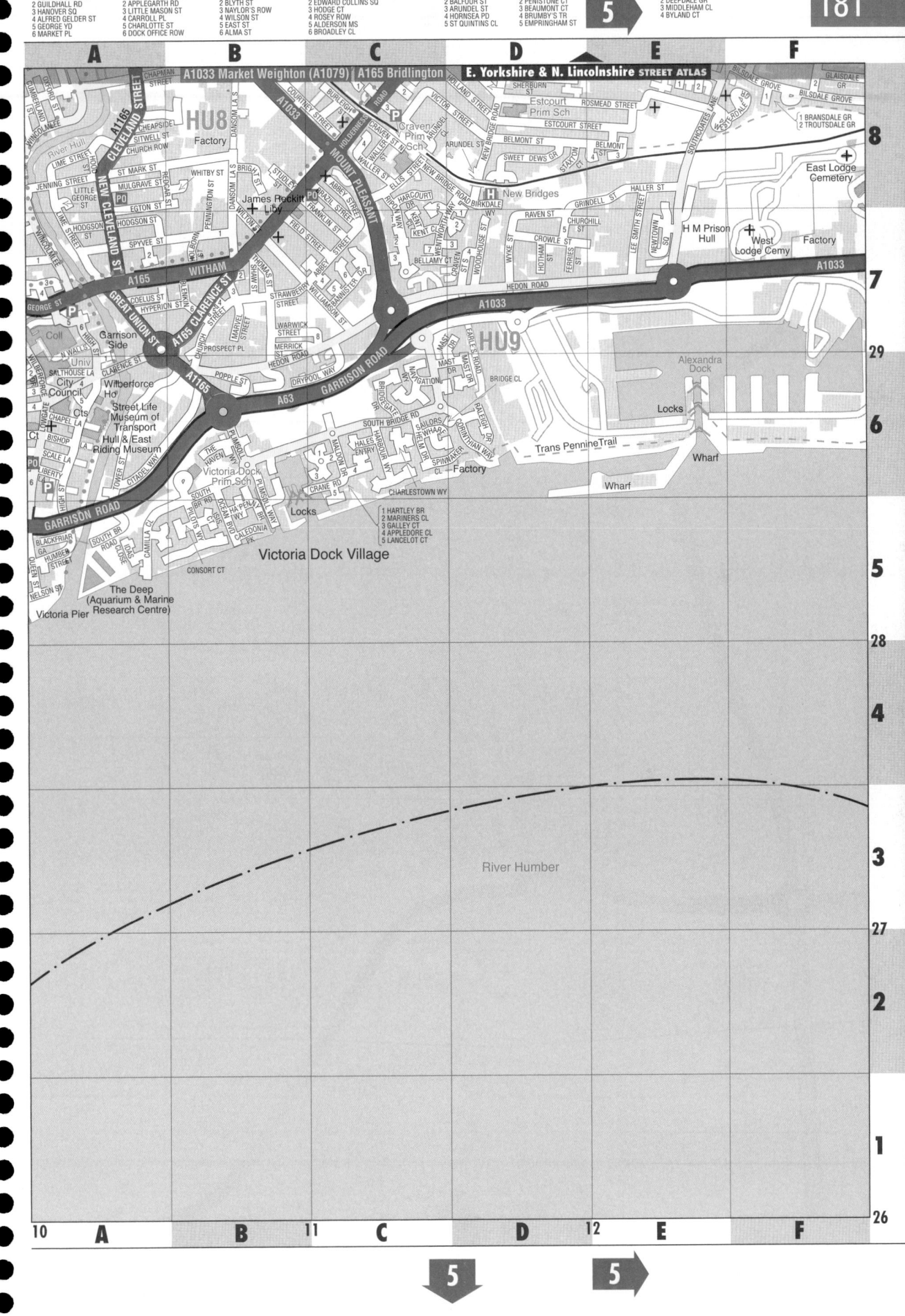

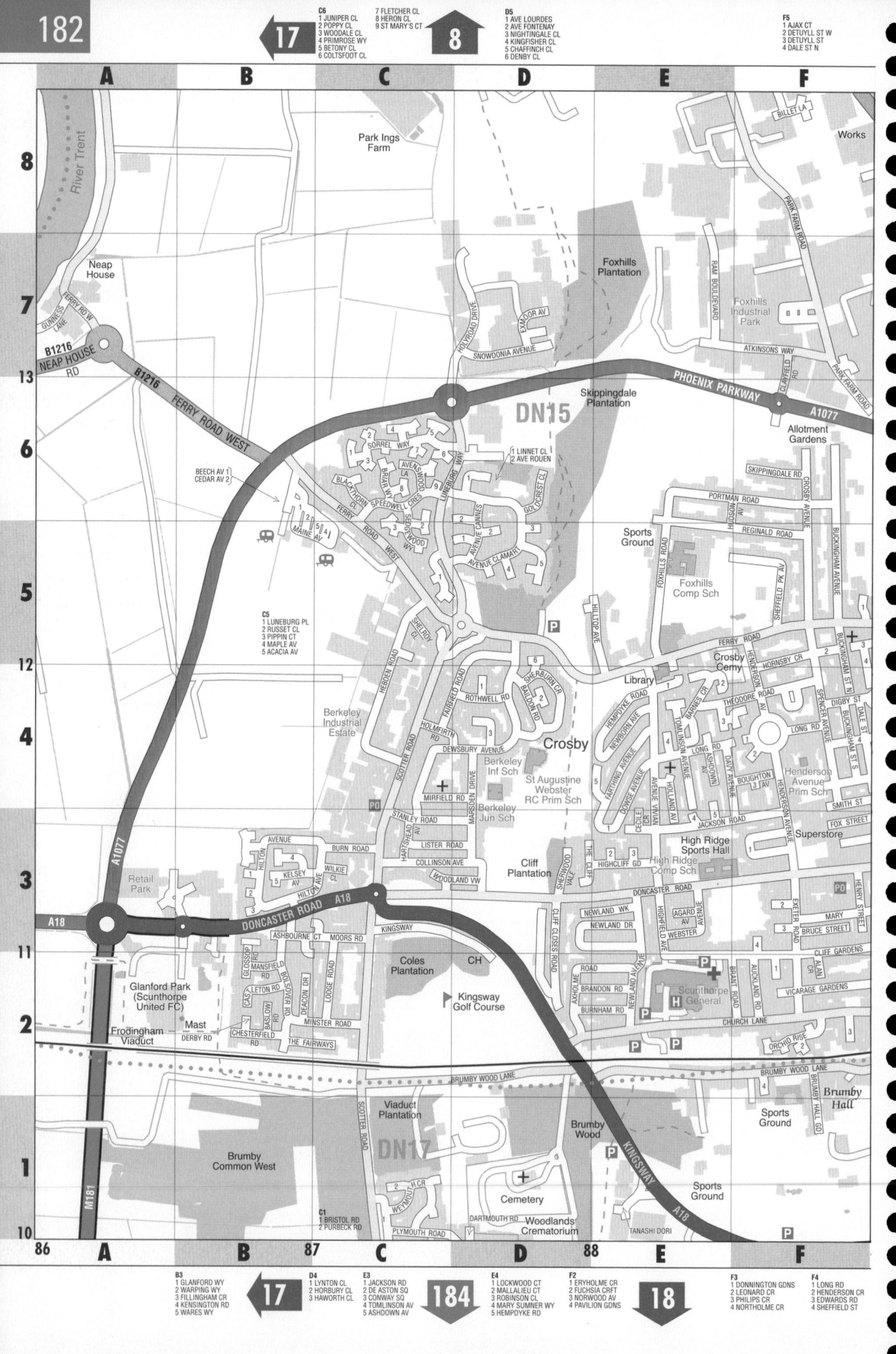

17   8

A   B   C   D   E   F

8

7

13

6

DN15

5

12

4

Crosby

3

11

2

1

10

86   A   87   B   C   88   D   E   F

17   184   18

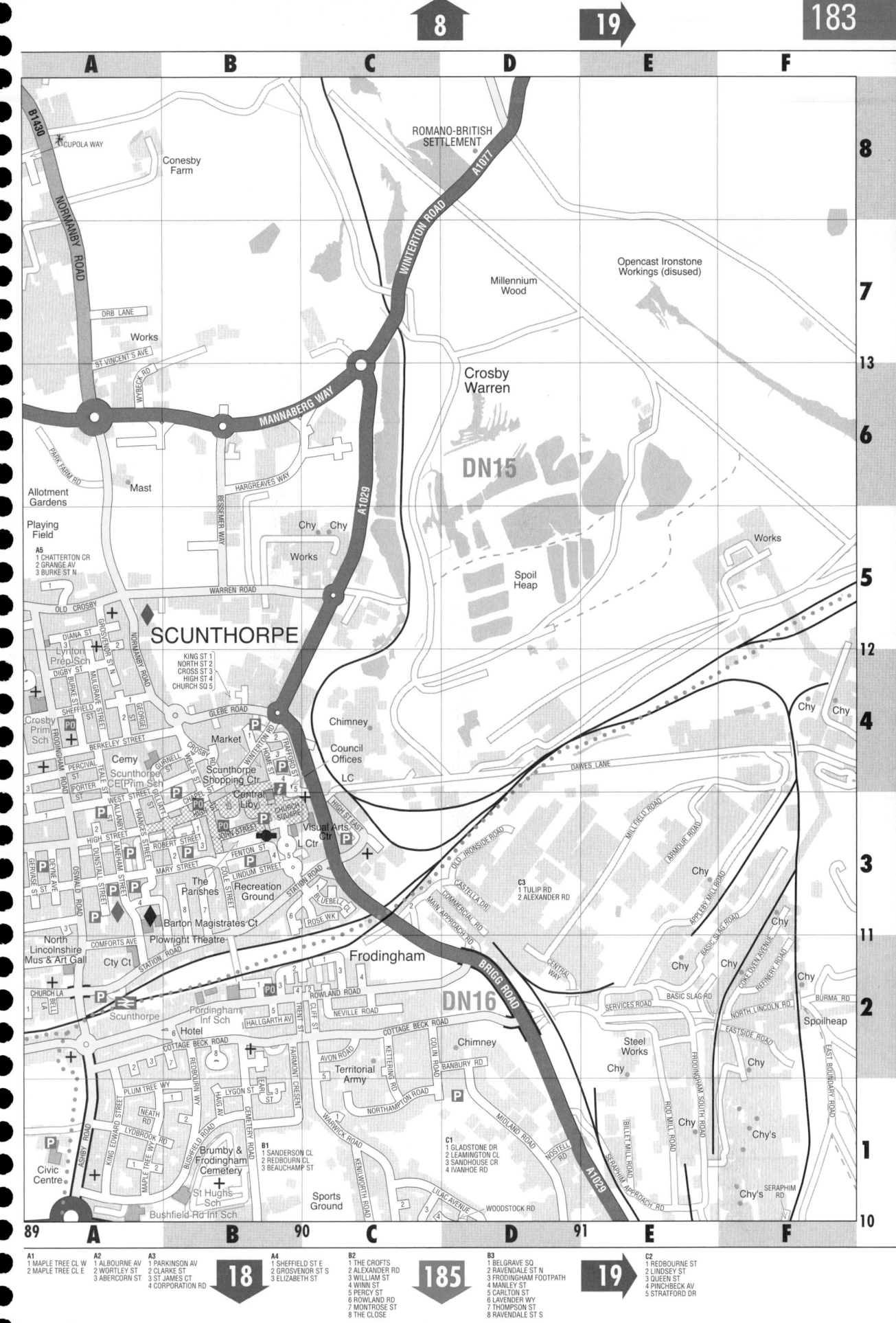

A1
1 MAPLE TREE CL W
2 MAPLE TREE CL E

A2
1 ALBOURNE AV
2 WORTLEY ST
3 ABERCORN ST

A3
1 PARKINSON AV
2 CLARKE ST
3 ST JAMES CT
4 CORPORATION RD

A4
1 SHEFFIELD ST E
2 GROSVENOR ST S
3 ELIZABETH ST

B1
1 SANDERSON CL
2 REDBOURN CL
3 BEAUCHAMP ST

B2
1 THE CROFTS
2 ALEXANDER RD
3 WILLIAM ST
4 WINN ST
5 PERCY ST
6 ROWLAND RD
7 MONTROSE ST
8 THE CLOSE

B3
1 BELGRAVE SQ
2 RAVENDALE ST N
3 FRODINGHAM FOOTPATH
4 MANLEY ST
5 CARLTON ST
6 LAVENDER WY
7 THOMPSON ST
8 RAVENDALE ST S

C1
1 GLADSTONE DR
2 LEAMINGTON CL
3 SANDHOUSE CR
4 IVANHOE RD

C2
1 REDBOURNE ST
2 LINDSEY ST
3 QUEEN ST
4 PINCHBECK AV
5 STRATFORD DR

C3
1 TULIP RD
2 ALEXANDER RD

A5
1 CHATTERTON CR
2 GRANGE AV
3 BURKE ST N

17

182

C5
1 BETULA WY
2 CONIFER CL
3 ACER GR

C6
1 FOURTH AV
2 THIRD AV
3 SECOND AV
4 SHAKESPEARE AV
5 SIDNEY RD

C7
1 ROCHESTER CL
2 SALISBURY CL
3 ST ALBANS CL

D7
1 CANTERBURY CL
2 NEWBOLT AV
3 LANDOR AV
4 KIPLING AV
5 COVENTRY CL

D8
1 QUANTOCK CL
2 CLEVELAND CL
3 BARNSTAPLE RD

E6
1 BROWNING CL
2 MAVIS RD
3 MALLARD RD
4 KIPLING AV
5 PHEASANT CL

F8
1 NORMAN CR
2 GLANVILLE CR
3 HAWTHORNE CR
4 HAWTHORNE AV

E3
1 WADDINGTON DR
2 THE OVAL
3 EDGBASTON AV
4 HEADINGLEY AV
5 JESMOND AV
6 LOW LEYS RD

F3
1 PRINCESS ALEXANDRA CT
2 SOUTHRIDGE CR
3 AUSTIN CR
4 THORNHILL CR
5 KIRMAN CR

F4
1 HARROW GD
2 KEDDINGTO RD

F2
1 LEE FAIR GDNS
2 ST ANDREWS AV

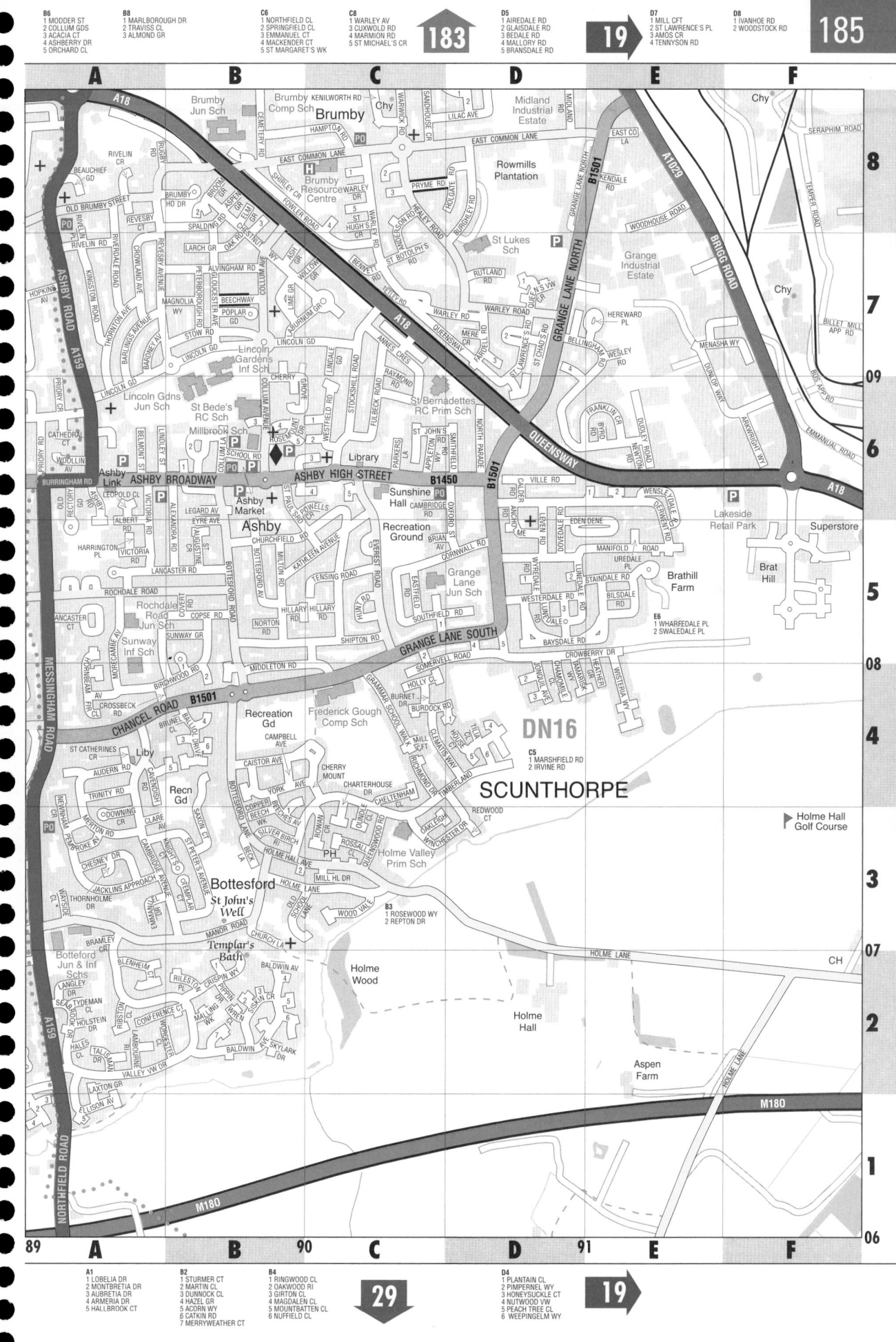
185
183
19
B6
1 MODDER ST
2 COLLUM GDS
3 ACACIA CT
4 ASHBERRY DR
5 ORCHARD CL
B8
1 MARLBOROUGH DR
2 TRAVISS CL
3 ALMOND GR
C6
1 NORTHFIELD CL
2 SPRINGFIELD CL
3 EMMANUEL CT
4 MACKENDER CT
5 ST MARGARET'S WK
C8
1 WARLEY AV
3 CUXWOLD RD
4 MARMION RD
5 ST MICHAEL'S CR
D5
1 AIREDALE RD
2 GLAISDALE RD
3 BEDALE RD
4 MALLORY RD
5 BRANSDALE RD
D7
1 MILL CFT
2 ST LAWRENCE'S PL
3 AMOS CR
4 TENNYSON RD
D8
1 IVANHOE RD
2 WOODSTOCK RD
Brumby
Brumby Jun Sch
Brumby Comp Sch
Midland Industrial Estate
Rowmills Plantation
Brumby Resource Centre
St Lukes Sch
Grange Industrial Estate
Lincoln Gardens Inf Sch
Lincoln Gdns Jun Sch
St Bede's RC Sch
Millbrook Sch
St Bernadettes RC Prim Sch
Library
Ashby Link
Ashby Market
Ashby
ASHBY BROADWAY
ASHBY HIGH STREET
Sunshine Hall
Recreation Ground
Grange Lane Jun Sch
Lakeside Retail Park
Superstore
Brat Hill
Brathill Farm
E6
1 WHARFEDALE PL
2 SWALEDALE PL
Rochdale Road Jun Sch
Sunway Inf Sch
GRANGE LANE SOUTH
CHANCEL ROAD
Recreation Gd
Frederick Gough Comp Sch
DN16
C5
1 MARSHFIELD RD
2 IRVINE RD
SCUNTHORPE
Liby
Recn Gd
Holme Hall Golf Course
Holme Valley Prim Sch
Bottesford
St John's Well
Templar's Bath
B3
1 ROSEWOOD WY
2 REPTON DR
Botteford Jun & Inf Schs
Holme Wood
Holme Hall
Aspen Farm
HOLME LANE
M180
MESSINGHAM ROAD
NORTHFIELD ROAD
ASHBY ROAD
QUEENSWAY
BRIGG ROAD
GRANGE LANE NORTH
89
90
91
06
07
08
09
A1
1 LOBELIA DR
2 MONTBRETIA DR
3 AUBRETIA DR
4 ARMERIA DR
5 HALLBROOK CT
B2
1 STURMER CT
2 MARTIN CL
3 DUNNOCK CL
4 HAZEL GR
5 ACORN WY
6 CATKIN RD
7 MERRYWEATHER CT
B4
1 RINGWOOD CL
2 OAKWOOD RI
3 GIRTON CL
4 MAGDALEN CL
5 MOUNTBATTEN CL
6 NUFFIELD CL
29
D4
1 PLANTAIN CL
2 PIMPERNEL WY
3 HONEYSUCKLE CT
4 NUTWOOD VW
5 PEACH TREE CL
6 WEEPINGELM WY

13   13

A   B   C   D   E   F

Rosper Road Pools Nature Reserve

ROSPER ROAD

HUMBER ROAD   A160

HUMBER ROAD

WEST HAVEN WAY

LC   LC   LC

Water Tower

Oil Storage Depot

A1173

Houlton's Covert

SOUTHERN WAY   SOUTHERN ROAD

SEVEN QUAY ROAD

ALEXANDRA ROAD SOUTH

Robinson RD

Works

MANBY ROAD

Pelham Industrial Estate

A1173

MIDDLEPLATT ROAD

Sports Ground

DN40

Immingham Golf Course

STANDISH LA 1
HINKLEY DR 2
WESTON GR 3
ATWOOD CL 4

Medieval Village of Immingham

WOODLANDS AVENUE

COPSE CL

WASHDYKE LANE

CHURCH LANE

CH

1 CEDAR DR
2 MAPLE GR
3 OAKLANDS RD

Football Ground

ASH TREE CL

Manby Hall Business Park

Mast

Mon

P   PO

1 HUMBERVILLE RD
2 LARCH CL
3 TRENCHARD CL

MILL LANE

VIKING CL

PILGRIMS WAY

WINSLOW DRIVE

MORTON

CLIFTON CRESCENT

Allerton Prim Sch

ROSS GDNS

PARK CL

Hotel

BEECHWOOD AV

SPINNEY CL

MAYFIELD CFT

BERKELEY CL

WICK CL

PELHAM ROAD

FERNDOWN DR

HUMBERVILLE ROAD

WATERWORKS ST

BATTERY ST

CHESTNUT AV

HAWTHORN AV

Washdyke Retail Park

Pelham Inf Sch

SPRING STREET

Sports Ctr

Civic Ctr

WORSLEY ROAD

Recreation Ground

ROYAL DRIVE

VALDA VALE

SONIA CREST

BRADFORD RD

ROBERT CL

ALLERTON DR

Kennedy Way Shopping Ctr

Mkt

Lib

ALDEN CL

WINSLOW CL

Swimming Pool

St Andrews CE Jun Sch

P

1 DEANE RD
2 SACKVILLE CL
3 WORSLEY CL
4 EATON RD

IMMINGHAM

KINGS ROAD

KINGS ROAD

Coomb Brigg Prim Sch

PH

BLUESTONE LANE

PELHAM ROAD

HUME BRAE

PO

HIGHLAND TARN

THORNTON PL

CRAIKHILL AV

MAYFLOWER AV

MARGARET STREET

PRINCESS STREET

CUSHMAN CR

Immingham Sch

Immingham Business Units

PATELA CL

CARVER ST

SACKVILLE RD

PILGRIM AVENUE

LYDFORD RD

TALBOT ROAD

SOMERTON ROAD

HADLEIGH ROAD

KENDAL RD

ANCHOLME AV 1
CALDER CL 2
STEEPING DR 3
AIRE CL 4

HABROUGH ROAD   B1210

Sports Gd

JASMINE WY

Resource Centre

1 COLLIER RD
2 BREWSTER AV
3 THORNBURY RD

KISHORN CT 1
PERTH WY 2
TUMMEL CT 3

KINLOCH

Eastfield Cty Inf & Jun Sch

GUERNSEY GR

ALDERNEY WY

SHETLAND WY

Highfield Farm

ANGLESEY DR

ARRAN CL

MULL WY

STALLINGBOROUGH ROAD

ORKNEY PL 1
FAIRISLE RI 2
LUNDY CT 3

A180

B1210

Mauxhall Farm

A1173

KILN LANE

DN41

17   A   B   18   C   D   19   E   F

A4
1 MAIDEN CL
2 CLEVELAND CL
3 LYDIA CT
4 HAZEL CFT
5 MILLHOUSE ST RI
6 JACKSON MS
7 ANDREWS WY
8 HELEN CR

B3
1 BLOSSOM WY
2 CLARENCE CL
3 LINDUM AV
4 HIGHFIELD AV
5 MACKENZIE PL
6 HUME BRAE
7 BOWMAN WY
8 HAMISH WK
9 JAMES WY

B4
1 HOLLINGSWORTH AV
2 HOLBECK PL
3 BALFOUR PL
4 LANSDOWN RD
5 AINSWORTH RD
6 LEYDEN CL
7 CHILTON CL
8 STAINTON DR

C3
1 PRINCESS ST
2 ROUNDWAY
3 JAPONICA HL
4 MAGNOLIA RI
5 PADDOCK CT
6 OBAN CT

23   23

A B C D E F

8

Immingham
Dock

7

Oil
Storage
Depot

16

LC

6

Oil
Storage
Depot

QUEENS RD

Chy

LC

DN40

A1173

LAPORTE ROAD

5

QUEENS ROAD

15

Chimney

Works
Humber Bank
Factories

Chimney

4

EUROPA WAY

SCANDINAVIAN WAY

NETHERLANDS WAY

LC

3

Spoil Heap

Kiln Lane
Ind Est

KILN LANE

WORLDWIDE WAY

WORLDWIDE WY

14

Kiln Lane
Ind Est

DN41

HOBSON WAY

South
Marsh Road
Ind Est

2

BEEL'S RD

OSBORNE RD

SOUTH MARSH ROAD

NORTH MOSS LANE

LC

SOUTH MARSH ROAD

Power
Station

Chimney

1

SOUTH MARSH ROAD

Poplar
Farm

13

20 A B 21 C D 22 E F

River Humber

Works

Works

Pyewipe

Chimney

Chimney

Chimney

Water
Reclamation
Works

Sports
Ground

LC

LC

Sports
Ground

LC

DN31

Sewage
Works

LAFOREY ROAD

MOODY LANE

MOODY LANE

A180

Mast

ESTATE ROAD NO 4

ESTATE ROAD NO 3

ESTATE ROAD NO 1

Europa
Business Park

LC

GATE WY

ALLINGTON DR 1
NAVENSBY CL 2

WOAD LANE

ESTATE ROAD NO 5

Hotel

APIAN WY

GILBEY ROAD

ESTUARY WAY

LC

WESTSIDE ROAD

NEWBURY AV

ESTATE ROAD NO 6

ESTATE ROAD NO 2

South Humberside
Industrial
Estate

WEST COATES RD

Alexandra Dock

DN37

PINE CL

ESTATE RD NO 7

CRANWELL DR

ESTATE RD NO 2

CROMWELL ROAD

ESTATE RD NO 8

HAVEN GDNS

Littlecoates
Prim Sch

ELSENHAM ROAD

HARLOW ST

NEW HAVEN TERRACE

GILBEY RD

HARGRAVE

DUMMOW ST

BIRCHIN WAY

PYEWIPE ROAD

BOULEVARD AV

GEESON ST

CHARLTON ST

ADAM SMITH ST

WATKIN ST NORTH

ARMSTRONG ST

RENDEL ST

ALEXANDRA ROAD

WESTGATE

Alexandra
Retail
Park

The Willows

West Marsh

190
24
24
191

	A	B	C	D	E	F	
							8
							7
							13
							6

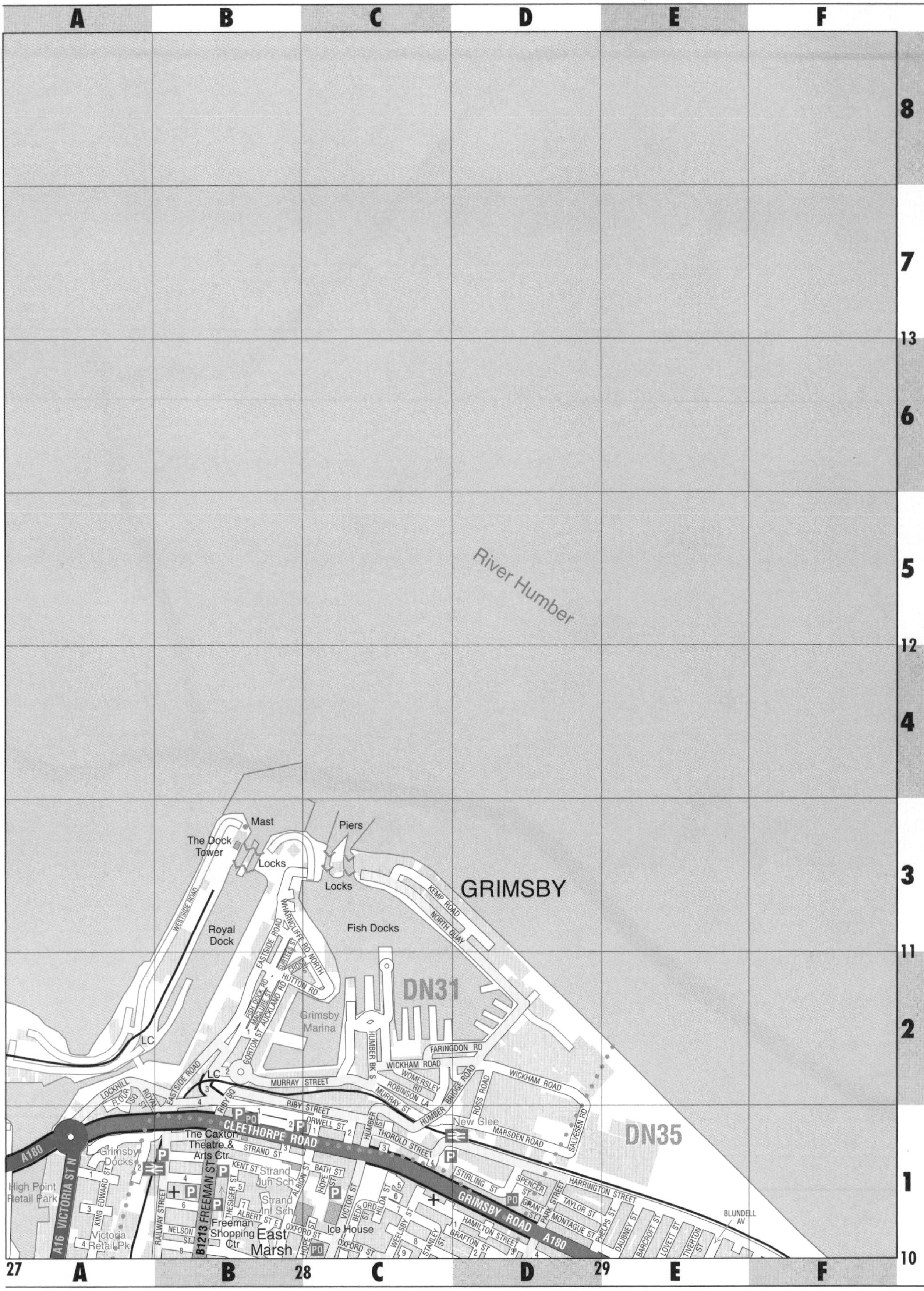

River Humber

							5
							12
							4

Mast

Piers

The Dock Tower

Locks

Locks

GRIMSBY

KEMP ROAD

WESTSIDE ROAD

Royal Dock

Fish Docks

NORTH QUAY

							3
							11

DN31

Grimsby Marina

HUTTON RD

FARINGDON RD

WICKHAM ROAD

WOMERSLEY RD

WICKHAM ROAD

ROBINSON LA

HUMBER BK S

MURRAY STREET

MURRAY ST

ROSS ROAD

HUMBER BRIDGE ROAD

SILVERGEN RD

MARSDEN ROAD

DN35

							2

RIBY SQ

RIBY STREET

ORWELL ST

THOROLD STREET

New Glee

The Caxton Theatre & Arts Ctr.

CLEETHORPE ROAD

STRAND ST

STIRLING ST

KENT ST Strand Jun Sch

Strand Inf Sch

BATH ST

HOPE ST

SPENCER ST

HARRINGTON STREET

Grimsby Docks

LOCKHILL

FLOTTERGATE

KING EDWARD ST

RAILWAY STREET

FREEMAN STREET

ALBERT ST E

ALBERT ST W

OXFORD ST

VICTOR RD

WELLS ST

STANLEY ST

HAMILTON STREET

GRANT ST

PARK STREET

TAYLOR ST

MONTAGUE ST

PHELPS ST

DAUBNEY ST

BARCROFT ST

LOVETT ST

TIVERTON ST

BLUNDELL AV

High Point Retail Park

A180

A16 VICTORIA ST N

Victoria Retail Pk

B1213

Freeman Shopping Ctr

East Marsh

Ice House

NELSON ST

GARIBALDI ST

GRAFTON ST

GRIMSBY ROAD

A180

LC

LC

							1
							10

 191

 25 **192** **25**

A1
1 LOWER SPRING ST
2 ALBERT GDNS
3 CRESSEY ST
4 FOTHERBY ST

B1
1 TOMLINE ST
2 NACTON ST
3 BRIDGE ST NORTH
4 CHURCH ST
5 SERVICE RD NO 1
6 ALBERT ST W
7 SERVICE RD NO 2
8 GARIBALDI ST

B2
1 STUART WORTLEY ST
2 MURRAY ST
3 ROWLANDSON ST
4 RAILWAY PL

D1
1 CASSWELL CL
2 RUTLAND ST
3 MANSEL ST
4 SIDNEY ST

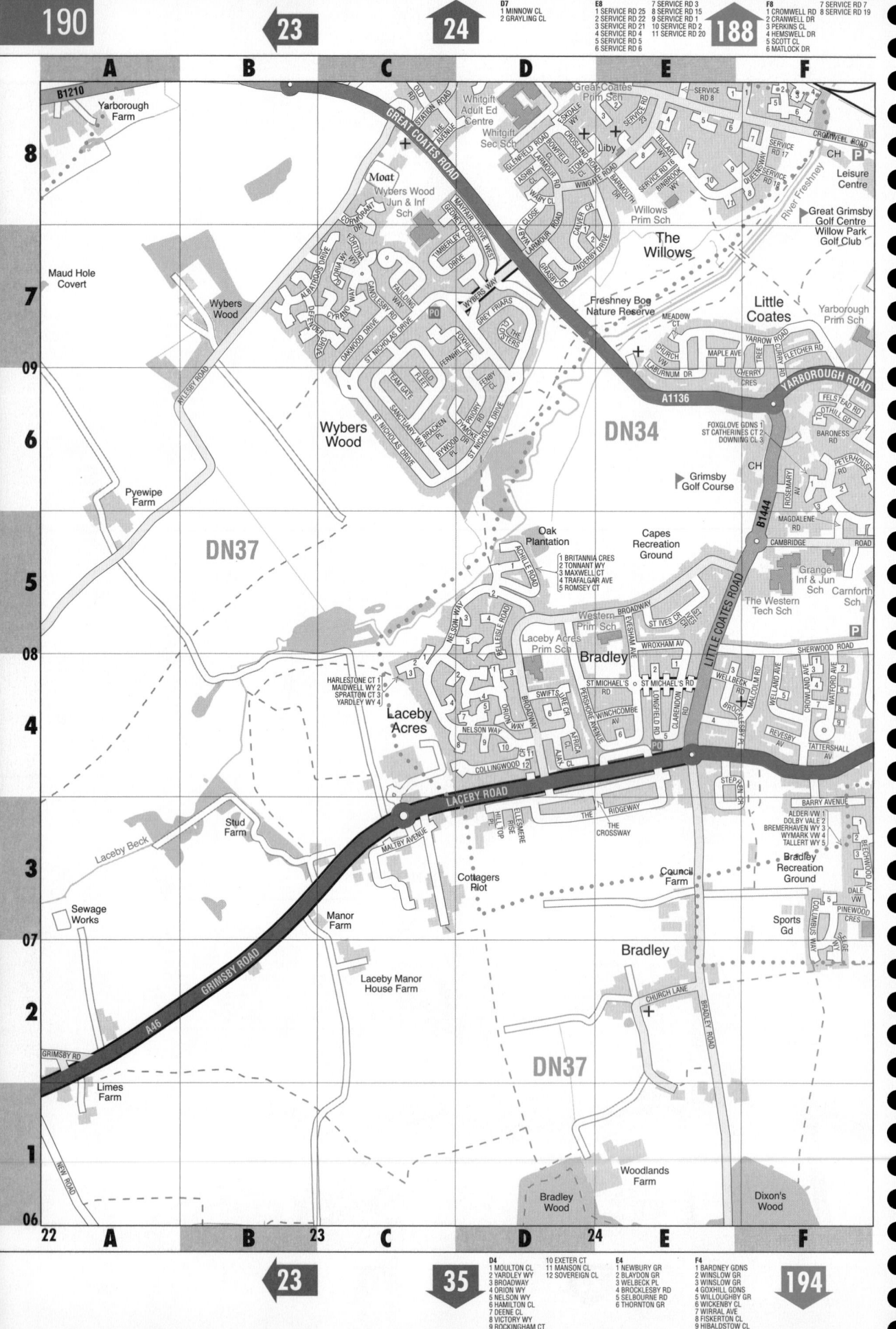

← 23

↑ 24

↑ 188

D7
1 MINNOW CL
2 GRAYLING CL

E8
1 SERVICE RD 25
2 SERVICE RD 22
3 SERVICE RD 21
4 SERVICE RD 4
5 SERVICE RD 5
6 SERVICE RD 6

7 SERVICE RD 3
8 SERVICE RD 15
9 SERVICE RD 1
10 SERVICE RD 2
11 SERVICE RD 20

F8
1 CROMWELL RD
2 CRANWELL DR
3 PERKINS CL
4 HEMSWELL DR
5 SCOTT CL
6 MATLOCK DR

7 SERVICE RD 7
8 SERVICE RD 19

← 23

↓ 35

↓ 194

D4
1 MOULTON CL
2 YARDLEY WY
3 BROADWAY
4 ORION WY
5 NELSON WY
6 HAMILTON CL
7 DEENE CL
8 VICTORY WY
9 ROCKINGHAM CT

10 EXETER CT
11 MANSON CL
12 SOVEREIGN CL

E4
1 NEWBURY GR
2 BLAYDON GR
3 WELBECK PL
4 BROCKLESBY RD
5 SELBOURNE RD
6 THORNTON GR

F4
1 BARDNEY GDNS
2 WINSLOW GR
3 WINSLOW GR
4 GOXHILL GDNS
5 WILLOUGHBY GR
6 WICKENBY CL
7 WIRRAL AVE
8 FISKERTON CL
9 HIBALDSTOW CL

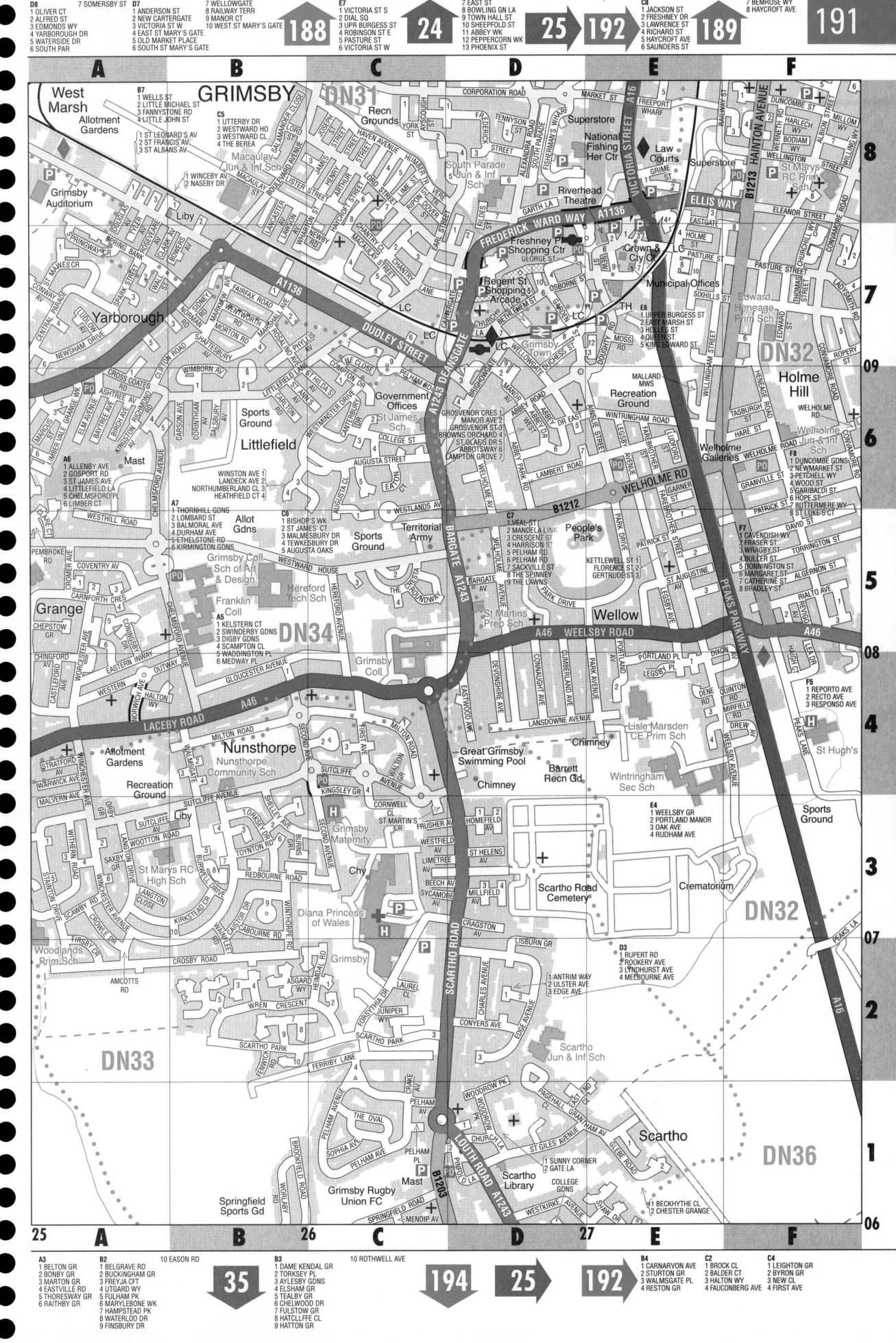
191
D8
1 OLIVER CT
2 ALFRED ST
3 EDMONDS WY
4 YARBOROUGH DR
5 WATERSIDE DR
6 SOUTH PAR
7 SOMERSBY ST
D7
1 ANDERSON ST
2 NEW CARTERGATE
3 VICTORIA ST W
4 EAST ST MARY'S GATE
5 OLD MARKET PLACE
6 SOUTH ST MARY'S GATE
7 WELLOWGATE
8 RAILWAY TERR
9 MANOR CT
10 WEST ST MARY'S GATE
188
E7
1 VICTORIA ST S
2 DIAL SQ
3 UPR BURGESS ST
4 ROBINSON ST E
5 PASTURE ST
6 VICTORIA ST W
24
7 EAST ST
8 BOWLING GN LA
9 TOWN HALL ST
10 SHEEPFOLD ST
11 ABBEY WK
12 PEPPERCORN WK
13 PHOENIX ST
25
192
C8
1 JACKSON ST
2 FRESHNEY DR
3 LAWRENCE ST
4 RICHARD ST
5 HAYCROFT AVE
6 SAUNDERS ST
189
7 BEMROSE WY
8 HAYCROFT AVE
A
B
C
D
E
F
West Marsh
Allotment Gardens
GRIMSBY
DN31
Recn Grounds
B7
1 WELLS ST
2 LITTLE MICHAEL ST
3 FANNYSTONE RD
4 LITTLE JOHN ST
C5
1 UTTERBY DR
2 WESTWARD HO
3 WESTWARD CL
4 THE BEREA
1 ST LEONARD'S AV
2 ST FRANCIS AV
3 ST ALBANS AV
1 WINCEBY AV
2 NASEBY DR
Grimsby Auditorium
Macaulay Jun & Inf Sch
South Parade Jun & Inf Sch
Superstore
National Fishing Her Ctr
Law Courts
Superstore
Riverhead Theatre
ELLIS WAY
FREDERICK WARD WAY
A1136
Freshney Pl Shopping Ctr
Crown & Cty Ct
Municipal Offices
Regent St Shopping Arcade
Grimsby Town
St Marys RC Prim Sch
Edward Heneage Prim Sch
E8
1 UPPER BURGESS ST
2 EAST MARSH ST
3 HOLLES ST
4 QUEEN ST
5 KING EDWARD ST
Yarborough
DUDLEY STREET
DN32
Holme Hill
Government Offices
St James Sch
Sports Ground
Littlefield
Mast
A1243 DEANSGATE
GROSVENOR CRES 1
MANOR AVE 2
GROSVENOR ST 3
BROWNS ORCHARD 4
ST OLAF'S DR 5
ABBOTSWAY 6
LAMPTON GROVE 7
Recreation Ground
Welholme Galleries
Welholme Jun & Inf Sch
A6
1 ALLENBY AVE
2 GOSPORT RD
3 ST JAMES AVE
4 LITTLEFIELD LA
5 CHELMSFORD PL
6 LIMBER CT
WINSTON AVE 1
LANDECK AVE 2
NORTHUMBERLAND CL 3
HEATHFIELD CT 4
F8
1 DUNCOMBE GDNS
2 NEWMARKET ST
3 PETCHELL WY
4 WOOD ST
5 GARIBALDI ST
6 HOPE ST
7 BUTTERMERE WY
8 ST LUKE'S CT
A7
1 THORNHILL GDNS
2 LOMBARD ST
3 BALMORAL AVE
4 DURHAM AVE
5 ETHELSTONE RD
6 KIRMINGTON GDNS
Allot Gdns
C6
1 BISHOP'S WK
2 ST JAMES' CT
3 MALMESBURY DR
4 TEWKESBURY DR
5 AUGUSTA OAKS
Territorial Army
Sports Ground
C7
1 VEAL ST
2 MANDELA LINK
3 CRESCENT ST
4 HARRISON ST
5 PELHAM RD
6 PELHAM RD
7 SACKVILLE ST
8 THE SPINNEY
9 THE LAWNS
People's Park
WELHOLME RD
B1212
F7
1 CAVENDISH WY
2 FRASER ST
3 WRAGBY ST
4 BULLER ST
5 DONNINGTON ST
6 MARGARET ST
7 CATHERINE ST
8 BRADLEY ST
KETTLEWELL ST 1
FLORENCE ST 2
GERTRUDE ST 3
Grimsby Coll Sch of Art & Design
Hereford Tech Sch
Franklin Coll
Grange
A5
1 KELSTERN CT
2 SWINDERBY GDNS
3 DIGBY GDNS
4 SCAMPTON CL
5 WADDINGTON PL
6 MEDWAY PL
DN34
St Martins Prep Sch
Wellow
A46 WEELSBY ROAD
BARGATE A1243
PEAKS PARKWAY
Grimsby Coll
F5
1 REPORTO AVE
2 RECTO AVE
3 RESPONSO AVE
LACEBY ROAD A46
Allotment Gardens
Nunsthorpe
Nunsthorpe Community Sch
Recreation Ground
Great Grimsby Swimming Pool
Chimney
Barrett Recn Gd
Lisle Marsden CE Prim Sch
St Hugh's
Wintringham Sec Sch
Liby
Grimsby Maternity
E4
1 WEELSBY GR
2 PORTLAND MANOR
3 OAK AVE
4 RUDHAM AVE
Sports Ground
St Marys RC High Sch
Chy
Scartho Road Cemetery
Crematorium
Diana Princess of Wales
SCARTHO ROAD
DN32
Woodlands Prim Sch
AMCOTTS RD
Grimsby
D3
1 RUPERT RD
2 ROOKERY AVE
3 LYNDHURST AVE
4 MELBOURNE AVE
1 ANTRIM WAY
2 ULSTER AVE
3 EDGE AVE
DN33
Scartho Jun & Inf Sch
A16
Scartho
DN36
1 SUNNY CORNER
2 GATE LA
Scartho Library
Grimsby Rugby Union FC
Mast
Springfield Sports Gd
LOUTH ROAD A1243
B1203
1 BECKHYTHE CL
2 CHESTER GRANGE
8
7
09
6
5
08
4
3
07
2
1
06
25
26
27
A
B
C
D
E
F
A3
1 BELTON GR
2 BONBY GR
3 MARTON GR
4 EASTVILLE RD
5 THORESWAY GR
6 RAITHBY GR
B2
1 BELGRAVE RD
2 BUCKINGHAM GR
3 FREYJA CFT
4 UTGARD WY
5 FULHAM PK
6 MARYLEBONE WK
7 HAMPSTEAD PK
8 WATERLOO DR
9 FINSBURY DR
10 EASON RD
35
B3
1 DAME KENDAL GR
2 TORKSEY PL
3 AYLESBY GDNS
4 ELSHAM GR
5 TEALBY GR
6 CHELWOOD DR
7 FULSTOW GR
8 HATCLIFFE CL
9 HATTON GR
10 ROTHWELL AVE
194
25
192
B4
1 CARNARVON AVE
2 STURTON GR
3 WALMSGATE PL
4 RESTON GR
C2
1 BROCK CL
2 BALDER CT
3 HALTON WY
4 FAUCONBERG AVE
C4
1 LEIGHTON GR
2 BYRON GR
3 NEW CL
4 FIRST AVE

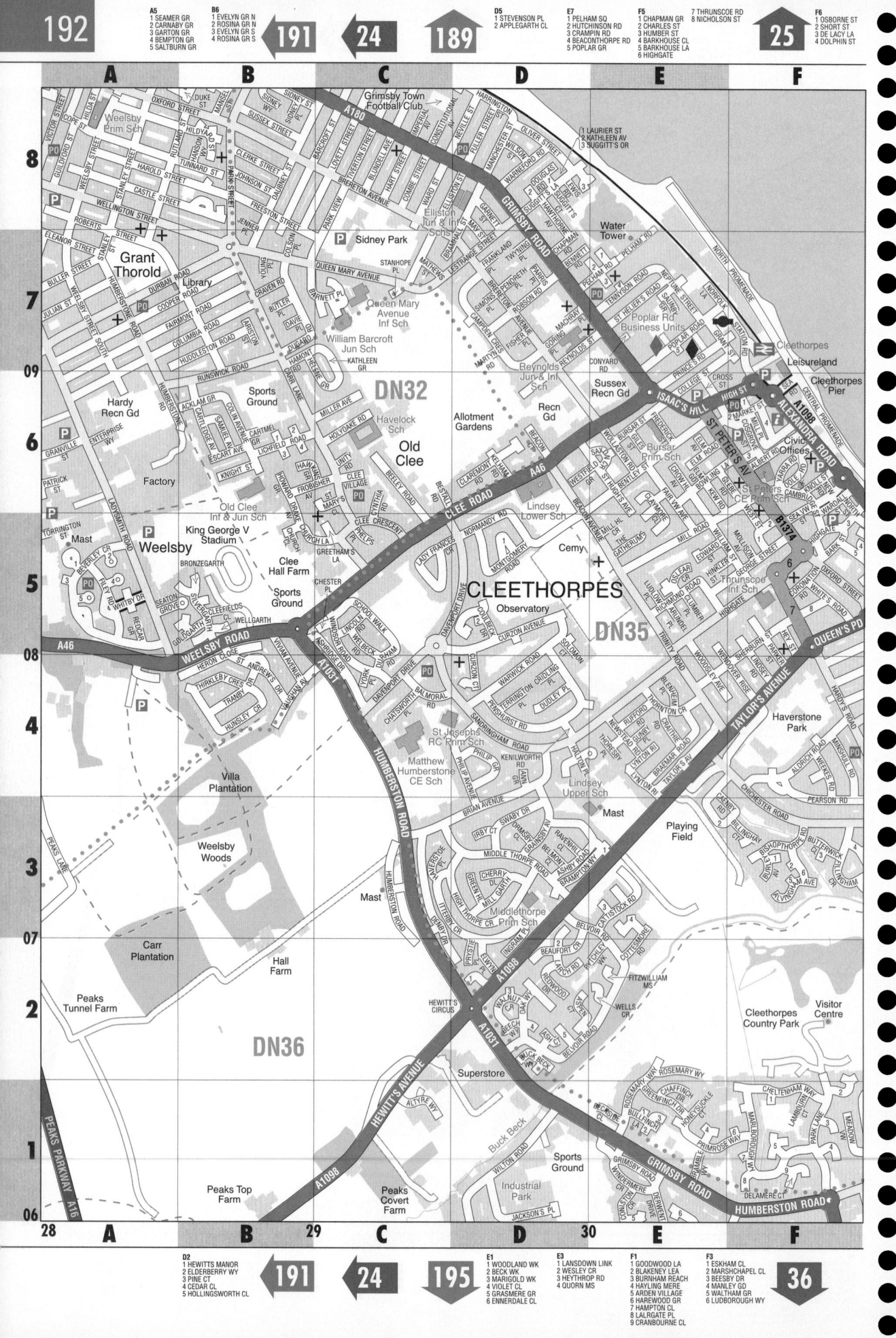
A5
1 SEAMER GR
2 CARNABY GR
3 GARTON GR
4 BEMPTON GR
5 SALTBURN GR
B6
1 EVELYN GR N
2 ROSINA GR N
3 EVELYN GR S
4 ROSINA GR S
191
24
189
D5
1 STEVENSON PL
2 APPLEGARTH CL
E7
1 PELHAM SQ
2 HUTCHINSON RD
3 CRAMPIN RD
4 BEACONTHORPE RD
5 POPLAR GR
F5
1 CHAPMAN GR
2 CHARLES ST
3 HUMBER ST
4 BARKHOUSE CL
5 BARKHOUSE LA
6 HIGHGATE
7 THRUNSCOE RD
8 NICHOLSON ST
25
F6
1 OSBORNE ST
2 SHORT ST
3 DE LACY LA
4 DOLPHIN ST
A B C D E F
8 7 6 5 4 3 2 1
09 08 07 06
Grimsby Town Football Club
Weelsby Prim Sch
Grant Thorold
Library
Sidney Park
Elliston Jun & Inf Schs
Queen Mary Avenue Inf Sch
William Barcroft Jun Sch
Water Tower
Poplar Rd Business Units
Cleethorpes
Leisureland
Cleethorpes Pier
Hardy Recn Gd
Sports Ground
DN32
Havelock Sch
Old Clee
Allotment Gardens
Reynolds Jun & Inf Sch
Sussex Recn Gd
Recn Gd
Bursar Prim Sch
Civic Offices
St Peters CE Prim Sch
Factory
Old Clee Inf & Jun Sch
King George V Stadium
Clee Hall Farm
Lindsey Lower Sch
Cemy
Mast
Weelsby
Sports Ground
CLEETHORPES
Observatory
DN35
Thrunscoe Inf Sch
A46
WEELSBY ROAD
CLEE ROAD
GRIMSBY ROAD
ISAAC'S HILL
ALEXANDRA ROAD
A1098
A180
A1031
B1374
TAYLOR'S AVENUE
HUMBERSTON ROAD
QUEEN'S PD
St Josephs RC Prim Sch
Matthew Humberstone CE Sch
Haverstone Park
Villa Plantation
Lindsey Upper Sch
Mast
Playing Field
Weelsby Woods
Mast
Middlethorpe Prim Sch
Carr Plantation
Hall Farm
Peaks Tunnel Farm
HEWITT'S CIRCUS
Cleethorpes Country Park
Visitor Centre
DN36
Superstore
HEWITT'S AVENUE
Buck Beck
Sports Ground
Industrial Park
Peaks Top Farm
Peaks Covert Farm
PEAKS PARKWAY A16
GRIMSBY ROAD
HUMBERSTON ROAD
28 A B 29 C D 30 E F
D2
1 HEWITTS MANOR
2 ELDERBERRY WY
3 PINE CT
4 CEDAR CL
5 HOLLINGSWORTH CL
191
24
195
E1
1 WOODLAND WK
2 BECK WK
3 MARIGOLD WK
4 VIOLET CL
5 GRASMERE GR
6 ENNERDALE CL
E3
1 LANSDOWN LINK
2 WESLEY CR
3 HEYTHROP RD
4 QUORN MS
F1
1 GOODWOOD LA
2 BLAKENEY LEA
3 BURNHAM REACH
4 HAYLING MERE
5 ARDEN VILLAGE
6 HAREWOOD GR
7 HAMPTON CL
8 LALRGATE PL
9 CRANBOURNE CL
F3
1 ESKHAM CL
2 MARSHCHAPEL CL
3 BEESBY DR
4 MANLEY GD
5 WALTHAM GR
6 LUDBOROUGH WY
36

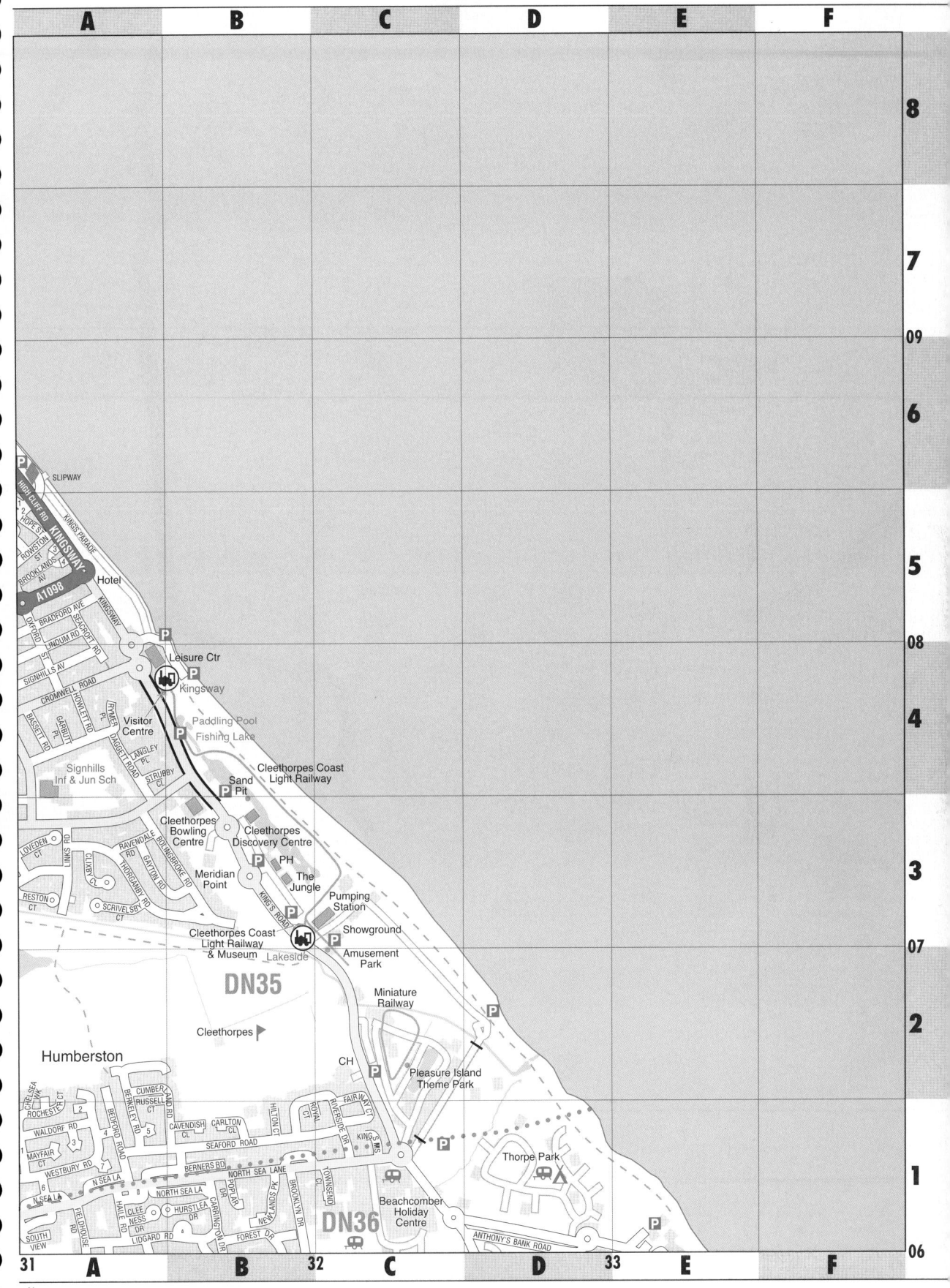

A5
1 SOUTH ST
2 BRIGHTON ST
3 SEGMERE ST
4 HAIGH ST

A1
1 WESTPORT RD
2 WESTBURY PK
3 FAIRFIELD CT
4 WEYFORD RD
5 GROVENOR CT
6 WHITEHALL RD
7 KINGSTON CL

190
35
C5
1 CORAL DR
2 PEACE HAVEN
3 CARDINAL CT
4 ALBERTINE CT
5 FOUNTAIN CL
6 SWEET BRIAR CL
7 WHEATFIELD DR
8 FRANCES CT
9 WRAY CL
D8
1 BAYSWATER PL
2 WELL VALE
3 MAYFIELD CL
4 CORNFIELD CL
5 SAGEFIELD CL
191
E7
1 CONISTON AV
2 FLEETWOOD CL
3 BARBARA CL
4 WINDERMERE AV
5 ORCHARD CFT
6 HEATHERDALE CL
E8
1 TONBRIDGE
2 GRAMPIAN WY
3 CHILTERN WY
4 LANCING WY
5 PURBECK RD
6 DOVEDALE DR
F8
1 GORDON GD
2 COLLEGE GD
3 LINDSEY RI
4 HAWTHORNE AV
5 LINWOOD AV
6 WESTBOURNE GR
Nature Reserve
Bradley Wood
Dixons Wood
Springfield Sports Gd
Fairfield Prim Sch
Scartho
DN33
Springfield Prim Sch
Netherwood Dairy
Bradley Gairs
Netherwood Farm
Grove Farm
BRADLEY ROAD
WALTHAM ROAD
GRIMSBY ROAD
B1203
A1243
B1219
DN36
DN37
Waltham
Corner Farm
The Leas Jun & Inf Sch
HIGH STREET
Recreation Ground
Cemetery
Poplar Farm
Grange Farm
Waltham Windmill
Waltham Museum of Rural Life
BRIGSLEY ROAD
Norman Corner
Mushroom Farm
Brigsley Top Farm
Mast
CHEAPSIDE
CH
Brigsley
TOTNES RD 1
DAWLISH RD 2
BRIXHAM CT 3
PAIGNTON CT 4
MEADOW CFT 1
NORSEFIELD AV 2
SUMMERFIELD CL 3
DOUGHTY CL 4
DOROTHY AV 5
24
25
26
C4
1 DRURY CL
2 HARVEST CR
3 BARKWORTH CT
4 OLD FARM CT
5 LINDRICK WK
6 ASHBOURNE
7 CARNOUSTIE
8 SUNNINGDALE
9 BIRKDALE
10 GLENEAGLES
11 MUIRFIELD
12 MAYFAIR CR
13 CHESTNUT CL
35
D4
1 NEVILLE TURNER WY
2 LUDGATE CL
3 ORCHARD CT
4 PEAR TREE CL
5 ASCOT RD
6 KIRKSIDE
7 LABURNHAM CL
8 SALISBURY DR
9 COTSWOLD DR
E4
1 HIGH ST
2 CHURCH VW
3 CROSS ST
4 CHEESEMANS CL
5 MILL VW
6 ATKINSON LA

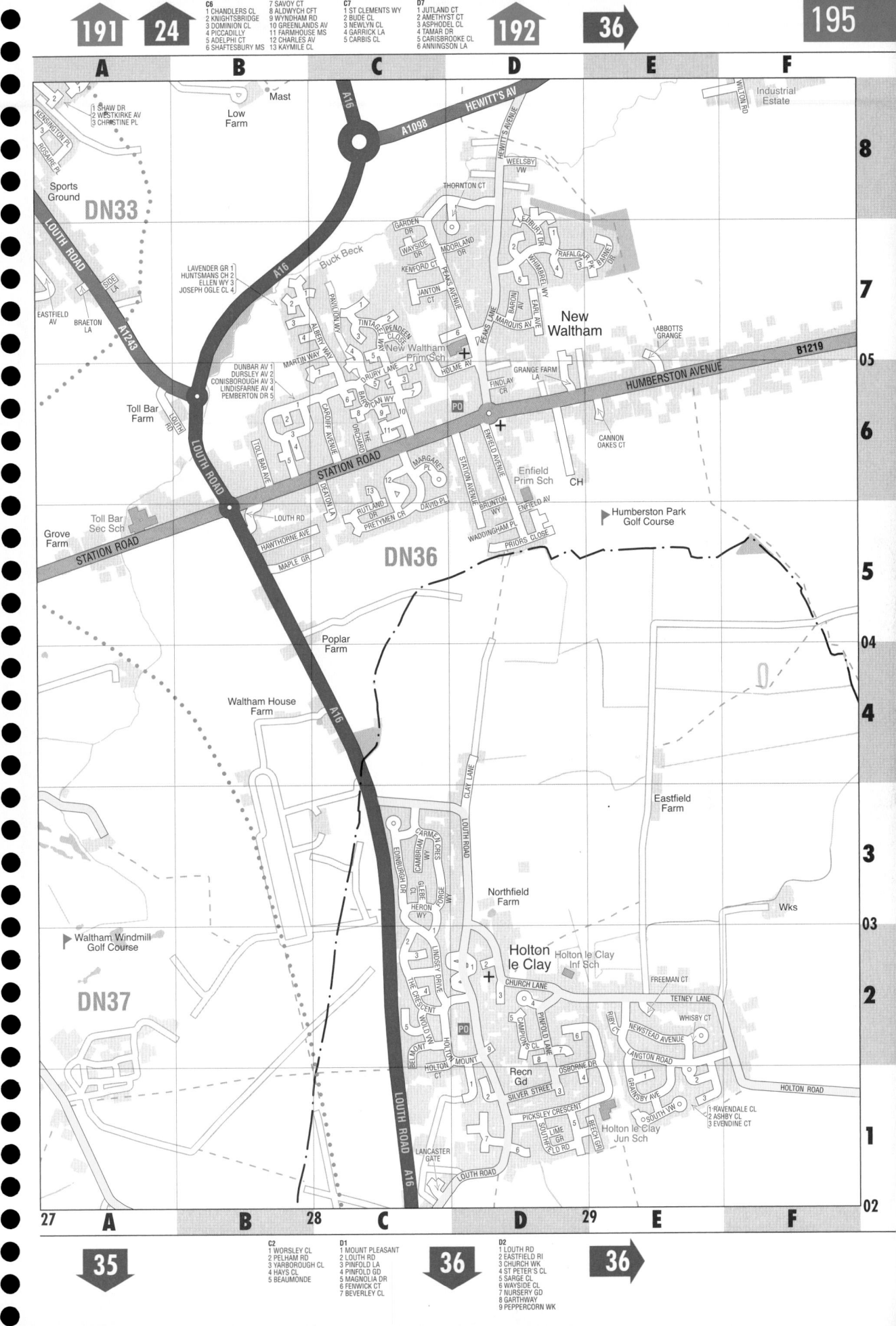

C6
1 CHANDLERS CL
2 KNIGHTSBRIDGE
3 DOMINION CL
4 PICCADILLY
5 ADELPHI CT
6 SHAFTESBURY MS

7 SAVOY CT
8 ALDWYCH CFT
9 WYNDHAM RD
10 GREENLANDS AV
11 FARMHOUSE MS
12 CHARLES AV
13 KAYMILE CL

C7
1 ST CLEMENTS WY
2 BUDE CL
3 NEWLYN CL
4 GARRICK LA
5 CARBIS CL

D7
1 JUTLAND CT
2 AMETHYST CT
3 ASPHODEL CL
4 TAMAR DR
5 CARISBROOKE CL
6 ANNINGSON LA

A B C D E F

8

Industrial Estate

WILTON RD

HEWITT'S AV

A1098

HEWITT'S AVENUE

Sports Ground

DN33

WEELSBY VW

Mast

Low Farm

A16

THORNTON CT

7

KENSINGTON PL

1 SHAW DR
2 WESTKIRKE AV
3 CHRISTINE PL

ROSMIE PL

Buck Beck

GARDEN DR

MOORLAND DR

DIDBURY DR

WHIMBREL WY

TRAFALGAR PK

BARNET DR

New Waltham

B1219

05

SIDE LA

EASTFIELD AV

BRAETON LA

A243

LAVENDER GR 1
HUNTSMANS CH 2
ELLEN WY 3
JOSEPH OGLE CL 4

PAVILION WY

ALBERT WAY

TINTAGEL

PENDEN CLOSE

KENFORD CT

JANTON CT

PEAKS AVENUE

BARON

EARL AV

MARQUIS AV

ABBOTTS GRANGE

HUMBERSTON AVENUE

Toll Bar Farm

LOUTH RD

DUNBAR AV 1
DURSLEY AV 2
CONISBOROUGH AV 3
LINDISFARNE AV 4
PEMBERTON DR 5

MARTIN WAY

DRURY LANE

New Waltham PrimSch

HOLME AV

GRANGE FARM LA

6

LOUTH ROAD

TOLL BAR AV

CARDIFF AVENUE

THE ORCHARD

BARCLAY WY

CAN WY

10

FINDLAY CR

PO

Enfield Prim Sch

CANNON OAKES CT

CH

Toll Bar Sec Sch

STATION ROAD

11

MARGARET PL

ENFIELD AVENUE

STATION AVENUE

Humberston Park Golf Course

Grove Farm

LOUTH RD

DEATON LA

RUTLAND DR

PRETYMEN CR

DAVID PL

12

13

BRUNTON WY

ENFIELD AV

STATION ROAD

HAWTHORNE AVE

WADDINGHAM PL

PRIORS CLOSE

DN36

MAPLE GR

5

Poplar Farm

04

Waltham House Farm

A16

4

Eastfield Farm

CLAY LANE

3

Waltham Windmill Golf Course

LOUTH ROAD

EDINBURGH DR

CAMBRIAN AV

GLEBE AV

CARMEN CRES

HERON WY

Northfield Farm

Wks

03

DN37

LINDSEY DRIVE

THE CRESCENT

WILLOW DR

Holton le Clay

Holton le Clay Inf Sch

FREEMAN CT

TETNEY LANE

WHISBY CT

2

CHURCH LANE

RUBY CL

NEWSTEAD AVENUE

BELMONT

HOLTON MOUNT

PINFOLD LANE

OSBORNE DR

GRAINSBY AVE

LANGTON ROAD

PO

CAMPION

Recn Gd

SILVER STREET

PICKSLEY CRESCENT

SOUTH VW

HOLTON ROAD

1

LIME GR

OLD RD

BEECH CL

SOUTH

Holton le Clay Jun Sch

1 RAVENDALE CL
2 ASHBY CL
3 EVENDINE CT

LANCASTER GATE

LOUTH ROAD

A16

02

27 A B 28 C D 29 E F

C2
1 WORSLEY CL
2 PELHAM RD
3 YARBOROUGH CL
4 HAYS CL
5 BEAUMONDE

D1
1 MOUNT PLEASANT
2 LOUTH RD
3 PINFOLD LA
4 PINFOLD GD
5 MAGNOLIA DR
6 FENWICK CT
7 BEVERLEY CL

D2
1 LOUTH RD
2 EASTFIELD RI
3 CHURCH WK
4 ST PETER'S CL
5 SARGE CL
6 WAYSIDE CL
7 NURSERY GD
8 GARTHWAY
9 PEPPERCORN WK

F6
1 FRANKLAND CL
2 VICARAGE AV
3 DOVECOTE MS

F7
1 GILLATTS CL
2 MARKHAM WY
3 ECCLES CT
4 CHAPEL LA

M180

B1206

Star Carr Lane

Wrawby
Farm

Three Tree
Farm

Star Carr Lane

Star Carr Lane

BARTON ROAD

BAKERSFIELD

TUNNEL ROAD

OLD MILL
LA

Wrawby

Wrawby
Carrs

Low
Farm

College
Farm

Carr
Farm

GRAMMAR SCHOOL LANE

Ashdale
Farm

Ivy House
Farm

BRICKYARD LANE

B1206

A18 BRIGG ROAD

HIGHFIELD RD

Manor
Farm

DN20

M180

Tongs
Farm

Barton Road
End

WESTERN AVE
NORTHERN AVE
ATKINSON AVE
POPLAR DR
HORSTEAD AVE

St Marys RC
Prim Sch

SUNNINGDALE AVE
DAVY CR
HIGHFIELD DRIVE

SPRINGBANK

SOUTH VIEW AVE

Recn Gd
Playing Field

St
Helens

Vale of
Ancholme Sch

Recreation
Ground

EUROPA WAY

Ancholme
Business Park

ATHERTON WAY

POPPYFIELD WY
FOXGLOVE CL

PRESTON DR
AVE

HAWTHORN

Brigg
Prim Sch

EAST
PARADE

Football
Gd

WOODBINE AV

WRAWBY ROAD

CHURCHILL AVENUE

BRIGG

Sewage
Works

REDCOMBE LANE
ELM WY

GRAMMAR SCHOOL ROAD

ASH GROVE

WESLEY

DIXON
CL

GLEBE ROAD

COLTON ST

Swimming
Pool

Sir John Nelthorpe
Sch

NICOLGATE
LA

Cemy

YORK ROAD

BIRCH AVE

BARNARD AVENUE

Mast

ANCHOLME WY

SPRINGS
WY

Liby

WRAWBY ST

DUDLEY

Clerk to
the Justices

EASTFIELD RD

ST JAMES RD

HARBOROUGH RD

KENNEDY
CL

O HANLON AVE

BURGESS RD

P

CARY

Glanford Road

St Helen's Road

KING'S AVENUE

MAPLE CL

WILLOWBROOK

KILN
LA

WATERS EDGE

ISLAND CARR RD

BRIDGE ST

ELWES
ST

JAMES ST

ST CLARES WK

BIGBY STREET

WRAWBY ST

A18

BIGBY ROAD

PRINCES ST

ALBERT STREET

BIGBY HIGH ROAD

A1084

Anchorholme
L Ctr

ENGINE
ST

WEST
TR

MANLEY GARDENS

ELWES STREET

Brigg
Pre Sch

LC

TENNYSON
CL

BIGBY HIGH

PINGLEY LANE

THE COPSE

Garden
Centre

SCAWBY ROAD

A18

BRIDGE STREET

MILL LANE

Brigg

WESTRUM LANE

Pingley
MD

Pingley
Farm

SILVERSIDES LA

Sports
Gd

RIVER
MEADOW

NEW RIVER ANCHOLME

Island
Carr

Windmill

Westrum

CAUNEY ROAD

Island
Carr Farm

Bentley
Farm

Chy Chy Chy

A3
1 THEMOORINGS
2 RIVERSIDE
3 THE NARROW BOATS
4 TEAL CL
5 MILL CL
6 MILLERS QUAY
7 ANCHORS WY

B3
1 FORRESTER ST
2 MARKET PL
3 CARY LA
4 ANCHORAGE ST
5 EXCHANGE PL
6 PARADISE PL

B4
1 BRAMBLE WY
2 KINGSWAY
3 CHERRY TREE AV

C3
1 MAGRATH CT
2 OLD COURTS RD
3 GRAMMAR SCHOOL RD
4 CROSS ST
5 GD ST
6 QUEEN ST
7 BIGBY RD
8 NEW ST
9 THE BOTTLINGS

10 ANCHOLME GD

D3
1 HEDGEROW LA
2 SPRINGFIELD RD

D4
1 WOLD VW
2 RIDGE VW
3 KETTLEBY VW
4 WELLBECOTE CL
5 WINSTON WY
6 CHAPEL WY

E3
1 SPRINGFIELD RI
2 OAKFIELD CL
3 ASHDOWN CL

MARGATE CLOSE

A159 – MANY NAMES

FRONT ST

QUEEN E HIGH SCH

VENESSA DR.

SPITAL HILL   B1433

NORTHOLME

SPITAL

TRAIN T.

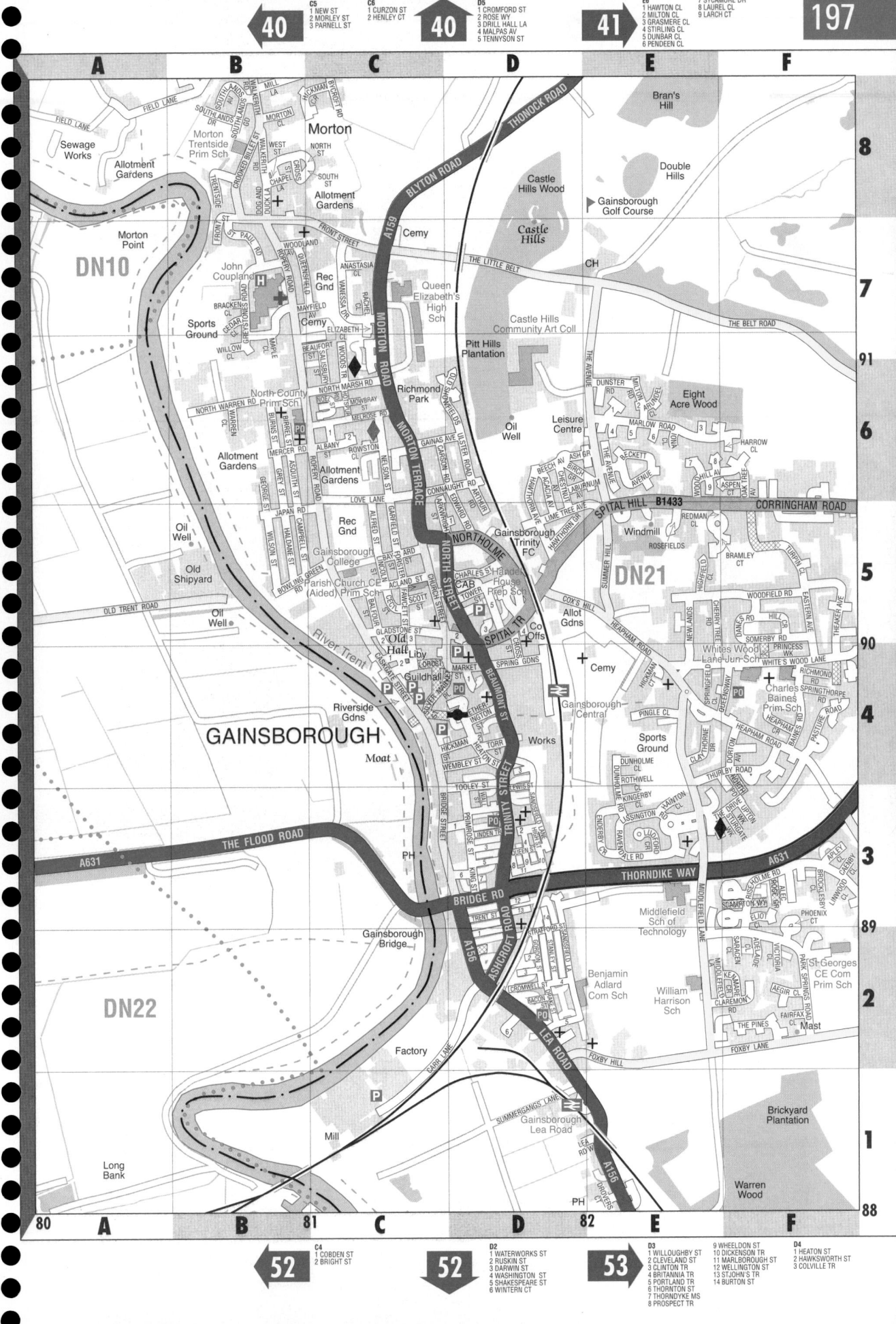

197
40
C5
1 NEW ST
2 MORLEY ST
3 PARNELL ST
C6
1 CURZON ST
2 HENLEY CT
40
D5
1 CROMFORD ST
2 ROSE WY
3 DRILL HALL LA
4 MALPAS AV
5 TENNYSON ST
41
E6
1 HAWTON CL
2 MILTON CL
3 GRASMERE CL
4 STIRLING CL
5 DUNBAR CL
6 PENDEEN CL
7 SYCAMORE DR
8 LAUREL CL
9 LARCH CT
A
B
C
D
E
F
8
7
91
6
5
90
4
3
89
2
1
88
80
81
82
Morton
Sewage Works
Allotment Gardens
Morton Trentside Prim Sch
FIELD LANE
THONOCK ROAD
BLYTON ROAD
A159
Bran's Hill
Double Hills
Castle Hills Wood
Castle Hills
Gainsborough Golf Course
Morton Point
DN10
FRONT STREET
Cemy
THE LITTLE BELT
CH
John Coupland
Rec Gnd
Queen Elizabeth's High Sch
MORTON ROAD
Sports Ground
Castle Hills Community Art Coll
Pitt Hills Plantation
THE BELT ROAD
THE AVENUE
Richmond Park
North County Prim Sch
NORTH WARREN RD
Oil Well
Leisure Centre
Eight Acre Wood
MARLOW ROAD
HARROW CL
Allotment Gardens
MORTON TERRACE
LOVE LANE
SPITAL HILL
B1433
CORRINGHAM ROAD
Windmill
ROSEFIELDS
Gainsborough Trinity FC
NORTHOLME
NORTH STREET
Oil Well
Old Shipyard
Gainsborough College
Parish Church CE (Aided) Prim Sch
DN21
WOODFIELD RD
OLD TRENT ROAD
Oil Well
CAB
Handel House Prep Sch
SPITAL TR
Co Offs
COX'S HILL
Allot Gdns
HEAPHAM ROAD
River Trent
Old Hall
Liby
Guildhall
Cemy
Whites Wood Lane Jun Sch
WHITE'S WOOD LANE
Charles Baines Prim Sch
Riverside Gdns
BEAUMONT ST
Gainsborough Central
PINGLE CL
GAINSBOROUGH
Works
Sports Ground
Moat
TRINITY STREET
THURLBY ROAD
BRIDGE STREET
THE FLOOD ROAD
A631
PH
THORNDIKE WAY
A631
BRIDGE RD
MIDDLEFIELD LANE
Middlefield Sch of Technology
Gainsborough Bridge
ASHCROFT ROAD
A156
DN22
Benjamin Adlard Com Sch
William Harrison Sch
St Georges CE Com Prim Sch
LEA ROAD
Mast
Factory
CARR LANE
FOXBY HILL
FOXBY LANE
SUMMERGANGS LANE
Gainsborough Lea Road
Brickyard Plantation
Mill
Long Bank
A156
Warren Wood
PH
52
C4
1 COBDEN ST
2 BRIGHT ST
52
D2
1 WATERWORKS ST
2 RUSKIN ST
3 DARWIN ST
4 WASHINGTON ST
5 SHAKESPEARE ST
6 WINTERN CT
53
D3
1 WILLOUGHBY ST
2 CLEVELAND ST
3 CLINTON TR
4 BRITANNIA TR
5 PORTLAND TR
6 THORNTON ST
7 THORNDYKE MS
8 PROSPECT TR
9 WHEELDON ST
10 DICKENSON TR
11 MARLBOROUGH ST
12 WELLINGTON ST
13 STJOHN'S TR
14 BURTON ST
D4
1 HEATON ST
2 HAWKSWORTH ST
3 COLVILLE TR

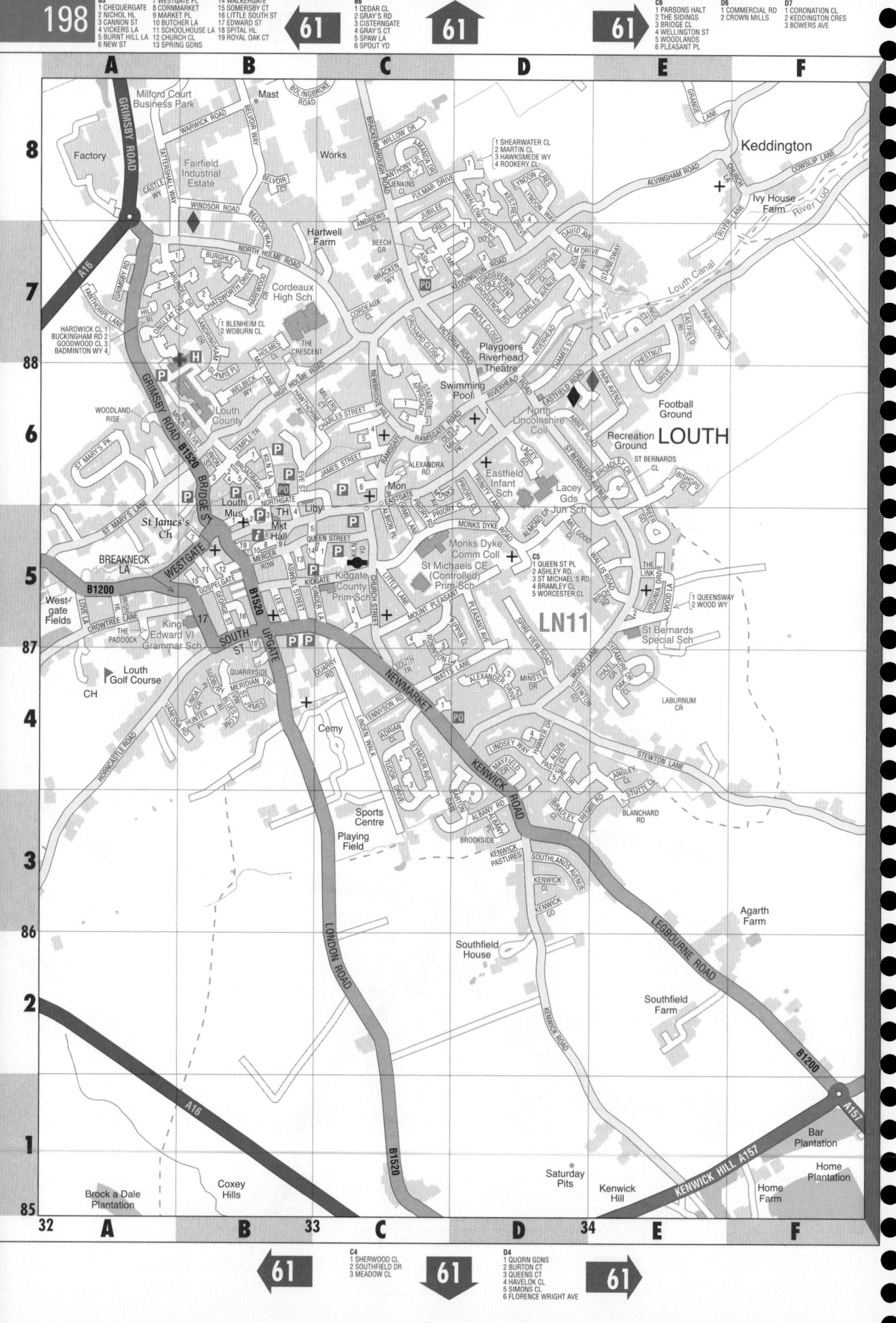

B5
1 CHEQUERGATE
2 NICHOL HL
3 CANNON ST
4 VICKERS LA
5 BURNT HILL LA
6 NEW ST

7 WESTGATE PL
8 CORNMARKET
9 MARKET PL
10 BUTCHER LA
11 SCHOOLHOUSE LA
12 CHURCH CL
13 SPRING GDNS

14 WALKERGATE
15 SOMERSGATE
16 LITTLE SOUTH ST
17 EDWARD ST
18 SPITAL HL
19 ROYAL OAK CT

B6
1 CEDAR CL
2 GRAY'S RD
3 CISTERNGATE
4 GRAY'S CT
5 SPAW LA
6 SPOUT YD

C6
1 PARSONS HALT
2 THE SIDINGS
3 BRIDGE CL
4 WELLINGTON ST
5 WOODLANDS
6 PLEASANT PL

D6
1 COMMERCIAL RD
2 CROWN MILLS

D7
1 CORONATION CL
2 KEDDINGTON CRES
3 BOWERS AVE

C4
1 SHERWOOD CL
2 SOUTHFIELD DR
3 MEADOW CL

D4
1 QUORN GDNS
2 BURTON CT
3 QUEENS CT
4 HAVELOK CL
5 SIMONS CL
6 FLORENCE WRIGHT AVE

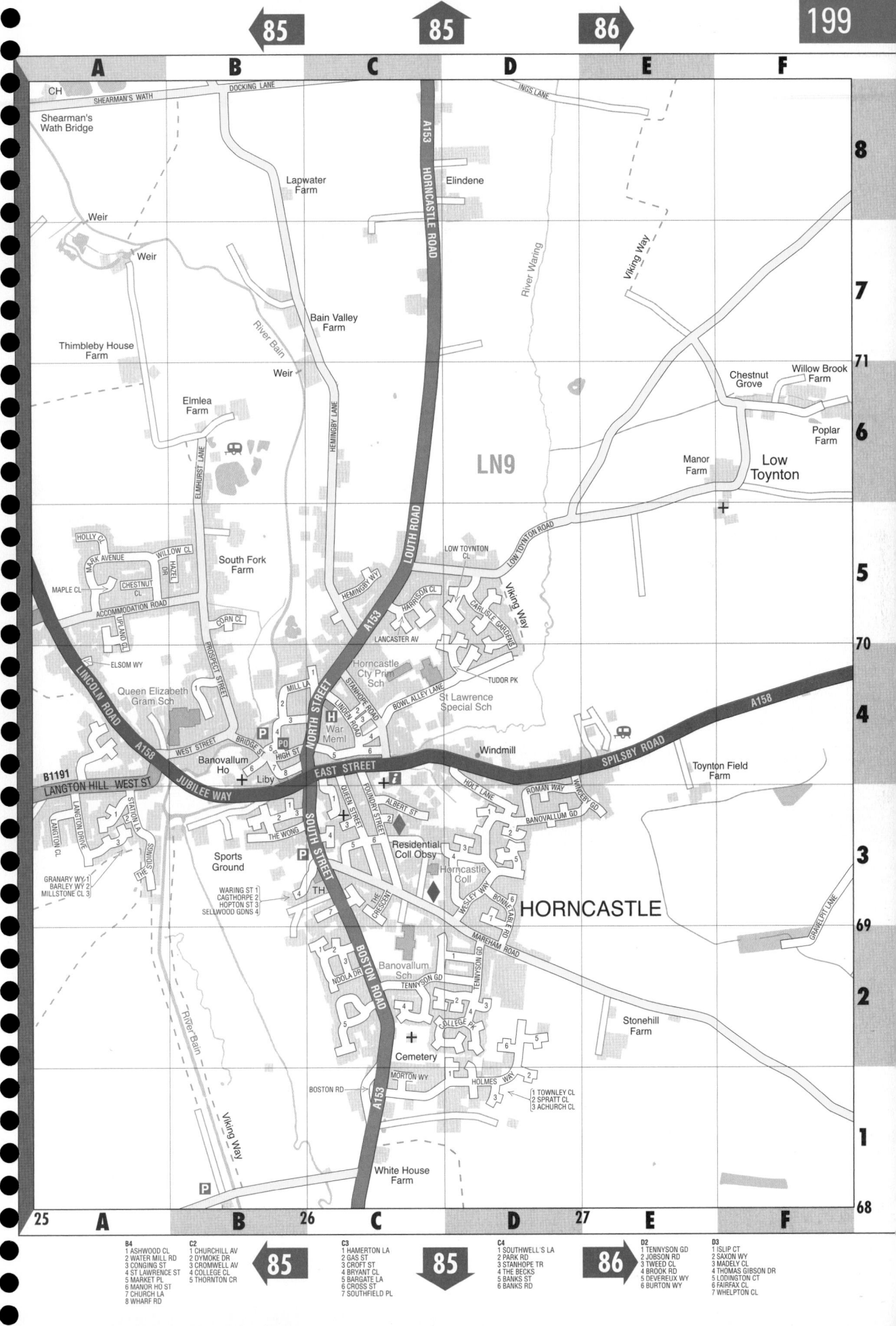

B4
1 ASHWOOD CL
2 WATER MILL RD
3 CONGING ST
4 ST LAWRENCE ST
5 MARKET PL
6 MANOR HO ST
7 CHURCH LA
8 WHARF RD

C2
1 CHURCHILL AV
2 DYMOKE DR
3 CROMWELL AV
4 COLLEGE CL
5 THORNTON CR

C3
1 HAMERTON LA
2 GAS ST
3 CROFT ST
4 BRYANT CL
5 BARGATE LA
6 CROSS ST
7 SOUTHFIELD PL

C4
1 SOUTHWELL'S LA
2 PARK RD
3 STANHOPE TR
4 THE BECKS
5 BANKS ST
6 BANKS RD

D2
1 TENNYSON GD
2 JOBSON RD
3 TWEED CL
4 BROOK RD
5 DEVEREUX WY
6 BURTON WY

D3
1 ISLIP CT
2 SAXON WY
3 MADELY CL
4 THOMAS GIBSON DR
5 LODINGTON CT
6 FAIRFAX CL
7 WHELPTON CL

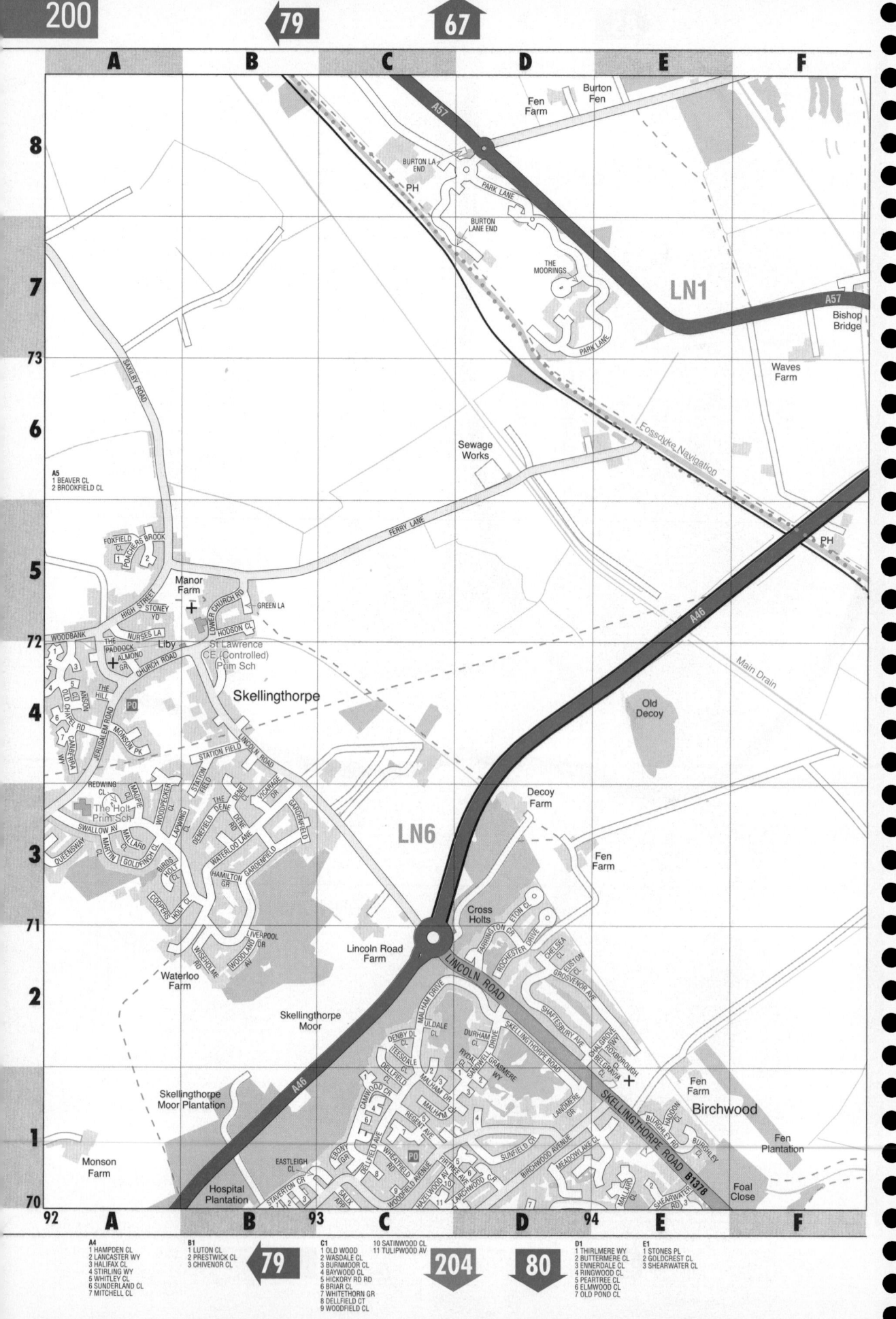

79
67

LN1

A57

Bishop Bridge

Waves Farm

Fen Farm

Burton Fen

PH

BURTON LA END

Park Lane

Burton Lane End

THE MOORINGS

Park Lane

Fossdyke Navigation

Sewage Works

Ferry Lane

A46

Main Drain

Old Decoy

A5
1 BEAVER CL
2 BROOKFIELD CL

FOXFIELD CL

POACHERS BROOK

Manor Farm

GREEN LA

HIGH STREET

STONEY YD

LOWER CHURCH RD

HODSON CL

CHURCH RD

WOODBANK

THE PADDOCK

NURSES LA

Liby

ALMOND GR

St Lawrence CE (Controlled) Prim Sch

SAXILBY ROAD

THE HILL

ANSON CL

OLD CHAPEL RD

JERUSALEM ROAD

MONSON PK

CARRER RD

CHURCH ROAD

Skellingthorpe

PO

STATION FIELD

LINCOLN ROAD

REDWING CL

The Holt Prim Sch

SWALLOW AV

QUEENSWAY

MARTIN

MALLARD

GOLDFINCH CL

MAGPIE

WOODPECKER CL

LAPWING CL

STATION FIELD

OERNFIELD

THE DENE

DENE DENE

VICARAGE DR

GARDENFIELD

GARDENFIELD

BIRDS HOLT

COOPERS HOLT CL

HAMILTON GR

WATERLOO LANE

LIVERPOOL RD

WISEHOLME

WOODLAND DR

AV

LN6

Decoy Farm

Cross Holts

Fen Farm

Waterloo Farm

Lincoln Road Farm

Skellingthorpe Moor

A46

Skellingthorpe Moor Plantation

Monson Farm

Hospital Plantation

EASTLEIGH CL

STAVERTON CR

SALIX APP

ELDON GR

DELLFIELD AVE

WHEATFIELD RD

REGENT AVE

CAMION CL

CAMION CL

WOODFIELD AVENUE

MALHAM

A46

PO

MALHAM DRIVE

ULDALE CL

DENBY DL

TEESDALE

DELLFIELD

RYDAL CL

DURHAM CL

GRASMERE WY

DOWNELL DRIVE

SKELLINGTHORPE ROAD

LINCOLN ROAD

FARRINGTON GR

ROCHESTER DRIVE

ETON CL

CHELSEA CL

ELSTON

GROSVENOR AVE

SHAFTESBURY AVE

MALGROVE WY

BOXBOROUGH

BELGRAVIA

LANTIMERE GR

LANGWOOD

HAZELWOOD AV

FIRTREE AV

SUNFIELD GR

BIRCHWOOD AVENUE

MEADOWLANE CL

LARCHWOOD

BURGHLEY

HADDON CL

MALLARD

Fen Farm

Birchwood

B1378

SKELLINGTHORPE ROAD

SHEARWATER RD

Foal Close

Fen Plantation

79
204
80

A4
1 HAMPDEN CL
2 LANCASTER WY
3 HALIFAX CL
4 STIRLING WY
5 WHITLEY CL
6 SUNDERLAND CL
7 MITCHELL CL

B1
1 LUTON CL
2 PRESTWICK CL
3 CHIVENOR CL

C1
1 OLD WOOD
2 WASDALE CL
3 BURNMOOR CL
4 BAYWOOD CL
5 HICKORY RD RD
6 BRIAR CL
7 WHITETHORN GR
8 DELLFIELD CT
9 WOODFIELD CL

10 SATINWOOD CL
11 TULIPWOOD AV

D1
1 THIRLMERE WY
2 BUTTERMERE CL
3 ENNERDALE CL
4 RINGWOOD CL
5 PEARTREE CL
6 ELMWOOD CL
7 OLD POND CL

E1
1 STONES PL
2 GOLDCREST CL
3 SHEARWATER CL

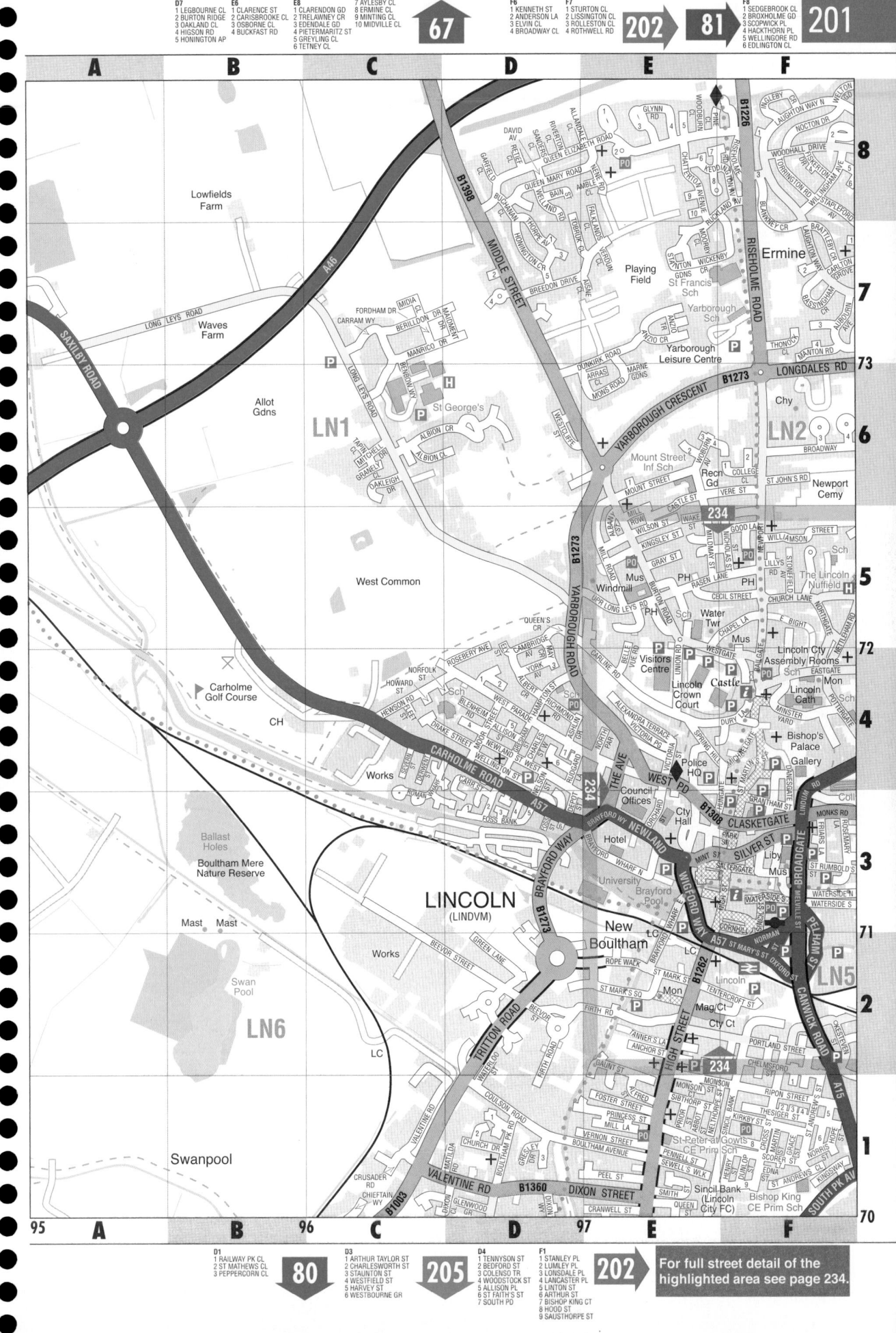
D7
1 LEGBOURNE CL
2 BURTON RIDGE
3 OAKLAND CL
4 HIGSON RD
5 HONINGTON AP
E6
1 CLARENCE ST
2 CARISBROOKE CL
3 OSBORNE CL
4 BUCKFAST RD
E8
1 CLARENDON GD
2 TRELAWNEY CR
3 EDENDALE GD
4 PIETERMARITZ ST
5 GREYLING CL
6 TETNEY CL
7 AYLESBY CL
8 ERMINE CL
9 MINTING CL
10 MIDVILLE CL
67
F6
1 KENNETH ST
2 ANDERSON LA
3 ELVIN CL
4 BROADWAY CL
F7
1 STURTON CL
2 LISSINGTON CL
3 ROLLESTON CL
4 ROTHWELL RD
202
81
F8
1 SEDGEBROOK CL
2 BROXHOLME GD
3 SCOPWICK PL
4 HACKTHORN PL
5 WELLINGORE RD
6 EDLINGTON CL
A B C D E F
Lowfields Farm
Waves Farm
LONG LEYS ROAD
SAXILBY ROAD
A46
Allot Gdns
LN1
St George's
West Common
MIDDLE STREET
B1398
Playing Field
St Francis Sch
Yarborough Sch
Yarborough Leisure Centre
Ermine
RISEHOLME ROAD
B1226
YARBOROUGH CRESCENT
B1273
LONGDALES RD
LN2
Mount Street Inf Sch
Recn Gd
Newport Cemy
234
Windmill
Mus
Water Twr
The Lincoln Nuffield
YARBOROUGH ROAD
Visitors Centre
Lincoln Crown Court
Castle
Lincoln Cty Assembly Rooms
Lincoln Cath
Bishop's Palace
Gallery
Police HQ
Council Offices
Cty Hall
CLASKETGATE
Carholme Golf Course
CH
Works
CARHOLME ROAD
A57
BRAYFORD WAY
NEWLAND
Hotel
University
Brayford Pool
SILVER ST
BROADGATE
Liby
Mus
Ballast Holes
Boultham Mere Nature Reserve
Mast
Mast
LINCOLN
(LINDVM)
New Boultham
WIGFORD WAY
B1262
PELHAM ST
LN5
Lincoln
Works
Swan Pool
LN6
TRITTON ROAD
HIGH STREET
Mag Ct
Cty Ct
CANWICK ROAD
A15
LC
Swanpool
VALENTINE RD
B1360
DIXON STREET
B1003
St Peter at Gowts CE Prim Sch
Sincil Bank (Lincoln City FC)
Bishop King CE Prim Sch
SOUTH PK AV
8
7
73
6
5
72
4
3
71
2
1
70
95
96
97
A B C D E F
D1
1 RAILWAY PK CL
2 ST MATHEWS CL
3 PEPPERCORN CL
80
D3
1 ARTHUR TAYLOR ST
2 CHARLESWORTH ST
3 STAUNTON ST
4 WESTFIELD ST
5 HARVEY ST
6 WESTBOURNE GR
205
D4
1 TENNYSON ST
2 BEDFORD ST
3 COLENSO TR
4 WOODSTOCK ST
5 ALLISON PL
6 ST FAITH'S ST
7 SOUTH PD
F1
1 STANLEY PL
2 LUMLEY PL
3 LONSDALE PL
4 LANCASTER PL
5 LINTON ST
6 ARTHUR ST
7 BISHOP KING CT
8 HOOD ST
9 SAUSTHORPE ST
202
For full street detail of the highlighted area see page 234.

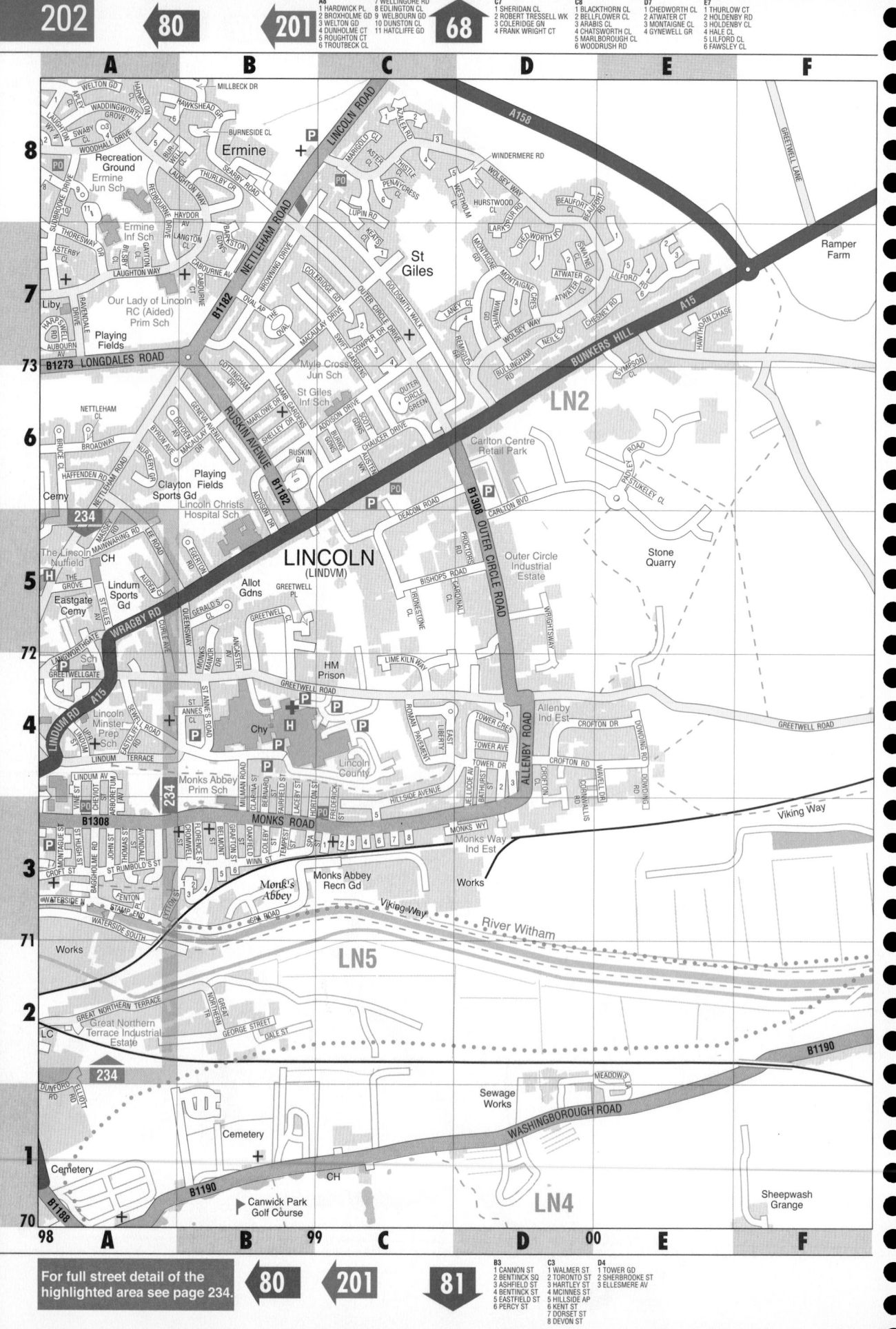

202
80
201
68
A8
1 HARDWICK PL
2 BROXHOLME GD
3 WELTON GD
4 DUNHOLME CT
5 ROUGHTON CT
6 TROUTBECK CL
7 WELLINGORE RD
8 EDLINGTON CL
9 WELBOURN GD
10 DUNSTON CL
11 HATCLIFFE GD
C7
1 SHERIDAN CL
2 ROBERT TRESSELL WK
3 COLERIDGE GN
4 FRANK WRIGHT CT
C8
1 BLACKTHORN CL
2 BELLFLOWER CL
3 ARABIS CL
4 CHATSWORTH CL
5 MARLBOROUGH CL
6 WOODRUSH RD
D7
1 CHEDWORTH CL
2 ATWATER CT
3 MONTAIGNE CL
4 GYNEWELL GR
E7
1 THURLOW CT
2 HOLDENBY RD
3 HOLDENBY CL
4 HALE CL
5 LILFORD CL
6 FAWSLEY CL
A
B
C
D
E
F
8
7
73
6
5
72
4
3
71
2
1
70
98
99
00
Ermine
Recreation Ground
Ermine Jun Sch
Ermine Inf Sch
Our Lady of Lincoln RC (Aided) Prim Sch
Playing Fields
Liby
LONGDALES ROAD
B1273
NETTLEHAM ROAD
B1182
LINCOLN ROAD
A158
St Giles
Myle Cross Jun Sch
St Giles Inf Sch
RUSKIN AVENUE
OUTER CIRCLE ROAD
B1308
BUNKERS HILL
A15
Ramper Farm
LN2
Carlton Centre Retail Park
Clayton Sports Gd
Playing Fields
Lincoln Christs Hospital Sch
Cemy
234
The Lincoln Nuffield
CH
Lindum Sports Gd
Eastgate Cemy
LINCOLN
(LINDVM)
Allot Gdns
Outer Circle Industrial Estate
Stone Quarry
WRAGBY RD
HM Prison
GREETWELL ROAD
Lincoln Minster Prep Sch
Chy
Lincoln County
Allenby Ind Est
ALLENBY ROAD
Monks Abbey Prim Sch
MONKS ROAD
Monks Way Ind Est
Viking Way
Works
Monks Abbey Recn Gd
Monk's Abbey
River Witham
LN5
Works
Great Northern Terrace Industrial Estate
GREAT NORTHERN TERRACE
GEORGE STREET
LC
B1190
Sewage Works
WASHINGBOROUGH ROAD
Cemetery
Cemetery
CH
Canwick Park Golf Course
B1188
LN4
Sheepwash Grange
For full street detail of the highlighted area see page 234.
80
201
81
B3
1 CANNON ST
2 BENTINCK SQ
3 ASHFIELD ST
4 BENTINCK ST
5 EASTFIELD ST
6 PERCY ST
C3
1 WALMER ST
2 TORONTO ST
3 HARTLEY ST
4 MCINNES ST
5 HILLSIDE AP
6 KENT ST
7 DORSET ST
8 DEVON ST
D4
1 TOWER GD
2 SHERBROOKE ST
3 ELLESMERE AV

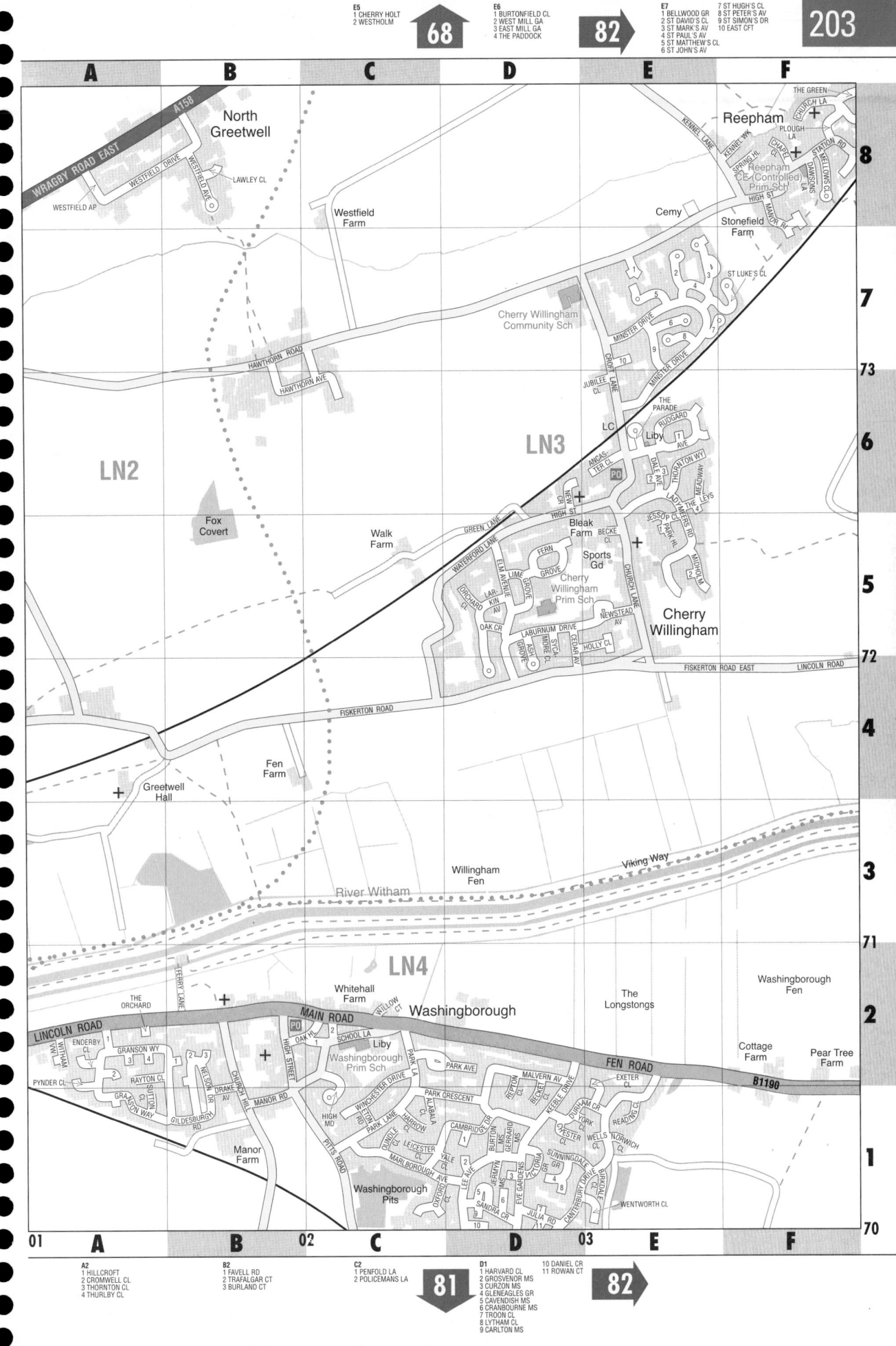

203
E5
1 CHERRY HOLT
2 WESTHOLM
68
E6
1 BURTONFIELD CL
2 WEST MILL GA
3 EAST MILL GA
4 THE PADDOCK
82
E7
1 BELLWOOD GR
2 ST DAVID'S CL
3 ST MARK'S AV
4 ST PAUL'S AV
5 ST MATTHEW'S CL
6 ST JOHN'S AV
7 ST HUGH'S CL
8 ST PETER'S AV
9 ST SIMON'S DR
10 EAST CFT
A
B
C
D
E
F
8
7
73
6
5
72
4
3
71
2
1
70
North Greetwell
A158
WRAGBY ROAD EAST
WESTFIELD DRIVE
WESTFIELD AVE
LAWLEY CL
WESTFIELD AP
Westfield Farm
Reepham
THE GREEN
CHURCH LA
PLOUGH LA
KENNEL LANE
KENNEL WK
SPRING HL
CHAPEL LA
STATION RD
MELLOWS CL
DAWSONS LA
Reepham CE (Controlled) Prim Sch
HIGH ST
MANOR RI
Cemy
Stonefield Farm
ST LUKE'S CL
Cherry Willingham Community Sch
MINSTER DRIVE
CROFT LANE
JUBILEE CL
HAWTHORN ROAD
HAWTHORN AVE
THE PARADE
RUDGARD AVE
LC
Liby
LN3
LN2
ANCASTER CL
PO
DALE AVE
THORNTON WY
MEADWAY
THE LEYS
NEW CR
HIGH ST
LADY MEERS RD
JESSOP CL
PARK HL
Fox Covert
Walk Farm
GREEN LANE
Bleak Farm
BECKE CL
WATERFORD LANE
ELM AVENUE
LIME GROVE
FERN GROVE
Sports Gd
MIDHOLM
Cherry Willingham Prim Sch
ORCHARD CL
LARKIN AV
NEWSTEAD AV
CHURCH LANE
Cherry Willingham
OAK CR
LABURNUM DRIVE
ASH GROVE
SYCAMORE CL
CEDAR AV
HOLLY CL
FISKERTON ROAD EAST
LINCOLN ROAD
FISKERTON ROAD
Fen Farm
Greetwell Hall
Willingham Fen
Viking Way
River Witham
LN4
FERRY LANE
THE ORCHARD
Whitehall Farm
WILLOW CT
Washingborough
The Longstongs
Washingborough Fen
LINCOLN ROAD
MAIN ROAD
PO
OAK HL
SCHOOL LA
Liby
Washingborough Prim Sch
Cottage Farm
Pear Tree Farm
ENDERBY CL
WITHAM VW
GRANSON WY
RAYTON CL
SUTTON CL
NELSON DR
DRAKE AV
CHURCH HILL
HIGH STREET
PARK LA
PARK AVE
MALVERN AV
REPTON CL
BECKET CL
KEBLE DRIVE
EXETER CL
FEN ROAD
B1190
PYNDER CL
GRANSON WAY
GILDESBURGH RD
MANOR RD
WINCHESTER DRIVE
PARK CRESCENT
HIGH MD
NEWTON RD
ALABALA CL
DURHAM CR
YORK CL
READING CL
PARK LANE
HARROW CL
CAMBRIDGE DR
BURTON MS
GERRARD MS
CHESTER CL
WELLS CL
NORWICH CL
DUNDLE CL
LEICESTER CL
YALE CL
VICTORIA GR
SUNNINGDALE GR
Manor Farm
PITTS ROAD
MARLBOROUGH AVE
LEE AVE
JERMYN MS
EVE GARDENS
CANTERBURY DRIVE
BIRKDALE CL
Washingborough Pits
OXFORD CL
SANDRA CR
JULIA RD
WENTWORTH CL
01
02
03
A2
1 HILLCROFT
2 CROMWELL CL
3 THORNTON CL
4 THURLBY CL
B2
1 FAVELL RD
2 TRAFALGAR CT
3 BURLAND CT
C2
1 PENFOLD LA
2 POLICEMANS LA
81
D1
1 HARVARD CL
2 GROSVENOR MS
3 CURZON MS
4 GLENEAGLES GR
5 CAVENDISH MS
6 CRANBOURNE MS
7 TROON CL
8 LYTHAM CL
9 CARLTON MS
10 DANIEL CR
11 ROWAN CT
82

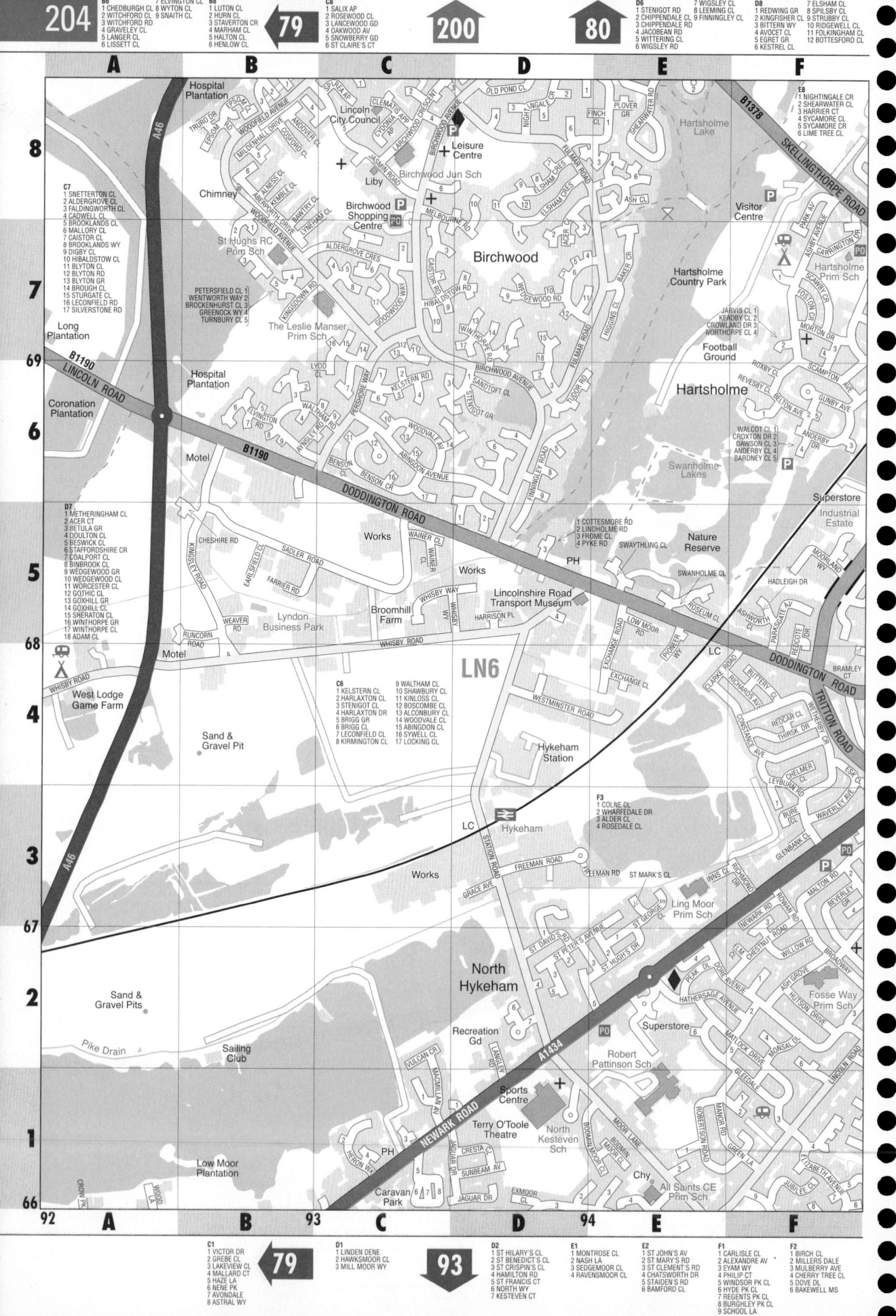

B6
1 CHEDBURGH CL
2 WITCHFORD CL
3 WITCHFORD RD
4 GRAVELEY CL
5 LANGER CL
6 LISSETT CL

7 ELVINGTON CL
8 WYTON CL
9 SNAITH CL

B8
1 LUTON CL
2 HURN CL
3 STAVERTON CR
4 MARHAM CL
5 HALTON CL
6 HENLOW CL

C8
1 SALIX AP
2 ROSEWOOD CL
3 LANCEWOOD GD
4 OAKWOOD AV
5 SNOWBERRY GD
6 ST CLAIRE'S CT

D6
1 STENIGOT RD
2 CHIPPENDALE CL
3 CHIPPENDALE RD
4 JACOBEAN RD
5 WITTERING RD
6 WIGSLEY RD

7 WIGSLEY CL
8 LEEMING CL
9 FINNINGLEY RD

D8
1 REDWING GR
2 KINGFISHER CL
3 BITTERN WY
4 AVOCET CL
5 EGRET GR
6 KESTREL CL

F7
1 ELSHAM CL
2 SPILSBY CL
3 STRUBBY CL
4 RIDGEWELL CL
5 FOLKINGHAM CL
6 BOTTESFORD CL

E8
1 NIGHTINGALE CR
2 SHEARWATER CL
3 HARRIER CT
4 SYCAMORE CR
5 SYCAMORE CL
6 LIME TREE CL

79 ← 200 80

C7
1 SNETTERTON CL
2 ALDERGROVE CL
3 FALDINGWORTH CL
4 CADWELL CL
5 BROOKLANDS CL
6 MALLORY CL
7 CAISTOR CL
8 BROOKLANDS WY
9 DIGBY CL
10 HIBALDSTOW CL
11 BLYTON CL
12 BLYTON RD
13 BLYTON GR
14 BROUGH CL
15 STURGATE CL
16 LECONFIELD RD
17 SILVERSTONE RD

D7
1 METHERINGHAM CL
2 ACER CT
3 BETULA GR
4 DOULTON CL
5 BESWICK CL
6 STAFFORDSHIRE CR
7 COALPORT CL
8 BINBROOK CL
9 WEDGEWOOD GR
10 WEDGEWOOD CL
11 WORCESTER CL
12 GOTHIC CL
13 GOXHILL GR
14 GOXHILL CL
15 SHERATON CL
16 WINTHORPE GR
17 WINTHORPE CL
18 ADAM CL

C6
1 KELSTERN CL
2 HARLAXTON CL
3 STENIGOT CL
4 HARLAXTON DR
5 BRIGG GR
6 BRIGG CL
7 LECONFIELD CL
8 KIRMINGTON CL

9 WALTHAM CL
10 SHAWBURY CL
11 KINLOSS CL
12 BOSCOMBE CL
13 ALCONBURY CL
14 WOODVALE CL
15 ABINGDON CL
16 SYWELL CL
17 LOCKING CL

F3
1 COLNE CL
2 WHARFEDALE DR
3 ALDER CL
4 ROSEDALE CL

LN6

C1
1 VICTOR DR
2 GREBE CL
3 LAKEVIEW CL
4 MALLARD CT
5 HAZE LA
6 NENE PK
7 AVONDALE
8 ASTRAL WY

D1
1 LINDEN DENE
2 HAWKSMOOR CL
3 MILL MOOR WY

79 ← 93

D2
1 ST HILARY'S CL
2 NASH LA
3 SEDGEMOOR CL
4 RAVENSMOOR CL

E1
1 MONTROSE CL
2 NASH LA
3 SEDGEMOOR CL

E2
1 ST JOHN'S AV
2 ST MARY'S RD
3 ST CLEMENT'S RD
4 CHATSWORTH DR
5 STAIDEN'S RD
6 BAMFORD CL

F1
1 CARLISLE CL
2 ALEXANDRE AV
3 EYAM WY
4 PHILIP CT
5 WINDSOR PK CL
6 HYDE PK CL
7 REGENTS PK CL
8 BURGHLEY PK CL
9 SCHOOL LA

F2
1 BIRCH CL
2 MILLERS DALE
3 MULBERRY AVE
4 CHERRY TREE CL
5 DOVE DL
6 BAKEWELL MS

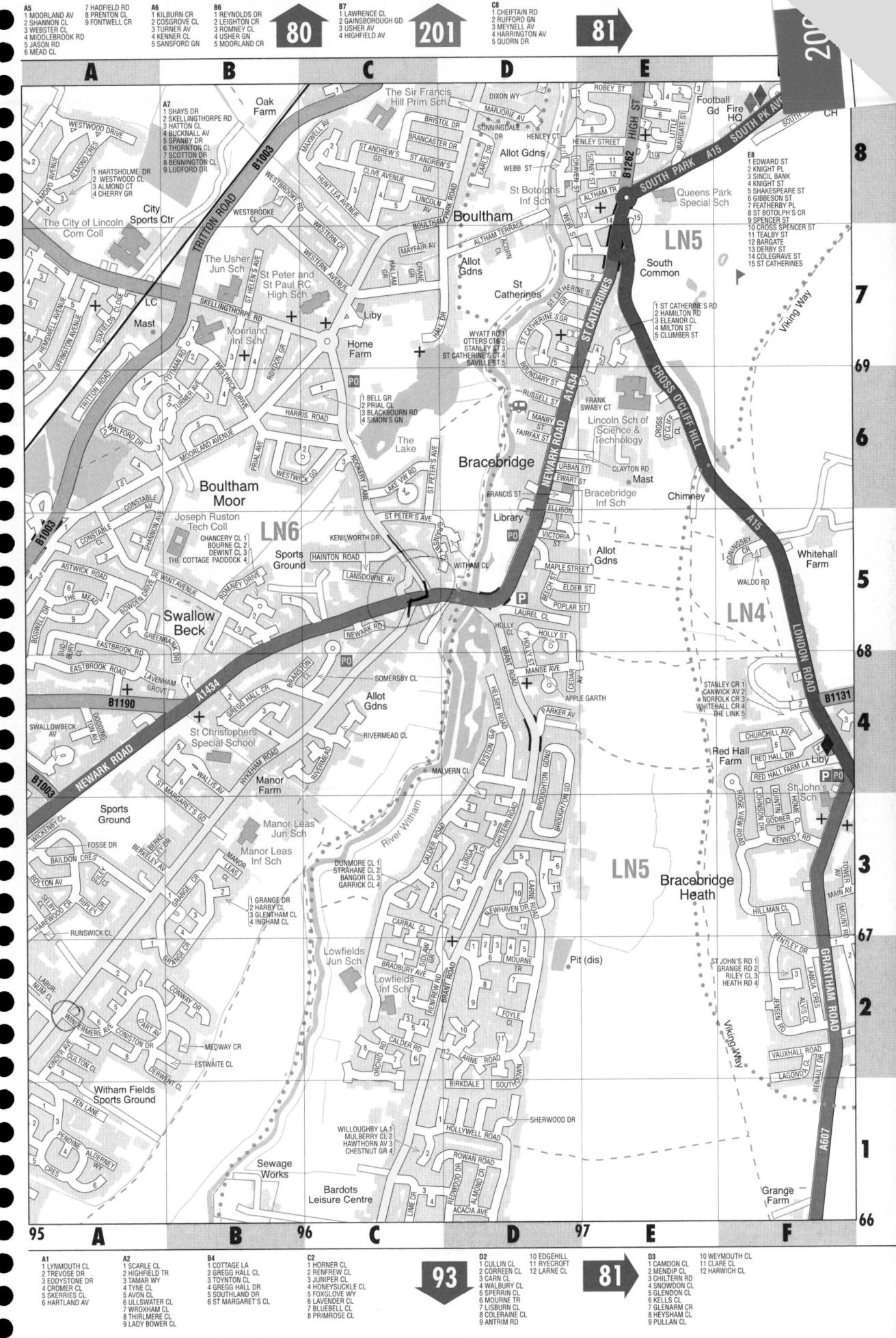

A5
1 MOORLAND AV
2 SHANNON CL
3 WEBSTER CL
4 MIDDLEBROOK RD
5 JASON RD
6 MEAD CL

7 HADFIELD RD
8 PRENTON CL
9 FONTWELL CR

A6
1 KILBURN CR
2 COSGROVE CL
3 TURNER AV
4 KENNER CL
5 SANSFORD GN

B6
1 REYNOLDS DR
2 LEIGHTON CR
3 ROMNEY CL
4 USHER AV
5 MOORLAND CR

B7
1 LAWRENCE CL
2 GAINSBOROUGH GD
3 USHER AV
4 HIGHFIELD AV

C8
1 CHEIFTAIN RD
2 RUFFORD GN
3 GIBBESON AV
4 HARRINGTON AV
5 QUORN DR

E8
1 EDWARD ST
2 KNIGHT PL
3 SINCIL BANK
4 KNIGHT ST
5 SHAKESPEARE ST
6 GIBBESON ST
7 FEATHERBY PL
8 ST BOTOLPH'S CR
9 SPENCER ST
10 CROSS SPENCER ST
11 TEALBY ST
12 BARGATE
13 DERBY ST
14 COLEGRAVE ST
15 ST CATHERINES

80   201   81

A1
1 LYNMOUTH CL
2 TREVOSE DR
3 EDDYSTONE DR
4 CROMER CL
5 SKERRIES CL
6 HARTLAND AV

A2
1 SCARLE CL
2 HIGHFIELD TR
3 TAMAR WY
4 TYNE CL
5 AVON CL
6 ULLSWATER CL
7 WROXHAM CL
8 THIRLMERE CL
9 LADY BOWER CL

B4
1 COTTAGE LA
2 GREGG HALL CL
3 TOYNTON CL
4 GREGG HALL DR
5 SOUTHLAND DR
6 ST MARGARET'S CL

C2
1 HORNER CL
2 RENFREW CL
3 JUNIPER CL
4 HONEYSUCKLE CL
5 FOXGLOVE WY
6 LAVENDER CL
7 BLUEBELL CL
8 PRIMROSE CL

D2
1 CULLIN CL
2 CORREEN CL
3 CARN CL
4 WALBURY CL
5 SPERRIN CL
6 MOURNE TR
7 LISBURN CL
8 COLERAINE CL
9 ANTRIM RD
10 EDGEHILL
11 RYECROFT
12 LARNE CL

D3
1 CAMDON CL
2 MENDIP CL
3 CHILTERN RD
4 SNOWDON CL
5 GLENDON CL
6 KELLS CL
7 GLENARM CR
8 HEYSHAM CL
9 PULLAN CL
10 WEYMOUTH CL
11 CLARE CL
12 HARWICH CL

93   81

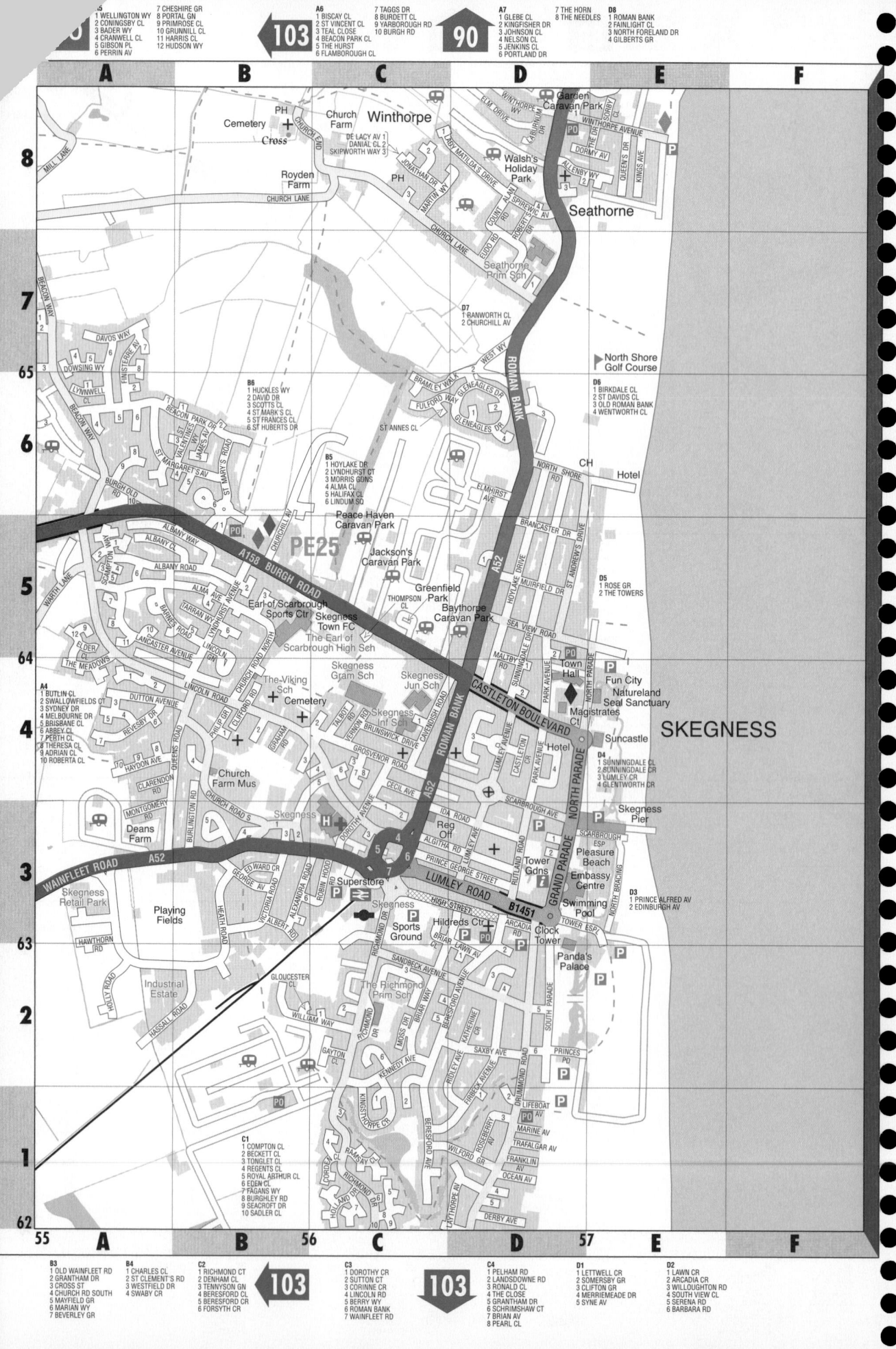

1 WELLINGTON WY
2 CONINGSBY CL
3 BADER WY
4 CRANWELL CL
5 GIBSON PL
6 PERRIN AV
7 CHESHIRE GR
8 PORTAL GN
9 PRIMROSE CL
10 GRUNNILL CL
11 HARRIS CL
12 HUDSON WY
103
A6
1 BISCAY CL
2 ST VINCENT CL
3 TEAL CLOSE
4 BEACON PARK CL
5 THE HURST
6 FLAMBOROUGH CL
7 TAGGS DR
8 BURDETT CL
9 YARBOROUGH RD
10 BURGH RD
90
A7
1 GLEBE CL
2 KINGFISHER DR
3 JOHNSON CL
4 NELSON CL
5 JENKINS CL
6 PORTLAND DR
7 THE HORN
8 THE NEEDLES
D8
1 ROMAN BANK
2 FAINLIGHT CL
3 NORTH FORELAND DR
4 GILBERTS GR
A B C D E F
Winthorpe
Seathorne
Garden Caravan Park
Walsh's Holiday Park
Cemetery
Cross
Church Farm
Royden Farm
Seathorne Prim Sch
North Shore Golf Course
D7
1 RANWORTH CL
2 CHURCHILL AV
B6
1 HUCKLES WY
2 DAVID DR
3 SCOTTS CL
4 ST MARK'S CL
5 ST FRANCES CL
6 ST HUBERTS DR
B5
1 HOYLAKE DR
2 LYNDHURST CT
3 MORRIS GDNS
4 ALMA CL
5 HALIFAX CL
6 LINDUM SQ
D6
1 BIRKDALE CL
2 ST DAVIDS CL
3 OLD ROMAN BANK
4 WENTWORTH CL
Peace Haven Caravan Park
Jackson's Caravan Park
PE25
Greenfield Park
Baythorpe Caravan Park
Earl of Scarbrough Sports Ctr
Skegness Town FC
The Earl of Scarbrough High Sch
A158 BURGH ROAD
ROMAN BANK
A52
D5
1 ROSE GR
2 THE TOWERS
Town Hall
Fun City
Natureland Seal Sanctuary
Magistrates Ct
SKEGNESS
Suncastle
A4
1 BUTLIN CL
2 SWALLOWFIELDS CT
3 SYDNEY DR
4 MELBOURNE DR
5 BRISBANE CL
6 ABBEY CL
7 PERTH CL
8 THERESA CL
9 ADRIAN CL
10 ROBERTA CL
Skegness Gram Sch
Skegness Jun Sch
Skegness Inf Sch
The Viking Sch
Cemetery
CASTLETON BOULEVARD
D4
1 SUNNINGDALE CL
2 SUNNINGDALE CR
3 LUMLEY CR
4 GLENTWORTH CR
Church Farm Mus
Deans Farm
Skegness Pier
Pleasure Beach
Embassy Centre
Swimming Pool
Tower Gdns
Reg Off
NORTH PARADE
GRAND PARADE
WAINFLEET ROAD
Skegness Retail Park
Playing Fields
Superstore
Skegness
Sports Ground
Hildreds Ctr
LUMLEY ROAD
B1451
Clock Tower
D3
1 PRINCE ALFRED AV
2 EDINBURGH AV
Panda's Palace
Industrial Estate
The Richmond Prim Sch
C1
1 COMPTON CL
2 BECKETT CL
3 TONGLET CL
4 REGENTS CL
5 ROYAL ARTHUR CL
6 EDEN CL
7 FAGANS WY
8 BURGHLEY RD
9 SEACROFT DR
10 SADLER CL
55 56 57
B3
1 OLD WAINFLEET RD
2 GRANTHAM DR
3 CROSS ST
4 CHURCH RD SOUTH
5 MAYFIELD GR
6 MARIAN WY
7 BEVERLEY GR
B4
1 CHARLES CL
2 ST CLEMENT'S RD
3 WESTFIELD DR
4 SWABY CR
C2
1 RICHMOND CT
2 DENHAM CL
3 TENNYSON GN
4 BERESFORD CL
5 BERESFORD CR
6 FORSYTH CR
103
C3
1 DOROTHY CR
2 SUTTON CT
3 CORINNE CR
4 LINCOLN RD
5 BERRY WY
6 ROMAN BANK
7 WAINFLEET RD
103
C4
1 PELHAM RD
2 LANDSDOWNE RD
3 RONALD CL
4 THE CLOSE
5 GRANTHAM DR
6 SCHRIMSHAW CT
7 BRIAN AV
8 PEARL CL
D1
1 LETTWELL CR
2 SOMERSBY GR
3 CLIFTON GR
4 MERRIEMEADE DR
5 SYNE AV
D2
1 LAWN CR
2 ARCADIA CR
3 WILLOUGHTON RD
4 SOUTH VIEW CL
5 SERENA RD
6 BARBARA RD

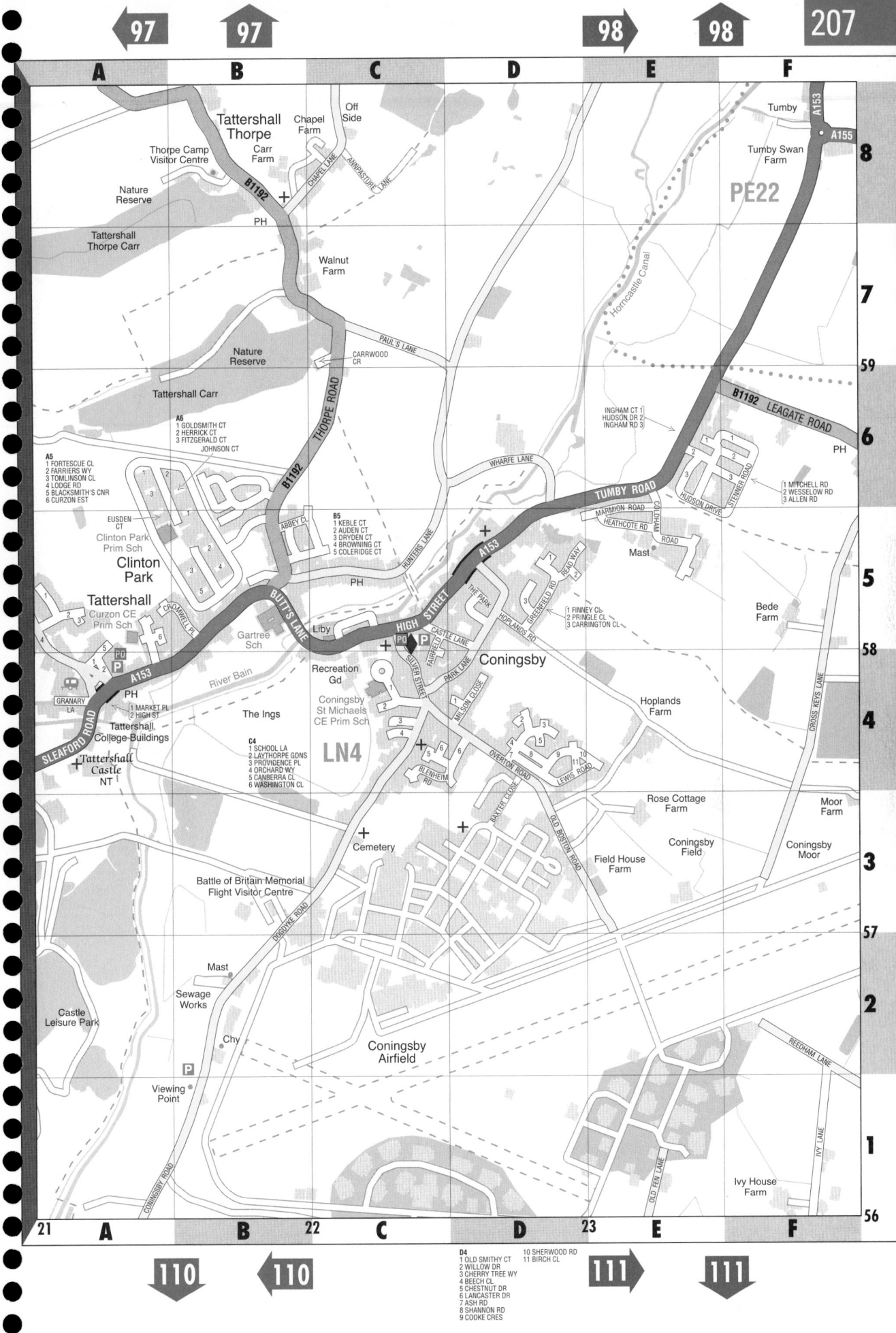

A B C D E F

Tattershall Thorpe

Off Side

Tumby

A153

A155

Thorpe Camp Visitor Centre

Chapel Farm

Carr Farm

Nature Reserve

B1192

Tumby Swan Farm

PE22

8

Tattershall Thorpe Carr

Walnut Farm

Chapel Lane

Annpasture Lane

Horncastle Canal

7

Nature Reserve

Paul's Lane

CARRWOOD CR

59

Thorpe Road

Tattershall Carr

Ingham Ct 1
Hudson Dr 2
Ingham Rd 3

B1192 LEAGATE ROAD

6

A5
1 GOLDSMITH CT
2 HERRICK CT
3 FITZGERALD CT
JOHNSON CT

Wharfe Lane

PH

A5
1 FORTESCUE CL
2 FARRIERS WY
3 TOMLINSON CL
4 LODGE RD
5 BLACKSMITH'S CNR
6 CURZON EST

EUSDEN CT

B1192

ABBEY CL

B5
1 KEBLE CT
2 AUDEN CT
3 DRYDEN CT
4 BROWNING CT
5 COLERIDGE CT

Tumby Road

Marmion Road

Heathcote Rd

Hudson Drive

Steiner Road

1 MITCHELL RD
2 WESSELOW RD
3 ALLEN RD

WHD CC ROAD

Mast

1 FINNEY CL
2 PRINGLE CL
3 CARRINGTON CL

Bede Farm

5

Clinton Park Prim Sch

Clinton Park

Tattershall

Curzon CE Prim Sch

CROMWELL PL

BUTT'S LANE

Gartree Sch

PH

Liby

Hunters Lane

A153

HIGH STREET

PO P

Castle Lane

The Park

Fairfield Rd

Greenfield Rd

Hoplands Rd

Coningsby

58

GRANARY LA

PH

A153

River Bain

1 MARKET PL
2 HIGH ST

Recreation Gd

Silver Street

Park Lane

Milson Close

Hoplands Farm

Cross Keys Lane

4

Tattershall College Buildings

The Ings

Coningsby St Michaels CE Prim Sch

C4
1 SCHOOL LA
2 LAYTHORPE GDNS
3 PROVIDENCE PL
4 ORCHARD WY
5 CANBERRA CL
6 WASHINGTON CL

LN4

BLENHEIM RD

Overton Road

Lewis Road

Rose Cottage Farm

Coningsby Field

Moor Farm

Tattershall Castle NT

Sleaford Road

Cemetery

Baxter Close

Old Boston Road

Field House Farm

Coningsby Moor

Coningsby Field

3

Battle of Britain Memorial Flight Visitor Centre

Dogdyke Road

57

Mast

Sewage Works

Chy

Castle Leisure Park

Coningsby Road

P

Coningsby Airfield

Reedham Lane

2

Viewing Point

Old Fen Lane

Ivy House Farm

Ivy Lane

1

21 A B 22 C D 23 E F 56

D4
1 OLD SMITHY CT
2 WILLOW DR
3 CHERRY TREE WY
4 BEECH CL
5 CHESTNUT DR
6 LANCASTER DR
7 ASH RD
8 SHANNON RD
9 COOKE CRES
10 SHERWOOD RD
11 BIRCH CL

125
125

E6
1 BRADY ST
2 WITHAM CT
3 FRACKNAL'S ROW
4 WITHAM BANK EAST

E7
1 DAVEY CL
2 BURROWS CL
3 PARSONS DR
4 TUDOR DR
5 RAYBROOK CL
6 LOCKSLEY CL

F5
1 UNION PL
2 UNION ST
3 WITHAM ST
4 CHAPEL ST
5 NORMAN AV
6 RED LION ST

7 PARK GATE
8 WIDE BARGATE
9 THREADNEEDLE ST
10 FOUNTAIN PL
11 COLLEY ST
12 ARCHER LA
13 FOUNTAIN LA

14 TOWER ST
15 PETTICOAT LA
16 MITRE LA
17 MARKET SQ
18 PUMP SQ
19 CHURCH ST
20 CHURCH ST

21 MARKET PL
22 TOWN BRIDGE
23 CRAYTHORNE LA

F6
1 GRAND SLUICE LA
2 NORTH ST
3 STAFFORD ST
4 NORFOLK PL
5 PARK LA

Boundary Farm
Washdyke Lane
Middle Drove
North Forty Foot Bank
Langrick Road
River Witham
High Hill Farm
White House Farm
Allot Gdns
Boston Rowing Club
Boston Cemetery
Crem
Memorial
The Haven High Sch
Norfolk Street Ind Est
Boston Ind Ctr
Central Park
Norfolk Street
Boston Marina
Boston City Ctr
Boston Park Com Prim Sch
Recn Gd
Mayflower Sports Ground
Shooting Range
Peter Paine Sports Centre
Eurosure Tennis Centre
Boston Tennis Club
Boston West Prim Sch
Wyberton Fen
PE21
Sleaford Road
A52
Boardsides A1121
Chain Bridge
Superstore
Alban Retail Park
Old Macdonalds Farm
Cherry Tree Farm
Windmill
New Hammond Beck Rd
Swineshead Rd A52
Endeavour Park Ind Est
Westfield Avenue
Cherry Walk
Hessle Avenue
Staniland County Prim Sch
Holland Park
Allot Gdns
Moat
Skirbeck Quarter
Water Tower
Garfit's Lane
Woodside
Abbey Dale
Hunter's Row
Five House Lane
West End Road
Wyberton West Road
London Road
Spalding Rd A16
Swing Bridge
John Adams Way
South End
St Thomas CE (Controlled) Prim Sch
Bayswood Ave
Allot Gdns
Argyle St A1137 Fydell St
St Botolphs Ch (The Stump)
Pescod Hall
Guildhall Mus
City H & Lib
Ass Rms
Queen St
Mast

125
136

D3
1 HEATHER CL
2 WOODVILLE GD W
3 WOODVILLE GD E
4 FRANCIS BERNARD CL

E4
1 WALDEN GD
2 ALBERT TR
3 TRAFALGAR PL
4 WEST ROW
5 GEORGE ST
6 BRAMLEY LA
7 BLUE ST
8 BROADFIELD LA
9 NELSON WY

F1
1 FLEMING CT
2 WHITTLE CL
3 SIR ISAAC NEWTON DR
4 STEPHENSON CL
5 BELL CT

F2
1 WYBERTON LOW RD
2 MIDDLECOTT CL
3 WYBERTON LOW RD
4 ELMWOOD AV

F4
1 BOND ST
2 BRIDGE ST
3 SIBSEY LA
4 SHODFRIARS LA
5 SPAIN LA
6 PADDOCK GR
7 QUAKER LA
8 VICTORIA PL
9 GREYFRIARS LA

9 GREYFRIARS LA
10 WHITEHORSE LA
11 LIQUORPOND ST
12 PULVERTOFT LA
13 EDWIN ST
14 ROSEGARTH ST

30 31 32

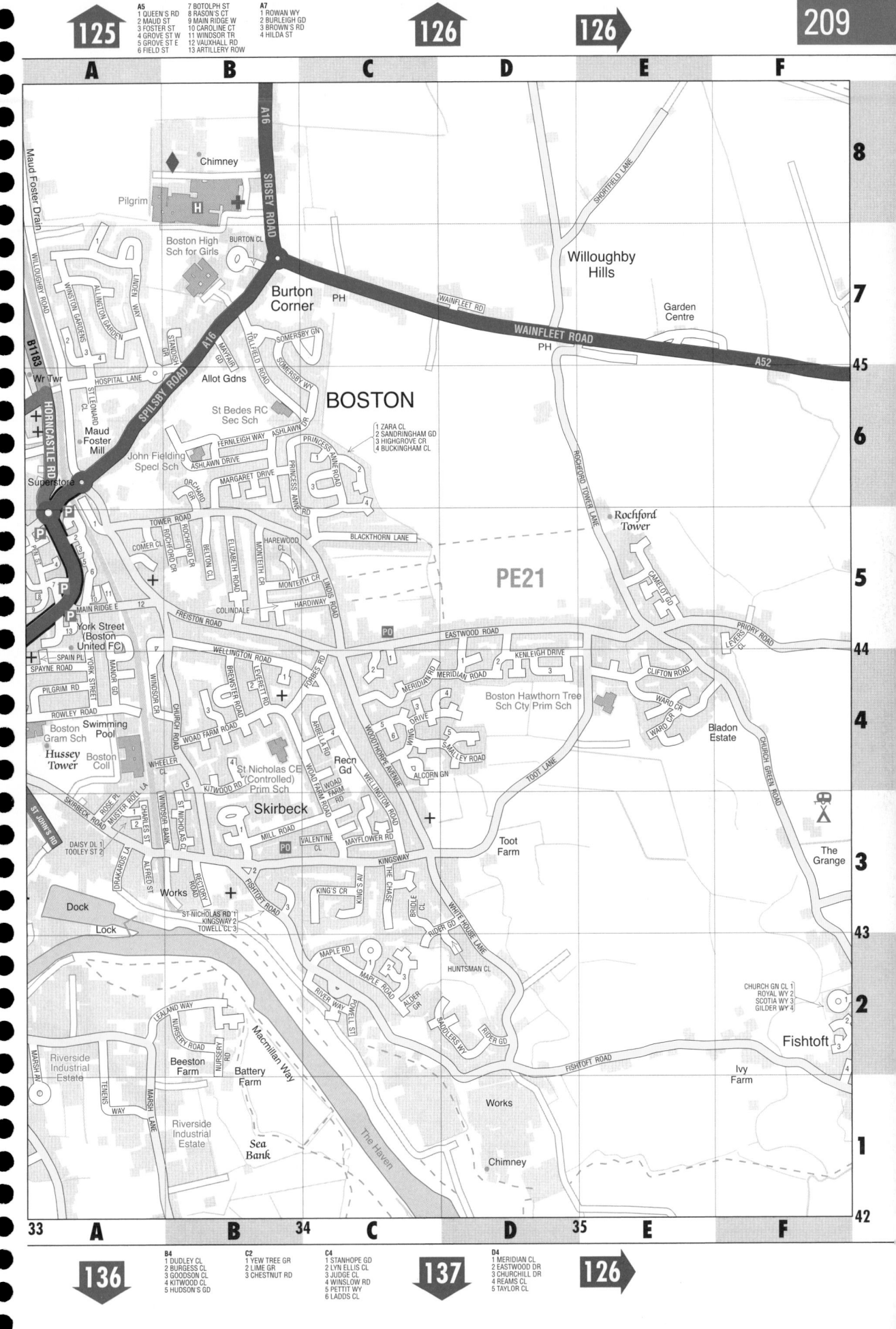

125

A5
1 QUEEN'S RD
2 MAUD ST
3 FOSTER ST
4 GROVE ST W
5 GROVE ST E
6 FIELD ST

7 BOTOLPH ST
8 RASON'S CT
9 MAIN RIDGE W
10 CAROLINE CT
11 WINDSOR TR
12 VAUXHALL RD
13 ARTILLERY ROW

A7
1 ROWAN WY
2 BURLEIGH GD
3 BROWN'S RD
4 HILDA ST

126

126

A B C D E F

8

7

45

6

BOSTON

1 ZARA CL
2 SANDRINGHAM GD
3 HIGHGROVE CR
4 BUCKINGHAM CL

Willoughby
Hills

Garden
Centre

WAINFLEET ROAD   A52

Rochford
Tower

PE21

5

44

Boston Hawthorn Tree
Sch Cty Prim Sch

Bladon
Estate

4

The
Grange

3

43

CHURCH GN CL 1
ROYAL WY 2
SCOTIA WY 3
GILDER WY 4

2

Fishtoft

Ivy
Farm

1

42

33 A B 34 C D 35 E F

136

B4
1 DUDLEY CL
2 BURGESS CL
3 GOODSON CL
4 KITWOOD CL
5 HUDSON'S GD

C2
1 YEW TREE GR
2 LIME GR
3 CHESTNUT RD

C4
1 STANHOPE GD
2 LYN ELLIS CL
3 JUDGE CL
4 WINSLOW RD
5 PETTIT WY
6 LADDS CL

D4
1 MERIDIAN CL
2 EASTWOOD DR
3 CHURCHILL DR
4 REAMS CL
5 TAYLOR CL

137

126

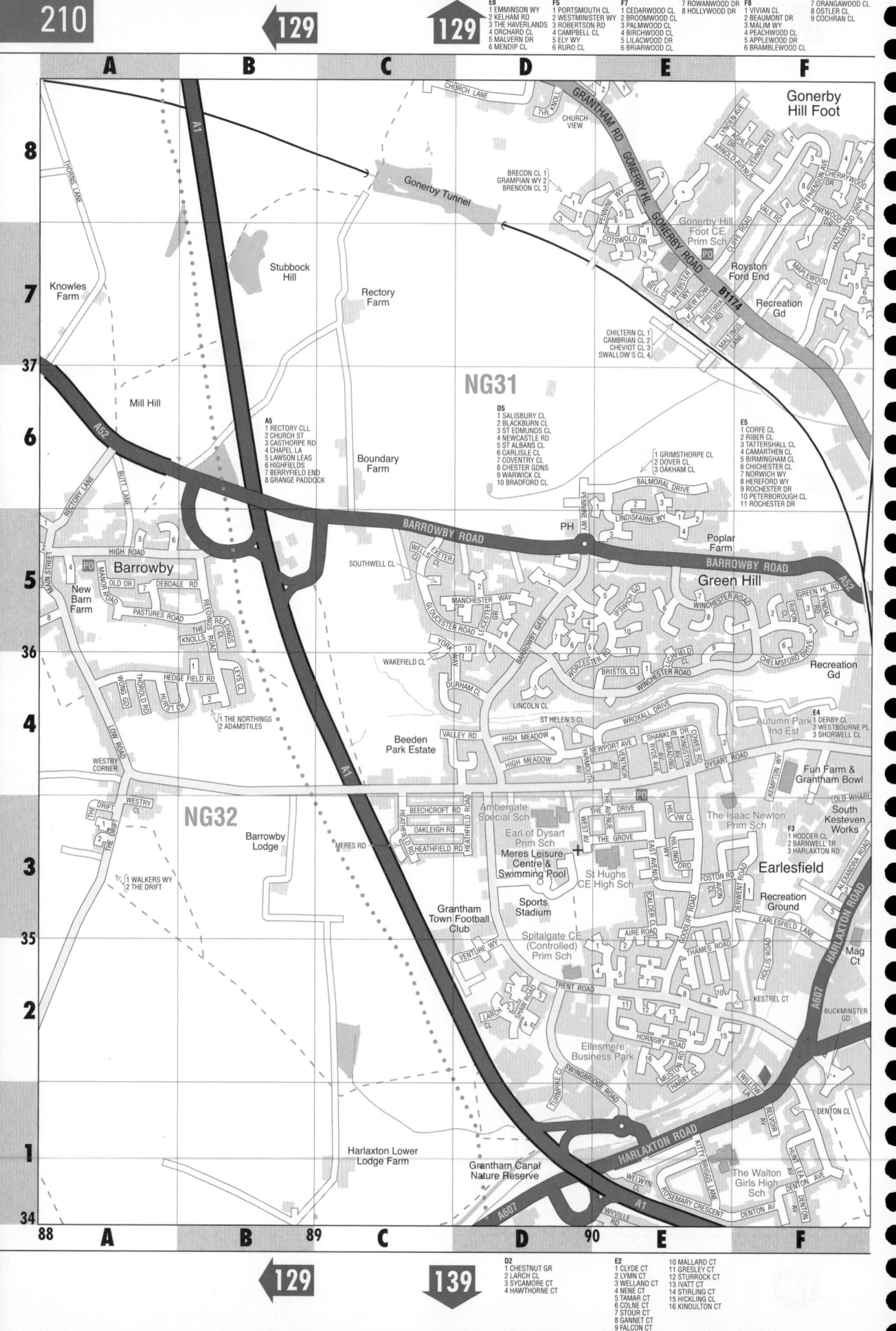

210

E8
1 EMMINSON WY
2 KELHAM RD
3 THE HAVERLANDS
4 ORCHARD CL
5 MALVERN DR
6 MENDIP CL

F5
1 PORTSMOUTH CL
2 WESTMINISTER WY
3 ROBERTSON RD
4 CAMPBELL CL
5 ELY WY
6 RURO CL

F7
1 CEDARWOOD CL
2 BROOMWOOD CL
3 PALMWOOD CL
4 BIRCHWOOD CL
5 LILACWOOD DR
6 BRIARWOOD CL

7 ROWANWOOD DR
8 HOLLYWOOD DR

F8
1 VIVIAN CL
2 BEAUMONT DR
3 MALIM WY
4 PEACHWOOD DR
5 APPLEWOOD DR
6 BRAMBLEWOOD CL

7 ORANGAWOOD CL
8 OSTLER CL
9 COCHRAN CL

Gonerby
Hill Foot

Knowles
Farm

Stubbock
Hill

Rectory
Farm

Gonerby Tunnel

BRECON CL 1
GRAMPIAN WY 2
BRENDON CL 3

Gonerby Hill
Foot CE
Prim Sch

Royston
Ford End

Recreation
Gd

CHILTERN CL 1
CAMBRIAN CL 2
CHEVIOT WY 3
SWALLOW'S CL 4

NG31

Mill Hill

A5
1 RECTORY CLL
2 CHURCH ST
3 CASTHORPE RD
4 CHAPEL LA
5 LAWSON LEAS
6 HIGHFIELDS
7 BERRYFIELD END
8 GRANGE PADDOCK

Boundary
Farm

D5
1 SALISBURY CL
2 BLACKBURN CL
3 ST EDMUNDS CL
4 NEWCASTLE RD
5 ST ALBANS CL
6 CARLISLE CL
7 COVENTRY CL
8 CHESTER GDNS
9 WARWICK CL
10 BRADFORD CL

1 GRIMSTHORPE CL
2 DOVER CL
3 OAKHAM CL

E5
1 CORFE CL
2 RIBER CL
3 TATTERSHALL CL
4 CAMARTHEN CL
5 BIRMINGHAM CL
6 CHICHESTER CL
7 NORWICH WY
8 HEREFORD WY
9 ROCHESTER DR
10 PETERBOROUGH CL
11 ROCHESTER DR

BALMORAL DRIVE

LINDISFARNE WY

Poplar
Farm

BARROWBY ROAD
PH

BARROWBY ROAD

Green Hill

High Road

New
Barn
Farm

Barrowby

DEBDALE RD

PASTURES ROAD

THE KNOLLS

HEDGE FIELD RD

SOUTHWELL CL

Manchester Way

Recreation
Gd

E4
1 DERBY CL
2 WESTBOURNE PL
3 SHORWELL CL

1 THE NORTHINGS
2 ADAMSTILES

WAKEFIELD CL

YORK WAY

DURHAM CL

LINCOLN CL

ST HELEN'S CL

WROXALL DRIVE

Autumn Park
Ind Est

Beeden
Park Estate

VALLEY RD

HIGH MEADOW

HIGH MEADOW

NEWPORT AVE

Fun Farm &
Grantham Bowl

NG32

1 WALKERS WY
2 THE DRIFT

THE DRIFT

WESTRY
CORNER

Barrowby
Lodge

MERES RD

BEECHCROFT RD

OAKLEIGH RD

HEATHFIELD RD

HEATHFIELD RD

Ambergate
Special Sch

Earl of Dysart
Prim Sch

Meres Leisure
Centre &
Swimming Pool

St Hughs
CE High Sch

The Isaac Newton
Prim Sch

South
Kesteven
Works

Earlesfield

Recreation
Ground

F3
1 HODDER CL
2 BARNWELL TR
3 HARLAXTON RD

Grantham
Town Football
Club

Sports
Stadium

Spitalgate CE
(Controlled)
Prim Sch

AIRE ROAD

THAMES ROAD

EARLESFIELD LANE

Mag
Ct

VENTURE WY

TRENT ROAD

SNOW ROAD

LARCH
CL

HORNSBY ROAD

KESTREL CT

BUCKMINSTER
GD

Ellesmere
Business Park

SWINGBRIDGE ROAD

TURNPIKE ROAD

Harlaxton Lower
Lodge Farm

Grantham Canal
Nature Reserve

HARLAXTON ROAD

DENTON CL

WELWYN
CL

ROSEMARY CRESCENT

WYVILLE
RD

A607

The Walton
Girls High
Sch

DENTON AV

D2
1 CHESTNUT GR
2 LARCH CL
3 SYCAMORE CT
4 HAWTHORNE CT

E2
1 CLYDE CT
2 LYMN CT
3 WELLAND CT
4 NENE CT
5 TAMAR CT
6 COLNE CT
7 STOUR CT
8 GANNET CT
9 FALCON CT

10 MALLARD CT
11 GRESLEY CT
12 STURROCK CT
13 IVATT CT
14 STIRLING CT
15 HICKLING CL
16 KINOULTON CT

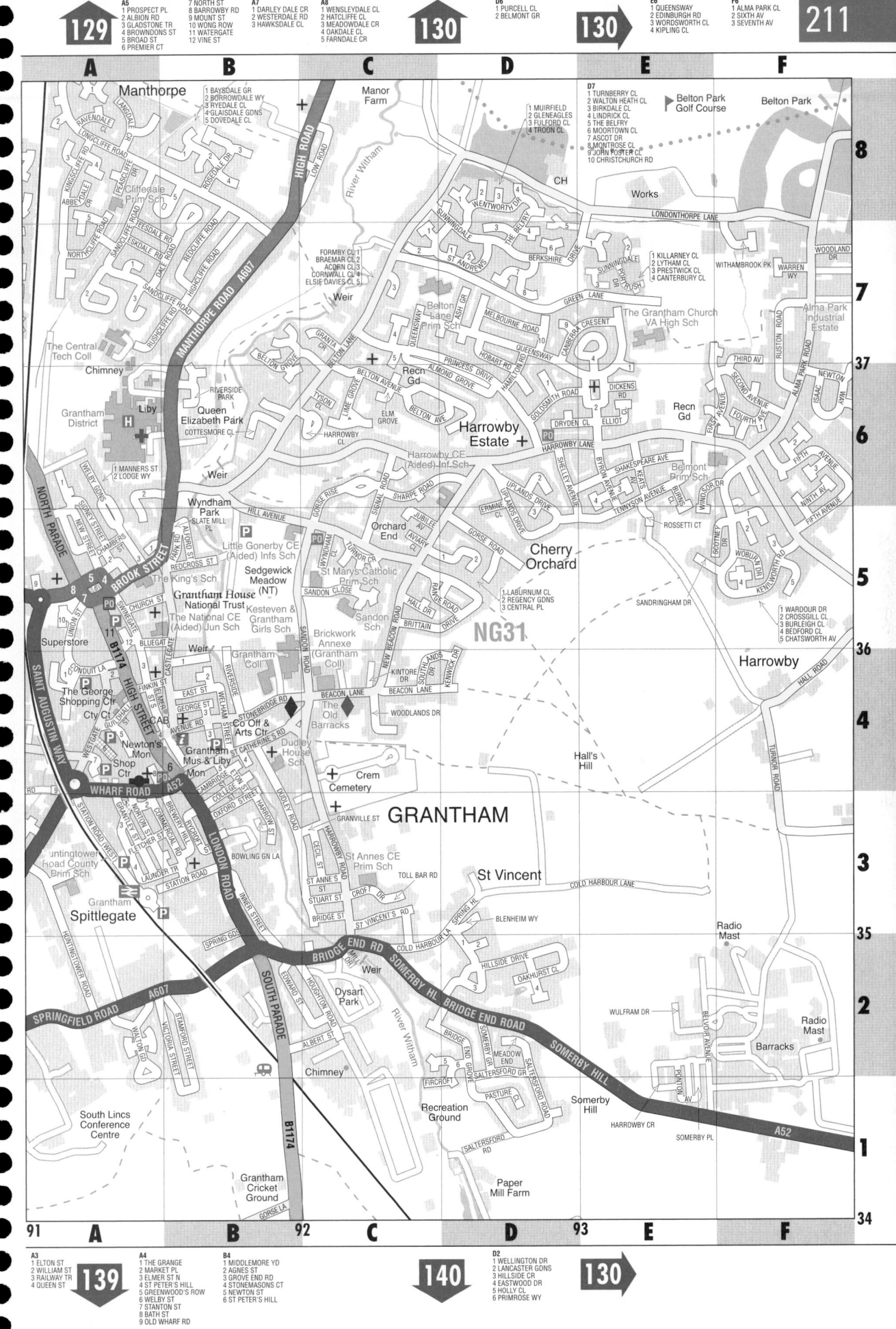

129

A5
1 PROSPECT PL
2 ALBION RD
3 GLADSTONE TR
4 BROWNDONS ST
5 BROAD ST
6 PREMIER CT

7 NORTH ST
8 BARROWBY RD
9 MOUNT ST
10 WONG ROW
11 WATERGATE
12 VINE ST

A7
1 DARLEY DALE CR
2 WESTERDALE RD
3 HAWKSDALE CL

A8
1 WENSLEYDALE CL
2 HATCLIFFE CL
3 MEADOWDALE CR
4 OAKDALE CL
5 FARNDALE CR

130

D6
1 PURCELL CL
2 BELMONT GR

130

E6
1 QUEENSWAY
2 EDINBURGH RD
3 WORDSWORTH CL
4 KIPLING CL

F6
1 ALMA PARK CL
2 SIXTH AV
3 SEVENTH AV

211

A   B   C   D   E   F

Manthorpe

B5
1 BAYSDALE GR
2 BORROWDALE WY
3 RYEDALE CL
4 GLAISDALE GDNS
5 DOVEDALE CL

Manor Farm

D7
1 MUIRFIELD
2 GLENEAGLES
3 FULFORD CL
4 TROON CL

Belton Park Golf Course

Belton Park

D7
1 TURNBERRY CL
2 WALTON HEATH CL
3 BIRKDALE CL
4 LINDRICK CL
5 THE BELFRY
6 MOORTOWN CL
7 ASCOT DR
8 MONTROSE CL
9 JOHN FOSTER CL
10 CHRISTCHURCH RD

CH

Works

Londonthorpe Lane

Woodland Dr

Warren Wy

Withambrook Pk

8

River Witham

Wentworth

The Belfry

Berkshire Drive

Green Lane

Sunningdale Pk Rush

Alma Park Road

Ruston Road

Newton Wy

Isaac

7

Weir

E6
1 KILLARNEY CL
2 LYTHAM CL
3 PRESTWICK CL
4 CANTERBURY CL

Alma Park Industrial Estate

The Central Tech Coll

St Andrews

Belton Lane Prim Sch

Melbourne Road

Queensway

Canberra Cresent

The Grantham Church VA High Sch

Third Av

37

Chimney

Granta Cr

Belton Lane

Recn Gd

Princess Drive

Hobart Rd

Dickens Rd

Recn Gd

Second Avenue

Fourth Av

6

Grantham District

Liby

Chimney

H

Queen Elizabeth Park

Belton Grove

Belton Avenue

Almond Grove

Elm Grove

Belton Ave

Goldsmith Road

Dryden Cl

Elliot

PO

Harrowby Lane

Shelley Avenue

Byron Avenue

Keats

Shakespeare Ave

First Avenue

Fifth Av

Ninth Av

Belmont Prim Sch

Goettre Dr

Second Av

Wobura Cl

Kenilworth Rd

Fifth Avenue

Harrowby Estate

Harrowby CE (Aided) Inf Sch

1 MANNERS ST
2 LODGE WY

Cottesmore Cl

Tyson Cl

Harrowby Rd

Lane Grove

Sharpe Road

Uplands Drive

Ermine Cl

Uplands Drive

Tennyson Avenue

Burns

Wingsor Dr

Rossetti Ct

F5
1 WARDOUR DR
2 CROSSGILL CL
3 BURLEIGH CL
4 BEDFORD CL
5 CHATSWORTH AV

Weir

Wyndham Park

Slate Mill Pl

Hill Avenue

Gorse Rise

Signal Rd

Jubilee Av

Gorse Road

Sandringham Dr

5

P

Little Gonerby CE (Aided) Infs Sch

Orchard End

Aviary

Cherry Orchard

North Parade

Brook Street

Sidney Street

New Street

Chambers

Redcross St

Park Rd

Castlegate

Sedgewick Meadow (NT)

PO

Wyndham Rd

St Marys Catholic Prim Sch

Turnor Road

Race Road

Hall Dr

D5
1 LABURNUM CL
2 REGENCY GDNS
3 CENTRAL PL

NG31

Superstore

B1174

Church St

PO

Bluegate

The King's Sch

Grantham House National Trust

The National CE (Aided) Jun Sch

Kesteven & Grantham Girls Sch

Sandon Cl

Sandon Sch

Brittain

Sandon Road

Hall Dr

Harrowby

36

Saint Augustin Way

High Street

Conduit La

Finkin St

Elmer

West St

George St

William Road

Riverside

Weir

Brickwork Annexe (Grantham Coll)

Grantham Coll

Kintore Dr

Southlands

Kenwick Dr

Beacon Lane

4

The George Shopping Ctr

Cty Ct

Guildhall St

P

East St

Welham St

Stonebridge Rd

St Catherine's Rd

Beacon Lane

The Old Barracks

Hall's Hill

Turnor Road

Newton's Mon

Shop Ctr

Grantham Mus & Liby Mon

PO

Avenue Rd

College

Dudley House Sch

Woodlands Dr

Wharf Road

A52

Cambridge

Oxford Street

Harrow Rd

Crem Cemetery

GRANTHAM

3

Huntingtower Road County Prim Sch

Station Road (West)

Grantley St

North St

London Road

Fletcher St

Commercial Rd

Brewery Hill

Eton

Dudley Road

Granville St

Cecil St

St Annes CE Prim Sch

Toll Bar Rd

St Vincent

Cold Harbour Lane

Radio Mast

P

Bowling Gn La

St Anne's St

Stuart St

Croft Dr

Spring Hl

35

Spittlegate

Launder Tr

Station Road

Inner Street

Spring Gdns

Bridge St

St Vincent's Rd

Blenheim Wy

Hillside Drive

Oakhurst Cl

Wulfram Dr

Belvoir Avenue

Radio Mast

2

Hunting Tower Road

A607

Springfield Road

Edward St

Houghton Road

South Parade

Bridge End Rd

Weir

Dysart Park

River Witham

Somerby Hl

Bridge End Road

Somerby Hill

Bridge End Grove

Meadow End

Saltersford Gr

Barracks

Ponton Av

Somerby Pl

A52

South Lincs Conference Centre

Stamford Street

Victoria Street

Walton Rd

Albert St

Chimney

Fircroft

Pasture

Saltersford Rd

Recreation Ground

Somerby Hill

Harrowby Cr

1

B1174

Grantham Cricket Ground

Gorse La

Paper Mill Farm

34

91   A   92   B   C   93   E   F

A3
1 ELTON ST
2 WILLIAM ST
3 RAILWAY TR
4 QUEEN ST

139

A4
1 THE GRANGE
2 MARKET PL
3 ELMER ST N
4 ST PETER'S HILL
5 GREENWOOD'S ROW
6 WELBY ST
7 STANTON ST
8 BATH ST
9 OLD WHARF RD

B4
1 MIDDLEMORE YD
2 AGNES ST
3 GROVE END RD
4 STONEMASONS CT
5 NEWTON ST
6 ST PETER'S HILL

140

D2
1 WELLINGTON DR
2 LANCASTER GDNS
3 HILLSIDE DR
4 EASTWOOD DR
5 HOLLY CL
6 PRIMROSE WY

130

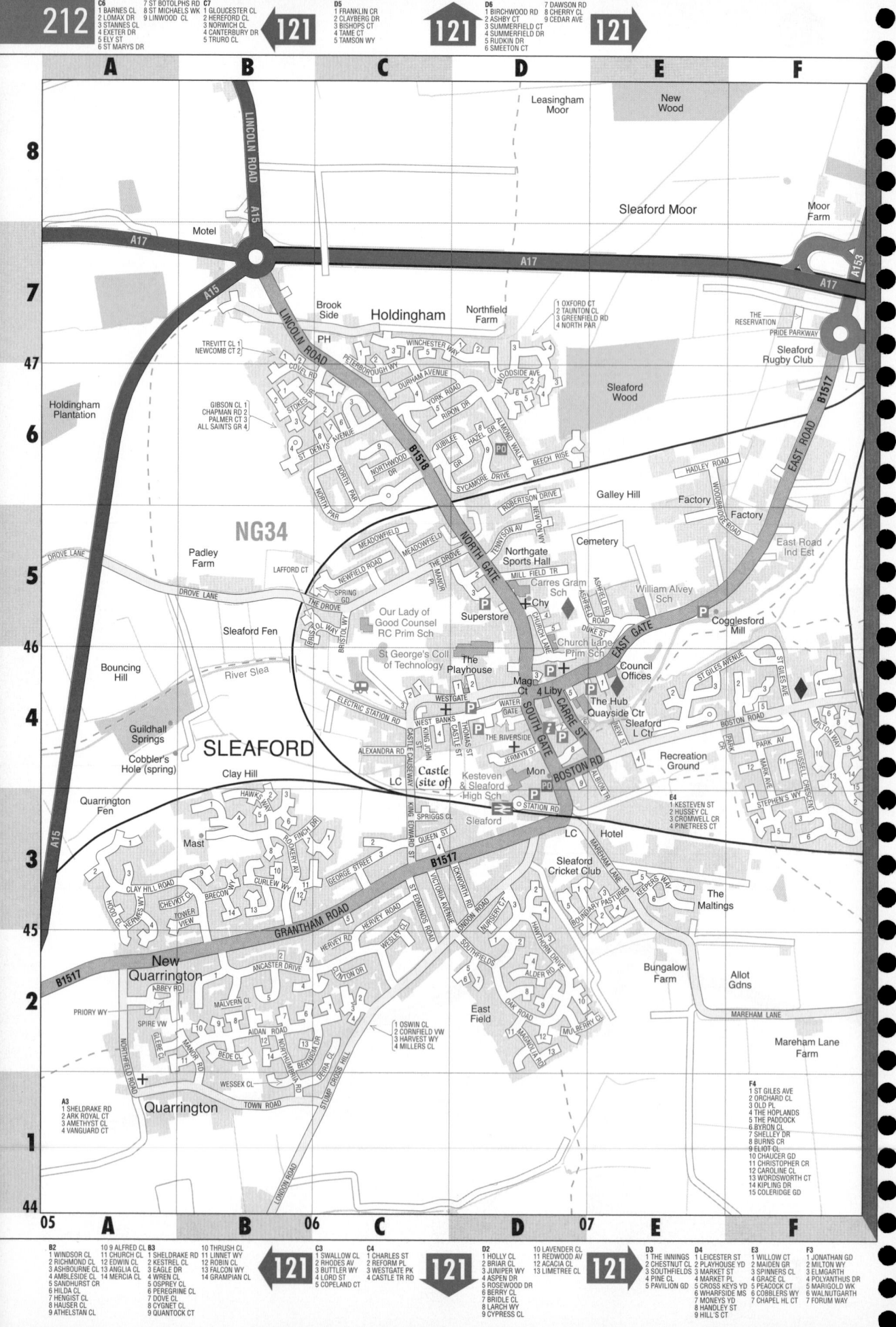
C6
1 BARNES CL
2 LOMAX DR
3 STANNES CL
4 EXETER DR
5 ELY ST
6 ST MARYS DR
7 ST BOTOLPHS RD
8 ST MICHAELS WK
9 LINWOOD CL
C7
1 GLOUCESTER CL
2 HEREFORD CL
3 NORWICH CL
4 CANTERBURY DR
5 TRURO CL
121
D5
1 FRANKLIN CR
2 CLAYBERG DR
3 BISHOPS CT
4 TAME CT
5 TAMSON WY
121
D6
1 BIRCHWOOD RD
2 ASHBY CT
3 SUMMERFIELD CT
4 SUMMERFIELD DR
5 RUDKIN DR
6 SMEETON CT
7 DAWSON RD
8 CHERRY CL
9 CEDAR AVE
121
A
B
C
D
E
F
8
7
47
6
5
46
4
3
45
2
1
44
05
06
07
Leasingham Moor
New Wood
LINCOLN ROAD
A15
Sleaford Moor
Moor Farm
Motel
A17
A17
A17
A153
A15
Brook Side
Holdingham
Northfield Farm
1 OXFORD CT
2 TAUNTON CL
3 GREENFIELD RD
4 NORTH PAR
THE RESERVATION
PRIDE PARKWAY
Sleaford Rugby Club
PH
TREVITT CL 1
NEWCOMB CT 2
WINCHESTER WAY
PETERBOROUGH WY
DURHAM AVENUE
WOODSIDE AVE
Sleaford Wood
Holdingham Plantation
GIBSON CL 1
CHAPMAN RD 2
PALMER CT 3
ALL SAINTS GR 4
COVEL RD
STOKES DR
AVENUE
YORK ROAD
RIPON DR
ALMOND WALK
B1517
EAST ROAD
ST DENYS
NORTHWOOD DR
B1518
JUBILEE GR
HAZEL GR
PO
BEECH RISE
SYCAMORE DRIVE
NORTH PAR
HADLEY ROAD
Galley Hill
Factory
Factory
WOODBRIDGE ROAD
ROBERTSON DRIVE
NEWTON WY
TENNYSON AV
NG34
MEADOWFIELD
MEADOWFIELD
NORTH GATE
Cemetery
East Road Ind Est
DROVE LANE
Padley Farm
LAFFORD CT
NEWFIELD ROAD
THE DROVE
MANOR PL
Northgate Sports Hall
MILL FIELD TR
Carres Gram Sch
ASHFIELD ROAD
William Alvey Sch
DROVE LANE
SPRING GD
THE DROVE
Superstore
Chy
CHURCH LANE
DUKE ST
EAST GATE
Cogglesford Mill
Sleaford Fen
IBBIS
OL WAY
BRISTOL WY
Our Lady of Good Counsel RC Prim Sch
Church Lane Prim Sch
St George's Coll of Technology
The Playhouse
Council Offices
ST GILES AVENUE
ST GILES AVE
Bouncing Hill
River Slea
Mag Ct
Liby
CARRE ST
The Hub
Quayside Ctr
Sleaford L Ctr
ELECTRIC STATION RD
WESTGATE
WEST BANKS
KING JOHN ST
CASTLE ST
WATER GATE
SOUTH GATE
NEW ST
BOSTON ROAD
MILTON WAY
Guildhall Springs
SLEAFORD
THOMAS ST
THE RIVERSIDE
PARK CR
PARK AV
Recreation Ground
Cobbler's Hole (spring)
ALEXANDRA RD
CASTLE CAUSEWAY
JERMYN ST
MARK AVE
RUSSELL CRESCENT
Clay Hill
LC
Castle (site of)
Kesteven & Sleaford High Sch
Mon
PO
BOSTON RD
ALBION TR
E4
1 KESTEVEN ST
2 HUSSEY CL
3 CROMWELL CR
4 PINETREES CT
STEPHEN'S WY
Quarrington Fen
HAWKS WAY
FINCH DR
ROOKERY AV
STATION RD
Sleaford
SPRIGGS CL
KING EDWARD ST
QUEEN ST
LC
Hotel
Mast
MAREHAM LANE
A15
GEORGE STREET
B1517
ICKWORTH RD
Sleaford Cricket Club
KEEPERS WAY
The Maltings
CLAY HILL ROAD
CHEVIOT CL
BRECON WY
CURLEW WY
ST EDMUNDS ROAD
VICTORIA AVENUE
LONDON ROAD
NURSERY CT
HAWTHORN DRIVE
BOUNDARY PASTURES
HOOD CL
HERMES WAY
TOWER VIEW
GRANTHAM ROAD
HERVEY ROAD
HERVEY RD
WESLEY CL
SOUTHFIELDS
New Quarrington
B1517
ANCASTER DRIVE
CLINTON DR
ALDER RD
Bungalow Farm
Allot Gdns
ABBEY RD
PRIORY WY
MALVERN CL
SPIRE VW
East Field
OAK ROAD
MULBERRY CL
MAREHAM LANE
AIDAN ROAD
1 OSWIN CL
2 CORNFIELD VW
3 HARVEST WY
4 MILLERS CL
MAGNOLIA RD
Mareham Lane Farm
GLEBE CL
MANOR RD
BEDE CL
NORTHUMBRIA RD
BERNICIA DR
DEIRA CL
STUMP CROSS HILL
NORTHFIELD ROAD
WESSEX CL
A3
1 SHELDRAKE RD
2 ARK ROYAL CT
3 AMETHYST CL
4 VANGUARD CT
Quarrington
TOWN ROAD
F4
1 ST GILES AVE
2 ORCHARD CL
3 OLD PL
4 THE HOPLANDS
5 THE PADDOCK
6 BYRON CL
7 SHELLEY DR
8 BURNS CR
9 ELIOT CL
10 CHAUCER GD
11 CHRISTOPHER CR
12 CAROLINE CL
13 WORDSWORTH CT
14 KIPLING DR
15 COLERIDGE GD
LONDON ROAD
A
B
C
D
E
F
B2
1 WINDSOR CL
2 RICHMOND CL
3 ASHBOURNE CL
4 AMBLESIDE CL
5 SANDHURST CR
6 HILDA CL
7 HENGIST CL
8 HAUSER CL
9 ATHELSTAN CL
10 9 ALFRED CL
11 CHURCH CL
12 EDWIN CL
13 ANGLIA CL
14 MERCIA CL
B3
1 SHELDRAKE RD
2 KESTREL CL
3 EAGLE DR
4 WREN CL
5 OSPREY CL
6 PEREGRINE CL
7 DOVE CL
8 CYGNET CL
9 QUANTOCK CT
10 THRUSH CL
11 LINNET WY
12 ROBIN CL
13 FALCON WY
14 GRAMPIAN CL
121
C3
1 SWALLOW CL
2 RHODES AV
3 BUTTLER WY
4 LORD ST
5 COPELAND CT
C4
1 CHARLES ST
2 REFORM PL
3 WESTGATE PK
4 CASTLE TR RD
121
D2
1 HOLLY CL
2 BRIAR CL
3 JUNIPER WY
4 ASPEN DR
5 ROSEWOOD DR
6 BERRY CL
7 BRIDLE CL
8 LARCH WY
9 CYPRESS CL
10 LAVENDER CL
11 REDWOOD AV
12 ACACIA CL
13 LIMETREE CL
121
D3
1 THE INNINGS
2 CHESTNUT CL
3 SOUTHFIELDS
4 PINE CL
5 PAVILION GD
D4
1 LEICESTER ST
2 PLAYHOUSE YD
3 MARKET ST
4 MARKET PL
5 CROSS KEYS YD
6 WHARFSIDE MS
7 MONEYS YD
8 HANDLEY ST
9 HILL'S CT
E3
1 WILLOW CT
2 MAIDEN GR
3 SPINNERS CL
4 GRACE CL
5 PEACOCK CT
6 COBBLERS WY
7 CHAPEL HL CT
F3
1 JONATHAN GD
2 MILTON WY
3 ELMGARTH
4 POLYANTHUS DR
5 MARIGOLD WK
6 WALNUTGARTH
7 FORUM WAY

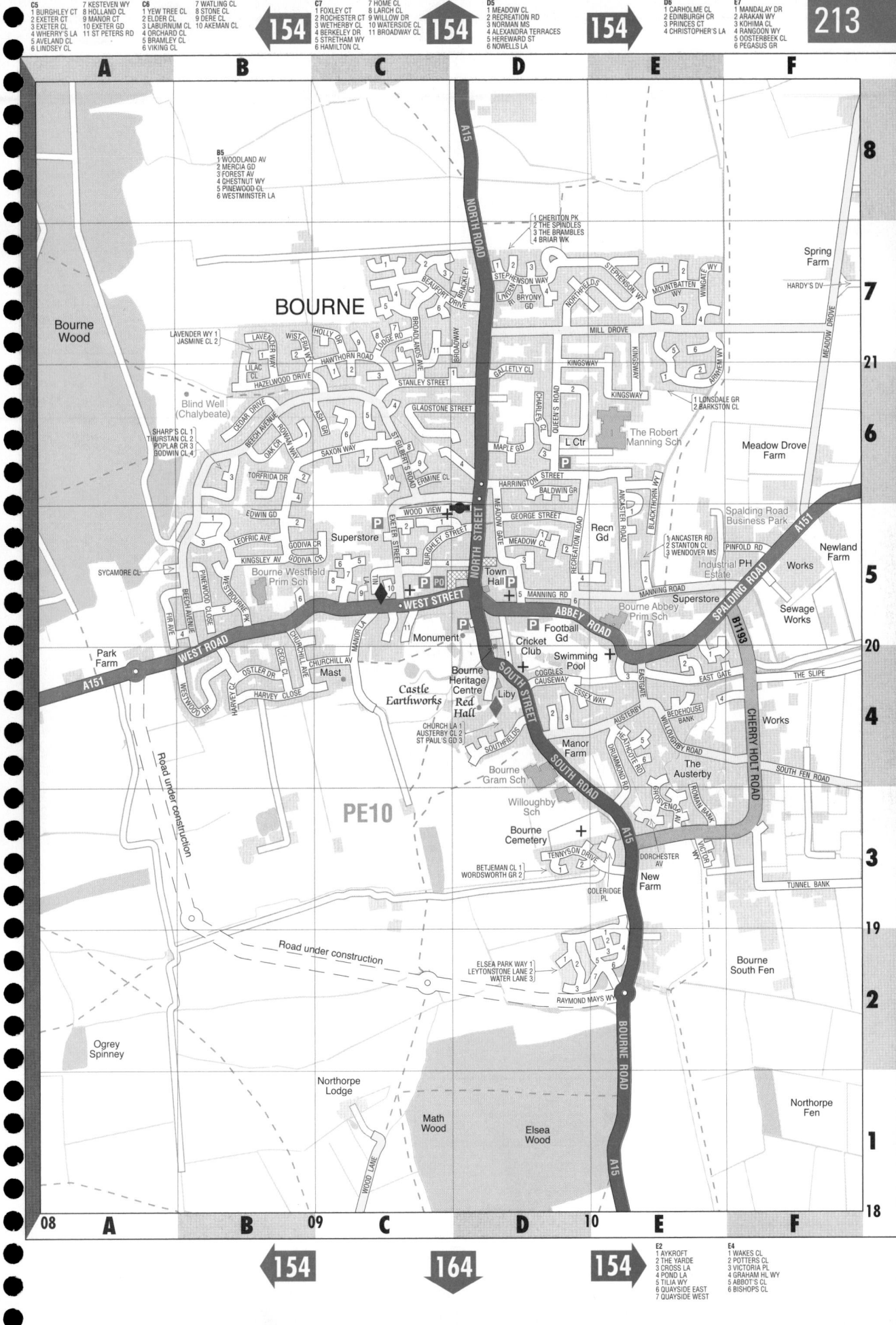

C5
1 BURGHLEY CT
2 EXETER CT
3 EXETER CL
4 WHERRY'S LA
5 AVELAND CL
6 LINDSEY CL
7 KESTEVEN WY
8 HOLLAND CL
9 MANOR CT
10 EXETER GD
11 ST PETERS RD

C6
1 YEW TREE CL
2 ELDER CL
3 LABURNUM CL
4 ORCHARD CL
5 BRAMLEY CL
6 VIKING CL
7 WATLING CL
8 STONE CL
9 DERE CL
10 AKEMAN CL

C7
1 FOXLEY CT
2 ROCHESTER CT
3 WETHERBY CL
4 BERKELEY DR
5 STRETHAM WY
6 HAMILTON CL
7 HOME CL
8 LARCH CL
9 WILLOW DR
10 WATERSIDE CL
11 BROADWAY CL

D5
1 MEADOW CL
2 RECREATION RD
3 NORMAN MS
4 ALEXANDRA TERRACES
5 HEREWARD ST
6 NOWELLS LA

D6
1 CARHOLME RD
2 EDINBURGH CR
3 PRINCES CT
4 CHRISTOPHER'S LA

E7
1 MANDALAY DR
2 ARAKAN WY
3 KOHIMA CL
4 RANGOON WY
5 OOSTERBEEK CL
6 PEGASUS GR

154 154 154

B5
1 WOODLAND AV
2 MERCIA GD
3 FOREST AV
4 CHESTNUT WY
5 PINEWOOD CL
6 WESTMINSTER LA

BOURNE

1 CHERITON PK
2 THE SPINDLES
3 THE BRAMBLES
4 BRIAR WK

Spring Farm
HARDY'S DV

Bourne Wood

LAVENDER WY 1
JASMINE CL 2

1 LONSDALE GR
2 BARKSTON CL

Meadow Drove Farm

SHARP'S CL 1
THURSTAN CL 2
POPLAR CR 3
GODWIN CL 4

The Robert Manning Sch

Blind Well (Chalybeate)

1 ANCASTER RD
2 STANTON CL
3 WENDOVER MS

Spalding Road Business Park

Newland Farm

SYCAMORE CL

Bourne Westfield Prim Sch

Superstore

Industrial Estate

Works

WEST STREET
Town Hall

Sewage Works

Bourne Abbey Prim Sch
Superstore

Park Farm

WEST ROAD

Monument

Mast

Football Gd
Cricket Club

Swimming Pool

THE SLIPE

Castle Earthworks
Bourne Heritage Centre
Red Hall
Liby

COGGLES CAUSEWAY

Works

CHURCH LA 1
AUSTERBY CL 2
ST PAUL'S GD 3

Manor Farm

The Austerby

SOUTH FEN ROAD

PE10

Bourne Gram Sch

Willoughby Sch

New Farm

Bourne Cemetery

BETJEMAN CL 1
WORDSWORTH GR 2

COLERIDGE PL

DORCHESTER AV

TUNNEL BANK

Ogrey Spinney

Road under construction

ELSEA PARK WAY 1
LEYTONSTONE LANE 2
WATER LANE 3

Bourne South Fen

RAYMOND MAYS WY

Northorpe Lodge

Math Wood

Elsea Wood

Northorpe Fen

154 164 154

E2
1 AYKROFT
2 THE YARDE
3 CROSS LA
4 POND LA
5 TILIA WY
6 QUAYSIDE EAST
7 QUAYSIDE WEST

E4
1 WAKES CL
2 POTTERS CL
3 VICTORIA PL
4 GRAHAM HL WY
5 ABBOT'S CL
6 BISHOPS CL

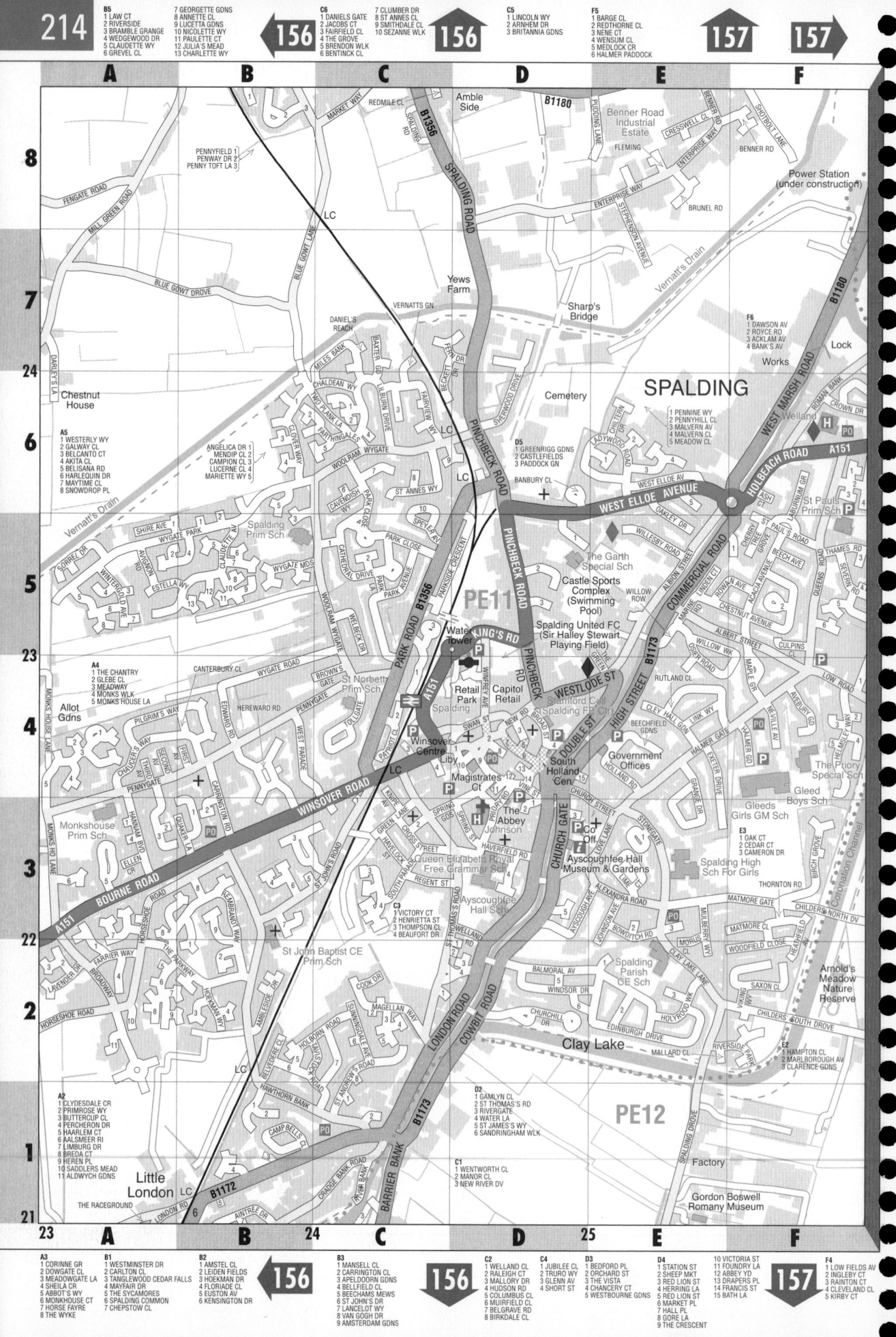

214
B5
1 LAW CT
2 RIVERSIDE
3 BRAMBLE GRANGE
4 WEDGEWOOD DR
5 CLAUDETTE WY
6 GREVEL CL
7 GEORGETTE GDNS
8 ANNETTE CL
9 LUCETTA GDNS
10 NICOLETTE WY
11 PAULETTE CT
12 JULIA'S MEAD
13 CHARLETTE WY
156
C6
1 DANIELS GATE
2 JACOBS CT
3 FAIRFIELD CL
4 THE GROVE
5 BRENDON WLK
6 BENTINCK CL
7 CLUMBER DR
8 ST ANNES CL
9 SMITHDALE CL
10 SEZANNE WLK
156
C5
1 LINCOLN WY
2 ARNHEM DR
3 BRITANNIA GDNS
F5
1 BARGE CL
2 REDTHORNE CL
3 NENE CT
4 WENSUM CL
5 MEDLOCK CR
6 HALMER PADDOCK
157
157
A B C D E F
8 7 24 6 5 23 4 3 22 2 1 21
SPALDING
PE11
PE12
Amble Side
Benner Road Industrial Estate
Power Station (under construction)
Yews Farm
Sharp's Bridge
Vernatt's Drain
Chestnut House
Cemetery
Welland
Lock
Works
St Pauls Prim Sch
Spalding Prim Sch
The Garth Special Sch
Castle Sports Complex (Swimming Pool)
Spalding United FC (Sir Halley Stewart Playing Field)
Water Tower
Retail Park
Capitol Retail
Spalding
Stamford Coll (Spalding FE Ctr)
St Norbetts Prim Sch
Allot Gdns
Winsover Centre
Liby
Magistrates Ct
South Holland Cen
Government Offices
The Priory Special Sch
Gleed Boys Sch
Gleeds Girls GM Sch
Monkshouse Prim Sch
The Abbey
Johnson
Queen Elizabeth Royal Free Grammar Sch
Ayscoughfee Hall Museum & Gardens
Ayscoughfee Hall Sch
Spalding High Sch For Girls
St John Baptist CE Prim Sch
Spalding Parish CE Sch
Arnold's Meadow Nature Reserve
Coronation Channel
Clay Lake
Little London
Factory
Gordon Boswell Romany Museum
THE RACEGROUND
A151 B1356 B1180 B1173 B1172
SPALDING ROAD
PINCHBECK ROAD
PARK ROAD
WINSOVER ROAD
BOURNE ROAD
WEST ELLOE AVENUE
HOLBEACH ROAD
WEST MARSH ROAD
COMMERCIAL ROAD
HIGH STREET
DOUBLE ST
CHURCH GATE
LONDON ROAD
COWBIT ROAD
BARRIER BANK
WESTLODE ST
FENGATE ROAD
MILL GREEN ROAD
BLUE GOWT DROVE
BLUE GOWT LANE
ENTERPRISE WAY
STEPHENSON AVENUE
A5
1 WESTERLY WY
2 GALWAY CL
3 BELCANTO CT
4 AKITA CL
5 BELISANA RD
6 HARLEQUIN DR
7 MAYTIME CL
8 SNOWDROP PL
D5
1 GREENRIGG GDNS
2 CASTLEFIELDS
3 PADDOCK GN
F6
1 DAWSON AV
2 ROYCE RD
3 ACKLAM AV
4 BANK'S AV
A4
1 THE CHANTRY
2 GLEBE CL
3 MEADWAY
4 MONKS WLK
5 MONKS HOUSE LA
C3
1 VICTORY CT
2 HENRIETTA ST
3 THOMPSON CL
4 BEAUFORT DR
E3
1 OAK CT
2 CEDAR CT
3 CAMERON DR
E2
1 HAMPTON CL
2 MARLBOROUGH AV
3 CLARENCE GDNS
A2
1 CLYDESDALE CR
2 PRIMROSE WY
3 BUTTERCUP CL
4 PERCHERON DR
5 HAARLEM CT
6 AALSMEER RI
7 LIMBURG DR
8 BREDA CT
9 HEREN PL
10 SADDLERS MEAD
11 ALDWYCH GDNS
D2
1 GAMLYN CL
2 ST THOMAS'S RD
3 RIVERGATE
4 WATER LA
5 ST JAMES'S WY
6 SANDRINGHAM WLK
C1
1 WENTWORTH CL
2 MANOR CL
3 NEW RIVER DV
1 PENNINE WY
2 PENNYHILL CL
3 MALVERN AV
4 MALVERN CL
5 MEADOW CL
PENNYFIELD 1
PENWAY DR 2
PENNY TOFT LA 3
ANGELICA DR 1
MENDIP CL 2
CAMPION CL 3
LUCERNE CL 4
MARIETTE WY 5
A3
1 CORINNE GR
2 DOWGATE CL
3 MEADOWGATE LA
4 SHEILA CR
5 ABBOT'S WY
6 MONKHOUSE CT
7 HORSE FAYRE
8 THE WYKE
B1
1 WESTMINSTER DR
2 CARLTON CL
3 TANGLEWOOD CEDAR FALLS
4 MAYFAIR DR
5 THE SYCAMORES
6 SPALDING COMMON
7 CHEPSTOW CL
B2
1 AMSTEL CL
2 LEIDEN FIELDS
3 HOEKMAN DR
4 FLORIADE CL
5 EUSTON AV
6 KENSINGTON DR
156
B3
1 MANSELL CL
2 CARRINGTON CL
3 APELDOORN GDNS
4 BELLFIELD CL
5 BEECHAMS MEWS
6 ST JOHN'S DR
7 LANCELOT WY
8 VAN GOGH DR
9 AMSTERDAM GDNS
156
C2
1 WELLAND CL
2 RALEIGH CT
3 MALLORY DR
4 HUDSON RD
5 COLUMBUS CL
6 MUIRFIELD CL
7 BELGRAVE RD
8 BIRKDALE CL
C4
1 JUBILEE CL
2 TRURO WY
3 GLENN AV
4 SHORT ST
D3
1 BEDFORD PL
2 ORCHARD ST
3 THE VISTA
4 CHANCERY CT
5 WESTBOURNE GDNS
D4
1 STATION ST
2 SHEEP MKT
3 RED LION ST
4 HERRING LA
5 RED LION ST
6 MARKET PL
7 HALL PL
8 GORE LA
9 THE CRESCENT
10 VICTORIA ST
11 FOUNDRY LA
12 ABBEY YD
13 DRAPERS PL
14 FRANCIS ST
15 BATH LA
157
F4
1 LOW FIELDS AV
2 INGLEBY CT
3 RAINTON CT
4 CLEVELAND CL
5 KIRBY CT

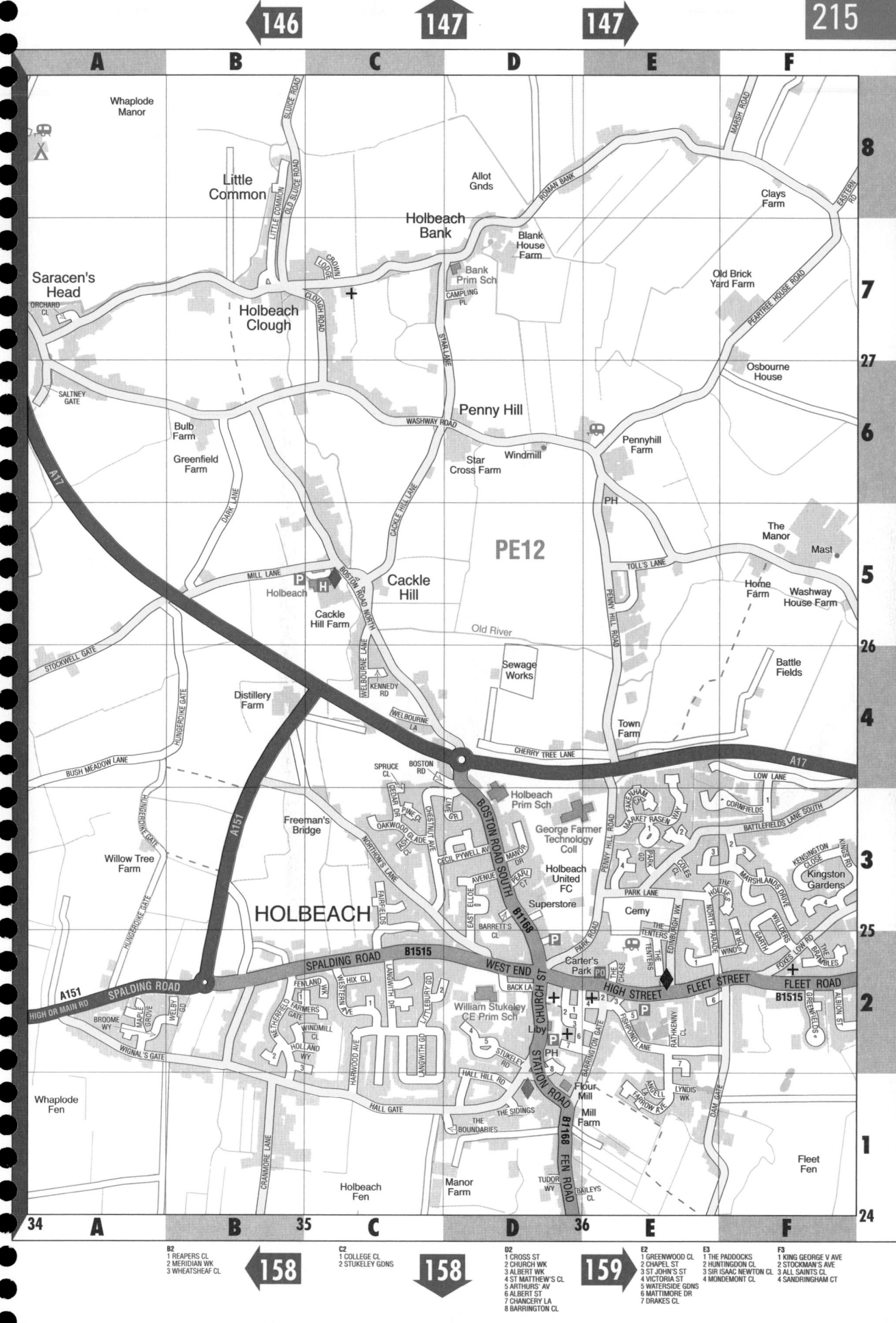

A B C D E F

8
7
27
6
5
26
4
3
25
2
1
24

34 A B 35 C D 36 E F

Whaplode Manor
Little Common
Holbeach Bank
Allot Gnds
Blank House Farm
Clays Farm
Old Brick Yard Farm
Saracen's Head
ORCHARD CL
Holbeach Clough
Bank Prim Sch
CAMPLING PL
Osbourne House
SALTNEY GATE
Penny Hill
Pennyhill Farm
Bulb Farm
Greenfield Farm
Washway Road
Star Cross Farm
Windmill
PH
The Manor
Mast
DARK LANE
Home Farm
Washway House Farm
STOCKWELL GATE
MILL LANE
Holbeach
Cackle Hill
PE12
Old River
TOLL'S LANE
PENNY HILL ROAD
Cackle Hill Farm
Sewage Works
Battle Fields
HUNGERDIKE GATE
Distillery Farm
KENNEDY RD
WELBOURNE LANE
WELBOURNE LA
Town Farm
BUSH MEADOW LANE
CHERRY TREE LANE
A17
Willow Tree Farm
HUNGERDIKE GATE
Freeman's Bridge
SPRUCE CL
BOSTON RD
Holbeach Prim Sch
LOW LANE
CORNFIELDS
BATTLEFIELDS LANE SOUTH
A151
CEDAR DR
PINE CL
OAKWOOD GLADE
CHESTNUT AV
LIME GR
George Farmer Technology Coll
FACKNAM WAY
MARKET RASEN
KENSINGTON CLOSE
KINGS RD
Kingston Gardens
HOLBEACH
CECIL PYWELL CT
MANOR DR
PEARL CT
Holbeach United FC
PARK RD
COLES
MARSHLANDS DRIVE
NORTHON'S LANE
AVENUE
Superstore
PARK LANE
THE HOLLIES
WILLBERRY
THE GARTH
FOXES COV RD
THE BRAMBLES
B1168
EAST ELLOE
Cerny
NORTH PARADE
WIND'S
FAIRFIELDS
BARRETT'S CL
Carter's Park
THE CHASE
THE TENTERS
ALBION ST
SPALDING ROAD
B1515
WEST END
HIGH STREET
FLEET STREET
FLEET ROAD
A151
SPALDING ROAD
BACK LA
Liby
B1515
GREENFIELDS
HIGH OR MAIN RD
FENLAND WK
HIX CL
LANGWITH DR
William Stukeley CE Prim Sch
CHURCH ST
PH
FISHPOND LANE
BROOME WY
MAPLE GROVE
WELBY GD
FARMERS GATE
WESTERN AV
LITTLEBURY GD
HOLLAND WY
WINDMILL CL
HARWOOD AV
LANGWITH GD
STUKELEY GD
BARRINGTON GATE
FATHKENNY
ANGELL
LYNDIS WK
WIGNAL'S GATE
HALL HILL RD
Flour Mill
STATION ROAD
ARROW AVE
DAM GATE
CRANMORE LANE
HALL GATE
THE SIDINGS
THE BOUNDARIES
Mill Farm
FEN ROAD
B1168
BAILEYS CL
Fleet Fen
Whaplode Fen
Holbeach Fen
Manor Farm
TUDOR WY

← 158 158 159 →

B2
1 REAPERS CL
2 MERIDIAN WK
3 WHEATSHEAF CL

C2
1 COLLEGE CL
2 STUKELEY GDNS

D2
1 CROSS ST
2 CHURCH WK
3 ALBERT WK
4 ST MATTHEW'S CL
5 ARTHURS' AV
6 ALBERT ST
7 CHANCERY LA
8 BARRINGTON CL

E2
1 GREENWOOD CL
2 CHAPEL ST
3 ST JOHN'S ST
4 VICTORIA ST
5 WATERSIDE GDNS
6 MATTIMORE DR
7 DRAKES CL

E3
1 THE PADDOCKS
2 HUNTINGDON CL
3 SIR ISAAC NEWTON CL
4 MONDEMONT CL

F3
1 KING GEORGE V AVE
2 STOCKMAN'S AVE
3 ALL SAINTS CL
4 SANDRINGHAM CT

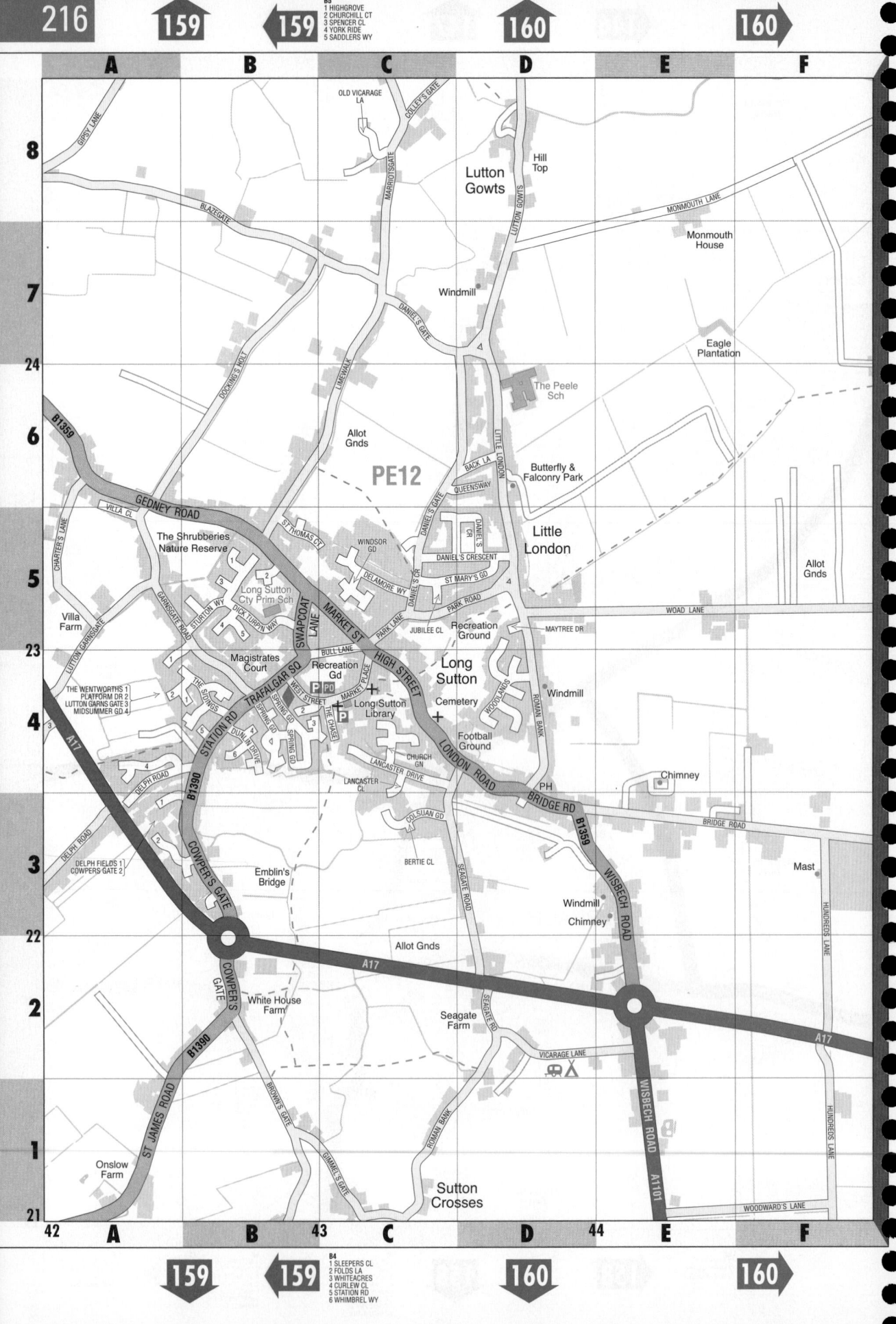

159   ◄159   160   160►

B5
1 HIGHGROVE
2 CHURCHILL CT
3 SPENCER CL
4 YORK RIDE
5 SADDLERS WY

A   B   C   D   E   F

OLD VICARAGE LA

Lutton Gowts

Hill Top

MONMOUTH LANE

Monmouth House

BLAZEGATE

Windmill

8

7

Eagle Plantation

24

B1359

The Peele Sch

6

Allot Gnds

PE12

Butterfly & Falconry Park

Little London

Allot Gnds

GEDNEY ROAD

VILLA CL

CHARTER'S LANE

The Shrubberies Nature Reserve

ST THOMAS CT

WINDSOR GD

DANIEL'S GATE

DANIEL'S CR

Little London

WOAD LANE

5

Villa Farm

Long Sutton Cty Prim Sch

DELAMORE WY

DANIEL'S CRESCENT

ST MARY'S GD

PARK ROAD

SWAPCOAT LANE

MARKET ST

DICK TURPIN WAY

STURTON WY

GARNSATE ROAD

LUTTON GARNSATE

JUBILEE CL

Recreation Ground

MAYTREE DR

23

THE WENTWORTHS 1
PLATFORM DR 2
LUTTON GARNS GATE 3
MIDSUMMER GD 4

Magistrates Court

THE SONGS

Recreation Gd

PARK LANE

HIGH STREET

Long Sutton

Windmill

BULL LANE

P PO

Market Place

Long Sutton Library

Cemetery

ROMAN BANK

WOODLANDS

A17

STATION RD

TRAFALGAR SQ

WEST STREET

SPRING GD

DUBLIN DRIVE

THE CHASE

P

Football Ground

4

B1390

DELPH ROAD

COWPER'S GATE

LANCASTER DRIVE

CHURCH GN

LONDON ROAD

PH

Chimney

Windmill

BRIDGE RD

B1359

BRIDGE ROAD

DELPH ROAD

DELPH FIELDS 1
COWPERS GATE 2

LANCASTER CL

COLSUAN GD

BERTIE CL

Emblin's Bridge

WISBECH ROAD

Mast

3

22

COWPER'S GATE

A17

Allot Gnds

HUNDREDS LANE

2

White House Farm

SEAGATE ROAD

Seagate Farm

SEAGATE RD

A17

B1390

ST JAMES ROAD

BROWN'S GATE

VICARAGE LANE

Onslow Farm

GIMMEL'S GATE

ROMAN BANK

Sutton Crosses

WISBECH ROAD

A1101

WOODWARD'S LANE

1

21

42   A   43   B   C   D   44   E   F

159   ◄159   160   160►

B4
1 SLEEPERS CL
2 FOLDS LA
3 WHITEACRES
4 CURLEW CL
5 STATION RD
6 WHIMBREL WY

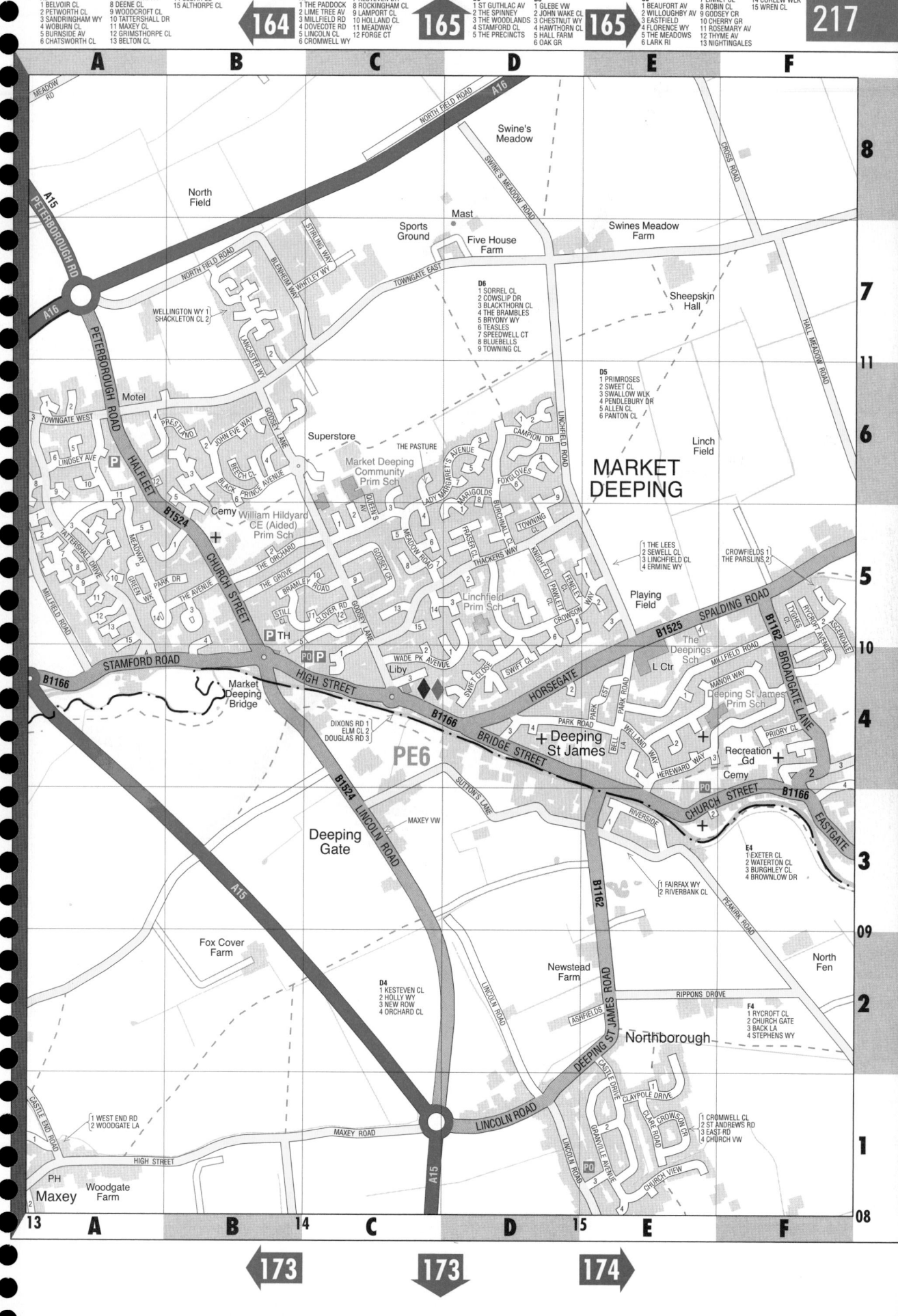

A5
1 BELVOIR CL
2 PETWORTH CL
3 SANDRINGHAM WY
4 WOBURN CL
5 BURNSIDE AV
6 CHATSWORTH CL

7 OSBOURNE WY
8 DEENE CL
9 WOODCROFT CL
10 TATTERSHALL DR
11 MAXEY CL
12 GRIMSTHORPE CL
13 BELTON CL

14 CEDAR CL
15 ALTHORPE CL

A6
1 THE PADDOCK
2 LIME TREE AV
3 MILLFIELD RD
4 DOVECOTE RD
5 LINCOLN CL
6 CROMWELL WY

7 KESTEVEN DR
8 ROCKINGHAM CL
9 LAMPORT CL
10 HOLLAND CL
11 MEADWAY
12 FORGE CT

B5
1 ST GUTHLAC AV
2 THE SPINNEY
3 THE WOODLANDS
4 STAMFORD CL
5 THE PRECINCTS

B6
1 GLEBE VW
2 JOHN WAKE CL
3 CHESTNUT WY
4 HAWTHORN CL
5 HALL FARM
6 OAK GR

C5
1 BEAUFORT AV
2 WILLOUGHBY AV
3 EASTFIELD
4 FLORENCE WY
5 THE MEADOWS
6 LARK RI

7 LINNET CL
8 ROBIN CL
9 GODSEY CR
10 CHERRY GR
11 ROSEMARY AV
12 THYME AV
13 NIGHTINGALES

14 CURLEW WLK
15 WREN CL

164 **165** **165**

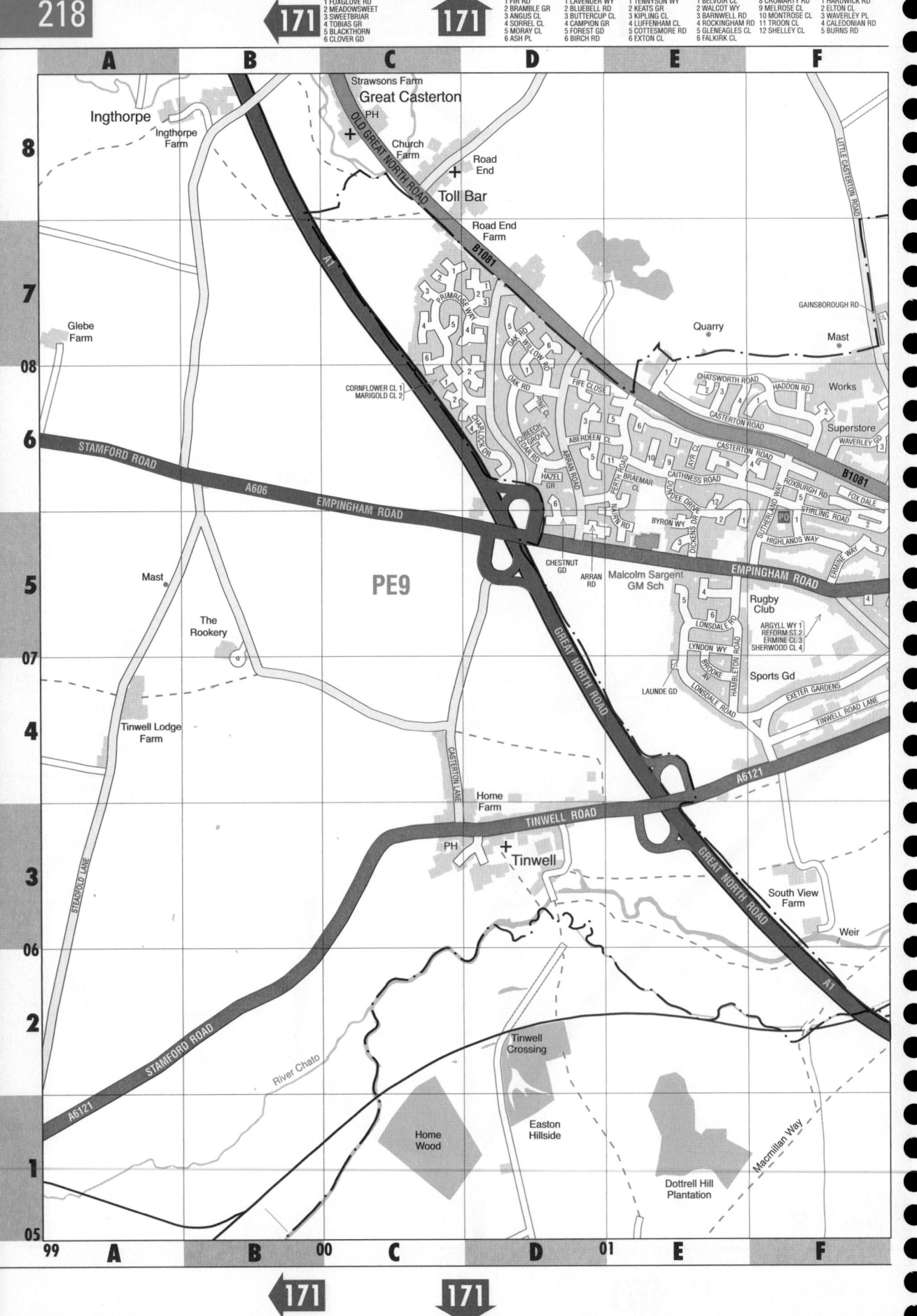

C7
1 FOXGLOVE RD
2 MEADOWSWEET
3 SWEETBRIAR
4 TOBIAS GR
5 BLACKTHORN
6 CLOVER GD

D6
1 FIR RD
2 BRAMBLE GR
3 ANGUS CL
4 SORREL CL
5 MORAY CL
6 ASH PL

D7
1 LAVENDER WY
2 BLUEBELL RD
3 BUTTERCUP CL
4 CAMPION GR
5 FOREST GD
6 BIRCH RD

E5
1 TENNYSON WY
2 KEATS GR
3 KIPLING CL
4 LUFFENHAM CL
5 COTTESMORE RD
6 EXTON CL

E6
1 BELVOIR CL
2 WALCOT WY
3 BARNWELL RD
4 ROCKINGHAM RD
5 GLENEAGLES CL
6 FALKIRK CL

7 OBAN CL
8 CROMARTY RD
9 MELROSE CL
10 MONTROSE CL
11 TROON CL
12 SHELLEY CL

F6
1 HARDWICK RD
2 ELTON CL
3 WAVERLEY PL
4 CALEDONIAN RD
5 BURNS RD

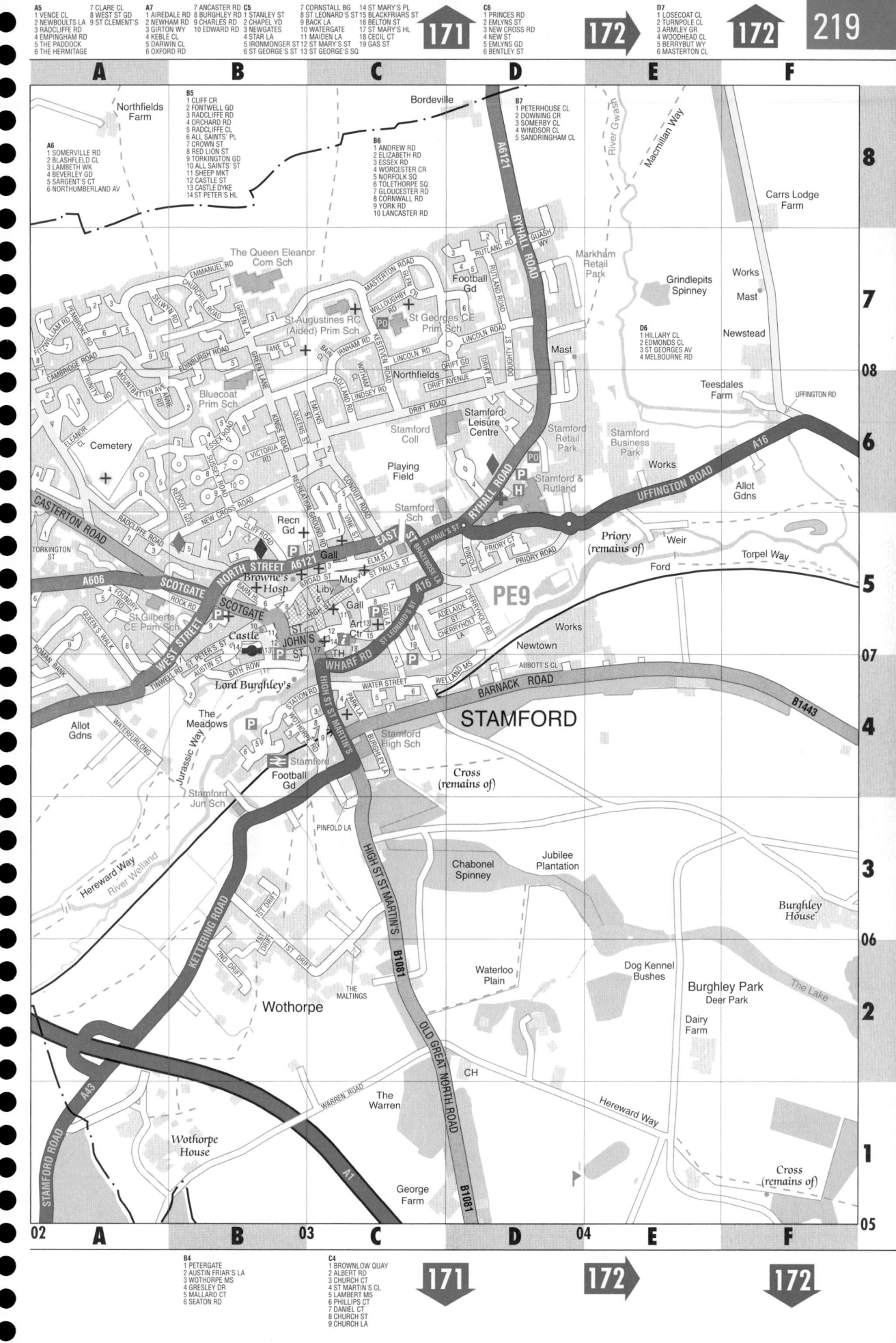
A5
1 VENCE CL
2 NEWBOULTS LA
3 RADCLIFFE RD
4 EMPINGHAM RD
5 THE PADDOCK
6 THE HERMITAGE
7 CLARE CL
8 WEST ST GD
9 ST CLEMENT'S
A7
1 AIREDALE RD
2 NEWHAM RD
3 GIRTON WY
4 KEBLE CL
5 DARWIN CL
6 OXFORD RD
7 ANCASTER RD
8 BURGHLEY RD
9 CHARLES RD
10 EDWARD RD
C5
1 STANLEY ST
2 CHAPEL YD
3 NEWGATES
4 STAR LA
5 IRONMONGER ST
6 ST GEORGE'S ST
7 CORNSTALL BG
8 ST LEONARD'S ST
9 BACK LA
10 WATERGATE
11 MAIDEN LA
12 ST MARY'S ST
13 ST GEORGE'S SQ
14 ST MARY'S PL
15 BLACKFRIARS ST
16 BELTON ST
17 ST MARY'S HL
18 CECIL CT
19 GAS ST
171
C6
1 PRINCES RD
2 EMLYNS ST
3 NEW CROSS RD
4 NEW ST
5 EMLYNS GD
6 BENTLEY ST
172
D7
1 LOSECOAT CL
2 TURNPOLE CL
3 ARMLEY GR
4 WOODHEAD CL
5 BERRYBUT WY
6 MASTERTON CL
172
A
B
C
D
E
F
B5
1 CLIFF CR
2 FONTWELL GD
3 RADCLIFFE RD
4 ORCHARD RD
5 RADCLIFFE CL
6 ALL SAINTS' PL
7 CROWN ST
8 RED LION ST
9 TORKINGTON GD
10 ALL SAINTS' ST
11 SHEEP MKT
12 CASTLE ST
13 CASTLE DYKE
14 ST PETER'S HL
A6
1 SOMERVILLE RD
2 BLASHFIELD CL
3 LAMBETH WK
4 BEVERLEY GD
5 SARGENT'S CT
6 NORTHUMBERLAND AV
B6
1 ANDREW RD
2 ELIZABETH RD
3 ESSEX RD
4 WORCESTER CR
5 NORFOLK SQ
6 TOLETHORPE SQ
7 GLOUCESTER RD
8 CORNWALL RD
9 YORK RD
10 LANCASTER RD
B7
1 PETERHOUSE CL
2 DOWNING CR
3 SOMERBY CL
4 WINDSOR CL
5 SANDRINGHAM CL
D6
1 HILLARY CL
2 EDMONDS CL
3 ST GEORGES AV
4 MELBOURNE RD
Northfields Farm
Bordeville
River Gwash
Macmillan Way
A6121
RYHALL ROAD
Carrs Lodge Farm
The Queen Eleanor Com Sch
Markham Retail Park
Football Gd
Grindlepits Spinney
Works
Mast
Newstead
St Augustines RC (Aided) Prim Sch
St Georges CE Prim Sch
Northfields
Bluecoat Prim Sch
Teesdales Farm
UFFINGTON RD
Stamford Coll
Stamford Leisure Centre
Stamford Retail Park
Stamford Business Park
Cemetery
Playing Field
Stamford & Rutland
UFFINGTON ROAD
A16
Allot Gdns
CASTERTON ROAD
Recn Gd
Stamford Sch
Priory (remains of)
Weir
Torpel Way
Ford
A606
SCOTGATE
NORTH STREET
A6121
EAST ST
Gall
Browne's Hosp
Mus
Liby
PE9
St Gilberts CE Prim Sch
WEST STREET
Castle
ST JOHN'S
TH
Art Ctr
WHARF RD
Works
Newtown
Lord Burghley's
BARNACK ROAD
B1443
The Meadows
Allot Gdns
STAMFORD
Stamford High Sch
Jurassic Way
Stamford
Football Gd
Cross (remains of)
Stamford Jun Sch
PINFOLD LA
HIGH ST ST MARTIN'S
Chabonel Spinney
Jubilee Plantation
Hereward Way
River Welland
KETTERING ROAD
Burghley House
1ST DRIFT
2ND DRIFT
B1081
Waterloo Plain
Dog Kennel Bushes
Burghley Park
Deer Park
The Lake
THE MALTINGS
Wothorpe
Dairy Farm
OLD GREAT NORTH ROAD
CH
A43
The Warren
WARREN ROAD
Hereward Way
STAMFORD ROAD
Wothorpe House
A1
George Farm
Cross (remains of)
8
7
08
6
5
07
4
3
06
2
1
05
02
03
04
B4
1 PETERGATE
2 AUSTIN FRIAR'S LA
3 WOTHORPE MS
4 GRESLEY DR
5 MALLARD CT
6 SEATON RD
C4
1 BROWNLOW QUAY
2 ALBERT RD
3 CHURCH CT
4 ST MARTIN'S CL
5 LAMBERT MS
6 PHILLIPS CT
7 DANIEL CT
8 CHURCH ST
9 CHURCH LA
171
172
172

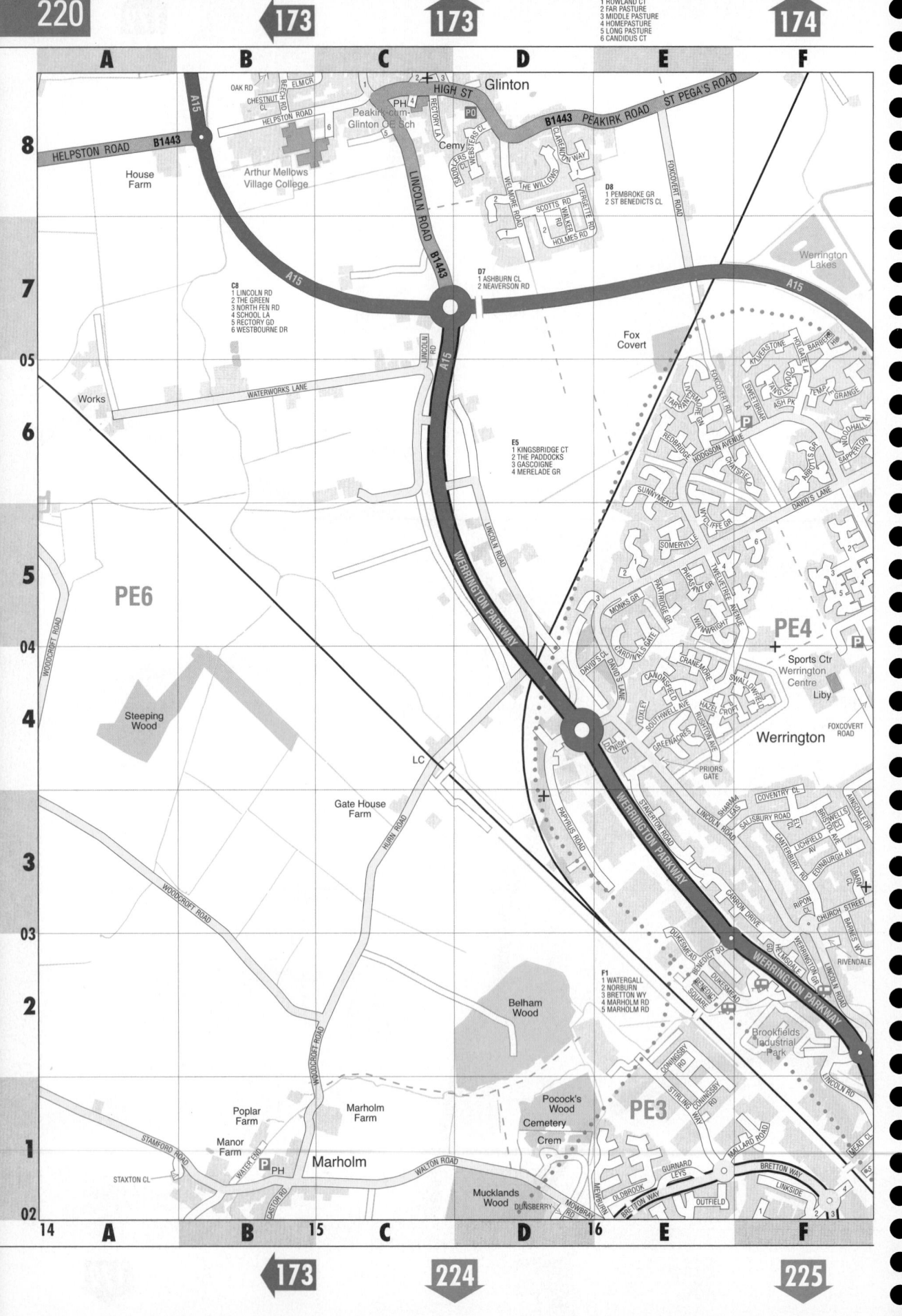

← 173
173
174
173 →
224
225

F5
1 ROWLAND CT
2 FAR PASTURE
3 MIDDLE PASTURE
4 HOMEPASTURE
5 LONG PASTURE
6 CANDIDUS CT

7 DERWOOD GR

Glinton

OAK RD
CHESTNUT CL
ELM CR
HELPSTON ROAD
PH
Peakirk-cum-
Glinton CE Sch
HIGH ST
PEAKIRK ROAD
ST PEGA'S ROAD
B1443
PO
CLARENDON WAY
THE WILLOWS
FOXCOVERT ROAD

HELPSTON ROAD B1443

House
Farm

Arthur Mellows
Village College

Cemy

LINCOLN ROAD

RECTORY LA
WEBSTERS CL
FRS CL
CROSS
WELMORE ROAD
SCOTTS RD
WALKER RD
HOLMES RD
VERRETTE RD

D8
1 PEMBROKE GR
2 ST BENEDICTS CL

Werrington
Lakes

A15

A15

C8
1 LINCOLN RD
2 THE GREEN
3 NORTH FEN RD
4 SCHOOL LA
5 RECTORY GD
6 WESTBOURNE DR

D7
1 ASHBURN CL
2 NEAVERSON RD

Fox
Covert

B1443

A15

WATERWORKS LANE

Works

LINCOLN RD

RIVERSTONE
KIRKSTONE
HOLME LA
BARBICAN
GRIP
FOXCOVERT ROAD
LIVERMORE
SWEETBRIAR
ASH PK
TEMPL
GRANGE
WOODHALL
SAPPERTON

E5
1 KINGSBRIDGE CT
2 THE PADDOCKS
3 GASCOIGNE
4 MERELADE GR

REDBRIDGE
HODGSON AVENUE
CHATSFIELD

SUNNYMEAD

WERRINGTON PARKWAY

LINCOLN ROAD

SOMERVILLE

WYCLIFFE GR

DAVID'S LANE

PE6

MONKS GR
PARTRIDGE GR
PHEASANT GR
TWELVETREE AVENUE
WAINWRIGHT

PE4

Steeping
Wood

CARDIN'S GATE
DAVID'S CT
DAVID'S LANE
CANONSFIELD
CRANEMORE
COXLEY
CANONGATE
SOUTHWELL AVE
GREENACRES
HAZEL CROFT
SWALLOWFIELD
RIGHTON AVE

Sports Ctr
Werrington
Centre
Liby

WOODCROFT ROAD

WOODCROFT ROAD

Gate House
Farm

LC

HURN ROAD

WERRINGTON PARKWAY

PRIORS
GATE

Werrington

FOXCOVERT
ROAD

STAVERTON ROAD
PAPYRUS ROAD

LISGHIGH
CT

COVENTRY CL.
SHARMA
LEAS
LINCOLN RD
SALISBURY ROAD
LICHFIELD
AV
ABSOLUTE
CANTERBURY RD
EDINBURGH AV
BARN
RIPON CL
CHURCH STREET
BARNES WY
ABBOTS
HELMSDALE RD
WERRINGTON SQ
LINCOLN ROAD
RIVENDALE

CARRON DRIVE

WERRINGTON PARKWAY

Belham
Wood

DUKESMEAD
DUKESMEAD
SQUARE

F1
1 WATERGALL
2 NORBURN
3 BRETTON WY
4 MARHOLM RD
5 MARHOLM RD

Brookfields
Industrial
Park

STAMFORD ROAD

Poplar
Farm

Marholm
Farm

Pocock's
Wood
Cemetery
Crem

PE3

CONINGSBY RD
STIRLING WAY
CONINGSBY RD

LINCOLN RD

Manor
Farm
P PH

Marholm

WALTON ROAD

Mucklands
Wood
DUNSBERRY

MOWBRAY RD
MELVERN
OLDBROOK
GURNARD
LEYS
BRETTON WAY

Bretton Way
MALLARD RD
BRETTON WAY
LINKSIDE

STAXTON CL

WATER END
CASTOR RD

OUTFIELD

MEAD CL

PE4

PE6

WOODCROFT ROAD

14
15
16

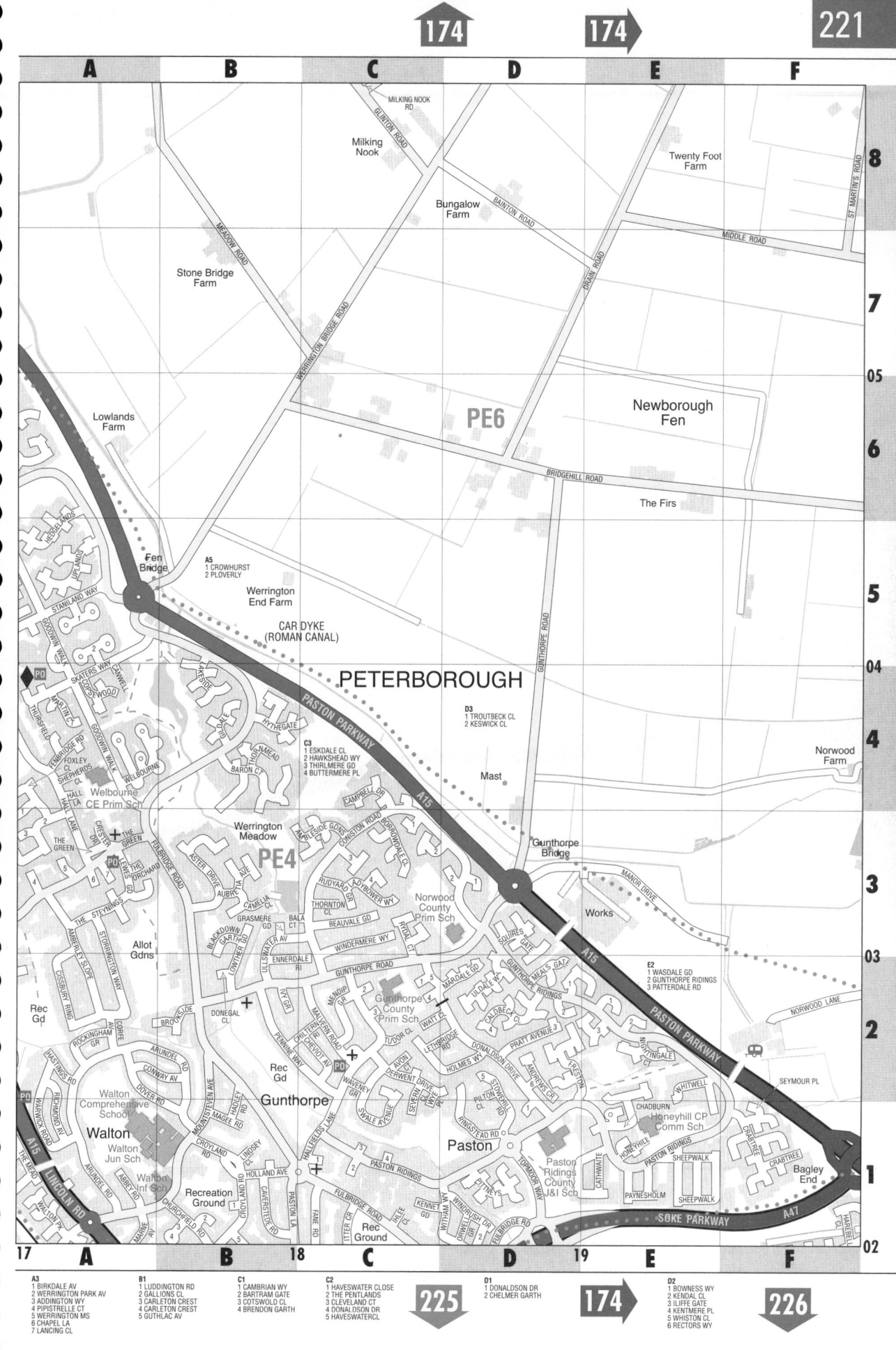

A B C D E F

MILKING NOOK RD

Milking Nook

GLINTON ROAD

BAINTON ROAD

Bungalow Farm

Twenty Foot Farm

MIDDLE ROAD

ST MARTINS ROAD

MEADOW ROAD

Stone Bridge Farm

DRAIN ROAD

WERRINGTON BRIDGE ROAD

PE6

Newborough Fen

BRIDGEHILL ROAD

Lowlands Farm

The Firs

HEDLANDS
UPLANDS

Fen Bridge

A5
1 CROWHURST
2 PLOVERLY

Werrington End Farm

GUNTHORPE ROAD

STANIAND WAY CANWELL

GOODWIN WALK

CAKESIDE

CAR DYKE
(ROMAN CANAL)

PO

SKATERS WAY

PASTON PARKWAY

PETERBOROUGH

Norwood Farm

MARTIN C
THURSFIELD

HYTHEGATE

A15

D3
1 TROUTBECK CL
2 KESWICK CL

FENBRIDGE RD
FOXLEY CL
SHEPHERDS
HALL

THE
GREEN

Welbourne CE Prim Sch

C3
1 ESKDALE CL
2 HAWKSHEAD WY
3 THIRLMERE GD
4 BUTTERMERE PL

Mast

GOODWIN WALK

WELBOURNE

Werrington Meadow

PE4

ASTER DRIVE

AUBRETIA AVE
CAMELIA CL

CAMPBELL OR

CONISTON ROAD
BORROWDALE CL

RUDYARD GR

Gunthorpe Bridge

MANOR DRIVE

Works

THE STEYINGS

AMBERLEY SLOPE

CISSBURY RING

Allot Gdns

CRESTA DR

THE ORCHARD

FULBRIDGE ROAD

BLACKDOWN GARTH

GRASMERE GD

THORNTON CL

BALA CT

BEAUVALE GD

WINDERMERE WY

Norwood County Prim Sch

SQUIRES GATE

A15

PASTON PARKWAY

E2
1 WASDALE GD
2 GUNTHORPE RIDINGS
3 PATTERDALE RD

NORWOOD LANE

Rec Gd

ROCKINGHAM GR

COPPE

BROOKSIDE

LOWTHER

ULLSWATER AV

ENNERDALE RI

GUNTHORPE ROAD

MCNDIP GR

DONEGAL CL

MAYFEN ROAD

CHILTERN RD

CHEVIOT AV

PENNINE WAY

IVY GRI

Gunthorpe County Prim Sch

MARDALE GD

ULDALE CL

CALDBECK CL

GUNTHORPE RIDINGS

PRATT AVENUE

MEALS GATE

NIGHTINGALE

SEYMOUR PL

Rec Gd

HASTINGS RD

ARUNDEL RD

CONWAY AV

DOVER RD

HADLEY RD

LINDSEY CL

WAVENEY GRI

WATT CL

TUDOR CL

AVON

DERWENT DRIVE

SEVERN

HOLMES W

ANDREWS CR

PRESTON

WHITWELL

Gunthorpe

PO

Walton Comprehensive School

MOUNTSTEVEN AVE

MAGEE RD

HOLLAND AVE

PASTON LA

SWALE AVENUE

STONEHILL

PILTON RD

Paston

CHADBURN

Honeyhill CP Comm Sch

NIGHTINGALE

PASTON RIDINGS

SHEEPWALK

CRABTREE

Bagley End

Walton

A15

THE READ

WALTON PK

Walton Jun Sch

CROYLAND RD

Walton Inf Sch

CHURCHFIELD

Recreation Ground

HALLBEDS LANE

CAVERSTEDE RD

PASTON LA

FANE RD

PASTON RIDINGS

FULBRIDGE ROAD

Rec Ground

KENNET W

WINDRUSH DR

FULBRIDGE RD

Paston Ridings County J&I Sch

CATHWAITE

PAYNESHOLM

SHEEPWALK

SOKE PARKWAY

A47

HAREBELL

LINCOLN RD

WARWICK RD

RICHMOND RD

PO

CAMBRIAN WY

WITHAM

TORMOR WY

A3
1 BIRKDALE AV
2 WERRINGTON PARK AV
3 ADDINGTON WY
4 PIPISTRELLE CT
5 WERRINGTON MS
6 CHAPEL LA
7 LANCING CL

B1
1 LUDDINGTON RD
2 GALLIONS CL
3 CARLETON CREST
4 CARLETON CREST
5 GUTHLAC AV

C1
1 CAMBRIAN WY
2 BARTRAM GATE
3 COTSWOLD CL
4 BRENDON GARTH

C2
1 HAVESWATER CLOSE
2 THE PENTLANDS
3 CLEVELAND CT
4 DONALDSON DR
5 HAVESWATERCL

D1
1 DONALDSON DR
2 CHELMER GARTH

D2
1 BOWNESS WY
2 KENDAL CL
3 ILIFFE GATE
4 KENTMERE PL
5 WHISTON CL
6 RECTORS WY

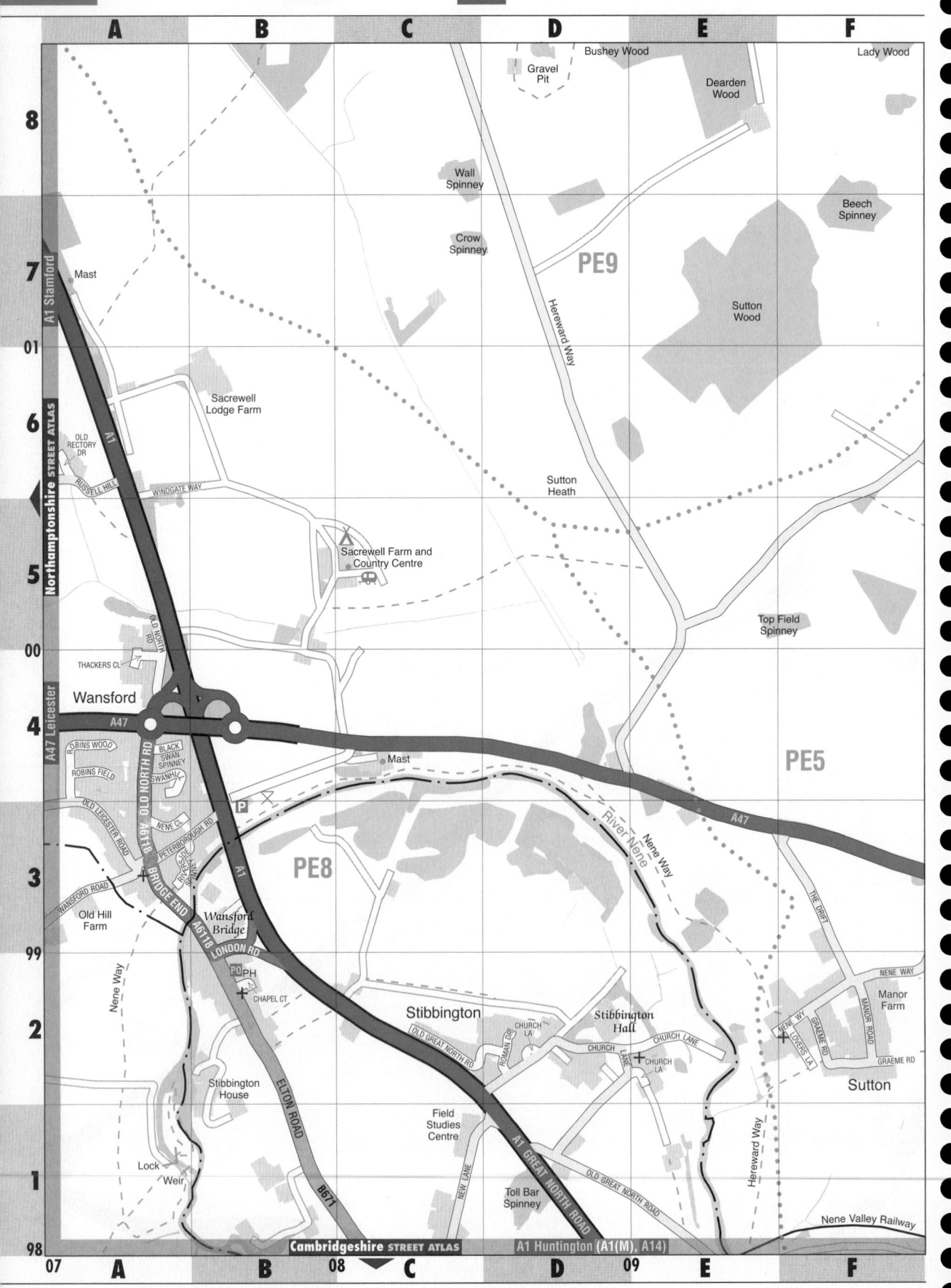

A   B   C   D   E   F

Bushey Wood

Gravel
Pit

Lady Wood

Dearden
Wood

8

Wall
Spinney

Beech
Spinney

Crow
Spinney

PE9

7

Mast

Hereward Way

Sutton
Wood

01

Sacrewell
Lodge Farm

6

OLD
RECTORY
DR

A1

Sutton
Heath

RUSSELL HILL

WINDGATE WAY

Top Field
Spinney

5

THACKERS CL

Sacrewell Farm and
Country Centre

00

OLD NORTH RD

Wansford

PE5

4

A47 Leicester

A47

A1

A47

Mast

River Nene

Nene Way

ROBINS WOOD

BLACK
SWAN
SPINNEY

THE DRIFT

ROBINS FIELD

SWANH'LL

P

PE8

3

A6118

OLD LEICESTER ROAD

NENE CL

PETERBOROUGH RD

A1

NENE WAY

Old Hill
Farm

BRIDGE END

Wansford
Road

Manor
Farm

Wansford
Bridge

MANOR ROAD

99

LONDON RD

A6118

Nene Way

PO PH

GRAEME RD

LOVERS LA

NENE WY

Stibbington
Hall

CHAPEL CT

2

Stibbington

CHURCH
LA

CHURCH
LANE

CHURCH LANE

GRAEME RD

Sutton

OLD GREAT NORTH RD

ROMAN DR

CHURCH
LA

CHURCH
LA

Stibbington
House

ELTON ROAD

Field
Studies
Centre

Hereward Way

1

Lock

Weir

NEW LANE

A1 GREAT NORTH ROAD

OLD GREAT NORTH ROAD

Nene Valley Railway

B671

Toll Bar
Spinney

98

07   A   B   08   C   D   09   E   F

A1 Stamford

Northamptonshire STREET ATLAS

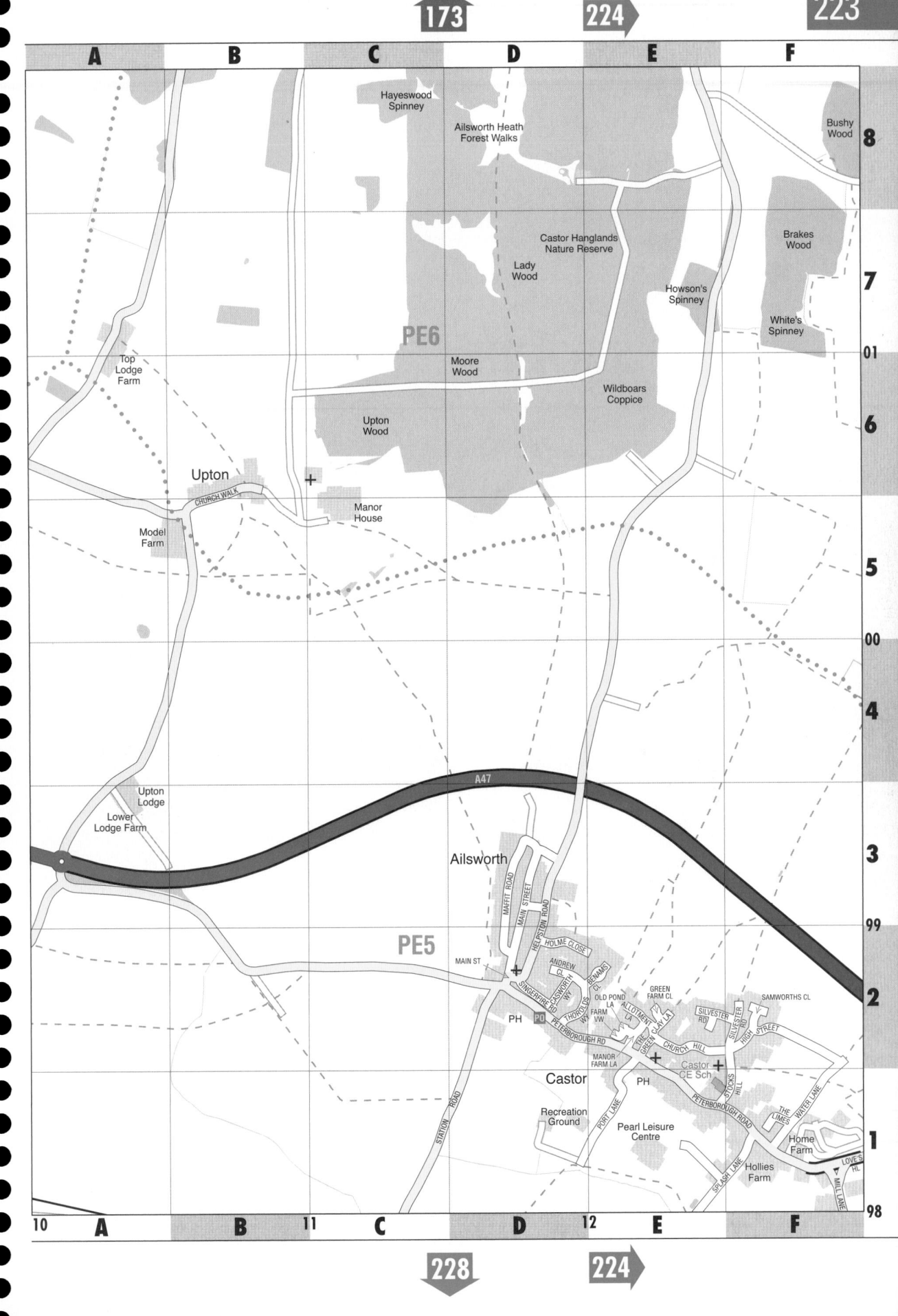

A B C D E F

8

Hayeswood
Spinney

Ailsworth Heath
Forest Walks

Bushy
Wood

Castor Hanglands
Nature Reserve

7

Brakes
Wood

Lady
Wood

Howson's
Spinney

PE6

White's
Spinney

01

Moore
Wood

Wildboars
Coppice

6

Top
Lodge
Farm

Upton
Wood

Upton

CHURCH WALK

5

Model
Farm

Manor
House

00

4

A47

Upton
Lodge

Lower
Lodge Farm

3

Ailsworth

99

PE5

MAIN ST

MAFFIT ROAD

MAIN STREET

HELPSTON ROAD

HOLME CLOSE

2

ANDREW
CL

BEMANS
CL

GREEN
FARM CL

SAMWORTHS CL

SINGERDIKE RD

CASHWORTH
WY

THOROLDS
WY

OLD POND
FARM
VW

ALLOTMENT
LA

SILVESTER
RD

HIGH STREET

PH

PO

PETERBOROUGH RD

GREEN
CLAY LA

CHURCH HILL

SILVESTER
RD

MANOR
FARM LA

Castor
CE Sch

STOCKS
HILL

Castor

PH

PETERBOROUGH ROAD

1

Recreation
Ground

PORT LANE

STATION
ROAD

Pearl Leisure
Centre

THE
LIMES

WATER LANE

Home
Farm

LOVE S
HL

SPLASH LANE

Hollies
Farm

MILL LANE

98

10 A B 11 C D 12 E F

173 223 220

A B C D E F
Foster's Coppice
Home Farm
Bushy Wood
Burmer Wood
Mucklands Wood
GULLYMORE
DUNSBERRY
BRETTON WAY
HYHOLMES
Marholm Lodges
PE3
WESTHAWE
PARK FARM ROAD
Popple's Coppice
Belsize Farm
Belsize Wood
CASTOR ROAD
Grimeshaw Wood
Park Farm
Thistlemoor Wood
Little Thistlemoor Wood
PE6
Stamford Plantations
Stamford Lodge
Oldfield Pond
New Park Farm
BRETTON GATE
STAMFORD LODGE ROAD
PARK FARM ROAD
Deer Park
Ten Acre Plantation
New Plantation
Salter's Wood
Milton Hall
MUSKHAM
SPRIGNALL
KENNELS ROAD
NICHOLAS TAYLOR GD 1
STAMPER ST 2
BRAILSFORD CL 3
JOROSE ST 4
TEANBY CT 5
CARTERS CL 6
THOMAS CL 7
GOODWOOD RD 8
BARNARD WY 9
HARRISON CL 10
LONGTHORPE HOUSE MEWS 11
Recreation Ground
MARHOLM ROAD
Milton Park
WALKERS WAY
RINGWOOD
HUNTSMANS GATE
Crickety Park
Sheep Park
LITTLE JOHNS CL
SEBRIGHTS WY
MILTON WAY
FERRY DRIVE
PETERBOROUGH DRIVE
Fitzwilliam
ROBIN HOOD CL
BRETTON WAY
EGAR WAY
HOLYWELL WY
ELLIOT AV
OAK
PELHAM CL
LODER AVENUE
PEACOCK WY
HERONRY DRIVE
Ferry House
Ferryhill Plantation
PETERBOROUGH DR
PE5
CH
A47
VIRGINIA CL 1
CYPRESS CL 2
LONGTHORPE CL 3
River Nene
FERRY HILL
Love's Hill
LOVE'S HILL
Little John
Robin Hood
Bluebell Walk Plantation
Playing Fields
Mast
Thorpe Wood
NENE PARKWAY A1260
THORPE WOOD
PE2
Hereward Way
Gunwade Lake
Nene Way
8 7 01 6 5 00 4 3 99 2 1 98
13 14 15

223 229

A B C D E F

8
7
01
6
5
00
4
99
2
1
98

PE4

Walton

New England

Bretton

Bretton Park

Ravensthorpe

PETERBOROUGH

PE1

Millfield

Westwood

PE3

Longthorpe

Thorpe Hall

Thorpe Park

Nene Valley Railway   Peterborough NV

Railworld Museum

Bourgess Retail Park

Mus & Art Gall

Peterborough District

Peterborough High Sch

West Town County Sch

Jack Hunt Sch

Jack Hunt Swimming Pool

Thorpe CP Sch

Edith Cavell

Sports Centre

Bretton Gate Ground

College

Highlees Prim Sch

Water Spinney

Ravensthorpe Prim Sch

Sacred Heart RC Prim Sch

Bretton Woods Com Sch

Eyrescroft CP Sch

Watergall CP Sch

Heltwate Special Sch

Playing Fields

Factory

Works

Brotherhood Retail Park

Boulevard Retail Park

Recreation Ground

Allotments

Fulbridge Jun/Inf Sch

Sports Club

Maskew Av Sports Club

Gladstone Prim Sch

The Beeches Prim Sch

Middleton Jun Sch

Longthorpe CP Sch

Tower Heritage Ctr

Holy Well

SOKE PARKWAY A47

BOURGES BOULEVARD A15

LONGTHORPE PARKWAY A1179

THORPE ROAD A1179

LINCOLN ROAD

A47

A15

BOURGES BVD

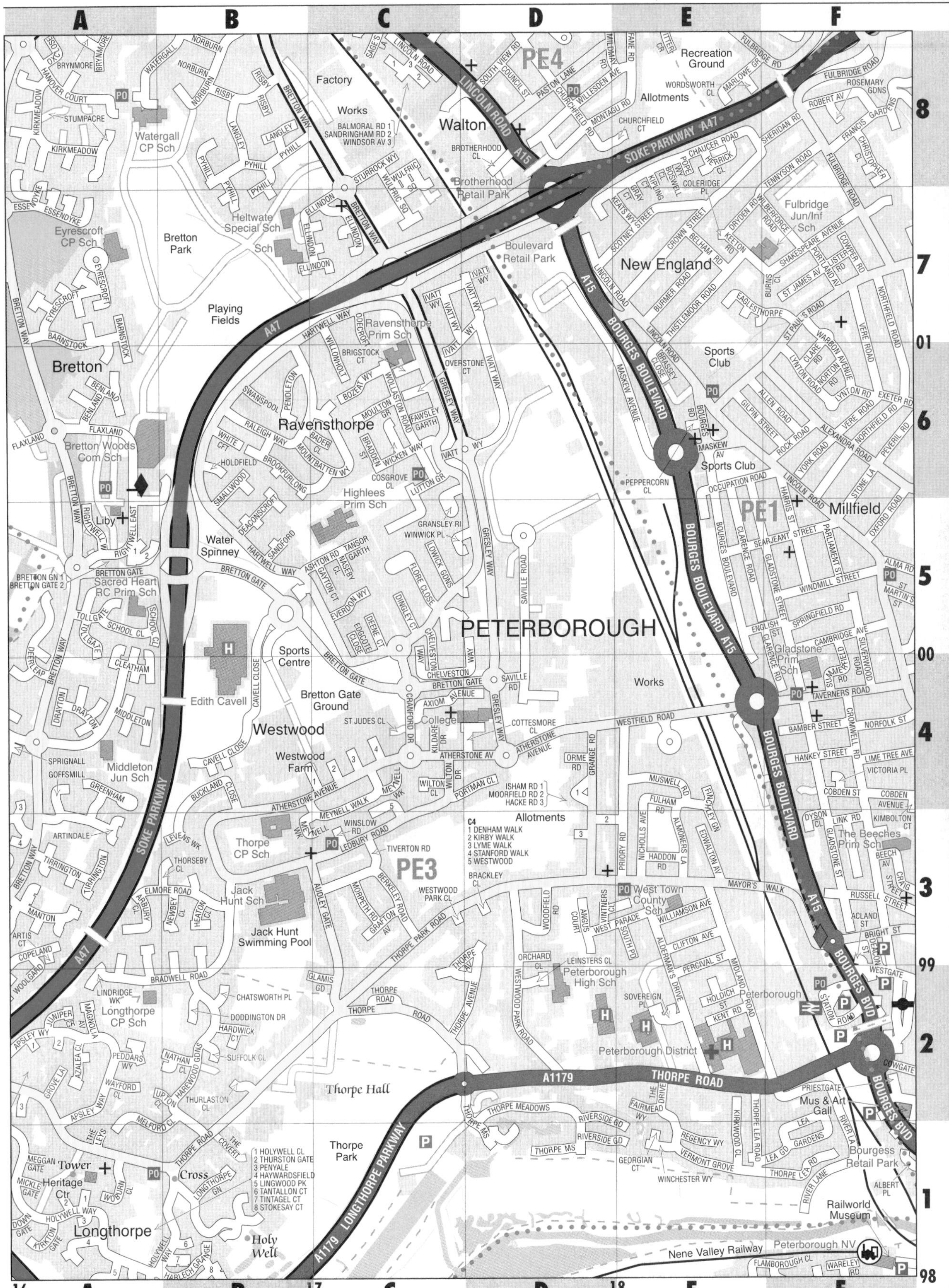

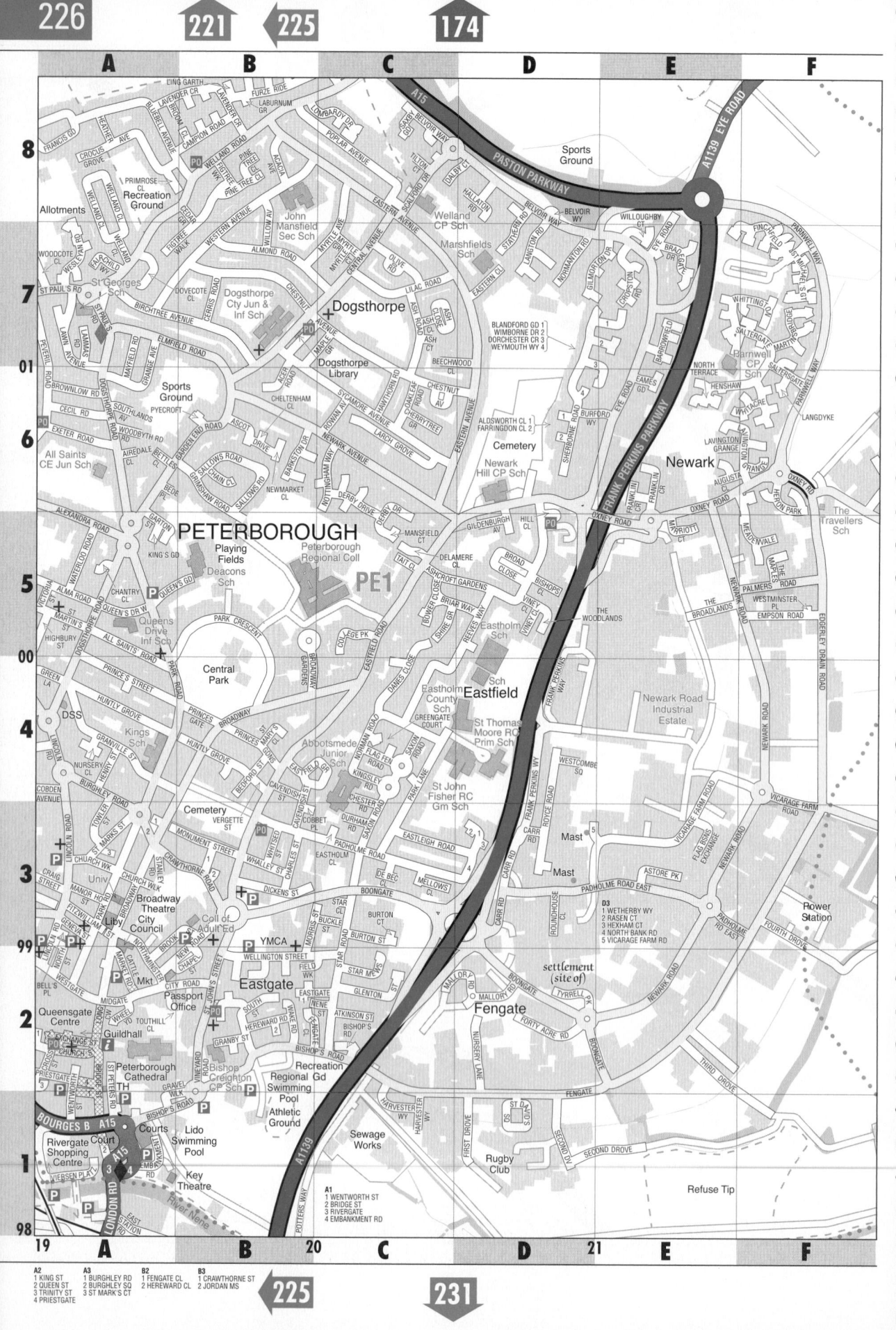

A   B   C   D   E   F

8   7   01   6   5   00   4   3   99   2   1   98

PETERBOROUGH
PE1

Dogsthorpe

Newark

Eastfield

Fengate

A2
1 KING ST
2 QUEEN ST
3 TRINITY ST
4 PRIESTGATE

A3
1 BURGHLEY RD
2 BURGHLEY SQ
3 ST MARK'S CT

B2
1 FENGATE CL
2 HEREWARD CL

B3
1 CRAWTHORNE ST
2 JORDAN MS

A1
1 WENTWORTH ST
2 BRIDGE ST
3 RIVERGATE
4 EMBANKMENT RD

D3
1 WETHERBY WY
2 RASEN CT
3 HEXHAM CT
4 NORTH BANK RD
5 VICARAGE FARM RD

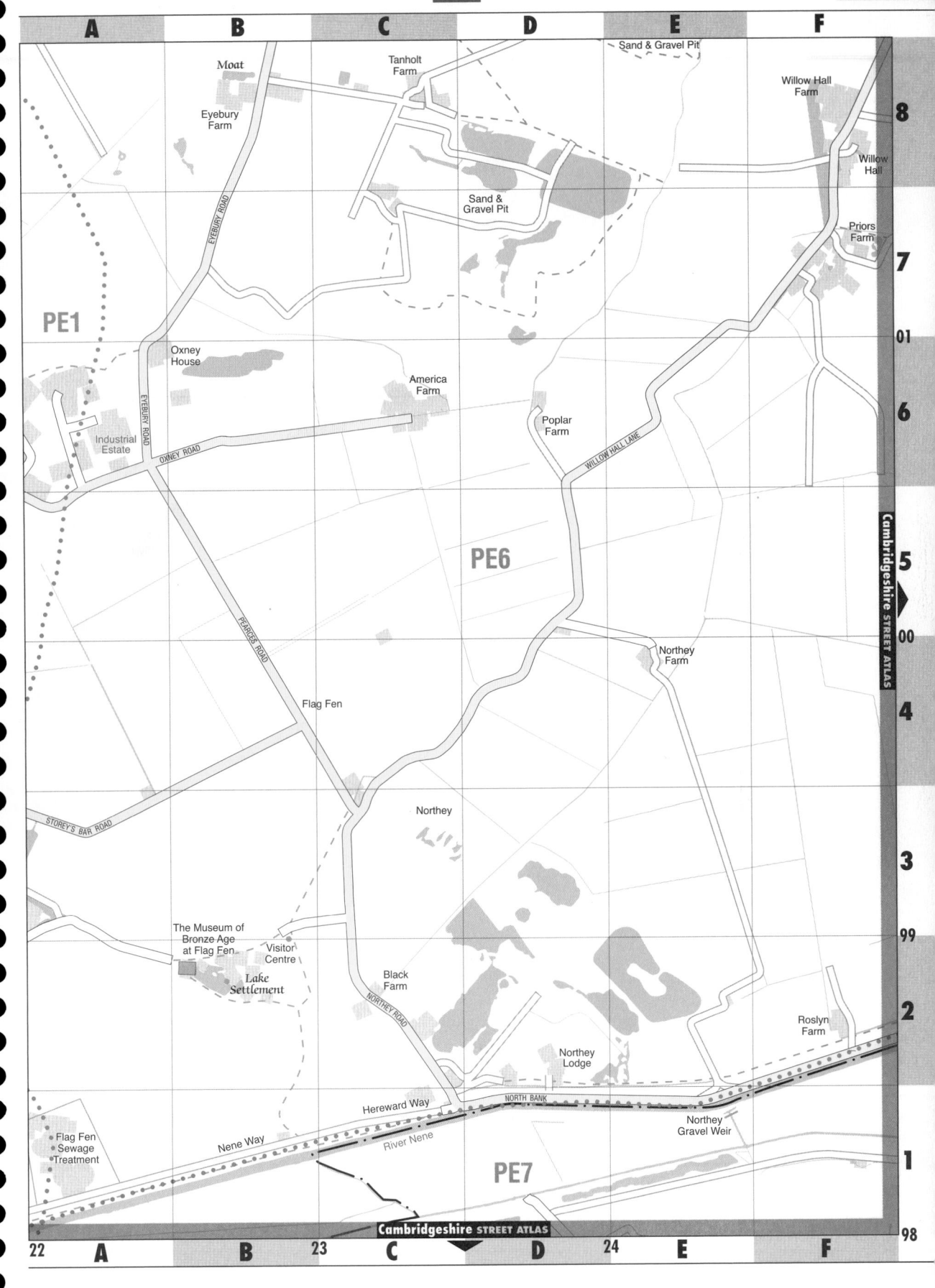

A B C D E F

Moat

Tanholt
Farm

Sand & Gravel Pit

Willow Hall
Farm

Eyebury
Farm

8

Willow
Hall

Sand &
Gravel Pit

Priors
Farm

7

PE1

01

Oxney
House

America
Farm

Poplar
Farm

6

Industrial
Estate

OXNEY ROAD

EYEBURY ROAD

WILLOW HALL LANE

PE6

5

Cambridgeshire STREET ATLAS

00

Northey
Farm

PEARCES ROAD

4

Flag Fen

STOREY'S BAR ROAD

Northey

3

99

The Museum of
Bronze Age
at Flag Fen

Visitor
Centre

Black
Farm

Roslyn
Farm

Lake
Settlement

NORTHEY ROAD

2

Northey
Lodge

Hereward Way

NORTH BANK

Northey
Gravel Weir

Flag Fen
Sewage
Treatment

Nene Way

River Nene

PE7

1

98

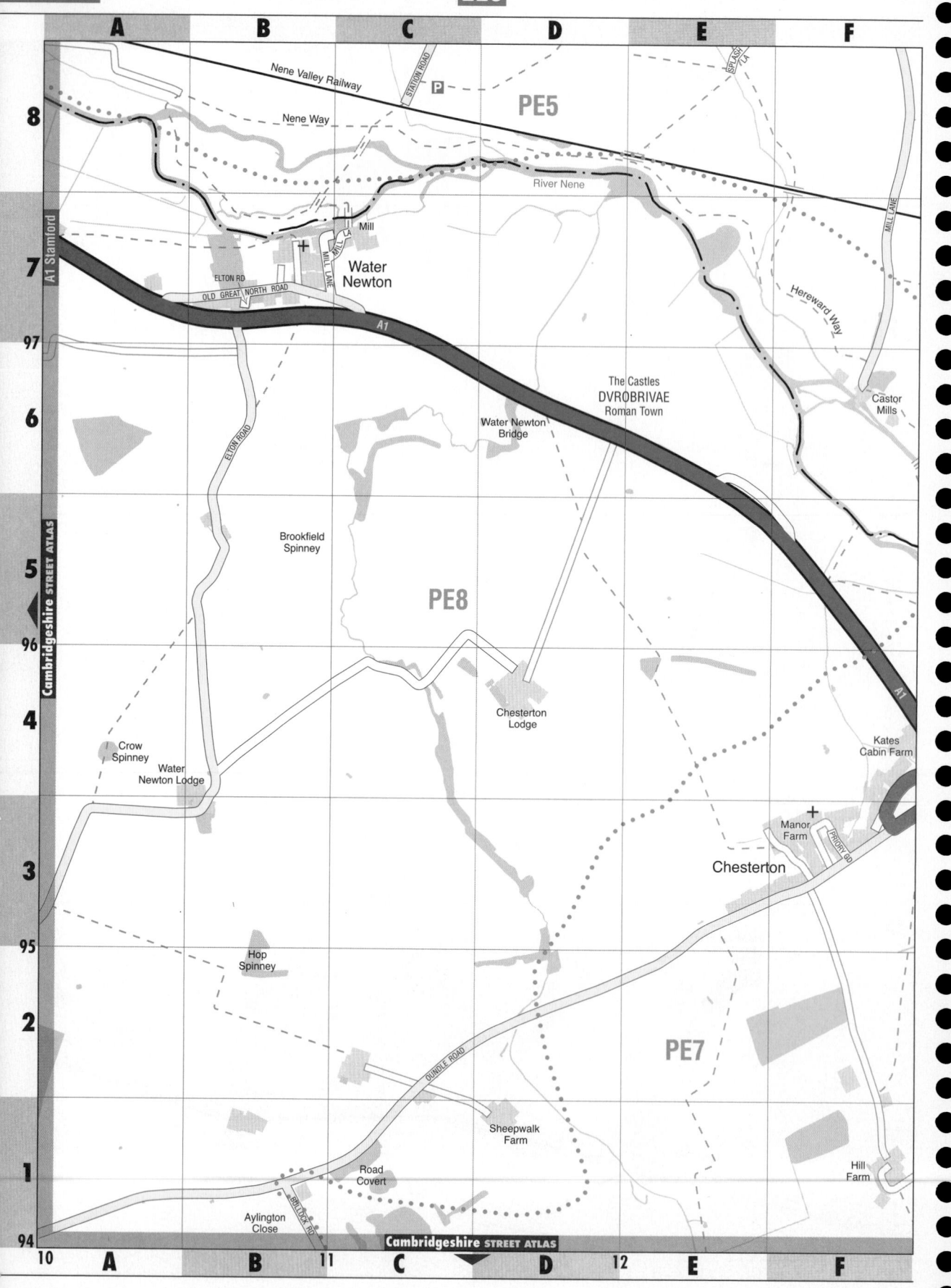

223

PE5

A1 Stamford

Nene Valley Railway

Nene Way

STATION ROAD

P

River Nene

Mill

MILL LA

MILL LANE

SPLASH LA

MILL LANE

Water
Newton

ELTON RD

OLD GREAT NORTH ROAD

A1

Hereward Way

Castor
Mills

The Castles
DVROBRIVAE
Roman Town

Water Newton
Bridge

ELTON ROAD

A1

Brookfield
Spinney

PE8

Chesterton
Lodge

Crow
Spinney

Water
Newton Lodge

Kates
Cabin Farm

Manor
Farm

PRIORY RD

Chesterton

Hop
Spinney

PE7

DUNDLE ROAD

Sheepwalk
Farm

Road
Covert

BULLOCK RD

Hill
Farm

Aylington
Close

Cambridgeshire STREET ATLAS

224
230
A
B
C
D
E
F
8
7
97
6
5
96
4
3
95
2
1
94
13
14
15
PETERBOROUGH
PE5
PE3
PE2
PE7
Gunwade Lake
Lynch Lake
Overton Lake
Ferry Meadows Country Park
Nene Park
Visitor Centre
Bluebell Bridge
ROMAN FORT
Ham Mere Bird Sanctuary
Hereward Way
Nene Valley Railway
Nene Way
River Nene
Lynch Bridge
Ferry Meadows
Orton Wistow
Orton Wistow Prim Sch
Back Dike
Lock
Manor House
Alwalton
Alwalton Hall
Business Park
Orton Brimbles
Orton Malley Prim Sch
Orton Waterville
Bushfield Sports Centre
Liby
Bushfield Com Coll
St Johns Church Sch CE Aided
Orton Goldhay
East of England Showground
Orton Southgate
Clynebury Lodge
Bottom Lodge Farm
Upper Lodge Farm
Mast
Service Area
Hotel
OUNDLE ROAD
A605
A1139
ORTON PARKWAY
FLETTON PARKWAY
A1(M)
17
232
230

229
225

PETERBOROUGH
PE3
PE2
PE7
Thorpe Meadows
Nene Valley Railway
River Nene
Nene Way
Orton Mere
Orton Water
OUNDLE ROAD
NENE PARKWAY
LONGTHORPE PARKWAY
Hotel
St Botolphs Prim Sch
Lakeside Leisure Centre
Orton Longueville
Orton Longueville Sch
Clayton Sch
Orton Malbourne
Leighton CP Sch
Braybrook CP Sch
Winyates Prim Sch
FLETTON PARKWAY
THE SERPENTINE
Botolph Bridge
Woodston
Cemy
Regional Coll
Mast
Works
Factory
Cold Storage
Busway
St Augustines Jun Sch
Brewster Avenue Inf Sch
Liby
TA Ctr
Fletton Prim Sch
LONDON ROAD
NEW ROAD
HICKS LANE
(Disused)
Reservoir
Cygnet Park
Serpentine Green Shopping Centre
Hampton Hargate
Hampton Hargate Prim Sch
PHORPRES WAY
1 CHIPPENHAM MEWS
2 GLEMSFORD RI
WESTBROOK AV 1
WESTBROOK PK CL 2
BARRY WK 3
SHERWOOD AV 4
ST MARGARETS RD 1
ST MARGARETS PL 2
A B C D E F
16 17 18

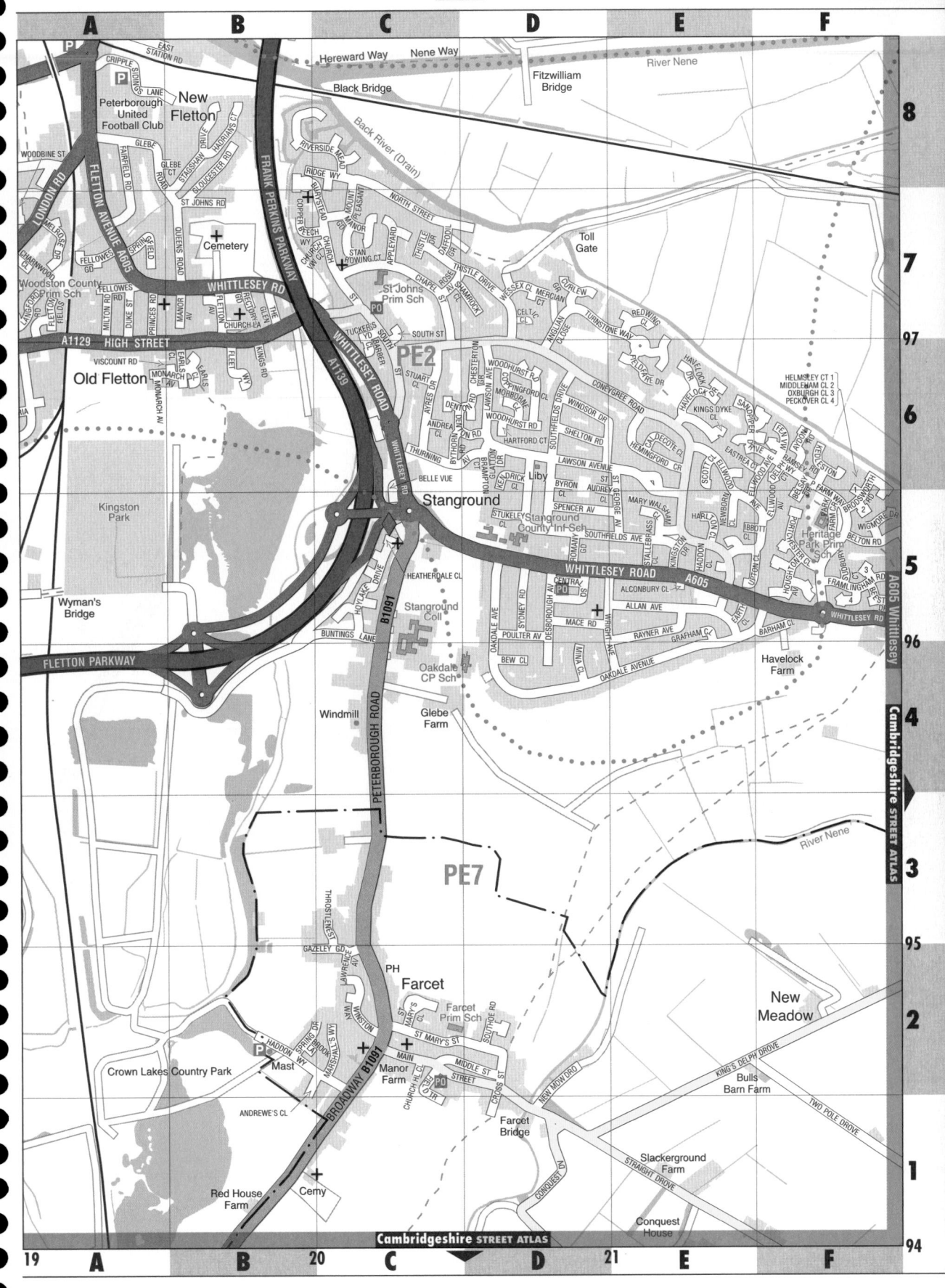

Hereward Way   Nene Way   River Nene

Black Bridge   Fitzwilliam
                            Bridge

EAST
STATION RD

CRIPPLE
SIDINGS
LANE

Peterborough
United
Football Club

New
Fletton

WOODBINE ST

Back River (Drain)

RIVERSIDE MEAD

Toll
Gate

RIDGE WY

NORTH STREET

FAIRFIELD RD

GLEBE
CT

GLEBE
ROAD

STASSHAW

GLOUCESTER RD

HADRIANS CT

ST JOHNS RD

BARTSTEAD

MOUNT PLEASANT

COPPER LN

CHURCH

MANOR

APPLEYARD

THISTLE DRIVE

Cemetery

CHAPEL
ROSSE

WESSEX CL

MERCIAN

CURLEW

REDWING

HELMSLEY CT 1
MIDDLEHAM CL 2
OXBURGH CL 3
PECKOVER CL 4

WHITTLESEY RD

St Johns
Prim Sch

SHAMROCK

ANGLIAN
CLOSE

CELT
CL

CL

TURNSTONE WAY

SANDPIPER

HAVELOCK
CL

KINGS DYKE

PE2

SOUTH ST

CHESTERTON
CL

WOODHURST DR

CONEYGREE ROAD

HAVELOCK
DRIVE

FIELDFARE DR

A1129   HIGH STREET

A1139

STUART
CL

AYRES CL

DENTON RD

DIPPINGFORD CL

WINDSOR DR

HEMINGFORD CR

SCOTT CL

RAMSEY

KEDLESTON

VISCOUNT RD

Old Fletton

ANDREA

BYTHORN

WOODHURST RD

SHELTON RD

DECOTE CL

ELLWOOD

EASTREA

BROADSWORTH

THURNING

HARTFORD CT

LAWSON AVENUE

UPTON

FARM WAY

BELTON RD

BELLE VUE

BRAMPTON

DRICK CL

Liby

BYRON CL

ST
AUDREY

ST GEORGE

MARY WALSHAM

HARL

IBBOTT
CL

WIGMORE

Kingston
Park

Stanground

STUKELEY
CL

SPENCER AV

SOUTHFIELDS DRIVE

ROMANY

STALLEBRASS

NEWBORN CL

Heritage
Park Prim
Sch

HOYLAKE DRIVE

Stanground
County Inf Sch

HADDON CL

KINGSTON

FRAMLINGHAM RD

WHITTLESEY ROAD   A605

HEATHERDALE CL

CENTRA
PO

ALCONBURY CL

ALLAN AVE

WHITTLESEY RD

3

Wyman's
Bridge

B1091

Stanground
Coll

SYDNEY RD

DESBOROUGH AV

MACE RD

WRIGHT AVE

RAYNER AVE

GRAFHAM CL

BARHAM CL

Havelock
Farm

FLETTON PARKWAY

BUNTINGS LANE

OAKDALE AVE

POULTER AV

BEW CL

Oakdale AVENUE

Windmill

Oakdale
CP Sch

Glebe
Farm

River Nene

PETERBOROUGH ROAD

THROSTLE NEST

PE7

GAZELEY GDNS

95

Farcet

New
Meadow

LAWRENCE

WINSTON

Farcet
Prim Sch

SOUTHOE RD

KING'S DELPH DROVE

WM ST

SPRING BROOK

MARSHALL

MANN ST

PH

ST
MARY'S

ST MARY'S ST

MAIN

MIDDLE ST

Bulls
Barn Farm

Crown Lakes Country Park

HADDON

Mast

Manor
Farm

CHURCH HL CL

STREET

TWO POLE DROVE

BROADWAY B1091

PO
STR

CROSS RD

NEW MOW DRO

ANDREWE'S CL

Farcet
Bridge

STRAIGHT DRIVE

Slackerground
Farm

Red House
Farm

Cerny

CONQUEST DV

Conquest
House

229

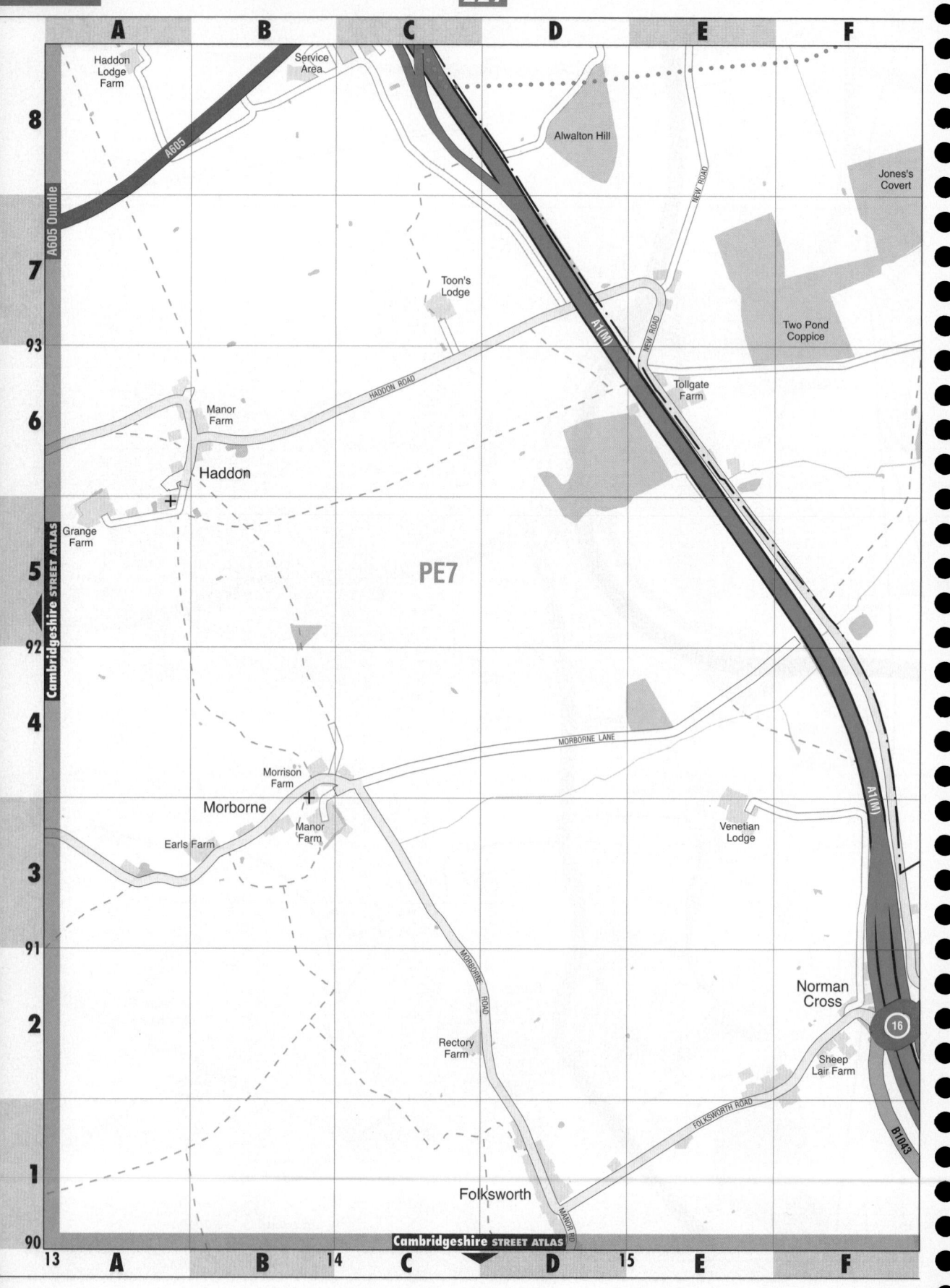

A B C D E F

8

93

7

6

5

92

4

3

91

2

91

1

90

13 A B 14 C D 15 E F

A605 Oundle

Cambridgeshire STREET ATLAS

Haddon Lodge Farm

Service Area

Alwalton Hill

Jones's Covert

NEW ROAD

Two Pond Coppice

Toon's Lodge

A1(M)

HADDON ROAD

Manor Farm

Tollgate Farm

Haddon

Grange Farm

PE7

Morborne Lane

Morrison Farm

Morborne

Earls Farm

Manor Farm

Venetian Lodge

MORBORNE ROAD

A1(M)

Norman Cross

16

Rectory Farm

Sheep Lair Farm

FOLKSWORTH ROAD

B1043

Folksworth

MANOR RD

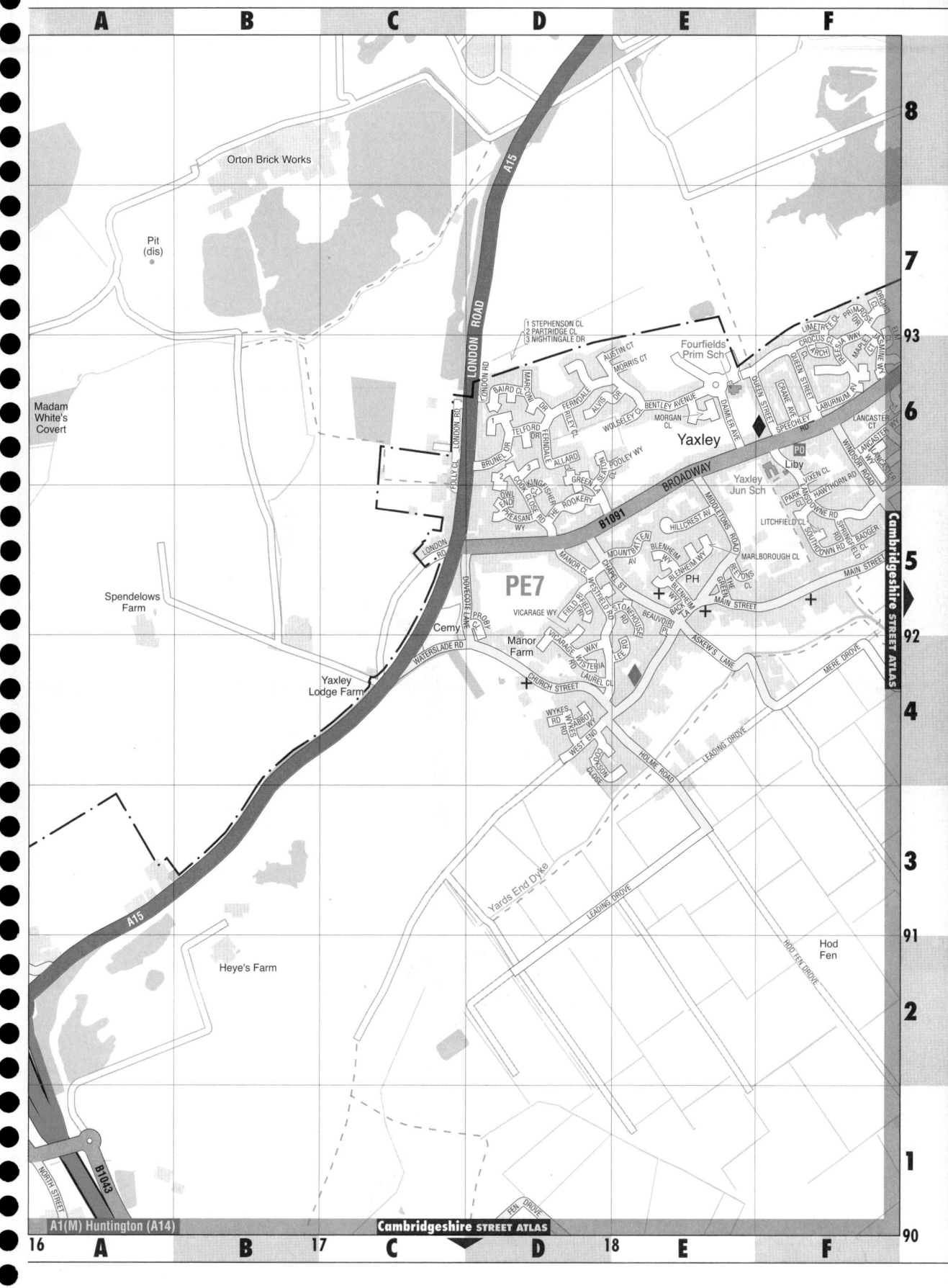

A B C D E F

8

7

93

6

Orton Brick Works

Pit
(dis)

Madam
White's
Covert

LONDON ROAD

A15

1 STEPHENSON CL
2 PARTRIDGE CL
3 NIGHTINGALE DR

AUSTIN CT

MORRIS CT

Fourfields
Prim Sch

LIMETREE CL

CROCUS CL

QUEEN STREET

CRANE AITCHLEY

PLUM CL

ORCHARD

FREESIA WAY

MAPLE

JASMINE DR

ARCH

LABURNUM

LONDON RD

BAIRD CL

MARSTON

TELFORD
DR

FERNVALE

ALVIS DR

WOLSELEY CL

BENTLEY AVENUE

MORGAN
CL

Yaxley

DAMMER AVE

SPEECHLEY

LANCASTER RD

WINDSOR RD

LANCASTER
WY

PO

Liby

VIXEN CL

HAWTHORN RD

Lancaster

6

FOLLY CL

BRUNEL DR

FERNDALE
DR

RILEY CL

NAUD

GREEN

POOLEY WY

SEATON

THE ROOKERY

BROADWAY

B1091

Yaxley
Jun Sch

LITCHFIELD CL

LANSDOWNE RD

SPRINGFIELD

SOUTHDOWN RD

BADGER
CL

MAIN STREET

5

92

LONDON
RD

OWL
END

KINGFISHER
WY

COOK CLOSE RD

PHEASANT
WY

MANOR CL

DOVECOTE LANE

PROB'

PE7

VICARAGE WY

MOUNTBATTEN
AV

CHAPEL ST

FIELD
RD

WESTFIELD

BLENHEIM
WY

HILLCREST AV

BLENHEIM WY

STONHOUSE RD

MIDDLETON ROAD

PH

BEAUVOIR
CL

GREEN
CL

MARLBOROUGH CL

BEE-ONS
CL

MAIN STREET

MERE GROVE

Spendelows
Farm

WATERSLADE RD

Cemy

Manor
Farm

VICARAGE
RD

WISTERIA
WAY

LAUREL CL

WY
DR
LEE

ASKEW'S LANE

4

3

91

Yaxley
Lodge Farm

CHURCH STREET

WYKES
RD

ABBOT
W
WEST END

WEST END
WY

COOKSON
CLOSE

HOLME ROAD

LEADING DROVE

Hod
Fen

HOD FEN DROVE

Heye's Farm

Yards End Dyke

LEADING DROVE

2

A15

1

B1043

NORTH STREET

FEN DROVE

FEN DROVE

90

Cambridgeshire STREET ATLAS

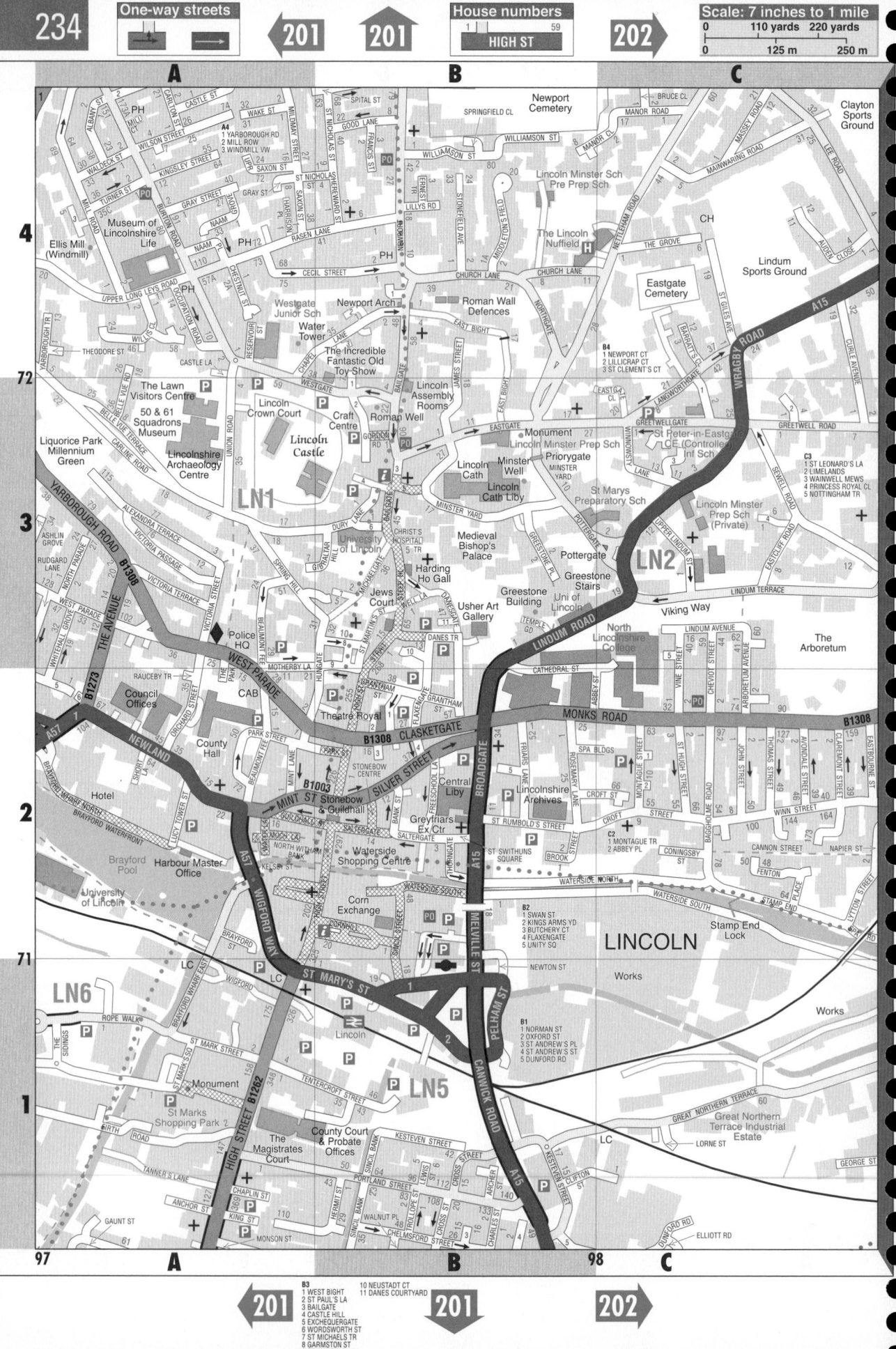

Church Rd 6 Beckenham BR2..........**53** C6

Place name	**Location number**	**Locality, town or village**	**Postcode district**	**Page and grid square**
May be abbreviated on the map	Present when a number indicates the place's position in a crowded area of mapping	Shown when more than one place has the same name	District for the indexed place	Page number and grid reference for the standard mapping

Public and commercial buildings are highlighted in magenta   **Places of interest** are highlighted in blue with a star★

Abbreviations used in the index

Acad	Academy	Comm	Common	Gd	Ground	L	Leisure	Prom	Prom
App	Approach	Cott	Cottage	Gdn	Garden	La	Lane	Rd	Road
Arc	Arcade	Cres	Crescent	Gn	Green	Liby	Library	Recn	Recreation
Ave	Avenue	Cswy	Causeway	Gr	Grove	Mdw	Meadow	Ret	Retail
Bglw	Bungalow	Ct	Court	H	Hall	Meml	Memorial	Sh	Shopping
Bldg	Building	Ctr	Centre	Ho	House	Mkt	Market	Sq	Square
Bsns, Bus	Business	Ctry	Country	Hospl	Hospital	Mus	Museum	St	Street
Bvd	Boulevard	Cty	County	HQ	Headquarters	Orch	Orchard	Sta	Station
Cath	Cathedral	Dr	Drive	Hts	Heights	Pal	Palace	Terr	Terrace
Cir	Circus	Dro	Drove	Ind	Industrial	Par	Parade	TH	Town Hall
Cl	Close	Ed	Education	Inst	Institute	Pas	Passage	Univ	University
Cnr	Corner	Emb	Embankment	Int	International	Pk	Park	Wk, Wlk	Walk
Coll	College	Est	Estate	Intc	Interchange	Pl	Place	Wr	Water
Com	Community	Ex	Exhibition	Junc	Junction	Prec	Precinct	Yd	Yard

Index of localities, towns and villages

A

Aby	75	B5
Addlethorpe	90	C3
Adlingfleet	7	E7
Ailby	75	D4
Ailsworth	223	D3
Aisby Heydour	131	D5
Aisby Pilham	41	D4
Aisthorpe	67	C7
Aldgate	171	A3
Alford	75	C2
Algakirk	136	B2
Alkborough	8	C8
Allington	128	F7
Althorpe	17	D5
Alvingham	49	E2
Alwalton	229	B4
Amcotts	7	F1
Ancaster	120	B2
Anderby	77	A2
Anderby Creek	77	C3
Anlaby	179	A6
Anlaby Park	179	C5
Anton's Gowt	125	B6
Anwick	109	B1
Apley	70	A2
Appleby	9	D1
Asgarby Asgarby and Howell	122	B4
Asgarby Lusby with Winceby	86	F1
Ashby Lusby with Winceby	185	B5
Ashby by Partney	88	D1
Ashby cum Fenby	35	D3
Ashby de la Launde	108	B6
Ashby Hill	35	C3
Ashby Puerorum	86	E6
Ashington End	90	B1
Ashton	173	A4
Aslackby	142	D6
Asperton	135	D4
Asserby	76	D4
Asterby	72	E6
Aswarby	132	D6
Aswardby	87	E5
Atterby	43	D3
Aubourn	93	A5
Aunby	163	B5
Aunsby	132	A5
Austendike	157	E4
Austen Fen	49	F5
Authorpe	74	F7
Aylesby	23	E2

B

Bag Enderby	87	B7
Bainton	172	F5
Balderton	104	C2
Bardney	83	C4
Barholm	164	C1
Barkston	130	B8
Barlings	69	D1
Barnack	172	E4
Barnby Dun	14	A4
Barnby in the Willows	104	F3
Barnetby le Wold	21	C4
Barnoldby le Beck	35	B6
Barrowby	210	A5
Barrow Hann	4	E1
Barrow Haven	4	B2
Barrow upon Humber	11	C8
Barton-Upon-Humber	10	F7
Barton Waterside	3	F2
Bassingham	92	F2
Bassingthorpe	140	E3
Baston	164	E4
Baumber	72	A1
Baythorpe	135	C8
Beacon Hill	104	B5
Beckingham Barnby in the Willows	105	A4
Beckingham	40	E4
Beelsby	34	E4
Beesby	76	A7
Belchford	73	B2
Belleau	75	A5
Bellmount	161	E4
Belmesthorpe	163	D1
Belnie	145	D5
Beltoft	17	B1
Belton Belton and Manthorpe	130	B6
Belton	16	E1
Belvoir	138	B8
Benington	126	F5
Benniworth	59	B1
Bescaby	138	B1
Besthorpe	91	C7
Bicker	135	A4
Bicker Gauntlet	134	F6
Bigby	21	C2
Billingborough	133	A1
Billinghay	109	F5
Bilsby	76	A3
Bilsby Field	76	A2
Binbrook	47	B4
Birchwood	204	D7
Birkholme	152	B6
Birthorpe	143	A8
Biscathorpe	59	D3
Bishopbridge	44	C1
Bishop Norton	43	D3
Bitchfield	141	B3
Blackjack	135	E6
Blankney	95	D3
Bleasby	58	A3
Bleasby Moor	57	F2
Bloxholm	108	C4
Blyborough	42	E5
Blyton	41	C5
Bole	52	C5
Bonby	10	C2
Bonthorpe	89	B7
Boothby Graffoe	94	A2
Boothby Pagnell	140	E5
Boston	209	C6
Boston Long Hedges	126	B6
Boston West	125	B4
Bottesford	128	A6
Bottesford Scunthorpe	185	B3
Boughton	122	C4
Boultham	205	D8
Boultham Moor	205	B6
Bourne	213	C7
Braceborough	164	B4
Bracebridge	205	D6
Bracebridge Heath	205	E3
Braceby	131	D2
Bracon	16	F2
Bradley	190	E2
Braithwaite	14	A7
Brampton	65	E6
Brand End	126	D4
Brandon	118	D7
Bransby	66	E6
Branston Branston and Mere	81	E2
Branston Croxton Kerrial	138	A4
Branston Booths	82	C4
Brant Broughton	105	F5
Brantingham	2	C8
Bratoft	102	B7
Brattleby	67	C8
Bretton	225	A6
Brigg	196	E4
Brigsley	35	D4
Brinkhill	87	C8
Broadholme	66	C1
Brocklesby	22	E6
Brookenby	47	B6

Broomfleet	1	B6
Brothertoft	124	F5
Brough	2	C5
Brough Collingham	91	E1
Broughton	19	D3
Broughton Common	19	F5
Broxholme	66	F5
Brumby	185	C8
Bucklegate	136	F3
Buckminster	150	E5
Bucknall	84	A4
Bulby	142	B1
Bullington	69	E4
Bunker's Hill	111	E4
Burgh le Marsh	102	E7
Burgh on Bain	59	D5
Burnham	11	C4
Burringham	17	E4
Burton	67	D1
Burton Corner	209	B7
Burton-le-Coggles	152	D8
Burton Pedwardine	122	B1
Burton Stather	8	B5
Burton upon Stather	8	A4
Burwell	74	B6
Buslingthorpe	57	A4
Butterwick	126	F4

C

Cabourne	33	D4
Cackle Hill	215	C5
Cadney	31	D6
Caenby	55	F8
Caistor	33	B4
Calceby	74	E2
Cammeringham	54	F1
Canal Side	15	A7
Candlesby	88	F2
Canwick	81	B4
Careby	163	B7
Carlby	163	D5
Carlton-le-Moorland	105	E8
Carlton Scroop	119	D3
Carrington	112	D6
Castle Bytham	152	D1
Castle Carlton	62	C2
Castlethorpe	20	A1
Castor	223	D1
Cawkwell	73	A6
Cawthorpe	154	B5
Caythorpe	119	C7

Chain Bridge	208	B3
Chapelgate	159	D7
Chapel Hill	110	E5
Chapel St Leonards	90	E7
Cherry Willingham	203	E5
Chesterton	228	F3
Church End	50	F6
Church Laneham	65	B3
Church Town	16	E1
Clark's Hill	159	B3
Claxby	45	D5
Claxby St Andrew	88	E6
Clay Lake	214	E2
Claypole	117	F7
Claythorpe	75	B6
Cleatham	30	B3
Cleethorpes	192	D5
Clinton Park	207	A5
Clipsham	162	B7
Clixby	33	A7
Coates North Leverton with Habblesthorpe	65	B8
Coates Stow	54	C2
Coddington	104	D5
Cold Hanworth	56	C2
Cold Harbour	130	D1
Coleby	93	F3
Coleby West Halton	8	E6
Collingham	91	C4
Collyweston	171	B1
Colsterworth	151	E2
Coningsby	207	D4
Conisholme	50	D6
Corby Glen	152	E8
Corringham	41	E2
Coston	150	C5
Cottam	65	C7
Covenham St Bartholomew	49	C5
Covenham St Mary	49	C5
Cowbit	157	B1
Cowbridge	125	E6
Cowbridge	125	E6
Cranwell	120	F8
Creeton	153	A2
Croft	102	F4
Crosby	182	D4
Crosby Warren	183	D6
Crossgate	145	C1
Crowland	166	E1
Crowle	16	D7
Croxby	34	D1
Croxton	21	F7
Croxton Kerrial	138	D4
Culverthorpe	131	E7

D

Cumberworth 89 F8
Cuxwold 34 B4

Dalby 88 B5
Dalderby 85 D1
Dawsmere 148 E5
Deeping Gate 217 C3
Deeping St James 217 D4
Deeping St Nicholas 166 C6
Dembleby 132 A4
Denton 139 B7
Derrythorpe 17 C3
Dickon Hills 114 D7
Digby 108 E6
Doddington 79 E5
Dogdyke 110 E6
Dogsthorpe 226 D2
Donington 134 F1
Donington Eaudike 135 A3
Donington on Bain 59 F1
Donna Nook 38 D2
Dorrington 108 E4
Dovendale 60 F1
Dowsby 143 B4
Dowsdale 167 D1
Dragonby 8 E1
Drayton 135 C6
Driby 74 E1
Dry Doddington 117 E5
Dunham on Trent 65 B1
Dunholme 68 E6
Dunsby 143 A1
Dunscroft 14 C4
Dunston 95 C5
Dunsville 14 C3
Dyke 154 D5

E

Eagle 79 C2
Eagle Barnsdale 92 C7
Eagle Moor 79 C2
Ealand 16 E6
Earlesfield 210 F3
East Barkwith 71 C4
East Butterwick 28 E8
East Ella 179 D7
East Ferry 28 B2
Eastfield 226 D4
East Firsby 55 F4
Eastgate 226 B2
East Halton 12 E6
East Heckington 123 D3
Easthorpe 128 B3
East Keal 100 C4
East Keal Fen Side 100 E4
East Kirkby 99 F5
East Lound 27 E2
East Marsh 189 B1
Eastoft 7 A3
Easton 140 E1
Easton on the Hill 171 C3
East Ravendale 35 C2
East Stockwith 40 C5
East Torrington 58 C2
Eastville 114 B8
Edenham 153 F4
Edenthorpe 14 A1
Edlington 85 B6
Ellerker 2 A8
Elloughton 2 B6
Elsham 20 F7
Emorsgate 161 E3
Epworth 27 E7
Epworth Turbary 27 C6
Ermine 202 B8
Eskham 37 C1
Essendine 163 D3
Etton 173 E5
Evedon 121 F6
Ewerby 122 B6
Ewerby Thorpe 122 D6
Eye 175 A1
Eye Green 175 B2

F

Faldingworth 56 F3
Far Bank 14 C8
Farcet 231 C2
Farforth 73 D5
Farlesthorpe 76 B1
Faxfleet 1 A2
Fengate 226 D2
Fenhouses 135 D7
Fen Side 100 A1
Fenton 65 E3
Fenton 105 B1
Ferriby Sluice 9 F7
Fillingham 54 F4
Firsby 101 E7
Fishlake 14 D8
Fishtoft 126 C1
Fishtoft Drove 125 D8
Fiskerton 82 A6

Fitton End 169 F3
Fledborough 78 A7
Fleet 159 C6
Fleet Hargate 159 C7
Flixborough 8 B1
Flixborough Stather 8 A1
Fockerby 7 E5
Fold Hill 115 A6
Folkingham 142 C8
Folksworth 232 D1
Fordington 88 C6
Fosdyke 146 D8
Fosdyke Bridge 146 E7
Foston 117 F2
Fotherby 49 A2
Foul Anchor 170 D8
Four Gotes 170 B7
Frampton 136 F6
Freiston 126 D2
Freiston Shore 126 F1
Friesthorpe 57 A2
Frieston 119 B6
Friskney 115 A6
Friskney Eaudyke 115 B7
Frith Bank 125 D5
Frithville 112 D1
Frodingham 183 C2
Frognall 165 D1
Fulbeck 106 C1
Fulletby 86 B8
Fulnetby 69 F6
Fulney 157 B6
Fulstow 49 B8

G

Gainsborough 197 B4
Galley Hill 75 E6
Garnsgate 159 E5
Garthorpe Garthorpe and Fockerby 7 F6
Garthorpe 150 A4
Gate Burton 53 B2
Gautby 84 B7
Gayton Engine 63 C6
Gayton le Marsh 62 F3
Gayton Le Wold 59 E4
Gedney 159 D7
Gedney Broadgate 159 D5
Gedney Drove End 149 A4
Gedney Dyke 148 B1
Gedney Hill 168 D2
Geeston 171 A2
Gelston 118 F4
Gipsey Bridge 124 E8
Gipsyville 179 E3
Girsby 59 C6
Girton 78 C1
Glentham 43 E1
Glentworth 54 E7
Glinton 220 D8
Gonerby Hill Foot 210 F8
Gorefield 169 E2
Gosberton 145 B6
Gosberton Cheal 145 A4
Gosberton Clough 144 D4
Goulceby 72 D6
Goxhill 12 A8
Graby 142 F4
Grainsby 35 F2
Grainthorpe 50 B8
Graiselound 27 C1
Grange 191 A5
Grantham 211 A5
Grant Thorold 192 A7
Grasby 32 F7
Grayingham 42 D7
Great Carlton 62 E4
Great Casterton 171 B8
Great Coates 24 B5
Greatford 164 B3
Great Gonerby 129 E5
Great Hale 122 F2
Great Limber 22 D3
Great Ponton 140 A5
Great Steeping 101 E7
Great Sturton 71 F3
Great Tows 47 D1
Grebby 88 D3
Green Hill 210 E5
Greetham 86 D5
Greetwell 30 C7
Grey Green 16 C2
Grimoldby 62 B7
Grimsby 191 B8
Grimsthorpe 153 E5
Gringley on the Hill 39 C1
Gunby Candlesby with Gunby 89 B1
Gunby Gunby and Stainby 151 C4
Gunnerby 34 F2
Gunness 17 E6
Gunthorpe Owston Ferry 40 D7
Gunthorpe Peterborough 221 B1
Guthram Gowt 155 E5
Guyhirn 177 F2

H

Habertoft 89 E4

Habrough 22 E8
Haceby 131 E3
Hackthorn 55 E1
Haconby 154 D8
Haddington 92 F6
Haddon 232 B6
Hagnaby East Kirkby 100 A5
Hagnaby Hannah cum Hagnaby 76 C6
Hagnaby Lock 99 F2
Hagworthingham 87 A4
Hainton 58 F3
Halesgate 146 E1
Hall End 114 D1
Hallington 60 F4
Haltham 98 C6
Haltoft End 126 C4
Halton Fenside 101 C6
Halton Holegate 101 B8
Hameringham 86 C2
Hampton Hargate 230 D2
Hanby 141 E7
Hannah 76 C4
Hanthorpe 154 B7
Harby 79 C5
Hardwick 66 A2
Hareby 99 F8
Harlaxton 139 C7
Harmston 93 F5
Harpswell 54 E8
Harrington 87 C7
Harrowby 211 F4
Harston 138 E6
Hartsholme 204 E6
Hasthorpe 89 C4
Hatcliffe 34 F3
Hatfield 14 D5
Hatfield Woodhouse 15 A3
Hatton 71 B3
Haugh 75 B2
Haugham 73 F8
Haven Bank 111 B3
Hawthorn Hill 110 F6
Hawthorpe 142 A2
Haxey 27 C2
Haxey Carr 27 B4
Hay Green 161 E1
Healing 23 F5
Heapham 53 E7
Heckdyke 40 C7
Heckington 122 D3
Hedgehog Bridge 124 E5
Heighington 81 E4
Helpringham 133 E7
Helpston 173 C4
Helsey 89 F7
Hemingby 72 B1
Hemswell 42 D1
Hemswell Cliff 55 A8
Hessle 178 D1
Heydour 131 D6
Hibaldstow 31 A5
High Ferry 126 A8
High Marnham 78 B5
High Risby 9 A1
High Toynton 86 A4
Hilldyke 126 A4
Hoffleet Stow 135 C4
Hogsthorpe 90 B6
Holbeach 215 C3
Holbeach Bank 215 C7
Holbeach Clough 215 B7
Holbeach Drove 168 B3
Holbeach Hurn 147 F2
Holbeach St Johns 158 E1
Holbeach St Marks 147 D6
Holbeach St Matthew 148 A2
Holdingham 212 C7
Holme 19 A1
Holme 91 A2
Holme Hill 191 F6
Holton cum Beckering 70 C8
Holton le Clay 195 D2
Holton le Moor 45 A8
Honington 119 C2
Hop Pole 165 F5
Horbling 133 C2
Horkstow 10 A5
Horncastle 199 D3
Horsington 84 C3
Hougham 118 C3
Hough-on-the-Hill 119 A5
Howell 122 D5
Howsham 32 A6
Hubbert's Bridge 124 F2
Humberston 193 A2
Humby 141 C7
Hundleby 87 F1
Hundle Houses 111 C4
Hungerton 139 B4
Hurn's End 127 C8
Huttoft 76 E3

I

Immingham 186 E4
Ingham 54 F2
Ingleborough 170 E5
Ingleby 66 C4
Ingoldmells 90 E4
Ingoldsby 141 D5

Ingthorpe 218 A8
Irby in the Marsh 102 B6
Irby upon Humber 34 D7
Irnham 141 E1
Island Carr 196 B2

K

Keadby 17 D7
Keal Cotes 100 C4
Keddington 198 F8
Keelby 23 C6
Keisby 141 F3
Kelby 131 C5
Kelfield 28 C4
Kelstern 48 A1
Ketsby 74 D3
Kettlethorpe 65 F2
Ketton 171 A3
Kexby 53 E5
Kilvington 117 A1
Kingerby 44 E3
Kingston upon Hull 180 F4
Kingthorpe 70 C2
Kirk Bramwith 14 A1
Kirkby 44 F3
Kirkby Fenside 99 E4
Kirkby Green 108 E4
Kirkby la Thorpe 121 F5
Kirkby on Bain 98 B5
Kirkby Underwood 142 D2
Kirk Ella 178 C8
Kirmington 22 A6
Kirmond le Mire 46 F3
Kirton 136 D5
Kirton End 136 B6
Kirton Holme 135 C4
Kirton in Lindsey 30 C2
Knaith 53 A3
Knaith Park 53 B4
Knipton 138 C6

L

Laceby 23 E1
Laceby Acres 190 C4
Lade Bank 113 F5
Laneham 65 A3
Langford 91 C1
Langholme 39 E8
Langrick 124 E7
Langrick Bridge 124 E6
Langtoft 164 F3
Langton Langton by Spilsby 87 F5
Langton 85 B3
Langton by Wragby 70 C3
Langworth 69 B3
Laughterton 65 D2
Laughton 41 C8
Lea 52 F5
Leadenham 106 C3
Leake 127 C8
Leake Commonside 113 F5
Leake Fold Hill 114 A2
Leasingham 121 B8
Legbourne 61 F3
Legsby 58 A4
Lenton 141 E5
Leverington 170 B3
Leverton 126 F6
Leverton Highgate 127 A6
Leverton Lucasgate 127 B6
Leverton Outgate 127 B7
Lincoln 234 C2
Linwood 57 D5
Lissington 57 E2
Listoft 89 F7
Littleborough 52 F1
Little Bytham 163 A4
Little Carlton 62 C4
Little Casterton 171 E8
Little Cawthorpe 61 E2
Little Coates 190 F7
Little Common 215 B8
Littlefield 191 B6
Little Grimsby 49 B2
Little Hale 133 E8
Little Limber 22 C5
Little London Legsby 58 A5
Little London Long Sutton 216 D8
Little London Spalding 156 E3
Little London Spalding 214 A1
Little London Tetford 73 F2
Little Ponton 140 A7
Little Steeping 101 D5
Little Sutton 160 C5
Little Welton 60 F6
Little Wisbeach 143 C6
Lobthorpe 152 A3
Londonthorpe 130 D4
Long Bennington 117 D3
Long Sutton 216 C4
Longthorpe 225 A1
Loosegate 158 A8
Louth 198 E6
Low Barlings 82 E8
Low Burnham 27 E5
Lower Bassingthorpe 140 E4
Lower Bitchfield 141 A3

Low Fulney 157 B4
Low Marnham 78 A4
Low Risby 9 A2
Low Toynton 199 F6
Ludborough 48 D6
Luddington 7 D3
Ludford 59 A8
Ludney 50 C6
Lusby 86 F2
Lutton 160 A8
Lutton Gowts 216 D8

M

Mablethorpe 64 C3
Maidenwell 73 E6
Maltby 60 F3
Maltby le Marsh 76 A8
Manby 62 D6
Manor Park 184 D6
Manthorpe Grantham 211 A8
Manthorpe Toft with Lound and Manthorpe 164 A7
Manton 30 B5
Manton Warren 30 B8
Mareham le Fen 99 A3
Mareham on the Hill 86 A2
Marfleet 5 E2
Marholm 220 C1
Markby 76 C5
Market Deeping 217 E6
Market Rasen 57 E8
Market Stainton 72 B6
Marlborough 93 B4
Marshchapel 37 B2
Marston 118 C2
Martin 96 C3
Martin Roughton 85 B1
Marton 65 D8
Mavis Enderby 87 C1
Mawthorpe 88 F8
Maxey 173 C7
Medlam 112 D7
Melton 2 F5
Melton Ross 21 D5
Messingham 29 D7
Metheringham 95 D4
Middle Rasen 57 B8
Midville 113 E8
Millfield 225 F5
Mill Hill 103 B8
Millthorpe 143 B6
Miningsby 99 D7
Minting 84 D8
Misterton 39 F5
Monksthorpe 101 E8
Moorby 99 B6
Moorhouses 112 A8
Moor Side 111 D8
Moortown 32 C2
Morborne 232 B3
Morton 197 C8
Morton 154 C6
Morton Thorpe on the Hill 92 C6
Moulton 157 F7
Moulton Chapel 157 E1
Moulton Eaugate 167 F8
Moulton Seas End 146 E2
Muckton 74 D8
Mumby 76 F1
Murrow 177 D5
Muston 128 C5

N

Navenby 107 A8
Nene Terrace 175 D6
Nettleham 68 D2
Nettleton 33 A3
Newark 226 E6
Newark-on-Trent 104 B4
New Balderton 104 A2
Newball 69 D3
New Barnetby 21 D5
New Bolingbroke 112 D8
Newborough 174 E4
New England Croft 102 E2
New England Peterborough 225 E7
New Fletton 231 B8
Newham 112 A1
New Holland 4 E2
New Leake 114 A8
New Meadow 231 F2
New Quarrington 212 A2
Newtoft 56 E5
Newton Newton and Haceby 132 A3
Newton 170 A5
Newton by Toft 56 E6
Newton on Trent 65 D1
New Waltham 195 D7
New York 111 C5
Nocton 95 B7
Normanby 8 C3
Normanby-by-Spital 55 E7
Normanby by Stow 53 E1
Normanby le Wold 45 F5
Norman Corner 194 C2

Norman Cross .232 F2
Normanton Bottesford .128 A7
Normanton .119 D5
Northbeck .132 F8
Northborough .217 E2
North Carlton .67 C4
North Carr .27 C3
North Clifton .78 C7
North Cockerington .50 A1
North Cotes .37 A3
North Elkington .48 D1
North End Alvingham .49 E3
North End Saltfleetby .62 F8
North End Swineshead .135 B8
North Ferriby .3 B4
Northfield .178 F2
Northgate .144 D1
North Greetwell .203 B8
North Harby .79 C7
North Hykeham .204 D2
North Kelsey .32 A4
North Kelsey Moor .32 D4
North Killingholme .12 D3
North Kyme .109 F4
Northlands .113 A4
North Leverton with Habblesthorpe .52 B1
North Ormsby .48 E4
Northorpe Donington .134 E3
Northorpe .42 A8
Northorpe Thurlby .164 C8
North Owersby .44 E5
North Rauceby .120 E5
North Reston .62 B2
North Scarle .78 F2
North Somercotes .50 F8
North Thoresby .36 B1
North Willingham .58 D7
North Witham .151 D4
Norton Disney .92 C2
Nunsthorpe .191 B4

O

Oasby .131 C6
Obthorpe .164 C6
Old Bolingbroke .100 B8
Old Clee .192 C6
Old Fletton .231 A6
Old Gate .159 F3
Old Leake .114 A1
Old Somerby .140 D8
Old Woodhall .85 A2
Orange Row .161 F3
Orby .89 C2
Orton Brimbles .229 D5
Orton Goldhay .229 F3
Orton Longueville .230 B5
Orton Malbourne .230 C4
Orton Southgate .229 C2
Orton Waterville .229 E4
Orton Wistow .229 C6
Osbournby .132 C4
Osgodby Lenton Keisby and Osgodby .141 E3
Osgodby .45 A3
Otby .46 A4
Owmby .32 D7
Owmby-by-Spital .55 F6
Owston Ferry .28 B3
Oxcombe .73 D4

P

Panton .71 B5
Parson Drove .177 D7
Partney .88 A3
Paston .221 D1
Peakirk .174 A5
Penny Hill .215 D6
Peterborough .225 D5
Pickworth .142 A8
Pickworth .162 E4
Pilham .41 D4
Pilsgate .172 C4
Pinchbeck .156 E8
Pinchbeck West .156 A7
Pode Hole .156 C5
Pointon .143 B7
Port Sutton Bridge .160 F4
Potterhanworth .82 B1
Potterhanworth Booths .82 C2
Pyewipe .188 C4

Q

Quadring .145 A8
Quadring Eaudike .145 C8
Quarrington .212 B1

R

Ragnall .78 A8
Raithby .60 F3
Raithby by Spilsby .87 D2
Rampton .65 A4
Ranby .72 B5
Rand .70 A5
Ravensthorpe .225 C6
Reasby .69 C6
Redbourne .30 F3
Reedham .111 C7
Reed Point .110 E2
Reepham .203 F8
Revesby .99 C3
Revesby Bridge .99 C3
Riby .23 C2
Riddings .184 F4
Rigsby .75 D2
Rippingale .142 F3
Risby .46 B3
Risegate .144 F4
Riseholme .68 A2
Ropsley .131 B1
Rothwell .33 F2
Roughton .98 B7
Roughton Moor .98 A7
Rowston .108 E7
Roxby .9 A3
Ruckland .73 F5
Ruskington .108 E2
Ryhall .163 C1

S

St Giles .202 C7
St Vincent .211 D3
Saleby .75 F6
Salmonby .86 E8
Saltby .138 F1
Saltfleet .51 B4
Saltfleetby All Saints .51 C1
Saltfleetby St Clement .51 C2
Saltfleetby St Peter .63 B8
Sandbraes .33 A4
Sandholme .136 F4
Sandilands .77 A8
Sandtoft .16 A3
Sandy Bank .111 E6
Santon .19 B7
Sapperton .141 E8
Saracen's Head .215 A7
Saundby .52 B7
Sausthorpe .87 E4
Saxby .55 F5
Saxby All Saints .10 A3
Saxilby .66 D3
Scamblesby .72 F5
Scampton .67 D6
Scartho .194 E8
Scawby .30 E8
Scopwick .95 D1
Scothern .68 E4
Scotland .141 C5
Scotter .29 B3
Scotterthorpe .29 B5
Scotton .29 C2
Scott Willoughby .132 B4
Scrafield .86 C3
Scrane End .137 F8
Scredington .132 E7
Scremby .88 E2
Scrivelsby .98 E8
Scrub Hill .111 B6
Scunthorpe .183 B5
Seacroft .103 E4
Seadyke .136 E3
Searby .32 C8
Seathorne .206 E8
Sedgebrook .128 F5
Sewstern .150 F4
Shepeau Stow .167 F3
Sibsey .113 B2
Silk Willoughby .121 C1
Sixhills .58 E6
Skegness .206 E4
Skeldyke .136 F4
Skellingthorpe .200 B4
Skendleby .88 D4
Skidbrooke .51 B3
Skillington .151 B8
Skinnand .106 C8
Skirbeck .209 B3
Skirbeck Quarter .208 D2
Sleaford .212 B4
Sloothby .89 D5
Snarford .56 D1
Snelland .69 D7
Snitterby .43 D5
Somerby .21 B1
Somersby .87 A7
Sotby .71 E5
Sots Hole .96 C7
South Bramwith .14 A6
South Carlton .67 D3
South Clifton .78 B5
South Cockerington .62 A8
South Elkington .60 E7
South End .12 B7
South Ferriby .10 B8
South Field .3 E4
South Green .161 E2
South Hykeham .93 B7
South Kelsey .32 A1
South Killingholme .12 E3
South Kyme .123 B8
South Ormsby .74 D2
Southorpe .172 E2
South Owersby .44 E4
South Rauceby .120 E4
South Reston .62 D1
Southrey .83 D1
South Scarle .91 E6
South Somercotes .50 E5
South Thoresby .75 A3
South Willingham .59 A2
South Witham .151 E2
Spalding .214 E6
Spalford .78 D4
Spanby .132 F4
Spilsby .101 A8
Spital in the Street .43 B1
Spittlegate .211 A3
Spridlington .55 F3
Springthorpe .53 E8
Sproxton .150 C7
Stainby .151 C5
Stainfield Haconby .154 A8
Stainfield .83 B8
Stainforth .14 C6
Stainsby .86 F6
Stainton by Langworth .69 C4
Stainton le Vale .46 E5
Stallingborough .23 E6
Stamford .219 D4
Stanground .231 C5
Stapleford .105 B8
Staunton in the Vale .117 A2
Stenigot .72 D8
Stenwith .128 D3
Stewton .61 E5
Stibbington .222 C2
Stickford .100 B2
Stickney .113 A8
Stixwould .97 B8
Stockholes Turbary .16 B2
Stoke Rochford .139 F2
Stone Hill .14 F4
Stow .66 C8
Stragglethorpe .105 E3
Stroxton .139 E5
Strubby .63 C1
Stubton .118 B7
Sturgate .53 F8
Sturton .30 F7
Sturton by Stow .66 C7
Sturton le Steeple .52 B3
Sudbrook .119 E3
Sudbrooke .68 F2
Sudthorpe .119 C8
Surfleet .145 C3
Surfleet Seas End .145 F3
Susworth .28 D5
Sutterby .87 E7
Sutterton .136 A3
Sutterton Dowdyke .146 A8
Sutton Beckingham .105 B3
Sutton .222 F2
Sutton Bridge .160 D4
Sutton Crosses .216 C1
Sutton on Sea .76 F8
Sutton on Trent .91 A8
Sutton St Edmund .168 F4
Sutton St James .159 D1
Swaby .74 E4
Swallow .34 B5
Swallow Beck .205 B5
Swanland .3 A7
Swarby .132 A7
Swaton .133 D4
Swayfield .152 D5
Swinderby .92 A5
Swineshead .135 B7
Swineshead Bridge .123 F1
Swinethorpe .79 B4
Swinhope .47 C7
Swinstead .153 A5
Syston .130 A7

T

Tallington .172 E7
Tamworth Green .126 E1
Tathwell .61 B2
Tattershall .207 A5
Tattershall Bridge .110 D7
Tattershall Thorpe .207 B8
Tealby .46 C1
Terrington St Clement .161 E3
Tetford .73 F1
Tetley .16 D6
Tetney .36 D4
Tetney Lock .37 A4
Thealby .8 D4
Theddlethorpe All Saints 63 D7
Theddlethorpe St Helen .63 E8
The Parks .14 C4
Thetford .164 E5
The Willows .190 E7
Thimbleby .85 B5
Thoresthorpe .75 F4
Thoresway .46 D7
Thorganby .47 B8
Thorne .15 B8
Thorney .78 F8
Thorney .176 A3
Thorney Toll .177 A2
Thornton .85 C2
Thornton Curtis .11 E4
Thornton le Moor .44 E7
Thorpe .64 A1
Thorpe Culvert .102 A3
Thorpe Fendykes .101 F3
Thorpe Latimer .133 C6
Thorpe le Vale .47 B1
Thorpe on the Hill .92 E8
Thorpe St Peter .102 B3
Thorpe Tilney .109 C8
Three Bridges .63 A7
Threekingham .132 E3
Throckenholt .177 B8
Thurlby Bilsby .76 D2
Thurlby .92 E4
Thurlby .164 C8
Tickencote .171 A8
Timberland .96 C1
Tinwell .218 D3
Toft .163 F8
Toft Hill .98 D5
Toft next Newton .56 C7
Toll Bar .218 C8
Torksey .65 E5
Torksey Lock .65 E5
Tothill .62 E1
Towngate .164 F1
Toynton All Saints .100 F6
Toynton Fen Side .100 F5
Toynton St Peter .101 A6
Trusthorpe .64 B2
Tumby Woodside .111 F8
Twenty .155 C3
Tydd St Giles .169 F7
Tydd St Mary .160 B1

U

Uffington .172 C6
Ufford .172 F3
Ulceby .12 B1
Ulceby Ulceby with Fordington .88 C7
Ulceby Skitter .12 C2
Upperthorpe .27 B3
Upton .53 E5
Upton .223 B6
Usselby .45 C4
Utterby .48 F4

V

Victoria Dock Village .181 C5

W

Waddingham .43 D7
Waddington .93 F7
Waddingworth .84 C6
Wainfleet All Saints .102 D2
Wainfleet Bank .102 B1
Wainfleet St Mary .115 E8
Wainfleet Tofts .115 C8
Waithe .36 A3
Walcot Alkborough .8 B8
Walcot Walcot Near Folkingham .132 C1
Walcott .109 D7
Walesby .46 A3
Walkeringham .39 F3
Walkerith .40 B4
Walmsgate .74 C5
Walpole Cross Keys .161 C3
Walpole Marsh .170 F8
Walsoken .170 E1
Waltham .194 D5
Walton .221 A1
Walton Highway .170 F3
Wansford .222 A4
Wargate .145 B5
Washingborough .203 D2
Wasps Nest .95 E7
Water Newton .228 C7
Waterside .14 E8
Weecar .78 D1
Weelsby .192 A5
Welbourn .106 F5
Welby .130 F5
Well .88 E8
Wellingore .107 A7
Wellow .191 E5
Welton .2 E6
Welton .68 C6
Welton Hill .69 A8
Welton le Marsh .89 B3
Welton le Wold .60 C6
Werrington .220 F4
West Ashby .85 E7
West Barkwith .70 F7
Westborough .117 E3
West Butterwick .28 D8
Westby .140 F3
Westcliff .184 E7
West Deeping .173 B8
West Ella .178 A8
West End .126 E6
West Field .12 C6
Westgate .16 D2
West Halton .8 E8
Westhorpe .144 F5
West Keal .100 C6
West Marsh .188 D1
Weston .157 D7
Weston Hills .157 C3
West Rasen .56 E8
West Ravendale .35 A2
Westrum .196 C1
West Stockwith .40 C6
West Torrington .58 A1
West Walton .170 E4
West Willoughby .119 E2
Westwood .225 B4
Westwoodside .27 A2
Whaplode .158 A7
Whaplode Drove .168 B4
Whaplode St Catherine 158 C2
Wharton .41 B4
Whisby .79 E2
White Pit .74 D4
Whitton .1 D3
Wickenby .69 F8
Wigsley .78 F5
Wigtoft .135 E3
Wike Well End .15 B7
Wildsworth .40 E8
Wilksby .99 A5
Willingham by Stow .53 F3
Willoughby .89 B7
Willoughby Hills .209 E7
Willoughby Moor .119 F2
Willoughton .42 D4
Will Row .63 C5
Wilsford .120 C1
Wilsthorpe .164 C4
Winceby .86 E3
Winteringham .2 A1
Winterton .9 A5
Winthorpe Langford .104 B8
Winthorpe Skegness .206 C8
Wisbech .170 B1
Wispington .84 E6
Witham on the Hill .163 D7
Witham St. Hughs .92 D5
Withcall .60 C2
Withern .63 A1
Wittering .172 B1
Wold Newton .47 F7
Wood Enderby .98 F6
Woodhall Spa .97 E5
Woodhouse .16 E3
Woodnook .140 C7
Woodside .26 D6
Woodston .230 E7
Woodthorpe .75 D7
Woolsthorpe by Belvoir 128 D1
Woolsthorpe-by-Colsterworth .151 D7
Wootton .11 F3
Worlaby Maidenwell .74 A4
Worlaby .20 D8
Wothorpe .219 B2
Wragby .70 E5
Wragholme .50 A8
Wrangle .114 C1
Wrangle Bank .114 C4
Wrangle Lowgate .114 D2
Wrangle Low Ground .114 D4
Wrawby .20 E4
Wressle .19 F4
Wroot .26 C6
Wybers Wood .190 C6
Wyberton .136 D8
Wykeham .145 F1
Wymondham .150 B1
Wyville .139 C4

Y

Yaddlethorpe .184 E3
Yarborough .191 A7
Yarburgh .49 E4
Yawthorpe .42 A2
Yaxley .233 E6

1

1st Drift PE9 ....219 B2
1st Main Rd DN36 ......36 F8

2

2nd Ave DN36 ....36 F8
2nd Drift PE9 ....219 B2

4

4th Ave DN36 ....36 F8

12

12th Ave DN36 ....36 F8

A

Aalsmeer Rise 6 PE11 .214 A2
Abbey Cl
  Coningsby LN4 ....207 B5
  6 Skegness PE25 ....206 A4
  5 Woodhall Spa LN10 ..97 C6
Abbey Cres 4 PE20 ...135 C7
Abbey Dr 20 Hatfield DN7 .14 D4
  13 Woodhall Spa LN10 ..97 C5
Abbey Dr E DN32 ......191 D6
Abbey Dr W DN32 ......191 D6
Abbey Gdns 22 DN7 .....14 D4
Abbey Gr 23 DN7 ......14 D4
Abbey La
  Sedgebrook NG32 ....128 F4
  Swineshead PE20 .....135 C6
  Woodhall Spa LN10 ...97 C5
Abbey Mews 11 PE6 ...166 F1
Abbey Pk Rd DN32 ....191 D6
Abbey Pl 2 Lincoln LN2 .234 C2
  10 Thorney PE6 ......176 A3
Abbey Rd
  Alvingham LN11 ....49 F2
  Bardney LN3 ....83 B4
  Bourne PE10 ....213 D5
  Grimsby DN32 ....191 D6
  Hatfield DN7 ....14 D4
  Louth LN11 ....198 D6
  Peterborough PE4 ....221 A1
  Revesby PE22 ....99 C5
  Scunthorpe DN17 .....184 F4
  Sleaford NG34 ....212 A2
  Swineshead PE20 .....135 C7
  Ulceby DN39 ....12 A1
Abbey Rise 20 DN19 ...11 D8
Abbey St
  Kingston upon Hull HU9 .181 C7
  Lincoln LN2 ....234 C2
Abbey Way DN7 ....14 D5
Abbey Wlk
  10 Crowland PE6 .....166 F1
  11 Grimsby DN32 .....191 D7
Abbey Yd 12 PE11 .....214 A2
Abbeydale Cres NG31 .211 A8
Abbeyfield Rd 1 DN7 ...14 C4
Abbot St LN5 ....201 E1
Abbot Way PE7 ....233 D4
Abbot's Cl 5 PE10 ....213 E4
Abbot's Way 5 PE11 ..214 A3
Abbots Dr 1 PE6 .....175 B8
Abbots Gdns 1 PE12 ..158 B6
Abbots Rd DN17 ......184 F6
Abbotsbury PE2 ....230 A3
Abbotsmede Jun Sch
  PE1 ....226 C4
Abbotsway DN32 ......191 D6
Abbott Cl 10 LN8 ......57 B8
Abbott's Cl PE9 ....219 D4
Abbotts Gr PE4 ....220 F6
Abbotts Grange DN36 .195 E7
Abercorn St 3 DN33 ..183 A2
Aberdeen Cl PE9 .....218 D6
Aberporth Dr LN6 .....204 B8
Abingdon Ave LN6 ....204 C6
Abingdon Cl 15 LN6 ..204 C6
Aboyne Ave PE2 ......229 F5
Abraham Cl 11 LN2 ...129 E5
Aby CE Prim Sch LN13 .75 B5
Acacia Ave
  Chapel St Leonard PE24 ..90 D8
  Gainsborough DN21 ..197 D6
  Peterborough PE1 ....225 B8
  5 Scunthorpe DN15 ..182 C5
  Spalding PE11 ....214 F5
  Waddington LN5 .....205 D1
  3 Wisbech PE13 .....170 C1
Acacia Cl 12 NG34 ...212 D2
Acacia Ct 3 DN16 ....185 B6
Acacia Way
  Boston PE21 ....208 C4
  Messingham DN17 ....29 C7
Acadia Gr HU13 ......178 F1
Accommodation Rd
  LN9 ....199 A5
Acer Cl LN6 ....204 D7
Acer Ct 2 LN4 ....204 D7
Acer Gr 3 DN17 .....184 C5
Acer Rd PE1 ....226 D5
Achille Rd DN34 .....190 D5
Achurch Cl LN9 ......199 D1

Acklam Ave 3 PE11 ...214 F6
Acklam Gr DN32 ......192 B6
Acklands La 13 NG23 ..117 D3
Acland St
  Gainsborough DN21 ..197 C5
  4 Kingston upon Hull
    HU3 ....180 A6
  Peterborough PE1 ....225 F3
Acomb Comm Rd DN7 ..14 F4
Acorn Cl Freiston PE21 .126 C4
  Grantham NG31 ......211 C7
  Lincoln LN5 ....205 D7
Acorn Way
  5 Bottesford DN16 ...185 B2
  Hessle HU13 ....178 B3
Acre Dyke La LN4 .....82 B4
Acre La Scopwick LN4 ..95 E1
  Threekingham NG34 ..132 E2
Acres La DN9 ....26 D7
Acres The 1 PE9 .....172 D4
Ada Way LN11 ....198 D7
Adam Cl 18 LN6 ......204 D7
Adam Smith St DN31 ..188 F1
Adams Way DN21 .....65 E8
Adamstiles 2 NG32 ...219 A8
Addington Way 3 PE4 .221 A3
Addison Cl 4 LN5 ....107 A8
Addison Dr LN2 ....202 B6
Addison Pl LN1 ......65 E3
Adelaide Cl
  Gainsborough DN21 ..197 F2
  13 Waddington LN5 ...93 E8
Adelaide Prim Sch
  HU3 ....180 D5
Adelaide Sch HU3 ....180 D5
Adelaide St
  Kingston upon Hull HU3 .180 D5
  Stamford PE9 ....219 D5
Adelphi Ct 5 DN36 ...195 C6
Adelphi Dr DN33 .....194 E7
Adlard Gr DN36 ......36 C7
Adlingfleet Rd DN17 ...7 E6
Admirals Dr 7 PE13 ..170 D2
Admiralty Rd 19 LN12 ..64 B4
Adrian St Louth LN11 ..198 C4
  9 Skegness PE25 ....206 A4
  9 Swineshead PE20 ..135 B7
Advent Ct 2 DN39 ....12 A1
Aegir Cl DN21 ....197 F2
Africa Cl DN34 ......190 D4
Agard Ave DN15 .....182 E3
Agnes St 2 NG31 ....211 B4
Aidan Rd NG34 ......212 B2
Aima Ct 2 LN2 ......68 C2
Ainsdale Dr PE4 .....220 F3
Ainslie St DN32 ......191 B5
Ainsworth Rd 5 DN40 .186 B4
Ainthorpe Gr HU5 ...179 C7
Ainthorpe Prim Sch
  HU5 ....179 C8
Aintree Dr PE11 .....214 B1
Aire Cl DN40 ....186 A3
Aire Rd NG31 ....210 E3
Airedale Cl
  12 Broughton DN20 ...19 E4
  Peterborough PE1 ....226 A6
Airedale Rd
  1 Scunthorpe DN16 ..185 D5
  1 Stamford PE9 .....219 A7
Airlie St HU3 ....180 B5
Airmanship Rd NG34 ..120 B8
Airmyn Ave 1 HU3 ...179 E6
Airship Rd NG34 .....107 C1
Aisne Cl LN1 ....201 E7
Aisne St HU5 ....180 A8
Ajax Cl DN34 ....190 D4
Ajax Ct DN15 ....182 F5
Akeferry Rd DN9 .....27 C1
Akeman Ct 10 PE10 ..213 C6
Akita Cl 4 PE11 .....214 A5
Alabala Cl LN4 ......203 C1
Alabala La LN4 ......81 F4
Alan Cres DN15 .....182 F2
Alba Cl DN17 ....184 D5
Alban Ret Pk PE21 ..208 B3
Albany Cl PE25 .....206 A5
Albany Pl LN11 .....198 D3
Albany Rd Louth LN11 .198 D3
  Skegness PE25 .....206 A5
  21 Wisbech PE13 ...170 D1
  3 Woodhall Spa LN10 ..97 C5
Albany St
  Gainsborough DN21 ..197 C6
  Kingston upon Hull HU3 .180 D8
  Lincoln LN1 ....234 A4
Albany Way PE25 ....206 A5
Albany Wlk PE2 .....230 D7
Albatross Dr DN37 ..190 B7
Albemarle Cl 5 HU15 ..2 B5
Albemarle St 1 DN35 .180 B5
Albert Ave
  Kingston upon Hull HU3 .180 A7
  Long Sutton PE12 ...159 E4
  1 Skegness PE25 ....103 E4
Albert Cres LN1 .....201 D4
Albert Pl PE3 ....225 F1
Albert Rd
  Cleethorpes DN35 ...192 F6
  Scunthorpe DN16 ....185 A5
  Skegness PE25 .....206 B3
  2 Stamford PE9 .....219 C4
Albert St Boston PE21 .208 D5
  15 Bottesford NG13 .128 A6
  Brigg DN20 ....196 C3
  Grantham NG31 .....211 C2
  6 Holbeach PE12 ....215 D2
  Horncastle LN9 .....199 C3
  7 New Holland DN19 ..4 E2

Albert St continued
  Spalding PE11 ....214 C6
  Thorne/Moorends DN8 ..15 B8
Albert St E DN32 .....189 B1
Albert St W 6 DN32 ..189 B1
Albert Terr 2 PE21 ..208 E4
Albert Wlk 3 PE12 ..215 D2
Alberta Cres DN17 ...184 E3
Albertine Ct 4 DN37 .194 C5
Albery Way DN36 ....195 C7
Albion Cl LN1 ....201 C6
Albion Cres LN1 .....201 C6
Albion Hill 8 DN9 ....27 E6
Albion Pl LN11 ......198 C5
Albion Rd 2 NG31 ...211 A5
Albion St
  8 Crowland PE6 .....166 F1
  Grimsby DN32 ......189 B1
  Holbeach PE12 .....215 F2
  10 Kingston upon Hull
    HU1 ....180 E7
  Spalding PE11 .....214 C5
Albion Terr
  4 Misterton DN10 ...40 A4
  Sleaford NG34 .....212 E4
Albourne Ave 1 DN15 .183 A2
Alconbury Cl
  13 Birchwood LN6 ...204 C6
  Peterborough PE2 ...231 E5
Alcorn Gn PE21 ....209 C4
Aldbro' St HU2 ......180 F8
Alden Cl DN40 ......186 C4
Alder Cl 3 Lincoln LN6 .204 F3
  Louth LN11 ....198 D4
Alder Gr PE21 ......209 C2
Alder Rd
  Peterborough PE7 ...230 C3
  Sleaford NG34 .....212 D2
Alder View DN33 ....190 F3
Aldergrove Cl 2 LN6 .204 C7
Aldergrove Cres LN6 .204 C7
Alderlands Cl 6 PE6 .175 B8
Alderley Edge DN37 .194 C4
Alderman's Dr PE3 ..225 E3
Alderney Way
  Immingham DN40 ....186 C2
  Lincoln LN6 ....205 A1
Alderson Mews 5 HU9 .181 C7
Aldrich Rd DN35 ....192 F4
Aldsworth Cl 1 PE1 ..226 D6
Aldwych Croft 8 DN36 .195 C6
Aldwych Ct HU5 .....179 E8
Aldwych Gdns 11 PE11 .214 A2
Alec Rose Gr DN21 ..197 F3
Alexander Ave
  NG24 ....104 A6
Alexander Cl 15 LN4 ..95 D4
Alexander Dr LN11 ...198 D4
Alexander Rd
  2 Scunthorpe DN16 .183 C3
  2 Scunthorpe DN16 .183 B2
Alexandra Cl 8 NG23 .117 D4
Alexandra Pk 22 LN12 .64 B4
Alexandra Rd
  Cleethorpes DN35 ...192 F6
  Grantham NG31 .....210 F3
  Grimsby DN31 ......188 F1
  Louth LN11 ....198 C6
  21 Mablethorpe/Sutton on Sea
    LN12 ....64 B4
  Peterborough PE1 ...225 F6
  Scunthorpe DN16 ...185 B6
  Skegness PE25 .....206 B3
  Sleaford NG34 .....212 C4
  3 Woodhall Spa LN10 .97 C6
Alexandra Rd S DN40 .186 E6
Alexandra Ret Pk
  DN31 ....188 F1
Alexandra St HU3 ...180 D7
Alexandra Terr LN1 ..234 A3
Alexandra Terraces 4
  PE10 ....213 D5
Alexandre Ave 2 LN6 .204 F1
Alexandria Rd LN8 ..56 D5
Alfonso St 5 HU3 ....180 B5
Alford Mill Cl 6 LN6 ..93 B8
Alford Pottery* LN13 .75 E3
Alford Prim Sch LN13 ..75 F2
Alford Rd 1 Alford LN13 .75 F3
  Bilsby LN13 ....76 A3
  Huttoft LN13 ....76 E3
  Mablethorpe/Sutton on Sea
    LN12 ....64 A3
Alford St NG31 ......211 B5
Alfred Ave LN4 ......95 C4
Alfred Cl 10 NG34 ...212 B2
Alfred Gelder St 6 HU1 180 F6
Alfred Smith Way 5
  LN11 ....61 F3
Alfred St Boston PE21 .209 A3
  Gainsborough DN21 ..197 C5
  2 Grimsby DN31 ....191 D8
  Kingston upon Hull HU3 .180 D5
  Lincoln LN5 ....201 E1
Alfric Sq PE2 ....230 D6
Algernon St DN32 ...191 F5
Algitha Rd PE25 ....206 C3
Alkborough La DN15 ..8 C7
Alkborough Prim Sch
  DN15 ....8 C8
All Saints Ave PE13 .170 E1
All Saints CE Jun Sch
  Kingston upon Hull
    HU13 ....178 F2
  Peterborough PE1 ...226 A1
All Saints CE Prim Sch
  LN6 ....204 E1

All Saints CE Sch Swinderby
  Prim School LN6 ....92 B6
All Saints' Cl 17 DN19 ..12 A8
All Saints Cl
  3 Holbeach PE12 ...215 F3
  7 Moulton PE12 ....157 F7
  4 Wainfleet All Saints
    PE24 ....102 D1
All Saints Cty Prim Sch
  LN5 ....93 F7
All Saints Gr 4 NG34 .212 B6
All Saints La 14 LN2 ..68 C2
All Saints' Pl 6 PE9 ..219 B5
All Saints' Rd PE1 ...226 A5
All Saints' St
  Kingston upon Hull HU3 .180 D8
  10 Stamford PE9 ....219 B5
Allan Ave PE2 ......231 E5
Allanby St DN15 ....183 A3
Allandale Cl LN1 ....201 D8
Allanhall Way HU10 ..178 B8
Allard Cl PE7 ....233 D6
Allen Cl
  7 Billingborough NG34 .133 B1
  4 Claypole NG23 ...117 E8
  5 Market Deeping PE6 .217 D5
  Fenton NG23 ....105 C1
  Peterborough PE1 ...225 E6
Allenby Ave 1 DN34 .191 A6
Allenby Cres LN11 ...49 A2
Allenby Ind Est LN2 .202 D4
Allenby Rd LN2 .....202 D5
Allenby Way PE25 ...206 D8
Allenby's Chase PE14 160 E4
Allen's Dro PE13 ...169 D1
Allertorpe Cres 19 HU15 .2 D5
Allerton Cl PE9 .....172 D3
Allerton Dr DN40 ...186 B4
Allerton Garth PE7 ..229 A4
Allerton Prim Sch
  DN40 ....186 A4
Allestree Dr DN33 ..194 E7
Alliance Ave HU3 ...179 F7
Alliance La HU3 ....179 F7
Allington Dr DN37 ..188 A2
Allington Gdn PE21 .209 A2
Allington La NG32 ..129 B4
Allington Rd NG32 ..128 F5
Allington with Sedgebrook
  CE Prim Sch NG32 .129 A7
Allison Cl 3 DN17 ...29 C7
Allison Pl 5 LN1 ....201 D4
Allison Rd 6 NG34 ..122 D3
Allison St LN1 ......201 D4
Allotment La PE5 ...223 E2
Allwood Rd 20 LN2 ..68 D6
Alma Ave PE25 .....206 B5
Alma Cl
  Kingston upon Hull
    HU10 ....178 D7
  4 Skegness PE25 ...206 B5
Alma Martin Way 13 LN3 .83 C4
Alma Pk Cl 1 NG31 .211 F6
Alma Pk Ind Est
  Grantham 211 F7
  Londonthorpe &
    Harrowby without NG31 .130 C4
Alma Pk Rd NG31 ..211 F6
Alma Rd PE1 ....225 F5
Alma St 6 HU9 .....181 B7
Almond Ave
  Heighington LN4 ....81 F4
  Lincoln LN6 ....205 A8
Almond Cl Boston PE21 .208 C5
  9 Saxilby LN1 ......66 D2
Almond Cres
  Lincoln LN6 ....205 A8
  Louth LN11 ....198 D5
  Waddington LN5 ...205 A8
Almond Gr Brigg DN20 .196 B4
  Grantham NG31 ....211 C6
  3 Kingston upon Hull
    HU3 ....180 D6
  5 Scunthorpe DN16 .185 B8
  Skellingthorpe LN6 .200 A4
Almond Rd PE1 .....226 B7
Almond Wlk
  Boston PE21 ....208 D5
  Sleaford NG34 .....212 D6
Almoners La PE3 ...225 E3
Alness Cl LN6 ......204 B8
Altham Terr LN5 ...205 D7
Althorpe & Keadby Prim Sch
  DN17 ....17 D5
Althorpe Cl 15 PE6 ..217 A5
Althorpe Sta DN17 ..17 D5
Altoft Cl 19 DN37 ...23 F1
Altyre Way DN36 ...192 C1
Alverston Ave LN10 ..97 C6
Alveston Rd DN17 ..184 D8
Alvingham Ave DN35 .192 F3
Alvingham Rd
  Keddington LN11 ...198 E8
  Scunthorpe DN16 ...185 B7
Alvis Cl LN4 ....205 F2
Alvis Dr PE7 ....233 D6
Alwyn Rd 10 DN6 ...15 B8
Amanda Dr Hatfield DN7 .14 D4
  Louth LN11 ....198 C8
Amber Hill Toftstead Prim
  Sch PE20 ....124 A5
Ambergate Specl Sch
  NG31 ....210 D3
Amberley Cres PE21 .208 C4
Amberley Slope PE4 .221 A3
Amble Cl LN1 ......201 E8

Ambleside Cl 4 NG34 .212 B2
Ambleside Dr PE11 ..214 B2
Ambleside Gdns PE4 .221 B3
Ambrose Ave 3 DN7 ..14 E4
Ambury Gdns 9 PE6 .166 F1
Amcott Ave DN10 ...40 A4
Amcotts Rd DN33 ...191 A2
Amesbury Ave DN33 .194 D7
Amethyst Cl 3 NG34 .212 A3
Amethyst Ct 2 DN36 .195 D7
Amman Sq 1 NG34 ..120 D8
Amos Cl NG23 .....91 E6
Amos Cres 3 DN16 ..185 D7
Amos La NG23 .....91 E6
Amos Way 8 PE22 ..113 B1
Ampleforth Gr HU5 ..179 D8
Amstel Cl 11 PE11 ..214 B2
Amsterdam Gdns 9
  PE11 ....214 B3
Amwell Gn 10 DN7 ..14 D3
Amy Johnson Sch
  HU3 ....179 F5
Anastasia Cl DN21 ..197 C7
Ancaster Ave
  Chapel St Leonard PE24 ..90 D7
  Grimsby DN33 .....194 D8
  Lincoln LN2 ....202 B5
  Spilsby PE23 ......100 F8
Ancaster CE Prim Sch
  NG32 ....120 A3
Ancaster Cl LN3 ....203 E6
Ancaster Ct DN16 ...185 A5
Ancaster Dr NG32 ..212 B2
Ancaster Rd
  Bourne PE10 ....213 E5
  17 Mablethorpe/Sutton on Sea
    LN12 ....64 B3
  7 Stamford PE9 ....219 A7
Ancaster Sta NG32 .120 A3
Ancaster Valley Nature
  Reserve* NG32 ....120 A2
Ancholme Ave DN40 .186 A3
Ancholme Bsns Pk
  DN20 ....196 A4
Ancholme Gdns 10
  DN20 ....196 C3
Ancholme Leisure Ctr
  DN20 ....196 A2
Ancholme Rd DN16 .185 D6
Ancholme Way DN20 .196 B3
Anchor La PE25 ....90 C2
Anchor Rd
  Scunthorpe DN16 ...19 B4
  Sutton Bridge PE34 .161 C4
Anchor St LN5 .....234 A1
Anchorage St 2 DN20 .196 B3
Anchors Way 7 DN20 .196 A3
Ancient La DN7 ....14 E3
Anderby Cl LN6 ....204 F6
Anderby Dr
  Grimsby DN37 .....190 D7
  Lincoln LN6 ....204 F6
Anderby Drainage Mus*
  PE24 ....77 C2
Anderby Rd PE24 ..77 D1
Anderson Cl 7 PE13 .170 C1
Anderson La 2 LN1 .201 F6
Anderson Rd
  2 Hemswell Cliff DN21 .55 A8
  Scunthorpe DN16 ...185 C7
Anderson St 1 DN31 .191 D7
Anderson Way DN21 .52 F5
Andover Cl LN6 ....204 B8
Andrea Cl PE2 .....231 C6
Andrew Ave 28 PE24 .90 D7
Andrew Cl PE5 .....223 C2
Andrew Rd
  9 Humberston DN36 ..36 D8
  1 Stamford PE9 ....219 B6
Andrewe's Cl PE7 ..231 B1
Andrews Cl LN11 ...198 C7
Andrews Cres PE4 ..221 C6
Andrews Rd LN18 ...10 A7
Andrews Way 7 DN40 .186 A4
Angel Ct 5 NG32 ...120 A2
Angelica Dr PE11 ..214 B6
Angell La PE12 .....215 E1
Angerstein Rd DN17 .184 F5
Anglesey Dr DN40 ..186 A6
Anglia Cl 13 NG34 .212 B2
Anglian Cl PE2 .....231 D6
Anglian Way 5 LN8 ..57 E8
Angus Cl 3 PE9 ....218 D6
Angus Ct PE3 ......225 D3
Anlaby Acre Head Cty Prim
  Sch HU4 ....179 A6
Anlaby Ave 7 HU4 ..179 B6
Anlaby High Rd HU4 .179 C6
Anlaby Jun Sch HU4 .179 A6
Anlaby Pk Rd N HU4 .179 B5
Anlaby Pk Rd S HU4 .179 B2
Anlaby Rd HU3 .....179 F6
Anlafgate 7 HU10 ..178 F4
Ann Gr DN35 ......192 D4
Annandale Rd HU10 .178 C8
Anne Rd Stamford PE9 .219 A6
  11 Sutton Bridge PE12 .160 E4
Annes Cres DN16 ...185 C7
Annesley St 1 DN31 .188 F1
Annette Cl 8 PE11 ..214 B5
Anningson La 6 DN36 .195 D7
Annpasture La LN4 ..207 C8
Anson Cl LN6 ......200 A4
Anthony Cres LN11 ..198 C8
Anthony Way 3 DN41 .23 D7
Anthony's Bank Rd
  DN36 ....193 D1

Antrim Rd 9 LN5 205 D2
Antrim Way DN33 191 D2
Anvil Cl PE12 148 B1
Anvil Wlk 2 DN15 8 F3
Anzio Cres LN1 201 E7
Anzio Terr LN1 201 E7
Apeldoorn Gdns 3
PE11 214 B3
Apley Cl
Gainsborough DN21 197 F3
Lincoln LN2 202 A8
Appian Way 8 PE6 164 E5
Apple Garth LN5 205 D4
Apple Tree Cl 19 LN4 95 C4
Apple Tree Ct 14 DN41 23 F5
Appleby Cl DN17 184 F5
Appleby Gdns DN20 19 D4
Appleby La DN20 19 D4
Appleby Mill Rd DN16 183 E3
Appledore Cl HU9 181 C6
Applegarth Cl 2 DN35 192 D5
Applegarth Rd 33 HU8 181 A7
Appleton Gate NG24 104 A5
Appleton Way DN16 185 C6
Applewood Dr 5 NG31 210 F8
Appleyard PE2 231 C7
Appleyard Dr 38 DN18 10 E8
Apsley Way PE3 225 A2
Aqua Dr LN12 64 B2
Aquila Way PE6 164 E2
Arabis Cl 3 LN2 202 C8
Arakan Way 2 PE10 213 E7
Arbella Rd PE21 209 C4
Arboretum Ave LN2 234 C2
Arboretum The* LN2 234 C3
Arborfield Cl 5 PE6 173 C4
Arbury Cl PE3 225 A3
Arcadia Cres 2 PE25 206 D2
Arcadia Rd PE25 206 D3
Archer La 12 PE21 208 F5
Archer Rd Branston LN4 81 E2
Waltham DN37 194 D4
Archer St
3 Bishop Norton LN8 43 D3
Lincoln LN5 234 B1
Archers Dro PE6 176 D6
Archers La PE20 136 C3
Archers Way NG33 140 A5
Archers Wood PE7 230 C3
Arcon Dr HU4 179 D6
Arcott Dr PE21 208 C5
Arden Cl 6 LN12 64 C3
Arden Moor Way 4 LN6 93 B8
Arden Village 5 DN35 192 F1
Ardent Rd DN18 4 A1
Argyle St Boston PE21 208 D5
Kingston upon Hull HU3 180 C7
Argyll Way PE9 218 F5
Ariston St DN32 192 B7
Ark Rd LN11 50 F8
Ark Royal Ct 2 NG34 212 A3
Arkley Cl 22 HU15 2 C5
Arkwright St DN21 197 C5
Arkwright Way DN16 185 F6
Arlington Rd 4 LN8 56 D5
Arlington St 2 HU3 180 D6
Armeria Dr 4 DN17 185 A1
Armley Gr 3 PE9 219 D7
Armour Rd DN16 183 E3
Armstrong Pl E 3 DN31 188 E1
Armstrong Pl W 2
DN31 188 E1
Armstrong St DN31 188 E1
Armstrong's Cl 2 PE12 157 D7
Armstrong's La PE22 115 B7
Armthorpe La DN3 14 A3
Armtree Rd PE22 124 E7
Arne Cl 10 NG31 120 A3
Arnhem Ave 1 NG34 108 D2
Arnhem Dr
10 Caythorpe NG32 119 B7
2 Spalding PE11 214 C5
Arnhem Way
Bourne PE10 213 E6
7 Woodhall Spa LN10 97 D5
Arnold Ave NG31 210 E8
Arnold Cl DN37 23 F2
Arnold La HU3 180 B6
Arnold St HU3 180 B6
Arnold's Mdw Nature
Reserve* PE12 214 F2
Arran Cl DN40 186 D2
Arran Rd PE9 218 D5
Arras Cl LN1 201 E6
Arthur Mellows Village Coll
PE6 220 B8
Arthur Rd DN21 197 D6
Arthur St
Grimsby DN31 191 C8
Kingston upon Hull HU3 180 A5
6 Lincoln LN5 201 F1
Arthur Taylor St 1 LN1 201 D3
Arthurs' Ave 5 PE12 215 D2
Artillery Row 13 PE21 209 A5
Artindale PE3 225 A3
Artis Ct PE3 225 A3
Arundel Cl
Gainsborough DN21 197 E6
Kingston upon Hull HU9 181 C8
Arundel Cres PE21 208 B4
Arundel Dr LN11 198 A7
Arundel Pl DN35 192 E5
Arundel Rd PE4 221 A1
Arundel St 3 HU9 181 C8
Ascendale PE6 217 F5
Ascot Cl 4 PE11 156 E3
Ascot Dr
7 Grantham NG31 211 D7
Ascot Dr continued
Peterborough PE1 226 B6
Ascot Rd 5 DN37 194 D4
Ascot Way 7 LN6 93 A8
Ascott Cl HU4 179 D5
Asgarby Rd NG34 122 B2
Asgard Way DN33 191 B2
Ash Ave 19 HU15 2 C6
Ash Cl
Burgh Le Marsh PE24 102 D7
5 Colsterworth NG33 151 E7
Fulbeck NG32 106 C1
Hessle HU13 178 C3
Holbeach PE12 215 C3
Langtoft PE6 164 E2
Lincoln LN6 204 E8
Louth LN11 198 C7
Peterborough PE1 226 C7
1 Thorney PE6 175 F3
Ash Ct
Cleethorpes DN35 192 D2
5 Donington PE11 134 E2
Peterborough PE1 226 C7
Spalding PE11 214 F6
Ash Dr
Kingston upon Hull
HU10 178 F8
3 Kirton PE20 136 C5
Ash Gr Bourne PE10 213 C6
Brigg DN20 196 B4
Cherry Willingham/Reepham
LN3 203 D5
Gainsborough DN21 197 D6
Grantham NG31 211 D7
Lincoln LN6 204 F2
32 Messingham DN17 29 D7
Scunthorpe DN16 185 B7
Ash Hill Cres DN7 14 D4
Ash Hill Rd DN7 14 D4
Ash La 26 LN5 93 F6
Ash Pk PE4 220 F6
Ash Pl 6 PE9 218 D6
Ash Rd 7 Coningsby LN4 207 D4
Peterborough PE1 226 C7
Ash Tree Ave 11 LN2 68 D2
Ash Tree Cl
Immingham DN40 186 C5
10 Market Rasen LN8 57 D7
Ash Tree Dr 5 DN9 27 D2
Ash Tree Rd 7 DN8 15 B7
Ashberry Dr
31 Messingham DN17 29 D7
4 Scunthorpe DN16 185 B6
Ashbourne 6 DN37 194 C4
Ashbourne Cl 3 NG34 212 B2
Ashbourne Ct DN15 182 B3
Ashburn Cl 1 PE6 220 D7
Ashburnham Rd 20 DN8 15 A8
Ashby Ave LN6 204 F7
Ashby Broadway
DN16 185 A6
Ashby Cl Grimsby DN37 190 D8
Holton le Clay DN36 195 E1
Kingston upon Hull HU4 179 B7
Ashby Ct 2 NG34 212 D6
Ashby Gdns 7 PE12 157 F6
Ashby High St DN16 185 B6
Ashby Hill DN37 35 C3
Ashby La DN37 35 D4
Ashby Rd
Cleethorpes DN35 192 D3
Kingston upon Hull HU4 179 B4
Scunthorpe DN16 183 A1
Spilsby PE23 88 A1
Ashcroft Gdns PE1 226 C5
Ashcroft Rd DN21 197 D2
Ashdale Cl 3 LN4 95 C4
Ashdale Pk 18 HU14 3 A5
Ashdene Cl HU10 178 E7
Ashdown Ave 5 DN15 182 E3
Ashdown Cl 3 DN20 196 E3
Ashdown Way 15 DN10 39 F5
Asheridge LN4 81 E2
Ashfield 2 LN1 66 D7
Ashfield Ave 2 DN8 15 A7
Ashfield Ct 20 DN17 16 D7
Ashfield Gr 1 DN7 14 C4
Ashfield Grange 5 LN1 66 C2
Ashfield Rd
8 Hatfield DN7 14 C4
Sleaford NG34 212 D5
Thorne DN8 14 F7
Ashfield St 3 LN2 202 B3
Ashfields PE6 217 D2
Ashing La LN2 68 F6
Ashlawn Dr PE21 209 B6
Ashlea 4 DN10 39 F5
Ashleigh PE2 229 C6
Ashleigh Ct 3 DN41 23 F5
Ashley Cl 1 LN12 64 C1
Ashley Dr NG31 210 E8
Ashley Pool La 5 PE6 176 A2
Ashley Rd 2 LN11 198 C5
Ashlin Gr LN1 234 A3
Ashridge Dr DN32 192 C5
Ashton Rd PE3 225 B5
Ashtree Ave DN34 191 A6
Ashtree Cl 1 Belton DN9 16 E2
12 Ruskington NG34 108 E1
Ashtree Gdns 5 PE9 171 B1
Ashwell Ave 2 HU9 5 E8
Ashwin Gate 2 PE11 145 A8
Ashwood Cl 1 LN9 199 B4
Ashwood Dr 10 DN36 36 D8
Ashworth Cl LN6 204 F5
Askew Ave HU4 179 E4
Askew's Dro PE6 166 D2
Askew's La PE7 233 E4
Aslackby Rd NG34 142 D3
Aspen Cl LN1 65 D2
Aspen Ct
Cleethorpes DN35 192 D2
Gainsborough DN21 197 F6
Aspen Dr 4 NG34 212 D2
Aspen Gr DN16 185 B8
Aspen Wlk 10 HU15 2 D5
Asperton Rd PE20 135 E4
Asphodel Cl 3 DN36 195 D7
Asquith St DN21 197 B6
Aster Cl LN2 202 C8
Aster Dr PE4 221 B3
Asterby Cl LN2 202 A7
Asterby End LN11 72 E6
Asterby La LN11 72 E5
Asterby Rd DN17 184 F5
Astley Cres 15 DN21 29 C3
Astley St HU3 179 F7
Aston Cl 4 LN5 93 F7
Aston Gn 5 DN7 14 D3
Aston Hall Dr 12 HU14 3 A5
Aston Rd HU10 178 F8
Astore Pk PE1 226 E3
Astral Cl HU13 178 F3
Astral Rd HU13 178 F3
Astral Way 8 LN6 204 C1
Astwick Rd LN6 205 A5
Aswell St LN11 198 B5
Athelstan Cl 9 NG34 212 B2
Athenian Way 1 DN31 188 A3
Atherstone Ave PE3 225 B4
Atherton Way DN20 196 B4
Athol St HU3 179 F4
Atholl Ave HU13 178 E3
Atkinson Ave DN20 196 C5
Atkinson Dr 24 HU15 2 C6
Atkinson La 6 DN37 194 E4
Atkinson St PE1 226 C2
Atkinsons Way DN15 182 F7
Atlas Rd DN17 184 F8
Atterby Carr La DN21 43 F4
Atterby La LN8 43 C3
Atton Ave 4 PE11 157 B6
Atwater Cl LN2 202 D7
Atwater Ct 2 LN2 202 D7
Atwater Gr LN2 202 D7
Atwood Cl DN40 186 B5
Aubourn Ave LN2 201 F7
Aubretia Ave PE4 221 B3
Aubretia Dr 3 DN17 185 A1
Auckland Cres 1 LN4 96 C1
Auckland Rd
Grimsby DN31 189 B2
Scunthorpe DN15 182 F2
Auden Cl LN2 234 C4
Auden Ct 2 LN4 207 B5
Audern Rd DN16 185 A4
Audley Gate PE3 225 C3
Augusta Cl
Grimsby DN34 191 C5
Peterborough PE1 226 E6
Augusta Oaks 5 DN34 191 C6
Augusta St DN34 191 C6
Augustus Dr 17 HU15 2 C5
Aunsby Rd NG34 132 A7
Austen Wlk LN2 202 C6
Austendike Rd PE12 157 C4
Austerby PE10 213 E4
Austerby Cl PE10 213 D4
Austerby The PE10 213 E4
Austin Cres 3 DN17 184 F3
Austin Ct PE7 233 D6
Austin Friar's La 2 PE9 219 B4
Austin Garth 5 DN37 23 F1
Austin St PE9 219 B4
Autumn Pk Ind Est
NG31 210 F4
Avebury Gdns PE11 214 F4
Aveland Cl
Aslackby & Laughton
NG34 142 E5
5 Bourne PE10 213 C5
Aveland Dr NG34 143 B8
Aveland High Sch The
NG34 143 B8
Aveland Way
Aslackby & Laughton
NG34 142 D5
3 Baston PE6 164 E4
Avenswood La DN15 182 C6
Avenue A DN21 53 D5
Avenue B DN21 53 D5
Avenue Cannes DN15 182 D5
Avenue Clamart DN15 182 D5
Avenue Farm Rd PE12 160 D6
Avenue Fontenay 2
DN15 182 D5
Avenue Lourdes 1
DN15 182 D5
Avenue Nozay 2 DN20 19 E4
Avenue Rd NG31 211 B4
Avenue Rouen DN15 182 D6
Avenue The
9 Blyton DN21 41 C5
Burton upon Stather DN15 8 B4
Carlby PE9 163 E4
Deeping St Nicholas
PE11 166 C7
East Ravendale DN37 35 C2
Friskney PE22 115 A6
Gainsborough DN21 197 E6
Grantham NG31 210 E4
6 Great Gonerby NG31 129 D5
Grimsby DN37 190 C8
Healing DN41 23 F5
7 Ingham LN1 54 F2
Avenue The continued
Kingston upon Hull
HU10 178 C7
Lincoln LN1 234 A3
Market Deeping PE6 217 B5
Newark-on-Trent NG24 104 A4
Nocton LN4 95 B7
Swinderby LN6 92 C6
Avenue Vivian DN15 182 E4
Aviary Cl NG31 211 C5
Avignon Rd PE11 214 A5
Avocet Cl
4 Birchwood LN6 204 D8
4 Essendine PE9 163 D3
Avon Cl Grantham NG31 210 E3
5 Lincoln LN6 205 A2
Avon Ct PE4 221 C2
Avon Rd DN16 183 C2
Avondale
1 Kingston upon Hull
HU4 179 B2
7 Lincoln LN6 204 C1
Avondale St LN2 234 C2
Axholme Ave 3 DN17 16 C7
Axholme Dr 6 DN9 27 D6
Axholme Gn 19 DN8 15 B7
Axholme Line Nature
Reserve* DN9 27 C4
Axholme Rd
Scunthorpe DN15 182 D2
2 Westwoodside DN9 27 A2
Axiom Ave PE3 225 C4
Ayam Cl 5 LN2 68 D6
Aydon Rd PE7 231 F6
Aykroft 1 PE10 213 E2
Aylesbury Gr HU5 179 D8
Aylesby Cl 7 LN1 201 E8
Aylesby Gdns 3 DN33 191 B3
Aylesby La DN37 23 F3
Aylesby Rd
Aylesby DN37 190 B6
Scunthorpe DN17 184 F5
Aylesford St 7 HU3 180 B5
Aylmer Ave PE24 103 D2
Aynsley Rd LN6 204 B6
Ayots Gn 14 DN7 14 D3
Ayr Cl PE9 218 E6
Ayres Dr PE2 231 C6
Ayscough Ave
Spalding PE11 214 D3
7 Stallingborough DN41 23 E6
Ayscough Gr 9 LN7 33 B4
Ayscough St 4 DN31 188 E1
Ayscoughfee Hall Mus &
Gdns* PE11 214 D3
Ayscoughfee Hall Sch
PE11 214 D3
Aysgarth Ave 18 DN17 29 D7
Azalea Cl PE3 225 A2
Azalea Rd LN2 202 C8

B

Bacheler St HU3 180 B5
Back Bank
Crowland PE12 167 F3
Whaplode PE12 168 A3
Back Field La DN7 14 E4
Back La
5 Allington NG32 128 F7
Aswarby & Swarby
NG34 132 A7
Barnby in the Willows
NG24 105 A3
Belvoir NG32 138 D6
Bicker PE20 134 F6
Bilsby LN13 76 A2
Bolingbroke PE23 100 A7
Buckminster NG33 151 A4
Burton Coggles NG33 152 C8
Cammeringham LN1 54 F1
Candlesby with Gunby
PE23 89 B1
Caythorpe NG32 119 B7
Claxby with Moorby PE22 99 B7
Claypole NG23 117 E7
Collyweston PE9 171 B1
Colsterworth NG33 151 E7
3 Deeping St James PE6 217 F4
Dunston LN4 95 C6
Eye PE6 175 A1
3 Foston NG32 117 F1
Garthorpe & Fockerby
DN17 7 F6
Heighington/Washingborough
LN4 81 F4
Holbeach PE12 215 D2
Ingoldsby NG33 141 C5
Leadenham LN5 106 C3
Long Bennington NG23 128 D8
Long Sutton PE12 216 D6
4 Lutton PE12 160 A8
Market Deeping PE6 174 A8
North Cockerington LN11 50 A1
1 Searby cum Owmby
DN38 32 D8
4 Skillington NG33 151 A8
4 Stainforth DN7 14 C6
9 Stamford PE9 219 C5
Stickford PE22 100 A3
Wainfleet All Saints
PE24 102 A2
Wilsford NG32 120 C2
Winteringham DN15 2 B1
Wood Enderby PE22 98 F6
Yaxley PE7 233 E5
Back Rd Gorefield PE13 169 E2
Back Rd continued
Murrow PE13 177 E6
Back St Alkborough DN15 8 C8
Buckminster NG33 150 E5
East Stockwith DN21 40 B5
Saltfleetby LN11 51 C1
South Clifton NG23 78 C5
Sproxton LE14 138 F1
Backgate PE12 167 B8
Bacon St DN21 197 D2
Bacon's La 1 PE11 145 C1
Bad Gate PE12 169 B6
Bader Cl PE3 225 B6
Bader Way 3 PE25 206 A5
Badgate PE11 134 F2
Badger Cl PE7 233 F5
Badger Way 1 DN20 19 E4
Badger's La PE20 136 B7
Badgers Oak 2 LN5 92 F3
Badinton La PE9 172 F5
Badminton Way LN11 198 A7
Baffen's La PE11 145 A4
Baggholme Rd LN2 234 C2
Baghdad Rd 2 NG34 120 D8
Bagsby Rd DN9 28 B3
Baildon Cres LN6 205 A3
Baildon Rd DN15 182 D4
Bailey La DN7 14 E6
Baileys Cl PE12 215 D1
Baileys La LN5 92 F5
Bailgate 3 LN2 234 B3
Baily's La PE12 147 F2
Bain Cl PE9 219 C7
Bain Rd PE21 208 C3
Bain Rise 3 LN8 59 A7
Bain St LN1 201 D8
Baines Ave NG24 104 B2
Baines Rd DN21 197 F4
Bainton Rd
Barnack PE9 172 D4
Newborough PE6 221 D8
Baird Cl PE7 233 D6
Baker Cres LN6 204 E7
Baker Dr 30 DN15 9 A5
Baker St HU2 180 E7
Baker's La
Candlesby with Gunby
PE23 89 A2
Fishtoft PE21 126 C4
Great Steeping PE23 101 E6
Westborough & Dry Doddington
NG23 117 E3
Bakers Cl DN38 21 B5
Bakers La
Bassingham LN5 92 E2
Peterborough PE2 230 E7
Bakers Way PE10 154 D6
Bakersfield DN20 196 F7
Bakestraw Gate PE12 157 F5
Bakewell Mews 6 LN6 204 F2
Bakewell Rd PE2 229 C2
Bala Ct PE4 221 B3
Balder Ct 2 DN33 191 C2
Balderton La NG24 104 D3
Baldwin Ave DN16 185 B2
Baldwin Cl PE8 172 C1
Baldwin Gr PE10 213 D6
Balfour Pl 3 DN40 186 B4
Balfour St
Gainsborough DN21 197 C5
2 Kingston upon Hull
HU9 181 C8
Balintore Rise PE2 229 D4
Balk Rd 8 PE9 163 C1
Ball's La PE12 159 A6
Balliol Dr DN16 185 B4
Balmoral Ave
3 Grimsby DN34 191 A7
Spalding PE11 214 D2
Balmoral Cl
12 Mablethorpe/Sutton on Sea
LN12 76 F8
2 Wragby LN8 70 D4
Balmoral Dr NG31 210 E6
Balmoral Rd
Cleethorpes DN35 192 C4
4 Hatfield DN7 14 D4
1 Peterborough PE4 225 C8
Balmoral Way PE12 159 A8
Bamber St PE1 225 F4
Bamford Ave 1 HU9 5 F8
Bamford Cl 6 LN6 204 E2
Banbury Cl PE11 214 D6
Banbury Rd DN16 183 D2
Bancroft Rd NG24 104 A3
Bangor Cl LN5 205 C3
Bank Dr
Ingoldmells PE25 90 F3
5 Wisbech PE13 170 C1
Bank End LN11 50 E8
Bank End Rd DN9 26 A3
Bank La 12 LN7 33 B4
Bank Prim Sch PE12 215 D7
Bank Side 1 PE21 136 D8
Bank St Boston PE21 208 F5
Kingston upon Hull HU3 180 C7
Lincoln LN2 234 B2
Bank The
Parson Drove PE13 177 C7
Swaton NG34 133 D4
Bank's Ave 4 PE11 214 F6
Banks La 4 NG34 122 E2
Banks Rd 6 LN9 199 C4
Banks St 5 LN9 199 C4
Bannister Dr HU9 181 C7

Bannister's La PE20 136 C7
Bannister's Row 6 PE13 170 C1
Banovallum Gdns LN9 199 D3
Banovallum Sch LN9 199 C2
Baptist Chapel La 4 DN40 12 F2
Baptist La 3 NG23 91 C4
Bar La 20 LN5 93 F7
Bar Rd DN10 52 B8
Bar Rd N 3 DN10 52 B8
Bar Rd S 7 DN10 52 B8
Barbara Cl 3 DN33 194 E7
Barbara Rd 6 PE25 206 D2
Barber Cl PE2 231 C7
Barberry Ct 3 HU3 180 C5
Barbers Dro PE6 175 C8
Barbers Hill PE4 220 F7
Barbican Way DN36 195 C6
Barcroft St DN35 189 E1
Bardling's Dro PE12 169 A7
Bardney PE2 230 A4
Bardney Ave DN16 185 A7
Bardney Cl LN6 204 F6
Bardney Gdns 1 DN34 190 F4
Bardney Joint CE/Methodist (Controlled) Sch LN3 83 C4
Bardney Rd
Branston & Mere LN4 82 C3
Wragby LN8 70 C4
Bardots Leisure Ctr LN5 205 C1
Barehams La PE11 145 A7
Barfen La LN13 63 B3
Barff La LN8 43 F2
Barff Rd LN4 82 B1
Barfields La LN3 68 F1
Barford Cl PE2 230 C7
Bargate Grimsby DN34 191 C5
12 Lincoln LN5 205 E8
Bargate Ave DN32 191 D5
Bargate Gr 3 HU5 179 D8
Bargate La 5 LN9 199 C3
Barge Cl 1 PE11 214 F5
Barge Rd PE12 148 A7
Barham Cl PE2 231 F5
Barholme Ave 7 PE12 160 A8
Bark St DN35 192 F5
Barkestone La NG13 128 A5
Barkham St 7 PE24 102 D2
Barkhouse Cl 4 DN35 192 F5
Barkhouse La 5 DN35 192 F5
Barkston & Syston CE (Aided) Prim Sch NG32 130 B8
Barkston Cl PE10 213 E6
Barkston Dr PE1 226 B6
Barkston Gdns LN2 202 B7
Barkston Rd NG32 118 D2
Barkwith Rd LN8 58 A1
Barkworth Cl HU10 178 D6
Barkworth Ct 3 DN37 194 C4
Barley Cl
Heckington NG34 122 D2
12 Hibaldstow DN20 31 A5
24 Metheringham LN4 95 C4
Barley Way LN9 199 A3
Barleycroft Rd NG33 152 E8
Barleyfield PE6 164 E2
Barlings Ave DN16 185 A7
Barlings Cl
1 Barlings LN3 69 C3
Scotter DN21 29 C4
Barlings La LN3 69 C2
Barmouth Dr DN37 190 E8
Barmston St HU2 180 F8
Barn Cl 2 Maxey PE6 173 C7
Peterborough PE4 220 F3
Barn Hill PE9 219 B5
Barn Owl Cl 1 PE6 164 F3
Barnack CE Prim Sch PE9 172 D4
Barnack Drift PE9 172 B3
Barnack Est 4 PE24 102 E7
Barnack Rd
Bainton PE9 172 E4
St Martin's without PE9 219 D4
Barnard Ave DN20 196 B3
Barnard Way 9 PE3 224 F3
Barnberry Way PE10 142 D2
Barnby Gate NG24 104 A4
Barnby La NG23 104 F1
Barnby Rd NG24 104 B3
Barnby Rd Prim Sch NG24 104 A4
Barnes Cl 1 NG34 212 C6
Barnes Cres DN15 182 E4
Barnes Dro PE10 154 F4
Barnes Gn DN21 29 C4
Barnes La LN5 106 F7
Barnes Rd
9 Donington PE11 134 E2
Skegness PE25 206 A5
Barnes Way PE4 220 F3
Barnet Dr DN36 195 E7
Barnet Gn 12 DN7 14 D3
Barnetby La DN20 20 F7
Barnetby Rd
1 Kingston upon Hull HU13 179 A3
Scunthorpe DN17 184 F5
Barnetby Sta DN38 21 B4
Barnett Pl DN35 192 B7
Barneyfield Rd PE22 126 E1
Barnfield Rd 22 NG23 91 D5
Barnoldby Rd DN37 194 C4
Barnside 6 DN20 30 F5
Barnstaple Rd 3 DN17 184 D8
Barnstock PE3 225 A7
Barnston Way 12 DN15 8 B4
Barnswallace Ct 15 LN2 68 D7
Barnwell Rd 3 PE9 218 E6
Barnwell Terr 2 NG31 210 F3
Baron Ave DN36 195 D7
Baron Ct PE4 221 B4
Baroness Rd DN34 190 F6
Barracks The PE13 169 E2
Barraclough's La 1 DN18 3 E1
Barr's La PE12 168 B4
Barratt's Cl LN2 234 C4
Barrett Gr 7 LN2 68 E6
Barrett's Cl PE12 215 D3
Barrick Cl 16 DN19 11 D8
Barrier Bank
Cowbit PE12 156 F2
Spalding PE12 214 C1
Barrington Cl 8 PE12 215 D2
Barrington Gate PE12 215 E1
Barrow Haven Sta DN19 4 C2
Barrow La HU13 178 D2
Barrow Rd
Barton-upon-Humber DN18 11 A8
New Holland DN19 4 E1
Barrowby CE (Controlled) Prim Sch NG32 129 B3
Barrowby Gate NG31 210 D4
Barrowby Rd 8 NG31 211 A5
Barrowden Rd PE9 171 A2
Barrowfield PE1 226 E7
Barrows Gate LN11 50 D6
Barry Ave DN34 190 F3
Barry Wlk 3 PE2 230 F7
Bars La Benington PE22 126 E5
Bicker PE20 135 A5
Bartholemew Cl 1 LN3 83 C4
Bartol Cres PE21 208 D5
Barton Dr HU13 178 D1
Barton Gate LN11 198 D4
Barton La
Barrow upon Humber DN19 11 C8
Tydd St Mary PE13 169 F8
Barton Outdoor Pursuits Ctr★ DN18 3 D2
Barton Rd
5 Wainfleet All Saints PE24 102 D1
Wrawby DN20 196 F6
Barton St Aylesby DN37 23 D2
Barrow upon Humber DN19 11 C8
Fotherby LN11 49 A2
Irby DN37 34 F7
Keelby DN41 23 A4
Ludborough DN36 48 C6
Barton St Peters CE Prim Sch DN18 3 F1
Barton-on-Humber Sta DN18 3 F1
Bartons La PE23 101 F6
Bartram Gate 2 PE4 221 C1
Bartrams 3 HU15 2 D6
Basic Slag Rd DN16 183 E2
Basil Gn PE2 230 D6
Baslow Rd DN15 182 B2
Bassett Cl 2 DN20 19 E3
Bassett Rd DN35 193 A4
Bassingham Cres LN2 201 F7
Bassingham Cty Prim Sch LN5 92 F2
Bassingham La PE23 88 E3
Bassingham Rd LN5 92 F5
Baston CE Prim Sch PE6 164 E5
Baston Edge Dro PE10 164 E7
Baston Fen Nature Reserve★ PE6 165 A8
Baston Outgang Rd PE6 165 A6
Bateman's Cl 3 PE12 159 D7
Batemans Ct 2 PE24 102 E2
Bath Gdns PE21 208 F3
Bath La 15 PE11 214 D4
Bath Rd
Bracebridge Heath LN4 81 A2
Wisbech PE13 170 D1
Bath Row PE9 219 B4
Bath St
8 Grantham NG31 211 A4
Grimsby DN32 189 C1
Bathurst PE2 230 A4
Bathurst St
8 Kingston upon Hull HU3 180 D5
Lincoln LN2 202 D3
Battery St DN40 186 D4
Battle Gn DN9 27 D7
Battle of Britain Meml Flight Visitor Ctr★ LN4 207 B3
Battlefields La N PE12 159 A8
Battlefields La S PE12 215 F3
Baulkin's Dro PE12 159 C1
Baumber Prim Sch LN9 72 A1
Bawtry Cl LN6 204 C8
Bawtry Rd DN7 14 F3
Baxter Cl
Coningsby LN4 207 D3
15 Wisbech PE13 170 E1
Baxter Gdns PE11 214 C7
Bayard St DN21 197 C5
Bayes Rd 6 PE25 103 E4
Bayfield Rd 4 LN4 96 B1
Bayons Ave DN33 194 D8
Baysdale Gr NG31 211 B8
Baysdale Rd DN16 185 D5
Baysgarth House Mus★ DN18 10 F8
Baysgarth Leisure Ctr DN18 10 F8
Baysgarth Sch DN18 10 F8
Baysgarth View DN18 10 F7
Bayswater Pl 1 DN33 194 D8
Bayswood Ave PE21 208 F1
Baytree Ave DN34 191 A6
Baytree Owl Ctr★ PE12 157 D7
Baywood Cl 4 LN6 200 C1
Beach Bank
Pinchbeck PE11 144 E3
Surfleet PE11 145 A3
Beach Holt La DN37 23 D2
Beach La PE11 144 F3
Beachcomber Holiday Ctr DN36 193 C1
Beachside 10 LN12 77 A8
Beacon Ave
16 Barton-upon-Humber DN18 10 E8
Cleethorpes DN35 192 D6
Beacon Ct DN35 192 D6
Beacon Hill La PE34 161 E3
Beacon Hill Rd
Gringley on the Hill DN10 39 D1
Newark-on-Trent NG24 104 B4
Beacon La NG31 211 C4
Beacon Pk Cl 4 PE25 206 A6
Beacon Pk Dr PE25 206 A6
Beacon Rd 7 NG34 107 C1
Beacon View 2 NG13 128 A6
Beacon Way PE25 206 A6
Beaconsfield Dr 3 NG24 104 C5
Beaconthorpe Rd 4 DN35 192 E7
Beagle Cl 16 DN20 19 E4
Beagle La NG34 107 C1
Bean St HU3 180 C6
Bear La 14 PE11 145 C1
Beatrice Rd 11 PE13 170 D2
Beatrice Way 27 PE24 90 D7
Beatty Ave DN33 194 F7
Beauchamp St 3 DN16 183 B1
Beauchief Gdns DN16 185 A8
Beaufort Ave 1 PE6 217 C5
Beaufort Cl
Kingston upon Hull HU3 180 D6
Lincoln LN2 202 D8
Beaufort Cres DN35 192 D2
Beaufort Dr
Bourne PE10 213 C7
4 Spalding PE11 214 C3
Beaufort Rd LN2 202 D8
Beaufort St DN21 197 B7
Beaulah Villas 9 DN18 10 A7
Beaulahland 8 DN18 10 A7
Beaulieu Ct 6 PE6 175 A1
Beaumonde 5 DN36 195 C2
Beaumont Cl 11 PE24 102 E7
Beaumont Ct 3 HU9 181 D7
Beaumont Dr 2 NG31 210 F8
Beaumont Fee LN1 234 A2
Beaumont St DN21 197 D4
Beauvale Gdns PE4 221 C3
Beauvoir Pl PE7 233 E5
Beaver Cl 1 LN6 200 A5
Beccelm Dr 9 PE6 175 B8
Beck Bank
Gosberton PE11 144 C3
Kirton PE20 124 E1
Beck Cl 5 Binbrook LN8 47 C5
13 Keelby DN41 23 A4
1 Ruskington NG34 108 D2
Beck Hill
6 Barton-upon-Humber DN18 10 F8
Tealby LN8 46 C1
Beck La Appleby DN15 9 D1
Aubourn Haddington & South Hykeham LN6 93 B7
10 Barrow upon Humber DN19 11 D8
7 Broughton DN20 19 E3
Fulbeck NG32 106 C1
Heighington/Washingborough LN4 81 F4
Ingoldmells PE25 90 E2
Redbourne DN21 30 F2
Scunthorpe DN16 185 B3
Welton Le Marsh PE23 89 A3
6 Welton/Dunholme LN2 68 E6
Beck Side 5 DN20 30 F5
Beck St Digby LN4 108 E5
Welbourn LN5 106 E4
Beck Way 5 PE10 164 C8
Beck Wlk 2 DN35 192 E1
Becke Cl LN3 203 E5
Becket Cl LN4 203 D1
Beckett Ave DN21 197 E6
Beckett Cl
9 Heckington NG34 122 D3
2 Skegness PE25 206 C1
Beckett Dr PE11 214 C6
Beckett Specl Sch DN21 53 A8
Beckhall LN2 68 D6
Beckhole Cl HU3 180 A6
Beckhythe Cl DN33 191 E1
Beckingham PE2 229 F3
Beckingham Rd
Coddington NG24 104 C5
Walkeringham DN10 40 A2
Beckingthorpe Dr 19 NG13 128 A6
Becks La DN21 29 A3
Becks The 4 LN9 199 C4
Beckside 11 Brough HU15 2 D6
Rothwell LN7 33 F2
Scopwick LN4 108 C8
Beckside Cl DN36 192 E1
Bedale Rd 3 DN16 185 D5
Bede Cl NG34 212 B2
Bede Cres PE22 126 F5
Bede Pl PE1 226 A6
Bede Rd 3 PE6 164 E5
Bedehouse Bank PE10 213 E4
Bedford Cl NG31 211 F5
Bedford Ct 16 PE6 176 A3
Bedford Pl 1 PE11 214 D3
Bedford Rd
Humberston DN35 193 A1
Kingston upon Hull HU13 178 F3
Bedford Row PE13 170 D8
Bedford St
Grimsby DN32 189 C1
2 Lincoln LN1 201 D4
Peterborough PE1 226 B4
Bee's La PE13 169 F6
Beech Ave
Bourne PE10 213 B5
Gainsborough DN21 197 D6
Grimsby DN33 191 C3
5 Gunness DN15 17 E6
Kingston upon Hull HU10 178 D8
24 Nettleham LN2 68 C2
Peterborough PE1 225 F3
Scunthorpe DN15 182 B6
Spalding PE11 214 F5
Beech Cl
5 Broughton DN20 19 D3
2 Colsterworth NG33 151 E7
4 Coningsby LN4 207 D4
Dunholme LN2 68 E5
3 Gringley on the Hill DN10 39 C1
7 Heckington NG34 122 D3
Kingston upon Hull HU3 180 C5
Market Deeping PE6 217 B6
RAF Cranwell NG34 107 D1
9 Sudbrooke LN2 68 F2
4 Thorney PE6 176 A3
Beech Cres 1 DN7 14 D6
Beech Dr
16 Bottesford NG13 128 A5
6 North Ferriby HU14 3 A4
15 Ryhall PE9 163 C1
Welton HU14 2 F5
Beech Garth 9 DN19 11 C7
Beech Gr
Anlaby with Anlaby Common HU13 178 C3
3 Burton-upon-Stather DN15 8 B5
Donington PE11 134 E2
Holton Le Clay DN36 195 E1
Louth LN11 198 C7
4 Scopwick Heath LN4 108 A7
Stamford PE9 218 D6
4 Swanland HU14 3 C7
Beech Hill Rd HU14 3 C7
Beech La 12 PE6 175 A1
Beech Lawn HU10 178 E6
Beech Rd Branston LN4 81 D2
6 Brough HU15 2 C6
Glinton PE6 220 B8
Beech Rise
Sleaford NG34 212 D6
2 South Rauceby NG34 120 E4
Beech St LN5 205 D5
Beech Tree Ave 17 DN8 15 B7
Beech Way DN35 192 D2
Beechams Mews 5 PE11 214 B3
Beechcroft Cl 6 LN6 93 A8
Beechcroft Rd NG31 210 C3
Beeches Ave DN16 185 B4
Beeches La PE22 112 C5
Beeches Prim Sch The PE1 225 F3
Beeches The 1 LN1 66 C7
Beechfield Rd 7 DN7 14 C4
Beechings Way 10 LN13 75 E2
Beechings Way Ind Est LN13 75 E2
Beechtree Cl 8 NG34 108 E1
Beechway DN16 185 B7
Beechwood Ave
Grimsby DN33 190 F3
Immingham DN40 186 C4
Beechwood Cl
16 Kirk Sandall DN3 14 A1
Peterborough PE1 226 C7
6 Wisbech PE13 170 D1
Beechwood Cres 4 DN20 19 E4
Beechwood Dr
12 Scawby DN20 30 F8
7 Scotter DN21 29 C3
Beechwood Rd 5 PE13 170 D1
Beeden Pk Est NG31 210 C4
Beehive La LN6 79 C1
Beel's Rd DN41 187 B2
Beeley Rd DN32 192 C6
Beelsby Rd LN7 34 C5
Bees Cnr 1 PE24 102 D2
Beesby Dr 3 DN35 192 F3
Beesby Rd
Maltby Le Marsh LN13 76 A7
Scunthorpe DN17 184 E5
Beesby Wlk LN13 76 A6
Beeson St DN31 188 E1
Beeston Dr PE7 231 F5
Beetons Cl PE7 233 E5
Beevor St LN6 201 C2
Beggar Hill Messingham Rd DN21 29 D4
Beggar's La PE22 98 F3
Begger's Bush La PE12 157 D7
Beilby St HU3 179 F4
Belcanto Ct 3 PE11 214 A5
Belchmire La PE11 145 B5
Belfry The 5 NG31 211 D7
Belgrave Cl 11 DN9 16 E1
Belgrave Dr HU4 179 D5
Belgrave Rd
1 Grimsby DN33 191 B2
7 Spalding PE11 214 C2
Belgrave Sq 1 DN15 183 B3
Belgravia Cl LN6 200 E1
Belham Rd PE1 225 E7
Belisana Rd 5 PE11 214 A5
Bell Cl NG31 210 E7
Bell Ct 5 PE21 208 F1
Bell Dro PE6 175 F6
Bell Gr LN6 205 C6
Bell La
4 Collingham NG23 91 C4
Fosdyke PE20 146 D8
Market Deeping PE6 217 E4
Moulton PE12 157 F7
Scunthorpe DN15 183 A2
Bell Wr Drain Bank
Eastville PE22 101 B1
New Leake PE22 100 E1
Bellamy Ct HU9 181 C7
Bellamy's La PE14 170 D4
Bell's Dro PE12 159 C1
Bell's Pl PE1 226 A2
Bellbutts View DN21 29 B3
Belle Vue PE2 231 C6
Belle Vue Rd LN1 234 A3
Belle Vue Terr
Lincoln LN1 234 A3
21 Thorne/Moorends DN8 15 A8
Belleisle Rd DN34 190 D4
Bellfield Cl 4 PE11 214 B3
Bellflower Cl 2 LN2 202 C8
Bellingham Rd DN16 185 D7
Bellingham's Dro PE11 166 F7
Bellview Rd 6 NG34 108 E1
Bellwin Dr DN15 8 A1
Bellwood Cres 5 DN8 15 A8
Bellwood Grange 1 LN3 203 E7
Belmesthorpe La PE9 163 D1
Belmont DN36 195 C1
Belmont Cl DN35 192 D3
Belmont Gr 2 NG31 211 D6
Belmont Prim Sch NG31 211 E6
Belmont St
Kingston upon Hull HU9 181 D8
Lincoln LN2 202 B3
Scunthorpe DN16 185 A6
Belnie La PE11 145 D5
Belsay Dr PE2 231 F5
Belshaw La DN9 16 D1
Belsize Ave PE2 230 E6
Belt Rd The DN21 197 F7
Belthorn Rd 2 DN17 7 F1
Belton All Saints CE Prim Sch DN9 16 E2
Belton Ave
Grantham NG31 211 C6
Lincoln LN6 204 F6
Belton Cl Boston PE21 209 B5
13 Market Deeping PE6 217 A5
Belton Fields 1 DN9 16 D1
Belton Gr
Grantham NG31 211 B7
1 Grimsby DN33 191 A3
Belton House (NT)★ NG32 130 B6
Belton La
Grantham NG31 211 C6
Great Gonerby NG31 129 E5
Belton La Prim Sch NG31 211 D7
Belton Pk★ NG32 211 F8
Belton Pk Dr 7 LN6 93 C8
Belton Rd Belton DN9 17 A1
Epworth DN9 27 E7
Peterborough PE7 231 F5
Sandtoft DN9 16 B3
Belton St 16 PE9 219 C5
Belvedere Cl PE11 214 B2
Belvedere Dr DN17 184 E7
Belvedere Rd HU13 178 F2
Belvoir Ave
12 Bottesford NG13 128 A5
Grantham NG31 210 F1
Spitalgate NG31 211 E2
Belvoir Castle★ NG32 138 B8
Belvoir Cl
4 Colsterworth NG33 151 E6
1 Market Deeping PE6 217 A5
1 Stamford PE9 218 E6
Belvoir Ct LN11 198 B8
Belvoir Gdns NG31 129 D5
Belvoir High Sch NG13 128 A5

Belvoir La NG32 ...128 D1
Belvoir Rd
Bottesford NG13 ...128 A4
Cleethorpes DN35 ...192 D2
Croxton Kerrial NG32 ...138 A6
Belvoir St HU5 ...180 C8
Belvoir Way Eye PE1 ...226 D8
Louth LN11 ...198 B8
Peterborough PE1 ...226 C8
Belwood Dr 7 DN9 ...16 E2
Bempton Gr
4 Grimsby DN32 ...192 A5
Kingston upon Hull HU5 ...179 D8
Bemrose Way 7 DN31 ...191 C8
Benams Cl PE5 ...223 E2
Ben's Gate PE12 ...159 B5
Benbow Way LN1 ...201 C6
Benderslough Dro
PE12 ...159 C3
Bendike La PE11 ...145 D4
Benedict Cl 2 HU4 ...179 A2
Benedict Rd HU4 ...179 A2
Benedict Sq PE4 ...220 E2
Benington Rd PE22 ...126 E3
Benjamin Adlard Com Sch
DN21 ...197 E2
Benland PE3 ...225 A6
Benner Rd PE11 ...214 E8
Benner Rd Ind Est
PE11 ...214 E8
Bennett Dr 28 DN15 ...9 A5
Bennett Rd
Cleethorpes DN35 ...192 D7
Scunthorpe DN16 ...185 C7
Bennington Cl
8 Lincoln LN6 ...205 A7
11 Long Bennington NG23 117 D3
Bennington La NG23 ...117 E4
Benson Cl LN6 ...204 C6
Benson Cres LN6 ...204 C6
Benson Ct LN11 ...48 F4
Bentinck Cl 6 PE11 ...214 C6
Bentinck Sq 2 LN2 ...202 B3
Bentinck St 4 LN2 ...202 B3
Bentley Ave PE7 ...233 E6
Bentley Ct HU3 ...180 A5
Bentley Dr LN4 ...205 F3
Bentley La 6 DN38 ...32 E7
Bentley St
Cleethorpes DN35 ...192 E6
6 Stamford PE9 ...219 C6
Bentley Way 1 LN4 ...95 C4
Benyon Gr PE2 ...230 B4
Berberis Cl 2 PE6 ...175 F3
Berea The 4 DN34 ...191 C5
Beresford Ave PE25 ...206 C2
Beresford Cl 4 PE25 ...206 C2
Beresford Cres 5 PE25 ...206 C2
Beresford Dr 5 LN2 ...68 F3
Beretun Gn 7 DN18 ...10 E8
Berilldon Dr LN1 ...201 C7
Berkeley Ave LN6 ...205 A3
Berkeley Dr
4 Bourne PE10 ...213 C7
Lincoln LN6 ...205 A3
Berkeley Ind Est DN15 ...182 C4
Berkeley Inf Sch
DN15 ...182 D4
Berkeley Jun Sch
DN15 ...182 D3
Berkeley Rd
Humberston DN35 ...193 A2
Peterborough PE3 ...225 C3
Berkeley St
1 Kingston upon Hull
HU3 ...180 D8
Scunthorpe DN15 ...183 A4
Berkshire Dr NG31 ...211 D7
Bermondsey Dr HU5 ...179 E8
Bernadette Ave HU4 ...179 B5
Bernard St LN2 ...202 B4
Berners Rd DN35 ...193 B1
Bernicia Dr NG34 ...212 B2
Berry Cl 6 NG34 ...212 D2
Berry Way 5 PE25 ...206 C3
Berrybut Way 5 PE9 ...219 D7
Berryfield End 7 NG32 ...210 A5
Berryman Way HU13 ...179 A3
Bert Allen Dr 1 PE22 ...114 A1
Bertie Cl
Long Sutton PE12 ...216 C3
Swinstead NG33 ...153 A5
Bertie La 8 PE9 ...172 C6
Berwick Ct DN40 ...186 C4
Besant Cl 10 PE22 ...113 B1
Bessemer Way DN15 ...183 B6
Bestall Rd DN32 ...192 C6
Besthorpe Cty Prim Sch
NG23 ...91 C7
Besthorpe Rd
Besthorpe NG23 ...91 C6
North Scarle NG23 ...78 D1
Beswick Cl 5 LN6 ...204 D7
Bethlehem St DN31 ...191 D7
Bethlem Cres 9 PE24 ...102 D1
Bethune Ave HU4 ...179 A3
Bethune Ave W HU13 ...179 A3
Bethune Pk Prim Sch
HU4 ...179 B3
Betjeman Cl PE10 ...213 D3
Betony Cl 5 DN15 ...182 C6
Bettesworth Rd DN21 ...54 F8
Bettles Cl PE1 ...226 A6
Betula Gr 3 LN6 ...204 D7
Betula Way 1 DN17 ...184 C5
Beverley Cl 7 DN36 ...195 D1
Beverley Cres DN32 ...192 A5
Beverley Ct 12 DN41 ...23 F5
Beverley Dr 5 NG24 ...104 C5
Beverley Gdns 4 PE9 ...219 A6
Beverley Gr
Lincoln LN6 ...204 F3
7 Skegness PE25 ...206 B3
Beverley Rd HU3 ...180 D8
Beverstone PE2 ...229 D5
Bew Cl PE2 ...231 D4
Bewholme Gr 3 HU9 ...5 D8
Bicker Dro PE20 ...134 D6
Bicker Rd PE11 ...134 F3
Bidwell La LE15 ...162 B6
Biergate LN11 ...49 F7
Bifield PE2 ...229 F3
Bigby Gr DN17 ...184 F4
Bigby High Rd DN20 ...196 D2
Bigby Hill DN38 ...21 C1
Bigby Rd 7 DN20 ...196 C3
Bigby St DN20 ...196 C3
Billet La DN15 ...182 F8
Billet Mill App Rd
DN16 ...19 A4
Billet Mill Rd DN16 ...183 E1
Billgate La PE24 ...102 E7
Billingborough Dro
NG34 ...143 E8
Billingborough Prim Sch
NG34 ...133 B1
Billingborough Rd
Billingborough NG34 ...133 B1
Folkingham NG34 ...132 E1
Billinghay CE Prim Sch
LN4 ...109 F6
Billinghay Ct DN35 ...192 F3
Billinghay Dales Head
LN4 ...110 B4
Billings Gate LN11 ...50 E5
Bilsby Cl LN2 ...202 A7
Bilsby Rd 2 LN13 ...75 F3
Bilsdale Gr HU9 ...181 F8
Bilsdale Rd DN16 ...185 E5
Binbrook (Controlled) Prim
Sch LN8 ...47 B5
Binbrook Cl 8 LN6 ...204 D7
Binbrook La LN8 ...47 B2
Binbrook Way DN37 ...190 E8
Birch Ave Brigg DN20 ...196 B4
Grimsby DN34 ...191 A6
Birch Cl
11 Coningsby LN4 ...207 D4
Kingston upon Hull HU5 ...179 B7
1 Lincoln LN6 ...204 F2
Wyberton PE21 ...136 E7
Birch Gr
Gainsborough DN21 ...197 D6
Spalding PE11 ...214 F3
Birch La 4 LN9 ...85 E7
Birch Leigh HU3 ...180 C6
Birch Rd Louth LN11 ...198 E5
6 Stamford PE9 ...218 D7
Birch Tree Cl 4 DN3 ...14 A4
Birch Way DN38 ...21 C5
Bircham Cres DN21 ...30 C1
Birchdale 31 DN18 ...10 E8
Birchen Cl PE7 ...230 C3
Birches The 8 DN9 ...27 A2
Birchfield Rd 8 DN9 ...27 D6
Birchin Way DN31 ...188 D1
Birchtree Ave PE1 ...226 A7
Birchwood PE2 ...230 A3
Birchwood Ave
Birchwood LN6 ...200 D1
Kingston upon Hull HU5 ...179 A7
Birchwood Cl 4 NG31 ...210 F7
Birchwood Jun Sch
LN6 ...204 C8
Birchwood Rd
Scunthorpe DN16 ...185 A4
1 Sleaford NG34 ...212 D6
Bird's Dro
Gorefield PE13 ...169 D1
Sutton St James PE12 ...169 B8
Birdcroft La DN10 ...40 A3
Birds Dro PE11 ...145 C4
Birds Holt Cl LN6 ...200 A3
Birds Wood Nature Reserve★
DN9 ...26 F4
Birkbeck Sch The LN11 ...50 E7
Birkdale Lincoln LN5 ...205 D1
9 Waltham DN37 ...194 C4
Birkdale Ave 1 PE4 ...221 A3
Birkdale Cl
3 Grantham NG31 ...211 D7
Heighington/Washingborough
LN4 ...203 E1
Kingston upon Hull
HU10 ...178 B8
1 Skegness PE25 ...206 D6
8 Spalding PE11 ...214 C2
8 Woodhall Spa LN10 ...97 C5
Birkdale Dr 3 DN40 ...186 D5
Birkdale Rd DN17 ...184 D3
Birkdale Way HU9 ...181 D8
Birketts La LN11 ...49 D5
Birkland La NG23 ...78 D5
Birkwood PE22 ...98 E2
Birkwood La PE22 ...98 E3
Birmingham Cl 5 NG31 210 E5
Birrel St DN21 ...197 B6
Birthorpe Rd NG34 ...143 A8
Biscay Cl 1 PE25 ...206 A6
Bishop Alexander Prim Sch
NG24 ...104 A6
Bishop Blunt Cl 2
HU13 ...178 F1
Bishop Creighton CP Sch
PE1 ...226 B2
Bishop Gurdon Cl 4
HU13 ...178 F1
Bishop Kempthorne Clo 3
HU13 ...178 F1
Bishop King CE (Aided) Prim
Sch LN5 ...201 F1
Bishop King Ct 7 LN5 ...201 F1
Bishop La HU1 ...181 A6
Bishop Norton Rd LN8 ...43 E1
Bishop Temple Ct
HU13 ...178 F3
Bishopdale Cl NG31 ...129 F5
Bishop's La LN8 ...47 D7
Bishop's Pl 5 LN2 ...68 C6
Bishop's Rd PE1 ...226 A1
Bishop's Wlk 1 DN34 ...191 C6
Bishops Cl
6 Bourne PE10 ...213 E4
Louth LN11 ...198 E6
Peterborough PE1 ...226 D5
Bishops Ct 3 NG34 ...212 D5
Bishop's Pal The★
LN2 ...234 B3
Bishops Rd
Leasingham NG34 ...121 B7
Lincoln LN2 ...202 C5
Bishops Wlk 5 PE9 ...172 D3
Bishopthorpe Rd
DN35 ...192 F3
Bittern Cl HU4 ...179 D2
Bittern Way 3 LN6 ...204 D8
Black Bank DN17 ...29 A6
Black Bear La PE13 ...170 F1
Black Dike PE13 ...169 E6
Black Dro Anwick LN4 ...109 D2
Baston PE6 ...165 B8
Ewerby & Evedon NG34 ...122 E8
Midville PE22 ...100 D2
Thorney PE6 ...175 F5
Wisbech St Mary PE13 ...177 B4
Black Dyke PE13 ...169 F4
Black Fen La LN4 ...82 C4
Black Hole Dro PE11 ...155 F8
Black Horse Dr 8 LN6 ...93 A8
Black La
Doddington & Whisby LN6 ...79 E3
Gorefield PE13 ...169 C2
Black Prince Ave PE6 ...217 B6
Black Swan Spinney
PE8 ...222 A4
Blackbourn Cl 20 NG23 ...91 D5
Blackbourn Rd LN6 ...205 C6
Blackburn Ave HU15 ...2 C5
Blackburn Cl 2 NG31 ...210 D5
Blackburn La DN22 ...52 D3
Blackdown Garth PE4 ...221 B3
Blackdykes Rd DN9 ...28 B4
Blackey La PE22 ...99 B4
Blackfriargate HU1 ...181 A5
Blackfriars St 15 PE9 ...219 C5
Blackhill La LN9 ...73 F1
Blackjack Rd PE20 ...135 C6
Blackmead PE2 ...230 B4
Blackmoor Rd
Aubourn Haddington &
South Hykeham LN5 ...93 C5
Haxey DN9 ...27 D2
Black's Cl 17 LN5 ...93 F7
Blacksmith Hill DN15 ...1 E3
Blacksmith La
Boothby Graffoe LN5 ...94 A2
East Keal PE23 ...100 D6
2 Harmston LN5 ...93 F5
Thorpe on the Hill LN6 ...92 E8
Blacksmith Rd 4 LN3 ...82 A7
Blacksmith Row 1 LN5 ...92 F3
Blacksmith's Cnr 5
LN4 ...207 A5
Blacksmith's La
13 Navenby/Wellingore
LN5 ...107 A7
Norton Disney LN6 ...92 B2
Blacksmith's Row
PE11 ...156 B7
Blacksmiths Cl 2 DN19 ...11 C7
Blacksmiths Ct 10 LN4 ...95 C4
Blacksmiths La
North Scarle LN6 ...78 E1
Welby NG32 ...130 F5
Blackthorn 5 PE9 ...218 C7
Blackthorn Cl
1 Lincoln LN2 ...202 C8
3 Market Deeping PE6 ...217 D6
13 Ruskington NG34 ...108 E1
Scunthorpe DN15 ...182 C6
Blackthorn Ct 4 HU3 ...180 D6
Blackthorn La
Boston PE21 ...209 C5
Cammeringham LN1 ...54 E1
Kingston upon Hull
HU10 ...178 F7
Blackthorn Way PE10 ...213 E5
Blackthorns The 4
DN20 ...19 D4
Blackwell Rd PE7 ...230 C2
Bladon Est PE21 ...209 F4
Bladons Wlk HU10 ...178 D8
Blaides Staithe 1 HU1 ...181 A6
Blake Ave DN17 ...184 E7
Blake Cl 2 HU2 ...180 E7
Blakeney Lea 2 DN35 ...192 F1
Blanchard Cl PE10 ...142 F2
Blanchard Rd LN11 ...198 E3
Blandford Gdns 1 PE1 ...226 E7
Blands Hill LN8 ...47 D5
Blanket Row HU1 ...180 F5
Blankney Cl 4 LN1 ...66 D2
Blankney Cres LN2 ...201 F8
Blankney Ct 13 DN15 ...9 A5
Blankney Dro LN10 ...96 E5
Blankney N Dro LN4 ...96 B5
Blashfield Cl 2 PE9 ...219 A6
Blatherwick Rd NG24 ...104 B4
Blaydon Gr 2 DN34 ...190 E4
Blazegate PE12 ...216 B8
Bledwick Dro PE13 ...170 C3
Blenheim Cl
17 Hatfield DN7 ...14 D3
Louth LN11 ...198 B7
Skellingthorpe LN6 ...79 F6
Blenheim Ct DN16 ...185 A2
Blenheim Pl DN35 ...192 E4
Blenheim Rd
Coningsby LN4 ...207 C4
Lincoln LN1 ...201 D4
Moorland Prison DN7 ...26 A8
Blenheim St HU5 ...180 B8
Blenheim Way
Londonthorpe &
Harrowby without NG31 ...211 D3
Market Deeping PE6 ...217 B7
Yaxley PE7 ...233 E5
Blenkin St HU9 ...181 B7
Blind La Coleby LN5 ...93 F3
Hough-on-the-Hill NG32 ...118 E7
4 Maxey PE6 ...173 C7
22 Waddington LN5 ...93 F7
Bloom La DN15 ...8 C1
Bloomfield Ave HU5 ...179 C8
Bloomsbury Ct 1 HU3 ...180 D6
Blossom Way 1 DN40 ...186 B3
Blow Row DN9 ...27 E6
Blow's La PE20 ...135 F3
Bloxholm La
Blankney LN4 ...95 A2
Bracebridge Heath LN4 ...81 B1
Nocton LN4 ...94 D6
Blue Gowt Dro PE11 ...214 A7
Blue Gowt La PE11 ...214 B7
Blue St 7 PE21 ...208 E4
Bluebell Ave PE1 ...226 A8
Bluebell Cl
7 Lincoln LN5 ...205 C2
Scunthorpe DN15 ...183 C3
Bluebell Rd 2 PE9 ...218 D7
Bluebells 8 PE6 ...217 D6
Blueberry Ct HU4 ...179 C4
Bluecoat Prim Sch
PE9 ...219 B6
Bluegate NG31 ...211 A5
Bluestone Heath Rd
Scamblesby LN11 ...73 A7
Skendleby PE23 ...88 D5
South Ormsby cum Ketsby
LN11 ...74 B3
South Thoresby LN13 ...75 A1
Tetford LN11 ...73 F3
Ulceby with Fordington
LN13 ...88 B8
Welton Le Wold LN11 ...60 A4
Bluestone La DN40 ...186 B4
Bluestone Rise LN11 ...198 B4
Bluestone Way 24 LN12 ...77 A7
Blundell Ave DN35 ...189 E1
Blyth Ct 28 DN18 ...10 F8
Blyth St 2 HU9 ...181 B7
Blyton CE (Aided) Prim Sch
DN21 ...41 C6
Blyton Cl 11 LN6 ...204 C7
Blyton Gr 13 LN6 ...204 C7
Blyton Rd
12 Birchwood LN6 ...204 C7
Laughton DN21 ...41 B8
Thonock DN21 ...197 C8
Boardsides
Frampton PE20 ...124 F2
Wyberton PE21 ...208 A3
Boating Dyke Way 19
DN8 ...15 A8
Boatswain Croft 7 HU1 180 F5
Bodiam Way DN32 ...191 F8
Bodmin Cl DN17 ...184 D8
Bodmin Moor Cl LN6 ...204 D1
Boggle La LN8 ...45 E5
Bolingbroke Castle (remains
of)★ PE23 ...100 A7
Bolingbroke Rd
Cleethorpes DN35 ...193 A3
Louth LN11 ...198 B8
Scunthorpe DN17 ...184 E4
Bolsover Rd DN15 ...182 B2
Bolton Ave LN6 ...205 A3
Bolton's La PE25 ...90 D2
Bomber Cty Aviation Mus★
DN21 ...42 F1
Bon Accord Rd HU13 ...178 E1
Bona La PE13 ...169 E1
Bonby Gr
2 Grimsby DN33 ...191 A3
Scunthorpe DN17 ...184 F5
Bonby Rd DN20 ...10 C1
Bond Hays La 3 PE23 ...87 A4
Bond St 1 Boston PE21 ...208 F4
Kingston upon Hull HU1 ...180 F7
Bonemill La NG34 ...121 E6
Bonnetable Rd LN9 ...199 D3
Bonnyhale Rd DN17 ...16 E6
Bonthorpe Rd LN13 ...89 B7
Boongate PE1 ...226 C3
Boonground La PE22 ...115 A3
Boot La PE20 ...136 E3
Booth Nooking La DN15 ...2 A2
Bootham Cl 6 DN7 ...14 D4
Bootham Cres 12 DN7 ...14 C6
Bootham La DN7 ...14 D5
Bootham Rd 11 DN7 ...14 C6
Boothferry Pk (Hull City AFC)
HU4 ...179 E5
Boothferry Rd HU13 ...178 B2
Borman's La 7 DN36 ...36 B1
Borrowdale Cl PE4 ...221 C3
Borrowdale Way
NG31 ...211 B8
Borthwick Pl PE2 ...229 D6
Bos App Rd DN16 ...185 F7
Boscombe Cl 12 LN6 ...204 C6
Boston Aerodrome
PE21 ...125 B2
Boston Coll PE21 ...209 A4
Boston Gram Sch
PE21 ...209 A4
Boston Hawthorn Tree Sch
Cty Prim School
PE21 ...209 D4
Boston High Sch for Girls
PE21 ...209 B7
Boston Ind Ctr PE21 ...208 F6
Boston Long Hedges
PE22 ...126 C6
Boston Pk Com Prim Sch
PE21 ...208 E7
Boston Rd
Algarkirk PE20 ...136 A3
Frithville PE22 ...125 E7
Gosberton PE11 ...145 C6
Heckington NG34 ...122 E2
Holbeach PE12 ...215 C4
Horncastle LN9 ...199 C1
Sleaford NG34 ...212 D4
14 Spilsby PE23 ...88 A1
Spilsby PE23 ...100 F8
Swineshead PE20 ...124 D1
Wainfleet St Mary PE24 ...102 D1
Boston Rd N PE12 ...215 C5
Boston Rd Pits Nature
Reserve★ PE11 ...145 C6
Boston Rd S PE12 ...215 D3
Boston Sta PE21 ...208 E5
Boston Stump (St Botolph's
Ch)★ PE21 ...208 F5
Boston W Prim Sch
PE21 ...208 B5
Boswell Cl PE1 ...225 E8
Boswell Dr LN6 ...205 A5
Bosworth Cl 18 DN7 ...14 D3
Botany Bay La DN3 ...14 B4
Bothwell Gr 3 HU9 ...5 E8
Botolph Gn PE2 ...230 C7
Botolph St 7 PE21 ...209 A5
Botolph's View 1 LN11 ...51 C4
Botteford Jun & Inf Schools
DN16 ...185 A2
Bottesford Ave DN16 ...185 B5
Bottesford Cl 12 LN6 ...204 D8
Bottesford La DN16 ...185 B4
Bottesford Rd
Allington NG32 ...128 E6
Scunthorpe DN16 ...185 B5
Bottesford Sports Ctr
DN17 ...184 C3
Bottesford Sta NG13 ...128 B6
Bottle La PE13 ...169 C7
Bottlings The 9 DN20 ...196 C3
Bottom St NG32 ...128 F7
Boughton Ave DN15 ...182 F4
Boulevard HU3 ...180 B5
Boulevard Ave DN31 ...188 E1
Boulevard Ret Pk PE1 ...225 D7
Boultham Ave LN5 ...201 D1
Boultham Pk Rd LN6 ...201 D1
Boundaries The PE12 ...215 D1
Boundary La LN6 ...93 A8
Boundary Paddock 1
LN5 ...107 A7
Boundary Pastures
NG34 ...212 D3
Boundary Rd DN33 ...194 E6
Boundary St LN5 ...205 D7
Bourges Bvd PE1 ...225 D7
Bourgess Ret Pk PE3 ...225 F1
Bourne Abbey Prim Sch
PE10 ...213 E5
Bourne Cl LN6 ...205 B5
Bourne Dro PE10 ...155 A5
Bourne Gram Sch
PE10 ...213 D4
Bourne Heritage Ctr★
PE10 ...213 D4
Bourne La 7 NG34 ...108 D2
Bourne Outdoor Swimming
Pool PE10 ...213 D4
Bourne Rd 20 Alford LN13 ...75 F2
Baston PE6 ...164 E3
Bourne PE10 ...213 E2
Colsterworth NG33 ...151 E6
Essendine PE9 ...163 E3
Folkingham NG34 ...142 D8
Morton PE10 ...154 C6
Old Somerby NG33 ...140 D8
Pinchbeck PE11 ...155 F5
Spalding PE11 ...214 A3
Swinstead NG33 ...153 A5
Thurlby PE10 ...164 D8
Bourne Rd Est 6 NG33 ...151 E6
Bourne Westfield Prim Sch
PE10 ...213 B5
Bow Gate PE11 ...145 B6
Bow Rd HU15 ...2 E6
Bowbridge Gdns 4
NG13 ...128 A6

Bowbridge La
10 Bottesford NG13 .....128 A6
Hawton NG24 .....104 A1
Bowbridge Rd NG24 ...104 A2
Bowden Dr LN6 .....205 A5
Bowditch Rd PE11 .....214 E3
Bower Cl PE1 .....226 C5
Bowers Ave
Grimsby DN31 .....191 B7
3 Louth LN11 .....198 D7
Bowfield Cl DN37 .....190 D8
Bowl Alley La LN9 .....199 C4
Bowlalley La 9 HU1 ...180 F6
Bowling Gn La
11 Crowle DN17 .....16 D8
Grantham NG31 .....211 B3
8 Grimsby DN32 .....191 E7
Bowling Gn Rd DN21 ..197 B5
Bowling La DN35 .....192 E6
Bowman Ave PE22 .....115 A6
Bowman Cl PE21 .....208 D6
Bowman Way 7 DN40 ..186 B3
Bowmandale 30 DN18 ...10 E8
Bowmandale Prim Sch
DN18 .....10 E8
Bowmans Ridge 1 PE23 .87 F1
Bowmans Way NG32 ..128 F4
Bowness Way 1 PE4 ...221 D2
Boxer Rd PE8 .....172 B1
Boxgrove Cl 8 PE6 .....175 A1
Boyfields 1 PE11 .....145 A8
Boynton Cres 9 DN15 .....9 A5
Boynton St 1 HU3 .....180 C4
Bozeat Way PE3 .....225 C6
Brabbs Ave 4 DN7 .....14 E4
Bracebridge Inf Sch
LN5 .....205 E6
Braceby Rd NG33 .....131 B1
Bracken Cl
Gainsborough DN21 .....197 B7
Leasingham NG34 .....121 C7
Bracken Heen Cl 2 DN7 .14 E4
Bracken La PE24 .....90 A7
Bracken Pk DN33 .....194 E8
Bracken Pl DN37 .....190 C6
Bracken Rd LN6 .....92 B7
Bracken Way LN11 .....198 C7
Brackenborough Rd
Brackenborough with
Little Grimsby LN11 .....49 C1
Keddington LN11 .....61 C8
Louth LN11 .....198 C8
Brackenburry Way
PE21 .....208 E8
Brackenbury Fields
NG33 .....140 F6
Brackenhill Rd DN9 .....27 E2
Brackenholmes Rd
DN15 .....9 A2
Brackley Cl
Bourne PE10 .....213 D7
Peterborough PE3 .....225 D3
Brackwood PE2 .....229 D6
Bracon Cl 9 DN9 .....16 E2
Bradbury Ave LN5 .....205 C2
Bradden St PE3 .....225 C6
Bradegate Dr PE1 .....226 E7
Bradford Ave DN35 .....193 A5
Bradford Cl 10 NG31 ...210 D5
Bradford Rd
Boston PE21 .....208 D3
Immingham DN40 .....186 B4
Brading Ave NG31 .....210 E4
Bradley Cl LN11 .....198 D3
Bradley La LE15 .....162 B7
Bradley Rd
Bradley DN37 .....194 B6
Grimsby DN37 .....190 E2
Bradley St 8 DN32 .....191 F7
Bradman Ct 6 DN32 ...189 C1
Bradshaw's La PE24 .....90 C7
Bradway 9 LN1 .....66 D7
Bradwell Cl 19 DN18 .....10 E8
Bradwell Rd PE3 .....225 A2
Brady St 1 PE21 .....208 E6
Braemar Cl
Grantham NG31 .....211 C7
1 Middle Rasen LN8 .....57 B8
Stamford PE9 .....218 E6
Braemar Rd
Cleethorpes DN35 .....192 E4
3 Mablethorpe/Sutton on Sea
LN12 .....76 F8
Braemer Rd NG23 .....91 D4
Braeton La DN33 .....195 A7
Braids Wlk HU10 .....178 B8
Brailsford Cl 3 PE3 .....225 A4
Braithwaite La DN7 .....14 A8
Bramar Rd 5 DN7 .....14 D4
Bramble Cl 4 LN2 .....68 D7
Bramble Ct 24 LN2 .....68 D2
Bramble Gr 2 PE9 .....218 D6
Bramble Grange 3
PE11 .....214 B5
Bramble Hills PE25 .....103 E3
Bramble Way
1 Brigg DN20 .....196 B4
Humberston DN36 .....192 E1
Brambleberry La PE24 .102 B7
Brambles The
3 Barrow upon Humber
DN19 .....11 C8
Bourne PE10 .....213 D7
Holbeach PE12 .....215 F2
4 Market Deeping PE6 ..217 D6

Brambles The *continued*
Newton on Trent LN1 .....65 D1
Bramblewood Cl 6
NG31 .....210 F8
Brambling Wlk PE10 ..143 A3
Bramhall St DN35 .....192 C7
Bramley Cl
5 Bourne PE10 .....213 C6
8 Fleet PE12 .....159 C7
2 Heckington NG34 .....122 E2
4 Louth LN11 .....198 C5
Bramley Cres DN16 ...185 A3
Bramley Ct
Gainsborough DN21 .....197 F5
Lincoln LN6 .....204 F4
Bramley Gr 1 DN21 .....29 C3
Bramley La 6 PE21 ...208 E4
Bramley Rd
Market Deeping PE6 .....217 B5
11 Wisbech PE13 .....170 D1
Bramley Wlk PE25 .....206 C6
Brampton Ct PE2 .....231 D6
Brampton Way DN35 ..192 D3
Bramwith La DN7 .....14 A6
Brancaster Dr
Lincoln LN6 .....205 C8
Skegness PE25 .....206 D5
Brancepeth Pl PE2 .....230 E7
Branches La PE12 .....159 A7
Brand End Rd PE22 .....126 E4
Brandesburton St
HU3 .....180 B7
Brandon Rd
Hough-on-the-Hill NG32 ..118 E6
Scunthorpe DN15 .....182 D2
Stubton NG23 .....118 C7
Brandy Wharf Cider Ctr*
DN21 .....44 A7
Brankwell Cres DN17 ..184 E3
Bransby Home of Rest for
Horses* LN1 .....66 D6
Bransdale Gr HU9 .....181 F8
Bransdale Rd 5 DN16 ..185 D5
Branston CE (Controlled) Inf
Sch LN4 .....81 D2
Branston Cl
Lincoln LN6 .....205 B4
4 Winthorpe NG24 .....104 B7
Branston Com Coll LN4 .81 E3
Branston Cswy LN3 .....82 F3
Branston Cty Jun Sch
LN4 .....81 E2
Branston La LN4 .....94 D7
Branston Rd LN4 .....81 E3
Brant Broughton CE
Methodist Prim Sch
LN5 .....105 F5
Brant Rd Fulbeck NG32 ..105 F1
Lincoln LN5 .....205 D2
Scunthorpe DN15 .....182 E2
Waddington LN5 .....93 D7
Brantingham Rd HU15 ...2 B7
Brassey Cl PE1 .....225 E6
Bratoft Cnr PE24 .....102 D7
Bratoft End PE24 .....102 C5
Brats La LN8 .....47 E5
Bratt Field Rd DN21 .....53 F8
Brattleby Cres LN2 .....201 F7
Brauncewell Cl 18
NG34 .....108 D2
Brauncewell Rd 6
NG34 .....107 C1
Bray Ave 5 LN12 .....64 C2
Braybrook PE2 .....230 A3
Braybrook CP Sch
PE2 .....230 B4
Braybrooks Way PE12 .157 E1
Brayfields 3 PE11 .....156 F8
Brayford St LN5 .....234 A2
Brayford Waterfront
LN1 .....234 A2
Brayford Way 1 LN1 ...234 A2
Brayford Wharf E LN5 .234 A1
Brayford Wharf N LN1 .234 A2
Braygate La PE23 .....100 E5
Brazenose La PE9 .....219 C5
Brazil St HU9 .....181 C8
Breakneck La LN11 .....198 A5
Brecks La
Kirk Sandall DN3 .....14 A2
Stapleford LN6 .....105 C8
Brecon Cl NG31 .....210 D8
Brecon Way NG34 .....212 B3
Breda Ct 8 PE11 .....214 A2
Breedon Dr LN1 .....201 D7
Breezemount Ct 2 DN7 .14 C6
Brellows Hill 7 PE34 ...161 F3
Bremerhaven Way
DN33 .....190 F3
Brendon Cl NG31 .....210 D8
Brendon Garth 4 PE4 ..221 C1
Brendon Wlk 5 PE11 ...214 C6
Brent Rd LN4 .....110 E8
Brentwood Cl HU15 .....2 B6
Brereton Ave DN35 .....192 C8
Brethergate DN9 .....27 B2
Bretton Cl 4 DN7 .....14 D3
Bretton Gate 2 PE3 .....225 A5
Bretton Gn 1 PE3 .....225 A5
Bretton Way
Bretton PE3 .....225 A7
3 Peterborough PE3 .....220 F1
Peterborough PE3 .....224 F2
Bretton Woods Com Sch
PE3 .....225 A6
Brewerne PE2 .....230 B4
Brewers La PE13 .....170 A5
Brewery Gdns 2 DN17 ..16 D8

Brewery Hill NG31 .....211 B3
Brewery La NG34 .....143 B8
Brewery Rd DN17 .....16 D8
Brewery St 6 PE24 .....102 E8
Brewster Ave
Immingham DN40 .....186 D3
Peterborough PE2 .....230 F8
Brewster Ave Inf Sch
PE2 .....230 F8
Brewster La PE24 .....102 C2
Brewster Rd PE21 .....209 B4
Breydon Ct 3 DN15 .....8 B4
Brian Ave
Cleethorpes DN35 .....192 D3
Scunthorpe DN16 .....185 C5
7 Skegness PE25 .....206 C4
Waltham DN37 .....194 D4
Briar Cl
6 Birchwood LN6 .....200 C1
5 Lincoln LN6 .....93 A8
Skegness PE25 .....206 C3
2 Sleaford NG34 .....212 D2
4 South Killingholme DN40 12 E3
Briar La Grimsby DN33 ..194 D8
Healing DN41 .....23 F5
Briar Way
Peterborough PE1 .....226 C5
Scunthorpe DN15 .....182 C6
Skegness PE25 .....206 C2
Briar Wlk PE10 .....213 D7
Briars La 6 DN7 .....14 C7
Briars The HU13 .....178 E3
Briarwood Cl 6 NG31 ..210 F7
Brick La
North Killingholme DN40 ...12 E5
Wrangle PE22 .....114 C1
Brickberry Cl PE7 .....230 C2
Bricken Field La LN9 .....84 C8
Brickenhole La 7 DN10 ..39 F3
Brickings Way 4 DN22 ..52 B3
Brickwork Annexe (Grantham
College) NG31 .....211 C5
Brickyard La
Folkingham NG34 .....142 D8
Hundleby PE23 .....87 E1
Mablethorpe & Sutton
LN12 .....76 E8
Melton HU14 .....2 F4
Navenby LN5 .....94 A1
Theddlethorpe St Helen
LN12 .....63 F7
Walkeringham DN10 .....39 E3
Wrawby DN20 .....196 D6
Bridge Cl
Kingston upon Hull HU9 ..181 D6
3 Louth LN11 .....198 C6
Bridge Dro PE13 .....177 B7
Bridge End
Colsterworth NG33 .....151 D7
Wansford PE8 .....222 A3
Bridge End Cswy
NG34 .....133 F3
Bridge End Gr NG31 ..211 D2
Bridge End Rd NG31 ..211 C2
Bridge Gdns 1 DN31 .....188 D1
Bridge La Cadney DN20 ..31 C6
Horkstow DN18 .....9 F5
Scopwick LN4 .....108 D8
Bridge Pl 22 LN1 .....66 D2
Bridge Rd
Aubourn Haddington &
South Hykeham LN5 .....92 F5
Gainsborough DN21 .....197 D3
Greetham with Somersby
LN9 .....86 F7
Long Sutton PE12 .....216 D3
6 Sutton Bridge PE12 .....160 F4
4 Sutton Bridge PE12 .....160 F4
Sutton Bridge PE12 .....160 C5
Bridge St
3 Billinghay LN4 .....109 F5
2 Boston PE21 .....208 F4
Brigg DN20 .....196 A3
Gainsborough DN21 .....197 C3
Grantham NG31 .....211 C3
Horncastle LN9 .....199 B4
Louth LN11 .....198 B6
Market Deeping PE6 .....217 D4
Marston NG32 .....118 D2
19 Nettleham LN2 .....68 C2
2 Peterborough PE1 .....226 A1
4 Ryhall PE9 .....163 C1
Saxilby LN1 .....66 D2
27 Thorne/Moorends DN8 .15 A8
Bridge St N 3 DN32 .....189 B1
Bridge View LN8 .....56 F8
Bridgegate Dr HU9 .....181 C6
Bridgehill Rd PE6 .....221 D6
Bridges Rd DN17 .....184 E7
Bridges The 24 DN18 .....10 F8
Bridgeview Sch HU13 .178 D1
Bridgewater Rd DN17 .184 D8
Bridle Cl Fishtoft PE21 ..209 C3
7 Sleaford NG34 .....212 D2
Bridle La LN5 .....105 E8
Bridle Way 7 LN8 .....70 D5
Bridle Way The LN4 .....95 B7
Bridles The 11 DN19 .....12 A8
Bridlington Ave HU2 ...180 F8
Brierholme Carr Rd
DN7 .....14 F5
Brierholme Cl DN7 .....14 F5
Brierholme Ings Rd
DN7 .....14 F5
Brigg Cl 6 LN6 .....204 C6
Brigg Dr HU13 .....178 F3
Brigg Gr 5 LN6 .....204 C6
Brigg La LN5 .....105 F8

Brigg Prep Sch DN20 ..196 C3
Brigg Prim Sch DN20 ..196 C4
Brigg Rd
Barton-upon-Humber
DN18 .....10 E5
Broughton DN20 .....19 E3
Cadney DN20 .....31 D7
Grasby LN7 .....33 A6
Hibaldstow DN20 .....30 F6
North Kelsey LN7 .....32 A5
Scawby DN20 .....30 F8
Scunthorpe DN16 .....183 D2
South Kelsey LN7 .....32 A1
Wrawby DN20 .....196 F5
Brigg Sta DN20 .....196 C2
Briggate Dr 19 DN17 .....29 D7
Brighowgate DN32 .....191 D6
Bright St
2 Gainsborough DN21 ..197 C4
Kingston upon Hull HU8 ..181 B8
Peterborough PE1 .....225 F3
Brighton St
2 Cleethorpes DN35 .....193 A5
Kingston upon Hull HU3 ..180 A3
Brigsley Rd DN37 .....194 D2
Brigstock Ct PE3 .....225 C6
Brigstock Rd PE13 .....170 C1
Brimbles Way PE2 .....229 E5
Bringhurst PE2 .....230 A4
Brinkhall Way 9 LN2 .....68 D7
Brinkhill Pottery*
LN11 .....87 D8
Brinkle Spring La LN4 ..82 A4
Brisbane Cl
5 Skegness PE25 .....206 A4
12 Waddington LN5 .....93 E8
Brisbane St HU3 .....180 D5
Bristol Ave PE4 .....220 F3
Bristol Cl NG31 .....210 E4
Bristol Dr LN6 .....205 C8
Bristol House Rd
NG34 .....107 C1
Bristol Rd
Kingston upon Hull HU5 ..179 C8
1 Scunthorpe DN17 .....182 C1
Scunthorpe DN17 .....184 C8
Bristol Way NG34 .....212 B5
Bristow Rd 3 NG34 .....120 E8
Bristows Yd NG32 .....118 D2
Britannia Cres DN34 ...190 D5
Britannia Gdns 3 PE11 .214 C5
Britannia Terr 4 DN21 .197 D3
Brittain Dr NG31 .....211 C5
Britton Cl DN17 .....7 D3
Brixham Ct
Grimsby DN33 .....194 E6
5 Kingston upon Hull
HU3 .....180 A5
Broach Rd LN5 .....106 B5
Broad Cl PE1 .....226 D5
Broad Dale Cl 4 LN2 .....68 F3
Broad Dro PE11 .....144 B5
Broad Dro E PE13 .....169 E6
Broad Dro W PE13 .....169 B4
Broad Fen La NG23 .....104 D1
Broad Gate
Sutton St James PE12 ...169 A8
Weston PE12 .....157 C1
Wrangle PE22 .....114 C3
Broad La Bicker PE20 ...135 B4
Moulton PE12 .....157 F6
South Leverton DN22 .....65 A7
Sutterton PE20 .....135 F1
Whaplode PE12 .....146 F1
Broad St
5 Grantham NG31 .....211 A5
Spalding PE11 .....214 D4
Stamford PE9 .....219 B5
Broad Wheel Rd PE6 ..173 B3
Broadacre Pk 2 HU15 .....2 D5
Broadbank LN11 .....198 B6
Broadbeck 2 DN21 .....43 D7
Broadbent Theatre*
LN3 .....69 E8
Broadfield La 8 PE21 ..208 E4
Broadfield St PE21 .....208 E4
Broadgate
Gedney PE12 .....159 D6
Lincoln LN2 .....234 B2
Whaplode PE12 .....168 A3
Broadgate Dro PE12 ...167 C8
Broadgate La PE6 .....217 F4
Broadgate Rd
South Witham NG33 .....151 E2
Sutton St Edmund PE12 ..168 F3
Broadholme Rd LN1 .....66 D1
Broadhurst Rd 18 PE8 ..172 B1
Broadings La DN22 .....65 A4
Broadlands Ave PE10 ..213 C7
Broadlands Cl
41 Hatfield DN7 .....14 D4
1 Hatfield DN7 .....14 D3
Broadlands The PE1 ...226 E5
Broadley Ave HU10 .....178 D6
Broadley Cl 6 HU9 .....181 C7
Broadley Cres LN11 ...198 E6
Broadley Croft 5 HU15 ...2 D5
Broadley Way 8 HU15 ....2 D5
Broadsyke La NG24 ....105 A4
Broadwater Dr
9 Hatfield DN7 .....14 D3
3 Hatfield DN7 .....14 D3
Broadwater La PE12 ...158 A4
Broadway
Crowland PE6 .....175 B8
Farcet PE7 .....231 C1
3 Grimsby DN34 .....190 D4
Hatfield DN7 .....14 C3

Broadway *continued*
2 Keelby DN41 .....23 A5
Lincoln LN2 .....201 F6
Mablethorpe/Sutton on Sea
LN12 .....77 A8
Peterborough PE1 .....226 A3
Spalding PE11 .....214 A2
Yaxley PE7 .....233 E5
Broadway Cl
11 Bourne PE10 .....213 C7
4 Lincoln LN2 .....201 F6
Broadway Gdns PE1 ...226 B5
Broadway Nook 1 DN7 ..14 C3
Broadway The
Morton PE10 .....154 B7
Woodhall Spa LN10 .....97 D6
Broadway Theatre*
PE1 .....226 A3
Brock Cl 1 DN33 .....191 C2
Brockenhurst Cl LN6 ..204 B7
Brockenhurst Rd 9 DN7 .14 E4
Brocklebank Cl LN5 .....92 F2
Brocklesby Cl
Gainsborough DN21 .....197 F3
5 Kingston upon Hull
HU13 .....179 A3
Brocklesby Pk Prim Sch
DN37 .....22 D4
Brocklesby Pl DN34 ...190 E4
Brocklesby Rd
Brocklesby DN41 .....22 E5
4 Grimsby DN34 .....190 E4
Habrough DN40 .....22 E8
Scunthorpe DN17 .....184 F4
Ulceby DN39 .....12 A1
Brocks Cl 21 PE24 .....90 D7
Brockton Cl HU3 .....179 F5
Brodsworth Rd PE7 .....231 F5
Bromwich Rd HU10 .....178 F8
Bronzegarth DN32 .....192 B5
Brook Dr 4 LN12 .....64 C3
Brook La Farcet PE7 .....231 B2
Scawby DN20 .....20 A1
Brook Rd 4 LN9 .....199 D2
Brook St
Grantham NG31 .....211 A5
Hemswell DN21 .....42 D2
Kingston upon Hull HU2 ..180 E7
Lincoln LN2 .....234 B2
Peterborough PE1 .....226 A2
Brook Way 5 NG34 .....108 D2
Brookdale Rd DN17 .....184 D6
Brooke Ave PE9 .....218 E4
Brooke St DN8 .....15 A8
Brookenby Bsns Pk
LN8 .....47 B6
Brookfield Ave LN2 .....68 D2
Brookfield Cl
2 Skellingthorpe LN6 ...200 A5
6 Thorne/Moorends DN8 .15 A8
Brookfield Rd DN33 ...191 B1
Brookfields Ind Pk
PE4 .....220 F2
Brookfurlong PE3 .....225 B6
Brooklands 1 DN20 .....19 E3
Brooklands Ave
Broughton DN20 .....19 D4
Cleethorpes DN35 .....193 A5
Brooklands Cl
5 Birchwood LN6 .....204 C7
3 Collingham NG23 .....91 D5
Brooklands Rd HU5 .....179 E8
Brooklands Way 8 LN6 204 C7
Brooklyn Dr DN36 .....193 B1
Brookside
8 Ancaster NG32 .....120 A3
4 Brough HU15 .....2 D6
Louth LN11 .....198 D3
Peterborough PE4 .....221 B2
Brookside Cl 7 NG32 ..120 A3
Broom Cl PE1 .....226 A8
Broom Ct 24 DN7 .....14 D4
Broom Gr DN16 .....185 B8
Broome Way PE12 .....215 A2
Broomfleet Sta HU15 .....1 B6
Broomston La DN9 .....26 F1
Broomwood Cl 2 NG31 .210 F7
Brosley Ave 1 DN3 .....14 A4
Brotherhood Cl PE4 ...225 D8
Brotherhood Ret Pk
PE4 .....225 D8
Brothertoft Rd PE21 ..208 D5
Brotts Rd NG23 .....78 A3
Brough Cl 14 LN6 .....204 C7
Brough Cty Prim Sch
HU15 .....2 C6
Brough La NG23 .....91 D2
Brough Rd LN6 .....105 A8
Brough Sta HU15 .....2 B5
Brougham St HU3 .....179 F7
Broughton Gdns LN5 ..205 D3
Broughton Inf Sch
DN20 .....19 E3
Broughton La LN5 .....93 C3
Broughton Rd
Carlton-le-Moorland LN5 ...92 E1
Stapleford LN6 .....105 C8
Broughton's La 1 PE22 126 E3
Brown La NG23 .....79 A7
Browndons St 4 NG31 .211 A5
Browne's Hosp* PE9 ...219 B5
Brownes Rd 7 PE8 .....172 B1
Browning Cl
3 Kingston upon Hull
HU3 .....180 D8
1 Scunthorpe DN17 .....184 E6
Browning Ct 4 LN4 .....207 B5
Browning Dr LN2 .....202 B7

Brownlow Cres 3 PE11 .145 B1
Brownlow Dr 4 PE6 ..217 E4
Brownlow Quay 1 PE9 .219 C4
Brownlow Rd PE1 .....226 A6
Brownlow's Dro PE12 .167 A8
Brownlow's Hill NG24 .104 D5
Browns CE (Aided) Prim Sch NG34 .....133 C2
Brown's Dro PE20 .....123 F2
Brown's Gate
Long Sutton PE12 ....216 B1
Spalding PE11 ....214 C4
Brown's Rd 3 PE21 ...209 A7
Browns La 13 DN8 ......15 A8
Browns Orch DN32 ....191 D6
Browntoft La 2 PE11 ...134 F2
Broxholme Gdns 2 LN2 201 F8
Broxholme La LN1 ......66 F3
Bruce Cl
7 Broughton DN20 ......19 D3
Lincoln LN2 ....234 C4
Bruce St DN15 ....182 F3
Brudenell PE2 ....229 E2
Brudenell Cl 1 PE6 ...164 E5
Brumby Comm La DN17 .....184 B7
Brumby Comp Sch DN16 .....185 B8
Brumby Cres 10 LN5 .....93 F7
Brumby Hall Gdns DN17 .....182 F2
Brumby House Dr DN16 .....185 A8
Brumby Jun Sch DN16 .....185 B8
Brumby Resource Ctr DN16 .....185 C8
Brumby Wood La DN15 .....182 C2
Brumby's Terr 4 HU9 ..181 D7
Brunel Cl DN16 ......185 B4
Brunel Dr
Newark NG24 ....104 B5
Yaxley PE7 ....233 D6
Brunel Rd PE11 ......214 E8
Brunslow Cl HU3 ......179 E5
Brunswick Ave HU2 ...180 E8
Brunswick Dr PE25 ...206 C4
Brunswick Gr 5 HU13 ..178 E2
Brunswick Sq 1 LN4 ..109 F6
Brunton Way DN36 ...195 D5
Brush Mdw La PE34 ...161 E3
Bryant Cl 4 LN9 ......199 C3
Brynmore PE3 ....225 A8
Bryony Gdns PE10 ...213 D7
Bryony Way 5 PE6 ...217 D6
Buccaneer Way 21 HU15 ..2 C5
Buchanan Cl LN1 .....201 D8
Buchanan Rd DN21 .....54 F8
Buck Beck Way DN36 ..192 D2
Buckfast Rd 4 LN1 ...201 E6
Buckingham Ave DN15 .....182 F5
Buckingham Cl
Fishtoft PE21 ....209 C6
15 Mablethorpe & Sutton LN12 .....76 F8
Buckingham Dr 15 PE24 .90 D7
Buckingham Gr 2 DN33 .....191 B2
Buckingham Rd LN11 ..198 A7
Buckingham St N DN15 .....182 F5
Buckingham St S DN15 .....182 F4
Buckland Cl PE3 ......225 B4
Buckle St PE1 ....226 C3
Bucklegate La PE20 ...136 F2
Buckminster Gdns NG31 .....210 F2
Buckminster La NG33 .151 A7
Buckminster Prim Sch NG33 .....150 F5
Buckminster Rd
Gunby & Stainby NG33 ...151 A5
Sproxton LE14 ....150 C7
Bucknall Ave 4 LN6 ...205 A7
Bucknall Rd LN10 ......84 C3
Bucknall's Mdw 5 LN12 .76 F8
Bucksholt Rd PE14 ...170 E3
Buckthorn Ave
8 Skegness PE25 ......103 E4
3 Skegness PE25 ......103 E4
Buddleia Cl DN41 ......23 E5
Buddleia Dr LN4 ......81 D3
Bude Cl 2 DN36 ......195 C7
Bukehorn Rd PE6 .....175 D4
Bulby La 1 NG32 ......106 C1
Bulham La NG23 ....78 A1
Bull Bank LN11 ....49 D7
Bull Dro PE22 ....114 B5
Bull La 1 Ketton PE9 ...171 A3
Long Sutton PE12 ....216 C4
North Witham NG33 .....151 E4
4 Peakirk PE6 ....174 A5
Bull Moor Rd DN7 ......15 A4
Bull Pasture PE22 .....126 D2
Bull's Bank PE11 ......144 E8
Bulldog Cres LN11 .....62 B6
Bullen's La PE20 ......135 C6
Buller Cl 16 NG23 ......91 D5
Buller St 4 DN32 ......191 F7
Bullfinch La DN35 .....192 E1
Bullingham Rd LN2 ....202 D6
Bullivant Rd DN7 ....14 E4
Bullock Rd
Terrington St Clement PE34 .....161 F1
Bullock Rd *continued*
Thorney PE8 ....228 B1
Bullock's Short Gate PE12 .....159 C4
Bullpit Rd NG24 ......104 C3
Bully Hill LN8 ....46 D2
Bulpit La LN6 ....91 F7
Bulwick Ave DN33 .....194 E7
Bungley La PE20 ......136 C6
Bunker's Hill La PE21 ..136 F8
Bunkers Hill
Hemswell DN21 ....42 E1
Lincoln LN2 ....202 D6
Bunkers Hill Cl 2 DN36 ..36 D4
BUPA Hull & E Riding Hospl HU10 .....178 E5
Burchnall Cl PE6 .....217 D6
Burchnall Dr 4 PE25 ...90 E3
Burcom Ave 3 DN36 ...36 D8
Burcott Garth HU4 ....179 B3
Burcroft Rd 17 PE13 ...170 C1
Burdett Cl 8 PE25 ....206 A6
Burdock Rd DN16 .....185 C4
Bure Cl LN6 ....204 F3
Burford Way PE1 .....226 D6
Burgar Rd 11 DN8 ......15 A7
Burgate 5 DN18 ....10 F8
Burgess Cl 2 PE21 ....209 B4
Burgess Dr 4 PE12 ....159 C7
Burgess Rd DN20 .....196 E3
Burgh Old Rd PE25 ...206 A6
Burgh Rd
Friskney PE22 ....115 A7
Skegness PE25 ....103 C7
Burghley Ave 14 PE8 ...172 B1
Burghley Cl
Birchwood LN6 ....200 E1
3 Market Deeping PE6 ..217 E4
3 Nettleton LN7 ....33 A3
Burghley Cres LN11 ...198 B7
Burghley Ct 1 PE10 ...213 C5
Burghley House* PE9 .219 F3
Burghley La PE9 ......219 C4
Burghley Pk Cl 8 LN6 ..204 F1
Burghley Rd
Birchwood LN6 ....200 E1
1 Peterborough PE1 ...226 A3
Scunthorpe DN16 ......185 D7
8 Skegness PE25 ......206 C1
8 Stamford PE9 ....219 A7
Burghley Sq 2 PE1 ....226 A3
Burghley St PE10 .....213 C5
Burgin Cl 6 NG32 ......117 F1
Burgon Cres 3 DN15 .....9 B5
Burke St (North) DN15 .....183 A5
Burke St DN15 ....183 A4
Burland Ct 3 LN4 .....203 B2
Burleigh Cl NG31 .....211 F5
Burleigh Gdns 2 PE21 .209 A7
Burleigh St HU8 ......181 C8
Burley Ave DN35 .....192 F3
Burley Rd 14 PE9 ......163 C1
Burlies' Gate PE12 ....159 E4
Burlington Rd PE25 ...206 B3
Burma Dr HU9 ....5 D8
Burma Rd DN16 ....183 F2
Burmer Rd PE1 ....225 E7
Burn Rd DN15 ....182 C3
Burneside Cl LN2 .....202 B8
Burnet Dr DN16 ....185 C4
Burnett's Yd LN7 ......33 C4
Burnham La
Kirton PE20 ....136 F4
Thornton Curtis DN39 ....11 E4
Burnham Rd
Barton-upon-Humber DN18 .....11 A6
Epworth DN9 ....27 E6
Kingston upon Hull HU4 ..179 B3
Owston Ferry DN9 ......28 A3
Scunthorpe DN15 ......182 D2
Burnham Reach 3 DN35 .....192 F1
Burnham Sq 2 DN9 .....28 A3
Burnmoor Cl 3 LN6 ...200 C1
Burns Cl
Grantham NG31 ....211 E6
Peterborough PE1 ......225 F7
Burns Cres 8 NG34 ....212 F4
Burns Gdns LN2 ......202 C6
Burns Gr DN33 ....191 B3
Burns Rd 5 PE9 ....218 F6
Burns St DN21 ....197 B6
Burnside DN20 ....19 D3
Burnside Ave 5 PE6 ...217 A5
Burnstone Gdns 4 PE12 .....157 F7
Burnt Hill La 5 LN11 ...198 B5
Burr La PE12 ....156 F3
Burrett Gdns PE13 ....170 F1
Burrett Rd PE13 ....170 F2
Burrettgate Rd 4 PE13 .170 F1
Burrill La HU15 ....2 B8
Burringham Rd
Burringham DN17 ....17 E5
Scunthorpe DN17 ......184 D5
Burrows Cl 2 PE21 ....208 E7
Burrs The HU15 ....2 B5
Bursar Prim Sch DN35 .....192 E6
Bursar St DN35 ......192 E6
Bursnells La 3 LE14 ...150 B1
Burswood PE2 ....229 F2
Burtey Fen La PE11 ...145 B2
Burtoft La PE20 ....135 E2
Burton Cl PE21 ....209 B7
Burton Ct 2 Louth LN11 .198 D4
Burton Ct *continued*
Peterborough PE1 ......226 C3
Burton La
8 Billingborough NG34 ..133 B1
Burton Coggles NG33 ....140 E1
Easton NG33 ....140 B1
Burton La End LN1 ....200 C8
Burton Mews LN4 .....203 D1
Burton Rd
Burton upon Stather DN15 ..8 C4
Heckington NG34 ......122 C2
Lincoln LN1 ....234 A4
Burton Ridge 2 LN1 ...201 D7
Burton St
14 Gainsborough DN21 ...197 D3
Peterborough PE1 ......226 C3
Burton Stather Prim Sch DN15 .....8 B4
Burton Way 6 LN9 ....199 D2
Burtonfield Cl 1 LN3 ..203 E6
Burwell Cl LN2 ....202 A8
Burwell Dr DN33 .....191 B3
Burwell Rd LN11 ....74 D7
Burwell Reach PE2 ....230 C7
Burystead PE2 ....231 B8
Bush Cl HU4 ....179 D3
Bush Gn La
Algarkirk PE20 ....146 C8
Fosdyke PE20 ....136 C1
Bush Mdw La PE12 ....215 A4
Bushfield Com Coll PE2 .....229 E3
Bushfield Rd DN16 ...183 B1
Bushfield Rd Inf Sch DN16 .....183 A1
Bushfield Sports Ctr PE2 .....229 E4
Buslingthorpe Rd LN8 ..57 A4
Bustards' La PE14 .....161 C1
Butcher La 10 LN11 ...198 B5
Butchery Ct 3 LN2 ....234 B2
Butforth La DN19 ......11 E8
Butler Pl DN35 ....192 B7
Butler's Way 14 PE20 ..135 B7
Butlin Cl 1 PE25 ......206 A4
Butt Gate LN11 ....50 B8
Butt La Barrowby NG32 .210 A6
Goulceby LN11 ....72 D6
Laceby DN37 ....23 F2
Norton Disney LN6 ......92 C2
Theddlethorpe All Saints LN12 .....63 E7
Walcott LN4 ....109 C7
Wymondham LE14 ......150 C2
Butter Mkt 11 LN7 ......33 B4
Buttercake La PE22 ...113 F2
Buttercross Cl 2 DN41 ..23 E6
Buttercup Cl
1 Kingston upon Hull HU9 .....181 D7
3 Spalding PE11 ....214 A2
3 Stamford PE9 ....218 D7
Buttercup Paddock 4 PE12 .....158 B6
Butterfield Cl 7 DN37 ...23 F1
Buttergate Hill LN9 ....71 F3
Buttermere Cl 2 LN6 ..200 D1
Buttermere Cres 2 DN36 .....36 C8
Buttermere Pl 4 PE4 ..221 C3
Buttermere Way 7 DN32 .....191 F8
Butterwick Cl DN35 ...192 F3
Butterwick Pinchbeck Endowed CE Sch PE22 .....126 E3
Butterwick Rd
Benington PE22 ....126 F4
Messingham DN17 ......29 A7
Buttery Cl LN6 ....204 F4
Buttfield Rd HU13 ....178 E1
Buttler Way 3 NG34 ...212 C3
Butts La LN5 ....92 F6
Butt's La LN4 ....207 B5
Butts Rd DN18 ....3 F1
Butts The LE14 ....138 F1
Bycroft Rd DN21 ......197 C8
Byfield Rd DN17 ......184 D6
Byland Ct 4 HU9 ......181 E8
Byrd Rd DN16 ....185 E6
Byron Ave
Grantham NG31 ....211 E6
Lincoln LN2 ....202 A6
Byron Cl
Peterborough PE2 .....231 D6
Scunthorpe DN17 ......184 E6
6 Sleaford NG34 ....212 F4
Byron Gr 2 DN33 .....191 C4
Byron Rd LN12 ....64 B4
Byron Way PE9 ....218 E5
Bytham Hts 3 NG33 ...162 E8
Bythams Cty Prim Sch The NG33 .....153 A2
Bythorn Rd PE2 ......231 C6
Bythorne Bank PE13 ..169 B6
Bywood Pl DN37 ......190 C6

C

Cabourne Ave LN2 ....202 B7
Cabourne Ct LN2 .....202 B7
Cabourne Rd DN33 ...191 B3
Cackle Hill La PE12 ..215 C5
Caddle Rd 11 DN41 ......23 A4
Cade Cl 12 LN2 ....68 F4
Cade Dro PE12 ....159 D4
Cade La DN21 ....53 D6
Cades Field Rd 24 LN12 ..77 A8
Cadman Way DN21 .....41 A1
Cadney Rd DN20 ......196 C1
Cadwell Cl 4 LN6 .....204 C7
Cadwell Pk Motor Racing Circuit* LN11 .....73 B8
Caenby Cl DN21 ......197 F3
Caenby Cnr LN8 ......55 B8
Caenby Rd Caenby LN8 ..43 F1
Cleethorpes DN35 ......192 E4
Scunthorpe DN17 ......184 E5
Caesar Cl 7 PE6 ......164 E5
Cagthorpe LN9 ....199 B3
Cairns Way 8 LN5 ......93 E8
Caistor Ave DN16 .....185 B4
Caistor By-Pass LN7 ...33 B3
Caistor Cl 7 LN6 .....204 C7
Caistor Dr
Bracebridge Heath LN4 ...81 A2
Grimsby DN33 ....191 B3
Caistor Gram Sch LN7 ..33 B4
Caistor La LN8 ....46 C3
Caistor Rd
Barton-upon-Humber DN18 .....11 A7
Birchwood LN6 ....204 C7
Cabourne LN7 ....33 F5
Caistor LN7 ....32 E4
Laceby DN37 ....23 E1
2 Market Rasen LN8 .....57 D8
Middle Rasen LN8 ......45 D2
Rothwell LN7 ....33 E2
South Kelsey LN7 ....32 A1
Swallow LN7 ....34 A5
Caistor Yarborough Sch LN7 .....33 C4
Caithness Rd PE9 .....218 E6
Caldbeck Cl PE4 ......221 D2
Caldecote Cl PE2 .....231 E6
Calder Cl
Grantham NG31 ....210 E3
Immingham DN40 ......186 A3
Calder Gn 24 DN17 .....29 D7
Calder Rd Lincoln LN5 ..205 C2
Scunthorpe DN16 ......185 D6
Caldervale PE2 ....230 C6
Caldicott Dr 8 DN21 ...53 A8
Caleb Hill La
Leake Commonside PE22 .....113 F3
Old Leake PE22 ....114 A3
Caledonia Pk HU9 .....181 B5
Caledonian Rd 4 PE9 ..218 F6
Callan's La PE10 .....142 C2
Calver Cres DN37 .....190 D7
Calvert La HU4 ....179 D7
Calvert Rd HU5 ....179 D8
Camargue Ave DN37 ..194 F4
Camarthen Cl 4 NG31 .210 E5
Cambrian Cl NG31 ....210 E7
Cambrian Way
Holton le Clay DN36 ...195 C3
11 North Hykeham LN6 ...93 B8
1 Peterborough PE4 ...221 C1
Cambridge Ave
Lincoln LN1 ....201 D4
Peterborough PE1 ......225 F5
Scunthorpe DN16 ......185 A3
Cambridge Cres 4 LN8 ..47 B6
Cambridge Dr
Heighington/Washingborough LN4 .....203 D1
Wisbech PE13 ....170 C1
Cambridge Gdns 4 PE11 .....145 B7
Cambridge Rd
Grimsby DN34 ....190 F5
Kingston upon Hull HU13 .....178 F3
Scunthorpe DN16 ......185 C6
Stamford PE9 ....219 A6
Cambridge Rd N 1 LN12 64 B5
Cambridge Rd S 3 LN12 .64 B5
Cambridge St
Cleethorpes DN35 ......192 F6
Grantham NG31 ....211 B3
Kingston upon Hull HU3 ..180 D6
Camden St 1 HU3 .....180 B5
Camdon Cl 1 LN5 .....205 D3
Camel Gate PE12 .....157 B7
Camelia Cl PE4 ....221 B3
Camelot Gdns
Boston PE21 ....209 E5
11 Mablethorpe/Sutton on Sea LN12 .....76 F8
Cameron Dr 3 PE11 ...214 E3
Cameron St 4 NG34 ...122 E3
Camilla Cl HU9 ....181 A5
Camm's La PE22 ......114 D2
Camp La NG33 ....141 B1
Campain's La PE11 ...166 C7
Campbell Ave DN16 ...185 B4
Campbell Cl 4 NG31 ..210 F5
Campbell Dr PE4 .....221 C4
Campbell St DN21 ....197 B5
Campbells Cl PE11 ....214 B1
Campbells Farm Ave 1 DN15 .....17 E6
Campden Cres DN35 ..192 D7
Campion Ave HU4 .....179 B2
Campion Cl PE11 .....214 B6
Campion Dr PE6 ......217 D6
Campion Gr 4 PE9 ....218 D7
Campion Rd PE1 .....226 B8
Campions Cl DN36 ....195 D2
Campions' La 11 DN36 ..36 B1
Campling Pl PE12 .....215 D7
Campney La LN10 ......83 F1
Camwood Cres LN6 ...200 C1
Canada La Caistor LN7 ...33 C4
Wildmore LN4 ....111 A4
Canal La DN10 ....40 B5
Canal View 12 DN8 .....15 A7
Canberra Ave DN7 .....26 A8
Canberra Cl 5 LN4 ....207 C4
Canberra Cres
11 Binbrook Tech Pk LN8 ..47 B6
Grantham NG31 ....211 D7
10 Manby LN11 ....62 C6
Canberra Dr 5 LN1 .....67 F5
Canberra Rd 8 NG24 ...104 C5
Canberra St HU3 ......180 D5
Canberra Way LN6 ....200 A4
Candidus Ct 6 PE4 ....220 F5
Candlehouse La 9 LN13 .75 F3
Candlesby Rd DN37 ...190 C7
Candy Bank DN9 ....26 B5
Canister La
Frithville PE22 ....112 C1
Langriville PE22 ....124 F8
Canning St HU1 ....180 E6
Cannon Cl NG24 ......104 C5
Cannon Oakes Ct DN36 .....195 E6
Cannon St
Kingston upon Hull HU2 ..180 F8
1 Lincoln LN2 ....202 B3
Lincoln LN2 ....234 C2
3 Louth LN11 ....198 B5
Cannonhill Dro PE12 ..167 A8
Canon Dr 6 PE9 ......172 D3
Canonsfield PE4 ......220 E4
Canterbury Cl
Grantham NG31 ....211 E7
1 Scunthorpe DN17 ....184 D7
Spalding PE11 ....214 B4
Canterbury Dr
Grimsby DN34 ....191 C6
Heighington/Washingborough LN4 .....203 D1
4 Sleaford NG34 ......212 C7
Canterbury Rd
1 Hatfield DN7 ....14 D4
Peterborough PE4 ......220 F3
Cant's Dro PE13 ......177 C4
Canturbury Cl 10 LN10 ..97 C5
Canty Nook 5 DN38 ....32 E7
Canwell PE4 ....221 A4
Canwick Ave LN4 .....205 F4
Canwick Hill LN4 ....81 A4
Canwick Rd
Canwick LN5 ....81 A4
Lincoln LN5 ....234 B1
Washingborough LN4 ....81 D4
Capes Entry PE12 .....157 A2
Capitol Pk DN8 ....14 F8
Capper Ave 3 DN21 .....55 A8
Cappitt Dr 2 PE10 ....164 C8
Capp's La 19 LN5 ......93 F7
Capstan Way 17 DN8 ....15 A8
Captain's Hill NG34 ...121 B7
Captains Beck 9 PE11 ..145 C1
Capthorne Cl PE7 .....230 C2
Caravan Pk LN6 ......204 C1
Carbis Cl 5 DN36 .....195 C7
Cardiff Ave DN36 .....195 C6
Cardigan Rd HU3 .....179 E6
Cardinal Cl LN2 ......202 D5
Cardinal Ct 3 DN37 ...194 C5
Cardinals Gate PE4 ...220 E4
Cardyke Dr 13 PE6 ...164 E5
Carew St HU3 ....179 F7
Carholme Cl 1 PE10 ..213 D6
Carholme Rd LN1 .....201 C4
Carisbrooke Cl
2 Lincoln LN1 ....201 E6
5 New Waltham DN36 ...195 D7
Carisbrooke Manor La DN17 .....184 A5
Carleton Crest 3 PE4 ..221 B1
Carline Rd LN1 ....234 A3
Carlisle Cl
6 Grantham NG31 ......210 D5
1 Lincoln LN6 ....204 F1
Carlisle Gdns LN9 ....199 D5
Carlisle Way LN4 ......81 A2
Carlton Ave DN41 ......23 F5
Carlton Bvd LN2 .....202 D5
Carlton Cl
Humberston DN35 ......193 B1
8 Leverington PE13 ....170 B2
2 Spalding PE11 ......214 B1
Carlton Ferry La NG23 ..91 A6
Carlton Gr LN2 ....201 F7
Carlton La
Broxholme LN1 ....67 A4
Sutton-on-Trent NG23 ....91 A7
Carlton Mews 9 LN4 ..203 D1
Carlton Pk LN11 ....62 C5
Carlton Rd
Ancaster NG32 ....119 E3
Bassingham LN5 ....92 E2
Boston PE21 ....208 D5
Grimsby DN34 ....191 B6
9 Healing DN41 ....23 F5
Hough-on-the-Hill NG32 ..119 B5
Manby LN11 ....62 C6
Carlton Rd Cty Prim Sch PE21 .....208 E5
Carlton St
Kingston upon Hull HU3 ..179 F4
Lincoln LN1 ....234 A4
5 Scunthorpe DN15 ....183 B3

Carmel Gn PE21 208 E2
Carmen Cres DN36 195 C3
Carn Cl 3 LN5 205 D2
Carnaby Gr 2 DN32 192 A5
Carnarvon Ave 1 DN34 191 B4
Carnegie Rd 21 PE8 172 B1
Carnegie St 6 HU3 180 A6
Carnforth Cres DN34 191 A5
Carnforth Sch DN34 190 F5
Carnoustie 7 DN37 194 C4
Carnoustie Cl 2 LN10 97 C5
Carol Dickson Ct 9 HU3 180 C5
Caroline Cl 12 NG34 212 F4
Caroline Ct 10 PE21 209 A5
Caroline Pl HU2 180 F7
Caroline Rd 5 LN4 95 D4
Caroline St 10 Alford LN13 75 F2
Kingston upon Hull HU2 180 F8
Carr Dike La HU15 1 C7
Carr Dyke Bank DN17 28 D5
Carr Dyke Rd DN17 17 D3
Carr La 6 Alford LN13 75 F2
Appleby DN15 9 D2
Bishop Norton LN8 43 F3
Blyton DN21 41 B5
Bonby DN20 10 B1
Broomfleet HU15 1 B7
Broughton DN20 196 A6
Burton upon Stather DN15 8 D4
Doddington & Whisby LN6 79 D6
Gainsborough DN21 197 C1
Garthorpe & Fockerby DN17 7 E4
Grimsby DN32 192 B7
Haxey DN9 27 E2
Healing DN41 23 F4
Hibaldstow DN20 31 A6
Horkstow DN18 9 F4
Kingston upon Hull HU1 180 E6
Luddington & Haldenby DN17 7 C1
3 Misterton DN10 39 F5
Redbourne DN21 30 F3
Stallingborough DN41 23 F7
Ulceby DN39 12 B3
West Butterwick DN17 28 C8
Wildsworth DN21 40 F8
Winterton DN15 9 D6
Worlaby DN20 20 B7
Carr Rd
Gringley on the Hill DN10 39 A4
North Kelsey LN7 31 E4
Peterborough PE1 226 D3
Carr Side La DN7 14 E2
Carr St LN1 201 D4
Carradale PE2 229 D5
Carral Cl LN5 205 C3
Carram Way LN1 201 C7
Carre St NG34 212 D4
Carres Gram Sch NG34 212 D5
Carre's Sq LN4 109 E6
Carrhouse Rd DN9 16 D1
Carrington Cl
Coningsby LN4 207 D5
2 Spalding PE11 214 B3
Carrington Dr
Deeping St Nicholas PE11 165 F5
8 Humberston DN36 36 D8
Humberston DN36 193 B1
Lincoln LN6 204 F7
Carrington Rd
Carrington PE22 112 D3
Moulton PE12 146 C3
Spalding PE11 214 B4
Carrington St 6 HU3 180 B5
Carrington's Dro PE6 175 C7
Carroll Pl 4 HU1 181 A7
Carron Cl 3 LN3 83 B4
Carron Dr PE4 220 E3
Carrside DN9 27 D6
Carrwood Cres LN4 207 C7
Carson Ave DN34 191 B6
Carson Cl 5 PE24 90 B7
Carson Rd DN21 197 C6
Carter's Garth Cl 4 LN11 50 B8
Cartergate DN32 191 C7
Carterplot Rd NG34 123 A2
Carters Cl 6 PE3 224 F3
Cartledge Ave DN32 192 B6
Cartmel Gr DN32 192 B6
Cartmel Way 14 PE6 175 A1
Carver Rd Boston PE21 208 D3
Immingham DN40 186 D3
Cary La 3 DN20 196 B3
Caryer Cl PE2 230 D6
Casewick La 4 PE9 172 F7
Casewick Rd PE9 172 E7
Caskgate St DN21 197 C4
Cassbrook Dr 2 LN11 49 B8
Cassons Cl PE12 157 D4
Casson's Rd 1 DN8 15 A8
Casswell Cl 1 DN32 189 D1
Casswell Cres 4 LN11 49 B8
Castella Dr DN16 183 D3
Casterton Com Coll PE9 171 C8
Casterton La PE9 218 C4
Casterton Rd PE9 218 E6
Casthorpe Rd
3 Barrowby NG32 210 A5
Denton NG32 139 A8
Castle Bytham Rd
Clipsham LE15 162 C7
Swayfield NG33 152 E5
Castle Cl 3 NG13 128 B5
Castle Cswy NG34 212 C4
Castle Ct 14 DN18 10 F8
Castle Dr Epworth DN9 27 E7
Northborough PE6 217 E2
Castle Dyke 13 PE9 219 B5
Castle Dyke Bank LN4 111 B4
Castle End Rd PE6 217 A1
Castle Hill 15 Caistor LN7 33 B4
4 Lincoln LN1 234 B3
3 Welbourn LN5 106 E5
Castle Hills Com Art Coll DN21 197 D7
Castle Keep DN20 30 F6
Castle La
Boothby Graffoe LN5 93 E1
Coningsby LN4 207 C5
Lincoln LN1 234 A4
Castle Rise PE9 163 D1
Castle Sports Complex PE11 214 E5
Castle St Boston PE21 208 D6
Grimsby DN32 192 A8
Kingston upon Hull HU1 180 E5
Lincoln LN1 234 A4
Sleaford NG34 212 D4
12 Stamford PE9 219 B5
Castle Terr Rd 4 NG34 212 C4
Castle View LN4 109 D7
Castle View Rd NG13 128 B4
Castle Way LN11 198 A8
Castledyke Bank PE22 125 A8
Castledyke Prim Sch DN18 3 E1
Castledyke S 13 DN18 10 F8
Castledyke W 7 DN18 3 E1
Castlefields 2 PE11 214 D5
Castleford Ave DN34 191 A4
Castlegate
Castle Bytham NG33 152 D1
Grantham NG31 211 B4
Thornton Le Fen PE22 111 F1
Castleton Bvd PE25 206 D4
Castleton Cres PE25 206 D4
Castleton Rd DN15 182 B2
Castleview
Coningsby LN4 110 E8
Tattershall LN4 97 E1
Castor CE Sch PE5 223 E2
Castor Hanglands Nature Reserve★ PE6 223 D7
Castor Rd Marholm PE6 220 B1
Peterborough PE6 224 C6
Casworth Way PE5 223 D2
Cater La LN7 44 F7
Cater Way PE21 208 D2
Cates's Cove Cnr PE6 167 F4
Cathedral Ct
13 Hatfield DN7 14 C2
Scunthorpe DN17 185 A6
Cathedral Dr PE11 214 C5
Cathedral St LN2 234 B2
Catherine Cl PE2 230 B7
Catherine Gr 6 DN20 19 E3
Catherine St
7 Grimsby DN32 191 F7
1 Kingston upon Hull HU2 180 F7
Cathwaite PE4 221 E1
Catkin Rd 6 DN16 185 B2
Catling's La PE13 170 C7
Catskin La LN8 46 A3
Cattistock Rd DN35 192 E3
Cattle Dike PE13 169 E2
Cattle Mkt Rd PE1 226 A2
Cattle Rd DN10 39 B5
Caughey St HU3 180 D7
Causeway
Burgh le Marsh PE24 102 E7
Wyberton PE21 136 E7
Causeway Bank La LN13 63 F1
Causeway La 3 DN21 52 F6
Causeway Rd LN4 109 E5
Causeway The
6 Northorpe PE10 164 C8
Revesby PE22 111 F7
Thorney PE6 175 E2
Cavalry Ct 2 LN4 95 D4
Cave Rd HU15 2 B6
Cave's Cl 8 PE34 161 F3
Cave's La DN10 39 E3
Cavell Cl PE3 225 B4
Cavendish Cl DN35 193 B1
Cavendish Dr
9 Boston PE21 136 D8
Gainsborough DN21 52 F5
Cavendish Mews 5 LN4 203 D1
Cavendish Pk 10 HU15 2 C5
Cavendish Rd
Scunthorpe DN16 185 A4
Skegness PE25 206 C4
Cavendish St PE1 226 B3
Cavendish Way
1 Grimsby DN32 191 F7
Spalding PE11 214 C6
Caverstede Rd PE4 221 B1
Cavill Pl HU3 180 D5
Cawkwell Cl 25 LN12 77 A7
Cawkwell Hill LN11 73 A6
Cawood La PE11 145 B5
Cawthorne Cl 18 NG23 91 D5
Cawthorne Dr HU4 179 C3
Cawthra Ct NG32 139 A7
Caxton Theatre & Arts Ctr The★ DN32 189 B1
Cayley Rd HU10 178 F6
Caythorpe Heath La NG32 119 D7
Caythorpe Prim Sch NG32 119 B7
Caythorpe Rd PE11 134 F2
Cecil Ave PE25 206 C4
Cecil Cl Bourne PE10 213 B4
16 Scotter DN21 29 C3
Cecil Ct 18 PE9 219 C5
Cecil Pywell Ave PE12 215 C3
Cecil Rd PE1 226 A6
Cecil St
Gainsborough DN21 197 C5
Grantham NG31 211 C3
Kingston upon Hull HU3 179 F5
Lincoln LN1 234 A4
Cecile Cres DN15 182 E3
Cedar Ave
Cherry Willingham/Reepham LN3 203 D5
Lincoln LN5 205 D4
Scunthorpe DN15 182 B6
9 Sleaford NG34 212 D6
2 Stainforth DN7 14 D6
Cedar Cl
4 Cleethorpes DN35 192 D2
Gainsborough DN21 197 B7
Kingston upon Hull HU10 178 D7
1 Louth LN11 198 B6
14 Market Deeping PE6 217 A5
6 Market Rasen LN8 57 D7
9 Ruskington NG34 108 D1
6 Scawby DN20 30 F8
2 Scotter DN21 29 C3
13 Sudbrooke LN2 68 F2
Cedar Ct 2 PE11 214 E3
Cedar Dr Bourne PE10 213 B6
Holbeach PE12 215 C4
Immingham DN40 186 C5
Cedar Gr PE1 226 B8
Cedar Rd PE9 218 D6
Cedarwood Cl 1 NG31 210 F7
Cedarwood Dr HU5 179 B7
Cedric Rd 10 DN3 14 A1
Cekhira Ave PE12 157 E1
Celta Rd PE2 230 F6
Celtic Cl PE2 231 D7
Cemetery Cres 10 DN37 23 F1
Cemetery La LN7 32 A5
Cemetery Rd
Hatfield DN7 14 F4
16 Laceby DN37 23 F1
North Somercotes LN11 50 E8
Scunthorpe DN16 185 B8
Winterton DN15 9 B5
4 Wragby LN8 70 D4
Centenary Cl 3 PE22 126 E3
Centenary Way PE12 160 F2
Central Ave
Ingoldmells PE25 90 F3
Peterborough PE1 226 C7
Central Dr 7 NG34 120 C8
Central Par DN34 191 A7
Central Pl NG31 211 D5
Central Prom DN35 192 F6
Central Sq PE2 231 D5
Central Tech Coll The NG31 211 A7
Central Way DN16 183 D2
Centurion Way 12 HU15 2 C5
Century La 1 LN1 66 D3
Cerris Rd PE1 226 B7
Ceylon St 9 HU9 5 D8
Chadburn PE4 221 E1
Chadwell Springs DN37 194 B4
Chaffinch Cl 5 DN15 182 D5
Chaffinch Dr DN35 192 E1
Chain Bridge Rd PE21 208 B3
Chain Cl PE1 226 B6
Chaintoft La PE11 145 A7
Chaldean Way PE11 214 B6
Chalfont Ave LN12 64 A5
Chalfont Cl HU13 178 D2
Chalfonts The LN4 81 E2
Chalgrove Way LN6 200 E2
Chalk La
Burgh Le Marsh PE24 89 F1
Sutton Bridge PE12 160 F3
Withern with Stain LN13 63 A1
Chalk Pit La PE23 88 F2
Chalk Rd PE13 169 D1
Chamber's Farm Wood Nature Reserve★ LN8 83 F8
Chambers St NG31 211 A5
Chamomile Cl DN16 185 D5
Champion Way LN12 64 B2
Chancel Rd DN16 185 A4
Chancel Wlk 13 DN20 19 E3
Chancery Cl LN6 205 B5
Chancery Ct 4 PE11 214 D3
Chancery La
3 Crowle DN17 16 D7
7 Eye PE6 175 A1
7 Holbeach PE12 215 D2
Chanctonbury Cl 20 LN12 77 A8
Chanctonbury Way 19 LN12 77 A8
Chandlers PE2 229 E5
Chandlers Cl 1 DN36 195 C6
Chandos Rd DN17 184 F7
Chanterlands Ave HU5 180 A8
Chantreys Dr 16 HU15 2 C6
Chantry Cl
Grimsby DN31 191 C7
Peterborough PE1 226 A5
Chantry La DN31 191 C7
Chantry The 1 PE11 214 A4
Chantry Way 16 HU14 3 B7
Chantry Way E 14 HU14 3 B7
Chapel Cl
Barrow upon Humber DN19 11 D7
Chapel St Leonard PE24 90 D8
Cherry Willingham/Reepham LN3 203 F8
10 Misterton DN10 39 F5
1 South Rauceby NG34 120 E4
2 Westwoodside DN9 27 B2
Chapel Ct
5 Alkborough DN15 8 C8
Wansford PE8 222 B2
Chapel Dro PE12 168 B2
Chapel Farm Dr 19 PE24 90 D7
Chapel Field Rd DN19 5 C1
Chapel Garth
Broomfleet HU15 1 B5
16 Tetney DN36 36 D4
Chapel Gate
Sutton St James PE12 159 B1
Sutton St James PE12 169 B7
Whaplode PE12 168 B5
Chapel Gdns
Moulton PE12 157 E1
2 Whaplode PE12 158 B7
Chapel Hill Brough HU15 2 D6
Ropsley NG33 131 B1
Whaplode PE12 168 A4
Woolsthorpe By Belvoir NG32 138 D8
Chapel Hill Ct 7 NG34 212 E3
Chapel Hill La HU15 2 E6
Chapel La
Addlethorpe PE24 90 C3
Amber Hill PE20 124 B5
Anwick NG34 109 B1
Ashby cum Fenby DN37 35 D3
3 Aubourn Haddington & South Hykeham LN5 93 A5
3 Barnetby Le Beck DN37 35 B6
4 Barrowby NG32 210 A5
1 Barton-upon-Humber DN18 10 F8
Belchford LN9 73 B2
Branston & Mere LN4 81 E2
Caythorpe NG32 119 B7
2 Claypole NG23 117 E8
1 Croxton Kerrial NG32 138 D4
5 Donington on Bain LN11 59 E1
Dunston LN4 95 C5
East Kirkby PE23 99 F5
4 Elsham DN20 20 F7
2 Folkingham NG34 142 D8
4 Foston NG32 117 F1
Foston NG32 118 A1
Friskney Eaudike PE22 115 A6
2 Fulletby LN9 86 B8
Gainsborough DN21 197 B8
Glentworth DN21 54 F7
3 Grainthorpe LN11 50 B8
Habrough DN40 12 E1
4 Harmston LN5 93 F5
Heckington NG34 122 F1
Heighington/Washingborough LN4 81 E4
2 Helpringham NG34 133 D7
Hemingby LN9 72 B1
Horkstow DN18 10 A5
Keadby with Althorpe DN17 17 C6
3 Ketton PE9 171 A3
Kingston upon Hull HU1 181 A6
2 Leasingham NG34 121 B7
6 Legbourne LN11 61 F3
2 Legbourne LN11 62 A3
Lincoln LN1 234 A4
Little Hale NG34 133 E8
Ludborough DN36 48 E6
Ludford LN8 59 A8
Manby LN11 62 C6
6 Mareham Le Fen PE22 99 A4
Messingham DN17 29 D7
Minting LN9 84 C8
11 Misterton DN10 39 F5
Navenby/Wellingore LN5 107 A8
13 Nettleham LN2 68 C2
7 Newark-on-Trent NG24 104 D5
Newton PE13 170 B5
Normanby By Spital LN8 55 F7
North Cockerington LN11 49 F1
North Scarle LN6 78 E2
Northorpe PE10 164 C8
6 Peterborough PE4 221 A3
Peterborough PE2 229 F5
Scamblesby LN11 73 A5
10 Scawby DN20 30 E8
14 Sibsey PE22 113 B1
Snitterby DN21 43 D5
South Cockerington LN11 62 A8
Spalford NG23 78 D4
Springthorpe DN21 53 E8
Swallow LN7 34 B5
Tattershall Thorpe LN4 207 C8
Thimbleby LN9 85 B4
14 Thorne/Moorends DN8 15 A8
Toynton St Peter PE23 101 A6
4 Tydd St Giles PE13 169 F7
Utterby LN11 48 F4
Welton/Dunholme LN2 68 C6
Chapel La *continued*
West/East Butterwick DN17 17 D1
Whitton DN15 1 E3
16 Winterton DN15 9 A5
2 Winthorpe NG24 104 B7
Wrawby DN20 20 E4
2 Wymondham LE14 150 C1
Chapel Lodge Dr LN8 55 F7
Chapel Mews 3 HU15 2 C6
Chapel Nook La LN5 93 B1
Chapel Rd Branston LN4 81 E2
4 Broughton DN20 19 E3
Carrington PE22 112 B8
Fillingham DN21 54 F4
Fiskerton LN3 82 A7
4 Habrough DN40 22 E8
Ingoldmells PE25 90 D4
Leake Commonside PE22 113 F3
Sutton St Edmund PE12 168 E4
Terrington St Clement PE34 161 F3
Chapel Row
Baumber LN9 72 A1
7 Skillington NG33 151 A8
Chapel St 10 Alford LN13 75 F3
3 Amcotts DN17 7 F1
Beckingham LN5 105 B4
6 Billingborough NG34 133 B1
4 Boston PE21 208 F5
16 Bottesford NG13 128 A6
13 Caistor LN7 33 B4
4 Crowland PE6 175 B8
12 Crowle DN17 16 D8
6 Epworth DN9 27 E6
Goxhill DN19 12 A8
Haconby PE10 154 D8
2 Holbeach PE12 215 E2
1 Market Rasen LN8 57 D7
7 North Kelsey LN7 32 A4
Peterborough PE1 226 B2
18 Ruskington NG34 108 E2
Scunthorpe DN15 183 B3
Yaxley PE7 233 D5
Chapel St Leonards Prim Sch
Chapel St Leonards PE24 90 D6
Collingham NG23 91 D4
Chapel Way 6 DN20 196 D3
Chapel Yd 2 PE9 219 C5
Chapelgate PE12 159 D7
Chaplin Cl 22 LN4 95 D4
Chaplin St LN5 234 A1
Chapman Ave
6 Burgh le Marsh PE24 102 E7
Scunthorpe DN17 184 D6
Chapman Cres 4 DN36 36 D8
Chapman Gr 1 DN35 192 F5
Chapman Rd
Cleethorpes DN35 192 D7
2 Sleaford NG34 212 B6
Chapman St
Kingston upon Hull HU8 181 A8
3 Market Rasen LN8 57 E7
Chapnall Cl 18 PE13 170 E1
Chapnall Rd PE13 170 E1
Chappell Rd PE11 166 C6
Chapter Wk 12 DN20 19 E3
Chariots Way 6 PE6 164 E5
Charity St NG32 119 D4
Charles Ave
11 Ancaster NG32 120 A2
Grimsby DN33 191 D2
3 Laceby DN37 23 E1
Louth LN11 198 D7
12 New Waltham DN36 195 C6
18 Scotter DN21 29 C3
Charles Baines Prim Sch DN21 197 F4
Charles Cl
Bourne PE10 213 D6
1 Skegness PE25 206 B4
Charles Cope Rd PE2 229 F5
Charles Gate LN11 63 A8
Charles Lovell Way DN17 184 D8
Charles Rd
5 Fleet Hargate PE12 159 C7
9 Stamford PE9 219 A7
12 Sutton Bridge PE12 160 E4
Charles Read High Sch The NG33 152 F7
Charles St Boston PE21 209 A3
2 Cleethorpes DN35 192 F5
Gainsborough DN21 197 D5
3 Kingston upon Hull HU2 180 F7
Lincoln LN5 234 B1
Louth LN11 198 C6
Newark-on-Trent NG24 104 A4
Peterborough PE1 226 B3
1 Sleaford NG34 212 C4
Wrange PE22 114 C2
Charles St W LN1 201 D4
Charles Wright Cl 15 LN12 64 B4
Charlestown Way HU9 181 C6
Charlesworth St 2 LN1 201 D3
Charlette Way 13 PE11 214 B5
Charlock Dr PE9 218 D6
Charlotte Cl 4 LN8 57 E8
Charlotte St 5 HU1 181 A7
Charlotte Wlk 5 PE11 145 A8
Charlton St DN31 188 E1
Charnwood Cl PE2 231 A7
Charter Cl PE21 208 E7

Charterhouse Dr
DN16 . . . . .185 C4
Charterhouse La 1
HU2 . . . . .181 A7
Charter's La PE12 . . . . .216 A5
Charters The 2 PE9 . . .172 C6
Chase Hill Rd DN40 . . . .12 E5
Chase St PE13 . . . . . . .170 D1
Chase The
Boston PE21 . . . . .209 C3
Crowland PE6 . . . . .166 F1
Holbeach PE12 . . . . . . .215 C2
Long Sutton PE12 . . . . .216 C4
9 Metheringham LN4 . . .95 C4
Pinchbeck PE11 . . . . . .156 E8
Ropsley NG33 . . . . .131 A1
Weston PE12 . . . . .145 C4
Whaplode PE12 . . . . . . .147 A6
Wisbech PE13 . . . . .170 C1
Chasm & Northorpe Slipe
Nature Reserve The ★
PE10 . . . . .165 B8
Chater Rd 5 PE8 . . . . . .172 B1
Chatham St HU3 . . . . . .179 F7
Chatsfield PE4 . . . . .220 E6
Chatsworth Ave NG31 . .211 F5
Chatsworth Cl
4 Lincoln LN2 . . . . . . .202 C8
6 Market Deeping PE6 . .217 A5
Chatsworth Dr
4 Lincoln LN6 . . . . . . .204 E2
Louth LN11 . . . . .198 B7
Chatsworth Pl
Cleethorpes DN35 . . . . .192 C4
Peterborough PE3 . . . . .225 C2
Chatsworth Rd PE9 . . . .218 E6
Chatsworth St HU5 . . . .180 B8
Chatterton Ave LN1 . . . .201 C8
Chatterton Cres DN15 . .183 A5
Chaucer Ave
12 Mablethorpe/Sutton on Sea
LN12 . . . . .64 B4
Scunthorpe DN17 . . . . .184 D7
Chaucer Cl 1 PE13 . . . .170 B1
Chaucer Dr LN2 . . . . . . .202 C6
Chaucer Gdns 10 NG34 .212 F4
Chaucer Rd PE1 . . . . . . .225 E8
Chaucer's Way PE11 . . .214 A4
Chauntry Rd 19 LN13 . . .75 F2
Cheal La PE11 . . . . .144 F2
Cheal Rd PE11 . . . . .144 F4
Cheapside
Kingston upon Hull HU8 . .181 A8
Waltham DN37 . . . . . . .194 B4
Cheapside Rd DN36 . . . . .36 A4
Chedburgh Cl 1 LN6 . . .204 B6
Chedworth Cl 1 LN2 . . .202 D7
Chedworth Rd LN2 . . . . .202 D7
Cheese Hill 10 PE20 . . .135 B7
Cheesemans Cl 4
DN37 . . . . .194 E4
Cheesemans La DN37 . . .194 E4
Cheethams La LN4 . . . . .110 F2
Chelmer Cl LN6 . . . . . . .204 F4
Chelmer Garth 2 PE4 . .221 D1
Chelmsford Ave DN34 . .191 A5
Chelmsford Dr NG31 . . .210 F4
Chelmsford Pl 5 DN34 . .191 A6
Chelmsford St LN5 . . . . .234 B1
Chelsea Cl LN6 . . . . . . .200 D2
Chelsea Wlk DN35 . . . .193 A1
Cheltenham Cl
Peterborough PE1 . . . . .226 B6
Scunthorpe DN16 . . . . .185 C4
Cheltenham Way
Humberston DN35 . . . . .192 F1
7 Mablethorpe/Sutton on Sea
LN12 . . . . .64 A3
Chelveston Way PE3 . . .225 C4
Chelwood Dr 6 DN33 . .191 B3
Chelwood Rd DN17 . . . .184 F7
Chepstow Cl
1 Spalding PE11 . . . . .156 E3
7 Spalding PE11 . . . . .214 B1
Chepstow Gr DN34 . . . .191 A5
Chequergate 1 LN11 . . .198 B5
Chequers La DN22 . . . . .65 A2
Cheriton Cl 1 LN3 . . . . .83 B4
Cheriton Pk PE10 . . . . .213 D7
Cherry Ave LN4 . . . . . . .81 D2
Cherry Cl 8 NG34 . . . . .212 D6
Cherry Cnr PE22 . . . . . .113 A5
Cherry Cobb Sands Rd
HU12 . . . . .13 F8
Cherry Dale DN35 . . . . .192 D3
Cherry Garth HU3 . . . . .180 A5
Cherry Gr 10 Belton DN9 . .16 E1
Lincoln LN6 . . . . .205 A8
10 Market Deeping PE6 . .217 C5
Scunthorpe DN16 . . . . .185 B6
Cherry Holt 1 LN3 . . . .203 E5
Cherry Holt La
13 Pinchbeck PE11 . . . .156 E8
Sutterton PE20 . . . . . . .136 A4
Cherry Holt Rd PE10 . . .213 F4
Cherry La
Barrow upon Humber
DN19 . . . . .11 D8
7 Fleet PE12 . . . . . . .159 C7
Stubton NG23 . . . . .118 B7
Wootton DN39 . . . . .11 E2
Cherry Mount DN16 . . .185 C4
Cherry Orch
21 Epworth DN9 . . . . . .27 E6
Grantham NG31 . . . . . .211 D5
Cherry Orton Rd PE2 . . .229 F5
Cherry Rd 9 PE13 . . . . .170 D2

Cherry Tree Ave 3
DN20 . . . . .196 B4
Cherry Tree Cl 4 LN6 . .204 D3
Cherry Tree Cres
DN34 . . . . .190 F6
Cherry Tree Dr 5 DN7 . .14 D5
Cherry Tree Gr
2 Hatfield DN7 . . . . . . .14 D5
Spalding PE11 . . . . . . .214 F5
Cherry Tree La
Holbeach PE12 . . . . . . .215 D4
23 Nettleham LN2 . . . . .68 C2
Cherry Tree Rd DN21 . . .197 E5
Cherry Tree Way
3 Coningsby LN4 . . . . .207 D4
17 Metheringham LN4 . . .95 C4
Cherry Way 34 DN17 . . . .29 D7
Cherry Willingham Com Sch
LN3 . . . . .203 D3
Cherry Willingham Prim Sch
LN3 . . . . .203 D3
Cherry Wlk PE21 . . . . . .208 D4
Cherryfields PE21 . . . . .229 E6
Cherryholt La PE9 . . . . .219 D5
Cherryholt Rd PE9 . . . . .219 D5
Cherrytree Ave PE25 . . . .90 E4
Cherrytree Gr PE1 . . . . .226 C6
Cherrywood Dr NG31 . . .210 F6
Chesboule La PE11 . . . .144 E5
Chesham Dr 7 PE6 . . . .164 E4
Cheshire Gr 7 PE25 . . .206 A5
Cheshire La LN6 . . . . . .92 E5
Cheshire Rd LN6 . . . . . .204 B5
Chesney Dr DN16 . . . . .185 A3
Chesney Rd LN2 . . . . . .202 D7
Chesnut Cl 11 LN2 . . . . . .68 F2
Chesnut Dr 12 LN2 . . . . .68 F2
Chesnut Way 4 DN19 . . .12 A8
Chesswick Ave DN17 . . . .17 D5
Chester Cl LN4 . . . . . . .203 D1
Chester Gdns 8 NG31 . .210 D5
Chester Grange DN33 . .191 E4
Chester Pl DN32 . . . . . .192 C5
Chester Rd PE1 . . . . . . .226 C3
Chester Way PE21 . . . . .208 C3
Chesterfield Rd LN5 . . . .182 B2
Chesterton Gr PE2 . . . . .231 B3
Chestnut Ave
7 Donington PE11 . . . .134 E4
Edenham PE10 . . . . . . .153 C2
Gainsborough DN21 . . . .197 D6
Holbeach PE12 . . . . . . .215 C3
Immingham DN40 . . . . .186 E5
Kingston upon Hull
HU3 . . . . .178 E1
Peterborough PE1 . . . . .226 B7
RAF Cranwell NG34 . . . .107 D1
Spalding PE11 . . . . . . .214 E5
3 Stainforth DN7 . . . . . .14 D6
6 Thorne/Moorends DN8 .15 B7
Chestnut Cl
Bottesford NG13 . . . . . .128 B6
Glinton PE6 . . . . .220 B8
Horncastle LN9 . . . . . . .199 A5
4 Metheringham LN4 . . .95 C4
1 Peakirk PE6 . . . . . . .174 A5
13 Scotter DN21 . . . . . .29 C3
1 Sleaford NG34 . . . . .212 D3
Swaton NG34 . . . . .133 D4
13 Waltham DN37 . . . .194 C4
Chestnut Cres 3 LN5 . . .92 F3
Chestnut Dr
5 Coningsby LN4 . . . .207 D4
Louth LN11 . . . . .198 E6
38 Messingham DN17 . . .29 D7
3 Thorney PE6 . . . . . . .176 A3
Chestnut Gdns PE9 . . . .218 E6
Chestnut Gr
8 Broughton DN20 . . . . .19 E4
4 Colsterworth NG33 . .151 E3
1 Grantham NG31 . . . .210 D2
Waddington LN5 . . . . . .205 D1
Chestnut La NG33 . . . . .152 C8
Chestnut Rd
3 Boston PE21 . . . . . .209 C2
Lincoln LN6 . . . . .204 F2
Waltham DN37 . . . . . . .194 C4
Chestnut Rise 1 DN19 . . .11 C8
Chestnut St
Lincoln LN1 . . . . .234 A4
5 Ruskington NG34 . . .108 E1
Chestnut St CE Prim Sch
NG34 . . . . .108 F1
Chestnut Terr 2 PE12 . .160 E4
Chestnut Way
6 Binbrook LN8 . . . . . .47 C5
4 Bourne PE10 . . . . . .213 B6
3 Market Deeping PE6 . .217 A5
Scunthorpe DN16 . . . . .185 B8
Chestnut Wlk 5 DN41 . . .24 A5
Chestnuts The 7 LN2 . . .68 C2
Cheviot Ave PE4 . . . . . .221 C4
Cheviot Cl
Gonerby Hill Foot NG31 . .210 E7
Sleaford NG34 . . . . . . .212 A3
6 Thorne/Moorends DN8 . .15 A7
Cheviot St LN2 . . . . . . .234 C4
Chichester Cl 6 NG31 . .210 E5
Chichester Dr 20 LN7 . . .33 B4
Chichester Rd
6 Bracebridge Heath LN4 .81 A1
Cleethorpes DN35 . . . . .192 F4
Chieftain Way 1 LN6 . . .205 C8
Childers' N Dro
Cowbit PE12 . . . . .157 B5
Spalding PE11 . . . . . . .214 F3
Childers' S Dro
Cowbit PE12 . . . . .157 B4

Childers' S Dro *continued*
Pinchbeck PE11 . . . . . .214 F2
Childersgate La PE12 . . .159 D2
Childrens Highway 6
NG24 . . . . .104 C1
Chiltern Cl NG31 . . . . . .210 E7
Chiltern Cres DN17 . . . .184 D8
Chiltern Dr
Spalding PE11 . . . . . . .214 E6
Waltham DN37 . . . . . . .194 D3
Chiltern Prim Sch
HU3 . . . . .180 B5
Chiltern Rd 3 LN5 . . . . .205 D3
Chiltern Rise PE4 . . . . .221 B2
Chiltern Way
3 Grimsby DN33 . . . . .194 E8
24 North Hykeham LN6 . .93 C8
Chilton Cl 7 DN40 . . . . .186 B4
China St PE22 . . . . .114 C4
Chingford Ave DN34 . . .191 A4
Chippendale Cl
2 Birchwood LN6 . . . .204 D6
2 Humberston DN36 . . .36 C8
Chippendale Rd 3 LN6 .204 D6
Chippenham Mews 1
PE2 . . . . .230 C7
Chisenhale PE2 . . . . . . .229 E6
Chivenor Cl 3 LN6 . . . . .200 B1
Cholmley St HU3 . . . . . .180 B5
Chopdike Dro PE11 . . . .144 D3
Christ's Hospl Terr
LN2 . . . . .234 B3
Christchurch Rd 10
NG31 . . . . .211 D7
Christine Pl DN33 . . . . .195 A8
Christopher Cl
5 Heckington NG34 . . .122 E3
Louth LN11 . . . . .198 D7
Peterborough PE1 . . . . .225 F8
Christopher Cres 11
NG34 . . . . .212 F4
Christopher Dr 6 PE13 .170 C1
Christopher Rd 6 LN3 . . .75 E2
Christopher's La 4
PE10 . . . . .213 D6
Church Ave
Ashby De La Launde & Bloxholm
LN4 . . . . .108 B5
Humberston DN36 . . . . .36 C8
7 North Ferriby HU14 . . .3 A4
Church Balk DN8 . . . . . .15 B8
Church Bank 2 PE34 . . .161 F3
Church Cl 2 Bonby DN20 . .10 C2
Donington on Bain LN11 . .59 E2
Grimsby DN32 . . . . .192 B5
12 Louth LN11 . . . . . . .198 B5
16 Mablethorpe/Sutton on Sea
LN12 . . . . .77 A8
1 Newborough PE6 . . . .174 E4
11 Sibsey PE22 . . . . . .113 B1
11 Sleaford NG34 . . . . .212 B2
Stoke Rochford NG33 . . .139 F2
3 Thorne/Moorends DN8 . .15 B8
Wrangle PE22 . . . . .114 C1
Church Cres 4 DN9 . . . .28 A3
Church Ct 3 PE9 . . . . . .219 C5
Church Dr Lincoln LN6 . .201 D1
9 Misterton DN10 . . . . .39 F5
Norton Disney LN6 . . . . .92 C1
Peterborough PE2 . . . . .229 F4
Church End
Gedney PE12 . . . . .159 D7
9 Leverington PE13 . . .170 B2
Skegness PE25 . . . . . . .206 B8
Wrangle PE22 . . . . .114 C1
Church End Dro PE11 . .134 F1
Church Farm Cl 22 PE24 . .90 D7
Church Farm Mus ★
PE25 . . . . .206 B4
Church Fields
Pickworth NG34 . . . . . .142 A8
Winterton DN15 . . . . . . .9 A5
Church Gate
Fleet PE12 . . . . .159 B6
2 Market Deeping PE6 . .217 F4
Spalding PE11 . . . . . . .214 D3
22 Sutton Bridge PE12 . .160 F4
Whaplode PE12 . . . . . .158 B6
Church Gn DN21 . . . . . .216 C4
Church Gn Cl PE21 . . . .209 F2
Church Gn La
Frampton PE20 . . . . . . .136 B7
Quadring PE11 . . . . . . .135 A1
Church Gn Rd PE21 . . . .209 F4
Church Hill
Belvoir NG32 . . . . .138 C6
1 Burgh le Marsh PE24 . .102 E1
Castor PE5 . . . . .223 E2
2 Grasby DN38 . . . . . .32 E7
Heighington/Washingborough
LN4 . . . . .203 B2
Ingham LN1 . . . . .55 A2
Riby DN37 . . . . .23 C2
Spridlington LN8 . . . . . .55 F3
Whitton DN15 . . . . .1 E3
Church Hill Cl PE7 . . . . .231 C1
Church La
Addlethorpe PE24 . . . . . .90 D4
Algarkirk PE20 . . . . . . .136 B1
Alvingham LN11 . . . . . . .49 F2
9 Ancaster NG32 . . . . .120 A2
Appleby DN15 . . . . .9 D1
Aylesby DN37 . . . . .23 E2
7 Bardney LN3 . . . . . . .83 B4
Baumber LN9 . . . . .72 B1
Benniworth LN8 . . . . . . .71 E8
Besthorpe NG23 . . . . . .91 D7

Church La *continued*
4 Billinghay LN4 . . . . .109 F5
Blyton DN21 . . . . .41 C5
Bonby DN20 . . . . .10 C2
19 Boston PE21 . . . . . .208 F3
Bottesford NG13 . . . . . .128 C4
Bourne PE10 . . . . .213 D4
Brant Broughton LN5 . . .105 F5
Brigsley DN37 . . . . .35 C4
15 Brough HU15 . . . . . .2 C7
15 Broughton DN20 . . . .19 E3
Buckminster NG33 . . . . .150 F4
Burton Coggles NG33 . . .152 D8
Cadney DN20 . . . . .31 D6
6 Carlton-le-Moorland
LN5 . . . . .105 E8
3 Caythorpe NG32 . . . .119 B7
28 Chapel St Leonard PE24 . .90 D7
Cherry Willingham/Reepham
LN3 . . . . .203 E5
Clipsham LE15 . . . . . . .162 B2
Coleby LN5 . . . . .93 F3
6 Collingham NG23 . . .91 D5
Corringham DN21 . . . . .41 E2
Counthorpe & Creeton
NG33 . . . . .153 A2
Croft PE24 . . . . .102 E5
7 Crowland PE6 . . . . . .166 F1
3 Croxton Kerrial NG32 .138 D4
1 Donington PE11 . . . .134 F2
Eagle & Swinethorpe LN6 . .79 B2
East Keal PE23 . . . . . . .100 E6
Edenham PE10 . . . . . . .153 F4
Elkington LN11 . . . . . . .60 E7
Ewerby & Evedon NG34 . .122 C6
5 Fishlake DN7 . . . . . .14 D8
1 Folkingham NG34 . . .142 D8
Fotherby LN11 . . . . .49 A2
Friesthorpe LN3 . . . . . . .57 A2
Friskney PE22 . . . . .114 F6
Frithville PE22 . . . . .125 D8
5 Glentham LN8 . . . . . .43 F1
Goulceby LN11 . . . . .72 D6
Grainthorpe LN11 . . . . .50 B7
Great Gonerby NG31 . . .210 C8
Great Limber DN37 . . . .22 D3
Grimsby DN37 . . . . .190 E2
1 Hagworthingham PE23 . .87 A4
Harmston LN5 . . . . .93 F5
Haxey DN9 . . . . .27 C2
Heckington NG34 . . . . .122 E1
3 Helpringham NG34 . .133 D7
1 Helpston PE6 . . . . . .173 C4
Holton le Clay DN36 . . .195 D2
Horbling NG34 . . . . . . .133 B2
7 Horncastle LN9 . . . .199 B4
Hougham NG32 . . . . . . .118 C3
Humberston DN36 . . . . .36 D8
Huttoft LN13 . . . . .76 E3
Immingham DN40 . . . . .186 B5
3 Ingham LN1 . . . . . . .54 F7
2 Irby DN37 . . . . .34 D7
4 Keadby with Althorpe
DN17 . . . . .17 D4
Keddington LN11 . . . . . .198 E8
4 Keelby DN41 . . . . . . .23 A4
Kingston upon Hull
HU10 . . . . .178 C8
Kirkby La Thorpe NG34 . .121 F3
Kirton PE20 . . . . .136 C5
12 Laceby DN37 . . . . . .23 F1
2 Legbourne LN11 . . . .61 F3
Lincoln LN2 . . . . .234 B4
3 Little Bytham NG33 . .163 A8
Londonthorpe &
Harrowby without NG31 . .130 D5
Long Bennington NG23 . .117 E2
Luddington & Haldenby
DN17 . . . . .7 D4
Lutton PE12 . . . . .160 A8
14 Mablethorpe/Sutton on Sea
LN12 . . . . .77 A8
3 Mareham Le Fen PE22 . .98 F4
Marshchapel DN36 . . . . .37 B1
17 Metheringham LN4 . .95 D4
Minting LN9 . . . . .84 C8
6 Misterton DN10 . . . . .39 F5
Misterton LN13 . . . . . . .89 B6
Moulton PE12 . . . . .157 F7
Navenby LN5 . . . . .107 A8
Newton NG34 . . . . .170 A5
North Carlton LN1 . . . . .67 C4
10 North Kelsey LN7 . . .32 A4
North Kyme LN4 . . . . . .109 F3
North Rauceby NG32 . . .120 C5
North Scarle LN6 . . . . . .78 E1
North Somercotes LN11 . .50 E6
Old Somerby NG33 . . . .140 E8
5 Owmby LN8 . . . . . . .55 F6
Peterborough PE2 . . . . .229 F5
Pickworth NG34 . . . . . .132 A1
6 Potterhanworth LN4 . .82 B1
Rand LN8 . . . . .70 A5
Ropsley & Humby NG33 . .131 B1
Roughton LN9 . . . . .85 B1
Saltfleetby LN12 . . . . . .63 B7
Saxby All Saints DN20 . . .10 B3
Saxby DN21 . . . . .42 F7
Saxilby with Ingleby LN1 . .66 C3
Scamblesby LN11 . . . . .72 F5
Scawby DN20 . . . . .20 A1
Scopwick LN4 . . . . .108 B8
9 Scotter DN21 . . . . . .29 C3
Scotton DN21 . . . . .29 D2
Scredington NG34 . . . . .132 F7
Scunthorpe DN15 . . . . .182 E2
Sedgebrook NG32 . . . . .128 F4

Church La *continued*
Silk Willoughby NG34 . . .121 B1
Skegness PE25 . . . . . . .206 B8
Skidbrooke with Saltfleet Haven
LN11 . . . . .51 B4
Sleaford NG34 . . . . . . .212 D5
Snitterby DN21 . . . . . . .43 D5
South Clifton NG23 . . . .78 C6
South Kyme LN4 . . . . . .123 A8
15 South Witham NG33 . .151 D2
Spilsby PE23 . . . . .87 E1
Springthorpe DN21 . . . .53 E8
Sproxton LE14 . . . . . . .150 C7
Stallingborough DN41 . . .23 D6
2 Stamford PE9 . . . . . .219 C4
Sudbrooke LN2 . . . . . . .68 F3
Swaby LN13 . . . . .74 E3
13 Swineshead PE20 . .135 B7
Tallington PE9 . . . . .172 F6
Tealby LN8 . . . . .46 C1
Tetford LN9 . . . . .73 F1
Tetney DN36 . . . . .36 D3
3 Timberland LN4 . . . . .96 C1
Toynton St Peter PE23 . .101 A6
Twin Rivers DN14 . . . . .7 A8
Tydd St Giles PE13 . . . .169 F7
Tydd St Mary PE13 . . . .160 B1
2 Ulceby DN39 . . . . . .12 A1
Utterby LN11 . . . . .48 F3
21 Waddington LN5 . . . .93 F7
Wainfleet St Mary PE24 . .102 B1
Waithe DN36 . . . . .36 A3
Waltham DN37 . . . . . . .194 E4
Wansford PE8 . . . . .222 D1
Welby NG32 . . . . .130 F3
2 Welton/Dunholme LN2 . .68 D6
West Keal PE23 . . . . . . .100 C6
3 Westborough & Dry
Doddington NG23 . . . .117 F3
Withern with Stain LN13 . .62 F1
Wood Enderby LN9 . . . . .98 F1
Wrangle PE22 . . . . .114 C1
Wyberton PE21 . . . . . . .136 F8
3 Wymondham LE14 . . .150 C1
Church La Prim Sch
NG34 . . . . .212 D5
Church Lees NG32 . . . . .131 C6
Church Mdw Dr 20 PE24 . .90 D7
Church Mews 7 PE20 . .136 A2
Church Pk 17 LN12 . . . . .77 A8
Church Rd
Auburn Haddington &
South Hykeham LN5 . . .93 A5
4 Bicker PE20 . . . . . . .135 A4
Boston PE21 . . . . .209 B4
4 Butterwick PE22 . . . .126 E3
Freiston PE22 . . . . .126 D2
Friskney PE22 . . . . .115 A6
Harby NG23 . . . . .79 B5
4 Ketton PE9 . . . . .171 A3
Laughton DN21 . . . . . . .41 C8
Leverington PE13 . . . . .170 C1
3 Mablethorpe/Sutton on Sea
LN12 . . . . .64 A3
North Ferriby HU14 . . . .3 A4
Old Leake PE22 . . . . . . .114 A1
Saxilby LN1 . . . . .66 C2
Skellingthorpe LN6 . . . .200 A4
Stainforth DN7 . . . . . . .14 C6
Stickford PE22 . . . . . . .100 B3
1 Stow LN1 . . . . .66 C8
Ulceby with Fordington
LN13 . . . . .88 C7
Upton DN21 . . . . .53 D5
Waddingham DN21 . . . .43 D7
Wigtoft PE20 . . . . .135 E3
Wisbech PE13 . . . . .170 B1
Wittering PE8 . . . . .172 B1
Church Rd N PE25 . . . . .206 B4
Church Rd S 4 PE25 . . .206 B3
Church Rise 5 PE22 . . . .98 F1
Church Row HU8 . . . . . .181 A8
Church Side
3 Alkborough DN15 . . . .8 C8
3 Appleby DN15 . . . . . .9 D1
19 Goxhill DN19 . . . . . .12 E8
3 Grasby DN38 . . . . . .32 E7
3 West Halton DN15 . . .8 E7
14 Winterton DN15 . . . .9 A5
Church Sq DN15 . . . . . .183 E8
Church St 4 Alford LN13 . .75 F3
Amcotts DN17 . . . . .7 F1
Barkston NG32 . . . . . . .130 B8
2 Barrowby NG32 . . . .210 A5
2 Baston PE6 . . . . . . .164 E4
Beckingham DN10 . . . . .40 A1
4 Billingborough NG34 .133 B1
2 Billinghay LN4 . . . . .109 F5
20 Boston PE21 . . . . . .208 F5
Bottesford NG13 . . . . . .128 A5
9 Brough HU15 . . . . . .2 D6
2 Brough HU15 . . . . . .2 C7
5 Burgh le Marsh PE24 .102 E8
14 Caistor LN7 . . . . . . .33 B4
Carlby PE9 . . . . .163 D5
4 Carlton-le-Moorland
LN5 . . . . .105 E8
Collingham NG23 . . . . .91 C4
Corby Glen NG33 . . . . .152 E8
2 Crowle DN17 . . . . . .16 D7
Denton NG32 . . . . .139 A7
Digby LN4 . . . . .108 D5
3 Donington PE11 . . . .134 E2
Easton on the Hill PE9 . .171 D3
Elsham DN20 . . . . .20 F7

Church St *continued*
1 Epworth DN9 .....27 E6
6 Fishlake DN7 .....14 D8
1 Foston NG32 .....117 F1
3 Fulletby LN9 .....86 B8
Gainsborough DN21 .....197 C5
Glentworth DN21 .....54 F6
4 Gosberton PE11 .....145 B6
16 Goxhill DN19 .....12 A8
Grantham NG31 .....211 A5
4 Grimsby DN32 .....189 B1
1 Haconby PE10 .....154 D8
5 Harlaxton NG32 .....139 C7
Haxey DN9 .....27 C2
6 Heckington NG34 .....122 E3
Heckington NG34 .....122 E1
Hemswell DN21 .....42 D1
7 Hibaldstow DN20 .....30 F5
Holbeach PE12 .....215 D2
Kingston upon Hull HU10 .....178 E6
7 Kirton in Lindsey DN21 .....30 B1
Long Bennington NG23 .....117 D3
Louth LN11 .....198 C5
Market Deeping PE6 .....217 B5
6 Market Rasen LN8 .....57 D8
Messingham DN17 .....29 D7
7 Middle Rasen LN8 .....57 B8
Misterton DN10 .....39 F5
20 Nettleham LN2 .....68 C2
Nettleton LN7 .....33 B3
12 North Kelsey LN7 .....32 A4
North Witham NG33 .....151 D4
Northborough PE6 .....173 F6
Owston Ferry DN9 .....28 A3
Peterborough PE4 .....220 F3
Peterborough PE7 .....229 A4
Peterborough PE2 .....231 C7
Pinchbeck PE11 .....145 C1
17 Ruskington NG34 .....108 E2
7 Ryhall PE9 .....163 C1
9 Scawby DN20 .....30 E8
10 Scothern LN2 .....68 F4
Skillington NG33 .....151 A8
10 South Witham NG33 .....151 D2
Spalding PE11 .....214 D4
11 Spilsby PE23 .....87 F1
9 Spilsby PE23 .....88 A1
8 Stamford PE9 .....219 C4
Sturton Le Steeple DN22 .....52 B2
21 Sutton Bridge PE12 .....160 E4
1 Sutton on Trent NG23 .....91 A8
Sutton-on-Trent NG23 .....78 A1
26 Thorne/Moorends DN8 .....15 A8
9 Thorney PE6 .....176 A3
Thurlby PE10 .....164 D7
Willoughton DN21 .....42 E4
1 Wragby LN8 .....70 D4
Yaxley PE7 .....233 D4
Church View
2 Alkborough DN15 .....8 C8
11 Barton-upon-Humber DN18 .....10 F8
1 Beckingham DN10 .....40 A1
13 Bottesford NG13 .....128 A6
9 Brough HU15 .....2 C7
Freiston PE22 .....126 D2
3 Gainsborough DN21 .....53 A5
8 Great Gonerby NG31 .....129 D5
Great Gonerby NG31 .....210 D8
Grimsby DN34 .....190 E7
Northborough PE6 .....217 E1
10 Ruskington NG34 .....108 E2
2 Waltham DN37 .....194 E4
Church View Cl
3 Belton DN9 .....16 E1
1 Donington PE11 .....134 E2
Peterborough PE2 .....231 B7
Church View Cres LN3 .....82 B7
Church Way PE13 .....160 A1
Church Wlk
Brant Broughton & Stragglethorpe LN5 .....105 F4
1 Dunham-on-Trent NG22 .....65 B1
2 Holbeach PE12 .....215 D2
3 Holton le Clay DN36 .....195 D2
1 Legbourne LN11 .....61 F3
1 Manby LN11 .....62 C6
21 Metheringham LN4 .....95 D4
27 Metheringham LN4 .....95 C4
1 Owston Ferry DN9 .....28 A3
Peterborough PE1 .....226 A3
2 Pinchbeck PE11 .....156 F8
Sibsey PE22 .....113 B2
Upton PE6 .....223 B5
Churchfield Ct PE4 .....225 E8
Churchfield Rd
Peterborough PE4 .....221 B1
Scunthorpe DN16 .....185 B5
Churchfields Rd NG34 .....142 C8
Churchfleet La PE11 .....145 B7
Churchgate PE12 .....159 D7
Churchgate Mews 5 PE12 .....159 D7
Churchill Ave
Bourne PE10 .....213 B4
Bracebridge Heath LN4 .....205 F4
Brigg DN20 .....196 D4
2 Hatfield DN7 .....14 F4
1 Horncastle LN9 .....199 C2
4 Keelby DN41 .....23 A5
4 Market Rasen LN8 .....57 D7
2 Skegness PE25 .....206 D7
Churchill Cl 6 LN11 .....50 F7
Churchill Ct 2 PE12 .....216 B5
Churchill Dr
3 Boston PE21 .....209 D4
2 Martin LN10 .....97 B4
Spalding PE11 .....214 D2
Churchill La LN12 .....63 E8
Churchill Rd
Gorefield PE13 .....169 F3
North Somercotes LN11 .....50 F7
Stamford PE9 .....219 B7
Churchill St HU9 .....181 D7
Churchill Way
Grimsby DN32 .....191 F7
Heckington NG34 .....122 D3
5 Lea DN21 .....52 F6
Churchthorpe 1 LN11 .....49 B8
Churchtown 9 DN9 .....16 E1
Churchview Cl 5 NG34 .....122 D3
Churchway PE22 .....127 A5
Chuter Ede Prim Sch NG24 .....104 C2
Cinder La LN11 .....198 B5
Circle The 4 HU13 .....178 E2
Cissbury Cl 12 LN12 .....77 A8
Cissbury Ring PE4 .....221 A2
Cissplatt La DN41 .....23 A5
Cisterngate 3 LN11 .....198 B6
Citadel Way HU9 .....181 A6
City of Lincoln Com Coll The LN6 .....205 A8
City Rd PE1 .....226 A2
City Sports Ctr LN6 .....205 A8
Clampgate Rd PE21 .....126 C1
Clapton Gate PE12 .....157 E5
Clare Ave DN17 .....184 D7
Clare Cl 11 Lincoln LN5 .....205 D3
7 Stamford PE9 .....219 A5
Clare Ct 4 Baston PE6 .....164 E4
Grimsby DN34 .....191 A5
Clare Rd
Northborough PE6 .....217 E1
Peterborough PE1 .....225 F6
Claremont Rd
1 Burgh le Marsh PE24 .....102 E8
Gainsborough DN21 .....197 E2
Grimsby DN32 .....192 D6
Claremont St LN2 .....234 C2
Clarence Cl 2 DN40 .....186 B3
Clarence Gdns 3 PE11 .....214 E2
Clarence Rd
Peterborough PE1 .....225 E5
28 Wisbech PE13 .....170 D1
3 Woodhall Spa LN10 .....97 D6
Clarence St
Kingston upon Hull HU1 .....181 A6
1 Lincoln LN1 .....201 E6
Clarendon Gdns 1 LN1 .....201 E8
Clarendon Rd
Grimsby DN34 .....190 E4
Scunthorpe DN17 .....184 F7
Skegness PE25 .....206 A4
Clarendon St HU3 .....180 D7
Clarendon Way PE6 .....220 D8
Clarina St LN2 .....202 B4
Clark Ave DN31 .....191 A7
Clarke Ct 10 PE21 .....136 D8
Clarke Rd 11 Lincoln LN6 .....93 C8
Lincoln LN6 .....204 E4
Clarke St 2 DN15 .....183 A3
Clarkes Rd 3 DN40 .....12 E4
Clarkson Ave 1 PE12 .....167 B8
Clarkson Ct 27 PE13 .....170 D1
Clarkson Infants Sch The PE13 .....170 E1
Clarksons Dr 3 DN41 .....23 E6
Clasketgate LN2 .....234 B2
Clatterdykes Rd PE20 .....136 E6
Claudette Ave PE11 .....214 B5
Claudette Way 5 PE11 .....214 B5
Clavering St 6 DN31 .....188 D1
Claxby Rd DN17 .....184 F5
Claxy Bank PE22 .....114 D6
Clay Bank LN4 .....123 C7
Clay Bank Rd DN8 .....15 C6
Clay Dro PE11 .....156 C5
Clay Hill Rd NG34 .....212 A3
Clay La
Carlton-le-Moorland LN5 .....105 D8
Castor PE5 .....223 E2
Fenton LN1 .....65 E4
Gate Burton DN21 .....53 B1
Harby NG23 .....79 C5
Holton le Clay DN36 .....195 D3
Kirton in Lindsey DN21 .....30 A1
Newark NG24 .....104 B4
Norton Disney LN5 .....92 D2
Stapleford LN6 .....105 B7
Tetford LN9 .....73 F2
Toft Newton LN8 .....56 C7
Waddingham DN21 .....43 D7
Clay Lake Bank PE12 .....157 A3
Clay Lake La PE11 .....214 E2
Clay Pit La NG34 .....122 C6
Clayberg Dr 2 NG34 .....212 D5
Clayden St 4 DN31 .....188 D1
Claydike Bank PE20 .....124 B4
Clayfield Rd DN15 .....182 F6
Clayhough La DN22 .....65 B3
Claymore Cl DN35 .....192 E6
Claypole CE (Controlled) Prim Sch NG23 .....117 F8
Claypole Dr PE6 .....217 E1
Claypole La NG23 .....117 E6
Claypole Rd NG23 .....118 A7
Claythorne Dr DN21 .....197 E4
Claythorpe Water Mill★ LN13 .....75 B5
Clayton Cl 16 PE13 .....170 E1
Clayton Cres PE12 .....157 C2
Clayton Rd LN5 .....205 E6
Clayton Sch PE2 .....230 B4
Clayworth Rd 6 DN10 .....39 C1
Cleatham PE3 .....225 A4
Cleatham Rd DN21 .....30 B3
Clee Cres DN32 .....192 C5
Clee Ness Dr DN36 .....193 A1
Clee Rd DN35 .....192 C5
Clee Village DN32 .....192 C6
Cleefields Cl DN32 .....192 B5
Cleethorpe Rd DN31 .....189 B1
Cleethorpes Coast Light Rly & Mus★ DN35 .....193 B3
Cleethorpes Ctry Pk★ DN35 .....192 F2
Cleethorpes Discovery Ctr★ DN35 .....193 B3
Cleethorpes Showground★ DN35 .....193 C3
Cleethorpes Sta DN35 .....192 F7
Clematis App LN6 .....204 C8
Clematis Ave 7 DN41 .....23 F5
Clematis Cl LN4 .....81 D2
Clematis Way DN16 .....185 C4
Clensey La NG23 .....117 F5
Clerke St DN35 .....192 B8
Cleve Pl 3 PE6 .....175 A1
Clevedon Rd DN17 .....184 D8
Cleveland Ave 26 LN6 .....93 C8
Cleveland Cl
2 Immingham DN40 .....186 A4
2 Scunthorpe DN17 .....184 D8
4 Spalding PE11 .....214 F4
Cleveland Ct 3 PE4 .....221 C2
Cleveland Gdns 2 DN31 .....188 D1
Cleveland St
2 Gainsborough DN21 .....197 D3
3 Grimsby DN31 .....188 D1
Kingston upon Hull HU8 .....181 A8
Cleveland Way 27 DN7 .....14 D4
Cley Hall Gdns PE11 .....214 E4
Cleymond Chase 2 PE20 .....136 C5
Cliff Ave 22 Nettleham LN2 .....68 C2
Winterton DN15 .....8 F5
Cliff Closes Rd DN15 .....182 D3
Cliff Cres 1 PE9 .....219 B5
Cliff Dr
Burton upon Stather DN15 .....8 B5
3 Kingston upon Hull HU13 .....3 E4
Cliff Gdns DN15 .....182 F2
Cliff Gr 9 DN18 .....10 E8
Cliff La Marston NG32 .....129 D8
Waddingham DN21 .....43 C6
Washingborough LN4 .....81 D4
Cliff Rd Fulbeck NG32 .....119 C8
Hessle HU13 .....3 E4
Leadenham LN5 .....106 D2
Snitterby DN21 .....43 C5
Spridlington LN8 .....55 F3
Stamford PE9 .....219 B5
Welbourn LN5 .....106 E4
Welton LN2 .....68 C6
Winteringham DN15 .....9 A8
Woolsthorpe By Belvoir NG32 .....128 D1
Cliff St DN16 .....183 C2
Cliff The DN15 .....182 D3
Cliff Top La 2 HU13 .....3 E4
Cliffe Ave 1 NG34 .....108 D1
Cliffe Cl 19 NG34 .....108 D2
Cliffe Rd
Easton on the Hill PE9 .....171 D2
Gonerby Hill Foot NG31 .....210 E7
Cliffe View NG34 .....120 E4
Cliffedale Prim Sch NG31 .....211 A8
Clifford Rd PE25 .....206 B4
Cliffside 3 LN5 .....107 A7
Clifton Ave PE3 .....225 E3
Clifton Ct 2 DN8 .....15 A8
Clifton Gr 3 PE25 .....206 D1
Clifton Prim Sch HU2 .....180 E8
Clifton Rd Boston PE21 .....209 E4
Grimsby DN34 .....191 A6
Clifton St LN5 .....234 B1
Clint La 9 LN5 .....107 A8
Clinton Dr NG34 .....212 C2
Clinton Pk Prim Sch LN4 .....207 A5
Clinton Terr 3 DN21 .....197 D3
Clinton Way LN10 .....97 B5
Clipseygap La PE10 .....154 B6
Clipsham Rd PE9 .....162 D8
Clive Ave LN6 .....205 C8
Clive Sullivan Way
Barton-upon-Humber DN19 .....4 A4
Kingston upon Hull HU4 .....179 C1
Clixby Cl DN35 .....193 A3
Clixby La DN38 .....32 E7
Cloddy Gate LN11 .....50 F5
Cloister Wk 14 DN20 .....19 E3
Cloisters The
Grimsby DN37 .....190 D7
17 Humberston DN36 .....36 D8
Cloot Dro PE6 .....166 F2
Close The
Barkston NG32 .....130 A8
1 Colsterworth NG33 .....151 D7
Easton on the Hill PE9 .....171 C3
2 Fiskerton LN3 .....82 A7
2 Goxhill DN19 .....5 A1
Grimsby DN34 .....191 C7
8 Scunthorpe DN16 .....183 B2
4 Skegness PE22 .....206 C4
5 Sturton by Stow LN1 .....66 D7
Close The *continued*
1 Woodhall Spa LN10 .....97 C6
Closshill La PE21 .....136 F8
Clouds La Belton DN9 .....17 B1
West Butterwick DN17 .....28 C8
Clough La Firsby PE23 .....101 F5
Kirton PE20 .....136 F2
Clough Rd
Gosberton PE11 .....144 D4
Holbeach PE12 .....215 B7
Cloven Ends 4 PE6 .....164 F3
Clover Gdns 6 PE9 .....218 C7
Clover La PE20 .....135 D4
Clover Rd
Market Deeping PE6 .....217 C5
Misterton LN13 .....89 A6
Clover Way PE11 .....214 B6
Cloverfields Prim Sch DN36 .....36 C8
Clowes Ct 4 HU13 .....178 E1
Clubhurn La PE11 .....145 D4
Clumber Ave NG24 .....104 A3
Clumber Dr 7 PE11 .....214 C6
Clumber Pl DN35 .....192 E5
Clumber St
Kingston upon Hull HU5 .....180 C8
Lincoln LN5 .....205 E7
Clutton's Cl 4 PE6 .....166 E1
Clyde Ct 1 NG31 .....210 E2
Clyde St HU3 .....179 F5
Clydesdale Cres 1 PE11 .....214 A2
Clyfton Cres DN40 .....186 B4
Coach House Gdns 8 DN20 .....30 E8
Coach Rd NG32 .....118 C3
Coachroad Hill DN21 .....54 F7
Coal Shore La LN11 .....37 D1
Coal Yd La NG23 .....78 C4
Coalbeach La 1 PE11 .....145 E3
Coalbeach La S PE11 .....145 E4
Coalport Cl 1 LN6 .....204 D7
Coates Ave 27 DN15 .....9 A5
Coates Rd DN22 .....65 B8
Cob Gate PE12 .....158 A6
Cobbet Pl PE1 .....226 B3
Cobblers Way 6 NG34 .....212 E3
Cobden Ave PE1 .....225 F4
Cobden St
1 Gainsborough DN21 .....197 C4
Kingston upon Hull HU3 .....179 F7
Peterborough PE1 .....225 F4
Cobgate Cl 2 PE12 .....158 B6
Cobham Cl 11 NG34 .....122 E3
Cobleas NG32 .....138 D8
Cochran Cl 9 NG31 .....210 F8
Cock Pit Cl HU10 .....178 C6
Cockbourn Fen Dike PE12 .....159 B2
Cockburn Way 6 LN5 .....93 F5
Cockerels Roost LN1 .....65 D1
Cocketts La 10 DN20 .....30 F5
Cocklehole Rd PE34 .....161 B5
Cockthorne La DN15 .....9 C7
Coddington CE Sch NG24 .....104 D5
Coddington La LN6 .....105 A7
Coddington Rd NG24 .....104 C3
Coelus St HU9 .....181 A7
Cogan St HU1 .....180 E5
Coggles Cswy PE10 .....213 D4
Coggles Way LN11 .....61 E3
Cogglesford Mill★ NG34 .....212 F5
Cohort Cl 18 HU15 .....2 C5
Coke Oven Ave DN16 .....183 F2
Cold Harbour La
Carrington PE22 .....112 B6
Covenham St Mary LN11 .....49 D5
Grantham NG31 .....211 C2
Cold Hurn La PE11 .....144 F6
Coldham Rd LN4 .....207 E6
Coldhorn Cres 14 PE13 .....170 D1
Cole La PE22 .....100 B3
Cole St DN15 .....183 B3
Coleby CE Prim Sch LN5 .....93 F3
Coleby Rd DN15 .....8 E7
Coleby St LN2 .....202 B3
Colegrave St 14 LN5 .....205 E8
Colenso Terr 3 LN1 .....201 D4
Coleraine Cl 8 LN5 .....205 D2
Coleridge Ave DN17 .....184 D7
Coleridge Ct 5 LN4 .....207 B5
Coleridge Gdns
Lincoln LN2 .....202 B7
15 Sleaford NG34 .....212 F4
Coleridge Gn 3 LN2 .....202 C7
Coleridge Pl
Bourne PE10 .....213 E3
Peterborough PE1 .....225 E8
Coles Ave LN13 .....75 E2
Coles Cl PE12 .....215 E3
Cole's La 1 PE20 .....135 B7
Colin Ave DN32 .....192 B6
Colin Rd DN16 .....183 C2
Colindale PE21 .....209 B5
Colins Wlk DN21 .....29 C4
College Ave DN33 .....194 F8
College Cl
6 Alkborough DN15 .....8 C8
1 Holbeach PE12 .....215 C2
4 Horncastle LN9 .....199 C2
Lincoln LN1 .....201 F6
Stamford PE9 .....171 C8
7 Wainfleet All Saints PE24 .....102 D1
College Gdns 2 DN33 .....194 F8
College Pk
Horncastle LN9 .....199 C2
Peterborough PE1 .....226 C5
College Rd
Barrow upon Humber DN19 .....11 E7
Cranwell & Byard's Leap NG34 .....120 E8
Thornton Curtis DN39 .....12 B6
College St
Cleethorpes DN35 .....192 E6
Grantham NG31 .....211 B3
Grimsby DN34 .....191 C6
1 Kingston upon Hull HU2 .....180 E7
Colley St 11 PE21 .....208 F5
Colley's Gate PE12 .....216 C8
Colleywell Cl 5 DN9 .....27 A2
Collier Cl 11 HU14 .....3 A4
Collier Rd 2 DN40 .....186 D5
Collier St HU1 .....180 E6
Collingham PE2 .....229 F3
Collingham Rd LN6 .....91 F5
Collingham Sta NG23 .....91 D4
Collingwood 21 LN6 .....93 C8
Collingwood Cres
3 Boston PE21 .....136 D8
Grimsby DN34 .....190 D4
Collingwood Prim Sch HU3 .....180 C7
Collingwood St HU3 .....180 D7
Collinson Ave DN15 .....182 C3
Collinson La
11 Balderton NG24 .....104 C1
Newport HU15 .....1 A8
Collison Gate PE24 .....102 C2
Collum Ave DN16 .....185 B6
Collum Gdns 2 DN16 .....185 B6
Collum La DN16 .....185 B6
Collynson Cl 1 HU10 .....178 E8
Collyweston Rd 1 PE8 .....172 B1
Colne Cl 11 LN6 .....204 F3
Colne Ct 6 NG31 .....210 E2
Colne Valley Visitor Ctr★ PE6 .....227 B2
Colonial St HU2 .....180 D7
Colson Pl DN35 .....192 B7
Colster Way 3 NG33 .....151 E6
Colsterworth CE Prim Sch NG33 .....151 E7
Colsterworth Rd NG33 .....151 C6
Colsuan Gdns PE12 .....216 C3
Coltman St HU3 .....180 C5
Colton Cl 6 PE6 .....164 E4
Colton St Brigg DN20 .....196 B4
2 Misterton DN10 .....39 F5
Coltsfoot Cl 6 DN15 .....182 C6
Coltsfoot Dr
Bradley DN37 .....194 B5
Peterborough PE2 .....230 E7
Columbia Rd DN32 .....192 A7
Columbus Cl 5 PE11 .....214 C2
Columbus Way DN33 .....190 F3
Colvile Rd PE13 .....170 A5
Colville Ave HU4 .....179 B6
Colville Terr 3 DN21 .....197 D4
Combe St DN35 .....192 C8
Comer Cl PE21 .....209 A5
Comforts Ave DN15 .....183 A2
Commerce La HU1 .....180 D4
Commercial Rd
2 Alford LN13 .....75 F2
Grantham NG31 .....211 A3
Kingston upon Hull HU1 .....180 E5
1 Louth LN11 .....198 D6
Scunthorpe DN16 .....183 D3
Spalding PE11 .....214 E5
Commodore Croft 6 HU1 .....180 F5
Common Balk LN13 .....76 C1
Common Dro
Crowland PE6 .....166 C3
Wrangle PE22 .....114 B5
Common La
7 Balderton NG24 .....104 C1
Bardney LN3 .....83 C4
Barnby Dun with Kirk Sandall DN3 .....14 B4
Burgh Le Marsh PE24 .....89 F1
Heapham DN21 .....53 F7
North Somercotes LN11 .....50 F8
Old Leake PE22 .....113 F4
Sturton Le Steeple DN22 .....52 C3
Twin Rivers DN14 .....7 B6
Welton HU15 .....2 D4
Common Mid Rd DN17 .....16 C8
Common Rd
Broughton DN20 .....19 E4
Gedney Hill PE12 .....176 F8
Moulton PE12 .....146 E3
Parson Drove PE12 .....176 F6
South Cave HU15 .....1 C7
Waddingham DN21 .....43 D7
Whaplode PE12 .....168 A2
Wrangle PE22 .....114 B3
Common Side Rd PE22 .....113 E4
Common Way PE13 .....160 B1
Commonside
2 Crowle DN17 .....16 C8
Westwoodside DN9 .....27 A2
Comper Swift Cl 1 LN12 .....77 A7
Compton Cl 1 PE25 .....206 C1
Compton Dr DN34 .....191 C7
Concast Rd DN16 .....19 A3
Conduit La NG31 .....211 A4
Conduit Rd PE9 .....219 C6

Coney Garth La PE11 ..145 F5
Coneygree Rd PE2 ....231 D6
Conference Ct DN16 ...185 A2
Conging St ⬛ LN9 ....199 B4
Congreves Cl ⬛ PE12 .160 A8
Conifer Cl
 ⬛ Kingston upon Hull
 HU5 ....179 C7
 ⬛ Scunthorpe DN17 ...184 C5
Conifers The PE2 .....229 F6
Coningsby Airfield
 LN4 ....207 C2
Coningsby Cl
 Boston PE21 ....208 D5
 ⬛ Skegness PE25 ....206 A5
Coningsby Cres LN4 ..205 F5
Coningsby Dr DN34 ...191 A5
Coningsby Rd
 Coningsby LN4 ......207 A1
 Peterborough PE3 ....220 E1
 Scunthorpe DN17 ....184 D5
Coningsby St LN2 ....234 C2
Coningsby St Michaels CE
 Prim Sch LN4 ......207 C4
Conisborough Ave
 DN36 ....195 B6
Conisholme Rd LN11 ..50 B7
Coniston Ave ⬛ DN33 .194 E7
Coniston Cres DN36 ..192 E1
Coniston Dr LN6 .....205 A2
Coniston Rd PE4 .....221 C3
Connaught Ave DN32 .191 D4
Connaught Dr
 ⬛ Chapel St Leonard PE24 .90 D7
 ⬛ Kirk Sandall DN3 ...14 C4
Connaught Rd DN21 ..197 C6
Conquest Dro PE7 ....231 D1
Consort Ct HU9 ......181 B5
Constable Ave LN6 ...205 A6
Constable Cl LN6 ....205 A5
Constable Prim Sch
 HU3 ....180 C5
Constable St HU3 ....180 C5
Constance Ave LN6 ...204 F4
Constitutional Ave
 DN35 ....192 C8
Convamore Rd DN32 ..191 F6
Convent La HU3 .....180 D6
Conway Ave
 Grimsby DN34 ......191 A7
 Peterborough PE4 ....221 A2
Conway Cl HU3 ......180 B5
Conway Dr LN6 ......205 B2
Conway Prep Sch
 PE21 ....208 F5
Conway Sq ⬛ DN15 ..182 E3
Conyard Rd DN35 ....192 E7
Conyers Ave DN33 ...191 D2
Cook Cl Rd PE7 .....233 D6
Cook Dr PE11 ....214 C2
Cooke Cres ⬛ LN4 ...207 D4
Cookridge Dr ⬛ DN7 ..14 D4
Cook's La PE23 ......88 E3
Cook's Rd PE11 .....145 E7
Cooks La Grimsby DN37 .24 B5
 ⬛ Nettleton LN7 .....33 A3
Cooks Lock PE21 .....208 C3
Cookson Cl PE7 .....233 D4
Coomb Brigg Prim Sch
 DN40 ....186 A3
Cooper Ave PE25 .....90 E4
Cooper La DN37 .....23 E1
Cooper Rd DN32 .....192 A7
Coopers Cl HU3 .....168 B4
Coopers Holt Cl LN6 .200 D3
Coots Cl PE25 ......103 C8
Coots La LN13 ......76 E1
Cope St DN32 ....192 A8
Copeland ⬛ PE3 ....225 A3
Copeland Ct ⬛ NG34 .212 C3
Copper Beech Cl
 ⬛ Gainsborough DN21 ..52 F6
 ⬛ Swanland HU14 ....3 B6
Copper Beech Way
 PE2 ....231 B7
Copper Beech Wlk
 DN16 ....185 B3
Copper St LN10 .....84 B3
Coppice Ave ⬛ DN7 ..14 D3
Coppice La ⬛ DN7 ...14 D3
Coppice Rd ⬛ PE9 ..163 C1
Coppice Side HU4 ...179 C6
Coppingford Cl PE2 ..231 D6
Copse Cl DN40 ......186 C5
Copse Rd DN16 .....185 B5
Copse The Brigg DN20 .196 B4
 Grimsby DN33 ....194 F8
 ⬛ Mablethorpe/Sutton on Sea
 LN12 ....77 A7
Copsewood PE4 .....221 A4
Copthill Sch PE9 ....172 C6
Coral Dr ⬛ LN6 ....194 C5
Corby Glen Com Prim Sch
 NG33 ....152 E8
Corby Pk HU14 .....3 A5
Corby Rd
 Burton Coggles NG33 .141 A1
 Irnham NG33 ....141 D1
 Swayfield NG33 .....152 D5
Cordeaux Cl LN11 ...198 C7
Cordeaux High Sch
 LN11 ....198 B7
Cordella Cl ⬛ HU3 ..180 A5
Corden Cl PE25 .....206 C1
Corfe Ave PE4 ......221 A2
Corfe Cl ⬛ NG31 ....210 E2
Corinne Cres ⬛ PE25 .206 C3
Corinne Gr ⬛ PE11 ..214 A3

Corinthian Ave DN34 .191 B6
Corinthian Way HU9 ..181 D6
Cork La PE24 ....102 B3
Cork Tree Cres PE21 ..208 E2
Cormorant Dr DN37 ..190 C8
Corn Cl Fiskerton LN3 ..82 B7
 Horncastle LN9 .....199 B5
Cornfield Cl ⬛ DN33 .194 D8
Cornfield View ⬛ NG34 .212 C2
Cornfields PE12 .....215 F3
Cornflower Cl
 ⬛ Healing DN41 .....23 F5
 Stamford PE9 ....218 C6
Cornflower Way ⬛ LN6 .93 A8
Cornhill LN5 ....234 B2
Cornhill Dr LN8 .....11 A8
Cornish Cres NG34 ..133 E7
Cornley Rd DN10 ....39 C7
Cornmarket ⬛ LN11 ..198 B5
Cornstall Bldgs ⬛ PE9 .219 C5
Cornwall Cl
 Grantham NG31 .....211 C7
 ⬛ Scampton LN1 ....67 E5
Cornwall Rd
 ⬛ Keadby DN17 .....17 D6
 Scunthorpe DN16 ...185 C5
 ⬛ Stamford PE9 .....219 B6
Cornwall St
 ⬛ Kirton in Lindsey DN21 .30 B1
 ⬛ Kirton in Lindsey DN21 .30 B1
Cornwall Way ⬛ NG34 .108 D2
Cornwallis Rd LN2 ...202 D4
Cornwell Cl DN33 ...191 C3
Corona Dr ⬛ DN8 ...15 A8
Coronation Ave
 ⬛ Crowland PE6 .....175 B8
 Deeping St Nicholas
 PE11 ....166 C2
 Parson Drove PE12 ..177 A7
Coronation Cl
 ⬛ Louth LN11 ....198 D7
 ⬛ Spalding PE11 .....157 B6
Coronation Cres
 Coleby LN5 ....93 F3
 ⬛ Epworth DN9 .....27 D7
 ⬛ Epworth DN9 .....27 D6
Coronation Gdns ⬛
 DN20 ....19 E3
Coronation Rd
 Cleethorpes DN35 ...192 F5
 Corby Glen NG33 ...152 E8
 Ingoldmells PE25 ...90 F3
 ⬛ Market Rasen LN8 ..57 D7
 ⬛ Stainforth DN7 ....14 C6
 ⬛ Ulceby DN39 .....12 A1
 Woodhall Spa LN10 ..97 D6
Corporation Bank
 ⬛ Crowland PE6 .....166 E1
 Crowland PE6 ......174 F4
Corporation Rd
 ⬛ Grimsby DN31 ....188 A2
 Grimsby DN31 ......191 D8
 ⬛ Kingston upon Hull HU9 ..5 D8
 ⬛ Scunthorpe DN15 ..183 A3
Corran Garth ⬛ HU4 ..179 A3
Correen Cl ⬛ LN5 ...205 C2
Corringham CE Prim Sch
 DN21 ....41 E2
Corringham Rd DN21 .197 F5
Corsair Gr ⬛ HU3 ...180 A4
Cosford Cl LN6 .....204 B8
Cosgrove Cl
 ⬛ Lincoln LN6 ......205 A6
 Peterborough PE3 ...225 C6
Cosgrove St DN35 ...192 F6
Costa Row NG23 ....117 D3
Coston Rd NG33 ....150 E5
Cot Garth La DN21 ..53 E3
Cotelands Sch LN8 ..108 E1
Cotham Gdns ⬛ DN41 .23 E4
Cotman Rd LN6 .....205 B6
Cotswold Cl
 ⬛ Lincoln LN6 ......93 C8
 ⬛ Peterborough PE4 ..221 C1
Cotswold Dr
 Great Gonerby NG31 ..210 E7
 ⬛ Waltham DN37 ....194 D4
Cotswold Rd DN8 ....15 A7
Cottage Beck Rd
 DN16 ....183 B2
Cottage Cl ⬛ DN20 ..30 D1
Cottage Dr HU10 ....178 B8
Cottage La
 Collingham NG23 ....91 B6
 ⬛ Lincoln LN6 ......205 B4
 North Clifton NG23 ..78 D7
Cottage Paddock The
 LN6 ....205 B6
Cottage Yd La DN36 ..36 C7
Cottesmore Cl
 Grantham NG31 .....211 B6
 Peterborough PE3 ...225 D4
Cottesmore Rd
 Birchwood LN6 .....204 D5
 Cleethorpes DN35 ...192 E2
 Kingston upon Hull
 HU13 ....178 F2
 ⬛ Stamford PE9 .....218 E5
Cottingham Dr LN2 ..202 B7
Cotton Rd PE21 .....208 D6
Cotton Smith Way ⬛
 LN2 ....68 C2
Coulam Pl LN36 ....36 D8
Coulbeck Dr DN35 ..192 D5
Coulby Cl NG23 ....117 F7
Coulman Rd DN8 ....15 A8
Coulman St DN8 ....15 B8
Coulson Cl ⬛ DN20 ..31 A5

Coulson Dr HU13 ....178 F2
Coult Ave LN6 ......201 D1
Coultas Ct
 ⬛ Kingston upon Hull
 HU3 ....180 A6
 ⬛ Kingston upon Hull
 HU3 ....180 A6
Council Ave HU4 ....179 E3
Council Rd ⬛ PE13 ..170 E1
Council St PE4 .....225 D8
Council Terr ⬛ DN18 ..3 E1
Count Alan Rd PE25 ..206 D8
Counter Drain Dro
 PE11 ....155 E2
Counterthorpe Rd NG33 .152 E2
Counthorpe Rd NG33 .152 F3
County Rd S ⬛ HU5 ..179 C8
Coupledyke La PE20 ..136 D5
Court The PE24 .....77 C3
Courtfield Cl ⬛ LN2 ..68 F2
Courtney St HU8 ....181 B8
Cove Rd DN9 ....26 F3
Covel Rd NG34 .....212 B6
Coventry Ave DN34 ..191 A5
Coventry Cl
 ⬛ Grantham NG31 ..210 D5
 Peterborough PE4 ...220 F3
 ⬛ Scunthorpe DN17 ..184 D7
Coventry Rd ⬛ DN18 ..15 B8
Coverley Rd ⬛ NG33 .151 D2
Covert Rd DN16 ....185 B5
Covert The PE3 .....225 B1
Covill Cl ⬛ NG31 ...129 D5
Covington ⬛ HU15 ..2 C6
Covin's La LN11 ....49 C8
Cow Dale La DN10 ..39 C3
Cow Dro LN4 ....123 B7
Cow Gate NG34 ....143 C8
Cow La Minting LN8 ..71 B1
 Swinderby LN6 .....92 B5
 Tealby LN8 ....46 C1
 Twin Rivers DN17 ...7 C6
 Upton DN21 ....53 F6
 Welbourn LN5 .....106 C5
Cow Marsh La DN36 ..36 E5
Cow Pasture La DN22 ..65 A7
Coward's La PE11 ...144 F2
Cowbit Dro PE11 ....144 C1
Cowbit Rd PE12 ....214 D2
Cowbit St Mary's Endowed
 Prim Sch PE12 .....167 A8
Cowbridge Bsns Pk
 PE22 ....125 E7
Cowbridge Rd PE20 ..134 E5
Cowbroads La PE22 ..113 E2
Cowdale La LN1 ....66 B6
Cowdale's Dro PE11 ..134 F1
Cowes Rd NG31 ....210 E4
Cowgate Brough HU15 ..2 D6
 ⬛ Heckington NG34 ..122 E3
 Peterborough PE1 ...225 F2
Cowhams La PE20 ...146 C8
Cowle La ⬛ LN11 ...62 A3
Cowley Cl PE20 .....135 C7
Cowley Endowed
 (Controlled) Prim Sch
 PE11 ....134 E2
Cowley's Rd ⬛ PE11 ..134 E2
Cowpaddle La LN4 ..82 A5
Cowpasture La DN22 ..52 D3
Cowper Ave DN17 ...184 D7
Cowper Dr LN2 .....202 C7
Cowper Rd PE1 .....225 F7
Cowpers Gate PE12 ..216 A3
Cowslip Dr ⬛ PE6 ...217 D6
Cowslip La LN11 ....198 F8
Cox La ⬛ DN17 .....16 D8
Cox's Ct ⬛ DN20 ...31 A5
Cox's Dro PE6 .....167 C1
Cox's Hill DN21 ....197 D5
Cox's Wlk ⬛ NG31 ..129 E5
Coxwold Gr HU4 ....179 E5
Crab La PE20 ......123 C4
Crab Marsh PE13 ...170 C2
Crabley La HU15 ....1 E7
Crabtree PE4 ......221 F1
Crabtree La
 Beckingham DN10 ...52 A8
 Mablethorpe & Sutton
 LN12 ....77 A7
 Saltfleetby LN12 ...51 D1
Crabtree Rd
 Colsterworth NG33 ..151 B7
 Easton NG33 ......140 A1
 ⬛ Hatfield DN7 .....14 C5
 Skillington NG33 ...139 F1
Crack Holt La PE22 ..126 E1
Cradge Bank Rd
 Deeping St Nicholas
 PE11 ....167 A7
 Spalding PE11 .....214 C1
Cragg Cl ⬛ PE20 ...135 C7
Cragmire La PE22 ...114 C3
Cragston Ave DN33 ..191 D3
Craig Cl ⬛ DN20 ...19 D3
Craig St PE1 ......225 F3
Craikbank La DN22 ..65 A8
Craikhill Ave DN40 ..186 C4
Craithie Rd DN35 ...192 E4
Crake Ave DN35 ....191 C1
Crakedale Rd ⬛ DN15 ..9 B5
Crampin Rd ⬛ DN35 .192 E7
Cranberry La PE22 ...114 F7
Cranberry Way HU4 ..179 C4
Cranbourne Mews ⬛
 LN4 ....203 D1

Cranbourne St HU3 ..180 C8
Crane Ave PE7 .....233 F6
Crane Cl ⬛ NG34 ...120 F8
Crane Rd HU9 ......181 C6
Cranemore PE4 ....220 E4
Cranepit La PE11 ...135 E1
Crane's Gate PE12 ..158 C1
Cranford Dr PE3 ...225 C4
Cranidge Cl ⬛ DN17 ..16 D8
Cranmore Dro PE6 ..165 F1
Cranmore PE12 ....215 B1
Cranwell Airfield
 NG34 ....120 D7
Cranwell Ave NG34 ..120 D8
Cranwell Aviation Heritage
 Cantre★ NG34 .....120 D6
Cranwell Cl
 ⬛ Kirton in Lindsey DN21 .42 F8
 ⬛ Skegness PE25 ....206 A5
Cranwell Dr ⬛ DN7 ..190 F8
Cranwell Prim Sch
 NG34 ....107 D1
Cranwell St LN5 ....201 E1
Crapple La DN21 ...29 C2
Craske La PE34 ....161 D3
Craven Ave ⬛ PE20 ..136 D5
Craven Prim Sch HU9 .181 C8
Craven Rd
 Cleethorpes DN35 ...192 E3
 ⬛ Hatfield DN7 .....14 C4
Craven St LN5 .....205 D8
Craven St N HU9 ...181 C8
Craven St S HU9 ...181 C8
Craven's La PE20 ...146 E7
Crawcroft La LN13 ..76 E5
Crawford Gdns ⬛ PE6 .175 C8
Crawthorne Rd PE1 .226 A3
Crawthorne St ⬛ PE1 .226 B3
Craycroft Rd ⬛ DN9 ..27 B2
Craypool La ⬛ LN2 ..68 F4
Craythorne La ⬛ PE5 .208 F5
Creampoke Cres ⬛
 DN21 ....55 A8
Crease Dro PE6 ....175 D4
Creaseyplot La PE20 .124 B1
Creeton Rd NG33 ...153 A1
Crescent Cl ⬛ LN2 ..68 D2
Crescent St ⬛ DN31 .191 C7
Crescent The
 Beckingham DN10 ...40 B1
 Bracebridge Heath LN4 .81 A2
 ⬛ Brough HU15 .....2 C6
 Easton on the Hill PE9 .171 C3
 ⬛ Eye PE6 ....175 A1
 Fiskerton LN3 ......82 B7
 Gainsborough DN21 ..52 F5
 Hatfield DN7 ......14 C5
 Holton le Clay DN36 ..195 C2
 Horncastle LN9 ....199 C3
 ⬛ Kirk Sandall DN3 ..14 A1
 Louth LN11 ....198 B7
 ⬛ Mablethorpe/Sutton on Sea
 LN12 ....77 A7
 Morton PE10 ......154 B7
 ⬛ Nettleham LN2 ...68 C2
 Peterborough PE2 ..230 C5
 Ryhall PE9 ....163 D1
 Sleaford NG34 .....121 A3
 ⬛ Spalding PE11 ....214 D4
 Swayfield NG33 ...152 E5
Cresent The ⬛ LN8 ..70 D4
Cressey St ⬛ DN31 ..189 A1
Cresswell Cl PE11 ..214 E8
Cresta Cl LN6 .....204 C1
Cresta Dr DN34 ....184 E4
Cresta The DN34 ...191 C5
Crester Dr PE4 ....221 A3
Crew Rd NG34 .....91 D5
Creyke La ⬛ HU15 ..2 D6
Cricketers Way ⬛ LN2 .170 C1
Cridling Pl DN35 ...192 D4
Cringle Rd NG33 ...139 F2
Cringleway NG33 ...140 A5
Cripple Sidings La
 PE2 ....231 A8
Crispin Cl ⬛ HU4 ...179 A4
Crispin Way DN16 ..185 B2
Croake Hill NG33 ...153 A5
Crocus Cl PE7 .....233 F6
Crocus Gr PE1 .....226 A3
Croft Bank Croft PE24 .102 F3
 ⬛ Croft PE24 ....102 E2
Croft Cl ⬛ PE24 ...102 E2
Croft Dr
 Grantham NG31 ...211 C3
 Kingston upon Hull
 HU10 ....178 C6
Croft La Bassingham LN5 .92 F3
 Cherry Willingham LN3 .203 E7
 Coningsby LN4 ....110 E8
 ⬛ Croft PE24 ....102 E2
 Scunthorpe DN17 ..184 E2
Croft Lodge ⬛ DN9 ..16 E1
Croft Marsh La PE24 .102 F3
Croft Pk ⬛ HU14 ..3 A5
Croft Rd Croft PE24 ..102 E3
 Finningley DN10 ...26 A1
Croft St
 ⬛ Horncastle LN9 ..199 C3
 Lincoln LN2 ....234 C3
Croft The
 ⬛ Beckingham DN10 ..52 B8
 ⬛ Nettleham LN2 ...68 C2
 ⬛ Thorne/Moorends DN8 .15 B7
 ⬛ West/East Butterwick
 DN17 ....28 D8
Croft View HU10 ....178 C6

Con - Cro 247

Croft Way PE7 .....230 C2
Crofton Cl LN2 ....202 D4
Crofton Dr LN2 ....202 D4
Crofton Rd LN2 ....202 D4
Croft's La DN9 ....28 B3
Crofts La DN7 .....14 B6
Crofts The
 ⬛ Humberston DN36 ..36 C8
 ⬛ Scunthorpe DN16 ..183 B2
Cromarty Rd ⬛ PE9 ..218 E6
Cromer Ave
 Grimsby DN34 .....191 A5
 Mablethorpe/Sutton on Sea
 LN12 ....64 D1
Cromer Cl ⬛ LN6 ...205 A1
Cromford St ⬛ DN21 .197 D5
Cromwell Ave
 ⬛ Gainsborough DN21 ..52 F6
 ⬛ Horncastle LN9 ...199 C2
 ⬛ Woodhall Spa LN10 .97 D5
Cromwell Cl
 Boston PE21 ....208 D7
 ⬛ Heighington/Washingborough
 LN4 ....203 A2
 ⬛ Kingston upon Hull
 HU3 ....180 D8
 Northborough PE6 ..217 E1
Cromwell Cres ⬛ NG34 .212 E4
Cromwell Ct ⬛ HU10 .178 E2
Cromwell Mews ⬛ PE6 .173 C4
Cromwell Pl LN4 ...207 A5
Cromwell Rd
 Cleethorpes DN35 ...193 A4
 Grimsby DN37 .....188 A1
 Peterborough PE1 ..225 F4
Cromwell St
 Gainsborough DN21 .197 D2
 Lincoln LN2 ....202 B3
Cromwell View ⬛ LN7 .33 B4
Cromwell Way ⬛ PE6 .217 A6
Crook Bank LN12 ...63 F6
Crook Hill HU15 ...2 C8
Crook Mill Rd DN40 .12 C4
Crook Tree La DN7 ..14 F5
Crooked Billet St
 DN21 ....197 B8
Crookes Broom Ave ⬛
 DN7 ....14 D4
Crookes Broom La
 DN7 ....14 D4
Cropper's La PE22 ..126 E1
Cropston Rd PE1 ...226 E2
Crosby Ave DN15 ...182 F6
Crosby La ⬛ LN5 ...106 E4
Crosby Prim Sch
 DN15 ....183 A4
Crosby Rd
 Grimsby DN33 .....191 B2
 Scunthorpe DN15 ..183 B4
Crosby Row PE12 ...160 D4
Crosland Rd DN37 ..190 D8
Cross Bank LN4 ....96 D8
Cross Carr Rd DN20 ..31 B5
Cross Coates Rd
 DN34 ....191 A6
Cross Comm La DN22 ..52 D3
Cross Dro Fleet PE12 .168 B2
 Holland Fen with Brothertoft
 PE20 ....125 B5
 Horbling NG34 ....133 F2
 Tydd St Giles PE13 .169 C5
Cross Gate
 Long Sutton PE12 ..159 F3
 Quadring PE11 ....135 A1
 Spalding PE12 ....157 B6
 Tydd St Mary PE13 ..160 A2
 Weston PE12 ......157 C7
Cross Hill
 Gringley on the Hill DN10 .39 C1
 Haxey DN9 ....27 C3
Cross Keys La LN4 ..207 F4
Cross Keys Yd ⬛ NG34 .212 D4
Cross La
 ⬛ Alkborough DN15 ..8 C8
 ⬛ Amcotts DN17 ....7 F1
 Balderton NG24 ...104 B1
 ⬛ Bourne PE10 .....213 E2
 Butterwick PE22 ...126 E3
 Collingham NG23 ..91 D5
 Flixborough DN15 ..8 B1
 Glentham LN8 .....44 A2
 Gringley on the Hill DN10 .39 A5
 Harby NG23 ....79 B3
 ⬛ Lincoln LN6 .....93 C8
 Long Bennington NG23 .117 D1
 North Kelsey LN7 ..32 B5
 Pinchbeck PE11 ...144 F1
 Wellingore LN5 ....106 E6
Cross O'Cliff Cl LN5 .205 E6
Cross O'Cliff Hill LN5 .205 E6
Cross Rd Hatfield DN7 ..15 B4
 Langtoft PE6 ......165 B4
 Market Deeping PE6 .217 F5
 Sutton St Edmund PE12 .169 A4
 Tydd St Mary PE13 .160 B2
 Ulceby DN39 ......12 B3
Cross Slack ⬛ DN17 ..16 C8
Cross Spencer St ⬛
 LN5 ....205 E8
Cross St
 Barnby in the Willows
 NG24 ....104 F3
 ⬛ Barrow upon Humber
 DN19 ....11 D8
 ⬛ Brigg DN20 ......196 C3

Cross St *continued*
Cleethorpes DN35 .....192 E6
13 Crowle DN17 .....16 D8
Gainsborough DN21 .....197 B8
Garthorpe & Fockerby DN17 .....7 E6
Grimsby DN31 .....189 B2
1 Holbeach PE12 .....215 D2
6 Horncastle LN9 .....199 C3
Lincoln LN5 .....234 B1
11 Nettleham LN2 .....68 C2
Peterborough PE1 .....226 A2
4 Potter Hanworth LN4 .....82 B1
Scunthorpe DN15 .....183 B4
3 Skegness PE25 .....206 B3
Spalding PE11 .....214 C3
Sturton Le Steeple DN22 .....52 B3
3 Waltham DN37 .....194 E4
2 West Halton DN15 .....8 E8
5 Whaplode PE12 .....158 B7
Cross Tree Rd 21 DN17 ...29 D7
Crossbeck Rd DN16 ...185 A4
Crossberry Way 1 PE6 .173 B4
Crosscliff Hill LN11 .....60 A8
Crossfield Rd
Kingston upon Hull HU13 .....178 E3
12 Navenby/Wellingore LN5 .....107 A8
Crossgate Cres 5 PE11 145 C1
Crossgate La 3 PE11 ..145 C1
Crossgill Cl NG31 .....211 F5
Crosslands 5 PE11 .....134 F2
Crossmoor Bank DN14 ....6 C5
Crossway The DN34 ...190 E3
Crossways 8 DN7 .....14 C6
Crow Hill Ave DN35 ...192 E6
Crow La Gedney PE12 ..159 D6
Great Hale NG34 .....122 F1
Leadenham LN5 .....106 D3
Crow Pk LN6 .....204 A1
Crow Tree Bank DN8 ....15 D4
Crowberry Dr DN16 ...185 D5
Crowdyke Gate PE12 ..158 B5
Crowfields PE6 .....217 F5
Crowhall La PE22 .....127 A4
Crowhurst 1 PE4 .....221 A5
Crowland Ave
Grimsby DN34 .....190 F4
Scunthorpe DN16 .....185 A7
Crowland Dr LN6 .....204 F7
Crowland Ponds Nature Reserve★ PE6 .....166 D2
Crowland Rd
14 Crowle DN17 .....16 D7
Deeping St James PE6 ...174 D7
Eye PE6 .....175 A3
Crowle Bank Rd DN17 ..17 C4
Crowle Dr DN33 .....191 A3
Crowle Moor Nature Reserve★ DN17 .....6 B1
Crowle Prim Sch DN17 .16 C7
Crowle Rd DN17 .....6 F2
Crowle St HU9 .....181 D7
Crowle Sta DN17 .....16 E5
Crown Ave
3 Chapel St Leonard PE24 .90 D7
Holbeach PE12 .....147 C6
Crown Cl 10 NG23 .....91 D5
Crown Ct 3 DN22 .....52 B3
Crown Dr PE11 .....214 F6
Crown Hill NG33 .....141 B8
Crown La 14 PE10 .....164 C8
Crown Lakes Ctry Pk★ PE7 .....231 B2
Crown Lodge PE12 ....215 C7
Crown Mills 2 LN11 ...198 D6
Crown St
Peterborough PE1 .....225 E7
Ryhall PE9 .....163 C2
7 Stamford PE9 .....219 B5
Crow's La PE24 .....102 C2
Crowson Cres PE6 .....217 E1
Crowson Way PE6 .....217 D5
Crowther Way 8 HU14 ...3 B7
Crowtree La LN11 .....198 A5
Croxby Ave DN33 .....194 F8
Croxby Gr DN33 .....194 F7
Croxton Dr LN6 .....204 F6
Croxton Kerrial CE Prim Sch NG32 .....138 D4
Croxton La NG32 .....138 D5
Croxton Rd
Croxton DN39 .....21 F7
Kirmington DN39 .....22 A5
Sproxton LE14 .....138 E2
Croyland Rd PE4 .....221 B1
Croyland Way 15 PE6 ...166 F1
Crusader Rd LN6 .....201 C1
Crystal St HU3 .....180 C7
Cuckoo La
Ashby De La Launde & Bloxholm LN4 .....107 F7
Hatfield DN7 .....14 E6
Pinchbeck PE11 .....145 C2
Cul-de-sac The PE22 ..100 B2
Cullin Cl 1 LN5 .....205 D2
Culpins Cl PE11 .....214 F5
Culvert Rd PE24 .....102 B3
Culverthorpe Hall★ NG32 .....131 D7
Culverthorpe Rd NG34 .....132 A7
Cumberland Ave
Grimsby DN32 .....191 D5
Cumberland Ave *continued*
14 Navenby/Wellingore LN5 .....107 A7
Cumberland Gdns NG33 .....152 D1
Cumberland Rd DN35 .193 A2
Cumberland St HU2 ...181 A8
Cumberland Terr 12 LN8 .47 B6
Cumberland Way 17 LN1 .67 E5
Cumberlidge Cl 10 PE24 102 E7
Cumberworth La 2 LN13 76 F1
Cumberworth Rd LN13 ..89 C7
Cunningham Rd 1 DN7 .26 A8
Cunsdike La PE11 .....145 D5
Cupola Way DN15 .....183 A8
Curle Ave LN2 .....234 C4
Curlew Cl 4 PE12 .....216 B4
Curlew Dr 8 PE12 .....167 B8
Curlew Gr PE2 .....231 D7
Curlew Lodge La PE12 .160 F8
Curlew Way NG34 .....212 B3
Curlew Wlk 14 PE6 .....217 C5
Curry Rd DN34 .....190 F7
Curtis Cl 13 NG23 .....91 D5
Curtis Dr LN4 .....81 E4
Curzen Cres 8 DN3 .....14 A2
Curzon Ave DN35 .....192 D5
Curzon CE (Controlled) Prim Sch LN4 .....207 A5
Curzon Ct DN35 .....192 D5
Curzon Est 6 LN4 .....207 A5
Curzon Mews 3 LN4 ...203 D1
Curzon St
1 Gainsborough DN21 ...197 C6
Kingston upon Hull HU3 ..179 F7
Cushman Cres DN40 ...186 C3
Customhouse St 2 PE12 .....160 F4
Cut Dike PE22 .....124 D8
Cut End Rd PE22 .....137 D7
Cuthbert Ave 6 DN38 ...21 B4
Cuthbert's La PE20 ....136 B8
Cuxwold Rd
3 Scunthorpe DN16 .....185 C8
Swallow LN7 .....34 B5
Cydonia App LN6 .....204 C8
Cygnet Cl 8 NG34 .....212 B3
Cygnet Pk PE7 .....230 E3
Cynthia Rd DN32 .....192 C5
Cypress Cl
2 Peterborough PE3 .....225 A2
9 Sleaford NG34 .....212 D2
Cyprus St 5 HU9 .....5 D8
Cyrano Way DN37 .....190 C7

D

Daffodil Gr PE2 .....231 C7
Dagger La HU1 .....180 F6
Daggett Rd DN35 .....193 A4
Daimler Ave PE7 .....233 E6
D'aincourt Pk LN4 .....81 D2
Dairy Cl 1 PE11 .....145 C6
Dairy Dro PE6 .....176 E2
Dairycoates Ave HU3 ..180 A4
Dairycoates Rd HU4 ...179 E3
Daisy Dale PE21 .....209 A3
Dalby Ct PE1 .....226 C8
Dalderby Cres 16 LN2 ...68 C2
Dale Ave LN3 .....203 E6
Dale Cl
Peterborough PE2 .....229 F5
10 Swanland HU14 .....3 B7
Dale Cres 1 NG24 .....104 C1
Dale Pit Rd 8 DN7 .....14 F3
Dale Pk Ave DN15 .....9 A5
Dale Rd 6 Brough HU15 ...2 C7
Grantham NG31 .....211 A7
Swanland HU14 .....3 B7
Welton HU15 .....2 E6
Dale St Lincoln LN5 .....202 B2
Scunthorpe DN15 .....182 F4
Dale St N DN15 .....182 F5
Dale View DN33 .....190 F3
Dale Way 9 NG24 .....104 C1
Dalehouse Dr 2 HU10 ..178 F6
Dales La DN10 .....39 A6
Dale's La PE20 .....135 D5
Dales The
25 Nettleham LN2 .....68 C2
Scunthorpe DN17 .....184 E3
Dalesway HU10 .....178 B6
Dallisons Rd 5 DN20 ....31 A5
Dallygate NG33 .....140 A5
Dallygate La NG33 .....140 B5
Dalmatian Way 14 DN20 .19 E4
Dam Gate PE12 .....215 E1
Dam Gn La 5 HU15 .....2 C7
Dam La DN39 .....11 E5
Dam Rd DN18 .....3 D1
Dame Kendal Gr 1 DN33 .....191 B3
Dams La LN9 .....73 B2
Danby Rd 16 DN17 .....29 D7
Dane Cl
15 Broughton DN20 .....19 E4
31 Metheringham LN4 .....95 C4
Danes Cl PE1 .....226 C4
Danes Ctyd 11 LN2 .....234 B3
Danes Rd DN21 .....197 F5
Danes Terr LN2 .....234 B3
Danesfield Ave DN37 ...194 E5
Danesgate LN2 .....234 B3
Danethorpe La NG24 ...104 D8
Danial Cl PE25 .....206 C8
Daniel Cres 10 LN4 .....203 D1
Daniel Ct 7 PE9 .....219 C4
Daniel's Cres PE12 .....216 C5
Daniel's Dro PE6 .....167 D1
Daniel's Gate PE12 ....216 C7
Daniel's Reach PE11 ..214 C7
Daniels Gate 1 PE11 ...214 C6
Danish Ct PE4 .....220 E4
Dansom La S HU8 .....181 B8
Danson Cl 19 DN18 .....10 F8
Danube Rd HU5 .....179 C8
Danum Cl 11 DN8 .....15 B8
Danum Rd
6 Hatfield DN7 .....14 D3
Scunthorpe DN17 .....184 F8
Dar Beck Rd DN21 .....29 C4
Darby Rd DN15 .....8 B4
Darbyshire Cl NG23 .....79 B5
Dark La Amcotts DN17 .....7 F1
Barnby in the Willows NG24 .....105 A3
Bicker PE20 .....135 A5
Bitchfield & Bassingthorpe NG33 .....141 A3
Burwell LN11 .....74 C6
Holbeach PE12 .....215 B5
Darley Cl PE8 .....172 C1
Darley Dale Cres 1 NG31 .....211 A7
Darley's La PE11 .....214 A6
Darnholme Cres
Epworth DN9 .....28 A8
15 Messingham DN17 .....29 D7
Darrismere Villas 4 HU3 .....180 A5
Dart Ave LN6 .....205 A2
Dartmouth Rd DN17 ...182 D1
Darwin Cl
5 Stamford PE9 .....219 A7
7 Sutton Bridge PE12 ...160 E4
10 Waddington LN5 .....93 E8
Darwin St
3 Gainsborough DN21 ...197 D2
6 Kirton in Lindsey DN21 ..30 B1
Dashwood Rd 7 LN13 ...75 E2
Datchet Garth 3 HU4 ..179 B2
Daubeney Ave LN1 .....66 D2
Daubney St DN35 .....189 E1
Davenport Ave HU13 ..178 D1
Davenport Dr DN35 ...192 C4
Davey Cl 1 PE21 .....208 E7
David Ave Lincoln LN1 ..201 D8
Louth LN11 .....198 D7
David Dr PE25 .....206 B6
David Pl DN36 .....195 C5
David St DN32 .....191 F5
David's Cl PE4 .....220 D4
David's La
Benington PE22 .....127 A5
Peterborough PE4 .....220 F5
Davie Pl DN35 .....192 B7
Davis's Cl HU10 .....178 C8
Davos Way PE25 .....206 A7
Davy Ave DN15 .....182 E4
Davy Cl 3 LN11 .....61 F3
Davy Cres DN20 .....196 C5
Dawber La
Claxby St Andrew LN13 ....88 F5
Thimbleby LN9 .....85 C5
Dawes La DN16 .....183 D4
Dawlish Rd DN33 .....194 E6
Dawnay Dr HU10 .....179 A6
Dawnhill La DN21 .....42 E2
Daws Gate
Moulton PE12 .....157 F2
Whaplode PE12 .....158 A2
Dawsmere Rd PE12 ....148 F4
Dawson Ave 1 PE11 ....214 F6
Dawson Cl Lincoln LN6 ..204 F6
6 Newborough PE6 .....174 E4
Dawson Dr 8 PE24 .....102 E7
Dawson Rd 7 NG34 .....212 D6
Dawsons La LN3 .....203 F8
Day Cl 6 Keadby DN17 ...17 D6
Wrawby DN20 .....20 E4
Daybell Cl 20 NG13 .....128 A6
Daybrook Cl NG32 .....139 C8
Day's La PE20 .....134 F3
De Aston Sch LN8 .....57 E7
De Aston Sq 2 DN15 ...182 E3
De Bec Cl PE1 .....226 C3
De Gravel Dr 5 NG34 ..107 F1
De Havilland Rd PE13 .170 D1
De La Bere Ave 25 LN12 .77 A8
De La Pole Ave HU3 ...179 F7
De Lacy Ave PE25 .....206 C8
De Lacy La 3 DN35 .....192 F6
De Lacy Way DN15 .....9 A5
De Ligne Dr 6 NG32 ...139 C7
De Wint Ave LN6 .....205 A5
De Wint Cl Lincoln LN6 .205 B5
6 Metheringham LN4 .....95 C4
Deacon Dr DN15 .....182 B2
Deacon Rd LN2 .....202 C5
Deacon St PE1 .....225 F3
Deacons Sch PE1 .....226 B5
Deaconscroft PE3 .....225 B5
Dealtry Cl DN21 .....53 D5
Dean Cl 3 NG34 .....121 B8
Dean Rd DN17 .....184 E6
Deane Cl 7 NG23 .....91 D5
Deane Rd DN40 .....186 D4
Deans Cl 7 DN10 .....39 F5
Deansgate DN32 .....191 C6
Dear Love Gate
1 Gedney PE12 .....160 A8
Lutton PE12 .....148 D1
Dear St 11 LN8 .....57 D8
Dearne Ct 9 HU15 .....2 D5
Deaton La DN36 .....195 C6
Debdale Rd NG32 .....210 A5
Debdhill Rd 1 DN10 ....39 F5
Decoy Rd
Borough Fen PE6 .....174 D6
Gorefield PE13 .....169 D2
Dee St 6 HU3 .....180 B4
Deene Cl
7 Grimsby DN34 .....190 D4
8 Market Deeping PE6 ..217 A5
Deene Ct PE3 .....225 C5
Deep (Aquarium & Marine Research Centre) The★ HU1 .....181 A5
Deep La PE23 .....87 A5
Deepdale Dr NG34 .....121 C7
Deepdale Gr 2 HU9 ....181 E8
Deepdale La LN2 .....68 C2
Deeping Rd PE6 .....164 E4
Deeping St James Prim Sch PE6 .....217 F4
Deeping St James Rd PE6 .....217 D2
Deeping St Nicholas Prim Sch PE11 .....166 B6
Deepings Leisure Ctr PE6 .....217 E4
Deepings Sch The PE6 .....217 E5
Deer Pk Rd 3 PE6 .....164 F3
Deerhurst Way 18 PE6 ..175 A1
Deerleap PE3 .....225 A5
Defender Dr DN37 .....190 B7
Deighton Cl Specl Sch LN11 .....61 A6
Deira Cl NG34 .....212 C1
Delamere Cl PE1 .....226 C5
Delamere Ct DN36 .....192 F1
Delamore Way PE12 ...216 C5
Delapre Ct 11 PE6 .....175 A1
Deldale Rd PE21 .....136 D8
Delfield Rd PE21 .....136 D8
Delgate Ave 3 PE12 .....157 E7
Delgate Bank PE12 ....157 D2
Delhi Sq 3 NG34 .....120 D8
Delhi St 7 HU9 .....5 D8
Delius Cl HU4 .....179 B4
Dell The
Peterborough PE2 .....230 E7
Scunthorpe DN17 .....184 D5
Dellfield Ave LN6 .....200 C1
Dellfield Cl LN6 .....200 C2
Dellfield Ct 8 LN6 .....200 C1
Delph Ct PE2 .....231 F6
Delph Fields PE12 .....216 A3
Delph Rd 18 Lincoln LN6 ..93 C8
Long Sutton PE12 .....216 A3
Delph The PE11 .....155 F4
Denbigh Ct 11 NG23 .....91 D5
Denby Cl 6 DN15 .....182 D5
Denby Dale Cl LN6 .....200 C2
Denby Dr DN35 .....192 C3
Dene Cl LN6 .....200 B3
Dene La LN4 .....109 C7
Dene Rd Grimsby DN32 .191 E4
Skellingthorpe LN6 .....200 B3
Dene The
6 Nettleham LN2 .....68 C2
Skellingthorpe LN6 .....200 B3
Denefield LN6 .....200 B3
Denehall Rd 14 DN3 .....14 A2
Denesway HU13 .....178 D2
Denham Cl 2 PE25 .....206 C2
Denham Wlk 1 PE3 .....225 C4
Denis Dr PE2 .....230 A4
Denmark Ct 7 HU9 .....181 C7
Denmark Dr PE2 .....230 A4
Dennett Cl PE23 .....100 F8
Dennor Cl 15 LN12 .....77 A8
Denshire Ct 5 PE6 .....164 E4
Denton Ave NG31 .....210 F1
Denton CE Prim Sch NG32 .....139 A7
Denton Cl NG31 .....210 F1
Denton La
Barrowby NG32 .....128 F3
Belvoir NG32 .....138 E6
Denton Rd PE2 .....231 C6
Denton's Way 11 DN20 ....31 A5
Depot St LN1 .....201 D3
Derby Ave PE25 .....206 D1
Derby Cl
1 Grantham NG31 .....210 E4
9 Grimsby DN32 .....189 C1
Derby Dr PE1 .....226 C5
Derby Rd DN15 .....182 B2
Derby St
Kingston upon Hull HU3 ..180 D8
13 Lincoln LN5 .....205 E8
Dere Cl 9 PE10 .....213 C6
Derringham Ave 5 HU4 179 B6
Derringham St HU3 ....180 C7
Derry Way DN33 .....194 E8
Derrythorpe Rd DN17 ...17 D4
Derwent Ave 18 HU14 ....3 A4
Derwent Cl LN6 .....205 A5
Derwent Dr
1 Humberston DN36 .....36 C8
Humberston DN36 .....192 E1
Peterborough PE4 .....221 C2
Derwent Rd
Grantham NG31 .....210 F3
Scunthorpe DN16 .....185 E6
Derwent St LN1 .....201 C4
Derwood Gr 7 PE4 .....220 F5
Desborough Ave PE2 ..231 D5
Detuyll St DN15 .....182 F5
Detuyll St W DN15 .....182 F5
Devereux Way 5 LN9 ..199 D2
Devon La 17 NG13 .....128 A6
Devon St
Kingston upon Hull HU4 ..179 F3
8 Lincoln LN2 .....202 C3
Devonshire Ave DN32 .191 D4
Devonshire Rd
2 Scampton Airfield LN1 ..67 E5
Scunthorpe DN17 .....184 F6
Dewberry Ct HU4 .....179 C4
Dewsbury Ave DN15 ...182 C4
Deyne Ave DN15 .....183 A3
Dial Sq 2 DN31 .....191 E7
Diana Princess of Wales Hospl DN33 .....191 C3
Diana St DN15 .....183 A5
Dick Turpin Way PE12 .216 B5
Dickens Dr PE9 .....218 E5
Dickens Rd NG31 .....211 E6
Dickens St PE1 .....226 B3
Dickenson Terr 10 DN21 .....197 D3
Dickinson Cl 11 DN20 ....30 F5
Dickinson's La 6 DN36 ...36 B1
Dickon Hill Rd PE22 ...114 D7
Digby CE Prim Sch LN4 .....108 D6
Digby Cl 9 LN6 .....204 C7
Digby Cnr Nature Reserve★ LN4 .....108 F5
Digby Gdns 3 DN34 .....191 A5
Digby Rd LN4 .....109 B6
Digby St DN15 .....182 F4
Dimmock Cl NG32 .....139 B7
Dingley Ct PE3 .....225 C5
Dirty La 4 DN7 .....14 D8
Disney Ct LN6 .....92 C2
Ditmas Ave 9 HU4 .....179 B6
Division Rd 1 HU3 .....180 B4
Dixon Ave
14 Broughton DN20 .....19 D3
Dorrington LN4 .....108 E3
Grimsby DN32 .....191 E4
Dixon Cl Brigg DN20 ...196 C4
Lincoln LN6 .....201 D1
12 Tetney DN36 .....36 D4
Dixon Dr LN13 .....75 E2
Dixon St LN5 .....201 D1
Dixon Way LN6 .....201 D1
Dixon's Dro PE14 .....170 F4
Dixons Rd PE6 .....217 C4
Dock Office Row 6 HU1 .....181 A7
Dock St HU1 .....180 F6
Dock Twr The★ DN31 ..189 B3
Dockholme Gate PE11 .145 A4
Docking La LN9 .....199 B8
Docking's Holt PE12 ..216 B6
Doctor's La PE10 .....143 A2
Doddington Ave LN6 ..205 A4
Doddington Dr PE3 ....225 B2
Doddington Hall★ LN6 .79 D5
Doddington La
Claypole NG23 .....117 E7
Stubton NG23 .....118 B7
Westborough & Dry Doddington NG23 .....117 E5
Doddington Rd
Birchwood LN6 .....204 C6
Doddington & Whisby LN6 ..79 E3
Lincoln LN6 .....204 F4
Dodswell Gr HU9 .....5 F8
Dog And Duck La DN21 .....197 B8
Dog Dro
Holbeach PE12 .....158 D2
Sutton St James PE12 ...159 A1
Dog Holes La DN22 .....52 A1
Dog Kennel Rd DN21 ....55 A8
Dogdyke Ppg Sta★ LN4 .....110 D7
Dogdyke Rd
Coningsby LN4 .....207 B2
Wildmore LN4 .....111 B6
Dogsthorpe Cty Jun & Inf Sch PE1 .....226 B7
Dogsthorpe Rd PE1 ...226 A5
Dolby Vale DN33 .....190 F3
Dole Rd DN17 .....6 B1
Dole Wood Nature Reserve★ PE10 .....164 C7
Doll La 1 DN20 .....20 F7
Doll's Bank PE12 .....159 A4
Dolman Cres DN17 .....184 F4
Dolphin St 4 DN35 ....192 F6
Dominion Cl 11 DN36 ...195 C6
Donaldson Dr 4 PE4 ...221 C2
Doncaster Gdns 14 LN5 .107 A8
Doncaster Rd
Gunness DN15 .....17 E6
Hatfield DN7 .....14 D3
Haxey DN9 .....26 F2
Scunthorpe DN15 .....182 B3
Stainforth DN7 .....14 B6
Doncaster St HU3 .....180 B6
Donegal Cl PE4 .....221 B2
Donington on Bain Prim Sch LN11 .....59 E1
Donington Rd
Bicker PE20 .....135 A4
Horbling NG34 .....133 C2
Kirton PE20 .....135 F6
Donnington Gdns 1 DN15 .....182 F3
Donnington Pk 1 PE13 170 A1
Donnington Rd LN8 ....59 B2
Donnington St 5 DN32 .191 F7
Donville Rd DN17 .....7 A2
Dooks Cl DN21 .....29 C1

Doon Garth HU4 179 A3
Dorado Cl 2 HU3 180 A5
Dorchester Ave PE10 213 E3
Dorchester Cres 3 PE1 226 D7
Dorchester Rd DN17 184 C8
Dorchester Way 10 LN6 93 B8
Dore Ave LN6 204 E2
Dormy Ave PE25 206 D8
Dorothy Ave
Skegness PE25 206 C3
Waltham DN37 194 E5
Dorothy Cl PE22 113 A1
Dorothy Cres 1 PE25 206 C3
Dorrington CE Sch LN4 108 D4
Dorset Cl E 6 DN15 8 B4
Dorset Cl W 5 DN15 8 B4
Dorset Pl 8 LN1 67 E5
Dorset St
Kingston upon Hull HU4 179 F3
7 Lincoln LN2 202 C3
Dorton Ave DN21 197 F4
Dotam's La PE22 126 D4
Double Bank PE22 126 D6
Double Bridges Rd DN8 15 B6
Double St PE11 214 D4
Doubledays La PE24 102 D8
Doubletwelves Dro PE20 134 D6
Doughty Cl DN37 194 E5
Doughty Rd DN32 191 E7
Doughty St PE9 219 D6
Douglas Ave
Grimsby DN31 191 A8
5 Ingoldmells PE25 90 D3
Douglas Rd
Cleethorpes DN35 192 D8
Market Deeping PE6 217 C4
Doulton Cl 4 LN6 204 D7
Dove Cl Louth LN11 198 D7
7 Sleaford NG34 212 B3
Dove Dale 5 LN6 204 F2
Dovecote
4 Middle Rasen LN8 57 B8
Rippingale PE10 143 A3
Dovecote Cl PE1 226 B7
Dovecote La
Aubourn Haddington & South Hykeham LN5 92 F5
Coleby LN5 93 F3
Wainfleet St Mary PE24 102 E1
Yaxley PE7 233 C5
Dovecote Mdws 3 DN20 196 F6
Dovecote Rd 4 PE6 217 A6
Dovecotes 3 PE11 145 A8
Dovedale Cl
Grantham NG31 211 B8
2 Winterton DN15 9 A6
Dovedale Dr 6 DN33 194 E8
Dovedale Gr 1 HU9 181 E8
Dovedale Rd DN16 185 D5
Dover Cl NG31 210 E6
Dover Rd PE4 221 A2
Dover St Grimsby DN31 191 C8
Kingston upon Hull HU3 180 C8
Doves' La PE22 126 E3
Dowding Rd LN2 202 E4
Dowdyke Dro PE20 146 B8
Dowdyke Rd PE20 145 F8
Dower Rise 11 HU14 3 B7
Dowgate Cl 2 PE11 214 A3
Dowgate Rd 4 PE13 170 B1
Dowlands Bsns Pk LN11 62 C5
Down Gate PE3 225 A1
Downing Cl DN34 190 F6
Downing Cres
Scunthorpe DN16 185 A3
2 Stamford PE9 219 B7
Dowsdale Bank
Thorney PE6 176 A8
Whaplode PE12 167 E2
Dowse Ave DN15 182 E3
Dowsing Way PE25 206 A6
Dozen's Bank PE11 156 B6
Dragonby Rd DN17 184 E4
Drain Bank
Cowbit PE12 157 A2
East Kirkby PE23 99 F3
Newport HU15 1 B8
Drain Rd PE6 221 E7
Drainside PE20 136 B5
Drainside S PE20 136 C4
Drakards La PE21 209 A3
Drake Ave
Grimsby DN32 192 B6
Heighington/Washingborough LN4 203 B1
Drake Rd PE25 103 E4
Drake St
Gainsborough DN21 197 D2
Lincoln LN1 201 C4
Drakes Cl
7 Holbeach PE12 215 E2
19 Mablethorpe & Sutton LN12 77 A7
Drapers Pl 18 PE11 214 D4
Draw Dike PE12 159 D1
Drax Ct 6 LN8 57 B8
Draycot 6 LN7 33 A3
Drayton PE3 225 A4
Drayton Rd PE20 135 C7
Drew Ave DN32 191 F4
Drewry La 10 DN9 27 A2
Driffil Way 28 DN15 9 A5
Drift Ave PE9 219 C6
Drift Gdns PE9 219 C6
Drift La NG32 119 A1
Drift Rd PE9 219 C6
Drift The
Barrowby NG32 210 A3
Belvoir NG32 138 F5
Buckminster NG33 151 A4
Collyweston PE9 171 B1
Croxton Kerrial NG32 138 F5
Harlaxton NG32 139 C8
Ryhall PE9 163 B3
Skillington NG33 151 A7
Syston NG32 130 A7
Walcott LN4 109 D7
Wansford PE5 222 F3
Drigh Rd 17 LN8 47 B6
Drill Hall La 3 DN21 197 D5
Dring La DN21 41 D7
Drinsey Nook La NG23 66 B1
Drive The
Gainsborough DN21 197 E3
Grantham NG31 210 D3
Ingoldmells PE25 206 E8
7 Kirk Sandall DN3 14 A1
2 Mablethorpe/Sutton on Sea LN12 64 A4
Peterborough PE3 225 E2
Waltham DN37 194 F3
1 Winthorpe NG24 104 B7
Drove End Prim Sch PE12 148 F3
Drove La
Coddington NG24 104 D7
Sleaford NG34 212 A5
Drove Rd
Crowland PE12 167 F3
Whaplode PE12 168 A3
Drove The
4 Aubourn Haddington & South Hykeham LN6 93 A8
Collyweston PE9 171 B1
Osbournby NG34 132 D5
Sleaford NG34 212 B5
Drovers Ct DN21 197 E1
Drovers Rise 1 HU15 2 C6
Drummond Rd
Bourne PE10 213 E4
Skegness PE25 206 D1
Drury Cl 1 DN37 194 C4
Drury La Bicker PE20 135 A4
New Waltham DN36 195 C6
Drury Pk 9 NG23 117 D3
Drury St LN4 95 D4
Dry Leys PE2 230 C6
Drydales HU10 178 C6
Dryden Ave LN2 202 B6
Dryden Cl NG31 211 D6
Dryden Ct 3 LN4 207 B5
Dryden Rd
Peterborough PE1 225 E7
Scunthorpe DN17 184 D6
Drypool Way HU9 181 B6
Duchess St DN32 191 D6
Ducie La DN22 52 C5
Duckpool La LN10 84 B1
Duckthorpe La DN36 37 B2
Dudley Cl 1 PE21 209 B4
Dudley House Sch NG31 211 B4
Dudley Pl DN35 192 D4
Dudley Rd Brigg DN20 196 C3
Grantham NG31 211 B4
Scunthorpe DN16 185 E6
Dudley St DN31 191 C7
Duesbery St HU3 180 C8
Dugard Rd DN32 192 B7
Duke of Bedford Sch PE6 176 A3
Duke Rd PE22 113 F3
Duke St Boston PE21 208 E4
8 Grimsby DN32 189 C1
Grimsby DN32 192 B8
Peterborough PE2 231 A7
Sleaford NG34 212 E5
14 Stainforth DN7 14 C6
Duke's Covert Nature Reserve★ NG32 120 A1
Dukesmead PE4 220 E2
Dunbar Ave DN36 195 B6
Dunbar Cl 5 DN21 197 E6
Dunblane Dr PE2 229 D4
Duncombe Gdns 1 DN32 191 F8
Duncombe St DN32 191 F8
Dundee Dr PE9 218 E6
Dundee St HU5 180 A8
Dunes Family Entertainment Ctr The★ LN12 64 C4
Dunford Rd 5 LN5 234 B1
Dunham Cl LN1 65 D1
Dunham on Trent Prim Sch NG22 65 A1
Dunham Rd DN22 65 A3
Dunholme Cl
Gainsborough DN21 197 E4
11 Welton/Dunholme LN2 68 D6
Dunholme Ct 4 LN2 202 A8
Dunholme Rd
Gainsborough DN21 197 E4
9 Welton/Dunholme LN2 68 D6
Dunholme St Chads CE Prim Sch LN2 68 E6
Dunkirk Rd LN1 201 D6
Dunlin Dr PE12 216 B4
Dunlin Rd 2 PE9 163 D3
Dunlop St LN5 201 F1
Dunlop Way DN16 185 E7
Dunmires La DN14 6 E8
Dunmore Cl LN5 205 C3
Dunmow St DN31 188 D1
Dunnegate Way PE11 145 D2
Dunnock Cl 3 DN16 185 B2
Dunns Paddock 3 DN20 20 F7
Dunsberry
Marholm PE6 220 D1
Peterborough PE3 224 F8
Dunsby Dro PE10 143 D1
Dunstall St DN15 183 A3
Dunstan Hill 26 DN21 30 B1
Dunstan Villas 29 DN21 30 B1
Dunster Rd DN21 197 E6
Dunston Cl 10 LN2 202 A8
Dunston Dr HU13 178 D1
Dunston Fen La LN4 83 D1
Dunston Heath La LN4 94 E5
Dunston Rd
Kingston upon Hull HU5 179 D7
Metheringham LN4 95 C5
Durban Rd DN32 192 A7
Durham Ave
4 Grimsby DN34 191 A7
Sleaford NG34 212 C6
Thorne/Moorends DN8 15 A8
Durham Cl
Birchwood LN6 200 D2
Grantham NG31 210 C4
Durham Cres LN4 203 D1
Durham Rd
Cleethorpes DN35 192 C4
Hatfield DN7 14 D4
Peterborough PE1 226 C3
Durham's Rd PE12 148 D5
Dursley Ave DN36 195 B6
Dury La LN1 234 B3
Dutton Ave PE25 206 A4
Dycote La LN5 106 D5
Dyke Cty Prim Sch PE10 154 D5
Dyke Dro PE10 154 E5
Dyke Rd 5 DN36 37 C5
Dykes End NG23 91 D4
Dymoke Cl 3 LN12 64 C3
Dymoke Dr
Grimsby DN37 190 C6
2 Horncastle LN9 199 C2
Dymoke Rd 5 LN12 64 C3
Dysart Rd NG31 210 E4
Dyson Cl PE1 225 F3

E

Eagle Cl 7 LN12 64 A4
Eagle Com Prim Sch LN6 79 B2
Eagle Dr
3 Sleaford NG34 212 B3
8 Welton/Dunholme LN2 68 D7
Eagle La LN6 79 D1
Eagle Moor LN6 79 C3
Eagle Rd
Doddington & Whisby LN6 79 D3
North Scarle LN6 78 F2
Spalford NG23 78 D4
Eaglesthorpe PE1 225 E7
Ealand Rd 3 DN17 17 C6
Eames Gdns PE1 226 E6
Earl Ave DN36 195 D7
Earl of Dysart Prim Sch NG31 210 D3
Earl of Scarbrough High Sch The PE25 206 C5
Earl of Scarbrough Sports Ctr PE25 206 B5
Earl Spencer Ct PE2 230 E8
Earl St Grimsby DN31 191 C7
Scunthorpe DN16 183 B1
Earle's Rd HU9 181 D7
Earlesfield La NG31 210 F3
Earls Cl PE2 231 B6
Earls Dr LN5 205 D8
Earlsfield Cl LN6 204 B5
Earlsgate Gdns 3 DN15 8 F5
Earlsgate Rd DN15 8 F5
Earlswood PE2 229 E5
Earth Cl PE2 231 E5
Ease La NG23 117 F3
Easenby Ave HU10 178 C6
Easenby Cl 2 HU14 3 C7
Eason Rd 10 DN33 191 B2
East Acridge
15 Barton-upon-Humber DN18 3 F1
8 Barton-upon-Humber DN18 10 F8
East Ave
Brant Broughton LN5 105 F5
Grantham NG31 210 E3
1 Stainforth DN7 14 C5
East Bank
2 Stainforth DN7 14 C7
Sutton Bridge PE12 160 F5
East Barkwith CE Sch LN8 71 A8
East Bight LN2 234 B3
East Boundary Rd DN16 183 F2
East Camp Rd 8 NG34 120 C8
East Cl 18 NG34 108 E2
East Cob Gate PE12 157 F6
East Comm La DN16 185 B8
East Croft 10 LN3 203 E7
East Cross St 25 DN21 30 B1
East Dale Dr 3 DN21 30 B2
East Dale Rd HU14 2 E5
East Dr LN4 110 E8
East Ella Dr HU4 179 C6
East Elloe Ave PE12 215 D3
East End
3 Burgh le Marsh PE24 102 E7
Humberside Airport DN39 22 A6
Langtoft PE6 164 F3
East End Cl DN33 191 D1
East Fen La PE22 113 B7
East Ferry Rd
East Ferry DN21 28 E3
Laughton DN21 41 B8
Wildsworth DN21 40 D8
East Field LN5 92 F2
East Field Rd DN7 14 C8
East Gate Bourne PE10 213 E4
Fleet PE12 159 C7
Moulton PE12 158 A7
Sleaford NG34 212 E4
Whaplode PE12 158 C7
East Gn 30 DN17 29 D7
East Gr
12 Barton-upon-Humber DN18 3 F1
8 Colsterworth NG33 151 E6
Kingston upon Hull HU4 179 D4
East Halton Prim Sch DN40 12 D6
East Halton Rd DN40 12 E3
East Hann La DN19 4 E1
East Heckington CE Sch PE20 123 E3
East La Corringham DN21 41 E2
Morton PE10 154 C7
Stainforth DN7 14 C6
East Liberty LN2 202 C4
East Lound Rd
Haxey DN9 27 D2
Owston Ferry DN9 28 A3
East Marsh Rd DN19 5 C3
East Marsh St 2 DN31 191 E8
East Mid Mere Rd
Immingham DN40 12 F4
South Killingholme DN40 13 A4
East Mill Gate 3 LN3 203 E6
East Mount 12 HU14 3 A4
East of England Showground★ PE2 229 C4
East Par DN20 196 C4
East Ravendale CE Prim Sch DN37 35 C2
East Rd
Deeping St Nicholas PE11 156 C4
4 Keadby with Althorpe DN17 17 C6
Navenby/Wellingore LN5 107 B8
Northborough PE6 217 E1
Sleaford NG34 212 F6
Tetford LN9 73 F1
Tydd St Mary PE13 170 C8
East Rd Ind Est NG34 212 F5
East Row LN11 50 E4
East St Alford LN13 75 F4
Bole DN22 52 C6
Crowland PE6 166 E1
Grantham NG31 211 B4
7 Grimsby DN32 191 E7
Helpringham NG34 133 E7
18 Hibaldstow DN20 30 F5
Horncastle LN9 199 C4
5 Kingston upon Hull HU9 181 B7
Nettleham LN2 68 C2
Rippingale PE10 143 A2
Roxby cum Risby DN15 9 A3
Stamford PE9 219 C5
East St Mary's Gate 4 DN31 191 D7
East Sta Rd PE2 231 B8
East View LN4 109 D7
East Wold CE Prim Sch LN11 62 A3
Eastbeck La LN9 86 A2
Eastbourne St
Kingston upon Hull HU3 180 A5
Lincoln LN2 234 C2
Eastbourne Way DN33 194 F7
Eastbrook Rd LN6 205 A5
Eastchurch Rd 4 NG34 120 D8
Eastcliff Rd LN2 234 C3
Eastcliffe Sq 9 NG32 119 B7
Eastcroft 5 LN1 66 D3
Eastern Ave
Gainsborough DN21 197 F5
Peterborough PE1 226 C8
Eastern Cl PE1 226 D7
Eastern Dr
3 Balderton NG24 104 C1
RAF Cranwell NG34 120 D8
Eastern Inway DN34 191 A4
Eastern Rd PE12 215 F8
Eastfield
14 Humberston DN36 36 D8
3 Market Deeping PE6 217 C5
11 Sturton by Stow LN1 66 D7
Eastfield Ave DN33 195 A7
Eastfield Cl
1 Dunholme LN2 68 E6
6 Sutterton PE20 136 A2
Eastfield Cty Inf & Jun Sch DN40 186 C2
Eastfield Gr PE1 226 B4
Eastfield Inf Sch LN11 198 D6
Eastfield La Manby LN11 62 C7
Welton LN2 68 E7
Eastfield N Ind Est DN40 12 F3
Eastfield Prim Sch HU4 179 D6
Eastfield Rd
Barton-upon-Humber DN18 10 F7
Brigg DN20 196 D3
Epworth DN9 27 E6
Firsby PE23 101 F7
Immingham DN40 12 F3
3 Keelby DN41 23 A5
Kingston upon Hull HU4 179 D6
Louth LN11 198 D6
40 Messingham DN17 29 D7
North Killingholme DN40 12 E5
Peterborough PE1 226 C4
Scunthorpe DN16 185 C5
1 Wisbech PE13 170 E1
Eastfield Rise
2 Holton le Clay DN36 195 D2
Louth LN11 198 E7
Eastfield S Ind Est DN40 12 F3
Eastfield St 5 LN2 202 B3
Eastfield Way 17 PE13 170 D1
Eastfields 2 LN8 43 D3
Eastgate
Bassingham LN5 92 F2
Bourne PE10 213 E4
Grimsby DN32 191 E8
Heckington NG34 122 E3
Kingston upon Hull HU13 178 E2
Lincoln LN2 234 B3
Louth LN11 198 C6
Market Deeping PE6 217 F3
Peterborough PE1 226 B2
Scotton DN21 29 C2
Eastgate Cl LN2 234 C3
Eastgate Gdns 3 PE12 159 C7
Eastgate La PE34 161 E2
Easthall Rd LN7 32 B4
Eastholm Cl PE1 226 C3
Eastholm Cty Sch PE1 226 C4
Eastholm Sch PE1 226 D5
Eastholme Gdns 10 DN15 8 B4
Easthorpe La NG13 128 C5
Easthorpe Rd
1 Bottesford NG13 128 B5
2 Great Gonerby NG31 129 E5
Easthorpe View 2 NG13 128 B5
Eastlands 4 PE6 166 F1
Eastlands Bank PE14 161 B1
Eastleigh Cl LN6 200 B1
Eastleigh Rd PE1 226 C3
Eastmoor Villas DN9 27 D3
Eastoft CE Prim Sch DN17 7 A3
Eastoft Rd Crowle DN17 16 D8
Luddington & Haldenby DN17 7 C3
Easton Garfords Charity Aided Sch PE9 171 D3
Easton La NG33 140 A2
Eastrea Ct PE2 231 E6
Eastside Rd
Grimsby DN31 189 B1
Scunthorpe DN16 183 F2
Eastview Cl PE24 90 E6
Eastville Rd
4 Grimsby DN33 191 A3
Toynton St Peter PE23 101 A6
Eastway 19 LN2 68 D2
Eastwood Ave DN32 191 D4
Eastwood Day Hospl NG24 104 A3
Eastwood Dr
2 Boston PE21 209 D4
10 Broughton DN20 19 E4
4 Grantham NG31 211 D2
Eastwood Rd PE21 209 D5
Easy Rd PE11 156 E1
Eaton Ct DN34 191 C6
Eaton Rd Boston PE21 208 E3
Immingham DN40 186 D4
Eau Bank LN11 50 D7
Eau Dike Rd PE22 115 A7
Eaudike Rd
Donington PE20 135 A3
Quadring PE11 145 C8
Eaudyke Bank 1 PE13 169 F7
Eaugate Rd PE12 157 F1
Ebony Gr LN6 200 C1
Ebrington Cl 3 LN10 97 E6
Eccles Ct 3 DN20 196 F7
Eccleston Rd 15 DN3 14 A3
Eddystone Dr 3 LN6 205 A1
Eden Cl 6 PE25 206 C1
Eden Dene DN16 185 D5
Eden Field Rd
20 Kirk Sandall DN3 14 A2
4 Kirk Sandall DN3 14 A1
Eden Gr Rd 8 DN3 14 A1
Edendale Gdns 3 LN1 201 E8
Edenfield PE2 230 C6
Edenham CE (Controlled) Prim Sch PE10 153 F5
Edenham Rd PE10 154 B6
Edenthorpe Hall Fst & Mid Sch DN3 14 A1
Edgar St HU3 180 D5
Edgbaston Ave 3 DN17 184 E3
Edgcote Cl PE3 225 C5

Edge Ave DN33 191 D2
Edgefield 4 PE12 157 E7
Edgehill 10 LN5 205 D2
Edgerley Drain Rd
PE1 226 F5
Edinburgh Ave
Peterborough PE4 220 F3
2 Skegness PE25 206 D3
Edinburgh Cl 13 PE20 136 C5
Edinburgh Cres
2 Bourne PE10 213 D6
12 Kirton PE20 136 C5
Edinburgh Dr
Holton le Clay DN36 195 C3
11 Kirton PE20 136 C5
Spalding PE11 214 E2
Wisbech PE13 170 D2
Edinburgh Rd
16 Binbrook Tech Pk LN8 47 B6
2 Grantham NG31 211 E6
3 Ruskington NG34 108 E2
Stamford PE9 219 B6
Edinburgh Sq 4 LN5 94 A7
Edinburgh St HU3 180 A5
Edinburgh Wlk
Holbeach PE12 215 E2
Pinchbeck PE11 156 B7
Edington Ct 3 DN21 53 A8
Edith Cavell PE3 225 B4
Edlington Cl 6 LN2 201 F8
Edmonds Cl 2 PE9 219 D6
Edmonds Way 3 DN31 191 D8
Edmondthorpe Drift
LE14 150 D1
Edmondthorpe Rd
LE14 150 C1
Edmund Cl DN21 41 D2
Edmunds Dr 7 PE9 171 A3
Edmunds Rd 3 NG34 107 F1
Edna St LN5 201 F1
Edwalton Ave
9 Mablethorpe/Sutton on Sea
LN12 77 A8
Peterborough PE3 225 E3
Edward Barker Rd LN4 81 F4
Edward Collins Sq 2
HU9 181 C7
Edward Cres PE25 206 B3
Edward Heneage Prim Sch
DN32 191 F7
Edward Rd
Gainsborough DN21 197 D6
Spalding PE11 214 B4
10 Stamford PE9 219 A7
Edward St
Cleethorpes DN35 192 E5
Grantham NG31 211 B2
Grimsby DN32 191 F7
Kingston upon Hull
HU13 178 F1
1 Lincoln LN5 205 E8
17 Louth LN11 198 B5
Edwards Rd 3 DN15 182 F4
Edwin Cl 12 NG34 212 B2
Edwin Gdns PE10 213 B5
Edwin St 13 PE21 208 F4
Edwina Ave 6 PE11 156 F8
Egar Way PE3 224 F2
Egerton Rd LN2 202 B5
Egginton Cl HU10 178 C7
Egginton St 4 HU2 180 F7
Egret Gr 5 LN6 204 D8
Egton Ave 17 DN17 29 D7
Egton St HU8 181 A8
Eighth Ave DN15 8 A1
Elan Cl PE21 208 E5
Elba St 6 HU9 5 E8
Elbow La PE13 177 F8
Elder Cl 2 Bourne PE10 213 C6
Skegness PE25 206 A5
Elder St LN5 205 D5
Elder Tree Way LN10 84 D3
Elderberry Dr HU4 179 C4
Elderberry Way 2
DN35 192 D2
Elder's Gate PE12 169 E8
Elderwood Ct 6 HU3 180 D5
Eleanor Cl Lincoln LN5 205 E7
Stamford PE9 219 A6
Eleanor St DN32 191 F8
Electric Sta Rd NG34 212 C4
Eleven Acre La PE20 136 D4
Eley's La PE20 136 B2
Elgar Rd HU4 179 B4
Eliot Cl
Gainsborough DN21 197 F3
9 Sleaford NG34 212 F4
Elizabeth Ave
Dogdyke LN4 110 D7
11 Kirk Sandall DN3 14 A2
6 Lincoln LN6 93 C8
Lincoln LN6 204 F1
Wrange PE22 114 C2
Elizabeth Cl
16 Chapel St Leonard PE24 90 D7
Gainsborough DN21 197 C7
Glentworth DN21 54 F6
Grimsby DN33 194 D7
Scotter DN21 29 C4
Elizabeth Cres
6 Ingoldmells PE25 90 E3
Pinchbeck PE11 144 D1
Elizabeth Ct 17 PE24 90 D7
Elizabeth Dr
Billingborough NG34 143 B8
Elizabeth Dr *continued*
12 Chapel St Leonard PE24 90 D7
Elizabeth Rd
Boston PE21 209 B5
2 Stamford PE9 219 B6
Elizabeth St 3 DN15 183 A4
Elizabeth Way 4 PE10 164 C8
Ella Pk HU10 178 D7
Ellen Cres PE11 214 A3
Ellen Way DN36 195 B7
Ellerby Mead NG33 152 D5
Ellesmere Ave 3 LN2 202 D4
Ellesmere Bsns Pk
NG31 210 E2
Ellesmere Gr 4 DN7 14 D6
Ellesmere Rise DN34 190 D3
Ellicar La DN10 39 A3
Ellindon PE3 225 B7
Elliot Ave PE3 224 F2
Elliot Cl NG31 211 E6
Elliott Rd LN5 234 C1
Elliott Way 11 PE24 90 D7
Ellis St HU9 181 C8
Ellis Way DN32 191 E8
Ellison Ave DN16 185 A1
Ellison Boulters CE (Con)
Prim Sch LN2 68 F4
Ellison Cl 5 LN2 68 F2
Ellison St Lincoln LN5 205 D5
Thorne/Moorends DN8 15 A7
Elliston Jun & Inf Schs
DN35 192 C8
Elliston St DN35 192 C8
Ellmore La LN7 32 C3
Elloe Bank PE13 169 B2
Elloughton Cty Prim Sch
HU15 2 B7
Elloughton Dale HU15 2 D8
Elloughton Rd HU15 2 C6
Elloughtonthorpe Way 15
HU15 2 D5
Ellwood Ave PE2 231 E5
Elm Ave 18 Brough HU15 2 C6
Cherry Willingham/Reepham
LN3 203 D5
Cleethorpes DN35 192 E6
Grimsby DN34 191 A6
21 Mablethorpe/Sutton on Sea
LN12 64 B3
Newark-on-Trent NG24 104 A3
Elm Cl Lincoln LN6 204 F2
17 Long Bennington NG23 117 D3
Market Deeping PE6 217 C4
13 Saxilby LN1 66 D2
Yaxley PE7 233 F7
Elm Cres
Burgh le Marsh PE24 102 D8
Glinton PE6 220 B8
Elm Dr
Ingoldmells PE25 206 D8
Louth LN11 198 D7
Skegness PE25 90 E1
3 Sudbrooke LN2 68 F2
Elm Gdns DN35 192 E6
Elm Gr Grantham NG31 211 C6
8 Healing DN41 24 A5
Scunthorpe DN16 185 B8
Elm La Goxhill DN19 5 A1
7 Laceby DN37 23 E1
Low Fulney PE12 157 C6
Elm Rd
Cleethorpes DN35 192 E6
Waltham DN37 194 E3
Elm St
Peterborough PE2 230 F7
Stamford PE9 219 C5
Elm Tree Cl 11 LN8 57 D7
Elm Tree Gr 8 DN8 15 B7
Elm Way Brigg DN20 196 B4
Messingham DN17 29 C7
Elmdale 29 DN18 10 E8
Elmdene 5 LN2 68 F4
Elmer St N 3 NG31 211 A4
Elmer St S NG31 211 A4
Elmfield Rd PE1 226 A7
Elmgarth 3 NG34 212 F3
Elmhirst Ave PE25 206 D6
Elmhirst Rd 5 DN8 15 B8
Elmhurst La LN9 199 B6
Elmore Rd PE3 225 A3
Elms Dr HU10 178 C8
Elms View 4 NG31 129 D5
Elmswood HU13 178 C2
Elmtree Ave 10 HU14 3 A4
Elmtree Rd NG34 108 D1
Elmwood Ave 4 PE21 208 F2
Elmwood Cl 6 LN6 200 D1
Elmwood Dr 6 PE25 90 D3
Elsea Dr 3 PE10 164 C8
Elsea Pk Way PE10 213 D2
Elsenham Rd DN31 188 D1
Elsham Cl 7 LN6 204 D8
Elsham Cres LN6 204 D8
Elsham Dr DN37 194 C3
Elsham Gr 4 DN33 191 B3
Elsham Rd DN20 20 D7
Elsham Rise HU13 178 D1
Elsham Wold Ind Est
DN20 21 A8
Elsie Davies Cl NG31 211 C7
Elsiemere Wlk 6 HU4 179 B6
Elsom Way LN9 199 A4
Elsthorpe Rd
Edenham PE10 153 E6
Haconby PE10 154 A7
Elstone PE2 230 A4
Elton Cl 2 PE9 218 F6
Elton Rd Thorney PE8 228 B6
Elton Rd *continued*
Wansford PE8 222 B2
Elton St 1 NG31 211 A3
Elveley Dr HU10 178 A7
Elvin Cl 3 LN2 201 F6
Elvington Cl 7 LN6 204 B6
Elvington Rd LN6 204 B6
Elwes St DN20 196 C2
Elwyn Pl DN35 192 D2
Ely Cl PE4 220 F3
Ely St Lincoln LN1 201 D4
5 Sleaford NG34 212 C6
Ely Way 5 NG31 210 F5
Embankment Rd 4 PE1 226 A1
Ember La
Chapel St Leonards PE24 77 B1
Hogsthorpe PE24 90 B8
Embry Rd 22 PE8 172 B1
Emerald Gr 8 HU3 180 A4
Emerson Ave DN7 14 C5
Emfield Gr DN33 194 E7
Emfield Rd DN33 194 D6
Emily St 8 HU9 181 C7
Eminson Cl DN21 29 C4
Emlyns Gdns 5 PE9 219 C6
Emlyns St 2 PE9 219 C6
Emmanual Rd DN16 185 F6
Emmanuel Ct 3 DN16 185 C6
Emmanuel Dr DN16 185 A3
Emmanuel Rd PE9 219 B7
Emmery Cl 2 DN20 19 D4
Emminson Way 1
NG31 210 E8
Emorsgate PE34 161 E3
Empingham Rd
4 Stamford PE9 219 A5
Tinwell PE9 218 B6
Emprinham St 5 HU9 181 D7
Empson Rd PE1 226 F5
Ena St HU3 180 B6
Endcliffe Ave DN17 184 F2
Endeavour Cres 1 HU9 5 D8
Endeavour Pk Ind Est
PE21 208 B4
Endeavour Way PE20 136 A2
Enderby Cl LN4 203 A2
Enderby Cres DN21 197 E3
Enderby Rd DN17 184 E4
Enderby Rd Inf Sch
DN17 184 D4
Endsleigh St HU3 180 A7
Enfield Ave DN36 195 D5
Enfield Prim Sch
DN36 195 D6
Enfield Rd 8 LN11 59 E1
Engaine PE2 230 B5
Engine Bank PE12 157 F2
Engine Dro NG34 134 B4
Engine Dyke PE12 148 B1
Engine St DN20 196 B3
English Cl HU3 180 E4
English Rd PE6 176 B5
English St
Kingston upon Hull HU3 180 E4
Peterborough PE1 225 E5
Ennerdale Cl
3 Birchwood LN6 200 D1
6 Humberston DN36 192 E1
Ennerdale Rise PE4 221 B2
Enterprise Rd
Caistor LN7 33 A4
3 Mablethorpe/Sutton on Sea
LN12 64 A4
Enterprise Way
Grimsby DN32 192 A6
Pinchbeck PE11 214 E8
4 Winterton DN15 8 F5
Ephams La DN41 23 E7
Epsom Cl LN6 204 B8
Epsom Rd LN6 204 B8
Epworth Cty Prim Sch
DN9 27 D6
Epworth Leisure Ctr
DN9 27 D6
Epworth Rd (West) 10
DN7 14 E4
Epworth Rd Hatfield DN7 14 F4
Haxey DN9 27 D3
Owston Ferry DN9 28 A4
Epworth Turbary Nature
Reserve★ DN9 27 B6
Erebus Cl 7 PE23 101 A8
Eresbie Rd LN11 198 D3
Eresby Ave
13 Spilsby PE23 87 F1
Spilsby PE23 100 F8
Eresby Specl Sch The
PE23 100 F8
Ermine Cl
5 Ancaster NG32 120 A3
Bourne PE10 213 C6
Grantham NG31 211 D5
8 Lincoln LN1 201 E8
Stamford PE9 218 F5
Ermine Dr 3 LN5 107 B8
Ermine Inf Sch LN2 202 A7
Ermine Jun Sch LN2 202 A8
Ermine Rise PE9 171 B8
Ermine St
Ancaster NG32 120 A2
Appleby DN15 9 C1
Winteringham DN15 9 B8
Ermine Way
Market Deeping PE6 217 E5
Stamford PE9 218 F5
Ernest Terr LN2 234 B4
Eryholme Cres 1 DN15 182 F2
Escart Ave DN32 192 B6
Esk Cl LN6 204 F4
Eskdale Cl 1 PE4 221 C3
Eskdale Rd NG31 211 A7
Eskdale Way DN37 190 D8
Eskham Cl 1 DN35 192 F3
Essendine Rd PE9 163 C2
Essendyke PE3 225 A7
Essex Dr 9 DN15 8 B4
Essex Rd 3 PE9 219 B6
Essex St HU4 179 E3
Essex Way PE10 213 D4
Estate Ave DN20 19 D3
Estate Rd No 1 DN31 188 B2
Estate Rd No 2 DN31 188 B1
Estate Rd No 3 DN31 188 B3
Estate Rd No 4 DN31 188 B2
Estate Rd No 5 DN31 188 B2
Estate Rd No 6 DN31 188 B2
Estate Rd No 7 DN31 188 B1
Estate Rd No 8 DN31 188 B1
Estcourt Prim Sch
HU9 181 D8
Estcourt St HU9 181 D8
Estella Way PE11 214 A5
Estuary Way DN31 188 D2
Estwaite Cl LN6 205 B2
Ethelstone Rd 5 DN34 191 A7
Etherington St DN21 197 D4
Eton Cl LN6 200 D3
Eton Dr DN17 184 F3
Eton Rd
Heighington/Washingborough
LN4 203 C1
6 Mablethorpe/Sutton on Sea
LN12 64 C2
Eton St Grantham NG31 211 B4
Kingston upon Hull HU3 180 C4
Eudo Rd PE25 206 D7
Eugate Rd PE6 167 F4
Europa Bsns Pk DN31 188 C2
Europa Way
Brigg DN20 196 A4
Immingham DN41 187 B3
Eurosure Tennis Ctr
PE21 208 C5
Eusden Ct LN4 207 A5
Euston Ave 5 PE11 214 B2
Euston Cl LN6 200 D2
Eve Gdns LN4 203 D1
Eve St LN11 198 B6
Evedon Rd NG34 121 F5
Evelyn Gr N 1 DN32 192 B6
Evelyn Gr S 3 DN32 192 B6
Evendine Ct DN36 195 E1
Ever Thorpe Cl 5 HU3 180 C5
Everard Rd PE11 155 C1
Everdon Way PE3 225 C5
Everest Rd DN16 185 C5
Everingham PE2 229 D5
Everington's La PE25 103 C8
Everthorpe Cl 16 HU15 2 D5
Eves Cl 9 PE6 174 E5
Evesham Ave DN34 190 E5
Evison Cres 2 LN13 75 E3
Evison Ct 12 PE22 113 B1
Evison Way LN11 50 E7
Ewart St LN5 205 D6
Ewerby Rd NG34 122 A5
Exchange Cl LN6 204 E4
Exchange Pl 5 DN20 196 B3
Exchange Rd LN6 204 E4
Exchange St PE1 226 A2
Exchequergate 5 LN2 234 B3
Exeter Cl 3 Bourne PE10 213 C5
Grantham NG31 210 C5
Heighington/Washingborough
LN4 203 E2
1 Market Deeping PE6 217 E4
Exeter Ct
2 Bourne PE10 213 C5
10 Grimsby DN34 190 D4
Exeter Dr
4 Sleaford NG34 212 C6
Spalding PE11 214 E4
Exeter Gdns
10 Bourne PE10 213 C5
Stamford PE9 218 F4
Exeter Rd
Peterborough PE1 225 F6
Scunthorpe DN15 182 F3
8 Wittering PE8 172 B1
Exeter St PE10 213 C5
Exmoor Ave DN15 182 D7
Exmoor Cl LN6 204 D1
Exmoor Rd DN17 184 C8
Exton Cl 6 PE9 218 E5
Eyam Way 3 LN6 204 F1
Eye CE (Controlled) Sch
PE6 175 B1
Eye Rd PE1 174 F1
Eyebury Rd Eye PE6 175 A1
Peterborough PE6 227 A6
Eyre Ave DN16 185 B5
Eyre's La LN6 78 F1
Eyrescroft PE3 225 A7
Eyrescroft CP Sch
PE3 225 A7

F

Fagans Way 7 PE25 206 C1
Fainlight Cl 2 PE25 206 D8
Fair View Ave DN35 192 E6
Fairburn Cl 9 PE24 90 D7
Fairchild Way PE1 226 A7
Fairfax Cl Boston PE21 208 D7
Gainsborough DN21 197 F2
Fairfax Cl *continued*
6 Horncastle LN9 199 D3
2 Toft Newton LN8 56 D5
Fairfax Rd DN31 191 B7
Fairfax St LN5 205 D6
Fairfax Way PE6 217 E3
Fairfield LN4 207 C4
Fairfield Ave
25 Chapel St Leonard PE24 90 D7
Grimsby DN33 194 E7
Fairfield Cl
8 Broughton DN20 19 E3
3 Spalding PE11 214 C6
Fairfield Croft 9 DN9 27 E6
Fairfield Ct 3 DN35 193 A1
Fairfield Dr
29 Barton-upon-Humber
DN18 10 F8
39 Messingham DN17 29 D7
Fairfield Est LN11 198 B8
Fairfield Prim Sch
DN33 194 E8
Fairfield Rd
Grimsby DN33 194 E7
Peterborough PE2 231 A8
Scunthorpe DN15 182 C4
Fairfield St LN2 202 B4
Fairfield View 11 HU15 2 D5
Fairfields
Holbeach PE12 215 C3
33 Kirton in Lindsey DN21 30 B1
Fairisle Rise DN40 186 C2
Fairleas LN4 81 E2
Fairmead Way PE3 225 E2
Fairmont Cres DN16 183 B2
Fairmont Rd DN32 192 A7
Fairtree Wlk 24 DN8 15 A8
Fairview Way PE11 214 C6
Fairway DN37 194 D5
Fairway Ct DN35 193 C1
Fairway The
Kingston upon Hull
HU10 178 A8
1 Mablethorpe/Sutton on Sea
LN12 64 A4
Fairways PE10 164 A8
Fairways The DN15 182 B2
Fakenham Chase
PE12 215 E3
Falcon Cl LN6 79 B2
Falcon Ct
9 Grantham NG31 210 E2
Kingston upon Hull HU4 179 D2
Falcon Rd 7 LN4 108 A7
Falcon Way 13 NG34 212 B3
Falconers The DN21 30 F2
Faldingworth Cl 3 LN6 204 C7
Faldingworth Prim Sch
LN8 56 F3
Faldingworth Rd LN8 55 F3
Falkirk Cl 6 PE9 218 E6
Falkland Rd 4 HU9 5 F8
Falkland Way DN18 3 F1
Falklands Cl LN1 201 E8
Falklands Rd PE12 160 D4
Fallodan Rd PE2 229 C3
Fallow La Foston NG32 118 A2
1 Westborough & Dry
Doddington NG23 117 F3
Fallowfield PE2 229 D5
Fallowfield Rd DN33 194 D7
Fall's Dro PE6 175 F7
Falsgrave Gr HU5 179 D7
Fane Cl PE9 219 B7
Fane Rd PE4 221 C1
Fanny Hands La 1 LN8 59 A7
Fannystone Rd 3 DN34 191 B7
Fantail Cl 2 PE11 156 E2
Fantasy Island★ PE25 90 E3
Fanthorpe La LN11 198 A7
Far Bank La DN7 14 C8
Far Comm Rd DN7 15 A3
Far Dro PE20 124 E2
Far End LN5 94 A2
Far Field Rd 22 DN3 14 A2
Far Holme La 5 NG23 91 A8
Far Hurn Dro LN4 110 B7
Far Ings La DN18 3 C1
Far Ings Nature Reserve★
DN18 3 D2
Far Ings Rd DN18 3 D1
Far La LN5 93 F3
Far Pasture 2 PE4 220 F5
Farcet Prim Sch PE7 231 C2
Fardell Rd DN16 185 D7
Farebrother St DN32 191 E6
Faringdon Rd DN31 189 C2
Farleigh Fields PE2 229 D6
Farlesthorpe Rd
Alford LN13 75 F2
Bilsby LN13 76 A2
Willoughby with Sloothby
LN13 89 B8
Farm Cl 2 Gunness DN15 17 E6
12 Kirk Sandall DN3 14 A1
Farm La 1 DN17 28 D8
Farm View Castor PE5 223 E2
18 Welton LN2 68 D7
Farmers Gate PE12 215 B2
Farmhouse Cl 12 NG13 128 A6
Farmhouse Mews 11
DN36 195 C6
Farndale Cres 5 NG31 211 A8
Farndale Way
26 Winterton DN15 9 A5
25 Winterton DN15 9 A5
1 Winterton DN15 9 A5
Farnella Cl HU3 180 A5

Farrier Rd LN6 ... 204 B5
Farrier Way PE11 ... 214 A2
Farriers Ct
Peterborough PE2 ... 230 D7
Scopwick LN4 ... 95 C1
Farriers Way
Carlby PE9 ... 163 D4
2 Tattershall LN4 ... 207 A5
Farringdon Cl 2 PE1 ... 226 D6
Farrington Cres LN6 ... 200 D2
Farrishes La DN18 ... 10 A8
Farrow Ave PE12 ... 215 E1
Farrow Rd PE12 ... 168 A4
Farrows Pond 3 DN19 ... 5 A1
Farthing Ave DN15 ... 182 E4
Farthingales PE11 ... 214 C6
Farthings Fold PE10 ... 154 B6
Fauconberg Ave 4
DN33 ... 191 C2
Faulding La DN40 ... 12 F2
Faulding Way DN37 ... 190 C7
Faulkers La PE24 ... 89 E1
Favell Rd 1 LN4 ... 203 B2
Faversham Ave HU4 ... 179 B6
Fawcett St DN21 ... 197 C5
Fawsley Cl 6 LN2 ... 202 E7
Fawsley Garth PE3 ... 225 C6
Faxfleet La DN14 ... 1 A3
Fayid La LN4 ... 95 C7
Feale Abbey PE34 ... 161 E1
Feather La 8 DN19 ... 11 C7
Featherby Pl 7 LN5 ... 205 E8
Fellands Gate PE22 ... 113 F3
Fellowes Gdns PE2 ... 231 E4
Fellowes Rd PE2 ... 231 A7
Felstead Rd DN34 ... 190 F6
Fen Cl 24 PE13 ... 170 D1
Fen Ct 1 DN3 ... 14 A1
Fen Dike PE12 ... 159 B3
Fen Dro PE7 ... 233 D1
Fen End La PE12 ... 156 F3
Fen Gate PE12 ... 157 E2
Fen La Balderton NG24 ... 104 D2
Bassingham LN5 ... 93 A3
Beesby with Saleby LN13 ... 76 A7
Conisholme LN11 ... 50 C5
Dunston LN4 ... 95 C6
East Keal PE23 ... 100 E5
Grainthorpe LN11 ... 49 F5
Lincoln LN6 ... 205 A1
Long Bennington NG23 ... 117 B6
Mablethorpe & Sutton
LN12 ... 64 A1
Maltby Le Marsh LN13 ... 63 E1
Mareham Le Fen PE22 ... 98 F2
North Somercotes LN11 ... 50 D6
North Thoresby DN36 ... 36 C1
South Carlton LN1 ... 67 C2
Tydd St Giles PE13 ... 169 B5
Fen Prep Sch The
NG34 ... 123 C3
Fen Rd Billinghay LN4 ... 109 F6
Dowsby PE10 ... 143 D4
East Kirkby PE23 ... 99 F4
Frampton PE20 ... 125 B1
Gosberton PE11 ... 144 A4
Heighington LN4 ... 82 A4
Heighington/Washingborough
LN4 ... 203 E2
Holbeach PE12 ... 215 D1
Little Hale NG34 ... 133 F8
Metheringham LN4 ... 95 C4
Newton PE13 ... 169 E4
Owmby LN8 ... 55 F6
Pointon & Sempringham
NG34 ... 143 D6
Ruskington NG34 ... 108 F2
Stickford PE22 ... 100 C2
Thurlby PE10 ... 154 E1
Timberland LN4 ... 96 C1
Toynton St Peter PE23 ... 101 A4
Wisbech St Mary PE13 ... 177 E2
Fen View
Heighington LN4 ... 81 F4
Peterborough PE2 ... 231 F6
Fen Wlk DN36 ... 37 C5
Fenbridge Rd PE4 ... 221 A4
Fenby Cl DN37 ... 190 D6
Fence Bank PE34 ... 161 D1
Fendike Bank PE24 ... 101 F3
Fendike La PE20 ... 135 B5
Fendyke End La PE22 ... 126 E5
Fendyke La PE13 ... 169 F1
Feneley Cl PE6 ... 217 D5
Fengate PE1 ... 226 D1
Fengate Cl 1 PE1 ... 226 B2
Fengate Dro PE12 ... 157 C3
Fengate Rd
Pinchbeck PE11 ... 214 A8
Walsoken PE14 ... 170 F1
Fenhouses Dro PE20 ... 135 D8
Fenhouses La PE20 ... 135 C7
Fenland Airfield PE12 ... 168 B8
Fenland Rd
13 Thorne/Moorends DN8 ... 15 B7
Wisbech PE13 ... 170 E1
Fenland Wlk PE12 ... 215 B2
Fennell Rd 5 PE11 ... 156 E8
Fenside
Halton Holegate PE23 ... 101 C6
Toynton All Saints PE23 ... 100 F4
Fenside Dr 5 PE6 ... 174 E5
Fenside Rd
Boston PE21 ... 208 C6
Holland Fen with Brothertoft
PE21 ... 125 C5
Fenton Dr PE9 ... 163 E5
Fenton La DN22 ... 52 C1
Fenton Pl LN2 ... 234 C2
Fenton Rd
Fenton NG23 ... 105 B1
Stubton NG23 ... 118 B8
Fenton St DN15 ... 183 B3
Fenwick Ct 6 DN36 ... 195 D1
Fenwick Rd DN33 ... 191 B2
Ferensway HU2 ... 180 E7
Fern Croft 10 DN9 ... 27 E6
Fern Ct HU13 ... 179 A1
Fern Dr PE11 ... 214 C7
Fern Gr LN3 ... 203 D5
Fernbank 2 DN9 ... 27 D7
Ferndale PE7 ... 233 D6
Ferndale Cl NG33 ... 152 F7
Ferndown 1 DN37 ... 188 A1
Ferndown Dr DN40 ... 186 D4
Ferneries La 3 DN38 ... 21 B4
Fernhall Cl 15 DN3 ... 14 A2
Fernhill DN37 ... 190 C7
Fernie Cl 3 PE6 ... 174 E4
Fernland Cl 18 HU15 ... 2 C5
Fernleigh Way PE21 ... 209 B6
Ferriby High Rd HU14 ... 3 B5
Ferriby La DN33 ... 191 C2
Ferriby Rd
Barton-upon-Humber
DN18 ... 10 E8
Hessle HU13 ... 178 B1
Scunthorpe DN17 ... 184 E5
Ferriby Sta HU14 ... 3 A4
Ferries St HU9 ... 181 D7
Ferry Dr PE6 ... 224 D3
Ferry Hill PE5 ... 224 B1
Ferry La
Holland Fen with Brothertoft
PE20 ... 124 D6
Newton PE13 ... 170 B5
North Kyme LN4 ... 109 F2
Skellingthorpe LN6 ... 200 C5
South Kyme LN4 ... 109 F1
Sturton Le Steeple DN22 ... 52 D3
Washingborough LN4 ... 203 B2
Winteringham DN15 ... 2 B1
Ferry Mdws Ctry Pk*
PE2 ... 229 D8
Ferry Mdws Sta PE2 ... 229 E7
Ferry Rd Bardney LN3 ... 83 D1
Barrow upon Humber DN19 ... 4 C1
Fiskerton LN3 ... 82 D6
Haxey DN9 ... 27 D1
2 Keadby with Althorpe
DN17 ... 17 D4
Kingston upon Hull
HU13 ... 178 E1
Langriville PE22 ... 124 D8
Scunthorpe DN15 ... 182 E5
Ferry Rd W DN15 ... 182 A6
Ferryside 2 LN3 ... 82 B6
Ferryside Gdns 3 LN3 ... 82 B6
Ferryview PE2 ... 229 E6
Festival Ave 3 PE25 ... 90 D3
Ffolkes Dr 12 PE34 ... 161 F3
Field Ave 6 PE13 ... 169 F7
Field Cl
6 Gosberton PE11 ... 145 B6
10 Laceby DN37 ... 23 F1
23 Nettleham LN2 ... 68 D2
14 Ruskington NG34 ... 108 D2
1 Welton LN2 ... 68 D7
Field Dr 2 NG24 ... 104 C1
Field Farm La 3 LN4 ... 95 D4
Field Head 5 DN37 ... 23 E1
Field La Bardney LN3 ... 83 C5
Eastoft DN17 ... 7 A3
Ewerby & Evedon NG34 ... 122 C6
Friskney PE22 ... 115 A6
Morton DN21 ... 197 A8
2 Normanby By Spital LN8 ... 55 F6
Strubby with Woodthorpe
LN13 ... 63 C1
Wroot DN9 ... 26 D5
Field Rd Billinghay LN4 ... 109 E6
Crowle DN17 ... 16 D7
Stainforth DN7 ... 14 C6
Thorne/Moorends DN8 ... 15 A8
Field Rise PE7 ... 233 D5
Field Side
Mareham Le Fen PE22 ... 98 F4
Thorne DN8 ... 15 A8
Field St 6 Boston PE21 ... 209 A5
Kingston upon Hull HU9 ... 181 B7
Field Terr PE7 ... 231 C2
Field View PE22 ... 111 F8
Field Wlk PE1 ... 226 B2
Fieldfare Croft PE21 ... 208 C6
Fieldfare Dr PE2 ... 231 E6
Fieldhouse Rd DN36 ... 193 A1
Fields Cl 3 DN9 ... 27 D7
Fields Rd DN9 ... 27 E2
Fieldside 6 Blyton DN21 ... 41 C5
11 Crowle DN17 ... 16 D7
Epworth DN9 ... 27 D6
Fieldside Cres 1 PE22 ... 99 A4
Fife Cl PE9 ... 218 D6
Fifth Ave
Fixborough Ind Est DN15 ... 8 A1
Grantham NG31 ... 211 F6
Scunthorpe DN17 ... 184 B6
Fifth Dro PE11 ... 144 A4
Fiftyeights Rd DN10 ... 26 B2
Figtree Wlk PE1 ... 226 A7
Fildes St DN31 ... 191 D7
Filey Cl LN6 ... 205 A3
Filey Rd DN32 ... 192 A5
Fillingham Cres
Cleethorpes DN35 ... 192 F3
3 Scunthorpe DN15 ... 182 B3
Fillingham La DN21 ... 53 F3
Finch Cl LN6 ... 204 D8
Finch Dr NG34 ... 212 B3
Finchfield PE1 ... 226 F7
Finchley Gn PE3 ... 225 E4
Findlay Cres DN36 ... 195 D6
Fingle St 3 DN22 ... 52 B1
Finisterre Ave PE25 ... 206 A6
Finkell St DN10 ... 39 C1
Finkin St NG31 ... 211 A4
Finkle La 11 DN18 ... 3 F1
Finkle St
Benington PE22 ... 127 A5
Stainforth DN7 ... 14 C7
Finney Cl LN4 ... 207 D5
Finningley Cl 9 LN6 ... 204 D6
Finningley Rd LN6 ... 204 D6
Finns La NG32 ... 138 C6
Finsbury Dr 9 DN33 ... 191 B2
Finsbury St 18 LN13 ... 75 F2
Fir Ave PE10 ... 213 A5
Fir Cl DN16 ... 185 A4
Fir Rd 1 PE9 ... 218 D6
Fir Tree Ave 5 LN5 ... 93 E8
Fir Tree Cl 4 LN2 ... 68 F2
Fir Tree La NG32 ... 119 F3
Fir Trees HU10 ... 178 D6
Firbeck Ave PE25 ... 206 D1
Fircroft NG31 ... 211 C1
Firdale Cl 3 PE6 ... 174 A5
Firebeacon La
Grainthorpe LN11 ... 49 E8
Marshchapel LN11 ... 37 D1
Firethorn Cl 3 HU3 ... 180 D5
Firs The 6 NG34 ... 108 D1
Firsby Cres DN33 ... 191 A2
First Ave
1 Fixborough Ind Est DN15 ... 7 F1
Grantham NG31 ... 211 E6
4 Grimsby DN33 ... 191 C4
6 Scampton Airfield LN1 ... 67 E5
Scunthorpe DN17 ... 184 C6
Spalding PE11 ... 214 B4
First Dro Crowland PE6 ... 166 E2
Gosberton PE11 ... 144 C3
Moulton PE12 ... 146 E6
Peterborough PE1 ... 226 D1
First Holme La 2 NG23 ... 91 A8
First Hurn Dro LN4 ... 110 A6
First La HU10 ... 179 A5
First Marsh Rd PE13 ... 170 C2
Firth Field Rd DN7 ... 14 F4
Firth La DN9 ... 26 D6
Firth Rd LN6 ... 234 A1
Firtree Ave LN6 ... 200 C1
Firtree Dr 6 DN20 ... 20 F7
Fish Dock Rd DN31 ... 189 B2
Fish Groom's La PE11 ... 145 E6
Fish St 1 HU1 ... 180 F5
Fish Well Cl 3 NG33 ... 151 A8
Fishemore Ave HU13 ... 178 F2
Fisher Cl 23 NG23 ... 91 D5
Fisher Pl DN35 ... 192 D7
Fishergate PE12 ... 159 B1
Fisherman's Wharf
DN31 ... 191 D8
Fishermans Wlk 2 HU3 ... 180 C4
Fishlake Nab DN7 ... 14 C7
Fishmere End Rd
Sutterton PE20 ... 136 A4
Wigtoft PE20 ... 135 F3
Fishmere Gate Rd LN11 ... 51 B1
Fishpond La PE12 ... 215 E2
Fishtoft Dro PE22 ... 125 C7
Fishtoft Rd PE21 ... 209 B3
Fishtoft Sch PE21 ... 126 C1
Fishwick Ave 5 HU13 ... 178 E1
Fiskerton CE (Controlled)
Prim Sch LN3 ... 82 B7
Fiskerton Cl 8 DN34 ... 190 F4
Fiskerton Dr LN2 ... 201 F8
Fiskerton Rd
Cherry Willingham LN3 ... 203 C4
Cherry Willingham/Reepham
LN3 ... 82 A8
Fiskerton Rd E LN3 ... 203 E4
Fiskerton Way 2 DN31 ... 188 A3
Fitties La 2 DN36 ... 37 C5
Fitton End Rd PE13 ... 169 F3
Fitzgerald Ct 3 LN4 ... 207 A6
Fitzjames Cl 2 PE23 ... 101 A8
Fitzwilliam Hospl PE6 ... 224 E2
Fitzwilliam Mews
DN35 ... 192 E2
Fitzwilliam Pl 6 LN4 ... 109 F5
Fitzwilliam Rd PE9 ... 219 A7
Fitzwilliam St
10 Mablethorpe/Sutton on Sea
LN12 ... 64 B4
Peterborough PE1 ... 226 A3
Five Arches PE2 ... 229 C6
Five Bell La PE20 ... 135 C4
Five House La
Frampton PE20 ... 136 C8
Wyberton PE21 ... 208 B1
Five La Ends NG23 ... 79 C8
Five Mile La LN4 ... 82 B5
Flag Bsns Exchange
PE1 ... 226 E3
Flag Fen Bronze Age Mus*
PE6 ... 227 B3
Flag Fen Rd PE1 ... 226 C4
Flag La PE12 ... 168 B7
Flamborough Cl
Peterborough PE2 ... 225 E1
6 Skegness PE25 ... 206 A6
Flaminian Way 8 NG32 ... 120 A2
Flarepath The DN20 ... 21 A8
Flaxengate 4 LN2 ... 234 B2
Flaxland PE3 ... 225 A6
Flaxmill La 6 PE11 ... 145 C1
Flaxwell Way 12 NG34 ... 121 B7
Fleet Rd Fleet PE12 ... 159 B7
Holbeach PE12 ... 215 F2
Fleet St Holbeach PE12 ... 215 E2
Lincoln LN1 ... 201 C4
Fleet Way PE2 ... 231 B6
Fleetgate 8 DN18 ... 3 E1
Fleets La LN1 ... 54 A1
Fleets Rd LN1 ... 66 D7
Fleetway DN36 ... 37 A3
Fleetwood Cl 2 DN33 ... 194 E7
Fleetwood Ct LE15 ... 162 A8
Fleming Ave NG13 ... 128 B6
Fleming Ct 1 PE21 ... 208 F1
Fleming Rd PE11 ... 214 E8
Fleming Wlk HU4 ... 179 D2
Fletcher Cl
Kingston upon Hull
HU13 ... 178 E2
7 Scunthorpe DN15 ... 182 C6
Fletcher Rd DN34 ... 190 F7
Fletcher St NG31 ... 211 A3
Fletton Ave PE2 ... 231 A8
Fletton Fields PE2 ... 231 A7
Fletton Parkway PE2 ... 229 F2
Fletton Prim Sch PE2 ... 230 F6
Flinders Cl 5 LN4 ... 95 C4
Flinders Rd 13 PE11 ... 134 E2
Flint Cl PE9 ... 163 D1
Flint Gate 23 PE12 ... 160 E4
Flint House Rd PE12 ... 147 C3
Flintham Cl 2 LN4 ... 95 C4
Flinton St HU3 ... 180 B3
Flixborough Rd DN15 ... 8 B4
Flood Rd The DN21 ... 197 B3
Flore Cl PE3 ... 225 C5
Florence Ave HU13 ... 178 F1
Florence St
Grimsby DN32 ... 191 E5
Lincoln LN2 ... 202 B3
Florence Way 4 PE6 ... 217 C5
Florence Wright Ave 6
LN11 ... 198 D4
Floriade Cl 4 PE11 ... 214 B2
Florins Field NG34 ... 132 F3
Floss La DN22 ... 65 B6
Flour Sq DN31 ... 189 A1
Flowerdown Ave 5
NG34 ... 120 D8
Foal Plats La LN13 ... 90 A8
Fodder Dike Bank
Eastville PE22 ... 114 C7
Midville PE22 ... 113 E7
Fold Hill Rd PE22 ... 114 A2
Fold La Moulton PE12 ... 157 F7
5 Tydd St Giles PE13 ... 169 F7
Folds La 2 PE12 ... 216 B4
Folgate La PE14 ... 170 F6
Folkingham Cl 11 LN6 ... 204 D8
Folkingham Rd
Billingborough NG34 ... 133 A1
1 Morton PE10 ... 154 C7
Pickworth NG34 ... 142 A8
Folksworth Rd PE7 ... 232 E1
Folly Cl PE7 ... 233 C5
Folly La
Branston & Mere LN4 ... 81 C2
Hough-on-the-Hill NG32 ... 118 F5
North Kelsey LN7 ... 32 C5
North Scarle NG23 ... 91 D8
West Fen PE22 ... 99 E1
Folly's Dro PE13 ... 177 F3
Fontwell Cres 9 LN6 ... 205 A5
Fontwell Gdns 2 PE9 ... 219 B5
Foote's Dro PE12 ... 167 C8
Forbes Rd PE21 ... 209 C4
Ford La
8 Hibaldstow DN20 ... 30 F5
Morton PE10 ... 154 C6
Ford Way LN11 ... 72 D6
Fordham Dr LN1 ... 201 C7
Fordingham Inf Sch
DN16 ... 183 B2
Ford's Ave 17 DN41 ... 23 F5
Fore La PE20 ... 135 A5
Foredyke Prim Sch HU9 ... 5 D8
Foreman Way 1 PE6 ... 166 E1
Forest Ave 3 PE10 ... 213 B5
Forest Dale PE21 ... 208 F7
Forest Dr DN36 ... 193 B1
Forest Dro PE6 ... 166 C2
Forest Gdns 5 PE9 ... 218 D7
Forest Pines La 11 LN10 ... 97 C5
Forest Way 7 DN36 ... 36 D8
Forester Way HU4 ... 179 D3
Forge Cl Freiston PE22 ... 126 C4
South Kelsey LN7 ... 32 A1
Forge Cres
3 Pinchbeck PE11 ... 156 E8
Ulceby DN39 ... 12 A1
Forge Ct 12 PE6 ... 217 A6
Forge End PE7 ... 229 A4
Forge La LN8 ... 56 F8
Forge Way DN36 ... 195 C3
Forkedale DN18 ... 10 E8
Forman's La NG34 ... 109 B1
Formby Cl NG31 ... 211 C7
Forrester St 1 DN20 ... 196 B3
Forrington Pl LN1 ... 66 E2
Forstedd Hill NG33 ... 153 B5
Forster St DN21 ... 197 C5
Forsyth Cres 6 PE25 ... 206 C2
Forsythia Dr DN33 ... 191 C2
Fortescue Cl 1 LN4 ... 207 A5
Fortuna Way DN37 ... 190 C7
Forty Acre HU10 ... 178 F7
Forty Acre Rd PE1 ... 226 D2
Forty Foot La
Humberside Airport DN39 ... 21 F6
Old Leake PE22 ... 113 D3
Forty Stps HU10 ... 178 F7
Forum Way 7 NG34 ... 212 F3
Foss Bank LN1 ... 201 D3
Foss St LN1 ... 201 D3
Fossdyke Gdns 18 LN1 ... 66 D2
Fosse Cl 9 PE6 ... 164 E5
Fosse Dr LN6 ... 205 A3
Fosse La
Thistleton LE15 ... 151 B1
Thorpe on the Hill LN6 ... 92 E7
Fosse Way Prim Sch
LN6 ... 204 F2
Foster Cl 2 LN4 ... 96 C1
Foster Rd
21 Collingham NG23 ... 91 D5
7 Thorne/Moorends DN8 ... 15 A8
Foster St 3 Boston PE21 ... 209 A5
Heckington NG34 ... 122 E3
Lincoln LN5 ... 201 E1
Foster's Dro PE10 ... 155 A3
Foster's Gdns 1 LN4 ... 82 B1
Fosters Cl 5 LN4 ... 107 A8
Foston by Pass NG32 ... 117 F1
Foston Cres LN6 ... 204 F7
Foston La NG32 ... 128 F7
Foston Rd NG31 ... 210 E3
Fotherby Rd DN17 ... 184 F4
Fotherby St 4 DN31 ... 189 A1
Fothergill Dr 17 DN3 ... 14 A2
Foundry La
11 Spalding PE11 ... 214 D4
12 Thorne/Moorends DN8 ... 15 A8
Foundry Rd
Bucknall LN10 ... 84 B3
Ryhall PE9 ... 163 C2
Stamford PE9 ... 219 A5
Foundry St LN9 ... 199 C4
Fountain Cl
Kingston upon Hull
HU13 ... 178 C3
5 Waltham DN37 ... 194 C5
Fountain Hill DN10 ... 39 E3
Fountain Hill Rd DN10 ... 39 E4
Fountain La 18 PE21 ... 208 F5
Fountain Pl 10 PE21 ... 208 F5
Fountain St
22 Caistor LN7 ... 33 B4
Kingston upon Hull HU3 ... 180 D6
Fountains Pl PE6 ... 175 B1
Four Acre Cl HU10 ... 178 C6
Fourfields CE Prim Sch
PE20 ... 136 A2
Fourfields Prim Sch
PE7 ... 233 E6
Fourth Ave
2 Fixborough Ind Est DN15 ... 8 A1
Grantham NG31 ... 211 F6
3 Scampton Airfield LN1 ... 67 E5
1 Scunthorpe DN17 ... 184 C6
Fourth Dro
Gosberton PE11 ... 144 B4
Peterborough PE1 ... 226 F3
Fourways 6 DN36 ... 36 D4
Fowler Rd DN16 ... 185 B8
Fox Cl PE21 ... 208 C6
Fox Covert 2 LN6 ... 93 A8
Fox Covert La DN10 ... 40 A4
Fox Ct 1 DN17 ... 16 D8
Fox Dale PE9 ... 218 F6
Fox Headings PE12 ... 158 C1
Fox St DN15 ... 182 F3
Foxby Hill DN21 ... 197 E2
Foxby La DN21 ... 197 F2
Foxcovert Rd PE6 ... 220 E8
Foxe End 12 LN12 ... 64 B3
Foxendale Hill LN9 ... 72 F1
Foxes Low Rd PE12 ... 215 F2
Foxfield Cl LN6 ... 200 A5
Foxglove Cl
Brigg DN20 ... 196 B4
1 Spilsby PE23 ... 101 A8
Foxglove Gdns DN34 ... 190 F6
Foxglove Rd 1 PE9 ... 218 C7
Foxglove Way 5 LN5 ... 205 C2
Foxgloves PE6 ... 217 D6
Foxhill DN37 ... 190 C7
Foxhill Rd DN8 ... 15 B7
Foxhills Comp Sch
DN15 ... 182 E5
Foxhills Ind Pk DN15 ... 182 F7
Foxhills Rd DN15 ... 182 E5
Foxhole La PE22 ... 126 D3
Foxley Cl PE4 ... 221 A4
Foxley Ct 1 PE10 ... 213 C7
Foyle Cl LN5 ... 205 D2
Fracknal's Row 3 PE21 ... 208 E6
Framlingham Rd PE7 ... 231 F5
Frampton Bank PE20 ... 136 B8
Frampton La PE20 ... 124 E2
Frampton Marsh Nature
Reserve* PE20 ... 137 D5
Frampton Pl PE21 ... 208 D4
Frampton Roads PE20 ... 136 F6
Frances Askew Prim Sch
HU4 ... 179 F4
Frances Ct 8 DN37 ... 194 C5
Frances St DN15 ... 183 A3
Francis Bernard Cl 4
PE21 ... 208 D3
Francis Gdns PE1 ... 225 F8

Francis St
Kingston upon Hull HU2 .. 180 F7
Lincoln LN1 .. 234 B4
14 Spalding PE11 .. 214 D4
Francklin Wlk 5 PE12 .. 158 B6
Frank Perkins Parkway
PE1 .. 226 E6
Frank Perkins Way
PE1 .. 226 D3
Frank Swaby Ct LN5 .. 205 E6
Frank Whittle Cl 1
NG34 .. 120 E8
Frank Wright Ct 4 LN2 202 C7
Frankland Cl
2 Wrawby DN20 .. 20 E3
1 Wrawby DN20 .. 196 F6
Frankland Pl DN35 .. 192 D7
Franklin Ave PE25 .. 206 D1
Franklin Cl
Boston PE21 .. 208 C6
7 Metheringham LN4 .. 95 C4
Franklin Coll DN34 .. 191 B5
Franklin Cres
Peterborough PE1 .. 226 E6
Scunthorpe DN16 .. 185 E6
1 Sleaford NG34 .. 212 D5
Franklin Rd DN21 .. 29 C4
Franklin St HU9 .. 181 C8
Franklin Way DN38 .. 21 F5
Franks Cl 2 PE20 .. 136 D5
Franks La PE13 .. 169 F5
Fraser Cl PE6 .. 217 D5
Fraser St 2 DN32 .. 191 F7
Fraserburgh Way 2
PE2 .. 229 D4
Frederica Rd
13 Skegness PE25 .. 103 E4
12 Skegness PE25 .. 103 E4
Frederick Gough Comp Sch
DN16 .. 185 C4
Frederick St
Cleethorpes DN35 .. 192 E6
Grimsby DN31 .. 191 D8
Lincoln LN2 .. 202 C3
Frederick Ward Way
DN31 .. 191 D7
Freehold St HU3 .. 180 D7
Freeman Ave 4 HU15 .. 2 C5
Freeman Cl 10 PE8 .. 172 B1
Freeman Ct DN36 .. 195 E2
Freeman Rd LN6 .. 204 D3
Freeman St DN32 .. 189 B1
Freeman's La DN22 .. 52 A2
Freemans La 6 DN20 .. 10 C2
Freeport Wharf DN31 .. 191 E8
Freer Gdns LN11 .. 198 E6
Freeschool La LN2 .. 234 B2
Freesia Way PE7 .. 233 F6
Freeston St DN35 .. 192 B8
Freetown Way HU2 .. 180 E7
Freightliner Rd HU3 .. 179 F2
Freiston Rd PE21 .. 209 B5
French Dro PE6 .. 175 E7
French's Rd PE14 .. 170 F8
Fresh Fields 14 HU15 .. 2 C5
Freshney Bog Nature
Reserve* DN37 .. 190 E7
Freshney Dr 2 DN31 .. 191 C8
Freshney Way PE21 .. 208 B3
Freston PE4 .. 221 D2
Freyja Croft 3 DN33 .. 191 B2
Friar Way PE21 .. 208 F6
Friars La LN2 .. 234 B2
Friars Rd DN17 .. 184 E6
Friest La 11 PE20 .. 135 A4
Frieston Heath La
NG32 .. 119 D6
Frieston Rd NG32 .. 119 B6
Frinkley La
Honington NG32 .. 119 B2
Hougham NG32 .. 118 D2
Frisby Cl PE6 .. 164 D4
Friskney All Saints CE
(Aided) Prim Sch
PE22 .. 115 A6
Friskney Decoy Wood Nature
Reserve* PE22 .. 115 A8
Frith Bank PE22 .. 125 D6
Friths La PE20 .. 125 B1
Frithville Cty Sch
PE22 .. 112 D1
Frithville Rd PE22 .. 113 A1
Frobisher Ave DN32 .. 192 B6
Frodingham Footpath 3
DN15 .. 183 B3
Frodingham Rd DN15 .. 183 A4
Frodingham S Rd
DN16 .. 183 E2
Frodsham St 8 HU9 .. 5 D8
Frognall PE6 .. 165 D1
Frog's Abbey Gate
PE12 .. 158 E4
Frome Cl LN6 .. 204 D5
Front Rd
Tydd St Mary PE13 .. 160 D1
Wisbech St Mary PE13 .. 177 D6
Front St Alkborough DN15 .. 8 C8
Barnby in the Willows
NG24 .. 104 F3
Dunston LN4 .. 95 C5
East Stockwith DN21 .. 40 B5
Elsham DN20 .. 20 F7
Gainsborough DN21 .. 197 B7
4 Grasby DN38 .. 32 E7
Normanby By Spital LN8 .. 55 E7
Front St *continued*
South Clifton NG23 .. 78 C5
Tealby LN8 .. 46 C1
Ulceby DN39 .. 12 A1
Frost Cl DN15 .. 2 A1
Frostley Gate PE12 .. 158 F3
Frusher Ave DN33 .. 191 C3
Fryston 28 HU15 .. 2 C6
Fuchsia Croft 2 DN15 .. 182 F2
Fuchsia Dr HU4 .. 179 B2
Fulbeck Rd DN16 .. 185 C6
Fulbridge Jun/Inf Sch
PE1 .. 225 F7
Fulbridge Rd PE4 .. 221 A3
Fulford Cl NG31 .. 211 D8
Fulford Cres
Kingston upon Hull
HU10 .. 179 A8
3 New Holland DN19 .. 4 E2
Fulford Way PE25 .. 206 C6
Fulham Pk 5 DN33 .. 191 B2
Fulham Rd PE3 .. 225 E4
Fuller St DN35 .. 192 D8
Fulmar Dr LN11 .. 198 C8
Fulmar Rd LN6 .. 204 D8
Fulney Dro PE12 .. 157 B3
Fulney La PE12 .. 157 B6
Fulstow Gr 7 DN33 .. 191 B3
Fulstow Prim Sch LN11 .. 49 B8
Fun Farm* PE12 .. 157 D7
Fundrey Rd PE13 .. 170 E1
Furlongs La
Belchford LN9 .. 73 B1
Old Leake PE22 .. 114 A1
Furlongs Rd LN12 .. 77 A8
Furniss Ct 2 DN18 .. 10 E8
Furrow Cl 16 LN2 .. 68 D6
Further Old Gate
PE12 .. 158 D5
Fury Ave LN11 .. 62 B6
Furze La LN11 .. 62 A5
Furze Ride PE1 .. 226 B8
Fussey Gdns DN20 .. 10 C1
Fydell Cres PE21 .. 208 E4
Fydell Ct PE21 .. 208 E6
Fydell St PE21 .. 208 E5
Fyson Way PE20 .. 136 C6

G

Gables Hospl The PE23 .. 87 F1
Gadd's La PE13 .. 170 A1
Gainas Ave DN21 .. 197 C6
Gainsborough Central Sta
DN21 .. 197 E4
Gainsborough Coll
DN21 .. 197 C5
Gainsborough Gdns 2
LN6 .. 205 B7
Gainsborough La DN20 .. 30 F8
Gainsborough Lea Rd Sta
DN21 .. 197 D1
Gainsborough Rd
Blyton DN21 .. 41 B4
Bole DN22 .. 52 A6
Girton NG23 .. 78 C2
32 Kirton in Lindsey DN21 .. 30 B1
Kirton in Lindsey DN21 .. 42 D8
Little Casterton PE9 .. 218 F7
Middle Rasen LN8 .. 57 B7
Saundby DN22 .. 52 B7
Saxilby with Ingleby LN1 .. 66 D2
Scotter DN21 .. 29 B3
Sturton Le Steeple DN22 .. 52 B3
West Rasen LN8 .. 57 A7
Willingham DN21 .. 53 E4
6 Winthorpe NG24 .. 104 B7
Wiseton DN10 .. 39 A1
Gainsthorpe Rd E
DN21 .. 30 D4
Gainsthorpe Rd W
DN21 .. 30 C4
Gallamore Ct 5 LN8 .. 57 C8
Gallamore La 6 LN8 .. 57 C8
Galletly Cl PE10 .. 213 D6
Galley Ct HU9 .. 181 C6
Gallions Cl 2 PE4 .. 221 B1
Galway Cl 2 PE11 .. 214 A5
Gamlyn Cl 1 PE11 .. 214 D2
Gannet Ct 8 NG31 .. 210 E2
Gannocks Cl PE2 .. 229 F5
Gannocks The PE2 .. 229 F5
Ganton Sch HU10 .. 179 A7
Ganton Way HU10 .. 178 F8
Garbutt Pl DN35 .. 193 A4
Garden Dr DN36 .. 195 C7
Garden End Rd PE1 .. 226 B6
Garden St 5 Brigg DN20 196 C3
Grimsby DN31 .. 191 D7
Gardeners Wlk PE21 .. 208 D2
Gardenfield LN6 .. 200 B3
Gardenia Dr DN17 .. 184 F1
Garfield Cl LN1 .. 201 D8
Garfield St DN21 .. 197 C5
Garfit's La PE21 .. 208 D1
Garibaldi St
8 Grimsby DN32 .. 189 B1
5 Grimsby DN32 .. 191 F8
Garmston St 8 LN1 .. 234 B3
Garner St DN32 .. 191 E6
Garner's La PE34 .. 161 A4
Garnet Gr 6 HU3 .. 180 A4
Garnett St DN35 .. 192 D8
Garnsgate Rd PE12 .. 216 A5
Garrick Cl LN5 .. 205 C3
Garrick La 4 DN36 .. 195 C7
Garrison Rd HU9 .. 181 C6
Garth La DN31 .. 191 D8
Garth Specl Sch The
PE11 .. 214 E5
Garthorpe Rd DN17 .. 7 C4
Garthway 8 DN36 .. 195 D2
Garton Gr
3 Grimsby DN32 .. 192 A5
3 Kingston upon Hull
HU5 .. 179 C7
Garton St PE1 .. 226 A5
Gartree Sch LN4 .. 207 B5
Gas House La 16 PE12 .. 160 E4
Gas La
7 Navenby/Wellingore
LN5 .. 107 A8
Stamford PE9 .. 219 C5
5 Thorney PE6 .. 176 A3
Gas St 2 Horncastle LN9 199 C3
19 Stamford PE9 .. 219 C5
Gascoigne 3 PE4 .. 220 E5
Gashouse La 3 DN9 .. 28 A3
Gate La DN33 .. 191 D1
Gate Way DN31 .. 188 E2
Gatehouse Rd DN19 .. 11 F7
Gateroom La PE22 .. 114 E3
Gatewood La DN7 .. 14 E1
Gatherums The DN35 .. 192 E5
Gatram Rd PE24 .. 90 D6
Gaunt St LN5 .. 234 A1
Gauntlet Dro PE20 .. 134 F6
Gauntlet Rd
3 Bicker PE20 .. 135 A4
Grimoldby LN11 .. 62 B6
Gautry La DN9 .. 28 B4
Gayle Rd LN4 .. 110 E8
Gaysfield Rd 6 PE21 .. 126 C1
Gayton Cl Lincoln LN2 .. 202 A7
Skegness PE25 .. 206 C2
Gayton Ct PE3 .. 225 C5
Gayton Rd DN35 .. 193 A3
Gazeley Gdns PE7 .. 231 B2
Gedney Church End Prim Sch
PE12 .. 159 D7
Gedney Cl DN37 .. 190 C8
Gedney Hill CE (Controlled)
Prim Sch PE12 .. 168 D2
Gedney Hill Gate PE12 .. 168 F7
Gedney Rd PE12 .. 216 A6
Gee St HU3 .. 180 C5
Gelder Beck Rd DN17 .. 29 D6
Gelder's La PE12 .. 158 A1
Gelston Rd NG32 .. 119 A4
Gemsbok Cl 3 HU4 .. 179 D2
Geneva Ave LN2 .. 202 B6
Geneva St PE1 .. 226 A3
George Ave
Gedney PE12 .. 148 F4
4 Keadby DN17 .. 17 D5
Skegness PE25 .. 206 B3
George Butler Cl 23
DN37 .. 23 F1
George Farmer Tech Coll
PE12 .. 215 D3
George Mews 2 LN7 .. 33 B4
George St
2 Barton-upon-Humber
DN18 .. 10 F8
5 Boston PE21 .. 208 E4
Bourne PE10 .. 213 D5
Broughton DN20 .. 19 D3
Cleethorpes DN35 .. 192 F5
Gainsborough DN21 .. 197 B6
Grantham NG31 .. 211 B4
Grimsby DN31 .. 191 D7
Helpringham NG34 .. 133 D7
5 Keadby DN17 .. 17 D5
Kingston upon Hull HU1 .. 180 F6
11 Kirton in Lindsey DN21 .. 30 B1
Lincoln LN5 .. 234 C1
Louth LN11 .. 198 B5
Mablethorpe/Sutton on Sea
LN12 .. 64 B3
7 Market Rasen LN8 .. 57 D8
Peterborough PE2 .. 230 F8
Scunthorpe DN15 .. 183 A4
Sleaford NG34 .. 212 C3
George Yd 5 HU1 .. 181 A6
Georgette Gdns 7
PE11 .. 214 B5
Georgian Ct PE3 .. 225 E1
Georgina Ct 27 DN18 .. 10 E8
Gerald's Cl LN2 .. 202 B5
German's La PE34 .. 161 D2
Gerrard Mews LN4 .. 203 D1
Gershwin Ave HU4 .. 179 B4
Gertrude St DN32 .. 191 E5
Gervase St DN15 .. 183 A3
Gibbeson St 6 LN5 .. 205 E8
Gibbet La LN8 .. 57 A5
Gibraltar Hill LN1 .. 234 A3
Gibraltar La 2 DN37 .. 23 F1
Gibraltar Point National
Nature Reserve*
PE24 .. 103 E2
Gibraltar Rd
Croft PE24 .. 103 D1
5 Hemswell Cliff DN21 .. 55 A8
Mablethorpe/Sutton on Sea
LN12 .. 64 B4
Gibson Cl Branston LN4 .. 81 E2
1 Sleaford NG34 .. 212 B6
Gibson Gn LN6 .. 92 E5
Gibson La HU14 .. 2 E4
Gibson Pl 5 PE25 .. 206 A5
Gibson Rd 2 DN7 .. 26 A8
Gibsons Gdn 2 LN11 .. 50 F7
Giddings Cl PE2 .. 229 F4
Gilberts Gr 4 PE25 .. 206 D8
Gilbey Rd DN31 .. 188 D1
Gildale PE4 .. 221 B4
Gildenburgh Ave PE1 .. 226 D5
Gilder Way PE21 .. 209 F2
Gildesburgh Rd LN4 .. 203 B1
Giles Sch The PE22 .. 114 A1
Giles St DN35 .. 192 E6
Gillatts Cl 1 DN20 .. 196 F7
Gillett St HU3 .. 180 B4
Gilliatt St DN15 .. 183 A4
Gilmores La 8 NG24 .. 104 C1
Gilmorton Dr PE1 .. 226 D7
Gilpin St PE1 .. 225 E6
Gimmel's Gate PE12 .. 216 C1
Gipsy Dro
Friskney PE22 .. 114 D7
Langriville PE22 .. 124 F8
Gipsy La Gedney PE12 .. 216 A8
Holton Le Moor LN7 .. 32 C1
Osgodby LN8 .. 45 D3
Owersby LN7 .. 44 F8
Owston Ferry DN9 .. 40 C8
South Kelsey LN7 .. 32 C1
Swineshead PE20 .. 124 A1
Tydd St Mary PE13 .. 160 A2
Wrangle PE22 .. 114 D2
Girdlestone Wlk 2 PE6 .. 166 F1
Girsby La LN8 .. 59 B6
Girton Cl 3 DN16 .. 185 B4
Girton La NG23 .. 78 D1
Girton Way 3 PE9 .. 219 A7
Gisburn Rd HU13 .. 178 F2
Glade The 8 LN12 .. 77 A7
Gladiator Rd LN11 .. 62 B6
Gladstone Dr 1 DN16 .. 183 C1
Gladstone Prim Sch
PE1 .. 225 F5
Gladstone St
Bourne PE10 .. 213 C6
Gainsborough DN21 .. 197 C5
Kingston upon Hull HU3 .. 180 C6
Peterborough PE1 .. 225 F3
Gladstone Terr 3 NG31 .. 211 A5
Glaisdale Gdns NG31 .. 211 B8
Glaisdale Gr HU9 .. 181 F8
Glaisdale Rd 2 DN16 .. 185 D5
Glamis Gdns PE3 .. 225 B2
Glamis Pl LN11 .. 198 B6
Glamis Rd HU13 .. 178 F2
Glanford Gr 12 DN19 .. 11 D8
Glanford Pk (Scunthorpe
United FC) DN15 .. 182 A2
Glanford Rd
Brigg DN20 .. 196 D3
Scunthorpe DN17 .. 184 F3
Glanford Way 1 DN15 .. 182 B3
Glanville Ave DN17 .. 184 F8
Glanville Cres 2 DN17 .. 184 F8
Glasgow St HU3 .. 180 A5
Glastonbury Cl 20 PE6 .. 175 A1
Glatton Dr PE2 .. 231 D6
Gleanings The 5 LN5 .. 107 B8
Glebe Ave PE2 .. 229 E4
Glebe Cl
Burton upon Stather DN15 .. 8 A5
3 Donington on Bain LN11 .. 59 E1
Gorefield PE13 .. 169 E3
Holton le Clay DN36 .. 195 C3
Humberston DN36 .. 36 C8
5 Ingham LN1 .. 54 F2
5 Sibsey PE22 .. 113 B1
1 Skegness PE25 .. 206 A7
Sleaford NG34 .. 212 A2
2 Spalding PE11 .. 214 A4
Glebe Ct PE2 .. 231 B8
Glebe Gdns 2 PE6 .. 175 B8
Glebe Rd Brigg DN20 .. 196 C4
Cleethorpes DN35 .. 192 E6
Grimsby DN33 .. 191 E1
Humberston DN36 .. 36 C7
Peterborough PE2 .. 231 A8
Scunthorpe DN15 .. 183 B4
Thorne/Moorends DN8 .. 15 B8
Wymondham LE14 .. 150 B1
Glebe The
Sturton By Stow LN1 .. 66 D8
Upton DN21 .. 53 D5
Glebe View 1 PE6 .. 217 B6
Glebe Way
Barton-upon-Humber
DN18 .. 11 A8
5 Sutterton PE20 .. 136 A2
Glebe Wlk 3 PE12 .. 167 B8
Gleed Ave PE11 .. 134 E2
Gleed Boys Sch PE11 .. 214 F4
Gleedale LN6 .. 204 F1
Gleeds Girls Gm Sch
PE11 .. 214 F3
Glemsford Rise 2 PE2 .. 230 C7
Glen Ave 4 PE11 .. 145 B1
Glen Cl NG33 .. 153 A1
Glen Cres
7 Essendine PE9 .. 163 D3
Stamford PE9 .. 219 C7
Glen Dr PE21 .. 208 B4
Glen Gdns 2 PE11 .. 145 E3
Glen Hall Rise 10 DN19 .. 11 C8
Glen Rd
Castle Bytham NG33 .. 152 D1
Counthorpe & Creeton
NG33 .. 153 A2
3 Wittering PE8 .. 172 B1
Glen The PE2 .. 231 B7
Glenarm Cres 7 LN5 .. 205 D3
Glenbank Cl LN6 .. 204 F3
Glencoe Cl 2 DN7 .. 14 D4
Glencoe St HU3 .. 179 F6
Glencoe Way PE2 .. 229 D3
Glendale PE2 .. 229 D6
Glendon Cl 5 LN5 .. 205 D3
Gleneagles
Grantham NG31 .. 211 D8
Peterborough PE2 .. 229 F6
10 Waltham DN37 .. 194 C4
Gleneagles Cl 5 PE9 .. 218 E6
Gleneagles Cres 6 DN19 .. 4 E2
Gleneagles Dr
Skegness PE25 .. 206 D6
12 Woodhall Spa LN10 .. 97 C5
Gleneagles Gr 4 LN4 .. 203 D1
Glenfield Rd DN37 .. 190 D8
Glenn Ave 3 PE11 .. 214 C4
Glenrock Pk HU15 .. 2 B6
Glenside NG33 .. 152 E1
Glenside N PE11 .. 156 C8
Glenside S PE11 .. 156 C8
Glentham Cl LN6 .. 205 B3
Glentham Ct 6 LN8 .. 43 F1
Glentham Rd
Bishop Norton LN8 .. 43 D3
5 Gainsborough DN21 .. 53 A8
Glenton St PE1 .. 226 C2
Glentworth Cres 4
PE25 .. 206 D4
Glentworth Rd DN21 .. 53 F4
Glenwood Dr 2 HU4 .. 179 B6
Glenwood Gr LN6 .. 201 D1
Glinton Rd
Helpston PE6 .. 173 C4
Newborough PE6 .. 221 C8
Gloria Way DN37 .. 190 C7
Glossop Rd DN15 .. 182 B2
Gloucester Ave
Grimsby DN34 .. 191 B4
Scunthorpe DN16 .. 185 B7
Gloucester Cl
Skegness PE25 .. 206 B2
1 Sleaford NG34 .. 212 C7
Gloucester Rd
Grantham NG31 .. 210 C5
Peterborough PE2 .. 231 B7
7 Stamford PE9 .. 219 B6
Gloucester St HU4 .. 179 E3
Glover Rd DN17 .. 184 E8
Glovers Ave 8 DN17 .. 17 D4
Glynn Rd LN1 .. 201 E8
Goathland Cl HU3 .. 180 A6
Godber Dr LN4 .. 205 F3
Goddam's La PE12 .. 146 F1
Goddard Cl 37 DN18 .. 10 E8
Goddard Cres 12 PE13 .. 170 D1
Godfrey Ave 6 PE11 .. 145 C6
Godfrey Cl 7 PE6 .. 174 E5
Godfrey Rd 11 DN8 .. 15 A8
Godiva Cl 16 PE6 .. 166 F1
Godiva Cres PE10 .. 213 B5
Godman's La HU10 .. 178 B8
Godnow Rd DN17 .. 16 C6
Godric Sq PE2 .. 230 D6
Godsey Cres 9 PE6 .. 217 C5
Godsey La PE6 .. 217 B6
Godson Ave 1 NG34 .. 122 D3
Godwin Cl PE10 .. 213 B6
Godwin Rd 13 PE13 .. 170 D1
Goffsmill PE3 .. 225 A4
Gold Fen Dike Bank
PE22 .. 114 D2
Gold La LN13 .. 63 A1
Goldcrest Cl
2 Birchwood LN6 .. 200 E1
Scunthorpe DN15 .. 182 D6
Golden Drop 2 PE6 .. 173 C4
Golden Gr PE20 .. 135 C5
Golden Harvest Way 6
PE12 .. 158 B6
Goldenholme La 4 DN22 65 A5
Goldfinch Cl LN6 .. 200 A3
Goldgarth DN32 .. 192 A5
Goldhay Way PE2 .. 229 F2
Goldie La PE2 .. 229 F6
Goldings The 10 DN9 .. 27 D2
Goldsmith Ct 1 LN4 .. 207 A6
Goldsmith Rd NG31 .. 211 D6
Goldsmith Wlk LN2 .. 202 C7
Goldson's La PE22 .. 126 F6
Golf Ct PE12 .. 160 F5
Golf Links Dr HU15 .. 2 B6
Golf Rd LN12 .. 64 A4
Gollands La DN9 .. 27 B2
Gonerby Hill NG31 .. 210 E8
Gonerby Hill Foot CE Prim
Sch NG31 .. 210 E8
Gonerby La NG32 .. 129 A7
Gonerby Rd NG31 .. 210 E8
Goochgate PE12 .. 169 A7
Good La LN1 .. 234 B4
Goodacre PE2 .. 230 A4
Goodens La PE13 .. 170 A5
Goodfellows CE Prim Sch
PE11 .. 156 E3
Goodfellows Rd 7
PE11 .. 156 E3
Goodhand Cl DN18 .. 11 A8
Goodliff Rd NG31 .. 210 E2
Goodman Cl 6 NG31 .. 129 E5
Goodson Cl 3 PE21 .. 209 B4
Goodwin Dr 7 PE24 .. 90 B7
Goodwin La 10 NG24 .. 104 C1
Goodwin Par 1 HU3 .. 180 D5
Goodwin Wlk PE4 .. 221 A4
Goodwood DN17 .. 184 D4
Goodwood Ct LN11 .. 198 A7
Goodwood La 1 DN35 .. 192 F1
Goodwood Rd 8 PE3 .. 224 F3
Goodwood Way LN6 .. 204 C7
Goole Rd DN14 .. 6 C8

Goose Gn 10 PE12 ....160 E4
Goose La PE23 ....87 D2
Gooseacre 33 DN17 ...29 D7
Goosegate La NG32 ..118 A2
Goose's La PE14 .....161 A1
Gordon Ave PE2 ......230 E7
Gordon Boswell Romany
Mus★ PE12 ....214 E1
Gordon Fendick Sch The
PE13 ....170 D2
Gordon Field 8 LN8 ...57 D7
Gordon Gdns 1 DN33 .194 F8
Gordon Rd LN1 ....234 B3
Gordon St
Gainsborough DN21 ...197 D2
4 Kingston upon Hull
HU3 ....180 B5
Gordon Way PE2 .....230 C7
Gore La 8 PE11 ......214 D4
Goredike Bank PE13 ..169 C2
Gorefield Cty Prim Sch
PE13 ....169 F2
Gorefield Rd PE13 ...169 F2
Gorehall Dr 10 LN2 ...68 D7
Goring Pl PE35 ......192 D7
Gorse Cl 5 Hatfield DN7 .14 C3
4 Woodhall Spa LN10 .97 E6
Gorse Dro NG34 .....133 A6
Gorse Hill La
Caythorpe NG32 .....119 A8
Wellingore LN5 ......107 C7
Gorse La
Gonerby Hill Foot NG31 .211 B1
Great Ponton NG31 ..139 F8
9 Leasingham NG34 ..121 B7
Scredington NG34 ...133 A7
Silk Willoughby NG34 .121 C1
Gorse Rd NG31 ......211 D5
Gorse Rise NG31 .....211 C5
Gorton Rd HU10 .....178 E7
Gorton St DN31 .....189 B2
Gorwick La LN1 ....66 B6
Gosberton Bank PE11 .145 E6
Gosberton Clough & Risegate
Prim Sch PE11 ......144 D4
Gosberton House Specl Sch
PE11 ....145 B6
Gosberton Prim Sch
PE11 ....145 B6
Gosberton Rd PE11 ..145 C4
Gospel La LN5 ....106 C3
Gospelgate LN11 ....198 B5
Gosport Rd 2 DN34 ..191 A6
Gostwick PE2 ....229 D5
Gote La PE13 ....169 E3
Gothic Cl 12 LN6 ....204 D7
Gouldeby La LN11 ....72 D6
Goulton St HU3 ......180 B3
Gover's Dro PE12 ....159 A2
Gower Rd HU4 ....179 B3
Gowt Bank PE22 .....114 C2
Gowts La PE12 ......159 E3
Goxhill Ave 4 PE11 ..134 E2
Goxhill Cl 14 LN6 ....204 D7
Goxhill Gdns 4 DN34 .190 F4
Goxhill Gr 13 LN6 ....204 D7
Goxhill Prim Sch DN19 .12 A8
Goxhill Rd DN19 .....11 E8
Goxhill Sta DN19 ....11 F8
Grace Ave LN6 ......204 D3
Grace Cl 4 NG34 ....212 E3
Grace Cres PE24 ....77 C3
Grace St LN5 ....201 F1
Gracefield La NG23 ...78 A4
Graeme Rd PE5 .....222 F2
Grafham Cl PE2 .....231 E4
Grafton Ave PE3 ....225 C3
Grafton St
Grimsby DN32 ....189 C1
Lincoln LN2 ....202 B3
Graham Ave HU4 ....179 C2
Graham Hill Way 4
PE10 ....213 E4
Graham Rd PE25 ....206 B4
Grains Gate LN11 ....37 E1
Grainsby Ave
Cleethorpes DN35 ...192 D3
Holton le Clay DN36 ..195 E1
Grainsby Cl LN6 ....205 C5
Grainsby La DN36 ...35 E1
Grainthorpe Sch LN11 .50 B7
Graizelound Fields Rd
DN9 ....27 D1
Grammar Sch La
DN20 ....196 C6
Grammar Sch Rd
DN20 ....196 C4
Grammar Sch Rd S 3
DN20 ....196 C3
Grammar Sch Wlk
DN16 ....185 C4
Grampian Cl 14 NG34 .212 B3
Grampian Way
Gonerby Hill Foot NG31 .210 D8
2 Grimsby DN33 .....194 E8
Thorne/Moorends DN8 .15 A7
Granary Cl
22 Metheringham LN4 .95 C4
5 Waddington LN5 ...93 F6
Granary Croft 7 DN9 ..27 D2
Granary La LN4 .....207 A4
Granary Way LN9 ....199 A3
Granby Dr 5 NG13 ..128 A5
Granby Rd LN8 ......47 B5
Granby St PE1 ......226 B2
Grand Par PE25 .....206 D3
Grand Sluice La 1
PE21 ....208 F6

Granely Cl LN1 ......201 C6
Grange Ave
15 Barton-upon-Humber
DN18 ....10 E8
Hatfield DN7 ....14 D4
24 Laceby DN37 ....23 F1
Misterton DN10 .....40 A4
Peterborough PE1 ...226 A6
Scunthorpe DN15 ...183 A5
Grange Cl 17 Hatfield DN7 .14 C4
1 Ingham LN1 ....54 F2
Misterton DN10 .....40 A5
Grange Cres
Kingston upon Hull
HU10 ....178 E6
Lincoln LN6 ....205 B3
Peterborough PE2 ...230 A5
Grange Ct 3 LN5 ....92 E1
Grange Dr Lincoln LN6 .205 B3
Misterton DN10 .....40 A4
Spalding PE11 ......214 E4
Stapleford LN6 .....105 A7
Grange Farm La DN36 .195 D6
Grange Field 2 DN20 .20 D8
Grange Ind Est DN16 .185 E7
Grange Inf & Jun Sch
DN34 ....190 F5
Grange La
Balderton NG24 .....104 A1
Canwick LN4 ....81 A4
Covenham St Bartholomew
LN11 ....49 D6
Garthorpe LE14 .....150 C4
Hough-on-the-Hill NG32 .118 E6
2 Ingham LN1 ......54 F2
Keddington LN11 ...198 E8
8 Manby LN11 ......62 C6
Nocton LN4 ....94 F6
North Cockerington LN11 .50 A1
North Kelsey LN7 ...32 A4
Stixwould & Woodhall
LN10 ....97 B6
Utterby LN11 ....49 A4
3 Willingham by Stow
DN21 ....53 E3
Grange La Jun Sch
DN16 ....185 D5
Grange La N DN16 ..185 D7
Grange La S DN16 ..185 C5
Grange Mdws PE22 ..113 A1
Grange Paddock 8
NG32 ....210 A5
Grange Pk 2 Brough HU15 .2 C5
17 Kirk Sandall DN3 .14 A3
8 Swanland HU14 ...3 B6
Grange Rd
Bracebridge Heath LN4 .205 F2
Gainsborough DN21 ..41 A1
Garthorpe & Fockerby
DN14 ....7 A5
14 Mablethorpe/Sutton on Sea
LN12 ....77 A7
4 Metheringham LN4 .95 D4
Peterborough PE3 ...225 D4
8 Ruskington NG34 ..108 D1
Sutton Bridge PE34 .161 B4
10 Wisbech PE13 ....170 C1
Grange St LN4 ......109 C7
Grange The 1 NG31 ..211 A4
Grange Wlk
Grimsby DN34 ......191 A6
6 Misterton DN10 ...40 A5
Grangehill Rd PE12 ..169 B6
Gransley Rise PE3 ...225 C5
Granson Way LN4 ...203 A2
Grant St
Cleethorpes DN35 ...192 E7
Grimsby DN31 ......189 D1
Granta Cres NG33 ...211 C7
Grantham Ave NG33 .191 D1
Grantham Canal Nature
Reserve★ NG13 ....210 D1
Grantham Church VA High
Sch The NG31 .....211 E7
Grantham Coll NG31 .211 B4
Grantham Cricket Gd
NG31 ....211 B1
Grantham District Hospl
NG31 ....211 A6
Grantham Dr
5 Skegness PE25 ...206 C4
2 Skegness PE25 ...206 B3
Grantham Fun Farm The★
NG31 ....210 F4
Grantham House (NT)★
NG31 ....211 B5
Grantham Mus★
NG31 ....211 B4
Grantham Prep Sch The
NG31 ....139 F8
Grantham Rd
Boothby Graffoe LN5 ..94 A2
Bottesford NG13 ....128 B5
Bracebridge Heath LN4 .205 F2
Carlton Scroop NG32 .119 C3
7 Great Gonerby NG31 .129 D5
Great Gonerby NG31 .210 D8
Harmston LN5 ......93 F6
Hough-on-the-Hill NG32 .119 A4
Ingoldsby NG33 ....141 C5
Navenby/Wellingore
LN5 ....107 A8
Old Somerby NG33 ..140 D8
Ropsley & Humby NG33 .131 A1
2 Skillington NG33 ..151 A8
Sleaford NG34 .....212 B2
Grantham St LN2 ...234 B2
Grantham Sta NG31 .211 A3

Grantham Town FC
NG31 ....210 D3
Granthams The 12 LN2 .68 E6
Grantley St NG31 ....211 A3
Granville Ave
12 Boston PE21 .....136 D8
Northborough PE6 ...217 E1
Granville St
Boston PE21 ....208 D5
Grantham NG31 .....211 C3
Grimsby DN32 ......191 F6
1 Kingston upon Hull
HU3 ....180 A6
Peterborough PE1 ..226 A4
Granville Terr PE12 ..160 D4
Grasby All Saints CE Prim
Sch DN38 ....32 E7
Grasby Cl 4 DN21 ...53 A8
Grasby Cres DN37 ...190 D7
Grasby Rd
Great Limber DN37 ..22 C3
North Kelsey LN7 ...32 D5
Scunthorpe DN17 ...184 E5
Grasby Wold La DN38 .21 F1
Grasmere Ave DN36 ..90 E6
Grasmere Cl 3 DN21 .197 E6
Grasmere Gdns PE4 ..221 B3
Grasmere Gr 5 DN36 .192 E1
Grasmere Way LN6 ..200 D1
Grassdale Pk 2 HU15 ..2 B5
Grassgate La PE14 ..170 E3
Grassmoor Cl 2 LN6 ..93 B8
Gravecoat La PE11 ..144 E6
Gravel Cswy PE6 ...166 D1
Gravel Pit Hill LN20 ..31 D6
Gravel Pit La 1 DN39 .22 A6
Gravel Pit Rd
Barton-upon-Humber DN18 .3 D1
Scotter DN21 ....29 C4
Gravel Pits La PE24 .102 C8
Gravel Rd
Market Deeping PE6 .165 D3
Revesby PE22 ......99 B4
Gravel Wlk PE1 .....226 A2
Graveley Cl 4 LN6 ..204 B6
Gravelhill Dro LN4 ...109 E7
Gravelholes La DN10 ..39 F5
Gravelpit La LN9 ....199 F2
Gray Ct PE1 ....225 E8
Gray Rd DN17 ......184 D6
Gray St LN1 ....234 A4
Grayingham Rd DN21 .42 E7
Grayling Cl 2 DN37 ..190 D7
Graylings The PE21 ..208 B6
Gray's Ct 4 LN11 ...198 B6
Gray's Rd 2 LN11 ...198 B6
Great Casterton CE Prim Sch
PE9 ....171 C8
Great Cl 1 NG33 ....151 D2
Great Coates Prim Sch
DN37 ....190 E8
Great Coates Rd
Grimsby DN37 ......190 C8
Healing DN41 ......23 F5
Great Coates Sta DN37 .24 B5
Great Field La 1 HU9 ..5 E8
Great Grimsby Swimming
Pool DN33 ....191 D4
Great Hale Dro NG34 .123 A2
Great N Rd
Balderton NG24 .....117 C8
Empingham PE9 ....162 B2
Great Gonerby NG32 .129 C6
Long Bennington NG23 .117 D2
Tinwell PE9 ....218 D5
Wansford PE8 ......222 D1
Great Northern Terr
LN5 ....234 C1
Great Northern Terr Ind Est
LN5 ....234 C1
Great Ponton CE (Aided)
Prim Sch NG33 ....140 A5
Great Steeping Prim Sch
PE23 ....101 E7
Great Thornton St
HU3 ....180 D6
Great Union St HU9 .181 A7
Greatford Gdns PE9 ..164 B3
Greatford Rd
Baston PE6 ....164 D4
5 Uffington PE9 ....172 C6
Grebe Cl 2 LN6 ....204 C1
Greek St HU3 ......179 F5
Green Acres HU10 ..178 C6
Green Bank DN8 ....15 D6
Green Dro
Billinghay LN4 .....109 F6
Crowland PE6 ......175 D8
Helpringham NG34 ..133 F7
Little Hale NG34 ...134 A7
Thorney PE6 ....175 F6
Green Dyke PE2 ....148 D1
Green Farm Cl PE5 ..223 E2
Green Gate PE22 ...114 D1
Green Hill DN35 ....192 D3
Green Hill Rd NG31 ..210 F5
Green La
Algarkirk PE20 .....136 B3
Aunsby & Dembleby
NG34 ....132 A4
18 Barrow upon Humber
DN19 ....11 D8
10 Barton-upon-Humber
DN18 ....10 D8
Beckingham LN5 ...105 C4
Belton DN9 ....16 D2
Belton & Manthorpe
NG32 ....130 B7

Green La continued
Boston PE21 ....208 E7
Bottesford NG13 ...128 B5
Bratoft PE24 ....102 C2
Brigsley DN37 .....35 D4
6 Broughton DN20 ..19 E3
5 Broughton DN20 ..19 E3
Cherry Willingham LN3 .203 D5
Collingham NG23 ...91 B3
Deeping St Nicholas
PE11 ....166 C8
Dunham-on-Trent NG22 .65 B1
Dunston LN4 ....95 D6
Eagle & Swinethorpe LN6 .79 C2
Eaton NG32 ....138 A2
Gedney PE12 ....159 A1
Girton NG23 ....78 C1
Gosberton PE11 ....145 C7
Grantham NG31 ....211 D7
Hatfield DN7 ....14 E1
Hemingby LN9 .....72 C3
Heydour NG32 .....131 D5
Hogsthorpe NG13 ..90 A8
Kingston upon Hull
HU13 ....179 A1
Kirton PE20 ....135 C6
Lea DN21 ....52 F5
Leake Commonside
PE22 ....113 C3
Leverington PE13 ...169 F2
Lincoln LN6 ....201 D2
Mablethorpe & Sutton
LN12 ....63 F4
Marston NG32 .....118 D1
Middle Rasen LN8 ..57 C7
Moulton PE12 ......146 E1
13 North Kelsey LN7 ..32 A4
North Somercotes LN11 .50 F7
Peterborough PE1 ..226 A4
Pilham DN21 ....41 D4
Pinchbeck PE11 ...145 C2
7 Skegness PE25 ..103 E4
3 Skegness PE25 ..103 E4
Skellingthorpe LN6 ..200 B5
Spalding PE11 .....214 C5
Stamford PE9 ......219 B7
Stickney PE22 .....113 A7
Stixwould & Woodhall
LN10 ....97 B8
Strubby with Woodthorpe
LN13 ....63 F6
Sutterton PE20 ....136 A2
Swinderby LN6 .....92 B5
Thimbleby LN9 .....85 C5
Threekingham NG34 .132 C4
Wainfleet St Mary PE24 .102 A1
18 Welton DN20 ....68 D6
Westborough & Dry Doddington
NG23 ....117 C5
Wigtoft PE20 ......135 E1
Willoughby with Sloothby
LN13 ....89 C5
Witham St Hughs LN6 .92 D5
Woodhall Spa LN10 ..97 C5
Wyberton PE21 ....136 F8
Yaxley PE7 ....233 D6
Green La Mid Sch DN8 .15 B7
Green Man La LN4 ..94 F1
Green Man Rd LN5 ..94 C1
Green Pastures 4 PE12 .158 B7
Green Rd
Aswarby & Swarby
NG34 ....131 F7
Newborough PE6 ...174 F2
Green St 1 NG31 ...129 D5
Green The
3 Allington NG32 ...128 F7
8 Brough HU15 .....2 D6
Castor PE5 ....223 E2
Cherry Willingham/Reepham
LN3 ....203 F8
1 Coddington NG24 .104 D5
Collingham NG23 ...91 C4
Corby Glen NG33 ...152 E7
Dunston LN4 ....95 D6
2 Glinton PE6 ......220 C8
6 Leasingham NG34 .121 B8
5 Mablethorpe/Sutton on Sea
LN12 ....64 A4
3 Minting LN9 ......84 C8
15 Navenby/Wellingore
LN5 ....107 A7
Peterborough PE4 ..221 A3
3 Reepham LN3 ....82 A8
Revesby PE22 .....99 B4
6 Scothern LN2 ....68 F4
Scotter DN21 ......29 C3
Spalding PE11 .....214 E5
4 Swanland HU14 ..3 B7
23 Thorne/Moorends DN8 .15 A8
11 Thorney PE6 ....176 A3
Thurlby PE10 ......164 C7
Welbourn LN5 .....106 E4
Yaxley PE7 ....233 E5
Green Wlk PE6 .....217 A5
Greenacre Cl 7 DN7 ..14 C4
Greenacres
6 Donington on Bain LN11 .59 E1
Peterborough PE4 ...220 E4
5 Swanland HU14 ...3 C7
Greenbank Dr LN6 ..205 A5
Greendyke La PE13 ..160 A2
Greenfield Cl 13 DN3 .14 A3
Greenfield Dr 9 DN20 .31 A5
Greenfield La LN13 ..75 D7
Greenfield Rd
Coningsby LN4 .....207 D1
3 Sleaford NG34 ...212 D7

Greenfields
3 Glentham LN8 ....43 F1
Holbeach PE12 .....215 F2
Greenfields La 5 NG34 .142 D8
Greenfinch Dr DN35 ..192 E1
Greengarth DN17 ...184 C2
Greengate 11 DN9 ...27 E6
Greengate Ct PE1 ..226 C4
Greengate La 14 DN19 .12 A8
Greengate Rd PE23 ..88 D3
Greenham PE3 .....225 A4
Greenhill 8 DN20 ...19 D3
Greenhill Dr 1 LN8 ..43 D3
Greenhill Rd DN9 ...27 C2
Greenhoe Rd DN17 ..184 D3
Greenlands Ave 10
DN36 ....195 C6
Greenock Way LN6 ..204 B7
Greenrigg Gdns 1
PE11 ....214 D5
Green's Rd 4 DN7 ...14 C3
Greenstiles La 5 HU14 .3 C7
Greenstock La PE13 ..170 A6
Greenway
7 Barton-upon-Humber
DN18 ....3 F1
Waltham DN37 .....194 E3
2 Welton/Dunholme LN2 .68 C7
Greenway The 1 HU4 .179 C6
Greenways 1 HU14 ..3 A5
Greenwood Cl PE21 .215 E2
Greenwood Dr PE21 .208 F6
Greenwood's Row 5
NG31 ....211 A4
Greestone Pl LN2 ...234 B3
Greestone Strs★ LN2 .234 B3
Greetham's La DN32 .192 C5
Greetwell Cl LN2 ....202 B5
Greetwell La LN2 ...202 F8
Greetwell Pl LN2 ...202 B5
Greetwell Rd LN2 ...234 C3
Greetwellgate LN2 ..234 C3
Gregg Hall Cl 2 LN6 .205 B4
Gregg Hall Cres LN6 .205 B4
Gregg Hall Dr 4 LN6 .205 B4
Gregory Cl 1 NG32 ..139 C7
Gresham St LN1 ....201 D4
Gresley Ct 11 NG31 ..210 E2
Gresley Dr Lincoln LN6 .201 D1
4 Stamford PE9 ....219 B4
Gresley Way
Immingham DN40 ..186 F5
Peterborough PE3 ..225 C6
Gretton Cl
1 Claypole NG23 ...117 E8
Peterborough PE2 ..230 C7
Grevel Cl 6 PE11 ...214 B5
Grey Friars DN37 ...190 D7
Grey St
Gainsborough DN21 .197 B6
Kingston upon Hull HU2 .180 D7
Greyfleet Bank 7 LN11 .51 C4
Greyfriars La 9 PE21 .208 F4
Greyfriars Rd 11 DN20 .19 C3
Greyling Cl 5 LN1 ...201 E8
Greystone Ave LN5 ..179 E7
Greystones Rd DN21 .197 B7
Gride Bank PE22 ...126 E8
Gride The PE22 ....113 E1
Griffins Cl 4 PE6 ...174 E5
Griffiths Ct PE2 ....229 E5
Grime St DN31 .....191 E8
Grimmer's Rd 12 PE13 .170 E1
Grimoldby Prim Sch
LN11 ....62 C6
Grimsby Auditorium
DN34 ....190 F8
Grimsby Coll DN34 ..191 C4
Grimsby Coll Sch of Art &
Design DN34 ......191 B5
Grimsby Docks Sta
DN31 ....189 A1
Grimsby Hospl DN33 .191 C4
Grimsby Leisure Ctr
DN34 ....190 F8
Grimsby Maternity Hospl
DN33 ....191 C3
Grimsby Rd
2 Binbrook LN8 ....47 C5
Brackenborough with
Little Grimsby LN11 ..61 A8
Cleethorpes DN35 ..192 D8
Fotherby LN11 .....49 A1
Grimsby DN32 .....189 D1
Humberston DN36 ..192 E1
Laceby DN37 ......190 A2
Louth LN11 ....198 A6
Swallow LN7 ....34 B6
Waltham DN37 .....194 F5
Grimsby Town Sta
DN32 ....191 D7
Grimshaw Rd PE1 ..226 B6
Grimsthorpe Castle★
PE10 ....153 D5
Grimsthorpe Cl
Grantham NG31 ....210 E6
12 Market Deeping PE6 .217 A5
Grimston Rd 6 HU10 .178 F6
Grindell St HU9 ....181 D8
Gringley Rd DN10 ..39 E4
Grinter Cl 3 LN6 ...93 C8
Groose La PE24 ....115 D8
Grosvenor Ave
Birchwood LN6 .....200 D2

Grosvenor Ave *continued*
Bourne PE10 .213 E4
Grosvenor Cres
Grimsby DN32 .191 D6
Louth LN11 .198 D7
Grosvenor Ct 3 DN7 .14 D8
Grosvenor Mews 2
LN4 .203 D1
Grosvenor Rd
9 Billingborough NG34 .133 B1
Kirton PE20 .136 C6
Louth LN11 .198 D7
Skegness PE25 .206 C4
Wisbech PE13 .170 D1
Grosvenor Sq 17 LN5 .107 A7
Grosvenor St (South) 2
DN15 .183 A4
Grosvenor St
Grimsby DN32 .191 D6
Kingston upon Hull HU3 .180 D8
Grosvenor St N DN15 .183 A5
Grove Cl 10 PE11 .145 C1
Grove Dr 9 LN10 .97 D5
Grove End Rd 3 NG31 .211 B4
Grove Hill HU13 .178 E1
Grove La
Peterborough PE3 .225 A2
Waltham DN37 .194 E4
Grove Leisure Ctr
NG24 .104 B3
Grove Pk 18 DN10 .39 F5
Grove Rd 1 Fishlake DN7 .14 D8
9 Mablethorpe/Sutton on Sea
LN12 .64 C1
Theddlethorpe All Saints
LN12 .63 D6
Grove Sch The NG24 .104 B3
Grove St
Heckington NG34 .122 E2
5 Kirton in Lindsey DN21 .30 B1
Newark-on-Trent NG24 .104 B3
Peterborough PE2 .230 F8
Grove St E 5 PE21 .209 A5
Grove St W 4 PE21 .209 A5
Grove The
14 Barrow upon Humber
DN19 .11 C8
4 Beckingham DN10 .40 A1
Edlington with Wispington
LN9 .85 B6
6 Gainsborough DN21 .53 A5
Grantham NG31 .210 E3
Lincoln LN2 .234 C4
Market Deeping PE6 .217 B5
Morton PE10 .154 B6
Newton on Trent LN1 .65 D1
4 Spalding PE11 .214 C6
4 Welton/Dunholme LN2 .68 D6
Grove Wood Rd DN10 .39 F5
Grove Wood Terr 17
DN10 .39 F5
Grovefield La PE22 .126 D1
Grovenor Ct 5 DN35 .193 A1
Grundale HU10 .178 C6
Grundy La LN3 .57 D2
Grundy's La LN9 .84 C8
Grunnill Cl 10 PE25 .206 A5
Gardens The 3 PE6 .166 F1
Guanockgate Rd PE12 .169 A2
Guash Way PE9 .219 D7
Gubbole's Dro PE11 .145 A3
Guernsey Gr DN40 .186 C2
Guild Rd PE13 .170 E1
Guildford Cl 11 NG31 .210 E5
Guildford La LN5 .105 F5
Guildford St DN32 .192 A8
Guildhall Dr 2 PE11 .156 E8
Guildhall Mus★ PE21 .208 F4
Guildhall Rd HU1 .180 F6
Guildhall St
Grantham NG31 .211 A4
Lincoln LN1 .234 A2
Guilicarr La LN7 .31 F4
Guisefield Rd 9 DN9 .27 D6
Gulham Rd LN8 .44 D5
Gull Bank
Whaplode PE12 .167 F5
Wisbech St Mary PE13 .177 E3
Gull Dro PE13 .177 D3
Gull La PE13 .170 A2
Gull Rd PE13 .177 F2
Gullymore PE3 .224 F8
Gunby Ave LN6 .204 F6
Gunby Hall (NT)★
PE23 .89 A1
Gunby La PE23 .89 A1
Gunby Pl DN35 .192 E4
Gunby Rd
Gunby & Stainby NG33 .151 A4
Scunthorpe DN17 .184 E5
Gunness & Burringham CE
Prim Sch DN17 .17 E5
Gunness La
Amcotts DN17 .17 F8
Flixborough DN15 .182 A7
Gunthorpe Cty Prim Sch
PE4 .221 C2
Gunthorpe Rd
Newborough PE6 .221 D4
Owston Ferry DN9 .40 C8
Peterborough PE4 .221 C2
Sutton Bridge PE14 .160 E1
1 Walpole PE14 .170 F8
Gunthorpe Ridings 2
PE4 .221 E2
Gunton's Rd PE6 .174 E3
Gurnard Leys PE3 .220 E1
Gurnell St DN15 .183 A4
Gurth Ave 6 DN3 .14 A1
Guthlac Ave 5 PE4 .221 B1
Guy's Head Rd
Sutton Bridge PE12 .160 F8
Lutton PE12 .149 C1
Guys Head Rd PE12 .160 E7
Gynewell Gr 4 LN2 .202 D7
Gypsy La Newton PE13 .170 C4
Whaplode PE12 .167 F3

H

Haalam Bank LN12 .63 C4
Haarlem Ct 5 PE11 .214 A2
Habbanya Rise LN4 .95 C7
Habblesthorpe Cl DN22 .52 C1
Habblesthorpe Rd
DN22 .52 C1
Habrough La DN39 .22 B6
Habrough Rd
Immingham DN40 .186 A3
South Killingholme DN40 .12 E2
Habrough Sta DN40 .22 E8
Hacconby Dro
Dunsby PE10 .144 A1
Haconby PE10 .155 A8
Hacconby La PE10 .154 C7
Hack's Dro PE6 .164 F6
Hacke Rd 3 PE3 .225 D3
Hackness Gr 2 HU5 .179 D8
Hackthorn CE (Controlled)
Prim Sch LN2 .55 F1
Hackthorn Pl 4 LN2 .201 F8
Hackthorn Rd LN2 .68 D8
Haddington La LN6 .92 F6
Haddon Cl
Birchwood LN6 .200 E1
Peterborough PE2 .231 E5
Haddon Rd
Peterborough PE3 .225 E3
Peterborough PE7 .232 C6
Stamford PE9 .218 F6
Haddon St HU3 .179 F4
Haddon Way PE7 .231 B2
Hadfield Rd 7 LN6 .205 A5
Hadleigh Dr LN6 .204 F5
Hadleigh Gn 7 DN17 .17 D4
Hadleigh Rd DN40 .186 D3
Hadley Rd
Peterborough PE4 .221 B1
Sleaford NG34 .212 E6
Hadrian Dr 10 PE6 .164 E5
Hadrians Ct PE2 .231 B8
Haff Cl 2 PE20 .135 C7
Haffenden Rd LN2 .202 A6
Hagbeach Dro PE12 .168 A5
Hagbeach Gate PE12 .158 C6
Hagg Cross Roads
PE23 .87 A4
Hagg La 1 DN17 .16 E3
Hagnaby Abbey LN13 .76 C7
Hagnaby Rd PE23 .100 A6
Haig Ave DN16 .183 B1
Haigh Ct DN32 .191 F5
Haigh St 4 DN35 .193 A5
Haile Rd DN36 .193 A1
Hainton Ave DN32 .191 F8
Hainton Cl DN21 .197 E3
Hainton Rd Hainton LN8 .58 F3
Lincoln LN6 .205 C5
Haith's La 4 DN36 .36 B1
Haldane St DN21 .197 B5
Hale Cl 4 LN2 .202 E7
Hale Hill La DN7 .14 E2
Hale House Rd PE10 .153 C2
Hale La PE22 .112 F1
Hale Rd
Heckington NG34 .122 E2
Helpringham NG34 .133 E7
Horsington LN10 .84 B2
Hales Cl DN16 .185 A2
Hales Entry HU9 .181 C6
Hales La 6 LN5 .107 B8
Haley Cl 6 PE13 .170 D2
Half Acre Wood 3 DN17 .17 D4
Halfleet PE6 .217 A6
Halford Cl 8 NG33 .151 D2
Halfpenny Cl 19 LN2 .68 D7
Halfway House La LN6 .92 C6
Halfway Houses LN6 .92 D5
Halifax App DN20 .21 A8
Halifax Cl
5 Skegness PE25 .206 B5
3 Skellingthorpe LN6 .200 A4
Halkon Cl DN17 .7 D3
Hall Bank 3 PE13 .169 F7
Hall Cl
Heckington NG34 .122 E3
Ropsley NG33 .131 B1
Hall Ct DN17 .7 A3
Hall Dr Canwick LN4 .81 A4
Grantham NG31 .211 C5
Lincoln LN6 .205 C7
Hall End Rd PE22 .114 C1
Hall Farm
5 Market Deeping PE6 .217 B6
6 Newark-on-Trent
NG24 .104 D5
Hall Gate Fleet PE12 .159 B6
Holbeach PE12 .215 C1
Moulton PE12 .157 F5
Wainfleet St Mary PE24 .102 C1
Weston PE12 .146 B1
Hall Gate Rd PE12 .168 E2
Hall Gdns 8 DN15 .9 B5
Hall Hill Rd PE12 .215 D1
Hall La Algarkirk PE20 .136 B3
Benington PE22 .126 F5
Branston & Mere LN4 .81 D1
Burgh Le Marsh PE24 .102 E7
Elsham DN20 .20 F7
Fiskerton LN3 .82 C7
Frampton PE20 .136 E6
Gunby & Stainby NG33 .151 B5
Hough-on-the-Hill NG32 .118 E7
Lenton Keisby & Osgodby
NG33 .141 E3
Moulton PE12 .146 D2
Nettleham LN2 .68 B2
Peterborough PE4 .221 A4
Stainforth DN7 .14 A6
Stenigot LN11 .72 D7
Stickney PE22 .112 F7
Welbourn LN5 .106 E4
West Keal PE23 .100 C6
Wrangle PE22 .114 D1
Hall Leas Dr 2 LN12 .64 C1
Hall Mdw 1 DN20 .10 C2
Hall Mdw Rd PE6 .217 F7
Hall Orch La 2 LN5 .106 E5
Hall Pk
Heckington NG34 .122 F1
Swanland HU14 .3 C7
Hall Pl 7 PE11 .214 D4
Hall Rd Haconby PE10 .154 D8
Heckington NG34 .122 E1
Hough-on-the-Hill NG32 .118 E7
Londonthorpe &
Harrowby without NG31 .211 F4
Hall Rise 7 DN17 .29 D7
Hall St Crowland PE6 .166 F1
Kingston upon Hull HU2 .180 D7
16 Navenby/Wellingore
LN5 .107 A7
Hall Wath LN5 .92 E2
Hall Way DN38 .21 F5
Hall Wlk 1 HU15 .2 D6
Hall Yd
2 Collyweston PE9 .171 B1
26 Metheringham LN4 .95 C4
Hallam Cl 3 LN13 .75 E2
Hallam Gr LN6 .205 C7
Hallam's Dro PE20 .123 F2
Hallam's La 3 LN4 .96 B1
Hallaton Rd PE1 .226 D8
Hallbrook Ct 5 DN16 .185 A1
Hallcroft 6 DN39 .12 A1
Hallcroft Rd 1 DN9 .27 D2
Haller St HU9 .181 E8
Hallfield Cres NG32 .119 C2
Hallfields La PE4 .221 C1
Hallgarth DN36 .37 B2
Hallgarth Ave DN16 .183 B2
Hallgate PE12 .159 E8
Halliwell Cl 5 HU9 .5 F8
Halls Ct LN4 .95 C6
Halls Hill LN11 .72 D6
Halls La 6 Keelby DN41 .23 A4
9 North Kelsey LN7 .32 A4
Hall's Rd DN10 .39 D2
Halmer Gate PE11 .214 E4
Halmer Gdns PE11 .214 F4
Halmer Paddock 6
PE11 .214 F5
Haltemprice Leisure Ctr
HU10 .178 E7
Haltemprice St HU3 .179 F5
Haltoft End Est PE22 .126 C3
Halton Cl
5 Birchwood LN6 .204 B8
4 Kirton in Lindsey DN21 .42 F8
Halton Holegate CE Prim Sch
PE23 .101 B7
Halton Pl DN35 .192 D4
Halton Rd PE23 .101 A8
Halton Way 3 DN33 .191 C2
Halyard Croft 8 HU1 .180 F5
Halycon Ave 1 HU13 .178 E2
Ham La PE2 .229 E7
Ham Mere Bird Sanctuary★
PE2 .229 E7
Hambleton La LN8 .57 E8
Hambleton Rd PE9 .218 E4
Hamerton La 1 LN9 .199 C3
Hamilton Cl
6 Bourne PE10 .213 C7
6 Grimsby DN34 .190 D4
Hamilton Gr LN6 .200 B3
Hamilton Rd Alford LN13 .75 F2
Grantham NG31 .211 D6
4 Lincoln LN6 .204 D2
Scunthorpe DN17 .184 F8
Hamilton St DN32 .189 D1
Hamish Wlk 8 DN40 .186 B3
Hamling Way HU4 .179 D2
Hamlyn Ave HU4 .179 E7
Hamlyn Dr HU4 .179 E6
Hammerton Rd DN17 .184 E4
Hammond Cl PE8 .172 C1
Hammond Ct 11 LN12 .64 B3
Hamont Rd DN32 .192 B7
Hampden Cl 1 LN6 .200 A4
Hampden Cres 3 DN7 .26 A8
Hampden Way 8 LN5 .94 A7
Hampshire St HU4 .179 E3
Hampson Gdns 18 DN3 .14 A2
Hampstead Pk 7 DN33 .191 B2
Hampton Cl
7 Humberston DN35 .192 F1
1 Spalding PE11 .214 E2
Hampton Hargate Prim Sch
PE7 .230 C2
Hampton La PE22 .127 B7
Hampton Rd
2 Hatfield DN7 .14 C4
Scunthorpe DN16 .185 C8
Hampton St LN1 .201 D4
Hanbury PE2 .229 F3
Hanby La 11 Alford LN13 .75 F2
Welton Le Marsh PE23 .89 B4
Handel House Prep Sch
DN21 .197 D5
Handley St
Heckington NG34 .122 E3
8 Sleaford NG34 .212 D4
Hands on History Mus★
HU1 .180 F6
Hangman's Cnr PE6 .175 F5
Hangman's La
Edenham PE10 .153 F7
Haconby PE10 .154 A7
Hankey St PE1 .225 F4
Hankinson's Est PE34 .161 D1
Hannah Cres LN6 .92 E5
Hannam Bvd PE11 .214 A3
Hannath Rd PE13 .170 B8
Hanover Ct PE3 .225 A8
Hanover Hill DN21 .54 F6
Hanover Sq
5 Kingston upon Hull
HU1 .180 F6
3 Kingston upon Hull
HU1 .181 A6
Hansard Cres 3 LN7 .33 B4
Hansard Way 8 PE20 .136 C5
Hansards Dr 2 LN8 .70 D5
Hanson Dr 2 LN12 .76 F8
Hanson Way DN32 .192 B8
Hanthorpe Rd PE10 .154 B7
Ha'penny Bridge Way
HU9 .181 B5
Harbour Way HU9 .181 C6
Harby Cl
Grantham NG31 .210 E1
Lincoln LN6 .205 B3
Harcourt Dr HU9 .181 C8
Harden's La LN9 .73 F1
Harding Cl
13 Mablethorpe & Sutton
LN12 .64 C1
6 Mablethorpe/Sutton on Sea
LN12 .76 F8
Harding House Gall★
LN2 .234 B3
Hardings La PE23 .88 B2
Hardings The 20 LN2 .68 D7
Hardiway PE21 .209 B5
Hardwick Cl
Louth LN11 .198 A7
3 Saxilby with Ingleby LN1 66 C2
Hardwick Ct PE3 .225 B2
Hardwick Pl 1 LN2 .202 A8
Hardwick Plot La
PE20 .124 C1
Hardwick Rd
5 Kirton PE20 .136 C5
1 Stamford PE9 .218 F6
Hardwick St HU5 .180 B8
Hardy Rd DN17 .184 D6
Hardy's Animal Farm★
PE25 .90 E5
Hardy's Dro PE10 .213 F7
Hardy's La PE6 .167 D4
Hardy's Rd DN35 .192 F4
Hare Cl 9 NG34 .122 E2
Hare St DN32 .191 F6
Harebell Cl PE1 .221 F1
Harecroft Rd PE13 .170 C1
Harewood Ave 7 DN3 .14 A2
Harewood Cl PE21 .209 B5
Harewood Cres
Lincoln LN6 .205 A3
Louth LN11 .198 B7
Harewood Gdns PE3 .225 B2
Harewood Gr 6 DN35 .192 F1
Harford Gate PE12 .159 D5
Hargate Cl 1 PE12 .159 C7
Hargate La PE34 .161 E2
Hargate Way PE7 .230 D3
Hargon La NG24 .104 B7
Hargrave St DN31 .188 D1
Hargreaves Way DN15 .183 B6
Harland Rd 9 HU15 .2 C6
Harlaxton CE Prim Sch
NG32 .139 C7
Harlaxton Cl 2 LN6 .204 C6
Harlaxton Coll NG32 .139 D7
Harlaxton Dr 4 LN6 .204 C6
Harlaxton Gdns★
NG32 .139 D7
Harlaxton Rd
3 Grantham NG31 .210 F3
Grantham NG31 .210 E1
Harlech Grange PE3 .225 B1
Harlech Way DN32 .191 F8
Harlequin Dr
23 Mablethorpe/Sutton on Sea
LN12 .64 B3
6 Spalding PE11 .214 A5
Harlestone Ct DN34 .190 C4
Harley St HU2 .180 E8
Harlow St DN31 .188 D1
Harlton Cl PE2 .231 E5
Harmston Cl LN2 .202 A8
Harmston Pk Ave LN5 .93 F4
Harmston Rd LN5 .93 A3
Harneis Cres DN37 .23 F2
Harold St DN32 .192 A8
Harold's Bank PE13 .169 B2
Harome Gr HU5 .179 C7
Harpe Cl 10 PE11 .156 E8
Harpenden Cl 15 DN7 .14 D3
Harpendon Dr 16 DN7 .14 D3
Harpham Rd
Gate Burton DN21 .53 A1
Marshchapel DN36 .37 B2
Harpswell Cl 7 DN21 .53 A8
Harpswell La DN21 .42 C1
Harpswell Rd LN2 .202 A7
Harrier Ct 3 LN6 .204 E8
Harrier Rd 3 DN18 .3 F1
Harriet Cl 5 PE12 .160 E4
Harrington Ave 4 LN6 .205 C8
Harrington Dr 7 PE6 .175 C8
Harrington Pl DN16 .185 A5
Harrington Rd 7 NG33 .151 D2
Harrington St
Bourne PE10 .213 D6
Cleethorpes DN35 .189 D1
Harrington Way 6 PE6 .175 C8
Harris Bvd 18 LN12 .64 B3
Harris Cl 11 PE25 .206 A5
Harris Rd LN6 .205 B6
Harris St
Kingston upon Hull HU3 .179 F5
Peterborough PE1 .225 F6
Harrison Cl
Horncastle LN9 .199 C5
10 Peterborough PE3 .224 F3
Winteringham DN15 .9 A8
Harrison Pl
Lincoln LN1 .234 A4
North Hykeham LN6 .204 D5
Harrison St 4 DN31 .191 C7
Harrison's Dro PE20 .124 B2
Harrison's La PE24 .101 F4
Harrolds Cl 3 PE13 .170 F1
Harrow Cl
Gainsborough DN21 .197 F6
Heighington/Washingborough
LN4 .203 C1
Harrow Gdns DN17 .184 F4
Harrow Rd
Deeping St Nicholas
PE11 .166 C7
6 Mablethorpe/Sutton on Sea
LN12 .64 B4
Harrow St
Grantham NG31 .211 B3
Kingston upon Hull HU3 .180 B4
Harrowby CE (Aided) Inf Sch
NG31 .211 C6
Harrowby Cl Digby LN4 .108 E5
Grantham NG31 .211 C6
Harrowby Cres NG31 .211 E1
Harrowby Est NG31 .211 D6
Harrowby La
Grantham NG31 .211 D6
Londonthorpe &
Harrowby without NG31 .130 C3
Harrowby Rd NG31 .211 C3
Harrowdyke 6 DN18 .10 E8
Harrows The 15 LN2 .68 D6
Harrox Rd 3 PE12 .157 F7
Harrox Sq 5 PE12 .157 F6
Harrys Dream 3 DN20 .19 E3
Harston Rd NG32 .138 F7
Hart La DN15 .9 B5
Hart St DN35 .192 C8
Hartford Ct PE2 .231 D6
Harthill Dr HU3 .180 C5
Hartland Ave 6 LN6 .205 A1
Hartley Bridge HU9 .181 C6
Hartley St Boston PE21 .208 F6
3 Lincoln LN2 .202 C3
Hartshead Ave DN15 .182 C3
Hartsholme Dr LN6 .205 A8
Hartsholme Prim Sch
LN6 .204 F7
Hartwell Way PE3 .225 B5
Harvard Cl 1 LN4 .203 D1
Harvest Ave 34 DN18 .10 E8
Harvest Cl
21 Kirk Sandall DN3 .14 A2
23 Metheringham LN4 .95 C4
Harvest Cres 2 DN37 .194 C4
Harvest Rise 2 DN19 .11 C8
Harvest Way 3 NG34 .212 C2
Harvester Cl 19 DN9 .27 E6
Harvester Way
Crowland PE6 .175 B8
Peterborough PE1 .226 C1
1 Sibsey PE22 .113 B1
Harvey Ave
10 Coddington NG24 .104 C5
14 Newark-on-Trent NG24 104 C5
Harvey Cl Bourne PE10 .213 B4
11 Wittering PE8 .172 B1
Harvey Kent Gdns 4
LN3 .83 C4
Harvey St 5 LN1 .201 D3
Harwich Cl 12 LN5 .205 D3
Harwood Ave PE12 .215 C1
Harwood Dr 1 HU4 .179 B6
Hassall Rd PE25 .206 A2
Hassock Hill Dro
PE13 .169 D3
Hasthorpe Rd LN13 .89 C5
Hastings Dr 4 PE24 .102 D2
Hastings Gr HU5 .179 E7
Hastings Rd PE4 .221 A2
Hatcliffe Cl 2 NG31 .211 A8
Hatcliffe Gdns 11 LN2 .202 A8
Hatcliffe Cl 8 DN33 .191 B3
Hatfield & Stainforth Sta
DN7 .14 C5
Hatfield Crookesbroom Prim
Sch DN7 .14 C4

Hatfield High Sch DN7 ..14 D3
Hatfield La DN3 ....14 A4
Hatfield Manor Mid Sch
  DN7 ....14 E5
Hatfield Rd Hatfield DN7 .14 F6
  Thorne/Moorends DN8 ...15 A7
Hatfield Water Pk★
  DN7 ....14 E5
Hathersage Ave LN6 ..204 C2
Hatt Cl 1 PE12 ....157 F7
Hatton Cl 3 LN6 ......205 A4
Hatton Gr 9 DN33 ....191 B3
Haugh La LN13 ....75 A3
Haugham Pastures
  LN11 ....61 E2
Hauser Cl 8 NG34 ....212 B2
Havelock Dr PE2 .....231 E6
Havelock Sch DN32 ...192 C6
Havelock St
  Kingston upon Hull HU3 ..180 A4
  Spalding PE11 ....214 C3
Havelok Cl 4 LN11 ...198 D4
Haven Ave Brough HU15 ...2 B5
  Grimsby DN31 ....191 C8
Haven Bank
  6 Skidbrooke with
  Saltfleet Haven LN11 ...51 C4
  Wildmore LN4 ....111 B2
Haven Cl 7 Blyton DN21 ..41 C5
  9 Fleet PE12 ....157 C2
Haven Ctry Pk★ PE21 .137 C7
Haven Garth HU15 .....2 B5
Haven Gdns DN31 ....188 C1
Haven High Sch The
  PE21 ....208 F7
Haven House Rd PE24 .102 F3
Haven Rd
  4 Barton-upon-Humber
  DN18 ....3 C1
  North Killingholme DN40 ..13 A6
Haven Side 8 DN18 ...102 C1
Haven The HU9 ......181 B6
Havenhouse Sta PE24 .102 F2
Haverfield Rd PE11 ...214 D3
Haverholme Cl 10 NG34 108 E1
Haverholme Dro PE12 .159 D5
Haverlands The 3
  NG31 ....210 E8
Haverstoe Pl DN35 ...192 C3
Haveswater Cl 1 PE4 .221 C2
Hawerby Rd 4 DN37 ..23 F1
Hawker Dr LN11 ......198 D4
Hawkins Dr 20 PE13 ..170 E1
Hawkins Gr DN32 ....192 B6
Hawkins Way 7 DN40 ..12 E3
Hawks Way NG34 ....212 B3
Hawksdale Cl 3 NG31 .211 A7
Hawkshead Gr LN2 ...202 A8
Hawkshead Way 2 PE4 221 C3
Hawksmede Way
  LN11 ....198 D8
Hawksmoor Cl 2 LN6 .204 D1
Hawksworth St 2
  DN21 ....197 D4
Haworth Cl 3 DN15 ...182 C4
Haworth Way PE21 ...208 D7
Haw's La PE11 ......134 F1
Hawthorn Ave
  Brigg DN20 ....196 C4
  Cherry Willingham LN3 ..203 B6
  Gainsborough DN21 ...197 D6
  Immingham DN40 .....186 E5
  Kingston upon Hull HU3 .179 F5
  Waddington LN5 .....205 C1
Hawthorn Bank PE11 .214 B1
Hawthorn Chase
  Lincoln LN2 ....202 E7
  1 Moulton PE12 ....157 F6
Hawthorn Cl
  Beckingham DN10 .....52 A8
  Healing DN41 ....23 F6
  4 Market Deeping PE6 .217 B6
  5 Newborough PE6 ...174 E5
  7 Ruskington NG34 ..108 E1
Hawthorn Ct 1 HU3 .179 F6
Hawthorn Dr .... .212 D3
Hawthorn Gate 26 DN18 .10 F8
Hawthorn Gr DN21 ...197 D5
Hawthorn Rd
  Bourne PE10 ....213 C6
  Cherry Willingham LN3 .203 B7
  4 Old Leake PE22 ...114 A1
  Peterborough PE1 ....226 C6
  Skegness PE25 ......206 A2
  Yaxley PE7 ....231 F5
Hawthorn Rise 4 DN19 .11 C8
Hawthorn Way 4 NG31 .92 F3
Hawthorn Wlk 1 LN1 ..66 D7
Hawthorne Ave
  Cleethorpes DN35 ....192 D8
  4 Grimsby DN33 .....194 F8
  9 Hatfield DN7 ......14 C2
  Louth LN11 ....198 B6
  New Waltham DN36 ...195 B5
  4 Scunthorpe DN17 ..184 C4
  8 Wisbech PE13 .....170 D2
Hawthorne Cl
  5 Manby LN11 ....62 C6
  6 Scopwick Heath LN4 .108 A7
  20 Winterton DN15 ...9 A5
  Wootton DN39 ....11 E4
Hawthorne Cres 3
  DN17 ....184 F8
Hawthorne Ct 4 NG31 .210 D2
Hawthorne Gdns 8
  DN19 ....12 A8
Hawthorne Rise HU13 .178 B3
Hawthorns The 14 LN2 .68 D2

Hawthorpe Rd NG33 ..141 E1
Hawton Cl 1 DN21 ...197 E6
Hawton La NG24 .....104 A2
Haxey CE Prim Sch
  DN9 ....27 D3
Haxey Gate Rd DN10 ..39 F7
Haxey Grange 9 DN9 ..27 D3
Haxey La DN9 ....27 D1
Haxey Rd DN10 ....39 F6
Hay Gn Rd (North)
  PE34 ....161 E2
Hay Gn Rd (South)
  PE34 ....161 D1
Haycroft Ave 8 DN31 .191 C8
Haycroft La PE12 .....159 B7
Haycroft St DN31 ....191 C7
Haydon Ave PE25 ....206 A4
Haydor Ave LN2 .....202 A8
Hayes Yd 4 LN1 .....54 F7
Hayfield Cl
  7 Barnby Dun DN3 ...14 A4
  Haxey DN9 ....27 D1
Hayling Mere 4 DN35 .192 F1
Haynes Cl 3 DN8 .....15 B7
Haynes Gdns 13 DN8 ..15 B8
Haynes Gn 6 DN8 ....15 B8
Haynes Gr 1 DN8 ....15 B7
Haynes Wlk 2 DN8 ...15 B8
Hays Cl 4 DN36 .....195 C4
Hayton Cl 2 DN15 ....9 B5
Hayton Gr HU4 ......179 D4
Haytons La 2 DN15 ...9 D1
Haywardsfield 4 PE3 .225 A4
Haze La 5 LN6 ......204 C1
Hazel Cl 4 LN9 ......29 C7
Hazel Croft
  4 Immingham DN40 ...186 A4
  Peterborough PE4 ....220 E4
Hazel Dr LN9 ....199 B5
Hazel Gr
  4 Bottesford DN16 ...185 B2
  2 Kingston upon Hull
  HU3 ....180 D5
  Louth LN11 ....198 E4
  Sleaford NG34 ....212 D6
  Stamford PE9 ....218 D6
  Welton/Dunholme LN2 .68 C3
Hazel Rd 6 DN7 .....14 C5
Hazeland Cl DN10 ....154 C6
Hazelbarrow Dr HU10 .178 F7
Hazelnut Cl 3 PE22 ..99 A4
Hazelwood Ave LN6 ..204 C8
Hazelwood Dr DN16 ..213 B6
Hazelwood La PE12 ..159 A4
Hazlewood Dr NG31 ..210 F7
Headingley Ave 4
  DN17 ....184 E3
Headland Way
  3 Haconby PE10 ....154 D8
  7 Navenby NG34 ....107 B8
Headlands Dr HU13 ..178 C2
Headquarters Cres 5
  NG34 ....120 C8
Heads La HU13 ......178 C1
Headstead Bank DN22 .65 B7
Healey Cl 5 NG23 ....91 D4
Healey La LN12 ......63 C4
Healey Rd DN16 .....185 C3
Healing Prim Sch DN41 .23 F5
Healing Sch DN41 ....23 D6
Healing Sta DN41 ....23 F6
Heapham Cres DN21 ..197 F4
Heapham La DN21 ....53 F7
Heapham Rd DN21 ...197 E5
Heath Cl 4 LN1 ......68 C7
Heath Farm Cl NG32 ..119 F3
Heath Farm Rd NG31 .130 C2
Heath La
  Ancaster NG32 ......119 F3
  Boothby Graffoe LN5 ..94 B2
  Carlton Scroop NG32 ..119 D4
  Great Ponton NG33 ...139 D4
  Honington NG32 .....119 C2
  Leasingham NG34 ....121 C7
  Normanton NG32 ....119 F6
  Syston NG32 ....130 D8
  Welton LN1 ....67 F6
  Wilsford NG32 ......120 B1
Heath Rd
  Bracebridge Heath LN4 .205 F2
  Coleby LN5 ....93 F3
  Helpston PE6 ....173 C2
  15 Navenby LN5 .....107 A8
  5 Nettleham LN2 ....68 C2
  Scopwick LN4 ....108 B8
  Scothern LN2 ....68 A4
  Skegness PE25 ......206 B3
Heathcote Rd
  Bourne PE10 ....213 E4
  Castle Bytham NG33 ..152 D1
  Coningsby LN4 ....207 E5
Heather Ave PE1 ....226 A8
Heather Cl
  1 Boston PE21 .....208 D3
  7 Woodhall Spa LN10 .97 E6
Heather Gr DN16 ....185 C6
Heatherdale Cl
  6 Grimsby DN33 ....194 E7
  Peterborough PE7 ...231 C5
Heathfield Ave
  Branston LN4 ....81 D4
  Spalding PE11 ......214 F2
Heathfield Cl 9 DN3 ..14 A3
Heathfield Ct DN34 ..191 B6
Heathfield Rd NG31 ..210 C3

Heathlea 11 LN2 .....68 F4
Heath's Mdw Nature
  Reserve★ PE24 ....102 C7
Heaton Cl PE3 ......225 B3
Heaton St 2 DN21 ...197 D4
Hebden Moor Way 8
  LN6 ....93 B8
Heckdyke La DN10 ...40 C7
Heckington 8 Sailed
  Windmill★ NG34 ....122 C2
Heckington Rd NG34 .122 C1
Heckington St Andrews CE
  Sch NG34 ....122 C2
Heckington Sta NG34 .122 E2
Hedge Field Rd NG32 .210 A4
Hedgefield Hurn PE11 .144 F4
Hedgehog La PE20 ...124 D4
Hedgelands
  Peterborough PE4 ...221 A5
  3 Wisbech PE13 ....170 D2
Hedgerow Cl 5 DN19 ..11 C8
Hedgerow La 5 DN20 .196 D3
Hedon Rd HU9 ......181 B6
Heighington La LN4 ..82 A5
Heighington Rd LN4 ..81 C4
Heimdal Rd DN31 ....191 C2
Helen Cres 8 DN40 ..186 A4
Helene Gr DN32 .....192 B7
Helenship La DN22 ...65 A4
Hell La NG33 ....140 C5
Hellyers Ct HU4 .....179 D2
Helm Dr HU9 ....181 C6
Helmsdale Gdns PE4 ..220 F7
Helmsley Ct 1 PE7 ..231 F5
Helmsley Gr HU5 ....179 C7
Helmsley Wlk PE11 ..214 F4
Helpringham Rd
  Burton Pedwardine
  NG34 ....122 B1
  Helpringham NG34 ...133 C8
Helpringham Sch
  NG34 ....133 D7
Helpston Rd
  Castor PE5 ....223 D2
  Etton PE6 ....220 A8
Helsby Rd LN5 ......205 D4
Helsey La PE24 .....89 F7
Heltwate Specl Sch
  PE3 ....225 B7
Hemingby La LN9 ....199 C6
Hemingby Way LN9 ..199 C5
Hemingford Cres PE2 .231 E6
Hemington Way 1
  PE20 ....136 C3
Hemmingway Wlk
  HU13 ....178 C3
Hempdyke Rd 5 DN15 .182 E4
Hemplands The 9 NG23 .91 D5
Hemswell Ave
  4 Kingston upon Hull HU9 .5 E8
  Lincoln LN6 ....205 A7
Hemswell Dr 4 DN31 .190 F8
Hemswell La DN21 ...42 D1
Hemswell Prim Sch
  LN8 ....43 A1
Henderson Ave 5 DN15 .182 F4
Henderson Ave Prim Sch
  DN15 ....182 F4
Henderson Cres 2
  DN15 ....182 F4
Henderson Way 5 NG9 .A5
Heneage Rd DN32 ...191 F6
Hengist Gr 7 NG34 ..212 B2
Henley Ct
  2 Gainsborough DN21 .197 C6
  Lincoln LN5 ....205 D8
Henley St 5 LN5 ....205 D8
Henlow Cl
  6 Birchwood LN6 ...204 B8
  3 Kirton in Lindsey DN21 .42 F8
Henrietta St 2 PE11 .214 C3
Henry Boot Way HU4 .83 D4
Henry La LN3 ....83 D4
Henry St Grimsby DN31 .191 C8
  Lincoln LN5 ....201 F1
  Peterborough PE1 ...226 A4
  Scunthorpe DN15 ....182 F3
Henshaw PE1 ....226 E6
Henshaw Ave 2 LN12 .77 A7
Henson Cl 5 PE13 ...170 C2
Henson Dr 18 LN5 ...107 A8
Herdgate La PE11 ...145 D2
Hereford Ave DN34 ..191 C5
Hereford Cl 2 NG34 ..212 C7
Hereford St HU4 ....179 D3
Hereford Tech Sch
  DN34 ....191 B5
Hereford Way 8 NG31 .210 E5
Heren Pl 2 PE11 ....214 A2
Hereward Cl 2 PE1 ..226 B2
Hereward Pl DN16 ...185 E7
Hereward Rd
  Peterborough PE1 ...226 B2
  Spalding PE11 ......214 B4
Hereward St
  3 Bourne PE10 .....213 D5
  Lincoln LN1 ....234 B4
Hereward Way
  21 Crowland PE6 ...166 E1
  Market Deeping PE6 .217 E4
Heritage Pk Prim Sch
  PE7 ....231 F5
Herlyn Cres 3 PE25 ..90 E3
Hermes Way NG34 ..212 A3
Hermit St LN5 ......201 F3
Hermitage The 6 PE9 .219 A5
Heron Cl Grimsby DN32 .192 B4

Heron Cl continued
  8 Scunthorpe DN15 ..182 C6
  Skegness PE25 .....103 C8
  3 Surfleet PE11 ....145 E2
Heron Holt 3 DN20 ..19 C4
Heron Pk PE1 ....226 F6
Heron St HU3 ....180 B5
Heron Way
  Holton le Clay DN36 .195 C3
  Wyberton PE21 .....136 D3
Heron Wlk LN6 .....204 C1
Heronry Dr PE6 .....224 C2
Herons Cl PE9 ......172 F6
Herrick Cl PE1 .....225 F5
Herrick Ct 2 LN4 ...207 A6
Herrick Rd DN17 ...184 D7
Herring La
  1 Pinchbeck PE11 ..145 A1
  4 Spalding PE11 ...214 C4
Herrington Ave 2 LN3 .68 C2
Hersey Rd 16 LN7 ...33 B4
Hervey Rd NG34 ....212 C2
Hesketh Cres
  12 Skegness PE25 ..103 E4
  11 Skegness PE25 ..103 E4
Hesketh Ct LE15 ...162 A8
Hesketh Dr 3 DN3 ..14 A2
Hessle Ave PE21 ...208 C3
Hessle Ct PE21 .....208 C3
Hessle Dr PE21 .....208 C3
Hessle High Sch
  HU13 ....178 C1
Hessle Lower Sch
  HU13 ....178 B1
Hessle Mount Sch
  HU13 ....178 C1
Hessle Penshurst Prim Sch
  HU13 ....178 F3
Hessle Rd HU3 .....179 D3
Hessle Sta HU13 ....3 D4
Hessle View 4 DN18 ..10 E8
Hetley PE2 ....230 A4
Hewde La DN15 .....2 A1
Hewitt's Ave
  Humberston DN36 ...192 C1
  New Waltham DN36 ..195 D8
Hewitt's Cir DN36 ...192 C2
Hewitts Ave 1 DN35 192 D2
Hewson Rd
  5 Humberston DN36 ..36 D8
  Lincoln LN1 ....201 C4
Hewson St 23 DN17 ..29 D7
Hewson's La NG23 ...91 D3
Hexham St 3 PE1 ...226 D3
Hey St DN35 ....192 F5
Heysham Cl 8 LN5 ..205 D3
Heythrop Rd 3 DN35 .192 C4
Hibaldstow Cl
  10 Birchwood LN6 ..204 C7
  9 Grimsby DN34 ...190 F4
Hibaldstow Prim Sch
  DN20 ....31 A5
Hibaldstow Rd LN6 ..204 C7
Hickling Cl 15 NG31 ..210 E2
Hickman Cres DN21 ..197 C8
Hickman Ct DN21 ...197 E4
Hickman Gr 2 DN21 ..41 B5
Hickman St DN21 ...197 C5
Hickory Rd Rd 5 LN6 .200 C1
Hicks La PE7 ....230 E3
Hide's La
  Addlethorpe PE24 ...90 B1
  Skegness PE25 .....103 B8
Higgins Cl LN6 .....204 E7
Higgins Rd 6 LN13 ..75 E2
High Bridge Rd DN6 ..15 C7
High Broadgate PE13 .169 F7
High Bunning La
  NG34 ....143 A7
High Burgage DN15 ..2 B1
High Cliff Rd DN35 ..193 A6
High Cres PE9 ......171 C4
High Dike
  Cranwell & Byard's Leap
  NG34 ....120 B8
  Easton NG33 ....151 C4
  Great Ponton NG33 ..140 C4
  Navenby/Wellingore LN5 .94 B1
  North Rauceby NG32 .120 A5
  Old Somerby NG33 ...130 D2
  Waddington LN5 ....93 F8
  Welby NG31 ....130 E5
  Wellingore LN5 .....107 B6
  Wilsford NG32 .....119 F1
High Dyke Rd 2 NG34 .107 C1
High Fen PE11 ......144 B4
High Ferry La PE22 ..113 A1
High Field Rd DN20 ..196 F6
High Fields La LN6 ..156 E8
High Garth DN17 ...184 F2
High Gate
  Helpringham NG34 ..133 D7
  Mablethorpe & Sutton
  LN12 ....64 C1
  Theddlethorpe St Helen
  LN12 ....63 D5
High Holme Rd LN11 .198 B6
High House Rd DN22 .52 A2
High La Croft PE24 ..102 D6
  Mareham on the Hill LN9 .85 F2
High Leas 1 LN2 ....68 D2
High Levels Bank
  Belton DN8 ....15 C5
  Hatfield DN8 ....15 E5
High Leys Rd DN17 ..184 F5
High Mdw
  Grantham NG31 .....210 D4

Hat - Hig 255

High Mdw continued
  Heighington/Washingborough
  LN4 ....203 C1
  Westborough & Dry Doddington
  NG23 ....117 F5
High Mdws
  1 Fiskerton LN3 .....82 A7
  Kingston upon Hull
  HU10 ....178 C8
High or Main Rd PE12 .215 A2
High Point Ret Pk
  DN31 ....189 A1
High Rd
  Barrowby NG32 .....210 A5
  Elloughton-cum-Brough
  HU15 ....2 D7
  Gorefield PE13 .....169 F2
  Grantham NG31 ....211 E2
  Hough-on-the-Hill NG32 .119 A5
  Londonthorpe &
  Harrowby without NG31 .130 D4
  Moulton PE12 ......158 A7
  Newton PE13 ......169 F5
  Weston PE12 ......157 C2
  Wisbech St Mary PE13 .177 F2
High Ridge Comp Sch
  DN15 ....182 E3
High Ridge Sports Hall
  DN15 ....182 E3
High Side PE13 .....169 E2
High St 8 Alford LN13 ..75 F3
  Alvingham LN11 .....49 C2
  Barrow upon Humber
  DN19 ....11 D8
  Barton-upon-Humber DN18 .3 E1
  Bassingham LN5 ....92 F2
  Baumber LN9 ....85 A8
  1 Beckingham DN10 .52 B8
  Belton DN9 ....16 E1
  Benniworth LN8 ....71 F8
  Bicker PE20 ....47 C4
  Blyton DN21 ....41 C5
  Boston PE21 ....208 F3
  Bottesford NG13 ...128 A5
  Branston LN4 ......81 E2
  Brant Broughton LN5 .105 F4
  Broughton DN20 ....19 D3
  Burgh le Marsh PE24 .102 E8
  Burringham DN17 ...17 D4
  Caistor LN7 ....33 B4
  Carlby PE9 ....163 D4
  Carlton-le-Moorland LN5 .105 E8
  Castle Bytham NG33 .152 D1
  Castor PE5 ....223 C2
  Caythorpe NG32 ...119 B7
  Cherry Willingham/Reepham
  LN3 ....203 D5
  Cleethorpes DN35 ...192 E6
  Collingham NG23 ...91 A4
  3 Collyweston PE9 ..171 B1
  Colsterworth NG33 ..151 D6
  Coningsby LN4 .....207 A4
  Corby Glen NG33 ...152 E8
  Corringham DN21 ...41 C1
  9 Crowle DN17 .....16 D7
  Donington PE11 ....134 E2
  Eagle & Swinethorpe LN6 .79 B2
  East Ferry DN21 ....28 B2
  Eastoft DN17 ......7 A3
  3 Easton on the Hill PE9 .171 D3
  Elkington LN11 .....60 D1
  Epworth DN9 ......27 D7
  Eye PE6 ....175 A1
  Faldingworth LN8 ...56 F3
  Fillingham DN21 ...54 F4
  3 Fiskerton LN3 ....82 A7
  Flixborough DN15 ..8 B2
  5 Fulbeck NG32 ...106 C1
  Fulletby LN9 ....86 B8
  Gainsborough DN21 .197 D3
  Garthorpe & Fockerby
  DN17 ....7 A3
  Gate Burton DN21 ..53 A1
  Girton NG23 ....78 C1
  Glentham LN8 .....43 F1
  Glinton PE6 ....220 C8
  Gosberton PE11 ...145 B6
  Grainthorpe LN11 ..50 B8
  Grantham NG31 ....211 A4
  Great Gonerby NG31 .129 D5
  Great Limber DN37 ..22 D3
  Gringley on the Hill DN10 .39 C3
  Hagworthingham PE23 .87 A4
  Harby NG23 ....79 C5
  Harlaxton NG32 ....139 C7
  Harmston LN5 .....93 F5
  Hatfield DN7 ....14 C2
  Haxey DN9 ....27 C2
  16 Heckington NG34 .122 D2
  Heighington/Washingborough
  LN4 ....203 B2
  Helpringham NG34 ..133 D7
  Hogsthorpe PE24 ...90 B2
  Holbeach PE12 ....215 E2
  Horbling PE11 .....133 B2
  Horncastle LN9 ....199 B4
  Humberside Airport DN39 .22 A6
  Ingham LN1 ....54 F2
  2 Ingoldmells PE25 .90 E3
  Ketton PE9 ....171 A2
  Kexby DN21 ....53 E5
  Kingston upon Hull HU1 .181 A5
  18 Kirton in Lindsey DN21 .30 B1
  Laceby DN37 ......23 F1

High St *continued*
Leadenham LN5 ....106 D3
Lincoln LN5 ....234 A1
2 Little Bytham NG33 ...163 A8
Long Sutton PE12 ....216 C4
Luddington & Haldenby DN17 ....7 C4
18 Mablethorpe/Sutton on Sea LN12 ....64 B4
Mablethorpe/Sutton on Sea LN12 ....76 F8
Market Deeping PE6 ....217 B4
Market Stainton LN8 ....72 A6
Martin LN4 ....96 C2
Marton DN21 ....65 D8
Maxey PE6 ....217 A1
Messingham DN17 ....29 D7
Metheringham LN4 ....95 C4
Misterton DN10 ....39 F5
5 Morton PE10 ....154 C7
Moulton PE12 ....157 F6
12 Navenby/Wellingore LN5 ....107 A7
Nettleham LN2 ....68 C2
Nettleton LN7 ....33 C2
Newton on Trent LN1 ....65 D1
North Ferriby HU14 ....3 A5
8 North Kelsey LN7 ....32 A4
North Scarle LN6 ....78 E1
North Thoresby DN36 ....36 A1
Northorpe PE10 ....164 C7
Osbournby NG34 ....132 C5
Owston Ferry DN9 ....28 B3
Peterborough PE2 ....231 A6
Pointon & Sempringham NG34 ....143 B7
Redbourne DN21 ....30 F2
Reepham LN3 ....203 F8
Rippingale PE10 ....142 F2
Ropsley NG33 ....131 B1
Roxby cum Risby DN15 ....8 E1
Saxilby LN1 ....66 D2
Scampton LN1 ....67 C6
Scotton DN21 ....29 C1
Scunthorpe DN15 ....183 A3
Sixhills LN8 ....59 A7
Skegness PE25 ....206 C3
Skellingthorpe LN6 ....200 A5
Snitterby DN21 ....43 D5
South Clifton NG23 ....78 C5
South Ferriby DN18 ....10 A7
South Kyme LN4 ....123 B8
South Witham NG33 ....151 D2
Spalding PE11 ....214 E4
7 Spilsby PE23 ....88 A1
Stamford PE9 ....219 C5
Staunton NG13 ....117 A2
Sturton by Stow LN1 ....66 C7
5 Sutton Bridge PE12 ...160 F4
Swayfield NG33 ....152 D5
Swinderby LN6 ....92 A5
Swineshead PE20 ....135 B7
Swinstead NG33 ....153 A5
Upton DN21 ....53 D5
3 Waddingham DN21 ....43 D7
Waddington LN5 ....93 F7
Wainfleet All Saints PE24 ....102 D1
Walcott LN4 ....109 D7
Walesby LN8 ....46 B5
Walkeringham DN10 ....39 F3
1 Waltham DN37 ....194 E4
Welbourn LN5 ....106 E5
West/East Butterwick DN17 ....17 D1
Willingham by Stow DN21 ..53 E3
11 Winterton DN15 ....9 A5
Wootton DN39 ....11 E2
Wroot DN9 ....26 D6
High St E DN15 ....183 C3
High St N 16 NG34 ....108 E2
High St S 3 NG34 ....108 E1
High St St Martin's PE9 ....219 C3
High St W DN21 ....29 B4
High Thorpe Cres DN35 ....192 D3
High Thorpe Rd LN3 ....83 D1
High Wash Dro 2 PE6 .166 E1
Higham Way 1 HU15 ....2 D5
Highbridge La PE11 ...145 C6
Highbridge Rd LN11 ....49 F2
Highbury St PE1 ....226 A5
Highclere Rd PE7 ....230 D3
Highcliff Gdns DN15 ...182 E3
Highcliffe 5 LN5 ....107 A7
Highcliffe Rd NG31 ....211 B7
Highdales HU10 ....178 C8
Highfield Ave
4 Immingham DN40 ....186 B3
4 Lincoln LN6 ....205 B7
5 Mablethorpe/Sutton on Sea LN12 ....64 C1
Scunthorpe DN15 ....182 E3
Highfield Cl
8 Barnby Dun DN3 ....14 A4
Foston NG32 ....117 F2
Gainsborough DN21 ....197 E5
8 North Thoresby DN36 ...36 B1
Osbournby NG34 ....132 C5
Highfield Cres
17 Barton-upon-Humber DN18 ....10 F8
Croxton Kerrial NG32 ....138 D3
4 Westwoodside DN9 ....27 B2
Highfield Dr
2 Kirton in Lindsey DN21 ..30 B1
Stapleford LN6 ....105 A6
Highfield Gr DN20 ....196 C5
Highfield La
Halton Holegate PE23 ....101 B8
Revesby PE22 ....99 B5
Highfield Rd
7 Donington PE11 ....134 F2
North Thoresby DN36 ....36 B1
14 Saxilby LN1 ....66 D2
Highfield Terr
4 Glentham LN8 ....43 F1
2 Lincoln LN6 ....205 A2
Highfields
1 Barrow upon Humber DN19 ....11 C7
6 Barrowby NG32 ....210 A5
17 Crowle DN17 ....16 D8
2 Nettleham LN2 ....68 D2
Highfields Rise 29 LN4 ..95 C4
Highfields Sch NG24 ...104 B3
Highgate 6 DN35 ....192 F5
Highgate Cl 4 LN12 ....64 C1
Highgate La
Claxby with Moorby PE22 ..99 B6
Normanby By Spital LN8 ...56 B7
Owmby LN8 ....55 F6
Highgrove
1 Long Sutton PE12 ....216 B5
4 Messingham DN17 ....29 D7
Highgrove Cres PE21 ..209 C6
Highland Tarn DN40 ...186 B3
Highlands 1 PE9 ....163 C1
Highlands Way PE9 ...218 F5
Highlees Prim Sch PE3 ....225 C6
Highstock La PE12 ....168 D1
Higson Rd 4 LN1 ....201 D7
Hilary Gr HU4 ....179 B2
Hilary Rd DN33 ....194 F7
Hilda Cl 6 NG34 ....212 B2
Hilda St 4 Boston PE21 .209 A7
Grimsby DN32 ....189 C1
Hildyard Cl 1 HU10 ....178 F6
Hildyard St DN32 ....192 B8
Hiles Ave 6 DN15 ....9 A5
Hill Abbey LN4 ....95 D7
Hill Ave NG31 ....211 B5
Hill Brow HU10 ....178 B6
Hill Cl PE1 ....226 D5
Hill Cres DN21 ....197 F5
Hill Field 3 PE24 ....102 D2
Hill La PE20 ....136 B5
Hill Rd DN21 ....41 E1
Hill Rise 8 Brough HU15 ...2 C6
Coleby LN5 ....93 F3
Louth LN11 ....198 A7
Hill The 4 Saltfleet LN11 ..51 C4
Skellingthorpe LN6 ....200 A4
Worlaby DN20 ....10 E1
Hill Top 1 LN5 ....93 E5
Hill Top La 1 DN21 ....41 B5
Hill Top Pl DN34 ....190 D3
Hill View Cl NG31 ....210 E3
Hill View Rd 14 NG33 ...151 D2
Hillary Cl 1 PE9 ....219 D6
Hillary Rd DN16 ....185 B5
Hillary Way DN37 ....190 E8
Hill's Ct 9 NG34 ....212 D4
Hillcrest NG34 ....107 C2
Hillcrest Ave
Kingston upon Hull HU13 ....178 C2
Yaxley PE7 ....233 E5
Hillcrest Dr 2 DN15 ....8 A4
Hillcrest Gdns 3 PE20 .135 B7
Hillcroft 1 LN4 ....203 A2
Hillfoot Dr DN17 ....184 E3
Hillgate PE12 ....168 C2
Hillgate St PE34 ....161 F3
Hillingford Way NG31 ..210 E3
Hillman Cl LN4 ....205 F3
Hillman Rd HU13 ....178 F3
Hills Dr 14 DN36 ....36 D4
Hillside
4 Ancaster NG32 ....120 A2
Marton DN21 ....65 E8
Hillside App 5 LN2 ....202 C3
Hillside Ave
Lincoln LN2 ....202 C3
7 Mablethorpe/Sutton on Sea LN12 ....77 A8
Hillside Cl PE9 ....172 F2
Hillside Cres
Barnetby le Wold DN38 ....21 B5
3 Grantham NG31 ....211 D2
Hillside Dr
5 Barton-upon-Humber DN18 ....10 E8
Grantham NG31 ....211 D2
Hillside Est NG34 ....108 F2
Hillside Rd
6 Broughton DN20 ....19 E4
Glentworth DN21 ....54 F7
Woolsthorpe By Belvoir NG32 ....128 D1
Hillstead Cl 13 DN36 ....36 D4
Hillsyde Ave
12 Misterton DN10 ....39 F5
2 Misterton DN21 ....40 A5
Hilltop Ave DN15 ....182 D5
Hilltop Cl LN6 ....79 B2
Hillward Cl PE2 ....230 C6
Hilton Ave DN15 ....182 B3
Hilton Cl 2 DN9 ....16 E2
Hilton Ct DN35 ....193 B1
Hilton's La PE20 ....136 E1
Hinaidi La LN4 ....95 C7
Hinchcliffe PE2 ....229 E2
Hine Ave NG24 ....104 B4
Hinkler St DN35 ....192 E5
Hinkley Dr DN40 ....186 B5
Hipper La PE20 ....135 D2
Hither Old Gate PE12 ..158 D6
Hives La LN6 ....78 E2
Hix Cl PE12 ....215 C2
Hix's La PE13 ....160 A1
Hobart Cl 11 LN5 ....93 E8
Hobart Rd NG31 ....211 D7
Hobart St HU3 ....180 D5
Hobb La 4 DN21 ....29 C3
Hobson Rd 7 HU15 ....2 C6
Hobson Way DN41 ....187 E2
Hockland Rd 2 PE13 ...169 F7
Hockle's Gate PE12 ...159 B7
Hockney Hole La PE12 ....158 A7
Hod Fen Dro PE7 ....233 F2
Hodder Cl 1 NG31 ....210 F3
Hoddesdon Cres 20 DN7 .14 D3
Hodge Ct 3 HU9 ....181 C7
Hodgetoft La LN13 ....63 E1
Hodgson Ave PE4 ....220 E6
Hodgson St HU8 ....181 A7
Hodgson Way 3 LN12 ...77 A8
Hodney Rd 5 PE6 ....175 A1
Hodson Cl LN6 ....200 B5
Hoekman Dr 3 PE11 ...214 B2
Hoekman Way PE11 ...214 B2
Hogens La PE13 ....170 A5
Hogg La HU10 ....178 B8
Hoggard La DN14 ....7 E8
Hog's Gate PE12 ....158 A6
Hogsthorpe Prim Sch PE24 ....90 B7
Hogsthorpe Rd LN13 ....76 F1
Holbeach Dro Gate PE12 ....168 C4
Holbeach Hospl PE12 ..215 B5
Holbeach Prim Sch PE12 ....215 D3
Holbeach Rd
1 Spalding PE12 ....157 B6
Spalding PE11 ....214 F6
Holbeach St Marks CE Prim Sch PE12 ....147 D6
Holbeck Pl 2 DN40 ....186 B4
Holborn Rd PE11 ....214 B2
Holborn St HU8 ....181 B7
Holcroft PE2 ....230 B3
Holden Dr 9 PE24 ....102 E7
Holden Way 7 NG31 ....129 E5
Holdenby Cl 3 LN2 ....202 E7
Holderness Rd HU9 ....181 C8
Holdfield PE3 ....225 B6
Holdich St PE3 ....225 E2
Holdingham La NG34 ...121 E7
Hole Gate PE23 ....101 C8
Holgate La PE4 ....220 F7
Holgate Pl 18 HU14 ....3 B7
Holgate Rd DN16 ....185 D8
Holkham Rd PE2 ....229 D3
Holland Ave
18 Crowle DN17 ....16 D8
Peterborough PE4 ....221 B1
Scunthorpe DN15 ....182 E4
Holland Cl
8 Bourne PE10 ....213 C5
10 Market Deeping PE6 ..217 A6
Holland Dr PE25 ....206 C1
Holland La PE22 ....114 F4
Holland Rd
Horbling NG34 ....133 B3
Spalding PE11 ....214 E4
Stamford PE9 ....219 C6
Swaton NG34 ....133 E3
Holland St HU9 ....181 D8
Holland Way PE12 ....215 B2
Holland's Chase PE11 .156 A6
Hollengs La 1 LN11 ....59 E1
Holles St 3 DN32 ....191 E8
Hollies The PE12 ....215 E3
Hollin Bridge La DN7 ...15 A3
Hollingsworth Ave 1 DN40 ....186 B4
Hollingsworth Cl 5 DN35 ....192 D2
Hollingsworth La DN9 ..27 E6
Hollis' Rd NG31 ....210 F2
Hollowbrook Cl 3 NG34 ....108 D2
Hollowdyke La NG24 ..104 C1
Hollowgate Hill DN21 ...42 E4
Hollowgate La NG23 ....78 A5
Hollows The 4 LN11 ....61 F3
Holly Cl
Cherry Willingham/Reepham LN3 ....203 E5
5 Grantham NG31 ....211 D2
Horncastle LN9 ....199 A5
Lincoln LN5 ....205 D5
2 Newborough PE6 ....174 E5
Scunthorpe DN16 ....185 C4
1 Sleaford NG34 ....212 D2
6 Stallingborough DN41 ...23 E6
Holly Dr PE10 ....213 C7
Holly Hill 1 HU15 ....2 E6
Holly Rd PE25 ....206 A2
Holly St LN5 ....205 D5
Holly Tree Cl 9 LN8 ....57 D7
Holly Way 2 PE6 ....217 D4
Holly Wlk PE7 ....230 D3
Hollytree Ave 2 HU5 ...179 B7
Hollywell Rd (The Rookery) 23 LN13 ....75 F2
Hollywell Rd LN5 ....205 D1
Hollywood Dr 8 NG31 ..210 F7
Holm La NG23 ....104 F1
Holm Rd DN9 ....27 B2
Holme Ave DN36 ....195 C6
Holme Cl Brigg DN20 ...196 D4
Castor PE5 ....223 D2
Thorpe on the Hill LN6 ....92 F8
Holme Dene 1 DN9 ....27 C2
Holme Dr
Burton-upon-Stather DN15 ..8 B5
Sudbrooke LN2 ....68 F2
Holme Gdns 7 DN7 ....14 C7
Holme Hall Ave DN16 ..185 B3
Holme La
Grassthorpe NG23 ....78 A2
Holme DN16 ....185 E2
Marnham NG23 ....78 A4
Messingham DN17 ....29 E8
4 Ruskington NG34 ....108 E1
Scunthorpe DN16 ....185 B3
Winthorpe NG24 ....104 B8
Holme Rd PE7 ....233 E4
Holme St DN32 ....191 E7
Holme Valley Prim Sch DN16 ....185 C3
Holme Wood Ct 5 DN3 ..14 A1
Holme Wood La
Claxby with Moorby LN9 ..99 B8
Hameringham LN9 ....86 B1
Holmes Cl Louth LN11 ..198 B7
2 Skidbrooke with Saltfleet Haven LN11 ....51 C4
Holmes Field 6 LN5 ....92 F3
Holmes La
North Somercotes LN11 ..38 A1
Roxby cum Risby DN15 ....9 D5
2 Welton/Dunholme LN2 ..68 E6
Holmes Rd
Frampton PE20 ....124 F1
Glinton PE6 ....220 D7
Horsington LN10 ....83 F1
Kirton PE20 ....136 A8
Stickney PE22 ....113 A7
Stixwould & Woodhall LN10 ....84 A1
Holmes Way
Horncastle LN9 ....199 D1
Peterborough PE4 ....221 D2
Wragby LN8 ....70 C5
Holmfirth Rd DN15 ....182 C4
Holstein Dr DN16 ....185 A2
Holt Cl 10 Lincoln LN6 ....93 C8
9 Wittering PE8 ....172 B1
Holt La Horncastle LN9 ..199 D4
Mareham Le Fen PE22 ....99 A3
Holt Prim Sch The LN6 ....200 A3
Holton Ct DN36 ....195 C1
Holton le Clay Jun Sch DN36 ....195 E1
Holton Mount DN36 ...195 C2
Holton Rd Nettleton LN7 .33 A2
South Kelsey LN7 ....32 D1
Tetney DN36 ....195 F1
Holton-le-Clay Jun Sch DN36 ....195 D2
Holy Family Prim Sch DN7 ....14 D7
Holy Well La LN11 ....49 A4
Holydyke DN18 ....10 E8
Holyoake Rd DN32 ....192 C6
Holyroad Dr DN15 ....182 D7
Holyrood Cl PE20 ....134 E3
Holyrood Wlk PE11 ....214 E2
Holywell Cl 1 PE3 ....225 A1
Holywell Rd PE9 ....162 E8
Holywell Way PE3 ....224 F2
Home Beat Dr DN20 ...19 C3
Home Cl 7 Bourne PE10 213 C7
Bracebridge Heath LN4 ..205 F3
Kingston upon Hull HU4 .179 C5
Home Ct 8 LN5 ....107 A7
Home Paddock DN37 ..194 E4
Home Pasture 4 PE4 ..220 F5
Home Pk 4 NG34 ....120 F8
Home St DN15 ....183 B4
Homefarm La NG23 ....79 A7
Homefield Ave DN33 ..191 D3
Homers La PE22 ....126 D4
Homestead Garth 11 DN7 ....14 D4
Honey Pot La NG33 ....151 F4
Honeyhill PE4 ....221 E1
Honeyhill CP Com Sch PE4 ....221 E1
Honeyhill Rd PE13 ....169 C2
Honeyholes La LN2 ....68 D6
Honeysuckle Cl
4 Lincoln LN5 ....205 C2
14 Mablethorpe & Sutton LN12 ....76 F8
Honeysuckle Ct
Humberston DN35 ....192 E1
Peterborough PE2 ....230 D7
3 Scunthorpe DN16 ....185 D4
Honeysuckle Pl 19 HU15 ..2 C5
Honington App 5 LN1 .201 D7
Honington Cres LN1 ..201 D7
Honington Rd 2 NG32 .130 B8
Hood Cl NG34 ....212 A3
Hood Rd DN17 ....184 D6
Hood St
Kingston upon Hull HU8 ..181 A8
8 Lincoln LN5 ....201 F1
Hook's Dro PE13 ....177 C4
Hooks La LN5 ....106 E6
Hoop End DN36 ....36 D4
Hoop La LN8 ....70 E2
Hoopers Cl 4 NG13 ....128 A5
Hop Hills La DN7 ....14 D5
Hope Gdns PE21 ....208 F6
Hope St
Cleethorpes DN35 ....193 A5
6 Grimsby DN32 ....191 F8
Lincoln LN5 ....201 F1
Hopfield DN20 ....31 A5
Hopgardens 1 DN21 ....53 E3
Hopgarth 11 DN9 ....27 D2
Hopkins Ave DN17 ....185 A7
Hoplands Rd LN4 ....207 D5
Hoplands The 4 NG34 ..212 F4
Hopton St LN9 ....199 B3
Hopwood Cl HU3 ....180 D8
Hopyard La
Bassingham LN5 ....93 B1
Normanton on Trent NG23 ....78 A3
Horace St PE21 ....208 E5
Horbling Fen Dro NG34 ....133 D2
Horbling La PE22 ....113 A7
Horbury Cl 2 DN15 ....182 D4
Horkstow Rd DN18 ....10 E7
Horn The 7 PE25 ....206 A7
Hornbeam Ave DN16 ..185 A5
Hornby Dr 20 LN12 ....77 A7
Horncastle Coll LN9 ..199 D3
Horncastle Cty Prim Sch LN9 ....199 C4
Horncastle Hill PE23 ....87 A1
Horncastle La
Dunholme LN2 ....68 B5
Grange De Lings LN1 ....67 F5
Horncastle Rd
Bardney LN3 ....83 C4
Boston PE21 ....208 F8
Fishtoft PE21 ....125 E5
Goulceby LN9 ....72 D5
Horsington LN10 ....84 D4
Louth LN11 ....198 A4
Mareham Le Fen PE22 ....98 F4
Raithby cum Maltby LN11 ..60 F2
Roughton LN9 ....85 C2
Tathwell LN11 ....73 A8
West Ashby LN9 ....199 C8
Woodhall Spa LN10 ....97 F6
Wragby LN8 ....70 D4
Horne La 3 NG22 ....65 B1
Horner Cl 1 LN5 ....205 C2
Hornsby Cres DN15 ....182 F4
Hornsby Rd NG31 ....210 E2
Hornsea Par 4 HU9 ...181 C8
Hornsey Hill Rd DN21 ..28 D1
Horse Fair Gn 25 DN8 ...15 A8
Horse Fayre 7 PE11 ...214 A3
Horse Mkt 24 LN7 ....33 B4
Horsegate PE6 ....217 D4
Horsegate Field Rd DN19 ....5 B2
Horseham's La PE20 ..135 A5
Horsemoor Dro PE12 ..159 B1
Horsemoor La LN9 ....72 C2
Horsepit La 12 PE11 ...145 C1
Horseshoe Cl 12 NG34 ..108 D2
Horseshoe La PE20 ...136 D5
Horseshoe Rd PE11 ...214 A2
Horseshoe Terr PE13 ..170 C1
Horseshoe Yd 11 PE6 ..166 E1
Horsewells St 1 DN10 ..39 C1
Horstead Ave DN20 ...196 D5
Horton St LN2 ....202 C3
Hospital Dro PE12 ...160 C3
Hospital La PE21 ...209 A6
Hospital Rd PE12 ...161 A5
Hotham Dr HU5 ....179 B8
Hotham Rd HU5 ....179 A8
Hotham Rd S HU5 ....179 B8
Hotham St HU9 ....181 D7
Hotspur Rd DN21 ....197 C6
Hough La
Carlton Scroop NG32 ...119 C4
Claypole NG23 ....117 F7
Hough Rd
Barkston NG32 ....130 B8
Carlton Scroop NG32 ...119 A3
Hough-on-the-Hill NG32 ..118 E7
Hougham Rd
Hougham NG32 ....118 B4
Westborough & Dry Doddington NG23 ....117 F5
Houghton Ave PE2 ....231 F5
Houghton Rd NG31 ....211 C2
Houlden Way 1 NG34 ...122 E3
Hounsfield Cl NG24 ...104 B5
Houps Rd 8 DN8 ....15 B8
Hourne The HU13 ....178 E2
House Ct DN16 ....185 D4
Howard Cl PE34 ....161 F2
Howard Gr DN32 ....192 B6
Howard Rd 10 LN4 ....108 A7
Howard St LN1 ....201 C4
Howdale La NG32 ....119 A3
Howden Croft Hill HU15 ..2 A8
Howe La
Ashby with Scremby PE23 ..88 C3
Goxhill DN19 ....11 F8
Howell Fen Dro NG34 .122 D5
Howell Rd NG34 ....122 E3
Howgarth La PE22 ....114 F5
Howitts Rd 14 NG13 ....128 A5
Howland PE2 ....230 A3
Howlett Rd DN35 ....193 A4
Howsham La 2 DN38 ...32 D8
Howville Ave 2 DN7 ....14 F3
Howville Rd 1 DN7 ....14 F3

Hoylake Dr
1 Immingham DN40 ....186 D5
Peterborough PE7 ......231 C5
1 Skegness PE25 ......206 B5
Hoylake Rd DN17 .....184 D3
Hubba Cres PE20 .....135 C6
Hubbard Cl 2 NG34 ...122 D3
Hubberts Bridge Sta
PE20 ....124 E2
Hubert's Cl PE12 ......168 C1
Huckles Way PE25 .....206 B6
Huddleston Rd DN32 ..192 B7
Hudson Ave DN15 .....182 E5
Hudson Cl PE23 ....88 B3
Hudson Dr LN4 ....207 E6
Hudson Rd 4 PE11 .....214 C2
Hudson St HU3 ....180 D8
Hudson Way 12 PE25 ...206 A5
Hudson's Gdns 5 PE21 .209 B4
Huggin Carr Rd DN7 ....14 F1
Hugh Hill La DN7 ....14 D6
Hughes Ford Way 20
LN1 ....66 D2
Hughson Wlk 3 LN2 ....68 E6
Hulberry Cl 10 DN41 .....23 A4
Hull & E Riding Mus★
HU9 ....181 A6
Hull Arena★ HU1 .....180 E4
Hull Coll HU3 ....179 F7
Hull Coll Pk St Ctr
HU2 ....180 D7
Hull High Sch for Girls
HU10 ....178 D5
Hull Maritime Mus★
HU1 ....180 F6
Hull Rd HU13 ....178 F1
Hull Royal Infmy HU3 ..180 C6
Hull Sta HU1 ....180 E6
Hull Trinity House Sch
HU1 ....180 F6
Hull Truck Theatre★
HU2 ....180 D7
Hull's Dro PE6 ....167 D3
Humber Bank Factories
DN41 ....187 D4
Humber Bank S DN31 .189 C2
Humber Bridge Rd
DN31 ....189 C1
Humber Cres
6 Brough HU15 ....2 C5
Scunthorpe DN17 ....184 F6
Humber Dock St HU1 ..180 F5
Humber Rd
Barton-upon-Humber DN18 ...3 E1
Immingham DN40 ....186 A8
North Ferriby HU14 ....3 A4
Humber St
3 Cleethorpes DN35 ....192 F5
Grimsby DN31 ....189 C1
Kingston upon Hull HU1 ..180 F5
Humber Terr DN31 ....191 C8
Humber View
3 Barton-upon-Humber
DN18 ....10 E8
Kingston upon Hull
HU13 ....178 C2
4 Swanland HU14 ....3 B6
Humberdale Cl 5 HU14 ...3 B6
Humberdale Dr HU14 ....3 C5
Humberside Int Airport
DN38 ....21 F5
Humberston Ave
DN36 ....195 E6
Humberston CE Prim Sch
DN36 ....36 D8
Humberston Comp Sch
DN36 ....36 C8
Humberston Pk Specl Sch
DN36 ....36 C8
Humberston Rd
Cleethorpes DN36 ......192 C3
Tetney DN36 ....36 C6
Humberstone Holt 1
LN11 ....50 F7
Humberstone Rd
DN32 ....192 A6
Humberville Rd DN40 .186 D4
Humby Rd NG33 ......141 B8
Hume Brae 6 DN40 ....186 B3
Hume St 5 DN31 ......191 C7
Hun Gate PE11 ....145 D3
Hunchback La PE13 ...170 E2
Hund Oak Dr 9 DN7 ....14 D4
Hundle Houses La
LN4 ....111 D4
Hundlehouse La LN4 ..111 D4
Hundred Acres La
NG24 ....104 B1
Hundreds La
Gringley on the Hill DN10 ..39 A5
Little Sutton PE12 ....216 F1
Hundreds Rd PE6 .....175 C6
Hungate LN1 ....234 B2
Hungate Rd NG32 .....139 A7
Hungerdike Gate
PE12 ....215 A2
Hungry Hill La LN11 ....62 C5
Hunsley Cres DN32 ....192 B4
Hunsley Dr 5 DN41 .....23 E6
Hunstan La PE22 ......113 F4
Hunston Rd 4 LN10 .....97 C5
Hunt Lea Ave
Grantham NG31 ....210 F1
Lincoln LN6 ....205 C8
Hunt Rd DN16 ....185 C5
Huntcliff Comp Sch
DN21 ....30 C1
Hunter Ave LN11 ....62 C6
Hunter Pl LN11 ....198 B4
Hunter Rd
Brookenby LN8 ....47 A6
Brough HU15 ....2 C6
Hunter's Croft 1 DN9 ...27 D3
Hunter's Dr 5 DN10 .....39 C1
Hunters Dr 13 LN4 ......95 C4
Hunters La Baumber LN9 .72 A1
Tattershall LN4 ....207 C5
Hunting Ave PE2 ......230 F7
Huntingdon Cl 2 PE12 .215 E3
Huntingdon Cres 8 DN15 .8 B4
Huntingdon St HU4 ...179 E3
Huntingtower Rd
NG31 ....211 A3
Huntingtower Rd Cty Prim
Sch NG31 ....211 A3
Huntly Gr PE1 ....226 A4
Huntly Rd PE2 ....230 E7
Hunts Cl 7 DN20 ....19 E4
Hunt's Gate PE12 .....159 E1
Hunts La 4 DN20 ....30 F5
Huntsgate PE12 ....159 D4
Huntsman Cl PE21 ....209 D2
Huntsmans Chase
DN36 ....195 B7
Huntsmans Gate PE3 ..224 F3
Hurdletree Bank PE12 .158 E4
Hurdman Way PE25 .....90 E3
Hurford Pl DN37 ......194 D7
Hurle Cres PE21 ......208 D6
Hurn Bank PE12 ....147 E2
Hurn Cl
2 Birchwood LN6 ....204 B8
7 Ruskington NG34 .....108 D1
Hurn Dro LN4 ....110 A8
Hurn La PE22 ....126 A7
Hurn Rd Holbeach PE12 .147 E1
Marholm PE6 ....220 C3
Hurn The
5 Billingborough NG34 ...133 B1
Digby LN4 ....108 E6
Hurnbridge Rd LN4 ...111 A4
Hurst Cres NG32 ......210 A4
Hurst La DN17 ....184 E3
Hurst The 5 PE25 .....206 A6
Hurstlea Dr DN36 .....193 B1
Hurstwood Cl LN2 ....202 D8
Hurton's La LN11 ....49 C6
Hussey Cl 2 NG34 .....212 E4
Hussey Twr★ PE21 ...209 A4
Husthwaite Rd 18 HU15 ...2 D5
Hutchinson Gdns 5
PE12 ....157 E7
Hutchinson Rd 2 DN35 192 E7
Huteson La DN15 ....8 C8
Hutson Dr LN6 ....204 F2
Hutt St HU3 ....180 D7
Huttoft Bank Pit nature
Reserve★ LN13 ....77 B6
Huttoft Prim Sch LN13 ..76 F3
Huttoft Rd 17 LN12 ......76 F8
Hutton Rd DN31 ......189 B2
Hyde Gdns PE6 ....164 F3
Hyde Pk Cl 6 LN6 .....204 F1
Hydes Ct DN40 ....186 E5
Hyholmes PE3 ....224 F7
Hykeham Rd LN6 .....205 B4
Hykeham Sta
Lincoln LN6 ....204 D3
North Hykeham LN6 .....204 D4
Hymers Ave HU3 ......180 B7
Hymers Coll HU3 .....180 B7
Hyperion St HU9 ......181 A7
Hythegate PE4 ....221 B4

I

Ibbott Cl PE2 ....231 E5
Icehouse Rd HU3 .....180 D6
Ickworth Rd NG34 ....212 D3
Ida Rd PE25 ....206 C3
Idas Cl HU9 ....181 A5
Iddesleigh Rd 4 LN10 ...97 D6
Idle Bank Epworth DN9 ...15 F1
Haxey DN9 ....26 E2
Misson DN9 ....26 E1
Ihlee Cl PE4 ....221 C1
Ilex Cl PE7 ....230 C3
Iliffe Gate 3 PE4 ......221 D2
Immingham Bsns Units
DN40 ....186 D3
Immingham Sch DN40 .186 C4
Impala Way HU4 ......179 D2
Imperial Ave DN35 ....192 C8
Incredible Fantastic Old Toy
Show The★ LN1 ......234 B4
Independence Dr 5
PE11 ....156 F8
Industrial Est DN36 ...195 F8
Ing Dro PE20 ....134 F4
Ingelow Ave PE21 .....208 C6
Ingham Cl LN6 ....205 B3
Ingham Ct LN4 ....207 E6
Ingham Hall Gdns
PE13 ....177 D7
Ingham Prim Sch LN1 ..54 F2
Ingham Rd
Coningsby LN4 ....207 E6
3 Stow LN1 ....66 C8
Inghams La 1 DN36 .....36 D4
Inghams Rd 3 DN36 ....36 D4
Ingle Ct 2 NG33 ......151 D7
Ingleby Cres LN2 .....201 F8
Ingleby Ct 2 PE11 .....214 F4
Ingleby Rd 14 DN17 ....29 D7
Ingledew Cl 8 NG34 ...122 E2
Inglenook Dr 2 DN8 ....15 B8
Ingleton Ave HU4 .....179 C6
Inglewood Dr 4 HU4 ..179 B5
Ingmires 7 HU15 ....2 D6
Ingoldmells Prim Sch
PE25 ....90 D4
Ingoldmells Rd
Burgh Le Marsh PE24 .....89 F1
Burgh le Marsh PE24 ....102 E8
Ingoldsby Prim Sch
NG33 ....141 D5
Ingoldsby Rd NG33 ...141 B3
Ingram Cres 9 DN7 .....14 C4
Ingram Gdns 11 DN20 ...30 E8
Ingram Gr 10 DN7 ......14 C4
Ingram La NG23 ....78 A1
Ingram Pl DN35 ......192 D2
Ingram Rd
Boston PE21 ....208 D6
Hatfield DN7 ....14 C3
Ings Bank PE22 ....126 E7
Ings Dro
Butterwick PE22 ....126 D7
Leverton PE22 ....113 E1
Ings La Belchford LN9 ...73 B2
Brackenborough with
Little Grimsby LN11 ......49 B4
Bratoft PE24 ....102 C6
Brough HU15 ....2 C5
Cumberworth LN13 ....89 E7
Ellerker HU15 ....1 F8
2 Hibaldstow DN20 ......31 A5
Horsington LN10 ....84 D2
1 Kirk Bramwith DN7 ....14 C7
Leverton PE22 ....126 F7
Little Steeping PE23 .....101 E5
North Coates DN36 ......37 A3
North Ferriby HU14 ....3 A4
Saltfleetby LN11 ....62 F8
Scamblesby LN11 ....73 A4
Skidbrooke with Saltfleet Haven
LN11 ....51 A3
South Cave HU15 ....1 E7
South Somercotes LN11 ...50 E3
Walkerith DN21 ....40 C3
Waltham DN37 ....194 F4
6 West Ashby LN9 ....85 E7
West Ashby LN9 ....199 D8
West Stockwith DN10 .....40 C6
Winterton DN15 ....9 D7
Ings Rd Benington PE22 .126 D8
Gringley on the Hill DN10 ..39 B3
Kirton in Lindsey DN21 ...29 F1
Mablethorpe & Sutton
LN12 ....76 E7
Inhams Cl PE13 ....177 D5
Inley Dro PE12 ....169 A8
Inner St NG31 ....211 B3
Innings The 1 NG34 ...212 D3
Inns Cl LN6 ....204 E3
Inverness Rd 14 DN7 ....14 D4
Iona Cl DN21 ....197 E6
Iona Dr DN36 ....36 D8
Ipswich Gdns NG31 ...210 E5
Irby Cres 9 PE12 ......158 B7
Irby Ct DN35 ....192 D3
Irby Pl PE21 ....208 F5
Irby Rd DN17 ....184 E5
Irby St PE21 ....208 E5
Irish Hill LN11 ....198 A5
Irnham Rd
Corby Glen NG33 ....141 C1
Stamford PE9 ....219 C7
Iron Bar Dro PE11 .....155 F4
Ironestone Cl LN2 .....202 C5
Ironmonger St 5 PE9 ..219 C5
Irvine Rd 2 DN16 .....185 C5
Isaac Newton Prim Sch The
NG31 ....210 F3
Isaac Newton Way
NG31 ....211 F6
Isaac's Hill DN35 .....192 E6
Isham Rd 1 PE3 ....225 D4
Isis Ct HU9 ....181 B5
Island Carr Rd DN20 ..196 A3
Island Rd DN17 ....7 E6
Isle Cl 3 DN17 ....16 D8
Islip Ct 1 LN9 ....199 D3
Ison Cl 4 NG34 ....120 E8
Itlings La HU13 ....178 F1
Itter Cres PE4 ....221 C1
Itterby Cres DN35 ....192 C3
Ivanhoe Rd
4 Scunthorpe DN16 .....183 C1
1 Scunthorpe DN16 .....185 D8
Ivatt Ct 13 NG31 ......210 E2
Ivatt Way PE3 ....225 C6
Ivel Cl 6 LN12 ....64 B5
Ivel Gr 4 LN12 ....64 B5
Ivery La PE22 ....114 D4
Ivesdyke Cl 3 PE13 ...170 B2
Ivy Cl DN7 ....14 E4
Ivy Cres PE21 ....208 D3
Ivy Farm Ct 20 DN41 ....23 F5
Ivy Gr PE4 ....221 B2
Ivy La Coningsby LN4 ...207 F1
Grainthorpe LN11 ....37 E1
Wainfleet St Mary PE24 ..115 C8

J

Jack Haws La 3 PE9 ...172 D4
Jack Hunt Sch PE3 ....225 B3
Jack Hunt Swimming Pool
PE3 ....225 B3
Jack Row La DN7 ....14 B8
Jacklin Cl 5 LN11 ....50 B8
Jacklin Cres 6 LN12 ....64 A4
Jacklin Dr 3 LN11 ....51 C4
Jacklin La DN17 ....7 C3
Jacklins App DN16 ....185 A3
Jackson Dr 3 PE20 ....136 C5
Jackson Mews 6 DN40 186 A4
Jackson Rd 1 DN15 ...182 E3
Jackson St
1 Grimsby DN31 ....191 C8
Kingston upon Hull HU3 ..180 D4
Jacksons La 4 PE24 ...102 E8
Jackson's Pl DN36 ....192 D1
Jacobean Rd 4 LN6 ...204 D6
Jacobs Ct 2 PE11 .....214 C6
Jade Gr 1 HU3 ....180 A4
Jaguar Dr LN6 ....204 D1
Jail La PE22 ....126 F2
James Ave
3 Mablethorpe/Sutton on Sea
LN12 ....64 C2
Skegness PE25 ....206 B6
James Pl DN39 ....12 B1
James Rd 1 DN21 ....55 A8
James St Boston PE21 ..208 E5
Brigg DN20 ....196 B3
Grimsby DN31 ....191 C8
Lincoln LN2 ....234 B3
Louth LN11 ....198 C6
James Way 9 DN40 ...186 B3
Jameson Bridge St 8
LN8 ....57 D8
Jameson St 2 HU1 ....180 F6
Jankin La PE34 ....161 F1
Janton Ct DN36 ....195 C7
Japan Rd DN21 ....197 B5
Japonica Hill 3 DN40 ..186 C3
Jaque's Bank DN8 ......16 A5
Jarratt Hill La HU15 .....1 D8
Jarratt St HU1 ....180 F7
Jarvis Cl LN6 ....204 F7
Jarvis's Gate PE12 ....159 C1
Jasmin Cl 9 PE13 .....170 E1
Jasmin Rd LN6 ....204 C8
Jasmine Cl PE10 ......213 B7
Jasmine Ct
2 Goxhill DN19 ....12 A8
Peterborough PE2 ....229 E2
Jasmine Way
Immingham DN40 ....186 C3
Yaxley PE7 ....233 F6
Jason Rd 5 LN6 ....205 A5
Javelin Ave 8 LN8 ......47 B6
Javelin Rd 12 LN11 .....62 C6
Jefferson Cl 24 PE8 ...172 B1
Jefferson Dr 23 HU15 ....2 C6
Jeffery Ave 6 PE13 ....170 E1
Jeffrey La DN9 ....16 E1
Jekil's Bank
Holbeach PE12 ....158 C1
Moulton PE12 ....167 F8
Whaplode PE12 ....168 B8
Jekil's Gate PE12 .....159 A5
Jellicoe Ave LN2 .....202 D3
Jenkins Cl Louth LN11 ..198 C8
5 Skegness PE25 ....206 A7
Jenkins' La PE22 ......127 A6
Jenner Pl DN35 ....192 B8
Jenning St HU8 ....181 A8
Jenny Brough La
HU13 ....178 B3
Jenny Cl HU13 ....178 B3
Jensen Rd LN4 ....205 F2
Jericho La DN40 ....12 D7
Jermyn Mews LN4 .....203 D1
Jermyn St NG34 ......212 D4
Jerusalem LN6 ....79 F5
Jerusalem Rd LN6 ....200 A4
Jesmond Ave 5 DN17 ..184 E3
Jessop Cl
Cherry Willingham/Reepham
LN3 ....203 E5
9 Leasingham NG34 ....121 B8
Jessop Way NG24 ....104 B5
Jiggle's Gate PE12 ....158 F1
Jill Gr HU13 ....178 F1
Job's La LN6 ....79 C1
Jobson Rd 2 LN9 .....199 D2
Jock Hedge PE24 .....102 E6
Joel Sq 8 NG34 ....107 F1
John Adams Way
PE21 ....208 F4
John Clare Cty Prim Sch The
PE6 ....173 B4
John Coupland Hospl
DN21 ....197 B7
John Eve Way PE6 ....217 B6
John Fielding Specl Sch
PE21 ....209 A6
John Foster Cl 9 NG31 211 D7
John Harrison CE Prim Sch
DN19 ....11 C8
John Harrison's Cl 3
DN19 ....11 D8
John Harrox Prim Sch The
PE12 ....157 F7
John Hunt Cty Jun Mix Sch
The NG24 ....104 B2
John Hunt Infants & Nursery
Sch NG24 ....104 B3
John Leggott Coll
DN17 ....184 E8
John Mansfield Sec Sch
PE1 ....226 B8
John Smith Cl LN13 ....89 A6
John Spendluffe Sch The
LN13 ....75 F2
John St Lincoln LN2 ...234 C2
13 Market Rasen LN8 .....57 D8
Scunthorpe DN15 ....183 B3
John Wake Cl 2 PE6 ...217 B6
Johnson Ave PE11 .....214 E2
Johnson Cl 8 Belton DN9 16 E2
3 Skegness PE25 ....206 A7
Johnson Ct LN4 ....207 B6
Johnson Dr LN4 ....205 F4
Johnson Hospl PE11 ..214 D3
Johnson St DN35 .....192 B8
Johnson Way 14 PE24 ..102 E7
Johnson's Dro PE13 ...177 B6
Johnson's La 7 DN17 ...16 D7
Johnston's Rd DN7 .....14 E7
Jolls La LN9 ....86 C5
Jolly Comm La LN13 ....77 A3
Jolly Farmer La PE21 .126 C3
Jonathan Dr PE25 .....206 C8
Jonathan Gdns 1 NG34 212 F3
Jonquil Ave DN16 .....185 D5
Jordan Mews 2 PE1 ...226 B3
Jordan's Cradge Bank Rd
PE11 ....156 C2
Jorose St 4 PE3 ....225 A3
Joseph Ogle Cl DN36 ..195 B7
Joseph Ruston Tech Coll
LN6 ....205 B5
Joseph St DN31 ....191 C8
Joshua Way 5 DN21 ....43 D7
Joy Paine Cl PE21 ....208 C6
Joy's Bank PE12 ......158 E1
Jubilee Ave
Boston PE21 ....208 E6
Grantham NG31 ....211 C5
Jubilee Cl 4 Bardney LN3 83 B4
Cherry Willingham/Reepham
LN3 ....203 E6
1 Hogsthorpe PE24 ......90 B7
Lincoln LN6 ....204 F1
Long Sutton PE12 ....216 C5
Martin LN4 ....96 C2
8 Morton PE10 ....154 C7
1 Spalding PE11 ....214 C4
Jubilee Cres LN11 .....198 C8
Jubilee Dr
3 Bardney LN3 ....83 C4
10 Wragby LN8 ....70 D4
Jubilee Gr NG34 ......212 C6
Jubilee Par 6 PE24 .....90 D7
Jubilee Rd LN11 ....50 E7
Jubilee St
Peterborough PE2 ....230 F8
2 Ruskington NG34 .....108 E1
Jubilee Way LN9 ......199 B4
Jude Gate PE22 ....114 E3
Judge Cl 3 PE21 ......209 C4
Judy Cross PE11 ......145 B8
Julia Rd LN4 ....203 D1
Julian Cl HU5 ....179 A7
Julian St DN32 ....192 A7
Julian's Wlk 8 HU10 ...178 F6
Julia's Mead 12 PE11 ..214 B5
Junction Rd 10 DN7 ....14 C6
Junella Cl HU3 ....180 A4
Jungle The★ DN35 ...193 B3
Junior Cadets Rd
NG34 ....120 B8
Juniper Cl
1 Flixborough DN15 ....182 C6
10 Leasingham NG34 ....121 B7
3 Lincoln LN5 ....205 C2
Juniper Cres PE3 .....225 A2
Juniper Dr 13 LN2 ......68 F4
Juniper Way
Grimsby DN33 ....191 C2
3 Sleaford NG34 ....212 D2
Justice Hall La 10 DN17 .16 D8
Justice La DN14 ....7 B8
Jutland Ct 1 DN36 ....195 D7

K

Karen Ave 12 DN41 .....23 A4
Katherine Cres PE25 ..206 D2
Kathleen Ave
Cleethorpes DN35 ......192 D8
Scunthorpe DN16 ....185 B5
Kathleen Gr DN32 ....192 C7
Kaymile Cl 13 DN36 ...195 C6
Keadby Cl LN6 ....204 F7
Keal Hill PE23 ....100 B7
Kealholme Rd DN17 ....29 D7
Keats Ave
Grantham NG31 ....211 E6
Scunthorpe DN17 ....184 D7
Keats Cl Lincoln LN2 ..202 C7
17 Mablethorpe/Sutton on Sea
LN12 ....77 A7
Keats Dr NG34 ....121 E4
Keats Gr 2 PE9 ....218 E5
Keats Way PE1 ....225 D7
Keb La DN15 ....9 D2
Keble Cl 4 PE9 ....219 A7
Keble Ct 1 LN4 ....207 B5
Keddington Ave LN1 ..201 E8
Keddington Cres 2
LN11 ....198 D7
Keddington Rd
Louth LN11 ....198 C7
Scunthorpe DN17 ....184 F4
Kedleston Rd PE7 .....231 F6
Keeble Dr LN4 ....203 D1
Keel Dr 9 NG13 ....128 A5
Keelby Prim Sch DN41 ..23 A5
Keelby Rd
6 Gainsborough DN21 ....53 A8

Keelby Rd *continued*
Scunthorpe DN17 ....184 F5
Stallingborough DN41 .....23 C6
Keeling St 7 LN11 ....50 F7
Keeper's Way 6 DN9 ....16 E1
Keepers Cl 2 LN2 ......68 D7
Keepers Way NG34 ....212 E3
Keeton Rd PE1 ....225 E7
Keightley Rd PE12 .....147 B5
Keith Cres 15 DN37 ......23 F1
Kelham Rd
9 Great Gonerby NG31 ..129 E5
2 Great Gonerby NG31 ..210 E8
Grimsby DN32 ....192 D6
Kellet Gate PE12 ......157 B5
Kells Cl 6 LN5 ....205 D3
Kell's Dro PE20 ....124 E1
Kelly Cl 14 PE11 ....156 E8
Kelsey Ave DN15 ......182 B3
Kelsey La 1 DN17 ......17 D4
Kelsey Prim Sch LN7 ...32 A4
Kelsey Rd LN7 ....32 C2
Kelsey St LN1 ....234 A2
Kelstern Cl 1 LN6 .....204 C6
Kelstern Ct 1 DN34 ....191 A5
Kelstern Rd LN6 ......204 C6
Kelston Dr 2 HU13 .....179 A3
Kelthorpe Cl PE9 ......171 A2
Kemble Cl LN6 ....204 B8
Kemp Rd
Grimsby DN31 ....189 C3
3 Swanland HU14 ....3 B6
Kemp St PE6 ....166 E1
Kempton Cl 3 PE11 ....156 E3
Kempton Dr 4 DN7 .....14 C2
Kempton Rd HU3 ....179 E6
Kempton Way NG31 ....210 F4
Kendal Cl 2 PE4 ......221 D2
Kendal Rd DN40 ....186 E3
Kendal Way HU5 ....179 C7
Kendale Rd DN16 .....185 E8
Kendon Gdns DN8 ......15 B8
Kendrick Cl PE2 ......231 D6
Kenford Ct DN36 ......195 C7
Kenilworth Cl 3 LN1 ....66 D2
Kenilworth Dr LN6 ....205 C5
Kenilworth Rd
Cleethorpes DN35 ......192 D4
Grantham NG31 ....211 F5
Scunthorpe DN16 ....183 C1
Kenlan Rd 23 PE13 .....170 D1
Kenleigh Dr PE21 ......209 D4
Kenmar Rd 20 DN37 .....23 F1
Kenmare Cres DN21 ...197 F2
Kennedy Ave
21 Alford LN13 ....75 F2
Skegness PE25 ....206 C2
Kennedy Cl DN20 .....196 E3
Kennedy Rd
Bracebridge Heath LN4 ...205 F3
Holbeach PE12 ....215 C4
Kennel La
Doddington & Whisby LN6 ..79 E5
Reepham LN3 ....203 E8
Kennel Wlk LN3 ....203 F8
Kennels Rd PE6 ....224 D4
Kenner Cl 4 LN6 ......205 A6
Kennet Gdns PE4 .....221 C1
Kenneth Ave
2 Burgh Le Marsh PE24 .102 E8
8 Hatfield DN7 ....14 C2
5 Stainforth DN7 ....14 C6
Kenneth Campbell Rd 4
DN36 ....37 C5
Kenneth St 1 LN1 .....201 F6
Kennington Cl LN2 .....68 E5
Kennulphs Cl 5 PE6 ...175 C8
Kensington Cl PE12 ....215 F3
Kensington Dr 6 PE11 .214 B2
Kensington Gdns 3
LN12 ....64 B3
Kensington Pl DN33 ...195 A8
Kensington Rd 4 DN15 .182 B3
Kent Ave LN12 ....63 F5
Kent Cl
Kingston upon Hull HU9 ..181 C7
3 Sutton Bridge PE12 ...160 E4
Kent Dr 4 DN20 ....31 A5
Kent Rd
9 Binbrook Tech Pk LN8 ...47 B6
Leake Commonside
PE22 ....113 F3
Peterborough PE3 ......225 E2
Kent St Grimsby DN32 ..189 B1
6 Lincoln LN2 ....202 C3
Kentmere Pl 4 PE4 ....221 D2
Kenwardly Rd HU10 ...178 E8
Kenwick Cl LN11 ......198 D3
Kenwick Dr NG31 .....211 D4
Kenwick Gdns LN11 ...198 D3
Kenwick Hill
Legbourne LN11 ....198 E1
Raithby cum Maltby LN11 ..61 C3
Kenwick Pastures
LN11 ....198 D3
Kenwick Rd LN11 .....198 D2
Kenya Dr DN17 ....184 F2
Kenyon Cl 8 DN8 ......15 A8
Kerries Wlk DN17 .....184 C7
Kerrison View 5 LN2 ....68 D2
Kerr's Cres NG32 ......118 D2
Kerry Dr HU10 ....178 C6
Kerry Pit Way HU10 ...178 C6
Kesgrave St 1 DN31 ...189 C1
Kesteven & Grantham Girls
Sch NG31 ....211 B5
Kesteven & Sleaford High
Sch NG34 ....212 D4
Kesteven Agricultural
College-Elms Farm
NG32 ....119 E6
Kesteven Cl 1 PE6 ....217 D4
Kesteven Ct
3 Habrough DN40 ....22 E8
7 Lincoln LN6 ....204 D2
Kesteven Dr 7 PE6 ....217 A6
Kesteven Gr 19 DN17 ....16 D8
Kesteven Rd PE9 ......219 C7
Kesteven St
Lincoln LN5 ....234 B1
1 Sleaford NG34 ....212 E4
Kesteven Way 7 PE10 ..213 C5
Kestrel Cl
6 Birchwood LN6 ......204 D8
2 Sleaford NG34 ....212 B3
Kestrel Ct NG31 ....210 F2
Kestrel Dr LN11 ....198 D8
Kestrel Rd
8 Scopwick Heath LN4 ..108 A7
Scunthorpe DN17 ....184 E6
Kestrel Rise LN6 ....79 B1
Keswick Cl 2 PE4 .....221 D3
Ketco Ave PE9 ....171 A4
Ketlock Hill La 1 DN22 ..52 B1
Kettering Rd
Scunthorpe DN16 ....183 C2
Wothorpe PE9 ....219 B2
Kettlebridge La DN40 ...12 E6
Kettleby La DN20 ......20 E3
Kettleby View 3 DN20 ..196 D4
Kettlethorpe Dr 17 HU15 ..2 D5
Kettlethorpe Rd LN1 ....65 E3
Kettlewell St DN32 ....191 E5
Ketton CE Prim Sch
PE9 ....171 A3
Ketton Rd PE9 ....171 B2
Kew Rd DN35 ....192 E6
Kexby La DN21 ....53 C4
Kexby Mill Cl 5 LN6 ....93 B8
Kexby Rd DN21 ....54 D6
Key Theatre* PE1 .....226 B1
Keyholme La DN36 .....37 D2
Keyworth Dr 10 LN7 .....33 B4
Khormaksar Dr LN4 ....95 C7
Kidd La HU15 ....2 D6
Kiddier Ave DN37 .....194 D7
Kidgate LN11 ....198 B5
Kidgate Cty Prim Sch
LN11 ....198 C5
Kilburn Cres 1 LN6 ...205 A6
Kildare Dr PE3 ....225 C4
Kilham PE2 ....229 E2
Killarney Cl NG31 .....211 E7
Killingholme Prim Sch
DN40 ....12 E3
Killingholme Rd DN40 ..12 F2
Kiln Hill 4 LN8 ....59 A7
Kiln La Brigg DN20 ....196 B3
Fulbeck NG32 ....106 C1
Immingham DN41 ......187 C2
Louth LN11 ....198 B6
Stallingborough DN41 ...186 F1
Kiln La Ind Est DN41 ..187 B3
Kiln Yd LN11 ....198 C5
Kilnwell Rd 12 LN8 .....57 D8
Kilverstone PE4 ....220 F6
Kimberley St HU3 .....180 C7
Kimbolton Ct PE1 .....225 F3
Kime Cl NG34 ....142 C8
Kime's La 6 PE22 ....98 F4
Kinder Ave LN6 ....205 A2
Kinderley Rd PE13 ....170 D2
King Charles Cl HU10 ..178 E7
King Edward Rd
Thorne/Moorends DN8 ....15 A8
2 Woodhall Spa LN10 ....97 C6
King Edward St
Belton DN9 ....16 E2
Grimsby DN31 ....189 A1
3 Kingston upon Hull
HU1 ....180 F6
Kingston upon Hull HU1 ..180 E7
Kirton in Lindsey DN21 ....30 B1
Scunthorpe DN16 ....183 A1
Sleaford NG34 ....212 C3
King Edward VI Gram Sch
LN11 ....198 A5
King Edwards Terr 4
HU15 ....2 B5
King George Ave 1
LN10 ....97 D6
King George V Ave 1
PE12 ....215 F3
King George V Stadium
DN32 ....192 B5
King Georges Ct 3 DN7 .14 C5
King John Bank
2 Sutton Bridge PE14 ...170 F8
Walpole PE14 ....161 A2
King John St NG34 ....212 C4
King Johns Rd 6 PE20 .135 B7
King St 1 Billinghay LN4 .109 F5
Boston PE21 ....208 E4
East Halton DN40 ....12 D7
Gainsborough DN21 ....197 D3
15 Goxhill DN19 ....12 A8
2 Keelby DN41 ....23 A4
10 Kirton PE20 ....136 C5
Lincoln LN5 ....234 A1
20 Mablethorpe/Sutton on Sea
LN12 ....64 B3
Market Rasen LN8 ....57 D8
King St *continued*
1 Peterborough PE1 ....226 A2
Scunthorpe DN15 ....183 B4
18 Sutton Bridge PE12 ...160 E4
Thorne/Moorends DN8 ....15 A8
Wainfleet All Saints
PE24 ....102 A2
West Deeping PE6 ......173 A8
Wilsford NG32 ....120 A1
Winterton DN15 ....9 A5
Yarburgh LN11 ....49 E4
King St La LE14 ....150 A6
King William Cl 4 PE34 161 F3
Kingerby Beck Mdws Nature
Reserve* LN8 ....44 E5
Kingerby Cl DN21 .....197 E3
Kingerby Rd DN17 .....184 E5
Kingfisher Cl
2 Birchwood LN6 ......204 D8
4 Scunthorpe DN15 ....182 D5
Yaxley PE7 ....233 D5
Kingfisher Dr
2 Skegness PE25 ......206 A7
4 Surfleet PE11 ....145 E3
Kingfishers PE2 ....229 D6
King's Ave Boston PE21 .209 C3
Brigg DN20 ....196 D3
King's Cl 15 DN7 ....14 D4
King's Bench St HU3 ..180 B5
King's Cres
Boston PE21 ....209 C3
Swineshead PE20 ......135 B8
King's Cross Cl 2 HU3 .180 C6
King's Cswy DN14 ....6 E8
King's Delph Dro PE7 .231 E2
King's Gdns PE1 ......226 A5
King's Rd
Barnetby Le Wold DN38 ....21 B5
Humberston DN35 ......193 B3
Spalding PE11 ....214 D5
King's Sch The NG31 ..211 B5
Kings Arms Yd 2 LN2 ..234 B2
Kings Ave PE25 ....206 E8
Kings Cl PE22 ....112 C8
Kings Croft 1 DN17 .....16 E6
Kings Ct Louth LN11 ...198 E7
9 Scawby DN20 ....30 F8
Kings Dyke Cl PE2 ....231 E6
Kings Hill 2 NG32 .....119 B7
Kings Leigh 1 HU3 ....180 C6
Kings Mews DN35 .....193 C1
Kings Par DN35 ....193 A5
Kings Rd
Holbeach PE12 ....215 F3
Immingham DN40 ....186 E5
Metheringham LN4 ....95 C4
Peterborough PE2 ......231 B6
Stamford PE9 ....219 B6
Kings Sch PE1 ....226 A4
Kings Way LN2 ....68 C7
Kingsbridge Ct 1 PE4 ..220 E5
Kingscliffe Rd NG31 ..211 A8
Kingsdale DN17 ....184 E2
Kingsdown Rd LN6 ....204 B7
Kingsgate PE12 ....159 E7
Kingsley Ave PE10 ....213 B5
Kingsley Cl
4 Barnack PE9 ....172 D3
6 Brough HU15 ....2 B5
Kingsley Gr DN33 .....191 C4
Kingsley Rd
14 Mablethorpe/Sutton on Sea
LN12 ....64 B4
North Hykeham LN6 .....204 B5
Peterborough PE1 ......226 C4
Kingsley St LN1 ....234 A4
Kingsline Cl 1 PE6 ....176 A3
Kingsport Cl HU3 .....180 A7
Kingsthorpe Cres
PE25 ....206 C1
Kingston Ave
Grantham NG31 ....210 E4
Grimsby DN34 ....191 A6
Kingston upon Hull
HU13 ....178 F1
Kingston Cl 7 DN35 ...193 A1
Kingston Dr PE2 ......231 E5
Kingston Lower Sch
HU4 ....179 C4
Kingston Rd
Kingston upon Hull
HU10 ....178 F8
Scunthorpe DN16 ....185 A7
Kingston Ret Pk HU1 ..180 E5
Kingston St HU1 ......180 E5
Kingston Upper Sch
HU4 ....179 C4
Kingston View 20 DN18 ..10 F8
Kingston Wharf 4 HU1 .180 F5
Kingsway Boston PE21 .209 B3
Bourne PE10 ....213 D6
2 Brigg DN20 ....196 B4
Cleethorpes DN35 ......193 A5
11 Leverington PE13 ....170 E1
Lincoln LN5 ....201 F1
Nettleham LN2 ....68 C2
Scunthorpe DN15 ....182 C3
Stainforth DN7 ....14 C6
Tealby LN8 ....46 C1
Kingsway Sta DN35 ....193 B4
Kinloch Way DN40 .....186 B2
Kinloss Cl 11 LN6 .....204 C6
Kinnears Wlk PE2 .....229 F2
Kinoulton Ct 16 NG31 ..210 E2
Kinsbourne Gn 40 DN7 ..14 D4
Kintore Dr NG31 ......211 C4
Kipling Ave 4 DN17 ...184 D7
Kipling Cl
4 Grantham NG31 ......211 E6
3 Stamford PE9 ....218 E5
Kipling Ct PE1 ....225 E8
Kipling Dr
4 Mablethorpe/Sutton on Sea
LN12 ....77 A7
14 Sleaford NG34 ......212 F4
Kipling Wlk 1 HU4 ....179 D2
Kiplington Cl HU3 ....180 A7
Kippings The 8 PE10 ..164 C8
Kirby Ct 5 PE11 ......214 F4
Kirby Wlk 2 PE3 ......225 C4
Kirk Gate
Waltham DN37 ....194 E4
6 Whaplode PE12 ......158 B7
Kirk Rise HU10 ....178 C7
Kirkby Bank PE23 ......99 E3
Kirkby Gravel Pit Nature
Reserve* LN4 ....207 A8
Kirkby La LN10 ....97 E6
Kirkby la Thorpe CE Prim Sch
NG34 ....121 F4
Kirkby Moor Nature
Reserve* LN10 ....98 A5
Kirkby Rd
Ewerby & Evedon NG34 ..122 B5
Scunthorpe DN17 ....184 E4
Kirkby St LN5 ....201 F1
Kirkby Underwood Rd
PE10 ....154 A8
Kirkby-on-Bain CE (Aided)
Prim Sch LN10 ....98 C5
Kirkdale Cl 4 NG34 ...121 B8
Kirkden Paddocks DN9 .16 C2
Kirkgate
Tydd St Giles PE13 .....169 F7
Tydd St Giles PE13 .....170 A7
Kirkgate St PE13 ......170 E1
Kirkham Cl HU13 .....178 F2
Kirkhouse Gn Rd DN7 ..14 A8
Kirklands Rd HU5 .....179 E8
Kirkmeadow PE3 ......225 A8
Kirkside 6 DN37 ......194 D4
Kirkstall PE2 ....230 B3
Kirkstead Bridge LN10 ..97 B4
Kirkstead Cres DN33 ..191 B3
Kirkstead Ct 8 LN10 ....97 D5
Kirkstone House Sch
PE6 ....164 E4
Kirkton Gate PE3 .....225 A1
Kirkway HU10 ....178 B7
Kirkwood Cl PE3 ......225 E2
Kirman Cres 5 DN17 ..184 F3
Kirmington CE Prim Sch
DN39 ....22 A6
Kirmington Cl 8 LN6 ..204 C6
Kirmington Gdns 6
DN34 ....191 A7
Kirmond Rd LN8 ....47 A4
Kirness Dro LN4 ......109 C6
Kirton Dro LN4 ....110 F1
Kirton Holme Rd
PE20 ....124 D1
Kirton La Hatfield DN8 ..14 E7
2 Long Bennington NG23 117 D4
Stainforth DN7 ....14 D6
Kirton Lindsey Prim Sch
DN21 ....30 B1
Kirton Lindsey Sta
DN21 ....30 B2
Kirton Rd Blyton DN21 ..41 D6
Holme DN16 ....19 B2
Manton DN21 ....30 A3
Messingham DN17 ....29 E6
Scawby DN20 ....30 C8
Scotter DN21 ....29 D3
Waddingham DN21 ....43 B7
Kisgate 10 LN1 ....66 D7
Kishorn Ct DN40 ......186 B2
Kisimul Sch LN6 ....92 A6
Kit Cat La PE20 ....145 F8
Kitty Briggs La NG31 ..210 E1
Kitwood Cl 4 PE21 ....209 B4
Kitwood Rd PE21 ......209 B4
Knaith Hall La DN22 ....52 E3
Knaith Hill DN21 ....53 A3
Knarr Fen Rd PE6 .....176 E2
Kneeland 24 LN2 ....68 D6
Knight Cl PE6 ....217 D5
Knight Pl 2 LN5 ....205 E8
Knight St
Grimsby DN32 ....192 B6
4 Lincoln LN5 ....205 E8
2 Pinchbeck PE11 ......145 B1
Pinchbeck PE11 ....156 E8
Knight's Ct DN16 ......185 A3
Knights Cl 5 Belton DN9 .16 E2
18 Laceby DN37 ....23 F1
Leverington PE13 ....170 B2
Knightsbridge 2 DN36 .195 C6
Knightsbridge Rd 41
DN17 ....29 D7
Knipe Ave PE11 ....214 C3
Knipton CE Prim Sch
NG32 ....138 C6
Knipton La NG32 ......138 D6
Knipton Rd NG32 ......138 B4
Knoll St DN35 ....192 F6
Knoll The NG31 ....210 D8
Knolls The NG32 ......210 B5
Knowle St 2 LN12 ......64 B3
Kohima Cl 3 PE10 .....213 E7
Kooreman Ave 19 PE13 .170 D1
Kyme Rd Boston PE21 ..208 D6
Heckington NG34 ....122 E3

L

La Milesse Way 1 PE20 135 C7
Labour In Vain Dro
LN4 ....110 A6
Labrador Dr 11 DN20 ....19 E4
Laburnham Ave DN37 .194 D4
Laburnham Cl 7 DN37 .194 D4
Laburnum Ave
Gainsborough DN21 .....197 D6
4 Gunness DN15 ....17 E6
Yaxley PE7 ....233 F6
Laburnum Cl
3 Bourne PE10 ....213 C6
Grantham NG31 ....211 D5
Lincoln LN6 ....205 A2
7 Wisbech PE13 ....170 E1
Laburnum Cres LN11 ..198 E4
Laburnum Ct 2 LN3 ....82 A8
Laburnum Dr
Cherry Willingham/Reepham
LN3 ....203 D5
Grimsby DN34 ....190 E7
Ingoldmells PE25 ....206 D8
3 Kingston upon Hull
HU5 ....179 B7
Morton PE10 ....154 B7
Laburnum Gr
8 Burton-upon-Stather
DN15 ....8 B5
16 Crowle DN17 ....16 D7
Peterborough PE1 ......226 B8
Scunthorpe DN16 ....185 B7
Spalding PE11 ....214 F5
Laburnum Rd NG34 ...107 C2
Laceby Acres Prim Sch
DN34 ....190 D5
Laceby Rd
Grimsby DN34 ....191 A4
Laceby DN37 ....190 C3
Scunthorpe DN17 ....184 E5
Laceby St LN2 ....202 B3
Lacey Gdns LN11 .....198 D6
Lacey Gdns Jun Sch
LN11 ....198 D6
Lacey's Cl PE22 ....126 F6
Lacey's Dr PE22 ....126 F6
Lacey's La PE22 ....126 F6
Lacy Cl 21 LN2 ....68 D2
Ladds Cl 6 PE21 ......209 C4
Ladd's Mill Cl 7 LN6 ....93 B8
Lade Bank
Old Leake PE22 ....113 F5
Wrangle PE22 ....114 B6
Lady Bower Cl 9 LN6 ..205 A2
Lady Charlotte Rd
PE7 ....230 D3
Lady Fen La LN13 ......76 B1
Lady Frances Cres
DN35 ....192 C5
Lady Frances Dr 1 LN8 .57 D8
Lady La PE24 ....102 A2
Lady Lodge Dr PE2 ...230 A5
Lady Margaret's Ave
PE6 ....217 C5
Lady Matilda's Dr
PE25 ....206 C8
Lady Meers Rd LN3 ...203 E6
Ladybower Way PE4 ...221 C3
Ladysmith Rd DN32 ...191 F7
Ladywell Gate 4 HU15 ....2 E6
Ladywood Rd PE11 ....214 E6
Lafford Ct NG34 ....212 B5
Lafford Dr 2 LN4 ......109 F6
Lafford High Sch The
LN4 ....109 F6
Laforey Rd DN31 ......188 A3
Lagonda Cl LN4 ....205 F1
Lagoon Rd DN17 ......184 B6
Laing Cl 2 LN3 ....83 B4
Lake View Rd LN6 .....205 C6
Lakeside Anderby PE24 ..77 C3
Peterborough PE4 ......221 B5
Peterborough PE7 ......230 C2
Lakeside Dr DN17 .....184 C5
Lakeside Gr HU4 ......179 D4
Lakeside Leisure Ctr
PE2 ....230 A5
Lakeside Ret Pk DN16 .185 F6
Lakeside Sta DN35 ....193 B2
Lakeview Cl 3 LN6 ....204 C1
Lairgate Pl 8 DN35 ....192 F1
Lamb Gdns LN2 ....202 B6
Lamb La
Benington PE22 ....127 A4
Newport HU15 ....1 B8
Lambert Ave 12 HU15 .....2 C6
Lambert Bank
Fleet PE12 ....158 D1
Holbeach PE12 ....168 D8
Lambert Mews 5 PE9 ..219 C4
Lambert Rd
4 Allington NG32 ....128 F7
Grimsby DN32 ....191 D6
Lambeth Wlk 3 PE9 ...219 A6
Lambourn Ct DN35 ....192 F1
Lambourne Rise DN16 .185 A2
Lambourne Way 5
NG34 ....122 D2
Lammas Leas Rd 4 LN8 .57 E7
Lammas Rd PE1 ....226 A7
Lammin's La 2 PE22 ....99 A4
Lamport Cl 9 PE6 .....217 A6
Lampton Gr DN32 .....191 D6
Lanark St 2 HU5 ......180 B8
Lancaster App DN40 ....12 D4

Lancaster Ave
Grimsby DN31 .... 191 B7
Horncastle LN9 .... 199 C5
Skegness PE25 .... 206 A5
Lancaster Cl
3 Great Steeping PE23 .. 101 D7
Long Sutton PE12 .... 216 C4
Stickney PE22 .... 113 A7
6 Waddington LN5 .... 94 A7
Lancaster Ct
14 Welton/Dunholme LN2 .. 68 D7
Yaxley PE7 .... 233 F6
Lancaster Dr
6 Coningsby LN4 .... 207 D4
Long Sutton PE12 .... 216 C4
Moorland Prison DN7 .... 26 A8
6 Scampton Airfield LN1 .. 67 F5
Lancaster Gate DN36 .. 195 C1
Lancaster Gdns 2 NG31 .... 211 D2
Lancaster Gn DN21 .... 54 F8
Lancaster Pl 4 LN5 .... 201 F1
Lancaster Rd
3 Binbrook Tech Pk LN8 .. 47 B6
Gringley on the Hill DN10 .. 39 D1
Scunthorpe DN16 .... 185 A5
10 Stamford PE9 .... 219 B6
Lancaster Way
Market Deeping PE6 .... 217 B7
2 Skellingthorpe LN6 .. 200 A4
Yaxley PE7 .... 233 F6
Lancelot Ct HU9 .... 181 C6
Lancelot Way 7 PE11 .. 214 B3
Lancewood Gdns 3 LN6 .... 204 C8
Lancia Cres LN4 .... 205 F2
Lancing Cl 7 PE4 .... 221 A3
Lancing Way 4 DN33 .. 194 E8
Land Dike LN11 .... 37 A1
Land of Gn Ginger 10 HU1 .... 180 F6
Landeck Ave DN34 .... 191 B6
Landing La HU15 .... 1 A7
Landmere Gr LN6 .... 200 D1
Landor Ave 3 DN17 .. 184 D7
Landsdowne Cl 22 LN12 .. 77 A8
Landsdowne Rd 2 PE25 .... 206 C4
Landseer Ave PE24 .... 90 D8
Lane The
1 Easton on the Hill PE9 .. 171 D3
West Deeping PE6 .... 173 B7
Laneham Rd NG22 .... 65 A1
Laneham St
Rampton DN22 .... 65 A5
Scunthorpe DN15 .... 183 A3
Lanes The 10 DN36 .... 36 D4
Laney Cl LN2 .... 202 C7
Langary Gate Rd PE12 .. 158 E1
Langdale Ave DN33 .. 194 D7
Langdale Cres NG31 .. 211 A8
Langdyke PE1 .... 226 F6
Langer Cl 5 LN6 .... 204 B6
Langford La NG23 .... 91 A2
Langford Rd PE2 .... 231 A7
Langford Wlk 1 HU4 .. 179 B7
Langham Rd PE24 .... 90 B7
Langhole Dro PE11 .... 145 B1
Langholme La DN9 .... 27 B1
Langholme Wood Nature Reserve* DN9 .... 39 D8
Langley PE3 .... 225 B8
Langley Cl LN11 .... 198 E4
Langley Dr DN16 .... 185 A2
Langley Pl DN35 .... 193 A4
Langley Rd LN6 .... 204 D2
Langrick Rd
Boston PE21 .... 208 C6
Coningsby LN4 .... 98 C1
Holland Fen with Brothertoft PE20 .... 124 E4
Langtoft Prim Sch PE6 .... 164 F3
Langtoft Drain Rd PE6 .... 165 C4
Langtoft Outgang Rd PE11 .... 165 D6
Langton Cl
Grimsby DN33 .... 191 A3
Horncastle LN9 .... 199 A3
Lincoln LN2 .... 202 B7
Langton Dr
Grimsby DN33 .... 191 A3
Horncastle LN9 .... 199 A3
Langton Hill LN9 .... 199 A3
Langton La LN9 .... 85 C4
Langton Rd
Holton le Clay DN36 .... 195 E2
Peterborough PE1 .... 226 D7
Langwith Dr PE12 .... 215 C2
Langwith Gdns PE12 .... 215 C1
Langworth Rd LN2 .... 69 B4
Langworthgate LN2 .... 234 C3
Lansdall Ave 4 DN21 .... 52 F6
Lansdown Link 1 DN35 192 E3
Lansdown Rd 4 DN40 .. 186 B4
Lansdowne Ave
Grimsby DN32 .... 191 D4
Lincoln LN6 .... 205 C5
Lansdowne Dr 21 LN12 .. 77 A8
Lansdowne Rd
8 Navenby/Wellingore LN5 .... 107 A8
Yaxley PE7 .... 233 F6
Lansdowne St HU3 .... 180 C6
Lansdowne Way PE2 .. 230 D7
Laporte Rd DN40 .... 187 C5
Lapwater La PE12 .... 147 C6
Lapwing Cl LN6 .... 200 A3
Larch Ave 16 LN2 .... 68 D2
Larch Cl 8 Bourne PE10 .. 213 C7
2 Grantham NG31 .... 210 D2
Immingham DN40 .... 186 E5
Yaxley PE7 .... 233 F6
Larch Ct 9 DN21 .... 197 E6
Larch Gn NG34 .... 107 D1
Larch Gr
Peterborough PE1 .... 226 C6
8 Scawby DN20 .... 30 F8
Scunthorpe DN16 .... 185 B7
Larch Rd DN35 .... 192 D2
Larch Way 8 NG34 .... 212 D2
Larchmont Cl 10 HU15 .... 2 C6
Larchwood Cres LN6 .. 200 D1
Larden Ave DN33 .... 194 E8
Lark Cl 13 LN8 .... 70 D4
Lark Dr 4 LN5 .... 107 A7
Lark Rise
6 Market Deeping PE6 .. 217 C5
Scotter DN21 .... 29 B3
Larkin Ave LN3 .... 203 D5
Larkspur Ave 6 DN41 .... 23 F5
Larkspur Croft PE21 .. 208 C6
Larkspur Rd LN2 .... 202 D7
Larmour Rd DN37 .... 190 D7
Larne Cl 12 LN5 .... 205 C2
Larne Rd LN5 .... 205 D2
Larners Fields 6 LN1 .... 66 C7
Lashbrook Garth HU4 .. 179 B4
Lastingham 30 HU15 .... 2 C6
Latham Ave PE2 .... 230 C7
Latimer Gdns 12 NG34 .. 122 E3
Laughton Endowed (Aided) DN21 .... 41 C8
Laughton Rd
Blyton DN21 .... 40 F5
Boston PE21 .... 208 D6
Laughton Way LN2 .... 201 F7
Laughton Way N LN2 .. 201 F8
Launde Gdns PE9 .... 218 E4
Launder Terr NG31 .... 211 A3
Laundon Rd NG34 .... 132 E3
Laura Ct 5 PE25 .... 90 E3
Laurel Cl
6 Donington PE11 .... 134 E2
8 Gainsborough DN21 .. 197 E6
Grimsby DN33 .... 191 C2
Kingston upon Hull HU5 .. 179 B7
Lincoln LN5 .... 205 D5
Yaxley PE7 .... 233 D4
Laurel Dr 7 PE6 .... 176 A3
Laurels Cl 1 DN40 .... 22 E8
Laurier St DN35 .... 192 D8
Laurold Ave 1 DN7 .... 15 A3
Lavender Cl
6 Lincoln LN5 .... 205 C2
10 Sleaford NG34 .... 212 D2
Lavender Cres PE1 .... 226 B8
Lavender Dr PE11 .... 214 A2
Lavender Gr DN36 .... 195 B7
Lavender Way
Bourne PE10 .... 213 B7
6 Scunthorpe DN15 .... 183 B3
1 Stamford PE9 .... 218 D7
Lavender Wlk 1 HU5 .. 179 C7
Lavenham Ct PE2 .... 230 C7
Lavenham Gr LN6 .... 205 A4
Lavenham Rd DN33 .. 194 D7
Lavington Grange PE1 .. 226 E6
Law Ct 1 PE11 .... 214 B5
Lawley Cl LN2 .... 203 B8
Lawn Ave
Peterborough PE1 .... 226 A7
Skegness PE25 .... 206 D2
Lawn Cres 1 PE25 .... 206 D2
Lawn La NG33 .... 152 F2
Lawn Wood Nature Reserve* NG33 .... 152 E2
Lawns The
Collingham NG23 .... 91 D5
9 Grimsby DN31 .... 191 C7
Kingston upon Hull HU10 .... 178 D7
18 Wisbech PE13 .... 170 C1
Lawnswood HU13 .... 178 D2
Lawrance Way 10 PE10 .. 164 C8
Lawrence Ave PE7 .... 231 C2
Lawrence Cl 1 LN6 .... 205 B7
Lawrence La 3 NG34 .. 120 C8
Lawrence Rd PE8 .... 172 C1
Lawrence St 3 DN31 .. 191 C8
Lawrence's Dro PE10 .. 164 F8
Law's Cl PE6 .... 174 C5
Lawson Ave
Grimsby DN31 .... 191 B7
Peterborough PE2 .... 231 D6
Lawson Leas 5 NG32 .. 210 A5
Laxton Gdns 7 PE11 .. 156 E8
Laxton Gr DN16 .... 185 A2
Laxton La NG33 .... 152 E7
Laycock Ave 2 DN10 .... 39 C1
Laythorpe Ave PE25 .. 206 D1
Laythorpe Gdns 2 LN4 .. 207 C4
Lea Dr DN32 .... 191 F5
Lea Frances Olive Anderson CE (Aided) Prim Sch DN21 .... 53 A5
Lea Garth 6 DN17 .... 29 D7
Lea Gdns PE3 .... 225 F1
Lea Gr 2 LN3 .... 83 C4
Lea Rd DN21 .... 197 D2
Lea Rd W DN21 .... 197 D1
Lea The NG34 .... 121 B8
Lea View 2 PE9 .... 163 C1
Leaburn Rd DN17 .... 29 D7
Leadenham CE Prim Sch LN5 .... 106 D3
Leading Dro PE7 .... 233 D3
Leafere Way 1 PE13 .. 170 B2
Leagate Rd
Coningsby LN4 .... 207 F6
Langriville PE22 .... 124 F8
Thornton Le Fen PE22 .... 111 F1
Lealand Way PE21 .... 209 A2
Leame Cl HU3 .... 180 A7
Leamington Cl 2 DN16 .. 183 C1
Leamlands La PE12 .. 149 B1
Leas Cl DN37 .... 194 E5
Leas Jun & Inf Sch The DN37 .... 194 E5
Leas Rd NG34 .... 122 F2
Leas The NG32 .... 119 B1
Lease La DN40 .... 12 D6
Leasingham La NG34 .. 108 D1
Leaver Gate PE24 .... 102 B2
Leaves Lake Dro PE11 .. 155 E7
Lebanon Dr 3 PE13 .... 170 E1
Lechler Cl LN2 .... 68 D3
Leconfield Cl 7 LN6 .. 204 C6
Leconfield Rd 16 LN6 .. 204 C7
Ledbury Dr DN36 .... 195 D7
Ledbury Rd PE3 .... 225 C3
Ledham PE2 .... 229 D4
Lee Ave
Heighington/Washingborough LN4 .... 203 D1
Sutterton PE20 .... 136 B2
Lee Fair Gdns 1 DN17 .. 184 F2
Lee Rd Lincoln LN2 .... 234 C4
Yaxley PE7 .... 233 E4
Lee Smith St HU9 .... 181 E7
Lee St LN11 .... 198 B5
Leek Hill 18 DN15 .... 9 A5
Leeming Cl 8 LN6 .... 204 D6
Lees The PE6 .... 217 E5
Lees Wlk HU3 .... 180 A7
Legard Ave DN16 .... 185 B6
Legard Dr HU10 .... 178 F6
Legarde Ave HU4 .... 179 C6
Legbourne Abbey LN11 .. 61 F3
Legbourne Cl 1 LN1 .. 201 D7
Legbourne Rd LN11 .. 198 E3
Leggott Way 8 DN41 .... 23 E6
Legion Cl 8 HU15 .... 2 C5
Legsby Ave DN32 .... 191 E5
Legsby Pl DN32 .... 191 E4
Legsby Prim Sch LN8 .. 58 A4
Legsby Rd LN8 .... 57 E7
Leicester Cl LN4 .... 203 C1
Leicester Gr NG31 .... 210 D5
Leicester St
Kingston upon Hull HU3 .. 180 D8
1 Sleaford NG34 .... 212 D4
Leiden Fields 2 PE11 .. 214 B2
Leighton PE2 .... 230 C4
Leighton CP Sch PE2 .. 230 C4
Leighton Cres 2 LN6 .. 205 B6
Leighton Gr 1 DN33 .. 191 C4
Leighton Wlk 4 PE12 .. 159 D7
Leinsters Cl PE3 .... 225 D3
Leiston Ct 21 PE6 .... 175 A1
Lemon Wong La LN5 .. 106 C3
Lenton Way 2 PE20 .. 136 D6
Lenton's La
Friskney PE22 .... 115 A5
Leverton PE22 .... 126 F6
Leofric Ave PE10 .... 213 B5
Leofric Cl 19 PE6 .... 166 F1
Leonard Cres 2 DN15 .. 182 F3
Leonard St 4 HU3 .... 180 D8
Leopold Cl DN16 .... 185 A6
Lerowe Rd PE13 .... 170 E1
Leslie Manser Prim Sch The LN6 .... 204 B7
Lessingham PE2 .... 229 D4
Lestrange St DN35 .. 192 C7
Lethbridge Rd PE4 .. 221 D2
Lettwell Cres 1 PE25 .. 206 D1
Levels La Blaxton DN9 .. 26 A4
Misson DN10 .... 39 A8
Leven Rd DN16 .... 185 D6
Levens Wlk PE3 .... 225 B3
Leverett Rd PE21 .... 209 B4
Leverington Comm
Gorefield PE13 .... 169 F1
Wisbech PE13 .... 170 A1
Leverington Cty Prim Sch PE13 .... 170 B2
Leverington Rd PE13 .. 170 C1
Levers Cl PE21 .... 209 F5
Leverstock Gn 38 DN7 .. 14 D4
Leverton Rd DN22 .... 52 B1
Levington St 2 DN31 .. 189 C1
Lewes Gdns PE4 .... 221 A3
Lewis Ave 13 LN12 .... 77 A8
Lewis Rd
Cleethorpes DN35 .... 192 D8
Coningsby LN4 .... 207 D4
Lewis St
Gainsborough DN21 .... 197 D3
Lincoln LN5 .... 234 B1
Lexington Dr HU4 .... 179 C5
Leyburn Rd LN6 .... 204 F4
Leyden Cl 6 DN40 .... 186 B4
Leyland Ave DN7 .... 14 E4
Leys Cl NG32 .... 210 B4
Leys Farm Cty Jun Sch DN17 .... 184 F4
Leys La DN15 .... 9 B6
Leys The
Cherry Willingham LN3 .. 203 E6
Peterborough PE3 .... 225 A1
Leytonstone La PE10 .. 213 D2
Liberty La HU1 .... 181 A6
Lichfield Ave
Peterborough PE4 .... 220 F3
Scunthorpe DN17 .... 184 C7
Lichfield Cl NG31 .... 210 E4
Lichfield Rd
Bracebridge Heath LN4 .... 81 A2
Grimsby DN32 .... 192 B6
12 Hatfield DN7 .... 14 D4
Liddell St HU2 .... 180 E7
Lidgard Rd DN36 .... 193 A1
Lidgate Cl PE2 .... 230 C7
Lidgett Cl 10 DN20 .... 30 F8
Lidgett The 7 DN9 .... 27 D6
Lifeboat Ave PE25 .... 206 D1
Lighter-than-air Rd
Cranwell & Byard's Leap NG34 .... 107 C1
2 RAF Cranwell NG34 .. 120 C8
Lighton Ave 4 PE20 .. 136 C5
Lila Dr 1 PE11 .... 145 B7
Lilac Ave DN16 .... 183 C1
Lilac Cl Bourne PE10 .. 213 B6
Wisbech PE13 .... 170 E1
Lilac Rd
9 Ellloughton-cum-Brough HU15 .... 2 C5
Peterborough PE1 .... 226 C7
Lilacwood Dr 5 NG31 .. 210 F7
Lilburn Cl 5 NG34 .... 121 B8
Lilburn Dr PE11 .... 214 C6
Lilford Cl 5 LN2 .... 202 E7
Lilford Rd LN2 .... 202 E7
Lilley St 6 NG23 .... 117 D3
Lillicrap Ct 2 LN1 .... 234 B4
Lillys Rd LN2 .... 234 B4
Lilywood Rd 12 DN20 .... 19 D3
Limber Cl 2 DN21 .... 53 A7
Limber Ct 6 DN34 .... 191 A6
Limber Hill LN8 .... 47 D4
Limber Rd
Humberside Airport DN39 .. 22 A6
Swallow LN7 .... 34 A7
Limber Vale DN34 .... 191 A6
Limburg Dr 7 PE11 .. 214 A2
Lime Ave
Scunthorpe DN16 .... 19 A3
Wisbech PE13 .... 170 D1
Lime Cl
Burgh Le Marsh PE24 .. 102 D7
2 Langtoft PE6 .... 164 F3
3 Old Leake PE22 .... 114 A1
RAF Cranwell NG34 .... 107 D1
Lime Cres LN5 .... 205 C1
Lime Ct PE11 .... 214 E3
Lime Gr 2 Boston PE21 .. 209 C2
2 Bottesford NG13 .... 128 A5
Caythorpe NG32 .... 119 C7
Cherry Willingham/Reepham LN3 .... 203 D5
9 Goxhill DN19 .... 12 A8
Grantham NG31 .... 211 C6
Holbeach PE12 .... 215 D3
Holton le Clay DN36 .... 195 D1
Humberston DN36 .... 36 C7
7 Ingoldmells PE25 .... 90 D3
Louth LN11 .... 198 C7
Scunthorpe DN16 .... 185 B7
Lime Kiln Way LN2 .. 202 C4
Lime St Grimsby DN31 .. 191 C8
Kingston upon Hull HU8 .. 181 A8
3 Sutton Bridge PE12 .. 160 F4
Lime Tree Ave
Gainsborough DN21 .... 197 D5
Kingston upon Hull HU13 .... 178 F2
2 Market Deeping PE6 .. 217 A6
20 Metheringham LN4 .... 95 C4
Peterborough PE1 .... 225 F4
Lime Tree Cl
1 Collingham NG23 .... 91 D4
6 Fulbeck NG32 .... 106 C1
6 Lincoln LN6 .... 204 E8
Lime Tree Gr 4 DN8 .... 15 A8
Lime Tree Paddock 2 LN2 .... 68 F4
Limedale View 2 DN3 .. 14 A3
Limelands 2 LN2 .... 234 C3
Limes The
7 Beckingham DN10 .... 40 A1
Castor PE5 .... 223 F1
4 Stallingborough DN41 .. 23 D6
12 Wittering PE8 .... 172 B1
Limetree Ave DN33 .... 191 C3
Limetree Cl
13 Sleaford NG34 .... 212 D2
Yaxley PE7 .... 233 F7
Limetree Wlk 1 NG34 .. 122 E2
Limewalk PE12 .... 216 C6
Linchfield Cl PE6 .... 217 E5
Linchfield Prim Sch PE6 .... 217 D5
Linchfield Rd PE6 .... 217 D6
Lincoln Ass Rm* LN2 .. 234 B3
Lincoln Ave LN6 .... 205 C8
Lincoln Castle* LN1 .. 234 A3
Lincoln Castle Way DN19 .... 4 D2
Lincoln Cath* LN2 .... 234 B3
Lincoln Christs Hospl Sch LN2 .... 202 B6
Lincoln Cl
4 Crowle DN17 .... 16 D7
Grantham NG31 .... 210 D4
5 Market Deeping PE6 .. 217 A6
Lincoln Cres 2 DN21 .... 42 F8
Lincoln Cty Hospl LN2 .. 202 C4
Lincoln Dr
27 Barton-upon-Humber DN18 .... 10 F8
30 Caistor LN7 .... 33 B4
3 Scampton Airfield LN1 .. 67 F5
5 Waddington LN5 .... 94 A7
24 Winterton DN15 .... 9 A5
Lincoln Gate DN36 .... 48 D5
Lincoln Gdns DN16 .... 185 A6
Lincoln Gdns Infants Sch DN16 .... 185 B7
Lincoln Gdns Jun Sch DN16 .... 185 A6
Lincoln Gn
Kingston upon Hull HU4 .. 179 C7
Skegness PE25 .... 206 B5
Lincoln La Boston PE21 .. 208 E5
Holbeach PE12 .... 147 D5
Kettlethorpe LN1 .... 65 F3
Osgodby LN8 .... 44 F2
Thorpe on the Hill LN6 .... 92 E8
Lincoln Minst Prep Sch (Private) LN2 .... 234 C3
Lincoln Minst Prep Sch LN2 .... 234 B3
Lincoln Minst Sch Pre Prep Sch LN2 .... 234 B4
Lincoln Nuffield Hospl The LN2 .... 234 B4
Lincoln Rd
Bassingham LN5 .... 92 F2
10 Binbrook Tech Pk LN8 .. 47 B6
Brant Broughton LN5 .... 105 F5
Brant Broughton & Stragglethorpe LN5 .... 106 A5
Canwick LN4 .... 81 B3
Caythorpe NG32 .... 119 B6
Cleethorpes DN35 .... 192 C5
Deeping Gate PE6 .... 217 C3
Digby LN4 .... 108 D6
Doddington & Whisby LN6 .... 204 A6
Dunholme LN2 .... 68 D6
Dunston LN4 .... 95 B5
Faldingworth LN8 .... 56 F3
Fenton LN1 .... 65 E3
Fiskerton LN3 .... 203 F4
1 Glinton PE6 .... 220 C8
Heighington/Washingborough LN4 .... 203 A2
Holton cum Beckering LN8 .... 70 B7
Honington NG32 .... 119 C2
Horncastle LN9 .... 199 A4
Ingham LN1 .... 54 F2
1 Leasingham NG34 .... 121 B8
3 Leasingham NG34 .... 121 B7
Lincoln LN6 .... 204 F1
Louth LN11 .... 61 B8
Metheringham LN4 .... 95 C4
Middle Rasen LN8 .... 57 B7
Moorland Prison DN7 .... 26 A8
Nettleham LN2 .... 68 B1
Newark-on-Trent NG24 .. 104 A6
Northborough PE6 .... 217 D1
Peterborough PE6 .... 220 D5
Ruskington NG34 .... 108 D2
Saxilby with Ingleby LN1 .. 66 E1
4 Skegness PE25 .... 206 C3
Skegness PE25 .... 206 B4
Skellingthorpe LN6 .... 200 B4
Sleaford NG34 .... 212 B7
Stamford PE9 .... 219 C7
West Barkwith LN8 .... 71 A7
Lincoln Rd Bridge NG24 .... 104 A5
Lincoln Rd Nocton LN4 .. 95 A7
Lincoln Sch of Science & Tech LN5 .... 205 E6
Lincoln St
Gainsborough DN21 .... 197 C5
Kingston upon Hull HU2 .. 180 F8
Lincoln Sta LN5 .... 234 B1
Lincoln Way 1 PE11 .. 214 C5
Lincoln's Ave PE12 .... 168 C2
Lincolnshire Aviation Heritage Ctr* PE23 .. 99 F5
Lincolnshire Coast Light Rly* PE25 .... 90 D1
Lincolnshire Coll of Ag & Hort NG32 .... 119 D7
Lincolnshire Rd Transport Mus* LN6 .... 204 D5
Lincolnshire Showground* LN1 .... 67 E4
Linda Cres LN11 .... 198 B4
Lindale Gdns DN16 .... 185 C7
Linden Cl 16 DN7 .... 14 D4
Linden Ct PE11 .... 214 E5
Linden Dene 1 LN6 .. 204 D1
Linden Dr PE24 .... 102 D7
Linden Rd LN9 .... 199 C4
Linden Rise PE10 .... 213 D7
Linden Terr DN21 .... 197 D3
Linden Way
Boston PE21 .... 209 A7
Pinchbeck PE11 .... 144 D1
Linden Wlk LN11 .... 198 C4
Lindens Cl PE13 .... 177 A3
Lindholme 5 DN21 .... 29 C3
Lindholme Bank Rd DN7 .... 15 B1
Lindholme Rd LN6 .... 204 D5
Lindis Rd PE21 .... 209 C5
Lindisfarne Ave DN36 .. 195 B6

Lindisfarne Rd PE6 ... 175 A1
Lindisfarne Way NG31 ... 210 E5
Lindley St DN16 ... 185 A6
Lindrick Cl 4 NG31 ... 211 D7
Lindrick Rd 6 DN7 ... 14 F3
Lindrick Wlk 5 DN37 ... 194 C4
Lindridge Wlk PE3 ... 225 A2
Lindsey Ave PE6 ... 217 A6
Lindsey Cl
6 Bourne PE10 ... 213 C5
Peterborough PE4 ... 221 B1
Lindsey Ct 12 DN9 ... 27 E6
Lindsey Dr Crowle DN17 ... 16 D8
6 Healing DN41 ... 24 A5
Holton le Clay DN36 ... 195 C2
Lindsey Lower Sch DN35 ... 192 D6
Lindsey Pl HU4 ... 179 D6
Lindsey Rd
Cleethorpes DN35 ... 192 F4
Stamford PE9 ... 219 C6
4 Uffington PE9 ... 172 C6
Lindsey Rise 3 DN33 ... 194 F8
Lindsey St 2 DN16 ... 183 C2
Lindsey Upper Sch DN35 ... 192 D4
Lindsey Way LN11 ... 198 D4
Lindum Ave
3 Immingham DN40 ... 186 B3
Lincoln LN2 ... 234 C3
Lindum Cotts PE13 ... 170 B2
Lindum Gr
Chapel St Leonard PE24 ... 90 E7
2 Crowle DN17 ... 16 C7
Lindum Rd
Cleethorpes DN35 ... 193 A4
Lincoln LN2 ... 234 B3
Lindum Sq 6 PE25 ... 206 B5
Lindum St DN15 ... 183 B3
Lindum Terr LN2 ... 234 C3
Lindum Way 9 PE11 ... 134 F2
Lindum Wlk 1 LN7 ... 32 A4
Linecroft La DN10 ... 40 B4
Ling Garth PE1 ... 226 B8
Ling House La DN7 ... 14 A5
Ling La NG33 ... 152 C5
Ling Moor Prim Sch LN6 ... 204 E3
Linga La LN5 ... 93 A3
Lingfield Cl 6 LN1 ... 66 D3
Linghall La LN4 ... 111 E5
Lings La DN7 ... 14 D3
Lingwood Pk
5 Peterborough PE3 ... 225 A1
Peterborough PE3 ... 230 A8
Link Rd PE1 ... 225 F3
Link The
Bracebridge Heath LN4 ... 205 F4
Kingston upon Hull HU4 ... 179 C5
2 Leasingham NG34 ... 121 B8
Louth LN11 ... 198 E5
2 Navenby/Wellingore LN5 ... 107 A7
Link Way PE11 ... 214 E4
Linkage Com Trust Sch PE23 ... 88 D2
Links Ave 2 LN12 ... 64 B5
Links Cres
8 Skegness PE25 ... 103 E4
4 Skegness PE25 ... 103 E4
Links Rd DN35 ... 193 A3
Linkside PE3 ... 220 F1
Linkway 7 DN7 ... 14 F3
Linley Cl 4 NG23 ... 91 D4
Linley Dr PE21 ... 208 E2
Linnaeus St HU3 ... 180 C6
Linnet PE2 ... 229 D6
Linnet Cl
7 Market Deeping PE6 ... 217 C5
Scunthorpe DN15 ... 182 D6
Linnet Dr PE10 ... 143 A3
Linnet Way 11 NG34 ... 212 B3
Linthorpe Gr HU10 ... 178 E8
Linton 21 HU15 ... 2 C6
Linton Cl PE22 ... 137 E7
Linton Rise 3 DN15 ... 8 A4
Linton St 5 LN5 ... 201 F1
Linwood Ave 5 DN33 ... 194 F8
Linwood Cl
Gainsborough DN21 ... 197 F3
9 Sleaford NG34 ... 212 C6
Linwood Rd
Lissington LN8 ... 57 D3
Martin LN4 ... 96 B3
Liquorpond St 11 PE21 ... 208 F4
Lisburn Cl 7 LN5 ... 205 D2
Lisburn Gr DN33 ... 191 D2
Lisle Marsden CE Prim Sch DN32 ... 191 E4
Lissett Cl 6 LN6 ... 204 B6
Lissington Cl 2 LN2 ... 201 F7
Lissington Rd
Gainsborough DN21 ... 197 E3
Wickenby LN3 ... 57 C1
Lister Rd
Peterborough PE1 ... 225 F7
Scunthorpe DN15 ... 182 C3
Lister St Grimsby DN31 ... 191 B8
Kingston upon Hull HU1 ... 180 E5
Listoft La PE24 ... 89 F7
Litchfield Cl PE7 ... 233 F5
Little Bargate St LN5 ... 205 E8
Little Belt The DN21 ... 197 D7
Little Bytham Rd
Castle Bytham NG33 ... 152 E1
Little Bytham Rd *continued*
Counthorpe & Creeton NG33 ... 153 A2
Little Casterton Rd PE9 ... 218 F8
Little Cl Edenham PE10 ... 153 D5
15 Eye PE6 ... 175 A1
Little Coates Rd DN34 ... 190 E4
Little Comm PE12 ... 215 B7
Little Dog Dro PE12 ... 158 C1
Little Dowgate PE13 ... 170 B1
Little Dro PE20 ... 124 C2
Little Gate La LN4 ... 82 A1
Little George St HU8 ... 181 A8
Little Gonerby CE (Aided) Infant's Sch NG31 ... 211 B5
Little Grimsby La LN11 ... 49 A1
Little Hale Dro NG34 ... 133 F8
Little Hale Rd NG34 ... 122 E1
Little Holme Rd PE34 ... 161 C2
Little John St 4 DN34 ... 191 B7
Little Johns Cl PE3 ... 224 F3
Little La Broomfleet HU15 ... 1 C6
6 Collingham NG23 ... 91 C4
Gringley on the Hill DN10 ... 39 C1
Louth LN11 ... 198 C5
Surfleet PE11 ... 145 B3
5 Welbourn LN5 ... 106 E5
Whaplode PE12 ... 158 A5
Wrawby DN20 ... 196 F6
Little London PE12 ... 216 D6
Little Marsh La PE12 ... 159 B7
Little Mason St 3 HU1 ... 181 A7
Little Merebalk La LN9 ... 86 B2
Little Michael St 2 DN31 ... 191 B7
Little Northfields PE9 ... 172 E4
Little Ramper PE13 ... 170 B4
Little S St 18 LN11 ... 198 B5
Little Side Rd PE20 ... 135 E8
Little Thorpe La LN6 ... 79 F1
Little Wlk DN21 ... 40 B5
Littlebeck Cl HU3 ... 180 A7
Littlebeck Rd 3 DN36 ... 36 C8
Littleborough La DN21 ... 53 A1
Littleborough Rd DN22 ... 52 C2
Littlebury Gdns PE12 ... 215 C2
Littlechild Dr 4 PE13 ... 170 B2
Littlecoates Prim Sch DN31 ... 188 D1
Littlefair Rd 6 HU9 ... 5 D8
Littlefield La
4 Grimsby DN34 ... 191 A6
Marshchapel DN36 ... 37 B2
Littlemeer PE2 ... 229 F4
Littlemoors La PE22 ... 113 A3
Littleport La
6 Sibsey PE22 ... 113 B1
3 Sibsey PE22 ... 113 B1
Littlewood Rd DN8 ... 15 B8
Littleworth Dro
Deeping St Nicholas PE11 ... 156 D1
Heckington NG34 ... 122 F4
Spalding PE11 ... 156 E2
Sutton St Edmund PE12 ... 176 F8
Livermore Gn PE4 ... 220 E6
Liverpool Dr LN6 ... 200 B2
Liverpool St HU3 ... 180 A3
Livesey Rd DN36 ... 48 E6
Lloyds Ave DN17 ... 184 F8
Lobelia Dr 1 DN17 ... 185 A1
Lock Hill 30 DN8 ... 15 A8
Lock La DN8 ... 15 A8
Lock Rd Alvingham LN11 ... 49 F2
North Coates DN36 ... 37 A3
Lockham Gate PE22 ... 114 B2
Lockhill DN31 ... 189 A2
Locking Cl 17 LN6 ... 204 C6
Locking Garth LN11 ... 49 D5
Locks Cl PE6 ... 174 A8
Locksley Christian Sch LN11 ... 62 C6
Locksley Cl
6 Boston PE21 ... 208 E7
4 North Somercotes LN11 ... 50 F7
Locksley Way 5 LN11 ... 50 F7
Lockton Cl 2 PE20 ... 135 B7
Lockton Gr 1 HU5 ... 179 D8
Lockwood Bank DN9 ... 27 E6
Lockwood Cl 12 DN8 ... 15 B8
Lockwood Ct 1 DN15 ... 182 E4
Lockwood St HU2 ... 180 F8
Loder Ave PE3 ... 224 F2
Lodge Ave 22 DN18 ... 10 F8
Lodge Cl 10 Brough HU15 ... 2 C7
Kingston upon Hull HU13 ... 178 F1
6 Welton/Dunholme LN2 ... 68 D7
Lodge Ct 37 DN7 ... 14 D4
Lodge Dr LN6 ... 105 A8
Lodge La
Flixborough DN15 ... 8 B2
Kirk Bramwith DN7 ... 14 A8
Nettleham LN2 ... 68 D1
Upton DN21 ... 53 D5
Lodge Rd Bourne PE10 ... 213 C7
6 Coningsby LN4 ... 207 A5
Scunthorpe DN15 ... 182 C2
Tattershall Thorpe LN10 ... 97 E3
Lodge Way NG31 ... 211 A6
Lodington Ct 5 LN9 ... 199 D3
Loganberry Dr HU4 ... 179 C4
Lomax Dr 2 NG34 ... 212 C6
Lombard St
2 Grimsby DN34 ... 191 A7
Kingston upon Hull HU1 ... 180 E6
Lombardy Dr PE1 ... 226 B8
Lomond Gr DN36 ... 36 C8
Lomond Rd HU5 ... 179 E8
Londesborough St HU3 ... 180 C7
Londesborough Way
19 Metheringham LN4 ... 95 D4
13 Metheringham LN4 ... 95 D4
London Rd
Boston PE21 ... 208 E1
Bracebridge Heath LN4 ... 205 F5
Frampton PE20 ... 136 D7
Grantham NG31 ... 211 B3
Haugham LN11 ... 74 A7
Long Sutton PE12 ... 216 C4
Louth LN11 ... 198 C3
Newark-on-Trent NG24 ... 104 B2
Osbournby NG34 ... 132 C5
Peterborough PE2 ... 226 A1
Sleaford NG34 ... 212 B1
Spalding PE11 ... 214 C2
Tathwell LN11 ... 61 C2
Wansford PE8 ... 222 B2
Yaxley PE7 ... 233 C5
Londonthorpe La NG31 ... 211 E8
Long Acre 1 LN12 ... 64 B4
Long Bennington CE Prim Sch NG23 ... 117 D3
Long Cl La LN3 ... 82 B7
Long Cswy PE1 ... 226 A2
Long Dro Bourne PE10 ... 155 B1
Gosberton PE11 ... 144 B6
Rippingale PE10 ... 143 D3
Thurlby PE10 ... 164 E7
Walcott LN4 ... 109 E8
Wisbech St Mary PE13 ... 177 D4
Long Farm La DN22 ... 52 E2
Long Field Dr 2 DN3 ... 14 A1
Long Field Rd 23 DN3 ... 14 A2
Long Gates LN11 ... 51 A1
Long Hedge La
Greetham with Somersby LN9 ... 86 C5
Swaby LN13 ... 74 E4
Long Hollow NG33 ... 131 C3
Long La
Aubourn Haddington & South Hykeham LN6 ... 93 B7
Barnby in the Willows NG24 ... 104 F4
Fleet PE12 ... 168 B3
Ingham LN1 ... 54 E2
Leadenham LN5 ... 107 A2
Moulton PE12 ... 157 E5
Mumby LN13 ... 76 E2
Redmile NG32 ... 128 A1
2 Westborough & Dry Doddington NG23 ... 117 F3
Willoughton DN21 ... 42 E3
Long Leys Rd LN1 ... 201 C6
Long Pasture 5 PE4 ... 220 F5
Long Rd
1 Scunthorpe DN15 ... 182 F4
Terrington St Clement PE34 ... 161 F5
3 Tydd St Mary PE13 ... 170 C8
Long St 2 Foston NG32 ... 117 F1
Great Gonerby NG31 ... 129 E5
Long Sutton Butterfly Pk* PE12 ... 216 D6
Long Sutton Cty Prim Sch PE12 ... 216 B5
Long Wood La LN4 ... 95 C2
Long Wood Rd DN21 ... 41 A1
Longcliffe Rd NG31 ... 211 A8
Longcroft Dr 1 NG34 ... 107 C1
Longdales Rd LN2 ... 201 F6
Longden St HU3 ... 180 A7
Longdon Cl 6 PE12 ... 160 E4
Longfield Rd DN34 ... 190 E4
Longhead La PE14 ... 170 D3
Longhedge Dro PE20 ... 134 E5
Longhorn Cl DN37 ... 194 B4
Longhurst Gdns PE21 ... 208 D7
Longlands LN13 ... 63 D3
Longleat Dr LN11 ... 198 A7
Longmeadow Rise 18 DN41 ... 23 A4
Longmeadows PE10 ... 154 B7
Longmeadows Dr DN37 ... 23 F2
Longthorpe Cl 3 PE3 ... 225 A2
Longthorpe CP Sch PE3 ... 225 A2
Longthorpe Gn PE3 ... 225 B1
Longthorpe House Mews 11 PE3 ... 224 F2
Longthorpe Parkway PE3 ... 225 C1
Longton Rd
18 Kirk Sandall DN3 ... 14 A3
4 Kirk Sandall DN3 ... 14 A2
Longueville Ct PE2 ... 230 B5
Longwater PE2 ... 230 B6
Lonsdale Cl 20 DN36 ... 36 D8
Lonsdale Gr PE10 ... 213 E6
Lonsdale Pl 3 LN5 ... 201 F1
Lonsdale Rd PE9 ... 218 E5
Lonsdale St 5 HU3 ... 180 A6
Loop La 1 PE12 ... 157 F7
Loosegate Rd PE12 ... 158 A8
Lopham La DN37 ... 34 F8
Lord Dr 4 NG31 ... 129 E5
Lord St
Gainsborough DN21 ... 197 C4
Grimsby DN31 ... 191 B8
4 Sleaford NG34 ... 212 C3
17 Stainforth DN7 ... 14 C6
Lord's La 6 NG33 ... 151 A8
Lords La 19 DN19 ... 11 D8
Lornas Field PE7 ... 230 D2
Lorne St LN5 ... 234 C1
Losecoat Cl 1 PE9 ... 219 D7
Lotus Cl 7 LN5 ... 93 F7
Lough Rd LN9 ... 72 F1
Loughborough Univ of Peterborough PE1 ... 226 A3
Louis Dr HU5 ... 179 B8
Louis St HU3 ... 180 C8
Louisberg Rd DN21 ... 54 F8
Louth Cty Hospl LN11 ... 198 B6
Louth Mus* LN11 ... 198 B5
Louth Playgoers Riverhead Theatre* LN11 ... 198 D7
Louth Rd
East Barkwith LN8 ... 58 E1
Fotherby LN11 ... 49 A3
Grimsby DN33 ... 191 D1
Holton Le Clay DN36 ... 36 A4
1 Holton le Clay DN36 ... 195 D2
2 Holton le Clay DN36 ... 195 D1
Horncastle LN9 ... 199 C5
New Waltham DN36 ... 195 B5
Skidbrooke with Saltfleet Haven LN11 ... 51 C4
2 West Ashby LN9 ... 85 E7
Wragby LN8 ... 70 D5
Lovat Cl HU3 ... 180 D5
Love La
Caythorpe NG32 ... 119 C7
Gainsborough DN21 ... 197 C6
Louth LN11 ... 198 A5
Spalding PE11 ... 214 E3
9 Sutterton PE20 ... 136 A2
Wrangle PE22 ... 114 C4
Loveden Ct DN35 ... 193 A3
Loveden View 6 NG32 ... 119 B7
Lovell Rd DN17 ... 184 E3
Lovell Way PE34 ... 161 F2
Lovers La PE5 ... 222 F2
Love's Hill Castor PE5 ... 223 F1
Peterborough PE5 ... 224 A1
Love's La PE20 ... 135 C8
Loves La LE15 ... 162 A1
Lovett St DN35 ... 189 E1
Low Burgage DN15 ... 2 B1
Low Church Rd 2 LN8 ... 57 C8
Low Comm La HU15 ... 2 D4
Low Cross St 6 DN17 ... 16 D8
Low Deeps La DN10 ... 26 C1
Low Farm Dr NG34 ... 142 C8
Low Field La HU15 ... 2 E5
Low Fields Ave 1 PE11 ... 214 F4
Low Fulney Est PE12 ... 157 C5
Low Garth DN17 ... 184 F2
Low Gate
Friskney PE22 ... 115 A6
Gosberton PE11 ... 145 C7
Marshchapel DN36 ... 37 C1
Moulton PE12 ... 146 C1
Surfleet PE11 ... 145 C3
Tydd St Mary PE13 ... 160 A1
Low Gate La 6 PE20 ... 135 A4
Low Holland La DN22 ... 52 C2
Low La Croft PE24 ... 102 D6
Holbeach PE12 ... 215 F4
Kirk Bramwith DN7 ... 14 A6
Middle Rasen LN8 ... 45 C1
Terrington St Clement PE34 ... 161 E3
Wrangle PE22 ... 114 B3
Low Levels Bank DN8 ... 15 D4
Low Leys Rd 6 DN17 ... 184 E3
Low Mill La PE20 ... 136 E1
Low Moor Rd LN6 ... 204 E5
Low Pk La LN4 ... 81 F4
Low Rd Barrowby NG32 ... 210 A4
Besthorpe NG23 ... 91 C7
Blyborough DN21 ... 42 E6
Croft PE24 ... 102 F5
Crowland PE6 ... 175 A8
Friskney PE22 ... 114 F4
Grantham NG31 ... 211 C8
Harmston LN5 ... 93 D6
Healing DN41 ... 23 F5
Holbeach PE12 ... 147 F2
Marshchapel DN36 ... 37 A1
Osgodby LN8 ... 45 B3
South Kyme LN4 ... 123 B8
Spalding PE11 ... 214 F4
Wainfleet St Mary PE24 ... 102 C1
Walpole Cross Keys PE34 ... 161 D3
Worlaby DN20 ... 20 C8
Wyberton PE21 ... 136 E7
Low St Beckingham DN10 ... 40 A1
Billingborough NG34 ... 133 B1
Collingham NG23 ... 91 C4
Dunham-on-Trent NG22 ... 65 A1
Harby NG23 ... 79 B5
Haxey DN9 ... 27 D2
North Ferriby HU14 ... 3 A4
5 South Ferriby DN18 ... 10 A7
Winterton DN15 ... 9 A5
Low Thorpe Rd LN3 ... 83 D1
Low Toynton Cl LN9 ... 199 D5
Low Toynton Rd LN9 ... 199 D5
Low Wood La LN6 ... 91 F8
Lowbridge La 4 PE11 ... 145 C6
Lowcroft Ave 3 DN9 ... 27 D2
Lowcroft Cl 4 DN9 ... 27 D2
Lower Church Rd LN6 ... 200 B5
Lower High St 9 LN5 ... 93 F7
Lower Kenyon St 10 DN8 ... 15 A8
Lower Rd NG32 ... 119 A5
Lower Spring St 1 DN31 ... 189 A1
Lowerdale 27 HU15 ... 2 C6
Lowfield Cl
4 Barnby Dun DN3 ... 14 A3
31 Kirton in Lindsey DN21 ... 30 B1
Lowfield La
Balderton NG24 ... 104 A1
Belchford LN9 ... 73 C2
Lowfield Rd HU10 ... 178 E5
Lowfields Inf Sch LN5 ... 205 C2
Lowfields Jun Sch LN5 ... 205 C2
Lowfields La
Allington NG32 ... 128 F7
Butterwick PE22 ... 126 E5
Lowfields Rd PE22 ... 126 E6
Lowgate Fleet PE12 ... 159 C8
Kingston upon Hull HU1 ... 181 A6
Lutton PE12 ... 160 A8
Lowgate Ave 7 PE20 ... 135 A4
Lowgate Cres PE12 ... 159 E8
Lowgate Rd
Ashby with Scremby PE23 ... 88 D2
Conisholme LN11 ... 50 C5
Hogsthorpe PE24 ... 90 B8
Lowick Gdns PE3 ... 225 C5
Lowmoor La LN9 ... 85 C3
Lowther Gdns PE4 ... 221 B2
Lowther St HU3 ... 180 A7
Loxley PE4 ... 220 E4
Loxley Gn HU4 ... 179 B7
Loxley Way 6 HU15 ... 2 D5
Loyd St HU10 ... 178 F6
Lucan Cl 13 PE22 ... 113 B1
Lucas Ct 4 DN41 ... 23 F5
Lucerne Cl PE11 ... 214 B6
Lucetta Gdns 9 PE11 ... 214 B5
Lucy Twr St LN1 ... 234 A2
Ludborough Pk DN36 ... 48 E6
Ludborough Rd
13 North Thoresby DN36 ... 36 B1
North Thoresby DN36 ... 48 D8
Ludborough Sta DN36 ... 48 F6
Ludborough Way 6 DN35 ... 192 F3
Luddington & Garthorpe Prim Sch DN17 ... 7 C3
Luddington Rd
Garthorpe & Fockerby DN17 ... 7 E5
1 Peterborough PE4 ... 221 B1
Ludford CE Sch LN8 ... 59 B8
Ludford Cres DN21 ... 197 E3
Ludford Dr 9 LN6 ... 205 A7
Ludford Rd LN8 ... 47 C4
Ludford St DN32 ... 191 E6
Ludgate Cl 2 DN37 ... 194 D4
Ludlow Ave DN34 ... 191 A7
Ludlow Gdns 4 PE11 ... 145 A8
Ludlow Pl DN35 ... 192 E5
Ludney La LN11 ... 50 C6
Luffenham Cl 4 PE9 ... 218 E5
Lulworth Ave HU4 ... 179 A3
Lumley Ave PE25 ... 206 D3
Lumley Cres 3 PE25 ... 206 D4
Lumley Pl 2 LN5 ... 201 F1
Lumley Rd PE25 ... 206 C3
Lunds The HU10 ... 178 C6
Lundy Ct DN40 ... 186 C2
Luneburg Pl 1 DN15 ... 182 C5
Luneburg Way DN15 ... 182 C6
Lunedale Rd DN16 ... 185 D5
Lunn La 5 NG23 ... 91 C4
Lunn's Cres 21 DN18 ... 10 E8
Lupin Rd LN2 ... 202 C8
Lurgan Cl LN5 ... 205 D3
Lusher Way DN21 ... 41 A1
Luton Cl
1 Birchwood LN6 ... 200 B1
1 Birchwood LN6 ... 204 B8
Luton Rd HU5 ... 179 F8
Lutton Bank PE12 ... 148 D1
Lutton Garnsgate PE12 ... 216 A4
Lutton Gate Rd PE12 ... 168 E4
Lutton Gowts PE12 ... 216 D7
Lutton Gr PE3 ... 225 C6
Lutton Lodge La PE12 ... 149 B2
Lych Gate 10 DN20 ... 19 D3
Lydbrook Rd DN16 ... 183 A1
Lydd Cl LN6 ... 204 C6
Lydford Rd DN40 ... 186 D3
Lydia Ct 3 DN40 ... 186 A4
Lygon St DN16 ... 183 B1
Lyle Cl 4 LN12 ... 64 A4
Lyme Wlk 3 PE3 ... 225 C4
Lymington Garth HU4 ... 179 A3
Lymn Bank PE24 ... 102 C4
Lynn Ct 2 NG31 ... 210 E2
Lyn Ellis Cl 2 PE21 ... 209 C4
Lynchwood PE2 ... 229 C5
Lyndale Ave 17 DN3 ... 14 A1
Lyndale Pk PE2 ... 229 C6
Lynden Ave NG31 ... 210 E8
Lyndhurst Ave
3 Grimsby DN33 ... 191 D3
Skegness PE25 ... 206 B5
Lyndhurst Ct 2 PE25 ... 206 B5
Lyndis Wlk PE12 ... 215 E1
Lyndon Bsns Pk LN6 ... 204 B5
Lyndon Cres LN11 ... 198 D8
Lyndon Way
Louth LN11 ... 198 D8
Stamford PE9 ... 218 E5
Lyneham Cl LN6 ... 204 B7
Lynmouth Cl 1 LN6 ... 205 A1
Lynmouth Dr DN17 ... 184 C8

Lynn Rd
Walpole Cross Keys PE34 161 C3
Walsoken PE13 170 E2
Lynnwell Cl PE25 206 A6
Lynton Ave HU4 179 B3
Lynton Cl 1 DN15 182 D4
Lynton Prep Sch DN15 183 A4
Lynton Rd PE1 225 F6
Lynton Rise DN35 192 E4
Lynwood Ave HU10 178 E6
Lyric Cl 1 HU3 180 C5
Lysaghts Way DN15 8 C1
Lytham Cl
8 Heighington/Washingborough LN4 203 D1
Londonthorpe & Harrowby without NG31 211 E7
Lytham Dr DN37 194 C3
Lythemere PE2 230 C4
Lytton St LN2 234 C2

M

Mablethorpe Com Prim Sch LN12 64 A4
Mablethorpe Rd
North Coates DN36 37 A3
Theddlethorpe St Helen LN12 63 F5
Macaulay Dr
Lincoln LN2 202 B6
Newark-on-Trent NG24 104 B3
Macaulay Jun & Inf Sch DN31 191 B8
Macaulay St DN31 191 B8
Mace Rd PE2 231 D5
Machray Pl DN35 192 D7
Mackender Ct 4 DN16 185 C6
Mackenzie Pl 5 DN40 186 B3
Maclure St DN31 189 B2
Macmillan Ave LN6 204 C2
Macphail Cres LN1 66 E2
Maddison La PE23 88 B3
Madeley St HU3 180 C4
Madely Cl 3 LN9 199 D3
Maffit Rd PE5 223 D3
Magdalen Cl 4 DN16 185 B4
Magdalen Rd PE24 102 D2
Magdalene Rd DN34 190 F5
Magee Rd PE4 221 B1
Magellan Dr 9 PE23 101 A8
Magellan Way PE11 214 C2
Magna Cres 15 NG34 122 E2
Magna Mile LN8 59 B8
Magnolia Ave PE3 225 A2
Magnolia Cl LN4 81 D2
Magnolia Dr 5 DN36 195 D1
Magnolia Rd NG34 212 D2
Magnolia Rise 4 DN40 186 C3
Magnolia Way DN16 185 B7
Magpie Cl LN6 200 A3
Magpie La DN22 52 C1
Magrath Ct 1 DN20 196 C3
Maiden Cl 1 DN40 186 A4
Maiden Ct 19 LN1 66 D2
Maiden Gr 2 NG34 212 E3
Maiden La
Hogsthorpe PE24 90 B7
11 Stamford PE9 219 C5
Maiden Well La 5 LN5 107 A8
Maidens Rd 10 PE20 136 A2
Maidenwell La 11 LN7 32 A4
Maidment Dr LN1 201 C7
Maidwell Way DN34 190 C4
Main App Rd DN16 183 C3
Main Ave
Bracebridge Heath LN4 205 F3
Scunthorpe DN17 184 C6
Main Rd Anwick NG34 109 B1
Ashby cum Fenby DN37 35 D3
Barkston NG32 130 B8
Belchford LN9 73 A2
Benniworth LN8 59 B1
Bourne PE10 154 C5
Carrington PE22 112 C7
Collyweston PE9 171 B1
2 Donington on Bain LN11 59 E1
Dunsby PE10 143 B2
East Kirkby PE23 99 F5
Etton PE6 173 E5
Friskney Eaudike PE22 115 C6
Gedney PE12 159 D7
Goulceby LN11 72 D6
Gunby & Stainby NG33 151 B5
Haconby PE10 154 C8
Heighington/Washingborough LN4 203 B2
Leadenham LN5 106 D3
Little Hale NG34 122 E1
Little Steeping PE23 101 D6
Long Bennington NG23 117 D3
Nocton LN4 95 B7
North Willingham LN8 58 D7
Parson Drove PE13 177 F8
3 Potterhanworth LN4 82 B1
Quadring PE11 134 F1
Saltfleet LN11 51 C4
Saltfleetby LN11 51 B1
2 Sibsey PE22 113 B1
Spilsby PE23 87 F1
Stickford PE22 100 B3
Stickney PE22 113 B5
Tallington PE9 172 E6
Thurlby PE10 164 D8
Toynton All Saints PE23 100 F6

Main Rd *continued*
Tydd St Giles PE13 170 C8
2 Tydd St Mary PE13 170 C8
7 Uffington PE9 172 C6
Utterby LN11 48 F5
West Keal PE23 100 C3
Wigtoft PE20 135 E3
Wisbech St Mary PE13 177 A2
Withern with Stain LN11 62 E1
Main Ridge E PE21 209 A5
Main Ridge W 9 PE21 209 A5
Main St (Southorpe) PE9 172 E2
Main St Ailsworth PE5 223 D2
Ancaster NG32 119 F3
Ashby De La Launde & Bloxholm LN4 108 B5
Barlings LN3 69 C3
Barnack PE9 172 D3
Barrowby NG32 210 A5
Baston PE6 164 E4
4 Bishop Norton LN8 43 D3
Bonby DN20 10 C2
Boothby Graffoe LN5 94 A2
Boothby Pagnell NG33 140 F5
Bottesford NG13 128 C4
Broomfleet HU15 1 C6
Brough HU15 2 C6
Buckminster NG33 150 E5
Cadney DN20 31 E6
Careby Aunby & Holywell PE9 163 B7
Carlton Scroop NG32 119 C4
Castor PE5 223 D3
Claypole NG23 117 F7
Clipsham LE15 162 C7
Crowle DN17 16 E6
Croxton Kerrial NG32 138 D3
Denton NG32 139 A7
Doddington & Whisby LN6 79 D5
Dorrington LN4 108 E3
Dunham-on-Trent NG22 65 B1
East/West Stockwith DN10 40 C5
Edenham PE10 153 F4
Ellerker HU15 2 A8
Ewerby & Evedon NG34 122 C6
Farcet PE7 231 C2
Fenton NG23 105 C1
Fishlake DN7 14 D8
Foston NG32 117 F1
Fulstow LN11 49 B8
Gedney PE12 148 B1
1 Grasby DN38 32 E7
Greatford PE9 164 C2
Gunby & Stainby NG33 151 B4
Hackthorn LN2 55 E1
Haconby PE10 154 D8
Hatfield DN7 14 F3
Honington NG32 119 C1
Horkstow DN18 10 A5
Horsington LN10 84 D3
Hougham NG32 118 C3
Ingoldsby NG33 141 D5
Laneham DN22 65 A3
Mablethorpe & Sutton LN12 64 B1
Mareham Le Fen PE22 98 F3
Marston NG32 118 D2
Newark-upon-Trent NG24 104 C2
Normanby By Spital LN8 55 F7
North Kyme LN4 109 F3
North Leverton with Habblesthorpe DN22 52 B1
North Rauceby NG34 120 E5
Norton Disney LN6 92 C2
Osgodby LN8 45 A3
RAF Cranwell NG34 120 C8
Ryhall PE9 163 D1
Scawby DN20 30 F7
Scopwick LN4 95 D1
Scothern LN2 68 F4
Scredington NG34 132 F7
South Rauceby NG34 120 E4
South Scarle NG23 91 E6
Southorpe PE9 172 E1
Sproxton LE14 138 F1
Sutton on Trent NG23 91 A8
Swanland HU14 3 B7
Syston NG32 130 A7
Thistleton LE15 151 C1
Thorney NG23 78 F7
Thornton Curtis DN39 11 E5
Thorpe on the Hill LN6 92 E8
1 Timberland LN4 96 B1
Torksey LN1 65 D6
Ufford PE9 172 F3
Upton DN21 53 D5
Welby NG32 130 F5
West Ashby LN9 85 E7
Westborough & Dry Doddington NG23 117 E5
Whitton DN15 1 E3
Wilsford NG32 120 C2
1 Worlaby DN20 20 D8
1 Wymondham LE14 150 C1
Yaxley PE7 233 E5
Maine Ave DN15 182 B5
Mainwaring Cl 5 LN2 68 E6
Mainwaring Rd LN2 234 C4
Maisdike La PE12 159 B5
Malborne Way PE2 230 B4
Malborough Dr 4 LN12 64 A3
Malborough La LN5 93 A4
Malcolm Ave NG34 107 C1
Malcolm Rd DN34 190 F4

Malcolm Sargent Gm Sch PE9 218 E5
Maldon Dr HU9 181 C6
Malham Ave HU4 179 C6
Malham Cl LN6 200 C1
Malham Dr LN6 200 C1
Malim Way 3 NG31 210 F8
Malkinson Cl
4 West Halton DN15 8 E7
21 Winterton DN15 9 A5
12 Winterton DN15 9 A5
Mallalieu Ct 2 DN15 182 E4
Mallard Ave
6 Barnby Dun DN3 14 A4
12 Barnby Dun DN3 14 A3
Mallard Cl
Birchwood LN6 200 E1
5 Essendine PE9 163 D3
19 Healing DN41 23 F5
Skellingthorpe LN6 200 A3
Spalding PE11 214 E2
Mallard Ct
10 Grantham NG31 210 E2
4 North Hykeham LN6 204 C1
5 Stamford PE9 219 B4
Mallard Dr 6 LN7 33 B4
Mallard Dro PE11 134 B1
Mallard Mews DN32 191 E6
Mallard Rd
Low Fulney PE12 157 C5
Peterborough PE3 220 E1
3 Scunthorpe DN17 184 E6
Mallard Way PE25 103 C7
Mallards Reach 8 PE11 134 F2
Mallards The 5 PE6 174 A5
Malling Wlk DN16 185 B2
Mallory Cl 6 LN6 204 C7
Mallory Dr 3 PE11 214 C2
Mallory Rd
1 Ashby De La Launde & Bloxholm LN4 108 A7
Peterborough PE1 226 C2
4 Scunthorpe DN16 185 D5
Mallowfield 2 LN8 57 B8
Mallows La PE22 113 C2
Malm St HU3 180 B6
Malmesbury Dr 3 DN34 191 C6
Malmsgate La PE20 135 F6
Malpas Ave 4 DN21 197 D5
Malt Kiln La 1 LN5 93 F6
Maltby Ave DN37 190 C3
Maltby Cl 20 PE8 172 B1
Maltby Dr PE6 164 D4
Maltby La 12 DN18 3 E1
Maltby Rd
Scunthorpe DN17 184 E5
Skegness PE25 206 D5
Malten La 8 PE12 158 B7
Malting La PE11 134 E2
Maltings La NG31 210 E7
Maltings The
5 Alford LN13 75 F3
1 Leasingham NG34 121 B7
6 Thorney PE6 176 A3
Wothorpe PE9 219 C2
Maltkiln La
Brant Broughton LN5 105 F5
2 Elsham DN20 20 F7
Maltkiln Rd
Barton-upon-Humber DN18 3 F1
Fenton LN1 65 E3
Malton Rd LN6 204 F3
Malvern Ave
Grimsby DN33 191 A3
Heighington/Washingborough LN4 203 D2
Spalding PE11 214 E6
Malvern Cl 20 Lincoln LN6 93 C8
15 Lincoln LN6 93 C8
Lincoln LN5 205 D4
Sleaford NG34 212 B2
Spalding PE11 214 E6
4 Thorne/Moorends DN8 15 A7
Malvern Dr 5 NG31 210 E8
Malvern Rd
5 Mablethorpe/Sutton on Sea LN12 64 B4
Peterborough PE4 221 C2
Scunthorpe DN17 184 F7
Manasty Rd PE2 229 C2
Manby Hall Bsns Pk DN40 186 D5
Manby Middlegate LN11 62 D7
Manby Rd
Immingham DN40 186 C6
Legbourne LN11 61 E4
Scunthorpe DN17 184 E4
Manby St LN5 205 D6
Manchester Rd 11 LN5 94 A7
Manchester St
Cleethorpes DN35 192 D8
Kingston upon Hull HU3 180 A4
Manchester Way
3 Donington PE11 134 F2
Grantham NG31 210 C5
Mandalay Dr 1 PE10 213 E7
Mandela Link 2 DN31 191 C7
Mandeville PE2 229 F4
Mandike Rd PE20 136 C2
Manifold Rd DN16 185 E5
Manlake Ave DN15 9 A5
Manley Ct 1 DN9 27 D6
Manley Gdns
Brigg DN20 196 B3
4 Cleethorpes DN35 192 F3
Manley St 4 DN15 183 B3

Mann La DN9 16 D2
Mannaberg Way DN15 183 B6
Manners Cl 3 PE9 172 C6
Manners Rd NG24 104 B2
Manners St NG31 211 A6
Manning Rd PE10 213 D5
Manor Ave
Grimsby DN32 191 D6
Peterborough PE2 231 B7
Manor Cl 6 Bardney LN3 83 C4
11 Baston PE6 164 E5
East Kirkby PE23 99 F4
3 Great Gonerby NG31 129 E5
11 Keelby DN41 23 A5
Langtoft PE6 164 E3
7 Leasingham NG34 121 B7
Lincoln LN2 234 B4
14 Metheringham LN4 95 D4
15 Ruskington NG34 108 D2
Ryhall PE9 163 C2
7 Sibsey PE22 113 B1
2 Spalding PE11 214 C1
6 Welbourn LN5 106 E5
13 Wittering PE8 172 B1
Yaxley PE7 233 D5
Manor Cliff 1 LN8 55 F6
Manor Ct
9 Bourne PE10 213 C5
2 Carlton-le-Moorland LN5 105 E8
9 Grimsby DN32 191 D7
17 Nettleham LN2 68 C2
Nocton LN4 95 B7
1 Stallingborough DN41 23 E6
2 Sudbrooke LN2 68 F3
Manor Ct Rd 7 DN9 27 E6
Manor Dr 12 Baston PE6 164 E5
2 Binbrook LN8 47 C4
3 Bonby DN20 10 C2
4 Brough HU15 2 C6
1 Great Gonerby NG31 129 E5
5 Great Gonerby NG31 129 D5
Halton Holegate PE23 101 B7
7 Harlaxton NG32 139 C7
Holbeach PE12 215 D3
1 Long Bennington NG23 117 D3
Peterborough PE6 221 E3
3 Scawby DN20 30 E8
2 Sudbrooke LN2 68 F2
Waltham DN37 194 E5
7 Wragby LN8 70 D4
Manor Farm Cl 43 DN17 29 D6
Manor Farm Dr 3 LN1 66 D7
Manor Farm La
Castor PE5 223 E2
3 Essendine PE9 163 D3
Manor Farm Rd DN17 184 E6
Manor Gdns
Boston PE21 209 A4
8 Hatfield DN7 14 E4
Peterborough PE2 231 C7
Manor Hill LN11 60 A1
Manor Hill Cnr PE12 169 D7
Manor House La NG23 117 E5
Manor House Mus★ LN13 75 F3
Manor House Rd PE12 146 F2
Manor House St
1 Fulletby LN9 86 B8
6 Horncastle LN9 199 B4
Peterborough PE1 226 A3
Manor La Aisthorpe LN1 67 C7
4 Barrow upon Humber DN19 11 D8
Bourne PE10 213 C4
Broadholme LN6 66 D1
5 Carlton-le-Moorland LN5 105 E8
Goxhill DN19 11 F8
Hougham NG32 118 C3
Threekingham NG34 132 E3
16 Waddington LN5 93 F7
1 Welton/Dunholme LN2 68 D6
Wrangle PE22 114 B2
Manor Leas Cl LN6 205 B3
Manor Leas Inf Sch LN6 205 B3
Manor Leas Jun Sch LN6 205 B3
Manor Paddock 6 NG32 128 F7
Manor Pk 7 LN11 61 F3
Manor Pl NG34 212 C5
Manor Rd
Barrowby NG32 210 A5
Bottesford NG13 128 A5
Burton Coggles NG33 152 C8
Carlby PE9 163 E4
2 Collingham NG23 91 D4
Coningsby LN4 110 E8
1 Crowle DN17 16 D7
Folksworth PE7 232 D1
4 Hagworthingham PE23 87 A4
Hatfield DN7 14 E4
Heighington/Washingborough LN4 203 B1
Kingston upon Hull HU5 179 B8
Kirton PE20 136 B5
Lincoln LN2 234 C4
Northorpe DN21 42 A8
Saxilby LN1 66 D2
Scunthorpe DN16 185 B3
Sleaford NG34 212 B2
5 Stainforth DN7 14 C7
Stretton LE15 162 A6
Swanland HU14 3 B6
Swinderby LN6 92 A5
Twin Rivers DN14 7 E7

Manor Rd *continued*
Wansford PE5 222 F2
Manor Rise LN3 203 F8
Manor St
7 Heckington NG34 122 E3
Keelby DN41 23 A5
8 Kingston upon Hull HU1 180 F6
Ruskington NG34 108 D2
Manor Stables Craft Ctr★ NG32 106 C1
Manor Way
Kingston upon Hull HU10 178 F6
6 Langtoft PE6 164 F3
Market Deeping PE6 217 E4
Manrico Dr LN1 201 C7
Manse Ave LN5 205 D4
Mansel St
3 Grimsby DN32 189 D1
Grimsby DN32 192 B8
Mansell Cl 1 PE11 214 B3
Mansfield Ct PE1 226 C5
Mansfield Rd DN15 182 B2
Mansgate Hill LN7 33 B3
Mansion Ct Gdns DN8 15 A8
Manson Cl 11 DN34 190 D4
Manthorpe Dro PE10 164 F8
Manthorpe Rd NG31 211 B7
Mantle Gn PE22 115 B6
Manton PE3 225 A3
Manton Ct DN20 30 F6
Manton La DN20 30 E6
Manton Rd Lincoln LN2 201 F7
Manton DN21 30 B4
Mantree Cross DN21 41 A8
Maple Ave
15 Crowle DN17 16 D7
Grimsby DN34 190 E7
Keelby DN41 23 A4
Kingston upon Hull HU10 178 F8
13 Northorpe PE10 164 C8
4 Scunthorpe DN15 182 C5
10 Wisbech PE13 170 D1
Woodhall Spa LN10 97 C6
Maple Cl Brigg DN20 196 E3
Gainsborough DN21 197 B7
9 Keelby DN41 23 A4
5 Kingston upon Hull HU5 179 C7
Leasingham NG34 121 C7
Louth LN11 198 D7
42 Messingham DN17 29 D7
Thimbleby LN9 199 A5
4 Waddington LN5 93 E8
Maple Ct PE7 233 F6
Maple Dr
5 Bassingham LN5 92 F3
1 Sudbrooke LN2 68 F2
Maple Gdns PE10 213 D6
Maple Gr 22 Healing DN41 23 F5
Holbeach PE12 215 A2
Immingham DN40 186 C5
New Waltham DN36 195 B5
Peterborough PE1 226 C7
3 Scopwick Heath LN4 108 A7
Spalding PE11 214 F4
Maple Rd PE21 209 C2
Maple St LN5 205 D5
Maple Tree Cl E 2 DN16 183 A1
Maple Tree Cl W 1 DN16 183 A1
Maple Tree Way DN16 183 A1
Maple Way 12 PE11 134 E2
Maple Wlk PE7 230 C2
Maples The PE1 226 F5
Maplewood Ave HU5 179 B7
Maplewood Cl NG31 210 F7
March Rd PE13 177 F1
March St 13 DN21 30 B1
Marconi Dr PE7 233 D6
Marcus St DN34 191 A6
Mardale Gdns PE4 221 D2
Mareham La
Aswarby & Swarby NG34 132 E7
Pointon & Sempringham NG34 142 F7
Sleaford NG34 212 F2
Threekingham NG34 132 F3
Mareham le Fen CE (Controlled) Prim Sch PE22 99 A4
Mareham Rd LN9 199 D2
Marfleet Ave 4 HU9 5 D8
Marfleet Cnr 9 DN36 36 B1
Marfleet La HU9 5 E8
Marfleet Prim Sch HU9 5 E8
Margaret Ave 1 DN17 17 D5
Margaret Dr PE21 209 B6
Margaret Gr 1 HU13 178 F1
Margaret Pl DN36 195 C6
Margaret St
6 Grimsby DN32 191 F7
Immingham DN40 186 C3
Margrave La
Garthorpe & Fockerby DN17 7 E5
Reedness DN14 6 E7
Marham Cl 4 LN6 204 B8
Marholm Rd
4 Peterborough PE3 220 F1
Peterborough PE6 224 B3

Marholm Rd continued
Ufford PE9 ....172 F2
Marian Ave 22 LN12 ....64 B3
Marian Rd PE21 ....208 F7
Marian Way
6 Skegness PE25 ....206 B3
Waltham DN37 ....194 B4
Mariette Way PE11 ....214 B6
Marigold Cl
Lincoln LN2 ....202 C8
Stamford PE9 ....218 C6
Marigold Wlk
3 Humberston DN35 ....192 E1
5 Sleaford NG34 ....212 F3
Marigolds PE6 ....217 D5
Marina Dr 19 LN12 ....64 B3
Marina View 8 DN8 ....15 A7
Marine Ave
12 Mablethorpe/Sutton on Sea LN12 ....64 C1
4 Mablethorpe/Sutton on Sea LN12 ....76 F8
North Ferriby HU14 ....3 A4
Skegness PE25 ....206 B3
Marine Ave W 8 LN12 ....76 F8
Marine Rd PE11 ....214 E5
Marine Wharf 5 HU1 ....180 F5
Mariners Arms Flats 2 DN17 ....17 D6
Mariners Cl HU9 ....181 C6
Marisco Ct 2 LN12 ....77 A8
Marjorie Ave LN6 ....205 D8
Mark Ave
Horncastle LN9 ....199 A5
Sleaford NG34 ....212 F4
Mark Rise 1 DN21 ....41 C5
Market Ct 8 DN17 ....16 D7
Market Deeping Com Prim Sch PE6 ....217 C6
Market Hall★ LN11 ....198 B5
Market Hill DN15 ....2 B1
Market La
Old Leake PE22 ....127 C8
Terrington St Clement PE34 ....161 E2
Market Pl 3 Alford LN13 ....75 F2
1 Binbrook LN8 ....47 C4
21 Boston PE21 ....208 F5
2 Brigg DN20 ....196 B3
Coningsby LN4 ....207 A4
2 Epworth DN9 ....27 E6
Gainsborough DN21 ....197 C4
2 Grantham NG31 ....211 A4
5 Horncastle LN9 ....199 B4
6 Kingston upon Hull HU1 ....181 A6
Long Sutton PE12 ....216 C4
2 Louth LN11 ....198 B5
10 Market Rasen LN8 ....57 D8
Owston Ferry DN9 ....28 B3
4 Sleaford NG34 ....212 D4
5 Spalding PE11 ....214 D4
Swineshead PE20 ....135 B7
4 Wragby LN8 ....70 D5
Market Rasen CE Prim Sch LN8 ....57 D7
Market Rasen Race Course LN8 ....57 F7
Market Rasen Rd
Dunholme LN2 ....68 E6
Holton cum Beckering LN8 ....70 B8
Lissington LN3 ....57 E1
Snarford LN8 ....56 E1
Welton/Dunholme LN2 ....68 E6
Market Rasen Sta LN8 ....57 D7
Market Rasen Way PE12 ....215 E3
Market Sq 17 PE21 ....208 F5
Market St
Bottesford NG13 ....128 A5
Cleethorpes DN35 ....192 F6
Gainsborough DN21 ....197 D4
Grimsby DN31 ....191 D8
Long Sutton PE12 ....216 C5
3 Sleaford NG34 ....212 D4
11 Spilsby PE23 ....88 A1
31 Winterton DN15 ....9 A5
Market Way PE11 ....214 C8
Markham Mews DN37 ....194 F4
Markham Ret Pk PE9 ....219 E7
Markham Orch DN20 ....196 F7
Markhams Orch DN37 ....194 F7
Markillie La PE12 ....160 A3
Marklew Ave DN34 ....191 B7
Marlborough Ave
2 Haxey DN9 ....27 D2
Heighington/Washingborough LN4 ....203 C1
Kingston upon Hull HU13 ....178 D2
2 Spalding PE11 ....214 E2
Marlborough Cl
5 Lincoln LN2 ....202 C8
Yaxley PE7 ....233 C5
Marlborough Dr 1 DN16 ....185 B8
Marlborough Rd 11 DN8 ....15 B7
Marlborough St 11 DN21 ....197 D3
Marlborough Terr 3 HU2 ....180 E7
Marlborough Way DN35 ....192 F1

Marlow Rd DN21 ....197 E6
Marlowe Dr LN2 ....202 B6
Marlowe Gr PE4 ....225 E8
Marlowe Rd DN17 ....184 D7
Marmaduke St 3 HU3 ....180 C4
Marmion Dr 7 DN15 ....9 A5
Marmion Rd
Coningsby LN4 ....207 E5
4 Scunthorpe DN16 ....185 C8
Marne Ave PE4 ....221 A1
Marne Gdns LN1 ....201 E6
Marne St HU5 ....180 A8
Marquis Ave DN36 ....195 D7
Marr La HU15 ....1 A7
Marratts La NG31 ....129 D5
Marriotsgate
6 Lutton PE12 ....160 A8
Lutton PE12 ....216 C8
Marriott Ct PE1 ....226 E5
Marris Dr 7 DN15 ....9 B5
Marsden Dr DN15 ....182 D3
Marsden Rd DN31 ....189 D1
Marsh Ave PE21 ....209 A2
Marsh Dro PE11 ....146 A5
Marsh La
Algarkirk PE20 ....146 B8
Barnetby le Wold DN38 ....21 B4
Barrow upon Humber DN19 ....4 C1
Barton-upon-Humber DN18 ....3 F1
Boston PE21 ....209 A1
Burgh Le Marsh PE24 ....102 E7
Carlton-le-Moorland LN5 ....106 A7
Dunham-on-Trent NG22 ....65 B1
Grainthorpe LN11 ....50 C7
Kettlethorpe LN1 ....65 C2
Middle Rasen LN8 ....57 B8
Misterton DN10 ....40 A5
New Holland DN19 ....4 D2
North Leverton with Habblesthorpe DN22 ....52 E1
North Somercotes LN11 ....38 C1
Orby PE24 ....89 C6
Saundby DN22 ....52 B7
Skidbrooke with Saltfleet Haven LN11 ....51 C5
South Cockerington LN11 ....62 B8
South Killingholme DN40 ....13 B4
Tattershall LN4 ....97 D1
Tattershall Thorpe LN4 ....97 D1
Winteringham DN15 ....2 A1
Wyberton PE21 ....136 F8
Marsh Rd 4 Crowle DN17 16 C8
Crowle DN17 ....16 B7
Gedney PE12 ....148 C2
Holbeach PE12 ....215 F6
Kirton PE20 ....137 A3
Orby PE24 ....90 B3
Spalding PE12 ....157 B7
Sutterton PE20 ....146 A7
Tydd St Mary PE13 ....160 C1
Walkeringham DN10 ....40 B3
Walpole PE14 ....170 F4
Weston PE12 ....145 F1
Marsh The PE14 ....170 E8
Marsh Way 3 DN36 ....37 C5
Marshall Ave
Grimsby DN34 ....191 B7
Kingston upon Hull HU10 ....178 E8
Marshall Cl 3 PE21 ....126 C1
Marshall Way 2 DN21 ....53 A8
Marshall's Bank PE13 ....177 D8
Marshall's Way PE7 ....231 C2
Marsham PE2 ....229 F3
Marshchapel Cl 2 DN35 ....192 F3
Marshchapel Prim Sch DN36 ....37 B2
Marshfield Rd 1 DN16 ....185 C2
Marshfields Sch PE1 ....226 D7
Marshland High Sch PE14 ....170 E4
Marshland St 10 PE34 ....161 F3
Marshlands Dr PE12 ....215 F3
Marston La NG32 ....129 A7
Martin Cl
2 Bottesford DN16 ....185 B2
Heighington/Washingborough LN4 ....81 E4
Louth LN11 ....198 D3
Skellingthorpe LN6 ....200 A3
Martin Ct PE4 ....221 A4
Martin Dales Dro 1 LN10 ....97 B4
Martin N Dro LN4 ....96 D3
Martin Rd LN4 ....96 C2
Martin S Dro LN4 ....96 D3
Martin St LN5 ....201 F1
Martin Way
Ingoldmells PE25 ....206 C8
New Waltham DN36 ....195 B6
Martin's Cl 5 DN19 ....11 D8
Martins Rd
Crowland PE6 ....167 E4
Ulceby DN39 ....12 B1
Martins Way PE2 ....229 F5
Martins Wlk 11 LN12 ....77 A8
Martinsbridge PE1 ....226 F7
Marton Gr
2 Grimsby DN33 ....191 A3
35 Hatfield DN7 ....14 D4
Marton Prim Sch DN21 ....65 E8
Marton Rd
Sturton By Stow LN1 ....66 B7
Willingham DN21 ....53 E2
Martyn Rd DN35 ....192 D7
Marvel St HU9 ....181 B7

Mary Armyne Rd PE2 ....230 B5
Mary La LE14 ....138 B1
Mary St DN15 ....182 F3
Mary Sumner Way 4 DN15 ....182 E4
Mary Walsham Cl PE2 ....231 E5
Marylebone Wlk 6 DN33 ....191 B2
Masefield Dr 10 LN12 ....77 A7
Maskew Ave PE1 ....225 E6
Mason Dr DN17 ....184 E3
Masonic La 5 PE23 ....87 F1
Masons Ct 25 DN18 ....10 E8
Massey Cl
11 Epworth DN9 ....27 D6
Kingston upon Hull HU3 ....180 A5
Massey Rd LN2 ....234 C4
Massey St HU3 ....180 A4
Mast Dr HU9 ....181 C6
Master Dike PE12 ....159 D1
Masterton Cl 6 PE9 ....219 D7
Masterton Rd PE9 ....219 C7
Mat Pitts La PE24 ....102 C1
Mathews St DN35 ....192 C7
Matilda Rd LN6 ....201 D1
Matley PE2 ....229 E5
Matlock Dr
Grimsby DN37 ....190 F8
Lincoln LN6 ....204 E2
Matmore Cl PE11 ....214 F3
Matmore Gate PE11 ....214 F3
Matthew Flinders Way PE21 ....208 D3
Matthew Humberstone CE Sch DN35 ....192 C4
Mattimore Dr 6 PE12 ....215 E2
Maud St 2 DN21 ....209 A5
Mavis Enderby Cross Roads PE23 ....87 D1
Mavis Rd 2 DN17 ....184 E6
Mawford Cl PE12 ....146 E2
Mawson Gdns 6 PE24 ....102 E2
Mawthorpe Hill Rd LN13 ....88 F8
Mawthorpe Mus★ LN13 ....88 F8
Maxey Cl 1 PE6 ....217 A5
Maxey Rd Maxey PE6 ....173 C6
Northborough PE6 ....217 C1
Maxey View PE6 ....217 C3
Maxham's Gn Rd PE6 ....173 D3
Maxwell Ave LN6 ....205 C8
Maxwell Ct DN34 ....190 D5
Maxwell Dr 1 LN12 ....64 B3
Maxwell Rd PE2 ....230 D6
May Cres LN1 ....201 D4
May Gr HU13 ....178 D2
May St DN35 ....192 D8
Mayall St 23 LN5 ....93 F7
Mayfair Ave LN6 ....205 C7
Mayfair Cres 12 DN37 ....194 C4
Mayfair Ct DN35 ....193 A1
Mayfair Dr 4 PE11 ....214 B1
Mayfair Dr W DN37 ....190 C8
Mayfair Gdns PE21 ....209 B7
Mayfield Ave
Gainsborough DN21 ....197 B7
3 South Killingholme DN40 12 F2
6 Stainforth DN7 ....14 D6
Mayfield Cl
3 Grimsby DN33 ....194 D8
15 Pinchbeck PE11 ....156 E8
Mayfield Cres
Louth LN11 ....198 D4
3 Middle Rasen LN8 ....57 C8
Mayfield Gr 5 PE25 ....206 B3
Mayfield Rd PE1 ....226 A6
Mayfield St HU3 ....180 C8
Mayflower Ave DN40 ....186 C3
Mayflower Cl
2 Gainsborough DN21 ....52 F6
6 South Killingholme DN40 12 E3
Mayflower Dr NG34 ....122 D2
Mayflower Rd PE21 ....209 C3
Mayflower Way 11 LN12 ....64 B3
Mayland Ave HU5 ....179 A8
Mayner's Dike PE12 ....169 F8
Mayor's Wlk PE3 ....225 E3
Maypole House Sch LN13 ....88 E8
Maypole St DN10 ....42 D2
May's La PE13 ....170 A2
Mays La LN1 ....66 E2
Maysfield Ct 10 DN10 ....31 A5
Maysfield Dr 6 PE13 ....170 B2
Maythorpe Cl HU3 ....180 A7
Maytime Cl 7 PE11 ....214 A5
Maytree Dr PE12 ....216 D5
McInnes St 4 LN2 ....202 C3
McVeigh Ct 13 DN41 ....23 F5
Meadow The 29 LN7 ....33 B4
Mead Cl 6 Lincoln LN6 ....205 A5
Peterborough PE3 ....220 F1
Mead The 11 Laceby DN37 ....23 F1
Lincoln LN6 ....205 A5
Peterborough PE4 ....221 A1
Mead Wlk HU4 ....179 C6
Meadenvale PE1 ....226 F5
Meadow Ave DN39 ....12 A2
Meadow Bank PE22 ....126 F6
Meadow Bank Ave 1 LN3 ....82 B6
Meadow Cl
1 Bourne PE10 ....213 D5
7 Cherry Willingham/Reepham LN3 ....82 A8
1 Colsterworth NG33 ....151 E6

Meadow Cl continued
5 Goxhill DN19 ....5 A1
Lincoln LN6 ....93 C8
1 Louth LN11 ....198 C4
6 Manby LN11 ....62 C6
6 Metheringham LN4 ....95 D4
2 Pinchbeck PE11 ....145 C1
4 Scothern LN2 ....68 F4
Spalding PE11 ....214 E6
Meadow Croft
6 Kirk Sandall DN3 ....14 A1
Waltham DN37 ....194 E5
Meadow Ct
Grimsby DN34 ....190 E7
15 Hibaldstow DN20 ....30 F5
Meadow Dr
Barton-upon-Humber DN18 ....10 F8
4 Binbrook LN8 ....47 C5
Grimsby DN33 ....194 D8
6 Healing DN41 ....24 A5
14 Misterton DN10 ....39 F5
Meadow Dro PE11 ....213 F7
Meadow End NG31 ....211 D2
Meadow Field Rd 6 DN3 14 A3
Meadow Gate PE11 ....213 D6
Meadow La
Auborn Haddington & South Hykeham LN6 ....93 B7
Benniworth LN8 ....59 B1
Girton NG23 ....78 C2
Leasingham NG34 ....121 B7
9 Lincoln LN6 ....93 C8
Normanton on Trent NG23 ....78 B3
North Cockerington LN11 ....50 A1
North Hykeham LN6 ....93 C8
North Scarle LN6 ....78 F1
Pointon & Sempringham NG34 ....143 C6
16 Ryhall PE9 ....163 C1
Meadow Rd
Dunston LN4 ....95 C5
Langtoft PE6 ....217 A8
Newark-on-Trent NG24 ....104 B2
Newborough PE6 ....221 B8
Scunthorpe DN17 ....184 C6
Meadow Rise
5 Barnby Dun DN3 ....14 A4
Blyton DN21 ....41 C6
1 Gainsborough DN21 ....53 A5
2 Saxilby LN1 ....66 D2
Meadow Vale 4 DN20 ....30 F8
Meadow View
Humberston DN35 ....192 F1
Morton DN21 ....154 D6
Swinderby LN6 ....92 A5
Meadow Way
Billinghay LN4 ....109 E6
Bracebridge Heath LN4 ....81 A1
7 Old Leake PE22 ....114 A1
6 Welton/Dunholme LN2 ....68 D6
Meadow Wlk
19 Kirk Sandall DN3 ....14 A2
6 Swanland HU14 ....3 B7
Meadowbank 5 DN9 ....16 E1
Meadowbank Rd HU3 ....179 E7
Meadowbrook
9 Ancaster NG32 ....120 A3
4 Ruskington NG34 ....108 D2
Meadowcroft 7 LN11 ....59 E1
Meadowdale Cres 3 NG31 ....211 A8
Meadowfield
4 Middle Rasen LN8 ....57 C8
Sleaford NG34 ....212 C5
Meadowgate PE9 ....172 F5
Meadowgate La 3 PE11 ....214 A3
Meadowlake Cl LN6 ....200 D1
Meadows Cl 7 NG23 ....117 D3
Meadows La
Lincoln LN4 ....202 E2
Reepham LN3 ....69 A1
Meadows Rise 1 LE14 ....150 B1
Meadows The
2 Beckingham DN10 ....52 B8
Burringham DN17 ....17 D4
8 Long Bennington NG23 117 D3
Mablethorpe/Sutton on Sea LN12 ....64 C2
5 Market Deeping PE6 ....217 C5
Messingham DN17 ....29 D8
7 Pinchbeck PE11 ....145 C1
Skegness PE25 ....206 A4
Westwoodside DN9 ....27 A2
Meadowsweet 2 PE9 ....218 C7
Meadway
Cherry Willingham/Reepham LN3 ....203 E6
11 Market Deeping PE6 ....217 A6
3 Spalding PE11 ....214 A4
Meakers Way LN13 ....76 F3
Meals Gate PE21 ....221 D2
Measham Dr 4 DN7 ....14 D7
Mechanic La 9 HU3 ....180 D5
Meden Ave 12 HU15 ....2 D5
Medeswell PE2 ....230 C3
Medforth La PE21 ....208 E8
Medina Gdns LN12 ....64 B2
Medium Section Rd DN16 ....19 A4
Medlam Cl PE22 ....112 C1
Medlam La PE22 ....112 D7
Medlam Rd PE21 ....208 C2
Medlar Dr 4 HU15 ....2 D5
Medlock Cres 5 PE11 ....214 F5
Medway 7 LN1 ....66 D7

Medway Cl 3 PE11 ....145 C6
Medway Cres LN6 ....205 B2
Medway Pl 6 DN34 ....191 A5
Medworth PE2 ....229 F3
Meeres' La PE20 ....136 A5
Meering Cl 12 NG23 ....91 D5
Meering La NG23 ....91 C7
Meers Bank LN12 ....64 A6
Meeting House La LN5 ....105 F5
Meggan Gate PE3 ....225 A1
Meggitt La DN15 ....2 A1
Megs La 10 LN5 ....107 A8
Melbourne Ave 4 DN33 ....191 D3
Melbourne Dr 4 PE25 ....206 A4
Melbourne Rd
Birchwood LN6 ....204 C8
Grantham NG31 ....211 D7
4 Stamford PE9 ....219 D6
Melbourne Way 6 LN5 ....93 E8
Melford PE3 ....225 A2
Melholme La LN11 ....50 A7
Mellows Cl
Cherry Willingham/Reepham LN3 ....203 F8
Peterborough PE1 ....226 C3
Mellwood View DN9 ....28 A3
Melrose Cl 9 PE9 ....218 E6
Melrose Dr PE2 ....231 A4
Melrose Rd DN21 ....197 C6
Melrose St HU3 ....179 F6
Melton Bottom HU14 ....2 F6
Melton Fields HU14 ....2 F5
Melton Old Rd HU14 ....2 E5
Melton Rd
North Ferriby HU14 ....3 A5
Wrawby DN20 ....20 F4
Wymondham LE14 ....150 B1
Melville St LN5 ....234 B2
Melwood Cl DN9 ....27 F6
Melwood Hill DN9 ....27 F6
Melwood View 18 DN9 ....27 E6
Memorial Hall Dr 9 LN5 ....107 A7
Menasha Way DN16 ....185 E7
Mendip Ave
Grimsby DN33 ....191 C1
25 Lincoln LN6 ....93 C8
Mendip Cl
6 Gonerby Hill Foot NG31 ....210 E8
2 Lincoln LN5 ....205 D3
Spalding PE11 ....214 B6
Mendip Gr PE4 ....221 C2
Mendip Rd DN17 ....184 D8
Menson Dr DN7 ....14 D4
Mercer Rd DN21 ....197 B6
Mercer Row LN11 ....198 B5
Mercia Cl 14 NG34 ....212 B2
Mercia Dr 3 NG32 ....120 A2
Mercia Gdns 2 PE10 ....213 B5
Mercia Gr 4 PE6 ....164 E5
Mercian Ct PE2 ....231 D7
Mere Balk La LN9 ....85 A7
Mere Booth Rd PE22 ....125 A2
Mere Cres DN16 ....185 D7
Mere Dro
Old Leake PE22 ....113 F4
Yaxley PE7 ....233 F4
Mere La Edenthorpe DN3 ....14 A1
Heydour NG32 ....131 D6
Winterton DN15 ....9 A7
Mere Rd
Branston & Mere LN4 ....81 E1
Waddington LN5 ....93 F7
Merebalk La LN9 ....86 B2
Meredith Ave DN17 ....184 D6
Meredyke Rd DN17 ....7 D3
Merelade Gr 4 PE4 ....220 E5
Meres Leisure Ctr & Swimming Pool NG31 ....210 D3
Meres Rd NG31 ....210 C3
Mereway The NG33 ....141 B3
Meridian Cl 1 PE21 ....209 D4
Meridian Rd PE21 ....209 C4
Meridian View LN11 ....198 B4
Meridian Wlk 2 PE12 ....215 B2
Merleswen LN2 ....68 D6
Merlin Dr 2 DN20 ....21 A8
Merlin Rd
14 Binbrook Tech Pk LN8 ....47 B6
Scunthorpe DN17 ....184 E6
Merrick St HU9 ....181 B7
Merriemeade Dr 4 PE25 ....206 D1
Merrifield Rd 7 PE24 ....102 E2
Merryweather Ct 7 DN16 ....185 B2
Merton Rd DN16 ....185 A3
Messingham La DN20 ....30 D8
Messingham Nature Reserve★ DN17 ....29 F6
Messingham Prim Sch DN17 ....29 D7
Messingham Rd
East Butterwick DN17 ....28 D8
Scotter DN21 ....29 C4
Scunthorpe DN17 ....184 D4
Metheringham Airfield Visitor Ctr★ LN4 ....96 A2
Metheringham Cl 1 LN6 ....204 D7
Metheringham Fen La LN4 ....95 E5
Metheringham Heath La LN4 ....94 E3

Metheringham Prim Sch LN4 95 C4
Metheringham Sta LN4 95 D4
Mewburn PE3 220 E1
Mews The HU3 180 C5
Meynell Ave 3 LN6 205 C8
Meynell St DN21 40 D8
Meynell Wlk PE3 225 B3
Michaelgate LN2 234 B3
Mickle Gate PE3 225 A1
Mid Gate PE22 113 E3
Middle Barn Hill DN20 10 D1
Middle Broad Dro PE13 169 D5
Middle Dro
Gedney PE12 148 C2
Holland Fen with Brothertoft PE21 208 A7
Kirton PE20 124 D2
Newton PE13 169 E4
Middle Fen Dro PE20 134 D4
Middle Fen La LN4 82 C5
Middle Holme La 3 NG23 91 A8
Middle La Amcotts DN17 7 E1
Sturton Le Steeple DN22 52 E3
Thorpe on the Hill LN6 92 F8
Middle Marsh Rd PE12 146 F7
Middle Pasture 3 PE4 220 F5
Middle Rasen Prim Sch LN8 57 B8
Middle Rd
Crowland PE6 166 E1
Newborough PE6 221 E7
Terrington St Clement PE34 161 D4
Tydd St Mary PE13 160 B1
7 Whaplode PE12 158 B7
Middle St Aisthorpe LN1 67 D7
Cammeringham LN1 55 A1
Corringham DN21 41 E2
Croxton Kerrial NG32 138 D4
Dunston LN4 95 C5
Farcet PE7 231 C2
Fillingham DN21 55 A5
Gunby & Stainby NG33 151 B5
5 Lincoln LN6 93 C8
Lincoln LN1 201 D7
7 Metheringham LN4 95 D4
14 North Kelsey LN7 32 A4
5 Potterhanworth LN4 82 B1
Rippingale PE10 142 F2
Scampton LN1 67 D6
Scotton DN21 29 C1
5 Skillington NG33 151 A8
South Carlton LN1 67 D3
Willoughton DN21 42 E3
Middle Thorpe Rd DN35 192 D3
Middlebridge Rd DN10 39 B3
Middlebrook La 1 DN8 15 A7
Middlebrook Rd 4 LN6 205 A5
Middlecott Cl 2 PE21 208 F2
Middlecott Sch The PE20 136 C5
Middlefield PE7 230 D3
Middlefield La
Gainsborough DN21 197 E2
1 Glentham LN8 43 F1
Middlefield Sch of Tech DN21 197 E3
Middlegate LN5 92 F2
Middlegate Cl 12 DN19 11 C8
Middlegate La
Bonby DN20 10 C3
Elsham DN20 21 A7
Orby PE24 89 D2
South Ferriby DN18 10 B7
Middlegate Rd (West) 1 PE20 136 D6
Middlegate Rd PE20 136 C6
Middlegate Rd E PE20 136 D5
Middleham Cl
3 Kingston upon Hull HU9 181 E8
2 Peterborough PE7 231 F5
Middlemarsh Rd PE24 103 A7
Middlemere Bank PE22 126 E7
Middlemore Yd 1 NG31 211 B4
Middleplatt Rd DN40 186 E5
Middlesykes La LN11 62 C7
Middlethorpe Prim Sch DN35 192 D3
Middleton PE3 225 A4
Middleton Cl 9 DN17 29 D7
Middleton Ct HU5 180 B8
Middleton Jun Sch PE3 225 A4
Middleton Rd
Newark NG24 104 B6
Scunthorpe DN16 185 B4
Middleton St HU3 180 C8
Middleton Way NG34 121 C7
Middleton's Field LN2 234 B4
Middletons Rd PE7 233 E5
Midfield Pl 16 DN36 36 D8
Midfield Rd DN36 36 D8
Midfield Way 14 DN41 23 A4
Midgate (East) PE22 113 E1
Midgate PE1 226 A2
Midgley Cl HU3 180 C5
Midholm LN3 203 E5
Midia Cl LN1 201 C7
Midland Ind Est DN16 185 D8
Midland Rd
Peterborough PE3 225 E3
Scunthorpe DN16 183 D1
Midsummer Gdns PE12 216 A4
Midthorpe La 3 LN9 85 E7
Midville Cl 10 LN1 201 E8
Midville La PE22 100 B1
Midville Rd
Midville PE22 113 B7
Toynton All Saints PE23 100 F4
Midway Cl 9 LN2 68 D2
Midway Gr HU4 179 E4
Milcroft Cres DN7 14 D4
Mildenhall Dr LN6 204 B8
Mildmay Rd PE4 225 D8
Mildmay St LN1 234 A4
Mile Dro PE6 173 F5
Mile End Ave 19 DN7 14 D3
Mile La LN12 64 A2
Miles Bank PE11 214 C7
Miles Cross Hill LN13 75 D1
Milestone La PE11 145 C1
Milfoil La 11 PE12 167 B8
Milford Ct Bsns Pk LN11 198 A8
Milking Nook Dro PE10 154 F3
Milking Nook Rd PE6 221 C8
Milkinghill La PE20 135 A5
Mill Bank PE12 159 A5
Mill Baulk Rd 3 DN10 39 F3
Mill Cl 7 Alford LN13 75 F3
Billinghay LN4 109 E5
5 Brigg DN20 196 A3
4 Croft PE24 102 E2
5 Marshchapel DN36 37 C2
Murrow PE13 177 D5
2 North Leverton with Habblesthorpe DN22 52 B1
Waltham DN37 194 E3
26 Wisbech PE13 170 D1
Mill Cres
Peterborough PE2 229 E4
20 Scotter DN21 29 C3
Mill Croft 3 Scawby DN20 30 F8
1 Scunthorpe DN16 185 D7
Mill Ct LN1 234 A4
Mill Dr NG31 211 C2
Mill Dro Bourne PE10 213 E7
Cowbit PE12 157 B2
Crowland PE6 175 A8
Deeping St Nicholas PE11 155 D1
Mill Field 1 LN12 64 C2
Mill Field Cl 6 PE6 173 C4
Mill Field Ct 11 DN3 14 A3
Mill Field Rd
8 Donington PE11 134 E2
Fishlake DN7 14 C8
Scunthorpe DN16 183 E3
Mill Field Terr NG34 212 D5
Mill Garth DN35 192 D3
Mill Gate PE12 158 B1
Mill Gn Rd PE11 214 A7
Mill Hill Ellerker HU15 2 A8
Friskney PE22 114 F6
Gringley on the Hill DN10 39 B1
Nettleham LN2 68 C2
Mill Hill Cres DN35 192 E5
Mill Hill Dr DN16 185 C3
Mill Hill Rd DN7 14 E3
Mill Hill Way LN11 62 A8
Mill House La 1 DN15 9 B5
Mill La Addlethorpe PE25 90 D1
Ashby with Scremby PE23 88 D3
Aubourn Haddington & South Hykeham LN5 92 F5
8 Barrow upon Humber DN19 11 C8
Beesby with Saleby LN13 75 F5
Bicker PE20 135 B4
Billinghay LN4 109 E5
Boston PE21 208 E4
Brant Broughton & Stragglethorpe LN5 105 E5
Bratoft PE24 102 C7
Brigg DN20 196 B2
Brough HU15 2 C6
9 Broughton DN20 19 E3
Burgh on Bain LN8 59 D5
Butterwick PE22 126 E4
Caistor LN7 33 C4
Castor PE5 223 F1
7 Croxton Kerrial NG32 138 D4
Donington PE11 134 F2
Eagle & Swinethorpe LN6 79 C2
East Halton DN40 12 D6
Firsby PE24 102 A7
Fleet PE12 168 C2
Fosdyke PE20 136 D1
Friskney PE22 115 C7
Gainsborough DN21 197 B8
Gorefield PE13 169 E1
Gosberton PE11 145 C6
4 Goxhill DN19 5 A1
Grainthorpe LN11 50 B8
Great Ponton NG33 140 A5
Hackthorn LN2 56 B1
Haxey DN9 27 B2
Heighington/Washingborough LN4 81 E4
Hemingby LN9 72 B1
Heydour NG32 131 B5
Hogsthorpe PE24 90 B7
Holbeach PE12 215 B5
Holton Le Clay DN36 36 B4
Horbling NG34 133 B3
Mill La *continued*
Horncastle LN9 199 B4
Huttoft LN13 76 E4
Immingham DN40 186 A4
8 Keelby DN41 23 A4
5 Ketton PE9 171 A3
Kingston upon Hull HU10 178 C6
Kirton PE20 136 A7
Kirton in Lindsey DN21 30 C1
Legbourne LN11 61 F3
Lincoln LN5 201 E1
Little Steeping PE23 101 C6
Louth LN11 198 B7
Maltby Le Marsh LN13 75 F8
Manby LN11 62 C7
4 Marshchapel DN36 37 C2
Marston NG32 118 D2
Martin LN4 96 C3
Middle Rasen LN8 57 C7
Minting LN8 71 B2
Mumby LN13 76 F1
Newton PE13 169 F5
North Clifton NG23 78 C7
3 North Kelsey LN7 32 A4
Osgodby LN8 45 A3
Owmby LN8 55 E6
Peterborough PE5 228 F7
Pickworth NG34 132 A1
Saltfleetby LN11 51 C1
Saxilby LN1 66 D2
Scamblesby LN11 72 F5
Scawby DN20 30 F8
Skegness PE25 206 A8
Skidbrooke with Saltfleet Haven LN11 51 C4
10 South Ferriby DN18 10 A7
South Somercotes LN11 50 D4
South Witham NG33 151 C1
Sturton By Stow LN1 66 C6
Sutterton PE20 135 F2
19 Sutton Bridge PE12 160 E4
Swineshead PE20 135 A8
Tallington PE9 172 F7
Tetford LN9 73 E1
Thorney PE8 228 B7
Tydd St Mary PE13 160 B1
Wainfleet All Saints PE24 102 C1
Walkeringham DN10 39 F3
Welbourn LN5 106 F4
Welton LN2 68 E8
Welton Le Marsh PE23 89 A3
West Keal PE23 100 B4
West Walton PE14 170 F4
Whaplode PE12 158 B7
Wigsley NG23 78 F4
Wildmore LN4 111 C4
Willoughby with Sloothby LN13 89 C6
Woodhall Spa LN10 97 B5
Wrangle PE22 114 D1
Wrawby DN20 20 E3
Mill La Cl 8 PE24 90 B7
Mill La W HU15 2 B6
Mill Marsh Rd PE12 146 D2
Mill Mere Rd
Corringham DN21 41 D2
5 Waddington LN5 93 F7
Mill Moor Way 3 LN6 204 D1
Mill Pl DN35 192 F6
Mill Race DN36 36 E4
Mill Rd Addlethorpe PE24 90 D2
Boston PE21 209 B3
Claypole NG23 117 E7
Cleethorpes DN35 192 E5
Crowle DN17 16 D8
Donington on Bain LN11 59 E2
Hibaldstow DN20 30 E4
2 Keadby DN17 17 D5
Lincoln LN1 234 A4
Luddington & Haldenby DN17 7 C4
Market Rasen LN8 57 D7
Maxey PE6 173 C7
Swanland HU14 3 A6
Walpole PE14 170 F6
Wisbech St Mary PE13 177 D5
Mill Rise
6 Navenby/Wellingore LN5 107 A7
14 Scothern LN2 68 F4
Swanland HU14 3 A6
Mill Row
Barrowby NG32 129 B3
2 Lincoln LN1 234 A4
Mill St
Kingston upon Hull HU1 180 E6
Ryhall PE9 163 C2
Scamblesby LN11 73 A4
Mill View
Peterborough PE7 229 A5
5 Waltham DN37 194 E4
Mill View Ct 12 LN8 70 D4
Mill View Rd 12 LN8 70 D4
Millard Ave DN7 14 D4
Millard Nook 30 DN7 14 D4
Millbeck Bank HU15 1 E8
Millbeck Dr LN2 202 B8
Millbrook Cl 3 LN6 93 B8
Millbrook Sch DN16 185 B6
Millbrook Way 30 DN18 10 F8
Miller Ave DN32 192 C6
Miller Cl 12 DN8 15 B7
Miller La DN8 15 B7
Miller's Cl PE10 143 A3
Millers Cl
Heighington/Washingborough LN4 81 E4
4 Sleaford NG34 212 C2
Millers Ct LN11 198 C6
Millers Dale 2 LN6 204 F2
Millers' Gate PE22 113 A2
Millers Quay 6 DN20 196 A3
Millers Rd LN5 93 F6
Millers Rest PE12 158 C7
Millers Way
6 Alford LN13 75 F3
6 Heckington NG34 122 E2
Millfield Ave
Grimsby DN33 191 D3
8 Saxilby LN1 66 D2
Millfield Cres NG32 119 B6
Millfield Gdns 6 PE6 166 F1
Millfield La E PE20 136 D7
Millfield La W PE20 136 D7
Millfield Prim Sch LN4 81 F4
Millfield Rd
Bratoft PE24 102 C7
3 Market Deeping PE6 217 A6
21 Metheringham LN4 95 C4
7 Morton PE10 154 C7
South Somercotes LN11 50 F5
Thorne/Moorends DN8 15 A8
Millfield The 1 DN20 31 A5
Millfields
22 Barton-upon-Humber DN18 10 E8
18 Caistor LN7 33 B4
Millfields Way 9 DN19 11 C8
Millgate 10 LN5 107 A7
Millgood Cl LN11 198 D5
Millhill La 12 PE20 135 B7
Millhouse St Rise 5 DN40 186 A4
Millom Way DN32 191 F8
Millport Dr HU4 179 B2
Mills Cl 15 NG23 117 D3
Mills Dr DN7 26 A8
Mills Service Rd DN16 19 A4
Millstone Cl LN9 199 A3
Millstone La 3 PE9 172 D3
Millstream Rd LN4 81 E4
Millthorpe Dro NG34 143 E5
Millthorpe Rd NG34 143 B5
Millview Gdns 3 DN20 20 E3
Millview Rd
11 Heckington NG34 122 E2
Ruskington NG34 108 D2
Milman Rd LN2 202 B4
Milne Gn 4 PE20 135 B7
Milner's La 2 PE23 87 F1
Milnyard Sq PE2 229 C2
Milson Cl
18 Barton-upon-Humber DN18 10 E8
7 Broughton DN20 19 D4
Coningsby LN4 207 D4
Milson Rd 17 DN41 23 A4
Milton Cl 2 DN21 197 E6
Milton Dr PE13 170 B1
Milton Rd
Gainsborough DN21 197 E6
Grimsby DN34 191 B4
Peterborough PE2 231 A7
Scunthorpe DN16 185 B5
Milton St Lincoln LN5 205 E7
Newark-on-Trent NG24 104 A3
Milton Way
Kirkby La Thorpe NG34 121 E4
Peterborough PE3 224 E3
2 Sleaford NG34 212 F3
Mina Cl PE2 231 D4
Minden Pl 4 DN21 55 A8
Minnett's Hill NG32 130 B8
Minnow Cl 1 DN37 190 D7
Minshull Rd DN35 192 F4
Minster Dr
Cherry Willingham/Reepham LN3 203 E7
Louth LN11 198 D4
Minster Rd
16 Misterton DN10 39 F5
Scunthorpe DN15 182 B2
Minster Yd LN2 234 B3
Mint La LN1 234 A2
Mint St LN1 234 A2
Minting Cl 9 LN1 201 E8
Minting La LN9 71 D1
Mirfield Rd
Grimsby DN32 191 F4
Scunthorpe DN15 182 C4
Misson Bank DN9 26 C3
Misterton Cty Prim Sch DN10 39 F4
Mitchel Ave 7 NG24 104 C5
Mitchell Cl
3 Hatfield DN7 14 D5
7 Skellingthorpe LN6 200 A4
Mitchell Dr LN1 201 C6
Mitchell Rd LN4 207 F6
Mitre La 16 PE21 208 F5
Moat House Rd 22 DN21 30 B1
Moat La
Bolingbroke PE23 100 A8
Old Leake PE22 114 B1
3 South Killingholme DN40 12 E3
4 Welbourn LN5 106 E5
Moat Rd Scunthorpe DN15 8 C1
Terrington St Clement PE34 161 F1
Modder St 1 DN16 185 B6
Moggswell La PE2 230 B4
Moira Cl 5 DN7 14 D7
Mole Dro PE12 168 C1
Mollison Ave DN35 192 F5
Mollison Rd HU4 179 A3
Monarch Ave PE2 231 A6
Monce Cl LN2 68 C7
Monckton Way LN2 68 D5
Mondemont Cl 4 PE12 215 E3
Money Bridge La PE11 144 F1
Moneys Yd 7 NG34 212 D4
Monic Ave HU13 178 F2
Monkfield Coll LN5 106 C2
Monkhouse Ct 6 PE11 214 A3
Monks Abbey Prim Sch LN2 202 B4
Monks Ave LN11 198 C6
Monks Cl 4 DN7 14 D5
Monks Dr 22 PE6 175 A1
Monks Dyke Com Coll LN11 198 D5
Monks Dyke Rd LN11 198 D5
Monks Gr PE4 220 E5
Monks House La 5 PE11 214 A4
Monks Manor Dr LN2 202 B4
Monks Mdw 5 PE6 175 B8
Monks Rd Lincoln LN2 234 B2
Scunthorpe DN17 184 F6
8 Swineshead PE20 135 B7
Monks Way LN2 202 C3
Monks Way Ind Est LN2 202 D3
Monks Wlk 4 PE11 214 A4
Monkshouse Prim Sch PE11 214 A3
Monksthorpe La PE23 88 F1
Monkton 2 HU15 2 D6
Monkwood Cl 17 NG23 91 D5
Monmouth La PE12 216 E8
Monmouth St HU4 179 E3
Mons Rd LN1 201 E6
Mons St HU5 180 A8
Monsal Dale LN6 204 F2
Monson CE Prim Sch LN1 67 C3
Monson Ct LN5 201 E1
Monson Pk LN6 200 A4
Monson Rd DN21 42 A8
Monson St LN5 234 A1
Montagu Rd PE4 225 D8
Montague St
Cleethorpes DN35 189 D1
Lincoln LN2 234 C2
Montague Terr 1 LN2 234 C2
Montaigne Cl 3 LN2 202 D7
Montaigne Cres LN2 202 D7
Montaigne Gdn LN2 202 D7
Montbretia Dr 2 DN17 185 A1
Monteith Cres PE21 209 B5
Montgomery Rd
Cleethorpes DN35 192 D5
Skegness PE25 206 A3
Montrose Cl
8 Grantham NG31 211 D7
1 Lincoln LN6 204 E1
10 Stamford PE9 218 E6
Montrose St 7 DN16 183 B2
Monument Rd 5 PE20 135 A4
Monument St PE1 226 A3
Moody La DN31 188 C3
Moon's Gn 3 PE12 157 F6
Moor Bank PE22 113 C3
Moor Closes Nature Reserve* NG32 120 A2
Moor Dike Rd DN7 26 A8
Moor Edges Rd DN8 15 B8
Moor Farm Nature Reserve* LN10 98 A6
Moor Gate PE12 159 A4
Moor Gn HU4 179 B7
Moor La
Ashby De La Launde & Bloxholm LN4 108 C3
Besthorpe NG23 91 D7
Blankney LN4 95 E4
Braceby & Sapperton NG34 131 E1
Branston & Mere LN4 81 F2
Caistor LN7 33 A5
5 Cherry Willingham/Reepham LN3 82 A8
Hatfield DN8 15 D3
Horsington LN10 84 D2
Kirkby on Bain LN10 97 F6
Laneham DN22 65 A3
Leasingham NG34 121 C7
Lincoln LN6 204 E1
Long Bennington NG23 117 C3
Martin LN4 96 A2
North Clifton NG23 78 D6
Potter Hanworth LN4 82 B2
Reepham LN3 69 B1
Roughton LN10 98 B7
South Clifton NG23 78 E5
South Witham NG33 151 B2
Stapleford LN6 105 B8
Thorpe on the Hill LN6 79 E1
Thurlby LN6 92 E4
Wroot DN9 26 C6
Moor Owners Rd DN8 15 D8
Moor Pk 5 NG34 108 D1
Moor Pk Dr 9 LN10 97 C5
Moor Rd
Bottesford DN17 184 C2
15 Collingham NG23 91 D5

Moor Rd *continued*
Crowle DN17 16 C8
Newborough PE6 174 C5
Owersby LN8 45 A5
Snitterby DN21 43 D5
Thorne DN8 15 C7
Walesby LN8 45 E3
Moor Side PE22 111 C8
Moor St LN1 201 D4
Moorby Cl LN1 201 E7
Moore Cl NG23 117 F7
Moore's La 1 PE6 175 A1
Moorfield Rd 2 PE3 225 D3
Moorfields La DN14 6 F7
Moorgate Cl PE10 154 D7
Moorhouse Rd HU5 179 B8
Moorhouses Rd PE22 111 F8
Moorings The
Broughton DN20 196 A3
Burton LN1 200 D7
Moorland Ave
1 Lincoln LN6 205 A5
4 Walkeringham DN10 39 F3
Moorland Cl
8 Carlton-le-Moorland LN5 105 E8
5 Walkeringham DN10 39 F3
Moorland Cres 5 LN6 205 B6
Moorland Dr DN36 195 C7
Moorland Inf Sch LN6 205 B7
Moorland Way
5 Epworth DN9 27 E6
Lincoln LN6 204 F5
Moorlands 9 DN9 27 A2
Moorlands The 23 LN4 95 D4
Moors Rd DN15 182 C3
Moorside PE22 98 E3
Moorswood Gate PE12 159 D3
Moortown Cl 6 NG31 211 D7
Moortown Rd LN7 33 A3
Moorwell Bsns Pk DN17 184 D3
Moorwell Rd DN17 184 E2
Moray Cl 5 PE9 218 D6
Morborn Rd PE7 230 C2
Morborne Cl PE2 231 D6
Morborne La PE7 232 D4
Morborne Rd PE7 232 C2
Mordaunt Ave DN33 194 D7
Morden Cl 12 LN4 95 D4
Morecambe Ave DN16 185 A4
Moreland Ave 1 LN12 77 A8
Morfield Gr 5 DN9 27 D6
Morgan Cl PE7 233 E6
Morgan Way 5 DN19 4 E2
Morgans Cl 2 NG24 104 D5
Morkery La
Castle Bytham NG33 152 B2
North Witham NG33 151 F2
Morley La 10 PE20 135 A4
Morley Rd DN17 184 F5
Morley St 2 DN21 197 C5
Morley Way PE2 230 D5
Morley's La NG33 152 F7
Morpeth Cl PE2 230 C6
Morpeth Rd PE3 225 C3
Morpeth St HU3 180 D7
Morris Cl 21 LN2 68 D6
Morris Ct PE7 233 E6
Morris Gdns 3 PE25 206 B5
Morris Rd HU3 179 E7
Morris St PE1 226 B3
Morrison Cl 10 LN12 76 F8
Mortal Ash Hill DN16 19 C2
Mortimer Dr HU10 178 F6
Morton CE (Controlled) Prim Sch PE10 154 D7
Morton Cl
Gainsborough DN21 197 B8
Immingham DN40 186 B5
Morton Dr LN6 204 F7
Morton Dro PE10 155 A6
Morton La LN6 92 C8
Morton N Dro PE10 155 B7
Morton Rd
Gainsborough DN21 197 C7
Grimsby DN34 191 B7
Laughton DN21 41 B8
Swinderby LN6 92 B7
Morton St HU3 180 C8
Morton Terr DN21 197 C6
Morton Trentside Prim Sch DN21 197 B8
Morton Way LN9 199 C1
Morus Cl PE11 214 E2
Moss Dr PE25 206 C2
Moss Rd Grimsby DN32 191 F7
Kirk Bramwith DN7 14 A8
Mosscroft La DN7 14 F3
Mossdale Cl NG31 129 F5
Mossop Dr PE6 164 E3
Motherby La LN1 234 A2
Moulton Chapel Prim Sch PE12 157 F1
Moulton Chapel Rd PE12 157 C1
Moulton Cl 1 DN34 190 D4
Moulton Gr PE3 225 C6
Moulton Marsh Nature Reserve★ PE12 146 F8
Moulton Mere Bank PE12 157 E3
Mount Ave
14 Barton-upon-Humber DN18 10 E8
Kingston upon Hull HU13 178 D2
10 Winterton DN15 9 B5
Mount La
Burton Pedwardine NG34 122 A2
Kirkby La Thorpe NG34 121 F3
Legsby LN8 58 A3
Mount Olivet LN11 198 A6
Mount Pleasant
9 Alford LN13 75 F2
Binbrook LN8 47 B4
1 Holton le Clay DN36 195 D1
Kingston upon Hull HU9 181 C8
Louth LN11 198 C5
8 New Holland DN19 4 E2
Peterborough PE2 231 C7
6 Wainfleet All Saints PE24 102 D2
Waltham DN37 194 D5
Mount Pleasant Cl DN21 53 B1
Mount Pleasant Rd PE13 170 D1
Mount Rd LN4 205 F3
Mount Royale Cl DN39 12 A1
Mount St
9 Grantham NG31 211 A5
Lincoln LN1 201 E6
Mount St Inf Sch LN1 201 E6
Mount The 15 DN3 14 A1
Mount Tumbledown Cl 9 PE12 160 E4
Mount View 5 HU14 3 A5
Mountbatten Ave
11 Pinchbeck PE11 156 E8
Stamford PE9 219 A6
Yaxley PE7 233 D5
Mountbatten Cl 5 DN16 185 B4
Mountbatten Dr 2 PE13 170 C1
Mountbatten Way
Bourne PE10 213 E7
Peterborough PE3 225 B6
Mountsteven Ave PE4 221 B1
Mourne Terr 6 LN5 205 D2
Mowbray Cl 3 DN9 27 D3
Mowbray Ct 23 DN9 27 E6
Mowbray Rd
Bretton PE3 220 D1
14 Thorne/Moorends DN8 15 B7
Mowbray St
Epworth DN9 27 E6
Gainsborough DN21 197 C6
Moxon's La 18 LN5 93 F7
Mrs Mary Kings CE (Controlled) Prim Sch LN4 96 B3
Mrs Smith's Cottage★ LN5 107 B8
Much La LN1 234 A2
Muckton Wood Nature Reserve★ LN11 74 E8
Muirfield
Grantham NG31 211 D8
11 Waltham DN37 194 C4
Muirfield Cl 6 PE11 214 C2
Muirfield Croft DN40 186 C4
Muirfield Dr PE25 206 D5
Mulberry Ave 3 LN6 204 F2
Mulberry Cl
5 North Thoresby DN36 36 B1
Sleaford NG34 212 D2
Waddington LN5 205 C1
Mulberry Ct 6 PE20 135 B6
Mulberry Dr 21 DN17 16 D7
Mulberry Rd LN8 45 E5
Mulberry Way PE11 214 E3
Mulgrave St
Kingston upon Hull HU8 181 A8
Scunthorpe DN15 183 A4
Mull Way DN40 186 C2
Multon Ings La PE20 136 B7
Mumby Cl 12 DN36 36 B1
Mumby Rd LN13 76 F2
Mumby's Bridge Rd PE22 98 F2
Munton Fields NG33 131 A1
Murray St 2 DN31 189 B2
Murrow Bank PE13 177 D6
Murrow Cty Prim Sch PE13 177 D5
Murrow La PE13 177 F5
Museum of Lincolnshire Life★ LN1 234 A4
Musgraves Orch LN2 68 E7
Muskham PE3 224 F4
Mussons Cl NG33 152 E7
Muster Roll La PE21 209 A3
Musticott Pl 17 PE13 170 E1
Muston La NG13 128 B5
Muston Rd NG31 210 E2
Muswell Rd PE3 225 E4
Mutton La DN10 39 F1
Myers Cl NG32 120 C1
Myle Cross Jun Sch LN2 202 C6
Myrtle Ave PE1 226 C7
Myrtle Ct PE1 226 C7
Myrtle Gr PE1 226 C7
Myrtle Rd 5 DN7 14 C4
Myrtle Way 16 HU15 2 C5
Myton St HU1 180 E6

N

Naam Gr LN1 234 A4
Naam Pl LN1 234 A4
Nab La DN7 14 C8
Nairn Rd PE9 218 E6
Nan Sampson Bank DN9 26 B4
Nandike Cl 4 HU10 178 F6
Nansicles Rd PE2 230 D6
Napier Pl PE2 229 C6
Napier St LN2 234 C2
Narrow Boats The 3 DN20 196 A3
Narrow La Belchford LN9 73 B2
Kirkby on Bain LN10 98 C5
Twin Rivers DN14 7 C8
Whaplode PE12 158 C4
Naseby Cl 21 Hatfield DN7 14 D3
Peterborough PE3 225 C5
Naseby Dr DN31 191 B8
Nash La 2 LN6 204 E1
Nathan Cl PE3 225 B2
National Ave HU5 179 F8
National CE (Aided) Jun Sch The NG31 211 B5
National Fishing Heritage Ctr★ DN31 191 E8
Natureland Seal Sanctuary★ PE25 206 E4
Navenby CE Prim Sch LN5 107 B8
Navenby La
Ashby De La Launde & Bloxholm LN4 107 F6
Bassingham LN5 93 A1
Navensby Cl DN31 188 A2
Navigation La 28 LN7 33 B4
Navigation Way HU9 181 C6
Naylors Dr 5 LN8 57 B8
Naylor's Row 3 HU9 181 B7
Ndola Dr LN9 199 C2
Neale Rd 10 LN6 93 C8
Neal's Gate PE12 158 E2
Neap House Rd
Flixborough DN15 182 A7
Gunness DN15 17 E6
Neatgangs La DN19 5 A3
Neath Rd DN16 183 A1
Neaverson Rd 2 PE6 220 D7
Needham Dr PE12 159 C1
Needham Rd PE10 154 C6
Needhams Mdw LN13 76 B3
Needles The 8 PE25 206 A7
Neile Cl LN2 202 D7
Nelson Cl
5 Crowland PE6 166 F1
4 Skegness PE25 206 A7
Nelson Dr LN4 203 B2
Nelson Gdns 31 PE13 170 D1
Nelson Rd Fiskerton LN3 82 A6
Kingston upon Hull HU5 179 B7
5 Mablethorpe/Sutton on Sea LN12 64 B3
Nelson St
Gainsborough DN21 197 C6
Grimsby DN32 189 B1
Kingston upon Hull HU1 181 A5
Lincoln LN1 201 D3
Nelson Way
9 Boston PE21 208 E4
5 Grimsby DN34 190 D4
Grimsby DN34 190 C5
Nelthorpe Cl 9 DN39 12 A1
Nelthorpe St LN5 201 E1
Nene Cl
10 Ruskington NG34 108 D2
Wansford PE8 222 A3
4 Wittering PE8 172 B1
Nene Ct
4 Grantham NG31 210 E2
3 Spalding PE11 214 F5
Nene Mdws 1 PE12 160 F4
Nene Par 9 PE13 170 C1
Nene Parkway PE3 224 F1
Nene Pk 6 LN6 204 C1
Nene Rd LN1 201 E8
Nene St PE1 226 B2
Nene Way PE5 222 F2
Nenelands 8 PE12 160 F4
Neptune St
Cleethorpes DN35 192 E7
Kingston upon Hull HU1 180 D4
Neslam Rd NG34 143 C7
Ness La DN17 7 E6
Netherfield PE12 215 B2
Nethergate DN9 27 B2
Netherlands Way DN41 187 B3
Netherton Rd HU4 179 B4
Nettleham CE (Aided) Jun Sch LN2 68 C2
Nettleham Cl LN2 202 A6
Nettleham Inf Sch LN2 68 C2
Nettleham Rd
Lincoln LN2 234 C4
Scothern LN2 68 E3
Nettleholme 10 DN7 14 D4
Nettleton Dr LN6 92 E5
Nettleton Prim Sch LN7 33 A3
Nettleton Rd LN7 33 B3
Neustadt Ct 10 LN2 234 B3
Neville Ave PE11 214 F4
Neville Cl
5 Keadby with Althorpe DN17 17 D4
Neville Cl *continued*
Kingston upon Hull HU3 180 D5
Neville Cres 5 DN15 9 A5
Neville La DN7 14 A8
Neville Rd DN16 183 C2
Neville St DN35 192 D8
Neville Turner Way 1 DN37 194 D4
New Beacon Rd NG31 211 C4
New Bridge Rd HU9 181 C8
New Bridges Hospl HU9 181 D8
New Cartergate 2 DN31 191 D7
New Chapel La 8 DN37 23 F1
New Cl 3 DN33 191 C4
New Clee Sta DN31 189 D1
New Cleveland St HU8 181 A8
New Cres LN3 203 D6
New Cross Rd 3 PE9 219 C6
New Cut PE6 176 D5
New End Hemingby LN9 72 B1
5 Wainfleet All Saints PE24 102 D2
New Est
1 Little Bytham NG33 163 A8
Swinstead NG33 153 A5
New Fen Dike PE12 169 A7
New Fen Dro PE12 168 B1
New Gdn St 5 HU1 180 F7
New George St HU2 180 F7
New Gn 3 DN7 14 C6
New Hammond Beck Rd
Boston PE21 208 A3
Wyberton PE21 208 A3
New Haven Terr DN31 188 D1
New Hill NG32 119 A5
New Holland CE Methodist Prim Sch DN19 4 E2
New Holland Rd DN19 4 E1
New Holland Sta DN19 4 E3
New Ings La DN22 52 E3
New Inn La 3 DN7 14 C7
New La Girton NG23 78 D2
Great Carlton LN11 62 E3
Reedness DN14 6 E8
Tathwell LN11 61 A1
Toynton St Peter PE23 101 A5
Wansford PE8 222 C1
New Leake Prim Sch PE22 113 F7
New Mdw Dro PE7 231 D1
New Mill Field Rd DN7 14 E3
New Pk Est 1 DN7 14 D7
New Rd Blankney LN10 96 F5
Brantingham HU15 2 C8
Cleethorpes DN35 192 F6
Clipsham LE15 162 B7
1 Collyweston PE9 171 B1
Croft PE24 103 C3
Deeping St Nicholas PE6 166 D5
5 Easton on the Hill PE9 171 D3
9 Eye PE6 175 A1
Folksworth PE7 232 E6
Laceby DN37 35 A8
Langtoft PE6 164 F3
Peterborough PE1 226 B2
Quadring PE11 145 C8
Ryhall PE9 163 C1
Scunthorpe DN17 184 B6
Silk Willoughby NG34 121 A1
Spalding PE11 214 D4
Staunton NG13 117 B2
Sutton Bridge PE12 160 F5
Swinefleet DN14 6 C4
Thistleton LE15 151 D1
Wainfleet All Saints PE24 101 E2
Waltham DN37 194 E4
Worlaby DN20 10 D1
New River Dro
Cowbit PE12 156 F3
3 Spalding PE12 214 C1
New River Gate PE12 168 D8
New Roman Bank PE34 161 D3
New Row
Gonerby Hill Foot NG31 210 E7
3 Market Deeping PE6 217 D4
8 Messingham DN17 29 D7
New St
Aby with Greenfield LN13 75 B5
8 Brigg DN20 196 C3
Elsham DN20 20 E7
1 Gainsborough DN21 197 C5
Grantham NG31 211 A5
Grimsby DN31 191 E7
5 Heckington NG34 122 E2
Helpringham NG34 133 D7
6 Louth LN11 198 B5
Osbournby NG34 132 D5
Sleaford NG34 212 E4
4 Stamford PE9 219 C6
New Town 6 PE9 171 D3
New Trent St DN17 16 E6
New Waltham Prim Sch DN36 195 C7
New Wlk HU14 3 A4
New York Prim Sch LN4 111 C4
New York Rd LN4 110 F6
Newark & Nottinghamshire Agricultural Society's Showground★ NG24 104 C7
Newark Air Mus★ NG24 104 D6
Newark Ave PE1 226 C6
Newark Hill
Foston NG23 117 F1
Great Gonerby NG31 129 D6
Newark Hill CP Sch PE1 226 D6
Newark Hospl NG24 104 A4
Newark La NG32 119 C4
Newark N Gate Sta NG24 104 A5
Newark Rd
Barnby in the Willows NG24 104 E3
Bassingham LN5 92 E2
Fenton LN1 65 D4
Leadenham LN5 106 C3
Lincoln LN6 204 F3
Newark-on-Trent NG24 104 C5
Norton Disney LN6 91 F2
Peterborough PE1 226 E2
Stapleford LN6 105 B8
Swinderby LN6 92 A4
Newark Rd Ind Est PE1 226 E4
Newbey Cl PE3 225 B3
Newbigg 1 Crowle DN17 16 C8
Westwoodside DN9 27 B2
Newbolt Ave 2 DN17 184 D7
Newbolt Cl 1 LN7 33 A3
Newborn Ave DN15 182 E4
Newborn Cl PE2 231 E5
Newborough Rd PE4 174 E1
Newboults La 2 PE9 219 A5
Newbridge Hill LN11 198 C6
Newbridge La LN11 49 E5
Newbury Ave DN37 188 A1
Newbury Gr 1 DN34 190 E4
Newbury Rd 15 NG24 104 C5
Newbury Terr DN37 188 A1
Newby Rd DN31 191 C7
Newcastle Dr PE2 230 D6
Newcastle Rd 4 NG31 210 D5
Newcomb Ct 2 NG34 212 B7
Newcombe Way PE2 229 D2
Newcot La LN4 81 F4
Newdike Gate PE12 158 C5
Newdown Rd DN17 184 D3
Newfield Cl 10 DN3 14 A4
Newfield Dr LN4 109 F3
Newfield Rd NG34 212 C5
Newfields PE13 169 D1
Newgate La NG31 130 D4
Newgate Rd PE13 169 F6
Newgates 3 PE9 219 C5
Newhall Rd
13 Kirk Sandall DN3 14 A2
10 Kirk Sandall DN3 14 A2
Newham La PE22 112 A1
Newham Rd 2 PE9 219 A7
Newhaven Dr LN5 205 D3
Newington Ave HU4 179 E5
Newington Prim Sch HU3 180 A4
Newington St HU3 179 F4
Newland LN1 234 A2
Newland Ave DN15 182 E2
Newland Dr DN15 182 D3
Newland St W 6 LN1 234 A2
Newland View 17 DN9 27 E6
Newland Wlk DN15 182 E3
Newlands DN21 197 E5
Newlands Pk DN36 193 B1
Newlands Rd
2 Haconby PE10 154 D8
Parson Drove PE13 177 D7
Surfleet PE11 145 F4
Newlyn Cl
4 Kingston upon Hull HU13 179 A2
3 New Waltham DN36 195 C7
Newman Cl 19 PE8 172 B1
Newmarket LN11 198 C4
Newmarket Cl PE1 226 B6
Newmarket St 2 DN32 191 F8
Newnham Cres DN16 185 A4
Newport LN2 234 B4
Newport Ave NG31 210 D4
Newport Cl 4 HU3 180 D5
Newport Cres 2 LN5 93 F7
Newport Ct 1 LN1 234 B4
Newport Dr DN15 9 A6
Newport St 8 DN18 3 F1
Newsham Dr DN34 191 A7
Newsham Garth HU4 179 B5
Newsham La DN39 22 D8
Newstead Ave
Cherry Willingham/Reepham LN3 203 E5
Holton le Clay DN36 195 E2
Newstead Cl PE6 175 A2
Newstead Rd
Cleethorpes DN35 192 E4
2 Mablethorpe/Sutton on Sea LN12 64 C3
Ryhall PE9 163 D1
Newstead St HU5 180 A8
Newton Bar NG34 132 A3
Newton Cl
8 Metheringham LN4 95 C4
Swinderby LN6 92 A5
5 Wragby LN8 70 D4
Newton Ct 6 NG33 151 E7
Newton La Binbrook LN8 47 D5
15 Ruskington NG34 108 E2
Newton Marsh La DN36 36 F6
Newton Pk 10 NG23 117 D3
Newton Rd DN16 185 E6
Newton St
5 Grantham NG31 211 B4

Newton St *continued*
3 Kingston upon Hull HU3 .....180 B4
Lincoln LN5 .....234 B1
Newark-on-Trent NG24 ...104 A4
Newton Way
5 Colsterworth NG33 ...151 D7
Sleaford NG34 .....212 D5
Newton-on-Trent CE Sch LN1 .....65 C1
Newtown
8 Spilsby PE23 .....101 A8
Stamford PE9 .....219 D5
Newtown Sq HU9 .....181 E7
Nichol Hill 2 LN11 .....198 B5
Nicholas Ct 26 DN18 .....10 E8
Nicholas Taylor Gdns 1 PE3 .....224 F3
Nicholls Ave PE3 .....225 E3
Nicholson Rd
3 Healing DN41 .....24 A5
Immingham DN40 .....12 E4
Nicholson St 8 DN35 ..192 F5
Nicholson Way 7 DN9 ..27 D7
Nicolette Way 10 PE11 ..214 B5
Nicolgate La DN20 ....196 D4
Nicolson Dr 18 DN18 ....10 F8
Nidd's La PE20 .....136 E4
Nightingale Cl 3 DN15 .182 D5
Nightingale Cres 1 LN6 .....204 E8
Nightingale Ct PE4 ....221 E2
Nightingale Dr PE7 ...233 D6
Nightingales 13 PE6 ...217 C5
Nightleys Rd DN22 .....65 B5
Ninescores La DN9 .....26 B4
Ninth Ave
3 Fixborough Ind Est DN15 .8 A1
Grantham NG31 .....211 F5
Nipcut Rd PE6 .....175 C2
Nocton Com Sch LN4 ...95 C7
Nocton Dr LN2 .....201 F8
Nocton Fen La LN4 .....83 A1
Nocton Rd
Potter Hanworth LN4 .....95 B8
7 Potterhanworth LN4 ....82 B1
Noel St DN21 .....197 C6
Nook The
Croxton Kerrial NG32 ....138 D3
7 Easton on the Hill PE9 .171 D3
4 Helpston PE6 .....173 C4
Sproxton LE14 .....150 C7
Nookin The 1 LN5 .....106 E5
Nooking La DN37 .....23 D2
Nooking The DN9 .....27 C3
Nookings Dr 3 DN20 ....31 A5
Norbeck La LN2 .....68 C6
Norburn
2 Peterborough PE3 ....220 F1
Peterborough PE3 .....225 B8
Norfolk Ave DN15 .....8 B4
Norfolk Bank La HU15 ...1 F8
Norfolk Cl 1 LN8 .....47 B6
Norfolk Cres
Bracebridge Heath LN4 ...205 F4
1 Scampton Airfield LN1 ..67 E5
Norfolk La DN35 .....192 E7
Norfolk Pl 4 PE21 .....208 F6
Norfolk Sq 5 PE9 .....219 B6
Norfolk St Boston PE21 .208 F6
Kingston upon Hull HU2 ..180 E7
Lincoln LN1 .....201 C4
Peterborough PE1 .....225 F4
Norfolk St Ind Est PE21 .....208 F7
Norland Ave HU4 .....179 C6
Norman Ave 5 PE21 ...208 F5
Norman Cl
9 Barton-upon-Humber DN18 .....10 F8
30 Metheringham LN4 .....95 C4
Norman Cres 1 DN17 ..184 F8
Norman Dr 7 DN7 .....14 D3
Norman Mews 3 PE10 .213 D5
Norman Rd
Grimsby DN34 .....191 B7
Hatfield DN7 .....14 D3
Peterborough PE1 .....226 C4
Norman St 1 LN5 .....234 B1
Normanby Cliff Rd LN8 .55 D7
Normanby Hall Ctry Pk★ DN15 .....8 C3
Normanby Prim Sch LN8 .....55 E7
Normanby Rd
Burton upon Stather DN15 ..8 C3
Nettleton LN7 .....33 B2
3 Owmby LN8 .....55 F6
Scunthorpe DN15 .....183 A5
Stow DN21 .....53 F1
Normanby Rise LN8 ....45 E5
Normandy Rd DN35 ...192 D5
Normanton La NG13 ...128 A6
Normanton Rd
1 Crowland PE6 .....166 F1
Peterborough PE1 .....226 D7
Normanton Rise HU4 ..179 C7
Nornabell St 1 HU8 ...181 C8
Norris Cl 10 NG34 .....122 D3
Norris St LN5 .....201 F1
Norsefield Ave DN37 ..194 E5
North Ave PE10 .....153 D6
North Axholme Comp Sch DN17 .....16 D7
North Bank
Crowland PE6 .....166 E1
Thorney PE6 .....227 D1
North Bank Rd 4 PE1 ..226 D3
North Beck La PE23 ....87 E1
North Bracing PE25 ...206 E3
North Carr La DN20 .....9 F3
North Carr Rd
Misterton DN10 .....39 F7
Scotter DN17 .....28 E5
West Stockwith DN10 .....40 B6
North Church Side 12 HU1 .....180 F6
North Cliff Rd DN21 ....30 C2
North Clifton Sch NG23 .78 C6
North Coates Rd DN36 ..37 A4
North Cockerington CE Prim Sch LN11 .....50 A1
North Cotes CE (Controlled) Prim Sch DN36 .....37 B3
North Cres 7 NG13 ....128 A5
North Cswy LN4 .....82 D4
North Ct 10 LN2 .....68 C2
North Cty Prim Sch DN21 .....197 B6
North Dales Rd LN4 ....82 A5
North Dr
2 Ancaster NG32 .....120 A3
Balderton NG24 .....104 C1
Kingston upon Hull HU10 .....178 E6
RAF Cranwell NG34 .....107 D1
Swanland HU14 .....3 B7
North Dro Bicker PE20 ..134 E6
Deeping St Nicholas PE11 .....155 F1
Helpringham NG34 .....133 E7
Lutton PE12 .....148 D1
Quadring PE11 .....144 C8
Swaton NG34 .....133 E4
North Eastern Rd DN8 ..15 A8
North Elkington La LN11 .....48 E1
North End 5 Goxhill DN19 12 A8
South Ferriby DN18 .....10 A8
Wisbech PE13 .....170 C1
North End Cres 9 DN36 .36 D4
North End La
2 Fulbeck NG32 .....106 C1
Saltfleetby LN11 .....62 F8
South Cockerington LN11 ..50 F1
South Kelsey LN7 .....32 A2
Sturton Le Steeple DN22 ...52 E4
North End Rd 7 DN36 ...36 D4
North Farm Rd DN17 ..184 D3
North Fen Dro PE20 ..134 E4
North Fen Rd
3 Glinton PE6 .....220 C8
Helpringham NG34 .....133 D7
North Field Rd PE6 ....217 B7
North Foreland Dr 3 PE25 .....206 D8
North Forty Foot Bank PE21 .....208 A6
North Gate
Gosberton PE11 .....145 A6
Newark-on-Trent NG24 ...104 A5
Pinchbeck PE11 .....144 E1
Sleaford NG34 .....212 D5
North Halls 1 LN8 .....47 C5
North Heath La NG32 ..106 D1
North Holme 8 DN36 ...36 D4
North Holme Rd LN11 .198 B7
North Ing Dro PE11 ...134 C4
North Ings La LN13 .....77 A5
North Ings Rd DN7 .....14 E5
North Intake La DN9 ....40 C8
North Kelsey Rd LN7 ...33 A4
North Kesteven Sch LN6 .....204 D1
North Kesteven Sports Ctr LN6 .....204 D1
North Kyme Cty Prim Sch LN4 .....109 E3
North La Coningsby LN4 .110 E8
Marshchapel DN36 .....37 C2
2 Navenby/Wellingore LN5 .....107 A8
Reepham LN3 .....68 F1
Swaby LN13 .....74 E4
North Leverton CE Sch DN22 .....52 B1
North Leys Rd DN22 ....52 E1
North Lincoln Rd DN16 .....183 F2
North Lincolnshire Coll
Lincoln LN2 .....234 C3
Louth LN11 .....198 D6
North Lincolnshire Mus & Art Gall★ DN15 .....183 A2
North Lindsey Coll DN17 .....184 E8
North Marsh Rd DN21 .197 C6
North Moor Dr 2 DN10 ..39 F3
North Moor La
Martin LN4 .....96 B3
Messingham DN17 .....29 B8
North Moor Rd
Scotter DN17 .....29 C5
Walkeringham DN10 .....39 F3
North Moss La DN41 ...187 B1
North Par
Gainsborough DN21 .....197 F4
Grantham NG31 .....211 A6
Holbeach PE12 .....215 E3
Lincoln LN1 .....234 A3
Scunthorpe DN16 .....185 D6
Skegness PE25 .....206 D3
4 Sleaford NG34 .....212 D7
North Prom DN35 .....192 E7
North Quay DN31 .....189 C3
North Ramper DN21 ....44 A7
North Rd Bourne PE10 ..213 D8
Bratoft PE24 .....102 B8
7 Cranwell NG34 .....107 F1
Gedney Hill PE12 .....168 D4
1 Keadby with Althorpe DN17 .....17 C6
Kingston upon Hull HU4 ..179 E4
Leadenham LN5 .....106 D3
Mablethorpe & Sutton LN12 .....64 B1
Sturton Le Steeple DN22 ...52 B4
Tattershall Thorpe LN4 .....97 F3
Tetford LN9 .....73 F1
Tydd St Mary PE13 .....160 B2
North Scaffold La NG23 .....91 D3
North Scarle Prim Sch LN6 .....78 E2
North Scarle Rd NG23 ..91 F8
North Sea La DN35 ....193 A1
North Shore Rd PE25 ..206 D6
North Somercotes CE (Controlled) Prim Sch LN11 .....50 F7
North St
7 Barrow upon Humber DN19 .....11 D8
1 Barrow upon Humber DN19 .....11 D8
2 Boston PE21 .....208 F6
Bourne PE10 .....213 D5
Caistor LN7 .....33 B4
Cleethorpes DN35 .....192 F6
3 Crowland PE6 .....166 E1
9 Crowle DN17 .....16 D8
Digby LN4 .....108 E6
Folksworth PE7 .....233 A1
Gainsborough DN21 .....197 C5
7 Grantham NG31 .....211 A5
Horncastle LN9 .....199 C4
Kingston upon Hull HU10 .....178 E6
Middle Rasen LN8 .....57 B8
Morton DN21 .....197 C8
8 Nettleham LN2 .....68 C2
Osbournby NG34 .....132 C5
Owston Ferry DN9 .....28 B3
Peterborough PE1 .....226 A2
Roxby cum Risby DN15 .....9 A4
Scunthorpe DN15 .....183 B4
Stamford PE9 .....219 B5
Sturton Le Steeple DN22 ...52 B3
Thimbleby LN9 .....85 B5
West Butterwick DN17 ....17 D1
West/East Butterwick DN17 .....28 D8
Winterton DN15 .....9 B6
North Terr PE1 .....226 E7
North Thoresby Prim Sch DN36 .....36 A1
North Walls HU1 .....181 A6
North Warren Rd DN21 .....197 B6
North Way
6 Lincoln LN6 .....204 D2
Marshchapel DN36 .....37 B2
North Witham Bank LN1 .....234 A2
North Witham Rd NG33 .....151 D3
Northam Cl PE6 .....175 B3
Northampton Rd DN16 .....183 C1
Northborough Cty Prim Sch PE6 .....173 F6
Northcliffe Rd NG31 ...211 A7
Northcroft 4 LN1 .....66 D3
Northcroft La NG23 .....91 C5
North-dale Ct 4 DN21 ..30 B2
Northdale Pk 1 HU14 .....3 B7
Northern Ave DN20 ....196 C5
Northern Rd NG24 ....104 A5
Northern's Cl NG33 ....151 D5
Northey Rd PE6 .....227 C2
Northferry La 2 DN9 ...16 D1
Northfield HU14 .....3 B7
Northfield Ave
Kingston upon Hull HU13 .....178 E3
3 Sudbrooke LN2 .....68 F3
Northfield Cl
1 Scunthorpe DN16 ....185 C6
11 Tetney DN36 .....36 D4
West Butterwick DN17 ....17 D1
Northfield La
Amcotts DN17 .....7 E2
North Clifton NG23 .....78 D7
Thornton Curtis DN39 .....11 D5
Willoughton DN21 .....42 C4
Northfield Rd
Ashby with Scremby PE23 ..88 D1
Kingston upon Hull HU3 ..179 F6
Messingham DN17 .....185 A1
North Leverton with Habblesthorpe DN22 ....52 D1
Peterborough PE1 .....225 F7
4 Ruskington NG34 .....108 E2
Sleaford NG34 .....212 A2
Northfield Rise 1 LN1 ..66 C2
Northfields
Bourne PE10 .....213 D7
Stamford PE9 .....219 C6
Northgate
Kingston upon Hull HU13 .....178 E2
Lincoln LN2 .....234 B4
Louth LN11 .....198 B5
Northgate La LN11 .....62 B7
Northgate Sports Hall NG34 .....212 D5
Northing La LN2 .....68 F5
Northings The 1 NG32 .210 B4
Northlands Ave 3 DN15 ..9 A5
Northlands La PE22 ...113 A4
Northlands Rd
Glentworth DN21 .....54 E6
Winterton DN15 .....9 A6
Northlands Rd S 10 DN15 .9 A5
Northminster PE1 .....226 A3
Northmoor Rd DN17 .....6 C1
Northolme
Gainsborough DN21 .....197 D5
Sutton St Edmund PE12 ...168 E5
Northolme Circ 2 HU13 .....178 E2
Northolme Cres
Kingston upon Hull HU13 .....178 E2
4 Scunthorpe DN15 .....182 F3
Northolme Rd HU13 ...178 E2
Northon's La PE12 ....215 C3
Northorpe Cl LN6 .....204 F7
Northorpe La PE10 ....164 C8
Northorpe Rd
Donington PE11 .....134 D3
Halton Holegate PE23 ....101 B8
Scotton DN21 .....29 D1
North's La DN37 .....34 D8
Northside 2 DN9 .....27 C2
Northside La DN22 .....52 C1
Northumberland Ave
13 Scampton Airfield LN1 ..67 E5
6 Stamford PE9 .....219 A6
Northumberland Cl DN34 .....191 B6
Northumbria Rd NG34 .212 B2
Northway 3 LN11 .....49 B8
Northwood Dr
Hessle HU13 .....178 B3
Sleaford NG34 .....212 C6
Norton Disney Rd LN5 ..92 D1
Norton Gr HU4 .....179 D4
Norton La
Bishop Norton LN8 .....43 C2
Thurlby LN6 .....92 C4
Norton Rd
Peterborough PE1 .....225 F6
Scunthorpe DN16 .....185 B5
Stapleford LN6 .....105 C8
Norton St NG31 .....211 A3
Norwell La NG23 .....91 E1
Norwich Ave DN34 ....191 A4
Norwich Cl
Heighington/Washingborough LN4 .....203 E1
3 Sleaford NG34 .....212 C7
Norwich Dr LN4 .....81 A2
Norwich Rd PE13 .....170 E1
Norwich Way 7 NG31 ..210 E5
Norwood Ave 3 DN15 ..182 F2
Norwood Cl 3 HU10 ...178 E7
Norwood Cty Prim Sch PE4 .....221 C3
Norwood La
Borough Fen PE6 .....174 E1
Peterborough PE4 .....221 F2
Norwood Rd
7 Hatfield DN7 .....14 C5
5 Skegness PE25 .....103 E4
4 Skegness PE25 .....103 E4
Norwood St HU3 .....180 C7
Nostell Rd DN16 .....183 D1
Nottingham Rd 1 NG13 128 A5
Nottingham Terr 5 LN2 .....234 C3
Nottingham Way PE1 ..226 C6
Nowells La 6 PE10 ....213 D5
Nuffield Cl 6 DN16 ....185 B4
Nunburnholme Ave 5 HU14 .....3 A4
Nunburnholme Pk HU5 .....179 B7
Nuns Rd DN17 .....184 F6
Nunsthorpe Com Sch DN33 .....191 B4
Nunthorpe Cl 36 DN7 ....14 D4
Nursery Cl
4 Barton-upon-Humber DN18 .....3 F1
Peterborough PE1 .....226 A4
10 Saxilby LN1 .....66 D2
Scunthorpe DN17 .....184 F3
Nursery Ct 15 Brough HU15 2 C5
Sleaford NG34 .....212 D2
Nursery Dr PE13 .....170 E2
Nursery Gdns 7 DN36 ..195 D2
Nursery Gr LN2 .....202 A6
Nursery La
Belvoir NG32 .....138 C6
Peterborough PE1 .....226 D2
Nursery Rd
Boston PE21 .....209 B2
Cranwell & Byard's Leap NG34 .....120 C8
Nursery St 2 LN8 .....57 D7
Nurses La
Skellingthorpe LN6 .....200 A5
4 Wymondham LE14 .....150 C1
Nut La PE22 .....114 C1
Nutfields Gr 7 DN7 .....14 C6
Nutwood View 4 DN16 .185 D4

O

Oak Ave 13 Brough HU15 ...2 C6
Oak Ave *continued*
3 Grimsby DN32 .....191 E4
5 Scawby DN20 .....30 F8
11 Welton/Dunholme LN2 ..68 E6
Oak Cl
8 Ingoldmells PE25 .....90 D3
Louth LN11 .....198 E4
14 Sudbrooke LN2 .....68 F2
5 Woodhall Spa LN10 ....97 E6
Oak Cres Boston PE21 ..208 E7
Bourne PE10 .....213 B6
Cherry Willingham/Reepham LN3 .....203 D5
Oak Ct 1 PE11 .....214 E3
Oak Dr HU5 .....179 B7
Oak Gr
3 Barrow upon Humber DN19 .....11 C7
6 Market Deeping PE6 ..217 B6
Oak Hill LN4 .....203 B2
Oak House La PE22 ...126 C4
Oak Rd Glinton PE6 .....220 B8
1 Healing DN41 .....24 A5
Scunthorpe DN16 .....185 B7
Sleaford NG34 .....212 D2
Stamford PE9 .....218 D7
Oak Tree Ave DN21 ....197 F6
Oak Tree Cl
3 Long Bennington NG23 117 D3
7 Market Rasen LN8 .....57 D7
Oak View
13 Dunholme LN2 .....68 E6
Peterborough PE3 .....224 F2
Oak Way
Cleethorpes DN35 .....192 D2
3 Heckington NG34 .....122 D3
Oakdale Ave
3 Kingston upon Hull HU10 .....178 E8
Peterborough PE2 .....231 D4
Oakdale Cl 4 NG31 ....211 A8
Oakdale CP Sch PE7 ..231 C4
Oakfield 16 LN1 .....66 D2
Oakfield Cl 2 DN20 ....196 E3
Oakfield St LN2 .....202 B3
Oakford Cl DN17 .....184 D8
Oakham Ave 5 LN12 ....64 A3
Oakham Cl NG31 .....210 E6
Oakhurst Cl NG31 .....211 D2
Oakland Ave 39 DN7 ....14 D4
Oakland Cl 3 LN1 .....201 D7
Oakland Way 13 PE11 ...145 C1
Oaklands
3 Beckingham DN10 .....40 A1
8 Collingham NG23 .....91 D4
5 Woodhall Spa LN10 ....97 D5
Oaklands Dr
Kingston upon Hull HU13 .....178 D3
4 Wisbech PE13 .....170 E1
Oaklands Rd DN40 ....186 C5
Oaklands The 6 LN8 ....70 D4
Oakleaf Rd PE1 .....226 C6
Oakleigh DN16 .....185 C3
Oakleigh Dr
Canwick LN1 .....201 C6
Peterborough PE2 .....230 C6
Oakleigh Rd NG31 ....210 C3
Oakley Dr PE11 .....214 E6
Oakley Pl PE12 .....147 F2
Oakroyd Cres 22 PE13 ...170 D1
Oaks La DN10 .....39 F2
Oaks The
15 Nettleham LN2 .....68 D2
1 Scothern LN2 .....68 F3
Oaktree Cl 3 PE11 .....145 B7
Oakwood Ave 4 LN6 ....204 C8
Oakwood Cl HU10 .....179 A7
Oakwood Dr DN37 .....190 C7
Oakwood Glade PE12 ...215 C3
Oakwood Rise 2 DN16 .185 B4
Oasby Rd NG32 .....131 C7
Oatfield Way NG34 ....122 D2
Oban Cl 7 PE9 .....218 E6
Oban Ct 6 DN40 .....186 C3
Obthorpe La PE10 .....164 C7
Occupation La
Anderby PE24 .....77 C3
Carrington PE22 .....99 C1
6 North Kelsey LN7 .....32 A4
Swanland HU14 .....3 B8
Occupation Rd
Great Gonerby NG32 .....129 C6
Lincoln LN1 .....234 A4
Peterborough PE1 .....225 E6
Ocean Ave PE25 .....206 D1
Ocean Bvd HU9 .....181 B6
Octagon Dr 14 PE13 ....170 C1
Octavia Cl 23 PE13 ....170 E1
Odecroft PE3 .....225 C7
Ogilvy Dr DN17 .....184 F3
O'hanlon Ave DN20 ....196 D3
Old Annandale Rd HU10 .....178 C8
Old Barracks The NG31 .....211 C4
Old Black Dro NG34 ...109 D1
Old Boston Rd LN4 ...207 D3
Old Bowling Gn 4 LN13 .75 F2
Old Brickkiln La LN5 ...92 F2
Old Brumby St DN16 ...185 A8
Old Carpenter's Yd 1 DN7 .....14 B6
Old Chapel La
2 Burgh le Marsh PE24 ..102 E7

Old Chapel La *continued*
9 Laceby DN37 ... 23 F1
Old Chapel Rd LN6 ... 200 A4
Old Church La 1 PE23 . 101 D7
Old Church Rd PE24 ... 90 D4
Old Clee Infants & Jun Sch DN32 ... 192 B6
Old Courts Rd 2 DN20 . 196 C3
Old Crosby DN15 ... 183 A5
Old Dairy 11 DN19 ... 11 D8
Old Epworth Rd (East) 1 DN7 ... 14 F4
Old Farm Ct 4 DN37 ... 194 C4
Old Fen Bank
Wainfleet All Saints PE24 ... 101 F2
Wainfleet St Mary PE24 .. 102 A1
Old Fen Dike
Gedney PE12 ... 158 F1
Sutton St James PE12 ... 169 B8
Old Fen La
Coningsby LN4 ... 207 E1
Pinchbeck PE11 ... 145 A1
Old Fen Rd PE22 ... 115 A8
Old Fendike Rd PE12 .. 157 B3
Old Field La DN7 ... 14 A5
Old Fleet DN37 ... 190 C6
Old Forge Rd 8 DN10 ... 39 F5
Old Forty Foot Bank NG34 ... 123 C1
Old Great N Rd
Stamford PE9 ... 218 C8
Thorney PE8 ... 228 B7
Wansford PE8 ... 222 C2
Wothorpe PE9 ... 219 C2
Old Hall Gdns 12 NG24 . 104 C5
Old Hall La 6 PE11 ... 145 D2
Old Hall Spinney NG32 ... 119 C2
Old Hammond Beck Rd PE21 ... 208 A2
Old Haxey Rd DN10 ... 39 F6
Old Hill The NG32 ... 138 C6
Old Hundred La PE12 .. 167 F2
Old Inn La PE12 ... 146 E7
Old Ironside Rd DN16 . 183 D3
Old Knarr Fen Dro PE6 ... 176 C2
Old La DN14 ... 6 F7
Old Leake Prim Sch PE22 ... 114 A1
Old Leicester Rd PE8 .. 222 A3
Old Leys La DN21 ... 43 A3
Old Lincoln Rd NG32 .. 119 B7
Old Lynn Rd 2 PE13 .. 170 E1
Old Main Rd
2 Barnetby Le Beck DN37 . 35 B6
Fosdyke PE20 ... 146 D8
Irby DN37 ... 34 D7
Old Leake PE22 ... 114 B1
Scamblesby LN11 ... 72 F5
Old Mill La
10 Broughton DN20 ... 19 E3
Grimoldby LN11 ... 62 B6
Whitton DN15 ... 1 E3
Wrawby DN20 ... 196 F7
Old Mill Pk LN11 ... 198 C6
Old Mkt Ave
4 Hundleby PE23 ... 87 F1
12 Spilsby PE23 ... 87 F1
Spilsby PE23 ... 100 F8
Old Mkt Pl 5 DN31 ... 191 D7
Old N Rd PE8 ... 222 A3
Old Orch NG32 ... 210 A5
Old Pl 3 NG34 ... 212 F4
Old Plumtree La 3 DN36 36 B1
Old Pond Cl
7 Birchwood LN6 ... 200 D1
Birchwood LN6 ... 204 D8
Old Pond La PE5 ... 223 E2
Old Pond Pl 20 HU14 ... 3 A4
Old Post La NG33 ... 151 D6
Old Post Office La
8 Barnetby le Wold DN38 . 21 B4
Butterwick PE22 ... 126 E4
4 South Ferriby DN18 ... 10 A7
Old Rd Grimsby DN37 .. 190 C8
Healing DN37 ... 24 B5
Old Rectory Dr
1 Tallington PE9 ... 172 F7
Wansford PE8 ... 222 A6
Old Rectory Gdns DN16 ... 185 A6
Old Rectory The* DN9 .. 27 E6
Old Roman Bank
3 Skegness PE25 ... 206 D6
Terrington St Clement PE34 ... 161 E3
Old S Eau Bank PE12 .. 168 A1
Old Sch CE (Controlled) The NG32 ... 119 A5
Old Sch Dr 14 DN20 ... 30 F5
Old Sch La
2 Cranwell NG34 ... 120 F8
Donington on Bain LN11 .. 59 E2
5 Fishtoft PE21 ... 126 C1
2 North Kelsey LN7 ... 32 A4
Scunthorpe DN16 ... 185 B3
Old Sch Mews 12 PE23 .. 88 A1
Old Sch Yd 17 DN21 ... 30 B1
Old Showfields DN21 .. 197 D6
Old Sluice Rd PE12 ... 215 B8
Old Smithy Ct 1 LN4 .. 207 D4
Old Sta Yd NG13 ... 128 B6
Old Thorne Rd DN7 ... 14 E4
Old Trent Rd DN21 ... 197 A5
Old Upper Ings La DN22 ... 52 D3
Old Vicarage La
12 Lutton PE12 ... 160 A8
Lutton PE12 ... 216 C8
Old Vicarage Pk 2 DN20 . 30 E8
Old Village St DN15 ... 17 E6
Old Wainfleet Rd 1 PE25 ... 206 B3
Old Warp La 11 DN18 ... 10 A7
Old Wharf Rd 9 NG31 .. 211 A4
Old Wood 1 LN6 ... 200 C1
Oldbrook PE3 ... 220 E1
Olde Curiosity Mus* LN12 ... 64 C3
Oldfield Cl
9 Barnby Dun DN3 ... 14 A4
1 Stainforth DN7 ... 14 B6
Oldfield Cres 16 DN7 ... 14 C6
Oldfield La PE22 ... 127 C6
Oldfield Rd 20 DN8 ... 15 B7
Oldham Dr 8 PE11 ... 145 C1
Oldlane Gate DN14 ... 6 D4
Olive Rd PE1 ... 226 C7
Oliver Ct 1 DN31 ... 191 D8
Oliver Quibell Cty Infants Sch NG24 ... 104 A3
Oliver Rd 16 NG23 ... 117 D3
Oliver St DN35 ... 192 D8
Olivier Ct HU4 ... 179 E3
Ollard Ave PE13 ... 170 D1
Omega Bvd DN8 ... 14 F8
On Hill 17 HU14 ... 3 B7
Ontario Rd DN17 ... 184 E3
Onyx Gr 2 HU3 ... 180 A4
Oole Rd DN35 ... 192 F6
Oosterbeek Cl 5 PE10 . 213 E7
Opportune Rd 25 PE13 . 170 D1
Orangawood Cl 7 NG31 ... 210 F8
Orange Row 3 PE34 ... 161 F3
Orange Row Rd 1 PE34 161 F3
Orb La DN15 ... 183 A7
Orby Bank PE24 ... 89 D3
Orby Gr DN33 ... 191 A3
Orby Holme Field La PE24 ... 89 D3
Orby Rd
Addlethorpe PE24 ... 90 B4
Burgh Le Marsh PE24 ... 89 D1
Orchard Ave 8 DN21 ... 29 C3
Orchard Cl
4 Barrow upon Humber DN19 ... 11 C7
23 Barton-upon-Humber DN18 ... 10 F8
4 Blyton DN21 ... 41 C5
4 Bourne PE10 ... 213 C6
6 Burringham DN17 ... 17 D4
9 Burton-upon-Stather DN15 ... 8 B5
Cherry Willingham/Reepham LN3 ... 203 D5
11 Donington PE11 ... 134 F2
4 Gonerby Hill Foot NG31 ... 210 E8
Great Hale NG34 ... 122 E1
2 Hatfield DN7 ... 14 C3
6 Helpringham NG34 ... 133 D7
Kingston upon Hull HU10 ... 178 F7
1 Kirton in Lindsey DN21 .. 30 B2
Louth LN11 ... 198 C7
2 Mablethorpe/Sutton on Sea LN12 ... 64 A3
4 Market Deeping PE6 .. 217 D4
12 Messingham DN17 ... 29 D7
25 Metheringham LN4 ... 95 C4
2 Morton PE10 ... 154 C7
4 Moulton PE12 ... 157 F6
Peterborough PE3 ... 225 D3
9 Pinchbeck PE11 ... 156 E8
3 Scothern LN2 ... 68 F4
5 Scunthorpe DN16 ... 185 B6
2 Sleaford NG34 ... 212 F4
7 Welton/Dunholme LN2 .. 68 D6
Whaplode PE12 ... 215 A7
Orchard Croft
4 Epworth DN9 ... 27 D7
5 Grimsby DN33 ... 194 E7
Orchard Ct
1 Thorney PE6 ... 175 F3
3 Waltham DN37 ... 194 D4
Orchard Dr
7 Burton-upon-Stather DN15 ... 8 B5
3 Gunness DN15 ... 17 E6
3 Hatfield DN7 ... 14 C3
12 Heckington NG34 ... 122 E2
Kingston upon Hull HU13 ... 178 E1
2 Rampton DN22 ... 65 A5
Winteringham DN15 ... 2 B1
Orchard Garth 16 LN5 ... 93 E8
Orchard Gr
Boston PE21 ... 209 B6
1 Hatfield DN7 ... 14 D5
Misterton DN10 ... 40 A4
Orchard La 12 LN1 ... 66 D2
Orchard Mews PE2 ... 230 F8
Orchard Pk 4 LN11 ... 62 C6
Orchard Rd
Barnack PE9 ... 172 E3
5 Fiskerton LN3 ... 82 A7
Kingston upon Hull HU4 .. 179 B5
4 Stamford PE9 ... 219 B5
Orchard Sch NG24 ... 104 B3
Orchard St
Boston PE21 ... 208 D6
Lincoln LN1 ... 234 A2
Peterborough PE2 ... 230 F7
2 Spalding PE11 ... 214 D3
22 Thorne/Moorends DN8 . 15 A8
Orchard The
Market Deeping PE6 ... 217 B5
New Waltham DN36 ... 195 C6
Peterborough PE4 ... 221 A3
Washingborough LN4 ... 203 A2
Orchard Way
4 Coningsby LN4 ... 207 C4
5 Cowbit PE12 ... 167 B8
Easton on the Hill PE9 ... 171 C3
1 Mablethorpe/Sutton on Sea LN12 ... 64 A3
3 Market Rasen LN8 ... 57 E8
6 Nettleham LN2 ... 68 D2
Orchards The
8 Middle Rasen LN8 ... 57 B8
Peterborough PE2 ... 229 F4
Orchid Cl PE7 ... 233 F7
Orchid Rd LN5 ... 205 C2
Orchid Rise DN15 ... 182 F2
Ordoyno Gr 4 NG24 .. 104 C5
Ore Blending Rd DN16 .. 19 A4
Orford Rd LN8 ... 47 B5
Oribi Cl HU4 ... 179 C2
Oriole Rd DN17 ... 184 E6
Orion Cl 8 HU3 ... 180 B5
Orion Way 4 DN34 ... 190 D4
Orkney Pl DN40 ... 186 C2
Orme La LN11 ... 198 C6
Orme Rd PE3 ... 225 D4
Ormsby Cl DN35 ... 192 D3
Ormsby Rd DN17 ... 184 E5
Ormsby Ring LN11 ... 74 C1
Orton Ave PE2 ... 230 E7
Orton Brick Works PE7 ... 233 B8
Orton Longueville Sch PE2 ... 230 A5
Orton Matley Prim Sch PE2 ... 229 E5
Orton Mere PE2 ... 230 B7
Orton Parkway PE2 ... 229 D4
Orton Wistow Prim Sch PE2 ... 229 C6
Orwell Gr PE4 ... 221 D1
Orwell St DN31 ... 189 C1
Osborn Way 9 NG34 ... 122 D3
Osborne Cl 3 LN1 ... 201 E6
Osborne Dr DN36 ... 195 D1
Osborne Pk 1 PE13 ... 170 C2
Osborne Rd
Immingham DN41 ... 187 B2
Wisbech PE13 ... 170 C2
Osborne St
1 Cleethorpes DN35 ... 192 F6
Grimsby DN31 ... 191 D7
Kingston upon Hull HU1 .. 180 E6
Osbournby Prim Sch NG34 ... 132 C5
Osbourne Way 7 PE6 .. 217 A5
Ose 3 PE25 ... 206 B6
Oseby La NG34 ... 133 A1
Osgodby Prim Sch LN8 . 45 A3
Osgodby Rd LN8 ... 44 E5
Osier Rd PE11 ... 214 E5
Oslear Cres DN35 ... 192 E5
Oslear's La LN11 ... 73 D5
Osprey PE2 ... 229 F2
Osprey Cl 5 NG34 ... 212 B3
Oster Fen La NG23 ... 104 F1
Ostler Cl 8 NG31 ... 210 F8
Ostler Dr PE10 ... 213 B4
Ostler's La DN18 ... 10 A5
Oswald Rd DN15 ... 183 A3
Oswin Cl 1 NG34 ... 212 C2
Otby La LN8 ... 46 A3
Ottawa Rd DN17 ... 184 E4
Otter Ave 11 LN1 ... 66 D2
Otterbrook PE2 ... 229 D5
Otterburn St 6 HU3 ... 180 A5
Otters Cotts LN5 ... 205 D7
Oulton Cl LN6 ... 205 A2
Oundle Cl
Heighington/Washingborough LN4 ... 203 C1
Scunthorpe DN16 ... 185 C3
Oundle Rd
8 Mablethorpe/Sutton on Sea LN12 ... 64 C1
Peterborough PE2 ... 229 E6
Our Lady of Good Counsel RC Prim Sch NG34 ... 212 C5
Our Lady of Lincoln RC (Aided) Prim Sch LN2 ... 202 A7
Out Holme La DN36 ... 36 E3
Outer Circ Dr LN2 ... 202 C7
Outer Circ Gn LN2 ... 202 C6
Outer Circ Ind Est LN2 ... 202 D5
Outer Circ Rd LN2 ... 202 D5
Outfield PE3 ... 220 E1
Outgang La DN22 ... 65 A6
Outgang The HU15 ... 2 B7
Outgate DN17 ... 16 E7
Oval App LN2 ... 202 B7
Oval The 5 Brough HU15 .. 2 C5
Grimsby DN33 ... 191 C1
5 Hatfield DN7 ... 14 C5
Kingston upon Hull HU10 ... 178 E8
Lincoln LN2 ... 202 B7
Scopwick LN4 ... 108 B7
Oval The *continued*
2 Scunthorpe DN17 ... 184 E3
Overcoat La DN22 ... 65 B7
Overgate Rd NG33 ... 152 D5
Overstone Ct PE3 ... 225 D6
Overton Ave HU10 ... 178 E8
Overton Cl 4 LN5 ... 107 B8
Overton Ct 9 DN18 ... 3 E1
Overton Rd LN4 ... 207 D4
Overton Way PE2 ... 229 F4
Owen Ave HU13 ... 179 A1
Owen Cl 7 PE9 ... 172 D3
Owe's La LN11 ... 51 A5
Owl End PE7 ... 233 D5
Owmby Cliff Rd LN8 ... 55 C5
Owmby Hill DN38 ... 32 D8
Owmby La LN7 ... 32 C5
Owmby Rd
4 Searby cum Owmby DN38 ... 32 D8
Spridlington LN8 ... 55 F3
Owmby Wold La DN38 .. 21 E1
Owston Ferry Rd DN9 ... 27 F1
Owston Rd DN10 ... 40 B6
Oxburgh Cl
3 Peterborough PE7 ... 231 F5
1 Wisbech PE13 ... 170 C1
Oxclose PE3 ... 225 A8
Oxcombe Cl DN33 ... 194 D7
Oxcroft Bank
Moulton PE12 ... 157 F1
Whaplode PE12 ... 158 A2
Oxeney Dr 2 LN3 ... 69 C3
Oxford Cl LN4 ... 203 C1
Oxford Ct 1 NG34 ... 212 D7
Oxford Rd
Peterborough PE1 ... 225 F5
6 Stamford PE9 ... 219 A7
Oxford St Boston PE21 .. 208 F3
Cleethorpes DN35 ... 192 F5
Grantham NG31 ... 211 B3
Grimsby DN32 ... 189 B1
Kingston upon Hull HU2 .. 181 A8
2 Lincoln LN5 ... 234 B1
Market Rasen LN8 ... 57 D8
Scunthorpe DN16 ... 185 D6
Oxlands La PE24 ... 102 B7
Oxmarsh La DN19 ... 4 E2
Oxney Rd PE1 ... 226 D5

P

Pacey Cl LN6 ... 92 A6
Packhorse Gdns PE20 . 135 B6
Packman La HU10 ... 178 B8
Paddington Way PE10 . 154 D7
Paddock Cl
6 Ancaster NG32 ... 120 A2
Ropsley NG33 ... 131 B1
Paddock Ct 5 DN40 ... 186 C3
Paddock Gn 3 PE11 .. 214 D5
Paddock Gr 6 PE21 ... 208 F4
Paddock La
5 Blyton DN21 ... 41 C5
1 Metheringham LN4 ... 95 D4
West Butterwick DN17 ... 17 C1
Paddock Rd NG34 ... 120 C8
Paddock Rise
11 Barrow upon Humber DN19 ... 11 C8
Ingoldsby NG33 ... 141 C5
Paddock The
3 Barkston NG32 ... 130 B8
2 Burton-upon-Stather DN15 ... 8 B4
4 Cherry Willingham LN3 . 203 E6
10 Collingham NG23 ... 91 D4
Kingston upon Hull HU4 .. 179 B5
Louth LN11 ... 198 A5
1 Market Deeping PE6 .. 217 A6
4 Morton PE10 ... 154 C7
2 North Ferriby HU14 ... 3 A5
16 Ruskington NG34 ... 108 D2
Skellingthorpe LN6 ... 200 A4
5 Sleaford NG34 ... 212 F4
5 Stamford PE9 ... 219 A5
16 Sudbrooke LN2 ... 68 F2
3 Swanland HU14 ... 3 C7
Paddock View PE22 ... 100 B2
Paddocks The
1 Barnetby Le Beck DN37 . 35 B6
5 Beckingham DN10 ... 40 A1
6 Bottesford NG13 ... 128 A5
7 Burgh Le Marsh PE24 . 102 E7
Carlton Scroop NG32 ... 119 C3
12 Crowle DN17 ... 16 D7
Gedney PE12 ... 159 E7
1 Holbeach PE12 ... 215 E3
Kingston upon Hull HU10 ... 178 B7
10 Long Bennington NG23 117 D4
Newton on Trent LN1 ... 65 C1
2 Peterborough PE4 ... 220 E5
Stapleford LN6 ... 105 C8
Swayfield NG33 ... 152 E5
4 Willingham DN21 ... 53 E3
Pademoor Terr DN17 ... 7 A2
Padholme Rd PE1 ... 226 C3
Padholme Rd E PE1 ... 226 D3
Padley Rd LN2 ... 202 E6
Padleys La PE23 ... 100 C4
Padmoor La DN21 ... 53 C5
Pado La LN13 ... 74 E4
Pagehall Cl DN33 ... 191 D1
Paignton Ct DN33 ... 194 E6
Pain La PE22 ... 113 E3
Painshall Cl 11 LN2 ... 68 D7
Paisley Prim Sch HU3 . 180 A6
Paisley St HU3 ... 180 A7
Palace Theatre* NG24 ... 104 A4
Palma Ct 2 PE24 ... 90 D7
Palmer Ave HU10 ... 178 D8
Palmer Ct 3 NG34 ... 212 B6
Palmer La 15 DN19 ... 11 D8
Palmer Rd NG32 ... 129 C6
Palmers Rd PE1 ... 226 F5
Palmerston Rd PE2 ... 230 F7
Palmwood Cl 3 NG31 .. 210 F7
Pamela Rd DN40 ... 186 D4
Pandyke La PE22 ... 113 F3
Panton Cl 6 PE6 ... 217 D5
Panton Rd LN8 ... 71 B8
Papermill La
Ewerby & Evedon NG34 .. 121 E7
Tealby LN8 ... 46 D2
Pape's La PE24 ... 101 F4
Papyrus Rd PE4 ... 220 D3
Parade The LN3 ... 203 E6
Paradise La
5 Fulletby LN9 ... 86 B8
Northborough PE6 ... 173 F6
Paradise Pl 6 DN20 ... 196 B3
Paragon St HU1 ... 180 E6
Parish Church CE (Aided) Prim Sch DN21 ... 197 C5
Parishes Sh Ctr The DN15 ... 183 B3
Parish's La PE22 ... 115 A4
Park Ave
Allington NG32 ... 128 F7
15 Barton-upon-Humber DN18 ... 10 E8
Billinghay LN4 ... 109 F5
17 Crowle DN17 ... 16 D7
Grimsby DN32 ... 191 E4
Heighington/Washingborough LN4 ... 203 D2
Kingston upon Hull HU13 ... 178 E3
Lincoln LN6 ... 204 F7
Louth LN11 ... 198 E6
13 Mablethorpe/Sutton on Sea LN12 ... 64 B3
Scunthorpe DN17 ... 184 F3
Skegness PE25 ... 206 D4
Sleaford NG34 ... 212 F4
Spalding PE11 ... 214 C5
3 Spilsby PE23 ... 87 F1
Sutterton PE20 ... 136 A2
Park Cl
1 Gosberton PE11 ... 145 B6
Immingham DN40 ... 186 C4
Lea DN21 ... 52 F5
Spalding PE11 ... 214 C5
8 Sudbrooke LN2 ... 68 F2
Thorney PE6 ... 176 B3
7 Westwoodside DN9 ... 27 A2
Yaxley PE7 ... 233 F5
Park Cres
Heighington/Washingborough LN4 ... 203 D1
16 Metheringham LN4 ... 95 D4
Peterborough PE1 ... 226 B5
Sleaford NG34 ... 212 F4
Swinderby LN6 ... 92 B6
Thorne/Moorends DN8 ... 15 A7
Thorney PE6 ... 176 B3
Park Ct 2 PE12 ... 157 E7
Park Dr Grimsby DN32 .. 191 E5
Market Deeping PE6 ... 217 A5
6 Westwoodside DN9 ... 27 A2
Park Est PE6 ... 217 E4
Park Farm Cres PE7 ... 231 F5
Park Farm Rd
Peterborough PE6 ... 224 E5
Scunthorpe DN15 ... 182 F7
Park Farm Way PE7 ... 231 F6
Park Gate 7 PE21 ... 208 F5
Park Gdns PE12 ... 215 E3
Park Hill
Cherry Willingham/Reepham LN3 ... 203 E5
28 Kirton in Lindsey DN21 .. 30 B1
Park La 12 Alford LN13 ... 75 F3
Billinghay LN4 ... 109 F5
5 Boston PE21 ... 208 F6
Burton LN1 ... 200 D7
Coningsby LN4 ... 207 C4
Denton NG32 ... 139 A7
2 Donington PE11 ... 134 E2
East Kirkby PE23 ... 99 E5
Ewerby & Evedon NG34 .. 122 B7
Freiston PE22 ... 126 D3
Gorefield PE13 ... 169 F3
Heighington/Washingborough LN4 ... 203 C2
Holbeach PE12 ... 215 E3
Humberston DN35 ... 192 F1
Leverington PE13 ... 170 A3
Long Sutton PE12 ... 216 C5
Manby LN11 ... 62 C5
Peterborough PE1 ... 226 C4
Pinchbeck PE11 ... 145 D3
Redbourne DN21 ... 30 F3
Saxby All Saints DN20 ... 10 A3
1 Scawby DN20 ... 30 F8
1 Skillington NG33 ... 151 A8
Spalding PE11 ... 214 C5
Stamford PE9 ... 219 C4
2 Surfleet PE11 ... 145 D2
Swineshead PE20 ... 135 A7
Westwoodside DN9 ... 27 A2
Wigsley NG23 ... 78 F5
Park La Cl 6 DN7 ... 14 C2

Park La E HU4 ....179 C6
Park La Rd 11 DN7 ......14 C2
Park La W HU4 ......179 C5
Park Rd 11 Alford LN13 ...75 F3
1 Allington NG32 ....128 F7
Boston PE21 ....208 E2
5 Brough HU15 ....2 E6
Claxby LN8 ....45 E4
Grantham NG31 ....211 B5
Holbeach PE12 ....215 D2
2 Horncastle LN9 ......199 C4
Long Sutton PE12 ....216 C5
Mablethorpe/Sutton on Sea
LN12 ....64 C1
Market Deeping PE6 .....217 D4
Peterborough PE1 ......226 A3
Spalding PE11 ....214 C4
Sutton St James PE12 ...169 D7
Swinstead NG33 ....153 A5
1 Weston PE12 ....157 E7
5 Willingham DN21 ......53 E3
Park Rd E LN12 ....64 D1
Park Rd W 10 LN12 ....64 C1
Park Row
Kingston upon Hull HU3 ..180 D7
Louth LN11 ....198 E7
Park Springs Rd DN21 .197 F2
Park St
Cleethorpes DN35 ......189 D1
Grimsby DN32 ....192 B8
Kingston upon Hull HU3 ..180 D6
Lincoln LN1 ....234 A2
11 Messingham DN17 .....29 D7
Peterborough PE2 ....230 F7
Swinefleet DN14 ....6 D8
Winterton DN15 ....9 B5
Park The
Coningsby LN4 ....207 D5
Lincoln LN1 ....234 A2
Potter Hanworth LN4 .....95 B8
Park View
25 Barton-upon-Humber
DN18 ....10 F8
Cleethorpes DN35 ......192 C8
Crowle DN17 ....16 D6
Kingston upon Hull HU4 ..179 E4
6 Mablethorpe/Sutton on Sea
LN12 ....64 C1
10 Messingham DN17 .....29 D7
15 Northorpe PE10 ......164 C8
13 Thorne/Moorends DN8 ..15 A7
Park View Ave LN4 .....81 D2
Park View Cl 7 DN19 ....11 C7
Park View Terr DN17 ....28 C8
Park Wlk
Easton on the Hill PE9 ..171 D3
Kingston upon Hull HU4 ..179 B5
Parker Ave LN5 ....205 D4
Parker Rd
Humberston DN36 ....36 D8
23 Wittering PE8 ....172 B1
Parker St DN35 ....192 F5
Parkers Cl 12 PE24 .....102 E7
Parkers La DN16 ......185 C6
Parkes Cl 4 NG24 ......104 D5
Parkfield Ave 14 HU14 ....3 A4
Parkfield Dr HU3 ......179 F6
Parkfield Rd
7 Ruskington NG34 .....108 E2
13 Ryhall PE9 ....163 C1
Parkhill Cres 3 DN3 ....14 A4
Parkhill Rd 2 DN3 ......14 A4
Parkhill Rise 7 DN15 .....9 B5
Parkin Rd
7 Cowbit PE12 ....167 B8
Scunthorpe DN17 ....184 F4
Parkinson Ave 1 DN15 .183 A3
Parkinson's Way 2 LN12 64 C2
Parklands
2 Fleet Hargate PE12 ....159 C7
6 Mablethorpe/Sutton on Sea
LN12 ....64 B3
1 Mumby LN13 ....76 F1
4 West/East Butterwick
DN17 ....28 D8
Parklands Cl 13 NG24 ..104 C5
Parklands Cres 11 HU14 ..3 A5
Parklands Dr
4 Harlaxton NG32 ......139 C7
10 North Ferriby HU14 .....3 A5
Park-lea 6 NG34 ......108 E2
Parks Cl 4 DN39 ....12 A1
Parks Rd 3 DN7 ....14 C4
Parksgate Ave LN6 ....204 F5
Parkside
17 Nettleham LN2 ....68 D2
Peterborough PE2 ....230 B6
Parkside Cres PE11 ...214 C5
Parkside Dr 13 PE24 .....90 D7
Parkside The 4 NG33 ..151 D2
Parkstone Gr 28 DN7 ....14 D4
Parkway The
Kingston upon Hull
HU10 ....178 E8
Spalding PE11 ....214 A2
Parkwood Inf & Jun Sch
DN17 ....184 D8
Parkwood Rise 14 DN3 ..14 A3
Parliament St
5 Brough HU15 ....2 D6
7 Kingston upon Hull
HU1 ....180 F6
Peterborough PE1 ....225 F5
Parnell St 3 DN21 .....197 C5
Parnwell CP Sch PE1 ..226 F7
Parnwell Way PE1 .....226 F6
Parris Pl DN35 ....192 D7
Parry Rd 14 LN12 ....64 B3
Parslins The PE6 ......217 F5
Parson Dro
Billinghay LN4 ....109 F7
Pinchbeck PE11 ....144 B2
Parson Dro La PE13 ...170 B2
Parson La LN5 ....106 C8
Parsonage La PE12 ....159 F1
Parson's Dro
Holland Fen with Brothertoft
PE20 ....124 A8
Swaton NG34 ....133 D4
Parson's La PE12 .....168 B4
Parsons Dr 3 PE21 .....208 E7
Parsons Halt 1 LN11 ...198 C6
Parsons La 18 LN13 ......75 F2
Parthian Ave PE21 ....136 D8
Partney CE (Aided) Prim Sch
PE23 ....88 B3
Partney Rd PE23 ....87 C4
Partridge Cl
4 Caistor LN7 ....33 B4
4 Scunthorpe DN17 .....184 E6
Yaxley PE7 ....233 D6
Partridge Dr LN7 ....33 F2
Partridge Gr PE4 ......220 E5
Pashley Rd DN8 ....15 B7
Paston La PE4 ....221 B1
Paston Parkway PE4 ..221 C4
Paston Ridings PE4 ..221 C1
Paston Ridings Cty Jun &
Infants' Sch PE4 .....221 D1
Pasture Ave 9 DN17 .....17 D4
Pasture Cl
7 Colsterworth NG33 ...151 E7
Grantham NG31 ....211 D1
Pasture Dr LN11 ......198 D4
Pasture Dro PE10 .....154 F7
Pasture La Amcotts DN17 ..7 D1
Bassingham LN5 ....93 B2
Belvoir NG32 ....138 C6
Garthorpe & Fockerby
DN17 ....7 D6
Market Rasen LN8 ....57 E8
Northborough PE6 ....173 F6
Pasture Rd DN21 ......197 F4
Pasture Rd N DN18 ......3 F1
Pasture Rd S DN18 ......4 A1
Pasture St 5 DN32 .....191 E7
Pasture The PE6 ......217 C6
Pastures Ct 36 DN17 ....29 D7
Pastures Rd NG32 .....210 A5
Pastures The
12 Long Bennington NG23 117 D3
Old Somerby NG33 ....140 E8
1 Rampton DN22 ....65 A5
12 Welton LN2 ....68 D6
Patch Rd LN6 ....92 D4
Pateley Moor Cl 13 LN6 ..93 C8
Patman's La PE22 .....114 E4
Patrick St DN32 ......191 E5
Patricks Cl 5 LN7 ......32 A4
Patriot Cl PE11 ....214 C4
Patten Ave 2 PE24 .....102 D1
Patterdale Rd
Kingston upon Hull HU5 ..179 E8
3 Peterborough PE4 .....221 E2
Paul Cres 4 DN36 ....36 C8
Paul La 1 DN15 ....9 D1
Paulette Ct 11 PE11 .....214 B5
Paul's La LN4 ....207 C7
Paulsgrove PE2 ....229 D5
Pavilion Gdns
4 Scunthorpe DN17 .....182 F2
5 Sleaford NG34 ....212 D3
Pavilion Way DN36 ....195 C7
Pawlett Cl PE6 ....217 D5
Paxton Rd PE2 ....229 D4
Payne Ave PE13 ....170 D1
Payne Sch PE13 ....177 D7
Paynell 23 LN2 ....68 D6
Paynells PE2 ....230 A3
Paynesholm PE4 ......221 E1
Pea Rm Craft Ctr &
Heckington Sta Rly Mus*
NG34 ....122 F2
Peace Haven 2 DN37 ..194 C5
Peach La NG32 ....128 F6
Peach Tree Cl 5 DN16 .185 D4
Peach Tree Ct 5 HU3 ..180 D5
Peachwood Cl 4 NG31 .210 F8
Peacock Ct 5 NG34 ....212 E3
Peacock St DN17 ......184 F5
Peacock Way PE3 .....224 F2
Peacock's Rd PE22 ....112 B1
Peacocks The 5 NG23 .117 D3
Peak Dale LN6 ....204 E2
Peake Cl PE2 ....230 F6
Peakirk Rd
Deeping Gate PE6 ....217 F3
Glinton PE6 ....220 D8
Northborough PE6 ....174 A7
Peakirk-cum-Glinton CE Sch
PE6 ....220 C8
Peaks Ave DN36 ......195 C7
Peaks La Grimsby DN36 .191 F2
New Waltham DN36 .....195 D7
Peaks Parkway
Grimsby DN32 ....191 E5
New Waltham DN36 .....192 A1
Pear Tree Cl
4 Epworth DN9 ....27 D6
4 Waltham DN37 ....194 D4
Pear Tree Cres 2 PE13 .170 B1
Pear Tree La
Covenham St Bartholomew
LN11 ....49 B6
Kirk Bramwith DN7 ......14 A8
Utterby DN36 ....48 E5
Pear Tree Rd PE20 ....136 D5
Pearces La 3 PE10 ....154 C7
Pearces Rd PE6 ....227 B5
Pearl Cl 8 PE25 ....206 C4
Pearl Ct PE12 ....215 D3
Pearl Leisure Ctr PE5 ..223 E1
Pearson Pk Prim Sch
HU3 ....180 D8
Pearson Rd DN35 .....192 F3
Pearson St 5 HU2 .....180 E7
Peartree Cl 5 LN6 .....200 D1
Peartree Hill Rd PE12 .168 B8
Peartree House Rd
PE12 ....215 F7
Peascliffe Dr NG31 ...211 A8
Peaseholme HU13 .....178 C1
Peasgate La
Toynton All Saints PE23 ..100 F6
Toynton St Peter PE23 ...101 A7
Peashill La NG32 .....139 B8
Peat Carr Bank DN9 ....26 C3
Peatlings La PE13 .....170 C1
Pebble Cl 4 PE12 ......160 E4
Peck Ave PE21 ....208 D4
Peck Hill NG33 ....131 B1
Peckover Cl 4 PE7 .....231 F5
Peckover Sch The
PE13 ....170 C1
Peddars Way PE3 .....225 A2
Pedlar La LN11 ....62 A7
Pedley La 15 PE13 .....170 C1
Peel Castle Rd 10 DN8 ...15 B7
Peel Hill Rd 9 DN8 ......15 B7
Peel St
Kingston upon Hull HU3 ..180 D8
Lincoln LN5 ....201 E1
Peele Sch The PE12 ...216 D6
Pegasus Gr 6 PE10 ....213 E7
Pegasus Rd DN20 ......21 A8
Pelham Ave DN33 .....191 C1
Pelham Cl
20 Barton-upon-Humber
DN18 ....10 E8
Peterborough PE3 ....224 F2
7 Sudbrooke LN2 ....68 F2
Pelham Cres 1 DN41 ....23 A4
Pelham Dr 1 HU9 ......181 C7
Pelham Ind Est DN40 ..186 D6
Pelham Inf Sch DN40 ..186 D4
Pelham Pl DN33 ......191 C1
Pelham Rd Claxby LN8 ...45 D6
Cleethorpes DN35 ......192 D7
6 Grimsby DN31 ....191 C7
2 Holton le Clay DN36 ...195 C2
Immingham DN40 ....186 B3
1 Skegness PE25 ....206 C4
Pelham Sq 1 DN35 .....192 E7
Pelham St LN5 ....234 B1
Pelham View 3 DN20 ....30 F5
Pell's Dr 5 PE20 ....136 D5
Pemberton Dr DN36 ...195 B6
Pemberton St 1 HU8 ..181 B7
Pembroke Ave
Peterborough PE2 ....229 F5
Scunthorpe DN16 ....185 A3
Pembroke Gr 1 PE6 ...220 D8
Pembroke Rd
Grimsby DN34 ....191 A5
Stamford PE9 ....219 A7
Pen St PE21 ....209 A5
Pendeen Cl
6 Gainsborough DN21 ...197 E6
New Waltham DN36 .....195 C7
Pendine Cres. LN6 ....205 A1
Pendlebury Dr 4 PE6 ..217 D5
Pendleton PE3 ....225 B6
Pendred Ave LN6 ....92 D4
Pendreth Pl DN35 ....192 D7
Pendula Rd PE13 ......170 E1
Penfold La 1 LN4 .....203 C2
Penistone Ct 2 HU9 ...181 D7
Pennell St LN5 ....201 E1
Pennine Rd 7 DN8 ......15 A7
Pennine Way
Gonerby Hill Foot NG31 ..210 E7
Peterborough PE4 ....221 B2
Spalding PE11 ....214 E6
Pennington PE2 ......229 E3
Pennington St HU8 ...181 B7
Penny Gdns 6 PE20 ....136 C5
Penny Hill Rd PE12 ...215 E3
Penny Toft La PE11 ...214 B8
Pennycress Cl LN2 ....202 C8
Pennyfield
16 Pinchbeck PE11 ....156 E8
Pinchbeck PE11 ....214 B8
Pennygate PE11 ......214 A4
Pennyhill Cl PE11 ....214 E6
Penrose Cl 19 LN6 ......93 C8
Penshurst Ave HU13 ..178 F3
Penshurst Rd DN35 ...192 D4
Penswick Gr 11 NG24 ..104 C5
Pentelow Cl PE13 .....177 D5
Pentland Dr 23 LN6 .....93 C8
Pentlands The 2 PE4 ..221 C2
Penwald Cl 7 PE6 .....175 B8
Penway Dr PE11 ......214 B8
Penwith Dr HU10 .....178 F7
Penyale 3 PE3 ....225 A1
Peploe Cres 10 DN19 .....4 E2
Peploe La 9 DN19 ....4 E2
Peppercorn Cl
3 Lincoln LN6 ....201 D1
Peterborough PE1 ....225 E6
Peppercorn Wlk
12 Grimsby DN32 ....191 E7
9 Holton le Clay DN36 ..195 D2
Pepper's La NG34 ....133 C4
Peppin La LN11 ....49 A2
Percheron Dr 4 PE11 ..214 A2
Percival St
Peterborough PE3 ....225 E2
Scunthorpe DN15 ....183 A4
Percy St
8 Kingston upon Hull
HU2 ....180 E7
6 Lincoln LN2 ....202 B3
5 Scunthorpe DN16 .....183 B2
Peregrine Cl
Kingston upon Hull HU4 ..179 D2
6 Sleaford NG34 ....212 B3
Perkin Field PE34 ....161 F2
Perkins Cl 3 DN37 ....190 F8
Perkins La PE6 ....173 C6
Perney Cres 17 LN6 .....93 C8
Pernys Cl PE7 ....230 D3
Perrin Ave 6 PE25 .....206 A5
Perry Rd PE13 ....170 B2
Perry St HU3 ....180 A6
Pershore Ave DN34 ...190 D4
Pershore Way LN6 ...204 C6
Perth Cl 7 PE25 ....206 A4
Perth Rd PE9 ....218 E6
Perth St HU5 ....179 F8
Perth Way DN40 ......186 B2
Petchell Way 3 DN32 ..191 F8
Peter Paine Cl PE22 ..126 F4
Peter Paine Sports Ctr
PE21 ....208 B5
Peter Seadike La
PE11 ....145 D5
Peterborough Cath*
PE1 ....226 A2
Peterborough Cl 10
NG31 ....210 E5
Peterborough Coll of Adult
Ed PE1 ....226 B3
Peterborough District
PE3 ....225 E2
Peterborough Dr PE6 ..224 E2
Peterborough Her Ctr*
PE3 ....225 A1
Peterborough High Sch
PE3 ....225 D2
Peterborough NV Sta
PE2 ....225 F1
Peterborough Rd
Castor PE5 ....223 E1
19 Collingham NG23 ......91 D5
23 Eye PE6 ....175 A1
Langtoft PE6 ....217 A8
Newborough PE6 ....174 E4
Peterborough PE7 ....231 C3
Scunthorpe DN16 ....185 B7
Wansford PE8 ....222 A3
Peterborough Regional Coll
PE1 ....226 B5
Peterborough Sta PE3 .225 F2
Peterborough Way
NG34 ....212 C7
Petergate 1 PE9 ....219 B4
Peterhouse Cl 1 PE9 ..219 B7
Peterhouse Rd DN34 ..190 F6
Peter's La LN13 ....63 B2
Petersfield Cl LN6 ....204 B7
Peterspoint PE12 .....160 D3
Pethley La NG34 ......143 A6
Petticoat La 15 PE21 ..208 F5
Pettit Way 5 PE21 .....209 C4
Petts Cl 5 PE13 ....170 E1
Petts La PE12 ....160 F5
Petuaria Cl HU15 ....2 B6
Petworth Cl 2 PE6 .....217 A5
Peveril Ave DN17 .....184 F8
Peveril Rd PE1 ....225 F6
Pheasant Cl 5 DN17 ...184 E6
Pheasant Ct 5 LN7 ......33 B4
Pheasant Gr PE4 .....220 E5
Pheasant Way PE7 ....233 D5
Phelps Pl DN32 ......192 C5
Phelps St DN35 ....189 D1
Philip Ave
Cleethorpes DN35 ......192 D4
Waltham DN37 ....194 E5
Philip Ct 4 LN6 ....204 F1
Philip Gr
Cleethorpes DN35 ......192 D4
Skegness PE25 ....206 B4
Philips Cres 3 DN15 ...182 F3
Phillips Ct 6 PE9 ......219 C4
Phillips La 6 DN37 .....23 F1
Phoenix Ct DN21 .....197 F3
Phoenix Parkway
DN15 ....182 E7
Phoenix St 13 DN32 ....191 D7
Phorpres Cl PE7 ......230 D3
Phorpres Way PE7 ....230 E3
Phyllis Ave DN34 .....191 B7
Piccadilly 4 DN36 .....195 C6
Piccadilly Way PE10 ..154 D6
Pick Hill La
Grimoldby LN11 ....62 C8
South Cockerington LN11 ..50 C1
Pickards Way PE13 ...170 C1
Pickathorpe La LN11 ...50 E6
Pickering Gr 15 DN8 ....15 A7
Pickering Rd HU4 .....179 C3
Pickerings The 19 HU14 ...3 A4
Picksley Cres DN36 ...195 D1
Pickworth Rd PE9 .....162 F2
Pickworth's Dro PE10 .155 A3
Pidgeon Cote La 20
DN19 ....12 A8
Pier St 9 HU1 ....180 F5
Pietermaritz St 4 LN1 .201 E8
Pike Dam La PE12 ....159 A6
Pilgrim Ave DN40 .....186 D3
Pilgrim Hospl PE21 ...209 A8
Pilgrim Rd PE21 ......209 A4
Pilgrim's Cl 5 DN40 ....12 E3
Pilgrim's Way PE11 ...214 A4
Pilgrims Way DN40 ...186 A4
Pilham La DN21 ....41 C4
Pilley's La PE21 ......125 F5
Pilmore La PE12 ......157 B6
Pilots Way HU9 ....181 B5
Pilton Cl PE4 ....221 D1
Pimpernel Way 2
DN16 ....185 D4
Pinchbeck Ave 4 DN16 183 C2
Pinchbeck E CE Prim Sch
PE11 ....156 E8
Pinchbeck Engine Mus*
PE11 ....145 E1
Pinchbeck La PE24 ...102 F4
Pinchbeck Rd
5 Butterwick PE22 ......126 E3
Spalding PE11 ....214 D5
Pinchbeck W CE (Controlled)
Prim Sch PE11 ....156 A8
Pinder La 10 PE11 ......134 F2
Pine Cl Grimsby DN37 ..188 A1
Holbeach PE12 ....215 C3
Lincoln LN1 ....201 E8
4 Sleaford NG34 ....212 D3
Stamford PE9 ....218 D6
7 Waddington LN5 ....93 E8
Pine Ct 3 DN35 ....192 D2
Pine Hall Rd DN3 ......14 A3
Pine Mdws HU10 ......178 B8
Pine Tree Cl PE1 .....226 B8
Pine Wlk 5 Brough HU15 ..2 C6
4 Healing DN41 ....24 A5
Pinefield Ave 7 DN3 ....14 A3
Pinefield Rd 8 DN3 .....14 A3
Pines The DN21 ......197 F2
Pinetree Ave 11 DN21 ...29 C3
Pinetree Cl 5 DN20 ......19 E4
Pinetrees Ct 4 NG34 ...212 E4
Pinewood Ave PE8 ....172 B1
Pinewood Cl 5 PE10 ...213 B5
Pinewood Cres DN33 ..190 F3
Pinewood Dr NG31 ....210 F8
Pinewood Gr 2 HU5 ....179 C7
Pinfold 15 DN9 ....27 E6
Pinfold Cl
7 Bottesford NG13 ......128 A6
8 Collingham NG23 ......91 D5
11 Northorpe PE10 ......164 C8
Osbournby NG34 ....132 D5
Pointon & Sempringham
NG34 ....143 B6
Rippingale PE10 ....142 F2
Pinfold Gdns 4 DN36 ..195 D1
Pinfold La
11 Bottesford NG13 ......128 A6
Fishlake DN7 ....14 D8
Fishtoft PE21 ....137 C8
Great Steeping PE23 ....101 E6
Grimsby DN33 ....191 D1
Halton Holegate PE23 ...101 C6
3 Holton le Clay DN36 ...195 D1
Legbourne LN11 ....61 E3
Marston NG32 ....118 D2
Minting LN9 ....71 C1
Pointon & Sempringham
NG34 ....143 B6
8 Ruskington NG34 .....108 E2
South Rauceby NG34 ....120 E4
2 Stallingborough DN41 ..23 D6
Stamford PE9 ....219 C3
Stickney PE22 ....113 A6
Swaby LN13 ....74 E4
Walcott LN4 ....109 C7
Weston PE12 ....157 D8
Pinfold Rd
Bourne PE10 ....213 F5
Castle Bytham NG33 ....152 D1
Pinfold The LN4 ......108 D5
Pinfold Way 11 NG34 ...108 E2
Pingle Cl DN21 ....197 E4
Pingle La
Bishop Norton LN8 ....43 D3
Northborough PE6 ....173 F6
20 Wellingore LN5 ......107 A7
Pingle The 2 NG34 .....133 B1
Pingles The 9 PE10 .....164 C8
Pingley La DN20 ......196 D2
Pingley Mdw DN20 ....196 D2
Pinney's Ct 21 DN41 .....23 F5
Pinnings La DN21 ......43 D6
Pinstock La 10 PE12 ....159 C7
Pioneer Way LN6 .....204 E4
Pipistrelle Ct 4 PE4 ...221 A3
Pippin Cl LN11 ....198 C5
Pippin Ct 3 DN15 ......182 C5
Pippin Dr DN16 ......185 B2
Pipwell Gate PE12 ....146 E1
Pit La Gedney PE12 ...149 A4
Great Ponton NG33 .....140 B4
Ketton PE9 ....171 A4
Pitcher Row La PE20 ..136 B1
Pitman Ave 23 DN18 .....10 E8
Pitmoor La 8 DN39 ......12 A1
Pitt La DN10 ....39 C2
Pitt St HU3 ....179 F7
Pittneys PE4 ....221 D1
Pitts Rd LN4 ....203 C1
Plains La DN8 ....15 F3
Plane St HU3 ....180 A5
Plank Dro PE6 ....175 B8

Plantain Cl **1** DN16 .....**185** D4
Plantation Dr HU14 ....**2** F5
Plantation Rd
  Cranwell & Byard's Leap
  NG34 ....**107** C1
  29 Thorne/Moorends DN8 .**15** A8
Planting Rd NG33 ....**140** B1
Plash Dro PE13 ....**177** F4
Plassey Rd **6** DN21 ......**55** A8
Platform Dr PE12 ....**216** A4
Platt's La NG32 ....**118** B4
Platts La Bucknall LN10 ..**84** B4
  Tetford LN9 ....**73** E1
Playgarth Est LN4 ....**108** E4
Playhouse Yd **2** LN3 ...**212** D4
Playing Field La **2** LN8 ..**59** A7
Pleasant Ave LN11 ....**198** D5
Pleasant Pl **6** LN3 .....**198** C6
Pleasure Island Theme Pk★
  DN35 ....**193** C2
Plimsoll Way HU9 ....**181** B6
Plot La NG23 ....**91** E6
Plough Hill **23** LN7 .....**33** B4
Plough La
  1 Cherry Willingham/Reepham
  LN3 ....**82** A8
  Cherry Willingham/Reepham
  LN3 ....**203** F8
  6 Fiskerton LN3 ....**82** A7
  6 Newborough PE6 ....**174** E5
Plover Dr **15** HU15 .....**2** C6
Plover Gr LN6 ....**204** E8
Plover Rd **1** PE9 ....**163** D3
Plover Sq **7** LN7 ....**33** B4
Ploverly **2** PE4 ....**221** A5
Plowden Rd HU3 ....**179** F5
Plowright Theatre★
  DN15 ....**183** A2
Plum Tree Dr **8** DN7 ....**37** C2
Plum Tree Way DN16 ....**183** A1
Plumtree Hill Rd DN7 ....**14** C7
Plumtree La **2** DN36 ....**36** B1
Plymouth Cl **23** DN15 ....**9** A5
Plymouth Rd DN17 ....**182** C1
Poacher's Croft **8** DN9 ..**16** E1
Poachers Brook LN6 ....**200** A5
Poachers Ct **28** LN1 .....**66** D2
Poachers Gate **4** PE11 .**145** C1
Poachers Hide **2** PE11 .**145** B7
Poachers La LN2 ....**68** F3
Poachers Mdw **20** LN2 ...**68** D2
Poachers Rest **3** LN2 ...**68** D7
Pocklington Cres **3**
  NG24 ....**104** B7
Pocklington Rd **24** NG23 .**91** D5
Pocklington Way **10**
  NG34 ....**122** C2
Pode La PE22 ....**113** F1
Poffinder Wood Rd
  DN7 ....**14** E7
Point Rd PE25 ....**90** F3
Pointon Rd NG34 ....**143** B8
Poles Bank DN9 ....**26** E6
Policemans La **2** LN4 ..**203** C2
Pollyplatt La LN1 ....**67** E5
Pollyplatt Prim Sch
  LN1 ....**67** F5
Polton Cl **3** DN7 ....**14** D7
Polton Toft **2** DN7 .....**14** D7
Polyanthus Dr **4** NG34 .**212** F3
Pond Cl **19** LN2 ....**68** D6
Pond La **4** PE10 ....**213** C4
Pond Side DN39 ....**11** E3
Pond St
  Great Gonerby NG31 ...**129** D5
  8 Harlaxton NG32 ....**139** C7
Ponds Way **10** DN18 .....**3** E1
Ponton Ave NG31 ....**211** E2
Ponton Rd NG33 ....**140** D5
Pool Dr DN17 ....**184** F4
Poolbank La HU15 ....**2** C5
Poole's La HU15 ....**87** F1
Pooley Way PE7 ....**233** D6
Pools La PE20 ....**136** C4
Poor Gdn Rd NG34 ......**132** F6
Poor Plat La LN13 ....**62** F3
Pope Way PE1 ....**225** E8
Pope's La
  Leverington PE13 ......**170** A2
  Terrington St Clement
  PE34 ....**161** E2
Poplar Ave
  Mablethorpe/Sutton on Sea
  LN12 ....**64** A5
  Peterborough PE1 .....**226** C8
Poplar Cl
  Anlaby with Anlaby Common
  HU4 ....**179** A5
  Boston PE21 ....**208** D2
Poplar Cres PE10 ....**213** B6
Poplar Ct **5** PE22 ......**114** A1
Poplar Dr Brigg DN20 ...**196** C5
  6 Broughton DN20 ....**19** D3
  2 Gosberton PE11 ...**145** C6
  Humberston DN36 .....**193** B1
Poplar Gdns DN16 .....**185** B7
Poplar Gr
  5 Cleethorpes DN35 ..**192** E7
  3 Scotter DN21 ....**29** C3
Poplar La DN21 ....**41** D2
Poplar Rd Bucknall LN10 .**84** A3
  Cleethorpes DN35 .....**192** E7
  6 Hatfield DN7 ....**14** C4
  2 Healing DN41 ......**23** F5

Raceground The
Bourne PE11 . . . . .214 A1
2 Spalding PE11 . . . . . . .156 E3
Rachel Cl DN21 . . . . . . .197 C7
Radcliffe Cl 5 PE9 . . . . .219 B5
Radcliffe Rd
7 Healing DN41 . . . . .24 A5
3 Stamford PE9 . . . . . . .219 B5
3 Stamford PE9 . . . . . . .219 A5
Radford Cl PE8 . . . . . . .172 C1
Railway Cl 17 NG33 . . . .151 D1
Railway La PE12 . . . . . .160 E3
Railway Pk Cl 1 LN6 . . .201 D1
Railway Pl 4 DN31 . . . .189 B2
Railway St
Barnetby le Wold DN38 . . . .21 B4
Grimsby DN32 . . . . .189 B1
Kingston upon Hull HU1 . . .180 F5
Railway Terr
3 Grantham NG31 . . . . . .211 A3
8 Grimsby DN32 . . . . . . .191 D7
Railworld Mus* PE3 . . .225 F1
Rainsbutt Rd DN17 . . . . . .6 C1
Rainton Ct 3 PE11 . . . .214 F4
Rainwall Ct 2 PE20 . . . .136 A2
Rainwall's La PE20 . . . .136 A3
Raithby Ave 20 DN41 . . . .23 A4
Raithby Cross Roads
PE23 . . . . .87 C2
Raithby Gr 6 DN33 . . . .191 A3
Raithby Hill PE23 . . . . . .87 D1
Raithby Rd PE23 . . . . . . .87 D1
Rake Bridge Bank DN7 .14 D2
Raleigh Ct 2 PE11 . . . .214 C2
Raleigh Dr HU9 . . . . . . .181 D6
Raleigh Way PE3 . . . . . .225 B6
Ralphs La PE20 . . . . . . .136 C7
Ram Bvd DN15 . . . . .182 E7
Ramper La LN1 . . . . .65 E4
Ramper Rd DN22 . . . . . . .52 B7
Ramper The 6 PE11 . . .156 E3
Rampton Rd DN22 . . . . . .65 A4
Ramsay Cl PE25 . . . . . .206 C1
Ramsden Ave 8 DN18 . . .10 E8
Ramsey Way PE2 . . . . . .231 F6
Ramsgate LN11 . . . . . . .198 C6
Ramsgate Rd LN11 . . . .198 C6
Ramskir La DN7 . . . . .14 C7
Ranby Rd DN17 . . . . . . .184 E5
Rand Farm Pk* LN8 . . .70 A5
Randall Bank PE12 . . . .158 A2
Randolph Rd PE20 . . . . .146 D7
Randsfield Ave 20 HU15 . . .2 C5
Range Rd NG31 . . . . . . .211 C5
Rangefield PE2 . . . . . . .229 E4
Rangell Gate PE12 . . . .157 B5
Rangoon Way 4 PE10 . .213 E7
Ransom Ct 4 DN39 . . . . .22 A6
Ransome Way 17 HU15 . . .2 C6
Ranters Row 8 LN13 . . . .75 F2
Ranville Cl 11 PE11 . . . .145 C1
Ranworth Cl 1 PE25 . . .206 D7
Ranyard La LN11 . . . . . . .72 E5
Rase La 5 LN8 . . . . .57 D8
Rasen Cl 3 LN8 . . . . . . .57 B8
Rasen Ct 2 PE1 . . . . . .226 D3
Rasen La LN1 . . . . .234 A4
Rasen Rd Tealby LN8 . . . .46 B1
Walesby LN8 . . . . .45 F1
Rason's Ct 8 PE21 . . . .209 A5
Rat Abbey DN15 . . . . .9 C4
Rathkenny Cl PE12 . . . .215 E2
Rats Pen La LN11 . . . . . .62 C1
Ratten Row PE22 . . . . . .127 A5
Rauceby CE Sch NG34 .120 E5
Rauceby Dro NG34 . . . .120 F3
Rauceby Sta NG34 . . . .120 F3
Rauceby Terr LN1 . . . . .234 A2
Rauceby Warren Nature
Reserve* NG34 . . . . . .120 F2
Raven Cl 1 DN20 . . . . . . .19 D4
Raven St HU9 . . . . .181 D7
Ravencroft La 6 DN10 . . .40 A1
Ravendale 31 DN18 . . . . .10 F8
Ravendale Cl
Gonerby Hill Foot NG31 . . .211 A8
Holton le Clay DN36 . . . . .195 E1
Ravendale Dr LN2 . . . . .202 A7
Ravendale Rd
Cleethorpes DN35 . . . . . .193 A3
Gainsborough DN21 . . . . .197 E3
Ravendale St N 2 DN15 183 B3
Ravendale St S 8 DN15 183 B3
Ravenhill Cl DN35 . . . . .192 D3
Raven's Bank PE12 . . . .158 B2
Raven's Dro PE12 . . . . .159 A3
Raven's Gate
Fleet PE12 . . . . .159 A3
Holbeach PE12 . . . . .158 E2
Ravenscar Rd 5 DN37 . .188 A1
Ravensfleet Rd DN21 . . . .40 C6
Ravensmoor Cl 4 LN6 . .204 E1
Ravensthorpe Prim Sch
PE3 . . . . .225 C7
Rawcliffe Gr HU4 . . . . .179 D5
Rawling Way HU3 . . . . .180 C5
Rawlinson Ave 27 LN7 . . .33 B3
Rawnsley Cl 15 LN13 . . . .75 F2
Rawsons La PE21 . . . . .125 E5
Raybrook Cl 5 PE21 . . .208 E7
Raymond Mays Way
PE10 . . . . .213 D2
Raymond Rd DN16 . . . . .185 C7
Rayner Ave PE2 . . . . . .231 E5
Raysor's La PE22 . . . . .114 A2
Rayton Cl LN4 . . . . .203 A2
Raywell Cl HU10 . . . . . .178 F7
Raywell St HU2 . . . . . . .180 E7
Reaches The PE6 . . . . . .175 C3
Read Way LN4 . . . . .207 D5
Reading Cl LN4 . . . . . . .203 E1
Reading Gate DN14 . . . . . .6 C4
Reading Rm Yd 2 HU14 . . .3 A4
Reads La 4 NG33 . . . . . .151 D7
Reams Cl 4 PE21 . . . . . .209 D4
Reapers Cl 1 PE12 . . . .215 B2
Reaper's Rise 20 DN9 . . . .27 E6
Reaper's Way 8 DN9 . . . .27 D2
Recreation Gd Rd PE9 .219 B6
Recreation Rd 2 PE10 .213 D5
Recto Ave DN32 . . . . . . .191 F5
Rectors Way 6 PE4 . . . .221 D2
Rectory Cl
1 Barrowby NG32 . . . . . .210 A5
7 Binbrook LN8 . . . . .47 C5
2 Fishtoft PE21 . . . . . . .126 C1
Rectory Gdns
2 Beckingham DN10 . . . . .40 A1
5 Glinton PE6 . . . . .220 C8
Peterborough PE2 . . . . . . .231 B7
Rectory La
Addlethorpe PE24 . . . . .90 C4
Barrowby NG32 . . . . .210 A5
Bottesford NG13 . . . . . . .128 A6
Claypole NG23 . . . . .117 F8
Etton PE6 . . . . .173 D5
3 Fulbeck NG32 . . . . . . .106 C1
Gainsborough DN21 . . . . . .52 F5
6 Gedney PE12 . . . . . . .159 D7
Glinton PE6 . . . . .220 C8
Harlaxton NG32 . . . . .139 C7
Leadenham LN5 . . . . .106 C2
2 Mareham Le Fen PE22 . .98 F4
North Witham NG33 . . . . .151 D4
4 Owmby LN8 . . . . .55 F6
2 Peakirk PE6 . . . . .174 A5
24 Waddington LN5 . . . . . .93 F7
Woolsthorpe By Belvoir
NG32 . . . . .138 D8
Rectory Rd
Anderby PE24 . . . . .76 F2
Boston PE21 . . . . .209 B3
Coleby LN5 . . . . .93 F3
Newton PE13 . . . . .170 B5
Ruskington NG34 . . . . . . .108 D1
Tydd St Mary PE13 . . . . . .160 B1
Rectory St
Beckingham LN5 . . . . .105 B4
Epworth DN9 . . . . .27 E6
Red Barn La PE20 . . . . .136 B3
Red Cap La PE21 . . . . . .208 E8
Red Cow Dro PE12 . . . .146 F6
Red Hall* PE10 . . . . . . .213 D4
Red Hall Dr LN4 . . . . . .205 F4
Red Hall Farm La LN4 .205 F4
Red Hill Nature Reserve*
LN11 . . . . .72 E7
Red La South Ferriby DN18 . .9 F7
Welby NG32 . . . . .130 F5
Red Leas La LN11 . . . . . .62 A8
Red Lion St
9 Bicker PE20 . . . . .135 A4
6 Boston PE21 . . . . .208 F5
5 Spalding PE11 . . . . . .214 D4
3 Spalding PE11 . . . . . .214 D4
8 Stamford PE9 . . . . . . .219 B5
Red Rd LN8 . . . . .84 B8
Redbourn Cl 2 DN16 . . .183 B1
Redbourn E Rd DN16 . . . .19 A6
Redbourn Way DN16 . . .183 B2
Redbourne Dr LN2 . . . . .202 A8
Redbourne Mere DN21 . . .30 E2
Redbourne Rd
Grimsby DN33 . . . . .191 B3
Hibaldstow DN20 . . . . .30 F4
Waddingham DN21 . . . . . . .43 C7
Redbourne St
Kingston upon Hull HU3 . . .180 B5
1 Scunthorpe DN16 . . . .183 C2
Redbridge PE4 . . . . . . .220 E6
Redcar Cl LN6 . . . . .204 F4
Redcar Gr DN32 . . . . . .192 A5
Redcar St HU8 . . . . . . .181 A8
Redcliff Dr 22 HU14 . . . . .3 A4
Redcliffe Rd NG31 . . . . .211 B7
Redcombe La DN20 . . . .196 B4
Redcot Gdns PE9 . . . . .219 B6
Redcote Dr LN6 . . . . . . .204 F4
Redcross St NG31 . . . . .211 B5
Redfern Cl HU3 . . . . . . .180 D5
Redgate Rd PE13 . . . . .170 C8
Redhall Cl 9 DN3 . . . . . .14 A2
Redhill La LN8 . . . . .59 A8
Redland Cres 1 DN8 . . . .15 B8
Redman Cl DN21 . . . . . .197 E5
Redmile Cl
Bourne PE10 . . . . .154 D5
Pinchbeck PE11 . . . . .214 C8
Redmile's La 2 PE9 . . . .171 A3
Redthorn Way NG23 . . . .117 F7
Redthorne Cl 2 PE11 . .214 F5
Redwing Cl
Peterborough PE2 . . . . . . .231 E7
Skellingthorpe LN6 . . . . . .200 A3
Redwing Gr 1 LN6 . . . .204 D8
Redwood Ave 11 NG34 .212 D2
Redwood Ct DN16 . . . . .185 D3
Redwood Cty Prim Sch
LN5 . . . . .93 E8
Redwood Dr
Cleethorpes DN35 . . . . . .192 D2
Waddington LN5 . . . . .205 D1
Reed St 7 HU2 . . . . . . .180 E7
Reedham La LN4 . . . . . .207 F2
Reedings Cl NG32 . . . . .210 B5
Reedings Rd NG32 . . . . .210 B5
Reedmace Cl 8 PE6 . . .174 E4
Reedmans Cl 5 PE6 . . .164 F3
Reepham PE2 . . . . .229 D4
Reepham CE (Controlled)
Prim Sch LN3 . . . . .203 F8
Reepham Rd LN3 . . . . . . .82 A7
Reet 2 DN31 . . . . .189 B1
Reeves Way PE1 . . . . . .226 D5
Refinery Rd DN16 . . . . .183 F2
Reform Pl 2 NG34 . . . . .212 C4
Reform St
9 Crowland PE6 . . . . . . .166 E1
Kingston upon Hull HU2 . .180 F7
Stamford PE9 . . . . .218 F5
Regal Gdns 2 NG33 . . . .162 E8
Regency Ct
13 Barton-upon-Humber
DN18 . . . . .3 E1
1 Barton-upon-Humber
DN18 . . . . .10 E8
Regency Gdns NG31 . . .211 D5
Regency Way PE3 . . . . .225 E1
Regent Ave LN6 . . . . . .200 C1
Regent Cl HU3 . . . . . . .180 C6
Regent Dr 18 DN17 . . . . .16 D7
Regent Rd LN12 . . . . . . .64 B4
Regent St PE11 . . . . . .214 C3
Regents Cl
6 Collingham NG23 . . . . . .91 D4
4 Skegness PE25 . . . . . .206 C1
Regents Pk Cl 7 LN6 . . .204 F1
Regina Wlk 10 PE24 . . . . .90 D7
Reginald Rd DN15 . . . . .182 F5
Regional Coll PE2 . . . . .230 D6
Reldene Dr HU5 . . . . . . .179 B7
Rembrandt Way PE11 . .214 B3
Remigius Gr LN2 . . . . . .202 C7
Remple Ave 2 DN7 . . . . .15 A3
Remple Comm Rd DN7 . .14 F2
Remple La 3 DN7 . . . . . .15 A3
Renault Dr LN4 . . . . . . .205 F1
Rendel St DN31 . . . . . . .188 F1
Renew's Dro PE6 . . . . . .166 D3
Renfrew Cl 2 LN5 . . . . .205 C2
Renfrew Rd LN5 . . . . . .205 C2
Reporto Ave DN32 . . . . .191 F5
Repton Cl LN4 . . . . .203 D1
Repton Dr 2 DN16 . . . . .185 B3
Repton Rd 7 LN12 . . . . . .64 B4
Reservation The NG34 .212 F7
Reservoir Rd PE11 . . . .145 F4
Reservoir St LN1 . . . . . .234 A4
Resolute Cl 6 PE23 . . . .101 A8
Responso Ave 3 DN32 . .191 F5
Reston Ct DN35 . . . . . . .193 A3
Reston Gr 4 DN33 . . . . .191 B4
Retief Cl LN1 . . . . .201 D8
Retreat The
Easton on the Hill PE9 . . .171 C3
6 Maxey PE6 . . . . .173 C6
Revesby Abbey PE22 . . . .99 C5
Revesby Ave
Boston PE21 . . . . .208 D4
Grimsby DN34 . . . . .190 F4
Scunthorpe DN16 . . . . . . .185 A7
Revesby Bank
Carrington PE22 . . . . .99 B1
Revesby PE22 . . . . .112 B8
Revesby Cl
Boston PE21 . . . . .208 D4
Lincoln LN6 . . . . .204 F6
Revesby Cnr 5 PE22 . . . .99 A4
Revesby Ct DN16 . . . . . .185 A8
Revesby Dr PE25 . . . . . .206 A4
Revigo Ave DN32 . . . . . .191 F5
Revill Cl
5 Claypole NG23 . . . . . . .117 E8
17 Scotter DN21 . . . . .29 C3
Reynard St 3 PE23 . . . . .88 A1
Reynold's Paddock 2
LN5 . . . . .93 A5
Reynolds Cl HU14 . . . . . . .2 F5
Reynolds Dr 1 LN6 . . . .205 B6
Reynolds Gdns 6 PE12 .157 F7
Reynolds Jun & Inf Sch
DN35 . . . . .192 D7
Reynolds St DN35 . . . . .192 D7
Rhodes Ave 2 NG34 . . .212 C3
Rhodes St HU3 . . . . . . .179 F5
Rialto Ave DN32 . . . . . .191 F5
Ribble St 4 HU3 . . . . . .180 B4
Riber Cl 2 NG31 . . . . . .210 E5
Ribston Cl DN16 . . . . . .185 A2
Riby Cl 3 DN21 . . . . .53 A7
Riby Cross Roads DN37 .23 C3
Riby Ct DN36 . . . . .195 E2
Riby Rd Cabourne LN7 . . .33 D6
Keelby DN41 . . . . .23 A4
Scunthorpe DN17 . . . . . . .184 E5
Stallingborough DN41 . . . . .23 C4
Swallow LN7 . . . . .34 A7
Riby Sq DN31 . . . . .189 B1
Riby St DN31 . . . . .189 B1
Richard St 4 DN31 . . . .191 C8
Richard Young Cl 4
PE13 . . . . .170 D2
Richards Ave LN6 . . . . .204 F4
Richardson Cl 18 DN36 . .36 D8
Richdale Ave 1 DN21 . . .30 B2
Richmond Ave PE4 . . . .221 A2
Richmond Cl
Caythorpe NG32 . . . . .119 B6
2 Sleaford NG34 . . . . . . .212 B2
Richmond Ct 1 PE25 . .206 C2
Richmond Dr
Lincoln LN6 . . . . .204 F3
Scunthorpe DN16 . . . . . . .185 C4
Skegness PE25 . . . . .206 C1
Richmond Prim Sch The
PE25 . . . . .206 C2
Richmond Rd
Cleethorpes DN35 . . . . . . .192 E5
Gainsborough DN21 . . . . .197 F4
Grimsby DN34 . . . . .191 A6
Kingston upon Hull
HU13 . . . . .178 E2
Lincoln LN1 . . . . .201 D4
Richmond Way PE13 . . .170 B2
Riddings Inf Sch
DN17 . . . . .184 E4
Riddings Jun Sch
DN17 . . . . .184 F4
Rider Gdns PE21 . . . . . .209 D2
Rides The 7 PE6 . . . . . .164 F3
Ridge Cl 14 LN2 . . . . .68 D6
Ridge View
2 Brigg DN20 . . . . .196 D4
Harmston LN5 . . . . .93 F4
Ridge View Rd LN4 . . . .205 F4
Ridge Way PE2 . . . . . . .231 B8
Ridgeway 13 LN2 . . . . . . .68 D2
Ridgeway Rd HU5 . . . . .179 B7
Ridgeway The DN34 . . .190 D3
Ridgewell Cl 10 LN6 . . .204 D8
Ridgewood Ave 14 DN3 . .14 A1
Ridgewood Dr 5 DN15 . . .8 A4
Ridings The
Kingston upon Hull HU5 . .179 A8
Market Rasen LN8 . . . . .57 E7
17 North Ferriby HU14 . . . . .3 A4
Ridley Ave PE25 . . . . . . .206 D2
Rightwell E PE3 . . . . . .225 A5
Rightwell W PE3 . . . . . .225 A5
Rigsby Wood Nature
Reserve* LN13 . . . . . . .75 C3
Rigsmoor Cl 2 LN6 . . . . .93 C8
Rileston Pl DN16 . . . . . .185 B2
Riley Cl
Bracebridge Heath LN4 . . .205 F2
Yaxley PE7 . . . . .233 D6
Rimac Rd LN11 . . . . .51 D2
Rimes La DN22 . . . . .65 A7
Rime's La LN10 . . . . .98 C6
Rimington Rd 4 PE21 . .126 C1
Ring Beck La HU15 . . . . . .2 A8
Ring Moor Cl 7 LN4 . . .109 F5
Ringers La PE13 . . . . . .170 B2
Ringrose St HU3 . . . . . .179 F5
Ringstead Rd PE4 . . . . .221 D1
Ringstone Chase PE10 .142 F1
Ringwood PE3 . . . . .224 F3
Ringwood Cl
4 Birchwood LN6 . . . . . .200 D1
1 Scunthorpe DN16 . . . .185 B4
Rinks La LN5 . . . . .92 E1
Rio Dr NG23 . . . . .91 D5
Ripley Dr LN6 . . . . .205 A3
Riplingham Rd HU10 . . .178 A8
Ripon Cl
Grantham NG31 . . . . .210 F5
Peterborough PE4 . . . . . . .220 F3
Scunthorpe DN17 . . . . . . .184 C7
Ripon Dr NG34 . . . . .212 C6
Ripon Pl 16 LN12 . . . . . .64 B3
Ripon St Grimsby DN31 .191 C8
Lincoln LN5 . . . . .201 F1
Ripon Way HU9 . . . . . . .181 C8
Rippingale CE (Controlled)
Prim Sch PE10 . . . . . . .142 F2
Rippingale Rd PE10 . . .142 D2
Rippons Dro PE6 . . . . . .217 E2
Risby PE3 . . . . .225 B8
Risby Rd DN15 . . . . .9 A1
Rise The
16 Navenby/Wellingore
LN5 . . . . .107 A8
8 North Ferriby HU14 . . . . .3 A5
Scunthorpe DN17 . . . . . . .184 E3
South Ferriby DN18 . . . . . .10 A8
Risedale 26 LN7 . . . . . . .33 B4
Risegate Rd PE11 . . . . .144 F4
Riseholme PE2 . . . . . . .229 E3
Riseholme La LN2 . . . . . .67 F2
Riseholme Rd
Gainsborough DN21 . . . . .197 F3
Lincoln LN2 . . . . .201 F7
Risewood La NG33 . . . . .130 F1
Riston St HU3 . . . . .180 C5
Rivan Ave DN33 . . . . . . .194 E7
Rivehall Ave 7 LN2 . . . . .68 D7
Rivelin Cres DN16 . . . .185 A8
Rivelin Pl DN16 . . . . . .185 A8
Rivelin Rd DN16 . . . . . .185 A7
Rivendale PE4 . . . . . . .220 F2
River Bank PE12 . . . . . .214 C1
River Gr HU4 . . . . .179 E3
River La Anwick NG34 . . .109 B1
Keddington LN11 . . . . . . .198 E7
Moulton PE12 . . . . .158 A8
Peterborough PE3 . . . . . . .225 F2
River Mdw DN20 . . . . . .196 A2
River Rd
West Burton DN22 . . . . . . .52 D4
West Walton PE14 . . . . . .170 C4
River Terr 4 PE13 . . . . .170 C1
River View 21 DN18 . . . . .10 F8
River Way PE21 . . . . . . .209 C2
Riverbank Cl PE6 . . . . . .217 E3
Riverdale 1 LN2 . . . . . . .68 D2
Riverdale Rd DN16 . . . .185 A7
Rivergate
3 Peterborough PE1 . . . .226 A1
3 Spalding PE11 . . . . . . .214 D2
Rivergate Sh Ctr PE1 . .226 A1
Riverhead LN11 . . . . . . .198 D7
Riverhead Rd LN11 . . . .198 D6
Riverhead Theatre*
DN31 . . . . .191 D8
Rivermead LN6 . . . . . . .205 C4
Rivermead Cl LN6 . . . . .205 C4
Riverside 2 Brigg DN20 .196 A3
Grantham NG31 . . . . .211 B4
Market Deeping PE6 . . . . .217 E3
Scotter DN21 . . . . .29 C4
2 Spalding PE11 . . . . . . .214 B5
Riverside Cl 14 NG13 . . .128 A6
Riverside Dr DN35 . . . .193 C2
Riverside Gdns
Parson Drove PE13 . . . . . .177 C7
Peterborough PE3 . . . . . . .225 D1
Riverside Ind Est
PE21 . . . . .209 A2
Riverside Mead PE2 . . .231 B8
Riverside Pk
Grantham NG31 . . . . .211 B6
Spalding PE11 . . . . .214 E2
Riverside Spinney
PE8 . . . . .222 A3
Riverside The NG34 . . .212 D4
Riverside Wlk 8 NG13 .128 A6
Riverton Cl LN1 . . . . . . .201 D8
Riverview Ave HU14 . . . . .3 A4
Roadwood La NG23 . . . . .78 F8
Robert Ave PE1 . . . . . . .225 F8
Robert Cl DN40 . . . . . . .186 B4
Robert Dukeson Ave
NG24 . . . . .104 A6
Robert Manning Sch The
PE10 . . . . .213 E6
Robert Pattinson Sch
LN6 . . . . .204 E2
Robert Rayner Cl PE2 .230 D6
Robert St DN15 . . . . . . .183 A3
Robert Tressell Wlk 2
LN2 . . . . .202 C7
Roberta Cl 10 PE25 . . . .206 A4
Robert's Gr PE25 . . . . . .206 D7
Robert's Field Nature
Reserve* PE9 . . . . . . .162 F5
Roberts St DN32 . . . . . .192 A8
Robertson Ave 6 NG34 .121 B8
Robertson Cl 14 LN5 . . . .93 F7
Robertson Dr NG34 . . . .212 D5
Robertson Rd
3 Grantham NG31 . . . . . .210 F5
Lincoln LN6 . . . . .204 E1
Robey St LN5 . . . . .205 E8
Robin Cl
8 Market Deeping PE6 . .217 C5
12 Sleaford NG34 . . . . . .212 B3
Robin Hood Cl PE3 . . . .224 F2
Robin Hood Cres 13 DN3 14 A1
Robin Hood Rd
11 Kirk Sandall DN3 . . . . . .14 A1
Skegness PE25 . . . . .206 C3
Robin Hood's Wlk
PE21 . . . . .208 F6
Robinia Dr HU4 . . . . . . .179 C2
Robins Cl PE2 . . . . .230 E8
Robins Field PE8 . . . . . .222 A4
Robins Wood PE8 . . . . .222 A4
Robinson Ave 4 LN13 . . .75 E2
Robinson Cl 3 DN15 . . .182 E4
Robinson La
Grimsby DN31 . . . . .189 C2
Louth LN11 . . . . .198 C5
Robinson Pl LN5 . . . . . .105 F5
Robinson Rd DN40 . . . .186 F6
Robinson St E 4 DN32 .191 E7
Robinson's Gr 8 DN20 . . .31 A5
Robinson's La 1 DN36 . . .36 B1
Robson Rd DN35 . . . . . .192 D7
Rochdale Rd DN16 . . . .185 A5
Rochdale Rd Jun Sch
DN16 . . . . .185 A5
Rochester Ave HU4 . . . .179 B3
Rochester Cl 1 DN17 . .184 C7
Rochester Ct
2 Bourne PE10 . . . . .213 C7
Humberston DN35 . . . . . .193 A1
Rochester Dr
Birchwood LN6 . . . . .200 D2
9 Grantham NG31 . . . . . .210 E5
Rochford Cres PE21 . . .209 B5
Rochford Twr* PE21 . . .209 E5
Rochford Twr La
PE21 . . . . .209 D6
Rock Rd
Peterborough PE1 . . . . . . .225 F6
Stamford PE9 . . . . .219 B5
Rock The NG32 . . . . . . .138 B4
Rockingham Cl 8 PE6 .217 A6
Rockingham Ct 9
DN34 . . . . .190 D4
Rockingham Gr PE4 . . .221 A2
Rockingham Rd 4 PE9 .218 E6
Rod Mill Rd DN16 . . . . .183 E1
Roegate La PE12 . . . . . .159 F1
Roeze Cl 14 LN10 . . . . . .97 C5
Rogues Alley PE13 . . . .177 C4
Rokeby Ave HU4 . . . . . .179 B5
Rokeby Cl HU4 . . . . . . .179 B5
Rokeby Pk HU4 . . . . . . .179 B5
Rokeby Pk Prim Sch
HU4 . . . . .179 B4
Rolleston Cl 3 LN2 . . . .201 F7
Roman Bank
Bourne PE10 . . . . .213 E4
Holbeach PE12 . . . . .215 D8
Huttoft PE24 . . . . .77 C4
1 Ingoldmells PE25 . . . .206 D8

Roman Bank *continued*
Moulton PE12 .... 146 E2
Newton PE13 .... 170 B4
6 Skegness PE25 ...... 206 C3
Spalding PE11 .... 214 F6
Stamford PE9 .... 219 A5
Roman Cl 9 LN4 .... 95 D4
Roman Dr PE8 .... 222 D2
Roman Pavement LN2 . 202 C4
Roman Rd PE12 .... 157 D1
Roman Way
7 Ancaster NG32 ...... 120 A2
Aubourn Haddington & South Hykeham LN6 ..... 93 A8
Horncastle LN9 .... 199 D3
Roman Wharf LN1 .... 201 C3
Romany Gdns PE2 .... 231 D5
Romney Cl 3 LN6 ..... 205 B6
Romney Dr LN6 .... 205 B5
Romsey Ct DN34 ...... 190 D5
Ronald Cl 3 PE25 ..... 206 C4
Rood's La PE12 .... 157 C8
Rookery Ave
2 Grimsby DN33 .... 191 D3
Sleaford NG34 .... 212 B3
Rookery Cl LN11 ...... 198 D8
Rookery Croft 14 DN9 ... 27 E6
Rookery La
Ancaster NG32 .... 119 F2
13 Leasingham NG34 .... 121 B7
Lincoln LN6 .... 205 C6
Wildmore LN4 .... 111 E2
Wymondham LE14 .... 150 B1
Rookery Rd
2 Bicker PE20 .... 135 A4
16 Healing DN41 .... 23 F5
Sutton Bridge PE12 ..... 160 D7
Rookery The
14 Collingham NG23 ...... 91 D5
Peterborough PE2 ...... 229 C7
2 Scawby DN20 .... 30 F8
Yaxley PE7 .... 233 D5
Rooklands 10 DN21 ..... 29 C3
Rook's La DN10 .... 39 F6
Roosdyke La PE22 .... 137 D7
Rope Wlk Lincoln LN6 .. 234 A1
15 Thorne/Moorends DN8 . 15 A8
Roper's Bridge La
PE20 .... 136 A4
Roper's Gate
Gedney PE12 .... 159 F8
2 Lutton PE12 .... 160 A8
Roper's La PE12 ...... 159 D1
Ropery La 2 DN18 .... 3 E1
Ropery Rd DN21 ...... 197 B7
Ropery St
Grimsby DN32 .... 191 F7
Kingston upon Hull HU3 .. 180 D4
Ropewalk 6 LN8 .... 70 D5
Ropewalk Gall★ DN18 ... 3 F1
Ropewalk The
1 Caistor LN7 .... 33 B4
8 Colsterworth NG33 ... 151 E6
Ropsley CE (Controlled) Prim Sch NG33 .... 131 A1
Ropsley Rd NG33 ..... 140 E8
Rosaire Pl DN33 ...... 195 A8
Rosalind Ave DN34 ... 191 B7
Rosamond St 7 HU3 ... 180 B4
Rose Ave PE2 .... 231 C7
Rose Cottage Gdn Ctr & Tropical Forest★
PE11 .... 156 D8
Rose Cottage La LN5 ... 94 A3
Rose Cres PE12 .... 158 D3
Rose Gdns DN40 ...... 186 C4
Rose Gr 1 PE25 .... 206 D5
Rose La
Beesby with Saleby LN13 .. 75 F5
Pinchbeck PE11 .... 156 E8
Rose Pl PE21 .... 209 A3
Rose Wlk
Scunthorpe DN15 .... 183 C3
11 Wisbech PE13 .... 170 C1
Roseberry Ave
26 Hatfield DN7 .... 14 D4
Skegness PE25 .... 206 D1
Rosebery Ave
Boston PE21 .... 208 C5
Lincoln LN1 .... 201 D4
Rosedale
Scunthorpe DN17 .... 184 E2
Waltham DN37 .... 194 C5
Rosedale Cl 4 LN6 .... 204 F3
Rosedale Dr NG31 .... 211 B8
Rosedale Gr HU5 ..... 179 D7
Rosefields DN21 ...... 197 E5
Rosegar Ave PE20 .... 135 F2
Rosegarth St 14 PE21 .. 208 F4
Rosehill Cl 6 LN1 ...... 66 D2
Rosehip Rd PE10 ..... 154 D6
Roselea Ave 8 LN2 ..... 68 D6
Rosemary Ave
Grimsby DN34 .... 190 F6
11 Market Deeping PE6 .. 217 C5
Rosemary Cres NG31 .. 210 E1
Rosemary Gdns PE1 ... 225 F8
Rosemary La LN2 ..... 234 B2
Rosemary Rise NG33 .. 141 D5
Rosemary Way DN35 .. 192 E1
Rosemount Dr DN16 .. 185 B6
Rosemount Grange
HU13 .... 178 C3
Rosemount La 6 DN21 .. 43 D7
Roseum Cl LN6 .... 204 E5
Roseveare Ave DN31 .. 191 A7
Roseway 2 DN21 ...... 197 D5
Rosewood Cl
2 Birchwood LN6 ...... 204 C8
4 Kingston upon Hull HU5 .... 179 B7
Rosewood Dr 5 NG34 .. 212 D2
Rosewood Way 1 DN16 185 B3
Rosey Row 4 HU9 ..... 181 C7
Rosina Gr N 2 DN32 .. 192 B6
Rosina Gr S 4 DN32 .. 192 B6
Roslyn Rd HU3 .... 179 E7
Rosmead St HU9 ..... 181 D8
Rosper Rd DN40 ...... 186 A8
Ross Cl 5 NG24 ...... 104 D5
Ross La 6 DN15 .... 9 B5
Ross Rd DN31 .... 189 D1
Rossa Rd LN13 .... 76 D7
Rossall Cl
9 Mablethorpe/Sutton on Sea LN12 .... 77 A7
Scunthorpe DN16 ...... 185 C3
Rossetti Ct NG31 ..... 211 E5
Rossington Cl 18 LN4 ... 95 C4
Rostrop Rd LN4 .... 95 C7
Rosyth Ave PE2 .... 229 D3
Rothbury Rd DN17 .... 184 F7
Rothwell Ave 10 DN33 .. 191 B3
Rothwell Cl DN21 ..... 197 E4
Rothwell Rd
Cabourne LN7 .... 33 C3
4 Lincoln LN2 .... 201 F7
Scunthorpe DN15 ...... 182 D4
Rothwell Way PE2 .... 230 C7
Rotten Row
Pinchbeck PE11 .... 156 E8
Theddlethorpe St Helen LN12 .... 63 E5
Rotton Sykes La DN15 .... 1 F2
Roughton Ct 5 LN2 .... 202 A8
Roundhouse Cl PE1 ... 226 D3
Roundway
Grimsby DN34 .... 191 C5
2 Immingham DN40 .... 186 C3
Roundway The HU4 ... 179 C5
Routland Cl 8 LN8 ...... 70 D4
Roval Dr DN40 .... 186 A4
Rowan Ave
Peterborough PE1 ..... 226 C6
Spalding PE11 .... 214 E5
Rowan Cl
6 Barrow upon Humber DN19 .... 11 C8
16 Keelby DN41 .... 23 A4
10 Wisbech PE13 .... 170 E1
Rowan Cres DN16 ..... 185 C3
Rowan Ct 3 Goxhill DN19 .12 A8
11 Heighington/Washingborough LN4 .... 203 D1
Rowan Dr 5 Healing DN41 23 F5
Silk Willoughby NG34 ... 121 B2
Rowan Rd Lincoln LN6 .. 204 F3
Waddington LN5 .... 205 D1
Rowan Way
1 Boston PE21 .... 209 A7
Bourne PE10 .... 213 B6
16 Metheringham LN4 ..... 95 C4
Rowans The
Holbeach PE12 .... 159 A7
9 Nettleham LN2 .... 68 C2
4 Westwoodside DN9 .... 27 A2
Rowanwood Dr 7 NG31 210 F7
Rowdyke Rd PE21 .... 136 F7
Rowe Ave PE2 .... 230 D7
Rowgate Rd LN11 .... 73 A5
Rowland Ct 1 PE4 ..... 220 F5
Rowland Rd 6 DN16 ... 183 B2
Rowlandson St 3 DN31 189 B2
Rowley Rd PE21 ...... 209 A4
Rowmills Rd 2 DN16 .. 185 C8
Rowston Cl DN21 ..... 197 C6
Rowston St DN35 ..... 193 A5
Roxborough Cl LN6 ... 200 E2
Roxburgh Rd PE9 ..... 218 F6
Roxburgh St 1 HU5 ... 180 B8
Roxby Cl LN6 .... 204 F6
Roxby Cswy DN15 .... 9 C4
Roxby Rd DN15 .... 8 F4
Roxholm Cl 2 NG34 ... 108 D1
Roxholme Rd NG34 ... 121 B8
Roxton Ave DN41 .... 23 A5
Roxton Hall Dr 15 HU14 ... 3 A5
Royal Air Force Coll The NG34 .... 120 B8
Royal Arthur Cl 5 PE25 206 C1
Royal Cl 15 PE12 ...... 160 E4
Royal Ct DN35 .... 193 B1
Royal Hull Hospitals NHS Trust HU3 .... 180 C6
Royal Oak Ct
13 Heckington NG34 .... 122 E3
19 Louth LN11 .... 198 B5
Royal Oak La 1 LN5 ..... 93 A5
Royal St DN31 .... 189 A2
Royal Way PE21 ...... 209 F2
Royalty Bank PE22 .... 101 B3
Royce Rd
Peterborough PE1 ..... 226 D3
Peterborough PE7 ..... 229 A4
2 Spalding PE11 ...... 214 F6
Roydon Gr LN6 .... 205 B6
Royle Cl PE2 .... 230 C5
Royston Ave PE2 ..... 230 C6
Ruards La DN19 .... 5 A1
Ruckland Ave LN1 .... 201 E7
Rudgard Ave LN3 ..... 203 E6
Rudgard La
Lincoln LN1 .... 201 D4
Rudgard La *continued*
Lincoln LN1 .... 234 A3
Rudham Ave 4 DN32 ... 191 E4
Rudkin Dr 5 NG34 .... 212 D6
Rudyard Cl 7 LN12 ...... 77 A7
Rudyard Gr PE4 ...... 221 C3
Rue De L'yonne 1 NG23 .91 D5
Rue De Nozay 3 DN20 ... 19 E4
Rufford Gn 2 LN6 .... 205 C8
Rufford Rd DN35 ..... 192 E4
Rugby Rd
4 Mablethorpe/Sutton on Sea LN12 .... 64 B4
Scunthorpe DN16 ...... 185 A8
Rugby St 5 HU3 ...... 180 B4
Rumbold La 3 PE24 ... 102 D1
Runcorn Garth HU4 ... 179 B3
Runcorn Rd LN6 ..... 204 B5
Running Post La PE20 .135 B4
Runswick Cl LN6 ..... 205 A3
Runswick Rd DN32 ... 192 B6
Rupert Rd 1 DN33 ... 191 D3
Rural Ave PE11 .... 144 D1
Rural Villages Sch Bucknall LN10 .... 84 B3
Rush Furlong Nature Reserve★ DN9 .... 27 E3
Rushcarr La DN17 ...... 17 C1
Rushcliffe Rd NG31 ... 211 A7
Rushmere PE2 .... 229 F6
Rushmore Ctry Pk★ LN11 .... 61 F8
Rushton Ave PE4 ..... 220 E4
Rushtons Way 12 DN20 .. 30 F5
Rushy Dro PE11 ...... 145 C8
Ruskin Ave LN2 ...... 202 B6
Ruskin Gn LN2 .... 202 B6
Ruskin Rd 13 LN12 ...... 64 B4
Ruskin St
2 Gainsborough DN21 .. 197 D2
Kingston upon Hull HU3 .. 180 B6
Ruskington Sta NG34 .. 108 E1
Russell Ave Lincoln LN6 .. 93 C8
Newark-on-Trent NG24 .. 104 A2
Russell Cl 12 PE6 ..... 176 A3
Russell Cres NG34 .... 212 F4
Russell Ct DN35 ...... 193 A1
Russell Dr 2 PE12 .... 167 B8
Russell Hill PE8 ...... 222 A6
Russell Rd 7 NG34 .... 121 B8
Russell St
Kingston upon Hull HU2 .. 180 E7
Lincoln LN5 .... 205 D6
Peterborough PE1 ..... 225 F3
Russell Wlk 2 DN17 .... 29 D7
Russet Cl 2 DN15 ..... 182 C5
Rustic La DN21 .... 41 C6
Ruston Rd NG31 ...... 211 F7
Rutland Cl 13 NG33 ... 151 D2
Rutland Dr DN36 ..... 195 C5
Rutland La 15 NG13 ... 128 A5
Rutland Rd
Kingston upon Hull HU5 .. 179 E8
Scunthorpe DN16 ...... 185 D7
Skegness PE25 .... 206 D3
Stamford PE9 .... 219 D7
Rutland St
2 Grimsby DN32 .... 189 D1
Grimsby DN32 .... 192 A8
Rutland Way
Ryhall PE9 .... 163 C1
15 Scampton Airfield LN1 .. 67 E5
Rycroft Ave PE6 ...... 217 F5
Rycroft Cl 1 PE6 ...... 217 F4
Rycroft St NG31 ...... 211 B3
Rydal Ave DN33 ...... 194 D7
Rydal Cl LN6 .... 200 D2
Rydal Ct PE4 .... 221 C3
Ryde Ave NG31 ...... 210 E4
Rye Cres 3 HU15 .... 2 D5
Rye La LN13 .... 75 D5
Ryecroft 11 LN5 ...... 205 D2
Ryedale 6 HU15 .... 2 D6
Ryedale Ave 1 DN15 ..... 9 A6
Ryedale Cl NG31 ..... 211 B8
Ryefield La PE12 ..... 159 B3
Ryhall CE Prim Sch PE9 .... 163 C1
Ryhall Rd
Great Casterton PE9 ..... 171 C8
Stamford PE9 .... 219 D5
Ryland Gdns 10 LN2 .... 68 D6
Ryland Rd LN2 .... 68 E6
Rymac Cres PE25 .... 90 E4
Rymer Pl DN35 .... 193 A4
Ryton Rd PE21 .... 208 B3

S

Sable Cl HU4 .... 179 C2
Sackville Cl DN40 .... 186 D4
Sackville Rd DN40 .... 186 D4
Sackville St 7 DN31 .. 191 C7
Sacred Heart RC Prim Sch PE3 .... 225 A5
Sacrewell Farm & Ctry Ctr★ PE8 .... 222 C5
Saddle Row NG34 .... 120 B8
Saddleback Rd
Skidbrooke with Saltfleet Haven LN11 .... 51 A3
South Cockerington LN11 .. 50 E1
Saddler Dr PE10 ..... 154 C6
Saddler's Cl 11 LN4 ..... 95 C4
Saddler's Way 2 DN9 ... 27 D3
Saddlers Cl
Glinton PE6 .... 220 D8
Saddlers Cl *continued*
Osbournby NG34 .... 132 D5
Saddlers Mead 10 PE11 .214 A2
Saddlers Way
Fishtoft PE21 .... 209 C2
5 Long Sutton PE12 .... 216 B5
Sadler Cl 9 PE25 ..... 206 C1
Sadler Rd LN6 .... 204 B5
Saffrondale HU10 .... 178 E7
Sagefield Cl 5 DN33 .. 194 D8
Sage's La PE4 .... 225 C8
Sailors Wharf HU9 ... 181 C6
Sainsbury Way HU4 ... 179 A1
St Aiden's Rd 5 LN6 .. 204 E2
St Alban's Dr 16 PE6 .. 175 A1
St Albans Ave DN31 .. 191 A8
St Albans Cl
5 Grantham NG31 ...... 210 D5
16 Hibaldstow DN20 ...... 30 F5
3 Scunthorpe DN17 .... 184 C7
St Andrew's Cl
4 Helpringham NG34 ... 133 D7
Redbourne DN21 .... 30 F3
St Andrew's Cres 6
NG34 .... 121 B7
St Andrew's Dr
1 Burton-upon-Stather DN15 .... 8 B4
Grimsby DN32 .... 192 B4
Lincoln LN6 .... 205 C8
Skegness PE25 .... 206 D5
St Andrew's Gdns LN6 .205 C8
St Andrew's Mount
HU10 .... 178 C8
St Andrew's Pl 3 LN5 .. 234 B1
St Andrew's Rd
6 Butterwick PE22 ..... 126 E3
Spalding PE11 .... 214 C1
St Andrew's St
8 Heckington NG34 .... 122 E3
10 Kirton in Lindsey DN21 .. 30 B1
4 Lincoln LN5 .... 234 B1
St Andrew's Way
8 Barnby Dun DN3 ...... 14 A3
Epworth DN9 .... 27 E7
4 RAF Cranwell NG34 ... 120 C8
St Andrews NG31 ..... 211 D7
St Andrews Ave 2
DN17 .... 184 F2
St Andrews CE (Controlled) Prim Sch NG34 .... 121 B7
St Andrews CE Jun Sch DN40 .... 186 D4
St Andrews CE Prim Sch LN10 .... 97 C6
St Andrews Cl LN5 .... 201 F1
St Andrews Ct 4 LN4 .... 96 C1
St Andrews Dr 6 LN1 ... 66 C2
St Andrews Gr 33 DN7 ... 14 D4
St Andrews Prim Sch HU10 .... 178 C7
St Andrews Rd
2 Mablethorpe/Sutton on Sea LN12 .... 64 B4
Northborough PE6 ..... 217 E1
St Andrews Wlk 5 LN10 .97 C5
St Ann's Ave DN34 .... 191 B6
St Ann's La PE21 ..... 208 F3
St Anne's Rd
9 Keelby DN41 .... 23 A5
Lincoln LN2 .... 202 B4
St Anne's Specl Sch HU15 .... 2 E5
St Anne's St NG31 .... 211 C3
St Anne's Wlk 13 HU15 ... 2 D6
St Annes Ave 8 LN11 ..... 50 F7
St Annes CE Prim Sch NG31 .... 211 C3
St Annes Cl
Lincoln LN2 .... 202 B4
Skegness PE25 .... 206 C6
3 Sleaford NG34 ...... 212 C6
8 Spalding PE11 ...... 214 C6
St Annes Way PE11 ... 214 C6
St Aubins Cres LN4 .... 81 F4
St Audrey Cl PE2 ..... 231 D6
St Augustin Way
NG31 .... 211 A4
St Augustine Ave
DN32 .... 191 E5
St Augustine Cres
DN16 .... 185 B5
St Augustine Webster RC Prim Sch DN15 .... 182 D4
St Augustine's CE Sch PE13 .... 170 D2
St Augustine's Wlk
PE2 .... 230 E8
St Augustines Jun Sch PE2 .... 230 F8
St Augustines RC (Aided) Prim Sch PE9 .... 219 C7
St Barbara's Cres 7 DN15 8 B4
St Barnabas CE Prim Sch DN38 .... 21 B4
St Barnabas Ct 4 HU3 .180 C4
St Barnabas Dr 1 HU14 ... 3 C7
St Barnabas Rd DN38 ... 21 B4
St Bartholomew's Cl 4
DN41 .... 23 A4
St Bede's RC Sch DN16 .... 185 B6
St Bedes RC Sec Sch PE21 .... 209 B6
St Bee's Dr 19 PE6 .... 175 A1
St Benedict Cl 18 PE6 .. 166 F1
St Benedict's Cl 2 LN6 204 D2
St Benedicts Cl 2 PE6 .220 D8
St Benet's Gdns 2 PE6 .175 A1
St Bernadettes RC Prim Sch DN16 .... 185 C6
St Bernard's Cl 13 DN20 .19 E4
St Bernards Ave LN11 . 198 D6
St Bernards Cl LN11 .. 198 E6
St Bernards Specl Sch LN11 .... 198 E5
St Botolph La PE2 .... 230 C6
St Botolph's Cres 8
LN5 .... 205 E8
St Botolph's Rd DN16 .. 185 C7
St Botolph's Way PE6 .. 176 A2
St Botolphs Cl 2 LN1 ... 66 D3
St Botolphs Infants Sch LN5 .... 205 D8
St Botolphs Prim Sch PE2 .... 230 B6
St Botolphs Rd 7 NG34 212 C6
St Catherine's Ct LN5 .205 D7
St Catherine's Dr 3 DN7 14 C2
St Catherine's Gr LN5 .205 D7
St Catherine's Rd
Grantham NG31 .... 211 B4
Lincoln LN5 .... 205 E7
St Catherines 15 LN5 ... 205 E8
St Catherines Cres
DN16 .... 185 A4
St Catherines Ct DN34 .190 F6
St Chad's Rd DN16 .... 185 D7
St Chads Ct 8 LN2 ...... 68 E6
St Charles RC Prim Sch HU2 .... 180 E8
St Christopher's Rd 11
DN36 .... 36 C8
St Christophers Cl 1
NG34 .... 107 F1
St Christophers Specl Sch LN6 .... 205 B4
St Claire's Ct 6 LN6 ... 204 C8
St Clares Wlk DN20 ... 196 C2
St Clement's 9 PE9 .... 219 A5
St Clement's Ct 3 LN1 . 234 B4
St Clement's Dr 4 LN3 .. 82 B6
St Clement's Rd
3 Lincoln LN6 .... 204 E2
2 Skegness PE25 ...... 206 B4
St Clements Cl LN4 .... 108 E7
St Clements Rd 17
NG34 .... 108 D2
St Clements Way 1
DN36 .... 195 C7
St Crispin's Cl 3 LN6 .. 204 D2
St Crispins Cl 2 DN40 ... 12 E4
St David's Cl 2 LN3 ... 203 E7
St David's Rd LN6 ..... 204 D2
St David's Sq PE1 .... 226 D1
St David's St 13 LN8 ..... 47 B6
St Davids Cl 2 PE25 ... 206 D6
St Davids Cres DN17 .. 184 E3
St Deny's Cl 2 DN40 ... 12 E3
St Denys Ave NG34 .... 212 B6
St Edith Gate 6 LN11 ... 62 C6
St Edmonds Cl PE24 .. 115 D8
St Edmunds Cl 3 NG31 210 D5
St Edmunds Rd NG34 . 212 C3
St Edward's Dr 15 LN2 ... 68 F2
St Edwins Cl 18 DN7 .... 14 D4
St Edwins Dr 19 DN7 .... 14 D4
St Faith & St Martin CE (Controlled) Jun Sch LN1 .... 201 D4
St Faith's St 6 LN1 ... 201 D4
St Faiths CE Inf Sch LN1 .... 201 D4
St Firmin's Way PE10 .. 164 D7
St Frances Cl PE25 .... 206 B6
St Francis Ave DN31 .. 191 A8
St Francis Ct 5 LN6 ... 204 D2
St Francis Gdns 23 LN12 .77 A7
St Francis Gr 1 DN37 ... 23 E1
St Francis Sch LN1 ..... 201 E7
St George Ave PE2 .... 231 E6
St George's Ave
6 Hatfield DN7 .... 14 C3
5 Hatfield DN7 .... 14 C2
St George's Cl LN6 ... 204 E2
St George's Coll of Tech NG34 .... 212 C4
St George's Ct DN21 .... 30 F3
St George's Hill DN21 ... 54 F7
St George's Hospl LN1 .... 201 C6
St George's Rd
Kingston upon Hull HU3 .. 180 A5
17 Wittering PE8 .... 172 B1
St George's Sq 13 PE9 .. 219 C5
St George's St 6 PE9 .. 219 C5
St Georges Ave 3 PE9 . 219 D6
St Georges CE Com Prim Sch DN21 .... 197 F2
St Georges CE Prim Sch PE9 .... 219 C7
St Georges Cl
4 Cranwell NG34 ...... 107 F1
22 Thorne/Moorends DN8 . 15 B7
St Georges Dr 3 LN10 ... 97 C5
St Georges La LN2 ...... 67 F1
St Georges Prim Sch HU3 .... 180 A6
St Georges Rd 21 DN8 ... 15 B7
St Georges Sch PE1 ... 226 A7
St Gilbert of Sempringham CE Prim Sch NG34 ..... 143 B7
St Gilbert's Cl NG34 ... 143 B6
St Gilbert's Rd PE10 .. 213 C6
St Gilberts CE Prim Sch PE9 .... 219 A5

St Giles' Ave DN33 ....191 D1
St Giles Ave
Lincoln LN2 ....234 C4
1 Sleaford NG34 ....212 F4
St Giles Inf Sch LN2 ...202 B6
St Guthlac Ave 1 PE6 ...217 B5
St Guthlac High Sch
PE6 ....166 F1
St Guthlac's Cl 8 PE6 ...166 F1
St Guthlac's Way 1
PE21 ....126 C1
St Helen's Ave LN6 .....205 B7
St Helenas CE Prim Sch
LN13 ....89 A7
St Helen's Cl NG31 .....210 D4
St Helen's Cres DN37 ..194 D1
St Helen's Dr 14 HU15 .....2 D6
St Helen's Rd DN20 ....196 D3
St Helens Ave DN33 ....191 D3
St Helens Way DN21 .....42 E2
St Helier's Rd DN35 ....192 E7
St Hilary's Cl 1 LN6 ...204 D2
St Hilda's Ave DN34 ....191 B6
St Huberts Dr PE25 .....206 B6
St Hugh St LN2 ....234 C2
St Hugh's Ave DN35 .....192 E6
St Hugh's Cl 7 LN3 .....203 E7
St Hugh's Cres DN16 ....185 C8
St Hugh's Dr
3 Barlings LN3 ....69 C3
Lincoln LN6 ....204 E2
St Hugh's Hospl DN32 .191 F4
St Hugh's Terr 3 LN1 ....66 C7
St Hughs CE High Sch
NG31 ....210 E3
St Hughs RC Prim Sch
LN6 ....204 B7
St Hughs Sch
Scunthorpe DN16 ....183 B1
Woodhall Spa LN10 ....97 D5
St Hybald's Gr 2 DN20 ...30 F7
St Ives Cres DN34 ......190 E5
St James Ave
3 Grimsby DN34 ....191 A6
7 Hatfield DN7 ....14 C3
Peterborough PE1 ......225 F7
St James Cl 19 DN17 .....16 D7
St James' Ct 2 DN34 ...191 C6
St James Ct 3 DN15 ....183 A3
St James Rd
Brigg DN20 ....196 D3
Long Sutton PE12 ......216 A1
Welton HU14 ....2 F5
St James Sch DN34 ....191 C6
St James St HU3 ....180 D5
St James View LN11 ...198 B4
St James Way PE12 ....157 E1
St James's Rd 6 DN20 ...30 E8
St James's Way 5 PE11 214 D2
St Joan's Dr 5 DN20 .....30 E8
St John Baptist CE (Aided)
Prim Sch PE11 ....214 C2
St John Fisher RC Gm Sch
PE1 ....226 C4
St John St 1 PE24 ......102 D1
St John's Sch LN4 ....205 F4
St John's Ave
6 Cherry Willingham/Reepham
LN3 ....203 E7
1 Lincoln LN6 ....204 E2
St John's Cl
11 Leasingham NG34 ....121 B7
6 Morton PE10 ....154 C7
6 Ryhall PE9 ....163 C1
St John's Dr
Corby Glen NG33 ....152 F7
6 Spalding PE11 ....214 B3
St John's Rd
Boston PE21 ....209 A3
Bracebridge Heath LN4 ..205 F2
9 Humberston DN36 .....36 C8
Lincoln LN2 ....201 F6
Scunthorpe DN16 ....185 C6
Spalding PE11 ....214 C3
Weston PE12 ....157 C2
15 Wittering PE8 ....172 B1
St John's St
3 Holbeach PE12 ....215 E2
Peterborough PE1 ......226 B2
Stamford PE9 ....219 B5
St John's Terr 13 DN21 .197 D3
St John's Wlk HU13 ...178 F2
St Johns Church Sch CE
Aided PE2 ....229 F3
St Johns Cl
2 Baston PE6 ....164 E5
21 Goxhill DN19 ....12 A8
Scampton LN1 ....67 C6
St Johns Prim Sch
PE2 ....231 C7
St Johns Rd PE2 ....231 B7
St Joseph Dr HU4 .....179 C5
St Josephs RC Prim Sch
DN35 ....192 D4
St Judes Cl PE3 ....225 C4
St Julian's Wells
HU10 ....178 D7
St Lamberts Gr 4 PE12 157 D7
St Lawrence CE (Controlled)
Prim Sch LN6 ....200 B4
St Lawrence Rd DN7 ....14 C4
St Lawrence Specl Sch
LN9 ....199 D4
St Lawrence St 4 LN9 .199 B4
St Lawrence Way 3
PE9 ....172 F7
St Lawrence's Pl 2
DN16 ....185 D7
St Lawrence's Rd
DN16 ....185 D6
St Leodegar's Cl PE20 .136 D7
St Leonard Cl PE21 ....209 A6
St Leonard's Ave
DN31 ....191 A8
St Leonard's Dr 6 LN10 .97 D5
St Leonard's La
1 Lincoln LN2 ....234 C3
South Cockerington LN11 ..62 B7
St Leonard's Rd 2 PE13 170 B2
St Leonard's St 8 PE9 .219 C5
St Leonards Dr PE24 .....90 D7
St Luke's Cl
Cherry Willingham/Reepham
LN3 ....203 F7
1 Hatfield DN7 ....14 C2
St Luke's Cres 8 DN36 ...36 C8
St Luke's Ct 8 DN32 ...191 F8
St Luke's St HU3 ......180 D6
St Lukes CE Prim Sch
LN7 ....45 B8
St Lukes Sch DN16 ....185 D7
St Margaret's 6 PE11 ..145 A8
St Margaret's Ave
PE25 ....206 A6
St Margaret's Cl
17 Laceby DN37 ....23 F1
6 Lincoln LN6 ....205 B4
St Margaret's Cres 6
DN40 ....22 E8
St Margaret's Dr PE22 .113 A2
St Margaret's Gdns
LN6 ....205 A4
St Margaret's Wlk 5
DN16 ....185 C6
St Margarets CE (Controlled)
Prim Sch LN13 ....63 A1
St Margarets Pl 2 PE2 .230 F6
St Margarets Rd 1 PE2 230 F6
St Mark St
Kingston upon Hull HU8 ..181 A8
Lincoln LN5 ....234 A1
St Mark's Ave 3 LN3 ...203 E7
St Mark's Cl
North Hykeham LN6 .....204 E3
Skegness PE25 ....206 B6
St Mark's Ct 3 PE1 ....226 A3
St Mark's Rd
Holbeach PE12 ....147 D6
10 Humberston DN36 .....36 C8
St Mark's Sq
Kingston upon Hull HU3 ..180 D4
Lincoln LN5 ....234 A1
St Marks Dr 6 PE6 .....166 E1
St Marks Rd PE13 ......169 E3
St Marks St PE1 ....226 A3
St Martin's Cl
8 Blyton DN21 ....41 C5
4 Stamford PE9 ....219 C4
St Martin's Cres
Grimsby DN33 ....191 C3
7 Scawby DN20 ....30 E8
St Martin's La LN1 ....234 B3
St Martin's Pl 5 DN41 ...23 A4
St Martin's Rd
Newborough PE6 ....221 F8
4 Scawby DN20 ....30 E8
1 Wisbech PE13 ....170 E2
St Martin's St
Lincoln LN2 ....234 B3
Peterborough PE1 ......225 F5
St Martin's Way 4
NG32 ....120 A3
St Martins NG33 ....152 E1
St Martins Ave 2 HU4 ..179 E6
St Martins CE Prim Sch
DN9 ....28 A3
St Martins Cl 2 NG34 ..107 F1
St Martins Prep Sch
DN32 ....191 D5
St Mary Cl 12 PE6 ......166 F1
St Mary's Ave
4 Barnetby le Wold DN38 .21 B4
4 Pinchbeck PE11 ....156 E8
12 Welton/Dunholme LN2 ..68 D7
Wittering PE8 ....172 C1
St Mary's Cl
Bainton PE9 ....172 F5
18 Bottesford NG13 .....128 A6
2 Brough HU15 ....2 C7
Farcet PE7 ....231 C2
Grimsby DN32 ....192 C6
Peterborough PE1 ......226 B4
Thorney PE6 ....176 A2
Wilsford NG32 ....120 C1
St Mary's Cres
9 Manby LN11 ....62 C6
5 Stow LN1 ....66 C8
Swineshead PE20 ....135 B6
St Mary's Ct 9 DN15 ...182 C6
St Mary's Dr
8 Hatfield DN7 ....14 C3
15 Hatfield DN7 ....14 C2
10 Hatfield DN7 ....14 C2
2 Hatfield DN7 ....14 C2
Peterborough PE2 ......229 F4
St Mary's Gdns
6 Cowbit PE12 ....167 B8
Long Sutton PE12 ......216 C5
3 Whaplode PE12 ....158 B7
St Mary's Hill 17 PE9 ..219 C5
St Mary's La
4 Barton-upon-Humber
DN18 ....10 F8
Binbrook LN8 ....47 C4
Claxby LN8 ....45 E5
Louth LN11 ....198 A5
St Mary's Mdws 2
PE12 ....159 D7
St Mary's Pk LN11 .....198 A6
St Mary's Pl 14 PE9 ....219 C5
St Mary's Rd
Hatfield DN7 ....14 C3
2 Lincoln LN6 ....204 E2
Skegness PE25 ....206 B6
West Walton PE14 ......170 E4
St Mary's St Farcet PE7 .231 C2
Lincoln LN5 ....234 A1
12 Stamford PE9 ....219 C5
St Mary's Way 2 PE22 ..114 A1
St Marys Cath Prim Sch
NG31 ....211 C5
St Marys CE (Controlled)
Prim Sch
Welton/Dunholme LN2 ....68 C6
Weston PE12 ....157 E7
St Marys Cl 5 PE12 ....157 D7
St Marys Dr 6 NG34 ...212 C6
St Marys Prep Sch
LN2 ....234 C3
St Marys RC High Sch
DN33 ....191 A3
St Marys RC Prim Sch
Brigg DN20 ....196 C5
Grimsby DN32 ....191 F8
St Mathews Cl 2 LN6 ..201 D1
St Matthew St HU3 ....180 B5
St Matthew's Cl
5 Cherry Willingham/Reepham
LN3 ....203 E7
4 Holbeach PE12 ....215 D2
St Matthew's Dr 13
PE12 ....160 E4
St Matthew's Rd 12 DN36 36 C8
St Mawes Cres DN34 ..191 A7
St Michael Cl 25 LN5 ....93 F7
St Michael's Ave PE13 .170 D1
St Michael's Cl 16 DN8 ..15 B7
St Michael's Cres 5
DN16 ....185 C8
St Michael's Ct 22 DN19 .12 A8
St Michael's Dr 15 DN8 ..15 B8
St Michael's Gate PE1 .226 F7
St Michael's La
11 Wainfleet St Mary
PE24 ....102 D1
Wainfleet St Mary PE24 ..115 D8
St Michael's Mount 18
HU14 ....3 B7
St Michael's Rd
Grimsby DN34 ....190 D4
3 Louth LN11 ....198 C5
16 Wittering PE8 ....172 B1
St Michael's Way 1
NG34 ....120 C8
St Michaels CE (Controlled)
Prim Sch LN11 ....198 D5
St Michaels Cl 8 LN4 ..109 F5
St Michaels Terr 7 LN1 234 B3
St Michaels Wlk 8
NG34 ....212 C6
St Nectan Cl 9 HU3 ...180 A4
St Nicholas Ave HU4 ..179 C2
St Nicholas CE (Controlled)
Prim Sch PE21 ....209 B4
St Nicholas CE Prim Sch
DN39 ....12 A1
St Nicholas Cl
4 Barkston NG32 ....130 B8
Boston PE21 ....209 B3
St Nicholas Dr DN37 ..190 C6
St Nicholas Prim Sch
PE12 ....160 A8
St Nicholas Rd
Boston PE21 ....209 B3
Thorne/Moorends DN8 ....15 A8
St Nicholas St LN1 ....234 A4
St Nicholas Way 10
PE12 ....160 A8
St Norberts RC Prim Sch
DN17 ....16 D7
St Norbett Sch Prim School
PE11 ....214 C4
St Olaf's Dr DN32 .....191 D6
St Olave's Dr 17 PE6 ...175 A1
St Paul Rd DN21 ....197 B7
St Paul's Ave 4 LN3 ...203 E7
St Paul's Cl PE13 .....169 E2
St Paul's Gdns PE10 ...213 D4
St Paul's La 2 LN1 ....234 B3
St Paul's Rd
Gainsborough DN21 .....197 B7
Peterborough PE1 ......225 F7
Scunthorpe DN16 ....185 B6
Spalding PE11 ....214 F5
St Paul's St PE9 ......219 C5
St Pauls Cl PE24 ......102 D7
St Pauls Prim Sch
PE11 ....214 F6
St Pega Cl 17 PE6 .....166 F1
St Pega's Rd
Glinton PE6 ....174 A6
Peakirk PE6 ....220 E8
St Peter & St Paul CE Prim
Sch PE24 ....102 D7
St Peter & St Paul RC High
Sch LN6 ....205 B7
St Peter at Gowts CE
(Controlled) Prim Sch
LN5 ....201 E1
St Peter's Ave
8 Cherry Willingham/Reepham
LN3 ....203 E7
Cleethorpes DN35 ......192 E6
St Peter's Ave *continued*
Kingston upon Hull
HU10 ....178 E6
Lincoln LN6 ....204 D2
Scunthorpe DN16 ....185 B3
St Peter's CE Jun Sch
PE13 ....170 E1
St Peter's Cl
Burgh le Marsh PE24 ....102 D8
4 Holton le Clay DN36 ..195 D2
St Peter's Cres 5 DN36 ..36 C8
St Peter's Dr 4 LN10 ....97 D5
St Peter's Gr 14 DN21 ...29 C3
St Peter's Hill
6 Grantham NG31 ....211 B4
4 Grantham NG31 ....211 A4
14 Stamford PE9 ....219 B5
St Peter's La 4 LN12 ....64 C2
St Peter's Rd 12 DN21 ...29 C3
St Peter's Sch DN10 ....39 B1
St Peter's St PE9 .....219 B4
St Peter's Way PE6 ....176 A2
St Peter-in-Eastgate CE
(Controlled) Inf Sch
LN2 ....234 C3
St Peters CE Prim Sch
Cleethorpes DN35 ......192 F6
Dunston LN4 ....95 C6
St Peters Cl DN21 ....40 B5
St Peters Gr 2 DN37 ....23 E1
St Peters Rd
11 Bourne PE10 ....213 C5
Peterborough PE1 ......226 A2
St Polycarp's Dr PE12 .168 B3
St Quintins Cl 5 HU9 ..181 C8
St Rumbold's St LN2 ..234 B2
St Sebastians CE (Aided)
Prim Sch NG31 ....129 E5
St Simon's Dr 9 LN3 ..203 E7
St Stephens St HU2 ....180 D6
St Swithuns Cl 1 PE20 .135 A4
St Swithuns Sq LN2 ...234 B2
St Thomas CE (Controlled)
Prim Sch PE21 ....208 F1
St Thomas Ct PE12 .....216 B5
St Thomas Dr PE21 ....208 E2
St Thomas Moore RC Prim
Sch PE1 ....226 D4
St Thomas Moore Rd
HU4 ....179 A4
St Thomas More RC Prim Sch
HU4 ....179 A4
St Thomas' Rd 13 DN36 ..36 C8
St Thomas's Rd 2 PE11 214 D2
St Tibba Way 12 PE9 ...163 C1
St Valentines Way
PE25 ....206 B6
St Vincent Cl 2 PE25 ..206 A6
St Vincent's Ave DN15 .183 A6
St Vincent's Rd NG31 ..211 C3
St Wilfrid's Cl 18 LN4 ...95 D4
Salacon Way 5 DN32 ...189 C1
Salamander Cl DN31 ...191 B8
Salem St 5 PE11 ......145 B6
Salisbury Ave 2 LN8 ....47 B6
Salisbury Cl
1 Grantham NG31 ....210 D5
1 Saxilby with Ingleby LN1 66 D2
2 Scunthorpe DN17 .....184 C7
Salisbury Dr
Canwick LN4 ....81 A2
8 Waltham DN37 ....194 D4
Salisbury Rd PE4 ......220 F3
Salisbury St
Gainsborough DN21 .....197 C7
Kingston upon Hull
HU13 ....178 D1
Salix App 1 LN6 ....204 C8
Sallie Bank La LN1 .....65 D2
Sallows Rd PE1 ....226 B6
Salmonby Rd DN17 .....184 E4
Salsbury Ave DN34 ....191 B6
Saltash Rd HU4 ....179 A2
Saltburn Gr 5 DN32 ...192 A5
Saltby Rd
Croxton Kerrial NG32 ...138 D3
Sproxton LE14 ....150 C7
Salter Gate LN11 ......51 A1
Saltergate Lincoln LN2 ..234 B2
Peterborough PE1 ......226 E7
Saltergate Rd 28 DN17 ..29 D7
Salters' La LN11 ....48 B4
Salters Way 14 PE11 ...134 E2
Saltersford Gr NG31 ..211 D1
Saltersford Rd NG31 ..211 D2
Saltersgate PE1 ......226 F7
Saltersway NG34 ......132 F3
Saltfleet La PE11 ....145 B4
Saltfleet Rd
Saltfleetby LN12 ....51 D1
Theddlethorpe All Saints
LN12 ....63 E8
Saltfleetby - Theddlethorpe
Dunes National Nature
Reserve* LN11 ....51 E3
Saltfleetby CE Prim Sch
LN11 ....51 A1
Saltford Ave 2 HU9 .....5 F8
Saltgrounds Rd HU15 ....2 B5
Salthouse La HU1 .....181 A6
Saltings The 6 PE34 ...161 F3
Saltmarsh PE2 ....230 C4
Saltney Gate PE12 ....215 A6
Salts Rd PE14 ....170 F4
Salvesen Rd DN35 .....189 D1
Salvesen Way HU3 ....180 A3
Samman Cl HU10 ......178 D6
Samphire Cl 6 DN36 ....37 C5
Sampson St DN17 ....7 A2
Samuel Ave DN32 ......192 B6
Samworths Cl PE5 .....223 F2
Sanbeds La DN9 ....27 B2
Sanctuary Way DN37 ..190 C6
Sand La Barkston NG32 .129 F8
Besthorpe NG23 ....91 C8
Broadholme LN6 ....66 D1
4 Broughton DN20 ....19 D3
Caistor LN7 ....32 E4
Fenton LN1 ....65 D3
Great Steeping PE23 .....101 C7
Hougham NG32 ....118 C5
Manton DN21 ....30 A5
Marston NG32 ....118 E1
Messingham DN17 ....29 A7
Osgodby LN8 ....45 B3
Spalford NG23 ....78 D4
Thorney NG23 ....79 B8
Torksey LN1 ....65 E5
Wroot DN9 ....26 C6
Sand Rd DN17 ....28 B8
Sandars Rd DN21 ....53 A8
Sandbeck Ave PE25 ....206 C2
Sandbeck La DN21 ....41 B6
Sandcliffe Rd NG31 ...211 A7
Sanderlings The 6 PE6 174 A5
Sanders Cl Lincoln LN1 .201 D8
15 Mablethorpe & Sutton
LN12 ....77 A7
Meering NG23 ....91 C8
Sanderson Cl 1 DN16 ..183 B1
Sanderson's Bank
DN10 ....26 C2
Sandfield Cl DN17 .....184 D5
Sandfield Dr 1 HU15 .....2 C5
Sandford PE3 ....225 B5
Sandford St 8 DN31 ....188 D1
Sandhill La 1 DN22 .....52 B3
Sandhill Rd DN14 ....7 B6
Sandholme La PE20 ....136 E5
Sandhouse Cres
3 Scunthorpe DN16 .....183 C1
Scunthorpe DN16 ....185 C8
Sandhurst Cres 5
NG34 ....212 B2
Sandhurst Ct 6 LN12 ....77 A7
Sandhurst Rd 5 LN12 ....77 A7
Sandilands Cl 22 LN12 ...77 A7
Sandilands Pit Nature
Reserve* LN12 ....77 A7
Sandlees La NG34 .....123 B4
Sandlemere Cl 3 HU3 ..180 A5
Sandon Cl NG31 ....211 C5
Sandon Rd NG31 ....211 B5
Sandon Sch NG31 ......211 C5
Sandown Cl 5 PE11 ....156 E3
Sandpiper Dr
Kingston upon Hull HU4 ..179 B1
Peterborough PE2 ......231 E6
Sandpit Rd 14 PE6 .....176 A3
Sandra Cres LN4 ......203 D1
Sandringham Ave 29
PE13 ....170 D1
Sandringham Cl
5 Stamford PE9 ....219 B7
3 Whaplode PE12 ....158 B6
Sandringham Cres
DN17 ....184 F3
Sandringham Ct 4
PE12 ....215 F3
Sandringham Dr
Londonthorpe &
Harrowby without NG31 .211 E5
Louth LN11 ....198 B7
13 Mablethorpe & Sutton
LN12 ....76 F8
Wragby LN8 ....70 D4
Sandringham Gdns
PE21 ....209 C6
Sandringham Rd
Cleethorpes DN35 ......192 D4
2 Peterborough PE4 ....225 C8
Sandringham St 2 HU3 180 A6
Sandringham Way 3
PE6 ....217 A5
Sandringham Wlk 6
PE11 ....214 D2
Sands Cl 3 DN17 ....17 D5
Sands Ct 1 HU14 ....3 A4
Sands La
Brantingham HU15 ....1 F7
Brough HU15 ....2 C6
Carlton-le-Moorland LN5 ...92 E1
Ellerker HU15 ....2 A6
Scotter DN21 ....29 B3
2 South Ferriby DN18 ....10 A7
Sandsfield La DN21 ....197 D2
Sandtoft Cl LN6 ....204 D6
Sandtoft Rd
Hatfield DN7 ....15 A4
Sandtoft DN9 ....16 B3
Sandwell Dr LN6 ....200 D1
Sandy Bank PE22 ....98 C1
Sandy Cl 1 DN36 ....37 C5
Sandy Gate
Quadring PE11 ....144 F7
Sutton St James PE12 ...169 A7
Sandy La Anderby PE24 ...77 C3
Belchford LN9 ....73 A2
Candlesby with Gunby
PE23 ....88 F1
Chapel St Leonard PE24 ...90 E7
Great Steeping PE23 ....101 D7
Lusby with Winceby PE23 ..86 F1

Sandy La *continued*
North Willingham LN8 ...58 C8
Tealby LN8 ...46 C1
Tydd St Giles PE13 ...170 A7
5 West Ashby LN9 ...85 E7
Woodhall Spa LN10 ...97 E7
Sandyford La PE22 ...113 E3
Sandygate Cl NG34 ...133 C1
Sandygate La NG34 ...133 C2
Saner St HU3 ...180 B6
Sansford Gn 5 LN6 ...205 A6
Sapperton PE4 ...220 F6
Sapphire Cl PE24 ...89 D2
Sapphire Gr 7 HU3 ...180 A4
Saracen Cl DN21 ...197 F2
Sarah Gate PE11 ...145 B8
Sarge Cl 5 DN36 ...195 D2
Sargeants Cl 9 PE22 ...113 B1
Sargent Cl 4 LN4 ...95 C4
Sargent's Ct 5 PE9 ...219 A6
Sargon Way 3 DN31 ...188 A3
Sarthe Cl 5 PE20 ...135 B7
Sassaby Cl HU4 ...179 C3
Satinwood Cl 10 LN6 ...200 C1
Satterley Cl LN6 ...92 D4
Saunby Gr DN35 ...192 E7
Saundby Rd DN22 ...52 B6
Saundergate La PE21 ..136 D8
Saundergate Pk 11
PE21 ...136 D8
Saunders St 6 DN31 ...191 C8
Sausthorpe CE Sch
PE23 ...87 E4
Sausthorpe Rd
Partney PE23 ...88 A3
Sausthorpe PE23 ...87 F3
Sausthorpe St 9 LN5 ..201 F1
Saville Rd PE3 ...225 D4
Saville St LN5 ...205 D7
Savory Rd 1 PE13 ...170 D1
Savoy Ct 7 DN36 ...195 C6
Sawmill La LN8 ...70 C5
Saxby Ave PE25 ...206 D2
Saxby Cliff Rd LN8 ...55 D4
Saxby Gdns PE1 ...226 C8
Saxby Gr DN33 ...191 A3
Saxby Hill DN20 ...10 B4
Saxby Rd Bonby DN20 ...10 B2
Scunthorpe DN17 ...184 E5
Saxilby CE (Controlled) Prim
Sch LN1 ...66 E2
Saxilby Rd Lincoln LN1 ..201 A7
Skellingthorpe LN6 ...200 A6
Sturton by Stow LN1 ...66 D6
Saxilby Sta LN1 ...66 D2
Saxon Cl
7 Barton-upon-Humber
DN18 ...10 F8
10 Metheringham LN4 ...95 D4
Spalding PE11 ...214 F2
Saxon Cres DN35 ...192 E6
Saxon Ct 2 Blyton DN21 ..41 C5
Scunthorpe DN16 ...185 B3
Saxon Rd
8 Barnack PE9 ...172 D3
Peterborough PE1 ...226 C3
Saxon St LN1 ...234 A4
Saxon Way
2 Ancaster NG32 ...120 A2
Bourne PE10 ...213 C6
17 Caistor LN7 ...33 B4
2 Horncastle LN9 ...199 D3
6 Ingham LN1 ...54 F2
Kingston upon Hull
HU13 ...178 F1
Saxondale HU4 ...179 B7
Saxonfield LN7 ...33 A4
Saxony Way 6 PE11 ...134 F2
Sayer Ct PE2 ...229 F2
Scalby Gr HU5 ...179 D8
Scald Gate PE22 ...115 B8
Scale La HU1 ...181 A6
Scalesgate Rd PE12 ...159 B1
Scalford Dr PE1 ...226 C8
Scallow La DN17 ...29 D6
Scalp Rd PE21 ...137 B7
Scamblesby CE (Controlled)
Prim Sch LN11 ...72 F5
Scamblesby Hill LN9 ...72 E4
Scampton Airfield LN1 ..67 E6
Scampton Ave LN6 ...204 F6
Scampton CE (Controlled)
Prim Sch LN1 ...67 D6
Scampton Cl 4 DN34 ..191 A5
Scampton Way
Gainsborough DN21 ...197 E3
Skegness PE25 ...206 A5
Scandinavian Way
DN41 ...187 B3
Scarborough Bank
PE22 ...100 B1
Scarborough Cl PE10 ..142 F2
Scarborough St HU3 ..180 A4
Scarbrough Ave PE25 .206 D4
Scarbrough Espl PE25 .206 E3
Scargate La LN4 ...108 F8
Scarle Cl 1 LN6 ...205 A2
Scarle La LN6 ...79 B2
Scarrington Cres HU4 .179 B6
Scarrow Cl HU3 ...180 A7
Scartho Jun & Inf Sch
DN33 ...191 D2
Scartho Pk DN33 ...191 B2
Scartho Rd DN33 ...191 D2
Scawby Cres LN6 ...204 F7
Scawby Prim Sch DN20 .30 E8
Scawby Rd Brigg DN20 .196 A2
Broughton DN20 ...19 E2
Grimsby DN33 ...191 A3
Scawby DN20 ...31 A7
Scunthorpe DN17 ...184 E5
Schiphol Way DN38 ...21 E5
Schofield Cl 7 DN19 ...11 C8
School Cl 1 Maxey PE6 .173 C7
Peterborough PE3 ...225 A5
School Cres
Anwick NG34 ...109 B1
1 Scothern LN2 ...68 F4
5 Surfleet PE11 ...145 E3
School Dr
27 Messingham DN17 ...29 D7
8 Welton/Dunholme LN2 ..68 C6
School Hill LE14 ...150 C7
School House La 6
DN10 ...39 F3
School Houses 9 DN20 ..19 E4
School La
Addlethorpe PE24 ...90 D3
Appleby DN15 ...9 D1
1 Baston PE6 ...164 E4
Beckingham LN5 ...105 B4
8 Bicker PE20 ...135 A4
Binbrook LN8 ...47 B5
5 Bonby DN20 ...10 C2
Boothby Pagnell NG33 ...140 F5
Buckminster NG33 ...150 F5
Butterwick PE22 ...126 E3
Cabourne LN7 ...33 D5
Canwick LN4 ...81 A4
Claypole NG23 ...117 F8
7 Colsterworth NG33 ...151 D7
1 Coningsby LN4 ...207 C4
5 Croxton Kerrial NG32 .138 D4
4 Donington PE11 ...134 F2
East Keal PE23 ...100 E6
Edenham PE10 ...153 F4
4 Glinton PE6 ...220 C8
18 Goxhill DN19 ...12 A8
Grayingham DN21 ...42 E7
Great Steeping PE23 ...101 E7
Hainton LN8 ...58 E3
3 Harmston LN5 ...93 F5
Heighington/Washingborough
LN4 ...203 C2
5 Helpringham NG34 ...133 D7
3 Irby DN37 ...34 D7
1 Irby DN37 ...34 D7
Kingston upon Hull
HU10 ...178 C8
9 Lincoln LN6 ...204 F1
5 Lutton PE12 ...160 A8
Maltby Le Marsh LN13 ...76 A8
4 Mareham Le Fen PE22 ..99 A4
Marston NG32 ...118 D2
3 Maxey PE6 ...173 C7
1 New Holland DN19 ...4 E2
North Cockerington LN11 ..49 F1
3 North Ferriby HU14 ...3 A4
4 North Kelsey LN7 ...32 A4
North Scarle LN6 ...78 E1
North Somercotes LN11 ...50 F7
Old Leake PE22 ...114 A1
Old Somerby NG33 ...140 E8
Raithby PE23 ...87 D2
Redbourne DN21 ...30 F3
Ropsley NG33 ...131 B1
Rothwell LN7 ...33 E2
1 Scampton Airfield LN1 ..67 F5
Sedgebrook NG32 ...128 F4
Silk Willoughby NG34 ...121 A1
Snitterby DN21 ...43 D5
South Carlton LN1 ...67 D3
7 South Ferriby DN18 ...10 A7
Springthorpe DN21 ...53 E8
2 Sturton by Stow LN1 ...66 C7
17 Tetney DN36 ...36 D4
Thistleton LE15 ...151 C1
Thorpe on the Hill LN6 ...92 E8
6 Uffington PE9 ...172 C6
Walcott LN4 ...109 C7
3 West/East Butterwick
DN17 ...28 D8
2 Willingham by Stow
DN21 ...53 E3
Wilsford NG32 ...120 C1
School Rd
1 Barnack PE9 ...172 D3
Newborough PE6 ...174 E5
Scunthorpe DN16 ...185 B6
8 South Killingholme DN40 12 E3
West Walton PE14 ...170 E4
Winteringham DN15 ...2 A1
School View 10 NG13 ...128 A5
School Wlk DN35 ...192 C5
Schoolhouse La 11
LN11 ...198 B5
Schooner Ct HU4 ...179 B3
Schrimshaw Ct 6 PE25 206 C4
Schrimshire's Rd DN22 .52 A1
Scoggins Way 4 NG34 .122 D3
Scoldall La PE11 ...145 E4
Scolding Dro PE6 ...176 E5
Scopwick Pl 3 LN2 ...201 F8
Scorer St LN5 ...201 F1
Scotenoon PE2 ...229 E3
Scotgate PE9 ...219 A5
Scothern La
Dunholme LN2 ...68 E5
Stainton By Langworth
LN2 ...69 B4
10 Welton/Dunholme LN2 ..68 E6
Scothern Rd LN2 ...68 D3
Scotia Way PE21 ...209 F2
Scotland La NG33 ...141 B5
Scotney Dr NG31 ...211 F5
Scotney St PE1 ...225 E7
Scott Ave DN17 ...184 C6
Scott Cl
6 Claypole NG23 ...117 E8
5 Grimsby DN37 ...190 F8
Peterborough PE2 ...231 E6
Scott Gdns LN2 ...202 C6
Scott St
Gainsborough DN21 ...197 C5
Kingston upon Hull HU2 ..180 F7
Scotten Dike Dro
PE10 ...154 E6
Scotter Prim Sch DN21 .29 C3
Scotter Rd
Laughton DN21 ...41 C8
Messingham DN17 ...29 D5
Scunthorpe DN17 ...182 C1
Scotter Rd S DN17 ...184 C3
Scotterthorpe Rd DN21 .29 B4
Scottlethorpe PE10 ...153 E4
Scottlethorpe Rd
PE10 ...153 D3
Scotton Comm Nature
Reserve★ DN9 ...27 B1
Scotton Dr 1 LN6 ...205 A7
Scotton Rd DN21 ...29 C3
Scott's Cl PE6 ...164 E3
Scott's Hill 4 NG32 ...106 C1
Scotts Rd PE6 ...220 D8
Scrap Bay Rd DN16 ...19 A3
Scredington Rd
Burton Pedwardine
NG34 ...122 B1
Helpringham NG34 ...133 C7
Scrivelsby Ct DN35 ...193 A3
Scrub La Authorpe LN11 ..75 A8
East Halton DN40 ...12 E5
Withern with Stain LN11 ..62 D1
Scullery La NG33 ...141 A5
Scunthorpe CE Prim Sch
DN15 ...183 A4
Scunthorpe General Hospl
DN15 ...182 E2
Scunthorpe Leisure Ctr
DN15 ...183 B3
Scunthorpe Sh Ctr
DN15 ...183 B4
Scunthorpe Sta DN16 ..183 A2
Sea Bank Rd PE24 ...90 E7
Sea Dyke PE22 ...114 B2
Sea Dyke Way 1 DN36 ..37 C2
Sea End Rd PE22 ...127 A4
Sea Front Rd
10 Skegness PE25 ...103 E4
9 Skegness PE25 ...103 E4
Sea La Benington PE22 ..127 B4
Butterwick PE22 ...126 F3
Friskney PE22 ...115 C5
Hogsthorpe PE24 ...90 C7
Huttoft LN13 ...77 A4
Ingoldmells PE25 ...90 E3
Leverton PE22 ...127 B6
Mablethorpe/Sutton on Sea
LN12 ...77 A7
North Coates DN36 ...37 B4
Old Leake PE22 ...114 C1
Saltfleet LN11 ...51 C5
Theddlethorpe St Helen
LN12 ...63 E7
Wrangle PE22 ...114 E1
Sea Rd Anderby PE24 ...77 B2
18 Chapel St Leonard PE24 .90 D7
Cleethorpes DN35 ...192 F6
Sea View LN11 ...51 D3
Sea View Rd PE25 ...206 D5
Sea View St DN35 ...192 F5
Seabank Rd 22 PE13 ...170 E1
Seabrook Dr DN16 ...185 A2
Seacroft Dr 10 PE25 ...206 C1
Seacroft Espl PE25 ...103 E4
Seacroft Rd
Cleethorpes DN35 ...193 A5
Mablethorpe/Sutton on Sea
LN12 ...64 B3
Seacroft Sq
11 Skegness PE25 ...103 E4
10 Skegness PE25 ...103 E4
Seadyke Rd
Kirton PE20 ...136 E3
Wisbech St Mary PE13 ...177 F6
Seafield Rd 5 PE13 ...170 B2
Seaford Rd DN35 ...193 B1
Seagate Rd PE12 ...216 D2
Seagull Cl HU4 ...179 E2
Seaholme Rd LN12 ...64 B2
Seal Sanctuary & Nature Ctr
The★ LN12 ...64 B5
Sealey's La PE13 ...177 D8
Seamer Gr 1 DN32 ...192 A5
Searby Hill DN38 ...32 D8
Searby Rd Lincoln LN2 ..202 B8
Scunthorpe DN17 ...184 E4
Searby Wold La DN38 ...21 E1
Seargeants Cl 1 PE6 ...174 E4
Searjeant St PE1 ...225 E5
Seas End Prim Sch
PE11 ...145 D3
Seas End Rd
Moulton PE12 ...146 D1
Surfleet PE11 ...145 E3
Seathorne Cres PE25 ...90 F1
Seathorne Prim Sch
PE25 ...206 D7
Seaton Cl PE7 ...233 D6
Seaton Gr
Grimsby DN32 ...192 A5
Seaton Gr *continued*
Kingston upon Hull HU4 ..179 E5
Seaton Rd
Kingston upon Hull
HU13 ...178 F2
Scunthorpe DN17 ...184 D8
6 Stamford PE9 ...219 B4
Seawall La DN36 ...37 C5
Sebrights Way PE3 ...224 F3
Second Ave
Fixborough Ind Est DN15 ...7 F1
Grantham NG31 ...211 F6
Grimsby DN33 ...191 B4
5 Scampton Airfield LN1 ..67 E5
3 Scunthorpe DN17 ...184 C6
Spalding PE11 ...214 A4
Second Dro
Crowland PE6 ...166 E3
Gosberton PE11 ...144 C3
Peterborough PE1 ...226 D1
Second Marsh Rd
PE14 ...170 C3
Sedge Cl
6 Barton-upon-Humber
DN18 ...3 F1
Leasingham NG34 ...121 C7
Sedge Hole Cl Nature
Reserve★ DN9 ...27 F2
Sedge Pl 9 PE12 ...167 B8
Sedgebrook Cl 1 LN2 ..201 F8
Sedgebrook Rd NG32 ..128 F6
Sedgemoor Cl 3 LN6 ..204 E1
Sedgewood Way
DN15 ...182 C6
Seed Cl La 4 DN37 ...23 F1
Sefton Ave PE13 ...170 E1
Sefton St 2 HU3 ...180 B4
Segmere St 3 DN35 ...193 A5
Segrave Gr HU5 ...179 D8
Selbourne Rd 5 DN34 ..190 E4
Selby Cl LN6 ...205 A3
Selby Rd DN8 ...14 F8
Selby St HU3 ...180 A5
Selge Way DN33 ...190 F3
Selkirk St HU5 ...180 A8
Sellers Grange PE2 ...230 B4
Sellwood Gdns LN9 ...199 B3
Selwyn Ave 16 HU14 ...3 A4
Selwyn Rd PE9 ...219 A7
Sempers Cl LN6 ...92 E8
Sentance Cres PE20 ...136 C6
Seraphim App Rd
DN16 ...183 E1
Seraphim Rd DN16 ...183 F1
Serena Rd 5 PE25 ...206 D2
Serpentine St 1 LN8 ...57 D7
Serpentine The PE7 ...230 D3
Service Rd 1 9 DN37 ..190 E8
Service Rd 2 10 DN37 ..190 E8
Service Rd 3 7 DN37 ..190 E8
Service Rd 4 4 DN37 ..190 E8
Service Rd 5 5 DN37 ..190 E8
Service Rd 6 6 DN37 ..190 E8
Service Rd 7 7 DN37 ..190 F8
Service Rd 8 8 DN37 ..188 A1
Service Rd 9 7 DN37 ..188 A1
Service Rd 10 6 DN37 .188 A1
Service Rd 12 2 DN37 .188 A1
Service Rd 13 4 DN37 .188 A1
Service Rd 14 3 DN37 .188 A1
Service Rd 15 8 DN37 .190 E8
Service Rd 16 DN37 ..190 E8
Service Rd 17 DN37 ..190 F8
Service Rd 18 DN37 ..190 F8
Service Rd 19 8 DN37 .190 F8
Service Rd 20 11 DN37 .190 E8
Service Rd 21 3 DN37 .190 E8
Service Rd 22 2 DN37 .190 E8
Service Rd 23 DN37 ..190 E8
Service Rd 25 1 DN37 .190 E8
Service Rd 26 9 DN37 .188 A1
Service Rd No 1 5
DN32 ...189 B1
Service Rd No 2 7
DN32 ...189 B1
Services Rd DN16 ...183 E2
Setchfield Pl PE2 ...230 F7
Setterwood Garth 2
HU10 ...178 E8
Seven Quay Rd DN40 ..186 E7
Sevenacres PE2 ...229 E5
Seventh Ave 3 NG31 ..211 F6
Severn Cl PE4 ...221 C1
Severn Rd PE11 ...214 F5
Severn St LN1 ...201 C4
Sewell Cl PE6 ...217 E5
Sewell Rd LN2 ...234 C3
Sewell's Wlk LN5 ...201 E1
Sewer La 3 HU1 ...180 F5
Sewstern La
Allington NG32 ...128 E7
Long Bennington NG23 ..117 E1
Sedgebrook NG32 ...128 D4
Sewstern Rd NG33 ...151 B4
Seymour Ave LN11 ...198 C4
Seymour La 14 LN13 ...75 F2
Seymour Pl PE4 ...221 F2
Seymour St HU3 ...179 F5
Sezanne Wlk 10 PE11 ..214 C6
Shackleton Cl PE6 ...217 B7
Shaddys Wlk LN13 ...88 E6
Shaftesbury Ave
Birchwood LN6 ...200 D2
Grimsby DN34 ...191 B7
Shaftesbury Mews 6
DN36 ...195 C6
Shaftesbury Way 2
NG23 ...91 D5
Shakespeare Ave
Grantham NG31 ...211 E6
Peterborough PE1 ...225 F7
4 Scunthorpe DN17 ...184 C6
Shakespeare Cl 6 HU3 .180 D8
Shakespeare St
5 Gainsborough DN21 ..197 D2
5 Lincoln LN5 ...205 E8
Shamfields Rd 3 PE23 .101 A8
Shamrock Cl PE2 ...231 C7
Shanklin Dr NG31 ...210 E4
Shannon Ave LN6 ...205 A5
Shannon Cl 2 LN6 ...205 A5
Shannon Rd 8 LN4 ...207 D4
Shardloes LN4 ...81 E2
Shardloes Rd 9 PE25 ..103 E4
Sharma Leas PE4 ...220 E3
Sharmans Cl 11 LN12 ...77 A7
Sharpe Cl 35 DN18 ...10 E8
Sharpe Rd NG31 ...211 C6
Sharpe's Rd PE6 ...165 C3
Sharp's Cl PE10 ...213 B6
Sharp's La PE22 ...127 A6
Shaw Dr DN33 ...191 E1
Shaw La PE22 ...127 B8
Shaw Rd Boston PE21 ..208 C7
Grantham NG31 ...210 D2
Gringley on the Hill DN10 ..39 C2
Shaw St HU9 ...181 B7
Shaw Way 4 LN2 ...68 C2
Shawbury Cl 10 LN6 ..204 C6
Shawfield Cl 10 DN3 ...14 A3
Shaws La PE12 ...160 B3
Shays Dr 1 LN6 ...205 A7
Shearman's Wath
Thimbleby LN9 ...85 C6
West Ashby LN9 ...199 A8
Shears Ct DN37 ...194 F4
Shearwater Cl
3 Birchwood LN6 ...200 E1
2 Birchwood LN6 ...204 E8
Louth LN11 ...198 D8
Shearwater Rd LN6 ...200 E1
Sheep Cote La DN7 ...14 D2
Sheep Dip La DN7 ...14 D4
Sheep Marsh La DN36 ..37 B3
Sheep Mkt
2 Spalding PE11 ...214 D4
11 Stamford PE9 ...219 B5
Sheepdyke La 4 DN20 ..10 C2
Sheepfold St 10 DN32 ..191 E7
Sheepgate PE22 ...127 A6
Sheepwalk
Aubourn Haddington &
South Hykeham LN5 ...92 E5
Peterborough PE4 ...221 E1
Sheepwash La LN4 ...81 E4
Sheffield Pk Ave
DN15 ...182 F5
Sheffield St (East) 1
DN15 ...183 A4
Sheffield St (West) 4
DN15 ...182 F4
Sheffield St DN15 ...183 A4
Sheila Cres 4 PE11 ...214 A3
Sheldrake Rd 1 NG34 ..212 B3
Shelley Ave
Grantham NG31 ...211 D6
Grimsby DN33 ...191 B4
Shelley Cl
3 Mablethorpe/Sutton on Sea
LN12 ...77 A7
12 Stamford PE9 ...218 E6
Shelley Dr Lincoln LN2 ..202 B6
7 Sleaford NG34 ...212 F4
Shelroy Cl DN15 ...182 C5
Shelton Rd PE2 ...231 D6
Shenley Cl 11 DN7 ...14 D3
Shepeau Stow Cty Prim Sch
PE12 ...167 F3
Shepherd's Croft 1 DN9 27 D7
Shepherd's La NG34 ...133 E7
Shepherds Cl PE4 ...221 A4
Sheppard's Dro PE6 ...167 B1
Shepperson's Ave
PE11 ...144 F5
Shepton La NG34 ...142 A8
Sheraton Cl 15 LN6 ...204 D7
Sheraton Dr 13 DN36 ...36 D8
Sherborne Rd PE1 ...226 D6
Sherbrooke St 2 LN2 ..202 D4
Sherburn Cres DN15 ..182 D4
Sherburn St
Cleethorpes DN35 ...192 F4
Kingston upon Hull HU9 ..181 D8
Sheridan Cl 1 LN2 ...202 C7
Sheridan Rd PE1 ...225 F8
Sheriff Way PE21 ...208 E7
Sheringham Way PE2 .230 C6
Sherwood Ave
Boston PE21 ...208 E7
Newark-on-Trent NG24 ..104 A4
4 Peterborough PE2 ...230 F7
7 Wisbech PE13 ...170 D1
Sherwood Cl
1 Louth LN11 ...198 C4
Stamford PE9 ...218 F5
Sherwood Dr
Kingston upon Hull HU4 ..179 A7
Spalding PE11 ...214 D6
Waddington LN5 ...205 D1
Sherwood Rd
10 Coningsby LN4 ...207 D4
Grimsby DN34 ...190 F5
3 Mablethorpe/Sutton on Sea
LN12 ...64 B4
Sherwood Rise 7 NG32 119 B7
Sherwood Vale DN15 ..182 D3

Shetland Way DN40 . . .186 C2
Shipton Rd DN16 . . . . . .185 C5
Shire Ave PE11 . . . . . . .214 A5
Shire Gr PE1 . . . . .226 C5
Shire La NG23 . . . . .117 D8
Shiregate 12 LN4 . . . . . . .95 C4
Shires Orch 6 NG32 . . .138 D4
Shirley Cres DN16 . . . . .185 B8
Shivean Gate 5 PE12 . . .157 F7
Shodfriars La 4 PE21 . .208 F4
Shoe La LN9 . . . . .72 C5
Shoemaker's La DN21 . . .29 E5
Shoff Dro PE11 . . . . . . .134 D1
Shoff Rd PE11 . . . . .134 D1
Sholt's Gate PE12 . . . . .158 C7
Shop Hill 7 PE22 . . . . . . .98 F4
Shop La LN11 . . . . .72 D6
Shore Rd
Freiston PE22 . . . . .126 D2
Garthorpe & Fockerby
DN17 . . . . .7 F5
Short Dro
Gosberton PE11 . . . . .144 C5
Pointon & Sempringham
NG34 . . . . .143 F4
Thurlby PE10 . . . . .164 E8
Short Ferry Rd LN3 . . . . .82 F6
Short Hollow NG33 . . . .131 C1
Short La Fotherby LN11 . .49 A2
Ingham LN1 . . . . .54 F3
Lincoln LN1 . . . . .234 A2
1 West Halton DN15 . . . . . .8 E8
3 Wisbech PE13 . . . . . . .170 A1
Short St
2 Cleethorpes DN35 . . . .192 F6
Kingston upon Hull HU1 . . .180 E6
4 Spalding PE11 . . . . . . .214 C4
Short Wheatley La
NG23 . . . . .91 D3
Shortacres Rd PE2 . . . .230 F7
Shortfen PE2 . . . . .230 C4
Shortfield La PE21 . . . .209 E8
Shortleys Rd DN22 . . . . .65 B5
Short's Cnr PE22 . . . . . .112 D3
Shortwood La
Bullington LN8 . . . . .69 F4
Friesthorpe LN3 . . . . .57 A2
Shorwell Cl 3 NG31 . . . .210 E4
Shotbolt La PE11 . . . . .214 F8
Shrewsbury Ave PE2 . .230 D5
Shropshire Rd 9 LN1 . . . .67 E5
Shrubberies Nature Reserve
The★ PE12 . . . . .216 B5
Shrubwood Cl 3 NG34 . .122 E2
Shuttlefield La PE20 . . . .135 F4
Shuttleworth Ct 12 LN6 . .93 C8
Sibelius Rd HU4 . . . . . .179 B4
Sibsey Drain Bank
PE22 . . . . .126 A6
Sibsey Free (Controlled)
Prim Sch PE22 . . . . . . .113 A2
Sibsey La 3 PE21 . . . . . .208 F4
Sibsey Rd Boston PE21 .209 B8
Fishtoft PE21 . . . . .125 F5
Sibthorp St LN5 . . . . . . .201 E1
Sibthorpe Dr LN2 . . . . . .68 F2
Sickling Gate Rd PE22 .115 B7
Side La DN33 . . . . .195 A7
Side St 2 NG32 . . . . .128 F7
Sidebar La NG34 . . . . . .123 C4
Sidings Ct 3 HU15 . . . . . . .2 B5
Sidings The
Holbeach PE12 . . . . .215 D1
Horncastle LN9 . . . . .199 A3
Lincoln LN6 . . . . .234 A1
Long Sutton PE12 . . . . . . .216 B4
2 Louth LN11 . . . . .198 C6
23 Mablethorpe/Sutton on Sea
LN12 . . . . .77 A8
Morton PE10 . . . . .154 D6
8 Moulton PE12 . . . . .157 F6
9 Ruskington NG34 . . . . . .108 E1
25 Saxilby LN1 . . . . .66 D2
Sidlaw Gr LN5 . . . . .205 C2
Sidney Pl DN35 . . . . . . .192 B8
Sidney Rd
Grimsby DN34 . . . . .191 B7
5 Scunthorpe DN17 . . . . .184 C6
Sidney St
4 Cleethorpes DN35 . . . .189 D1
Cleethorpes DN35 . . . . . . .192 B8
Grantham NG31 . . . . .211 A6
Lincoln LN5 . . . . .205 E8
Sidney Way DN35 . . . . .192 B8
Signal Rd NG31 . . . . . . .211 C5
Signhills Ave DN35 . . . .193 A4
Signhills Inf & Jun Sch
DN35 . . . . .193 A4
Silica Cres DN17 . . . . . .184 C5
Silt La PE20 . . . . .136 E3
Silt Pit La PE21 . . . . . . .137 A7
Siltside PE11 . . . . .144 D4
Silver Birch Rise
DN16 . . . . .185 B3
Silver Hill PE7 . . . . .230 D3
Silver St Bardney LN3 . . . .83 C4
Barnetby le Wold DN38 . . . .21 B4
Barrow upon Humber
DN19 . . . . .11 C7
Baumber LN9 . . . . .72 A1
Benniworth LN8 . . . . .71 F8
Branston LN4 . . . . .81 E2
Coningsby LN4 . . . . .207 C4
Gainsborough DN21 . . . . .197 C4
Holton le Clay DN36 . . . . .195 D1
11 Kingston upon Hull
HU1 . . . . .180 F6
Lincoln LN2 . . . . .234 B2
Silver St *continued*
Minting LN9 . . . . .84 C8
North Clifton NG23 . . . . . . .78 C7
Owston Ferry DN9 . . . . .28 B2
Peterborough PE2 . . . . . . .230 F7
1 Ruskington NG34 . . . . .108 E1
Stainforth DN7 . . . . .14 C6
Theddlethorpe St Helen
LN12 . . . . .63 E5
4 Waddingham DN21 . . . .43 D7
6 Wainfleet All Saints
PE24 . . . . .102 D1
Winteringham DN15 . . . . . . .2 B1
Wisbech PE13 . . . . .170 D1
5 Wragby LN8 . . . . .70 D5
Silvergarth DN32 . . . . . .192 B5
Silverines Mdws Nature
Reserve★ LN11 . . . . . . .72 E5
Silver's La PE13 . . . . . .177 E7
Silversides La DN20 . . . .196 A2
Silverstone Rd 17 LN6 . .204 C7
Silvertoft La PE20 . . . . .136 B8
Silverwood Rd
8 Bottesford NG13 . . . . .128 A5
Peterborough PE1 . . . . . . .225 F5
Silvester Rd PE5 . . . . . .223 E2
Simon Weir La PE20 . . . .135 D8
Simons Cl
4 Donington on Bain LN11 .59 E1
5 Louth LN11 . . . . .198 D4
Simon's Gn LN6 . . . . . . .205 C6
Simons Pl DN35 . . . . . .192 D7
Simpson Cl 17 DN19 . . . . .11 D8
Sincil Bank (Lincoln City FC)
LN5 . . . . .201 E1
Sincil Bank LN5 . . . . . . .234 B1
Sincil St LN5 . . . . .234 B2
Sinclair Cl PE21 . . . . . . .208 E8
Sinderson Rd DN36 . . . . .36 D8
Singerfire Rd PE5 . . . . .223 D2
Sir Francis Hill Prim Sch The
LN6 . . . . .205 C8
Sir Isaac Newton Cl 3
PE12 . . . . .215 E3
Sir Isaac Newton Dr 3
PE21 . . . . .208 F1
Sir John Nelthorpe Sch
DN20 . . . . .196 C3
Sir William Robertson High
Sch LN5 . . . . .106 E4
Sirius Cl 3 HU3 . . . . . . .180 B5
Siskin Cl PE10 . . . . .143 A3
Siskin Cres DN16 . . . . . .185 B2
Sitwell St HU8 . . . . .181 A8
Six House Bank PE11 . . .144 D1
Six Hundreds Dro
PE20 . . . . .123 E3
Sixfields Cl LN6 . . . . . . .205 A7
Sixhills La LN8 . . . . .59 A7
Sixhills Rd LN8 . . . . .58 D6
Sixhills St DN32 . . . . . . .191 E7
Sixth Ave
Fixborough Ind Est DN15 . . . .8 A1
2 Grantham NG31 . . . . . .211 F6
Scunthorpe DN17 . . . . . . .184 B6
Skaters Way PE4 . . . . . .221 A4
Skayman Fields 7 LN5 . .105 E8
Skegness & District Hospl
PE25 . . . . .206 B3
Skegness (Ingoldmells)
Aerodrome PE25 . . . . . .90 D1
Skegness Gram Sch
PE25 . . . . .206 C4
Skegness Inf Sch
PE25 . . . . .206 C4
Skegness Jun Sch
PE25 . . . . .206 C4
Skegness Motor Racing
Stadium PE24 . . . . .90 A2
Skegness Rd
Burgh Le Marsh PE24 . . . .103 A7
Chapel St Leonards PE24 . .90 D6
Partney PE23 . . . . .88 B3
5 Wainfleet All Saints
PE24 . . . . .102 E2
Skegness Ret Pk
PE25 . . . . .206 A3
Skegness Sta PE25 . . . .206 C3
Skegness Water Leisure Pk★
PE25 . . . . .90 E1
Skeldyke Rd PE20 . . . . .136 D5
Skellingthorpe Rd
LN6 . . . . .200 D2
Skelton Rd DN17 . . . . . .184 C7
Skerries Cl 5 LN6 . . . . .205 A1
Skerry La NG13 . . . . . . .128 C5
Skillings La HU15 . . . . .2 C5
Skillington Rd NG33 . . . .151 B6
Skinnand La LN5 . . . . . .106 D7
Skinner's La
Middle Rasen LN8 . . . . .45 C1
South Kyme LN4 . . . . .110 B1
Skinners La
6 South Ferriby DN18 . . . .10 A7
Waltham DN37 . . . . .194 E4
Skipmarsh La
Leverton PE22 . . . . .126 E8
Old Leake PE22 . . . . .113 E1
Skippingdale Rd DN15 .182 F6
Skipwith Cres 20 LN4 . . . .95 D4
Skipworth Way PE25 . . .206 C8
Skirbeck Dr 15 LN1 . . . . .66 D2
Skirbeck Rd PE21 . . . . . .209 A3
Skirmore Rd PE22 . . . . .114 E5
Skirth Rd LN4 . . . . .109 F6
Skitter Rd DN40 . . . . .5 D1
Skylark Dr DN16 . . . . . .185 B2
Slack The 4 DN17 . . . . . .16 D8
Slash La LN9 . . . . .86 D3
Slate Drift 2 PE9 . . . . . .171 C2
Slate Mill Pl NG31 . . . . .211 B5
Slay Pit Cl 3 DN7 . . . . . . .14 F4
Slay Pit La DN7 . . . . .14 F3
Sleaford Leisure Ctr
NG34 . . . . .212 E4
Sleaford Rd
Ancaster NG32 . . . . .120 A2
Barnby in the Willows
NG24 . . . . .104 F5
Boston PE21 . . . . .208 B4
Bracebridge Heath LN4 . . . .81 A1
Branston & Mere LN4 . . . . .81 E1
Coningsby LN4 . . . . .207 A4
Cranwell NG34 . . . . .120 F8
East Kirkby PE23 . . . . .99 E4
Folkingham NG34 . . . . . . .142 D8
Heckington NG34 . . . . . . .122 D3
Honington NG32 . . . . .119 C2
Leadenham LN5 . . . . .106 D2
14 Leasingham NG34 . . . . .121 B7
Metheringham LN4 . . . . . . .95 B4
18 Navenby/Wellingore
LN5 . . . . .107 A7
Newark-on-Trent NG24 . . .104 A5
North Kyme LN4 . . . . .109 E2
Ruskington NG34 . . . . . . .108 E1
Tattershall LN4 . . . . .110 D7
Walcot Near Folkingham
NG34 . . . . .132 D2
Sleaford Sta NG34 . . . . .212 D3
Sledge La LN8 . . . . .59 B8
Sledmere Gr HU4 . . . . . .179 E5
Sleepers Cl 1 PE12 . . . .216 B4
Sleights Cl HU3 . . . . . . .180 A7
Sleights Dr 2 PE14 . . . .170 F1
Sleights La HU15 . . . . .1 B6
Slessor St 2 LN5 . . . . . . .94 A7
Slipe Dro PE11 . . . . .155 F5
Slipe The PE10 . . . . .213 F4
Slippery Gowt La
PE21 . . . . .136 F8
Slipway DN35 . . . . .193 A6
Sloothby High La
Hogsthorpe PE24 . . . . .90 A6
Willoughby with Sloothby
PE24 . . . . .89 F6
Sluice La DN18 . . . . .9 E8
Sluice Rd
Holbeach PE12 . . . . .215 B8
South Ferriby DN18 . . . . . . .9 F8
Sutton Bridge PE12 . . . . . .161 A6
Whaplode PE12 . . . . .147 B4
Small Dro PE12 . . . . . . .157 E7
Small Dro La PE11 . . . . .144 E1
Small End Rd PE22 . . . .114 E6
Smalley Rd PE21 . . . . . .209 D4
Smallwood PE3 . . . . .225 B5
Smeeton Ct 6 NG34 . . . .212 D6
Smeeton's La PE20 . . . .146 C7
Smith Field 10 DN36 . . . . .36 B1
Smith St Lincoln LN5 . . . .201 E1
Scunthorpe DN15 . . . . . . .182 F4
Smithdale Cl 9 PE11 . . .214 C6
Smithfield PE6 . . . . .176 B3
Smithfield Rd DN16 . . . .185 D6
Smithy La
7 Barnetby le Wold DN38 . .21 B4
Friskney PE22 . . . . .115 A6
Smooting La 4 LN3 . . . . .82 A8
Smooting The LN8 . . . . . .46 C1
Smythe La DN22 . . . . .52 D1
Snaffer's La PE12 . . . . . .158 C5
Snainton Gr 4 HU5 . . . . .179 D8
Snaith Ave PE20 . . . . . .146 D7
Snaith Cl 9 LN6 . . . . . . .204 B6
Snarford Rd LN3 . . . . .69 D8
Snelland Rd LN3 . . . . .69 E8
Snetterton Cl 1 LN6 . . . .204 C7
Snipe Dales Ctry Pk★
PE23 . . . . .86 F3
Snitterby Carr La DN21 .43 F5
Snitterby Rd DN21 . . . . . .43 D6
Snowberry Gdns 5 LN6 204 C8
Snowden Cl 1 PE6 . . . . .175 C8
Snowdon Cl 4 LN5 . . . . .205 D3
Snowdon Rd 3 NG23 . . . .91 D4
Snowdonia Ave DN15 . . .182 D7
Snowdrop Cl 10 DN41 . . . .23 F5
Snowdrop Pl 8 PE11 . . . .214 A5
Sods La PE11 . . . . .145 D5
Soff La DN19 . . . . .12 A6
Soke Parkway PE1 . . . . .221 E1
Soke Rd PE6 . . . . .174 D5
Solhem Ave 13 PE21 . . . .136 D8
Solomon Ct DN35 . . . . . .192 D5
Solway Ave PE21 . . . . . .136 E8
Somerby Cl
8 Moulton PE12 . . . . .157 F7
3 Stamford PE9 . . . . .219 B7
Somerby Gr NG31 . . . . .211 D2
Somerby Hill NG31 . . . . .211 C2
Somerby Pl NG31 . . . . . .211 E1
Somerby Rd
Gainsborough DN21 . . . . . .197 F5
Ropsley & Humby NG33 . . .141 A8
Scunthorpe DN17 . . . . . . .184 D5
Somerby Wold La
DN38 . . . . .21 C1
Somerden Rd HU9 . . . . . . .5 F8
Somersby Ave 9 LN12 . . .64 B4
Somersby Cl LN6 . . . . . .205 C4
Somersby Ct 15 LN11 . . .198 B5
Somersby Gn PE21 . . . .209 B7
Somersby Gr 2 PE25 . . .206 D1
Somersby St 7 DN31 . . .191 D8
Somersby Way PE21 . . .209 B7
Somerset Dr 4 DN15 . . . . .8 B4
Somerset St HU3 . . . . . .180 A5
Somerton Dr 3 DN7 . . . . .14 F3
Somerton Gate La LN5 . .93 D7
Somerton Rd DN40 . . . .186 D3
Somervell Rd DN16 . . . .185 C4
Somerville PE4 . . . . .220 E5
Somerville Cl 15 LN5 . . . .93 E8
Somerville Ct 14 LN5 . . . .93 E8
Somerville Rd 1 PE9 . . .219 A6
Somes Cl 1 PE9 . . . . . . .172 C6
Sonia Crest DN40 . . . . .186 B4
Sophia Ave DN33 . . . . . .191 C1
Sorbus Ct 5 HU3 . . . . . .180 D6
Sorbus View 4 HU5 . . . .179 C7
Sorby Cl PE25 . . . . .206 E8
Sorrel Cl 3 Binbrook LN8 .47 C5
1 Market Deeping PE6 . . .217 D6
4 Stamford PE9 . . . . .218 D6
Sorrel Dr PE11 . . . . .214 A5
Sorrel Way DN15 . . . . . .182 C6
Soss La DN10 . . . . .40 A5
Sour La DN7 . . . . .14 E8
Soutergate 13 DN18 . . . . . .3 F1
South Airfield Rd
NG34 . . . . .120 C8
South Axholme Com Sch
DN9 . . . . .27 D6
South Bank 3 DN17 . . . . .17 D6
South Brick Lines
NG34 . . . . .120 B8
South Bridge Rd HU1 . .181 A5
South Carr Rd DN20 . . . .31 A4
South Church Side 14
HU1 . . . . .180 F6
South Cliff Rd 27 DN21 . .30 B1
South Cres
11 Bottesford NG13 . . . . . .128 A5
1 Chapel St Leonards
PE24 . . . . .90 D7
South Dale LN7 . . . . .33 B4
South Dr
5 Balderton NG24 . . . . . .104 C1
4 Stow LN1 . . . . .66 C8
South Dro Bicker PE20 . .134 E4
Helpringham NG34 . . . . . .133 E6
Lutton PE12 . . . . .149 A1
Quadring PE11 . . . . .144 A8
Spalding PE11 . . . . .156 E2
South Ella Dr HU10 . . . .178 D7
South Ella Way HU10 . .178 D7
South End Boston PE21 .208 F4
Collingham NG23 . . . . .91 C4
Hogsthorpe PE24 . . . . .90 B6
Thorne/Moorends DN8 . . . .15 A7
South End La DN22 . . . . .52 E3
South Fen Rd
Bourne PE10 . . . . .213 F4
Helpringham NG34 . . . . . .133 D6
South Ferriby Prim Sch
DN18 . . . . .10 A7
South Furlong Croft 22
DN9 . . . . .27 E6
South Gate NG34 . . . . .212 D4
South Heath La NG32 .106 D1
South Holland Ctr★
PE11 . . . . .214 D4
South Humberside Ind Est
DN31 . . . . .188 B2
South Hunsley Sch HU14 .2 E5
South Hykeham Cty Prim Sch
LN6 . . . . .93 B7
South Ing Dro PE11 . . .134 E1
South Ings La PE24 . . . . .90 B5
South Intake La DN9 . . .40 C7
South Kesteven Works
NG31 . . . . .210 F3
South La
Kingston upon Hull
HU13 . . . . .178 E1
Willingham DN21 . . . . .54 A3
South Leys Sch DN17 . .184 D4
South Lincs Con Ctr
NG31 . . . . .211 A1
South Marsh Rd
Immingham Power St
DN41 . . . . .187 F1
Stallingborough DN41 . . . . .23 F7
South Marsh Rd Ind Est
DN41 . . . . .187 F2
South Mkt Pl 7 LN13 . . . .75 F2
South Moor Rd DN10 . . .39 F3
South Par Boston PE21 .208 C4
11 Caythorpe NG32 . . . . . .119 B7
Grantham NG31 . . . . .211 B2
6 Grimsby DN31 . . . . .191 D8
7 Lincoln LN1 . . . . .201 D4
Peterborough PE3 . . . . . . .225 E3
5 Saxilby LN1 . . . . .66 D2
Skegness PE25 . . . . .206 D2
South Kyme LN4 . . . . .123 B8
Spalding PE11 . . . . .214 C3
Thorne/Moorends DN8 . . . .15 A7
South Par Jun Sch
DN31 . . . . .191 D8
South Pk LN5 . . . . .205 F8
South Pk Ave
Bracebridge Heath LN5 . . .205 F8
Lincoln LN5 . . . . .201 F1
South Pk Rd DN17 . . . . .184 D3
South Ramper DN21 . . . .44 A5
South Rd Bourne PE10 . .213 D4
Chapel St Leonard PE24 . . .90 E6
5 Keadby with Althorpe
DN17 . . . . .17 C6
Mablethorpe/Sutton on Sea
LN12 . . . . .64 C1
North Somercotes LN11 . . .50 E7
South Rd *continued*
Sturton Le Steeple DN22 . . .52 C4
Tetford LN9 . . . . .73 F1
South Ridge Cres 2
DN17 . . . . .184 F3
South Rise 6 LN8 . . . . . .47 C4
South Scaffold La
NG23 . . . . .91 E3
South Scarle La LN6 . . . .78 E1
South Scarle Rd NG23 . .91 E6
South Sea La DN36 . . . . .36 D7
South Side DN15 . . . . .2 A1
South St 17 Alford LN13 . . .75 F2
12 Alford LN13 . . . . .75 F2
10 Barnetby le Wold DN38 .21 B4
Bole DN22 . . . . .52 C5
Boston PE21 . . . . .208 F4
Bourne PE10 . . . . .213 D4
Caistor LN7 . . . . .33 B4
1 Cleethorpes DN35 . . . .193 A5
20 Crowland PE6 . . . . . . .166 F1
Horncastle LN9 . . . . .199 B3
Keelby DN41 . . . . .23 A5
Louth LN11 . . . . .198 B5
Morton DN21 . . . . .197 C8
15 North Kelsey LN7 . . . . . .32 A4
Owston Ferry DN9 . . . . .28 B2
Peterborough PE1 . . . . . . .226 B2
Roxby cum Risby DN15 . . . . .8 F3
Scamblesby LN11 . . . . .72 F5
Swineshead PE20 . . . . . . .135 B7
West Butterwick DN17 . . . .28 D8
17 Winterton DN15 . . . . .9 A5
South St Mary's Gate 6
DN31 . . . . .191 D7
South Terr
Boston PE21 . . . . .208 F3
Louth LN11 . . . . .198 C4
South View
Broughton DN20 . . . . .19 D4
Fillingham DN21 . . . . .54 F4
Holton le Clay DN36 . . . . .195 E1
Humberston DN36 . . . . . .193 A1
Peterborough PE2 . . . . . . .230 F7
South View Ave
Brigg DN20 . . . . .196 C5
Burringham DN17 . . . . .17 D4
South View Cl 4 PE25 . .206 D2
South View La LN11 . . . .62 A7
South View Prim Sch
PE6 . . . . .166 E1
South View Rd PE4 . . . .225 D8
South Witham Nature
Reserve★ NG33 . . . . . .151 F2
South Witham Prim Sch
NG33 . . . . .151 D2
South Wood Dr 10 DN8 . .15 A7
Southburn Ave HU5 . . .179 E7
Southcliffe Rd 19 DN21 . .29 C3
Southcoates La HU9 . . .181 E8
South-Dale Cl 3 DN21 . . .30 B2
Southdown LN5 . . . . . . .205 D1
Southdown Rd PE7 . . . .233 F5
Southern Dr HU4 . . . . . .179 C5
Southern La LN6 . . . . . . .92 B7
Southern Rd DN40 . . . . .186 D7
Southern Way DN40 . . .186 C7
Southern Wlk DN33 . . . .194 F7
Southfield 7 Belton DN9 .16 E1
4 Kingston upon Hull HU13 .3 E4
Southfield Ave DN33 . . .194 F7
Southfield Cl
18 Thorne/Moorends DN8 .15 B7
Ulceby DN39 . . . . .12 B1
Southfield Dr
10 Epworth DN9 . . . . .27 D6
2 Louth LN11 . . . . .198 C4
21 North Ferriby HU14 . . . . .3 A4
Southfield La
Fishtoft PE21 . . . . .137 C8
6 Old Leake PE22 . . . . . .114 A1
Old Leake PE22 . . . . .127 A8
Willoughton DN21 . . . . .42 D3
Southfield Pl 7 LN9 . . .199 C3
Southfield Rd
1 Broughton DN20 . . . . . . .19 D3
13 Crowle DN17 . . . . .16 D7
Grimsby DN33 . . . . .194 F7
Holton le Clay DN36 . . . . .195 D1
North Kelsey LN7 . . . . .31 F3
Scunthorpe DN16 . . . . . . .185 C5
Thorne/Moorends DN8 . . . .15 B7
1 Winterton DN15 . . . . .8 F5
Southfields
7 Binbrook LN8 . . . . .47 C4
Bourne PE10 . . . . .213 D4
3 Sleaford NG34 . . . . . . .212 D3
Southfields Ave PE2 . . .231 D5
Southfields Cl 10 PE13 . .170 D2
Southfields Dr PE2 . . . .231 D6
Southgate
Kingston upon Hull
HU13 . . . . .178 E1
12 Pinchbeck PE11 . . . . . .156 E8
Southgate Spinneys 3
NG34 . . . . .120 E4
Southgate Way PE2 . . .229 C2
Southland Dr 5 LN6 . . .205 B4
Southlands Ave
Gainsborough DN21 . . . . .197 B8
Louth LN11 . . . . .198 D3
Peterborough PE1 . . . . . .226 A6
Southlands Dr
Grantham NG31 . . . . .211 C4
Morton DN21 . . . . .197 B8

Southlands Gdns
  DN21 ....197 B8
Southmoor La
  Newton on Trent LN1 ....78 D8
  Snitterby DN21 ....43 E5
Southmoor Rd
  Crowle DN17 ....16 C8
  Newton on Trent LN1 ....78 D8
Southoe Rd PE7 ....231 D2
Southorpe La DN21 ......42 A7
Southorpe Mdw Nature
  Reserve★ PE9 ....172 D3
Southorpe Paddock Nature
  Reserve★ PE9 ....172 E1
Southview Leisure Ctr
  PE25 ....103 C8
Southwell Ave
  3 Kingston upon Hull HU9 ..5 C8
  Peterborough PE4 ....220 E4
Southwell Cl NG31 ......210 C5
Southwell Rd
  9 Wisbech PE13 ....170 D1
  2 Wisbech PE13 ....170 C1
Southwell's La LN9 ......199 C4
Southwold Cres DN33 ..194 E8
Sovereign Cl
  12 Grimsby DN34 ....190 D4
  12 Wisbech PE13 ....170 C1
Sovereign Pl PE23 ....225 E2
Sovereign St NG34 ......142 C4
Sowers La DN15 ....9 A5
Spa Bldgs LN2 ....234 B2
Spa Hill **9** DN21 ....30 B1
Spa Rd Lincoln LN5 ......234 C2
  2 Woodhall Spa LN10 ..97 D6
Spa St LN2 ....202 B3
Spafford Cl DN21 ....65 E8
Spain La **5** PE21 ....208 F4
Spain Pl PE21 ....209 A4
Spalding Bulb Mus★
  PE11 ....145 C1
Spalding Comm **6**
  PE11 ....214 B1
Spalding Dro
  Cowbit PE12 ....157 A3
  Spalding PE12 ....214 E1
Spalding Gate PE12 ...158 B8
Spalding High Sch For Girls
  PE11 ....214 F3
Spalding Parish CE Sch
  PE11 ....214 E2
Spalding Prim Sch
  PE11 ....214 B5
Spalding Rd
  Boston PE21 ....208 E3
  Bourne PE10 ....213 E5
  Deeping St James PE6 ..165 D1
  Gosberton PE11 ....145 C5
  Holbeach PE12 ....215 A2
  Market Deeping PE6 ....217 E5
  Pinchbeck PE11 ....214 C8
  Scunthorpe DN16 ....185 B8
  Wigtoft PE20 ....135 E1
Spalding Rd Bsns Pk
  PE10 ....213 F5
Spalding Sta PE11 ......214 C4
Spalford La LN6 ....78 E2
Spalford Rd LN6 ....78 E3
Spalford Warren Nature
  Reserve★ NG23 ....78 D2
Spanby Dr **5** LN6 ....205 A7
Spanning Dr **22** LN13 ..75 F2
Spark St DN34 ....191 A4
Spark's La PE12 ....158 A4
Sparrow La
  2 Long Bennington NG23 117 D3
  Marnham NG23 ....78 A5
  Newball LN8 ....69 F2
Sparrowgate Rd PE14 ..170 F1
Spaw La **5** LN11 ....198 B6
Spayne Rd PE21 ....209 A4
Speechley Rd PE7 ....233 F6
Speechley's Dro PE6 ....174 F7
Speedwell Cres DN15 ..182 C6
Speedwell Ct **7** PE17 217 D6
Speight Cl **5** NG24 ....104 B7
Spence St **10** PE23 .....87 F1
Spencer Ave
  Peterborough PE2 ....231 D5
  Scunthorpe DN15 ....182 F4
Spencer Cl
  3 Long Sutton PE12 ...216 B5
  West Walton PE14 ....170 E4
Spencer Gdns **7** PE22 126 C2
Spencer St
  Grimsby DN31 ....189 D1
  6 Kingston upon Hull
    HU2 ....180 E7
  9 Lincoln LN5 ....205 E8
Spendla's La PE12 ....159 F3
Spendluffe Ave **3** LN13 ..75 F3
Spennymoor Cl **1** LN6 ..93 B8
Sperrin Cl **5** LN5 ....205 D2
Speyer Ave PE11 ....214 C5
Speyside Ct **1** PE2 ...229 D4
Spice Ave PE21 ....136 D8
Spicer's La PE22 ....127 B5
Spilsby Cl **8** LN6 ......204 D8
Spilsby Hill PE23 ....100 B8
Spilsby Prim Sch PE23 ..88 A1
Spilsby Rd
  Boston PE21 ....209 A6
  Eastville PE22 ....101 A1
  High Toynton LN9 ....86 B4
  Horncastle LN9 ....199 E4

Spilsby Rd continued
  Scunthorpe DN17 ....184 E5
  Spilsby PE23 ....101 A8
  Thorpe St Peter PE24 ..102 B4
Spindles The PE10 ......213 D7
Spindlewood **1** HU15 ....2 C7
Spinnaker Cl **1** HU5 ..181 C6
Spinners Cl **3** NG34 ..212 E3
Spinney Cl
  Immingham DN40 ....186 A4
  1 Manby LN11 ....62 C6
  9 Ryhall PE9 ....163 C1
Spinney Croft Cl **14** HU14 ..3 A5
Spinney La **10** Ryhall PE9 163 C1
  2 Scopwick Heath LN4 ..108 A7
Spinney The
  1 Barnby Dun DN3 ....14 A3
  13 Barrow upon Humber
    DN19 ....11 D8
  8 Grimsby DN31 ....191 C7
  2 Market Deeping PE6 ..217 B5
  7 Swanland HU14 ....3 B7
  4 Winthorpe NG24 ......104 B7
Spinney Wlk HU4 ....179 C6
Spinneys The **5** LN2 ...68 D7
Spion Kop La PE20 ......135 E3
Spire View
  1 Bottesford NG13 .....128 A6
  1 Kingston upon Hull
    HU13 ....178 E1
  Sleaford NG34 ....212 A2
Spire View Rd LN11 .....198 D5
Spirea App LN6 ....204 C8
Spirewic Ave PE25 ......206 D8
Spital Hill
  Gainsborough DN21 .....197 E5
  18 Louth LN11 ....198 B5
Spital La LN11 ....55 B8
Spital St LN1 ....234 B4
Spital Terr DN21 ....197 D4
Spitalgate CE (Controlled)
  Prim Sch NG31 ....210 D3
Spitfire Ave LN11 ....62 B6
Spittal Hill Rd PE22 ....126 D4
Splash La
  Ailsworth PE5 ....228 E8
  Castor PE5 ....223 E1
Spotfield La PE20 ....136 C7
Spout Hill HU15 ....2 C8
Spout Yd **6** LN11 ....198 B6
Spratt Cl LN9 ....199 D1
Spratton Ct DN34 ....190 C4
Spridlington Rd LN8 ......56 D3
Spriggs Cl NG34 ....212 C3
Spignall PE3 ....224 F4
Spring Bank
  5 Binbrook LN8 ....47 C4
  Grimsby DN34 ....191 A4
  Kingston upon Hull HU3 ..180 D7
Spring Bank W HU5 .....179 D7
Spring Cl **9** LN9 ....68 A4
Spring Ct Dunston LN4 ..95 C5
  13 Welton/Dunholme LN2 ..68 D7
Spring Dr
  Balderton NG24 ....104 C1
  Farcet PE7 ....231 B2
Spring End **3** NG31 ....129 D5
Spring Gdns
  Gainsborough DN21 .....197 D4
  Grantham NG31 ....211 B3
  Long Sutton PE12 ....216 B4
  13 Louth LN11 ....198 B5
  Sleaford NG34 ....212 C5
  Spalding PE11 ....214 C3
Spring Gdns E HU4 .....179 B6
Spring Gdns S HU4 .....179 B5
Spring Gdns W HU4 .....179 B6
Spring Gr
  Kingston upon Hull HU3 ..180 A7
  Terrington St Clement
    PE34 ....161 F2
Spring Hill
  3 Binbrook LN8 ....47 C4
  Cherry Willingham/Reepham
    LN3 ....203 F8
  Grantham NG31 ....211 D3
  Lincoln LN1 ....234 A3
Spring La
  Balderton NG24 ....104 C2
  8 Colsterworth NG33 ..151 D7
  4 Folkingham NG34 ....142 D8
  Horbling NG34 ....133 B2
  14 Laceby DN37 ....23 F1
  5 Leasingham NG34 ....121 B7
  4 Wymondham LE14 ...150 B1
Spring St
  Immingham DN40 ....186 D4
  Kingston upon Hull HU2 ..180 D7
  Spalding PE11 ....214 D3
Spring View **4** LN8 .....47 C4
Springbank DN20 ....196 D5
Springbok Cl HU4 ....179 D2
Springburn St HU3 ......180 A5
Springdale Cl
  2 Kingston upon Hull HU9 ..5 D8
  Kingston upon Hull
    HU10 ....178 F7
Springfield PE2 ....231 A7
Springfield Ave
  Brough HU15 ....2 C6
  7 Hatfield DN7 ....14 E4
Springfield Cl
  Gainsborough DN21 .....197 A4
  Lincoln LN2 ....234 B4
  2 Scunthorpe DN16 ....185 C6
Springfield Est
  DN33 ....194 D7

Springfield Rd
  2 Brigg DN20 ....196 D3
  Grantham NG31 ....211 A4
  Grimsby DN33 ....191 C1
  Kingston upon Hull HU3 ..179 F6
  Parson Drove PE13 ......177 D7
  Peterborough PE1 ....225 F5
  6 Ruskington NG34 ....108 C2
  Yaxley PE7 ....233 F5
Springfield Rise **1**
  DN20 ....196 B3
Springfield Way HU10 ..178 E7
Springfields LN8 ....46 B1
Springfields Ex Ctr
  PE12 ....157 B7
Springhead Ave HU5 ...179 A6
Springhead Ct HU10 ....179 A6
Springhead Gdns
  HU10 ....179 A7
Springhead La HU5 .....179 A7
Springhead Prim Sch
  HU10 ....178 E7
Springs La DN22 ....52 A2
Springs Rd DN10 ....26 C1
Springs Way DN20 ......196 B3
Springthorpe Rd
  Corringham DN21 ....41 E1
  Gainsborough DN21 .....197 F4
Springville Ave HU13 ..178 F2
Springway Cres DN34 ..191 A7
Springwood Cres
  DN33 ....194 D7
Sprite La LN4 ....109 D5
Sproxton Rd
  Buckminster NG33 ....150 D2
  Skillington NG33 ....151 A8
Spruce Cl PE12 ....215 C4
Spruce La DN39 ....12 A1
Spurn Ave DN33 ....194 F8
Spurn Lightship★
  HU1 ....180 F5
Spurr The **7** LN5 ....107 A7
Spyvee St HU8 ....181 A7
Square The
  2 Barnack PE9 ....172 D3
  Barrowby NG32 ....129 B3
  12 Goxhill DN19 ....12 A8
  Kingston upon Hull
    HU13 ....178 E1
  4 Leasingham NG34 ....121 B7
  5 Ryhall PE9 ....163 C1
  Toynton All Saints PE23 ..100 F6
Squires Gate PE4 ....221 D3
Stable La **3** DN18 ....3 E1
Stacey Cl **2** PE25 ....90 D3
Stackyard The PE2 ....229 E5
Stafford Ave NG24 ......104 A2
Stafford St
  3 Boston PE21 ....208 F6
  Kingston upon Hull HU2 ..180 E8
Staffordshire Cres **6**
  LN6 ....204 D7
Stagsden PE2 ....229 F4
Stagshaw Dr PE2 ....231 B8
Stain La LN12 ....63 E3
Stainby Rd
  Buckminster NG33 ....150 F5
  Gunby & Stainby NG33 ..151 C4
Staindale DN16 ....185 D5
Stainesway LN11 ....198 E7
Stainfield Rd
  Kirkby Underwood PE10 ..142 D1
  Morton PE10 ....154 B7
Stainforth Inf Sch DN7 ..14 C7
Stainforth Kirton La Prim Sch
  DN7 ....14 C7
Stainforth Moor Rd
  DN7 ....15 C3
Stainforth Rd DN7 ....14 A5
Stainton Ave **1** DN21 ..43 D7
Stainton Cl **5** DN21 .....53 A5
Stainton Dr
  Grimsby DN33 ....191 A3
  8 Immingham DN40 ....186 B4
  Scunthorpe DN17 ....184 E4
Stainton Gdns DN1 ......201 E7
Stainton La LN2 ....69 D4
Stallebrass Cl PE2 ......231 E5
Stallingborough CE Prim Sch
  DN41 ....23 E6
Stallingborough Rd
  Immingham DN40 ....186 B2
  Keelby DN41 ....23 A5
Stallingborough Sta
  DN41 ....23 E6
Stamford & Rutland Hospl
  PE9 ....219 D6
Stamford Bsns Pk
  PE9 ....219 E6
Stamford Cl **4** PE6 ....217 B5
Stamford Coll (Spalding FE
  Centre)** PE11 ....214 D4
Stamford Coll PE9 ....219 C4
Stamford High Sch
  PE9 ....219 C4
Stamford Jun Sch
  PE9 ....219 B3
Stamford Leisure Ctr
  PE9 ....219 D6
Stamford Lodge Rd
  PE6 ....224 C5
Stamford Mus★ PE9 ..219 C5
Stamford Rd
  Barnack PE9 ....172 C4
  Buckminster NG33 ....151 A4
  Collyweston PE9 ....171 C2
  Colsterworth NG33 ......151 E5
  Easton on the Hill PE9 ..219 A1

Stamford Rd continued
  Essendine PE9 ....163 D2
  Helpston PE6 ....173 C1
  Ketton PE9 ....218 A2
  Marholm PE6 ....220 A1
  Market Deeping PE6 ....217 A4
  Tinwell PE9 ....218 A6
  West Deeping PE9 ....173 A4
Stamford Ret Pk PE9 ..219 C6
Stamford Sch PE9 ....219 C6
Stamford St **1** PE3 ....211 B2
Stamford Sta PE9 ....219 C4
Stamfords Art Ctr★
  PE9 ....219 C5
Stamp End LN2 ....234 C2
Stamper St **2** PE3 .....224 F3
Stan Rowing Ct PE2 ....231 C7
Standard La **1** PE9 ....93 A2
Standish Gr PE21 ....209 B7
Standish La DN40 ....186 A5
Stanfield Rd **2** DN9 ....27 D6
Stanford Cl **1** DN37 ....23 F1
Stanford Jun & Inf Sch
  DN37 ....23 E1
Stanford Wlk **4** PE3 ..225 C4
Stanground Coll PE7 ..231 C5
Stanground Cty Inf Sch
  PE2 ....231 D5
Stanholme La DN36 ......36 A1
Stanhope Ave
  4 Balderton NG24 ......104 C1
  7 Woodhall Spa LN10 ..97 D6
Stanhope Gdns **1** PE21 209 C4
Stanhope Pl DN35 ....192 C7
Stanhope Rd LN9 ....199 C4
Stanhope Terr **3** LN9 ..199 C4
Stanhurst La PE7 ....15 A5
Staniland Cty Prim Sch
  PE21 ....208 D4
Staniland Rd PE21 ....208 D3
Staniland Way
  1 Humberston DN36 .....36 D8
  Peterborough PE4 ....221 A5
Staniwell Rise DN17 ....184 D7
Staniwells Dr **11** DN20 ..19 D3
Stanley Ave **4** LN11 .....64 B3
Stanley Cl **2** PE24 ......102 D2
Stanley Cres LN4 ....205 F4
Stanley Dr
  11 Sutterton PE20 ......136 A2
  Sutton Bridge PE12 ....160 E4
Stanley Gdns **13** DN7 ..14 C6
Stanley Pl **1** LN5 ....201 F1
Stanley Rd
  Peterborough PE1 ....226 A3
  Scunthorpe DN15 ....182 C3
  18 Stainforth DN7 ....14 C6
Stanley St Bourne PE10 213 C6
  Gainsborough DN21 .....197 D2
  Grimsby DN32 ....189 C1
  Kingston upon Hull HU3 ..180 C7
  Lincoln LN5 ....205 D7
  1 Stamford PE9 ....219 C5
Stansted St **5** DN31 ..188 D1
Stanton Cl PE10 ....213 E5
Stanton Rd **4** LN12 .....77 A8
Stanton Sq PE7 ....230 D2
Stanton St **7** NG31 ....211 A4
Stanton's Pit Nature
  Reserve★ PE10 ....163 C8
Stapes Garth **1** LN11 ....50 B8
Staple La NG24 ....104 B1
Staple Rd DN40 ....12 F3
Stapledon Rd PE2 ....229 D2
Stapleford Ave LN2 ......201 F8
Stapleford La
  Coddington NG24 ....104 E6
  Collingham NG23 ....91 E1
Staples La LN5 ....93 F7
Star Carr La DN20 ....196 D8
Star Cl PE1 ....226 C3
Star Fen Dro NG34 ......123 A4
Star La Holbeach PE12 ..215 C7
  4 Stamford PE9 ....219 C5
Star Lode Dro PE11 .....144 B1
Star Mews PE1 ....226 C2
Star Rd PE1 ....226 C2
Starella Gr HU3 ....180 A4
Starham Rd LN7 ....31 C4
Starks La LN8 ....58 D7
Stather Rd DN15 ....8 A1
Stathern Rd PE1 ....226 D7
Stathers Wlk **3** HU10 ..178 F6
Station App
  6 Ancaster NG32 ....120 A3
  Boston PE21 ....208 A4
  11 Donington PE11 ....134 E2
  Louth LN11 ....198 C6
Station Ave
  New Waltham DN36 ......195 D6
  16 South Witham NG33 ..151 D2
  Wisbech St Mary PE13 ..177 D5
Station Cl **9** NG23 ....91 D4
Station Ct **3** DN7 ....14 D4
Station Field LN6 ....200 B3
Station La
  Horncastle LN9 ....199 A3
  Searby cum Owmby DN38 ..32 D7
Station Rd (West)
  NG31 ....211 A3
Station Rd
  Ailsworth PE5 ....223 C1
  Alford LN13 ....75 E2
  Algarkirk PE20 ....146 B8
  Bardney LN3 ....83 B4
  Barkston NG32 ....129 F8
  Barlings LN3 ....69 B3
  Barnack PE9 ....172 E4

Station Rd continued
  Beckingham DN10 ....52 B8
  1 Billingborough NG34 ..133 B1
  Blyton DN21 ....41 C5
  Bottesford NG13 ....128 A6
  Bourne PE10 ....155 C3
  Branston LN4 ....81 E2
  Brough HU15 ....2 B5
  Burgh Le Marsh PE24 ..102 C8
  Burringham DN17 ....17 E4
  Candlesby with Gunby
    PE24 ....89 B1
  Careby Aunby & Holywell
    PE9 ....163 A8
  Castle Bytham NG33 .....152 D1
  6 Cherry Willingham/Reepham
    LN3 ....82 A8
  Cherry Willingham/Reepham
    LN3 ....203 F8
  Cleethorpes DN35 ....192 F7
  Collingham LN6 ....91 D4
  Corby Glen NG33 ....152 D7
  Deeping St James PE6 ..174 B7
  Digby LN4 ....108 E5
  Donington on Bain LN11 ..59 E1
  East Halton DN40 ....12 D7
  Epworth DN9 ....27 D7
  6 Essendine PE9 ....163 D3
  Fulstow LN11 ....49 A7
  Garthorpe & Fockerby
    DN17 ....7 E6
  Gedney Hill PE12 ....168 C1
  Gosberton PE11 ....145 A5
  Grantham NG31 ....211 B3
  Grasby DN38 ....32 E6
  Great Steeping PE23 ....101 F6
  Grimsby DN37 ....190 C8
  Gunness DN15 ....17 E5
  Habrough DN40 ....12 F1
  Halton Holegate PE23 ..101 B8
  Harby NG23 ....79 B5
  Harmston LN5 ....93 E5
  Hatfield DN7 ....14 D4
  Haxey DN9 ....27 D1
  Healing DN41 ....23 F5
  Heckington NG34 ....122 E2
  Heighington LN4 ....81 E4
  Helpringham NG34 ....133 D7
  9 Hibaldstow DN20 ....30 F5
  Holbeach PE12 ....215 D2
  Holton Le Clay DN36 ......36 B4
  Keadby with Althorpe
    DN17 ....17 D6
  6 Ketton PE9 ....171 A3
  Kingston upon Hull
    HU13 ....178 E1
  Kirton PE20 ....124 E1
  Kirton in Lindsey DN21 ..30 B2
  Knaith DN21 ....53 A4
  Legbourne LN11 ....61 E3
  Lincoln LN6 ....204 D3
  Little Steeping PE23 .....101 D5
  5 Long Sutton PE12 ...216 B4
  Ludborough DN36 ....48 E6
  16 Mablethorpe & Sutton
    LN12 ....76 F8
  20 Mablethorpe/Sutton on Sea
    LN12 ....64 B4
  Metheringham LN4 ....95 D4
  Midville PE22 ....113 E8
  1 Misterton DN10 ....40 A5
  Misterton LN13 ....89 A6
  Morton PE10 ....154 D6
  Moulton PE12 ....157 F6
  Mumby LN13 ....76 F1
  North Kelsey LN7 ....32 B4
  North Thoresby DN36 .....36 B1
  Northorpe PE10 ....164 C7
  Owston Ferry DN9 ....28 A2
  Peterborough PE3 ....225 F2
  Potter Hanworth LN4 .....82 A1
  Ruskington NG34 ....108 C2
  Scawby DN20 ....30 F7
  Scredington NG34 ....132 F7
  Scunthorpe DN15 ....183 C4
  Sibsey PE22 ....113 C1
  Sleaford NG34 ....212 D3
  South Kelsey LN7 ....32 D2
  South Killingholme DN40 ..13 A5
  South Willingham LN8 .....59 A1
  Stallingborough DN41 .....23 E6
  Stamford PE9 ....219 B3
  Stixwould & Woodhall
    LN10 ....97 A8
  Sturton Le Steeple DN22 ..52 B3
  Surfleet PE11 ....145 E3
  Sutterton PE20 ....136 A1
  Swinderby LN6 ....92 A6
  Swineshead PE20 ....123 F2
  Theddlethorpe All Saints
    LN12 ....63 D7
  Thorney PE6 ....176 A3
  Thornton Curtis DN39 ....11 F5
  Thorpe on the Hill LN6 ..79 E1
  Thorpe St Peter PE24 ..102 B3
  Timberland LN4 ....96 B1
  Torksey LN1 ....65 D6
  Tydd St Mary PE13 ....170 C8
  Ulceby DN39 ....12 B1
  Waddington LN5 ....93 F7
  Wainfleet All Saints
    PE24 ....102 D1
  Walkeringham DN10 ......40 A3
  Walpole Cross Keys
    PE34 ....161 C2
  Waltham LE14 ....138 A1
  Waltham DN36 ....195 A5
  Whitton DN15 ....1 D3

Station Rd *continued*
Wickenby LN3 .. 57 B1
Woodhall Spa LN10 .. 97 D6
Station St Boston PE21 .. 208 E5
Donington PE11 .. 134 E2
Rippingale PE10 .. 143 A3
1 Spalding PE11 .. 214 D4
Station Terr LN5 .. 106 D3
Staunt Rd PE22 .. 112 E2
Staunton St 3 LN1 .. 201 D3
Staveley Rd 8 LN13 .. 75 E2
Staverton Cres LN6 .. 200 B1
Staverton Rd PE4 .. 220 E3
Staves Ct 5 DN36 .. 36 D4
Staxton Cl PE6 .. 220 A1
Staxton Ct HU9 .. 181 D8
Steadfold La PE9 .. 218 A3
Steadings The DN15 .. 8 B2
Steamer Point Rd LN4 .. 95 C7
Steapas Cl 2 PE23 .. 101 D7
Steep Hill LN2 .. 234 B3
Steepers The 4 LN2 .. 68 D2
Steeping Dr DN40 .. 186 A3
Steeping Rd PE23 .. 101 C6
Stells La PE21 .. 208 F3
Stenigot Cl 3 LN6 .. 204 C6
Stenigot Gr LN6 .. 204 D6
Stenigot Rd 1 LN6 .. 204 D6
Stenner Rd LN4 .. 207 F6
Stennett Ave 1 PE11 .. 156 E2
Stephen Cl 3 DN39 .. 12 A1
Stephen Cres
16 Barton-upon-Humber DN18 .. 10 F8
Grimsby DN34 .. 190 E4
Humberston DN36 .. 36 C8
Stephen Rd NG24 .. 104 A6
Stephen's Way NG34 .. 212 F3
Stephens Way 4 PE6 .. 217 F4
Stephenson Ave
Gonerby Hill Foot NG31 .. 210 F8
Pinchbeck PE11 .. 214 E8
Stephenson Cl
9 Alford LN13 .. 75 E2
4 Boston PE21 .. 208 F1
Yaxley PE7 .. 233 D6
Stephenson Way PE10 .. 213 D7
Stepping Stones Sch PE4 .. 221 B1
Sterling Cres DN37 .. 194 C4
Sterne Ave 9 DN20 .. 19 D3
Stevenson Pl 1 DN35 .. 192 D5
Stevenson's Way 33 DN18 .. 10 E8
Stewton Gdns LN11 .. 198 D4
Stewton La LN11 .. 198 E4
Steyning La PE20 .. 135 A7
Steynings The PE4 .. 221 A3
Stickney CE (Aided) Prim Sch PE22 .. 113 A8
Stickney La PE22 .. 112 D7
Still Cl PE6 .. 217 B5
Still The PE13 .. 170 B1
Stirling Cl 4 DN21 .. 197 E6
Stirling Ct
14 Grantham NG31 .. 210 E2
Heckington NG34 .. 122 D2
Stirling Rd PE9 .. 218 F5
Stirling St
Grimsby DN31 .. 189 D1
Kingston upon Hull HU3 .. 179 F6
Stirling Way
Market Deeping PE6 .. 217 C7
Peterborough PE3 .. 220 E1
4 Skellingthorpe LN6 .. 200 A4
Stixwould Rd LN10 .. 97 C7
Stockbridge Pk 3 HU15 .. 2 C7
Stockbridge Rd HU15 .. 2 C7
Stockhouse La PE11 .. 145 B3
Stockman's Ave 2 PE12 215 F3
Stockmoor La LN8 .. 57 A8
Stocks Hill 4 Belton DN9 .. 16 E1
Castor PE5 .. 223 F1
Stocks La LN8 .. 56 F3
Stockshill Rd DN16 .. 185 C6
Stockwell Gate PE12 .. 215 A4
Stockwell Gr 6 HU9 .. 5 F8
Stockwell Prim Sch HU9 .. 5 F8
Stockwith Mill* PE23 .. 87 B5
Stockwith Rd
Haxey DN9 .. 27 E1
Walkeringham DN10 .. 40 A3
Stokes Dr NG34 .. 212 B6
Stokesay Ct 8 PE3 .. 225 B1
Stone Cl 8 PE10 .. 213 C6
Stone Dr LE15 .. 152 A1
Stone Gate
Cowbit PE12 .. 157 B1
Weston PE12 .. 145 F2
Stone Hill DN7 .. 15 A4
Stone Hill Rd DN7 .. 15 A4
Stone La
Aubourn Haddington & South Hykeham LN5 .. 92 E6
Burringham DN17 .. 17 E4
Peterborough PE1 .. 225 F5
Sutterton PE20 .. 135 F1
6 Waddington LN5 .. 93 F7
Stone Moor Rd 14 LN6 .. 93 B8
Stone Pit La
Skendleby PE23 .. 88 D4
Willingham DN21 .. 53 F3
Stonebow Ctr LN2 .. 234 B2
Stonebridge PE2 .. 230 C5
Stonebridge Lea PE2 .. 230 C5
Stonebridge Rd NG31 .. 211 B4
Stonefield Ave LN2 .. 234 B4
Stonefield Pk LN2 .. 68 C7
Stonegate •
Gedney PE12 .. 159 D6
Spalding PE11 .. 214 E3
28 Thorne/Moorends DN8 .. 15 A8
Stonehouse Rd PE7 .. 233 E5
Stonemasons Ct 4 NG31 .. 211 B4
Stonepit La
Marston NG32 .. 118 C2
8 Skillington NG33 .. 151 A8
Stonepit Rd HU15 .. 2 E6
Stones Cl 3 PE24 .. 90 B7
Stone's La PE24 .. 77 C1
Stones La 13 Spilsby PE23 .. 88 A1
West Keal PE23 .. 100 C5
Stones Pl 1 LN6 .. 200 E1
Stonesby Rd LE14 .. 138 E1
Stoney La DN21 .. 54 F7
Stoney Way 15 DN36 .. 36 D4
Stoney Yd LN6 .. 200 A5
Stong's Dro PE11 .. 144 F8
Stool Cl Rd 2 DN9 .. 16 E1
Storbeck Rd 15 PE13 .. 170 D1
Storey's Bar Rd PE6 .. 227 A3
Storey's La PE24 .. 102 E7
Storrington Way PE4 .. 221 A3
Stortford St 7 DN31 .. 188 D1
Story St 11 HU1 .. 180 E7
Stothards La 7 DN19 .. 12 A8
Stoton's Gate PE12 .. 158 E2
Stour Ct 7 NG31 .. 210 E2
Stove Ct LE15 .. 162 A8
Stovin Cres DN15 .. 9 A5
Stow Cl DN37 .. 190 D8
Stow Hill LE14 .. 150 C7
Stow La NG34 .. 133 A1
Stow Pk Rd
Marton DN21 .. 65 E8
Stow LN1 .. 66 B8
Stow Rd
Scunthorpe DN16 .. 185 B7
Sturton By Stow LN1 .. 66 C8
Willingham DN21 .. 53 E2
Wisbech PE13 .. 170 E1
Stowe Rd PE6 .. 164 E2
Stowehill Rd PE4 .. 221 D2
Stowgate Rd PE6 .. 174 A8
Strafford St DN21 .. 197 D2
Stragglethorpe La
Caythorpe NG32 .. 118 E8
Fulbeck NG32 .. 105 E2
Strahane Cl LN5 .. 205 C3
Straight Dro PE7 .. 231 E1
Strait LN2 .. 234 B3
Strand Cl 10 LN12 .. 64 B3
Strand Infants Sch DN32 .. 189 B1
Strand Jun Sch DN32 .. 189 B1
Strand St DN32 .. 189 B1
Strand The 9 LN12 .. 64 B3
Stratford Ave DN34 .. 191 A4
Stratford Dr 5 DN16 .. 183 C1
Stratten Cl 5 NG34 .. 107 C1
Stratton Pk 1 HU14 .. 3 C6
Strawberry Cl 13 PE13 .. 170 C1
Strawberry Hill DN37 .. 194 B4
Strawberry St HU9 .. 181 B7
Stray Gn 12 NG34 .. 108 E2
Strayfleets La PE22 .. 126 D5
Street La
North Kelsey LN7 .. 32 B4
North Leverton with Habblesthorpe DN22 .. 65 A8
Street La Rd DN22 .. 52 C1
Street Life Mus of Transport* HU9 .. 181 A6
Streetway PE21 .. 136 E7
Stretham Way 5 PE10 .. 213 C7
Stretton Cl 4 LN1 .. 66 C7
Stretton Rd LE15 .. 162 B6
Strickland Rd DN17 .. 7 A3
Strickland St HU3 .. 180 C4
Stricklands Dr 4 PE6 .. 175 C8
Strong's Bank PE12 .. 158 F4
Strong's Gate PE12 .. 158 F3
Stroxton La NG33 .. 139 F5
Strubby Airfield LN13 .. 75 E8
Strubby Cl
9 Birchwood LN6 .. 204 D8
Cleethorpes DN35 .. 193 A4
Strugg's Hill La PE20 .. 136 B3
Stuart Cl
Peterborough PE2 .. 231 C6
Scunthorpe DN17 .. 184 F2
Stuart St NG31 .. 211 C3
Stuart Wortley St 1 DN31 .. 189 B2
Stubton Hall Boarding Sch NG23 .. 118 B7
Stubton Rd NG23 .. 117 F7
Studcross DN9 .. 27 D6
Studley St HU8 .. 181 B8
Stukeley Cl Lincoln LN2 .. 202 E6
Peterborough PE2 .. 231 D5
Stukeley Gdns 2 PE12 .. 215 C2
Stukeley Rd PE12 .. 215 D2
Stump Cross Hill NG34 .. 212 C1
Stumpacre PE3 .. 225 A8
Stumpcross La PE20 .. 135 B6
Stumps La PE12 .. 157 B7
Sturdy Hill LN11 .. 62 E4
Sturgate Airfield DN21 .. 53 E6
Sturgate Cl 15 LN6 .. 204 C7
Sturgate Wlk DN21 .. 197 F3
Sturmer Ct 1 DN16 .. 185 B2
Sturrock Ct 12 NG31 .. 210 E2
Sturrock Way PE3 .. 225 C8
Sturton by Stow Prim Sch LN1 .. 66 D8
Sturton CE Prim Sch DN22 .. 52 C2
Sturton Cl 1 LN2 .. 201 F7
Sturton Gr 2 DN33 .. 191 B4
Sturton La DN20 .. 30 E7
Sturton Rd
North Leverton with Habblesthorpe DN22 .. 52 B1
Stow LN1 .. 66 C8
Sturton Way PE12 .. 216 B5
Stutte Cl LN11 .. 198 E3
Styles Croft 6 HU14 .. 3 C6
Subway St HU3 .. 180 B3
Subway The DN16 .. 19 A4
Sudbeck La 17 LN2 .. 68 D6
Sudbrook Rd NG32 .. 119 D4
Sudbrooke Dr LN2 .. 202 A7
Sudbrooke La LN2 .. 68 E2
Sudbrooke Rd LN2 .. 68 F3
Sudbury Cl LN6 .. 205 A5
Sudbury Ct PE7 .. 231 F5
Sudbury Pl LN11 .. 198 B4
Suddle Way 19 DN41 .. 23 A4
Sudthorpe Hill
8 Fulbeck NG32 .. 106 C1
Fulbeck NG32 .. 119 C8
Suffolk Cl PE3 .. 225 B2
Suffolk Rd 10 LN1 .. 67 E5
Suggitt's Ct DN35 .. 192 D8
Suggitt's La DN35 .. 192 D8
Suggitt's Orch DN35 .. 192 D8
Sullivan Rd HU4 .. 179 B4
Summer Hill DN21 .. 197 E5
Summer Lesure La PE12 .. 159 F2
Summerdale 28 DN18 .. 10 E8
Summerfield Ave DN37 .. 194 E5
Summerfield Cl
Waltham DN37 .. 194 E5
16 Wisbech PE13 .. 170 C1
Summerfield Ct 3 NG34 .. 212 D6
Summerfield Dr 4 NG34 .. 212 D6
Summerfield Rd PE1 .. 225 F4
Summerfields PE22 .. 114 B1
Summergangs La DN21 .. 197 D1
Summergates La PE24 .. 102 C7
Summergroves Way HU4 .. 179 B2
Sunbeam Ave LN6 .. 204 D1
Sunbeam Rd HU4 .. 179 D5
Suncastle* PE25 .. 206 E4
Sunderfleet La LN11 .. 51 A5
Sunderland Cl 6 LN6 .. 200 A4
Sunfield Cres LN6 .. 200 D1
Sunfields Cl PE12 .. 157 C3
Sunningdale
Grantham NG31 .. 211 C8
Peterborough PE2 .. 229 E6
8 Waltham DN37 .. 194 C4
Sunningdale Ave
Brigg DN20 .. 196 C5
Spalding PE11 .. 214 C2
Sunningdale Cl
Chapel St Leonard PE24 .. 90 E7
1 Skegness PE25 .. 206 D4
6 Woodhall Spa LN10 .. 97 C5
Sunningdale Cres 2 PE25 .. 206 D4
Sunningdale Dr
Boston PE21 .. 208 C6
Chapel St Leonard PE24 .. 90 E7
4 Immingham DN40 .. 186 D5
Lincoln LN5 .. 205 D8
Skegness PE25 .. 206 D4
Sunningdale Gr LN4 .. 203 D1
Sunningdale Rd
5 Hatfield DN7 .. 14 F3
Kingston upon Hull HU13 .. 178 F2
Scunthorpe DN17 .. 184 D4
Sunny Bank HU3 .. 180 B7
Sunny Bank Gdns DN10 .. 39 C2
Sunny Cnr DN33 .. 191 D1
Sunny Hill 8 DN21 .. 30 B1
Sunnybank 11 DN18 .. 10 E8
Sunnydale Cl 1 PE11 .. 145 D2
Sunnymead PE4 .. 220 E6
Sunway Gr DN16 .. 185 B5
Sunway Inf Sch DN16 .. 185 A5
Surfleet Bank PE11 .. 145 F5
Surfleet Lows Nature Reserve* PE11 .. 145 D3
Surfleet Rd 5 PE11 .. 145 D2
Surfside 5 LN12 .. 77 A8
Surrey Garth HU4 .. 179 B4
Surtees St DN31 .. 189 B2
Sussex Ave PE21 .. 208 B4
Sussex Cl 7 LN8 .. 47 B6
Sussex Gdns 16 LN1 .. 67 E5
Sussex Rd PE9 .. 219 B6
Sussex St DN35 .. 192 B8
Susworth Rd DN17 .. 28 E4
Sutcliffe Ave DN33 .. 191 A3
Sutherland Way PE9 .. 218 F5
Sutterton Dro LN4 .. 110 E1
Suttling Dales La PE22 .. 126 B8
Sutton Cl
Heighington/Washingborough LN4 .. 203 A1
Sutton Cl *continued*
15 Nettleham LN2 .. 68 C2
Sutton Cl 2 PE25 .. 206 C3
Sutton Gate PE12 .. 159 D1
Sutton Mdws PE13 .. 170 C2
Sutton on Sea Prim Sch LN12 .. 76 F8
Sutton Pl 4 DN20 .. 30 F7
Sutton Rd
Beckingham LN5 .. 105 B4
Bilsby LN13 .. 76 C4
16 Kirk Sandall DN3 .. 14 A3
Mablethorpe/Sutton on Sea LN12 .. 64 C2
Newton PE13 .. 170 B6
Sutton St James PE12 .. 159 D2
Terrington St Clement PE34 .. 161 F2
Sutton St James Prim Sch PE12 .. 159 C1
Sutton's La PE6 .. 217 D4
Svenskaby PE2 .. 229 B6
Swaby Cl LN2 .. 202 A8
Swaby Cres 4 PE25 .. 206 B4
Swaby Dr DN35 .. 192 D3
Swaby Valley Nature Reserve* LN13 .. 74 F4
Swadales Cl 11 NG31 .. 129 E5
Swain's Dro PE13 .. 170 C8
Swale Ave PE4 .. 221 C1
Swale Bank PE11 .. 144 D5
Swale Rd 14 HU15 .. 2 D5
Swaledale 10 HU15 .. 2 D6
Swaledale Pl 2 DN16 .. 185 E6
Swales Rd 12 DN36 .. 36 D8
Swallow Ave LN6 .. 200 A3
Swallow Cl
5 Chapel St Leonard PE24 .. 90 D7
4 Gainsborough DN21 .. 53 A7
1 Sleaford NG34 .. 212 C3
Swallow Ct 6 DN9 .. 27 D7
Swallow Dr
3 Claypole NG23 .. 117 E8
15 Healing DN41 .. 23 F5
Louth LN11 .. 198 D8
Swallow Gate Rd LN11 .. 51 B2
Swallow Hill PE10 .. 164 B7
Swallow La
Tydd St Giles PE13 .. 170 B8
Wootton DN39 .. 11 E2
Swallow Wlk 3 PE6 .. 217 D5
Swallowbeck Ave LN6 .. 205 A4
Swallowfield PE4 .. 220 E4
Swallowfield Dr HU4 .. 179 B2
Swallowfields Ct 2 PE25 .. 206 A4
Swallow's Cl NG31 .. 210 E7
Swan Dr
Skegness PE25 .. 103 C7
6 Sturton by Stow LN1 .. 66 D7
Swan Moor Bank PE22 .. 114 C3
Swan St 1 Lincoln LN2 .. 234 B2
Spalding PE11 .. 214 D4
Swanella Gr HU3 .. 180 A4
Swanhill PE8 .. 222 A4
Swanhole La PE22 .. 126 D4
Swanholme Cl LN6 .. 204 E5
Swanland Butts Cl HU10 .. 178 C6
Swanland Cl 25 DN8 .. 15 B7
Swanland Ct 24 DN8 .. 15 B7
Swanland Cty Prim Sch HU14 .. 3 B6
Swanland Dale HU14 .. 3 B8
Swanland Garth 6 HU14 .. 3 A5
Swanland Hill HU14 .. 3 B5
Swanland Rd HU13 .. 178 C2
Swannacks View 3 DN20 .. 30 F7
Swan's La LN5 .. 105 F5
Swanspool PE3 .. 225 B6
Swapcoat La PE12 .. 216 B5
Swarby La NG34 .. 132 A7
Swaton La NG34 .. 133 C3
Swayne Cl LN2 .. 202 D7
Swaythling Cl LN6 .. 204 E5
Sweet Briar Cl 6 DN37 .. 194 C5
Sweet Cl 2 PE6 .. 217 D5
Sweet Dews Gr HU9 .. 181 D8
Sweetbriar 3 PE9 .. 218 C7
Sweetbriar La PE4 .. 220 F6
Sweetlands Way PE11 .. 145 B5
Swen Cl 17 LN2 .. 68 D7
Swift Cl PE6 .. 217 D4
Swift Gdns LN2 .. 202 C7
Swift Rd DN17 .. 184 D6
Swift Way PE10 .. 164 B7
Swiftsure Cres DN34 .. 190 D4
Swin Cl PE20 .. 135 C6
Swinburne La DN17 .. 184 D7
Swinderby Gdns 2 DN34 .. 191 A5
Swinderby Rd
Collingham NG23 .. 91 E4
Eagle & Swinethorpe LN6 .. 79 B1
North Scarle LN6 .. 78 F1
Norton Disney LN6 .. 92 C2
South Scarle NG23 .. 91 F7
Swinderby Sta LN6 .. 92 B7
Swindler's Dro PE12 .. 157 C6
Swine Hill NG32 .. 139 C7
Swine's Mdw Rd PE6 .. 217 D8
Swinefleet Rd DN14 .. 6 B8
Swinegate
Grantham NG31 .. 211 A5
Kingston upon Hull HU13 .. 178 E1
Swineshead Cowleys Foundation CE VC Prim Sch PE20 .. 135 C7
Swineshead Rd
Boston PE21 .. 208 A3
Frampton PE20 .. 124 E1
Swineshead Sta PE20 .. 123 F1
Swingbridge Rd NG31 .. 210 D2
Swinhope Hill LN8 .. 47 C5
Swinhope Rd LN8 .. 47 B6
Swinstead (CE) Prim Sch NG33 .. 153 B5
Swinstead Rd
Corby Glen NG33 .. 152 F7
Counthorpe & Creeton NG33 .. 153 A3
Irnham NG33 .. 141 E1
Swinster La DN40 .. 12 E6
Switchback LN8 .. 47 C2
Swithin Cl HU13 .. 179 A2
Swynford Cl LN1 .. 65 D2
Sybil Rd 18 PE13 .. 170 D1
Sycamore Ave
Grimsby DN33 .. 191 C3
Peterborough PE1 .. 226 C6
Sycamore Cl
1 Barnetby Le Wold DN38 .. 21 B4
4 Birchwood LN6 .. 204 E8
Bourne PE10 .. 213 A5
2 Broughton DN20 .. 19 D3
Cherry Willingham/Reepham LN3 .. 203 D5
Croft PE24 .. 102 E4
Kingston upon Hull HU5 .. 179 C7
5 Scopwick Heath LN4 .. 108 A7
Sycamore Cres 5 LN6 .. 204 E8
Sycamore Ct 3 NG31 .. 210 D2
Sycamore Dr
7 Gainsborough DN21 .. 197 E6
Louth LN11 .. 198 E5
9 Newark-on-Trent NG24 104 C5
Sleaford NG34 .. 212 D6
6 Waddington LN5 .. 93 E8
3 Waddington LN5 .. 93 E8
Sycamore Gr LN4 .. 81 A1
Sycamore La 2 LE14 .. 150 B1
Sycamores The 5 PE11 .. 214 B1
Sydney Dr 3 PE25 .. 206 A4
Sydney Rd PE2 .. 231 D5
Sydney Smith Sch HU10 .. 179 A5
Sydney St PE21 .. 208 D5
Sykemouth Dro PE20 .. 124 C1
Sykes Cl
6 Kingston upon Hull HU10 .. 178 F6
15 Swanland HU14 .. 3 B7
Sykes La Goxhill DN19 .. 5 A2
Saxilby with Ingleby LN1 .. 66 C3
Sykes St 2 HU2 .. 180 F7
Sylvan Ave 5 LN10 .. 97 D6
Sylvden Dr 24 PE13 .. 170 E1
Sylvester St 12 DN21 .. 30 B1
Symmington Cl PE2 .. 230 F8
Sympson Cl LN2 .. 202 E6
Syne Ave 5 PE25 .. 206 D1
Syston Gr LN5 .. 205 D4
Sywell Cl 16 LN6 .. 204 C6

T

Tadman St HU3 .. 180 D4
Taggs Dr 7 PE25 .. 206 A6
Tait Cl PE1 .. 226 C5
Talbot Ave PE2 .. 230 D6
Talbot Cl 4 PE23 .. 101 A8
Talbot Rd
Immingham DN40 .. 186 D3
Skegness PE25 .. 206 C4
Talisman Dr DN16 .. 185 A2
Tall Gables 2 NG22 .. 65 B1
Tall Trees HU13 .. 178 C3
Tallert Way DN33 .. 190 F3
Tallington Dry Ski Ctr* PE9 .. 172 F7
Tamar Ct 5 NG31 .. 210 E2
Tamar Dr 4 DN36 .. 195 D7
Tamar Way 3 LN6 .. 205 A2
Tamarisk Way DN16 .. 185 D5
Tame Ct 4 NG34 .. 212 D5
Tamson Way 5 NG34 .. 212 D5
Tanashi Dori DN17 .. 182 E1
Tanglewood PE4 .. 220 F6
Tanglewood Cedar Falls 3 PE11 .. 214 B1
Tanhouse PE2 .. 230 C5
Tanners' La NG33 .. 152 E8
Tanner's La LN5 .. 234 A1
Tannery La 3 NG34 .. 142 D8
Tansor Garth PE3 .. 225 C5
Tantallon Ct 6 PE3 .. 225 B1
Tapin Cl LN1 .. 201 C6
Tarleton Ave 1 LN10 .. 97 E6
Tarleton Cl 2 DN3 .. 14 A2
Tarran Way PE25 .. 206 B5
Tarrant PE4 .. 220 E6
Tasburgh St DN32 .. 191 F6
Tasman Rd 5 PE23 .. 101 A8
Tathwell CE Sch LN11 .. 61 B2
Tattershall Ave DN34 .. 190 F4
Tattershall Castle (NT)* LN4 .. 207 A4
Tattershall Cl 3 NG31 .. 210 E5

Tattershall Coll Bldgs★ LN4 .... 207 A4
Tattershall Dr 10 PE6 ... 217 A5
Tattershall Rd
Billinghay LN4 .... 109 F5
Boston PE21 .... 208 D7
Fishtoft PE21 .... 125 C5
Woodhall Spa LN10 .... 97 D5
Tattershall Sta Gall & Pottery★ LN4 .... 110 E7
Tattershall Way LN11 .. 198 A8
Tatwin Dr 8 PE6 .... 175 B8
Taunton Cl 2 NG34 .. 212 D7
Taunton Rd HU4 .... 179 A3
Taunton Way DN33 .... 194 E8
Tavella Ct 1 DN9 .... 27 B2
Tavern Cl LN13 .... 89 A6
Tavern La 6 PE24 .... 90 B7
Taverner Rd PE21 .... 208 D6
Taverners Rd PE1 .... 225 F4
Tavistock Cl 15 PE6 .... 176 A3
Tavistock Rd PE11 .... 214 B2
Tawney St PE21 .... 208 F6
Taylor Cl 6 Belton DN9 .... 16 E2
5 Boston PE21 .... 209 D4
Taylor St DN35 .... 189 D1
Taylor's Ave DN35 .... 192 E4
Taylor's Dro PE12 .... 159 C1
Teal Cl 4 Brigg DN20 ... 196 A3
3 Skegness PE25 .... 206 A6
Teal Gr 10 PE12 .... 167 B8
Teal Pl LN7 .... 33 A4
Teal Rd LN4 .... 110 E8
Tealby Cl 1 DN21 .... 53 A7
Tealby Gr 5 DN33 .... 191 B3
Tealby Rd
Middle Rasen LN8 .... 57 E8
Scunthorpe DN17 .... 184 D5
Tealby Sch LN8 .... 46 D1
Tealby St 11 LN5 .... 205 E8
Teale St DN15 .... 183 A4
Team Gate DN37 .... 190 C6
Teanby Ct 5 PE3 .... 224 F3
Teanby Dr 8 DN15 .... 9 A5
Teasles 6 PE6 .... 217 D6
Tedder Dr
3 Waddington LN5 .... 93 F7
3 Waddington LN5 .... 94 A7
Tedder Prim Sch The LN4 .... 108 B7
Teddy's Farm★ LN5 ... 105 C4
Tee La DN15 .... 8 B5
Teesdale Cl LN6 .... 200 C2
Teesdale Rd NG31 .... 211 A7
Telford Dr
Newark NG24 .... 104 B6
Yaxley PE7 .... 233 D6
Temper Rd DN16 .... 185 F8
Temperance Ave 5 DN17 .... 29 D7
Temperance La 2 NG23 . 91 C4
Temperton's La 5 DN9 .. 28 A3
Tempest St LN2 .... 202 B3
Templar Ct DN16 .... 185 B3
Templars Way 2 NG33 . 151 D2
Temple Cl 2 Alford LN13 . 75 E2
4 Belton DN9 .... 16 E2
3 Brough HU15 .... 2 E6
Temple Gdns LN2 .... 234 B3
Temple Grange PE4 ... 220 F6
Temple La DN37 .... 23 E1
Temple Rd
Aslackby & Laughton NG34 .... 142 E5
Welbourn LN5 .... 107 A4
Temple Terr LN11 .... 198 B6
Temple Wlk 2 HU15 .... 2 E6
Templefield Rd DN21 ... 42 D6
Templeman Dr PE9 .... 163 E5
Templemans La DN36 ... 36 A1
Templemeads Cl PE10 .... 154 D6
Temples Ct 3 PE6 .... 173 B4
Templeway Cl 5 NG32 . 119 B7
Templeway Sq 8 NG32 . 119 B7
Ten Acre Dro PE11 .... 135 C1
Ten Acre La
Pinchbeck PE11 .... 145 C1
Wyville cum Hungerton NG32 .... 139 B5
Tenens Way PE21 .... 209 A1
Tennyson Ave
Grantham NG31 .... 211 E5
16 Mablethorpe/Sutton on Sea LN12 .... 64 B4
Sleaford NG34 .... 212 D5
4 Thorne/Moorends DN8 . 15 B8
Tennyson Cl
Benniworth LN8 .... 59 B1
Brigg DN20 .... 196 D2
2 Caistor LN7 .... 33 A3
12 Mablethorpe/Sutton on Sea LN12 .... 77 A7
14 Metheringham LN4 .... 95 C4
Tennyson Dr
Bourne PE10 .... 213 D3
22 Welton/Dunholme LN2 .. 68 D6
Tennyson Gdns 1 LN9 . 199 D2
Tennyson Gn 3 PE25 .. 206 C2
Tennyson High Sch The LN12 .... 64 C3
Tennyson Rd
Cleethorpes DN35 .... 192 E7
Louth LN11 .... 198 C4
Tennyson Rd *continued*
17 Mablethorpe/Sutton on Sea LN12 .... 64 B4
Peterborough PE1 .... 225 F7
2 Ruskington NG34 .... 108 E2
Scunthorpe DN16 .... 185 D7
Tennyson St
5 Gainsborough DN21 .. 197 D5
Grimsby DN31 .... 191 D8
1 Lincoln LN1 .... 201 D4
Tennyson Way 1 PE9 .. 218 E5
Tensing Rd DN16 .... 185 C5
Tenter La 6 LN5 .... 107 A8
Tentercroft St LN5 .... 234 A1
Tenters The PE12 .... 215 E2
Terrace La PE22 .... 99 C5
Terrace The
Great Ponton NG33 .... 140 A5
10 Spilsby PE23 .... 88 A1
Terrington Pl DN35 .... 192 D4
Terry O'Toole Theatre★ LN6 .... 204 D1
Tetford Hill LN9 .... 73 E3
Tetford Prim Sch LN9 ... 73 F1
Tetford Rd LN9 .... 86 A5
Tethering La DN10 .... 39 A2
Tetley Rd DN16 .... 185 C7
Tetley View 3 DN17 .... 16 E6
Tetney Blow Wells Nature Reserve★ DN36 .... 36 E3
Tetney Cl 6 LN1 .... 201 E8
Tetney La DN36 .... 195 E2
Tetney Lock Rd DN36 ... 36 E4
Tetney Marshes Nature Reserve★ DN36 .... 37 C7
Tetney Prim Sch DN36 .. 36 D4
Tetney Rd DN36 .... 36 C7
Tewkesbury Dr 4 DN34 191 C6
Thacker Bank LN12 .... 63 B7
Thackers Cl PE8 .... 222 A4
Thackers La LN4 .... 81 D2
Thacker's Rd PE22 .... 112 B2
Thackers Way PE6 .... 217 D5
Thames Cl 2 PE24 .... 90 B7
Thames Cres 4 PE24 .... 90 B7
Thames Rd
Grantham NG31 .... 210 E2
Spalding PE11 .... 214 F5
Thames St
Hogsthorpe PE24 .... 90 B7
Louth LN11 .... 198 D6
Thary La PE11 .... 145 E4
Thatchers Wlk PE22 ... 113 B2
Theaker Ave DN21 .... 197 F5
Thealby La DN15 .... 8 E5
Theatre Royal★ LN2 ... 234 B2
Theddlethorpe Com Prim Sch LN12 .... 63 D6
Theddlethorpe Rd LN12 . 63 F4
Theodore Rd DN15 .... 182 E4
Theodore St LN1 .... 234 A4
Theresa Cl 8 PE25 .... 206 A4
Thesiger St
Grimsby DN32 .... 189 B1
Lincoln LN5 .... 201 F1
Thetford Ave 5 PE6 .... 164 E5
Thimbleby Hill LN9 .... 85 C5
Thinholme La DN9 .... 27 A1
Third Ave
1 Fixborough Ind Est DN15 . 8 A1
Grantham NG31 .... 211 F7
4 Scampton Airfield LN1 .. 67 E5
2 Scunthorpe DN17 .... 184 C6
Spalding PE11 .... 214 A4
Third Dro
Gosberton PE11 .... 144 B4
Moulton PE12 .... 146 F7
Peterborough PE1 .... 226 E2
Third Hill Rd LN4 .... 81 F3
Third La DN37 .... 35 D3
Third Marsh Rd PE14 .. 170 C3
Thirkleby Cres DN32 ... 192 B4
Thirlmere Ave DN33 .... 194 E7
Thirlmere Cl 8 LN6 .... 205 A2
Thirlmere Gdns 3 PE4 . 221 C3
Thirlmere Way 1 LN6 .. 200 D1
Thirsk Dr LN6 .... 204 F4
Thistle Cl LN2 .... 202 C8
Thistle Dr PE2 .... 231 C7
Thistlemoor Rd PE1 .... 225 E7
Thistleton La LE15 .... 151 D1
Thomas Cl 7 PE3 .... 224 F3
Thomas Cowley Sch The PE11 .... 134 F2
Thomas Gibson Dr 4 LN9 .... 199 D3
Thomas Magnus Sch NG24 .... 104 A4
Thomas Rd DN17 .... 184 F8
Thomas St
Grimsby DN32 .... 191 F7
Kingston upon Hull HU9 .. 181 B7
Lincoln LN2 .... 234 C2
Sleaford NG34 .... 212 D4
Thomas Sumpter Sch DN17 .... 184 E7
Thompson Cl
Skegness PE25 .... 206 C5
3 Spalding PE11 .... 214 C3
Thompson Dr 25 DN7 .... 14 D4
Thompson St 7 DN15 .. 183 B3
Thompsons Gd PE7 .... 230 D3
Thompson's La
Fosdyke PE20 .... 146 E8
Hough-on-the-Hill NG32 .. 119 A5
Thonock Cl LN2 .... 201 F7
Thonock Dr 7 LN1 .... 66 C2
Thonock Rd DN21 .... 197 D8
Thoresby Pl DN35 .... 192 E4
Thoresby Prim Sch HU5 .... 180 B8
Thoresby Rd
Fulstow LN11 .... 49 A8
Scunthorpe DN17 .... 184 D5
Tetney DN36 .... 36 D3
Thoresby St HU5 .... 180 B8
Thoresway Dr LN2 .... 202 A7
Thoresway Gr 5 DN33 . 191 A3
Thorganby Rd DN35 ... 193 A3
Thorn Bank DN9 .... 26 E4
Thorn La DN19 .... 12 A8
Thorn Leigh 3 HU3 .... 180 C6
Thornbury Rd DN40 .... 186 D3
Thorndales La PE22 .... 113 A5
Thorndike Way DN21 .. 197 E3
Thorndyke Mews 7 DN21 .... 197 D3
Thorne King Edward Fst Sch DN8 .... 15 B8
Thorne N Sta DN8 .... 14 F8
Thorne Rd
Edenthorpe DN3 .... 14 A2
Sandtoft DN8 .... 16 A3
8 Stainforth DN7 .... 14 C7
Thorne S Sta DN8 .... 15 B7
Thorne Swimming Baths DN8 .... 15 B8
Thorne Waste Drain Rd DN8 .... 15 E8
Thorne Way PE20 .... 136 C4
Thorney Heritage Mus★ PE6 .... 176 A3
Thorney Rd
2 Crowland PE6 .... 175 C8
Newborough PE6 .... 174 D5
Wisbech St Mary PE13 ... 177 C2
Thorngarth La 9 DN19 .. 11 D8
Thorngate LN5 .... 234 B2
Thornham's Way 8 HU15 . 2 C7
Thornhill Cres 4 DN17 . 184 F3
Thornhill Gdns 1 DN34 191 A7
Thornhill La DN22 .... 52 E1
Thornholme Dr DN16 .. 185 A3
Thorniman La PE20 .... 136 E6
Thornleigh Dr PE2 .... 230 C6
Thornmead PE4 .... 221 B4
Thorns La NG32 .... 210 A8
Thornton 20 HU15 .... 2 C6
Thornton Abbey★ DN39 .... 12 B5
Thornton Abbey Sta DN39 .... 12 A5
Thornton Ave
Boston PE21 .... 208 D3
Scunthorpe DN16 .... 185 A7
Thornton Cl
3 Heighington/Washingborough LN4 .... 203 A2
Kingston upon Hull HU13 .... 178 D1
Langriville PE22 .... 124 F8
6 Lincoln LN6 .... 205 A7
Peterborough PE4 .... 221 C3
Thornton Cres
Cleethorpes DN35 .... 192 E4
5 Horncastle LN9 .... 199 C2
Thornton Ct DN36 .... 195 D8
Thornton Gdns 21 DN41 . 23 A4
Thornton Gr 6 DN34 ... 190 E4
Thornton Pl DN40 .... 186 B3
Thornton Rd
Barrow upon Humber DN19 .... 11 D6
7 Collingham NG23 .... 91 D4
Goxhill DN19 .... 11 F6
Owersby LN7 .... 44 E7
South Kelsey LN7 .... 32 A1
Spalding PE11 .... 214 F3
Thornton Curtis DN39 .... 11 E4
Thornton St
Barrow upon Humber DN19 .... 11 C7
6 Gainsborough DN21 .. 197 D3
Thornton Way LN3 .... 203 E6
Thornwell La 2 PE23 ... 87 A4
Thornwick Ave HU10 ... 178 E8
Thornwick Cl 2 HU3 ... 180 C5
Thorold Ave
5 Cranwell NG34 .... 120 E8
Cranwell & Byard's Leap NG34 .... 107 E1
Thorold Gdns 1 NG32 .. 130 B8
Thorold Pl 1 DN3 .... 14 A2
Thorold Rd NG32 .... 210 A4
Thorold St Boston PE21 . 208 F6
Grimsby DN31 .... 189 C1
Thorold Way LN5 .... 93 F4
Thorolds Charity CE (Aided) Prim Sch NG32 .... 118 D2
Thorolds Way PE5 .... 223 D2
Thorpe Ave
Lincoln LN1 .... 201 D8
Moulton PE12 .... 157 E2
Peterborough PE3 .... 225 C2
Thorpe Bank PE22 .... 101 B3
Thorpe Camp Visitor Ctr★ LN4 .... 207 B8
Thorpe Cl 3 NG24 .... 104 D5
Thorpe CP Sch PE3 ... 225 B3
Thorpe Culvert Sta PE24 .... 102 B3
Thorpe Dr NG34 .... 120 E2
Thorpe Dro NG34 .... 120 E3
Thorpe La
Aubourn Haddington & South Hykeham LN6 .... 93 A8
Thorpe La *continued*
Brattleby LN1 .... 67 B7
Eagle & Swinethorpe LN6 .. 79 C1
Tealby LN8 .... 46 B1
Thorpe Lea Rd PE3 .... 225 E2
Thorpe Mdws PE3 .... 225 C2
Thorpe Pk Rd PE3 .... 225 C3
Thorpe Rd
Doddington & Whisby LN6 .. 79 E2
Ewerby & Evedon NG34 .. 122 C6
Peterborough PE3 .... 225 B1
Tattershall LN4 .... 207 C6
Thorpe St Peter Cty Sch PE24 .... 102 B4
Thorpe Tilney Dro
Timberland LN4 .... 97 A1
Walcott LN4 .... 109 C8
Thorpe Wood PE3 .... 224 F1
Thorpehall Rd
16 Kirk Sandall DN3 .... 14 A2
12 Kirk Sandall DN3 .... 14 A2
Thorpe-on-the-Hill CE (Controlled) Prim Sch LN6 .... 92 E8
Thorpes La 3 NG32 ... 138 D4
Thorpe's La PE12 .... 158 B6
Thorseby Cl PE3 .... 225 B3
Threadneedle St 9 PE21 .... 208 F5
Three Bridge La LN11 .. 63 A7
Three Leys La DN22 .... 52 B2
Threekingham Bar NG34 .... 132 D3
Throstlenest PE7 .... 231 C3
Thrumber Marsh La LN13 .... 76 F1
Thrunscoe Infants Sch DN35 .... 192 F5
Thrunscoe Rd 7 DN35 . 192 F5
Thrush Cl 10 NG34 .... 212 B3
Thurlaston Cl PE3 .... 225 B2
Thurlby Cl 1 LN4 .... 203 A2
Thurlby Com Prim Sch PE10 .... 164 C8
Thurlby Cres LN2 .... 202 B8
Thurlby Fen Nature Reserve★ PE10 .... 164 F7
Thurlby Rd
Bassingham LN5 .... 92 F3
Bilsby LN13 .... 76 B3
Gainsborough DN21 .... 197 E4
Thurlow Ct 1 LN2 .... 202 E7
Thurning Ave PE2 .... 231 C6
Thuro Gr PE2 .... 230 A3
Thursfield PE4 .... 221 A4
Thurstan Cl PE10 .... 213 B6
Thurston Gate 2 PE3 .. 225 A1
Thyme Ave 12 PE6 .... 217 C5
Tichbourne Cl 6 HU3 .. 180 C5
Tilbury Prim Sch HU4 . 179 B3
Tilbury Rd HU4 .... 179 B3
Tilebarn La PE20 .... 134 F7
Tilia Cl
Kingston upon Hull HU4 .. 179 B2
Scunthorpe DN16 .... 185 D4
Tilia Way 5 PE10 .... 213 E2
Till Bridge La
Marton LN1 .... 65 F8
Scampton LN1 .... 67 A6
Stow LN1 .... 66 A8
Tillbridge Rd LN1 .... 66 D7
Tilley Gate LN11 .... 51 B3
Tilney Ave PE21 .... 208 D6
Tilney The 10 PE12 .... 158 B7
Tilton Ct PE1 .... 226 C8
Timber Hill NG33 .... 151 A4
Timberland DN16 .... 185 C4
Timberland Dro LN4 .... 96 E2
Timberland Rd LN4 .... 96 C2
Timberley Dr DN37 .... 190 C7
Timm's La 18 LN5 .... 93 F7
Timms's Dro PE20 .... 134 E8
Timson Ct 5 DN10 .... 52 B8
Tin La PE10 .... 213 C5
Tindale Bank Rd
Haxey DN9 .... 39 C8
West Stockwith DN10 .... 40 A7
Tindall Cl 2 PE13 .... 170 D2
Tindall Way 10 PE24 ... 102 D1
Tinkermere Cl 3 LN2 ... 68 D6
Tinker's Dro PE13 .... 170 D1
Tinker's La Girton NG23 .. 91 C8
2 Waddington LN5 .... 93 F6
Tinkle St LN11 .... 62 C7
Tinsley Cl NG23 .... 117 F7
Tintagel Ct 7 PE3 .... 225 B1
Tintagel Way DN36 .... 195 C7
Tintern Rise 4 PE6 .... 175 A1
Tinwell Rd
Stamford PE9 .... 219 A4
Tinwell PE9 .... 218 D3
Tinwell Rd La PE9 .... 218 F4
Tip La PE24 .... 102 B4
Tirrington PE3 .... 225 A3
Tison Garth HU10 .... 178 F6
Tithe Barn La 9 DN8 .... 15 B8
Tiverton Rd PE3 .... 225 C3
Tiverton St DN35 .... 189 E1
Tobias Gr 4 PE9 .... 218 C7
Tobruk Cl LN1 .... 201 D8
Toby's Hill Nature Reserve★ LN11 .... 51 C5
Todd La DN21 .... 41 C4
Todds Cl 1 HU14 .... 3 C6
Todds Ct 26 DN17 .... 29 D7
Todds La 1 DN15 .... 8 A4
Todd's La HU15 .... 2 A8
Todkill's La 7 PE12 .... 160 F4
Toft Cl PE24 .... 115 D8
Toft Field La PE22 .... 114 A3
Toft Hurn 1 PE22 .... 98 F4
Toft La LN8 .... 56 E7
Toft Tunnel Nature Reserve★ PE10 .... 154 A1
Toftland PE2 .... 230 C5
Tofts Rd 10 DN18 .... 10 E8
Tolethorpe Sq 6 PE9 .. 219 B6
Toll Bar Ave
6 Bottesford NG13 .... 128 A6
New Waltham DN36 .... 195 B6
Toll Bar Rd Croft PE24 .. 103 D3
Grantham NG31 .... 211 C3
Toll Bar Sec Sch DN36 .... 195 A5
Toll House Rd PE2 .... 230 C7
Tollbar Rd
Great Gonerby NG32 .... 129 B8
Marston NG32 .... 118 C1
Tollemach Rd (South) NG31 .... 139 F8
Tollemache Fields 9 NG33 .... 151 D2
Tollemache Rd (North) NG31 .... 139 F8
Tollesby La 34 DN7 .... 14 D4
Tollfield Rd PE21 .... 209 B7
Tollgate
Peterborough PE3 .... 225 A5
Spalding PE11 .... 214 C4
Toll's La PE12 .... 215 E5
Tom La NG34 .... 120 E5
Tom Otter's La LN1 .... 66 B1
Tomline Rd 5 DN41 .... 23 A5
Tomline St 1 DN31 .... 189 B1
Tomlinson Ave 4 DN15 . 182 E3
Tomlinson Cl 3 LN4 ... 207 A5
Tomlinson Way 5 NG34 .... 108 E2
Tonbridge 1 DN33 .... 194 E8
Toneham La PE6 .... 175 F2
Tonglet Cl 3 PE25 .... 206 C1
Tonnant Way DN34 .... 190 D5
Tooley La PE22 .... 114 C2
Tooley St Boston PE21 .. 209 A3
Gainsborough DN21 .... 197 D3
Toot La PE21 .... 209 D4
Toothill Gdns DN34 .... 190 F6
Top La Goulceby LN11 .... 72 C6
Kirk Bramwith DN7 .... 14 A6
Top Rd
4 Croxton Kerrial NG32 . 138 D4
Little Cawthorpe LN11 .... 61 E2
Osgodby LN8 .... 45 A2
South Killingholme DN40 .... 12 E3
Thorney NG23 .... 78 F7
Winterton DN15 .... 8 F6
Worlaby DN20 .... 10 D1
Topaz Gr 3 HU3 .... 180 A4
Topham Cres 13 PE6 ... 176 A3
Topmoor Way PE4 .... 221 D1
Topsgate PE12 .... 159 C7
Torbay Dr DN33 .... 194 E6
Torchil Cl HU10 .... 178 C6
Torfrid Cl 14 PE6 .... 166 F1
Torfrida Dr PE10 .... 213 B6
Torgate Ave LN5 .... 92 F2
Torgate La LN5 .... 93 A2
Torkington Gdns 9 PE9 .... 219 B5
Torkington St PE9 .... 219 A5
Torksey Ave LN1 .... 66 C2
Torksey Dr DN33 .... 191 B3
Torksey Ferry Rd DN22 .. 65 B5
Torksey Pl 2 DN33 .... 191 B3
Torksey St
14 Kirton in Lindsey DN21 .. 30 B1
Rampton DN22 .... 65 A5
Tor-o-moor Gdns 2 LN10 .... 97 E6
Tor-o-moor Rd LN10 .... 97 D5
Toronto St 2 LN2 .... 202 C3
Torpel Way 5 PE6 .... 173 C7
Torr St DN21 .... 197 D4
Torrington La
East Barkwith LN8 .... 71 A8
Fleet PE12 .... 159 B5
Legsby LN8 .... 58 C1
Torrington Rd
Lincoln LN2 .... 201 F8
Scunthorpe DN17 .... 184 C8
Torrington St DN32 .... 191 F5
Torskey Castle★ LN1 ... 65 D5
Tortoiseshell Wood Nature Reserve★ NG33 .... 152 B2
Tossey La LN11 .... 50 B2
Tothby Cl 1 LN13 .... 75 E3
Tothby La LN13 .... 75 E2
Totnes Rd DN33 .... 194 E6
Tottermire La 5 DN9 .... 27 D7
Touthill Cl PE1 .... 226 A2
Tow La 5 NG32 .... 117 F1
Towell Cl PE21 .... 209 B3
Tower Ave
Bracebridge Heath LN4 ... 205 F3
Lincoln LN2 .... 202 D4
Tower Cl
24 Mablethorpe & Sutton LN12 .... 64 B3
Woodhall Spa LN10 .... 97 F7
Tower Cres LN2 .... 202 D4
Tower Dr Lincoln LN2 ... 202 D4
Woodhall Spa LN10 .... 97 F7
Tower Espl PE25 .... 206 D3
Tower Gdns 1 LN2 .... 202 D4

Tower Hill
Kingston upon Hull
HU13 ....178 E1
Westwoodside DN9 ......27 B2
Tower Hill Dr HU13 ....178 E1
Tower Hill Mews 2
HU13 ....178 E1
Tower House La 7 HU12 ..5 F8
Tower La LN4 ....94 B4
Tower Rd PE21 ......209 A5
Tower St 14 Boston PE21 .208 F5
Gainsborough DN21 ....197 D5
Kingston upon Hull HU9 .181 A6
Peterborough PE2 ......230 F8
Tower View
Kingston upon Hull
HU10 ....178 C5
Sleaford NG34 ....212 B3
Towers The 2 PE25 ....206 D5
Towler St PE1 ....226 A3
Town Bridge 22 PE21 ..208 F5
Town Dam Dro PE11 ...144 F8
Town Dam La PE11 ....134 F2
Town Dro PE11 ......144 F8
Town End NG32 ......120 B2
Town Farm Cl 1 PE11 .156 E8
Town Hall St 9 DN31 ..191 E7
Town Hill DN20 ......19 E4
Town Hill Dr DN20 ....19 E4
Town Rd Sleaford NG34 .212 B1
Tetney DN36 ....36 D4
Town St Cottam DN22 ..65 B6
Immingham DN40 ......12 E4
South Somercotes LN11 ..50 E4
Westborough & Dry Doddington
NG23 ....117 F3
Townfield La 5 PE6 ...135 C7
Towngate E PE6 ......217 A6
Towngate W PE6 ......217 A6
Towning Cl 9 PE6 ....217 D6
Townley LN9 ....199 D1
Townsend Cl DN36 ....193 C1
Townsend Rd 6 PE8 ..172 B1
Townside DN40 ......12 D6
Toynton All Saints Prim Sch
PE23 ....100 F6
Toynton Cl 3 LN6 ....205 B4
Toynton La PE23 .....101 B6
Toynton Rd DN33 ....191 B3
Trader Bank
Frithville PE22 ....125 F8
Sibsey PE22 ....113 A2
Trafalgar Ave
Grimsby DN34 ....190 D5
Skegness PE25 ....206 D1
Trafalgar Ct 4 LN4 ...203 B2
Trafalgar Pk DN36 ....195 D7
Trafalgar Pl 3 PE21 ..208 E4
Trafalgar Sq
Long Sutton PE12 .....216 B4
4 Sutton on Trent NG23 .91 A4
Trafalgar St 5 HU3 ...180 D7
Trafford Rd
Kingston upon Hull
HU10 ....178 E8
18 Wisbech PE13 .....170 C1
Trafford St DN15 ......183 B4
Traffords Way DN20 ...30 F6
Train Gate 28 DN21 ...30 B1
Tranby Ave HU13 .....178 D2
Tranby Dr DN32 ......192 B4
Tranby La
Anlaby with Anlaby Common
HU10 ....178 B5
Swanland HU14 ....3 C6
Tranby Mdws Pk
HU13 ....178 C3
Tranby Ride HU10 ....178 C5
Tranmere Ct HU3 .....180 B5
Travellers Sch The
PE1 ....226 F6
Travis Ave 16 DN8 ....15 B8
Travis CE Fst Sch DN7 .14 E4
Travis Cl 14 DN8 .....15 B8
Travis Gr 15 DN8 .....15 B8
Traviss Cl 2 DN16 ....185 B8
Treadgold Ave 10 NG31 .129 E5
Treading Bank PE13 ...169 C4
Treasure La LN11 .....49 F5
Treece Gdns 10 DN18 ..3 F1
Trehampton Dr 4 DN21 .53 A5
Trelawney Cres LN1 ...201 E8
Tremayne Ave 1 HU15 ..2 C5
Trenchard Ave 1 NG24 .104 C5
Trenchard Cl DN40 ....186 E1
Trenchard Rd
9 Ashby De La Launde &
Bloxholm LN4 ....108 A7
8 Mablethorpe/Sutton on Sea
LN12 ....64 B3
Trenchard Sq
2 Scampton Airfield LN1 .67 F5
1 Waddington LN5 .....94 A7
Trent La Besthorpe NG23 .91 B3
Girton NG23 ....78 B1
Newton on Trent LN1 ...65 C1
South Clifton NG23 ....78 B5
Trent Port Rd DN21 ...65 D8
Trent Rd
Grantham NG31 ......210 D4
Keadby with Althorpe
DN17 ....17 D6
Trent Side
Gainsborough DN21 ....197 D3
Scunthorpe DN16 .....183 B4
Trent View
Keadby DN17 ....17 D5

Trent View continued
Marton DN21 ....65 E8
Trent Wlk 13 HU15 ....2 C1
Trentholme Dr 37 DN17 .29 D7
Trenton Ave HU4 .....179 B6
Trentside
Gainsborough DN21 ....197 B8
Keadby with Althorpe
DN17 ....17 C3
Trentvale Prep Sch
DN17 ....17 D6
Tresham Rd PE2 ......229 D3
Trevitt Cl 1 NG34 ....212 B7
Trevor Cl 22 DN37 ....23 F1
Trevose Dr 2 LN6 ....205 A1
Triangle Dr HU4 ......3 A4
Triangle The 18 HU14 ..3 A4
Trienna PE2 ....230 B5
Trinity Cl
10 Crowland PE6 ......166 E1
10 Goxhill DN19 ......12 A4
Trinity Ct 9 DN20 .....19 D4
Trinity Gr HU13 ......178 E2
Trinity La LN11 ......198 D6
Trinity Rd
Cleethorpes DN35 .....192 E5
Newark-on-Trent NG24 ..104 A2
Scunthorpe DN16 .....185 A4
Stamford PE9 ....219 A6
Wisbech PE13 ....170 C1
Trinity St Boston PE21 .208 E4
Gainsborough DN21 ....197 D3
3 Grimsby DN31 ......189 C1
Kingston upon Hull HU3 .180 C7
3 Peterborough PE1 ...226 A2
Trinity Wlk 1 DN18 ...3 F1
Tritton Rd LN6 ......201 D2
Trollope St LN5 ......234 B1
Troon Cl
Grantham NG31 ......211 D8
7 Heighington/Washingborough
LN4 ....203 D1
11 Stamford PE9 ......218 E6
Troon Rd DN7 ....14 D4
Trotters La 2 NG32 ...139 C2
Troughton Way 10 PE13 .170 B2
Troutbeck Cl
6 Lincoln LN6 ....202 A8
1 Peterborough PE4 ...221 D3
Troutsdale Gr HU9 ....181 F8
Truesdale Gdns PE6 ..164 E3
Trunch La PE24 ......90 C5
Trundle La 2 DN7 ....14 D8
Trunkass La DN37 ....34 D7
Truro Cl
6 Grantham NG31 ....210 F5
5 Sleaford NG34 .....212 C7
Truro Dr LN6 ....204 B8
Truro Way 2 PE11 ....214 C4
Trusthorpe Rd 3 LN12 .64 C1
Tucker's Yd PE2 .....231 C2
Tuckers Nook PE6 ....173 C7
Tudor Cl
Northorpe PE10 ......164 C7
Peterborough PE4 .....221 C2
4 Sutterton PE20 .....136 A2
1 Toft Newton LN8 ...56 D5
Tudor Dr 4 Boston PE21 .208 E2
Louth LN11 ....198 C4
Tudor Pk LN9 ....199 D4
Tudor Rd LN6 ....204 D6
Tudor Way PE21 .....215 D5
Tudorth Field Rd DN7 .15 B5
Tudworth Rd DN7 ....15 A5
Tulip Rd 2 DN15 .....183 C3
Tulipwood Ave 11 LN6 .200 C1
Tumby PE22 ....207 F8
Tumby La PE22 ......98 D2
Tumby Rd LN4 ......207 E6
Tummel Ct DN40 ....186 B2
Tunnard St
Boston PE21 ....208 F6
Grimsby DN32 ....192 B8
Tunnel Bank PE10 ....213 F3
Tunnel Rd DN20 .....196 F7
Turbary Rd DN9 .....27 B6
Turf Moor Rd 4 DN7 ..15 A3
Turnberry App DN37 ..194 C4
Turnberry Cl 1 NG31 ..211 D7
Turnberry Dr 4 LN10 ..97 C6
Turnbury Cl LN6 .....204 B7
Turner Ave 3 LN6 ....205 A6
Turner Cl 2 LN5 .....107 B8
Turner St
15 Kirton in Lindsey DN21 .30 B1
Lincoln LN1 ....234 A4
Turner's La 17 HU14 ..3 A5
Turnor Cl 5 NG33 ....151 E6
Turnor Cres NG31 ....211 C5
Turnor Rd NG31 .....211 F4
Turnpike Cl
Great Gonerby NG31 ...210 F5
21 Wisbech PE13 .....170 C1
Turnpike Rd PE9 .....163 C2
Turnpole Cl 2 PE9 ...219 D7
Turnstone Way PE2 ..231 D7
Turpin Cl PE21 ......197 F5
Turves Rd PE6 ....175 A2
Tut Hole PE9 ....100 F7
Tuxhill Rd PE34 .....161 E1
Tweed Ct 8 LN6 .....199 D2
Twelve Foot Bank
LN4 ....109 C5
Twelvetree Ave PE4 ..220 E4
Twenty Dro PE10 .....155 C3
Twenty Foot Bank
LN4 ....110 C6
Twitchell 4 LN1 .....66 D7

Two Plank La PE11 ...214 B6
Two Pole Dro PE7 ....231 F1
Two Sisters Cl 8 PE11 .160 E4
Twyford Cl 2 NG33 ...151 E6
Twyning Pl DN35 .....192 D7
Tydd Low Rd PE12 ....160 A3
Tydd Rd PE11 ....156 C6
Tydd St Giles Sch
PE13 ....169 F6
**Tydd St Mary CE (Aided)
Prim Sch** PE13 ......160 A1
Tydeman Cl DN16 ....185 A2
Tye's Dro PE11 ......165 D2
Tyghes Cl PE6 ......217 F5
Tyler Ave DN31 ......191 A7
Tyler Cres 2 PE22 ...126 E3
Tylers Cl PE24 ......90 D7
Tyndal Rd NG31 .....210 F5
Tyne Cl 4 LN6 ......205 A2
Tyne St HU3 ....180 B4
Tynedale Ct 5 DN3 ...14 A2
Tyrrell Pk PE1 ......226 D2
Tyson Cl NG31 ......211 C6
Tytton Cl 2 PE21 ....136 D8
Tytton La E PE21 ....136 D8
Tytton La W PE21 ...136 D8

U

Uffington Ave LN6 ...205 A6
Uffington Rd
2 Barnack PE9 ....172 D4
Stamford PE9 ....219 E6
Ulceby Cross LN13 ...88 B8
Ulceby Rd
Scunthorpe DN17 .....184 D5
South Killingholme DN39 .12 C2
Wootton DN39 ....11 F3
Ulceby Sta DN39 .....12 C2
Uldale Cl LN6 ....200 C2
Uldale Way PE4 .....221 D2
Ullswater Ave PE4 ...221 B2
Ullswater Cl 6 LN6 ...205 A2
Ulster Ave DN33 .....191 D2
Ulster Rd DN21 .....197 D6
Ulverston Rd HU4 ....179 A3
Ulyett La DN17 ......28 C8
Unicorn Row 10 DN21 .30 B1
Union Pl 1 PE21 .....208 F5
Union Rd Lincoln LN1 .234 A3
Thorne/Moorends DN8 ..15 A8
Union St 2 Boston PE21 .208 F5
Grantham NG31 ......211 A5
Holbeach PE12 ....159 A7
Louth LN11 ....198 B6
Market Rasen LN8 .....57 D8
Unity Ave HU13 ......178 F1
Unity Rd DN32 ......192 C6
Unity Sq 5 LN2 ......234 B2
University of Humberside
HU1 ....180 F7
University of Lincoln
LN6 ....234 A2
**University of Lincolnshire &
Humberside City Ctr**
Campus HU1 ....180 E6
Upgate LN11 ....198 B5
Upland Cl LN9 ......199 A5
Uplands PE4 ....221 A5
Uplands DN21 ......211 D6
Upper Burgess St
1 Grimsby DN31 ......191 E8
3 Grimsby DN31 ......191 E7
Upper Cl The 8 LN1 ..66 D7
Upper Ings La DN22 ..52 D2
Upper Kenyon St 9 DN8 .15 A8
Upper Lindum St LN2 .234 C3
Upper Long Leys Rd
LN1 ....234 A4
Upper Row NG22 .....65 A1
Upper Saxon St LN1 ..234 A4
Upperthorpe Hill DN9 .27 A2
Uppingham Rd 7 LN12 .64 C1
Upsall Rd 9 PE22 ....126 E3
Upton Cl
Peterborough PE3 .....225 A2
Peterborough PE2 .....231 E5
Upton Rd DN21 ......53 B4
Upton Wlk DN21 .....197 F3
Urban St LN5 ....205 D6
Uredale Pl DN16 .....185 E5
Usher Art Gall★ LN2 .234 B3
Usher Gn 3 Lincoln LN6 .205 B7
4 Wellingore LN5 .....205 B6
Usher Jun Sch The
LN6 ....205 B7
Utgard Way 4 DN33 ..191 B2
Utterby Dr 1 DN34 ...191 C5
Utterby Prim Sch DN36 .48 D5

V

Vacherie La LN4 .....109 F3
Valda Vale DN40 .....186 A4
Vale of Ancholme Sch
DN20 ....196 B4
Vale Rd
Gonerby Hill Foot NG31 .210 F8
10 Spilsby PE23 ......101 A8
Vale The HU10 ......178 B7
Vale View NG23 .....117 F5
Valence Rd PE2 .....229 D4
Valentine Cl
Boston PE21 ....209 C3
1 Kingston upon Hull
HU4 ....179 A2

Valentine Rd LN6 ....201 C1
Valiant Rd
6 Coddington NG24 ...104 C5
Manby LN11 ....62 C5
Valletta St HU9 ......5 E8
Valley Dr HU10 ......178 B7
Valley La
Long Bennington NG23 .117 B4
Swaby LN13 ....74 E4
Valley Rd
Grantham NG31 ......210 C4
1 Waddington LN5 ....93 E8
Valley View 8 NG34 ..104 D5
Valley View Dr DN16 ..185 A2
Valliant St 7 LN5 ....94 A7
Vampire Dr LN6 .....62 C5
Van Gogh Dr 8 PE11 .214 B4
Vancouver Cres DN17 .184 E4
Vane St HU3 ....180 D7
Vanessa Dr DN21 ....197 C7
Vanessa Rd LN11 ....198 A4
Vanguard Ct 4 NG34 .212 A3
Vanwall Dr 8 LN5 ....93 F7
Varah Cl 39 DN18 ...10 E8
Varlow Rd 8 LN7 ....33 B4
Varsity Cl 4 DN7 ....26 A4
Vasey Cl LN1 ....66 C2
Vaughan Ave
Bottesford NG13 .....128 B6
Grimsby DN36 ....192 B4
Vauxhall Rd
12 Boston PE21 ......209 A5
Bracebridge Heath LN4 .205 D2
Veal St DN31 ....191 C7
Velden Way 5 LN8 ...57 D7
Venables Cl 13 PE24 .102 E7
Vence Cl 7 PE9 .....219 A5
Venom Rd LN11 .....62 C5
Ventnor Ave LN6 ....210 E4
Venture Way NG31 ..210 D2
Verdun Cl LN1 ......201 E7
Vere Rd PE1 ....225 F7
Vere St LN1 ....201 F6
Vere Terr LN1 ......191 C8
Vergette Rd PE6 .....220 D8
Vergette St PE1 .....226 B3
Vermont Gr PE3 .....225 E1
Vernatts Gn PE11 ...214 C7
Vernon Ave NG31 ...210 F8
Vernon Rd DN35 ....206 C4
Vernon St LN5 ......201 D1
Vicar La 2 HU1 .....180 F5
Vicarage Ave
4 Wrawby DN20 .....20 E3
2 Wrawby DN20 .....196 F6
Vicarage Cl
5 Collingham NG23 ...91 D5
4 Cowbit PE12 ......167 B8
Holbeach PE12 ....158 D1
Vicarage Cres 4 DN15 ..8 B5
Vicarage Dr LN6 .....200 B3
Vicarage Dro PE20 ..134 D5
Vicarage Farm Rd 5
PE1 ....226 D3
Vicarage Gdns
2 Brough HU15 ......2 C6
Scunthorpe DN15 .....182 F2
1 Wrawby DN20 .....20 E3
Vicarage La
Beckingham DN10 ....40 B1
Broughton DN20 .....19 E1
Cadney DN20 ....31 D6
4 Carlton-le-Moorland LN5 .92 E1
3 Carlton-le-Moorland
LN5 ....105 E8
Dunston LN4 ....95 C6
Elsham DN20 ....20 F7
Grasby DN38 ....32 E7
Harmston LN5 ....93 F5
1 Helpringham NG34 .133 D7
1 Immingham DN40 ...12 E4
3 Kingston upon Hull
HU13 ....178 E1
4 Long Bennington NG23 .117 D3
Long Sutton PE12 .....216 D2
11 Lutton PE12 ......160 A8
21 Nettleham LN2 .....68 C2
1 Scawby DN20 ......30 E8
Scopwick LN4 ....95 C1
4 Scothern LN2 ......68 F4
4 Sibsey PE22 ....113 B1
South Clifton NG23 ...78 C5
Wainfleet All Saints
PE24 ....102 D1
19 Wellingore LN5 ...107 A7
Wootton DN39 ....11 B3
Vicarage Pk 4 DN15 ..9 D1
Vicarage Rd
3 Heckington NG34 ...122 C3
Willoughton DN21 ....42 E4
Wrawby DN20 ....196 F6
Vicarage Way PE7 ...233 D5
Vicar's Wlk 6 DN17 ..16 D7
Viceroy Dr PE11 ....156 F8
Vickers La 4 LN11 ...198 B5
Victor Dr 1 LN6 .....204 C1
Victor St Grimsby DN32 .189 C1
Kingston upon Hull HU9 .181 C8
Victor Way
Bourne PE10 ....213 E6
10 Waddington LN5 ...94 A7
Victoria Ave
1 Hatfield DN7 ......14 C4
Sleaford NG34 ....212 C4
1 Woodhall Spa LN10 ..97 D5
Victoria Bank NG34 ..133 C1
Victoria Cl
Gainsborough DN21 ....197 F2

Victoria Cl continued
2 Marshchapel DN36 ...37 C2
2 Stainforth DN7 .....14 C5
Victoria Ct 5 DN15 ...8 B5
Victoria Dock Prim Sch
HU9 ....181 B6
Victoria Dr 5 DN18 ...3 E1
Victoria Gr
Heighington/Washingborough
LN4 ....203 D1
Morton PE10 ....154 D7
Victoria Pas LN1 .....234 A3
Victoria Pier★ HU1 ...181 A5
Victoria Pl
8 Boston PE21 ......208 F4
1 Bourne PE10 ......213 E4
Peterborough PE1 .....225 F4
Victoria Rd
Barnetby le Wold DN38 .21 B4
10 Keelby DN41 .....23 A5
Louth LN11 ....198 C7
Mablethorpe/Sutton on Sea
LN12 ....64 B3
2 Market Rasen LN8 ..57 E8
Scunthorpe DN16 .....185 A5
Skegness PE25 ....206 B3
Stamford PE9 ....219 B6
Victoria Ret Pk DN31 ..189 A1
Victoria St
Billingborough NG34 ..133 B1
3 Billinghay LN4 .....109 F6
Grantham NG31 ......211 A2
4 Holbeach PE12 ....215 E2
Kingston upon Hull
HU13 ....179 A1
Lincoln LN1 ....234 A3
Peterborough PE1 .....226 A5
Peterborough PE2 .....230 F6
10 Spalding PE11 ....214 A4
3 Wragby LN8 ......70 D5
Victoria St N DN31 ...189 A1
Victoria St S 1 DN31 .191 E7
Victoria St W
3 Grimsby DN31 .....191 E7
3 Grimsby DN31 .....191 D7
Victoria Terr LN1 .....234 A3
Victoria Way DN31 ...188 D2
Victory Cl 6 PE12 ....157 F6
Victory Ct 1 PE11 ....214 C3
Victory Way
2 Barton-upon-Humber
DN18 ....3 F1
8 Grimsby DN34 .....190 D4
Viersen Platz PE1 ....226 A1
Viking Cl 6 Bourne PE10 .213 C6
Immingham DN40 ....186 A4
11 Swineshead PE20 .135 B7
11 Waddington LN5 ...93 F7
Viking Sch The PE25 .206 B4
Viking Way
32 Metheringham LN4 ..95 C3
7 Northorpe PE10 ....164 C6
Spalding PE11 ....214 F2
Villa Cl PE12 ....216 A5
Villa La PE20 ....135 B7
Village Farm Dr 5 LN1 .66 C7
Village St
Burton Coggles NG33 ..152 C8
Easton NG33 ....139 F2
Pickworth NG34 ......142 A8
Sedgebrook NG32 ....128 F4
Woolsthorpe By Belvoir
NG32 ....128 D1
Village The PE2 .....230 B5
Ville Rd DN16 ....185 D6
Vincent Cl 3 HU4 ....179 A2
Vine Cl 13 NG13 .....128 A5
Vine Cres 8 PE21 ....136 D8
Vine Ct 3 NG34 .....133 B1
Vine Rd
6 Skegness PE25 .....103 E4
2 Skegness PE25 .....103 E4
Vine St
Billingborough NG34 ..133 C1
12 Grantham NG31 ...211 A5
Lincoln LN2 ....234 C2
Spalding PE11 ....214 D4
Stamford PE9 ....219 C5
Vinegarth 3 DN9 ....27 E6
Vinehall Rd 3 DN9 ...27 C2
Viney Cl PE1 ....226 D5
Vineyard Rd PE1 ....226 B2
Vinters Way PE22 ...126 E3
Vintners Ct PE3 .....225 D3
Violet Cl
4 Humberston DN35 ..192 E1
Morton PE10 ....154 D6
Virginia Cl 1 PE3 ....225 A2
Virginia Dr LN11 .....198 E5
Viscount Ct PE2 .....231 A6
Viscount Way 8 DN36 ..36 D8
Vista The 3 PE11 ....214 D3
Visual Arts Ctr★
DN15 ....183 C3
Vivian Ave DN32 ....192 B5
Vivian Cl 3 HU4 .....210 F8
Vixen Cl PE7 ....233 F6
Voases Cl HU10 .....178 E6
Voases La HU10 .....178 E6
Vulcan Cres LN6 .....204 C2
Vulcan Dr 4 LN1 ....67 F5
Vulcan St 9 LN5 .....94 A7
Vulcan Way DN7 ....15 A1
Vyner Cl 15 LN12 ....64 B3

W

Waby Cl DN37 190 D7
Waddingham Pl
5 Habrough DN40 22 E8
New Waltham DN36 195 D5
Waddingham Prim Sch
DN21 43 D7
Waddingham Rd LN7 31 F1
Waddington Dr 1 DN17 184 E3
Waddington La NG23 91 C7
Waddington Pl 5 DN34 191 A5
Waddingworth Gr
LN2 202 A8
Wade Pk Ave PE6 217 C4
Waggoners Way PE10 154 C6
Waggoners Wlk PE22 113 B1
Waggons Way 4 DN7 14 C5
Wainer Cl LN6 204 C5
Wainfleet Magdalen Sec Sch
PE24 102 D2
Wainfleet Rd
Boston PE21 209 D7
Croft PE24 102 D7
Firsby PE23 101 F6
Fishtoft PE21 209 D7
Grimsby DN33 191 B3
Irby in the Marsh PE24 102 B6
Skegness PE25 206 A3
Thorpe St Peter PE24 102 C3
Wainfleet Sta PE24 102 D1
Wainman Rd PE2 230 D5
Wainwell Mews 3 LN2 234 C3
Wainwright PE4 220 E5
Waithe La DN37 35 E4
Wake Rd PE1 226 B2
Wake St LN1 234 A4
Wakefield Ave DN21 29 D4
Wakefield Cl NG31 210 C4
Wakerley Dr PE2 230 C7
Wakerley Rd 6 DN21 29 C3
Wakes Cl 1 PE10 213 E4
Walbury Cl 4 LN5 205 D2
Walcot Bar NG34 132 D2
Walcot Cl LN6 204 F6
Walcot La NG34 142 C8
Walcot Rd
Alkborough DN15 8 B8
Ufford PE9 172 F3
Walcot Way 2 PE9 218 E6
Walcott Prim Sch LN4 109 C7
Walcott Rd LN4 109 E6
Walcott St HU3 180 C4
Waldeck St LN1 234 A4
Walden Gdns 1 PE21 208 E4
Waldo Rd LN4 205 F5
Waldorf Rd DN35 193 A1
Walesby Cl DN33 194 D8
Walesby Hill LN8 46 B3
Walesby La LN8 46 B2
Walesby Rd
Market Rasen LN8 57 E8
Middle Rasen LN8 45 E1
Scunthorpe DN17 184 E4
Walford Cl 2 NG13 128 A5
Walford Dr LN6 205 A6
Walgrave PE2 230 B4
Walk La
Humberston DN36 36 C7
4 Irby DN37 34 D7
Langton By Wragby LN8 70 F4
Walker Ave DN33 194 F8
Walker Cl 1 DN15 8 E7
Walker Dr 4 DN15 9 A5
Walker Rd PE6 220 D7
Walker St HU3 180 C5
Walkergate 14 LN11 198 B5
Walkeringham Prim Sch
DN10 39 F3
Walkeringham Rd
Beckingham DN10 40 A2
Gringley on the Hill DN10 39 D2
Walkerith Rd
East Stockwith DN21 40 B5
Gainsborough DN21 197 B8
Morton DN21 40 D3
Walker's Cl 5 DN38 21 B4
Walkers Cl 4 NG13 128 B5
Walkers Ct 20 DN17 29 D7
Walkers Way
Barrowby NG32 210 A3
Peterborough PE3 224 F3
Ulceby DN39 12 B2
Walkington Way 18 LN12 77 A7
Walks Rd NG34 120 F1
Walks The 4 PE9 171 B1
Wall St
Gainsborough DN21 197 D3
Grimsby DN34 191 A7
Wallace's Dro PE6 176 D4
Walled Gdn The 5 LN5 93 F5
Waller St HU9 181 C8
Walliker St HU3 180 A6
Wallingfen La HU15 1 B8
Wallis Ave LN6 205 B4
Wallis Rd LN11 198 D5
Wallisgate PE12 158 C7
Walls Ave 5 PE24 102 E7
Wall's La PE25 90 E2
Walmer St 1 LN2 202 C3
Walmgate DN34 191 B4
Walmsgate Pl 3 DN33 191 B4
Walmsley St HU3 180 D7
Walnut Cl
5 Newborough PE6 174 E4
14 Ruskington NG34 108 E2
2 Waddington LN5 93 E8
Walnut Cres DN35 192 D2
Walnut Dr 1 DN20 30 F7
Walnut Gr 3 NG33 151 E7
Walnut Pl LN5 234 B1
Walnut Rd
3 Bottesford NG13 128 A5
Kirton PE20 136 C6
Walnut Way DN17 29 C7
Walnutgarth 6 NG34 212 F3
Walpole Bank PE14 170 F7
Walsall Garth HU4 179 B4
Walsingham Ct 3 PE13 170 C1
Walsingham Way 13
PE6 175 A1
Waltham Cl 9 LN6 204 C6
Waltham Grange 5
DN35 192 F3
Waltham Mus of Rural Life*
DN37 194 D3
Waltham Rd
Barnoldby Le Beck DN37 194 A3
Birchwood LN6 204 B6
Brigsley DN37 194 C1
Croxton Kerrial NG32 138 A4
Grimsby DN33 194 F8
Waltham St 1 HU1 180 F6
Waltham Windmill*
DN37 194 E3
Walton Comp Sch
PE4 221 A2
Walton Gdns NG31 211 A2
Walton Girls High Sch The
NG31 210 F1
Walton Gr DN33 191 C4
Walton Heath Cl 2
NG31 211 D7
Walton Infants Sch
PE4 221 A1
Walton Jun Sch Cty
PE4 221 A1
Walton Pk PE4 221 A1
Walton Rd
7 Leverington PE13 170 B2
Marholm PE6 220 C1
Wisbech PE13 170 E1
Walton St HU3 180 A7
Walton St Leisure Ctr
HU3 180 A6
Walton Way 3 NG32 139 C7
Wandell's View HU15 2 C8
Wansbeck Rd 8 NG34 121 B7
Wansford Rd PE8 222 A3
Wanton La PE34 161 F3
Wanton's Cross Gate
PE12 159 D2
Wanton's La PE12 159 E2
Wapping La DN21 65 E8
War Meml Hospl LN9 199 C4
Warbon Ave PE1 225 F7
Ward Cres PE21 209 E4
Ward St DN35 192 C8
Wardall St DN35 192 F6
Wardentree La PE11 157 A8
Wardour Dr NG31 211 F5
Ward's La PE22 114 A3
Wareley Rd PE2 225 F1
Wares Way 5 DN15 182 B3
Wargate Field La
PE11 145 C5
Wargate Way PE11 145 B6
Waring St LN9 199 B3
Warley Ave 1 DN16 185 C8
Warley Dr DN16 185 C8
Warley Rd DN16 185 C7
Warneford Rd DN35 192 D8
Warping Way 2 DN15 182 B3
Warren Cl DN21 197 B6
Warren Rd
North Somercotes LN11 51 A6
Scunthorpe DN15 183 B5
5 Thorne/Moorends DN8 15 B7
Wothorpe PE9 219 C1
Warren Way NG31 211 F7
Warrendale 12 DN18 10 E8
Warrenne Cl 21 DN7 14 D4
Warrenne Rd DN7 14 D4
Warth La PE25 206 A5
Warwick Ave DN33 191 A4
Warwick Cl
9 Grantham NG31 210 D5
4 Hatfield DN7 14 F3
2 Saxilby with Ingleby LN1 66 C2
Warwick Dr 24 DN18 10 E8
Warwick Rd
7 Chapel St Leonard PE24 90 D7
Cleethorpes DN35 192 D4
Louth LN11 198 B8
Newark-on-Trent NG24 104 B2
Peterborough PE4 221 A2
Scunthorpe DN16 183 C1
Warwick St HU9 181 B7
Wascana Cl HU4 179 B3
Wasdale Cl 2 LN6 200 C1
Wasdale Gdns 1 PE4 221 E2
Wash Bank PE12 167 A5
Wash Dike La PE22 115 A6
Wash Rd Fosdyke PE20 146 D7
Kirton PE20 136 D4
Washdike Dro PE11 135 C1
Washdike La
Croft PE24 102 E4
Donington PE11 135 A1
Stoke Rochford NG33 140 A3
Toynton St Peter PE23 101 B6
Washdike La *continued*
Wainfleet St Mary PE24 102 C1
Washdike Rd
Algarkirk PE20 136 B1
Kirton PE20 136 A6
Washdyke La
Belton & Manthorpe
NG32 130 A6
Boston PE21 208 B7
Cumberworth LN13 89 E8
Elsham DN20 20 D6
2 Glentham LN8 43 F1
Immingham DN40 186 B5
Leasingham NG34 121 B7
Mumby LN13 76 F1
Nettleham LN2 68 B2
Old Leake PE22 113 F4
Osgodby LN8 45 A3
Washdyke Rd 7 NG32 106 C1
Washdyke Ret Pk
DN40 186 C4
Washingborough Prim Sch
LN4 203 C2
Washingborough Rd
Heighington/Washingborough
LN4 81 E4
Lincoln LN4 202 D1
Washinghall La DN17 7 A2
Washington Cl 6 LN4 207 C4
Washington Dr 5 LN8 56 D5
Washington St 4 DN21 197 D2
Washtub La NG23 91 E6
Washway Rd
Fleet PE12 159 B8
Holbeach PE12 215 C6
Moulton PE12 146 F4
Wass La LN8 71 E5
Wassand St HU3 180 C4
Waste Gn La PE20 146 C7
Water Bank DN9 26 E5
Water End
Marholm PE6 220 B1
Peterborough PE7 229 A5
Water Gate
Quadring PE11 145 B8
Sleaford NG34 212 D4
Water La
1 Ancaster NG32 120 A2
Bourne PE10 213 D2
Castle Bytham NG33 152 D1
Castor PE5 223 F1
6 Colsterworth NG33 151 D7
Gunby & Stainby NG33 151 B5
5 Hagworthingham PE23 87 A4
4 Lincoln LN6 93 C8
Lincoln LN1 234 A2
1 Long Bennington NG23 117 D4
12 South Witham NG33 151 D2
4 Spalding PE11 214 D2
Threekingham NG34 132 F3
Thurlby LN5 92 E3
Thurlby PE10 164 C8
2 West Halton DN15 8 E7
Water Mill La PE23 100 F6
Water Mill Rd 2 LN9 199 B4
Water Side DN15 2 B1
Water St PE9 219 C4
Waterbelly La PE20 136 A1
Waterfall Gdns 2 PE6 174 E4
Waterford La LN3 203 D5
Waterfurlong PE9 219 A4
Watergall
1 Peterborough PE3 220 F1
Peterborough PE3 225 A8
Watergall CP Sch PE3 225 B8
Watergate
11 Grantham NG31 211 A5
10 Stamford PE9 219 C5
Waterhouse La HU1 180 E5
Watering Dyke Houses
LN2 67 F4
Waterlees Rd PE13 170 D1
Waterloo Cl 1 NG32 119 B7
Waterloo Dr
8 Grimsby DN33 191 B2
Morton PE10 154 D6
Waterloo La LN6 200 B3
Waterloo Paddock
LN5 106 D3
Waterloo Rd
Mablethorpe/Sutton on Sea
LN12 64 B4
Peterborough PE1 226 A5
Waterloo St
Kingston upon Hull HU2 180 E8
Lincoln LN6 201 D2
4 Market Rasen LN8 57 D8
Waterlow Dr 22 DN15 9 A5
Watermill La 18 LN2 68 C2
Waters Edge DN20 196 A3
Waters' Edge Ctry Pk*
DN18 3 F2
Waterside
5 Billinghay LN4 109 F5
8 Ryhall PE9 163 C1
Thorne DN8 14 F8
Waterside Bsns Pk HU13 3 F4
Waterside Cl 10 PE10 213 C7
Waterside Dr 5 DN31 191 D8
Waterside Gdns 5
PE12 215 E2
Waterside N LN5 234 B2
Waterside Rd DN18 3 E2
Waterside S LN5 234 B2
Waterslade Rd PE7 233 C4
Waterton Cl 2 PE6 217 E4
Waterton La DN7 14 D2
Waterwell La NG32 120 C4
Waterworks La PE6 220 B6
Waterworks St
1 Gainsborough DN21 197 D2
Immingham DN40 186 D5
Watery La Asterby LN11 72 F5
Butterwick PE22 126 F3
Goulceby LN11 72 D6
Lissington LN3 57 D1
Little Cawthorpe LN11 61 E2
Mareham Le Fen PE22 98 F4
Swaby LN13 74 E4
4 Welton/Dunholme LN2 68 E6
1 West Ashby LN9 85 E7
Wickenby LN3 70 A8
Watford Ave DN34 190 F4
Watkin St N DN31 188 F1
Watkin St S 2 DN31 188 F1
Watkins La 2 DN22 52 B3
Watling Cl 7 PE10 213 C6
Watson Pk 4 DN10 52 B8
Watsons Croft 5 DN7 14 D6
Watt Cl PE4 221 C2
Watts La LN11 198 C4
Wauldby Cl 4 HU10 178 E7
Wauldby View 2 HU14 3 B7
Waumsley Way 1 LN13 75 E2
Wavell Dr LN2 202 E4
Waveney Cl 1 DN15 8 B5
Waveney Gr PE4 221 C2
Waverley Ave LN6 204 F3
Waverley Gdns
3 Leverington PE13 170 B1
Stamford PE9 218 F6
Waverley Pl 3 PE9 218 F6
Waverley St HU1 180 E5
Waverly Cl PE10 154 D7
Wayet Rd 6 PE11 156 E8
Wayford Cl PE3 225 A2
Wayside Cl
6 Holton le Clay DN36 195 D2
Scunthorpe DN16 185 A3
Wayside Dr DN36 195 C7
Weatherthorn PE2 230 C5
Weaver Rd LN6 204 B5
Weavers Croft 11 DN9 27 A2
Webb Cl 36 DN18 10 E8
Webb St LN5 205 D8
Webster Ave DN15 182 E3
Webster Cl 3 LN6 205 A5
Webster Way NG31 210 E7
Websters Cl PE6 220 D8
Wedgewood Cl 10 LN6 204 D7
Wedgewood Dr 4 PE11 214 B5
Wedgewood Gr 9 LN6 204 D7
Wedgewood Rd LN6 204 D7
Wedland La PE24 102 D3
Weekes Rd DN35 192 F4
Weelsby Ave DN32 191 F4
Weelsby Gr 1 DN32 191 E4
Weelsby Prim Sch
DN32 192 A8
Weelsby Rd DN32 191 D5
Weelsby St
4 Grimsby DN31 189 C1
Grimsby DN32 192 A8
Weelsby St S DN32 192 A7
Weelsby View DN36 195 D8
Weelsby Way HU13 178 C2
Weeping Elm Way 6
DN16 185 D4
Weeton Way 5 HU10 178 E7
Wegberg Rd LN4 95 C7
Weir Cl 3 DN9 27 A2
Weir Farm 3 LN2 68 F4
Weir Rd DN9 27 A2
Weir St LN5 205 D8
Weir The HU13 178 E1
Weirs La PE22 126 D4
Wel Fen La NG23 117 E8
Welbeck Dr PE11 214 C5
Welbeck Pl 3 DN34 190 E4
Welbeck Rd DN35 192 C5
Welbeck St HU5 180 B8
Welbeck Way
Louth LN11 198 B6
Peterborough PE2 230 D7
Welbourn CE (Controlled)
Prim Sch PE4 221 A4
Welbourn Gdns 9 LN2 202 A8
Welbourn Rd LN5 106 A5
Welbourn Wlk HU4 179 B6
Welbourne PE4 221 A4
Welbourne La PE12 215 C4
Welbourne's Cl 6
NG23 117 D4
Welbourne's La 7
NG23 117 D4
Welby Dr 3 PE11 145 B6
Welby Gdns
Grantham NG31 211 A6
Holbeach PE12 215 B2
Welby St 6 NG31 211 A4
Weldon Rd DN21 42 E1
Welham St NG31 211 B4
Welholme Ave DN32 191 D5
Welholme Jun & Inf Sch
DN32 191 F6
Welholme Rd DN32 191 E6
Well High La LN13 75 D1
Well La LN2 234 B3
Well St
5 Bishop Norton LN8 43 D3
Messingham DN17 29 C7
Well Turn LN13 75 F1
Well Vale 2 DN33 194 D8
Well Vale Cl 28 PE24 90 D7
Welland Ave DN34 190 F4
Welland Bank PE6 166 C1
Welland Cl
Peterborough PE1 226 A7
9 Ruskington NG34 108 D2
1 Spalding PE11 214 C2
Welland CP Sch PE1 226 C8
Welland Ct 3 NG31 210 E2
Welland Dr 2 DN15 8 B5
Welland Hospl PE11 214 F6
Welland Mews PE9 219 C4
Welland Rd
Borough Fen PE1 174 E1
Boston PE21 208 B3
Lincoln LN1 201 D8
Peterborough PE1 226 B8
Spalding PE11 214 D3
2 Wittering PE8 172 B1
Welland Way PE6 217 E4
Wellbeck Cl 4 DN20 196 D4
Wellbeck Rd DN34 190 E4
Wellesley Cl 3 LN8 57 D8
Wellesley Way NG34 120 B8
Wellfield Cl 6 NG33 151 D2
Wellgarth DN32 192 B5
Wellhead La LN4 95 B7
Wellingore Rd
5 Lincoln LN2 201 F8
7 Lincoln LN2 202 A8
Wellington Ave 11 LN12 64 B4
Wellington Cl
7 Heckington NG34 122 E2
Skellingthorpe LN6 79 F6
Wellington Dr 1 NG31 211 D2
Wellington La HU3 180 D8
Wellington Rd
Boston PE21 209 B4
Mablethorpe/Sutton on Sea
LN12 64 B4
Wellington Sq 12 LN5 94 A7
Wellington St
12 Gainsborough DN21 197 D3
Grimsby DN32 191 F8
Kingston upon Hull HU1 180 F5
Lincoln LN1 201 D4
4 Louth LN11 198 C6
Peterborough PE1 226 B2
7 Scampton Airfield LN1 67 E5
Wellington St Wes
HU1 180 E5
Wellington Way
1 Elsham Wold Ind Est
DN20 21 A8
Market Deeping PE6 217 B7
1 Skegness PE25 206 A5
Wellington Yd 4 PE23 88 A1
Wellowgate 7 DN32 191 D7
Wells Cl
Grantham NG31 210 C5
Heighington/Washingborough
LN4 203 E1
Peterborough PE4 220 F3
Wells Cres DN35 192 E2
Wells Dr 5 LN8 57 E7
Wells La DN22 65 B7
Wells Rd DN37 23 D4
Wells St
1 Grimsby DN31 191 B7
Kingston upon Hull HU3 180 A5
Scunthorpe DN15 183 B4
Wells The 13 LN2 68 D6
Wellsted St HU3 180 C5
Wellsyke La LN10 98 A6
Welmore Rd PE6 220 D8
Welsdale Rd LN11 59 E2
Welton Cl 32 DN18 10 E8
Welton Gdns LN2 201 F8
Welton Low Rd HU15 2 C6
Welton Old Rd HU15 2 E6
Welton Rd Brough HU15 2 C5
Nettleham LN2 68 C3
Welton Wold View 9
HU14 3 B7
Welwyn Cl NG31 210 E1
Wembley Rd LN11 50 F7
Wembley St DN21 197 C4
Wendan Rd 9 DN8 15 A7
Wendover Cl
19 Humberston DN36 36 D8
Messingham DN17 29 D7
Rippingale PE10 142 F2
Wendover Mews PE10 213 E5
Wendover Rd 13 DN17 29 D7
Wendover Rise DN35 192 E5
Wenlock St HU3 180 C7
Wensleydale Cl 1
NG31 211 A8
Wensleydale Rd DN16 185 E6
Wensum Cl 4 PE11 214 F5
Wentworth Cl
Heighington LN4 203 E1
4 Skegness PE25 206 D6
1 Spalding PE11 214 C1
Willerby HU10 178 F8
Wentworth Cres 2 DN19 4 E2
Wentworth Dr
Dunholme LN2 68 E5
Grantham NG31 211 D8
25 Messingham DN17 29 D7
2 Saxilby with Ingleby LN1 66 D2
Wentworth Rd
Grimsby DN34 191 B7
Scunthorpe DN17 184 D2
Wentworth St 1 PE1 226 A1
Wentworth Way
Kingston upon Hull HU9 181 C7
7 Woodhall Spa LN10 97 C5
Wentworths The PE12 216 A4
Werneth Rd DN32 191 F8

Werrington Bridge Rd
PE6 .... .221 B6
Werrington Ctr PE4 ....220 F4
Werrington Gr PE4 ....220 F2
Werrington Mews 5
PE4 .... .221 A3
Werrington Parkway
PE6 .... .220 C5
Werrington Pk Ave 2
PE4 .... .221 A3
Werrington Sports Ctr
PE4 .... .220 F4
Werry's Cl 4 PE10 ....213 C5
Wesley Ave 5 PE34 ...161 F3
Wesley Cl 4 Epworth DN9 27 E6
15 Metheringham LN4 ...95 C4
Sleaford NG34 ...... .212 C2
11 Terrington St Clement
PE34 .... .161 F3
2 Winterton DN15 ..... .9 A5
Wesley Cres 2 DN35 ...192 A3
Wesley Ct 8 HU3 .....180 C5
Wesley Rd Brigg DN20 .196 C3
Scunthorpe DN16 .... .185 E7
9 Terrington St Clement
PE34 .... .161 F3
Whaplode PE12 ...... .158 C7
Wesley St 19 DN21 .... .30 B1
Wesley Way LN9 .....199 D3
Wesleyan Rd PE1 ....226 A7
Wesselow Rd LN4 ....207 F6
Wessex Cl
Peterborough PE2 .....231 D7
Sleaford NG34 ...... .212 B1
West Acridge DN18 ....3 E1
West Ave
Cranwell & Byard's Leap
NG34 .... .120 B8
Grantham NG31 ..... .210 D3
6 Stainforth DN7 ..... .14 C6
West Bank
Crowland PE6 .... .166 E1
Saxilby with Ingleby LN1 ..66 C2
Stainforth DN7 ...... .14 B7
Strubby with Woodthorpe
LN13 .... .63 E2
West Bank Rd PE12 ...161 A8
West Banks NG34 ....212 C4
West Bight 1 LN1 ....234 B3
West Brook La NG23 ..91 D3
West Butterwick CE Prim Sch
DN17 .... .28 D8
West Coates Rd DN17 .188 D2
West Cob Gate PE12 ..157 F6
West Comm Cres
DN17 .... .184 F8
West Comm Gdns
DN17 .... .184 F7
West Comm La DN17 ..184 E7
West Comm N Rd DN17 .29 A8
West Comm Sports Hall
DN17 .... .184 E8
West Cross St 24 DN21 .30 B1
West Ct 14 DN8 ...... .15 A4
West Dock Ave HU3 ...180 B4
West Dock St HU3 ....180 B3
West Dr Coningsby LN4 .110 E8
Sudbrooke LN2 ...... .68 F3
West Dro PE12 ....168 C2
West Dro N PE12 .....168 C3
West Dro S PE12 .....168 C2
West Ella Rd
Kingston upon Hull
HU10 .... .178 A7
Swanland HU14 ...... .3 C7
West Ella Way HU10 ..178 C7
West Elloe Ave PE11 ..214 E6
West End
Burgh le Marsh PE24 ..102 D8
Garthorpe & Fockerby
DN17 .... .7 E5
Gorefield PE13 ...... .169 E3
Harlaxton NG32 ..... .139 B7
Hogsthorpe PE24 .... .90 B7
Holbeach PE12 ...... .215 D2
Ingham LN1 .... .54 F7
Langtoft PE6 .... .164 E3
7 Spilsby PE23 ...... .87 F1
Swanland HU14 ...... .3 B6
Walcott LN4 .... .109 C7
Winteringham DN15 ... .2 A1
Yaxley PE7 .... .233 D4
West End Cl 9 NG13 ..128 A6
West End Cres 9 PE23 .87 F1
West End La DN36 .... .37 B1
West End Rd
Boston PE21 .... .136 D8
Epworth DN9 .... .27 C8
2 Habrough DN40 .... .22 E8
Kirton PE20 .... .136 B7
Maxey PE6 .... .217 A1
Ulceby DN39 .... .11 F1
Wyberton PE21 ..... .208 B2
West Fen Drain Bank
PE22 .... .112 D1
West Fen La PE22 ....100 A1
West Field La
1 Swanland HU14 .... .3 B6
Thorpe on the Hill LN6 .92 E8
West Gate
9 Ruskington NG34 ...108 E2
Wainfleet All Saints
PE24 .... .101 E2
Weston PE12 .... .157 D2
West Glanford Leisure Ctr
DN17 .... .184 D3
West Gn
Kingston upon Hull HU10 .3 C8

West Gn continued
29 Messingham DN17 ...29 D7
West Gr
7 Colsterworth NG33 ...151 E6
Kingston upon Hull HU4 .179 D4
West Halton La DN15 ..8 C8
West Hann La DN19 ....4 C1
West Haven Way
DN40 .... .186 B8
West Hill 1 HU13 .....3 E4
West La Baumber LN9 ..72 A1
Girton NG23 .... .78 C1
Haltham LN9 .... .98 C6
7 Keelby DN41 ..... .23 A4
Skidbrooke with Saltfleet Haven
LN11 .... .51 A2
3 Winterton DN15 .... .9 B5
West Lea NG33 ......194 F7
West Leys Pk 7 HU14 ..3 B6
West Leys Rd HU14 ....3 B6
West Marsh La
Barrow upon Humber DN19 .4 B1
Goxhill DN19 .... .5 A3
West Marsh Rd
Pinchbeck PE11 ......145 E1
Spalding PE11 ...... .214 F6
West Mid Mere Rd
DN40 .... .12 D3
West Mill 1 PE9 .....171 C2
West Mill Gate 2 LN3 .203 E6
West Moor Rd 1 DN10 ..39 F3
West Par
Kingston upon Hull HU3 .180 C7
Lincoln LN1 .... .234 A3
Peterborough PE3 .... .225 D4
Spalding PE11 ...... .214 B4
Wisbech PE13 ...... .170 C1
West Parklands Dr 9
HU14 .... .3 A5
West Rd
Billingborough NG34 ...133 B3
Bourne PE10 .... .213 B4
Deeping St Nicholas
PE11 .... .156 D3
Haconby PE10 ...... .154 C4
2 Keadby with Althorpe
DN17 .... .17 C4
Pointon & Sempringham
NG34 .... .143 A6
4 Ruskington NG34 ...108 D1
3 Ruskington NG34 ...108 D1
2 Tallington PE9 .....172 F7
Tetford LN9 .... .73 E1
Thorney NG23 ...... .78 B4
1 Tydd St Mary PE13 ..170 C8
West Row 4 PE21 ....208 E4
West St Alford LN13 ...75 E2
Barkston NG32 ...... .119 A1
Barnetby le Wold DN38 .21 B4
Billinghay LN4 ...... .109 F6
Boston PE21 .... .208 E4
Bourne PE10 .... .213 C5
Brant Broughton LN5 ..105 F5
Cleethorpes DN35 .... .192 F6
Clipsham LE15 ...... .162 B7
Easton on the Hill PE9 .171 C3
Folkingham NG34 .... .142 C8
Gainsborough DN21 ...197 B8
Hagworthingham PE23 ..87 A4
Helpston PE6 ...... .173 B4
Hibaldstow DN20 .... .30 F5
Horncastle LN9 ..... .199 A3
Kingston upon Hull HU1 .180 E6
Long Sutton PE12 .... .216 B4
11 Navenby/Wellingore
LN5 .... .107 A7
North Kelsey LN7 .... .32 A4
Osbournby NG34 .... .132 C5
1 Roxby cum Risby DN15 ..8 F3
Scawby DN20 .... .30 E8
Scunthorpe DN15 .... .183 A3
Stamford PE9 ...... .219 A4
Swaton NG34 ...... .133 C4
Thorne/Moorends DN8 ..15 A7
2 Timberland LN4 .... .96 B1
West/East Butterwick
DN17 .... .28 C8
Winterton DN15 ..... .9 A5
West St Gdns 8 PE9 ..219 A5
West St Mary's Gate 10
DN31 .... .191 D7
West Stonebridge
PE2 .... .230 C5
West Syke La LN1 .....66 B7
West Terr PE20 ......196 B3
West Terr St 10 DN17 ..16 D7
West Town Cty Sch
PE3 .... .225 E3
West View
3 Ancaster NG32 ....120 A3
1 Bardney LN3 ...... .83 B4
Messingham DN17 .... .29 C7
15 North Ferriby HU14 ..3 A4
Scunthorpe DN16 .... .184 D3
West View Cl 8 DN41 ..23 A5
West View Cres 24 PE24 .90 D7
West Way PE25 ......206 D7
West Wells La 4 DN10 .39 C1
Westbeck 2 NG34 ....108 D2
Westbeck La DN21 ....42 C5
Westborough La
NG23 .... .117 D3
Westborough Way
HU4 .... .179 B6
Westbourne Ave 3
HU13 .... .178 E2

Westbourne Dr
22 Crowle DN17 ...... .16 D7
6 Glinton PE6 ...... .220 C8
Westbourne Gdns 5
PE11 .... .214 D3
Westbourne Gr
6 Grimsby DN33 .....194 F8
Kingston upon Hull
HU3 .... .178 D2
6 Lincoln LN1 ......201 D3
Westbourne Pk PE10 ..213 B5
Westbourne Pl 2 NG31 .210 E4
Westbourne St 5 HU3 .180 A4
Westbrecks La DN22 ...65 A7
Westbridge Rd PE21 ..208 A3
Westbrook Ave 1 PE2 .230 F7
Westbrook Pk Cl 2 PE2 230 F7
Westbrook Pk Rd PE2 .230 F7
Westbrooke Cl LN6 ...205 B8
Westbrooke Rd LN6 ...205 B8
Westburn Ave 4 DN19 ..4 E2
Westbury Pk 2 DN35 ..193 A1
Westbury Rd DN35 ...193 A1
Westby Rd
Bitchfield & Bassingthorpe
NG33 .... .140 F2
Burton Coggles NG33 ..152 C8
Westcliff Gdns DN17 ..184 F7
Westcliffe Prim Sch
DN17 .... .184 D6
Westcliffe Rd
Ruskington NG34 .....108 C2
21 Scotter DN21 .... .29 C3
Westcliffe St LN1 ....201 D6
Westcombe Sq 1 PE2 ..226 D4
Westcroft Dr 3 LN1 ...66 D3
West-dale Cres 2 DN21 .30 B2
Westdale Dro PE11 ...134 C2
Westerdale 1 DN35 ....3 B7
Westerdale Gr HU9 ...181 E8
Westerdale Rd
2 Grantham NG31 ....211 A7
Scunthorpe DN16 .... .185 D5
Westerly Way 1 PE11 .214 A5
Western Ave
Brigg DN20 .... .196 C5
Easton on the Hill PE9 .171 C3
Holbeach PE12 ...... .215 C2
Lincoln LN6 .... .205 C7
Peterborough PE1 .... .226 B7
3 Saxilby LN1 ..... .66 C2
Western Cres LN6 ....205 C8
Western Dr
Balderton NG24 ......104 C1
11 Barton-upon-Humber
DN18 .... .3 E1
9 RAF Cranwell NG34 .120 C8
Western Gn DN15 .....2 A1
Western Outway
DN34 .... .191 A4
Western Prim Sch
DN34 .... .190 E5
Western Tech Sch The
DN34 .... .190 F5
Westfield App LN2 ...203 A8
Westfield Ave
Boston PE21 .... .208 D4
Greetwell LN2 ...... .203 B8
Grimsby DN33 ...... .191 C3
Westfield Cl 8 LN4 ...95 D4
Westfield Dr
Greetwell LN2 ......203 A8
22 Messingham DN17 ..29 D7
1 Pinchbeck PE11 ...156 E8
3 Skegness PE25 ....206 B4
11 Swineshead PE20 ..135 B7
Westfield Garth 2 DN17 16 E6
Westfield Gr DN35 ...192 D6
Westfield La
Collingham NG23 .... .91 B4
Cumberworth LN13 ....89 D8
Kirk Bramwith DN7 ... .14 B8
Westfield Pk 11 HU15 ..2 C6
Westfield Rd
Bardney LN3 .... .83 D1
Barton-upon-Humber DN18 .3 C1
Fishlake DN7 ...... .14 B8
13 Goxhill DN19 .... .12 A8
6 Hatfield DN7 ..... .14 E4
Kingston upon Hull HU4 .179 D5
Newton PE13 ...... .169 F5
Peterborough PE3 .... .225 E4
Scunthorpe DN17 .... .184 B6
Waltham DN37 ...... .194 C4
Yarburgh LN11 ..... .49 D3
Yaxley PE7 .... .233 D5
Westfield Rise HU13 ..178 D2
Westfield St 4 LN1 ...201 D3
Westfield Villas 5 DN7 ..14 E4
Westfield Way PE6 ...164 E2
Westfields 1 Alford LN13 .75 F2
Easton on the Hill PE9 .171 C3
Westgate
Grantham NG31 .....211 A4
Grimsby DN31 ...... .188 F1
Kexby DN21 .... .53 E4
Lincoln LN1 .... .234 A3
Louth LN11 .... .198 A5
Peterborough PE1 .... .225 F2
Scotton DN21 ...... .29 C1
Sleaford NG34 ...... .212 C4
Westgate Jun Sch
LN1 .... .234 A4
Westgate Pk 3 NG34 .212 C4
Westgate Rd 7 LN11 ..198 B5
Westgate Rd DN9 .... .16 D2
Westhall Cl 1 LN5 .....92 E1

Westhall Rd 16 LN2 ....68 D7
Westhaven 2 PE9 ....171 D3
Westhawe PE3 ......224 F7
Westhill Rd DN34 ....191 A5
Westholm 2 LN3 .....203 E5
Westholme Cl 11 DN15 ..8 A5
Westholme La DN38 ...21 C5
Westhorpe Rd PE11 ..144 F5
Westhouses PE22 ....112 F5
Westkirke Ave DN33 ..191 D1
Westland Rd
Kingston upon Hull
HU10 .... .178 B7
5 Westwoodside DN9 ..27 B2
Westlands Ave
Grimsby DN34 ......191 C5
4 Tetney DN36 ..... .36 D4
Westlands Rd HU5 ...179 B8
Westlode St PE11 ....214 C4
Westmere Cty Prim Sch
PE12 .... .160 E4
Westminister Way 2
NG31 .... .210 D5
Westminster Dr
Grimsby DN34 ......191 C6
14 Hatfield DN7 ... .14 C2
1 Spalding PE11 ....214 A4
Westminster Gdns 24
PE6 .... .175 A1
Westminster La 6 PE10 213 B5
Westminster Pl PE1 ..226 F5
Westminster Rd
5 Broughton DN20 ...19 D4
Lincoln LN6 .... .204 D4
Westmoor La LN1 .....65 E2
Westmoreland Ave 14
LN1 .... .67 E5
Westmoreland Cl 1 DN9 27 A2
Westmoreland Rd 2
PE12 .... .157 F6
Westoby La DN19 .....11 C7
Weston Gr DN40 .....186 B5
Weston Hills CE (VC) Prim
Sch PE12 .... .157 D2
Weston Hills Rd PE12 .157 B4
Weston Miller Dr 8
PE13 .... .170 D1
Westonville 6 PE9 ...171 B1
Westover Dr 4 DN15 ..8 A4
Westport Rd 1 DN35 ..193 A1
Westrum La DN20 ....196 D2
Westry Cl
Barrowby NG32 ......210 A3
1 Leverington PE13 ..170 F1
Westry Cnr NG32 ....210 A4
Westside Ave NG31 ..139 E8
Westside Rd
Cranwell & Byard's Leap
NG34 .... .107 E1
Grimsby DN31 ...... .188 F2
Westville Rd PE22 ...112 B5
Westward Cl 3 DN34 ..191 C5
Westward Ho 2 DN34 .191 C5
Westward House
DN34 .... .191 B5
Westway 18 LN2 ..... .68 D7
Westwick Dr LN6 ....205 B7
Westwick Gdns LN6 ..205 B6
Westwinds Gdns 19 DN15 .9 A5
Westwold Rd 25 DN7 ..33 B4
Westwood
6 Broughton DN20 ...19 D4
5 Peterborough PE3 ..225 C4
Westwood Cl LN6 ....205 A8
Westwood Dr
Bourne PE10 ......213 C4
3 Kingston upon Hull
HU4 .... .179 B6
Westwood Pk Cl PE3 ..225 C4
Westwood Pk Rd PE3 .225 D5
Westwood Rd 1 DN41 ..23 D7
Westwoodside CE Prim Sch
DN9 .... .27 B2
Wetherby Cl
3 Bourne PE10 .....213 C7
6 Market Rasen LN8 ..57 E7
Wetherby Cres LN6 ...204 F4
Wetherby Way 1 PE1 .226 D3
Wetmoor La LN2 .... .56 C1
Weydike Bank PE12 ..159 A4
Weyford Rd 4 DN35 ..193 A1
Weymouth Cl 10 LN5 ..205 D3
Weymouth Cres DN17 .182 C1
Weymouth Way 4 PE1 226 D6
Whale Dro
Holbeach PE12 ......168 A1
Whaplode PE6 ...... .167 E1
Whalebone La NG31 ..140 B7
Whalley St 7 PE1 ....226 B3
Whaplode CE Controlled
Prim Sch PE12 ..... .158 C7
Wharf Rd Crowle DN17 .16 D7
Grantham NG31 .... .211 A4
8 Horncastle LN9 ...199 B4
13 Misterton DN10 ...39 F5
Stamford PE9 ...... .219 C4
Wharf St 20 PE12 ....160 C4
Wharf The DN36 .....37 A5
Wharfdale Cl 6 DN35 ..17 E6
Wharfe La
Kirkby on Bain LN10 ..98 C5
Tattershall LN4 ..... .207 D6
Wharfedale Dr 2 LN6 .204 F3
Wharfedale Pl DN16 ..185 E6

Wharfside Mews 6
NG34 .... .212 D4
Wharncliffe Rd N
DN31 .... .189 B3
Wharncliffe St HU5 ..180 A8
Wharton Rd DN21 ....41 A5
Wharton St DN31 ....191 B7
Whattoff Way PE6 ...164 D4
Whatton's Cl NG32 ...128 F5
Wheatfield
5 Barnby Dun DN3 ...14 A4
Epworth DN9 ...... .27 F6
2 Kingston upon Hull
HU4 .... .179 D2
Wheatfield Dr 7 DN37 .194 C5
Wheatfield Rd LN6 ...200 C1
Wheatfields 1 PE12 ..158 B7
Wheatfield PE6 ......164 E2
Wheatgrass La NG32 ..119 B7
Wheatholme La 3 ....78 C6
Wheatley Bank PE14 ..170 F1
Wheatley La
2 Carlton-le-Moorland LN5 92 E1
1 Carlton-le-Moorland
LN5 .... .105 E8
Collingham NG23 .... .91 D2
Wheatley Rd DN22 ...52 A3
Wheatmere Dro PE12 .157 B5
Wheatsheaf Cl
3 Holbeach PE12 ....215 B2
Sibsey PE22 .... .113 B2
Wheatsheaf La 4 NG23 117 D4
Wheel Yd PE1 ......226 A2
Wheeldon St 9 DN21 ..197 D3
Wheeler Cl PE21 ....209 A4
Wheeler Prim Sch
HU3 .... .179 F5
Wheeler St HU3 .....179 F6
Wheelwright Cl PE10 .154 C6
Wheelwrights Ct
NG34 .... .109 B1
Whelpton Cl 7 LN9 ..199 D3
Whichcote Rd PE6 ...174 C7
Whimbrel Way
6 Long Sutton PE12 ..216 B4
New Waltham DN36 ...195 D7
Whin Moor La HU15 ...2 A7
Whins Gate DN17 ....7 A4
Whipchicken Rd PE6 .167 B3
Whisby Cl DN36 .....195 E2
Whisby Nature Pk*
LN6 .... .79 F1
Whisby Rd LN6 ......204 A4
Whisby Way LN6 ....204 C5
Whiston Cl 5 PE4 ....221 D2
Whiston Way 9 DN18 ..3 F1
Whitacre PE1 ......226 E6
Whitby Dr DN32 ....192 A3
Whitby St HU8 ......181 B8
White Croft PE3 ....225 B6
White Cross La 4 PE11 145 D2
White Gate NG23 ....73 E2
White Hart La 1 NG23 .91 C4
White House Cl
29 Hatfield DN7 ..... .14 D4
4 Stainforth DN7 ... .14 C7
White House Garth 19
HU14 .... .3 A5
White House La
Boston PE21 .... .209 D3
3 West Halton DN15 ..8 E8
White House Mews 16
HU14 .... .3 A5
White La Harmston LN5 .93 C3
Thorne DN8 .... .15 A8
White Leather Sq
NG34 .... .133 C1
White Row La LN12 ...64 C1
White St HU3 ....179 F5
White Wlk HU10 ....178 C6
Whiteacres 3 PE12 ...216 B4
Whitebeam Cl HU3 ...180 D5
Whitebread Rd PE20 .136 A7
Whitecross Gate PE20 146 D8
Whitecross La NG34 ..121 F1
Whitecross St 12 DN18 ..10 F8
Whitefriargate HU1 ..180 F6
Whitegate Hill LN7 ...33 C3
Whitehall 5 PE11 ....145 C6
Whitehall Cres LN4 ..205 F4
Whitehall Gr LN1 ....234 A3
Whitehall Rd 6 DN35 .193 A1
Whitehead Cl 5 LN12 ..64 B4
Whitehorse La 10 PE21 208 F4
Whitehouse Rd 1 NG34 108 E2
Whitemoor La NG23 ...91 C3
Whitepit Way LN13 ...74 D4
Whitepost Rd PE6 ...174 F3
Whites La LN5 ......92 E2
White's Rd DN35 ....192 F5
White's Wood La
1 Corringham DN21 ...53 A8
Gainsborough DN21 ...197 A4
Whites Wood La Jun Sch
DN21 .... .197 F4
Whitestone Rd DN17 .184 C6
Whitethorn Gr 7 LN6 .200 C1
Whiteways PE2 .....229 D6
Whitewell Cl 4 DN21 ..30 B1
Whitfield Rd DN17 ...184 D6
Whitgift Cl 21 DN37 ..23 F1
Whitgift Sec Sch
DN37 .... .190 D8
Whiting Sq PE21 ....208 F6
Whitley Cl 5 LN6 ....200 A4

Whitley St **11** LN1 . . . . .67 E5
Whitley Way PE6 . . . . .217 B7
Whitman Cl **9** PE9 . . . . . .172 D3
Whitman Rd DN17 . . . . . .184 C6
Whitsed Rd **8** PE6 . . . . . .174 E5
Whitsed St 226 B3
Whittington PE1 . . . . .226 E7
Whittle Cl **2** PE21 . . . . . .208 F1
Whittlesey Rd
  Peterborough PE2 . . . . .231 B7
  Thorney PE6 . . . . .175 F1
Whitton Rd
  Alkborough DN15 . . . . .1 C1
  Whitton DN15 . . . . .1 E2
Whitwell PE4 . . . . .221 E2
Whitworth Way **12** LN8 . .57 D7
Whoofer La DN21 . . . . .40 E8
Whyalla Cl **2** LN11 . . . . . .50 B8
Whyche The LN4 . . . . . . .109 E5
Wicken La PE22 . . . . .113 F3
Wicken Way PE3 . . . . . . .225 C6
Wickenby Airport LN3 . . . .69 F8
Wickenby Cl
  6 Grimsby DN34 . . . . . .190 F4
  Lincoln LN6 . . . . .205 A3
Wickenby Cres LN1 . . . . .201 E7
Wickenby Rd LN3 . . . . .57 D1
Wickham Rd DN31 . . . . . .189 C2
Wicklow Ave LN8 . . . . . . .194 E8
Wide Bargate **8** PE21 . . .208 F5
Widford Gn **3** DN7 . . . . . .14 C3
Widow Fen La LN13 . . . . . .76 C3
Wigford LN5 . . . . .234 A1
Wigford Way LN5 . . . . . . .234 A2
Wigg La PE24 . . . . .90 D8
Wigmore Dr PE7 . . . . . . .231 F5
Wignal's Gate PE12 . . . . .215 D4
Wigsley Cl **7** LN6 . . . . . .204 D6
Wigsley Rd
  6 Birchwood LN6 . . . . .204 D6
  Harby NG23 . . . . .79 B5
  North Scarle LN6 . . . . . . .78 E3
Wigtoft Bank PE20 . . . . . .135 D1
Wigtoft Rd PE20 . . . . . . .135 F2
Wike Gate Cl **4** DN8 . . . . .15 B7
Wike Gate Gr **2** DN8 . . . . .15 B7
Wike Gate Rd DN8 . . . . . . .15 B8
Wilberforce Dr **6** HU1 . . .180 F7
Wilberforce House ★
  HU1 . . . . .181 A6
Wilberforce Rd PE1 . . . . .225 C7
Wilberforce St HU3 . . . . .180 D6
Wildfowlers Way
  PE12 . . . . .148 F4
Wildlake PE2 . . . . .230 C5
Wildmore Cl LN4 . . . . . . .111 C6
Wildmore Cres PE22 . . . . .114 F6
Wildshed La PE24 . . . . . .102 D7
Wiles's La DN17 . . . . .135 B4
Wilford Gr PE25 . . . . .206 C1
Wilfred Ave NG24 . . . . . .104 B2
Wilkie Cl DN15 . . . . .182 C3
Wilkie Dr NG34 . . . . .142 C8
Wilkinson Dr **9** LN8 . . . . .57 B8
Wilkinson Rd **7** NG32 . . .117 F1
Will Row LN12 . . . . .63 C5
Willders Garth PE12 . . . . .215 F2
Willerton Rd **3** LN11 . . . . .50 F7
Willesby Rd PE11 . . . . . . .214 E5
Willesden Ave PE4 . . . . . .225 D8
Willey's La PE24 . . . . .90 B8
William Alvey Sch
  NG34 . . . . .212 E5
William Barcroft Jun Sch
  DN32 . . . . .192 C7
William Farr CE Comp Sch
  LN2 . . . . .68 D6
William Gn Cl **9** LN12 . . . .76 F8
William Harrison Sch
  DN21 . . . . .197 E2
William Hildyard CE (Aided)
  Prim Sch PE6 . . . . .217 B5
William Lovell CE Sch
  PE22 . . . . .113 A7
William St
  Cleethorpes DN35 . . . . .192 E5
  2 Grantham NG31 . . . . .211 A3
  Kingston upon Hull HU1 . .180 E5
  24 Saxilby LN1 . . . . . . .66 D2
  3 Scunthorpe DN16 . . . .183 B2
William Stukeley CE Prim
  Sch PE12 . . . . .215 D2
William Tow Cl **7** LN12 . . .76 F8
William Way PE25 . . . . . .206 B2
Williams Cl **1** PE6 . . . . . .174 E5
Williams Dr DN39 . . . . . . .12 B1
Williamson Ave PE3 . . . . .225 E3
Williamson St
  Kingston upon Hull HU9 . .181 C7
  Lincoln LN2 . . . . .234 B4
Williamson's Dro LN4 . . . .110 A7
Willing Way DN32 . . . . . .191 F8
Willingham Ave **1** LN1 . .201 F8
Willingham Hill LN8 . . . . . .58 E7
Willingham La LN8 . . . . . . .57 F6
Willingham Rd
  East Barkwith LN8 . . . . . .58 E1
  Fillingham DN21 . . . . .54 D4
  Lea DN21 . . . . .53 A5
  Market Rasen LN8 . . . . . .57 E7
  Marton DN21 . . . . .53 B1
  Tealby LN8 . . . . .58 E8
Willingham St DN32 . . . . .191 E6
Willington Rd PE20 . . . . .136 A7

Willis Cl LN1 . . . . .234 A4
Willonholt PE3 . . . . . . .225 C7
Willoughby Ave **2** PE6 . .217 C5
Willoughby Branch Line
  Nature Reserve ★
  LN13 . . . . .89 A7
Willoughby Cl
  Corby Glen NG33 . . . . . .152 E3
  Helpringham NG34 . . . . .133 C7
  Silk Willoughby NG34 . . .121 B1
Willoughby Ct PE1 . . . . . .226 E8
Willoughby Dr **1** PE23 . . .88 A1
Willoughby Gall The ★
  NG33 . . . . .152 F8
Willoughby Gr **5** DN34 . .190 F4
Willoughby La
  Authorpe LN11 . . . . .74 F8
  Muckton LN11 . . . . .62 C1
  Waddington LN5 . . . . . .205 C1
Willoughby Rd
  18 Alford LN13 . . . . .75 F2
  Ancaster NG32 . . . . . . .119 C2
  Aunsby & Dembleby
    NG34 . . . . .132 B4
  Boston PE21 . . . . .209 A7
  Bourne PE10 . . . . .213 E4
  Cumberworth LN13 . . . . .89 C8
  14 Hibaldstow DN20 . . . .31 A5
  11 Mablethorpe/Sutton on Sea
    LN12 . . . . .64 C1
  Scunthorpe DN17 . . . . . .184 E5
  Sleaford NG34 . . . . .120 F3
  Stamford PE9 . . . . .219 C7
Willoughby Specl Sch
  PE10 . . . . .213 D3
Willoughby St **1** DN21 . .197 D3
Willoughton Prim Sch
  DN21 . . . . .42 D4
Willoughton Rd **3**
  PE25 . . . . .206 D2
Willow Ave
  5 Misterton DN10 . . . . . .39 F5
  Peterborough PE1 . . . . .226 B7
Willow Cl
  Gainsborough DN21 . . . .197 B5
  10 Holton le Moor NG34 .122 C3
  Horncastle LN9 . . . . . . .199 A5
  1 Laceby DN37 . . . . . . .23 C1
  17 Saxilby LN1 . . . . . . .66 D2
  Scopwick LN4 . . . . .95 D1
Willow Ct
  Heighington/Washingborough
    LN4 . . . . .203 C2
  1 Sleaford NG34 . . . . . .212 E3
Willow Dr
  14 Barton-upon-Humber
    DN18 . . . . .3 F1
  9 Bourne PE10 . . . . . . .213 C7
  2 Coningsby LN4 . . . . .207 D4
  Kingston upon Hull
    HU10 . . . . .178 D8
  Louth LN11 . . . . .198 C8
  35 Messingham DN17 . . .29 D7
Willow Dro PE6 . . . . .174 E6
Willow Gdns **2** DN19 . . . .11 D8
Willow Gr
  1 Keadby with Althorpe
    DN17 . . . . .17 D6
  7 Scawby DN20 . . . . . . .30 F8
  Scunthorpe DN16 . . . . . .185 C7
Willow Hall La PE6 . . .227 D6
Willow Holt PE7 . . . . . .230 C3
Willow La
  9 Cranwell NG34 . . . . .107 F1
  3 Cranwell NG34 . . . . .120 F8
  Dunston LN4 . . . . .95 C6
  6 Goxhill DN19 . . . . .5 A1
  1 Goxhill DN19 . . . . . . .12 A8
  Grantham NG31 . . . . . . .210 F2
  Ruskington LN4 . . . . . . .109 B3
Willow Rd Lincoln LN6 . .204 F2
  Stamford PE9 . . . . .218 D7
Willow Row PE11 . . . . . . .214 E5
Willow Row Bank LN11 . .62 F6
Willow Wlk PE11 . . . . . . .214 E5
Willowbrook Dr DN20 . .196 E3
Willowfield Ave **12** LN2 . .68 D2
Willows Cl PE13 . . . . . . .160 A1
Willows La PE22 . . . . . . .125 F7
Willows Prim Sch
  DN37 . . . . .190 E8
Willows The
  6 Cranwell NG34 . . . . .107 F1
  5 Crowland PE6 . . . . . .166 E1
  Glinton PE6 . . . . .220 D8
  Kingston upon Hull
    HU13 . . . . .178 E4
Wilmington Dr **18** LN12 . .77 A8
Wilsford La NG32 . . . . . . .120 A1
Wilson Cl **8** HU14 . . . . . . .3 A4
Wilson Ct LE15 . . . . .162 A8
Wilson St
  Cleethorpes DN35 . . . . .192 D8
  Gainsborough DN21 . . . .197 B5
  Kingston upon Hull
    HU10 . . . . .178 E6
  4 Kingston upon Hull
    HU9 . . . . .181 B7
  Lincoln LN1 . . . . .234 A4
Wilton Ave **14** PE24 . . . . .90 D7
Wilton Cl PE3 . . . . .225 C4
Wilton Dr PE3 . . . . .225 C4
Wilton Rd DN36 . . . . .192 D1
Wilton St HU8 . . . . .181 B8
Wiltshire Ave DN15 . . . . . .8 B4
Wiltshire Rd HU4 . . . . . . .179 E2
Wilyman Cl **21** LN12 . . . . .77 A7
Wimberley Cl **3** PE12 . . .157 D7

Wimberley Way 156 E8
  3 South Witham NG33 . .151 D2
Wimbishthorpe Cl **3**
  NG13 . . . . .128 A6
Wimborn Ave DN34 . . . . .191 B6
Wimborne Dr **2** PE1 . . . .226 E7
Winceby Ave DN31 . . . . . .191 B8
Winceby Gdns LN9 . . . . . .199 D4
Winchcombe Ave
  DN34 . . . . .108 D1
Winchelsea Prim Sch The
  NG34 . . . . .108 D1
Winchelsea Rd **14** NG34 .108 E1
Winchester Ave DN33 . . . .191 A3
Winchester Ct **9** LN6 . . . .93 B8
Winchester Dr
  Bottesford DN16 . . . . . .185 C3
  Heighington/Washingborough
    LN4 . . . . .203 C1
  8 Mablethorpe/Sutton on Sea
    LN12 . . . . .64 A3
Winchester Rd
  Grantham NG31 . . . . . . .210 E4
  13 Hatfield DN7 . . . . . . .14 D4
  8 Wainfleet All Saints
    PE24 . . . . .102 D2
Winchester Way
  Peterborough PE3 . . . . .225 E1
  Sleaford NG34 . . . . .212 C7
Wincolmlee HU2 . . . . . . .181 A7
Windermere Ave
  4 Grimsby DN33 . . . . .194 E7
  Lincoln LN6 . . . . .205 A2
Windermere Cres
  DN36 . . . . .192 E1
Windermere Rd LN2 . . . . .202 D8
Windermere Way PE4 . . . .221 C3
Windgate Way PE8 . . . . . .222 A6
Windlass Cl **16** DN8 . . . . .15 A8
Windlesham Ave
  DN33 . . . . .194 D7
Windmill Cl
  Holbeach PE12 . . . . .215 B2
  4 Waddington LN5 . . . . .93 F6
Windmill Dr
  Burgh le Marsh PE24 . . .102 D8
  18 Heckington NG34 . . .122 E2
Windmill Gdns **3** PE13 .170 E2
Windmill La
  8 Alford LN13 . . . . .75 F2
  Gosberton PE11 . . . . . . .144 F6
Windmill St PE1 . . . . .225 F5
Windmill View **3** LN1 . . .234 A4
Windmill Way HU13 . . . . .178 F1
Windrush Dr PE4 . . . . . . .221 D4
Windsmoor Rd **15** LN8 . . .47 B6
Windsor Ave
  Holbeach PE12 . . . . .215 F2
  Kingston upon Hull
    HU10 . . . . .178 E7
  3 Peterborough PE4 . . .225 C8
Windsor Bank PE21 . . . . .209 A3
Windsor Cl
  Collingham NG23 . . . . . .91 D4
  6 Keelby DN41 . . . . . . .23 A5
  1 Sleaford NG34 . . . . .212 B2
  4 Stamford PE9 . . . . . .219 B7
  6 Subbrooke LN2 . . . . . .68 F2
Windsor Cres
  Boston PE21 . . . . .209 A4
  1 Crowle DN17 . . . . . . .16 C7
  4 Ingoldmells PE25 . . . .90 D3
  Scunthorpe DN17 . . . . . .184 F2
Windsor Ct **12** DN7 . . . . .14 C2
Windsor Dr **19** Caistor LN7 33 B4
  Grantham NG31 . . . . . . .211 E5
  Peterborough PE2 . . . . .231 D6
  Spalding PE11 . . . . .214 D2
  Wisbech PE13 . . . . .170 D2
Windsor Gdns PE12 . . . . .216 C5
Windsor Gr **1** DN19 . . . . .5 A1
Windsor La DN17 . . . . . . .16 C7
Windsor Pk Cl **5** LN6 . . .204 F1
Windsor Rd
  Cleethorpes DN35 . . . . .192 C5
  Crowle DN17 . . . . .16 C7
  Louth LN11 . . . . .198 B8
  Yaxley PE7 . . . . .233 F6
Windsor Terr **11** PE21 . . .209 A5
Windsor Way
  Barnetby le Wold DN38 . . .21 B5
  Broughton DN20 . . . . . . .19 E4
Wine Hill La LN11 . . . . . . .51 B5
Winfrey Ave PE11 . . . . . .214 D4
Wing Dr PE21 . . . . .209 C4
Wingate Rd DN17 . . . . . .190 D8
Wingate Way PE10 . . . . .213 E7
Wingfield PE2 . . . . .229 F3
Winn La LN9 . . . . .86 B8
Winn St Lincoln LN2 . . . .234 C2
Winniffe Gdns LN2 . . . . . .202 D7
Winnowsty La LN2 . . . . . .234 C3
Winship Cl **4** HU3 . . . . . .180 C5
Winslow Dr DN40 . . . . . . .186 B5
Winslow Gate PE12 . . . . .159 B8
Winslow Gr
  3 Grimsby DN34 . . . . .190 F4
  2 Grimsby DN34 . . . . .190 F4
Winslow Rd
  4 Boston PE21 . . . . . . .209 C4
  Peterborough PE3 . . . . .225 C3
Winsover Rd PE11 . . . . . .214 C4
Winston Ave DN34 . . . . . .191 B6
Winston Gdns PE21 . . . . .209 A7
Winston Dr PE23 . . . . . . .100 F8

Winston Way
  5 Brigg DN20 . . . . . . .196 D4
  Farcet PE7 . . . . .231 C2
Winterbeck Cl **5** NG13 . .128 A6
Wintergold Ave PE11 . . . .214 A5
Winteringham La DN15 . . .8 E8
Winteringham Prim Sch
  DN15 . . . . .2 A1
Winteringham Rd DN15 . .9 B6
Wintern Ct **6** DN21 . . . . .197 D2
Winter's La
  9 Long Bennington NG23 117 D4
  Long Sutton PE12 . . . . .160 A3
Winterton CE Inf Sch
  DN15 . . . . .9 A5
Winterton Comp Sch
  DN15 . . . . .9 A6
Winterton Cty Jun Sch
  DN15 . . . . .9 A5
Winterton Rd
  Roxby cum Risby DN15 . . .8 F2
  Scunthorpe DN15 . . . . . .183 B4
  Winteringham DN15 . . . . . .9 B8
Winthorpe Ave PE25 . . . .206 D8
Winthorpe Cl **17** LN6 . . .204 D7
Winthorpe Gr **16** LN6 . . .204 D7
Winthorpe Prim Sch
  NG23 . . . . .104 C8
Winthorpe Rd
  Birchwood LN6 . . . . . . .204 D7
  Grimsby DN33 . . . . .191 B3
  4 Kingston upon Hull
    HU13 . . . . .179 A3
  8 Newark NG24 . . . . . .104 C3
Winthorpe Way
  Ingoldmells PE25 . . . . . .206 D8
  Skegness PE25 . . . . .90 C1
Winton Rd **11** LN5 . . . . .107 A8
Wintringham **26** HU15 . . . .2 D4
Wintringham Rd NG32 . . .191 E6
Wintringham Sec Sch
  DN32 . . . . .191 E4
Winwick Pl PE3 . . . . .225 C5
Winyates Prim Sch
  PE2 . . . . .230 A3
Wire Hill La LN8 . . . . .70 E5
Wirral Ave **7** DN34 . . . . .190 F4
Wisbech Rd
  Long Sutton PE12 . . . . .216 E1
  Thorney PE6 . . . . .176 A3
  Walpole PE14 . . . . .161 C1
  Walsoken PE14 . . . . . . .170 E2
  Wisbech St Mary PE13 . .177 A2
Wiseholme Rd LN6 . . . . . .200 B2
Wiseman's Gate **1**
  PE12 . . . . .157 D7
Wiske Ave **7** HU15 . . . . . .2 D5
Wistaria Cl PE13 . . . . . . .170 E1
Wisteria Ave LN4 . . . . . . .81 D2
Wisteria Dr DN41 . . . . . . .23 F5
Wisteria Rd PE7 . . . . .233 D4
Wisteria Way
  Bourne PE10 . . . . .213 B7
  Scunthorpe DN16 . . . . . .185 E4
Wistow Gr HU4 . . . . .179 D5
Wistow Way PE2 . . . . . . .229 D6
Witchford Cl **2** LN6 . . . . .204 B6
Witchford Rd **3** LN6 . . . .204 B6
Witham HU9 . . . . .181 B7
Witham Bank
  Dogdyke LN4 . . . . .110 D8
  Timberland LN4 . . . . .97 C3
Witham Bank E **4** PE21 208 D5
Witham Cl Lincoln LN6 . . .205 D5
  11 Ruskington NG34 . . .108 D2
  Stamford PE9 . . . . .219 C6
Witham Ct **2** PE21 . . . . .208 E6
Witham Dr **6** DN15 . . . . . .8 B5
Witham Gdns PE21 . . . . .208 E6
Witham Gn PE21 . . . . . . .208 E6
Witham Hall Prep Sch
  PE10 . . . . .163 D7
Witham Pl PE21 . . . . .208 E5
Witham Rd
  Gunby & Stainby NG33 . .151 C4
  5 Long Bennington NG23 117 D4
  Thistleton LE15 . . . . . . .151 C1
  Woodhall Spa LN10 . . . . .97 B5
Witham St PE21 . . . . .208 E5
Witham Town PE21 . . . . .208 E6
Witham View LN4 . . . . . .203 A2
Witham Way PE4 . . . . . . .221 D1
Witham/Haven Mouth Nature
  Reserve ★ PE22 . . . . . .137 F6
Withambrook Pk
  NG31 . . . . .211 F7
Withern Rd DN15 . . . . . . .191 A3
Withington St **1** PE12 . . .160 E4
Wittering Airfield PE8 . . .171 F1
Wittering Cl **5** LN6 . . . . .204 D6
Wittering Rd PE9 . . . . . . .172 D3
Witty St HU3 . . . . .180 A3
Wivell Dr **1** DN41 . . . . . . .23 A5
Woad Farm Rd PE21 . . . .209 B4
Woad La Fishtoft PE22 . . .137 C7
  Grimsby DN31 . . . . .188 C4
Woburn Ave LN1 . . . . . . .201 E6
Woburn Cl **7** Louth LN11 .198 B7
  4 Market Deeping PE6 . .217 A5
  Peterborough PE3 . . . . .225 C5
Woburn Dr
  Grantham NG31 . . . . . . .211 F5
  Thorney PE6 . . . . .176 A2
Woburn Gr **1** LN10 . . . . .97 C5
Woburn St HU3 . . . . .179 F4
Woffindin Cl **12** NG31 . . .129 C5

Wold Rd
  Barrow upon Humber
    DN19 . . . . .11 D7
  Kingston upon Hull HU5 . .179 C8
  Worlaby DN20 . . . . .10 E1
Wold View
  1 Brigg DN20 . . . . . . .196 D4
  25 Brough HU15 . . . . . . .2 C6
  Caistor LN7 . . . . .33 C4
  Fotherby LN11 . . . . .49 A2
  Holton le Clay DN36 . . . .195 C2
  3 Nettleham LN2 . . . . . .68 D2
  Rothwell LN7 . . . . .33 F2
Woldcarr Rd HU3 . . . . . . .179 F6
Wolds Cl **5** DN17 . . . . . . .16 D7
Wolf La PE13 . . . . .169 F1
Wolfreton Dr HU10 . . . . . .178 F6
Wolfreton Garth
  HU10 . . . . .178 D8
Wolfreton La HU10 . . . . . .178 F8
Wolfreton Rd HU10 . . . . . .178 F7
Wolfreton Sch HU10 . . . . .178 C7
Wolla Bank Nature
  Reserves ★ PE24 . . . . . .77 D1
Wollaston Rd
  Cleethorpes DN35 . . . . .192 E6
  Peterborough PE3 . . . . .225 C6
Wolseley Cl PE7 . . . . . . .233 D6
Wolsey Dr **6** DN19 . . . . . .11 C7
Wolsey Rd NG24 . . . . . . .104 A6
Wolsey Way LN2 . . . . . . .202 D8
Womersley Rd DN31 . . . .189 C2
Wong Gdns NG32 . . . . . .210 A4
Wong Row **10** NG31 . . . .211 A5
Wong The LN9 . . . . .199 B3
Wongs La PE24 . . . . .102 B7
Wood Carr La DN9 . . . . . .16 C1
Wood Cl
  14 Barton-upon-Humber
    DN18 . . . . .3 E1
  Grimsby DN33 . . . . .194 F7
Wood Dr **4** HU14 . . . . . . .3 A4
Wood End NG33 . . . . . . .131 A1
Wood Hill Rd DN21 . . . . . .29 B3
Wood La Bardney LN3 . . . .83 B4
  Beckingham DN10 . . . . . .52 A8
  Croxton Kerrial NG32 . . .138 A6
  Gringley on the Hill DN10 . .39 C2
  1 Lincoln LN6 . . . . . . .204 A1
  Little Cawthorpe LN11 . . .61 F2
  Louth LN11 . . . . .198 D4
  Moulton PE12 . . . . .158 A7
  Norton Disney LN6 . . . . . .92 B3
  Quadring PE11 . . . . . . .135 C1
  South Kyme LN4 . . . . . .109 F1
  South Kyme LN4 . . . . . .123 B8
  South Scarle NG23 . . . . .91 F7
  Sturton Le Steeple DN22 . .52 A3
  Thurlby PE10 . . . . .213 C1
Wood La Prim Sch
  PE12 . . . . .159 B6
Wood Rd **24** LN13 . . . . . .75 F2
Wood St **4** DN32 . . . . . .191 F8
Wood Vale DN16 . . . . . . .185 C3
Wood View
  Bourne PE10 . . . . .213 C5
  1 Messingham DN17 . . .29 D7
  3 Swanland HU14 . . . . . .3 B7
Wood Way LN11 . . . . . . .198 E5
Woodale Cl **3** DN15 . . . .182 C6
Woodapple Ct **4** DN41 . .23 E6
Woodbank
  Deeping St Nicholas
    PE11 . . . . .166 C6
  Skellingthorpe LN6 . . . . .200 A5
Woodbine Ave DN20 . . . .196 C4
Woodbine St PE2 . . . . . . .231 A8
Woodbridge Rd NG34 . . .212 C6
Woodburn Cl LN1 . . . . . .201 E8
Woodbyth Rd PE1 . . . . . .226 A6
Woodclose Rd DN17 . . . .184 D6
Woodcock St HU3 . . . . . .180 A4
Woodcote Cl PE1 . . . . . . .226 A7
Woodcroft Cl **9** PE6 . . . .217 C5
Woodcroft Rd
  Marholm PE6 . . . . .220 A3
  4 Saxilby LN1 . . . . . . .66 C2
Wooden Beck Hill
  DN10 . . . . .39 E2
Woodfield **7** PE9 . . . . . .171 B1
Woodfield Ave LN6 . . . . .200 C1
Woodfield Cl
  9 Birchwood LN6 . . . . .200 C1
  15 Humberston DN36 . . .36 D8
  Spalding PE11 . . . . .214 F2
Woodfield La HU13 . . . . .178 C1
Woodfield Rd
  Gainsborough DN21 . . . .197 F5
  Peterborough PE3 . . . . .225 D3
Woodgarr Ave **4** DN17 . .17 D6
Woodgate PE6 . . . . .173 C4
Woodgate La
  Beckingham LN5 . . . . . .105 C4
  Kingston upon Hull HU5 . .179 F8
  Maxey PE6 . . . . .217 A1
Woodgate Rd
  Kingston upon Hull HU5 . .179 F7
  Leverington PE13 . . . . . .170 A2
  Moulton PE12 . . . . .157 C2
Woodgates Cl **13** HU14 . . .3 A5
Woodgates La HU14 . . . . . .3 A6
Woodgates Mount **3**
  HU14 . . . . .3 A5
Woodhall Cl PE21 . . . . . .208 C5
Woodhall Cres **9** LN1 . . .66 C2
Woodhall Dr
  Lincoln LN2 . . . . .201 F8

Woodhall Dr continued
Waltham DN37 . . . . .194 C4
Woodhall Rd LN9 . . . . .85 C3
Woodhall Rise PE4 . . . . . .220 F6
Woodhall Spa Cottage Mus★
LN10 . . . . .97 D6
Woodhead Cl 4 PE9 . . . .219 D7
Woodhill Ave DN21 . . . . . .197 E6
Woodhill Cl 2 HU10 . . . . .178 E7
Woodhill Rise HU13 . . . . .178 C2
Woodhill Gn Rd DN7 .14 B8
Woodhouse La
2 Belton DN9 . . . . .16 E3
Hatfield DN7 . . . . .14 D2
Holbeach PE12 . . . . . . .159 A8
Moulton PE12 . . . . .146 E1
Woodhouse Rd DN16 . . . .185 E8
Woodhouse St HU9 . . . . .181 D7
Woodhurst Rd PE2 . . . . .231 D6
Woodland Ave
1 Bourne PE10 . . . . . . .213 B5
22 Brough HU15 . . . . . .2 C6
15 Crowle DN17 . . . . . .16 D8
Gainsborough DN21 . . . .197 B7
Skellingthorpe LN6 . . . .200 B2
Woodland Dr
8 Broughton DN20 . . . .19 D4
5 Elsham DN20 . . . . . .20 F7
Grantham NG31 . . . . . . .211 F7
Kingston upon Hull
HU10 . . . . .178 C6
6 Woodhall Spa LN10 . . .97 E6
Woodland End HU4 . . . . .179 C5
Woodland Lea 2 PE6 . . .173 B4
Woodland Rise LN11 . . . .198 A6
Woodland View
2 Barnetby Le Wold DN38 . .21 B4
Scunthorpe DN15 . . . . . .182 C3
Woodland Way 16 DN9 . . .27 E6
Woodland Wlk 1 DN35 . .192 E1
Woodlands
Langford NG24 . . . . . . .104 B8
Long Sutton PE12 . . . . .216 D4
5 Louth LN11 . . . . . . .198 C6
Woodlands Ave
Immingham DN40 . . . . .186 C5
15 Keelby DN41 . . . . . .23 A4
6 Spilsby PE23 . . . . . .87 F1
2 Spilsby PE23 . . . . . .88 A1
Woodlands Cl 5 DN19 . .11 C7
Woodlands Dr
1 Colsterworth NG33 . .151 E7
Grantham NG31 . . . . . . .211 C4
Woodlands La 14 HU15 . .2 C6
Woodlands Prim Sch
DN33 . . . . .191 A2
Woodlands Rd HU5 . . . .179 B7
Woodlands Rise 7 HU14 . .3 A5
Woodlands The
3 Market Deeping PE6 . .217 B5
Peterborough PE1 . . . . .226 E5
1 Stallingborough DN41 . .23 D6
Woodman's Ct 4 PE22 . .98 F4
Woodmill Bank PE12 . . . .159 F2
Woodpecker Cl LN6 . . . .200 A3
Woodrow Pk DN33 . . . . .191 D1
Woodrush Rd LN2 . . . . .202 C8
Woods Cl 14 NG23 . . . . .117 D3
Wood's La
Kingston upon Hull HU1 .180 E5
3 Pinchbeck PE11 . . . .145 D2
Woods La 2 DN40 . . . . . .12 F2
Woods Terr DN21 . . . . . .197 C7
Woodside Boston PE21 . .208 E1
Branston & Mere LN4 . . . .81 D2
Kingston upon Hull
HU13 . . . . .178 D1

Woodside Ave NG34 . . . .212 D6
Woodside Cl 1 PE10 . . . .164 C8
Woodside E PE10 . . . . . .164 D8
**Woodside Falconry &
Conservation Ctr**★
LN3 . . . . .69 D3
Woodside La DN9 . . . . . .26 D6
Woodside Rd PE20 . . . . .136 B5
Woodsley Ave DN35 . . . .192 E5
Woodstock Rd DN16 . . . .183 D1
Woodstock St LN1 . . . . .201 D4
Woodston Cty Prim Sch
PE2 . . . . .231 A7
Woodthorpe Ave
PE21 . . . . .209 C4
Woodvale Ave LN6 . . . . .204 C6
Woodvale Cl 14 LN6 . . . .204 C6
Woodville Gdns E 3
PE21 . . . . .208 D3
Woodville Gdns W 2
PE21 . . . . .208 D3
Woodville Rd PE21 . . . . .208 D4
Woodward's La
Little Sutton PE12 . . . . .160 B3
Long Sutton PE12 . . . . .216 F1
Woodyard The 4 NG32 . .119 B2
Woolcroft Cl 2 PE13 . . .170 A1
Woolfellhill Rd PE6 . . . .174 F1
Woolgard PE3 . . . . .225 A3
Woolley's La
Castle Bytham NG33 . . . .152 A4
North Witham NG33 . . . .151 F4
Woollin Ave DN17 . . . . .185 A6
Woolram Wygate
PE11 . . . . .214 C5
Woolsthorpe La
Belvoir NG32 . . . . .138 D7
Bottesford NG13 . . . . . .128 C4
Woolsthorpe Manor (NT)★
NG33 . . . . .151 D7
Woolsthorpe Rd 3
NG33 . . . . .151 D7
Woolwich Dr 2 HU4 . . . .179 B2
Wootton Ave PE2 . . . . .230 F6
Wootton Rd
Grimsby DN33 . . . . .191 A3
Wootton DN39 . . . . .11 F2
**Wootton St Andrews CE Prim
Sch** DN39 . . . . .11 E3
Worcester Ave DN34 . . . .191 A4
Worcester Cl
11 Birchwood LN6 . . . .204 D7
Bracebridge Heath LN4 . .81 A2
5 Louth LN11 . . . . . . .198 C5
Scunthorpe DN16 . . . . . .185 A2
Worcester Cres 4 PE9 . .219 B6
Worcester Rd
Grantham NG31 . . . . . . .210 D4
4 Wisbech PE13 . . . . .170 D1
Wordsworth Cl
3 Grantham NG31 . . . .211 E6
Peterborough PE4 . . . . .225 E8
Wordsworth Ct 13 NG34 212 F4
Wordsworth Gr PE10 . . .213 D3
Wordsworth Rd DN17 . . .184 D6
Wordsworth St 6 LN2 . .234 B3
Workhouse La
Algarkirk PE20 . . . . . . .136 B1
Hogsthorpe PE24 . . . . . .90 C7
Workington Ave 8 HU4 179 B6
Worlaby Prim Sch
DN20 . . . . .20 D8
Worlaby Rd DN33 . . . . .191 B1
World's End Rd LN8 . . . .160 A1
Worldwide Way DN41 . . .187 C5
Wormgate PE21 . . . . . . .208 F5
Worship St HU2 . . . . . . .180 F7
Worsley PE2 . . . . .230 A4

Worsley Cl
1 Holton le Clay DN36 . .195 C2
Immingham DN40 . . . . .186 D4
Worsley Rd DN40 . . . . . .186 D4
Worthington La NG32 . . .128 D1
Wortley St 2 DN16 . . . . .183 A2
Wortley's La PE21 . . . . .208 A2
Wothorpe Mews 3 PE9 .219 B4
Wothorpe Rd PE9 . . . . . .219 B4
Wragby Prim Sch LN8 . .70 D5
Wragby Rd Bardney LN3 .83 C4
Holton cum Beckering
LN8 . . . . .70 C7
Lincoln LN2 . . . . .234 C3
Lissington LN3 . . . . .57 E2
Reepham LN3 . . . . .68 F1
Scunthorpe DN17 . . . . . .184 D5
Wragby Rd E
Greetwell LN2 . . . . .203 A8
Reepham LN3 . . . . .68 C1
Wragby St 3 DN32 . . . . .191 F7
Wragholme La LN11 . . . .50 A8
Wragholme Rd LN11 . . . .50 A8
Wrangle Bank PE22 . . . .114 B4
Wrangle Prim Sch
PE22 . . . . .114 D2
Wrawby CE Prim Sch
DN20 . . . . .20 E4
Wrawby Rd
Brigg DN20 . . . . .196 D4
Scunthorpe DN17 . . . . . .184 E5
Wrawby St DN20 . . . . . .196 C3
Wray Cl 9 DN37 . . . . . . .194 C5
Wray St 20 DN21 . . . . . .30 B1
Wren Cl
Deeping St Nicholas
PE11 . . . . .166 B6
11 Healing DN41 . . . . .23 F5
15 Market Deeping PE6 .217 C5
Scunthorpe DN16 . . . . . .185 B2
4 Sleaford NG34 . . . . .212 B3
Wren Cres DN33 . . . . . .191 B2
Wressle Rd DN20 . . . . . .19 E3
Wright Ave PE2 . . . . . . .231 D5
Wright St HU2 . . . . .180 E7
Wright's Dro PE6 . . . . . .175 B7
Wright's La
Friskney PE22 . . . . .115 A5
Sutton Bridge PE12 . . . .160 E4
Wrights Gdns DN10 . . . . .40 A3
Wrights La 5 LE14 . . . . .150 C1
Wrightsway LN2 . . . . . . .202 D5
Wroot Rd DN9 . . . . .26 A3
**Wroot Travis Charity Prim
Sch** DN9 . . . . .26 D5
Wroxall Dr NG31 . . . . . .210 E4
Wroxham Ave DN34 . . . .190 E5
Wroxham Cl 7 LN6 . . . . .205 A2
Wrygarth Ave 7 HU15 . .2 C5
Wulfram Dr NG31 . . . . . .211 E2
Wulfric Sq PE3 . . . . . . .225 C8
Wyatt Ave 13 DN20 . . . .19 D3
Wyatt Cl LN4 . . . . .96 B2
Wyatt Rd LN5 . . . . .205 D7
Wybeck Rd DN15 . . . . . .183 A6
Wybers Way DN37 . . . . .190 D7
Wybers Wood Jun & Inf Sch
DN37 . . . . .190 C8
Wybert Cres 6 PE21 . . .136 D8
Wybert La PE21 . . . . . . .136 F8
Wyberton Low Rd
3 Boston PE21 . . . . . .208 F2
1 Boston PE21 . . . . . .208 F2
Wyberton Prim Sch
PE21 . . . . .136 E7
Wyberton Roads PE20 . .137 A7
Wyberton W Rd PE21 . . .208 C2
Wyche Ave 13 PE6 . . . . .166 F1

Wycliffe Gr PE4 . . . . . . .220 E5
Wydham Pk PE2 . . . . . . .229 D6
Wye Pl PE4 . . . . .221 C1
Wygate Mdws PE11 . . . .214 B5
Wygate Pk PE11 . . . . . . .214 A5
Wygate Rd PE11 . . . . . . .214 B4
Wyggeston Ave 22
NG13 . . . . .128 A6
Wyggeston Rd 21 NG13 .128 A6
Wyke St HU9 . . . . .181 D7
Wyke The 8 PE11 . . . . . .214 A3
Wykeham La
Burgh on Bain LN8 . . . . .59 C6
Weston PE12 . . . . .145 F1
Wykes La PE11 . . . . .135 A2
Wykes Rd
Donington PE11 . . . . . . .135 B1
Yaxley PE7 . . . . .233 D4
Wylson Cl 5 NG34 . . . . .120 F8
Wyman Way PE2 . . . . . .229 F5
Wymark View DN33 . . . . .190 F3
Wymersley Rd HU5 . . . . .179 A8
Wyndham Cl NG31 . . . . .211 C5
Wyndham Rd 9 DN36 . . .195 C6
Wyndham St HU3 . . . . . .180 C2
Wynmoor Rd DN17 . . . . .184 F7
Wyredale Rd DN16 . . . . .185 D5
Wythes La PE21 . . . . . . .126 C2
Wyton Cl 8 LN6 . . . . . . .204 B6
Wyvern Cl 16 DN17 . . . .16 D8
Wyville Rd
Grantham NG31 . . . . . . .210 E1
Little Ponton & Stroxton
NG31 . . . . .139 E8

Y

Yale Cl LN4 . . . . .203 D1
Yarborough Cl 3 DN36 . .195 C2
Yarborough Cres
17 Broughton DN20 . . .19 E4
Lincoln LN1 . . . . .201 E6
Yarborough Dr 4 DN31 191 D8
Yarborough Leisure Ctr
LN1 . . . . .201 E7
Yarborough Prim Sch
DN34 . . . . .190 F7
Yarborough Rd
Boston PE21 . . . . .136 E8
Brigg DN20 . . . . .196 D3
Grimsby DN34 . . . . .190 F6
Keelby DN41 . . . . .23 A5
1 Lincoln LN1 . . . . . . .234 A4
Scunthorpe DN16 . . . . . .19 A4
9 Skegness PE25 . . . .206 A6
Yarborough Sch LN1 . . .201 E7
Yarborough Terr LN1 . . .234 A4
Yarburgh Rd LN11 . . . . .49 E2
Yarde The 2 PE10 . . . . .213 E2
Yardley Way 2 DN34 . . .190 D4
Yarmouth Ave
Grantham NG31 . . . . . . .210 D4
3 Kingston upon Hull
HU4 . . . . .179 A3
Yarra Rd DN35 . . . . .192 F6
Yarrow Rd DN34 . . . . . . .190 F7
Yarwell Cl PE2 . . . . .230 D7
Yawling Gate Rd PE22 . .114 F5
Yaxley Jun Sch PE7 . . . .233 E6
Yew Tree Cl 1 PE10 . . . .213 C6
Yew Tree Gr 1 PE21 . . . .209 C2
Yew Tree Way 2 NG24 . .104 C5
Yews La DN37 . . . . .23 E1
Yewtree Dr HU5 . . . . . . .179 B7
York Ave Lincoln LN1 . . .201 D4
Scunthorpe DN16 . . . . . .185 B4
York Cl LN4 . . . . .203 D1

York Gdns
2 Gosberton PE11 . . . .145 B6
30 Wisbech PE13 . . . . .170 D1
York House Rd 6 NG34 120 C8
York Pl DN35 . . . . .192 C4
York Rd
5 Binbrook Tech Pk LN8 . .47 B6
Brigg DN20 . . . . .196 D4
Hatfield DN7 . . . . .14 C4
Kirton in Lindsey DN21 . .30 C1
Mablethorpe/Sutton on Sea
LN12 . . . . .64 D1
Peterborough PE1 . . . . .225 F6
RAF Cranwell NG34 . . . .107 C1
Sleaford NG34 . . . . .212 C6
Wisbech PE13 . . . . .170 D1
York Ride 4 PE12 . . . . . .216 B5
York St (Boston United FC)
PE21 . . . . .209 A5
York St Boston PE21 . . . .209 A4
Grimsby DN31 . . . . .191 C8
York Terr 3 DN10 . . . . . .40 A5
York Way NG31 . . . . . . .210 C5
Yorkshireside DN17 . . . . .7 A3
Youlgrave Ave 6 LN12 . .77 A8
Young Pl DN35 . . . . .192 B7
Younger's La PE24 . . . . .103 A8

Z

Zara Cl PE21 . . . . .209 C6
Zetland St HU3 . . . . .180 A5

NG NH NJ NK

NM NN NO NP

NR NS NT NU

NX NY NZ

SC SD SE TA

SH SJ SK TF TG

SM SN SO SP TL TM

SR SS ST SU TQ TR

SW SX SY SZ TV

Any feature in this atlas can be given a unique reference to help you find the same feature on other Ordnance Survey maps of the area, or to help someone else locate you if they do not have a Street Atlas.

The grid squares in this atlas match the Ordnance Survey National Grid and are at 500 metre intervals. The small figures at the bottom and sides of every other grid line are the National Grid kilometre values (**00** to **99** km) and are repeated across the country every 100 km (see left).

To give a unique National Grid reference you need to locate where in the country you are. The country is divided into 100 km squares with each square given a unique two-letter reference. Use the administrative map to determine in which 100 km square a particular page of this atlas falls.

The bold letters and numbers between each grid line (**A** to **F**, **1** to **8**) are for use within a specific Street Atlas only, and when used with the page number, are a convenient way of referencing these grid squares.

Example   The railway bridge over DARLEY GREEN RD in grid square B1

Step 1: Identify the two-letter reference, in this example the page is in **SP**

Step 2: Identify the 1 km square in which the railway bridge falls. Use the figures in the southwest corner of this square: Eastings **17**, Northings **74**. This gives a unique reference: **SP 17 74**, accurate to 1 km.

Step 3: To give a more precise reference accurate to 100 m you need to estimate how many tenths along and how many tenths up this 1 km square the feature is (to help with this the 1 km square is divided into four 500 m squares). This makes the bridge about **8** tenths along and about **1** tenth up from the southwest corner.

This gives a unique reference: **SP 178 741**, accurate to 100 m.

Eastings (read from left to right along the bottom) come before Northings (read from bottom to top). If you have trouble remembering say to yourself "Along the hall, THEN up the stairs"!

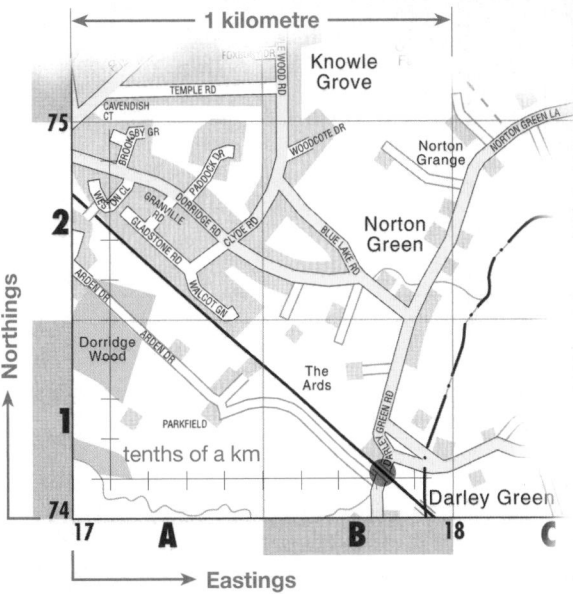

Addresses

Name and Address	Telephone	Page	Grid reference

Name and Address	Telephone	Page	Grid reference